Chinese Law: Context and Transformation

Chinese Law: Context and Transformation

by

Jianfu Chen, PhD

Professor of Law
La Trobe University
Australia

LEIDEN • BOSTON
2008

A C.I.P. Catalogue record for this book is available from the Library of Congress.

ISBN 978 90 04 16504 5 – hardback
ISBN 978 90 04 16505 2 – paperback

Koninklijke Brill NV incorporates the imprints Brill, Hotei Publishers, IDC Publishers, Martinus Nijhoff Publishers and VSP.

Contents

Chapter Two

Experience of Law in the PRC

Chapter Three

Constitutional Law

Chapter Seven

Criminal Law

Chapter Ten
Civil Law: Property

Chapter Eleven
Civil Law: Family

Chapter Fourteen

Securities Law

Chapter Fifteen

Enterprise Bankruptcy Law

Chapter Sixteen
Intellectual Property Law

Chapter Seventeen
Foreign Trade and Investment Law

Preface

Two years ago, urged by my publishers and readers, I decided that my book, *Chinese Law: Towards an Understanding of Chinese Law, Its Nature and Development* (The Hague/London/Boston, Kluwer Law International, 1999), needed to be updated. However, as soon as the updating work started it became clear that six to seven years was far too long a period for the purpose of merely updating a text on Chinese law. Chinese law is no longer the same; it has been transformed, just as the country has been. Meanwhile hundreds, if not thousands, of articles and many books have also been published on the subject. With so much time and energy invested by so many brilliant scholars in this 'enterprise', it would have been presumptuous to continue to call this substantially new book 'Towards an Understanding …'.

No one denies the fact that Chinese law has undergone significant changes, but scholars by no means agree on the nature of the changes and, in particular, on whether such changes are cosmetic or directional. Scholars continue to assess Chinese law and its development according to different criteria and from different perspectives, each of which, of course, contributes to our understanding of this subject. With some exceptions many such assessments have been made on the basis of the study of a specific area of law, or of a particular topic, but the conclusions are nevertheless often extrapolated to Chinese law in general. I myself have engaged in this endeavour to achieve an understanding of the nature of the Chinese law and its development. Increasingly, however, I have come to the conclusion that it is neither feasible nor necessarily desirable that scholars come to a consensus on this phenomenal development; a better approach is to lay down the context in which Chinese law has evolved and to leave the readers to judge for themselves. And that is primarily what this book intends to do.

The Wade-Giles romanisation is used in this book for the Chinese names of authors of publications appearing in Taiwan, and of those published before 1949. Otherwise the *pinyin* system is used throughout.

The Chinese laws and materials cited are those that have been available to me as at 15 August 2007, unless another date is given.

Jianfu Chen
August 2007
Melbourne, Australia

Acknowledgments

Needless to say a book like this is the result of many years of labour, but it has not been a lonely individual pursuit. It is a task that could never have been completed without the generous support, assistance, and friendship of many friends and colleagues in China, Australia and other countries. There are also many research institutes in Asia, Australasia, North America and Europe that have hosted my visits and research, and many people who have assisted my fieldwork and research. There are others who have read parts or the whole of the manuscript and have generously offered their constructive comments and criticisms. And there are also many who have attended my classes or conference presentations and offered their honest views and opinions. Among these, many have asked to remain anonymous. In any case, to even try to list them here is to run the risk of omission, so I can only say that I have drawn inspiration from many sources, both inside and outside China, and I am indebted to all these colleagues, friends and participants.

I must however specifically acknowledge the support of the School of Law, La Trobe University in Melbourne, Australia, and its successive Heads of School (Associate Professor Oliver Mendelsohn, Professors Martin Chanock and Gordon Walker) for providing me with excellent working and research conditions. I also gratefully acknowledge the financial support of the Australian Research Council for the research, and especially for fieldwork in China.

My special thanks go to Ms Gabi Duigu, a long-time friend, who constantly reminds me that law is not just an academic subject but one affecting the daily life of the ordinary people. On this occasion she has most generously agreed to undertake the final language polishing and proof-reading of the whole manuscript within an extremely tight schedule. I am deeply indebted to her for her kindness. I also wish to express my sincere thanks to my publisher, Martinus Nijhoff Publishers, especially Ms Lindy Melman and her assistant, Ms Bea Timmer, for their assistance and support.

Last but not least, I would like to express my special gratitude to my wife, Suiwa Ke (who also proofread the whole manuscript), and my son, Eugene, for their support, understanding and tolerance.

It is acknowledged that some of the original material contained in this book has previously been published, although not in its present form, in various international forums and edited volumes. These are indicated in the Select Bibliography at the end of the book.

August 2007
Melbourne

Abbreviations

ADR: Alternative Dispute Resolution
ALL: Administrative Litigation Law
APL: Administrative Penalty Law
ARL: Administrative Reconsideration Law
CASS: Chinese Academy of Social Sciences
CCCPC: Central Committee of the Communist Party of China
CDIC: Central Discipline Inspection Commission (of the CPC)
CJV: Contractual Joint Venture
CPC: Communist Party of China
CPD: Central Propaganda Department (of the CPC)
CPL: Civil Procedure Law
CPPCC: Chinese People's Political Consultative Conference
ECL: Economic Contract Law
EJV: Equity Joint Venture
FECL: Foreign Economic Contract Law
FTL: Foreign Trade Law
GAC: General Administration of Customs
GPCL: General Principles of Civil Law
HKSAR: Hong Kong Special Administrative Region
IP: Intellectual Property
KMT: Kuomintang (Guomindang)
LAC: Legislative Affairs Committee (of the SCNPC)
LAL: Law on Administrative Licensing
LAO: Legislative Affairs Office (of the State Council)
LAS: Law on Administrative Supervision

MII:	Ministry of Information Industry
MOC:	Ministry of Commerce
MOFTEC:	Ministry for Foreign Trade and Economic Cooperation
MOJ (MoJ):	Ministry of Justice
NAA:	National Autonomous Areas
NABSP:	National Administrative Bureau of State-owned Property
NCA:	National Copyright Administration
NCCPC:	National Congress of the Communist Party of China
NPC:	National People's Congress
PBOC:	People's Bank of China
PLC:	Political and Legal Committee (of the CPC)
PRC:	People's Republic of China
RSFSR:	Russian Soviet Federated Socialist Republic
SAIC:	State Administration for Industry and Commerce
SARFT:	State Administration of Film, Radio and Television
SCL:	State Compensation Law
SCNPC:	Standing Committee of the National People's Congress
SEPA:	State Environmental Protection Administration
SIPO:	State Intellectual Property Office
SOE:	State-owned Enterprise
SPC:	Supreme People's Court (of the PRC)
SPPA:	State Press and Publication Administration
TVE:	Township and Village Enterprise
VC:	Villagers' Committee
WFOE:	Wholly Foreign Owned Enterprises
WTO:	World Trade Organization

Introduction

1. The Transformation of Chinese Law in Context

Six years after the publication of *The Coming Collapse of China*,[1] China still stands; in fact it is getting stronger and its development is accelerating. Wherever one is, one can almost feel the heat emanating from economic development in China.

China did not collapse because it is a transformed and still rapidly changing society. Never in modern history has China enjoyed such economic prosperity and social stability. Never have the Chinese people felt so confident nor has their future looked so promising. And never has China been so outward looking, nor has the world paid so much attention to her. We have watched China, largely as bystanders, with amazement, bewilderment, and sometimes dismay.

These continuing changes in China have not just been about economic development. There has been another quiet, peaceful, and largely successful 'revolution' in the area of law, whose deficiencies have been more often mercilessly examined and documented than have its historical achievements and significance. This legal 'revolution' is the subject matter of the present book.

While people like to talk about the post-Mao economic 'miracle', the word 'miracle' is perhaps misleading. There is no doubt that pragmatic economic reforms and open door policies have been largely responsible for the success of post-Mao economic development. Common sense would inform us that the release and transformation of the national wealth in heavy industries, and the commercialisation of state-owned land and real property values, the wealth of which was accumulated during the first 30 years of the PRC, are critical factors that have ensured and sustained the economic successes of post-Mao China. The point here is this: history might be ignored but it is not a ghost – it is real and constantly within the present, and it always contributes to or hampers present development. This is also true of legal development.

Often scholars both inside and outside China see contemporary Chinese law as principally developed since the late 1970s. This is neither entirely accurate, nor is it possible. Beyond the mask of ideological differences the present legal development

---

1 By Gordon G. Chang, published by Random House, 2001.

is a continuing process of modernisation that was started at the turn of the 20th century. This is a view that was initially rejected but is increasingly subscribed to by Mainland Chinese scholars.[2] From this perspective, an evaluation of the 'revolution' or evolution of Chinese law only makes sense if it is positioned along the historical and political trajectory of China's modernisation.

Anyone who is familiar with Chinese history and Chinese legal tradition can see that Chinese law is no longer recognisable from the point of view of traditional law, since contemporary Chinese law is now western in its form. But which kind of western law? we are not so sure. Perhaps much more critical is the transformation of the society's and the government's perceptions of the role of law. Is law still merely a tool for the ruling class, as Marxism would have us believe? If not, is China moving towards the rule of law as understood in the west? Are Chinese people now living in an age of rights and freedoms, as the government in Beijing would like us to believe? Perhaps the truth lies somewhere in between. These are the questions this book attempts to answer.

However, this book is not about passing judgement on legal development in China in the last 28 years, or even in the last 100 years, although judgement is inevitable in the course of analysis. It is more about examining the context in which Chinese law has developed, whether adequately or not. In law, as Lord Steyn recently so succinctly put it, 'context is everything'.[3] While Lord Steyn was at that time discussing different approaches to Convention rights, the statement is equally valid for the study of law in general. While no judgement is entirely objective or value-free, judging a matter in its context is perhaps the closest we can come towards 'objectivity'. This context necessarily includes the Chinese legal traditions, the prevailing politico-economic situations, Party policies on politico-economic reform and tolerance towards politico-economic liberalisation, and scholarly discourse and debate. In short, the aim of this book is to put Chinese law and its development 'in context': providing the context of Chinese law and its development, but leaving the readers to make their own judgement on this phenomenal development in contemporary China.

---

2 See e.g. He Qinghua & Li Xiuqing, *Foreign Law and Chinese Law – An Examination of Transplanting Foreign Law into China in the 20th Century* (*Zhongguofa Yu Waiguofa – Ershishiji Zhongguo Yizhi Waiguofa Fansi*) (Beijing: Press of the China University of Political Science and Law, 2003); and Cao Quanlai, *Internationalisation and Localisation: the Formation of the Modern Chinese Legal System* (*Guojihua yu Bentuhua – Zhongguo Jindai falü Tixi de Xingcheng*), Beijing: Beijing University Press (2005).

3 See *R (Daly) v Secretary of State for the Home Department* [2001] 2 AC 532, at 548.

2. Structure of the Present Study

This book makes no claim to be completely comprehensive in coverage nor does it imply that the areas not covered are negligible or underdeveloped. It does, however, cover all the principal branches of law in China.[4] As such, the coverage is reasonably comprehensive and the conclusions that can be drawn from this study are generally applicable to other areas not covered in the book.

Chapter One provides a historical background to traditional Chinese 'legal culture' and modern law reform. Its aim is to outline the major features of the Chinese legal heritage as well as early efforts to modernise Chinese law. The historical background of specific topics will be further examined as they arise in the following chapters. Chapter Two deals with the changing fate of law in the PRC. Its focus is on the underlying factors and justifications for changes. Chapters One and Two, together, also attempt to sketch the main trends in legal modernisation in China. In this way it is hoped that the main features of contemporary Chinese law can be outlined and the nature of contemporary Chinese law can be better understood from a developmental perspective. From Chapter Three onward there are analyses of specific branches of law, from public law (constitutional law, legal institutions, law-making, administrative law, criminal law, criminal procedure law) to 'private' law (civil law, property, family law, contracts, law on business entities, securities, bankruptcy, intellectual property, and law on foreign investment and trade). Most of the topics are dealt with in separate chapters, with the exception of legal institutions and intellectual property. Specifically, Chapter 4 provides an outline of legal institutions in China, but their reforms (especially judicial reforms) are examined in the context of implementation and enforcement of law in Chapter 18. Similarly, the remarkable development of intellectual property law is examined in Chapter 16, but the practical reality of intellectual property protection is also analysed in Chapter 18. While each chapter contains its own conclusions, an overall conclusion is provided separately, attempting to assess the overall development of Chinese law and its future prospects.

---

4 According to the Standing Committee of the National People's Congress, a 'complete' legal system, to be established by 2010, will include seven major divisions: constitutional law, civil and commercial law, administrative law, economic law, social law, criminal law, and procedural law. See 'Chinese Legal System Will Be Established on Schedule', available from <www.legaldaily.com.cn/2007-3/13/content_557642htm> (last accessed 14 March 2007). Each of these seven divisions is represented in this book.

Chapter One

Legal Culture, State Orthodoxy and the Modernisation of Law

1. Introduction

The features of law in a given society and at a particular historical stage are shaped not only by the prevailing environment of that time, but also by the cultural heritage of the society, although the role of culture and tradition in shaping the law may be muted, implicit and even unconscious. Thus a study of current Chinese law requires some basic understanding of legal traditions in China.

Obviously we will not be able to deal with a legal heritage that spans some three to four thousand years[1] in any detail in one chapter, nor will we be able to do real justice to this legal heritage by treating it briefly.[2] What this chapter attempts to do

---

1 See *infra* notes 16-18.

2 There is a vast body of scholarship in the West on Chinese cultural history and legal tradition. See e.g. Joseph Needham, *Science and Civilisation in China*, multi-volume (Cambridge University Press, since 1954); Jacques Gernet, *A History of Chinese Civilisation*, 2nd edition translated from French by J.R. Foster & Charles Hartman (New York: Cambridge University Press, 1996); Fung Yu-lan, *A Short History of Chinese Philosophy* (New York: The Free Press, 1966); Benjamin I. Schwartz, *The World of Thought in Ancient China* (Cambridge, Massachusetts: Harvard University Press, 1985); James T. C. Liu & Wei-ming Tu (eds.), *Traditional China* (Englewood Cliffs: Prentice-Hall, Inc., 1970); T'ung-tsu Ch'ü, *Law and Society in Traditional China* (Paris: Mouton & Co., 1961); W.L. Idema & E. Zürcher (eds), *Thought and Law in Qin and Han China* (Leiden: E.J. Brill, 1990); Kathryn Bernhardt & Philip C.C Huang, *Civil Law in Qing and Republican China* (Stanford: Stanford University Press, 1994); Derk Bodde, & Clarence Morris, *Law in Imperial China* (Cambridge, Mass: Harvard University Press, 1967), 3-51; Jean Escarra, *Chinese Law: Conception and Evolution, Legislative and Judicial Institutions, Science and Teaching*, translated from a 1936 French edition by Gertrude R. Browne (Seattle: University of Washington, 1961); R. P. Peerenboom, *Law and Morality in Ancient China: The Silk Manuscripts of Huang-Lao* (Albany: State University of New York Press, 1993); Chung-ying Cheng, *New Dimensions of Confucian and Neo-Confucian Philosophy* (Albany, State University of New York Press, 1991); *Great Qing Code*, translated by William C Jones (Oxford, Clarendon Press, 1994); and Geoffrey MacCormack, *The Spirit of Traditional Chinese Law* (Athens/London: The University of Georgia Press, 1996).

is to outline the main typical, but by no means universal, features of that tradition,[3] on the basis of available scholarship.

There are several methodological factors that may do further injustice to an appreciation of Chinese legal culture and heritage when treating the subject in a brief and general section.

First, history, particularly foreign history, makes sense only when it is explained or interpreted by the notions, concepts and terms in which we are trained, and with which we are acquainted. This immediately brings us to a dilemma. On the one hand, we are wearing contemporary glasses in looking at a history whose environment was drastically different from ours. On the other hand, save for those well trained in the language and history of the society concerned, the use of contemporary terms to explain and interpret a history for contemporary students is inevitable.[4] It is therefore necessary to exercise caution and sensitivity in interpreting all history, whether foreign or native. This is particularly true when one is tempted to apply contemporary Western liberal conceptions and assumptions about law and justice to a traditional legal system that preceded the Western liberal tradition itself. It is particularly inappropriate to apply these conceptions and assumptions to judge and evaluate the 'progressiveness' of other legal systems and traditions.[5] A legal system must be assessed within its historical and cultural context. We therefore must consciously 'unpack' or discard many of the implicit assumptions that underlie the

---

3 The nature of traditional Chinese law and its social functions have been a subject of controversy, both in and outside China. This should not be surprising. With such a long history, vast area, and rich philosophical traditions, one can easily find all kinds of theories, philosophical teachings, schools of thought, and practices to support all kinds of contentions, just as one can find numerous texts to support the conventional/traditional views about China and Chinese law. In other words, almost all propositions on the nature and features of traditional Chinese law and its functions can be proven right and wrong, and true and false, at the same time. For instance, in relation to civil law in traditional China, as Liang Zhiping points out, a positive answer to the question of whether there was civil law could be both right and wrong, depending on whether one was considering simply the existence of civil law provisions, or the nature and the actual functions of such provisions in society. See Liang Zhiping, in 'The Sixth Civil Law Forum – Chinese Culture and Chinese Civil Code', 13 May 2004, China University of Political Science and Law, available at <www.ccelaws.com/mjlt/default.asp> (last accessed 10 June 2004). Yet this does not mean that any generalised statement about traditional Chinese law is necessarily unreliable.

4 On this point, see Hugh T. Scogin, Jr., 'Civil "Law" in Traditional China: History and Theory', in Bernhardt & Huang, *supra* note 2, at 13-14.

5 For a criticism of the approaches taken by Montesquieu, Unger and Maine, see Scogin, *id.*, at 24-32. See also MacCormack, *supra* note 2, at xiii. On the other hand, there are also many examples in which western laws are examined, without analysing the cultural and historical context of the selected legal provisions, to support the argument that certain elements in the Chinese tradition are universal. See, for instance, Fan Zhongxin, 'A Comparative Approach to Crimes Against Family Relatives', (no. 3, 1997) *CASS Journal of Law* (*Faxue Yanjiu*) 117.

use of modern (western) terminologies.[6]

Secondly, there is always a danger of over-generalisation and over-simplification when dealing with a tradition and a civilisation spanning several thousand years. In the case of China, the traditional society and legal culture are often described as 'Confucian'. However, Confucian teachings, as reflected in the Confucian Classics, have been the subject of endless interpretation and reinterpretation by both philosophers and the ruling elites in China. Views on and attitudes towards the governance of society and law within one school of thought are often as diverse as those between different schools of philosophy. In this sense, the term 'Confucianism' is perhaps quite misleading. Indeed, as de Bary has pointed out, if Confucianism means the original teachings of Confucius in the *Analects*, then 'almost nothing said about Confucianism today speaks to that. Indeed even the anti-Confucian diatribes earlier in this century spoke rarely to Confucius' own view but only to later adaptations or distortions of them.'[7] In short, Chinese culture, like that in any other nation, is not monolithic. However, the term Confucianism is not entirely useless or incorrect. The dominant force of state ideology since the Han Dynasty (206 BC) has been, at least in name, Confucianism. It is also true that Confucian teachings were embodied in traditional Chinese codes which were passed on from one dynasty to another, although they were supplemented and revised by each dynasty. This then suggests that certain premises have been common in various schools of Confucian philosophy. For this reason, we shall continue to use the term Confucianism in describing those typical features, attitudes and concepts. But at the same time we must see Confucianism as a 'multi-dimensional structure and a multi-stage process of creative change and creative transformation that includes heights of innovation and near-heights of renovation.'[8]

Finally, every legal system is built upon some kind of philosophical foundation. However, philosophical teachings, even though they might be incorporated into codes of law, generally represent an ideal order rather than a practical stipulation. This is particularly true in the case of Confucianism in China. The incorporation of some of the Confucian teachings into law might have been intended to be more for symbolic purposes than to have any practical use,[9] at least not until after other less punitive dispute resolution methods than state positive law had been

---

6 Scogin, *supra* note 4, at 14; H.C. Darby, 'The Chinese Legal and Political System: Historical Background', in Bhatia & Chung, *supra* note 2, at 25; William C. Jones, 'Introduction' in The *Great Qing Code*, *supra* note 2, at 4-12. This is not to argue for cultural relativism, but to urge caution, sensitivity and sensibility.

7 Wm. Theodore de Bary, *The Trouble with Confucianism* (Cambridge: Harvard University Press, 1991), at xi. See also Yang Jingfan and Yu Ronggen, *Confucius' Legal Thoughts* (*Kongzi de Falü Sixiang*) (Beijing: Press of the Masses, 1984), at 9.

8 Chung-ying Cheng, *supra* note 2, at vii.

9 See Scogin, *supra* note 3, at 30; MacCormack, *supra* note 2, ch. 3.

exhausted.[10] In any case, the function of philosophical teachings in the tradition of Chinese philosophy, especially of Confucianism, has not been the increase of positive knowledge, but rather the elevation of the mind – a reaching out for what is beyond the present actual world, and for values that are higher than those being practised.[11] This explains the lack of specific discussion of the notions of justice, rights and so forth. It also means that Chinese philosophies were often divorced from reality and monopolised by certain social elites. More importantly, once a philosophy was adopted by the imperial government it became the state orthodoxy, with the result that philosophical teachings were often manipulated, distorted, and sometimes abused by the ruling elites for their own political purposes. Traditional philosophy thus has to be distinguished from state ideology in practice. Indeed, recent archaeological discoveries of ancient covenant texts, and the opening of archives for scholarly scrutiny and study have brought into question previous assumptions about early Chinese law, which were based on philosophical teachings and thus confused the expression of ideals with actual social practice and social reality.[12] However, as this revaluation has just begun, more scholarly studies are still wanting. Many of the new conclusions are thus necessarily tentative.

Bearing in mind these points, in this chapter we will first briefly review the traditional legal culture through an examination of the basic premises of major philosophies in traditional China, and outline certain fundamental features of the traditional legal system.[13] This will then be followed by an examination of the modern legal reforms in the Qing Dynasty and under the Kuomintang (KMT). The experience of law in the PRC since 1949 will be dealt with in the next chapter.

2. Legal Culture and Heritage

2.1. An Overview

One of the early misconceptions about traditional Chinese society is that there was no law in traditional China.[14] On the contrary, law in China has a long history and

---

10 See Dodde & Morris, *supra* note 2, at 3. There were, however, occasions when Confucian teachings were directly applied to judging cases. See discussions on the Confucianisation of law below.

11 Fung Yu-lan, *supra* note 2, at 5.

12 In particular, see Bernhardt & Huang, *supra* note 2; MacCormack, *supra* note 2; and Karen Turner, 'A Case for Contemporary Studies of Classical Chinese Legal History', (vol. 22, no. 4, 1994) *China Exchange News* 25.

13 A more detailed history of specific legal institutions will be examined in the following chapters when the issues are under consideration.

14 According to MacCormack, a leading authority on traditional Chinese law, Montesquieu's

rich sources. The Tang Code (*Tanlü Shuyi*), first promulgated in AD 652 with 502 articles in total, contained not only legal provisions, but also commentaries which traced the historical origins of various provisions.[15] The earliest published law is believed to have been the 'Book of Punishment' (*Xingshu*), which was inscribed on a set of bronze tripod vessels probably in 536 BC.[16] More recently, archaeologists have unearthed covenant texts dating back to the Spring and Autumn Period (770–481 BC),[17] thus confirming the existence of written law during that period.[18] The bamboo strips found in 1975 contain strikingly sophisticated laws and institutions from the Qin Dynasty (221–206 BC). These legal arrangements, it is claimed,[19] perhaps represent the most advanced stage of legal development of the time in the world. It has been demonstrated by these discoveries that law in traditional China was much more prominent in social life than was previously understood.[20]

The traditional legal system, which continued from one dynasty to another for several thousand years, was seemingly deliberately broken off by modern legal reforms at the turn of the 20th century. It was further repudiated from 1949 onwards as

---

L'esprit des lois has played a large role in inducing such a misconception, which is common in the West and has not been entirely dispelled even among the writings of well-informed scholars. See MacCormack, *supra* note 2, at xiii-xiv.

15 *Chinese Encyclopaedia – Law* (*Zhongguo Dabaike Quanshu – Faxue*) (Beijing/Shanghai: The Chinese Encyclopaedia Press, 1984), at 579-80.

16 The texts have been lost. The belief in their existence is based on references and discussions in many historical records and Chinese classics. See Bodde & Morris, *supra* note 2, at 16; Zhang Jinfan, *et al.* (eds.), *A Chinese Legal History* (*Zhongguo Fazhi Shi*) (Beijing: Press of the Masses, 1986), at 58. On the basis of these references, Chinese scholars often trace Chinese legal history back to the 23rd – 21st century BC. See Zhang Jinfan, *et al.* (eds.), *id.*, at 13; Chen Guyuan, *An Outline of Chinese History* (*Zhongguo Fazhishi Gaiyao*), 4th edition (Taipei: Sanmin Shuju, 1970), at 43-44; Dai Yanhui, *A Chinese Legal History* (*Zhongguo Fazhishi*), 3rd edition (Taipei: Sanmin Shuju, 1971), at 1. Some western scholars also believe that Chinese legal tradition can be traced back to Shang (1766–1122 BC), see H.G. Creel, 'Legal Institutions and Procedures during the Chou Dynasty', in J. A. Cohen, R.R. Edwards & F-M. C. Chen (eds.), *Essays on China's Legal Tradition* (NJ: Princeton, 1980), at 28-29.

17 Turner, *supra* note 12, at 26.

18 On the basis of a study of these unearthed covenant texts, a prominent legal historian, Professor Zhang Jinfan, has argued that Chinese legal history can be traced back to much earlier than the 21st century BC, the date commonly accepted by Chinese scholars. See Zhang Jinfan, *A Collection of Papers on Legal History* (*Fashi Jianlüe*) (Beijing: Press of the Masses, 1988), at 1 & 27-28.

19 Zhang Jinfan (1988), *id.*, at 2.

20 Turner, *supra* note 12, at 25. This is particularly true if we not only see law as being state positive law. As will be shown below, civil matters in traditional China were often left not unregulated but to be dealt with largely by local customary laws.

being a feudalist remnant.[21] However, certain fundamental features of the traditional legal culture clearly persist in the contemporary legal system and in social attitudes towards law. The past, as Tu Wei-ming reminds us, 'lives on in China, muted and transformed in certain ways, vital and persistent in others.'[22]

Traditional Chinese conceptions of law have been largely influenced by the writings of traditional schools of philosophy.[23] Of these, three have had a particular influence, namely *Ru Jia* (Confucianism); *Fa Jia* (Legalism); and *Yin-Yang Jia*, with Confucianism being the dominant force since the Han Dynasty (206 BC).

2.2. Confucianism

The starting point of Confucianism was its emphasis on the educational function of morality (*li*) in governing a state. That is, Confucianists believed that people were educable and, by education through *li*, an ideal social order could be created on the basis of virtue (*de*). Regarding the role of law (*fa*), Confucianists strongly opposed the Legalists who emphasised the necessity of using severe punishment for maintaining a desired social order. According to Confucianism, only a government based on virtue could truly win the hearts of men.[24] This idea is reflected in one of the most cited Confucian passages:

> Lead the people by regulations, keep them in order by punishments (*xing*), and they will flee from you and lose all self-respect. But lead them by virtue and keep them in order by the established morality (*li*), and they will keep their self-respect and come to you.[25]

In short, a good government was seen as a government based on virtue (*de*) and *li*.

---

21 Until quite recently, scholars in the PRC had insisted that traditional legal culture was a part of the 'feudalist tradition' that was only abolished in 1949 when the PRC was established. See *Chinese Encyclopaedia – Law, supra* note 15, at 4-7. See also *infra* note 183. It is only more recently that traditional legal culture has been treated more seriously as part of a cultural heritage that still has some value in shaping the future of Chinese law. See e.g. 'Taking Traditions Seriously in Creating the Future – A Report on the Seminar on Recent American Academic Writings on Traditional Chinese Law', (no. 3, 1995) *Studies in Law* (*Faxue Yanjiu*) 84.

22 Tu Wei-ming (ed.), *China in Transformation* (Cambridge, Massachusetts: Harvard University Press, 1994), at x.

23 For an excellent summary of Chinese philosophy, see Fung Yu-lan, *supra* note 2.

24 Bodde & Morris, *supra* note 2, at 20-21. It should be pointed out that Confucianism is not a gender neutral philosophy; thus the use of gender neutral words may in fact distort Confucian doctrines. I have used the past tense here and below in describing the main features of the traditional philosophies. I am however not suggesting that they are totally irrelevant in China today. See *supra* note 22.

25 Cited in Bodde & Morris, *supra* note 2, at 21-22.

In Confucianism, a government based on virtue meant that the ruler was a sage who observed benevolence (*ren*) and social rightness (*yi*) as the basic roots of government; and that the ruler himself possessed all morality and set an example for his subjects. Thus, in reply to a question concerning the conduct of good government, Confucius said: 'Set yourself as an example to the people both in conduct and in physical labour'.[26] As such, the Confucian idea of government has been described as a government of 'rule by man'.[27] But perhaps this should be understood to be 'government lies in man'.[28]

The word *li* expressed a very comprehensive idea and had an extraordinarily wide range of meanings.[29] It can be translated as ceremonies, rituals, or rules of social conduct.[30] It regulated social relations, curbed the natural desires of man, and cultivated moral habits. In fact, 'Confucianists called all rules which upheld moral habits and served to maintain social order by the generic name of *li*'.[31]

Li thus was a set of general rules governing proper conduct and behaviour by which rulers could maintain an ideal social order.[32] It was never a body of detailed rules designed to deal with all situations, but a general instrument for training character and nourishing moral force.[33] However, *li* was not a set of rules universally applicable to all men, but rather varied according to one's status in society and in the family. This was a very basic principle of government in Confucianism. To Confucianists, to govern was to 'rectify names' (*zheng ming*), i.e. each class of things should be given a name which had certain implications attached to it, in order to regulate a society in an orderly and hierarchical fashion. Confucius once replied to his disciple concerning the question of ruling a state: 'The one thing needed first [to rule a state] is the rectification of names'.[34]

---

26 Cited in Chang Chi-yun, 'Confucianism vs. Communism', (no. 2, 1959) 2 *Chinese Culture* 1, at 32. For many similar Confucian passages, see Chang Chin-tsen, '*Li* and Law', (no. 2, 1960) 2 *Chinese Culture*, at 6.

27 Yu Ronggen, 'Questioning the Theory of Rule by Man in Confucianism and Rule of Law in Legalism', (no. 4, 1984) *Law Science Quarterly* (*Faxue Jikan*) 60.

28 T'ung-tsu Ch'ü, *supra* note 2, at 257.

29 Indeed, Confucianists saw it as their duty to dedicate their whole lives to studying and interpreting the meaning of *li*, which they believed was created by the ancient sage.

30 Fung Yu-lan, *supra* note 2, at 147; T'ung-tsu Ch'ü, *supra* note 2, at 230.

31 Chang Chin-tsen, *supra* note 26, at 4. For further discussions on the concept of *li* in Confucianism, see T'ung-tsu Ch'ü, *supra* note 2, at 226-241.

32 T'ung-tsu Ch'ü, *supra* note 2, at 230.

33 Benjamin Schwartz, 'On Attitudes Toward Law in China', reprinted in J.A. Cohen, *The Criminal Process of the People's Republic of China 1949 – 1963: An Introduction* (Cambridge: Harvard University Press, 1968), at 64.

34 Fung Yu-lan, *supra* note 2, at 41.

This well-ordered society, according to Confucianism, consisted of five cardinal relations of men. They were the relationship of ruler and minister; of father and son; of husband and wife; of elder brother and younger brother; and of friend and friend. Out of the five, three clearly belonged to the family, but the remaining two could also be conceived of in terms of the family: The relationship between the ruler and the minister could be seen as analogous to that between the father and son, while that between friend and friend was like the one between elder and younger brother.[35] In fact, the concept of family was one of the fundamental concepts in Confucianism, and the concept of state was only an extension of that of family. Individuals were no more than members of a family or a social group; there was little significance for their separate and independent existence, least of all the appreciation of liberty and individual rights.[36] To govern a state was similar to regulating a family, which was achieved through the cultivation of individual morality, as the Confucian social formula suggested: cultivating the personality – regulating family life – ordering a state – ensuring world peace (*xiushen – qijia – zhiguo – pingtianxia*).[37] The fusion of the concept of family with that of state thus provided a basis for elevating morality to the status of state law.[38]

Corresponding to the concept of *li*, the Chinese family system was a hierarchical system. Members were differentiated according to criteria of generation, age, degree of relationship and sex, with one's status determining one's different obligations and duties.[39] Citizens of a state, like members in an extended family, were similarly ranked as noble and humble, with varying levels of superordination and subordination.[40]

---

35 *Ibid.*, at 21.

36 See Lucian W. Pye, 'The State and the Individual: An Overview Interpretation', in Brian Hook (ed.), *The Individual and the State in China* (Oxford: Clarendon Press, 1996), at 16-24.

37 It is stated in the Great Learning, one of the Confucian classics, that: 'The ancients who wished to illustrate illustrious virtue through the kingdom, first ordered well their own states. Wishing to order well their states, they regulated their families. Wishing to regulate their families, they first cultivated their persons'. Cited in T'ung-tsu Ch'ü, *supra* note 2, at 255.

38 In fact, a great part of Confucianism is the rational justification or theoretical expression of the Chinese family system as a social system. See Fung Yu-lan, *supra* note 2, at 21-22. Xun-zi (Hsun tzu), also a great Confucian scholar, once replied when asked about ways of governing a country: 'I have heard only about self-cultivation, but never about ways of governing a country'. Cited in T'ung-tsu Ch'ü, *supra* note 2, at 255.

39 A Confucian passage says: 'The father should be kind, the son filial, the elder brother affectionate, the younger brother respectful, the husband good-natured, the wife gentle, the mother-in-law kind, the daughter-in-law obedient – all in conformity to *li*'. Cited in Chang Chin-tsen, *supra* note 26, at 2. For further discussions on the hierarchical relationship, see T'ung-Tsu Ch'ü, *supra* note 2, at 226-231.

40 One Confucian passage states: 'there must be gradations of the noble and the ignoble, differences of dress for different people, and different positions for high and low officials at court'. Cited in Chang Chin-tsen, *supra* note 26, at 2.

Therefore, to rectify names was to differentiate 'family' members, and hence social status, by means of *li*, or in other words, to rule a state was '[to] let the ruler be ruler, the minister be minister, the father be father, and the son be son.'[41] To achieve this, it was necessary to have *li* for 'without *li* it would be impossible to tell the difference between the position of a prince and that of his minister, between the position of a superior and that of an inferior, or between the position of an elder person and that of a younger one. Without *li* it would be impossible to fix the degrees of relationship between the sexes, between father and son, and between brothers',[42] and to be without these differences, 'it is to be like the beasts'.[43] In other words, the final goal of good government was the correct operation of hierarchical human relationships.[44]

However, it would be wrong to conclude that Confucianists abandoned law completely even though the concept of law was rarely deliberated by Chinese philosophers.[45] What Confucianists opposed was the replacement of moral influence by punishment and the improper application of punishment. This was because Confucianists believed that human beings, whether their nature is good or bad, were educable and, thus moral education and influence should be the first priority in maintaining an ideal social order. Confucius himself did not refuse to hear litigation; he was alleged to have said that: 'In hearing cases I am as good as anyone else, but what is really needed is to bring about that there are no cases!'[46] Nor did he absolutely oppose punishment. Rather, he held moral influence to be basic and punishment supplementary.[47] This point was made even more clearly by his follower, Xun-zi (Hsun Tsu), who said: 'If people are punished without education, penalties will be enormous and evil cannot be overcome; if they are educated without punishment, evil people will not be punished.'[48] The proper relationship between law and *li* was discussed in the most important Confucian classics, the *Li Ji* (*Li Chi*),[49] as follows: '*li* forbids trespasses before they are committed, whereas law punishes criminal acts

---

41 Cited in Fung Yu-lan, *supra* note 2, at 41.

42 Cited in Chang Chin-tsen, *supra* note 26, at 2.

43 Mencius, cited in Fung Yu-lan, *supra* note 2, at 151.

44 T'ung-Tsu Ch'ü, *supra* note 2, at 239.

45 The character of '*fa*' (law), however, was commonly used interchangeable with the character '*xing*'. (punishment). See further discussions of the concept of law in sections 2.3 and 2.5 below.

46 Confucius, cited in Bodde & Morris, *supra* note 2, at 21.

47 T'ung-Tsu Ch'ü, *supra* note 2, at 268.

48 *Xun-zi*, cited in T'ung-tsu Ch'ü, *supra* note 2, at 269.

49 See T'ung-tsu Ch'ü, *supra* note 2, at 271.

after their commission'.[50] To a Confucianist, law had only short-term effects whereas *li* had a broad and permanent influence on members of the society.

Confucianists also opposed the improper application of laws, requiring that people should be educated before they could be punished by law. Confucius once said: 'To put the people to death without having instructed them; – this is called cruelty. To require from them, suddenly, the full task of work, without having given them warning; – this is called oppression'.[51] To him, not to instruct people and to put them on trial was to kill the innocent. He insisted that if the law was improper the people should not be punished, for the guilt was then not on the side of the people.[52]

2.3. Legalism

In strong contrast to the Confucian conception that all men are educable, Legalists believed that man was naturally evil.[53] Their main concern was thus primarily with evil behaviour, and the primary function of law in their conception was to prevent evil, not to encourage good behaviour.[54] Thus Legalism was primarily associated with the concept of punishment, indeed, severe punishment.

To a Legalist, neither moral influence could determine the social order, nor the virtue of the ruler be powerful enough to transform society or create order or disorder.[55] To him, a uniform law was the only means to govern a state, and law must be universally applicable to all.[56] The commonly cited Legalist idea of government is summarised as 'ignoring the [difference between] the close, the remote, the noble, the humble, and evaluating all by the law'.[57] On the basis of the face value of this idea of government, many Chinese scholars have since the 1920s held the view that the historical struggle between Confucianism and Legalism was the struggle between

---

50 Cited in Chang Chin-tsen, *supra* note 26, at 4.

51 Cited in T'ung-tsu Ch'ü, *supra* note 2, at 252.

52 See T'ung-tsu Ch'ü, *supra* note 2, at 252.

53 Fung Yu-lan, *supra* note 2, at 162.

54 Thus, a good ruler 'seeks offences and not virtue' and 'punishes the bad people, but does not reward the virtuous ones.' See T'ung-tsu Ch'ü, *supra* note 2, at 261. There were however also Legalists who emphasised equally the importance of rewards in ruling a country. See Wu Chunlei, 'On Different Conceptions of Law in Different Historical Periods in Our Country', (no. 1, 1996) *Journal of Gansu Institute of Political Science and Law* (*Gansu Zhengfa Xueyuan Xuebao*) 7.

55 T'ung-tsu Ch'ü, *supra* note 2, at 257.

56 One of the famous teachings of Legalism is that '[o]rder cannot be changed because of the will of the ruler. Order is more important than the ruler.' See T'ung-tsu Ch'ü, *supra* note 2, at 244.

57 Cited in *Chinese Encyclopedia – Law*, *supra* note 15, at 97.

the idea of rule by man and the rule of law.[58] However, this interpretation is not without major problems. Firstly, Legalists neither opposed social differentiation between the noble and the humble or between the ruler and the ruled, nor did they reject privileges for the nobles and rulers; though they considered such matters minor, irrelevant and even a hindrance to the governing of a state.[59] Equality before the law had its own specific connotation: 'The ruler creates the law; the ministers abide by the law; and subjects are punished by the law. All (the ruler, the minister, the superior, the inferior, the noble, and the humble) are subject to law'.[60] Indeed, the real objectives of Legalist theory were 'to respect the position and prerogative of the prince and to support authoritarian policies'.[61] Secondly, although Legalists defined law in many ways, such as 'measures', 'rules', and 'codified books',[62] they all emphasised severe punishment, and some even advocated that 'bad law is better than no law'.[63] This conception was derived from their belief that human nature was inherently evil and that, therefore, only 'force and power can suppress violence and that kindness and leniency cannot put an end to social anarchy'.[64] One of the most famous Legalists, Han Fei Zi, once said that: 'It is by means of strict penalties and heavy punishments that the affairs of state are managed'.[65] Shang Yang, whose reform helped the Qin State to conquer other states and unify China, said: 'Nothing is more basic for putting an end to crimes than the imposition of heavy punishment',[66] and 'in applying punishments, light offences should be punished heavily'.[67] The Legalists believed that law was the order imposed by the state to suppress individuals' desires on the grounds that it was the nature of man to seek profit and avoid harm and that, therefore, rewards and punishments were two effective ways of governing, i.e. to establish the interdicts and commands of the state.[68]

As Legalists diametrically opposed the Confucian idea of 'rule by man', they also advocated strict regulation of and control over government officials (backed

---

58 See Yu Ronggen, *supra* note 27, at 60-61.

59 T'ung-tsu Ch'ü, *supra* note 2, at 241-2.

60 Guan Zi (Kuan Tzu), cited in Yu Ronggen, *supra* note 27, at 62.

61 Chang Chin-tsen, *supra* note 26, at 7.

62 See *Chinese Encyclopedia – Law*, *supra* note 15, at 97.

63 Ji Zi, cited in Yu Ronggen, *supra* note 27, at 62.

64 Cited in Chang Chin-tsen, *supra* note 26, at 12. See also Bodde & Morris, *supra* note 2, at 18.

65 Cited in Chang Chin-tsen, *supra* note 26.

66 Cited in Chang Chin-tsen, *supra* note 26.

67 *The Book of Lord Shang*, translated by Dr. J.J.L. Duyvendak (the University of Chicago Press, 1928), at 258.

68 Fung Yu-lan, *supra* note 2, at 162.

by severe punishment) and, thus, the establishment of a sophisticated and complex system of administrative law.[69]

Not only did the Legalists reject the Confucian idea of government by virtue, they also believed power and terror were the only tools that a ruler needed to govern a state.[70] The only dynasty established with the help of Legalism, the Qin Dynasty (221–207 BC), was a short-lived reign of terror,[71] which ended the first (and only) period of 'a hundred schools of thought contending with each other' in Chinese history, when all books of teaching of other philosophical schools were burned, and when Confucianists were buried alive *en masse*.

In short, the legacy left by the Legalists are the concept of law as severe punishment and the need for detailed regulation and control of government officials. Its important principle of equality before the law, however it was interpreted, disappeared entirely after the end of the Qin Dynasty.[72]

2.4. State Orthodoxy and Practice – the Confucianisation of Law

Confucianists are often described as educators and moralists, but they were also statesmen.[73] Legalists too were largely politicians who had a keen understanding of real and practical politics and provided practical solutions to rulers for the problems they faced. They were thus known as 'men of methods' (*fashu zhishi*).[74] Thus, the dispute between Confucianism and Legalism was more than philosophical contention; it was a political struggle for supremacy and domination in state ideology and hence state politics.

The struggle for ideological supremacy must be understood within the framework of the Chinese concept of 'Great Uniformity' (*dayitong*). This was first associated

---

69 MacCormack, *supra* note 2, at 4-5.

70 Yu Ronggen, *supra* note 27, at 63.

71 Qin is also known as 'the state of tiger and wolf'. Its unification of China was based on its military power and the brutal and ruthless ideology of Legalists. See Fung Yu-lan, *supra* note 2, at 191.

72 MacCormack, *supra* note 2, at 5.

73 T'ung-tsu Ch'ü, *supra* note 2, at 263. One of the well-known Confucian teachings is 'academic excellence leads to officialdom'. Indeed, Confucius himself spent 14 years travelling to different kingdoms seeking official appointment. See Kuang Yamin, *A Critical Biography of Confucius* (*Kunazi Pingzhuan*) (Jinan: Qiru Press, 1985), ch. 2.

74 See Fung Yu-lan, *supra* note 2, at 156. As pragmatic politicians, their rejection of the ideas of various schools of philosophy was for appearances only; they actually took whatever they found useful from these ideas for the purpose of government. Indeed, two of the most famous Legalists, Li Shi and Han Fei Zi (Li Ssu and Han Fei Tzu) were students of one of the most famous Confucianists, Xun Zi (Tsun Tsu). For a brief account of the origin of Legalism, see Fung Yu-lan, *supra* note 2, at 30-37. For the relations between Legalism and other schools of philosophy, see Fung Yu-lan, *id.*, 155-165.

with political or territorial unity, which was said to be a desire of all people long before the first unification of China by the First Emperor of Qin.[75] In order to achieve political unity, Qin took the measure, among others, of imposing unification of thought. With the help of the Legalists, in particular that of Li Si (Li Ssu), this idea of political unity was extended to include the imposition of one government, one history, and one way of thinking.[76] Thus the unity achieved by Qin also meant the end of the political and ideological pluralism found during the preceding Warring Period, and philosophical contention became a struggle for survival.

The succeeding dynasty, the Han Dynasty (206 BC – AD 220), inherited the concept of political unity of the Qin and continued its unfinished work of building up a new political and social order.[77] This resulted in the second attempt at 'Great Uniformity' in Chinese history, though the approach taken was somewhat different.[78]

While Qin rule only allowed the existence of one school of thought, during the Han Dynasty only one 'ideology' was supposed to be dominant in state teaching, but private teaching of different philosophies was still allowed. However, the study of Confucianism was required as a compulsory qualification for candidature for official positions.[79] Thus came about the so-called 'Confucianisation of law', that is, the incorporation of the spirit, and sometimes the actual practice, of Confucian teaching into legal form.[80]

While Emperor Wu (140–87 BC) of the Han Dynasty elevated Confucianism to the level of the only state teaching, it was the Confucian attitude of treating law as a supplementary or secondary tool for governing a state that facilitated the process of the Confucianisation of law. Gradually, the supplementary function of punishment was increasingly emphasised by Confucianists, and thus eventually the ultimate Confucianisation of law in the Han period occurred.[81] This process is closely associated with the philosopher Dong Zhongshu (Tung Chung-Shu, 179–104 BC) and his philosophy.

The philosophy of Dong Zhongshu is a mixture of theories of Confucianism, *Yin-Yang*, the third of the major schools of philosophy to influence China's legal

---

75 Fung Yu-lan, *supra* note 2, at 180.

76 Hence the above-mentioned burning of all books other than Legalist teachings, and the killing of Confucianists. Books of medicine and other technologies were spared as they were seen as having nothing to do with 'ideology'. See Fung Yu-lan, *supra* note 2, at 205.

77 Fung Yu-lan, *supra* note 2, at 191.

78 Fung Yu-lan, *supra* note 2, at 205.

79 Fung Yu-lan, *supra* note 2, at 206.

80 For further discussions on this political background, see Fung Yu-lan, *supra* note 2, at 204-206.

81 See T'ung-tsu Ch'ü, *supra* note 2, at 267-273.

tradition, and that of the Five Elements.[82] According to him, the five elements of the universe corresponded with the five human relations,[83] thus justifying the differentiated social relations within Confucianism. The theory of *Yin-Yang* meanwhile justified the supplementary function of punishment in governing a state, with *li*, being *Yang*, as the first instrument, and punishment, being *Yin*, as a supplementary tool for governing a state.[84] In this way he laid down the theoretical foundation for the harmonisation between Confucianism and Legalism.

Dong Zhongshu persuaded Emperor Wu to unify state ideology by placing Confucianism in a dominant position, and it was to remain the state orthodoxy in China for nearly two thousand years. However, this Confucianism was now very different from that of the previous Chou and Warring States periods, having absorbed many ideas from other rival schools, including, of course, Legalism.[85]

Eventually the gap between *li* and law (punishment) was filled during a later dynasty, when the Tang (T'ang) Code was enacted in AD 653, bringing about the ultimate completion of the process of Confucianisation of law.[86] This process was further reinforced by the direct influence of Confucianism on the administration of justice. Since official positions required the study of Confucianism, and judicial and administrative functions were not separated, Confucian scholars thus controlled the interpretation of the law in addition to controlling its formulation and revision.[87]

---

82 Fung Yu-lan, *supra* note 2, at 192-193. The philosophy of *Yin-Yang* and that of the Five Elements are inter-related; they are both theories of cosmology. The Chinese *Yin-Yang* philosophy explains the origin of the world: the interaction of *Yang* (originally meaning sunshine, and later developed to represent masculinity, activity, heat, brightness, dryness, hardness, etc.) and *Yin* (originally meaning absence of sunshine, later developed to represent femininity, passivity, cold, darkness, wetness, softness, etc.) produces all phenomena of the universe. The philosophy of the Five Elements explains the structure of the world: the universe consists of five powers (Wood, Fire, Soil, Metal, and Water). For further discussion on the very complicated philosophy of *Yin-Yang* and the Five Elements, see Fung Yu-lan, *supra* note 2, at 129-142.

83 That is ruler and minister, father and son, husband and wife, elder brother and younger brother, and friend and friend.

84 For further discussion of the philosophy of Dong Zhongshu, see Fung Yu-lan, *supra* note 2, at 191-206. Dong Zhongshu was however not the first philosopher to approach law with Yin-Yang and Five Elements philosophies. See Wang Limin, 'Yin-Yang and Five Elements and Ancient Law in Our Country', (no. 4, 1994) *Law Review* (*Faxue Pinglun*) 74.

85 For a discussion of changes of Confucianism in Chinese history, see Ting Wei-chih, 'The Phases of Changes in Confucianism', (no. 12, 1978) *Studies in History* (*Lishi Yangjiu*) 25; Duan Qinguan, 'A Brief Discussion on the Evolution of Legal Ideology in Qin and Han Dynasties', (no. 5, 1980) *Studies in Law* (*Faxue Yanjiu*) 45; and Bodde & Morris, *supra* note 2, at 27. Some scholars have thus declared that Confucianism since Han was no longer genuine Confucian teaching, but fake, distorted and imposed 'Confucianism' manipulated by the ruling elites. See Kuang Yamin, *supra* note 73, at 29.

86 See T'ung-tsu Ch'ü, *supra* note 2, at 267-279, and Bodde & Morris, *supra* note 2, at 27-29.

87 T'ung-tsu Ch'ü, *supra* note 2, at 275-276.

The most extreme practice of Confucianisation of law was the direct application of the Confucian classics in judging cases, the *Chunqiu Jueyu* (Judging Cases by *Chunqiu*) initially started by Dong Zhongshu and followed, to various degrees, in later dynasties.[88]

The outcome of all this was that the Legalists' concept of equality before the law (with, of course, the ruler being above the law) was replaced by the Confucianist differentiation of social status. Law increasingly became an administrative tool for determining and maintaining social order, with the state at the centre. Because the concept of law remained that of punishment, the Confucianisation of law led to the establishment of a harsh and detailed system of penal law, and the enactment of an enormous number of regulations, which may be called law for administration in Chinese history. Thus the Chinese concept of *Fa Zhi* (literally means 'rule of law' or 'rule by law') came to be associated with harsh despotism, heavy reliance on force, and oppressive demands on the people by an interventionist state.[89]

Although Confucianism remained enshrined as the state orthodoxy from the Han Dynasty until the late Qing reform of law at the turn of the 20th century, in practice Legalism was never entirely discarded. Hence rulers were said to be 'Confucianist in appearance but Legalist in reality.'[90] In other words, in state practice Legalism continued to provide its methods and solutions for government, while Confucianism was upheld as a desired and ideal order for the society.

2.5. The Legacy of History

The influence of legal and cultural heritage on contemporary China does not, perhaps, derive directly from the specific teaching of Confucianism or Legalism, but rather from the traditional patterns of thinking (morality v. punishment), the structure of institutions (the family as a central unit), conceptions and assumption about law (law as punishment), and the function of law (law as a political and administrative tool for maintaining social order). Confucianism, and indeed all traditional teachings, have been out of fashion ever since the May 4th Movement in 1919. In other words, contemporary Chinese law has few direct links with the imperial legal heritage.[91] Hence, traditional legal cultures cannot explain the structure and contents of contemporary Chinese laws. These are based on the immediate circumstances (what

---

88 *Chunqiu* (*Ch'un-chiu*) was a Confucian classic. See T'ung-tsu Ch'ü, *supra* note 2, at 275-276.

89 See Schwartz, *supra* note 33, at 65; and, Duo Fu & Liu Fan, 'On Chinese Orthodox Legal Culture and Its Modernisation', (no. 2, 1988) *Journal of the South-Central Institute of Political Science and Law* (*Zhongnan Zhengfa Xueyun Xuebao*), at 61-69.

90 Fung Yu-lan, *supra* note 2, at 215.

91 Thus one Chinese scholar has asserted that if Confucius was now given a copy of the western code and a Chinese code for him to identify which one was Chinese law, he would now mistake the western code as Chinese law and *vice versa*. See Fan Zhongxin, *supra* note 5, at 138.

the Chinese call 'reality'). The prevailing political ideology of the time in question will better explain the meaning of any specific legal provisions, but the values and techniques of traditional Chinese law continue to influence contemporary legal thinking and practice.

In this section, we will outline the fundamental features of traditional Chinese law as evidenced in state positive law,[92] which has continued to influence and even shape contemporary Chinese law.

(1) Law as a political tool: In contrast to Western legal tradition, traditional Chinese law was not attributed to any divine origin, although Taoism and Buddhism did have some influence.[93] Both Confucianism and Legalism were primarily concerned with determining and maintaining a desired social order.[94] Thus law in China was first and foremost a political tool, operating in a vertical direction, with its primary concern being state interests, rather than on a horizontal plane between individuals. As such it was not very interested in social regulations among autonomous individuals, and least of all in defending individual rights against the state.[95] In this sense the initial stimulus of traditional Chinese law was therefore also unrelated to economic

---

92 As alluded to earlier (*supra* note 20), a large part of social life in civil relations was dealt with by customary laws in traditional China. However, because of their scattered nature and informal operation, it is difficult to draw any general conclusions from these customary laws. For studies on customary laws in traditional China, see Liang Zhiping, *Customary Law in Qing Dynasty: Society and State* (*Qingdai Xiguan Fa: Shehui yu Guojiao*) (Beijing: China University of Political Science and Law Press, 1996); Liang Zhiping, *The Pursuit of Harmony in Natural Orders: A Study on Chinese Traditional Legal Culture* (*Xunqiu Ziran Zhixu Zhong De Hexie: Zhongguo Chuantong Falü Wenhua Yanjiu*) (Beijing: China University of Political Science and Law Press, 1997); Gao Qicai, *On Chinese Customary Law* (*Zhongguo Xiguan Fa Lun*) (Changsha: Hunan Press, 1995); Li Zhimi, *Ancient Chinese Civil Law* (*Zhongguo Gudai Minfa*) (Beijing: Publishing House of Law, 1988); Gao Huanyue, 'The Uniqueness of Ancient Chinese Civil Law', (no. 3, 1997) *China Law* 90; Kong Qingming, Hu Liuyuan & Sun Jiping (eds.), *A History of Chinese Civil Law* (*Zhongguo Minfa Shi*) (Changchun: Jilin People's Press, 1996); Hui-chen Wang Liu, *The Traditional Chinese Clan Rules* (New York: Association for Asian Studies, 1959); Mark Elvin, *The Pattern of the Chinese Past* (Stanford: Stanford University Press, 1973); Francis L.K. Hsu, *Under the Ancestors' Shadow* (New York: Columbia University Press, 1948); Zhao Xudong, *Power and Justice: Dispute Resolution in Rural Societies and Plurality of Authorities* (*Quanli Yu Gongzheng – Xiangtu Shehui de Jiufen Yu Quanwei Duoyuan*) (Tianjin: Tianjin Ancient Books Publishing House, 2003); Su Li, *Roads to Cities – Rule of Law in Transitional China* (*Daolu Tongxiang Chengshi – Zhuanxing Zhongguo de Fazhi*) (Beijing: Law Press, 2004); and Tian Chengyou, *Local Customary Law in Rural Societies (Xiangtu Shehui Zhong de Minjianfa)* (Beijing: Law Press, 2005).

93 Bodde & Morris, *supra* note 2, at 10 & 12-13; Zhang Jinfan (1988), *supra* note 18, at 36; and Pye, *supre* note 36, at 17. Whether Chinese law was comparable to natural law is however controversial. See Turner, *supra* note 12, at 27; Peerenboom, *supra* note 2.

94 T'ung-tsu Ch'ü, *supra* note 2, at 226.

95 Bodde & Morris, *supra* note 2, at 4; Jones, *supra* note 6, at 4.

development,[96] although some contemporary Chinese scholars have argued that law was often used to implement 'economic reforms' in traditional China.[97]

(2) Law as an administrative tool: Largely as a legacy of the influence of Legalism,[98] traditional Chinese positive law was also a tool for state administration. The sophisticated and complex bureaucracy established and developed since the Qin period facilitated the development of, and was backed by, an equally sophisticated and highly developed system of administrative law, with its primary attention on punishment rather than on adjudication. It was the belief of Chinese rulers that 'the wise emperor governs his officials, not his subjects'.[99] Thus detailed rules on officials' obligations and powers, such as the *Tang Liu Dian*, *Ming Hui Dian*, and *Qing Hui Dian* were codified separately and systematically.[100]

With law as an administrative tool, it is not surprising to note that there was no concept of the separation of powers. The administration of justice was always a part of general administration and judicial personnel were a part of the 'executive'.[101] Further, as administration was within the domain of the emperor and his officials, the activities of legal specialists and the development of a legal profession were strongly discouraged, if not prohibited, by all dynasties. Indeed, lawyers were politely described as 'litigation tricksters' or 'pettifoggers' and less politely as tigers, wolves or demons.[102]

(3) Law as a supplementary/secondary tool: With Confucianism as the state orthodoxy, state positive law was not seen as a primary regulator for state affairs, much less as a regulator for affairs among individuals. *Li* was the primary regulator. Indeed, the invention of *fa* (law) was attributed to a 'barbarian' people, the Miao people, who, it was alleged, 'made no use of spiritual cultivation, but controlled by means

96 Bodde & Morris, *supra* note 2, at 10-11.

97 See e.g. Zhang Jinfan (1988), *supra* note 18, at 12 & 42-43; Wang Qianghua, 'On the Role of Law in Reform and the Three Legal Reforms in Our History', (no. 5, 1982) *Studies in Law (Faxue Yanjiu)* 58.

98 See *supra* note 69.

99 Zhang Jinfan (1988), *supra* note 18, at 19; Jones, *supra* note 6, at 6.

100 For further discussion see Zhang Jinfan, 'Administration and Administrative Law in Ancient China', in Zhang Jinfan (1988), *supra* note 18, at 171-217; Alice Erh-Soon Tay, 'Law in Communist China – Part I', (1969) 6 *Syd.L.Rev.* 153, at 157-160; and Gao Huanyue, 'Ruling Government Officials through Laws: the Essence of Rule by Law in Ancient China', (no. 4, 1997) *China Law* 98.

101 A local magistrate was 'the judge, the tax collector and the general administrator. He had charge of the postal service, salt administration, pao-chia, police, public works, granaries, social welfare, education, and religious and ceremonial functions.' See T'ung-tsu Chü, *Local Government in China under the Ch'ing*, quoted in Jones, *supra* note 6, at 10.

102 MacCormack, *supra* note 2, at 25.

of punishments.'[103] The ancient character for *fa* represented a fierce animal.[104] As a supplementary means for social control, the word *fa* (law) is more a synonym for the word punishment, with its first and primary meaning being penal law.[105] Civil matters were seen as trivial (*xigu*) and the claims and suits of citizens between themselves were of secondary interest to the state;[106] they were largely left to be regulated by customary law.[107] When they were regulated by state law, penal sanctions were always attached to prevent the breakdown of the desired social order. The best summary of the attitude towards law as a supplementary means for social control is the Chinese saying *chuli ruxing* ('Outside the *li* are punishments').[108]

(4) Law as a tool for social stability: The Confucianisation of law also produced two distinctive features of Chinese law. First, the upholding of Confucianism as state orthodoxy led to the remarkably long continuation of a core group of legal provisions, which survived many centuries of development with little change.[109] Secondly, it also led to the upholding of a hierarchical relationship, with the family as the basic unit.[110] The abstract concept of the individual was conspicuously lacking in traditional Chinese law. Since rules were seen as laid down by ancestors and inherited by generations, it is not surprising that modern law reforms, which were

---

103 Quoted in Bodde & Morris, *supra* note 2, at 13.

104 See *Chinese Encyclopedia – Law, supra* note 15, at 76.

105 Schwartz, *supra* note 33, at 65.

106 Bodde & Morris, *supra* note 2, at 4; Zhang Jinfan, 'Chinese Legal Tradition and the Beginning of Modernisation', (no. 5, 1996) *Journal of China University of Political Science and Law (Zhengfa Luntan)* 77, at 78; and Gao Huanyue, 'The Uniqueness of Ancient Chinese Civil Law', (no. 3, 1997) *China Law* 90, at 92.

107 There are disagreements among scholars as to whether the imperial state saw civil matters as trivial and that thus customary laws were not part of state law. For instance, Alford insists that it is wrong to believe that the imperial state was indifferent to civil law matters and the regulation of these matters by local customs should be seen as a kind of controlled delegation of authority. See William P. Alford, *To Steal a Book Is an Elegant Offence: Intellectual Property Law in Chinese Civilisation* (Stanford: Stanford University Press, 1995), at 11. A prominent Chinese scholar, Liang Zhiping, however declares that, if understood in the Chinese cultural context and compared to the notion of 'civil law' or 'private law' as understood in the West, there was only one law in traditional China, and that was penal law. See Liang Zhiping (1997), *supra* note 92, at 249. This disagreement seems to be more about characterising traditional Chinese customary law than about its function in society. In fact, most scholars agree that customary law was officially recognised as having legal effect by authorities and played an important role in Chinese traditional society. See Zhang Jinfan (1988), *supra* note 18, at 6; Bodde & Morris, *supra* note 2, at 5-6; and MacCormack, *supra* note 2, at 23-27.

108 Zhang Jinfan (1988), *supra* note 18, at 36.

109 MacCormack, *supra* note 2, at 1.

110 Zhang Jinfan (1988), *supra* note 18, at 51-53.

later to undermine the foundation of the traditional institutions and structure, as discussed below, were strongly resisted by conservative forces in the society.

In short, traditional Chinese positive law was mainly conceived of as penal law, operated in a vertical direction, and used as a supplementary means for maintaining a hierarchical social relationship that continued for centuries.

3. The Beginning of Modernisation – The Wholesale Westernisation of Chinese Law

3.1. Constitutional and Political Reform at Gunpoint

Modern law reform, a process initially mainly concerned with the revision and making of law, started in the late nineteenth century when traditional values and systems were facing strong internal and external challenges and pressures for reform. Internally, a commodity economy had emerged and, at the same time, there was widespread social unrest (e.g. the Taiping Rebellion of 1851–1864 and the Boxer Rebellion of 1900) and official corruption. Externally, Western economic, cultural and political ideas had penetrated into China, and with the invasion of foreign ideas China also suffered from repeated humiliations at the hands of outside powers, including the defeat by Japan in the Sino-Japanese war of 1895 and, consequently, had to concede to demands of extra-territoriality by these powers. In response, intellectuals and other social elites began attempts to modernise (such as the Self-Strengthening Movement of 1860–1894), to press for reform (such as the Hundred Days Reform of 1898) or even to call for revolution.[111] These challenges and pressures both weakened the central government and at the same time made the Chinese even more aware of the serious defects of their societal structures. A climate for change was thus created which was to undermine the foundations of traditional ideology, culture and social structure.[112] More importantly for legal transplant, the Western

---

[111] For detailed studies of political, economic and social conditions as well as reform movements in China in the late 19th and early 20th centuries, see John K. Fairbank, *The Cambridge History of China*, vol. 10, Late Ch'ing, 1800–1911, Part I (Cambridge: Cambridge University Press, 1978); John K. Fairbank & Kwang-ching Liu, *The Cambridge History of China*, vol. 11, Late Ch'ing, 1800–1911, Part 2 (Cambridge: Cambridge University Press, 1980); Meribeth E. Cameron, *The Reform Movement in China 1898–1912* (New York: Octagon Books, 1963); Immanuel C.Y. Hsü, *The Rise of Modern China*, 5th ed, (New York: Oxford University Press, 1995). For a collection of original documents (including edicts, orders, submissions, draft documents etc.), see Xia Xinhua & Hu Xucheng (eds), *Modern Chinese Constitutional Movements: A Collection of Historical Records* (*Jindai Zhongguo Xianzheng Licheng: Shiliao Huicui*) (Beijing: Press of China University of Political Science and Law, 2004).

[112] M.J. Meijer, *Marriage Law and Policy in the Chinese People's Republic* (Hong Kong: Hong Kong University Press, 1971), at 21.

Powers' promise to relinquish extra-territorial rights and to assist in law reform along western lines propelled a concentrated effort to adopt or adapt Western law at the turn of the 20th century.[113]

In January 1901 the Empress Dowager, then in exile in Xi'an while the Western powers occupied the capital Beijing, issued an edict appealing to high officials in the Imperial Court and provinces for suggestions for the reform of Chinese law along the lines of Western models.[114] In March 1902, the Imperial Court again appealed to all ambassadors residing abroad to examine the laws in various countries and report back to the Ministry of Foreign Affairs.[115] In May 1902, Shen Chia-pen (Shen Jiaben), Junior Vice-President of the Board of Punishments,[116] and Wu T'ing-fang (Wu Tingfang), a former ambassador to the United States,[117] were appointed by the Imperial Court to carefully examine and re-edit all the laws then in force, to bring them into accord with the conditions resulting from international commercial negotiations, to consult the laws of various countries, and to ensure that new laws would be commonly applicable to both Chinese and foreigners and for the benefit of the Government.[118] In May 1904, a Law Codification Commission was established – an event seen by a former Chinese judge at the Permanent Court of International Justice, Tien-Hsi Cheng, as the commencement of a new era.[119] Shen and Wu were appointed commissioners to the Commission.[120]

---

113 See Tay, *supra* note 100, at 163.

114 For an English translation of the Edict, see Cameron, *supra* note 111, at 57-58. For a full text in Chinese, see Xia & Hu, *supra* note 111, at 35-36.

115 For an English translation of the Imperial Edict, see M.J. Meijer, *The Introduction of Modern Criminal Law in China*, 2nd edition (Hong Kong: Lung Men Bookstore, 1967), at 10.

116 For a brief biographical background on Shen Chia-pen, see *Chinese Encyclopaedia*, *supra* note 15, at 525-526; and China University of Political Science and Law, *A Study on the Legal Thought of Shen Jiaben* (*Shen Jiaben Falü Sixiang Yanjiu*) (Beijing: Publishing House of Law, 1990).

117 For a brief biographical background on Wu T'ing-fang, see *Chinese Encyclopedia – Law*, *id.*, at 627.

118 For a Chinese text of the Edict, see Yang Hunglieh, *A History of Chinese Legal Thought* (*Zhongguo Falü Sixiangshi*), vol. II (Beijing: Commercial Publishing House, 1937), reprinted by Shanghai Publishing House, 1984, at 305; for an English translation of the Edict, see Meijer, *supra* note 115, at 10-11.

119 Tien-Hsi Cheng, 'The Development and Reform of Chinese Law', 1948 (1) *Current Legal Problems* 170, at 179.

120 Although Wu was appointed commissioner, he became vice-president of the Board of Commerce soon after his return from overseas. His position as commissioner passed to Ying Jui (Ying Rui), but Ying died soon after his appointment. This position was then taken up by Yü Liensan (Yu Liansan), an ex-governor of Shanxi. Therefore, it was Shen Chia-pen who played the major role in the Law Codification Commission. See Zhang Jinfan, 'On the Legal Thought of Shen Jiaben – Part II', (no. 5, 1981) *Studies in Law* (*Faxue Yanjiu*), at 47.

At the same time constitutional reform also began, aimed at transforming the autocratic empire into a constitutional monarchy. In 1905 a commission was despatched to Japan, Europe and the United States to study constitutional methods in various countries.[121] On the commission's return in 1906 it recommended that the Japanese model be adopted as the two countries had many comparable conditions,[122] and an imperial decree was subsequently issued commanding high officials to prepare for a constitutional government.[123] In 1907 a constitutional committee, named the Committee for Investigating and Drawing up Regulations of Constitutional Government (*Xianzhen Biancha Guan*) was established.[124] In the following years until the final collapse of the Qing Dynasty in 1912, a series of edicts concerning the establishment of a constitutional government and a series of constitutional projects and documents were issued by the Throne.[125]

3.2. An Overview of the Reform

With the establishment of the Law Codification Commission the reform of Chinese law and the study of foreign law became a 'new cause' for the Imperial Court.[126] A two-stage approach was taken by the Commission. The first stage was to revise the old law, with a focus on abolishing the cruel punishments which then existed. This revision was to serve a two-fold purpose: to pave the way for the transition from traditional law to modern Western law; and to respond to Western criticisms on the cruelty of certain provisions in traditional Chinese law as reflected in the Great Qing Code (*Ta Ch'ing Lü Li*). In particular, the Commission was fully aware of the possibility of strong opposition towards such a transition, and thus of the need for measures to prepare the people for the introduction of modern Western laws into China.[127] The revision was done very swiftly and abolition of cruel punishment

---

121 H.G.W. Woodhead (ed.), *The China Year Book 1925–1926* (Tientsin: Tientsin Press Limited), at 615. See further discussions in Chapter 3.

122 Cameron, *supra* note 111, at 102.

123 An English translation of the Decree can be found in Cameron, *supra* note 111, at 103.

124 This Committee was re-organised on the basis of a previous committee, the Committee for Studying the Ways of Government (*Kaocha Zhenzhi Guan*), established in late 1905, see Meijer (1967), *supra* note 115, 40-41.

125 English texts of many of these edicts concerning the establishment of Western-style parliament can be found in Hawking L. Yen, *A Survey of Constitutional Development in China* (New York: AMS Press, 1968); these constitutional documents included Principles of Constitution (1908), Nine Year Programs of Constitutional Preparation (1908), A Three-Year Program of Constitutional Preparation (1911), A Constitutional Framework (1911), and Nineteen Articles of Constitution (1911). English translations of these documents can be found in *China Year Book 1925–1926*, *supra* note 121. See also further discussions in Chapter 3.

126 Yang Hunglieh, *supra* note 118, at 305.

127 See Meijer, *supra* note 115, at 14-15.

and reform of the police and prison systems were all carried out between 1902 and 1907.[128] By 1910 the very ancient *Ta Ch'ing Lü Li* had been completely revised and re-promulgated as a 'Current Criminal Code',[129] to serve as a transitional code before the promulgation of a new one.[130]

The second-stage reform, the making of new codes in line with Western laws, was carried out almost simultaneously, although the codes were only to be implemented after an unspecified transitional period. Thus within the space of a few years several new codes were drafted and issued: the General Principles for Merchants, the Company Law, and the Bankruptcy Law were promulgated in 1903;[131] the Law for the Organisation of the Supreme Court was issued in 1906, and in 1910 the Law for the Organisation of the Courts was also promulgated. The latter two laws established a judicature system separate from administrative organs.[132] Drafts of codes on criminal and civil procedural law, commercial law, civil law, as well as a new criminal code were all completed between 1910 and 1912.[133] Many foreign codes were translated into Chinese.[134] Finally, a modern law school was established in Beijing with the Japanese scholars, Dr. Okada Asataro and Dr. Matsuoka Yoshitada, as principal lecturers teaching several hundred students in 1906.[135] It is particularly worth noting that the Draft Law Governing Procedures in Civil and Criminal Cases, presented to the Throne in April 1906, attempted for the first time in Chinese history to distinguish civil from criminal cases, and such a distinction was finally established when the above-mentioned 'Current Criminal Code' was issued in 1910.[136]

---

128 For detailed studies of the revisions, see Meijer (1967), *supra* note 115, ch. 2.

129 Zhang Jinfan (1986), *supra* note 16, at 340.

130 Beijing University (ed.), *Chinese Legal History* (*Zhongguo Fazhi Shi*) (Beijing: Beijing University Press, 1979), vol. 2, at 39.

131 Zhang Jinfan (1986), *supra* note 16, at 341.

132 Zhang Jinfan, *id.*, at 342.

133 Zhang Jinfan, *id.*, at 339-342.

134 According to Chinese scholars, more than thirty codes were translated: Zhang Jinfan (1986), *supra* note 16, at 346. These codes included the German Criminal Law and Law of Civil Procedure; the Russian Criminal Law; the Japanese Criminal Law in Force, Revised Criminal Law, Criminal Law of the Army, Criminal Law of the Navy, Criminal Procedural Law, Prison Law, Law of Judicial Organisation, Explanation of Meanings in the Criminal Law; and the French Criminal Law. English and American criminal laws were also compiled and translated by the Law Codification Commission. See Memorial of Shen Chia-pen Concerning the Deletion of Severe Punishments in Old Laws, in Yang Hunglieh, *supra* note 118, at 307; an English translation of the Memorial can be found in Meijer (1967), *supra* note 115, 163. According to Chinese scholars, the German Civil Code, the Italian Criminal Law, the Finnish Criminal Law, and the American procedural laws were also translated. See Zhang Jinfan (1986), *supra* note 16, at 346.

135 Yang Hunglieh, *supra* note 118, at 321-322.

136 See Meijer, *supra* note 16, at 43-53.

In the first few years the law reform was focused on the area of criminal law while private law was totally ignored. The reform of civil law did not begin until 1907 when the above-mentioned constitutional committee was established and a general plan of codification was drawn up by the newly re-organised Committee for the Revision of Laws (*Falü Xiuding Guan*).[137] Under this general plan a civil code in five books was to be drafted. The Japanese scholar, Dr. Matsuoka Yoshitada, was put in charge of drafting the first three Books (General Principles, Obligations, and Rights *in rem*), and the Chinese scholars Chu Hsienwen (Zhu Xienwen) and Kao Chungho (Gao Zhonghe) of drafting the last two Books (Family and Succession).[138] The draft of the whole civil code was completed by 1911. Thus, with borrowings from Western legal institutions, the first draft in China's history of a distinct civil code came into being, though it was never promulgated.

3.3. The Choice of Foreign Model

The Qing reform, particularly in the second stage, thus began a process of westernisation of Chinese law. As mentioned above,[139] Japan was recommended by the commission despatched to study constitutional methods in various countries as a model for this process. The choice of Japan was no accident. Japan's success in reversing extra-territoriality and in becoming a mighty power in the Asian area was seen to be a result of its having a constitution and a legal system based on Western models. The similarity of the two countries in historical, ideological, and cultural features as well as in written language was seen as a further reason for the emulation of the Japanese model.[140] These factors prompted the concentrated study of Japanese law, including the translation of a large number of Japanese codes, and many young scholars went to Japan to study law, among other disciplines, well before legal reform started.[141] Thus there was a pool of Japan-trained scholars available and

---

137 Escarra, *supra* note 2, at 154.

138 Chang Hanchu, *A History of the Modern Chinese Legal System* (*Zhongguo Jindai Fazhishi*) (Taipei: The Commercial Press, 1973), at 34.

139 *Supra* note 122.

140 Foo Ping-sheung, 'Introduction', in *The Civil Code of the Republic of China* (Shanghai: Kelly & Walsh, Ltd., 1930), at xi; F.T. Cheng, 'Law Codification in China', 1924 (6) *J. of Comp. Leg.* 283, at 285; Li Guilian, 'Legal Reforms in Modern China and the Japanese Influence', (no. 1, 1994) *Studies in Comparative Law* (*Bijiaofa Yanjiu*) 24.

141 Li Guilian, *ibid*. It is difficult to determine the exact number of students studying law in Japan. According to some recent studies it is clear that the overwhelming majority of students who went abroad at the turn of the 20th century went to Japan and a majority of these studied law there. See Zhou Yiliang (ed.), *A History of Sino-Japan Cultural Exchange* (*Zhong Ri Wenhua Jiaoliu Shi Daxi*) vol. 2 (*Legal System*) (*Fazhi Juan*) (Hangzhou: Zhejiang People's Press, 1996), at 207; Hao Tiechuan, 'Law Students Studying Abroad in Modern Chinese History and the Modernisation of Chinese Law', (no. 6, 1997) *CASS Journal of Law* (*Faxue Yanjiu*) 3.

in favour of emulating the Japanese legal system. Also important is the fact that the Continental European, mainly German, system, which the Japanese legal system was modelled on, was seen as a form of Western jurisprudence that had been tested in an oriental society.[142]

Little attention was given to Common law by the early reformers. This neglect can be attributed to many causes. Technically, as Roscoe Pound has pointed out, materials in Common law are too unsystematic, too bulky, and too scattered, and its technique is too hard to acquire, to make its adoption possible.[143] More fundamentally, the early Romanist Continental law was based on the central concept of two authorities, that of the state over the citizen and that of the *pater familias* over his dependents.[144] This concept fitted well into the traditional Chinese conception of law and the prevailing social conditions. As one of the early authorities on Chinese law has observed:

> Anglo-American law emphasises the individual as against the family, while the Continental system inherits something of the old Roman *familia*. The unit of Chinese society being the family, reform naturally seeks to preserve this institution and to modernise it as far as possible.[145]

Moreover, the concept of state authority over its citizens as inherited from Roman law also fitted well into the ultimate goals of legal reform: to secure the emperor's position permanently, to ameliorate foreign aggression and to quell internal disturbance.[146]

3.4. The Persistence of Conservatism

Clearly the introduction of Western law was going to further undermine the structures and the values of traditional China. This was hardly the intention of the high officials who advised the Throne to undertake constitutional and legal

---

142 Cheng Hanchu, *supra* note 138, at 285. For a more detailed study of Japanese influence on early Chinese legal reform, see Zhou Yiliang, *id.*, chs. 7 & 8.

143 See Roscoe Pound, 'The Chinese Civil Code in Action', 1955 (29) *Tulane L. Rev.* 277, at 289.

144 Alice E.-S. Tay and Eugene Kamenka, 'Public Law – Private Law', in S.I. Benn & G.F. Gaus (eds.), *Public and Private in Social Life* (London/New York: Croom Helm St. Martin's Press, 1983), at 68.

145 Wang Chung-hui, 'Legal Reform in China', in *Chinese Social and Political Review*, June 1917, quoted in Cameron, *supra* note 111, at 174.

146 See the Report on Constitutional Government by the Commissioner (Zai Ze) for Investigating Foreign Government. For a full text of the report in Chinese, see Xia & Hu, *supra* note 111, at 40-42. Zai Ze is seen as the 'architect' of the Qing constitutional reform (Xia & Hu, *id.*, at 40).

reforms. It is therefore not surprising that the Qing reforms met strong opposition from within the Imperial Court.

Shen Jiaben apparently recognised the possible opposition to his reform. He was thus cautious in approaching the reform by dividing it into a two-stage process. He was apparently also cautious in appointing foreign experts in drafting new codes. Thus in drafting the civil code he only appointed one Japanese scholar to draft the general principles, obligations and rights *in rem* – legal areas that were not clearly codified in traditional Chinese law – but left the more traditional topics of family and succession to be drafted by Chinese scholars.[147] Mere precautions, however, did not stop fierce opposition to his reform. Indeed, virtually every major reform introduced by the Law Codification Commission, including the establishment of an independent judiciary, the introduction of procedural laws, and the revision of criminal laws was opposed by high officials, including Zhang Zhitong (Zhang Chih-tung), one of the three high officials who nominated Shen Jiaben for appointment to the Commission. Fundamentally, the reforms were seen as challenging the traditional institutions and structures, ignoring the traditional values as embodied in Confucian *li*, and undermining the social foundation built on centuries-old social morality and customs.[148] To the opponents to the reforms legal reforms were inevitable, but they had to be built upon Confucian doctrines of virtue, loyalty and filial piety.[149] Clearly, without a revolution in ideology, the reform was not going to succeed.

4. The Continuing Reform under the KMT – The Modernisation of Chinese Law

4.1. An Overview – the Continuity of Reform

The belated Qing reform efforts did not save the Dynasty; a Republic was established in 1912 by the revolutionaries led by Sun Yatsen. Although it overthrew the Dynasty, the Republican government allowed the continued use of the Qing laws: all imperial laws formerly in force were repeatedly declared to remain effective unless they were modified by new laws or were contrary to the principles of the Republic.[150]

---

147 See *supra* note 138.

148 See Meijer (1967), *supra* note 115, chs. 2 & 5; Guo Chengwei, 'Legal Thought of Shen Jiaben and the Controversies during the Qing Legal Reform', in *A Study on the Legal Thought of Shen Jiaben*, *supra* note 116, at 103-121.

149 Meijer (1967), *supra* note 115, at 44.

150 See Presidential Decree of March 10, 1912, in Escarra, *supra* note 2, at 169; Resolution of the Provisional Government of April 3, 1912, in Zhang Jinfan (1986), *supra* note 16, at 394; and Resolution of the Central Political Council (*Zhongyan Zhengzhi Huiyi*) of 1927, in Meredith P.

The legitimacy of the Republic was built upon revolutionary ideas and thus the need for continuing legal reform was assumed. Despite frequent changes of government and constitutions in the early period of the Republic,[151] the legal reform efforts of the late Qing were not abandoned. They were in fact greatly accelerated after the establishment of the Nationalist Government in Nanking (Nanjing) in 1927. An extensive program of legislation by the Kuomintang (KMT) government was carried out, in which draft codes prepared during the Qing reform were re-examined, revised and in some cases promulgated after re-evaluation in accordance with KMT guiding ideology.[152] This continuation of the Qing reform also meant the continuation of westernisation of Chinese law along the lines of the Continental European models. When the reform ultimately resulted in the 'Six Codes' of the Republic,[153] together with the establishment of a Continental-style judicial system in China, Chinese law was transformed and began to be Western law in its form, terminology, and notions.[154] Since then Continental European models have been firmly embedded in Chinese law and law reforms, despite differences in ideologies and political principles.

4.2. Guiding Principles – San Min Zhu Yi

However, KMT laws were made in accordance with some unique political principles – those of the *San Min Chu I* (*San Min Zhu Yi*) of Dr. Sun Yatsen. These principles are often translated into English as the Three Principles of the People – National-

Gilpatrick, 'The Status of Law and Law-making Procedures Under the Kuomintang 1925–46', 1950–1951 (10) *Far Eastern Q.* 39, at 45.

151 For discussions of changes in government, see Ch'ien Tuan-Sheng, *The Government and Politics of China* (Cambridge: Harvard University Press, 1950), at 57-69; and William L. Tung, *The Political Institutions of Modern China* (The Hague: Martinus Nijhoff, 1964), at 22-117. For a history of the making of the Constitution under the Republic, see W.Y. Tsao, *The Constitutional Structure of Modern China* (Melbourne: Melbourne University Press, 1947), at 1-22; and Pan Wei-Tung, *The Chinese Constitution: A Study of Forty Years of Constitution-making in China* (Washington: Institute of Chinese Culture, 1954).

152 For detailed studies of legislation by the KMT, see Escarra, *supra* note 2, particularly at 152-346; Meijer, *supra* note 115; Roscoe Pound, 'Law and Courts in China: Progress in the Administration of Justice', 1948 (34) *ABAJ* 273. For a historical study of KMT laws in the Chinese language, see Chang Hanchu, *supra* note 138, particularly ch. 7.

153 The term 'Six Codes' does not necessarily connote six separate codes, but is often used to mean the collective body of laws of the KMT Government. See *Chinese Encyclopedia – Law*, *supra* note 15, at 393.

154 Tay, *supra* note 100, at 164.

ism (*Minzu*), Democracy (*Minquan*)[155] and People's Livelihood (*Minsheng*).[156] They laid down the ideological and theoretical foundation of KMT laws and were institutionalised in all KMT constitutional documents.[157]

In general, the doctrine of nationalism meant the reconstruction of China into a unified state internally and a strong country on an equal footing with other nations externally; the doctrine of people's sovereignty (democracy) was the practice of Western democratic ideas within a Chinese context; and the doctrine of people's livelihood referred to the establishment of a welfare system for the nation and an improvement in the life of the masses, mainly by means of equalisation of land ownership and control of capital.

Although Dr. Sun saw his *San Min Chu I* as being equivalent to government 'of the people, by the people, and for the people' as declared by President Abraham Lincoln in his famous Gettysburg Address,[158] and he compared his doctrine with the catchwords of the French Revolution – Liberty, Equality, and Fraternity,[159] his doctrines were both authoritarian and instrumentalist. He said:

> Although democratic ideas came to us from Europe and America, yet the administration of democracy has not been successfully worked out there. We know a way now to make use of democracy and we know how to change the attitude of people towards government, but yet the majority of people are without vision. We who have prevision must lead them and guide them into the right way if we want to escape the confusions of Western democracy and not follow in the tracks of the West.[160]

---

155 *Minquan* literally means people's sovereignty or people's rights. However, as Dr. Sun Yatsen mainly referred to the issue of democracy when he was talking about *Minquan*, the term has thus more often been translated as 'democracy'.

156 The principal means of Dr. Sun Yatsen for elaborating his theory of *San Min Chu I* were his lectures delivered in 1924 to popular audiences: Sun Yatsen, *The Three Principles of the People: San Min Chu I* (With two supplementary chapters by Chiang Kai-shek) (Taipei: China Publishing Co., undated). For some English studies on *San Min Chu I*, see e.g. Paul M. A. Linebarger, *The Political Doctrine of Sun Yat-sen: An Exposition of the San Min Chu I* (Baltimore: John Hopkins University Press, 1937); and Chu-yuan Cheng (ed.), *Sun Yat-sen's Doctrine in the Modern World* (Doulder/London: Westview Press, 1989).

157 See the Preamble of the Organic Law of the National Government of China (October 4, 1928); the Preamble of the Provisional Constitution of the Republic of China for the Period of Political Tutelage (June 1, 1931), and Article 1 of the Constitution of the Republic of China (December 25, 1946). The Organic Law and the Provisional Constitution can be found in Pan Wei-tung, *supra* note 151, at 241 and 247 respectively; and the Constitution can be found in W.Y. Tsao, *supra* note 151, at 275.

158 Sun Yatsen, *Fundamentals of National Reconstruction* (published by China Culture Service and printed by Sino-America Publishing Co. Ltd., Taipei, 1953), at 43.

159 Sun Yatsen, *supra* note 156, at 77.

160 *Id.*, at 128-129.

Indeed, Dr. Sun divided mankind into three groups on the basis of the individual's natural intelligence and ability: those to guide, those to follow and those to be guided.[161] Individuals, according to him, 'should not have too much liberty, but the nation should have complete liberty.'[162]

The application of Sun's political doctrines in KMT law-making and their implications for KMT law were clearly explained by the first president of the Legislative *Yuan*, Mr. Hu Han-min, in his speech at the opening of the Legislative *Yuan* in November 1928.[163] This speech was seen as laying down the guiding principles of KMT legislation.[164]

According to Hu Han-min, *San Min Chu I* legislation was a revolutionary legislation which was both progressive and creative. Compared with traditional Chinese law, *San Min Chu I* legislation was designed to protect national interests in place of the family and clan system; to safeguard all new organisations which protected the national spirit, democratic ideas and happiness of the people instead of the autocratic monarchy; and to promote a national economy based on both industry and agriculture instead of a family economy based solely on agriculture. *San Min Chu I* legislation also separated private law from public law. Unlike Western laws, it was designed primarily to protect social interests as a whole rather than individual freedoms and private interests. According to Hu Han-min, a legal system [that is the Western legal system] which took individuals as its basic unit was more backward than the Chinese traditional legal system for which the family and clan were the basic units. This Western law was even more backward when compared with *San Min Chu I* legislation, which took the society as the basic unit.[165] Individuals were to be protected, not because of concern for the safety of individuals, but for the safety of the society.[166] The guiding principles of *San Min Chu I* legislation were to maintain social stability, to protect economic development and to adjust and balance social interests.[167]

The implementation of KMT ideology was carried out through the Party, which controlled the making of law. The making of the Civil Code clearly illustrates this practice. Drafting members of the Civil Codification Commission first formulated fundamental points of law in the form of 'preliminary questions of law' for the Legisla-

---

161 See *id.*, at 115.

162 *Id.*, at 76.

163 The full text of the speech was printed in the *Journal of the Legislative Yuan* (*Li-fa Ch'uan K'an*), vol. 1, 1929, 1-13.

164 See Escarra, *supra* note 2, at 200-201; M.H. van der Valk, *An Outline of Modern Chinese Family Law* (Peking: Henri Vetch, 1939, reprinted by Ch'eng Wen Publishing Co., Taipei, 1969), at 45-49.

165 Hu Han-min, *supra* note 163, at 4-6.

166 *Id.*, at 9.

167 *Id.*, at 11.

tive *Yuan,* which in turn submitted them to the Central Political Council. Within the Council, the 'preliminary questions' were first discussed by the Council and then transmitted to the Legal Department within the Council for further examination. After this they were returned to the Council with a statement of opinions and a request for an official decision on the statement. Final decisions were then resolved by the Council in the form of *Li Fa Yuanze* (general principles of legislation). Final drafts of the code were first presented for approval to the Central Executive Committee of the KMT (of which the Central Political Council was a permanent organ and the highest authority), before they were submitted to the National Government for adoption and promulgation as required by legislative procedures.[168]

It is also worth noting that KMT law not only incorporated KMT principles, it also created a legal basis for the possible future implementation of KMT principles in further laws and regulations, a practice later also to be found in the PRC. The most obvious example is the registration of land. One of the major goals of the principle of people's livelihood was the equalisation of land ownership. However, when the Civil Code was drawn up land reform could still not be effectively carried out, since the land reform law was not yet enacted. Nevertheless, Article 758 of the Civil Code made registration a compulsory requirement for ownership of immovables. This requirement, according to Hu Han-min, established a legal basis for future land registration legislation. This, in turn, was to serve the KMT land reform policy, which consisted of three elements: equalisation of ownership, land to the tiller, and state ownership of land. Land registration thus served to pave the way for possible future compulsory purchase of land by the government.[169]

4.3. Between Westernisation and Modernisation of Chinese Law

In supporting the *San Min Chu I* as guiding principles for KMT legislation, Hu Han-min seems to have rejected the idea of a wholesale import of foreign laws when he said:

> Those who do not know *San Min Chu I* believe that we should borrow from European and American laws and institutions to make our legislation. That is in truth an error.[170]

However, the actual implementation of these guiding principles seems to have been quite different and much more utilitarian and instrumentalist than he implied. Foo

---

168 See, for example, the making of Book IV, in van der Valk, *supra* note 164, at 54-58, and English translations of Preliminary Questions of Law of the Family and Statement of Opinion on the Preliminary Problems of Family Law, in Appendixes I and III of the same book.

169 See Yang Hunglieh, *supra* note 118, at 353.

170 Hu Han-min, *supra* note 163, at 13.

Ping-sheung, then Chairman of the Civil Codification Commission of the Legislative *Yuan*, later explained:

> Whilst in Europe and America they try to adjust the opposing interests of different classes of [the] population, the *Kuomintang* tries to make the notion of social order prevail. In practice the legal forms through which the conceptions are expressed do not differ, and in order to execute the intention of the Party the Commission had only to combine on that matter precedent derived from various foreign legislations.[171]

The result of the law-making, as illustrated by the Civil Code, was explained by one of the prominent Chinese legal scholars of that time, Dr. John C. H. Wu:

> If the Civil Code is studied carefully from Article 1 to Article 1225, and then compared with the German Civil Code, the Swiss Civil Code and the Swiss Code of Obligations, we will find that ninety-five percent of the provisions [in the KMT Civil Code] have their origin there: they are either copied directly or copied with some changes of expressions [from these foreign codes].[172]

The justification for using foreign laws while upholding the *San Min Chu I* was explained by Dr. Wu. He argued that the *San Min Chu I* legislation was a kind of creative legislation and that creation was nothing more than selection. Therefore, if the choice was appropriate, then selecting foreign laws and making them parts of Chinese law was not an action of simple blind copying of foreign laws. He argued that the prevailing legal thoughts and legislative trends in the West at that time happened to match perfectly the Chinese national sentiments. It was therefore natural for the revolutionary legislators to make selections from among foreign codes.[173]

However, the *San Min Chu I* ideology tilted the process of reform more towards modernisation than total westernisation: Whilst the Qing reform tried to incorporate Western laws by adopting the most recent developments, the Kuomintang took account of many of the latest developments of Western jurisprudence, but only adopted them if they were in harmony with *San Min Chu I* principles. Both had a utilitarian and instrumentalist approach to foreign laws and legal systems. A specific example of the ideological difference in action was in attitudes towards Chinese traditions and customs. Besides its conservative approach to family and succession matters, the Qing reform largely failed to preserve certain ancient and deep-rooted customs, such as the civil law institutions of *Yung-tien* (a long-term lease) and *Dien* (a kind of *usufructuary* mortgage). The Kuomintang Codification

---

171 Foo Ping-sheung, *supra* note 140, at xxi.

172 Cited in Yang Hunglieh, *supra* note 118, at 369.

173 *Id.*, at 369-370.

Commission took a different approach. It believed that in a vast country with a large population it was impossible to impose uniform and detailed rules on every sort of human activity. In cases of the absence of express provisions and expression of intentions of parties, the best interpreter was established local practice.[174] The Kuomintang also took into consideration Chinese traditions and customs in adopting and adapting Western legal doctrines and institutions.[175] The Kuomintang law reform was thus notably more progressive than the late Qing reform in balancing the process of westernisation and modernisation of Chinese law, while preserving Chinese traditions and customs.[176]

That is not to say that KMT law was of a conservative nature. On the contrary, it was the KMT revolutionary ideology that contributed substantially to the introduction of the modern family and succession law in China. One of the key KMT social and political programs of reconstruction was to reform the Chinese family and inheritance system, which was seen as being feudal and backward. The task of the reform was to 'superimpose on the primitive notion of the unity of the clan or the family that of the unity of the nation composed of the whole body of these families and these clans.'[177] Thus the KMT Party Congress of 1924 passed resolutions concerning equality of the sexes.[178] These resolutions, for the first time in Chinese history, formally established equal status for women with men. More and more foreign law provisions, largely attributable to the political ideas of the KMT, were incorporated into Books IV and V (on Family and Succession) of the 1925 Draft. When the KMT Political Council resolved the principles governing family and succession, equality of the sexes was no longer an empty principle: the actual equality of rights in the spheres of economic, political as well as private rights was stressed. In its Resolution, Point III provided that:

> It seems, however, that with regard to the equality of the sexes we should stress the actual situation, such as economic and political equality as well as equality of private rights, rather than appearances.[179]

---

174 Foo Fing-sheung, *supra* note 140, at xvi.

175 For instance, in the case of civil law, two devices were applied in the Code. One was generally to uphold the validity of customs in so far as they were not contrary to public order and good morals; the other was expressly to preserve some traditional legal institutions and customs and practices thereunder. See further discussions in Jianfu Chen, *From Administrative Authorisation to Private Law: A Comparative Perspective of the Developing Civil Law in the PRC* (Dordrecht/Boston/London: Martinus Nijhoff Publishers, 1995), at 25-27.

176 See a detailed discussion in Chen, *id.*, ch. 1.

177 Introduction of the French translation (of the Civil Code), vols. II, III, cited in Escarra, *supra* note 2, at 256.

178 Escarra, *supra* note 2, at 165.

179 For an English translation of the Resolution, see van der Valk, *supra* note 164, at 175-194.

Indeed, such issues as freedom of marriage, common property during marriage, and the equal right of male and female heirs to share inheritance were all addressed in these resolutions. When Books IV and V were drawn up, all the above KMT principles were embedded in the Code, and thus the traditional family system – the basic unit of traditional China – was formally broken, at least on paper.

5. Concluding Remarks

It is clear that modern legal reforms, started by the Qing Dynasty during its dying days and continued by the Nationalist Government, broke down the traditional institutions and structures that had continued for centuries. However, there is no universal agreement on the evaluation of the significance of these reforms and of the continuing influence of the traditional conceptions of law.

For instance, regarding the progress of legislation under the KMT, which clearly was a continuing process from the Qing reform, Pound has remarked:

> Thus in twenty-four years, from the overthrow of the Empire and setting up of the Republic, the work of providing a modern Constitution, modern codes, and a modern organisation of Courts was done, and well done. This would have been a remarkable achievement in any case, seeing that it had to be done with little to build on, by study of foreign institutions and laws and adaptation of new ideas to an old country in a time of profound changes, even if there had been propitious conditions of peace and stability. To do it under the actual conditions is an achievement without parallel.[180]

In contrast, and until quite recently, many scholars in mainland China tended to belittle the achievements of KMT legislation and institution-building, as well as the late Qing reform of law. According to a standard textbook in the 1980s, written jointly by major law institutes and departments in China, the KMT legislation (from 1927 to 1949) was 'a combination of reactionary law inherited from feudal China, bourgeois laws copied from foreign countries and the terrorist policies of a Fascist dictatorship.'[181] The KMT judicature system was labelled as an institution through which property-owners can use reactionary laws to wantonly persecute

---

[180] Pound, *supra* note 152, at 274.

[181] Zhang Jinfan (1986), *supra* note 16, at 422. See also Qiao Congqi, *A Study on Sun Yatsen's Legal Thoughts* (*Sun Zhongsan Falü Shixiang Tixi Yanjiu*) (Beijing: Publishing House of Law, 1992), at 206; Zhang Jinfan (ed.), *A Summary of Research in the History of the Chinese Legal System* (*Zhongguo Fazhishi Yanjiu Zongshu*) (Beijing: Press of Chinese People's University of Public Security, 1990), at 478. The latter is a general report of views expressed in published research, 1949–1989, in the area of Chinese legal history.

the working people.[182] The late Qing reform of law was also described as a 'political hoax' or a 'political farce'.[183]

It seems that criticisms by these scholars from mainland China have been more political than academic,[184] as the scholars have not given due credit to the Qing and KMT efforts in reforming Chinese law and Chinese legal institutions. Pound, on the other hand, seems to have ignored the reality of China under Chiang Kai-shek. Under Chiang China was to become a One-Party-State (*Tang Chih*, *Tang Zhi*), both *de facto* and *de jure*, through the imposition of political tutelage, first announced in 1929 and lasting until 1946 when a Constitution was drawn up.[185] During this period, certain specific writings of Sun Yatsen were declared to have the force of formal law.[186] Law, seen as an instrument for social change, was used largely as a tool for implementing the KMT doctrines and goals. Moreover, the KMT law and legal institutions were far from reaching the Chinese people and had no substantial impact on the society at large.[187]

These legal reforms have to be assessed from a historical perspective: They introduced, for the first time, Western law and legal systems into China. As a result, they broke down traditional systems, values and practices and separated private law from public law, civil law from criminal law, and the legal system from the administrative hierarchy. Most importantly, they laid down a foundation for Western law and legal systems to be further studied, developed and adapted in China. In this sense, the late Qing and KMT legal reforms may well be said to have brought

---

182 Zhang Jinfan (1986), *supra* note 16, at 448.

183 *Id.*, at 332; Zhang Jinfan (1990), *supra* note 181, at 414 & 416-417. This attitude began to change in the late 1980s when some scholars began to give limited acknowledgment to the historical contribution of the late Qing and KMT reforms in legal development in China. See e.g. Hua Yougen, 'The Guiding Principles and Ideological Influence of the Qing Draft of a Civil Code', (no. 5, 1988) *Political Science and Law* (*Zhnegzhi Yu Falü*), at 46-48; Xu Lizhi, 'Commercial Legislation in the Late Qing and Its Characteristics', (no. 3, 1989) *Studies in Law* (*Faxue Yanjiu*), at 89-94; A Tao & Zhu Huan, 'The Import of Legal Science in the Late Qing Dynasty and its Historical Significance', (no. 6, 1990) *Journal of China University of Political Science and Law* (*Zhengfa Luntan*), at 52-56; and Jiang Ping & Mi Jian, 'On Civil Law Tradition and Contemporary Chinese Law – Part II', (no. 3, 1993) *Journal of China University of Political Science and Law* (*Zhengfa Luntan*), at 1-8. See also *supra* note 21.

184 Although many academic works have been published on the late Qing and KMT legal reforms in general, little detailed work has been done on specific legislation made during the reforms. There was, until 1990, only one article specifically on the KMT Civil Code (published in *Hebei Law Science* (*Hebei Faxue*), no. 6, 1984) in the PRC. See Zhang Jinfan (1990), *supra* note 181, at 414-491.

185 See Ch'ien Tuan-Sheng, *supra* note 151, at 297; and Paul M.A. Linebarger, *The China of Chiang Kai-shek: A Political Study* (Boston: World Peace Foundation, 1943), at 23-24.

186 Van der Valk, *supra* note 164, at 47.

187 See Tay, *supra* note 100, at 165.

about a revolution in Chinese legal thought and to have provided a foundation upon which modern Chinese law is being developed in the PRC.

The breakdown of the traditional institutions and structures does not, however, necessarily mean the total disappearance of the influence of traditional conceptions of law on contemporary development of law. Indeed, the instrumentalist, utilitarian and authoritarian approach to law and law reform, both under the Qing and the KMT, clearly reflected and continued the influence of the traditional conception of law as an instrument for the authoritarian state, with its focus on state interests as defined by the state itself. It is in this conception of law that we find the link between modern and traditional Chinese law. We will see, in the next chapter, how this has continued throughout the history of the PRC until very recently.

Chapter Two

Experience of Law in the PRC

1. Introduction

The legal history of the PRC did not start in 1949. It is frankly admitted by many Chinese officials and scholars that the legal system of the PRC was established on the basis of the pre-1949 experience of communist justice and on the Soviet model.[1] Soviet influence or Marxist theories of law did not, however, lead to any significant activities in law-making or institution-building in China. Instead, the early communist experience and Soviet practice led, in the first 30 years of communism in China, to not only the use of law as a terrorising means for class struggle, with complete disregard for formal enactments and for formal procedures, but also to the popularisation of justice, to politicisation of law, and to the *ad hoc* nature of legal provisions.[2]

---

1 Dong Biwu (a principal member of the first generation CPC leadership in charge of political and legal work and, later, the President of the Supreme People's Court) in his speech to the Eighth National Congress of the CPC explicitly stated that the establishment of the PRC's legal system was based on the experience of revolutionary justice before 1949 and the Soviet experience of law. See *A Collection of Works of Dong Biwu on Politics and Law* (*Dong Biwu Zhengzhi FalüWenji*) (Beijing: Publishing House of Law, 1986), at 480. Chinese scholars plainly hold the same view. See Zhang Youyu & Wang Shuwen, (eds), *Forty Years of the PRC's Legal Science* (*Zhongguo Faxue Sishi Nian*) (Shanghai: Shanghai People's Publishing House, 1989), *passim*; Zhang Xibao (ed.), *A Legal History of Revolutionary Base Areas* (*Geming Genjudi Fazhi Shi*) (Beijing: Publishing House of Law, 1994), at 1; and Yang Yifan & Chen Hanfeng, *A Legal History of the People's Republic of China* (*Zhonghua Renmin Gongheguo Fazhishi*) (Haerbin: Helongjiang People's Press, 1997), at 2.

2 See an excellent three-part study on Law in Communist China by Alice E-S. Tay, in (1969) 6 *Syd.L.Rev.* 153 (Part 1), (1973–1976) 6 *Syd. L. Rev.* 335 (Part 2); and (1976) 6 *Syd.L.Rev.* 400 (Part 3). See also W.E. Butler (ed.), *The Legal System of the Chinese Soviet Republic 1931–1934* (New York: Transnational Publishers Inc., 1983); Shao-chuan Leng, *Justice in Communist China: A Survey of the Judicial System of the Chinese People's Republic* (New York: Oceana Publications, Inc., 1967); and Shao-chuan Leng & Hungdah Chiu, *Criminal Justice in Post-Mao China: Analysis and Documents* (Albany: State University of New York Press, 1985). See further discussions below.

While the rapid legal development in post-Mao China may have produced an entirely new body of law, the structure, style, terminology and notions of the new laws (with, perhaps, the exception of laws on foreign trade and investment) are no stranger to those who are familiar with the modern legal system established by the Qing and KMT legal reforms. In fact, the pre-1949 experience of communist justice is more relevant in explaining the lawlessness of the first 30 years of the PRC than the present legal developments.[3] It is the reliance on the Soviet experience during the early period of the PRC that has contributed, indirectly, to the continuation of the legal style established during the Qing and KMT reforms. As such and in terms of legislative style, structure and terminology, the present legal development can be seen as a continuing process of modernisation that was started at the turn of the 20th century.[4]

This Chapter will first review, briefly, the communist experience of law before 1949. It will then examine, again briefly, the troubled fate of the law in China under Mao's rule. This is followed by an analysis of the changing perceptions of the role of law in present-day China and the broad trends in the rapid legal developments since the launch of post-Mao reforms in 1978. These analyses will reveal the fundamental features of the contemporary Chinese law and its development since the late 1970s.

2. The Pre-PRC Communist Experience of Law

Chinese communism is associated with peasant revolution and the policy of 'circling the cities from the countryside', although Marxism was upheld as its guiding ideology and the Soviet model was to be followed from its inception. Its origin was the intellectual movement in cities, as part of the search for solutions to China's reform and modernisation. The early leaders of the communist movement in China were all city intellectuals who first accepted and believed in Western constitutionalism but later shifted to the Left. Initially it was the Russian October Revolution that caused the split among intellectuals regarding the pace and path for a Chinese reform. In this sense, the May Fourth Movement of 1919[5] was fundamentally a struggle

---

3 There are disagreements as to the influence of the pre-1949 experience on the legal developments in the first 30 years of the PRC. See Tay (1973), *supra* note 2, at 345.

4 See e.g. He Qinghua & Li Xiuqing, *Foreign Law and Chinese Law – An Examination of Transplanting Foreign Law into China in the 20th Century* (*Zhongguofa Yu Waiguofa – Ershiji Zhongguo Yizhi Waiguofa Fansi*) (Beijing: Press of China University of Political Science and Law, 2003); and Cao Quanlai, *Internationalisation and Localisation: the Formation of the Modern Chinese Legal System* (*Guojihua yu Bentuhua – Zhongguo Jindai falü Tixi de Xingcheng*) (Beijing: Beijing University Press, 2005).

5 The May Fourth Movement, the initial impetus of which was the 1919 Versailles Peace Conference at which the Chinese government failed to stand up to Japan and the West and to obtain

between the 'Russian School' and the 'Western School' of intellectuals and marked the systematic introduction of Marxism to China.[6] Mao and his followers were influenced by the May Fourth Movement, but were not the leaders of it. The early leaders in the communist movement were Chen Duxiu and Li Dazhao, who were supporters of Western constitutionalism but later led the 'Russian School' against the 'Western School' represented by Hu Shi. It was under the strong influence of Chen Duxiu and Li Dazhao that the Communist Party of China (CPC), born in Shanghai in 1921, came to the conclusion that the direction of the Chinese revolution was 'to follow the Russian road'.[7] Dr. Sun Yatsen's acceptance of the Comintern's advice for reform of the Kuomintang (KMT) and the subsequent cooperation between the KMT and the CPC in the first 'United Front' of 1923–1927 further spread Soviet influence in China.[8]

However, massive Soviet influence was only institutionalised after the establishment of a Soviet government in Hailufeng (Haifeng and Lufeng Counties in Guangdong Province) and later in the Chinese Soviet Republic (1931–1934) in Jiangxi Province. The first constitutional document by the CPC, the Constitutional Program of the Chinese Soviet Republic (*Zhonghua Su-Wei-Ai Xianfa Dagang*), issued in November 1931 and revised in January 1934,[9] was, as Hazard has pointed out, a product of a Moscow-derived formula (through the 'Russian returned students', the

---

the nation's due in the First World War settlement, has two aspects. First, it denotes the 'May Fourth Students' National Salvation Movement', a nationwide movement initiated to save China from imperialism and feudalism in 1919. Secondly, it indicates the 'May Fourth New Cultural Movement', an anti-tradition movement which led to strong criticism of the culture, philosophies and traditions of China, and the reform of the written Chinese language from its archaic classical style to the use of the vernacular form. However, these two movements were closely inter-locked under the common theme of science and democracy. See Wang Yanhua, 'Defending the Spirit of the May Fourth Movement', in Lin Yusheng (ed.), *The May Fourth Movement: A Pluralistic Retrospect* (*Wushi: Duoyuan Di Fansi*) (Hong Kong: Joint Publishing Co., 1989), at 1; and Wang Renbo, *Modern China and Its Constitutional Culture* (*Xianzheng Wenhua yu Jindai Zhongguo*) (Beijing: Law Press, 1997), at 385-429.

6 See Wang Dexian, 'The May Fourth Movement and Democratic Constitutionalism', (no. 3, 1989) *Studies in Law* (*Faxue Yanjiu*) 11, at 11-12.

7 *Id.*, at 13.

8 See Immanuel C. Y. Hsü, *The Rise of Modern China*, 5th edition (New York: Oxford University Press, 1995), at 518-531.

9 The main revision was in Article 2, by adding a call for strengthening the alliance with middle-class peasants. See Jiang Bikun, *al et.* (eds), *Constitutional Law (Xinfa Xue)* (Beijing: China University of Political Science and Law, 1993), at 59; and Zhang Jinfan (ed.), *A History of the Chinese Legal System* (*Zhonggu Fazhi Shi*) (Beijing: Press of the Masses, 1982), at 460. For an English translation of the 1934 revised Constitutional Program, see Butler, *supra* note 2, at 123-125.

'28 Bolsheviks') not of Mao's peasant revolutionary ideas.[10] The provisions of this document were largely copied from the 1918 Constitution of the Soviet Federated Socialist Republics and the Soviet influence was described as 'overpowering'.[11] Although it is a short document of only 17 articles in total, the basic state system or its variations (i.e. democratic dictatorship of workers and peasants) and the basic state power structure (i.e. the All Chinese Congress of Soviets of Workers', Peasants', and Soldiers' Deputies) were to be found in later constitutions.

As a peasant revolution, its goals were to confiscate land, to improve the working people's life, and to exterminate 'local bullies' and 'bad gentry'.[12] These goals were, however, not to be achieved through constitutional methods, but through ruthless violence and terror as Mao clearly spelt out in describing the basic spirit of the revolution:

> ... a revolution is not the same as inviting people to dinner, or writing an essay, or painting a picture, or doing fancy needlework. ... A revolution is an uprising, an act of violence whereby one class overthrows another. A rural revolution is a revolution by which the peasantry overthrows the authority of the feudal landlord class. ... To put it bluntly, it was necessary to bring about a brief reign of terror in every rural area; otherwise one could never suppress the activities of the counter-revolutionaries in the countryside or overthrow the authority of the gentry. To right a wrong it is necessary to exceed the proper limits and the wrong cannot be righted without the proper limits being exceeded.[13]

Thus terror and excesses against the landlords and 'counter-revolutionaries' became the marked features of the beginning of revolutionary justice.

The Japanese invasion in 1937 led to the second 'United Front' with the Kuomintang, during which time the areas controlled by the Communist Party were, theoretically, a part of the KMT Government.[14] By then, the CPC's policy was 'to

---

10 For detailed discussions, see John N. Hazard, 'The Experience with Constitutionalism', in Butler, *supra* note 2, at 21-45. See also William B. Simons, 'Reflections on State Administration in the Chinese Soviet Republic and the Soviet Union', in Butler, *id.*, at 47-52.

11 Hazard, *id.*, at 44.

12 Leng, *supra* note 2, at 2.

13 Quoted in Leng, *supra* note 2, at 2.

14 The Preamble of the Program of Government of the Shan-Gan-Ning Border Area During the Anti-Japanese War (*Shan-Gan-Ning Bianqu Kangzhan Shiqi Shizheng Gangling*) issued in 1939, for instance, specifically declared that the Border Area was to be under the leadership of the KMT Government and Jiang Kaishek. The text of the Program can be found in the South-West Institute of Political Science and Law (ed.), *A Selection of Materials on Legal Construction during the New Democratic Period* (*Zhongguo Xin Minzhu Zhuyi Geming Shiqi Fazhi Jianshe Ziliao Xuanbian*), Vol. I (Chongqing: South-West Institute of Political Science and Law, 1982), at 8-10. See also Leng, *supra* note 2, at 11.

facilitate the overall task of uniting to resist Japan'.[15] Laws applied during the period were comparatively moderate and in some cases KMT codes were simply adopted for application in the Border Area. The Program of Government also reflected the same policy. Thus private property was to be protected, private enterprise to be promoted, and human rights, both political and economic rights and all political freedoms were to be accorded to all people (including the landlords and capitalists) who opposed the Japanese invasion.[16] Thus some Chinese scholars hold that the period of the Shan-Gan-Ning Border Area represents the best of the pre-1949 communist experience of law.[17]

The victory over the Japanese also spelt the end of the second 'United Front'. By now both the KMT and the CPC were ready and determined to conquer the whole nation. The Constitutional Principles of the Shan-Gan-Ning Border Area (*San-Gan-Ning Bianqu Xianfa Yuanze*) of 1946,[18] the third and final constitutional document issued by the Communist Party before taking over China from the KMT, clearly reflected a return to the Soviet style of government and constitution. Again, violence and terror often became the pattern of 'people's justice' during this period.[19]

Although the pre-1949 communist legal developments were largely experimental and localised in nature, certain features of 'people's justice' were emerging and being shaped during these years. To start with, the Marxist concept of law as a tool to remould the society and to suppress class enemies, to enforce party policy rather than to protect individual rights, was taking root. Secondly, justice was politicised, such as in the enforcement of 'class justice' in which distinctions in administering justice were made according to class membership. It was also popularised, such as in the implementation of a 'mass line' under which mass trials were organised, not so much for the administration of justice but for political education and indoctrination. Thirdly, extrajudicial organisations and procedures and extralegal measures were often utilised to impose sanctions and to settle disputes.[20] These

---

15 Mao Zedong, 'The Task of the Chinese Communist Party in the Period of Resistance against Japan', in *Selected Works of Mao Tse-tung*, vol. III (Beijing: Foreign Languages Press, 1975), at 315.

16 Jiang Bikun, *supra* note 9, at 60; Zhang Jinfan (1982), *supra* note 9, at 187-189.

17 Zhang Jinfan, *et al.* (eds), *A Summary of Research in the History of the Legal System* (*Zhongguo Fazhishi Yanjiu Zongshu*) (Beijing: Press of Chinese People's University of Public Security, 1990), at 495.

18 This document served only for a short period as a provisional constitution. It was soon superseded by Government Programs issued by various Liberated Areas. See Zhang Jinfan (1982), *supra* note 9, at 513.

19 Leng, *supra* note 2, at 21.

20 See Leng, *supra* note 2, ch. 1; Tay (1969), *supra* note 2, at 165-72; and James P. Brady, *Justice and Politics in People's China: Legal Order or Continuing Revolution?* (London/New York: Academic Press, 1982), ch. 4.

features were to re-appear, from time to time, for the next 30 years in the PRC under Mao's leadership.

3. The Triumph of Ideology

Unlike the KMT, which overthrew the Qing Dynasty but allowed the continuation of its legal order, the People's Republic of China was determined not only to end the KMT's political rule, but also to dismantle the KMT's legal system and to abolish the KMT codes.

The intention to abolish KMT laws was first announced by Mao Zedong on 14th January 1949 as one of the eight fundamental conditions for a negotiation with the KMT to stop the civil war which followed the Japanese defeat in 1945.[21] The CPC insisted that the Constitution of the KMT Government as well as 'all reactionary laws and decrees' were to be abolished and a new constitution by a New Political Consultative Conference and the Democratic Coalition Government was to be formulated and promulgated.[22]

Neither the Statement by Mao, nor the draft Agreement, contained any explanation for the insistence on abolishing the KMT laws. This was to be found in an 'Instruction of the Central Committee of the CPC to Abolish the Kuomintang Six Codes and to Define the Judicial Principles for the Liberated Areas' issued in February 1949.[23] Item Two of the Instruction stated that:

> Law is the will of the state compulsorily and openly enforced through military forces by the ruling class. Law, like the state, is a tool for the protection of the interests of certain ruling classes. The Six Codes of the Kuomintang, like bourgeois law in general, were framed in such a way as to conceal their class character. But in reality, since there can be no state above classes, there certainly can be no law above classes. Like bourgeois law generally, the Six Codes give the appearance that people are all equal before the law. But in reality, since there can be no real common interests between the ruling classes and the ruled, between the exploiting classes and the exploited, between the appropriator and the expropriated, between the

21 'Statement on the Present Situation by Mao Tse-tung, Chairman of the Central Committee of the Communist Party of China', in *Selected Works of Mao Tse-tung*, vol. IV (Beijing: Foreign Languages Press, 1975), at 315-319.

22 See Articles 3-6 of the draft Agreement on Internal Peace, in *Selected Works of Mao Tse-tung*, *id.*, at 390-396.

23 For a full Chinese text of the Instruction, see *Reference Materials on Basic Legal Theories* (*Faxue Jichu Lilun Bufen Cankao Ziliao*) (edited and published by North-West Institute of Political Science and Law, 1982), at 11-13. For discussions of the Instruction, see Tay (1976) *supra* note 2, at 403-404.

> creditor and the debtor, there certainly can be no real equal legal rights. Thus all Kuomintang laws are nothing but instruments designed to protect the reactionary rule of the landlords, the compradores, the bureaucrats, and the bourgeoisie, and weapons to suppress and coerce the vast masses of the people. ... Therefore, the Six Codes cannot be the applicable law in both the areas controlled by Chiang Kai-shek and the liberated areas.

Together with the abolition of the KMT codes, instructions were also given to the judiciary to change its practice. Item Five of the Instruction continued:

> People's judicial work cannot be based on the Six Codes of the Kuomintang, but should be based on new laws of the people. Before the new laws of the people have been systematically promulgated, people's judicial work shall be based on policies of the Communist Party and various fundamental principles, laws, decrees, resolutions issued by the People's Government and the People's Liberation Army. ... In the meantime, the judicial organs should educate and reform their judicial cadres through scorning and criticising the Six Codes and all laws and decrees of the Kuomintang, all bourgeois anti-people's statutes and laws of Europe, America and Japan, through the learning of attitudes towards state and law of Marxism, Leninism and Mao Zedong Thought, as well as through the learning of policies, fundamental principles, orders, laws, decrees, and resolutions of the New Democracy.

This Instruction was issued as an opinion of the Central Committee of the CPC to governments at different levels and to judicial cadres for further discussion. Opinions and conclusions were sought, but the Instruction was immediately implemented in March 1949 by an 'Order of the North China People's Government to Abolish the Six Codes and All Reactionary Laws'.[24] This Order was identical to the Instruction. In September 1949 it was further implemented by the Common Program of the Chinese People's Political Consultative Conference, a document which served as a provisional constitution until the first constitution of the PRC was promulgated in 1954.[25] This 'Common Program', however, went further in directly and explicitly dismantling the KMT legal system as well.[26] The KMT legal system and its laws were thus abolished for ideological reasons.

---

24 The Order was issued on 31 March 1949. When the People's Republic of China was founded in October 1949, the North China People's Government was replaced by the Central People's Government. A full Chinese text can be found in *A Collection of Works of Dong Biwu on Politics and Law*, *supra* note 1, at 45-47.

25 An English translation of the 'Common Program' can be found in Albert P. Blaustein, (ed.), *Fundamental Legal Documents of Communist China* (New Jersey: Fred B. Rothman & Co., 1962), at 34-53.

26 See Article 17 of the 'Common Program'.

4. Legal Experience under Mao's Leadership

When the KMT legal system and its Six Codes were abolished, this virtually left a legal vacuum in China. The need to make new laws and to establish a new judicial system was recognised by the above mentioned 'Common Program',[27] but the urgency to fill the vacuum was not felt by the authorities in the first three to four years of the PRC. This is partly because of the heavy reliance on the pre-1949 Communist experience of law in which, as discussed above, law was basically used as a political weapon, with the terrorising threat of force, and partly because the first three to four years following the founding of the PRC were still a period for the new government to consolidate its newly-gained power and control over China through political campaigns.[28] Indeed, it was emphasised by some CPC leaders that law was 'an extension of military force',[29] being subordinate to politics,[30] and that judicial tasks were equivalent to those of the army and the police.[31] It was also emphasised that during the transitional period (from New Democracy to Socialism) and before the basic completion of the transformation of private ownership and the full establishment of socialist ownership, it was impossible to make such fundamental laws as a civil code and a criminal code.[32] It is therefore not surprising that during the first three years of the PRC only a handful of laws that were urgently needed for the political transformation of the society and for consolidation of political powers were issued,[33] although during the same period no less than 376 'legal documents' were issued by

---

27 *Ibid.*

28 These campaigns included the Movement to Suppress and Punish Counter-revolutionaries (*Shufan Yundong*, 1949–1952); the 'Three Antis' (anti-corruption, waste and bureaucracy) and 'Five Antis' (anti-bribery, tax evasion, theft of state property, cheating on government contracts, and stealing state economic information) campaigns (1951–1952). For discussions of these political campaigns, see Brady, *supra* note 20, at 74-112; and Bill Brugger, *China: Liberation and Transformation 1942–1962* (London: Croom Helm, 1981), at 50-88.

29 In a speech to cadres attending judicial training courses in 1949, Xie Juepei, who later became the first Minister for Internal Affairs of the PRC, stressed that law was the extension of the army, the state power vested in the organs for punishment. See *Reference Materials on Basic Legal Theories*, *supra* note 23, at 74.

30 Xie in the same speech declared that '[l]aw should provide whatever politics needs, and before the law is made, policies, as usual, should be applied.', *id.*, at 94.

31 See the Instruction of the Government Administration Council to Strengthen People's Judicial Work (3 November 1950), signed by Zhou Enlai, in *Reference Materials on Basic Legal Theories*, *supra* note 23, at 40.

32 Zhou Enlai, 'Government Report to the Fourth Session of the First National People's Congress', (extract), 26 June 1957, in *Selected Materials on Introduction to Law* (*Faxue Gailun Ziliao Xuanbian*) (Beijing: Publishing House of Law, 1984), at 84.

33 These laws included the Marriage Law (1950), the Agrarian Reform Law (1950), the Trade Union Law (1950), Regulations for the Punishment of Counter-revolutionaries (1951), and Regulations for the Punishment of Corruption (1952). See Tay (1976), *supra* note 2, at 406.

various central government departments and commissions.[34] Judicial reform was also carried out for these political purposes, during which former KMT judicial personnel were purged and traditional legal concepts and doctrines, such as the independence of the judiciary, equality before the law, the rule against retroactive application of criminal law, and the maxim *nullum crimen sine lege*, were all repudiated.[35]

Towards the end of 1952 when power consolidation was deemed to have been achieved, the Party appeared to shift its focus towards economic construction. Mao first proposed to the Central Committee of the CPC a general line for the transitional period, and elaborated this in June 1953 at the Politburo of the CPC. This stipulated that:

> During the transition the general line and fundamental task of the Party is to bring about, step by step, over a fairly long period of time the socialist industrialisation of the country and to accomplish, step by step, the socialist transformation of agriculture, handicraft and capitalist industry and commerce.[36]

This policy was first adopted by the Party in 1953[37] and then incorporated into the 1954 Constitution of the PRC.[38] The necessary conditions for a planned economy and a gradual transition to socialism were deemed to have been created after the large-scale political movements in the previous three years.[39] The first Five-Year Plan was thus adopted in 1953.

More important for legal construction was the official recognition by the Party of the inadequacy of the pre-1949 experience of law for the establishment of a socialist legal system. Liu Shaoqi, then the President of the State, in his Report to the Eighth National Congress of the CPC in 1956, said:

> During the period of revolutionary war and in the early days after the liberation of the country, in order to weed out the remnants of our enemies, to suppress the resistance of all counter-revolutionaries, to destroy the reactionary order and to establish a revolutionary order, the only expedient thing to do was to draw up some temporary laws in the nature of general principles in accordance with the policy of the Party and the

---

34 Wu Jianfan, 'Building New China's Legal System', (1983) 22 *Colum. J. Transnat'l L.* 1, at 8.

35 See Tay (1976), *supra* note 2, at 407.

36 *Selected Readings of Mao Zedong's Works* (*Mao Zedong Zhuzuo Xuandu*), vol. 2 (Beijing: People's Press, 1986), at 704.

37 *Ibid.*, see the note accompanied the text.

38 See the Preamble of the 1954 Constitution. An English text of the Constitution can be found in Blaustein, *supra* note 25, at 1-33. The only change in the Constitution was the term 'State', replacing the term 'Party'.

39 See the Preamble of the 1954 Constitution.

> People's Government. During this period, the chief aim of the struggle was to liberate the people from reactionary rule and to free the productive forces of society from the bondage of the old relations of production. The principal method of struggle was to lead the masses in direct action. Such laws in the form of general principles were thus suited to the needs of the time. Now, however, the period of revolutionary storm and stress is past, new relations of production have been set up, and the aim of our struggle is changed into one of safeguarding the successful development of the productive forces of society; a corresponding change in the methods of struggle will consequently have to follow, and a complete legal system has become an absolute necessity.[40]

In the same Report, Liu stressed that one of the urgent tasks of the state was to start systematically making laws and perfecting the legal system.[41] The then President of the Supreme People's Court, Dong Biwu, in his speech to the same Congress, specifically pointed out that:

> The problem today is that we still lack several urgently-needed, fairly complete basic statutes such as a criminal code, a civil code, procedural laws, a labour law, a law governing the use of land and the like.[42]

The first serious efforts to rebuild a legal system and to make comprehensive codes thus began, introducing what the Chinese scholars have called the 'golden period' of the 1950s. As the pre-1949 experience was seen as inappropriate for the prevailing circumstances, Soviet models were taken as the main sources. Indeed, many young students were sent to study in the Soviet Union and many Soviet scholars came to lecture in China. A large number of Soviet law textbooks and codes were also translated into Chinese.[43]

With this policy in place, the Constitution, organic laws for courts and procuracy, as well as regulations on arrest and detention were duly adopted in 1954. Drafting work on major codes, including the civil code and criminal code, also started. Before the completion of these major codes, individual laws, regulations, and decrees, though unsystematic, incoherent and inconsistent, were issued.[44]

---

40 Liu Shaoqi, 'The Political Report of the Central Committee of the CPC to the Eighth National Congress of the Party', in *Selected Works of Liu Shaoqi* (*Liu Shaoqi Xuanji*), vol II (Beijing: People's Press, 1985), at 253.

41 *Ibid.*

42 *A Collection of Works of Dong Biwu on Politics and Law*, *supra* note 1, at 481.

43 By 1957, 165 legal texts and monographs had been translated into Chinese. The great majority were from the Soviet Union. See Zhang & Wang, *supra* note 1, at 5.

44 All together 4,072 individual laws, regulations and decrees were passed from October 1949 to October 1957. See Tay (1976), *supra* note 2, at 411.

The first effort to draft comprehensive codes was abruptly ended by what scholars in China now term 'leftist errors' or a 'communist wind', i.e. the Anti-rightist Movement of 1957 and the 'Great Leap Forward' of 1958.[45] Efforts to develop stable and comprehensive codes were in fact openly criticised. For instance, the then Premier, Zhou Enlai, in a speech made on 16 September 1958, said:

> Why should we proletarians be restrained by laws?! ... Since 1954, emphasis has been put on standardisation and legal institutionalisation of plans through law. This in fact is regularisation. We wrote a large number of regulations and rules which then hindered our development. ... Our law should be developed in pace with the changes of the economic base. Institutions, rules and regulations should not be fixed. We should not be afraid of changes. We have advocated uninterrupted revolutions and the law should be in the service of the continuing revolutions. ... It does not matter if we make a law today and change it tomorrow.[46]

The political climate changed again, however, in 1961. After the disaster of the 'Great Leap Forward', a policy of 'readjusting (*Tiaozheng*), consolidating (*Gonggu*), strengthening (*Chongshi*) and enhancement (*Tigao*)' – a policy basically advocating a better controlled and more realistic economic plan for national economic development and, in today's terminology, economic reform – was adopted by the Party's Central Committee in early 1961. More importantly, at an enlarged meeting of the Central Committee of the CPC in February 1962, the necessity for the development of a commodity economy was recognised.[47] In Communist ideology this meant the need for law and social order.[48] It was under these circumstances that Mao was reported to have said in 1962 that '[l]aw is needed – not only a criminal code, but also a civil code'.[49]

---

45 See Wu Jianfan, *supra* note 34, at 11; Zhang & Wang, *supra* note 1, at 328, and Zhao Zhenjiang, (ed.), *Forty Years of the Chinese Legal System* (*Zhongguo Fazhi Jianshinian*) (Beijing: Beijing University Press, 1990), at 232. For a brief discussion of these movements, see Brugger, *supra* note 28, at 174-206; and Liu Suinian & Wu Qungan, (eds), *China's Socialist Economy: An Outline History (1949–1984)* (Beijing: Beijing Review Press, 1986), at 215-243.

46 A Chinese text of the speech can be found in *Reference Materials on Basic Legal Theories*, *supra* note 23, at 39.

47 Gu Angran, *The Socialist Legal System and Legislative Work* (*Shehui Zhuyi Fazhi He Lifa Gongzuo*) (Beijing: China University of Political Science and Law Press, 1989), at 102.

48 See John Hazard, 'The Abortive Codes of the Pashukanis School', in Donald D. Barry, F.J. M. Feldbrugge & Dominik Lasok, (eds), *Codification in the Communist World* (Leiden: A.W. Sijthoff, 1975), at 145-175.

49 See, for instance, Gu Angran, *supra* note 47, at 102; and Zhang & Wang, *supra* note 1, at 328.

This second effort to make laws and re-build a legal system lasted an even shorter time than the previous one had.[50] It was first interrupted by the so-called 'Four Clean-ups' Movement of 1963–1965 (clean-up of politics, the economy, organisation and ideology, also called 'Socialist Education').[51] This was then followed by the so-called 'Cultural Revolution' of 1966–1976 during which virtually all laws and the entire legal system were destroyed.[52] Personal pronouncements and party policies replaced law. Efforts to draft codes were only resumed after the end of the 'Cultural Revolution'.

While the two attempts at legal development were short-lived, they nevertheless consolidated the Soviet influence, first introduced in the 1930s, in the PRC's legal system. In terms of legislation, the most notable examples of the Soviet influence on specific legislation include the 1954 Constitution, various organic laws governing the National People's Congress, the court and the procuratorate, and the draft codes on criminal law, criminal procedural law, and civil law.[53] Most importantly, as will be shown in chapters below, all of these were to become the foundation upon which post-Mao China has re-established law in contemporary China.

5. Legal Experience in Post-Mao China

5.1. The Need for Law to Institutionalise and Generalise Ad Hoc Policies

1978 is seen by Chinese scholars as a new epoch in modern Chinese history and a turning point in legal development in China. In that year the Third Plenary Session of the Eleventh Central Committee of the CPC declared that large-scale nationwide mass political movements should be stopped and 'the emphasis of the Party's work

50 Therefore no significant laws were issued during these efforts, though some provisional measures or regulations on technical standards, forest protection and economic contracts were issued by the State Council. See Lan Quanpu, *Thirty Years of the Development of Law and Regulations in Our Country* (*Sanshi Nian Lai Woguo Fagui Yange Gaikuang*) (Beijing: Press of the Masses, 1982), at 5-6.

51 For a brief discussion of the political situation during the period between 1962–1965, see Bill Brugger, *China: Radicalism to Revisionism 1962–1979* (London: Croom Helm, 1981), at 21-42.

52 See detailed discussions in Tay (1976), *supra* note 2, at 417-423.

53 Institutionally, the procuratorate system is a distinct Soviet-imported institution that still exists in China. For other specific examples, see Albert Chen, 'Socialist Law, Civil Law, Common Law, and the Classification of Contemporary Chinese Law', in J M Otto, M V Polak, J Chen & Y Li (eds), *Law-Making in the People's Republic of China* (The Hague/London/Boston: Klewer Law International, 2000), at 57-59.

should be shifted to socialist modernisation as of 1979'.[54] A legal system was declared a necessity for socialist modernisation.[55] The then Party leaders also repeatedly emphasised the importance of law for providing a social order conducive to economic development.[56] This was summarised by Deng Xiaoping as a 'Two-Hands' policy: On the one hand, the economy must be developed; and on the other hand, the legal system must be strengthened.[57]

This new policy under the leadership of Deng Xiaoping thus apparently differed greatly from the practice under Mao's leadership. As discussed above, in the early part of the PRC's history under Mao (1949–1976), China was a country virtually without law or a legal system. Law under Mao's leadership did not 'wither away'[58] – there was little law to wither away – but was simply denounced and rejected. Under Deng's leadership in the 1980s and 1990s, in sharp contrast, China witnessed the massive and rapid enactment of laws and regulations, particularly laws and administrative rules regulating economic and commercial relations.[59] However one must not be misled by this apparent difference.

The changing fate of law was based directly on the need, as perceived by the Party leadership, for national development. Mao not only said that '[we must] depend on

---

54 See the Communiqué of the Third Plenary Session of the Eleventh Central Committee of the CPC. An English translation of the Communiqué appears in Liu & Wu, *supra* note 45, at 564-577.

55 *Id.*, at 573.

56 See e.g. Ye Jianying, then Chairman of the Standing Committee of the NPC, 'Opening Speech at the Second Session of the Fifth National People's Congress on June 18, 1979', in *Main Documents of the Second Session of the Fifth National People's Congress of the People's Republic of China* (Beijing: Foreign Languages Press, 1979), at 3; and Hua Guofeng, then Chairman of the Party and Premier of the State Council, 'Report on the Work of the Government', in *id.*, see particularly Part I (A Historical Turning Point) and Part III (Strengthening Socialist Democracy and the Socialist Legal System).

57 See Wang Jiafu *et al.*, 'On the Rule of Law', (no. 2, 1996) *Studies in Law* (*Faxue Yanjiu*) 3, at 7. See also Qiao Wei, 'Guidelines for Building Up a Legal System in the New Era – Comrade Deng Xiaoping's Writings on Building a Legal System', (no. 2, 1984) *Legal Science in China* (*Zhongguo Faxue*) 67.

58 Under the Marxist theory of law, both the state and the law as a coercive apparatus are to wither away in a communist society once antagonistic classes are eliminated. For discussions and analyses of Marxist theory of law and socialist attitudes towards the 'withering away of law', see Eugene Kamenka & Alice E.-S. Tay, 'Marxism, Socialism and the Theory of Law', (1985) 23 *Colum. J. Transnat'l L.* 217; and Eugene Kamenka & Alice E.-S. Tay, 'Beyond the French Revolution: Communist Socialism and the Concept of Law', (1971) 21 *U. Toronto L.J.* 109.

59 By March 1998, the National People's Congress (NPC) and its Standing Committee had promulgated 328 statutes and decisions. The State Council had issued more than 700 regulations and the local legislatures had adopted over 5,000 local rules. See *People's Daily* (*Renmin Ribao*), internet edition, 14 March 1998.

the rule of man, not the rule of law',[60] he on occasion also emphasised the need for law.[61] What is important is the fact that when he advocated law, it was at a time when the 'storming revolution' was perceived to be over and orderly economic development was considered necessary. When he repudiated law, it was at a time when he was advocating the 'uninterrupted revolution' which aimed at destroying 'old' orders. When Deng took over leadership, the 'uninterrupted revolution' had pushed the Chinese economy to the edge of collapse and the legitimacy of the Party leadership had to be re-built on the basis of economic development. For him, therefore, law had to be *used* to establish stability and order for economic development.[62] It was against this background that the Party in 1978 made the now famous declaration:

> There must be laws for people to follow; these laws must be observed; their enforcement must be strict; and law-breakers must be dealt with.[63]

From Deng's various speeches on law, it is clear that both he and Mao unambiguously saw law as an instrument of Party policy. Neither took the establishment of the rule of law to be an end in itself. One of the most prominent and influential jurists at that time, Zhang Youyu, once clearly spelt out the role of law in the PRC thus:

> Socialist democracy and the legal system [*fazhi*, sometimes translated as 'rule of law'] are inseparable; both of them are [to be used] to consolidate socialist economic bases and to enhance socialist development. At present, they are powerful tools for promoting the Four Modernisations. Neither of them is an end but both of them are means.[64]

If law is seen as designed to facilitate economic development, the question arises: why does China need law in addition to Party policies, since it is Party policy that decides the direction of economic reform? Well, according to Peng Zhen, then Chairman of the Standing Committee of the NPC, law is an important and necessary tool for implementing Party policies:

---

60 See Shao-chuan Leng, 'The Role of Law in the People's Republic of China as Reflecting Mao Tse-tung's Influence', (1977) 68 *J. Criminal L. & Criminology* 356, at 356.

61 See *supra* note 49.

62 See e.g. Deng Xiaoping, 'Implement the Policy of Readjustment, Ensure Stability and Unity', in *Selected Works of Deng Xiaoping (1975–1982)* (Beijing: Foreign Languages Press, 1984), at 335-355. See also Communiqué of the Third Plenary Session of the Eleventh Central Committee of the CPC, in Liu & Wu, *supra* note 45, at 574.

63 Communiqué of the Third Plenary Session of the Eleventh Central Committee of the CPC, *supra* note 45, at 574.

64 Zhang Youyu, 'On Strengthening the Socialist Legal System', first published in (no. 6, 1981) *Social Sciences in China* (*Zhongguo Shehui Kexue*), reprinted in *A Collection of Articles on Chinese Legal Science* (*Zhongguo Faxue Wenji*) (Beijing: Press of the Masses, 1984), at 41.

> Law is the fixation of the Party's fundamental principles and policies, that is the codification of the Party's fundamental principles and policies. These fundamental principles and policies are those that have in practice proven effective and correct.[65]

Instrumentalist this attitude might be, but as he himself was twice the victim of the lawless days, Deng was different from Mao in one crucial respect: he and the Party under his leadership saw law as a *better tool* than policy, capable of securing and institutionalising *ad hoc* policies in a more universal manner, of providing stability and order through state coercive forces for economic development, and of defining rights and duties in relation to the state as represented by various administrative authorities.[66] As such, the nature and the extent of legal development essentially depended on the parameters set by the reform program.[67] That is, policy was the foundation of law and law was the mature form of policy.[68]

As this economic reform had no clear direction,[69] it is not surprising that legal development occurred in an *ad hoc* and piecemeal fashion. Indeed, among the first casualties in pursuit of economic development was the stability and continuity of law. When the need for law first emerged, it was also recognised that:

---

65 Peng Zhen, 'Several Issues Concerning Socialist Legality', in *Selected Materials on Introduction to Law* (*Faxue Gailun Ziliao Xuanbian*), *supra* note 32, at 160-161. Identical views were then echoed by prominent Chinese scholars. See e.g. Chen Shouyi, 'A Review of Thirty Years of Legal Studies in New China', (1988) 2 *J.Chinese L.* 181, at 196. Chen was one of China's most prominent scholars. His article was originally published in Chinese in (no. 1, 1980) *Studies of Law* (*Faxue Yanjiu*), then reprinted in *A Collection of Articles on Chinese Legal Science*, *supra* note 17, at 13-31. See also Yu Xingzhong, 'Legal Pragmatism in the People's Republic of China', (1989) 3 *J. of Chinese L.* 29, at 46-47.

66 See e.g. Law Department of Beijing University, (ed.), *Basic Theories of Legal Science* (*Faxue Jichu Lilun*) (Beijing: Beijing University Press, 1984), at 212-221; Wu Daying & Shen Zhongling, *A Basic Theory of Chinese Socialist Legal Science* (*Zhongguo Shehui Zhuyi Falü Jiben Lilun*) (Beijing: Publishing House of Law, 1987), 165-177; Zhang Youyu, *supra* note 64, at 41.

67 I have discussed elsewhere in detail the relationship and interaction between legal development and economic reform in the context of civil and commercial law. See Jianfu Chen, *From Administrative Authorisation to Private Law: A Comparative Perspective of the Developing Civil Law in the People's Republic of China* (Dordrecht/Boston/London: Martinus Nijhoff Publisher, 1995), esp. ch. 3.

68 For further discussions, see Perry Keller, 'Legislation in the People's Republic of China', (1989) 23 (3) *U.B.C. Law Rev.* 643, at 658; Frances Hoar Foster, 'Codification in Post-Mao China', (1982) 30 *Am. J. Comp. L.* 395, esp. 395-413.

69 This is characterised by the Chinese phrase 'Crossing the river by touching the stones underneath (*Mozhuo Shitou Guohe*)'.

> Laws, rules and regulations, once they are framed and adopted, must be stable, have continuity, and enjoy full authority.[70]

However, the urgent need for laws to facilitate economic development took precedence over the importance of stability and continuity of law. A piecemeal approach to law-making was quickly adopted in line with the 'pragmatic' view of law held by Deng Xiaoping. He maintained in 1978:

> There is a lot of legislative work to do, and we do not have enough trained people. Therefore, legal provisions will inevitably be rough to start with, then be gradually improved upon. Some laws and statutes can be tried out in particular localities and later enacted nationally after experience has been evaluated and improvements have been made. In terms of revision and supplementation of law, once one provision is ripe, it should be revised or supplemented; we should not wait for a 'complete set of equipment'. In short, it is better to have some laws than none, and better to have them sooner than later.[71]

This unsystematic legal development then produced a large body of law consisting of many individual statutes, decisions and orders, and of administrative regulations and rules made under different *ad hoc* policy orientations.

5.2. The Need for 'Rational' Law for a Market Economy

While specific legal measures in relation to economic reform and their changes in post-Mao China have been closely examined, the politico-economic ideology behind these measures has not. Not surprisingly, the *ad hoc* and piecemeal approach to law and legal development has been easy to identify, as for a long time economic reform did not seem to have a clear direction. However, close examination of the politico-economic policies of the Party, in retrospect, indicates a gradual and incremental development towards liberalisation, directly in economic areas

---

70 Ye Jianying, 'Closing Address at the Second Session of the Fifth National People's Congress on July 1, 1979', in *Main Documents of the Second Session of the Fifth National People's Congress of the People's Republic of China, supra* note 56, at 224.

71 Deng Xiaoping, 'Emancipate the Mind, Seek Truth from Facts and Unite as One in Looking to the Future', in *Selected Works of Deng Xiaoping (1975–1982), supra* note 62, at 158. The English translation has been amended by myself according to Deng's original works published in Chinese under the same title in July 1983. These views were, however, not novel; Peng Zhen in 1951 expressed similar views, so did the *People's Daily* editorial. See Peng Zhen, 'On the Current Situation and Tasks of Political and Legal Work – a report delivered at the Government Administration Council on May 11, 1951', in Peng Zhen, *On Political and Legal Works in New China* (*Lun Xinzhongguo De Zhengfa Gongzuo*) (Beijing: Press of CPC Documents, 1992), at 26. See also Tay (1976), *supra* note 2, at 406 in her footnote 12; Gu Angran, *supra* note 47, 175.

and indirectly in political and legal spheres. The evolution of such policies is the underlying force that propels not only the formal but also the substantial changes in law in post-Mao China.

The initial reform policies during 1978–1984 were largely repetitions of policies from the 1950s and 60s.[72] However, a new politico-economic theory which justified the introduction of various reform measures was rapidly established, mainly by Chinese theorists working in the area of political economy from 1978 to 1980.[73] It did not take very long for the new 'Socialist Planned Commodity Economy' theory to dominate ideological thinking in China. The establishment of this 'new thinking' effectively led to the first transition from a totally mandatory planning system to a partly mandatory and partly guided one.[74] This transition was not just economic; it was politico-economic, and the liberal thinking that was tolerated in the economic sphere naturally flowed to law, which had always been seen as part of the 'political'. Hence we saw the initial discussions about, and introduction of, western liberal legal ideas. However, the concept of a 'socialist planned commodity economy' was not a complete break from the traditional understanding of 'socialism'. At the same time the memory of the Anti-rightist Movement and the Cultural Revolution in the 1950s and 1960s was still fresh. Thus, liberalisation of legal thinking was necessarily tentative, hesitant and limited.[75]

A major ideological breakthrough was made during Deng Xiaoping's surprise visit to Shenzhen and Zhuhai in January 1992 (now commonly referred to as the 'Southern Tour'). During his visit, Deng was reported as saying that 'reforms and greater openness are China's only way out' and that 'if capitalism has something good, then socialism should bring it over and use it.'[76] Subsequently, the *People's Daily* was flooded with editorials and articles calling for the speeding up of reform.

---

72 See Peter N.S Lee, *Industrial Management and Economic Reform in China, 1949–1984* (Hong Kong: Oxford University Press, 1987), at 177.

73 Among the most influential scholars in this area are: Hu Qiaomu, Yu Guangyuan (both were then viewed in China as top economists), Ma Hong (then president of the Chinese Academy of Social Sciences from 1979 to 1985), and Jiang Yiwei (former director of the Institute of Industrial Economics of the Chinese Academy of Social Sciences).

74 See Jianfu Chen, 'China: Constitutional Changes and Legal Developments', in Alice E-S Tay & Conita S. Leung, *Greater China: Law, Society and Trade* (Sydney: the Law Book Company, 1995), at 142-148.

75 See Chen, *supra* note 67, ch. 2.

76 *The Sydney Morning Herald*, 31 January 1992, at 6. An edited version of Deng's speech was later published in the Chinese media: 'Major Points of Speech Made in Wuchang, Shenzhen, Zhuhai and Shanghai [by Deng Xiaoping]', *People's Daily* (*Renmin Ribao*), 6 November 1993, at 1; and translated as 'Gist of Speeches Made in Wuchang, Shenzhen, Zhuhai and Shanghai [by Deng Xiaoping]', *Beijing Review*, 7-20 February 1994, at 9-20.

Using capitalism for building socialism began to be openly called for.[77] Party Secretary-General Jiang Zemin then proclaimed that the market and planning were both means of regulating the economy, but not criteria for distinguishing between socialism and capitalism.[78] The ruling Politburo also promised that the policies of reform and opening up to the world would remain for one hundred years and called for, among other things, a fast development of the socialist commodity economy.[79] Finally, the 14th Party Congress in 1992 set the tone for reform by declaring that economic reform would be accelerated towards achieving the central task of establishing a 'socialist market economy'.[80] So, not long after the Central Committee of the CPC formally submitted its 'Suggestions on Amending Certain Contents of the Constitution', the NPC dutifully adopted these suggestions and translated the new Party policy into law in March 1993.[81] As a result of the revision, the term 'socialist market economy' replaced that of 'planned economy' in the Constitution.

There was little new in the notion of a 'socialist market economy' as far as reform measures were concerned. The real significance lay in the justification for introducing the notion, rather than in the notion itself. The Political Report declared that theoretical and ideological innovations for reform should not be constrained by the abstract question of whether such innovations were capitalist or socialist – all modern business and enterprise operating mechanisms, foreign capital, resources, technologies and talented personnel, no matter whether socialist or capitalist, should be made use of for socialism.[82] The significance thus lay in the

77 Fang Sheng, 'Open Up to the World and Utilise Capitalism', *People's Daily* (*Renmin Ribao*), (overseas edition), 24 February 1992, at 1 & 4. It was later revealed by the author of the article that the article had actually been written three years earlier but was only allowed publication after Deng's Southern visit. See 'Market Economy and the Opening to the Outside – An Interview with Professor Fang Sheng', *Economic Daily* (*Jingji Ribao*), 11 March 1994, at 5.

78 *People's Daily* (*Renmin Ribao*), (overseas edition), 14 March 1992, at 1. According to the *People's Daily*, the concept came directly from Deng Xiaoping: at the end of 1990 Deng Xiaoping pointed out that 'planning and markets are not criteria for distinguishing socialism from capitalism'. Deng re-stressed this point during his tour to Shenzhen and Zhuhai Special Economic Zones in February 1992. See 'Great Practice, Bright Chapter – the Birth of the Political Report of the 14th Congress of the Party', in *People's Daily* (*Renmin Ribao*) (overseas edition) 24 October 1992, at 3. According to other scholars, Deng had in 1979 said that socialism could also practise a market economy. See Gao Lu, 'The Emergence of the Notion of "Socialist market Economy"' (no. 1, 1993) *Xinhua Digest* (*Xinhua Wenzhai*) 40, at 40-41.

79 *People's Daily* (*Renmin Ribao*) (overseas edition), 12 March 1992, at 1.

80 *Id.*, at 1.

81 Thus, according to Chinese scholars, Party policy was translated, through legal procedure, into state will. See Liu Zheng, 'Further Constitutional Protection for the Construction of Socialism with Chinese Characteristics', (no. 2, 1993) *Legal Science in China* (*Zhongguo Faxue*) 5, at 6. See further discussions in Chapter 3.

82 See 'Accelerating the Reform, the Opening to the Outside World and the Drive for Modernisation, so as to Achieve Great Successes in Building Socialism with Chinese Characteristics', a

abandonment of the requirement for ideological correctness in introducing reform measures. In other words, the notion of a 'socialist market economy' is first and foremost to be seen as a licence to practise capitalism in the economic sphere and to introduce capitalist mechanisms and measures (including legal measures) to facilitate economic development. It is in this sense that economic reform and the 'open door' policy brought about a new phase in China, and set new parameters for legal development.

Symbolic though it might seem to be, the new direction for economic reform has since had enormous implications for legal development. It has allowed scholars and officials to abandon any pretence of upholding socialism, as an ideology or a politico-economic system, when new ideas or practices are to be introduced. This explains, and is evidenced in, the lively discussions held in legal circles regarding the reform of legal ideologies and legal development since the remarks made by Deng Xiaoping during his 'Southern Tour' and the 14th Party Congress.

Thus as a consequence of the new policy Chinese scholars began to openly argue that a 'market economy' was a result of human wisdom; it was not a 'privilege' (*tequan*) for the West.[83] A socialist market economy, it was now often asserted, was an economy under rule of law (*fazhi jingji*).[84] The establishment and perfecting of a socialist market was thus said to be a process of establishing the rule of law.[85] To establish a market economy in China therefore demanded a revolution in legal theory and legal thought.[86]

Political Report delivered by Jiang Zemin to the 14th Congress of the CPC, in *People's Daily* (*Renmin Ribao*) (overseas edition), 21 October 1992, at 1-3, at 2.

83 Liu Jinghua, 'Globalisation: An Historical Process Full of Paradoxes', (no. 1, 1995) *Pacific Studies* (*Taipingyan Xuebao*) 70, at 70.

84 See e.g. Xiao Yang, *Market Economy and Legal Construction* (*Shichang Jingji yu Fazhi Jianshe*) (Beijing: Publishing House of Law, 1994); Chen Shixi, 'Our Legislative Trend in the 1990s', *Guangming Daily* (*Guangming Ribao*), 9 March 1994, at 5; 'The Legislative Train is Speeding Up towards the Market Economy', *Legal Daily* (*Fazhi Ribao*), 2 January 1994, at 3; 'A History of Economic Legislation by the NPC', *Economic Daily* (*Jingji Ribao*), 7 March 1994, at 1; and Min Xianwei, 'A Socialist Market Economy Is Naturally an Economy Under the Rule of Law', (Special Issue, 1994) *Journal of Shandong Normal University* (*Shandong Shifan Daxuebao*) 93. Such an assertion is not without challenges (though rather isolated), see e.g. Lin Jie, 'A Question on the Proposition "A Market Economy Is an Economy Under the Rule of Law"' (no. 1, 1994) *Legal Science in China* (*Zhongguo Faxue*) 68, at 68.

85 Wang Jiafu, *et al.*, *supra* note 57, at 3.

86 See Guo Daoxu, 'The Market Economy and the Changes in Legal Theory and Legal Thought', (no. 2, 1994) *Jurisprudence* (*Faxue*) 2; Xie Hui, 'From a Planned Economy to a Market Economy: A Revolution in Legal Theory', (no. 4, 1994) *Gansu Journal of Theoretical Research* (*Gansu Lilun Xuekang*) 53; Wen Zhengbang, 'Some Legal and Philosophical Thoughts on the Market Economy', (no. 4, 1995) *Legal System and Social Development* (*Fazhi Yu Shehui Fazhang*) 1; and Zhang Wenxian, 'The Market-oriented Economy and the Spirit of Modern Law', a paper

Though far short of such a revolution,[87] this 'second tide of academic thoughts' in post Mao-China[88] swept all areas of Chinese law,[89] and certain changes in legal theory have indeed occurred since then in China. For instance, legal discourse in jurisprudence is now strongly rights-based, as evidenced in the general debate on the relationship between rights and duties, namely, whether law should emphasise rights rather than duties.[90] Although this debate has been a continuing one since 1978, the discussion that began in the 1990s was on the issue of whether law should take rights or duties or both as its main concern. Many scholars took the view that law must first deal with rights and that duties would naturally follow as a consequence of protecting these rights. They argued that the emphasis on rights would liberate people from constraints imposed by traditional duties, status and dictatorship. This debate, according to some jurists, is essentially an argument for and against a shift from an emphasis on duties to the state, to an emphasis on rights against the state.[91]

Jurists also openly criticised the 'piecemeal' approach towards law-making. They argued that such guiding principles as 'a law can be rough to start with', 'a law should be made only when there is the need' and 'a law should be made when an issue is ripe',[92] had played a positive historical role but were no longer appropriate for the

---

presented to the 1995 International Sociological Association Conference, Tokyo, 1-4 August 1995.

87 Indeed, as Albert Chen has pointed out, the ideas advocated by the Chinese scholars are neither intellectually sophisticated, theoretically refined or rich in philosophical depth, nor are they original. See Albert Chen, 'Towards a Legal Enlightenment: Discussions in Contemporary China on the Rule of Law' (2000) 17 *UCLA Pacific Basin Law Journal* 125, at 163. This does not however mean, as is also emphasised by Albert Chen, that these academic thoughts have no practical significance.

88 Chinese scholars often refer to an academic debate and discussion as a 'tide of academic thoughts' or a 'liberation of thought'. In post-Mao China, the debate in the late 1970s was seen as the first 'liberation of thought', the second started in 1992 and the third from 1996–1997 onwards. Scholars are now anticipating a fourth 'liberation of thought', pending a Party decision to deepen political reforms. See Guo Daohui, Li Buyun, Hao Tiechuan (eds), *A Record of the Contentions on the Science of Law in Contemporary China* (*Zhongguo Dangdai Faxue Zhengming Shilu*), Changsha: Hunan People's Press (1998), at 1.

89 For an excellent summary of academic debates on this topic, see Albert Chen, *supra* note 87. For a more comprehensive study, see Randall Peerenboom, *China's Long March toward Rule of Law* (Cambridge: Cambridge University Press, 2002).

90 For a summary of views in the debate, see 'Jurisprudential Debate on the Relationship Between Rights and Duties', in (no. 4, 1991) *Xinhua Digest* (*Xinhua Wenzhai*) 16.

91 *Ibid.*

92 As discussed above, these are in fact instructions concerning legislative work given by Deng Xiaoping in 1978 and have been held as guiding principles in legislative work ever since. See *supra* note 71.

current situation in China.[93] Others urged the government to halt the practice of making policies for experimentation purposes and then translating them into law after gaining experience.[94] To secure the legitimacy of reform, such scholars argued, law, not policy, must be relied upon.[95]

There were similar debates on specific fronts. It is not surprising that the most notable changes occurred in civil and commercial law circles as a response to the notion of a 'socialist market economy'.

First, legal theories and civil and commercial legislation were now subject to sharp criticism for being too restricted by 'traditional doctrines' and for being too often compromised by the politico-economic system and ideology.[96] Many Chinese jurists declared that these 'traditional doctrines', namely, theories largely based on those of A.Y. Vyshinsky and imported from the former Soviet Union in the 1950s, were the first legal ideologies that had to be abandoned.[97] Existing laws governing civil law matters were also seen as being too unsystematic and unsophisticated and in many cases dated. Urgent revisions and the making of comprehensive laws governing civil and commercial matters were therefore demanded.[98]

---

93 See 'Summary of the 1992 Annual Conference of the Institute of Civil and Economic Law of the China Law Society', (no. 5, 1992) *Legal Science in China* (*Zhongguo Faxue*), at 118-119; and Fang Shaokun, 'On Correcting Civil Legislation Deficiencies', (no. 1, 1993) *Legal Science in China* (*Zhongguo Faxue*), at 29-30.

94 Gan Zangchuan, 'How to Secure the Legitimacy of Reform – From Reliance on Policy to Reliance on Law', (no. 6, 1991) *Studies in Law* (*Faxue Yanjiu*), at 3.

95 *Ibid.*

96 See e.g. 'Further Emancipating Minds and Making Great Efforts for the Prosperity of Legal Science – A Discussion in Commemorating the 10th Anniversary of the Re-establishment of the China Law Society', (no. 4, 1992) *Legal Science in China* (*Zhongguo Faxue*), at 13-24; Zhang Wenxian, 'Three Points on the Market Economy and Legal Construction', (no. 3, 1993) *Legal Science in China* (*Zhongguo Faxue*), at 12-19; Liu Shengping *et al.*, 'The Market Economy and Changes in Legal Ideologies', (no. 4, 1993) *Legal Science in China* (*Zhongguo Faxue*), at 3-9; 'A Summary Report of the Symposium on New Topics for Civil and Economic Law in a Socialist Market Economy', (no. 4, 1993) *Legal Science in China* (*Zhongguo Faxue*), at 119-122; and Project Group (Law Institute, Chinese Academy of Social Sciences), 'Some Theoretical Considerations and Practical Suggestions Regarding the Establishment of a Legal System for a Socialist Market Economy', (no. 6, 1993) *Studies in Law* (*Faxue Yanjiu*), at 3-19.

97 See e.g. Project Group, *id*; and Zhang Junhao, 'Market System and Private Law in China', (no. 6, 1994) *Journal of China University of Political Science and Law* (*Zhangfa Luntan*) 34. Some scholars have, however, offered some qualified defence for Vishinsky, see Sun Guohua & Zeng Bing, 'On the Definition of Law by Vishinsky', (no. 2, 1996) *Jurists* (*Faxue Jia*) 38.

98 See 'A Summary of Views Expressed at the Symposium on the Study of Chinese Civil Law-making', (no. 3, 1992) *Legal Science in China* (*Zhongguo Faxue*), at 120; 'Legal Science Must Serve Economic Development and Reform', (no. 1, 1992) *Legal Science in China* (*Zhongguo Faxue*), at 3-12; 'Political Reform, Next Target', *Beijing Review*, 21-27 December 1992, at 4; and Fang Shaokun, *supra* note 93, at 27-32.

Secondly, some Chinese scholars strongly attacked the fusion of public and private law – a long-standing controversial issue in China and other (former) socialist countries.[99] To these scholars, the separation of public and private law was not merely an academic issue, it challenged the fundamental politico-economic system in China. It concerned the very foundation of establishing a rule of law.[100] Thus Liang Huixin, a prominent civil law scholar in China, pointed out that the fusion reflected the 'old' administrative-economic system and the influence of Soviet civil law theories. It provided a theoretical basis for state interference through administrative measures in civil law activities. He argued that in order to establish a legal order for a market economy the government must be separated from enterprises, that economic and political functions of government must be distinguished, and that enterprises must become truly independent civil law subjects capable of resisting undue intervention from state administrative authorities. In short, the autonomy of private law must be upheld.[101] Liang further argued that not only public and private law had to be separated and distinguished from each other, but also that private law had to take precedence over public law. He asserted that public law taking precedence over private law was a product of dictatorship, of a natural [agrarian] economy (*ziran jingji*) and of a centralised administrative-economic system. In his view, public law had been in a dominant position in China until then and that, in order to build a modern legal system in China, private law had to have precedence.[102] Other scholars also saw the denial of the existence of private law as an 'extremist leftist' practice and strongly emphasised the importance of the distinction between public and private law.[103] Some scholars claimed that the fusion of public and private law was responsible for the interference of government in enterprises and for many forms of

---

99 See Jianfu Chen, *supra* note 76, at 52-56; Li Maoguan, 'The Legal Controversy Concerning the Separation of Public and Private Law', (no. 22, 1995) *Seeking Truth* (*Qiushi*) 44.

100 *Ibid.*

101 Liang Huixin, 'To Make a Perfect and Modern Civil Code', in 'Further Emancipating Minds and Making Great Efforts for the Prosperity of Legal Research – A Discussion on Deng Xiaoping's Talk during His Southern Tour', (no. 5, 1992) *Studies in Law* (*Faxue Yanjiu*), at 5.

102 See 'A Market Economy and the Modernisation of a Legal System – Speeches Given at the Symposium on a Market Economy and the Modernisation of the Legal System', (no. 6, 1992) *Studies in Law* (*Faxue Yanjiu*), at 2-3.

103 Li Jingbing, 'On the Significance of and Current Barriers to the Making of a Civil Code', (no. 5, 1992) *Law Science* (*Falü Kexue*), at 37; Project Group, *supra* note 96, at 6-7; Liu Shengping *et al.*, *supra* note 96, at 5; 'A Summary Report of the Symposium on New Topics for Civil and Economic Law in a Socialist Market Economy', *supra* note 93, at 119-120; Zhou Yongkun, 'A Market Economy Demands Equality in Legislation', (no. 4, 1993) *Legal Science in China* (*Zhongguo Faxue*), at 16.

corruption, such as officials conducting profit-seeking business.[104] It is not surprising therefore that some scholars argued that central to the establishment of a rule of law was the establishment of private law in China.[105]

Finally, it was strongly urged that all economic participants must be treated equally and that law must be made universally applicable to all kinds of economic actors.[106] Further, if public property was upheld as sacred and not to be violated, then private property also had to be elevated to the same level for protection, and not merely be allowed to have 'lawful existence'.[107]

In short, for Chinese scholars, the catchwords since then have become 'equality', 'universality', 'private rights', 'freedom of contract', 'supremacy of law', and 'humanity'.[108] A market economy, for these scholars, demands 'rational' law in the sense defined by Max Weber. It can therefore be said that with this ideological breakthrough the shackles of the Soviet conception of law in China have been finally, though not necessarily completely, thrown off.[109]

---

104 Fang Liufang, 'The Company Examination and Approval System and Administrative Monopoly', (no. 4, 1992) *Legal Science in China* (*Zhongguo Faxue*), at 56-58; Wang Chengguang & Liu Wen, 'The Market Economy and the Separation of Public and Private Law', (no. 4, 1993) *Legal Science in China* (*Zhongguo Faxue*), at 28-36; Xie Guisheng, 'The Market Economy and the Separation of Public and Private Law', (no. 1, 1994) *Studies in Finance* (*Caimao Yanjiu*), at 62-66.

105 Zhang Junhao, *supra* note 97; and Yang Zhengshan, 'The Central Point for Chinese Legal Reform is the Civil Law', (no. 1, 1995) *Journal of China University of Political Science and Law (Zhangfa Luntan)* 48.

106 See e.g. 'A Market Economy and the Modernisation of a Legal System – Speeches Given at the Symposium on a Market Economy and the Modernisation of the Legal System', *supra* note 102, at 3; Dong Kaijun & Li Cheng, 'On Legal Forms of Enterprises', (no. 4, 1992) *Legal Science in China* (*Zhongguo Faxue*), at 65-67; Wang Baoshu, 'The Fundamental Task of Economic Law Is to Establish and Maintain Freedom and Equality for Socialist Market Competition', in 'Further Emancipating Minds and Making Great Efforts for the Prosperity of Legal Research – A Discussion on Deng Xiaoping's Talk during His Southern Tour', *supra* note 101, at 3-4; Zhao Xudong, 'A New Thought on Ownership, Ownership Rights and Enterprise Legislation', in 'Further Emancipating Minds and Making Great Efforts for the Prosperity of Legal Science – A Discussion in Commemorating the 10th Anniversary of the Re-establishment of the China Law Society', *supra* note 95, at 21-23; Xie Huaishi, 'On Establishing a Civil-Economic Law System Appropriate to the Needs of a Socialist Market Economy', (no. 1, 1993) *Studies in Law* (*Faxue Yanjiu*), at 12-14; and Lu Yun, 'The Transformation of Legal Models: A Deep Revolutionary Change', (no. 1, 1994) *Legal Science in China* (*Zhongguo Faxue*) 27.

107 'A Market Economy and the Modernisation of a Legal System – Speeches Given at the Symposium on a Market Economy and the Modernisation of the Legal System', *supra* note 102, at 3; Zhang Wenxian, *supra* note 96, 18-19. Indeed, this was done in 2004 through a constitutional amendment. See further discussions in Chapter 3.

108 See *supra* note 96.

109 As I have argued earlier, the revision in the 2004 Constitution to article 13 (on protection of private property) was intended to do away with one of the last remnants of the influence of the

This pursuit of 'rational' law was also reflected in the legislative agenda of the National People's Congress. The NPC made it clear that the establishment of a socialist market economy must be guided, promoted and protected by law. Not only were new laws to be made, existing laws and regulations were to be revised, consolidated or repealed.[110] To this end, an ambitious, first ever five-year legislative plan was instituted after one year of deliberation in 1993: Within the five-year term of the 8th NPC (1992–1997), 152 laws were to be drafted and deliberated, 125 of them to be guaranteed full deliberation; that is, to be adopted. Of the 125 laws, 54 directly related to the socialist market economy and many of them were to be consolidated codes of existing laws.[111]

5.3. Ruling the Country According to Law

Although the search for 'rational' law had led to what Chinese scholars described as the 'second tide of academic thoughts' in post Mao-China, and the 'rational law' discourse swept all areas of Chinese law, significant legal development was still largely confined to civil and commercial law, or areas related to a 'socialist market economy'. More importantly, legal scholars were not in the forefront of theoretical innovation or ideological battlegrounds, and legal reform was still led by the needs of economic reform. Attitudes towards law remained fundamentally instrumentalist in nature. A legal revolution was yet to begin. China was in need of another ideological or political breakthrough to ensure that 'rational' law was also available for protecting human rights and upholding justice and equality of the law. Two major events soon occurred that pushed the transformation of law in this direction.

First, in early 1996, the then Party Secretary-General, Jiang Zemin initiated a seminar, given by prominent Chinese scholars to the Party and state leaders, on the topic of Ruling the Country according to Law (*Yifa Zhiguo*, 依法治国, sometimes translated as the Rule of Law). At the conclusion of the seminar, Jiang made a speech entitled *To Rule the Country according to Law and To Guarantee the Long-Term*

Soviet law. See Jianfu Chen, 'Conceptual Evolution of Socialism with Chinese Characteristics – the Revision of the Constitution in the PRC', 1999 (24) *China Perspectives* 66; and 'A Great Leap Forward or a Symbolic Gesture? – The Revision of the Constitution in the PRC', 2004 (53) *China Perspectives* 15. See also Chapter 3 below.

110 See 'Speech at the 2nd Session of the 8th NPC, delivered by Qiao Shi on 22 March 1994', *Economic Daily* (*Jingji Ribao*), 23 March 1994, at 1.

111 For a full list of the 152 laws, see *Economic Daily* (*Jingji Ribao*), 14 March 1994, at 5. This plan was particularly ambitious considering that from 1949 to 1992 only 170 statutes were made and adopted. See 'Legislation on a Fast Track', *People's Daily (Renmin Ribao)*, 20 March 1994, at 2. By the end of the 8th NPC (March 1998), 129 bills were examined and deliberated and 118 of them were adopted. See Tian Jiyuan, 'Work Report of the Standing Committee of the NPC, delivered at the First Session of the 9th NPC on 10 March 1998', in *People's Daily (Renmin Ribao)*, internet edition, 23 March 1998. A full list of these laws and decisions was annexed to the Report.

Stability of the Country.[112] Thereafter the Ninth Five-Year National Economic and Social Development Plan and the Outline of Goals by the Year 2010, adopted by the Fourth Plenary Session of the 8th NPC on 17 March 1996, formally decided that Ruling the Country According to Law was to be a long term development strategy.[113] Soon, the phrase 'Ruling the Country According to Law and Building a Socialist Country Governed by Law' was formally incorporated into Article 5 of the Constitution during the 1999 revision of the Constitution.[114]

Once again, as I have argued elsewhere,[115] there is little substance in the official documents, and technically it involved a mere linguistic change of terminology from 法制 to 法治 (both Romanised as *fazhi*). However, as in the adoption of the notion of 'socialist market economy', it signified the emergence of a new wave of 'liberation of legal thought'.[116] But, unlike the ideological breakthrough involved in adopting a 'socialist market economy', this time it was no longer confined to economic and commercial law; it has had the potential for development in the traditionally understood public law areas which have major implications for the protection of human rights and individual liberties.

In fact, the Party's strategy of 'Ruling the Country according to Law', though lacking specific substance, has provided the skeleton of principles. As in the previous ideological breakthrough, it is now up to scholars to supply flesh for the skeleton. This is done through academic debate, discussions and advocacy. Thus in the criminal law and criminal procedural law areas the debate on several long rejected criminal justice principles, such as the presumption of innocence, timely and adequate access to legal counsel, *nullum crimen, nulla poena sine lege* (and the consequential Abolition of Analogy in criminal law), judicial independence, equality before the law (and the consequential rejection of the class nature of the criminal law), and proportionality, have resumed their much deserved prominence in legal discourse. So has the debate on the abolition of the extra-judicial practice of the preliminary detention and the shelter and investigation system, of the exemption

---

112 I have not been able to locate a copy of the full text of the Speech, but the main contents were published in *People's Daily* (*Renmin Ribao*), internet edition, 9 February 1996.

113 The text of the Ninth Five Year National Economic and Social Development Plan and the Outline of Goals by Year 2010 can be found in *Guangming Daily* (*Guangming Ribao*), 20 March 1996, at 1.

114 The 1999 revision of the Constitution added the following to Article 5: 'The People's Republic of China practises Ruling the Country according to Law and is building a socialist country governed by law'. For a discussion of the 1999 constitutional revision, see Chen, *supra* note 109. Later in 2002 at the 16th Party Congress, the same phrase was also added to the Party Constitution.

115 Jianfu Chen, 'To Have the Cake and Eat It Too? China and the Rule of Law', in Guenther Doeker-Mach & Klaus A Ziegert (eds), *Law, Legal Culture and Politics in the Twenty First Century* (Munich: Franz Steiner Verlag Stuttgart, 2004), at 250-272.

116 See further discussions in Chapter 3.

from prosecution, of counter-revolutionary crimes, and on the reform of trial processes, and the strict application of the death penalty.[117] In the most important area for checks and balances, namely administrative reform, the underlying rationale was until recently the improvement of bureaucratic productivity and efficiency, rather than accountability. Now scholars have begun to advocate strongly the idea of administrative law being first and foremost a law for controlling government and its activities, rather than merely providing a legal basis for government control and management or for legitimising government actions. Administrative justice, it is argued, entails much more than substantive justice; procedural justice is no less important, if not more, in securing justice and equality for all and in controlling government behaviour.[118]The promulgation of the Administrative Penalty Law in 1996 and the Administrative Licensing Law in 2003 represented the beginning of the government's efforts to reduce and restrict powers that might be exercised by administrative authorities, in part as measures to curb widespread corruption and abuse of power. These measures have introduced some checks on administrative powers, though not so much balances. Finally, the protection of human rights was written into the Constitution by the 2004 Constitutional Amendment.

While scholarly debate may be seen as an academic exercise in nature (which is not strictly true as academics are nowadays heavily involved in law-making, especially in the initial drafting of law codes and revisions to existing laws), the second event that has propelled the current legal reform imposes certain binding obligations upon the Chinese Government under the international law principle of *pacta sund servanda*. This second event relates to China's membership of the WTO. The WTO-related legal reforms are seen by some as a new, third wave of legal reform, following the 'first wave' from 1978 to the early 1990s and the 'second wave' from the mid-1990s.[119] On the surface, this 'third wave' does no more than necessitate some legal and institutional reforms so as to ensure that Chinese laws and regulations conform with WTO regulatory requirements. Perhaps more by coincidence than by design, some WTO Agreements demand national laws to be transparent, readily accessible, relatively stable and universal in their application, and that national judicial and other dispute resolution mechanisms are independ-

[117] For detailed discussion on the development of the criminal law and criminal procedural law in the 1990s, see Chapters 7 and 8 below. For an English translation of the revised Criminal Law and Criminal Procedure Law, see Jianfu Chen & Suiwa Ke, *China Criminal Law: Commentary and Legislation* (Singapore: CCH Asia, 2000).

[118] For detailed discussions, see Chapter 6 below.

[119] See Jerome A. Cohen, 'Opening Statement Before the First Public Hearing of the US-China Security Review Commission', Washington, DC, 14 June 2001 (copy on file with author). It should be noted here that this 'definition' of the 'third wave' is different from the Chinese notion; the latter defines the 'third wave' to have started in 1996. See *supra* note 88.

ent, impartial and transparent.[120] Herein lies the significance of the WTO-related reforms, as a country cannot be expected to maintain a legal system which only guarantees fairness and justice in one area but not in others, and so these *ad hoc* requirements are often seen as requirements for a whole legal system for WTO members.[121] That is to say that if law reform in post-Mao China can be said to be divided into three waves, this present wave of reform has the potential to be very different from the previous two and to have a more direct and greater actual impact on the ordinary people and on the future of the rule of law in the country. Most importantly, together with the efforts to establish a rule of law, the transformation of law, especially in the perception of its role, has now gained a momentum in which legal scholars play a pivotal role – they are no longer passively led by economists or historians. Consequently legal theoretical breakthroughs are no longer confined to areas of economic and commercial law.

6. After Ideology – Continuing Westernisation/Modernisation of Chinese Law

6.1. Legal Transplant and the Modernisation of Chinese Law

Without ideological constraints and with ambitious five-year legislative plans in place, it is not surprising that great attention has been paid by scholars and law-makers to foreign legal models. Indeed, since 1992 when the Party adopted the notion of a 'socialist market economy', the new and most frequently used catchwords have become 'assimilation or harmonisation with international practice' or 'doing things in accordance with international practice', and they are the topics most frequently

---

120 Specifically, while the WTO does not lay down comprehensive and systematic requirements on law and the administration of law, WTO rules contain various *ad hoc* requirements in specific areas, such as Article X (Publication and administration of trade regulations) of the General Agreement on Tariffs and Trade (GATT), and Articles III (Transparency) and VI (Domestic regulation) of the General Agreement on Trade in Services (GATS), with the most comprehensive requirements being contained in the Agreement on Trade-Related Aspects of Intellectual Property Rights (TRIPS), including, for example, Part III (Articles 41-61) on enforcement of intellectual property rights and Part V (Articles 63-64) on dispute prevention and settlement See Cohen, *id.*, and Donald C. Clarke, 'Statement Before the US-China Security Review Commission', Washington, DC, 18 January 2002 (copy on file with the author). On China's membership specifically, Article 2 (Administration of the Trade Regime) of the Protocol on the Accession of the People's Republic of China does provide some basic principles on transparency of law, reasonable administration of law, and effectiveness of judicial review. For a more detailed discussion on WTO and legal reform requirements for China, see Stanley Lubman, 'Keynote Speech' (delivered at the international conference *Legal and Political Reform in the People's Republic of China,* Lund, Sweden, 3-4 June 2002) (copy on file with author).

121 See Clarke, *id.*

discussed in socio-legal studies in Chinese journals and newspapers.[122] Some Chinese scholars thus claim that studies in China on assimilating or harmonising Chinese law with international practice only began in 1992.[123]

However, internationalising Chinese law, in the sense of transplanting foreign (Western) laws, did not start in the 1990s. As discussed in Chapter One, modern reform of Chinese law during the dying days of the Qing Dynasty was, essentially, a process of wholesale westernisation with a clearly utilitarian and instrumentalist approach. From the very beginning officials were instructed to carry out legal reforms along the lines of Western models. The KMT legal reform was essentially a continuation of the Qing reform, although the process of westernising Chinese law under the KMT was a better balanced process, in which foreign laws were not selected because they were foreign and new, but because they were appropriate for adoption and adaptation in China. Equally, communist legal efforts relied heavily on foreign experience, but the practice of seeking foreign experience before 1992 was severely restrained by ideological considerations. What is particularly remarkable in the present process of seeking foreign assistance is the abandonment of any ideological requirement in choosing and adopting foreign legal institutions and theories. Further, the abandonment of ideology has allowed Chinese scholars and law-makers to make use not only of foreign legal experience but also of the results of KMT legal reform.

The continuing reliance on foreign experience thus leads to one of the most prominent features of Chinese law at present, which is the westernisation of its development. The changing perception of the role of foreign legal experience in developing a modern Chinese law since 1949 reflects and further reveals the nature of law in the PRC.

6.2. Using Foreign Law for Reference

As already noted, when the communists took over in 1949, law was abolished first and foremost for ideological reasons. What followed after the abolition of the KMT law and legal system was a few short-lived attempts to re-build a legal system when the Party's focus shifted from political struggle to economic development during

---

[122] See Li Shenzhi, 'Promoting the Study of Globalisation', unpublished paper. Professor Li Shenzhi, a former vice-president of the Chinese Academy of Social Sciences (CASS), is perhaps the most prominent scholar among the Chinese academics publishing on globalisation issues. The present author thanks Professor Wang Yizhou of CASS for supplying me with several unpublished papers by Professor Li Shenzhi.

[123] See Li Shuanyuan, Zhang Mao & Du Jian, 'A Study on the Assimilation of Chinese Law [with International Practice]', (no. 3, 1994) *Journal of Wuhan University* (*Wuhan Daxue Xuebao*) (Philosophy & Social Sciences) 3, at 3; and He Hangzhou, 'On Legal Transplant and the Construction of an Economic Legal System', (no. 5, 1992) *Legal Science in China* (*Zhongguo Faxue*) 50, at 53.

the first 30 years of socialism. It was during those short periods of legal effort that the overwhelming Soviet influence came and stayed in China.

The influence of the Soviet model led to a continuation, though fragmentary, of a Civil law style legal system, but also installed a formidable barrier to the importation of any other western influence. Fundamentally, Marxist legal theories, as introduced to China from the former Soviet Union, strongly emphasises the class nature of law.[124] This emphasis led to an almost automatic denial of any usefulness of 'feudalist' (a coded word for anything traditional) and 'capitalist' (a coded word for anything western or foreign) law.[125] Nevertheless, the ideological emphasis on the class nature of law could only help to justify the destruction of 'old' law but was unable to offer anything to fill the legal vacuum left. It was to history and foreign laws that China turned for ideas and assistance for legal construction. Clearly, neither history nor foreign influence can easily be ignored.[126] It is therefore not surprising that during the first serious efforts to re-build a legal system the question of heritability of law arose. The more daring jurists, probably misinterpreting the intention of the Party's invitation to participate in the '100 flowers' debate in 1956–1957, began to tackle the legal taboo and argued that there were laws of a technical nature which were 'internationally common' and thus could be 'critically inherited'.[127]

With the reform and 'open door' policy in place in the late 1970s came the slogans 'old things must be put to the use of the present' and 'foreign things must be put to Chinese use'. Such political slogans then led to a renewed discussion of and debate on the question of heritability of law when legislative programs and legal research resumed around 1977–1978.[128] That discussion and debate was hesitant, ambivalent, and sometimes confusing. The central issue was whether there were technical norms in the 'old' law (both in history and from foreign countries) that could be used as 'reference' or be 'critically inherited'. Both arguments for and against the heritability of law subscribed to and upheld the Marxist ideology of the class nature of law.[129]

---

124 Li Shuanyuan and Xiao Beigen, 'Socialist Market Economy and the Direction of Legal Modernisation', 1994 (6) *Hunan Normal University Social Science Journal* (*Hunan Shifan Daxue Shehui Xuebao*) 11, at 14-15; and A.E-S. Tay, and E. Kamenka 'Marxism-Leninism and the Heritability of Law', 1980 (6) *Review of Socialist Law* 261.

125 F. Münzel, 'Chinese Thoughts on the Heritability of Law: Translations', 1980 (6: 3) *Review of Socialist Law* 275, at 275.

126 After all, Marxism is also an alien concept to China.

127 Münzel, *supra* note 125, at 275-7.

128 R. Lin, 'A Little Discussion of the Heritability of Law', 1979 (1) *Studies in Law* (*Faxue Yanjiu*) 13, translated in (1980) (6) *Review of Socialist Law* 280, at 280-86.

129 Lin, *id*; and C Li, 'The Old Law Cannot Be Critically Inherited, It Can Only Be Used as a Mirror', originally published in (No. 3, 1979) *Studies in Law* (*Faxue Yanjiu*) 45, translated in (1980) (6) *Review of Socialist Law* 287. 'To be used for reference' in the debate was to serve the

While scholars continued their debate on the heritability of law, law-makers were facing the more pressing task of building a new legal system and making laws, almost from scratch. Thus the law-makers took a much more pragmatic approach towards 'old' laws – both 'feudalist' and 'capitalist'. In the early 1980s leading members of the Legislative Affairs Committee of the NPC's Standing Committee (SCNPC) frequently stressed the importance of foreign experience, to be used as 'reference' for building a socialist law with Chinese characteristics.[130] Even the more conservative forces recognised the usefulness of foreign legal experience. Thus, Peng Zhen, then the Chairman of the SCNPC, held that foreign experience, whether socialist or capitalist, from the Anglo-American or the Continental legal system, as well as from Chinese historical experience, should be consulted in making Chinese law.[131] Foreign legal terminologies, structures, and methodologies thus found their way into the Chinese laws of the 1980s, while rhetoric continued about the 'socialist' nature and 'Chinese characteristics' of the new law. Indeed, as mentioned above, some Chinese scholars have rightly observed that transplanting foreign laws and assimilating Chinese law to international practice started immediately with the reconstruction of the legal system in the post-Mao era,[132] although the practice in the 1980s was not as pronounced as it is today.

Further and stronger emphasis was placed on foreign experience in 1987 when the Chinese Communist Party (CPC) declared that China was at a primary stage of socialism.[133] This ideology implied that certain 'capitalist' aspects were useful for advancing socialism in China; thus, a clearer 'utilitarian' approach towards foreign laws and legal experience began to emerge. Legislation, it was emphasised, must be based on Chinese reality but foreign experience must also be used as 'reference'.[134]

---

purpose of pointing out what a socialist state must not do. 'To critically inherit' was to adapt the 'old' laws to the principles of socialism and assimilate them into the new laws (Münzel, *supra* note 125, at 277-278).

130 Xiang Chunyi, Yang Jingyu & Gu Angran, 'Strive to Build a Socialist Legal System with Chinese Characteristics', in *A Collection of Articles on Chinese Legal Science* (*Zhongguo Faxue Wenji*) (Beijing: Publishing House of Law, 1984), at 6-8. Xiang and Gu were then Vice-Chairmen of the Legislative Affairs Committee of the SCNPC, and Yang was Deputy Secretary of the Committee.

131 Peng Zhen, 'Advancing Socialist Democracy and Strengthening the Socialist Legal System', a speech given to the China Law Society on 22 July 1982, reprinted in Peng, *supra* note 70, at 294-95.

132 Li, Zhang, and Du, *supra* note 123, at 28.

133 Zhao Ziyang, 'Advance Along the Road of Socialism with Chinese Characteristics – Report Delivered at the Thirteenth National Congress of the Communist Party of China on 25 October 1987', in *Documents of the Thirteenth National Congress of the Communist Party of China* (Beijing: Foreign Languages Press, 1987), at 10.

134 Gu Angran, *supra* note 47, at 29.

The fundamental Chinese reality, the then Vice-Chairman of the Legislative Affairs Committee of the SCNPC, Gu Angran explained, was that China was a socialist country and socialism in China was at a primary stage.[135] He did not directly explain what this meant in relation to legislation. Instead, he emphasised that Chinese socialism was not built on an advanced economic base and that extensive investigation had to be carried out before a law could be made. Using foreign experience, he continued, was recognising that foreign laws could still be useful for China while socialism was at a primary stage. He justified using foreign laws in building a *Chinese socialist* legal system by explaining that laws which supported capitalism were to be rejected, but those concerning economic management and legislative techniques could be used. Furthermore, recognition of international practice and customs was seen as a necessity for attracting foreign investment and advanced foreign technologies.[136] With this legislative policy in place, systematic transplantation of foreign laws was also trialled in the late 1980s: In 1988, the State Commission for Structural Reform proposed that 'the experience in Hong Kong be transplanted into Shenzhen, thus establishing an inland Hong Kong'. Accordingly, the Shenzhen Government established a 'Leading Group for Drawing on and Transplanting Hong Kong and Other Foreign Legal Rules' to adopt Hong Kong law and other foreign legal experiences.[137]

Despite the ambivalent recognition of the relevance of foreign law and international practice, laws made in the 1980s, especially those regulating commercial transactions and economic relationships, were distinctly western in style, form, structure and language. The Equity and Cooperative Joint Venture Laws (1979 and 1988 respectively), the Foreign Economic Contract Law (1986), and individual statutes for the protection of intellectual property (e.g. Trade Marks Law (1982) and Patent Law (1984)) are some examples which clearly reflect the influence of Western law.[138] The revision of the Constitution in 1982 was reported to have only been carried out after a systematic study of the constitutions of 35 countries.[139] Most strikingly, the General Principles of Civil Law (GPCL), adopted in 1986, are seen in their form as

---

135 *Ibid.*

136 *Id.*, at 31.

137 Zhang Wenxian, 'Inheritance, Transplant and Reform: A Necessity for Legal Development', (no. 2, 1995) *Social Science Fronts* (*Shehui Kexue Zhanxian*) 9, at 13; He Hangzhou, *supra* note 123, at 52-53.

138 Guiguo Wang, 'Economic Integration in Quest of Law', 1995 (29: (2) *Journal of World Trade* 5; and Li, Zhang & Du, *supra* note 123.

139 Chengguan Wang, 'Cross Reference and Absorption Among Laws in Different Countries – An Important Topic for Comparative Law', (1992) (4) *Legal Science in China* (*Zhongguo Faxue*) 39, at 42; Guo Daoxu, *Law-Making in China* (*Zhongguo Lifa Zhidu*) (Beijing: People's Press, 1988), at 126-127.

a 'general part of a civil code constructed on the German or pandectist model', and the structure of the provisions 'follows the German model exactly.'[140]

The initial drafting of laws in the reconstruction of Chinese law after the Cultural Revolution relied heavily on the various laws and law drafts completed in the 1950s and 1960s.[141] As a result of ideological constraints, lack of experience in dealing with foreign-related business transactions, and the predominance of Soviet-trained scholars and officials in official positions, the first countries China looked to for foreign legislation were former Eastern (socialist) European countries and those in neighbouring South East Asia.[142] This once again ensured the continuation of the Soviet influence. Soon, however, Deng Xiaoping's pragmatism, notably expressed in his famous black-white cat statement,[143] was to dominate the legislative agenda. Together with ideological relaxation, the focus on foreign experience shifted to advanced (another coded word for western) law and no clear preference was given to any particular foreign law. Nevertheless, the legal drafting technique has been of a Continental Civil Law style, preferring general principles to minute details, and the language has been western in nature.

6.3. Beyond Ideology: Globalisation and 'Rational' Law

If phrases such as 'using foreign experience as a reference' were ambiguous, symptomatic of an obvious ideological constraint at the time, this was soon to be changed in 1992 when the Party decided to establish a 'socialist market economy'.

Together with the argument for 'rational' law for a market economy came the direct call for 'legal transplant', 'assimilation', 'harmonisation with international practice' and 'internationalisation' of Chinese law. Chinese law-makers and scholars forcefully called for the comprehensive and systematic study of foreign laws and basic legal theories. Some foreign laws, it was argued, could simply be transplanted into Chinese legislation.[144] Many Chinese scholars began to ignore criticisms that

---

140 W.C. Jones, 'Some Questions Regarding the Significance of the General Provisions of Civil Law of the People's Republic of China', (1987) 28 (2) *Harvard International Law Journal* 309, at 310-311. The GPCL was based on an earlier draft, which in turn was based on Soviet and East European models. Thus, the German tradition as evidenced in the GPCL is once again second-hand. See further discussions in Chapter 9.

141 See also Peng Zhen, 'Explanations on the Seven Law Drafts', delivered at the 2nd Session of the Fifth NPC, 26 June 1979, available at <www.npc.gov.cn/zgrdw/common/zw.jsp?label=WXZLK&id=1111> (last accessed 12 Nov 2006).

142 See Yao Meizheng, *International Investment Law* (*Guoji Touzifa*) (Wuhan: Wuhan University Press, 1984).

143 It does not matter whether the cat is black or white, as long as it catches mice.

144 Tian Jiyuan, 'Report of the Work of the Standing Committee of the NPC delivered by to the NPC on 15 March 1994', in *People's Daily* (*Renmin Ribao*) 26 March 1994, at 3; 'Major Tasks of the Standing Committee of the 8th NPC', *People's Daily* (*Renmin Ribao*) 3 July 1993, at 4; 'To

China was making its law by borrowing Western laws and that Chinese law had lost its socialist and Chinese characteristics.[145] Instead, jurists and law-makers argued that to build a legal system for a market economy, legislation had to be foresighted, systematic, and close to international practice.[146] 'Chinese characteristics', some urged, should not be overemphasised, or simply should not be pursued at all.[147]

If there was ambivalence in the admission of the usefulness of foreign law and international practice in building a Chinese legal system in the 1980s and thus a tendency to offer different interpretations, the language by the 1990s had become unambiguous. Now deputies to the National Congress called for the bold absorption of foreign laws.[148] The official organ for law-making formally adopted such an approach for fulfilling its tasks.[149] The leaders of the law-making authorities also explicitly endorsed bold adoption and the direct transplant of foreign laws.[150] With such a legislative policy in place, the Maritime Code which had been in the making for over ten years and was primarily composed of borrowings from international conventions and practice, was not only adopted in 1992, but its adoption was heralded as an excellent example for harmonising Chinese law with international practice.[151] Many long awaited codes, e.g. the Company Law (1993),

---

Boldly Borrow Legislative Experience from Developed Countries in Order to Perfect Chinese Market Legislation', *People's Daily* (*Renmin Ribao*) 5 December 1992 (overseas edition), at 3; Meng Qingguo, 'On Studying and Using Western Civil Law', 1993 (2) *Studies in Law* (*Faxue Yanjiu*) 79, at 79-81; 'Deputies to the People's Congress on Legislative Work', 1992 (6) *Legal Science in China* (*Zhongguo Faxue*) 28, at 28-29.

145 See Ronald C. Keith, *China's Struggle for the Rule of Law* (New York: St. Martin's Press, 1994), at 99-100.

146 'A Perfect Legal System Must Be Established in Order to Build a Socialist Market Economy', *People's Daily* (*Renmin Ribao*) (overseas edition), 7 November 1992, at 3; 'Market Economy and the Modernisation of a Legal System – Speeches Given at the Symposium on a Market Economy and the Modernisation of the Legal System', *supra* note 102, at 2; 'Further Emancipating Minds and Making Great Efforts for the Prosperity of Legal Research – A Discussion on Deng Xiaoping's Talk during his Southern Tour' (Southern Tour Symposium), 1992 (5) *Studies in Law* (*Faxue Yanjiu*) 1, at 4-5.

147 Junhao Zhang, 'The Market System and Private Law in China', 1994 (6) *Journal of the China University of Political Science and Law* (*Zhangfa Luntan*) 34; Sun Xiaoxia, 'On Internationalisation and Nationalisation of Law in a Market Economy Society', 1993 (4) *Journal of Hangzhou University* (*Hanzhou Daxue Xuebao*) 79; 'Market Economy and the Modernisation of a Legal System – Speeches Given at the Symposium on a Market Economy and the Modernisation of the Legal System', *supra* note 102; and Southern Tour Symposium, *id.*

148 'Deputies to the People's Congress on Legislative Work', *supra* note 144.

149 *People's Daily* (*Renmin Ribao*), 3 July 1993, *supra* note 144.

150 'Establishing an Economic Legal Structure for a Socialist Market Economy – Chairman of the Standing Committee of the NPC, Qiao Shi Answers Questions from [Journal of] Chinese Law', *Legal Daily* (*Fazhi Ribao*), 16 December 1994, at 1.

151 Li, Zhang & Du, *supra* note 123, at 30.

the Foreign Trade Law (1994), the Arbitration Law (1994), the Audit Law (1994), the Securities Law (1995), the People's Bank Law (1995), the Law on Commercial Banks (1995), the Law on Accounting (1995), and the Insurance Law (1995) were all adopted. Speedy revisions or additions were made to existing laws which were deemed inconsistent with international practice. Taxation laws, joint venture laws, intellectual property protection laws, the Criminal Procedure Law and the Criminal Law, and most recently, the Company Law, the Securities Law, all underwent major revisions. Further, China has now ratified a large number of international conventions dealing with international economic relations, especially intellectual property protection.[152]

What is now emphasised is the urgency of assimilating Chinese law to or harmonising it with international practice. It is therefore unsurprising to note the frequency of the words 'transplant', 'assimilation' and 'harmonisation' appearing in all Chinese legal literature. 'Internationalising' Chinese law, it is argued, is a matter of necessity, and the direction for modernising Chinese law and its rationale is determined by the nature of the market economy and the 'open door' policy.[153] Features of a modern market economy included its internationalisation and openness, as do those of a socialist market economy. Thus, the modern development of the market economy requires that the Chinese economy be part of and competing in the internationalised market. To do so, all economic activities, domestic or international, must be regulated in accordance with internationally accepted norms, customs, practices and rules. Harmonising Chinese law with international practices is thus a logical necessity.[154] Still some scholars go further to suggest that the internationalisation of Chinese law is required because of the common activities and common rational nature of human beings.[155] Even those who keep to a traditional Marxist line accept that the decision to establish a market economy in China has thus provided a foundation for legal transplant, assimilation and harmonisation.[156]

---

152 China is a party to most major international commercial agreements. As of November 2006, the People's Congress website contained 110 multilateral treaties and 207 bilateral agreements. See <www.npc.gov.cn/zgrdw/wxzl/wxzl_gbxx.jsp?lmid=0106&dm=010608&pdmc=010608> (last accessed 16 November 2006).

153 See e.g. Geng Cheng, 'The Market Economy and Internationalisation of the Legal System', 1994 (11) *Economic Law* (*Jingji Fazhi*) 2; Fang Jian, 'Internationalisation of Law and the Development of Jurisprudence', 1993 (3) *Law Science* (*Falü Kexue*) 9; He Hangzhou, 'On Legal Transplant and the Construction of an Economic Legal System', 1992 (5) *Legal Science in China* (*Zhongguo Faxue*) 50; and Sun, *supra* note 147.

154 Geng Cheng, *id.*, at 2; Li, Zhang & Du, *supra* note 123, at 3-4.

155 Sun, *supra* note 147, at 79.

156 Cong Xuangong, 'Applying Foreign Things for Chinese Use through Reference and Creation', 1992 (1) *Journal of the China University of Political Science and Law* (*Zhangfa Luntan*) 69, at 70; He Hangzhou, *supra* note 153, at 50-1.

The liberal attitude towards foreign law and the hunger for advanced (western) experience has made it almost impossible to trace the specific foreign sources of Chinese legislation as, in the making of each of the specific laws, scholars and law-makers have consulted practically all of the available foreign (Civil or Common) laws on the subject-matter under consideration.[157] Thus, the best we can say is that Chinese law, in its forms, structure and methodologies, has undoubtedly become Western[158] and is largely fashioned in a Continental style in its legislative techniques.[159]

6.4. Beyond Specific Western Models: Harmonisation with International Practice

While the movement towards the westernisation of Chinese law is easy to recognise, there has also been a rather subtle and incremental shift in recent years to a model based more on international practice and international treaties. Three principal factors underpin this shift. First, while the ideological breakthrough in 1992 allowed a liberal approach towards legal transplant, concerns were raised that modernisation was becoming a process of westernising Chinese law. To defuse this fear, many scholars stressed the importance of international conventions and practice in the process.[160] Much of the recent Chinese literature therefore concentrates on the necessity of harmonising Chinese law with international practice and conventions

157 As early as in 1990, in order to determine the terms of joint ventures, China consulted no less than 18 countries/regions, namely the USA, Japan, France, (then) West Germany, The Netherlands, Italy, Belgium, Luxemburg, the (former) Soviet Union, Romania, Poland, Egypt, Chile, Indonesia, Thailand, Singapore, Malaysia, South Korea, and Taiwan. See Song Rufeng, *Recollections on Participation in Law-making* (*Canjia Lifa Gongzuo Suoji*) (Beijing: Press of China Legal System, 1994), vol 1, at 22-24. Of course one can still generally see whether some specific legal institutions and mechanisms are based on Civil or Common law.

158 See Liang Zhiping, in 'The Sixth Civil Law Forum – Chinese Culture and Chinese Civil Code', 13 May 2004, China University of Political Science and Law, available at <www.ccelaws.com/mjlt/default.asp> (accessed 10 June 2004).

159 I should add that what I emphasise here is the word 'techniques' as opposed to legal classification. Indeed, as Mattei has recently pointed out, the traditional classification of legal families into Civil law, Common law, and Socialist law is losing its significance as a result of the convergence of legal traditions and legal transplant. See Ugo Mattei, 'Three Patterns of Law: Taxonomy and Change in the World's Legal Systems', 1997 (45) *Am. J. Comp. L.* 5.

160 Some scholars have specifically called for the bold and massive use of conventions to avoid the question of whether they are socialist or capitalist. See Cao Jianming, Sun Chao, and Gu Changhao, 'The Socialist Legal System Has to Favour the Liberation and Development of the Productive Forces', 1992 (4) *Legal Science in China* (*Zhongguo Faxue*) 8, at 3; He Hangzhou, *supra* note 153, at 52. 'International practice' is of course a two-edged sword: it could mean common practice among countries, or international law (both treaty based law and customary law).

in the process of transplanting western laws on market-related mechanisms.[161] In fact, the movement towards international practice had already emerged earlier in law-making. Thus, while the 1981 Contract Law (repealed in 1999) and the 1986 GPCL had the strong flavour of the Soviet and former Eastern European countries, the 1985 Foreign Contract Law (repealed in 1999) and the 1999 Contract Law signified the beginning of a 'pluralist' approach to drawing experience from many foreign countries and international treaty and customary law sources. In these two cases, while there were continuing influences from the former Eastern European countries, evidence of Common law influence is apparent (e.g. the notion of consideration in contract law). In the case of the 1999 Contract Law, while the German Civil Code, the Japanese Civil Code and the KMT Civil Code were all studied carefully and followed to varying degrees,[162] the UNIDROIT Principles of International Commercial Contracts (1994) and the UN Convention on Contracts for the International Sale of Goods (1980) were the actual models, and in some places were copied article by article.[163]

Secondly, as Potter has pointed out, the involvement of international agencies such as UNDP and the World Bank etc., and bilateral development programs with the USA, EU, Japan, Canada, Australia and other countries have played a significant role in broadening Chinese perspectives on foreign models and international development. With the assistance of these programs, large numbers of Chinese scholars and officials visited and studied in different countries in the west, and many of them soon returned to work in China,[164] replacing those retiring scholars and officials who had been trained in the former Soviet Union.

Finally, and more importantly, China's determination to join the WTO, and its efforts to comply with WTO requirements after being admitted, resulted in a huge effort to make new laws and revise existing laws in line with its WTO negotiations and agreements, and with WTO-related negotiations (such as IP protection).[165] Indeed,

---

161 Gong Pixiong, 'Four Great Contradictions Facing the Modernisation of Chinese Law', 1995 *Research and Debate* (*Tansuo Yu Zhengming*) 3; Geng Cheng, *supra* note 153; Li & Xiao, *supra* note 124; Li, Zhang & Du, *supra* note 123, and He Hangzhou, *supra* note 153.

162 See Liang Huixing, 'The Chinese Inheritance of Foreign Civil Laws' (undated), published in <www.iolaw.org.paper32.asp> (accessed 27 July 2004).

163 See Liang Huixing, *id.* Some Chinese scholars thus claim that studies in China on assimilating or harmonising Chinese law with international practice began in 1992. See Li, Zhang & Du, *supra* note 123, at 3; and He Hangzhou, *supra* note 153, at 53.

164 See Pitman B Potter, *The Chinese Legal System: Globalization and Local Legal Culture* (London & New York: Routledge Cuzon, 2001), ch. 1.

165 In fact, the present IP protection system (from its very initial development to its gradual improvement) in China could be seen as a product of Sino-US negotiations. See Richard L. Thurston, 'Country Risk Management: China and Intellectual Property Protection', 1993 (27) *Int'l Lawyer* 51; and Andrew Mertha, *The Politics of Piracy: Intellectual Property in Contemporary China* (Ithaca/London: Cornell University Press, 2005). See also discussion in Chapter 16.

the legislative tasks have been massive, and are ongoing, involving the revision of practically every piece of law concerning market entry and regulation in line with WTO agreements. And five years later, though much improvement is still desired, one can say that China has largely kept to its bargain, at least in terms of law in the statute books.[166] As a result, Chinese law is further internationalised.

What we have then seen in the last few years is a concentrated period when international law (both treaty-based and customary law), international practice, and the results of international negotiations have been rapidly absorbed into Chinese law, and no longer only in areas of market regulation and economic development. Here one has also seen some fundamentally significant developments in relation to the rule of law and the protection of human rights in conformity with commonly accepted international standards, such as the proclamation in the 1982 Constitution of the establishment of a rule of law and the protection of human rights. Equally significantly, the 1996–1997 revisions to the Criminal Procedural Law and Criminal Law were aimed at absorbing commonly accepted international standards on justice and the rule of law, rather than following any particularly legal tradition. With these developments, the process is thus better described as the internationalisation, rather than the westernisation, of Chinese law.

7. Concluding Remarks

Legal developments and the experience of law in China under communist rule started with the introduction and domination of a Chinese-style Marxist ideology. The genesis of the legal system lies, without much doubt, in the Soviet model. However, after some 80 years of trial and error, legal developments in the present China depend more on breaking off the shackles of ideological domination than on being guided by it. Indeed, the major breakthrough in legal developments in post-Mao China can largely be attributed to the abandonment of ideology.

Without this strong ideological constraint, it is equally clear that Chinese legal developments are now also moving away from the domination of Soviet law and jurisprudence, as will be shown in the discussions on specific areas of Chinese law in the following chapters. Since the 1990s law-makers in China have been looking for experience and models in Western countries, particularly in the pursuit for 'rational' law and in efforts to establish a country ruled according to law. In this way Chinese law is increasingly becoming 'Weberian' rather than 'Marxist'. Also importantly, great efforts have been made to ensure that Chinese law will conform to commonly accepted international practices and standards. Most importantly,

166 Indeed, the very critical analyses found in the annual reviews of the US seem to agree that China has kept its promises, at least in terms of law on paper. See US Trade Representative annual reports to the Congress on China's WTO compliance, available at <www.ustr.gov>.

a pure instrumentalist attitude towards law is losing its appeal in China, and the strong advocacy of a genuine rule of law is gaining momentum.

Chapter Three

Constitutional Law

1. Introduction

A constitution (*xianfa*), according to the Preamble of the Constitution of the PRC (1982), affirms the achievements of the struggles of the Chinese people and defines the basic system and basic tasks of the nation in a legal form. It is a set of general rules and serves the state as a fundamental charter of organisation.[1] It is therefore not surprising that over half of the provisions, precisely 78 of the 138 articles in the present (1982) Constitution, deal with the structure of state organisations.[2] Chinese law-makers also insist that a constitution should only contain the 'very fundamental and necessary' provisions that can be decided at the time.[3] In other

---

1 In 1954 when the first constitution of the PRC was adopted, Mao Zedong declared that 'An organisation must have rules, and a state also must have rules; the Constitution is a set of general rules and is a fundamental charter [of the state]'. See Chang Chun-chiao (one of the Gang of Four), 'Report on the Revision of the Constitution (delivered at the First Session of the Fourth National People's Congress, 1975)', in Joseph En-pao Wang (ed.), *Selected Legal Documents of the PRC* (University Publications of America, 1976), at 93. Despite the official repudiation of the Cultural Revolution and parts of Mao Zedong Thought, Mao's idea of the constitution is still followed by the contemporary leadership and law-makers in the PRC. See Gu Angran, *The Construction of a Socialist Legal System and Legislative Work* (*Shehui Zhuyi Fazhi Jianshe He Lifa Gongzuo*) (Beijing: China University of Political Science and Law Press, 1989), at 50. It should be pointed out, however, that especially since the mid-1990s scholars' views on the nature of a constitution have become much more sophisticated and most of them would include the stipulation of fundamental rights and freedoms as part of the important functions of a constitution. See e.g. Li Buyun (ed.), *A Comparative Study of Constitutional Law* (*Xianfa Bijiao Yanjiu*) (Beijing: Law Press, 1998), at 7-23.

2 See Jiang Bikun *et al.* (ed.), *Constitutional Law* (*Xianfa Xue*) (Beijing: China University of Political Science and Law Press, 1993), at 4. While the 1982 Constitution has so far undergone four revisions in 1988, 1993, 1999 & 2004, the total number of provisions has remained unchanged.

3 Gu Angran, *supra* note 1, at 57; and Zhang Youyu, 'To Discuss Seriously and Practically', in Zhang Youyu (ed.), *A Collection of Papers on the Constitution* (*Xianfa Lunwen Ji*) (Supplementary Volume) (Beijing: Press of the Masses, 1982), at 5.

words, a constitution is seen as a document about the future as it is perceived by 'the people' of the present time. In the Chinese reality a constitution is thus a document about the future as perceived by the present leadership of the Communist Party of China (CPC).[4] As such, the constitution in China has been in a constant state of flux, reflecting changes in the CPC leadership and in its policies about the kind of future society envisaged. It is not surprising, therefore, that in a history of less than 60 years the PRC has had four different constitutions, the fourth one being amended four times already since its adoption in 1982.[5]

In short, Chinese constitutional law has concerned itself more with state organisational structure than with the checks and balances of governmental powers, more with the future direction of the society than the protection of fundamental rights of citizens, and more with general principles than with detailed rules capable of implementation. However, one must not dismiss the Chinese Constitution out of hand. Seen as the 'mother of all laws',[6] the Chinese Constitution does set parameters for social and legal developments.[7] More importantly, after nearly three decades of legal reform, a series of administrative laws and regulations have been issued implementing various aspects of the Constitution, thus making the Constitution much more relevant in practical terms.

In this chapter we will first review constitutional developments in modern China. We will then examine the fundamental principles and state structures as provided by the present Constitution. Legal institutions (the judiciary, the legal profession etc.) will be dealt with in the next chapter.

---

4 Chinese leadership has never denied the fact that the Party has a heavy-handed involvement and exercises strong leadership in and control over the making and revision of the constitutions of the PRC. See Gu Angran, *supra* note 1, at 53-60. All amendments to the Constitution have been initiated and drafted by the Party despite recent calls for the separation of the Party and the State. See further discussions below.

5 Making frequent changes to the constitution is not however unique to the Communist Party. From 1900 to 1949, several 'constitutions' were promulgated by the imperial governments, by the warlords and by the Nationalist Government. See further historical review below.

6 Jiang Bikun, *supra* note 2, at 5.

7 It is not unusual these days, when discussing specific legal reforms with Chinese scholars, to hear them arguing that certain reforms are constrained by the present constitutional arrangement.

2. A Brief Historical Review

2.1. Constitutional Monarchy through Transformation v. Republic through Revolution – The Path and Pace of Reform

Modern constitutional law in China is a result of Western influence introduced by the legal reforms started at the turn of the 20th century; it is not a natural development of indigenous legal institutions.[8] Indeed, for all practical purposes, constitutional issues did not arise in China until the last dynasty, the Qing Dynasty, was facing downfall, and China faced the possibility of partition by the European powers.[9] It was during the dying days of this dynasty and after a series of humiliations brought about by foreign aggression and unequal treaties that the Imperial Court came to the belief that one of the main sources of influence of the world powers was the fact that they all had constitutional governments and, in particular, that the greatest reason for the Japanese success was its having a constitution.[10] Thus, together with modern law reform came constitutional reform, aimed at transforming the autocratic empire into a constitutional monarchy.[11]

The first move towards constitutional reform was the appointment, in June 1905, of a Special Commission of five high-ranking officials to travel to Austria, Belgium, England, France, Germany, Italy, Japan, Russia and the United States to examine their constitutions and political systems.[12] In the same year a Committee for Studying the Ways of Government (*Kaocha Zhengzhi Guan*) was established.[13] Upon the return of the Commissioners a unanimous recommendation in favour of

---

8 Although the Chinese term '*xianfa*' did appear in ancient texts, its meaning differed little from the term '*fa*' (law). See Jiang Bikun, *supra* note 2, at 9-10; Li Buyun, *supra* note 1, at 8-9; Xie Shiwen, 'The New Constitution Signifies the New Development in Socialist Democracy', in Chinese Society of Legal Science (ed.), *A Selection of Papers on the Constitution* (*Xianfa Lunwen Xuan*) (Beijing: Press of the Masses, 1983), at 97. There were also ideas comparable to Western notions of constitutionalism – the limitation of government powers – in various schools of philosophical thought, but there was hardly a tradition of such. See detailed discussion in Wm. Theodore de Bary, 'The "Constitutional Tradition" in China', (no. 1, 1995) 9 *J. of Chinese L.* 7.

9 See H.G.W. Woodhead (ed.), *The China Year Book 1925–1926* (Tientsin: The Tientsin Press, 1927), ch. XXIII (China's Constitutions and Election Laws); and Pan Wei-tung, *The Chinese Constitution: A Study of Forty Years of Constitution-Making in China* (Washington, DC: Institute of Chinese Culture, 1945), at 1.

10 Pan, *id.*, at 3-4.

11 For a detailed and excellent study of modern constitutional movements in China, see Wang Renbo, *Modern China and Its Constitutional Culture* (*Xianzheng Wenhua Yu Jingdai Zhongguo*) (Beijing: Publishing House of Law, 1997).

12 Pan, *supra* note 9, at 4.

13 In 1907 the Committee was renamed the Committee for Investigating and Drawing up Regulations of Constitutional Government (*Xianzhen Biancha Guan*). See M.J. Meijer, *The*

a constitutional government was made to the Imperial Court, which agreed with the recommendations in principle but was reluctant to act immediately.[14] Nevertheless, a series of Imperial Edicts concerning the establishment of a constitutional government and of Provincial Assemblies was soon issued.[15]

The first document in China that defined the principles of a constitutional government,[16] the Principles of Constitution (*Qinding Xianfa Dagang*), together with the Outlines of Parliamentary Procedure and Outlines of Election Law, was issued on 27 August 1908. However, the first modern constitutional document in China was a product of 'plagiarism' of the Japanese Constitution of 1889,[17] with the omission of provisions limiting the powers of the Emperor.[18] A nine-year program to transform the autocratic empire into a constitutional monarchy was also announced in 1908.[19] However, the Imperial Court was not to have the time to implement the Program. The revolutionaries, led by Dr. Sun Yat-sen, had neither faith in, nor patience for, the slow process of constitutional transformation. By August 1911, when an uprising was organised by the revolutionaries with the complicity of Imperial troops, revolution was sweeping the whole nation.[20] As a last effort to save the Empire, a constitution, known as the Nineteen Articles (*Zhongda Xintiao Shijiu Tiao*), aimed at establishing a British style system of ministerial responsibility and a parliament, was drafted in three days and issued for immediate implementation on 3 November 1911.[21] These Articles were however not able to save the Empire.

Introduction of Modern Criminal Law in China (2nd edition) (Hong Kong: Lun Men Bookstore, 1967), at 40-41.

14 Pan, *supra* note 9, at 5.

15 The texts of these Edicts can be found in *The China Year Book 1925–1926*, *supra* note 9; Hawking L. Yen, *A Survey of Constitutional Development in China* (New York: AMS Press, 1968). For Chinese texts of constitutional documents (from Qing to KMT reforms), see Xia Xinhua & Hu Xucheng (eds), *Modern Chinese Constitutional Movements: A Collection of Historical Records* (*Jindai Zhongguo Xianzheng Licheng: Shiliao Huicui*) (Beijing: Press of China University of Political Science and Law, 2004).

16 Jean Escarra, *Chinese Law: Conception and Evolution, Legislative and Judicial Institutions, Science and teaching*, translated from French by Gertrude R. Browne and published by the University of Washington (1961), at 185.

17 W.Y. Tsao, *The Constitutional Structure of Modern China* (Melbourne: Melbourne University Press, 1947), at 1; Pan, *supra* note 9, at 6-7. For an English translation of the Principles, see William L. Tung, *The Political Institutions of Modern China* (The Hague: Martinus Nijhoff, 1964), at 318-319.

18 Jiang Bikun, *supra* note 2, at 54.

19 For details of the plan, see *The China Year Book 1925–1926, supra* note 9, at 616-617,

20 Pan, *supra* note 9, at 10.

21 See Jiang Bikun, *supra* note 2, at 55; and Pan, *supra* note 9, at 11. For an English translation of the Articles, see *The China Year Book 1925–1926, supra* note 9, at 628-629.

2.2. Presidential System v. Cabinet System – The Struggle for the Control of Government Powers

While the Imperial government was trying to transform itself into a constitutional monarchy, a provisional government was being established by the revolutionaries. Within a month of the promulgation of the Nineteen Articles the revolutionaries themselves had promulgated the General Plan for the Organisation of the Provisional Government (*Linshi Zhengfu Zhuzhi Dagang*).[22] This General Plan was to establish an American-style presidential system in China. Dr. Sun was to be elected the Provisional President upon his return from the United States a month later. On 11 March 1912, the Provisional Constitution (*Linshi Yuefa*) of the Republic was promulgated.[23] This Provisional Constitution was to change the presidential system (as originally envisaged in the General Plan) to a cabinet system.[24] The reason for this change was that when the Provisional Constitution was being drafted by the members of the Council of State it had become clear that Yuan Shih-kai, the most powerful warlord of the time, was to succeed Dr. Sun as the provisional president and the members obviously feared that Yuan might abuse the presidential powers, a fear that proved later to have been well founded.[25]

Under the Provisional Constitution, the Provisional President was to convene the Parliament (a bicameral National Assembly) within ten months, and the Parliament was then to adopt a permanent constitution.[26] The National Assembly was convened fourteen months after the promulgation of the Provisional Constitution. A drafting committee, composed of sixty members (thirty members elected from each House) met at the Temple of Heaven in Beijing from 10 July to 31 October 1913 and produced a constitution in 113 articles, commonly refereed to as the 'Temple of Heaven Draft' (*Tientang Xiancao*).[27] This draft was again designed to restrict the power of the president and to institute a cabinet system of government. The Draft was modelled on the French Constitution in making the cabinet members responsible to the House of Representatives.[28]

---

22 Issued on 3 December 1911. An English translation (translated as 'Temporary Constitution of the Republic of China') can be found in *The China Year Book 1925–1926, supra* note 9, at 629-630.

23 An English translation can be found in *The China Year Book 1925–1926, supra* note 9, at 633-637.

24 Pan, *supra* note 9, at 15; and Tsao, *supra* note 17, at 2.

25 Tsao, *supra* note 17, at 2.

26 See Articles 53-54 of the Provisional Constitution.

27 An English translation of the Draft can be found in *The China Year Book 1925–1926, supra* note 9, at 658-665.

28 See Pan, *supra* note 9, at 21; Tsao, *supra* note 17; and Article 81 of the Draft.

The underlying principle of the Temple of Heaven Draft clearly conflicted with Yuan's ambition to be the new emperor – an ambition he later fulfilled. As the parliament was opposed to his move towards an American presidential system, Yuan established his own drafting committee and promulgated his own Constitutional Compact (*Zhonghua Minguo Yuefa*) on 1 May 1914.[29] This document was not only intended to restore the American style presidential system, it also gave the Chinese president much wider powers than those of the American president, especially in abolishing the restrictions on the powers of the president as contained in the Provisional Constitution, and in granting absolute control to the president over the legislature and the administration.[30] Even such a Constitution soon proved to be useless for Yuan's ambition, if not an obstacle to it. By December 1915 Yuan had the monarchy restored and made himself the emperor.

2.3. Centralism v. Federalism – The Struggle among the Warlords

Yuan's monarchy, however, lasted only 83 days.[31] After his death the then vice-president succeeded to the presidency and declared that the Provisional Constitution was still the valid supreme law of the land and the parliament, which had been dissolved by Yuan, was summoned and reconvened on 1 August 1916 to resume the work of constitution-making. The Temple of Heaven Draft was used as a basis for drafting.[32] However, this effort ran into many serious problems, chief among them being the issue of the division of powers between the central and local (provincial) governments. At the central level there was the struggle for supremacy between the new president and his premier, each backed by a different faction of warlords. At the provincial level the military governors were trying to establish their own kingdoms in the name of federalism. Thus at the central level the National Assembly was once again dissolved and, for a short period of a few days, the monarchy was restored. At the local level one province after another declared its independence and issued its

---

29 Dr. Frank J. Goodnow, then a professor at Columbia University and a counsellor to Yuan, exerted considerable influence on the preparation of the Constitution. Thus the document is sometimes referred to as the Goodnow Constitution. See Escarra, *supra* note 16, at 187. An English translation of the Constitution can be found in *The China Year Book 1925–1926*, *supra* note 9, at 665-670.

30 See Pan, *supra* note 9, at 25-26; Tsao, *supra* note 17, at 3-4; and Jiang Bikun, *supra* note 2, at 55.

31 The monarchy with Yuan as the emperor was restored on 11 December 1915. Yuan renounced the throne in the following March after several provinces declared their independence from the Central Government in protest against the restoration of the monarchy. Yuan himself died on 6 June 1916. See Pan, *supra* note 9, at 30-31; and *The China Year Book 1925–1926*, *supra* note 9, at 623-624.

32 See Pan, *supra* note 9, at 31; Tsao, *supra* note 17, at 4

own constitutions.[33] Instead of becoming a unified country under one constitution, China was divided by warlords and dominated by military feudalism.

However, the political climate had changed. Whatever the motivation of the warlords, they all wanted to use a constitution to legitimise their claims. Thus, besides the various constitutions issued by provincial governments, the Central Government also promulgated a new constitution, the Constitution of the Republic of China (*Zhonghua Minguo Xianfa*) on 10 October 1923, commonly referred to as the 'Bribery Constitution' as its passage through the National Assembly occurred through bribery. This Constitution,[34] technically well-framed and somewhat resembling a federal system,[35] was almost immediately denounced by the whole nation and was never put into operation.[36]

2.4. Political Elitism and Party Ideology – The Distorted Version of Chinese Constitutionalism

While the warlords were struggling for power in Beijing (known as the Northern Government), the revolutionaries led by Dr Sun had retreated to the South in Guangzhou, where they convened the dissolved National Assembly and established their own Southern Government (or Canton Government). The conflict between the North and the South was then settled by military means. Through the now famous Northern Expedition, the Southern Government defeated the warlords and once again reunited the nation under one banner – that of the Kuomintang.

The struggle against the warlords also led to the first collaboration between the Kuomintang and the Communist Party of China (CPC), with the latter agreeing to accept the political ideology of the Kuomintang, i.e. the Three Principles of the People and the Five-Power constitutional idea of Dr. Sun Yatsen. When the Northern Expedition came to a successful end in 1927, the Southern Government promulgated the Organic Law of the National Government of China. Although this Law was to serve as a provisional constitution, it was fundamentally a one-party rule document. Its Preamble stated:

> The Kuomintang of China, in order to establish the Republic of China on the basis of the Three Principles of the People and the Constitution of the Five Powers, which form the underlying principle of the Revolution, having conquered all opposition by military force and having now brought the

---

33 See Pan, *supra* note 9, at 31-33; Tsao, *supra* note 17, at 4-6.

34 An English translation of the Constitution can be found in *The China Year Book 1925–1926*, *supra* note 9, at 694-705.

35 In terms of foreign borrowings, it is said that the Constitution was largely modelled upon that of the French Republic with variations borrowed from the German and American Constitutions. See Pan, *supra* note 9, at 42.

36 Pan, *supra* note 9, at 34-42; Tsao, *supra* note 17, at 6-7.

> revolution from the military period to the political tutelage period, deem it necessary to construct a framework for the Constitution of Five Powers with a view to developing the ability of the people to exercise political power, so that constitutional government may soon come into existence and political power be restored to the people; and, further, in virtue of the responsibilities hitherto entrusted to the Party for the guidance and supervision of the government, do hereby ordain and promulgate the following Organic Law of the National Government.[37]

The Organic Law was subject to further revision, and indeed was revised several times, by the Central Executive Committee of the Kuomintang.[38] Here the Kuomintang, influenced by the Soviet experience, established the precedent of putting the Party above the state.

Under Sun's idea, as discussed in Chapter Two, after the military success of the Northern Expedition the nation was to undergo political tutelage during which the people would be trained and guided to exercise political powers. Thus, before a permanent Constitution of the Five Powers was to be created, a provisional constitution was deemed necessary for this political tutelage. Hence the Provisional Constitution for the Political Tutelage Period (*Xunzheng Shiqi Yuefa*) was duly promulgated and came into immediate effect on 1 June 1931.[39] This Provisional Constitution further entrenched Party rule in the national constitution. According to Article 30, during the period of political tutelage the Kuomintang was to exercise all governing powers on behalf of the National Assembly. On the subject of party supremacy, as evidenced in the document, one commentator had this to say:

> It is undeniable that the Provisional Constitution is a written testimony of the supremacy of the Kuomintang. The People's Convention which was summoned to enact and ordain the Provisional Constitution was largely under the influence of the party. The election of the delegates to the convention was far from being similar to popular suffrage. Candidates for election were selected and supported by various Kuomintang branches to ensure that desirable candidates be elected and those undesirable and hostile to the Kuomintang be ousted. It is evident that the convention, though nominally not subject to the party, was, in reality, bound to observe the policies and principles of the Kuomintang.[40]

---

[37] Quoted in Tsao, *supra* note 17, at 9.

[38] Tsao, *supra* note 17, at 9-10.

[39] For an English translation of the Provisional Constitution, see Tung, *supra* note 17, at 344-349.

[40] Tsao, *supra* note 17, at 12.

Thus the Constitution and its practice continued, and re-affirmed, the precedent of the domination of the Party over the state, as instituted by the 1927 Organic Law.

Political tutelage was to last for a period of six years.[41] Efforts were indeed made to draft a permanent constitution.[42] A draft was issued on 5 May 1936 by the Central Government, a document commonly referred to as the Double Fifth Draft Constitution. However the People's Congress, which was to adopt the Constitution, was not convened, in part due to the Japanese invasion which started in September of the same year.

A permanent constitution, the Constitution of the Republic of China (*Zhonghua Mingguo Xianfa*) was only adopted after the war, on 25 December 1946[43] and formally terminated the period of political tutelage in China. This Constitution again formally instituted the Kuomintang ideology as formulated by Dr. Sun Yatsen as the supreme law of the land. Political powers were far from reverting to the people. An indefinite period of Communist Rebellion, during which military rule was to be imposed, was formally declared by the Temporary Provisions Effective During the Period of Communist Rebellion attached to the Constitution.[44] This Period of Communist Rebellion was only formally terminated in 1991, and thus democracy, in the form of multi-party free elections, was only returned to the people in Taiwan after nearly half a century of military rule.

3. The Search for Socialist Solutions with Chinese Characteristics

As discussed in Chapter Two, the pre-Liberation practice of justice under communism was the foundation of that in the PRC, even though the experience was provisional in nature. In fact, the pre-1949 communist constitutional law was declared to be not yet of a socialist nature.[45] However, certain fundamental political principles, as

---

41 Pan, *supra* note 9, at 48.

42 See detailed discussions in Pan, *supra* note 9, at 51-63; and Tsao, *supra* note 17, at 17-22.

43 An English translation of the Constitution can be found in Tung, *supra* note 17, at 350-366.

44 These Provisions were abolished in July 1991. See Michael C H Kwang, 'Taiwan – The Republic of China: A Profile of Recent Constitutional Changes and Legal Developments', in Alice E-S Tay & Conita S C Leung (eds.), *Greater China: Law, Society and Trade* (Sydney: The Law Book Company, 1995), at 66. Various constitutional reforms had, however, occurred before 1991, most notably the lifting of the 38-year-old martial law in July 1987, and the legalisation of opposition parties in January 1989. For detailed discussions, see Yeh Jiunn-Rong, 'Changing Forces of Constitutional and Regulatory Reform in Taiwan', (1990) 4 *J. of Chinese L* 83, at 85-90.

45 Mao Zedong, 'On the New Democratic Constitutionalism', quoted in Zhao Zhenjiang (ed.), *Forty Years of the Chinese Legal System* (*Zhongguo Fazhi Sishinian*) (Beijing: Beijing University Press, 1989), at 31. The pre-1949 communist constitutional documents include the Constitutional Program of the Chinese Soviet Republic (first issued in November 1931 and

they now exist in the present Constitution, evolved from the pre-1949 experience through borrowings from the Soviet experience. Most notably, the systems of the People's Democratic Dictatorship, the People's Congress, and public ownership all have their roots in the pre-1949 communist constitutional documents, although they have often been formulated in different ways.[46] Also importantly, the Soviet model, which was first adopted during the Chinese Soviet Republic, was modified to suit the then prevailing political needs. This fundamentally utilitarian approach to socialist ideology was to define later constitutional developments in the PRC.[47]

One of the first legal documents issued by the new authority under the CPC leadership was the Common Program,[48] adopted by the Chinese People's Political Consultative Conference in September 1949, a month before the proclamation of the founding of the PRC. Serving as a provisional constitution it was not a radical document; in fact, it was a natural development of the pre-1949 experience. Thus the state was defined as a republic of the People's Democratic Dictatorship and its powers were to be vested with the People's Congress. Three related features are particularly notable. First, it continued its pre-1949 advocacy of a united front composed of the Chinese working class, peasantry, petty bourgeoisie, national bourgeoisie and other patriotic democratic elements, based on the alliance of workers and peasants and led by the working class. For this united front a People's Political Consultative Conference, composed of the representatives of the CPC, of all democratic parties and groups and people's organisations, of all regions, of the People's Liberation Army, of all national minorities, of overseas Chinese and of other patriotic democratic elements, was created as the organisational form of this united front.[49] The creation of this organisation was a clear deviation from the Soviet model to suit the political needs of the time.[50] Secondly, the need for a united front also necessitated the protection of private property, as many 'democratic elements' were of the property-owning class. Thus protection was given to the economic interests and private property of

---

revised in January 1934); the Program of Government of the Shan-Gan-Ning Border Area During the Anti-Japanese War (1939); the Program of Government of the Shan-Gan-Ning Border Area (1941); and the Constitutional Principles of the Shan-Gan-Ning Border Area (1946).

46 See discussions below. See also Zhao Zhenjiang, *supra* note 45, at 35.

47 The utilitarian approach towards the Soviet model as first adopted during the 1920–1930s thus prompting disagreement among Western scholars as to the significance of the pre-1949 experience in assessing or explaining post-1949 legal developments. See Alice E-S. Tay, 'Law in Communist China – Part 2', (1971) 6 *Syd. L. Rev.* 335, at 345.

48 An English translation can be found in Albert P. Blaustein (ed.), *Fundamental Legal Documents of Communist China* (New Jersey: Fred B. Rothman & Co., 1962), at 34-53.

49 See Paragraph 2 of the Preamble of the Common Program.

50 See John N. Hazard, *Communists and Their Law: A Search for the Common Core of the Legal Systems of the Marxian Socialist States* (Chicago/London: The University of Chicago Press, 1969), at 42-43.

workers, peasants, the petty bourgeoisie and the national bourgeoisie.[51] Further, the state-owned economy, the co-operative economy, the individual economy of peasants and handicraftsmen, the private capitalist economy and the state capitalist economy were all to co-exist, though under the leadership of the state-owned economy.[52] Again, such a moderate approach towards private property was much more tolerant than the Soviet practice.[53] Finally, the protection of citizens' rights featured prominently;[54] these rights, for the only time in the PRC, were located in chapter one of a constitutional document.

The Common Program was a provisional, not a transitional, constitution. Although a communist type constitution, it did not even mention the goal of socialism, or whether China would eventually practise it. Liu Shaoqi, in explaining the adoption of the Common Program, made it clear that whether China would practise socialism was a future matter to be decided by the people. A similar statement was made by Zhou Enlai in explaining the nature of the Common Program, although both Liu and Zhou also contradicted themselves by declaring that socialism would be adopted in China in the future.[55]

Socialism as a goal was to be enshrined in the first formal constitution of the PRC,[56] adopted in September 1954. This Constitution represented a first attempt by the CPC leadership to formalise and institutionalise the administration of the state. It also continued the moderate policy of social transformation.[57] This policy was particularly evident in the advocacy of a *step by step* process of social transformation from New Democracy to socialism.[58] The Common Program provisions regarding the nature of the state, the state power structure and the economic system were all inherited by the 1954 Constitution. As such, Soviet influence continued.[59] Indeed, scholars now complain that too much, both in terms of form and substance, was copied from the Soviet Union without sufficient regard to China's own situation.[60] There

---

51 Article 3 of the Common Program.

52 Article 26 of the Common Program.

53 See Hazard, *supra* note 50, chapters 8 & 9.

54 See Articles 4-6 and 9 of the Common Program.

55 Jiang Bikun, *supra* note 2, at 64-65.

56 An English translation can be found in Joseph En-pao Wang, *supra* note 1, at 65-89.

57 The continuation was specifically acknowledged in Para. 3 of the 1954 Constitution.

58 See Para. 2 of the Preamble of the 1954 Constitution.

59 Indeed, the Preamble of the Constitution declared that China had already built an indestructible friendship with the great Union of Soviet Socialist Republic and the People's Democracies.

60 Zhang Youyu & Wang Shuwen (eds.), *Forty Years of PRC's Legal Science* (*Zhonggu Faxue Sishinian*) (Shanghai: Shanghai People's Press, 1989), at 151.

was, however, an innovation in the creation of the office of 'Chairman of the People's Republic of China', an office which never existed in the Soviet Constitution.[61]

The 1954 Constitution was not intended to be permanent, but was a transitional constitution.[62] Indeed, by 1956 the transitional period was deemed over and the Constitution was seen as being out of date.[63] The need for constitutional revision was formally recognised by the Party at its Eighth Congress in 1956.[64] However, it was not to happen. The 'Anti-Rightists Movement' of 1957 spelt the end of the moderate policy towards social transformation and marked a return to mass campaigns, popular justice and political turmoil, culminating in the now infamous Cultural Revolution (1966–1977).[65]

The next constitution was the 1975 Constitution,[66] written during the Cultural Revolution. But, as some Chinese scholars have rightly pointed out, there was no need for a constitution, nor did the Constitution serve any meaningful purpose other than political propaganda.[67] The whole document was, as Hazard shows, simply a skeleton of the previous constitutions,[68] consisting of only 30 brief articles. Thus Western scholars were sceptical when Taiwan claimed to have found the draft constitution and had it published.[69] However, the 1975 Constitution may be said to represent the final triumph of Mao over the Russian School of ideologues in that it embodied his revolutionary ideas in place of those of the Soviets.[70] Although generally denounced by Chinese academics and officials as representing an extremist Left ideology, the provisions in the 1975 Constitution were more honest in reflecting the Chinese reality than other constitutions in the PRC, as they expressly affirmed the direct rule of the Party over the legislature, the government and the armed forces, abolished the Public Procuracy and advocated a wholesale dictatorship by

61 Hazard, *supra* note 50, at 43.

62 Gu Angran, *supra* note 1, at 54. Mao himself had said that the 1954 Constitution would be a transitional one. See Jiang Bikun, *supra* note 2, at 67.

63 Jiang Bikun, *supra* note 2, at 67.

64 Zhang & Wang, *supra* note 60, at 152.

65 See Alice Tay, 'The Struggle for Law in China', (1987) 21 *U.B.C. Law Rev.* 561, at 570-572.

66 An English translation of the 1975 Constitution can be found in Joseph Wang, *supra* note 1, at 65-89.

67 Zhao Zhenjiang, *supra* note 45, at 179-180.

68 Hazard, *supra* note 50, at 45.

69 *Ibid.*

70 *Ibid.* Indeed, it was Mao who first initiated the revision of the Constitution in March 1970. In July of the same year, a Constitutional Revision Committee was established with Mao as the Chairman. See Dong Chengmei, 'The Historical Developments of Our Constitution', in Chinese Society of Legal Science, *supra* note 8, at 56.

the proletariat. This brief and flexible document also reflected more honestly Mao's disregard for legalism and constitutional constraints.[71]

Changes in leadership after the fall of the so-called 'Gang of Four' produced yet another constitution, the 1978 Constitution.[72] This Constitution, in spite of the distrust, if not hatred, of the Soviet Union expressed by Mao's successors, restored much of the Soviet Russian type of constitutional structure.[73] More precisely, much of the constitutional structure as provided in the 1954 Constitution was restored,[74] and certain more radical provisions were abolished.[75] However, the 1978 Constitution was not a complete return to that of 1954; much of the radical ideology remained in the document. In particular the 1978 Constitution continued to advocate 'class struggle' and 'continuing revolution under the dictatorship of the proletariat'. The political and social turmoil of 1966–1976 was still affirmed as the first Great Proletarian Cultural Revolution, though declared to have been triumphantly concluded.[76] Certain explicit provisions granting direct Party control over the executive and the armed forces, as formally established in the 1975 Constitution, were also retained.[77] The continuation of these fundamental lines of the Cultural Revolution is not surprising. The Party was then headed by Hua Guofeng, claimed to be a wise leader chosen personally by Mao. Hua's continuing legitimacy lay not in repudiating the Cultural Revolution, but in upholding it. Thus Hua's rapid demise also sealed the fate of the 1978 Constitution.

In sharp contrast to Hua, Deng Xiaoping's ascendancy depended on the repudiation of the Cultural Revolution rather than the continuation of it; he was twice its victim. Deng also clearly saw the continuing legitimacy of the Party leadership as lying in the restoration of social order and economic development. Thus his initial strategy was to have the Cultural Revolution repudiated and 'Order and Development' back on the political agenda. This he achieved rapidly. At the Third Plenary Session of the Eleventh Party Central Committee in December 1978 he triumphed over Hua and managed to have his emphasis on social order and economic development written into the Communiqué issued after the Plenary Session. Soon at the Sixth Plenary Session of the Party in 1979 he had the history of the Communist Party

---

71 For an analysis of the 1975 Constitution, see Chün-tu Hsüeh, 'The New Constitution', (no. 3, 1975) 24 *Problems of Communism* 11.

72 An English translation can be found in Joseph Wang, *supra* note 1, at 124-170.

73 Hazard, *supra* note 50, at 45.

74 For instance, the restoration of the People's Procuratorate. See further discussions in Jiang Bikun, *supra* note 2, at 69.

75 For instance, the advocacy of total dictatorship was abolished.

76 See the Preamble of the 1978 Constitution.

77 See Arts. 19 and 22 (4).

rewritten and had the Cultural Revolution totally repudiated.[78] By now he had had the ideological foundation of the Chinese constitution changed; consequently, the need for further constitutional revision was not surprising.

Indeed, the first revision to the 1978 Constitution was made in 1979. This revision, among other things, re-established People's Governments to replace the Revolutionary Committees. Further, in line with Deng's emphasis on establishing a stable social order conducive to economic development, a second revision was made in 1980 to abolish Article 45, which provided the 'Four Great Rights', i.e. the right to speak out freely, air views fully, hold great debates, and write big-character posters.

4. Constitutional Law in Present-day China

4.1. Development of the 1982 Constitution

The radical change in the Party leadership after the defeat of Hua by Deng Xiaoping necessarily demanded a more fundamental revision of the Constitution.[79] Officially, the repudiation of the Cultural Revolution and the shift of the Party's work from political movements to economic development were advanced as the primary reasons for a comprehensive revision of the Constitution.[80]

Deng Xiaoping first outlined his basic idea for the revision of the 1978 Constitution when in August 1980 he reported to an enlarged meeting of the Politburo of the Central Committee of the Party:

> … the Central Committee will submit proposals for revising the Constitution of the People's Republic of China to the Third Session of the Fifth National People's Congress. Our Constitution should be made more complete and precise so as to really ensure the people's right to manage the state organs at all levels as well as the various enterprises and institutions, to guarantee to our people the full enjoyment of their rights as citizens, to enable the different nationalities to exercise genuine regional autonomy, to improve the multi-level system of people's congresses, and so on. The principle of

78 See 'On the Question of Party History – Resolution on Certain Questions in the History of Our Party Since the Founding of the People's Republic of China', adopted by the Sixth Plenary Session of the 11th Central Committee of the CPC on June 27, 1981. An English translation appears in Liu Suinian & Wu Qungan (ed.), *China's Socialist Economy: An Outline History (1949–1984)* (Beijing: Beijing Review Press, 1986), at 578-636.

79 See *supra* note 4.

80 See Jiang Bikun, *supra* note 2, at 69-70; Gu Angran, *supra* note 1, at 55; and Peng Zhen, 'Report on the Draft of the Revised Constitution of the People's Republic of China', in *Fifth Session of the Fifth National People's Congress* (*Main Documents*) (*November – December 1982*) (Beijing: Foreign Languages Press, 1993), at 69-70.

> preventing the over-concentration of power will also be reflected in the revised Constitution.[81]

The formal decision was made by the Central Committee of the Party, whose decision was dutifully accepted by the Fifth NPC at its third session in September 1980.[82] As with the previous revisions, the process was heavily controlled by the Party.[83] The same session also decided to establish a Constitutional Revision Committee headed by Ye Jianying, then the Chairman of the Standing Committee of the NPC, and composed of 103 members, including all members of the Politburo and the Secretariat of the Central Committee of the Party.[84] One of the major concerns for the Revision Committee was the prevention of a repetition of the Cultural Revolution. However, major disagreements soon emerged as to whether the new constitution should include the 'Four Fundamental Principles',[85] whether the doctrine of separation of powers or the People's Congress system should be adopted, and whether a federal system or national minority autonomy system should be provided by the constitution.[86] In July 1981, the Central Committee of the Party decided that Peng Zhen should take direct control of the revision. In October of the same year he then outlined four principles for the revision: first, the Constitution had to address the Chinese reality but at the same time take into consideration foreign experience and absorb all positive aspects of constitutions in foreign countries. Secondly, the Constitution should only contain the very fundamental and necessary provisions that could be decided at the time, with a focus on strengthening national unity and social stability and facilitating the construction of the Four Modernisations. Thirdly, the 1954 Constitution should be used as the foundation for the revision, but necessary improvements had to be made to reflect the present reality. Finally, the 'Four Fundamental Principles' must be used as the ultimate guideline for the revision.[87] With these guidelines in place, the revision was carried out swiftly. By April 1982 a draft was published for nationwide discussion, which lasted about four months. By November 1982 the final draft was submitted to the National People's

81 See *Selected Works of Deng Xiaoping (1875–1982)* (Beijing: Foreign Languages Press, 1984), at 322.

82 Peng Zhen, *supra* note 80, at 69.

83 In addition to the direct involvement of Party members in the drafting process and in the taking of its policies since the Third Plenary Session of the 11th Party Congress as the guidelines for the revision, the Politburo and the Secretariat convened eight sessions to specifically discuss various drafts of the constitution. See Gu Angran, *supra* note 1, at 59-60.

84 See Gu Angran, *supra* note 1, at 56.

85 See discussions on fundamental principles below.

86 Gu Angran, *supra* note 1, at 57.

87 *Id.*, at 57-58.

Congress for adoption. Among the 3,040 delegates, three abstained and the rest unanimously adopted the Constitution.[88]

The 1982 Constitution is essentially a Dengist constitution, reflecting Deng Xiaoping's ideas for modernising China, i.e. social stability, economic development and opening to the outside. Thus, the Preamble upholds the so-called 'Four Fundamental Principles' and emphasises the construction of socialist modernisation as a fundamental national task. Article 18 of the new Constitution formally provides a constitutional basis for foreign investment and its protection in China. Article 11 of the Constitution allows the development, within the limits prescribed by law, of an individual economy as a complement to the socialist economy. Article 10, for the first time in a PRC constitution,[89] defines the ownership of land in China. Certain institutions and provisions from the 1950s are restored. The position of the Chairperson of the State, with reduced power,[90] is re-established. The office of Chairperson of the Military Commission is also re-established, thus ending the situation where the armed forces had no constitutional status under the 1975 and 1978 Constitutions. Equality before the law is also restored, though with slightly different wording.[91]

Although hailed as 'the best since the founding of the PRC',[92] the 1982 Constitution was soon amended, in April 1988, to legitimise the existence of the rapidly developing private economy as well as to provide a constitutional basis for the commercial transfer of land use rights, both of which were the results of economic reform and prerequisites for further economic development.

In 1992 more ideologically significant revision was necessitated by the adoption by the Party at its 14th Congress of the notion of a 'socialist market economy'. So, not long after the Central Committee of the CPC formally submitted its 'Suggestions on Amending Certain Contents of the Constitution', the NPC dutifully adopted the suggestions and translated the new Party policy into law in March 1993.[93] As a

88 *Id.*, at 58-59.

89 *Id.*, at 70.

90 As compared with the 1954 Constitution, the Chairperson no longer had the power to convene the State Council nor the power to command the armed forces.

91 The difference in wording has certain implications for the interpretation of this principle. See the discussion on fundamental rights below.

92 Pu Zengyuan, 'The Movement for Constitutionalism and Constitutions in Twentieth-Century China', in Alice E-S. Tay & Conita Leung (eds.), *Constitution-making and Restructuring in the Present and Former Communist World*, being a special issue of the *Bulletin of Australian Society of Legal Philosophy* (Vol. 17, nos 58/59, 1992) 162, at 169. See also Jiang Bikun, *supra* note 2, at 3-4; and Zhang Youyu, 'Strengthening the Research on Constitutional Theories', in Chinese Society of Legal Science, *supra* note 8, at 2.

93 Thus, according to Chinese scholars, Party policy is translated, through legal procedure, into state will. See Liu Zheng, 'Further Constitutional Protection for the Construction of Socialism with Chinese Characteristics', (no. 2, 1993) *Legal Science in China* (*Zhongguo Faxue*) 5, at 6.

result of the revision, the term 'socialist market economy' replaced that of 'planned economy'. Similarly the terms 'state-owned (*guoyou*) economy' and 'state-owned enterprises' replaced 'state-run (*guoying*) economy' and 'state-run enterprises' respectively. Provisions on state planning were also removed and in their place were put provisions that required the state to strengthen economic legislation and macro-economic control. On the whole the 1993 Amendments provided flexibility, though not specific direction, for future development.

The 15th Party Congress in 1997 laid down certain political foundations for post-Deng China[94] by adopting a policy to continue the reform policy launched by Deng Xiaoping in 1979 and incorporating a Dengist version of socialism in the constitution.[95] Once again efforts were made to transform Party policy into constitutional provisions through constitutional revision. This revision was undertaken by a Revision Group of the Central Committee of the Party, headed by Li Peng. After its first draft, issued on 5 December 1998 for internal Party discussion, the drafting work proceeded swiftly. By 22 January 1999 a formal proposal had already been made by the Party to the Standing Committee of the NPC (SCNPC) for consideration and adoption.[96] Its formal adoption at the 2nd Session of the Ninth NPC was a pure formality; the proposal was adopted word for word.[97]

The 1999 revision was rather more sophisticated than those of 1988 and 1993. It involved six amendments falling into three categories: further supplementation to the 'Four Fundamental Principles', a Chinese version of the 'Rule of Law', and a politico-economic version of 'socialism with Chinese characteristics'.[98] On the whole the 1999 revision of the Constitution was essentially designed to carry out the conversion of the adopted ideology of the 15th Party Congress of 1997 into the form of fundamental state law. The revisions reflected the Party's determination

---

A full text of these 'suggestions' can be found in *Legal Daily* (*Fazhi Ribao*), 16 February 1993, at 1. The Constitutional Amendment was adopted by the First Session of the Eighth NPC on 29 March 1993.

94 See, 'Explanations on the Constitutional Amendment Bill', delivered by Tian Jiyun to the Ninth NPC on 9 March 1999, in *People's Daily* (*Renmin Ribao*), 9 March 1999, at 1.

95 See Political Report to the 15th Party Congress, delivered by Jiang Zemin on 12 September 1997. An English translation of the Report appears in <www.chinadaily.net/cndy/history/15/fulltext.html>.

96 The Proposal was published in full in the *People's Daily* (*Renmin Ribao*), 31 January 1999, at 1.

97 Although there were 21 votes against the adoption and 24 abstentions, there were no dissenting views published in any public media in China.

98 Each of these is to be discussed below. There is one amendment in 1999 which does not sit well with the above categories; that is, the replacement of the term 'counter-revolutionary activities' with the term 'criminal activities jeopardising the state security' in Article 28 – a change that occurred earlier in 1997 when the Criminal Law of the PRC was comprehensively revised.

to continue reform and opening-up to the world and to administer the country according to law. Examined from a development perspective, these revisions indicate the then understanding of the notion of socialism with Chinese characteristics among the Party leadership, while signalling its intention to continue the economic reforms initially launched in 1978, and to maintain stability in economic policies in post-Deng China.

The First Plenary Session of the16th CPC Congress (2002) began the changeover of Party leadership, which continued until the Third Plenary Session of the 10th National People's Congress in March 2005. These congresses saw the gradual handover of leadership power from Jiang Zemin to Hu Jintao.[99] The 16th Party Congress was therefore intended to sum up the Party's experience (or to record its achievements) in the previous five years, and to set out a policy direction for the new leadership. Not surprisingly, and as has routinely been the case in post-Mao China, the policy 'spirit' as adopted by the 16th Party Congress needed to be incorporated into the Constitution; hence a new round of constitutional revision was required.

The latest round of constitutional revision thus occurred in 2003–2004, aimed at setting out a new direction for the current leadership. As early as on 27 March 2003 a Constitutional Revision Group was established, headed by Wu Bangguo (the new Chairman of the Standing Committee of the NPC) and under the direct leadership of the Standing Committee of the Politburo of the Party. At the same time, the principles for the revision were also set down by the Standing Committee of the Politburo.[100] Official consultations were swiftly conducted in the next several months within limited circles of authorities and personnel, such as of provincial leaders, leaders of the democratic parties, and selected groups of local leaders and prominent scholars.[101] The draft Suggestion on Amending Certain Contents of the Constitution was soon taking shape by August 2003. It is at this time that the on-going revision was first officially reported,[102] but although this was the first announcement of it, there was no mention of such a Group, even though it was said that the plenary session would discuss the proposals for constitutional reform.[103]

---

99 Jiang passed his positions as Party Secretary-General and the President of the State to Hu Jintao in 2002 (at the Party Congress) and 2003 (at the NPC) respectively. However, Jiang only handed over to Hu Jintao the Chairmanship of the CPC Central Military Commission in September 2004 and the Chairmanship of the State Central Military Commission in March 2005.

100 See 'Explanation on the Draft Bill of the Constitutional Amendments', presented to the 2nd Plenary Session of the 10th National People's Congress by Wang Zhaoguo, 8 March 2004. The full text was published in the *Renmin Ribao*, 8 March 2004, <www.peopledaily.com.cn/GB/14576/28329/32383/32412/2380890.html>.

101 *Id.*

102 See *People's Daily* (*Renmin Ribao*), 12 August 2003, at 1.

103 *Id.*

As was the previous practice, the recommendations were dutifully and faithfully adopted by the NPC, making itself once again a rubber stamp for the Party. Sadly, this practice is patently undemocratic: If the people have no right to participate in such fundamentally important political matters, it is unrealistic, if not insulting, to tell the people that they enjoy democracy and rule of law.

Even though the on-going revision was not officially reported until August 2003, Chinese media began to break the news unofficially around June 2003.[104] It was clear that prominent Chinese scholars were consulted at a rather early stage, and certainly no later than June 2003. Not surprisingly, academics began to express a wide range of views and opinions, suggesting far reaching revisions to the Constitution.[105] Academic symposiums devoted to the revision were also organised, with the most notable ones convened in Qingdao City,[106] and in Shanghai,[107] both in June 2003, and both of which were attended by prominent scholars consulted by the Politburo on the revision, such as Professors Jiang Ping and Wu Jinlian. However, enthusiasm among academics was to be quickly dampened. A secret instruction was soon issued by the Party to stop all conferences and publication of academic papers on constitutional reform, and leading economists and legal scholars actively involved in presenting their views were reported to have been harassed by the security forces.[108] Thus, contrary to the assertion by the Chinese authorities that the revision of the constitution was carried out on a democratic basis with wide consultation,[109]

---

104 Thus, the *Caijing Weekly* (<www.Caijing.com.cn>) reported, on 20 June 2003, a meeting between Wu Bangguo as head of the Constitutional Group with several prominent Chinese economists and jurists, at which he solicited opinions from these scholars on the pending constitutional revision. Based on a *Caijing Weekly* report, Western media (such as Agence France Presse) then reported, on 23 June 2003, the 'secret' establishment of a constitutional revision group.

105 For an excellent overview of academic studies on constitutional revision that have emerged since 2001, see Zeng Ping, 'A Summary of Research on Issues relating to Constitutional Revision', in *Renmin Ribao* website: <www.peopledaily.com.cn/GB/14576/14841/2084188.htm>.

106 A detailed summary of views expressed at the Qingdao conference is available from <www.usc.cuhk.edu.hk/wk_wzdetails.asp?id=2550.>

107 A detailed summary of views expressed at the Shanghai conference is available from <www.usc.cuhk.edu.hk/wk_wzdetails.asp?id=2368>.

108 See John Pomfret, 'China Orders Halt to Debate on Reforms', *Washington Post*, 27 August 2003, at p. 01. Although there were rumours that there was a written document to the effect of banning further debate on constitutional and political reform, interviews with Chinese scholars seem to suggest that only an oral instruction (*Da Zhaohu*) was circulated to this effect. Since academic papers continued to appear in journals, newspapers and websites, it seems that it is more likely that the instruction was in an oral form with limited effect.

109 See 'Explanation on the Draft Bill of the Constitutional Amendments', *supra* note 100.

consultation was only conducted within strictly limited circles of authorities and the elite in the society.

Nevertheless, the drafting proceeded swiftly. By mid-October 2003 the Suggestions on Amending Certain Contents of the Constitution had been adopted by the 3rd Session of the Central Committee of the 16th Party Congress, which also decided to pass the Suggestions to the SCNPC to be converted into a constitutional amendment bill in accordance with constitutional procedures. As usual, the SCNPC dutifully did so at its 6th Meeting of the 10th NPC, held during 22-27 December 2003. Also on 22 December 2003 the Suggestions on Amending Certain Contents of the Constitution were, for the first time, published in full in the Chinese media. Theoretically, the Amendment Bill finally adopted by the full NPC on 14 March 2004 was no longer a Party document, but a formal legislative bill, except that the Bill was a verbatim copy of the Suggestions.

As with the 1999 revision, the 2004 revision was designed to incorporate policy decisions made at the 16th Party Congress in 2002. It was meant to be a partial, not comprehensive, revision.[110] It was expressly decided that only the matters that had to be regulated by the Constitution and only the provisions that had to be revised immediately would be dealt with by the revision. Other matters, though desirable for revision, would be clarified later by constitutional interpretations, rather than by this revision.[111] In other words, the 2004 revision was little more than an implementation of the Party policies as adopted at the 16th Party Congress in 2002. Nevertheless, the 2004 revision did include some significant, though not completely coherent, amendments, including the adoption of the 'Three Represents' idea, along with the 'Four Fundamental Principles' and Deng Xiaoping's Theory, as guiding principles of the Party, a declaration on the protection of human rights, further protection of private property, and other technical changes.

4.2. Fundamental Principles

(1) Political Ideological Guidance

The most prominent underlying principles in the 1982 Constitution are the supremacy of the Constitution, as provided in Article 5, and the 'Four Fundamental Principles' as loosely stated in the Preamble.[112] These two sets of principles are potentially conflicting.

Article 5 of the Constitution provides that no law or administrative rules or regulations shall contravene the Constitution and that all state organs, the armed

---

110 See *id.*

111 *Id.*

112 Paragraph 7 of the Preamble provides that '[t]he Chinese people of all nationalities will continue to be led by the Communist Party of China, guided by Marxism-Leninism and Mao Zedong Thought, adhere to the people's democratic dictatorship and follow the socialist road.'

forces, all political parties, all social organisations, all enterprises and all institutions must abide by the Constitution and the law. The Party's Constitution, as adopted at its 12th Congress on 6 September 1982, also specifically provides that the Party must conduct its affairs and activities within the boundaries of the Constitution and the law.[113] It seems, at least theoretically, that the Communist Party must operate under, not just with, the Constitution and the law.

As pointed out above and discussed in Chapter Two, the 1999 Constitutional revision formally incorporated the phrase 'Ruling the Country according to Law' into Article 5 of the 1982 Constitution. At the 16th Party Congress in 2002 the phrase 'Ruling the Country According to Law' was also added to the Party Constitution. To this effect, Paragraph 12 of the Preamble of the revised Party Constitution now states:

> The Communist Party of China leads the people in promoting socialist democracy and building socialist political civilisation. It keeps expanding socialist democracy, strengthens the socialist legal system, rules the country according to law, builds a socialist country ruled according to law, and consolidates the people's democratic dictatorship.

The adoption of the terminology of 'Ruling the Country according to Law' immediately aroused much enthusiasm among scholars in China. To Chinese scholars, the formal adoption of the phrase 'Ruling the Country according to Law' meant the final acceptance of the notion of Rule of Law and thus represented a new landmark in legal construction.[114] Indeed, discussions on the phrase 'Ruling the Country according to Law' have all been based on the Western notion of Rule of Law, embracing the concepts of supremacy of law, judicial independence, equality before the law, separation of powers, checks and balances, a parliamentary system and the protection of human rights.[115] Similarly, official propaganda machines also emphasised that the adoption of such a term indicated a deeper understanding of

---

113 Preamble of the Party Constitution (1982). Although the Party Constitution has undergone a number of revisions (including the latest in November 2002 at the 16th Party Congress), there has been no change to this requirement. An English translation of the original Party's Constitution can be found in Peter P. F. Chan, *People's Republic of China: Modernisation and Legal Development,* (London: Oyez Longman, 1983), at 275-288. An English text of the amended Party Constitution is available at <www.china.org.cn/english/features/49109.htm> (last accessed 8 June 2007).

114 Liu Hainian, 'Ruling the Country according to Law: A New Landmark in Socialist Legal Construction in China', in Liu Hainian, Li Buyuan & Li Lin (eds.), *To Rule the Country according to Law and to Establish a Socialist Rule of Law Country* (*Yifa Zhiguo Jianshe Shehui Zhuyi Fazhi Guojia*) (Beijing: Press of Chinese Legal System, 1996), at 73.

115 See various contributions to Liu, Li & Li, *id*. This book is a collection of papers presented to the Symposium on *Ruling the Country according to Law and Establishing a Socialist Rule of Law Country*, organised by the Chinese Academy of Social Sciences, 13-15 April 1996.

the socialist political system, imposed a higher standard for socialist democracy and a socialist legal system, and signified a new era in socialist democracy and legal construction.[116] Whatever the phrase might mean in practice, it should be seen as re-enforcing and crystallising the idea of the supremacy of the Constitution over the government and the Party.

However, together with the principle of supremacy of the Constitution there is that of the upholding of the 'Four Fundamental Principles'. The latter may undermine the former, if not conflict with it.

The 'Four Fundamental Principles' were first systematically laid down, supposedly on behalf of the Central Committee of the Party,[117] by Deng Xiaoping in his address to a Party conference in March 1979 at which he said:

> The Central Committee [of the Party] maintains that, to carry out China's four modernisations, we must uphold the four cardinal principles ideologically and politically. This is the basic prerequisite for achieving modernisation. The four principles are: 1. We must keep to the socialist road. 2. We must uphold the dictatorship of the proletariat. 3. We must uphold the leadership of the Communist Party. 4. We must uphold Marxism-Leninism and Mao Zedong Thought.[118]

Among the Four Principles, the most important ones are to uphold Party leadership and to adhere to the socialist road, with the central emphasis on the Party leadership.[119] With the deepening of economic reform and the adoption of the 'socialist market economy' as the direction for economic reform and development, perhaps the only practically significant principle is the upholding of Party leadership. Thus the potential conflict is between constitutional supremacy and Party leadership.

This problem was appreciated at the beginning of the constitutional revision and thus the incorporation of the 'Four Fundamental Principles' into the Constitution was not without opposition.[120] There were apparently arguments that if the 'Four Fundamental Principles' were to be incorporated into the Constitution it would be

---

116 'To Greatly Push the Process of Ruling a Country according to Law', *People's Daily* (*Renmin Ribao*) Editorial, internet edition, 17 October 1997; Lin Chengdong, 'The Development of Democracy Must Be Closely Linked with the Improvement of the Legal System', *People's Daily* (*Renmin Ribao*), internet edition, 18 October 1997; and Xue Ju & Wang Jiafu, 'Towards Ruling the Country according to Law', *People's Daily* (*Renmin Ribao*), internet edition, 1 November 1997.

117 See Gu Angran, *supra* note 1, at 60.

118 In *Selected Works of Deng Xiaoping (1875–1982), supra* note 81, at 172.

119 Gu Angran, *supra* note 1, at 62; Xie Fei, 'The Adherence to Four Fundamental Principles Are the Fundamental Guarantee for a Victory of the Socialist Course', in Zhang Youyu, *supra* note 3, at 21.

120 See *supra* note 85. See also Zhang Youyu, *supra* note 92, at 5.

more appropriate to retain the provisions on Party leadership as provided in the 1975 and 1978 Constitutions.[121] Deng Xiaoping was, however, firm that these principles must be written into law, but at the same time that the Party and the Government must be separated.[122] Thus the 1982 Constitution returned to the practice found in other socialist countries, i.e. the leadership role of the Party was to be recognised in the Preamble, with its actual exercise of power to be carried out through extra-constitutional methods.[123] The omission of specific provisions on Party leadership as contained in the 1975 and 1978 Constitutions seemed also to reflect the realisation among some Party leaders that Party membership comprised only a tiny part of the Chinese population; it thus would seem to be more legitimate and democratic to translate Party policies into law through legislatures rather than the direct control of state functions by the Party.[124] A congress or a parliament, as Zhang Youyu saw it, is no more than a rubber stamp for the ruling Party in any country.[125] Thus general, vague and ambiguous as it might be, a recognition of the Party's leadership role would suffice for all practical purposes. Indeed, it is now suggested that one of the unwritten constitutional conventions (*guanli*) in China is that major issues concerning the State, such as the revision of the Constitution, are to be initiated by the Party, though nominally decided by the Legislature.[126]

These constitutional arrangements and the unwritten conventions and practices suggest that the real power is vested with the Party, but exercised in the name of the state. Such an arrangement, according to some prominent constitutional scholars in China,[127] is no different from a parliamentary system of government in the West. Fundamental differences, however, do exist. First, the Party's control over the state legislature is not a result of popular election, but a pre-imposition by the Party itself. This contradicts any doctrine of democratic government. Secondly, the revision of the Constitution is firmly vested in the Party, not with the people.

---

121 Zhang Youyu, *id.*, at 5-6.

122 See Jiang Bikun, *supra* note 2, at 71.

123 The 1954 Constitution followed this practice; the 1982 Constitution thus simply restores the 1954 arrangement. See Wang Jingrong, 'On Strengthening and Improving the Party Leadership', in Zhang Youyu, *supra* note 3, at 40-1; Huang Fangjing & Lian Xisheng, 'On the Historical Developments of the Guiding Principles in Our Constitutions', in Chinese Society of Legal Science, *supra* note 8, at 36. Huang & Lian (at 32) argue that the Four Fundamental Principles were also embodied in the 1954 Constitution, though not concisely summarised in the Preamble. For the status of the Communist Party in socialist constitutions, see William B. Simons, 'The Communist Party in State Constitutions', in Dietrich André Loeber, *et al.* (eds.), *Ruling Communist Parties and Their Status under Law* (Dordrecht/Boston/Lancaster: Martinus Nijhoff Publishers, 1986), at 437-449.

124 See Gu Angran, *supra* note 1, at 62-63.

125 Zhang Youyu, *supra* note 92, at 6.

126 Jiang Bikun, *supra* note 2, at 38.

127 See *supra* note 92.

Indeed, in the history of constitutional revision in the PRC, there has been no case of any revision that was not initiated and strictly controlled by the Party. Thirdly, the Party operates with the Constitution rather than under the Constitution. The Constitution, its interpretation and implementation, is designed to uphold the Party leadership, not to provide a mechanism for challenging it, as it is made clear that the 'Four Fundamental Principles' are not to be questioned, let alone challenged, and the interpretation and implementation of the Constitution must be made in accordance with the Four Fundamental Principles.[128] In this context one should not be surprised that the Chairperson of the SCNPC emphasised that Chinese law is effectively the institutionalised form of the Party's policies and guidelines.[129] One should not be surprised either by the fact that there are still many Party members who cannot decide whether it is the Constitution or the Party that is superior in authority.[130]

Nevertheless, the Four Fundamental Principles are not stagnant; there have been further developments since, necessitated either by economic development or by a change of leadership.[131] Thus, to assure the world, and particularly foreign investors, of the continuation of China's open door policy, the 'Four Fundamental Principles' were supplemented in 1993 to include the principle of 'Keeping up reform and opening up',[132] thus effectively becoming 'Five Fundamental Principles'.

The death of Deng Xiaoping in February 1997 raised the question of the continuation and stability of Deng Xiaoping's pragmatic policies for economic reform and development, which virtually blur the distinction between capitalism and socialism. The Party's answer to this question was to uphold 'Deng Xiaoping Theory' as a fundamental guideline for the Party's ideology in its Party Constitution in 1997.[133] The 1999 constitutional revision then had this 'enshrined' into the state Constitution as a national guiding ideology. With the 1993 and 1999 amendments to the Preamble, we may henceforth consider the 'Four Fundamental Principles' to be the 'Six Fundamental Principles'.

---

128 See Zhang Youyu, *supra* note 92, at 5; Gu Angran, *supra* note 1, at 61.

129 See Li Peng, 'Speech at the Second Meeting of the Standing Committee of the 9th NPC', 29 April 1998, in *People's Daily* (*Renmin RiBao*), internet edition, 1 May 1998.

130 Chen Yunsheng, 'Ruling the Country according to the Constitution is the Core of Ruling the Country by Law', in *People's Daily* (*Renmin RiBao*), internet edition, 15 November 1997.

131 It is worth noting that each constitutional revision has coincided with the completion of the five-year term of the Party Congress (1982–1987, 1987–1992, 1992–1997, 1997–2002, 2002–2007) and the beginning of a new five-year term of the National People's Congress (1983–1988, 1988–1993, 1993–1998, 1998–2003, 2003–2008), and leadership changes take place at the end of the five-year term.

132 See the 1993 Amendment to the Preamble.

133 This was done through an amendment to the Party Constitution at the 15th Party Congress in 1997.

When Jiang Zemin was retiring he wanted to leave a personal stamp on the Constitution too. So he began, in February 2000, to talk about and promote his awkwardly worded 'Three Represents' in a piecemeal fashion as a 'new thinking'.[134] He managed to wage a major political campaign during 2000 through to the end of 2002, and most importantly, he managed to have the Party Constitution amended at the 16th Party Congress in 2002. In addition to upholding the Four Fundamental Principles and Deng Xiaoping's Theory, the revision adds Jiang Zemin's 'Three Represents' as an important 'Thought' to guide the action of the Party.[135] 'The Three Represents' means, according to the revised Party Constitution, that the Party represents the development trends of China's advanced productive forces, the orientation of China's advanced culture and the fundamental interests of the overwhelming majority of the Chinese People. In other words, the Party represents what are perceived by the Party as the 'advanced' forces of the society at a given time. The political rationale for this 'new thinking' is thus clear: that is, that the Party, as an embodiment of the 'advanced' forces, should continue to maintain its control of, legitimacy in, and relevance to the society.

The 2004 constitutional revision therefore incorporated the changes to the Party Constitution into the State Constitution. Thus the amended Constitution (Para 7 of the Preamble) now stipulates that the 'important thinking' of the 'Three Represents' is a national guiding ideology.

With these frequent changes/additions of political phrases, one may be inclined to dismiss the importance of such political ideologies. However, we must remember that there is in fact a 'tendency for ruling the country by slogans' in China.[136] As examined above, the 'Four Fundamental Principles' certainly have their practical implications, and awkward as they might be in their wording, the 'Three Represents' as a form of 'new thinking' are not completely devoid of practical implications either.[137] Indeed, that the Party must represent the development trend of China's advanced productive forces is nothing more than an ideologically coated phrase to

---

134 Interestingly, the most comprehensive statement on the 'Three Represents' is contained in the much anticipated and widely publicised first major speech by the new Party Secretary-General, Hu Jingtao on commemorating the 82nd anniversary of the founding of the CPC on 1 July 2003. The full speech was published in the *People's Daily* (*Renmin Ribao*), 2 July 2003, accompanied by a *People's Daily* (*Renmin Ribao*) editorial.

135 See Paragraph One of the revised Party Constitution.

136 He Weifang, 'Difficulties in Establishing the Rule of Law and Solutions', published in <www.sinoliberal.com/hwf/hwf2003010502.htm>.

137 Here I am not endorsing the practice of imposing a Party ideology upon the will of the people, however well the ideology is formulated. It certainly has little foundation in asserting that it is the desire or aspiration of the people to incorporate the 'Three Represents' in the Constitution, as some deputies to the NPC would like us to believe. See 'It is the desire of the people to incorporate the "Three Represents" thinking into the Constitution', Xinhua News Agency: <www.xinhuanet.com.newscenter/2004-03/11/content_1358308.htm>; and

say that capitalism is not inherently contradictory to communism. It is under this 'new thinking' that the Party invites 'capitalists' to join the Party, thus effectively telling the Chinese people that the Party does not only want capitalists as a new force (builders in the cause of socialist construction) in the United Front,[138] but also as a part of the Party. That is to say, 'getting rich is not only glorious (being in the United Front) but also prestigious (being part of the Party)'. Further, the added protection for private property, to be discussed below, may also be seen as a consequence of this 'new thinking'.

(2) The Nature of the Politico-Economic System

Ideological guidance has not been the only political struggle for China in the last 28 years or so; economic development and opening up to foreign investment has challenged another important and central tenet of socialism, namely the insistence on public ownership and its priority protection by law. In fact, the most substantial revisions since 1988, though only made incrementally, have been those defining the nature of the politico-economic system in China. These changes clearly reflect the gradual transformation of the Chinese politico-economic system, a process short of full privatisation but nevertheless allowing the gradual introduction of 'capitalist' practices in economic spheres. Here significant changes have occurred in relation to the description of socialism and to equal protection of public and private property.

The original 1982 Constitution heavily emphasised public ownership and state planning. Economic liberalisation under Deng Xiaoping allowed various 'capitalist' practices, including the tolerance of private ownership of businesses and their operations. The version of 'socialism' introduced from the Soviet Union, which was characterised by public ownership and state planning, clearly did not match the Chinese reality, nor was it conducive to economic reform and development.

In the 1993 constitutional revision the following sentences were added to the Preamble: 'Our country is in the primary stage of socialism. The basic task of the nation is to concentrate its efforts on socialist modernisation in accordance with the theory of building socialism with Chinese characteristics.' That was an ingenious invention to justify 'capitalist' practices in a socialist country.[139] However, in the Chinese language the phrase adopted in the 1993 amendment implied a temporary or a transitional status. Thus in the 1999 constitutional revision these two sentences were further changed to: 'Our country will over a long period of time be in the

---

'Lawmakers Discuss Party's Constitution-amending Proposal', in <www.xinhuanet.com.newscenter/2003-12/23/content_1333115.htm>.

138 See 2004 Amendment to Paragraph 10 of the Preamble.

139 See Jianfu Chen, *From Administrative Authorisation to Private Law: A Comparative Perspective of the Developing Civil Law in the PRC* (Dordrecht/Boston/London: Martinus Nijhoff Publishers, 1995), Chapter 3.

primary stage of socialism. The basic task of the nation is to concentrate its efforts on socialist modernisation in pursuing the construction of socialism with Chinese characteristics.' This was to signal to the world that capitalism would be tolerated on a long-term basis, if not permanently, and to declare that building socialism with Chinese characteristics was no longer a theory but a practice as well. In the 2004 constitutional revision, the phrase 'in pursuing the construction of socialism with Chinese characteristics' was further changed to that of 'along the road of Chinese-style socialism', thus indicating the confidence of the leadership that the Party and the State were no longer hesitating in their search for an original Chinese version of socialism,[140] just as it has become increasingly assertive in international affairs with the strengthening of its economic power in the world.

Corresponding to the changed nature of 'socialism with Chinese characteristics', as mentioned earlier, the state-run economy was re-defined as a state-owned economy, independent management rights in the state sector economy were confirmed, and the contractual responsibility system was upheld.[141]

These changes to the description of socialism were to provide a foundation for the search for justifications for the protection of private property in a socialist country.

Initially, Article 11 of the 1982 Constitution allowed and protected the individual economy of urban and rural working people as a complement to the socialist public economy. Article 13 further protected the rights of citizens to own lawfully earned income, savings, houses and other lawful property, as well as the right to inherit private property. Here, the individual economy of urban and rural working people referred to the economy in the form of Individual Industrial and Commercial Households and Rural Contracting Households (the so-called 'Two Households').[142] This was the only private economy allowed by the Chinese law at the time. The post-Mao economic reforms saw the emergence of private enterprise, defined as 'a privately funded economic entity which employs at least eight persons.'[143] Article 11 of the Constitution was then amended in 1988 to 'permit the private economy to exist and to develop within the limits prescribed by law' and defined such an economy as a complement to the socialist public economy. Here, the private economy refers to the economy in the form of private enterprises as defined by law. The rapid

---

[140] It is a quiet change as it has attracted little discussion in the Chinese media. Indeed, the 'Explanation on the Draft Bill of the Constitutional Amendments' (*supra* note 100) does not even explain the reasons for the change at all.

[141] See the 1993 Amendment to the Preamble.

[142] For further discussions on the 'Two Households', see Chapter 13.

[143] See Article 2 of the Provisional Regulations of the PRC on Private Enterprises (1988). See further discussions in Chapter 13.

development of the private economy[144] again necessitated further elevation of the role of the non-public economy in the state economic system. Through the 1999 constitutional revision the individual and private economies were no longer defined as a complement to the socialist public economy but were treated as 'an important component of the country's socialist market economy.'[145] Further, the 1999 revision tried to treat the individual and private economies on an equal footing, whereas the previous provisions seemed to accord a different degree of state control over each.[146]

Because of the specific meanings of the individual and private economies and the continued flourishing of the private sector[147] in different business forms and structures, such as sole proprietorship and partnerships, there was a clear need to accord constitutional protection to these new forms of the private economy; hence the phrase 'other non-public economy' was inserted into Article 11 through the 2004 constitutional revision. Though the phrase is an ambiguous one, it is meant to embrace the various existing and emerging forms of private business, including foreign investment in China. In addition to providing protection, the 2004 revision further added that the state would also provide encouragement and support to the development of the non-public economy. In this way the private sector finally achieved equal status with its public counterpart in most economic activities.[148]

On appearance these changes seem to be largely cosmetic. But in the context of socialism they amount to no less than an extremely bold approach to re-defining socialism. Not surprisingly, controversy soon erupted in relation to the revision of Article 13 during the 2004 constitutional revision.[149] As mentioned above, original Article 13 provided protection to lawful income, houses and other private property

---

144 By early 1999, it accounted for 15 per cent of the national GDP. See 'Constitutional Amendments Propel China's Reform and Opening-up', *China Daily*, 17 March 1999.

145 See 1999 amendment to Article 11.

146 See Article 11 as amended in 1988. It should also be pointed out that the distinction of the two sectors, depending on whether private employment involves eight or more people, is artificial and arbitrary. Such a distinction is increasingly blurred in practice. See Jianfu Chen, *supra* note 139, at 113-116.

147 By November 2003, there were some 2.97 million registered private businesses with a registered capital of more than US$ 40 billion, and contributing half of China's economic growth. See 'Private Firms Need Support, Understanding', *China Daily*, internet edition, 10 March 2004, <www.chinadaily.com.cn/english/doc/2003-03/10/content_313233.htm>.

148 Article 7 of the Constitution still states that '[T]he state-owned economy, i.e. the sector of the socialist economy under the ownership of the whole people, is the leading force in the national economy. The State ensures the consolidation and growth of the State-owned economy.' And indeed, in some important economic activities, such as obtaining bank loans, the state sectors continue to have priority over the private sectors.

149 It should be pointed out that this controversy was to re-occur in 2005–2007 during the enactment of a Law on Rights *in rem*. See further discussions in Chapter 10.

and the right to inheritance. There had long been uncertainties about Article 13. First, the listing of lawful income, wages, houses etc. came from the socialist distinction of means of production and means for livelihood,[150] with only the latter being allowed to be owned privately. Secondly, public property is declared sacred and inviolable by the Constitution (Article 12), while the state only offered protection for limited private property. This implicitly indicated a different degree of protection for the two types of property. Further, in line with the preoccupation with the notion of ownership in socialist countries,[151] Article 13 referred to ownership rights to property (*Suoyouquan*) instead of the more universally understood term of property rights (*Caichanquan*).

Under the 2004 revision, while private property is not deemed sacred, as is the case with public property, it is now declared inviolable.[152] Further, if private property is expropriated or taken over for state use, compensation must be paid by the state under the revised Constitution. Similarly, as land use rights have been commercialised, compensation for expropriation or taking over for use by the State is also guaranteed by the revised Constitution.[153] And finally, the term 'property rights' (*Caichanquan*) instead of 'ownership rights to property' (*Suoyouquan*) is now used in Article 13. Thus one can say quite comfortably that for most practical purposes equal protection is now provided for both public and private property, and so the revision in 2004 did away with one of the last remnants of the influence of Soviet law. For practical purposes this then clears away one of the most difficult aspects of enacting a civil code in China: how to deal with the differentiated treatment of public and private property under a unified notion of property rights.[154]

Being a socialist country and having provided constitutional protection to private property, China now faces an obvious question, namely that of social justice, or more practically, the establishment of a minimum social safety net in the face of the increasingly widening gap between the rich and poor. This the Chinese

---

150 For socialist conceptions of property, see Viktor Knapp, 'Socialist Countries' and F.H. Lawson, 'Comparative Conclusions' in *Int'l Enc. Comp. L.*, vol. vi (Property and Trust), ch. 2 (Structural Variations in Property Law), S.3 and S.8 respectively; Hazard, *supra* note 50, chapters 8 & 9; and Jianfu Chen, *supra* note 139, at 144-149. See also 'Explanation on the Draft Bill of the Constitutional Amendments', *supra* note 100.

151 See Jianfu Chen, *supra* note 139, at 144-149.

152 See Article 13 as amended in 2004. It should be pointed out here that the controversy, on appearances at least, was not about protection for private property *per se*, it was the concern about the legalisation of illegally acquired property, such as that acquired through corruption, embezzlement of public property by various means, and other illegal means. Not surprisingly, the adjective 'lawful' was used in front of private property. This adjective is therefore not redundant; it is used to address the fear that illegally acquired property might become untouchable.

153 See revised Article 10 of the Constitution.

154 See further discussions in Chapters 9 & 10.

government in fact began to address several years ago.[155] The 2004 revision now makes it a constitutional obligation of the state to establish a social security system appropriate to the level of national economic development.[156] Once again it is a positive development that should provide the poor, at least theoretically, with a constitutional claim, or a moral claim, against the government, should the government fail to deliver a minimum social safety net.

4.3. The Party System

There is no doubt that the Communist Party of China (CPC) has firm control over state affairs. It is however also clear that major efforts have been made for such control to be exercised through state mechanisms. Thus express constitutional provisions in the 1975 and 1978 Constitutions, which declared that the Party was the 'core of leadership', and which imposed an express obligation on the citizens to support the Party leadership, were abolished.[157] The requirement that the Premier of the State Council be nominated by the Central Committee of the Party was also dropped.[158] Further, a State Central Military Commission was established to command the armed forces.[159] This establishment nominally makes the armed forces the army of the state, not that of the Party. Although such changes to the Constitution may not have changed the nature of Party control over state affairs[160] – indeed there is

---

155 In the last ten years or so China has gradually established a social security structure, composed of retirement insurance, medical insurance, unemployment insurance, insurance for work-related injuries, and birth insurance, and covering a total population of some 187 million people. However, other than some rudimentary medical, poverty and old pension insurance for rural populations in coastal regions, the social security system is yet to reach the great majority of the rural population. See '2006 Statistics on the Development of Labour and Social Securities', jointly issued by the Ministry of Labour and Social Securities and the State Bureau of Statistics, available from <www.molss.gov.cn/gb/news/2007-05/18/content_178167.htm> (last accessed 16 June 2007). See also Press Conference given by the Minister for Labour and Social Security, 11 March 2004, Xinhua News Agency: <www.xinhuanet.com/zhibo/20040309b/wz.htm> (last accessed 18 April 2004).

156 See revised Article 14 of the Constitution.

157 These provisions included Articles 2 & 3 of both the 1975 and 1978 Constitutions, Article 26 of the 1975 Constitutions and Article 56 of the 1978 Constitution.

158 See Article 17 of the 1975 Constitution and Article 22 of the 1978 Constitution.

159 Under the 1975 and 1978 Constitutions, the armed forces were under the command of the Chairperson of the Party. See Article 15 of the 1975 Constitution and Article 19 of the 1978 Constitution.

160 In the case of the establishment of the Central Military Commission, Peng Zhen made it clear that the leadership of the Party over the army would not change as the affirmation of Party leadership in the Preamble would also include its leadership of the armed forces. See Peng Zhen, *supra* note 80, at 20. In fact, the Party organisation has always maintained its own Central Military Commission. As suggested by Hu Qiaomu (who presided over the

the argument that there is an unwritten constitutional convention that it is in the power of the Party to recommend (though not to make) the appointment of state leaders[161] – it changed the mechanism of control, thus making it possible for a gradual separation of the Party and Government, in the sense that Party policies would have to be translated into state law through legal procedures.[162]

Despite the firm control of the CPC over state affairs, China has insisted that its Constitution does not uphold a one-party or a multi-party system. The Constitution institutes a multi-party cooperation and political consultation system – the Chinese People's Political Consultative Conference – said to be a socialist party system with Chinese characteristics and an alternative to the bourgeois multi-party system.[163] This system of multi-party cooperation and political consultation means that the CPC will consult the democratic parties on major policy issues and, in return, the

---

revision of the Party Constitution at the 12th Congress of the Party), such control may be even tighter if the chairpersons of both the commissions are identical. See Tony Saich, 'The Fourth Constitution of the People's Republic of China', (1983) 2 *Rev. of Soc. L* 113, at 118. Indeed, it has been so: Jiang Zemin occupied both of the posts and now Hu Jintao does as well.

161 See Guo Daohui, 'Authority, Power or Rights: Some Considerations on the Relationship between the Party and the People's Congress', in (no. 1, 1994) *Studies in Law* (*Faxue Yanjiu*) 3, at 6; Qing Qianhong & Li Yuan, 'The Influence of the Chinese Communist Party on Law-making', initially published in 2003 in <www.chinapublaw.com/emphases/20030613120104htm>, reprinted in <www.usc.cuhk.edu.hk/wk.asp> (last accessed 25 September 2006); and Hang Li, 'On the Informality and Political Functions of Law-making in China', first published in (no. 2, 2002) *Research in Contemporary China* (*Dandai Zhongguo Yanjiu*), reprinted in <www.usc.cuhk.edu.hk/wk_wzdetails.asp?id=1685> (last accessed 10 May 2004).

162 This point has been emphasised from time to time. For instance, the Political Report of the Party at the 14th Party Congress specifically stated that 'the main method for the Party to exercise its political leadership over state affairs is to translate Party policies into state will through legal procedures'. See 'Accelerating the Reform, the Opening to the Outside World and the Drive for Modernisation, so as to Achieve Great Successes in Building Socialism with Chinese Characteristics', a political report delivered by Jiang Zemin to the 14th Congress of the CPC, in *People's Daily* (*Renmin Ribao*) (overseas edition), 21 October 1992, at 1-3. See also Li Peng, *supra* note 129.

163 See e.g. 'Opinions of the Central Committee of the Communist Party of China on Maintaining and Perfecting the Multi-Party Cooperation and Political Consultation System (December 30, 1989)', in *A Selection of Important Documents Since the 13th Congress* (*Shisanda Yilai Zhongyao Wenxian Xuanbian*) (vol. II) (Beijing: People's Press, 1991), at 821. These Opinions are translated into English as 'Guidelines Proposed by the Central Committee of the Communist Party of China for Upholding and Improving the System of Multi-Party Co-operation and Political Consultation Under the Leadership of the Communist Party', in (5-11 March 1990) *Beijing Review* 14-18. See also Yu Jianze, 'On the Multi-party Cooperation and Political Consultation System under the Leadership of Communist Party of China', in (no. 6, 1990) *Legal Science in China* (*Zhonggu Faxue*) 3, at 3; and Jiang Bikun, *supra* note 2, at 90.

democratic parties will support the CPC in making and implementing these policies. It is a part of, and evolved from, the United Front policy of the CPC.[164]

The democratic parties are elitist groups, consisting of elite intellectuals and prominent business persons, formed mainly during the 1930s and 1940s.[165] Although they were seen, historically, as a third force and organised in the form of political parties, they did not contend for political power, nor organise with a modern political party structure.[166] They were, however, important partners with the CPC during the Anti-Japanese Invasion period and in the first communist provisional government, the Central Government under the 1949 Common Program.

At the time of the founding of the PRC there were 11 democratic parties, but in the next two months the China Revolutionary Committee of the Kuomintang absorbed two other Left parties, and the National Salvation Party dismembered itself.[167] Subsequently there were, and still are, eight democratic parties.[168] When the first provisional Central Government was formed, three of the six vice-chairmen and two of the four vice-premiers of the Central Government were members of these parties. Further, eleven of the twenty-one State Councillors and 42 of the 93 ministers and vice-ministers were also members of these democratic parties, or persons without party affiliation (i.e. non-party members). The first president of the Supreme People's Court was also a member of the democratic parties (Shen Junru

---

[164] Initially, the CPC rejected any collaboration with any other political parties and organisations. Later, the United Front, initiated and promoted by the Soviet Union, was mainly formed between the CPC and the Kuomintang. Democratic Parties did not play any important role until the Anti-Japanese Invasion War (1938–1945). For a detailed history of the United Front, see Hu Zhixin (ed.), *A History of the United Front of the Communist Party of China* (*Zhongguo Gongchandang Tongyi Zhanxian Shi*) (Beijing: Huaxia Press, 1988); and Lu Yun, 'Formation and Development of the System of Multi-Party Cooperation', (19-25 March 1990) *Beijing Review 16*

[165] See Hu Zhixin, *supra* note 164, at 263-266. See also Lu Yun, *supra* note 164, at 18-19.

[166] See Anita Chan, 'The Changing Ruling Elite and Political Opposition in China', in Garry Rodan (ed.), *Political Oppositions in Industrialising Asia* (London/New York: Routledge, 1996), at 165.

[167] Ye Yonglie, *The History of the Anti-Rightists Movement* (*Fan Youpai Shimo*) (Xining: Qinghai People's Press, 1995), at 98.

[168] They are the China Revolutionary Committee of the Kuomintang (founded in 1948), the China Democratic League (founded in 1941), the China Democratic National Construction Association (founded in 1945), the China Association for Promoting Democracy (founded in 1945), the Chinese Peasants' and Workers' Democratic Party (founded in 1930 as the Provisional Action Committee of the Kuomintang and renamed in 1947), the China Zhi Gong Dang (founded in 1925), the Jiu San Society (founded in 1946), and the Taiwan Democratic Self-Government League (founded in 1947). For a brief description of these parties, see *Beijing Review* (19-25 March 1990), at 18-19; and Jiang Bikun, *supra* note 2, at 96-100. For a detailed study on the democratic parties, see James D. Seymour, *China's Satellite Parties* (New York/London: M.E. Sharpe, Inc., 1987).

of the China Democratic League).[169] Again, at the first National People's Congress, 668 (45%) of the 1226 deputies were members of the democratic parties or non-party members. Among the 79 members of the SCNPC, 39 were non-Communist Party members. Of the 13 vice-chairpersons of the SCNPC, eight were members of the democratic parties or non-party members. And of the 35 ministers, 13 were non-Communist Party members.[170] These proportions were significant, considering that at the time the membership of all democratic parties was only 11,540, whereas the CPC had a membership of five million.[171]

At the time the Communist Party's policy towards these democratic parties, as proposed by Mao, was 'long-term co-existence and mutual supervision'.[172] However, this policy was not to last too long: members of the democratic parties and the prominent non-party members were soon to become major victims of the Anti-Rightists Movement launched in 1957. They were to be humiliated, demoted or dismissed from government, and effectively silenced for the next 20 years.[173]

Deng Xiaoping's ascendancy to power also revived the democratic parties, membership of which expanded from 65,000 in 1979 to just over half a million in 2006.[174] Deng also wanted to institute multi-party cooperation under the leadership of the CPC.[175] Thus, the 1982 Constitution for the first time uses the term 'political parties', instead of the traditional term of 'democratic parties', in implicit recognition that along with the CPC, there are also other political parties which can no longer be seen as just other social organisations.[176] In 1987 the 13th Congress of the CPC declared that the provisions in the Preamble of the 1982 Constitution had established a fundamental political system which needed to be improved.[177] In

---

169 See Hu Zhixin, *supra* note 164, at 295-296; and Ye Yonglie, *supra* note 167, at 135.

170 Hu Zhixin, *supra* note 164, at 287-288.

171 See Hu Zhixin, *supra* note 164, at 311-312. It is however not unusual for prominent members of the Democratic Parties to concurrently hold membership of the Communist Party.

172 See Lu Yun, *supra* note 164, at 19.

173 Anita Chan, *supra* note 166, at 166-167. For a detailed history of the Anti-Rightists Movement, see Ye Yonglie, *supra* note 167.

174 Calculated on the basis of memberships for each of the democratic parties according to Xinhua News Agency statistics: <news.xinhuanet.com/ziliao/2002-01/28/content_256326.htm> (last accessed 25 September 2006). At the same time, the membership of the CPC had reached 70.8 million. See <news.xinhuanet.com/ziliao/2004-11/24/content_2255749.htm> (last assessed 25 September 2006). For post-Mao development (up to 1995) see Chen Chunlong, 'A Study on the System of Multi-party Cooperation under the Leadership of the Communist Party and Its Legal Problems', (no. 3, 1995) *Studies in Law & Commerce* (*Fashang Yanjiu*) 8.

175 Anita Chan, *supra* note 166, at 167.

176 See Article 5 of the 1982 Constitution. See also Chen Chunlong, *supra* note 174, at 13.

177 See 'Advance Along the Road of Socialism with Chinese Characteristics', a Political Report delivered by Zhao Ziyang at the 13th National Congress of the Communist Party of China,

December 1989, the Party issued its Opinions on Maintaining and Perfecting the Multi-Party Cooperation and Political Consultation System,[178] which laid down some basic principles for multi-party cooperation and provided some general and vague mechanisms for political consultation. In 1993 the Constitutional Amendment specifically declared that the system of multi-party cooperation and political consultation would be a long-term policy.[179] In February 2005 the CPC issued another set of Opinions on Further Strengthening the Construction of the Multi-Party Cooperation and Political Consultation System under the Leadership of the Communist Party of China.[180] Once again, the document talks about non-binding consultation, but unambiguously emphasises the leadership of the CPC and the required support of this leadership.

The basic principles are that the CPC is the party-in-power (*zhizhengdang*) and the democratic parties are parties participating in government affairs (*canzhengdang*), with the latter being led by the CPC and keeping to the Four Fundamental Principles.[181] The democratic parties are not opposition parties. Indeed, as the 1989 Opinions declared, 'political organisations that oppose the Four Fundamental Principles and endanger state power are absolutely not allowed to exist. Such organisations must be banned according to law as soon as they are discovered.'[182] Although the CPC's policy is summarised as being 'long-term coexistence, mutual supervision, treating each other with all sincerity, and sharing each other's weal and woe',[183] the membership of the democratic parties is to be mainly confined to persons that have some influence among certain types of people in medium-sized and large cities.[184] Only under these conditions will the democratic parties be consulted and participate in state affairs through irregular meetings with CPC leaders, representation in people's congresses, and appointment to government posts.

The principal mechanism for political participation and consultation, other than direct representation in the legislatures and direct appointment to government posts,

---

in *Documents of the Thirteenth National Congress of the Communist Party of China (1987)* (Beijing: Foreign Languages Press, 1987), at 56.

178 Issued on 30 December 1989. A Chinese copy can be found in *A Selection of Important Documents Since the 13th Congress, supra* note 163, at 821-830; an English translation can be found in (March 5-11, 1990) *Beijing Review*, at 14-18.

179 According to Chinese scholars, this amendment was proposed by the China Democratic National Construction Association. See Chen Chunlong, *supra* note 174, at 14.

180 See White Paper on Democracy: Building of Political Democracy in China, issued by the Information Office of the State Council, October 2005, available from <news.xinhuanet.com/politics/2005-10/19/content_3645697.htm> (last accessed 26 September 2006).

181 See the Preamble of the 1989 Opinions, *supra* note 178, at 14.

182 Preamble of the 1989 Opinions, *id.*, at 15.

183 Preamble of the 1989 Opinions, *id.*, at 15.

184 Para 22 of the 1989 Opinions, *id.*, at 18.

is the Chinese People's Political Consultative Conference (CPPCC). Though claimed to be an important organisational form of multi-party cooperation and political consultation,[185] the CPPCC is not a constitutional institution. The CPPCC did not appear in the 1954, 1975 and 1978 Constitutions.[186] It is only mentioned in the Preamble of the 1982 Constitution as a broadly based representative organisation of the United Front. The Constitution does not define its legal status or its functions or powers. As is the party leadership, it is effectively an extra-constitutional institution that has existed since the 1940s.

As far as the CPC's policy is concerned, the purpose of the CPPCC is to strengthen political consultation and democratic supervision with regard to major policies of the state, important local affairs, the implementation of policies, laws and decrees, and major issues concerning the people's livelihood and United Front work.[187] Nothing can be more vague than such functions for the CPPCC. What is clear is that the CPPCC is not an organ of state power,[188] nor is it an independent organisation.[189] Its usefulness depends entirely on the parameters set by the CPC of the time. It is therefore not entirely unfair to characterise the multi-party cooperation and political consultation as being 'flower vases', 'window-dressing' or 'loyal opposition'.[190] It is also clear that these democratic parties 'have travelled on a road from cooperating with the Communist Party to accepting its leadership, and from standing for patriotism to serving socialism.'[191] One Chinese scholar thus has this to ask: 'By appointing a few members of the democratic parties to the legislature, the judicial organs and the government, and holding a few meetings with the democratic parties, can we therefore say that multi-party cooperation is being practised?'[192]

---

185 See Para 15 of the 1989 Opinions, *id.*, at 17.

186 Liu Hang, 'Continuing to Strengthen and Expand the United Front', in Zhang Youyu, *supra* note 3, at 52; and Chen Chunlong, *supra* note 174, at 11.

187 See Para 15 of the 1989 Opinions. Similarly, the CPC issued a set of Opinions on Strengthening the Work of the CPPCC on 8 February 2006, which talks about non-binding consultation but unambiguously emphasises CPC leadership. The 2006 Opinions are available from <news.xinhuanet.com/misc/2006-03/01/content_4243798.htm> (last assessed 25 September 2006).

188 Jiang Bikun, *supra* note 2, at 106.

189 The Constitution of the CPPCC specifically provides that it is under the leadership of the Communist Party. It was argued that the CPC was the original promoter and member; it is now its organiser and leader. Liu Hang, *supra* note 186, at 55.

190 See Anita Chan, *supra* note 166, at 165-171.

191 Lu Yun, *supra* note 164, at 21.

192 Xiu Menyou, 'Legislation on Party System in the Western Countries and the Legal Institutionalisation of Our Multi-Party Cooperation', (no. 4, 1993) *Journal of Northwest University (Xibei Daxue Xuebao)* 23, at 26.

4.4. People's Congress

(1) The National People's Congress

Constitutional textbooks in China have often drawn a distinction between the 'form of state' (*guoti*) and the 'form of the political system' (*zhengti*). The 'form of state', according to Mao, means the status of different classes in the nation.[193] According to some Chinese scholars the nature of a state is a dictatorship of one class over another. This nature is concealed in bourgeois constitutions but openly declared in socialist constitutions.[194] The present 'form of state' is defined by Article 1 of the Constitution: 'The People's Republic of China is a socialist state under the people's democratic dictatorship led by the working class and based on the alliance of workers and peasants.'[195] Democratic dictatorship refers to democracy being practised among the 'people' and dictatorship against the 'enemies'.[196] Since the democratic dictatorship is to be led by the working class and such leadership is to be exercised through its vanguard, the CPC,[197] such a definition of the 'form of state' is designed to legitimise the domination of the CPC in Chinese political life.[198]

The 'form of political system', according to Mao, is the method through which class dictatorship is exercised.[199] It refers to the fundamental principles underlying state powers, including the methods of power distribution, the structure, organisation and inter-relations among the powers, and procedures for their exercise.[200] According to Chinese scholars, the nature of the state (i.e. the 'form of state') determines the 'form of political system', and the latter must serve the former.[201] The present 'form of political system' is the people's congress system.[202]

---

193 See Jiang Bikun, *supra* note 2, at 74. See also 'Studying the Constitution: What is the form of state?', in <news.xinhuanet.com/newscenter/2004-04/19/content_1427955.htm> (last accessed 16 June 2007).

194 Jiang Bikun, *supra* note 2, at 75.

195 According to the Preamble of the Constitution, people's democratic dictatorship means the same as dictatorship of the proletariat. The latter term was used in the 1975 and 1978 Constitutions. The 1982 Constitution restored the phrase used in the 1954 Constitution to reflect the repudiation of the Cultural Revolution. See Gu Angran, *supra* note 1, at 64-65.

196 See Jiang Bikun, *supra* note 2, at 76-82; Albert H.Y. Chen, *An Introduction to the Legal System of the People's Republic of China*, 3rd edition (Singapore: LexisNexix/Butterworths Asia, 2004), at 49.

197 Jiang Bikun, *supra* note 2, at 82.

198 Albert Chen, *supra* note 196, at 49.

199 See Gu Angran, *supra* note 1, at 73.

200 Jiang Bikun, *supra* note 2, at 110.

201 Jiang Bikun, *supra* note 2, at 113-114.

202 Jiang Bikun, *supra* note 2, at 115; Gu Angran, *supra* note 1, at 73.

The origin of the people's congress was the Representative Congress of the Peasants' Associations during the 1920s.[203] In the 1930s, in line with the introduction of the Soviet system, came the establishment of the Congress of Soviets. In the early 1940s Mao began to advocate the establishment of a people's congress system at all levels, from townships to the national level, and the election of governments by these people's congresses. The Common Program envisaged the establishment of the people's congress system and vested the state powers with the people's congress, but to be exercised by the CPPCC until the people's congress was elected.[204] The first congress was, by indirect election, formed in early 1953. It convened its first Plenary Session in September 1954, at which the 1954 Constitution was adopted, but it was non-functioning and irregularly convened after 1957.[205] From 1966 to 1975 the National People's Congress did not convene at all.[206]

When the 1978 Constitution was under review there was a suggestion to adopt a two-chamber system. This was rejected; it was claimed that the problem for China was not checks and balances, but work efficiency, and thus a single chamber, the people's congress system, was retained.[207]

Under the 1982 Constitution all power in the PRC belongs to the people and is to be exercised through the National People's Congress (NPC) and local people's congresses at various levels.[208] The people's congresses are established at the township, county, provincial and national levels. The NPC at the national level is defined as the 'supreme organ of state power'.[209] It consists of about 3,000 deputies,[210] elected for a term of five years by the people's congresses at provincial level in accordance with the Electoral Law of the NPC and Local People's Congresses,[211] and by the People's Liberation Army according to the Measures on the Election by the People's

---

203 Chang Xin, 'The Birth and Historical Evolution of the People's Congress System', *Economic Daily (Jingji Ribao)*, 19 September 1994, at 5.

204 See Chang Xin, *id.*; Kevin J. O'Brien, *Reform Without Liberalisation: China's National People's Congress and the Politics of Institutional Change* (New York: Cambridge University Press, 1990), at 20-25.

205 Zhao Zhenjiang, *supra* note 45, at 182-183.

206 Chang Xin, *supra* note 203.

207 Zhang Youyu, *supra* note 92, at 3-4.

208 Article 2 of the 1982 Constitution.

209 Article 57 of the 1982 Constitution.

210 The Number of deputies to the NPC has varied at each Congress. The Fifth NPC (1978–1982) had the largest number of deputies (3,497). See Albert Chen, *supra* note 196, at 55. Article 15 of the 1979 Electoral Law of the NPC and Local People's Congresses limits the total number to 3,000. The total number of deputies nationwide in the five-level system is about four million. See Kevin J. O'Brien, 'Agents and Remonstrators: Role Accumulation by Chinese People's Congress Deputies', (June 1994) *The China Quarterly* 359, at 363.

211 Originally adopted in 1979, revised in 1982, 1986, 1995 and 2004.

Liberation Army of Deputies to the NPC and to Local People's Congresses.[212] Under the Electoral Law direct elections are only held at the township and county level; deputies to higher congresses are elected by the congress at the level immediately below.[213]

The powers of the NPC are provided by Articles 62 and 63 of the Constitution, and include the powers to revise the Constitution and to supervise its implementation, to make fundamental laws, to appoint and remove top government officials (including all officials at the rank of minister), to examine and approve government budgets and economic and social development plans, and to supervise their implementation, and to exercise all other (undefined) supreme powers of the state. The structures, functions and the operation of the NPC are governed by the Organic Law of the NPC (1982),[214] the Procedural Rules of the NPC (1989), and the Law on Deputies of the NPC and the Local People's Congress (1992).

The NPC only meets once a year, usually for several weeks, unless extraordinary sessions are convened by the SCNPC or at the request of more than one-fifth of the deputies to the NPC.[215] When in session, two methods are employed. Plenary sessions are chaired by a presidium elected at a preparatory meeting before each annual meeting. The presidium itself is chaired, in turn, by one of the several executive chairpersons elected by the presidium.[216] Major powers of the presidium include the exclusive power to decide the agenda of the annual meeting and to nominate candidates for membership of the SCNPC and its official positions, for Chairperson and Vice-chairpersons of the PRC and the Central Military Commission, as well as for the presidents of the Supreme People's Court and Supreme People's Procuratorate.[217] The plenary session, attended by the large number of deputies, is apparently not seen as an appropriate venue for debate and discussion. Thus discussions are held in group meetings organised according to the electoral units of the NPC, i.e. groups of provinces, the Army, minorities' representatives, etc.[218] To further facilitate the work of the NPC specialised commissions are established, which examine, discuss

---

212 Originally adopted by the Standing Committee of the NPC in 1981, revised in 1996. In addition to these two sets of electoral law, the SCNPC also issues special rules for election of deputies representing Hong Kong, Macao, and Taiwan.

213 Article 2 of the Law on the Election of Deputies to the NPC and Local People's Congresses. This is an expansion of direct election from the township level, as provided in the 1953 Electoral Law, to a higher level, the county level.

214 Which has been revised three times (1986, 1995 & 2004).

215 Article 61 of the 1982 Constitution. Until now, this has not happened in the history of the PRC.

216 Article 5 of the Organic Law of the NPC.

217 Articles 10 & 13 of the Organic Law of the NPC.

218 These groups may be divided into further sub-groups. See Article 4 of the Organic Law of the NPC and Article 7 of the Procedural Rules of the NPC.

and draw up relevant bills and resolutions under the direction of the SCNPC.[219] These commissions are, however, not organs of state power, but auxiliary organs established purely to facilitate the operation of the NPC and its Standing Committee.[220] The NPC or its Standing Committee may also establish special investigatory commissions on specific issues.[221]

(2) The Standing Committee of the NPC

The large number of deputies in the NPC and the infrequency of its meetings clearly prevent the NPC from exercising its 'supreme power of the state'. There were discussions in the early 1980s as to whether to reduce the number of deputies. However, it was felt that the size of the Chinese population required a corresponding number of deputies in order to represent various interests in the society. Therefore it was decided that the solution lay in the strengthening and expansion of the powers of the SCNPC.[222]

The Constitution defines the SCNPC, elected by the NPC and composed of around 175 members,[223] as the permanent body of the NPC,[224] with extensive powers, including the power to interpret the Constitution and to supervise its implementation, to make and revise laws other than those that must be made by the NPC itself,[225] to interpret laws, to examine and approve, when the NPC is not in session, partial adjustments to the plans for national economic and social development and to the state budget that are necessitated during their implementation, to supervise the work of the State Council, the Central Military Commission, the Supreme People's Court and the Supreme People's Procuratorate, as well as certain powers to ap-

---

219 Article 70 of the 1982 Constitution establishes the Nationalities Commission, the Law Commission, the Finance and Economic Commission, the Education, Science, Culture and Public Health Commission, the Foreign Affairs Commission, and the Overseas Chinese Commission. The same Article also authorises the establishment of other Commissions deemed necessary by the NPC. Accordingly, three more Commissions, on Internal and Judicial Affairs, on Environment Protection and Resources, and on Agriculture and Rural Affairs have also been established. See *People's Daily* (*Renmin Ribao*), internet edition, 19 March 1998. For the current NPC (the Tenth NPC), these Commissions remain unchanged. See Decision on the Establishment of Specialised Commissions for the Tenth NPC, adopted 6 March 2003 by the First Session of the Tenth NPC.

220 Jiang Bikun, *supra* note 2, at 254-255.

221 Article 71 of the 1982 Constitution and Article 38 of the Organic Law of the NPC.

222 See Gu Anagran, *supra* note 1, at 82.

223 Among them are the Chairperson, 15 vice-chairpersons and a Secretary-General of the Committee. See 2005 White Paper on Democracy, Section 3.

224 Article 57 of the 1982 Constitution.

225 This power will be further discussed in the next chapter on law-making.

point top government and judicial officials.[226] In order for the SCNPC to function properly and to avoid conflicts of interest,[227] the Constitution prohibits members of the Committee from holding any post in any of the administrative, judicial or procuratorial organs of the state during their terms of office,[228] and the Standing Committee's Organic Law and Procedural Rules require the convening of meetings once every two months,[229] with each meeting lasting about two weeks.

The work of the SCNPC is facilitated by its specialised working committees, whose establishment is authorised by the Organic Law of the Standing Committee. The committees are composed of professionals and specialists and their members need not be deputies to the NPC. For the purpose of law-making, the most important committee is the Legislative Affairs Committee.

The SCNPC sees its own task as mainly to speed up economic law-making and to improve its mechanisms for supervising the implementation of the Constitution and laws.[230] For the first major task the SCNPC has been both effective and efficient.[231] For the second task, it is still in an embryonic stage of development.[232]

(3) The NPC and the CPC

Although the large number of deputies to the NPC and its infrequent meeting are seen as major problems in the state power structure, the establishment of the SCNPC and delegation of powers to it seem to quite effectively remedy these shortcomings. The major problem in improving the system of the people's congress, as clearly seen by Chinese scholars,[233] is how to regularise the relationship between the NPC and the CPC. Although, as discussed above, it is a common understanding that party

226 Article 67 of the 1982 Constitution.

227 Gu Angran, *supra* note 1, at 82-83.

228 Article 65 of the 1982 Constitution.

229 Article 29 of the Organic Law of the NPC; and Article 3 of the Procedural Rules of the Standing Committee of the NPC.

230 See 'Major Tasks of the Standing Committee of the 8th NPC', in *People's Daily* (*Renmin Ribao*), 3 July 1993, at 4. See also, Cai Dingjian, 'Some Considerations on Improving the System of the People's Congress', *People's Daily* (*Renmin Ribao*), 16 September 1994, at 5; Peng Chong, 'The Important Task of the NPC is to Strengthen Legal Construction', *People's Daily* (*Renmin Ribao*), 4 Sept. 1994, at 3; Li Peng, 'Working Hard to Promote the Rule by Law and to Strengthen Socialist Democracy and the Legal System – Speech at the First Meeting of the Standing Committee of the 9th NPC', in *People's Daily* (*Renmin Ribao*), internet edition, 22 March 1998.

231 See further discussions in the next chapter on law-making.

232 See further discussions in section 4.8 below.

233 See e.g. Chen Yanqing & Xu Anbiao, 'Clarify the NPC's External Relations and Invigorate the NPC', (no. 6, 1990) *Legal Science in China* (*Zhongguo Faxue*) 10; Guo Daohui, *supra* note 161.

leadership over the state is to be exercised through the practice of translating party policies into state will through legal procedures,[234] this common understanding has not prevented Party intervention in the actual and specific operation and functioning of the NPC. To start with, it is the constitutional power of the NPC to revise the constitution and to elect or appoint state leaders. However, it is now claimed to be a constitutional convention – said to be a privilege of the party in power (*zhizhengdang*) – that constitutional revision can only be initiated and proposed by the Party.[235] Further, the Central Committee of the Party can give direct orders, including 'recommendations' of candidates for state positions, to the Party organisations in the NPC; these organisations then must carry through these orders.[236] It is therefore said that while constitutionally the NPC is not under the leadership of the Party, in terms of Party organisation it is so.[237]

Indeed Party control over the NPC, and thus its domination in political, economic and social life, is well institutionalised. First is the well-known communist institution of *nomenklatura* (*zhiwu mingchen biao*) which 'consists of lists of leading positions, over which party units exercise the power to make appointments and dismissals; lists of reserves or candidates for these positions; and institutions and processes for making the appropriate personnel changes'.[238] The positions covered by these lists are both appointive and elective.[239] This *nomenklatura* system is carried out through the Party committees established in all state authorities.[240] Secondly,

---

234 See *supra* note 162. On CPC and law-making, see Chapter 5.

235 According to Chinese scholars it is an express requirement of the Party that the revision of the Constitution must first be reported by the Party Committee in the NPC to the Politburo for discussion and to the Central Committee of the Party for approval. It must then be initiated by the Central Committee to the CPC. Further, drafts of all other important laws dealing with political, administrative and economic affairs must also be discussed and approved by the Politburo. See Guo Daohui, *supra* note 161, at 6-7, Qing & Li, *supra* note 161; and Hang Li, *supra* note 161. See also previous discussions on the fundamental principles and the Party system.

236 *Id.*

237 *Id.*, at 7.

238 See John Burns (ed.), *The Chinese Communist Party's Nomenklatura System: A Documentary Study of Party Control of Leadership Selection 1979–1984* (Armonk, New York/London: M.E.Sharpe, Inc., 1989), at ix.

239 *Id.*, at xxix.

240 For a detailed study on the *nomenklatura* system in China, see Burns, *supra* note 238. For a recent Party document on *nomenklatura*, see Interim Regulations of the Central Committee of the CPC on Selecting and Appointing Party and Government Officials (1995), in *Gazette of the State Council of the PRC* (*Zhonghua Renmin Gongheguo Guowuyuan Gongbao*), no. 12, 1995, at 438-449. These regulations, applicable to selection and appointment to the Central Committee of the CPC, the Standing Committee of the NPC, the State Council, the Chinese People's Political Consultative Conference, the Discipline Inspection Committee of the CPC, the Supreme People's Court, the Supreme People's Procuratorate, and their corresponding organs

there is also institutional control over the election of the deputies to the people's congresses at all levels. The 1979 Electoral Law of the NPC and Local People's Congress, for the first time, introduced the notion of competitive election, i.e. the number of candidates exceeds the number of vacancies.[241] Under the Electoral Law the number of candidates must be 30-100% greater than the vacancies for direct election at township and county level and 20-50% greater for election at a higher level.[242] Candidates may be nominated by all political parties or people's organisations, or jointly nominated by 10 voters.[243] The Electoral Law, however, at the same time introduced a system for screening candidates. For direct election the local electoral group is 'to conduct deliberation, discussion and consultation' in order to produce a 'formal list of candidates'.[244] For elections of a lower people's congress to a higher people's congress, the presidium was to do the same until 1995.[245] The Electoral Law, by an amendment in 1986, also requires that candidates will only be introduced to the voters by the electoral committee or the presidium, not by the candidates themselves. This control mechanism, although it has the positive aspect of ensuring the representation of democratic parties, minorities and women in the

---

at or above county level (Article 4), specifically emphasise that the selection and appointment of leading personnel must uphold the principle of party leadership (article 2). The specific mechanism for party leadership is through the control of selection and appointment by the party committees in the relevant organisations (Articles 9 & 27). While the various reforms in the personnel system and the institution of a civil servant system in the last many years have reduced the scope of the *nomenklatura* system and the Party has emphasised that the appointment and dismissal of state leadership must be carried out through legal procedures, it is unrealistic, at least in the near future, to expect that the Party will one day abolish the whole *nomenklatura* system. On the other hand, these reforms seem to have resulted in the concentration of personnel powers in the individual hands of the Party Secretary at different levels (hence the serious question of corruption). See 'Dividing the Personnel Nomination Power of the "First Hands"', (no. 10, 2007) *Democracy and the Legal System* (*Minzhu yu Fazhi*) 1. My own various interviews through years in China also confirm that there would be little chance for anyone to be appointed to important government or judicial organisations without the support and endorsement of the 'core leadership' of the Party committee at the corresponding level.

241 Such a method of election was said to have been adopted from experimentation within the Party system before 1979. See Gu Angran, *supra* note 1, at 86.

242 Article 30 of the Electoral Law as amended in 1986, 1995 and 2004.

243 Article 29 of the Electoral Law.

244 Article 31 of the Electoral Law. By the 2004 revision a preliminary election will now be held if a consensus on the formal list of candidates cannot be formed by the electoral group after 'deliberation, discussion and consultation'.

245 See Article 28 of the Electoral Law (as revised 1986). The 1995 Decision to Revise the Electoral Law introduces a preliminary election system under which a preliminary election will be held if the number of candidates exceeds the '20-50%' rule. See Article 31 of the Electoral Law (as revised in 1995).

state authorities,[246] provides the opportunity for the Party to mobilise its members to ensure that the desired candidates are on the 'formal list of candidates' and, hence to control the election of deputies.[247]

As to the main function of the NPC and its Standing Committee, namely law-making, Party control is equally strict, at least in the enactment and revision of major laws.[248]

4.5. The State Council

China does not accept the theory of 'separation of powers'. Instead it practises the principle of 'unity of deliberation and execution' (*yixing heyi*). This principle means that all state powers are vested in one system, the people's congress system, which deliberates and makes decisions; these decisions are then executed by administrative, adjudicative and procuratorial organs which are created by, responsible and subordinate to, and supervised by the people's congress.[249] Under this principle, it is not surprising that the State Council, composed of the Premier, Vice-Premiers and State Councillors, Ministers, the Auditor-General and the Secretary-General, is defined as the executive body of the highest organ of state power and the highest organ of state administration.[250] Theoretically, the NPC and its Standing Committee are the organs of state power and the originator of powers for other state organisations. In reality however, the State Council seems to be much more powerful than is suggested by the Constitution.

The 1982 Constitution contains a number of reforms in relation to the State Council. First, unlike the previous constitutions which emphasised collective leadership, the 1982 Constitution introduced a system of the premier being responsible for the whole State Council, and a minister being responsible for ministries and commissions of

---

246 Appropriate representation of minorities at the NPC and its Standing Committee is required by Articles 59 and 65 of the Constitution. The Opinions of the Central Committee of the CPC on Maintaining and Perfecting the Multi-Party Cooperation and Political Consultation System (1989) calls for appropriate representation of democratic parties. The 1995 Decision to Revise the Electoral Law of the NPC and Local People's Congresses further requires proper representation of women in the NPC and local people's congresses. See Article 6 of the Electoral Law of the NPC and Local People's Congresses (as revised in 1995). A specific quota is set aside for minorities' representation and special procedures are laid down for election of minorities. See Article 17 and Chapter 4 of the Electoral Law. However, no such mechanisms exist for the representation of democratic parties and women; such a proportion of representation is mainly achieved through the control mechanisms.

247 See Albert Chen, *supra* note 196, at 68.

248 See Qing & Li, *supra* note 161; and Hang Li, *supra* note 161. See also further discussions in Chapter 5 on Law-making.

249 See Zhang & Wang, *supra* note 60, at 188; Albert Chen, *supra* note 196, at 67-68.

250 Articles 85 & 86 of the 1982 Constitution.

the Council.[251] The premier's responsibility was specifically introduced to improve work efficiency.[252] Under this system the premier and ministers have the power of decision-making, while also being held responsible for their decisions. Although major decisions are discussed in the Executive Meeting or the Plenary Meeting of the Council,[253] the premier makes the final decisions after deliberation; the majority voting rule does not apply.[254] Secondly, the Constitution provides that the premier, vice-premiers and state councillors shall not serve more than two consecutive terms of office. Thus the Constitution effectively abolishes the *de facto* life tenure practised ever since the founding of the PRC. This abolition appears to accord with the general reform policy of 'smashing the iron bowls'. Thirdly, in strong contrast to the 1975 and 1978 Constitutions where the premier was to be nominated by the CPC, the premier is now to be nominated by the Chairman of the State; the rest of the members of the State Council are nominated by the premier. All nominations are to be approved by the NPC, or its Standing Committee in the case of ministers or when the NPC is not in session, and appointed by the Chairman of the State.[255] Fourthly, the Constitution also establishes the office of Auditor-General,[256] an office that existed in the 1930s in the Soviet Border Areas but was not established in the PRC until the 1982 Constitution.[257] Although the Auditor-General's is not an independent office, but is under the leadership of the premier, it is empowered to exercise supervision through independent auditing, and subject to no interference by any other administrative organ or any public organisation or individual.[258] A proper functioning of the Auditor-General's office would thus have the potential to make the State Council and other governmental organisations more accountable financially and, indeed, it has been very visible in recent years and is becoming increasingly powerful in the fight against corruption. Finally, the State Council is now authorised to make administrative laws, whereas it was only empowered to issue administrative measures in the previous constitutions.[259]

---

251 Article 86 of the 1982 Constitution.

252 Zhang Youyu, *supra* note 3, at 3; Gu Angran, *supra* note 1, at 87-88.

253 The Executive Meeting is composed of the premier, vice-premier, state councillors and the Secretary-General, while a Plenary Meeting is composed of all members of the Council including all ministers. See Article 88 of the Constitution. Theoretically these are the two major decision-making organs of the State Council.

254 Jiang Bikun, *supra* note 2, at 267.

255 See Articles 62 (5), 67 (9) and 80 of the 1982 Constitution.

256 Article 91 of the 1982 Constitution.

257 See Wang Liming & Chen Xingbo, 'The Auditor-General in Foreign Countries and Its Provisions in the Constitution', in Chinese Society of Legal Science, *supra* note 8, at 238-239.

258 Article 91 of the 1982 Constitution.

259 The rule-making power of the State Council is further discussed in Chapter 5 on law-making.

The State Council has been subject to continuing structural adjustment since the 1980s. After the last round of adjustments in March 2003, the State Council now has 28 ministries/commissions and a General Office.[260] In addition, the State Council is responsible for many subordinate organisations, which are established and re-structured from time to time, including the Xinhua News Agency, the Academy of Sciences, the Academy of Social Sciences, and the Legal Office of the State Council.[261]

4.6. The Unitary System and Central-Local Relations

The Preamble of the 1982 Constitution declares:

> The People's Republic of China is a unitary multi-national state created jointly by the people of all its nationalities. Socialist relations of equality, unity and mutual assistance have been established among the nationalities and will continue to be strengthened. In the struggle to safeguard the unity of the nationalities, it is necessary to combat big-national chauvinism, mainly Han chauvinism, and to combat local national chauvinism. The state will do its utmost to promote the common prosperity of all the nationalities.

Article 52 of the Constitution also imposes an obligation on citizens to safeguard the unification of the country and the unity of all nationalities. The Constitution appears to uphold unitarianism. Appreciating the diversity of its ethnic composition[262] and the large size of the land and the population, and anticipating the need for economic reform in terms of decentralisation,[263] the Constitution also provides for a certain amount of flexibility to its unitarian principle, including limited regional autonomy for areas mainly inhabited by ethnic minorities.[264] This flexibility may

---

260 For a full list of the ministries and commissions, see Decision on the State Council Structural Reform Plan, adopted by the First Session of the Tenth NPC on 10 March 2003.

261 For a full list of these organisations, see Chinese Government on-line: <www.gov.cn/gjjg/2005-08/01/content_18608.htm> (last accessed 25 September 2006).

262 According to the 2000 census there are 56 ethnic nationalities with a total population of 1.265 billion. Among them, the Han population is 1.159 billion and the 55 ethnic minorities have a total population of 106.4 million. See <www.gov.cn/test/2005-07/26/content_17366.htm> (last accessed 8 June 2007).

263 Administratively, China is presently divided into four directly administered municipalities (*zhixia shi*, Beijing, Tianjin, Shanghai, and the latest addition of Chongqing in 1996), 22 provinces (*shen*, with Hainan being the most recent addition in 1988) and five autonomous regions (*zizhi qu*). In addition, there is the Hong Kong Special Administrative Region, with Macau being added into this special category in 1999. Taiwan is not included in the above.

264 It is therefore said that the current system is a unitary system with multi-forms, combining principle with flexibility. See Zhange & Wang, *supra* note 60, at 169.

reflect uncertainties in the search for a modern state structure that have arisen since the movement for constitutionalism began.

As discussed above, one of the major difficulties in the constitutionalism movement in China has been the struggle between unitarianism and federalism. The 1923 Constitution, commonly referred to as the 'Bribery Constitution', adopted a federal system, with powers for the central and local governments specifically listed in the Constitution.[265] It is however doubtful whether this was the result of a genuine desire for federalism or a reflection of the lust for power among the warlords.[266] In any case, this Constitution was almost universally denounced in China.[267] Dr. Sun Yatsen, in the early days of the revolution, advocated a federal system in line with the American model.[268] By the time he published his Fundamentals of National Reconstruction in 1924 he had changed his mind and began to advocate a system of equilibrium of powers in a unitary system. He made it clear that:

> during the Period of Constitutional Government, the powers of the Central Government and those of the provinces shall be evenly distributed. Affairs of a national character shall be reserved for the Central Government, and those of a local character shall be reserved for the district (*hsien*). The system is neither centralisation nor decentralisation.[269]

The Kuomintang under Chiang Kai-Shek effectively rejected the idea of federalism. The 1931 Provisional Constitution for the Political Tutelage Period not only established the supremacy of the Kuomintang, but also made local governments subsidiaries directly under the leadership of the Central Government.[270] Dr. Sun's idea of equilibrium of powers was only restored in the 1946 Constitution, which expressly listed the powers of Central and local governments[271] and empowered the Judicial *Yuan* to adjudicate and interpret the distribution of powers between the Central and local governments.[272] This Constitution was hardly implemented in China before the Kuomintang was defeated and retreated to Taiwan.

The Common Program was internally a self-contradictory document. On the one hand governments of all levels were to be appointed by a government at a higher level

---

265 See Chapter Five of the 1923 Constitution.

266 See W.Y. Tsao, *supra* note 17, at 215.

267 See *supra* note 36.

268 See Tong Zhiwei & Guo Yanjun, 'An Important Topic for Constitutional Studies – Comparative Study on State Structure', (no. 5, 1993) *Studies in Law* (*Faxue Yanjiu*) 10, at 13.

269 Article 17 of the Fundamentals of National Reconstruction, cited in Tsao, *supra* note 17, at 216.

270 See Article 78 of the Provisional Constitution for the Political Tutelage Period.

271 See Chapters 10 and 11 of the 1946 Constitution.

272 See Article 117 of the 1946 Constitution.

and all lower level governments were to obey the government at a higher level and ultimately the Central Government.[273] On the other hand the Central Government was to prescribe powers to the central and local governments 'so as to satisfy the requirements of both national unity and local expediency',[274] to 'give full play to local governments for their creativeness and initiative' in economic development,[275] to define 'the spheres of financial administration of central and local government',[276] and to establish regional autonomy in areas mainly occupied by ethnic minorities.[277] Fundamentally, the legitimacy and powers of the local governments were to be granted by the Central Government. It is interesting to note that the issue of federalism was discussed at the 7th Party Congress in 1945, and that federalism was rejected after an examination of the Soviet experience.[278]

The 1954 Constitution was again a self-contradictory document. The local governments were defined as the executive organs of the local people's congresses, and the latter were to be directly elected by the people at the township level and indirectly elected by the lower level congress.[279] This seemed to suggest that the legitimacy of the local governments came from the people. However, the local governments were also defined as state organs directly under the unitary leadership of the State Council, and had to obey the State Council.[280] Further, local governments also had to carry out resolutions and orders of the people's congress at the same level, as well as of administrative organs at higher levels.[281] Apparently the Constitution assumed that the interests of governments at all levels were identical. Again, the Constitution allowed the establishment of regional autonomy for areas occupied by ethnic minorities, but at the same time it elevated territorial integrity to a constitutional principle.[282]

The Organic Law of the Local People's Congress and the Local People's Committees, adopted at the same time as the 1954 Constitution, further provided that departments of local governments at a lower level were subject to the leadership

---

273 Article 15 of the Common Program.

274 Article 16 of the Common Program.

275 Article 33 of the Common Program.

276 Article 40 of the Common Program.

277 Article 51 of the Common Program.

278 See Gu Angran, *supra* note 1, at 77.

279 See Articles 56 & 62 of the 1954 Constitution.

280 Article 66 of the 1954 Constitution.

281 Article 64 of the 1954 Constitution.

282 Article of the 1954 Constitution. As the 1954 Constitution had a strong Soviet influence it is interesting to note that in the USSR the component Republics were allowed secession. See Tay, *supra* note 47, at 354.

of the same departments at a higher level.[283] Thus local governments were made effectively the outlets of the Central Government. Chinese scholars therefore correctly point out that the 1954 Constitution established a highly centralised system of state power.[284]

The 1975 and 1978 Constitutions did not offer anything new in regard to central-local relations; they continued the centralised system of power as established by the 1954 Constitution.

By the time the 1978 Constitution was under revision the Third Plenary Session of the 11th Party Congress had decided to deal with the issue of over-concentration of powers and of allowing a certain degree of autonomy for local authorities.[285] Thus the issue of federalism was again raised and discussed.[286] A federal system was however rejected as it was thought that such a system would weaken the economic ties between various parts of China.[287] Instead a certain amount of flexibility was incorporated into the 1982 Constitution, while unitarianism was firmly upheld.[288]

First, this Constitution expressly declares that China is a unitary state and imposes an obligation upon its citizens to safeguard the integrity of the state and the unity of all nationalities.[289] Further, the Constitution adopts the principle of democratic centralism.[290] This principle is not defined in the Constitution.[291] Contemporary

---

[283] Articles 24, 39 and 40 of Organic Law of the Local People's Congress and Local People's Committees.

[284] Liu Xiaobing, 'Some Legal Considerations on Central-Local Relations', (no. 2, 1995) *Legal Science in China* (*Zhongguo Faxue*) 24, at 25.

[285] See Liu Xiaobing, *id.*, at 25; and *supra* note 81.

[286] See *supra* note 86.

[287] See Gu Angran, *supra* note 1, at 77.

[288] The following outlines, briefly, the major features of the contemporary centre-local relations under the Constitution. For a detailed study on this subject, see Jianfu Chen & Lijian Hong, *China Local Business Law Guide* (Singapore: CCH Asia Pacific, loose-leaf services, first published in 1999).

[289] The Preamble and Article 52 of the 1982 Constitution. This constitutional principle is implemented by Chapter One of Part II (Specific Provisions) of the Criminal Law (1997). More recently a highly controversial law, the Anti-Secession Law, was adopted by the Third Plenary Session of the Tenth NPC on 14 March 2005. This Anti-Secession Law, which took immediate effect upon adoption and promulgation, is explicitly aimed at Taiwan and, for the first time, specifically authorises the use of 'non-peaceful' means to resolve the 'Taiwan issue' if Taiwan in any manner declares its independence or if there is a danger of China losing the possibility of peaceful re-unification (Article 8 of the Anti-Secession Law).

[290] Article 3 of the 1982 Constitution.

[291] It was defined in the 1949 Common Program to mean that 'the People's Congresses shall be responsible and accountable to the people; the People's Government Councils shall be responsible and accountable to the People's Congresses. Within the People's Congresses and within the People's Councils, the minority shall abide by the decisions of the majority;

constitutional scholars interpret it to mean a combination of centralisation of state power (*zhongyang jiquan*) and decentralisation through central authorisation (*zhongyang shouquan*). This means that, first, all state powers and authorities are subject to unified leadership by central authorities – state authorities at lower levels must abide by the decisions and leadership of those at higher levels – and secondly, while local initiative and enthusiasm are to be encouraged, local interests must not be put above national interests and local authorities must obey the central authorities.[292] The principle of democratic centralism seems to suggest that all local powers are generated from and authorised by central authorities. Such centralism, though defined as 'democratic', runs directly into conflict with other constitutional provisions which define the source of state power. According to Article 2 of the Constitution all powers belong to the people and are exercised by the people's congresses at various levels. Under the Electoral Law of the NPC and Local People's Congresses, as discussed above, people's congresses at township and county levels are elected directly by the people and all higher people's congresses are then elected by the congress at the immediately lower level. These provisions thus suggest, if interpreted correctly, that the state powers for the central authorities are generated by the lower authorities, not *vice versa*.

Secondly, while affirming the principle of unified leadership under the central authorities, state powers and functions are to be divided between central and local state organs in order to give full play to the initiative and enthusiasm of the local authorities.[293] These powers and functions, including law-making, are indeed divided among the governments but in very general and vague terms.[294] One of the significant improvements over the previous constitutions is the abolition of the power of higher-level government departments to give orders to the same departments at a lower level, although the power to direct their work and to reverse their 'inappropriate' decisions is retained.[295]

The redistribution of powers between central and local authorities has been a major aspect of political, administrative and, especially, economic reforms, and the effect of certain reforms has been far-reaching, namely reforms in taxation and finance

---

the appointment of the People's Governments of each level shall be ratified by the People's government of the higher level; the People's Governments of the lower levels shall obey the People's Governments of the higher levels and all local People's Governments throughout the country shall obey the Central People's Governments'. See Article 15 of the Common Program.

292 See Jiang Bikun, *supra* note 2, at 146. See also Albert Chen, *supra* note 196, at 51.

293 Article 3 of the 1982 Constitution.

294 See Chapter 3 on the Structure of the State of the 1982 Constitution.

295 See Article 108 of the 1982 Constitution.

systems and special powers granted to Special Economic Zones.[296] However, these reforms are not constitutional reforms. They are, as defined by Chinese scholars,[297] administrative reforms by way of power granted from the Centre to local authorities through administrative authorisation, driven mainly by considerations of economic efficiency and productivity.[298] So far the powers exercised by local authorities are *de facto*, not institutionalised in the Constitution or in any other laws.[299] The granting of powers to local authorities thus depends purely on the willingness of the central authorities and on their prevailing policies. Powers so granted may, at their will, be re-centralised at any time, as has often happened in the history of the PRC.[300]

Thirdly, provisions for regional autonomy for minority areas have been largely expanded and expressed in much clearer terms,[301] and further codified in, and complemented by, the Law of the PRC on Minority Regional Autonomy (1984).[302] Limited rights of autonomy are provided by the Constitution, which include the power of autonomous regions to issue autonomous regulations, to independently administer finances, to organise and maintain local police forces, to use local languages, and to independently administer and manage the local economy, education, science, culture, public health and cultural heritage. In addition to these rights of autonomy, special arrangements are made for minorities in some national laws,[303] or special concessions, modifications or considerations are required to be given in

296 Some scholars have claimed that economic reforms in taxation and finance have led to the existence of a *de facto* financial federalism in China. See Tong & Guo, *supra* note 268, at 11. Others believe that these reforms have led to the existence of 'economies by lords' (*zhuhou jingji*). See Liu Xiaobing, *supra* note 284, at 28. Both terms refer to the continuing decrease of revenue collecting at the central level and the corresponding increase at local levels. See also Chen & Hong, *supra* note 288.

297 Liu Xiaobing, *supra* note 284 and Tong & Guo, *supra* note 268.

298 See Jianfu Chen, *supra* note 139, Chapter 3. See also Chen & Hong, *supra* note 288.

299 There are calls to institutionalise the power distribution through a special law, a Law on Central-Local Relations. See e.g. Liu Xiaobing, *supra* note 284.

300 See Liu Xiaobing, *supra* note 284; and Tong & Guo, *supra* note 268. See also Chen & Hong, *supra* note 288.

301 See Section VI of Chapter 3 of the 1982 Constitution.

302 Last revised on 28 February 2001. Under Article 112 of the Constitution and Article 2 of the Law on Minority Regional Autonomy, regional autonomy is granted to areas where minority nationalities live in large communities. These areas are classified into autonomous regions (*zizhiqu*), autonomous prefectures (*zizhizhou*) and autonomous counties (*zizhixien*). In 1983, the State Council issued its Notice Regarding the Establishment of Nationalities Villages, which authorised the establishment of nationalities villages (*minzh xiang*) which also enjoy limited autonomy.

303 E.g. Organic Law of the Local People's Congresses and the Local People's Governments of the PRC at Various Levels (1979, as amended 1982, 1986, 1995 & 2004).

implementing national laws in regional minority autonomous areas.[304] Finally, there are various policies issued by the Party or state authorities dealing with regional minority autonomy.[305]

The right to autonomy and its related legal framework should not be taken at face value.[306] They are provided for within a specific constitutional framework and with constraints. To start with, the principle of democratic centralism applies also to regional minority autonomy. The Constitution not only opposes Han chauvinism, it also opposes local-national chauvinism.[307] Further, the Constitution and other laws in the PRC talk of autonomy, not self-determination. It was only in the early days of communist history that the Party supported the right of self-determination (*zhijuequan*) for minority nationalities.[308] Since the late 1930s the term 'self-determination' has been dropped and replaced by the term 'autonomy' (*zizhiquan*) within a unified state.[309] Further, the Constitution grants regional autonomy to areas occupied by minorities, not the right of autonomy for minorities. This effectively means that minorities have no right to claim independence or separation from

---

304 E.g. the Marriage Law of the PRC (1980); the Forestry Law of the PRC (1984); the Grassland Law of the PRC (1985), and the Law of the PRC on Mineral Resources and Products (1986). Article 20 of the Law of the PRC on Minority Regional Autonomy further grants the power for national autonomous authorities to modify or terminate implementation of resolutions, decisions, instructions or orders of a state authority at a higher level, provided such modification or termination is approved by the latter. For more detailed examination on the implementation of national law and the Minority Regional Autonomy Law, see Zhang Xiaohui (ed.), *The Implementation of Chinese [National] Law in National Minority Areas* (*Zhongguo Falü zai Shaoshu Minzu Diqu de Shishi*) (Kunming: Yunnan University Press, 1994); and Xu Jiexun & Wu Shuxing (eds), *A Study on the Implementation of Autonomy Law* (*Shishi Zizhi Fa Yanjiu*), Guilin: Guangxi Nationalities Press (1997).

305 See e.g. State Council Notice Concerning Certain Questions on Further Implementing the Regional Minority Autonomy Law (1991).

306 For more detailed discussions, see Sander G. Tideman, 'Tibetans and Other Minorities in China's Legal System'. (1988) 14 *Rev. of Soc. L.* 5; Franz Michael, 'Non-Chinese Nationalities and Religious Communities', in Yuan-li Wu, *et al.*, *Human Rights in the People's Republic of China* (Boulder/London: Westview Press, 1988), 268-286; and Arthur Rosett, 'Legal Structures for Special Treatment of Minorities in the People's Republic of China, (1991) 66 *Notre Dame L. Rev.* 1503.

307 In contrast, the 1954 Constitution only mentioned the opposition to Han chauvinism.

308 For instance, Article 14 of the Constitutional Outline of the Chinese Soviet (1934) provided that 'The Soviet government of China acknowledges the right of national self-determination of the national minorities in the territory of China, up to and including the right of all national minorities to separation from China and the creation of their own independent state'.

309 See Rosett, *supra* note 306, at 1510.

China.[310] Indeed, it is made clear that all national autonomous areas are inalienable parts of the PRC.[311]

Fourthly, an innovation was incorporated into the Constitution to deal with the difficult issue of national unification, i.e. the authorisation to establish special administrative regions when such establishment is deemed necessary.[312] Although the incorporation of this innovation was originally aimed at Taiwan, it is now applied to Hong Kong and Macau with no express constitutional barrier for it to be applied to other cases.[313] The central formula in establishing special administrative regions is the notion of 'one country, two systems'.

Again, the idea of 'one country, two systems' was also first aimed at the unification of Taiwan. In the Message to Compatriots in Taiwan, issued by the SCNPC on 1 January 1979, the Committee talked of respect for the reality of Taiwan. Later in the same year Deng Xiaoping, during his visit to the United States, also talked of respect for the reality and current system of Taiwan. In a policy statement on Taiwan announced by Ye Jianying, then the Chairman of the SCNPC, it was announced that, once re-united, Taiwan would become a special administrative region which would retain its existing socio-economic system and life style, and its existing economic and cultural ties with other countries would not be changed. Ye did not use the term 'one country, two systems'; the concept was later summarised in this term by Deng Xiaoping who also suggested that the formula could be applied to Hong Kong.[314] The term is said to have been first used by Deng Xiaoping during his talk with the then British Prime Minister, Margaret Thatcher in 1982. It was then used as a basis for negotiation with British authorities for the return of Hong Kong to China.[315] It acquired the status of state policy when it was reported to and approved by the NPC in 1984 as part of the Report of Government Work.[316]

The Concept of 'Special Administrative Region' (SAR) and the formula of 'one country, two systems' basically means that within a unified country the fundamental political, socio-economic and legal systems in an SAR may be allowed to be different

---

310 Gu Angran, *supra* note 1, at 78.

311 Article 4 of the 1982 Constitution.

312 Article 31 of the 1982 Constitution.

313 In the drafting of the special administrative region provisions there were suggestions to specifically mention Taiwan. Taiwan was omitted after some consideration to allow for future flexibility. See Zhang Youyu, *supra* note 92, at 11-12. See also Gu Angran, *supra* note 1, at 91-92. So far, there has been no official suggestion that this concept might be applied to areas other than the three regions.

314 See Jiang Bikun, *supra* note 2, at 166-167; Wen Qing, '"One Country, Two Systems" – The Best Way to Peaceful Reunification', (13-19 August 1990), *Beijing Review* 14, at 14-15.

315 Xiao Weiyun (ed.), *One Country Two Systems and the Basic Legal System in Hong Kong* (*Yiguo Liangzhi Yu Xianggang Jiben Falu Zhidu*) (Beijing: Beijing University Press, 1990), at 3.

316 Xiao Weiyun, *id.*, at 3-4.

from the rest of the country. However, the concept and the formula present some major problems. Article 31 of the Constitution allows the establishment of SARs, but it does not define the concept of SAR or its contents, nor grants any special powers to SARs. Instead, it provides that the systems to be instituted in SARs are to be prescribed by the NPC according to the specific conditions of the case. Thus the 'specialness' of a particular SAR depends on negotiation and bargaining between Beijing and the potential SAR, and the permission of the NPC;[317] the autonomy of the SAR is authorised by and subject to the unified leadership of the Central authority.[318] Further, the emphasis on, and a precondition of, the formula of 'one country, two systems' is 'one country'; it is only within one unified country that a different system, that is, a capitalist system, is allowed to be practised in an SAR, within a specific time frame.[319] Even here, the two systems are not parallel, nor mutually exclusive, but intended to promote each other and facilitate mutual development.[320] Despite all these potential problems, this system seems to have operated reasonably well since Hong Kong and Macao returned to China in 1997 and 1999 respectively.

In sum, all decentralisation and local autonomy are allowed on the premise of upholding territorial integrity. Further, decentralisation of powers has been largely carried out through administrative authorisation with no formal changes to the Constitution (with the exception of the SARs). The extent of such decentralisation depends on the will of the central government as well as the bargaining powers of the local government. There is no constitutional guarantee that decentralised power may not again be centralised, though in reality it would be very difficult to do so after nearly three decades of reform.[321] There has been no clear pattern emerging from decentralisation, nor any clear direction for future development. Central-local relations and relations among various nationalities will continue to be a major issue confronting Chinese constitutional lawyers and policy makers, just as it has confronted the modern movement towards constitutionalism in China.

4.7. Fundamental Rights and Duties

Chapter Two of the Constitution is entitled Fundamental Rights and Duties of Citizens. The provisions on citizens' rights appear to be compatible with international

---

317 For instance, one cannot assume that the Basic Law of Hong Kong will be a model for Taiwan, as China has made it clear that the situation of Taiwan is different in that it is treated as an internal issue, whereas in the case of Hong Kong, it has been an international issue between China and Great Britain, if not also Hong Kong. See Wen Qing, *supra* note 314, at 15-16.

318 Jiang Bikun, *supra* note 2, at 168. This point was reiterated in 2007 by Wu Bangguo when he delivered the keynote speech at a ceremony celebrating the 10th anniversary of the return of Hong Kong. See *People's Daily* (*Renmin Ribao*) (overseas edition), 7 June 2007, at 1.

319 Xiao Weiyun, *supra* note 315, at 5.

320 Jiang Bikun, *supra* note 2, at 166.

321 See Liu Xiaobing, *supra* note 284.

human rights standards. At face value it forms a mini Bill of Rights. It largely restores and expands the provisions in the 1954 Constitution.[322] These provisions start with the principle of equality before the law, followed by the political right to vote and to stand for election, and freedom of speech, of the press, of assembly, of association, of procession and of demonstration, and of religious belief. They then turn to the protection of personal security and dignity as well as personal freedom of communication. They further provide for the right to work and rest, to social security after retirement, and to education. Equal rights for women are specifically protected and the protection of rights and interests of overseas and returned overseas Chinese is emphasised.[323] Although the list of rights and duties is not meant to be exhaustive, there is no such concept as 'residue rights'; all rights are legal rights and must be provided by law.

While Chapter Two of the Constitution may be seen as a version of a bill of rights, the term 'human rights' was not used until the 2004 Constitutional revision.[324] Indeed, the term 'human rights' has had a rather bumpy history in the PRC. Although there have been many lively debates on issues commonly understood as human rights throughout the history of the PRC, the term was rarely applied as official language. Instead, all Chinese constitutions in the PRC have consistently used the term 'citizen's rights', which implicitly rejects the universality of human rights and implies the class nature of such rights; that is, citizens may be differentiated according to their class backgrounds. It may also imply the exclusion of foreigners and stateless persons in China.[325] Ironically, the term 'human rights' was only officially used after the June 4 Tiananmen Square Event in 1989, particularly after the State Council issued its white paper, *Human Rights in China,* in 1991.[326]

---

[322] There is a notable omission of the right to free movement within China. This omission reflects a more realistic and honest attitude of the authorities towards fundamental rights, as there has alway been restriction on migration from the countryside to the cities. See Gu Angran, *supra* note 1, at 95.

[323] See Articles 33-50 of the 1982 Constitutions. For a detailed analysis of constitutional rights in China, see Ann Kent, *Between Freedom and Subsistence: China and Human Rights* (Hong Kong: Oxford University Press, 1993).

[324] By a new insert in Article 33 of the Constitution through the 2004 Constitutional Revision, the Constitution now declares, without any qualification, that '[t]he state respects and protects human rights'.

[325] See Ronald C. Keith, *China's Struggle for the Rule of Law* (New York: St. Martin's Press, 1994), at 66-67; 'Recent Human Rights Studies in the PRC', being Annex II to the *Report of the Second Australian Human Rights Delegation to China 8-20 November 1992*, Canberra: AGPS (1993), at 99-100.

[326] See Keith, *id.*, at 66-72. The White Paper was published in several languages. For an English version, see *Beijing Review*, 4-10 November 1991. Since then, new White Papers on human rights have been issued in 1995, 1997, 1999, 2000, 2001, 2004, and 2005. All these White

This 2004 constitutional declaration on the protection of human rights can have some very significant practical implications. First, this unqualified declaration could mean that China has now finally come to accept universal human rights, rather than insisting on an 'Asian' or 'Chinese' conception of human rights. Secondly, also as a consequence of this unqualified declaration, the scope of human rights could be interpreted to include not only the fundamental rights as codified in Chapter Two of the Constitution, but also those contained in at least the two International Covenants and other international human rights treaties that China has agreed to abide by,[327] such as the right to strike which was dropped during the making of the 1982 Constitution. Thirdly, the insertion of this declaration in Article 33 bears some significant practical implications. Article 33 defines the nature of rights in China: that is, all citizens are equal before the law and citizens, while enjoying rights, must also perform the duties as prescribed by the Constitution and the law. Here the meaning of the principle of equality before the law had long been uncertain. 'Equality before the law' was first provided by Article 4 of the 1934 Constitutional Outline, but that article was only applied to working people. The 1949 Common Program talked of gender and racial equality in law.[328] The 1954 Constitution provided a general principle: 'All citizens are equal in law'. This general principle was abolished in the 1975 and 1978 Constitutions, but restored in the 1982 Constitution.[329] In the restoring of the principle the wording was changed. Instead of 'all citizens are equal in law (*zai falü shang*)' it declares that 'all citizens are equal before the law (*zai falü mianqian*)'. The change of wording was said to specifically mean equality in the implementation of laws, not in law-making.[330] The declaration on the respect for, and protection of, human rights could potentially allow the court to interpret 'all citizens are equal before the law' to mean 'all *people* are equal before the law'; otherwise the provisions in Article 33 would be inherently inconsistent. Finally, with calls from academics and officials to pay attention to the actual implementation of

---

Papers are available from <www.gov.cn/zwgk/2005-06/02/content_3618.htm> (last accessed 16 June 2007).

327 China signed the International Covenant on Political and Civil Rights on 5 October 1998, and the International Covenant on Economic, Social and Cultural Rights on 27 October 1997, with the latter having already been ratified by the SCNPC on 28 February 2001 and the ratification of the former being likely in the future. China has also ratified many other UN conventions on human rights, such as the International Convention on the Elimination of All Forms of Racial Discrimination, the International Convention on the Elimination of All Forms of Discrimination against Women etc.

328 See Articles 6, 9 and 50 of the Common Program.

329 Article 33 of the 1982 Constitution.

330 Zhang Youyu, *supra* note 92, at 8-9; Gu Angran, *supra* note 1, at 92-93; Sun Yamin, 'The New Developments in Socialist Democracy and Socialist Legality', in Zhang Youyu, *supra* note 3, at 19; and Wu Jie & Xu Xiuyi, 'On the Principle of Equality before the Law', in Chinese Society of Legal Science, *supra* note 8, at 134-141.

the Constitution,[331] Chinese courts can and should take protection of human rights as a major consideration in their adjudications, at least when the relevant Chinese law is not clear or is ambiguous on particular matters.[332] In short, as Xu Xianming, a jurist and a deputy to the NPC, has rightly pointed out, this declaration may ultimately bring about changes to the State's value system.[333]

However we are not seeing the coming of age of rights in China as yet. Through the efforts of many international human rights organisations, human rights activists, and Chinese dissidents[334] it has become clear that there is a huge gap between the law and reality.[335] Even the rights on paper are not without major flaws in their

---

331 For instance, on the occasion of the commemoration of the 20th anniversary of the promulgation of the Constitution on 4 December 2002, Hu Jintao emphasised that '[I]t is desirable to promote the Constitution extensively in society so that it is known to every household and penetrates to the people's heart, which will lead the broad masses of people to the notion that the Constitution is not only a norm every citizen should observe in behaviour, but also a legal weapon with which they can safeguard their citizens' rights.' An English translation of his speech is available from 2 (3) 2003 *Human Rights*, 1-5. (*Human Rights* is published by the China Society for Human Rights Studies, Beijing).

332 Some jurists in China clearly hold the same view. See 'Top legislators consider amending constitution again', *China Daily*, internet edition, 8 March 2004, <www.chinadaily.com.cn/english/doc/2004-03/08/content_312874.htm> (last accessed 12 March 2004).

333 'Top legislators consider amending constitution again', *id*. In mid-March 2004, for the first time, Chinese media reported that some 10,000 people were sentenced to immediate execution each year in China, not including people sentenced to death with a two-year suspension. See '41 deputies suggested that the Supreme People's Court should re-centralise the approval power over the death penalty', originally published in the *Zhongguo Qingnian Bao* (*China Youth Daily*), and re-published in the *Renmin Ribao*, 16 March 2004, website edition: <www.people.com.cn/GB/shehui/1060/2388561.html> (last accessed 22 March 2004). In this context, any positive change in the state value system is potentially life-saving.

334 There are numerous reports on human rights violations in China by international human rights organisations, such as Asia Watch and Amnesty International. There is also an increasing number of personal accounts of human rights abuses in China by Chinese dissidents now residing overseas. There are also many reports by Western governments, notably the US State Department's annual reports. Reports by these organisations, while praised for documenting individual cases of human rights, have been criticised for failing to assess human rights performance on a society-wide basis or in comparison with other countries with a compatible level of development. See Keith, *supra* note 325, at 55-58; and Randy Peerenboom, 'Assessing Human Rights in China: Why the Double Standard?', (2005) 38:1 *Cornell International Law Journal* 71.

335 There is a large number of scholarly analyses of law and human rights practices in China. See e.g. R. Randle Edward, Louis Henkin & Andrew J. Nathan, *Human Rights in Contemporary China*, New York: Columbia University Press (1986); Yuan-li Wu, Ta-ling Lee, Franz Michael, Maria Hsi Chang, John F. Cooper & A. James Gregor, *Human Rights in the People's Republic of China* (Boulder/London: Westview Press, 1988); and numerous articles published in major international scholarly journals.

conceptual and theoretical foundations, and in the constraints imposed upon their exercise. One must be cautious in analysing these rights.

First, there is no doubt that the protection of fundamental rights gained increasing importance in the 1982 Constitution, and especially since the 2004 Revision. Provisions on citizen's rights were moved from Chapter Three to Chapter Two, immediately following the General Principles. Provisions on citizens' rights have also been expanded considerably. The 1954 Constitution contained 19 articles on the subject. There were only 4 articles in the 1975 Constitution. The 1978 Constitution devoted 16 articles to the question, whereas the 1982 Constitution contains 24 articles on it. Further, informal freedoms, particularly in economic spheres, have been expanded quite considerably since 1978 with the blessing of economic liberalisation.[336] While acknowledging these positive developments one must not overlook the initial motivations for such development. Although the inclusion of provisions on personal security and dignity was a result of genuine concern about the possible repetition of the cruel treatment suffered by millions of Chinese people, including the top officials of the Chinese leadership, during the Cultural Revolution,[337] the emphasis on the protection of citizen's rights was largely motivated by consideration for rebuilding party legitimacy, strengthening party domination, as well as establishing a stable social order for smooth economic development – all relevant considerations in the actual human rights practice in contemporary China.[338]

Secondly, until very recently Chinese jurisprudence has emphasised the 'unity of rights and duties'. Although there has been a long-standing debate on the relationship between rights and duties, the central issue of controversy has been on the relative importance of rights or duties. While increasing numbers of scholars now emphasise the importance 'rights', the 'Marxist' principle of 'unity of rights and duties' itself has not been challenged,[339] at least not by officials or government authorities. This principle is directly reflected in the Constitution. In addition to Article 33, the Constitution further specifically provides that the exercise of freedoms and rights 'may not infringe upon the interests of the state, of society and of the collective, or upon the lawful freedoms and rights of other citizens.'[340] Above this, of course, any exercise of rights in violation of the Four Fundamental Principles would also be unconstitutional. Some provisions simply treat a right as a duty at the same time. For instance, Article 42 specifically provides that citizens have a right as well as duty

336 On the expansion of informal freedoms, see Kent, *supra* note 323.

337 See Keith, *supra* note 325, at 68 & 77; Kent, *supra* note 323, at 85.

338 See discussions in Chapter 2 on the experience of law in the PRC. See also Keith, *supra* note 325, at 69.

339 See Keith, *supra* note 325, at 69-79. For a recent Chinese summary of views in the debate, see 'Jurisprudential Debate on the Relationship Between Rights and Duties', (no. 4, 1991), *Xinhua Digest* (*Xinhua wenzhai*) 16. See also discussions in Chapter 2.

340 Article 51 of the 1982 Constitution.

to work. Still other provisions contain some ambiguous restrictions. For instance, while the Constitution provides for freedom of religious belief, it only protects 'normal' religious activities.[341]

The emphasis on 'unity of rights and duties' can be, and has been, applied to firmly restrict the exercise of constitutional rights. For instance the 1989 demonstrations in Tiananmen Square were condemned by the authorities on the grounds that these demonstrations infringed the rights of personal security, destroyed state property and violated state interests. Thus 'patriotic' activities were turned into 'counter-revolutionary' ones.[342] The emphasis on collective interests can also be stretched widely. For instance, the abolition of the 'right to strike', a provision incorporated in the 1978 Constitution, though clearly reflecting the emphasis on social order conducive to economic development, was done in the name of protecting the collective interests of the whole nation.[343]

Thirdly, the positive conferral of rights on citizens by the Constitution, by its nature, imposes few restrictions on the State. Indeed, there is little evidence to suggest that the control of state powers was the concern behind the making of the Constitution, other than the limited effort to divide powers among various state organs. On the other hand the Constitution makes it clear that the interests of the state, which are to be interpreted by the state authorities themselves, are above those of individuals.[344] Thus, if the rights contained in the Constitution appear to be similar to those in Western constitutions, they are, in effect, of a different quality.[345]

Finally, there is no mention of the right of citizens or organisations to challenge the constitutionality of government actions, nor any mechanism established for the enforcement of constitutional rights. Indeed, there have been suggestions that the provisions of the Constitution may not be directly enforced in a court of law.[346] Thus the protection and enjoyment of citizen's rights depends more on the

---

[341] Article 36 of the 1982 Constitution.

[342] See Keith, *supra* note 325, at 70. See also 'A Joint Statement of the Central Committee of the Chinese Communist Party and the State Council to All Party Members and All Nationals', (6 June 1989) *People's Daily* (*Renmin Ribao*) (overseas edition), at 1.

[343] Gu Angran, *supra* note 1, at 94-95.

[344] Article 51 of the 1982 Constitution.

[345] On this point, see two very different perspectives on Chinese constitutional rights: Pu Zengyuan, 'A Comparative Perspective on the United States and Chinese Constitutions' (1989) 30 *Williiam and Mary L. Rev.* 867; and Owen M. Fiss, 'Two Constitutions', (1986) 11 *Yale J. of Int'l L.* 492.

[346] See Zhang & Wang, *supra* note 60, at 160; Chen Yunsheng, *supra* note 130. As will be shown in the next section, these views are being questioned and challenged by many scholars of a younger generation. In fact, more recent studies on constitutional law are often placed in the context of specific political, social and legal problems, aimed at constitutional solutions. See e.g. Cai Dingjian, 'The Development of Constitutionalism in the Chinese Transitional

development of individual statutes such as, in particular, administrative law, than on the Constitution.

4.8. Interpretation, Supervision and Enforcement

It has been suggested that one of the reasons that the Constitution is not taken seriously by citizens or by Party and state leaders is that it is thought that the Constitution has no direct legal force. This perception has as much to do with Chinese constitutional practice as with the provisions of the Constitution itself. Indeed, the provision '[a]ll acts in violation of the Constitution and the law must be investigated' was only added to Article 5 of the Constitution at the NPC's Fifth Session at which the Constitution was adopted.[347]

Theoretically the 1982 Constitution for the first time expressly declares that the Constitution has the supreme authority of law.[348] It further declares that the state upholds the uniformity and dignity of the socialist legal system and that no law or administrative or local regulation shall contravene the Constitution.[349] It reserves the power of constitutional amendment to the NPC and requires that any amendment must be proposed by the SCNPC or one-fifth of the deputies of the NPC and adopted by a majority vote of more than two-thirds of all deputies.[350] However, in practice, all amendments to the Constitution have been proposed by the Party and no suggestion to amend the Constitution proposed by the Party has ever been rejected by the NPC.

The power to supervise the enforcement of the Constitution is vested with the NPC and its Standing Committee[351] – both of which are legislative organs. The Constitution, however, establishes no mechanisms for either its enforcement or its supervision. The SCNPC is further entrusted with the power to interpret the Constitution,[352] yet it rarely does so.[353] The Constitution also prohibits any laws or administrative

---

Period', (no. 4, 2006) *Journal of East China University of Political Science and Law* (*Huadong Zhengfa Xueyuan Xuebao*) 3.

347 See Gu Angran, *supra* note 1, at 59; Zhang Youyu, *supra* note 92, at 4.

348 See the Preamble of the 1982 Constitution.

349 Article 5 of the 1982 Constitution.

350 See Articles 62 (1) and 64 of the 1982 Constitution.

351 See Articles 62(2) and 67(1) of the 1982 Constitution.

352 Article 67(1) of the 1982 Constitution.

353 Jilin People's Press in 1993–1994 published a large collection of normative interpretations of laws; it does not even contain a section on constitutional interpretation. See *A Collection of Normative Interpretations of Laws in the PRC* (*Zhonghua Renmin gonghe Guo Falü Guifanxing Jieshi Jicheng*) (Changchun: Jilin People's Press, 1990, further supplemented in 1993). However, some Chinese scholars have argued that certain decisions of the SCNPC on specific issues may be interpreted as constitutional interpretations by the SCNPC. See Wang Lei, 'On Constitutional Interpretation Organs in Our Country', (no. 6, 1993) *Journal of Chinese*

or local regulations from contravening the Constitution, but as mentioned above, there are no mechanisms nor procedures established by the Constitution for citizens to challenge the constitutionality or legality of these laws and regulations, nor has the SCNPC ever invalidated any such laws or regulations.[354]

On the whole, the Constitution has been a rather weak one for practical purposes. As one prominent Chinese scholar recently conceded: 'the supervision and enforcement mechanisms are still imperfect. ... The power of constitutional supervision has not been sufficiently exercised; constitutional interpretation has yet to be developed; education in the constitution is still being carried out, and special institutions are yet to be established.'[355] While many scholars insist that the 1982 Constitution is the 'best' among the four Constitutions adopted in the PRC, other scholars and officials do recognise the weakness in the present Constitution. Thus the SCNPC has recently decided that one of its major tasks is to strengthen the supervision of legal enforcement,[356] and many congress deputies then began to call for the making of a law on supervision.[357] Certain measures have been taken, though not specifically for the enforcement of the Constitution.[358] Various proposals for strengthening constitutional interpretation and supervision, including the establishment of a Constitutional Committee within the NPC, the establishment of a Constitutional Court, or the granting of constitutional review powers to the

---

and Foreign Legal Science (*Zhongwai Faxue*) 21, at 21, Wang Shuwen, 'On the Guarantee of Constitutional Enforcement', (no. 6, 1992) *Legal Science in China* (*Zhongguo Faxue*) 15, at 19. If this interpretation is accepted, then, logically, all legislation by the SCNPC would have to be interpreted as constitutional interpretations by the SCNPC.

354 See Wang Shuwen, *supra* note 353, at 18; Hu Jianmiao & Gao Chunyan, 'Constitutional Review of Law and Regulation in China – Problems and Solutions', in (no. 3, 2006), *Printed Newspaper and Journal Articles (D411 Constitutional & Administrative Law)* 46, at 46. See further discussion in Chapter 5.

355 Jiang Bikun, *supra* note 2, at 43. For a similar statement, see also Cai Dingjian, 'Constitutional Supervision and Interpretation in the People's Republic of China', (1995) 9 *Journal of Chinese Law* 219, at 223.

356 See Major Tasks of the Standing Committee of the 8th NPC, *supra* note 230; 'Work Report of the Standing Committee', delivered by Tian Jiyun at the 1st Plenary Session of the 9th NPC on 10 March 1998, in *People's Daily* (*Renmin Ribao*), internet edition, 23 March 1998; and Li Peng, *supra* note 230.

357 See *People's Daily* (*Renmin Ribao*), internet edition, 19 March 1998. Such a law was indeed adopted in 2006. See discussions below.

358 See Certain Provisions on Strengthening the Inspection and Supervision of Legal Enforcement, adopted on 2 September 1993 by the Standing Committee, in *People's Daily* (*Renmin Ribao*), 4 September 1993, at 2. See also Jin Ren, 'New Approaches of People's Congresses in China to Supervise Law Enforcement', (no. 1, 1997) *China Law* 53.

Supreme People's Court, have been discussed and debated in China in the last few years.[359]

Though short of the aspirations of scholars, there have been some major developments in jurisprudence and judicial attitudes towards the Constitution, and in establishing mechanisms for the actual implementation of the Constitution since 2001.

First, there has been a change of attitude towards the enforceability of the constitutional provisions, with increasing numbers of Chinese scholars shifting to an affirmative view on this point.[360] Thus, with or without a practical mechanism for enforcing the supreme law, attempts have been made by Chinese scholars and the Supreme People's Court to use the Constitution as a document with practical consequences. In a 2001 case, which was widely reported as the first instance where constitutional rights were directly enforced by a court, the Supreme People's Court gave a clear and positive reply in relation to a request from Shandong High Court concerning whether the right to education as contained in the Constitution could be directly enforced and, if so, used as a legal basis for damages.[361] While this was a very positive development in constitutional law in China, the case raised many practical questions regarding whether the Supreme People's Court has a proper constitutional power to undertake such implementation through interpretation and, if so, whether there are any procedures that the Court must follow.[362] In

---

359 See Cai Dingjian, *supra* note 355; 'Considerations and Proposals for Strengthening the Work of Supervision by the NPC – A Summary of Newspaper and Journal Discussions', (no. 6, 1990) *Legal Science in China* (*Zhonggu Faxue*) 13; Wu Xieying, Li Zhiyong & Wang Ruihe, 'On a Constitutional Ligation System in China', (no. 5, 1989) *Legal Science in China* (*Zhonggu Faxue*) 62; Wang Shuwen, *supra* note 353; Wang Lei, *supra* note 353; Zhu Weijiu, *Legal Supervision Over Government* (*Zhengfu Fazhi Jiandu Lun*) (Beijing: China University of Political Science and Law Press, 1994); and Chen Yunsheng, *supra* note 130.

360 Whether the Preamble has any direct legal force remains a controversial issue in China. See Zhang & Wang, *supra* note 60, at 181; Li Buyun (ed.), *Comparative Constitutional Law* (*Xianfa Bijiao Yanjiu*) (Beijing: Law Press, 1998), at 182-195.

361 For a summary of the case, see *Nanfang Zhoumo* (*Nanfang Weekend*), internet edition, 17 August 2001, and *Renmin Ribao*, internet edition, 5 September 2001. The Supreme People's Court reply was issued on 24 July 2001, as Interpretation [2001] No. 25, containing merely one short paragraph.

362 For detailed academic analysis of the two cases, see Shen Kui, 'The Beginning of the Age of Constitutionalism – Questions regarding the First Constitutional Case', published in the Beijing University Law website: <www.law-dimension.com/details.asp?id=758> (last accessed 12 November 2004); and Li Huawei, 'A New Light in Constitutional Review in Mainland China?' available from the China Constitutionalism web: <www.calaw.cn/include/shownews.asp?newsid=2001> (last accessed 12 November 2004). Technically, it is also questioned whether the people's court should instead apply the Law on Education (for a right to education) and the General Principles of Civil Law (for remedies). See Cai Dingjian, 'Towards a Private Law Approach to the Implementation of the Chinese Constitution', originally published in (no.

2003, a university graduate named Sun Zhigang was detained in a Southern city in Guangdong Province under the then State Council Measures on Detention and Repatriation and was apparently beaten to death. Several scholars then petitioned the SCNPC to start a constitutional review of the Measures. However, the Measures were quickly repealed by the State Council before any SCNPC procedure was actually activated.[363] There have also been several other unsuccessful attempts by citizens to use the Constitution for the protection of their rights.[364] In all these cases and attempts many scholars have urged the government to consider the establishment of practical constitutional mechanisms.

Although the Supreme People's Court interpretation in the education case caused some considerable controversy, it is in fact not surprising, even though the Court had never directly dealt with issues of constitutionality nor claimed to have done so until this education case.[365] It has been argued for some time that the Supreme People's Court is in fact exercising certain powers to interpret and supervise the enforcement of the Constitution, though the Court has no such powers in the Constitution. This has been done through the publication of selected cases and opinions on legal issues.[366] There is no doubt that certain cases and legal opinions endorsed by the Supreme People's Court involved, indirectly, the interpretation and even the enforcement of the Constitution, by limiting or extending the application of constitutional provisions. However, the ability of the Court to do so is a result

---

2, 2004) *Social Science in China* (*Zhongguo Shehui Kexue*), re-published in <www.usc.cuhk.edu.hk/wk.asp> (last accessed 12 November 2004); Michael C. Dorf, 'What a Chinese Height Discrimination Case Says about Chinese (and American) Constitutional Law, FindLaw's Legal Docomentary, 26 May 2004, available <writ.findlaw.com/dorf/20040526.html> (last accessed 29 May 2004).

363 For a summary of the petition, see 'Five jurists requested the Standing Committee to activate constitutional review process on Sun Zhigang case', in <www.chinalaw.gov.cn> (last accessed 12 January 2004). According to Cai Dingjian, a prominent scholar in China, the repeal of the Measures by the State Council was in fact undertaken after the leaders of the SCNPC transmitted the petition to the State Council for processing. Thus Cai suggests that Chinese politicians attempted to avoid the establishment and use of a constitutional review mechanism. See Cai Dingjian, *supra* note 362.

364 See Cai Dingjian, *id.* Interestingly the Legislative Affairs Committee of the SCNPC has insisted that it never received any petition from citizens for constitutional review of laws and regulations. See 'The Leader of the Legislative Affairs Commission of the Standing Committee of the NPC Answers Journalist Questions concerning the Draft of a Law on Rights in rem and Review of Laws and Regulations Filed-for-Record', 1 March 2006, available from <www.lawbook.com.cn/fzdt/newshtml/20/20006030292112.htm> (last accessed 23 March 2006).

365 Indeed, in its *Complete Collection of Judicial Interpretation*, it has avoided completely the issue of constitutional law. See Supreme People's Court of the PRC, *A Complete Collection of Judicial Interpretation* (*Sifa Jieshi Quanji*) (Beijing: Press of the People's Court, 1994).

366 See Liu Nanping, '"Judicial Review" in China: A Comparative Perspective', (1988) 14 *Rev. of Soc. L.* 241.

of the lack of mechanisms and procedures for constitutional interpretation and supervision of its enforcement, rather than with any particular constitutional grounds or procedures.

Secondly, some significant progress has been made in maintaining consistency in law-making at central and local levels and in supervision over the work of the government and judiciary (including the courts and the procuratorates). In 2001, the *Law on Law-Making* was enacted. This Law has now established some mechanisms for systematic reviews of laws and regulations. A specialised unit within the Legislative Affairs Committee of the SCNPC was established in May 2004 to strengthen the work of the filing for the record of laws and regulations and of reviewing these laws and regulations.[367] In December 2005, the Working Procedures on Filing for Record and Review of Administrative Regulations, Local Regulations, and of Regulations of Autonomous Regions and Special Economic Zones, initially issued in 2003, were revised and a new set of Working Procedures on Filing for Record and Review of Judicial Interpretations was issued by the SCNPC.[368] These working procedures further established some specific procedures for the constitutional review of regulations and rules.[369]

Finally, and most importantly, some formal mechanisms for the exercise of the powers of constitutional supervision have now been established, though they have taken a long time to develop. Under the Constitution the supervisory power may be implemented or realised through different constitutional mechanisms and, among others, through interpreting the law, inspecting the implementation of selected laws, and supervising the work of the administrative and judicial organs.[370] Although the power to interpret the law is not uncontroversial, as it clearly contravenes the basic principles of the separation of powers, such power is solidly established by the Chinese constitution. Until quite recently most scholars have not been overly concerned about this constitutional arrangement, and criticisms of this power have been more about the 'neglect of duty' by the NPC and its Standing Committee in exercising the power than about its use.[371] The controversy over the interpretation

---

367 While the establishment of the specialised unit was widely publicised, we know very little about the functions and working procedures of the unit, as some Chinese scholars have pointed out. See Hu Jianmiao & Gao Chunyan, *supra* note 354, at 52.

368 These are seen as internal working procedures (Hu Jianmiao & Gao Chunyan, *supra* note 354, at 52) and none of them has been published.

369 See Hu Jianmiao & Gao Chunyan, *supra* note 354, at 52; and 'The Standing Committee of the NPC Clarifies Constitutional Review Procedures', in <news.xinhuanet.com/politics/2005-12/20/content_3944117.htm> (last accessed 20 December 2005).

370 For a detailed discussion, see Cai Dingjian, 'Functions of the People's Congress in the Process of Implementation of Law', in Jianfu Chen, Yuwen Li & Jan Michiel Otto, *Implementation of Law in the PRC* (The Hague/London/New York: Kluwer Law International, 2002), 35-54.

371 See Perry Keller, 'Sources of Order in Chinese Law', (1994) 42 *Am. J. Comp. L.* 711.

by the SCNPC of the Basic Law of Hong Kong in relation to the right of abode in Hong Kong in 1999 led scholars, especially those outside China, to have second thoughts about this power. Clearly the exercise of this interpretive power has the potential to interfere with judicial independence in Hong Kong.[372] The inspection of the implementation of selected laws by the NPC and the SCNPC is perhaps the least controversial part of the involvement of the legislatures in the implementation of law, and its practice is generally seen as positively contributing to the establishment of a genuine rule of law in China.

However, the most controversial aspect of the supervisory functions of the legislature in the implementation of law is the attempt by the various legislatures to 'supervise' individual cases handled by the judiciary. Although there were some guidelines formulated by the SCNPC in 1989 for the exercise of this supervision,[373] the constitutional basis for such a power is questionable. Even though the principle of separation of powers is not formally recognised in China, the 1982 Constitution clearly stipulates that the power of adjudication may only be exercised independently by the people's courts. The involvement of the legislatures in individual cases thus raises serious questions and concerns about judicial independence in China.[374] In a widely publicised case, now often referred to as the 'Seeds Case', a judge in a local court (Luoyang Intermediate Court in Henan Province) invalidated a local regulation on the basis of its being in conflict with the national Seeds Law. This decision quickly attracted intervention from the Standing Committee of the Henan People's Congress. The intervention was extraordinary in that the local Standing Committee

---

372 The interpretation in 1999 of the Basic Law of Hong Kong on the right to abode is seen by a prominent Chinese scholar, Professor Cai Dingjian, as one of the positive examples of the exercise of the supervisory power by the SCNPC, but by others as the first perceived constitutional crisis in Hong Kong since the handover of sovereignty in 1997. For different views on this, see Cai Dingjian, 'Functions of the People's Congress in the Process of Implementation of Law', and Albert Chen, 'Hong Kong's Legal System in the New Constitutional Order: The Experience of 1997–2000', both in Chen, Li & Otto, *supra* note 370, at 35-54 and 213-246 respectively.

373 Basically, such supervision may only start after a case is completed and it may not try to influence or intervene in on-going judicial work; secondly, the supervision shall focus on legal procedures and interpretation; and finally, the supervisory body may request the court to re-try or review the case but it must not substitute its own judgement for that of the courts. See Michael W. Dowdle, 'The Constitutional Development and Operations of the National People's Congress', (1997) 11 (1) *Columbia Journal of Asian Law* 1, at 110. Some local authorities have also issued their rules for implementing such supervision. See, for instance, *Working Rules for Supervision of the Judicial Organs by the Standing Committee of the Zhejiang Provincial People's Congress*, adopted and issued by the Standing Committee of the Zhejiang Provincial People's Congress on 28 December 2000 and effective on promulgation.

374 It should be pointed out that a controversial draft law on supervision of major violations of law in adjudication and procuratorate work, submitted to the 12th Meeting of the Standing Committee of the NPC (October 1999) seems to have now been shelved.

demanded the rectification of the decision and severe punishment of the judges even before an appeal had been dealt with by a higher court.[375] This simple contractual dispute, and especially its subsequent intervention by the local legislature, reveals a great deal (though not all) of the systemic problems in the Chinese legal system concerning implementation of law, as well as the sensitivity of constitutional issues, namely the existence of a hierarchy of law but the almost total absence of mechanisms and procedures for dealing with conflict of laws in the hierarchy, the ambiguous constitutional and institutional division of powers, the tension between judicial independence and accountability, the focus on substantive justice at the expense of due process, the conflict of local and national interests, and, of course, the constant power struggles between and among institutions and personnel. Clearly, some of these issues need to be addressed through the Constitution. In this context and after some twenty years of debate and discussion, a law – the Law on Supervision by Standing Committees of the People's Congresses at Various Levels – was finally adopted in August 2006 to address some of these issues.[376]

The idea of enacting a supervision law emerged during the sixth NPC in 1986 and it has never been off the agenda for the SCNPC since then.[377] The first deliberation

---

375 Despite the controversy and major debates in legal circles, the original judgement has not been published. There were however many media reports on the case and its decision: 'Judge holds local regulation invalid: a violation of law or a support for law', *Nanfang Zhoumo (Southern Weekly)*, internet edition <www.nanfandaily.com.cn/zm/20031120/xw/fz/200311200861.asp> (last accessed 20 November 2003); 'Judge sows seeds of lawmaking dispute', *China Daily*, internet edition <www.chinadaily.com.cn/en/doc/2003-11/24/content_283973.htm> (last accessed 24 November 2003); 'Lawyers request the National Congress to undertake legislative review over "Luoyang Seed Case"', Phoenix TV, internet edition <www.phoenixtv.com/home/news/society/200311/21/151034.html> (last accessed 21 November 2003); and articles collected in <www.law-thinker.com> (last accessed 21 November 2003). After the intervention by the provincial legislature, the Luoyang Intermediary Court Party Committee then decided to remove Judge Zhao from the position of Deputy Head of the Economic Chamber, Judge Li from Presiding Judge as well as dismissing her from the position of assistant judge, both pending formal legal procedures with the Standing Committee of the Luoyang People's Congress. However, according to follow-up reports in February 2004, the decisions to dismiss the judges were never actually submitted to the Standing Committee of the Luoyang People's Congress for deliberation and approval, apparently because of the controversy, and Judge Li, on sick leave since then, was notified to resume her work in the court. See 'Conflict of law shall not be dealt with by "cool handling"', *Nanfang Doushi Bao (Southern Urban Daily)*, internet edition <www.nanfandaily.com.cn/southnews/spqy/zy/2000402070066.asp> (last accessed 7 February 2004), and 'Further controversy concerning Li Huijun Incident in Henan', *Zhongguo Qingnianbao*, internet edition <www.cyol.com/zqb/gb/zqb/2004-02/06/content_813990.htm> (last accessed 6 February 2004).

376 The Law, adopted on 27 August 2006 by the 23rd Session of the Standing Committee of the Tenth NPC, took effect on 1 January 2007.

377 See 'Twenty Years in the Making – An Interview with Chairman Yang Jingyu of the Law Commission of the NPC on the Supervision Law Draft', in <www.npc.gov.cn/zgrdw/com-

of the draft law was in August 2002, but it took another two years before a second deliberation by the SCNPC was conducted in August 2004. Thereafter the legislative process sped up, leading to its adoption in 2006.[378]

The difficulties in drafting the law were clearly summarised by the Chairman of the Law Commission of the NPC: it is a politically sensitive law concerning the political and state system. It needs to balance the strengthening of NPC supervisory power and the maintenance of Party leadership. It needs to exercise supervision over, yet support the work of, the government, the courts and the procuratorates.[379] As such it is not surprising that the Party leadership took a very direct interest in the drafting process: the CPC itself formally recommended to the NPC the making of the law, and the Party Committee of the SCNPC reported, as a special topic, to the Politburo of the Central Committee of CPC three times in November 2003, December 2005 and May 2006.[380]

Even though the drafting work was apparently strongly supported by the Party, the final Law is not an ambitious piece of legislation. As the law-makers made clear after its adoption, where experience is 'ripe' the Law provides detailed and concrete provisions, but where experience is not yet 'ripe', only certain principles are laid down for future development, and where there is no existing experience or consensus is not reached, the Law is silent.[381] Indeed, the Law manages to avoid all controversial issues and only codifies the existing practice under the Law on Law-making (2001) and other NPC procedures. Further, instead of a NPC supervision law, it is now a law on supervision by the standing committees at the various levels.[382] While the official reasoning was that the infrequency of meetings of the people's congresses (once a

---

mon/zw.jsp?label=WXZLK&ID=351389&pdmc=110118> (last accessed 27 August 2006); 'Twenty Years in the Making – On the Background of the Supervision Law', in <www.npc.gov.cn/zgrdw/common/zw.jsp?label=WXZLK&ID=352052&pdmc=1516> (last accessed 19 September 2006);

378 *Id.*

379 'Twenty Years in the Making – An Interview with Chairman Yang Jingyu of the Law Commission of the NPC on the Supervision Law Draft', *supra* note 377.

380 'Twenty Years in the Making – On the Background of the Supervision Law', *supra* note 377.

381 See Wu Zeng (Legislative Commission of the Standing Committee of the NPC), 'On Several Principal Issues of the Supervision Law', <www.npc.gov.cn/zgrdw/common/zw.jsp?label=WXZLK&ID=352052&pdmc=110124> (last accessed 31 August 2006).

382 According to the Chairman of the Law Commission of the NPC, it was in April/May 2006 that it was decided that, instead of a Law on Supervision by People's Congresses at Various Levels, the scope was narrowed down to supervision by standing committees of the people's congresses at various levels and there was a consequential change of the law's title. See 'Twenty Years in the Making – An Interview with Chairman Yang Jingyu of the Law Commission of the NPC on the Supervision Law Draft' *supra* note 377.

year for a short period of a few weeks) makes routine supervision impractical,[383] the narrowing of the scope was perhaps to avoid the issue of the Party-State relationship by avoiding addressing the nature of 'supreme power' of the people's congresses. Finally, the Law is largely procedural, thus avoiding any need to address the question of separation of powers.[384]

The new Supervision Law elaborates the supervisory powers of the standing committees at various levels to include the following:

- deliberation on and review of specific work reports by the people's governments, the courts and the procuratorates;
- review and approval of final accounts (of revenue and expenditure), deliberation on and review of the implementation reports on national economic and social development plans, budgets, and auditing reports;
- inspection of implementation of laws and regulations;
- review of laws that have been filed-for-record;
- enquiry and consultation;
- inspection of specific issues; and
- deliberation and decision on selection and recall of personnel appointments.

There is little doubt that each of the above has already been granted by the Constitution, the Organic Law of the National People's Congress ('NPC'), and the Organic Law of the Local People's Congresses and Local Governments.[385] The Supervision Law therefore focuses on laying down specific working procedures, as well as the scope of the powers. Importantly, after much debate during the drafting process, the Supervision Law avoids the more contentious issue of standing committees supervis-

383 See 'Twenty Years in the Making – An Interview with Chairman Yang Jingyu of the Law Commission of the NPC on the Supervision Law Draft', *supra* note 377.

384 It is nevertheless emphasised that China does not practise separation of powers, and all state authorities – the people's congresses, the government, the courts and the procuratorates – are all state authorities under one leadership, that is, the Party leadership. See *People's Daily* editorial on the passage of the Law: 'Supervision Powers now Regularised and with Procedures', *People's Daily* (*Renmin Ribao*), 28 August 2006, also available from <www.law-lib.com> (last accessed 28 August 2006); 'The Leader of the Law Commission of the NPC Answers Questions relating to the Supervision Law', available from <www.law-lib.com> (last accessed 27 August 2006). See also deliberation speeches at the 23rd Session of the Standing Committee of the NPC available from <www.npc.gov.cn/zgrdw/common/zw.jsp?label=WXZLK&ID=352140&pdmc=1516> (last accessed 19 September 2006) & <news.xinhuanet.com/politics/2006-08/27/content_5013837.htm> (last accessed 28 August 2006).

385 For a detailed discussion of these supervisory powers before the enactment of the Supervision Law, see Cai Dingjian, *supra* note 370, 35-54.

ing specific cases handled by courts and procuratorates by opting for inspection of specific issues[386] and emphasising the collective exercise of the supervisory power.[387] The Law does not specify the meaning of 'specific issues', but law-makers made it clear that 'specific issues' refers to issues in the nature of common concerns, not individual cases.[388] This, on the whole, represents a sensitive and practical compromise for allocating powers between the legislature and the judiciary.[389]

All in all, while far from establishing a comprehensive constitutional review mechanism or other mechanisms for checks and balances in China, these developments represent significant progress towards making the Constitution a practical document.

5. Concluding Remarks

The movement towards constitutionalism has had a troubled history ever since its inception in China at the turn of the 20th Century. The constitutions and their practice before 1949 had had little effect on the life of ordinary people in China. However, the constitutionalism movement does establish firmly the idea that the legitimacy of government, be it the warlords, the Kuomintang or the communists, must be established by a document called a 'constitution'.

In terms of constitutions after 1949, the above discussion suggests that understanding the constitutions lies in understanding what is not in the constitutions, rather than what is in them. These analyses also suggest that the significance of the constitutions does not lie in their provisions, but in the parameters they set. Further, the realisation of constitutional rights largely depends on the developments of individual statutes besides the Constitution itself. There is evidence to suggest that Party leadership and state authorities are no longer the only driving forces for reform in contemporary

---

[386] See Chapter 7 of the Supervision Law.

[387] See Article 4 of the Supervision Law.

[388] See Chen Sixi (Legislative Affairs Committee of the SCNPC), 'Strengthening Supervision while Maintaining Judicial Authority', available from <www.npc.gov.cn/zgrdw/commn/zw.jsp?label=WXZLKK&id=352329&pdmc=1516> (last accessed 19 September 2006); 'The Leader of the Law Commission of the NPC Answers Questions relating to the Supervision Law', *supra* note 384; Wu Zeng (Legislative Affairs Committee of the SCNPC), 'On Several Principal Issues of the Supervision Law', *supra* note 381. See also deliberation speeches at the 23rd Session of the SCNPC, *supra* note 384.

[389] For further background on the need for compromise, see Cai Dingjian, *supra* note 370, 35-54.

China; ordinary people[390] and, especially, intellectuals[391] are important and active agents that often push against the constitutional parameters for further political, legal and economic reform.

The present Constitution is not one that is already 'perfect' and needing no further revision; indeed, it is a document riddled with many fundamental flaws. The problem with the various revisions is, therefore, not what has been revised, but what has not been addressed. Thus the question is: what are the problems that require urgent action. The answer to this question is not difficult; after all, the Constitution has been studied inside and outside China for some 25 years, and the list could be very long.[392] Many Chinese scholars now recognise that what is needed for China to have a rule of law is for certain fundamental premises of the Constitution to be changed, and not just a few simple minimalist amendments to be made to incorporate new Party policies[393] Chief among these are the need to address the lack of implementation procedures and a meaningful mechanism of checks and balances.[394] The former may be achieved through other basic laws – and

---

390 Indeed, barely two weeks after the adoption of the 2004 revision, an elderly resident in Beijing had already used the revised constitutional provisions on the protection of private property to stop the demolition of his old house that was built more than a hundred years ago in Beijing. See Xinhuanet: <news.xinhuanet.com/comments/2004-04/07/content_1405016.htm> (last accessed 28 August 2006).

391 Almost immediately after the 2004 revision of the Constitution a group of 30 prominent scholars produced some 18 suggestions for constitutional reforms to implement human rights protection as now enshrined in the Constitution. See He Weifang, Ji Weidong *et al.*, 'Suggestions for the Improvement of the Constitutional Protection of Human Rights in Our Country', available at <www.law-thinker.com/details.asp?id=2078> (last accessed 28 August 2006). Even though these suggestions are unlikely to be implemented any time soon by the government, such academic activities keep constitutional reform alive and on the agenda of national debate and discussion.

392 Indeed, Chinese scholars have identified many constitutional issues that need urgent solutions if the Constitution is to be effective in fulfilling its intended functions. See views expressed at Qingdao and Shanghai seminars on constitutional reform, *supra* notes 106 & 107; Zeng Ping, *supra* note 105. See also special collections of articles on constitutional revision: (no. 2, 2003) *Journal of the China University of Political Science and Law (Zhengfa Luntan)*; (no. 3, 2003) *Political Science and Law (Zhengzhi yu Falǘ)*; (no. 3, 2003) *China Legal Science (Zhongguo Faxue)*; and (no. 5, 2003) *Peking University Law Journal (Zhongwai Faxue)*.

393 See e.g. Zhou Yezhong, 'The Supremacy of the Constitution: The Spirit for the Chinese Movement towards a Rule of Law', (no. 6, 1995) *Review of Law* (*Faxue Pinglun*) 1.

394 See views expressed at Qingdao and Shanghai seminars on constitutional reform, *supra* notes 106 & 107. See also He Weifang, 'The Force and Obstacles to Constitutionalism', published in <law-thinker.com/details.asp?id=1754> (last accessed 21 November 2004); Cao Siyuan, '"Ten Major Proposals" for the revision of the Constitution', published at <www.usc.cuhk.edu.hk/wk_wzdetails.asp?id=2373>; Wang Xiaoping, 'The Protection of Constitutional Rights and the Realisation of a Constitutional Order', *People's Daily* (*Renmin Ribao*), internet edition, 18 November 2003, <www.peopledaily.com.cn/GB/14576/14841/2084205.htm> (last accessed

some significant progress has indeed been made – but the latter has to be dealt with in the Constitution.[395]

It is also important to note that, after some 25 years since the promulgation of the Constitution, the knowledge of the Constitution, as least in terms of knowing the existence of the Constitution, is high among the Chinese people, and their expectation of the actual implementation of the Constitution must not be disregarded in the making of constitutional reforms. In a survey conducted recently by a group of Suzhou University scholars[396] it was revealed that 97% of the people surveyed knew of the existence of the Constitution, 66% believed that a constitution was supposed to impose constraints on government and to provide protection for the rights of citizens, 66% believed that the main cause of corruption was the lack of checks and balances; and 54% of them did not believe that the Constitution had any major effect in real life. This survey perhaps indicates that the Constitution may well gain its real position in the not too distant future. In this context, there are reasons to be cautiously optimistic about the future of the rule of law and of constitutionalism in China.

---

21 November 2004); Xia Yong, 'Several Theoretical Questions concerning Constitutional Reform in China', *Social Sciences in China* (*Zhongguo Shehui Kexue*), no. 2, 2003, reproduced in <www.usc.cuhk.edu.hk/wk_wzdetails.asp?id=2150> (last accessed 21 November 2004); Ji Weigong, 'What do we expect of the fourth constitutional revision', in <www.law-thinker.com/detial.asp?id=1710> (last accessed 21 November 2004).

395 In a 2004 internet survey conducted by the Xinhua News Agency, anti-corruption was the top concern among the people participating in the web survey conducted before and during the 2nd Session of the 10th NPC (2003–2008). See <www.xinhuanet.com/newscenter/2004-02/17/content_1317652.htm> (last accessed 21 November 2003). In 2003, the *People's Daily* conducted a similar survey, which received responses from more than 200,000 people, and indicated that anti-corruption and the establishment of checks and balances were nominated as the top issues that people expected the 10th NPC to address. See 'Top ten issues selected by netizens for the NPC to address', *People's Daily* (*Renmin Ribao*), internet edition, 26 February 2003. Also according to Xinhua News Agency, as of October 2003 there were no fewer than 4,000 corrupt officials who had fled China, with more than US$ 5 billion having been stolen by them and transferred overseas and that, in the last three years alone, no less than US$ 53 billion has been illegally transferred overseas due to corruption. See <www.xinhuanet.com/newscenter/2003-10/13/content_1119999.htm> (last accessed 21 November 2003).

396 The survey was conducted by Shangguan Piliang in collaboration with many doctoral and other students in eastern coastal cities in November – December 2002. Altogether, 1001 copies of questionaries were distributed and collected in public places. A full report of the survey is published on the website of the Law Institute of the Chinese Academy of Social Sciences: <www.iolaw.org.cn/shownes.asp?id=3813> (last accessed 21 November 2003).

Chapter Four

Legal Institutions

1. Introduction

Modern legal institutions have had a short but much troubled history in China since the Continental-style legal system was introduced into the country at the turn of the 20th century. As discussed in Chapter Two, at the same time as the Nationalist (KMT) government was trying to establish a legal system, its destruction was being undertaken in all areas occupied by the Communist Party of China, well before 1949. Then, in September 1949, the KMT legal system as a whole was abolished by the Common Program of the Chinese People's Political Consultative Conference.[1] As also discussed in Chapter Two, an adjudication system separate from, and independent of, the administrative hierarchy was only introduced to China during the Qing reforms. And while the contemporary legal institutions are largely of a European Continental style, certain features introduced from the former Soviet Union in the 1950s are still maintained, most notably the procuratorate system that still forms an important part of the Chinese judiciary.

The Common Program first promised to establish a new legal system and, indeed, the establishment of a new court and procuratorate system began in 1949. The Organic Law of the People's Courts was adopted in 1951, and a similar law for People's Procuratorates in 1954. The 1954 Constitution solemnly provided for 'independent adjudication' by the courts. However, the endeavour to build a new legal system did not last long; the courts and procuratorates began to be merged into the public security organs at the county level in 1958, and later at higher levels. In 1959, the newly established Ministry of Justice was abolished, as was the People's Procuratorate in 1969.[2] Similarly, efforts to establish a lawyer system first appeared

---

1 See Article 17 of the Common Program. An English text of the Common Program can be found in Albert P. Blaustein (ed.), *Fundamental Legal Documents of Communist China* (New Jersey: Fred B. Rothman & Co., 1962), at 34-53.

2 Zhao Zhenjiang (ed.), *Forty Years of the Chinese Legal System* (*Zhongguo Fazhi Sishi Nian*), (Beijing: Beijing University Press, 1990), at 116; and *China Law Yearbook 1987* (*Zhongguo Falü Nianjian*) (Beijing: Law Publishing House, 1988), at 8-30. For further discussion see

in 1955, but were soon terminated in 1957.[3]

It was not until 1979, when two organic laws were promulgated, on courts and procuratorates respectively, that the systematic establishment of courts and procuratorates began again. Legal education also resumed in 1978 at the tertiary level and soon expanded into the vocational education system.[4] This has been supplemented by professional training mechanisms established by the court and procuratorate systems themselves. In 1980 the Provisional Regulations on Lawyers were issued, which formally established the present lawyer system in China. All these legal institutions have undergone major reforms and re-structuring in the last 28 years or so, a process which continues to this day. In strong contrast to 'reforms' in the 1950s and the destruction during the 'Cultural Revolution', these reforms have been carried out within each institution, and are aimed at strengthening each institution and making each of them more professional, independent, and accountable.

In short, the legal institutions in China are essentially a product of the post-Mao era and continue to evolve. This Chapter provides an overview of the legal system of the PRC and its recent reforms. It describes the structure and basic functions of the Chinese judicial institutions, the legal profession and other relevant legal institutions.

2. An Overview of Legal Institutions in China

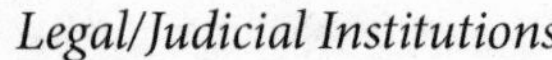
Legal/Judicial Institutions

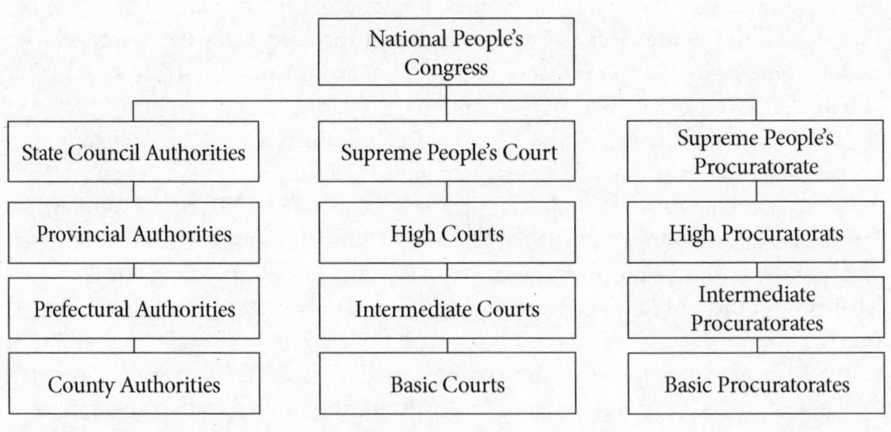

Alice E.-S. Tay, 'Law in Communist China', Part 1 & 2, in (1969) 6 *Syd.L.Rev.* at 125-172 and 335-423 respectively.

3 *China Law Yearbook 1987*, *supra* note 2, at 24.

4 *China Law Yearbook 1987*, *supra* note 2, at 20-22. For further discussion see Han Depei & Stephen Kanter, 'Legal Education in China', (1984) 32 *Am. J. Comp. L.* 543; & Alice E.-S. Tay and Eugene Kamenka, 'Law, Legal Theory and Legal Education in the People's Republic of China', (1986) *N.Y.L.S.J. Int'l & Comp. L.* 1.

Several points need to be explained regarding the above schematic outline of the structure of legal institutions in China.

First, the term 'judicial institutions' (*Sifa Jiguan*) is often broadly used in China to refer to the courts, the procuratorates and the public security force (police) as a whole. In a narrow sense, 'judicial institutions' mainly refers to the court and the procuratorate systems and in this book we use the term in its narrow sense. These institutions are, however, not the only authorities involved in the administration of law. In the State Council at least four ministries are directly involved in this task, namely the Ministry of Justice, the Ministry of Supervision, the Ministry of State Security, and the Ministry of Public Security (police), and many of these authorities are also established at the lower levels of the administrative hierarchy.[5] Further, the legal profession, notary public, and arbitration institutions are increasingly becoming self-regulated organisations which do not fit well into the above schematic outline, nor are they included in the term 'judicial institutions'. In this Chapter, we use the term 'legal institutions' to cover those authorities directly involved in and charged with the administration of law, each of which will be further discussed in some detail.

Secondly, China is governed as both a party state and a bureaucratic one, and the legal institutions are no exception. This simply means that the relationship between the Party and the administrative authorities and the hierarchical relationship among the bureaucratic authorities are largely identical to the relationship between the Party and the legal institutions, and to the hierarchical and bureaucratic structures within the legal institutions.[6]

Finally, as discussed in Chapter Three, the National People's Congress (NPC) is nominally defined by the 1982 Constitution as the supreme power of the state, which creates the legal institutions and makes them accountable to the NPC (or its local counterparts for local institutions). However, the NPC or its local counterparts are not the same as parliaments in many western countries. The Communist Party and the administrative (executive) authorities still exercise some very significant powers over the 'judicial' branch (i.e courts and procuratorates), particularly in financial allocation and appointment of personnel.

---

5 Of course, in a broad sense, all government authorities in China, just as in other countries, are heavily involved in the administration and implementation of law. We single out the four ministries here simply because their principal functions are about the administration of laws, whereas other government authorities are involved in the administration of law in particular areas under their respective administrative jurisdictions.

6 On the administrative (bureaucratic) hierarchical system, see Benjamin van Rooij, 'China's System of Public Administration', in J Chen, Y Li, and J.M. Otto, *Implementation of Law in the People's Republic of China* (The Hague/London/New York: Kluwer Law International, 2002), at 323-342.

3. The People's Courts

3.1. Hierarchy and Organisation

While the systematic establishment of courts only began in 1979, their development has been extraordinarily rapid: by the end of 1986, 29 high courts, 337 intermediate courts, 2907 basic courts and 14,000 people's tribunals as well as 132 specialised courts had been established throughout China.[7] At the end of 2004 there were 3,548 general and specialised courts (e.g. maritime, railway transport and military courts) nationwide.[8] These courts form a hierarchical structure as defined by the Organic Law of the People's Courts of the PRC,[9] which is illustrated below:[10]

The Supreme People's Court

High People's Courts
which are established at provincial level, a total of 31 in number

Intermediate People's Courts
set up in cities and prefectures within provinces, with a total number of 404

Basic People's Courts
which comprise more than 3,111 basic-level people's courts at county level and approximately 10,345 sub-divisions known as people's tribunals (*renmin fating*) in towns and villages

---

7 *China Law Yearbook 1987*, *supra* note 2, at 11. People's tribunals are outlets of the basic courts in rural areas.

8 See White Paper on Democracy: *Building of Political Democracy in China*, issued by the Information Office of the State Council, October 2005, available from <news.xinhuanet.com/politics/2005-10/19/content_3645697.htm> (last accessed 26 September 2006).

9 Adopted at the 2nd Plenary Session of the Fifth National People's Congress on 1 July 1979, and revised by the Standing Committee of the NPC on 2 September 1983 and 31 October 2006.

10 The statistical numbers (as of the end of 2004) contained in the schematic outline below are drawn from Table 4-01 (Chapter 4) in Zhu Jingwen (ed.), *A Report on Legal Development in China: Data Bank and Assessment Criteria* (*Zhongguo Falü Fazheng Baogao: Shujuku Yu Zhibiao Tixi*) (Beijing: Renmin University Press, 2007).

Included in the courts listed in the above schematic outline are also special courts, such as the military courts, railway transport courts and maritime courts.[11] Apart from the military courts, the special courts are generally established at the intermediate level (maritime courts; railway transport courts) and at the basic level (railway transport courts, also at the intermediate level), and are subject to the supervision of the High Court of the locality. Courts other than the Supreme People's Court are often referred to as local courts.

Courts are responsible and accountable to the people's congresses at the corresponding levels. They are, at least theoretically, required to exercise independent adjudication in accordance with the law, and guaranteed freedom from interference by administrative bodies, social organisations and individuals. Other than for simple civil and minor criminal cases, trials are conducted by a collegiate bench consisting of judges and layperson assessors (or judges alone for appeal cases).[12] With only limited exceptions,[13] judgement at the second instance trial is final, and judgments rendered therefrom are immediately effective.[14]

Judicial committees are established by people's courts at various levels.[15] These committees, consisting of senior judges and heads of divisions, are responsible for summing up adjudication experiences, discussing major or difficult cases, and other adjudication-related matters. The existence of these committees has been highly controversial and has often been seen as a barrier to justice and judicial independence.[16]

Under the Organic Law of the People's Courts, the People's Courts at various levels are made up of a president, a number of vice presidents, division heads (*tingchang*),[17] deputy division heads,[18] adjudicators (*shenpan yuan*), assistant adjudicators (*zhuli*

---

11 Initially Article 2 of the Organic Law of the People's Courts provided the establishment of military courts, railway transport courts, water transport courts, forestry courts and other special courts. The 1983 Revision omitted the specific mentioning of other special courts except for the military courts. This however was not designed to abolish the special courts, but to allow flexibility in the establishment of special courts according to specific needs.

12 Article 10 of the Organic Law of the People's Courts.

13 These include the finality of first and second instance judgement of the Supreme People's Court and an extra supervision process for all death sentences after the second instance decisions.

14 See Articles 12 & 14 of the Organic Law of the People's Courts.

15 This is legally required by Article 11 of the Organic Law of the People's Courts.

16 On this, see discussions in Chapter 18; and Randall Peerenboom, *China Modernizes: Threat to the West or Model for the Rest?* (New York: Oxford University Press, 2007), at 212-216.

17 The Chinese term '*tingzhang*' is sometimes translated as 'chief judge'.

18 Or 'deputy chief judges', see *ibid*.

shenpan yuan), and court clerks.[19] They are often collectively referred to as 'adjudication personnel' or 'judicial personnel'. A court consists of at least three divisions (*shenpan ting*) – the criminal, civil, and economic divisions.[20] Other divisions to deal with matters such as administrative law, real estate, forestry, intellectual property, juvenile cases, petitions etc. may also be set up when required.

3.2. Judges and Other Personnel of the People's Courts

The development of judicial personnel in the Chinese courts has been equally remarkable. In 1979 there were around 59,000 judicial personnel in the Chinese court system.[21] By the end of 1986 the total number had reached 98,518,[22] and by the end of 2004 there were 190,627 judicial personnel.[23]

More important, however, are the improvements in the professional qualifications of the judicial personnel. In 1987, only 17% of Chinese judges had post-secondary education (including vocational training) qualifications. By 1992, this percentage had increased to 66.6, and by 2000, 100% of Chinese judges had 'basically' completed their post-secondary education or training.[24] Gone are the days when demobilised army officers were transferred to the judicial system *en masse*[25] and when the judiciary was one of the professions in which it was most easy for non-professionals to be employed.[26] The qualifications of judicial personnel are now regulated by

---

19 *Shenpan Yuan* and *Zhuli Shenpan Yuan* have always been translated into English as judges and assistant judges. However, the 1995 Law on Judges introduces a new term '*faguan*' who is, appropriately, a judge. Even though the Organic Law of the People's Courts was revised for the second time in 2006, those terms remain unchanged in the Law. In a sense, *Shenpan Yuan* and *Zhuli Shenpan Yuan* denote the position a person holds in a trial case, whereas '*faguan*' means someone with a professional qualification. This perhaps explains why the Organic Law has not been amended in line with the Law on Judges.

20 See Articles 19-31 of the Organic Law of the People's Courts (since the revision in 1983).

21 See Chapter 4 in Zhu Jingwen, *supra* note 10.

22 *China Law Yearbook 1987*, *supra* note 2, at 11.

23 See White Paper on Democracy, *supra* note 8.

24 See Chart 1-32 in Zhu Jingwen, *supra* note 10.

25 See 'Expansion by 200,000 in Three Years for the Court and Procuratorate Systems', *Legal Daily* (*Fazhi Ribao*), 7 January 1994, at 1

26 See He Weifang, 'To Realise Social Justice Through the Judiciary', in Xia Yong (ed.) *Towards an Age of Rights: A Perspective on Civil Rights Development in China* (*Zouxiang Quanli de Shidai: Zhongguo Gongmin Quanli Fazhan Yanjiu*) (Beijing: Press of China University of Political Science and Law, 1995), at 288. The first casualty of this practice is, of course, the quality of court professional work. Indeed, the professional qualifications and education of some judges were so poor that many legal documents prepared by them became unenforceable (because of bad drafting, in terms of both general language and legal reasoning) and hence became a serious problem of enforcement in themselves. See 'On Internal Causes Leading to Difficulties in Enforcement', *People's Court Daily* (*Renmin Fayuan Bao*), internet edition, 18 August 2000;

national laws[27] and national judicial examination.[28] As mentioned above, even the conventional term 'judicial personnel' is increasingly becoming an ambiguous phrase, as the Law on Judges now clearly distinguishes court judges from other judicial personnel such as court clerks.

Judges are defined by the Law on Judges as those who exercise state adjudication powers in accordance with the law,[29] and they include the president, vice presidents, members of the judicial committees, division heads, deputy division heads, adjudicators and assistant adjudicators in various courts. The Law on Judges defines the qualifications for a judge, requiring that a candidate must:

- be a Chinese citizen;
- be over 23 years old;
- uphold the Constitution;
- possess good political, professional and moral character;
- be healthy;
- be a law graduate or a non-law graduate with professional legal knowledge, with at least two years' legal work experience, or, for a judge in a High Court or in the Supreme People's Court, with at least three years' legal work experience.[30]

Perhaps the most important reform towards professionalism has been the introduction of a national judicial examination. Under the 2001 revision of the Law on Judges a unified national judicial examination was to be implemented, to serve as the examination for lawyers' qualifications and for the initial selection and appointment of judges and prosecutors. The first unified national judicial examination was held in 2002.[31] Under this system, all new appointees as judges and prosecutors must

---

and Luo Shuping, 'The Quality of Court Adjudicating Documents Is Worrying', (no. 3, 1998) *Sichuan Adjudication* (*Sichuan Shenpang*) 22, at 22.

27 Law on Judges (initially promulgated by the Standing Committee of the NPC on 28 February 1995 and revised and re-promulgated on 30 June 2001), and Law on Prosecutors (initially promulgated by the Standing Committee of the NPC on 28 February 1995 and revised and re-promulgated on 30 June 2001).

28 See discussion below.

29 See Article 2 of the Law on Judges.

30 Article 9 of the Law on Judges (as revised in 2001).

31 See Public Announcement on Certain Questions concerning the Unified National Judicial Examination, jointly issued by the Ministry of Justice, the Supreme People's Court and the Supreme People's Procuratorate in July 2001. The first national judicial examination was held in March 2002 with some 360,000 candidates participating. See *Legal Daily* (*Fazhi Ribao*), internet edition, 31 March 2002. To ensure that such examinations are conducted properly,

first pass this national examination. The examination is now commonly referred to as 'The Examination', meaning it is the most difficult examination to pass in China today, with national average pass rates of 6.7% (2002), 8.7% (2003), 11.2% (2004), and 14.3% (2005).[32] However, to this day there has been no published data to indicate the percentage of judges in the Chinese courts who have passed the national judicial examination.

The selection, appointment and removal of judges of the people's courts is prescribed in the Law on Judges and the Organic Law of the People's Courts.

For the Supreme People's Court the president is elected and removed by the NPC while vice-presidents, members of the Judicial Committee, division heads, deputy division heads and judges are nominated by the president of the Court to the Standing Committee of the NPC for appointment or removal.[33]

For local people's courts at various levels the president is elected and removed by the people's congress at the corresponding level. Vice-presidents, members of the Judicial Committee, division head, deputy division heads and judges are nominated by the president to the Standing Committee of the people's congress at the corresponding level for appointment or removal.[34]

A judge may be dismissed if he/she:

- loses his/her Chinese citizenship;
- is transferred out of the court system;
- has no need to maintain his/her position after a change of position;
- is determined through examination not to be competent to hold the position;
- fails to perform a judge's duties due to poor health;
- has retired;
- had resigned or been dismissed; or

---

two sets of interim rules were issued by the Ministry of Justice: Interim Provisions on the Supervision of the Unified National Judicial Examination (28 March 2002), and Measures on the Handling of Discipline Violations in the Unified National Judicial Examination (for trial implementation) (13 March 2002). These are no doubt welcome developments; however, it will take some time before such examinations have any substantial impact on professional qualifications.

32 See Gao Yifei, 'China's Judicial Examination Pass Rate Needs to Be Dramatically Increased', available at <www.dffy.com/sifakaoshi/xx/200512/20051205072719.htm> (last accessed 1 January 2007). See also 'Fourth Judicial Examination Started', *Legal Daily* (*Fazhi Ribao*), 18 September 2005, at 1.

33 Article 11 of the Law on Judges (as revised in 2001).

34 Article 11 of the Law on Judges (as revised in 2001).

- is unsuitable for continuing appointment because of a violation of discipline or law.[35]

Judges are graded into 12 levels. The only judge at level 1 is the president of the Supreme People's Court, i.e. the Chief Justice. Other judges are graded from level 2 to level 12 under the titles of Grand Justices, Senior Judges, and Judges.[36] Although such ranking was provided in the initial 1995 Law on Judges, the actual ranking of judges did not start until 1999.[37]

As in other countries, courts also appoint clerks to keep trial records and marshals to execute judgments, decisions and rulings. Legal medical experts and bailiffs are also appointed. These auxiliary persons are sometimes also referred to as 'adjudication personnel' or 'judicial personnel'.

3.3. Judicial Reforms

Both the courts and the procuratorates have been subject to extensive and continuing reforms.[38] Initially judicial reform measures were largely *ad hoc*, aimed at improving the quality of judicial work. After much media publicity about the need for systematic judicial reform,[39] 1999 saw the start of such reform being introduced. In October 1999 the Supreme People's Court formally unveiled its comprehensive and clearly ambitious five-year (1999–2003) court reform plans.[40]

According to the 50-article document, the reform was to be carried out in accordance with the following principles:

- upholding the leadership of the Communist Party of China;
- upholding the people's proletarian dictatorship as the basic system of the State and the people's congress system as the basic political system;
- upholding the independent exercise of judicial powers;
- upholding the unity of the legal system; and

---

35 Article 13 of the Law on Judges.

36 Article 18 of the Law on Judges.

37 See Jianfu Chen, 'China Watch' (1998) (12) *China Law Update* 1, at 13.

38 For an overview of recent judicial reform efforts, see Li Yuwen, 'Court Reform in China: Problems, Progress and Prospects', in Chen, Li, and Otto, *supra* note 6, at 55-84; Chris X Lin, 'A Quiet Revolution: An Overview of China's Judicial Reform', 4 (2003) *Asian-Pacific Law & Policy Journal* 180; and Son Jian & Zheng Chengliang (ed.), *A Report on Judicial Reforms: Procuratorate and Court Reforms in China* (Beijing: Law Press, 2004). The most comprehensive treatment on this topic is Zhu Jingwen, *supra* note 10, Chapter 4.

39 See Yuwen Li, *supra* note 38. See also Jianfu Chen, 'Judicial Reform in China', (2000) 3 (5) *China Law Update* 3.

40 Five-Year Reform Outline of the People's Court, issued by the Supreme People's Court on 22 October 1999.

- absorbing overseas experience in court and personnel management while paying attention to China's own circumstance.

Specifically, the reform involved the improvement or the establishment of the following:

- functions, forms and procedures of the litigation systems;
- evidence rules and rules of proof;
- public trial by court;
- court documents;
- a quasi-precedent system through the issuing of model cases by the Supreme People's Court;
- rights of defendants and victims;
- criminal procedures and second instance trials;
- administrative litigation procedures;
- the jury (people's assessors) system;
- internal division and structure of the court system;
- supervision of court works; and
- court personnel training and management system.

Clearly, it was an ambitious plan, involving both institutional and organisational aspects of the judiciary as well as procedural matters. The overall objectives of the reform were stated as follows:

- a substantial improvement in the court management system, including the establishment of a system for regular examination, open competition and selection, and promotion on merit of judicial personnel;
- further reform of the trial process so as to strengthen the functions of the collegiate bench, to limit the role of adjudication committees, and to separate the work of adjudication, enforcement and supervision;
- the reform of evidence rules so as to ensure that all facts and evidence are debated and proven in courts before being admitted by courts;
- to improve the quality of court documents so that all judgements will contain not only brief facts and legal provisions for decisions, but also the reasoning for the particular application of the law.

There is little doubt that these initiatives could substantially improve the quality of the work of the judiciary as well as the judiciary itself. Also importantly, all these initiatives were specific and in relatively detailed form and hence practical. Finally, many individual measures were issued by the Supreme People's Court to implement its five-year reform plans,[41] and many of these reform measures have now been incorporated into the 2001 revised Law on Judges.

In October 2005 the Supreme People's Court further launched its Second Five-Year Court Reform Outline (2004–2008).[42] This Outline is said to be the result of a three-year investigation and consultation.[43] Once again it is a far-reaching and ambitious plan, including 50 specific measures and aimed at achieving seven broad objectives. According to the Outline, these objectives are:

- reform and improvement of the litigation processes, so as to ensure justice, efficiency and judicial respect;
- reform and improvement of the execution process and its working mechanisms so as to further resolve the difficulties in implementation of law;
- reform and improvement of trial organisation and trial processes so as to ensure the 'unity' of trial and judgement;
- reform and improvement of the judicial administration system;
- reform and improvement of the personnel system;
- reform and improvement of internal and external supervision over the courts; and
- enhancement of the reform of the court system in general and its working mechanisms.

As in the first five-year reform plan, the present Outline also contains very practical measures to improve the judiciary as a whole, and some of them have been swiftly

41 See e.g. Certain Provisions on the Strict Implementation of an Open Trial System (1999), Certain Provisions on the Strict Implementation of the System of Withdrawal of Adjudicating Personnel (2000), Provisions on Certain Issues concerning a Centralised Administration of Enforcement Work by Higher People's Courts (2000), Certain Provisions on Strengthening and Improving the Entrustment of Execution Work (8 March 2000), Certain Opinions on Basic-Level Construction of the People's Courts (2000), and Measures for the Selection and Appointment of Presiding Judges (2000).

42 Issued as *Fafa* (2005) No. 18. A Chinese copy of the Outline is available from <www.lawbook.com.cn/law_view.asp?id=120832> (last accessed 19 December 2005).

43 See 'Person-in-Charge of the Supreme People's Court Answering Questions from Journalists Regarding the Second Five-Year Reform Outline', available from <www.lawbook.com.cn/fzdt/newshtml/21/20051027092457htm> (last accessed 5 December 2005).

implemented.[44] Some are to significantly change the judicial practice in China,[45] while others appear to continue the reform measures of the first five-year plan.

So far there has been no published assessment of these reforms.[46] In any case one must realistically recognise that many problems with the judiciary and its work are deeply rooted in the politico-economic system and are not of a nature to be easily changed by the judiciary itself.

4. The People's Procuratorates

The procuratorate system is the authority in charge of initiating public prosecution on behalf of the state. Additionally, the procuratorates also exercise the functions and powers of supervising the implementation of law as well as undertaking direct investigation of certain crimes such as those involving graft, infringement of citizens' democratic rights, dereliction of duty and other cases which they deem it necessary to handle directly.[47]

As in the case of the courts, the procuratorate system has developed rapidly since its re-establishment in 1979, but its development has not been as steady as that of the court system. By the end of 1986 there were 3491 procuratorates established in China.[48] The total number then reached 4,052 in 1996 but receded to 3721 in 1998. In 1999 the number once again climbed to 4,142 and again declined to 3624 in 2002.[49] This contraction seems to puzzle Chinese researchers. Nevertheless they suggest that possible explanations are changes in administrative structures, in legal functions and in statistical reporting criteria.[50] At the end of 2004 there were 3,630 procuratorates, with 140,077 prosecutors nationwide.[51] Educational qualifications of

---

44 E.g. the restoration of the review power for all death penalties to the Supreme People's Court, which was carried out immediately after the issuance of the Outline, and most recently the Supreme People's Court issued its Certain Opinions on Strengthening the Open Trial System on 4 June 2007.

45 E.g. the establishment of a guidance system by legal precedents, and the gradual elimination of the practice of seeking guidance from superior courts in specific adjudication cases.

46 Again, one of the most comprehensive assessments of the court system, its current status and its existing problems is contained in Zhu Jingwen (*supra* note 10, chapter 4), but that assessment is not a direct assessment of the recent reforms.

47 The jurisdiction of direct investigation is defined by the Criminal Procedure Law and the Provisions Governing the Scope of Direct Investigations by People's Procuratorates, issued by the Supreme People's Procuratorate in 1998.

48 *China Law Yearbook 1987*, *supra* note 2, at 12.

49 See Chart 5-02 and its accompanying explanations in Zhu Jingwen, *supra* note 10.

50 *Ibid.*

51 See White Paper on Democracy, *supra* note 8.

the prosecutors have also improved significantly: in 1985, only 10% of the Chinese prosecutors had post-secondary education (including vocational training) qualifications. By 1993, this percentage had increased to 63, and by 2005, 86% of Chinese prosecutors had obtained post-secondary education or training qualifications (but some 31% of these qualifications are not law-related).[52]

The Organic Law of the People's Procuratorates of the PRC, issued in 1979 and revised in 1983, establishes a procuratorate system which is similar to the court system. The procuratorate system is structured as follows:[53]

The Supreme People's Procuratorate

High People's Procuratorates
which are established at provincial level, a total of 33 in number

Intermediate People's Procuratorates
with a total number of 384, set up in cities and prefectures within provinces

Basic People's Procuratorates
comprising more than 3,026 basic-level people's procuratorates at county level

As in the case of the courts, there are also special procuratorates established at the intermediate level. As part of the 'judiciary' in a broad sense, most aspects of the procuratorate system are similar to those of the people's court system, such as the organisational structure, rules regarding removal and appointment of personnel, qualifications and other matters. However, there is a unique feature of the procuratorates, namely that all procuratorates are under dual leadership: that of the superior procuratorate and that of the state authorities (local people's congress and government) at the same level. Like in the court system, the local Party committee, local people's congress and local government control the appointment and financial matters and thus the leadership by superior procuratorates is in fact rather weak.

The qualifications, rights and obligations, and the selection and promotion of, as well as ongoing training for, prosecutors in China are governed by the Law

52 See Chart 1-34 in Zhu Jingwen, *supra* note 10.

53 Statistical numbers contained in the schematic outline below are drawn from *China Law Yearbook 2004* (Beijing: China Law Yearbook Press, 2004), at 1057.

on Prosecutors. Article 2 of the Law on Prosecutors defines prosecutors as those who exercise state prosecution powers, including presidents, deputy presidents, members of procuratorate committees, and prosecutors and assistant prosecutors in the procuratorates at various levels. Again, the requirements set out in the Law on Prosecutors on the qualification, selection, removal, dismissal as well as the grades of prosecutors are similar to those set out in the Law on Judges.

In the same way as the court reform, and following the unveiling of a five-year court reform plan by the Supreme People's Court in 1999, the Supreme People's Procuratorate issued its Implementation Opinions for a Three-year Reform of the Procuratorates on 17 February 2000. The 35-article document outlines six major reforms:

- improvement of internal mechanisms within the procuratorate system and the supervision of prosecutors;
- reform of the leadership and organisational structure of the procuratorate system;
- establishment of a chief prosecutors' responsibility system and an expert consultancy system;
- reform of the personnel system and improvements in the professional qualifications of prosecutors;
- establishment of a power control and anti-corruption mechanism; and
- reform of the funding system and improvements in the use of new technologies.

As outlined in the document, these six areas of reform encompassed all aspects of the daily work of the Chinese procuratorate system, but the focus was on the practice of 'not to prosecute' cases, presentation of evidence, preparation of prosecution documents, handling of summary procedures and criminal cases involving children. Many of these were clearly required to implement the 1996 revised Criminal Procedural Law.[54]

Although the document stressed that the goals of the reform were to ensure justice, openness and fairness, as expected the procurotorial reform is required to be carried out in such a way as to ensure the strengthening of the leadership of the Communist Party.

On 12 September 2005, the Supreme People's Procuratorate further issued its Implementation Opinions for Further Deepening a Three-year Reform of the Procuratorates, to be implemented from 2005 to 2008, and focusing on its procuratorial supervision functions including:

---

[54] See further discussion in Chapter 8.

- strengthening supervision over trial processes;
- strengthening internal supervision and control over the procuratorial system;
- undertaking innovative measures to regulate implementation of laws;
- strengthening organisational leadership and restructuring;
- strengthening personnel management towards increasing professionalism; and
- exploring new methods of financial allocation for procuratorates.

As compared to the court reform measures, the measures contained in documents of the Supreme People's Procuratorate tend to be much more vague and general. However, the idea of exploring new methods for financial allocation is rather bold. It requires the budget to be guaranteed by the central financial authorities and listed as separate items in both central government and provincial government budgets. If this is to be achieved it will have a major impact on the fight against local protectionism.

5. Other Government Institutions

As mentioned earlier, it is important to note that besides the court and the procuratorate system there are other state organs which are involved in the administration of law, as well as the exercise of quasi-judicial powers. The most obvious examples are the Ministry of Justice and the Ministry of Public Security.[55]

The history of the Ministry of Justice dates back to the 1949 Organic Law of the Central People's Government. It was abolished in 1959 but re-established in 1979 to assume responsibility for the administration of China's judicial system. Like in all bureaucratic systems, there are various justice bureaus responsible for judicial administration at provincial and local levels, responsible to both the Ministry and the local governments.

As its principal functions the Ministry of Justice is responsible for the administration of Labour Reform Institutions (that is, prisons), the People's Mediation Committees at various levels, the Institute of Forensics, overseeing the lawyer system and the notary system, and publicising the legal system through legal training, legal education and the dissemination of legal knowledge to the general public (e.g. *Pufa* (Popularising Law) campaigns).

The Ministry of Public Security may be better named the Ministry of Police, as it is the country's central police authority. Its policing activities are carried out

55 The Ministry of Supervision will be discussed in Chapter 6.

through its various bureaus and offices at local levels. Until quite recently the police force had been subject to a set of regulations issued in 1957. In 1995 the Standing Committee of the NPC finally adopted and promulgated the Law on the People's Police, which became effective on 1 July 1995. This Law on Police is applicable to all police forces in organs in charge of public security, state security, prisons and organs for re-education through labour, as well as to judicial police established within people's courts and procuratorates. It defines the functions and powers, obligations and discipline, and organisations and administration of the police force. One of the underlying objectives of the Law is to transform the police force into a more respectable professional law enforcement institution.

6. The Legal Profession

The lawyer system has also encountered some fundamental changes. As mentioned earlier, efforts to establish a lawyer system first appeared in 1955 but were short-lived and ended in 1957.[56] They were only re-established in 1980 when the Provisional Regulations on Lawyers were issued.[57] In 1979–1980 there were fewer than 300 lawyers working in a dozen or so law firms.[58] By the end of 2004 there were more than 118,000 practising lawyers working in some 11,691 law firms.[59]

While the growth in the number of lawyers in China is important, more important are the changes in the nature of the lawyer system, with its trend firmly towards professionalism.

Initially, lawyers were defined by the 1980 Provisional Regulations as 'state legal workers'.[60] Such a definition, in theory and often in practice, deprived Chinese lawyers of the independent status enjoyed by their Western counterparts. Major reforms have been introduced since 1986, when the State Council approved a Ministry of

---

56 *China Law Yearbook 1987*, *supra* note 2, at 24. See also Zhao Zenghai & Fang Wei, 'The Tenth Five-Year Plan and the Development Strategy of the Chinese Legal Profession', 23 October 2006, available from <www.acla.org.cn/pages/2006-10-23/s36871.html> (last accessed 15 November 2006).

57 Adopted on 26 August 1980. These regulations have now been repealed and replaced by the Law on Lawyers, adopted 15 May 1996, effective on 1 January 1997 and revised on 31 December 2001. The Law on Lawyers is currently under review.

58 Zhao & Fang, *supra* note 56. Another source however put the number of lawyers in 1979 at around 2,000. See 'Reforms Demand More Lawyer Services', *Beijing Review* (21-27 September 1992), at 7.

59 See White Paper on Democracy, *supra* note 8. The total number of people who have passed practical qualification tests is however close to 300,000. See Zhao Bing, 'Problems in the Chinese Lawyer and Professional System and the Direction of Reform', available at <www.iolaw.org.cn/whownews.asp?id=15335> (last accessed 15 March 2007).

60 Article 1 of the 1980 Provisional Regulations.

Justice report on strengthening lawyers' work, including aiming to start national entry examinations for appointing lawyers and gradually allowing the establishment of financially independent law firms.[61] A critical reform was the proposal to establish cooperative law firms as 'socialist organisations with the status of institutional legal person'.[62] In the same year these non-state-run, financially independent firms began to appear in Shenzhen and Beijing, and later in other cities. Beginning in 1994, a shareholding system was also introduced for the establishment of law firms in Shenzhen and Sichuan Province.[63] New reforms continued to appear thereafter, mostly initiated by the Ministry of Justice. By 1994 a reform approved in principle by the State Council was to have law firms transformed from administrative organs into social service organisations, from state organs into a voluntary, financially independent and self-regulation profession, and from being controlled by the Ministry of Justice to being regulated by lawyers' associations.[64] The 'open door' policy was also incorporated into the reform plan, by which the establishment of foreign law firms was to be allowed under certain conditions.[65]

In 1996, a new Law on Lawyers was introduced,[66] which consolidated the various reforms undertaken in the 1980s and 1990s and has since changed the nature of the legal profession in China. Although defined as providers of legal services to society, not to clients, Chinese lawyers are now nevertheless allowed by Chinese law to perform similar functions to those of lawyers in other countries. Similarly, lawyers in China are also subject to certain prohibitions. They are prohibited from acting as a representative for both parties to the same case; revealing private matters of the client; accepting commissions without permission, privately collecting fees from clients or accepting money or other benefits from them; taking advantage of their position to seek gains from the disputed rights and interests of the party concerned; meeting judges, prosecutors or arbitrators in violation of regulations; sending gifts or offering bribes to these people or inciting or inducing the party

---

61 A text of the Report appears in *A Selection of Administrative Laws and Regulations* (Beijing: Law Publishing House, 1990), at 135-6. The first national examination was indeed held in September 1986, attended by 11,024 candidates nationwide. Of these, 3,707 (30%) passed the examination. See 'Lawyers on the Reform Road', *Economic Daily*, 14 March 1994, at 5. As mentioned earlier, this examination has now been merged with the national judicial examinations.

62 See the Proposals for the Experiment of Cooperative Law Firms, issued in June 1988 by the Ministry of Justice. These Proposals can be found in *China Law Yearbook 1989* (Beijing: China Law Yearbook Press, 1990), at 710-711.

63 'Appearance of Shareholding Law Firms", *Legal Daily* (*Fazhi Ribao*), 4 January 1994, at 1.

64 'State Council Approves Lawyer Reform Plan in Principle', *Legal Daily* (*Fazhi Ribao*), 5 January 1994, at 1.

65 'The Future is not a Dream – The Trend for Lawyer Reform (Part II)', *Legal Daily*, 21 March 1994, at 3.

66 The Law was passed on 15 May 1996 and became effective on 1 January 1997.

concerned to offer bribes; providing false evidence, concealing facts, threatening or inducing others to do so, or hindering the other party concerned from legally obtaining evidence; and disturbing the order of a court or arbitration tribunal or interrupting the normal litigation or arbitration procedures.[67]

These reforms have now completely changed the situation of the legal profession in China and, importantly, law firms are no longer monopolised by state-owned firms. Three major types of law firms now co-exist: State-funded,[68] cooperative,[69] and partnership.[70] Even the state-funded law firms are in fact largely self-funded through fees for legal services,[71] and partnership law firms now comprise almost 70 per cent of all law firms in China.[72]

An important aspect in this development has been the introduction of foreign law firms to China. The establishment of foreign law firms was initially allowed in 1992 when the Provisional Regulations concerning Foreign Law Firms Establishing Branches within China's Territory were promulgated and took effect.[73] Although such

---

67 See further discussion in Jianfu Chen (ed.), *China Business Law Guide* (loose-leaf service) (Singapore: CCH International), paras 4-600 – 4-660.

68 Although they are established with State investment, they are now mostly required to take responsibility for balancing their own books and to assume liability for their debts to the extent of the entirety of their assets.

69 They have been permitted since 1988 and are formed voluntarily by members of the firms responsible for day-to-day management. All assets of a firm are contributed by members. The firm balances its own books and assumes responsibility for profits and losses.

70 This kind of firm has been permitted since 1993 on a trial basis. All assets of the firm are contributed by the partners and belong to the firm. Partners in a partnership firm bear unlimited joint and several liability.

71 See further discussion in Jianfu Chen, *supra* note 67, para. 4-650.

72 See White Paper on Democracy, *supra* note 8.

73 Jointly issued by the Ministry of Justice and State Administration for Industry and Commerce on 26 May 1992 and becoming effective on promulgation. Since then, a series of regulations and measures have been issued to regulate foreign law firms in China: Provisions of the Ministry of Justice on Implementation of the 'Regulations on the Administration of Representative Offices in China of Foreign Law Firms' (initially issued on 4 July 2002 and revised on 2 September 2004); Regulations on the Administration of Representative Offices in China of Law Firms From Hong Kong and Macao (issued initially on 13 March 2002 by the Ministry of Justice (Order No. 70), first revised on 30 November 2003 (Order No. 84) and again on 22 December 2006 (Order No. 104) by the same body); Administrative Measures on the Co-operation of Law Firms between Law Firms from Hong Kong and Macao, and Law Firms in Mainland China (Ministry of Justice, [2003] Order No. 83), which were revised slightly on 28 December 2005 (Order No. 100) and again on 22 December 2006 (Order No. 106) by the Ministry of Justice); the Measures on the Administration of Residents from Hong Kong Special Administrative Region and from Macao Special Administrative Region who Obtain Mainland Legal Profession Qualifications to Practice as Lawyers on the Mainland (first issued on 27 November 2003 by the Ministry of Justice, and revised by the same body on 28 December 2005 and again on 1 December 2006); and Measures for the Registration

establishment is still subject to certain strict approval procedures, and the business scope for practising is restricted, the number of foreign law firms has gradually increased. As of September 2001 more than 100 foreign law firms (including Hong Kong law firms) had opened branch offices in China. By September 2006 there were 149 foreign law branches from 17 countries and 54 law branches from Hong Kong and Macao operating in China.[74] These firms represent a broad range of jurisdictions including Canada, Japan, USA, Australia, Germany, Singapore, The Netherlands, UK, and Hong Kong, etc. As in all other countries, foreign lawyers in China are not permitted to practice Chinese law, or to perform the functions of a Chinese lawyer. However, foreign lawyers are permitted to appear in arbitration proceedings conducted by the China International Economic and Trade Arbitration Commission and the China International Maritime Arbitration Commission. They also operate in some wide areas of law, from securities and banking to project finance, commercial arbitration, property, tax, maritime law, direct investment, intellectual property law, and general corporate consulting. Most importantly, foreign lawyers and foreign law firms in China bring in international experience, an internationally accepted code of conduct, and much needed managerial skills for Chinese law firms.[75]

Also importantly, a legal aid system began trial operations in 1994 and has developed rapidly since then. At the end of 2004 some 3,023 legal aid organisations had been established by governments at different levels, with 10,458 personnel (among whom 4,768 were practicing lawyers).[76]

The requirements for becoming a lawyer in China are, in theory, not radically different from those in most western countries. Generally, a candidate must have a law degree from a university or possess equivalent professional work experience in legal research or education at a senior professional level, must have passed a national examination and obtained a certificate to practice law, and must have undertaken a traineeship with a law firm for more than one year. In addition to these, the

---

of Permanent Resident Lawyers of the Offices of Foreign Law Firms in China (issued by the All-China Lawyers' Association on 18 September 1999).

74 See Public Notice of the Ministry of Justice, No. 57, 11 September 2006; and Public Notice of the Ministry of Justice, No. 58, 11 September 2006. It should be pointed out that while law firms from Hong Kong and Macao are in general treated as 'foreign' law firms in China, they are given certain more favourable treatments than their foreign counterparts, one of these being to allow them to establish a co-operative relationship with mainland law firms and to engage in activities within the business scope of co-operation. This differentiated treatment is a result of the 'Closer Economic Partnership Arrangement between China and Hong Kong' and the 'Closer Economic Partnership Arrangement between China and Macao' signed between Mainland China and Hong Kong and Macao respectively. See different regulations in *supra* note 73.

75 For further discussion on foreign law firms and foreign lawyers in China, see Jianfu Chen, *supra* note 67, paras 4-670 and 4-675.

76 See White Paper on Democracy, *supra* note 8.

person must be of good character (that is without a criminal record etc.) and must support the Constitution. In certain areas of specialist practice, such as securities, commercial bidding, and corporate restructuring involving State-owned assets, lawyers are required to undergo special training, to obtain additional qualifications or to meet additional conditions.[77]

Although lawyering in China is not deemed to be a 'free profession', today's lawyers are increasingly independent and willing to take on the State. Taking advantage of the amendments made to the Criminal Procedure Law of the PRC in 1996 (effective 1 January 1997) that afford defence counsels a greater role in discovery, the examination of witnesses and the presentation of evidence, criminal lawyers are becoming more aggressive in defending their clients. Similarly, lawyers are making use of a variety of means provided by administrative laws such as the Administrative Litigation Law of the PRC (effective 1 October, 1990), and the Administrative Supervision Law (effective 9 May, 1997) to sue the government and challenge administrative decisions. As China's economy is continuously developing, lawyers are playing a more and more important role in handling commercial litigation and non-litigation matters.[78]

The semi-independence of the legal profession is also reflected in the definition of lawyers' associations as incorporated self-regulating social organisations of lawyers.[79] Since the first establishment of the All-China Lawyers' Association in Beijing on 7 July 1986, local lawyers' associations have been set up at provincial and municipality level. However, unlike law societies or bars in many western countries, lawyers' associations in China do not control the admission of lawyers to practice, and the associations are under the supervision and guidance of the Ministry of Justice or its local bureaus.[80]

Also important in the examination of the lawyer system is the emerging professionalisation of the 'basic-level legal services' (*Jiceng falü fuwu*). These basic-level legal service offices emerged in the 1980s at the township and village level to fill a vacuum left by the shortage of lawyers.[81] The offices were staffed by legal workers without lawyers' qualifications. They are involved in all kinds of non-litigation matters, ranging from conducting the mediation of disputes to assisting in legal

---

77 See for instance the Administrative Measures Governing Securities Business Conducted by Lawyers, jointly issued by the China Securities Regulatory Commission and the Ministry of Justice, 9 March 2007. For detailed examination, see, Jianfu Chen, *supra* note 67, para. 4-630.

78 See further discussions in Randall Peerenboom, 'Law Enforcement and the Legal Profession in China', in Chen, Li & Otto, *supra* note 6, at 125-148.

79 See Article 37 of the Law on Lawyers.

80 See Jianfu Chen, *supra* note 67, para. 4-660.

81 See Fu Hualing, 'Shifting Landscape of Dispute Resolution in Rural China', in Chen, Li & Otto, *supra* note 6, at 179-195.

consultation and enquiries. Although there was a set of Interim Provisions on Legal Service Offices at Township and Village Level issued by the Ministry of Justice in 1987, their activities remained largely un-regulated until March 2000, when the Ministry of Justice issued the Administrative Measures Governing Basic-Level Legal Service Offices and the Administrative Measures Governing Workers in the Basic-Level Legal Service Offices.[82] Under the new Measures, a qualification system is to be established and these legal workers are to be required to pass a national examination to be qualified for practice. This national examination was conducted once in 2000 but up to the time of writing has since not been held. In the absence of a national examination and in light of the requirement for a qualification for practice, many local rules have been issued for the purpose of registration and recognition of a qualification.[83] As at the end of 2003 there were some 25,836 such offices with 93,970 legal workers.[84]

7. Legal Education

Sharing a similar fate to other legal institutions, law schools were closed down completely during the Cultural Revolution (1966–1976) and their rebuilding only began in 1978. The progress in this rebuilding has been rapid. Initially, there were only six political-legal institutions under the jurisdiction of the Ministry of Justice and a handful of other universities providing legal education in post-Mao China. This changed quickly, and as at the end of 2003 there were 560,916 undergraduate and 10,876 postgraduate students enrolled in several hundred law faculties/ schools established within universities.[85] These tertiary educational institutions provide 4-year Bachelor of Laws programs as well as further 2-3 year programs for Master of Laws and Ph.D. (called Doctor of Laws in China). Although university law departments/schools/faculties were traditionally seen as placing emphasis on legal theory studies and on preparing law students for government positions, or for teaching and research, while political-legal universities focused on the training of

---

82 Both were issued on 31 March 2000.

83 See Chapter 7 in Zhu Jingwen, *supra* note 10.

84 See Charts 7-41 and 7-42 in Zhu Jingwen, *supra* note 10.

85 See website of the Ministry of Education: <www.moe.edu.cn/edoas/website18/level2.jsp?tablename=1060> (last accessed 16 November 2006). According to China Campus website, as of 2005, there were 415 tertiary institutes in China that provided LLB education. See <campus.eol.cn/20050609/3140337.shtml> (last accessed 16 November 2006). The total number of tertiary institutions of law in China, as of 2005, was 559. See Chart 1-39 in Zhu Jingwen, *supra* note 10. According to State Council Degrees Committee data, as of 2006 there were 284 tertiary institutes in China that were qualified to provide legal education at Masters and Doctoral degree levels. See <edu.sina.com.cn/l/2006-09-13/1520135306.html> (last accessed 16 November 2006).

practitioners to serve in procuratorates, public security organs, courts, law firms and organs of judicial administration, such distinctions have now largely disappeared.

In addition to formal tertiary legal education, the public security system, the court and the procuratorate systems have each developed their own professional training centres, variously called 'universities' or 'colleges.[86] The Ministry of Justice itself also operates the Central School for Political-legal Management and the Central School for Labour Reform Management Cadres for professional training purposes. Significantly, all these universities, colleges and training centres have one kind or another of cooperative agreement with overseas universities and academic institutions for providing learning, research and training collaboration. At the same time, legal research is flourishing.[87]

The importance of these professional training centres is best illustrated by the case of the State College for Judges. In 1985 the Supreme People's Court established its Judicial Cadres' Vocational University, which trained some 170,000 judicial cadres and produced some 50,000 graduates with a Bachelor of Laws degree. In 1988 the China Training Centre for Senior Judges was established in conjunction with the State Education Commission.[88] In ten years of existence the Centre trained some 7,000 senior judges and produced some 590 graduates with Master of Laws or Doctor of Laws degrees. In 1997, the State College for Judges was established on the basis of the above Vocational University and Training Centre. From the time of its establishment until 2000 more than 3,000 senior judges, including many presidents of intermediate courts, had been through the College for professional training.[89] According to the Supreme People's Court, all judges are now required to undertake professional training at least once every three years.[90] Considering that a large number of Chinese judges are originally transferred demobilised army personnel or without any formal legal training, such professional education is perhaps not adequate, but certainly valuable in terms of raising the overall standards of the courts and their personnel.

---

86 These include the China University of Public Security (under the Ministry of Public Security), the State College for Judges (under the Supreme People's Court), and the State College for Prosecutors (under the Supreme People's Procuratorate). This kind of centre has also been established at the various levels of government.

87 For an excellent review of the current status of legal research in China, see Su Li, *Maybe It Is Happening – Legal Science in Transitional China* (*Yexu Zhengzai Fasheng – Zhuanxing Zhongguo de Faxue*) (Beijing: Law Press, 2004). See also Zhu Jingwen, *supra* note 10.

88 Following this practice, judge training centres were established by High Courts (courts at provincial level) in various locations. See Supreme People's Court Report 1993, *Gazette of the Supreme People's Court* (*Zhonghua Renmin Gongheguo Zuigao Faxuan Gongbao*) (no. 2, 1993), at 58. A similar training system for prosecutors also exists in the procuratorate system.

89 See *Legal Daily* (*Faxhi Ribao*), internet edition, 18 September 2000.

90 See *Legal Daily* (*Faxhi Ribao*), internet edition, 19 September 2000.

8. Concluding Remarks

There is little doubt that there has been a major transformation in all legal institutions and that the reforms of these institutions will continue. Furthermore, with China now being a member of the WTO, which demands legal transparency, impartial administration of law, and efficient and effective legal remedies, we can probably expect that the future reforms will be more systematic and in line with international practice.

There is no doubt either that the legal institutions of today are a far cry from those existing in 1979. While acknowledging the achievement, one must not ignore the fact that these institutions are still plagued by a number of fundamental problems. To start with, the development has been in strong favour of strengthening the state apparatus (though the (private) legal profession is catching up with the development), as clearly indicated in the following comparative table:[91]

Total Number of Judges, Prosecutors and Lawyers in China (1981–2004)

	Judges	*Prosecutors*	*Lawyers*
1981	60,439	n/a	8,571
1986	99,820	97,330	21,546
1990	131,460	126,334	34,379
1991	138,459	130,885	30,581
1998	170,000	168,780	68,966
2002	210,000	133,570	102,198
2003	194,622	129,230	106,643
2004	190,961	126,246	107,841

Further, because of the widespread corruption and the much talked about and seriously persistent problems of the implementation of law in China, the judicial institutions are yet to command high respect among the people.[92] There is also the lack of substantial independence of the judiciary. Lawyers too are facing serious problems in moving towards professionalism and, especially, independence.[93]

91 Compiled on the basis of Figure 1-12 in Zhu Jingwen, *supra* note 10. It should be pointed out that the numbers in the Figure do not exactly match the numbers I have quoted throughout this chapter. The choice of the particular years is made on the basis of availability of the relevant statistics.

92 See further discussion in Chapter 18.

93 See Fu Hualing, 'When Lawyers are Prosecuted: The Struggle of a Profession in Transition', available from <ssrn.com/abstract=956500> (last accessed 12 June 2007). See also Peerenboom, *supra* note 78.

It should also be recognised that many of the reform efforts so far have been largely technical in their nature and internal to each institution. That is to say that, although the reform measures that have been carried out are important for practical purposes and have indeed achieved some practical results, for the rule of law to be firmly established in China, deeper and more fundamental reforms will be required, not just within the legal institutions, but especially in the fundamental political system. In particular the question of judicial independence is not one that can easily be resolved by the judiciary itself, and the continuing emphasis on political and ideological correctness over professional qualifications will only prolong the process.[94] In other words, after some 28 years of legal and institutional reform the future of the Chinese legal institutions will now largely be decided and shaped by reforms from outside rather than inside the system.

94 Speaking at the National Judicial Education Conference, Wei Jianxing, a member of the Standing Committee of the Politburo of the Central Committee of the Communist Party of China, made it clear that the most important qualifications for judicial personnel were political quality and ideological standing. See *People's Daily* (*Renmin Ribao*), internet edition, 17 September 2000. See also 'The Central Political Legal Committee Demands an Overall Rise in the Quality of Judicial Forces under the Guidance of the "Three Representatives"', *Legal Daily* (*Fazhi Ribao*), internet edition, 27 September 2000; and 'Work Report of the Supreme People's Court', delivered at the Fifth Plenary Session of the Ninth National People's Congress, 11 March 2002, in *People's Daily*, internet edition, 20 March 2002. See also Chapter 18 on Implementation of Law, where the problems with the judiciary are further discussed.

Chapter Five

Sources of Law and Law-Making

1. Introduction

As already discussed in Chapter Two, one of the great contrasts between China under Mao and post-Mao has been the massive and rapid but, until recently, unsystematic, enactment of laws and regulations in the post-Mao period, aimed at creating a stable social order for smooth economic development.

When the economic reform and open door policy was officially launched in 1978 there was virtually no law in China; the only 'laws' being a few statutes and some provisional regulations or orders made in the 1950s. During a period of 20 years (between 1957–1976), the NPC only adopted the National Outline for Agricultural Development (1958–1967) and the 1975 Constitution. Its Standing Committee managed to enact seven regulations regarding public order, household registration, and agricultural tax. Local legislation was virtually non-existent.[1]

Rapid economic development since 1978 has not only created opportunities for foreign investment, but has also led to great activities in law-making. By the end of 1989 about 150 national statutes, more than 500 administrative regulations and rules, and more than 1000 local rules were issued, covering all major aspects of social and economic life. In addition, China had by then ratified more than 120 bilateral agreements.[2] A relatively comprehensive legal regime for foreign investment was established by 1986, though many improvements were only made in the 1990s, and especially after 2001 when China was admitted to the WTO. Law-making was

---

1 Zhao Zhenjiang (ed.), *Forty Years of the Chinese Legal System* (*Zhongguo Fazhi Sishinian*) (Beijing: Beijing University Press, 1990).

2 See Yu Ma, 'Our Socialist Legal System Has Been Basically Established', *People's Daily* (*Renmin Ribao*) (overseas edition), 28 June 1990, at 2. The message behind this title soon turned out to be a premature declaration. In accordance with the instructions issued by the Party's 15th National Congress (1997), a socialist legal system was to be 'preliminarily established' by the end of the 9th NPC (1997–2002), 'basically established' by the end of 10th NPC (2003–2008) and established by 2010. See 'Chinese Legal System to Be Established on Schedule', available at <www.legaldaily.com.cn/misc/2007-03/13/content_557642.htm> (last accessed 14 March 2007).

further accelerated with the adoption of the notion of a 'socialist market economy' in 1992, with specific and ambitious five-year legislative plans adopted by the NPC, the State Council and local legislatures and governments. The achievement is thus remarkable. By June 2004 the NPC and its Standing Committee had in total adopted 323 laws (with 212 laws remaining effective at that time), 138 resolutions and ten sets of legislative interpretation. The State Council had issued 970 administrative regulations (with 650 of them still effective at that time). At the same time local legislatures at the provincial level had issued more than 10,000 local rules (with 7,500 of them still effective), and some 480 sets of autonomous regulations had been issued by the various autonomous regions. Further, there were also some 260 local regulations by legislatures of the Special Economic Zones.[3] In addition, hundreds of multilateral and bilateral agreements had been ratified by the Chinese government and legislature.[4]

The following two Tables give an overview of the achievements in law-making in post-Mao China:[5]

---

3 See Xinhui Li, 'Fifty Years of Remarkable Legislative Process', *Legal Daily* (*Fazhi Ribao*), 14 October 2004, at 14; and Liu Zheng, 'Supervisory Work of the Standing Committee of the NPC – being the second seminar presented at the Standing Committee of the 10th NPC', July 2003, available from the *People's Daily,* internet edition: <www.peopledaily.com.cn> (accessed 30 September 2003). As of February 2007 there were 223 effective national laws promulgated by the NPC or its Standing Committee. See 'Chinese Legal System to Be Established on Schedule', *supra* note 2. The extra-ordinary growth of local law and the problems arising therefrom are discussed in Cui Zhuolan, Son Bo & Luo Mengyan, 'An Empirical Analysis of the Growth Trend of Local Legislation', originally published in (no. 5, 2005) *Jilin University Journal of Social Sciences* (*Jilin Daxue Shehuixue Xuebao*), reprinted in <www.usc.cuhk.edu.hk/wk.asp> (last accessed 17 July 2006).

4 In addition to being a member of the WTO, China is also a party to most major international commercial agreements. As of November 2006 the People's Congress website contained 110 multilateral treaties and 207 bilateral agreements. See <www.npc.gov.cn/zgrdw/wxzl/wxzl_gbxx.jsp?lmid=0106&dm=010608&pdmc=010608> (last accessed 16 November 2006).

5 Compiled on the basis of Chart 1-01 & Chart 1-03 in Zhu Jingwen (ed.), *A Report on Legal Development in China: Data Bank and Assessment Criteria* (*Zhongguo Falü Fazheng Baogao: Shujuku Yu Zhibiao Tixi*) (Beijing: Renmin University Press, 2007). I am most grateful to Professor Zhu who has kindly supplied me with the manuscripts before their publication. Clearly the statistics contained in the two tables differ significantly from the statistics I have just quoted above. The differences are largely caused by the inclusion of normative documents under the categories of Law, Administrative Regulations and Departmental Rules, and under Local Rules by the inclusion of 'legislative' authorities below the level of provinces.

Number of Laws, Regulations & Rules (1949–1978 & 1979–2005)

	National Laws	Administrative Regulations	Departmental Rules	Local Rules
1949–1978	127	319	586	118
1979–2005	762	3,985	55,714	110,122

Enactment, Revision & Repeal (1979–2004)

	Laws	Administrative Regulations	Departmental Rules	Local Rules	Judicial Interpretations
Total	727	3,809	51,554	91,334	2,889
Valid	220	3,457	44,870	77,663	2,577
Repealed	35	309	6,523	9,062	309
Revised	85	43	160	4,062	3

Clearly the days of 'lawlessness' have gone, at least as far as law on paper is concerned.

Theoretically, the Chinese Constitution upholds a unitary system under which all state powers are vested with the NPC and the local people's congresses. The reality is not so straight-forward; the state law-making power is effectively exercised by a multi-level and multi-dimensional system of authorities and, as a result, legislative enactments in China arise from many sources, both national and local. Indeed, when the NPC set itself an ambitious legislative task in 1993[6] the State Council also decided to enact no less than 500 regulations[7] and at the same time called upon local governments to put economic law-making at the top of their government agenda.[8] From the 'achievements' quoted above it is clear that the State Council and

6 See 'A Legislative Plan of the Standing Committee of the 8th NPC', in *Economic Daily* (*Jingji Ribao*), 14 March 1994, at 5. Under the plan 152 laws were to be drafted and deliberated within the five-year term of the 8th NPC (1992–1997), 125 of them to be guaranteed full deliberation, that is, to be adopted. It was truly an ambitious plan considering that from 1949 to 1992 only 170 statutes were made and adopted. See 'Legislation on a Fast Track', *People's Daily* (*Renmin Ribao*), 20 March 1994, at 2. This was the first time that a legislative plan was adopted. See 'Major Adjustment Made by National Legislative Authority Regarding the Law-Making System', available at <www.legaldaily.com.cn/misc/2007-03/01/content_547023.htm> (last accessed 2 March 2007).

7 Liu Shengrong, 'The Present Situation of the Legislative Process and Methods to Perfect It', (no. 2, 1995) *Journal of the Central Administrative College for Prosecutors* (*Zhongyang Jianchaguan Guanli Xueyuan Xuebao*) 24, at 25.

8 'State Council Decide to Further Strengthen Government Legal Work in Order to Enhance the Establishment of a System of Socialist Market Economy', *People's Daily* (*Renmin Ribao*),

local authorities are at least as important in law-making as the NPC, if not more so. Further, many state institutions, apparently without constitutional authorisation for law-making, are also heavily involved in such activities. The Supreme People's Court and the Supreme People's Procuratorate are two clear examples. Finally, laws made by these competing authorities, each of which clearly has its own vested interests, have now increasingly come into conflict with each other.

In this chapter we will first review the historical changes in law-making in China under the Chinese constitutions. We will then examine the Chinese sources and hierarchy of law and law-making under the Constitution and the Law on Law-making. This will be followed by an analysis of legal interpretation and the law-making processes. Finally, the mechanisms to ensure law-making quality, consistency and coherence will be discussed.

2. A Changing Constitutional Framework for Law-Making

The legal foundation for law-making is, theoretically, established by the Chinese Constitution. As has been the case with constitutional law, the practice of law-making has undergone some significant changes since 1949 and has often deviated considerably from the constitutional stipulation.

The Common Program, a provisional constitution enacted in 1949, anticipated the establishment of a people's congress system to exercise state powers. Before this, the powers of the people's congress were exercised by the Chinese People's Political Consultative Conference (CPPCC), and when it was not in session, by the Central Government. In terms of law-making, the CPPCC only exercised such power at its first session in September 1949 when it adopted the Common Program and several other 'basic laws'. The Central Government was not only a law-making organ, it also exercised the power of interpretation of laws as well as approving many 'normative documents'. Further, the State Affairs Council (the predecessor of the State Council and the executive branch of the Central Government), though not granted legislative powers by the Common Program or the Organic Law of Central Government, issued many 'normative documents' which were treated, in practice, as legal rules. It further approved many local rules and regulations.[9] Although the Common Program established a strict system under which the Central Government controlled all local governments, a *de facto* two-level law-making system – central and local – was practiced and sanctioned by various government organic laws issued by the Central Government.[10] Indeed, it has now been claimed that, other than the

---

28 October 1993, at 1.

9 See Zhao Zhenjiang (ed.) *supra* note 1. at 89.

10 Wu Daying & Shen Zongling, *A Basic Theory of Chinese Socialist Law* (*Zhongguo Shehui Zhuyi Falü Jiben lilun*) (Beijing: Publishing House of Law, 1987), at 179-180.

'basic laws' promulgated by the Central Government, most laws in the first few years of the PRC were issued by local governments.[11]

The first formal constitution of the PRC, the 1954 Constitution, vested law-making powers exclusively in the NPC.[12] The law-making powers of the local authorities and the Standing Committee of the National People's Congress (SCNPC) were severely restricted. Indeed, the SCNPC lost its general law-making power, though retaining the power to issue orders and decrees. The national autonomous regions continued to enjoy the power to make autonomous regulations, but this power was not effectively exercised by these regions, as they had only local people's congresses which held infrequent meetings, and had no standing committees or full-time members.[13] The impracticality of such a centralised system was soon felt, and so in July 1955, less than a year after the promulgation of the 1954 Constitution, the SCNPC was authorised by the NPC to issue laws on single subject matters (*danxing fagui*).[14] It was further authorised in April 1959 to revise laws.[15] These powers were, however, only exercisable when the NPC was not in session. The State Council, as an executive branch, lost its law-making power altogether, but it nevertheless issued many administrative measures, resolutions, orders and decrees, which were in fact treated as national laws and collected, together with the laws issued by the NPC, and orders and decrees issued by the SCNPC, in the *Collection of Laws and Regulations of the PRC*.[16] With the constitutional centralisation of legislative powers, local legislation began to disappear.[17]

This problem of centralisation of law-making power was soon recognised by Mao Zedong and he proffered the following solution: 'Under our Constitution, the law-making power is centralised with the central authority. However, without undermining the policies of the central authority, local authorities should be allowed

---

11 Wu & Shen, *ibid.*, at 180; and Zhao Zhenjiang, *supra* note 1, at 89.

12 Article 22 of the 1954 Constitution provided that 'The NPC is the sole organ exercising the state law-making power.' This provision was said to be a direct copy of Article 32 of the 1936 Soviet Constitution which provided that 'The Soviet Law-making power is to be exercised exclusively by the Supreme Soviet of the Union of Soviet Republics'. See Wu & Shen, *supra* note 10, at 181.

13 See Articles 22 & 27 of the 1954 Constitution. See further Zhao Zhenjiang, *supra* note 1, at 90.

14 See Decision on Authorising the Standing Committee to Issue Laws and Regulations governing Single Subject Matter, adopted by the 2nd Plenary Session of the First NPC on 30 July 1955. A copy of the decision can be found in <www.peoplesdaily.com.cn/focus/rd/newfiles/a1040htm>.

15 Wu & Shen, *supra* note 10, at 182; Wang Xiangming, 'Major Reform at the Supreme State Power Organs', in Chinese Society of Legal Science (ed.), *Selected Papers on Constitutional Law* (*Xianfa Lunwen Xuan*) (Beijing: Publishing House of Law, 1983), at 188-189.

16 Zhao Zhenjiang, *supra* note 1, at 90.

17 Zhao Zhenjiang, *supra* note 1, at 90.

to make rules, regulations and measures in accordance with their own circumstances. The Constitution does not prohibit this.'[18] Although Mao's statement was taken as a new interpretation of the Constitution, decentralisation did not occur.[19] In fact, Mao was about to embark on his continuing revolution and thus began his rejection of rigid rules and regulations. Thus, in the 20 years between 1957 and 1976 there was little to talk about in terms of law-making by the NPC or its Standing Committee. During the same period the State Council issued no more regulations than it did during the first seven years of the PRC, and local legislation became virtually non-existent after the 1954 Constitution.[20]

The provisions for exclusive law-making power in the 1954 Constitution were abolished in the 1975 and 1978 Constitutions, but the latter did not authorise the SCNPC to make laws either. Legislative power for autonomous regions was also abolished by the latter constitutions. During the time of the 1975 Constitution there was little perceived need for law, while the 1978 Constitution simply continued the arrangements under the 1975 Constitution without much thought being given to any actual difficulties there might be in implementing the constitutional provisions.

Although it had no solid constitutional foundation, the 1979 Organic Law on Local People's Congresses and Local People's Governments nevertheless granted local law-making powers to people's congresses and their standing committees at the level of province.[21] This power was confirmed by the 1982 Constitution. This Constitution also grants law-making power to the SCNPC as well as the State Council. Thus the 1982 Constitution has not only reverted to the practice of the 1950s, but also legally recognises the constitutional capacity of law-making of the bodies that had exercised law-making powers on a *de facto* basis. Also importantly, the 1982 Constitution has established a hierarchical system of law and law-making.[22]

---

18 Mao Zedong, *On the Ten Relations,* quoted in Wu & Shen, *supra* note 10, at 182.

19 Wu & Shen, *supra* note 10, at 182-183.

20 Zhao Zhenjiang, *supra* note 1, at 93.

21 See Articles 6 & 27 of the 1979 Organic Law of Local People's Congresses and Local People's Governments at Various Levels (since revised in 1982, 1986, 1995, and 2004).

22 See discussions below. See also J. M. Otto & Y. Li, 'An Overview of Law-making in China', Perry Keller, 'The National People's Congress and the Making of National Law', Li Shishi, 'The State Council and Law-making', Sun Chao, 'Local Law-making in China – A Case Study of Shanghai', and Shi Wenzheng & Bu Xiaolin, 'Legislation in National Autonomous Areas in the PRC', in J M Otto, M V. Polak, J. Chen & Y. Li (eds), *Law-Making in the People's Republic of China* (The Hague/London/Boston: Kluwer Law International, 2000), at 1-18, 75-90, 91-104, 117-130, and 131-140 respectively.

3. The Law on Law-Making

Although the 1982 Constitution has established a general legal framework governing law-making in China, particularly through its general division of legislative powers, the rapid development of law-making by various national and local authorities soon created many problems in terms of consistency and integrity of the legal system. Put simply, the constitutional provisions on law-making and the division of legislative powers were only implemented by *ad hoc* and piecemeal legal documents, without consistency and coherence. Laws and regulations were often issued by authorities whose legislative competence was questionable and some of these laws and regulations also came into conflict. There was also an absence of institutionalised procedures for law-making. The general lack of public input also attracted the particular criticism that law-making was 'secretive and mysterious'.[23] It is therefore not surprising that suggestions by scholars and officials to enact a law on law-making (*lifafa*) as an institutional solution to these practical problems began to emerge in the early 1990s.

The making of a law on law-making was on the legislative agenda for the 8th NPC (1993–1998), but remained one of the tasks not fully completed during that five-year period. Formal drafting by the Legislative Affairs Committee (LAC) started in the latter half of 1993,[24] although the preparatory work had apparently started much earlier.[25] By the end of 1993 the LAC had produced its first draft, with the actual task undertaken by its State and Administrative Law Office in consultation with the Legislative Affairs Office (LAO) (then Bureau) of the State Council and the Administrative Law Research Group under the LAC.[26] A group of academics, under the direction of Professor Li Buyun of the Law Institute at the Chinese Academy of Social Sciences, also began work in late 1993 to produce an 'expert' draft'.[27] This group of academics produced their 'expert draft' in October 1996.[28] By early June

---

23 See Peter Corne, 'Legal System Reforms Promise Substantive – but Limited – Improvement', (June 1997) *China Law & Practice* 29, at 31. See more generally Otto, Polak, Chen & Li, *supra* note 22.

24 See Gu Angran, 'Explanations on the Bill on the Law on Law-making', delivered at the Third Plenary Session of the Ninth NPC, 9 March 2000, (no. 2 2000) *Gazette of the Standing Committee of the NPC of the PRC* (*Zhonghua Renmin Gongheguo Quanguo Renmin Daibiaodahui Changwuweiyuan hui Gongbiao*), at 128.

25 The present author had received visiting scholars and officials from the NPC to investigate law-making processes in Australia well before 1993.

26 Qiao Xiaoyang, 'To Enact a Law on Law-making and to Promote the Ruling of the Country by Law – a speech at the symposium on the draft law on law-making', (no. 3, 1997) *Administrative Law Review* (*Xingzheng Fa Yanjiu*) 1, at 3.

27 *Ibid.*

28 Document on personal file. For an explanation of the 'expert draft', see Li Buyun, 'Explanations on the Proposed Law on Law-Making of the PRC', in Otto, Polak, Chen & Li, *supra* note 22, at

1997, the LAC had issued its fifth draft.[29] The last official draft available to the present author was dated 18 October 1999.[30]

The draft law was first planned to be submitted to the SCNPC for deliberation at the end of 1995 and to be adopted in early 1996.[31] Having failed to meet this schedule, the LAC decided to submit it to the SCNPC at the December 1997 meeting of the SCNPC and to have it adopted by the first plenary session of the 9th NPC in March 1998.[32] Continuing disagreements among major law-making authorities on key provisions again delayed the submission. From interviews with some staff members at the LAC in 1998, it seemed that the chance of submitting the draft law to the full NPC for adoption was seen by many as remote and thus the decision of the SCNPC to submit it to the NPC, made at its 12th meeting in October 1999, came to many as a surprise.[33]

157-173. See also Li Buyun, 'Several Questions on Drafting the Law on Law-making (Expert Draft)' (no. 1, 1997) *Legal Science in China* (*Zhongguo Faxue*) 11.

29 The draft on my personal file is dated 5 June 1997. According to the vice-chairman of the LAC, Mr Qiao Xiaoyang, the draft for discussion at the symposium on the draft law on law-making in April 1997 was the fourth draft. See Qiao Xiaoyang, *supra* note 26, at 3.

30 Document on personal file. This was the draft submitted to the SCNPC for deliberation and, after its deliberation at its 12th Meeting, held in late October 1999, the draft was recommended by the SCNPC to be submitted to a full NPC session for adoption. When the texts of the Law, the 'Report on the Examination and Deliberation by the Law Commission of the Ninth NPC on the Draft Bill of the Law on Law-making', and the October 1999 Draft are compared, it is clear that the draft submitted by the SCNPC to the full NPC already contained some further revisions. In the following discussion three drafts are selected for comparison in analysing the Law on Law-making. These are: The Basic Law on Law-making (dated 1 August 1995), the Expert Draft as mentioned above, and the draft dated 18 October 1999. These three drafts will respectively be referred to as the 1995 Draft, the Expert Draft and the 1999 Draft.

31 See Chen Sixi, 'Formulate a Law on Legislation to Regulate Legislative Activities', (no. 2, 1995) *China Law* 74, at 74. Chen was then a division chief of the State and Administrative Law Office of the LAC.

32 Qiao Xiaoyang, *supra* note 26, at 1.

33 Once it was submitted to the NPC the adoption of the Law was to be expected as by then the full sessions (held annually) of the NPC had never rejected any bills submitted for adoption. In fact, in the last 28 years or so there have been very few instances in which draft laws were submitted to the NPC and SCNPC for voting and adoption that failed to be adopted. Two highly publicised instances both occurred at the SCNPC, one related to the Organic Law for Urban Resident Committees in October 1989, and the other the revision of the Highway Law in April 1999. See 'An Important Step for the Promotion of Rule of Law – the Adoption of the Law on Law-making', *People's Court Daily* (*Renmin Fayuan Bao*) (internet edition), 16 March 2000. There are of course many instances in which draft bills were hotly debated at the SCNPC without being put to the vote.

The disagreements over the draft among law-makers and scholars indicate the complexity as well as the significance of the proposed law.[34] Indeed, if the Law was to properly deal with the existing problems in the law-making system in China, it had to address not merely technical issues relating to law-making, but also to attack some fundamental constitutional law issues.

Despite all the problems, after some seven years in the making the Law on Law-making was finally adopted by the Third Plenary Session of the Ninth National People's Congress (NPC) on 15 March 2000.[35] The Law took effect on 1 July 2000.[36]

The Law, consisting of six chapters and 94 articles, is relatively comprehensive in scope; it attempts to define and delimit legislative powers for various legislatures at the central and local levels, and administrative rule-making powers of various administrative authorities, as well as laying down law-making and rule-making procedures. In line with the 1982 Constitution it classifies legislative documents into law, administrative regulations, local regulations, autonomous regulations, departmental rules, and local government rules. Law-making powers are to be exercised by the NPC and its Standing Committee. The former is responsible for basic laws governing criminal and civil matters, basic economic systems and state structures, and the latter for other laws as well as partial supplementation and revision of basic laws when the NPC is not in session. The State Council is empowered to issue administrative regulations. Local legislatures at provincial level[37] are in charge of making local regulations and autonomous regulations. Governments at provincial level[38] and ministries and commissions under the State Council may issue local government rules (*difang zhengfu guizhang*) and departmental rules (*bumen*

[34] There were serious disagreements about almost every major issue the proposed law was intended to address. See Li Buyun, *supra* note 28. See also Qiao Xiaoyang, *supra* note 26; 'A Summary of the Symposium on the Draft Law on Law-Making', (no. 3, 1997) *Legal Science in China* (*Zhongguo Faxue*) 123; and Li Buyun (ed.), *Studies in Law on Law-making* (*Lifafa Yanjiu*) (Changsha: Hunan People's Press, 1998).

[35] The Law was overwhelmingly but not unanimously adopted by the NPC. Among the 2678 voting members of the Congress, 89 voted against the adoption and 129 abstained. See 'An Important Step for the Promotion of Rule of Law – the Adoption of the Law on Law-making', *supra* note 33.

[36] The effective date of the Law was a result of last minute changes made by the NPC. The Bill submitted to the NPC would make the Law effective immediately after promulgation by the President of the PRC. Deputies to the NPC believed, quite rightly, that a period of preparation would be required before the Law could be properly implemented and their suggestion was accepted by the Law Commission of the NPC and so the date of effect was subsequently changed. See 'Report on the Examination and Deliberation by the Law Commission of the Ninth NPC on the Draft Bill of the Law on Law-making', in *People's Daily* (*Renmin Ribao*) (internet edition), 14 March 2000.

[37] Including the authorities in Special Economic Zones and relatively large cities approved by the State Council.

[38] As above.

guizhang) respectively. These laws, regulations and rules also form a legislative hierarchy, similar to that under the Constitution.

Essentially, the Law addresses the following issues: the vertical division of central and local legislative powers, and the horizontal distribution of legislative powers among legislative and administrative authorities (judicial law-making is not addressed by the Law); inter-relations among 'laws' issued by various authorities; supervision over law, administrative regulations and rules; delegation of legislative powers; legislative processes; and interpretation of laws. Clearly, apart from procedures on law-making, all other issues are, one way or another, related to the fundamental design of the current constitution.

Just before the draft Bill was put to the vote the proposed Law was declared by deputies to the NPC to be yet another milestone in China's legislative history.[39] Indeed, it is a unique product among the world's major legal families.[40] Important as it might be and novel as it is, the Law on Law-making as adopted by the NPC essentially consolidates the existing practices, many of which had already been codified in procedural rules issued by the NPC and its Standing Committee, the State Council and its ministries and commissions, and governments and legislatures at the provincial level.

4. Substantive Issues

4.1. Integrity of the Legal System and Unity of Law

As mentioned above, the Chinese Constitution upholds a unitary system under which all state powers are vested in the NPC and the local people's congresses. It also grants the State Council the power to adopt administrative measures, to enact administrative rules and regulations, and to issue decisions and orders in accordance with the Constitution and laws.[41] Ministries and Commissions under the State Council are also authorised to issue orders, directives and regulations within their respective jurisdictions and in accordance with the laws and administrative

39 See *People's Daily* (*Renmin Ribao*) (internet edition), 14 March 2000.

40 As Otto has pointed out, there does not exist any similar product in the major legal systems in the world. In many countries there are, however, procedural rules for parliamentary debate and deliberation, and such documents as 'cabinet handbooks', which provide guidance on legislative procedures. The division of legislative powers and control of legislative products are fundamental matters dealt with by constitutional laws in the major legal systems. See J. M. Otto, 'Conclusion: A Comparativst's Outlook on Law-Making in China', in Otto, Polak, Chen & Li, *supra* note 22, at 223-224.

41 Article 89 of the Constitution. Its law-making power was further expanded by the delegation of several law-making powers from the SCNPC. See further discussion below.

rules and regulations, decisions and orders issued by the State Council.[42] Further, the people's congresses and their standing committees at the level of province and municipality directly under the Central Government may adopt local regulations, which must not contravene the Constitution, as well as laws and administrative rules and regulations. Finally, the people's congresses of national autonomous regions are empowered to enact autonomy regulations and specific regulations in the light of the political, economic and cultural characteristics of the nationality or nationalities in the areas concerned.

As alluded to earlier, the actual practice is much more complicated as a result of the delegation and authorisation of law-making powers, largely for economic reform purposes.[43] The structure is so complicated that Chinese scholars often find great difficulty in qualitatively defining the law-making system. Some describe the system as a 'one level unitary system', while others believe it to be a 'two level system' or a 'two level, multi-layered system', and still others define it as a 'multi-type and multi-level system under unified central leadership'.[44]

There is, however, a general agreement among scholars in China and abroad that laws and regulations issued by this 'unitary' system can be divided into three levels: primary (national law, *falü*), secondary (national administrative regulations, *xingzheng fagui*) and tertiary (local regulations, *difangxing fagui*).[45] Major problems exist at each level.

At the top of this hierarchy is the Constitution, followed by basic laws (*jiben falü*). The revision of the former and the enactment of the latter fall into the exclusive domain of the NPC.[46] The term 'basic law' is not defined by the Constitution, nor by any other Chinese legislation. The Constitution speaks of basic laws concerning criminal and civil matters, state organisation and other fundamental matters.[47] Although Chinese scholars too have failed to clearly define the term, they generally take it to mean statutes which have a fundamental effect on the whole society, including laws concerning state organisation and structure; minority autonomy and

42 Article 90 of the Constitution.

43 See discussion below.

44 For an analysis of these disagreements among scholars, see Zhou Wangsheng, *The Science of Legislation* (*Lifa Xue*) (Beijing: Beijing University Press, 1988), 259-274; Guo Daohui, *The Law-making System in China* (*Zhongguo Lifa Zhidu*) (Beijing: People's Press, 1988), at 16-30; Shen Zongling (ed.), *Studies in Jurisprudence* (*Falixue Yanjiu*) (Shanghai: Shanghai People's Press, 1990), at 153-166.

45 It should be pointed out that, although there seems to be agreement on the classification of the three-level division, there are different views as to which contents belong to which level. See Perry Keller, 'Sources of Order in Chinese Law', (1994) 42 *Am. J. Comp. L.* 711, at 726-727; Otto & Li, *supra* note 22.

46 Article 62 (1) and 62 (3) of the Constitution.

47 Article 62 (2) of the Constitution.

special administrative regions; criminal, civil and marriage codes and procedural codes; laws dealing with citizens' political and civil rights and personal liberties and freedoms; and other laws establishing state and social systems.[48]

At the next level are the 'other laws' (*qita falü*) enacted by the SCNPC in accordance with Article 67 (2) of the Constitution. Theoretically these laws have an effect only on a particular aspect of the society.[49] The SCNPC also has the power to revise or supplement statutes made by the NPC when the NPC is not in session, provided that they do not contravene the basic principles of these statutes.[50]

The NPC and its Standing Committee thus enjoy the primary legislative power, subject only to the Constitution.[51] The laws they make form the primary sources of legislation and enjoy, theoretically at least, the highest status in the hierarchy of law in China.

At this level the law-making powers seem to be reasonably clearly set out by the Constitution. However, as just mentioned, the distinction between 'basic law' (which must only be enacted by the NPC itself) and 'other laws' (which can be enacted by the SCNPC) is not always clear either in theory or in practice. This has often led to a situation where the SCNPC legislates in an *ultra vires* fashion, and what may be considered to be 'basic laws' have sometimes been enacted by the SCNPC.[52] Further, the Constitution provides that the NPC may alter or annul inappropriate decisions of the Standing Committee,[53] but is silent on laws adopted by the SCNPC. It is thus unclear what would happen if a law enacted by the SCNPC was in conflict with another law enacted by the full NPC.

At the secondary level administrative measures, rules and regulations, orders and decrees, referred to in their totality as administrative regulations and rules (*xingzheng fagui*), issued by the State Council in accordance with the Constitution

---

48 See Law Department of Beijing University, *Basic Theories of Law* (*Faxue Jichu Lilun*) (Beijing: Beijing University Press, 1986), at 361; Shen Zongling (ed.), *Basic Theories of Law* (*Faxue Jichu Lilun*) (Beijing: Beijing University Press, 1988), at 342; and Liu Hehai & Gao Xingwen, 'On Several Questions concerning Our State Law-making', (no. 2, 1995) *Journal on Politics and Law* (*Zhengfa Luncong*) 3, at 5. See also Keller, 'Legislation in the People's Republic of China', (1989) 23 *U.B.C. Law Rev.* 653, at 661.

49 Law Department of Beijing University, *id.*, at 361; and Shen Zongling (1988), *id.*, at 342.

50 Art 67 (3) of the Constitution.

51 As discussed in the previous chapter, the Constitution is the supreme law in China and, consequently, law-making by the NPC and its Standing Committee should be subject to it. However, as the NPC has the power to amend, and the SCNPC has the power to interpret, the Constitution, a constitutional constraint on law-making is clearly difficult to achieve.

52 In terms of *ultra vires* legislation the frequent revision of the Criminal Law and Criminal Procedure Law between 1979 and 1996 is one of the many examples, while the enactment of the Civil Procedure Law by the SCNPC is an example of the 'basic law' being enacted by the SCNPC. See further analyses in Otto & Li, *supra* note 22, and Li Buyun, *supra* note 28.

53 Article 62 (11) of the Constitution.

and national laws, are ranked immediately below those enacted by the SCNPC.[54] These administrative regulations and rules are supplemented by instructions, orders and rules (*guizhang*) issued by commissions and ministries of the State Council.[55]

The express constitutional granting of law-making power to the State Council is supplemented by several open-ended delegations of legislative power by the NPC and its Standing Committee.[56] First, in 1984 the State Council was authorised to enact regulations affecting national economic problems.[57] Later in the same year it was authorised to issue draft laws on industrial and commercial taxation for trial implementation.[58] In 1985, the NPC itself authorised the State Council to issue provisional rules and regulations concerning economic reform and the open door policy.[59] It should be noted that these delegations of legislative power are not subject-specific, but rather plenary in vaguely defined areas of activities. There are, of course, more specific delegations of legislative power by the SCNPC to amend specific laws.[60]

The extensive legislative powers granted to the State Council have thus made the Council the *de facto* most powerful law-making institution in China, which explains the huge number of administrative regulations issued by it, as illustrated in the table at the beginning of this chapter. In addition to thousands of rules and regulations it

---

54 See Article 89 (1) of the 1982 Constitution.

55 Article 90 of the 1982 Constitution. The nature and the relative status of these *guizhang* in the hierarchy is unclear. See further discussion below.

56 The authority to delegate the law-making power of the NPC and its Standing Committee to administrative organs is implied, but not made explicit, in the Constitution. Article 89 (18) specifically authorises the State Council 'to exercise such other functions and powers as the National People's Congress or its Standing Committee may assign it.'

57 Resolution on Government Work Report, 31 May 1984, in Conita Leung & Sun Chao, 'Law-making in China', paper presented to the Conference, *Citizenship, Accountability and the Law*, University of Melbourne and La Trobe University, 17-19 June 1996, at 7.

58 Resolution of the Standing Committee on Authorising the State Council to Issue Draft Regulations on Industrial and Commercial Taxes for Trial Implementation in Order to Reform Industrial and Commercial Taxes, adopted on 18 September 1984, in *A Collection of Administrative Laws in the People's Republic of China* (*Zhonghua Renmin Gongheguo Xingzhengfa Xuanbian*) (vol. I) (Beijing: Publishing House of Law, 1991), at 59.

59 Resolution of the NPC to Authorise the State Council to Issue Provisional Rules and Regulations Concerning Economic Reform and the Open Door Policy, adopted by the Third Plenary Session of the Sixth NPC, on 10 April 1985, in *A Collection of Administrative Laws in the People's Republic of China* (vol. I), *id.*, at 59.

60 For instance, in 1983, the State Council was authorised to amend two regulations which had earlier been approved in principle by the SCNPC, on the resignation and retirement of workers. See Standing Committee's Decision to Authorise the State Council to Amend and Supplement Measures on the Resignation and Retirement of Workers, adopted by the Standing Committee on 2 September 1983, in *China Law Yearbook* (*Zhongguo Falü Nianjian*) (1987) (Beijing: Publishing House of Law, 1987), at 228.

has itself issued, which touch almost every aspect of political, social and economic life in China, over 70% of laws considered by the NPC or the SCNPC are initiated, and often drafted, by the State Council.[61] This position is further strengthened by the fact that the State Council and its bureaucracies hold a superior position in the leadership of the Communist Party, which in many ways still has control over all spheres of state affairs. Finally, the State Council and its bureaucracies hold extensive authority over the interpretation of laws.[62]

Essentially the nature and extent of the legislative powers granted by the Constitution to the State Council are unclear. As a result there is a 'functional theory' among some Chinese scholars who believe that the State Council has the power to make any administrative regulations in fulfilling its functions as provided by Article 89 of the Constitution, without the need for any specific enabling legislation.[63] If this were true, the NPC and SCNPC would become redundant in terms of law-making. Partly in response to this theory, the Law on Law-making (Articles 8 & 9) now contains an extensive list of exclusive legislative powers reserved for the NPC or the SCNPC.

At the tertiary level local law-making was first legitimised by the Organic Law of the Local People's Congresses and Local People's Governments at Various Levels (1979), and later sanctioned by the 1982 Constitution. Since then four amendments have been made to this Law and thus local law-making powers have been gradually extended to other authorities.

Under the provisions of the original 1979 Organic Law and of the 1982 Constitution, people's congresses at the level of province and their standing committees are empowered to enact local rules and regulations (*difangxing fagui*), which must not contravene the Constitution or the laws and regulations promulgated by the NPC, its Standing Committee and the State Council, and must be reported to the Standing

---

61 Mao Di, 'China's Present Legislation', (no. 1, 1995) *China Law* 60, at 61; and Zhu Jingwen, *supra* note 5. For instance, during its five-year term (1993–1998) the 8th NPC adopted 85 laws (excluding resolutions or decisions). Among these, 66 (78%) were drafted and presented by the State Council. See 'Work Report of the Standing Committee', delivered at the First Session of the 9th NPC on 10 March 1998, in *People's Daily* (*Renmin Ribao), 23 March* 1998; 1998 Government Work Report, in *China Daily*, internet edition, 24 March 1998.

62 Thus one Chinese scholar comments: 'Major laws are initiated by the CPC, but end up with the State Council or its ministries and commissions; the majority of laws are initiated by the State Council or its ministries and commissions, adopted by the NPC or the SCNPC after deliberation, but their implementing details have to come from the State Council. Thus, there are few laws that are truly determined by the NPC or SCNPC'. See Hang Li, 'On the Informality and Political Functions of Law-making in China', first published in (no. 2, 2002) *Research in Contemporary China* (*Dandai Zhongguo Yanjiu*), reprinted in <www.usc.cuhk.hk/wk_wzdetails.asp?id=1685> (last accessed 10 May 2004).

63 See Chen Sixi, 'On the Division of Legislative Powers in Our Country', (no. 1, 1995) *Legal Science in China* (*Zhongguo Faxue*) 12, at 16.

Committee of the NPC and the State Council for recording.[64] In 1982, through an amendment to the 1979 Organic Law, Standing Committees of the people's congresses of capital cities of provinces and autonomous regions, and large cities approved by the State Council were authorised to draft local rules and regulations to be approved and enacted by standing committees of the people's congresses at provincial level. The 1982 amendment also allowed people's governments of provinces, autonomous regions, directly administered municipalities, capital cities and large cities approved by the State Council to enact local government rules (*guizhang*).[65] By a 1986 amendment, the congresses and their standing committees of capital cities and large cities further gained the power to directly enact local rules and regulations without the need to submit drafts to the legislative authorities at provincial level for enactment.[66]

Further, through three decisions of the NPC or its Standing Committee, the people's congresses and their standing committees in the four Special Economic Zones (SEZs) have also been authorised to make regulations (*fagui*), which should not contravene the Constitution, national laws and the basic principles of administrative rules and regulations, and their governments have been authorised to issue government rules (*guizhang*).[67]

---

64 Articles 6 and 27 of the 1979 Organic Law and Article 100 of the 1982 Constitution.

65 See the Decision of the NPC on Revising Certain Provisions of the Organic Law of Local People's Congresses and Local People's Governments at Various Levels, adopted by the Fifth Session of the Sixth NPC on 10 December 1982. Under a 1995 amendment these local administrative rules are to be reported to the State Council and the standing committees at the same level for the record. See Item 27 of the Decision of the Standing Committee of the NPC to Amend the Organic Law of Local People's Congresses and Local People's Governments at Various Levels, adopted at the 12th Meeting of the Standing Committee of the Eighth NPC on 28 February 1995, in (no. 1, 1995) *Gazette of the Standing Committee of the NPC* (*Zhonghua Renmin Gongheguo Quanguao Renmin Daibiao Dahui Changwu Wuyuanhui Gongbao*), at 42

66 See Item 1 of the Decision of the Standing Committee of the NPC to Amend the Organic Law of Local People's Congresses and Local People's Governments at Various Levels, adopted at the 18th Meeting of the Standing Committee of the NPC on 2 December 1986, in *China Law Yearbook* (1987), *supra* note 60, at 93.

67 See the Decision of the Standing Committee of the NPC Authorising Shenzhen Municipal People's Congress and its Standing Committee and the Shenzhen Municipal People's Government to Make Respective Laws and Regulations to be Implemented in the Shenzhen Special Economic Zone, adopted 1 July 1992, at the 26th Meeting of the Standing Committee of the 7th NPC, in (no. 21, 1992) *State Council Gazette* (*Zhonghua Renmin Gongheguo Guowuyuan Gongbao*) 786; the Decision of the NPC Authorising Xiamen Municipal People's Congress and its Standing Committee and the Xiamen Municipal People's Government to Make Respective Laws and Regulations to be Implemented in the Xiamen Special Economic Zone, adopted 22 March 1994, at the 2nd Session of the 8th NPC, in (no. 7, 1994) *State Council Gazette*, 258; and the Decision of the Standing Committee of the NPC on Authorising the Municipal People's Congresses and Their Standing Committees, the People's Governments of Shantou

As a result of delegation and authorisation the local law-making system is highly complicated, yet still mirrors the division of legislative power at the central level. In a nutshell, it can be said that legislative powers have only been granted to provincial authorities:[68] to the provincial people's congresses and to their standing committees to issue local regulations (*difangxing fagui*) on any subject that meets local needs, and for local implementation, as long as they do not contravene national laws and national administrative rules and regulations, and provincial governments are empowered to issue local government rules (*difang guizhang*) in accordance with national laws, national administrative rules and regulations and local *fagui*. This structure does not, however, prevent lower authorities from issuing local rules and local *guizhang*. In fact, as long as *fagui* issued below provincial level have the approval of higher authorities, they are valid local rules.

Interestingly, much stricter control has been imposed on a special category of local legislation, namely autonomous rules and regulations (*zizhi tiaoli*) issued by the autonomous regions, prefectures and counties in accordance with the Constitution and the Law on Minority Regional Autonomy.[69] Although these rules and regulations are clearly in the nature of local legislation in terms of their geographic applicability, there are a number of important, but ambiguous, differences between these rules and the local legislation described above. To start with, autonomous rules and regulations made at the regional level must be approved by the SCNPC, and those made by lower level autonomous authorities must be approved by the standing committees of the people's congresses of the autonomous region or the province concerned, before they acquire legal effect. This approval requirement seems to suggest that autonomous rules and regulations are different from local regulations (*difangxing fagui*) as autonomous regions have already had the power to enact local regulations without the need for approval by the SCNPC.[70] This requirement also suggests that the central authorities expect to have tighter control over autonomous regions than over provinces. On the other hand, autonomous rules and regulations are to be made in accordance with local political, economic and cultural circumstances, whereas local regulations are made in accordance with the Constitution, national laws and

---

and Zhuhai Cities to Make and Enforce Laws and Regulations in Their Respective Special Economic Zones, adopted at the 4th Session of the 8th NPC on 17 March 1996, (no. 9, 1996) *State Council Gazette*, at 336.

68 In the Chinese administrative hierarchy there is a concept of deputy provincial authorities, which are those in provincial capital cities, large cities with independent planning, and SEZs. These authorities are also granted law-making powers. See Jianfu Chen & Lijian Hong, *China Local Business Law Guide*, loose-leaf service (Singapore: CCH Asia Pacific), para. 1-105.

69 See Articles 115 & 116 of the Constitution and Article 19 of the Law on Minority Regional Autonomy.

70 In the Chinese administrative hierarchy an autonomous region is equivalent to a province.

national administrative rules and regulations.[71] It is therefore suggested by some Chinese scholars that the fundamental feature of autonomous rules and regulations is their flexibility in contents and scope.[72] Some scholars have even gone so far as to suggest that autonomous rules and regulations may determine the applicability of the Constitution and national laws in autonomous areas.[73] The reality probably is that autonomous regions may make modifications to the application of national law if a particular law allows such modification, and may make their own autonomous rules and regulations if there is no national legislation on a specific subject matter.[74] In short, the making of autonomous rules and regulations is more flexible than the making of local regulations in order to meet local conditions, but, at the same time, this flexibility is more tightly controlled by the central authorities.

At this tertiary level local rule-making powers are, by their nature, plenary. Unless a particular subject-matter has been enacted into national law, there are few mechanisms to control local regulations.[75] The Constitution has little to say about this. In fact, it seems to suggest that local legislation is valid as long as it does not contravene the existing central legislation and is within the administrative competence of the relevant issuing authorities. As authorities and functions of local legislatures and governments mirror those of the central authorities, local authorities are therefore competent to legislate in any areas in which the central authorities have not yet legislated, or where exclusive legislative powers have not been reserved by the national legislative authorities.[76] Theoretically, the higher authority can disallow

71 See Article 116 of the 1982 Constitution and Article 19 of the Law on Minority Regional Autonomy. It is suggested by some Chinese scholars that, precisely because of this lack of constitutional or legal control over the scope and contents of autonomous legislation, the requirement for approval was instituted as a mechanism for control. See Chen Yanqing, 'On the Procedures and Limitations of Legislative Supervision in Our Country', (no. 3, 1995) *Legal Science in China* (*Zhongguo Faxue*) 27, at 28.

72 See Chen Sixi, *supra* note 63, at 18.

73 See Chen Sixi, *id.*, at 18; and Chen Yanqing, *supra* note 71, at 28. This interpretation is, of course, wrong, as autonomous rights are required to be exercised in accordance with the Constitution, the Law on Minority Autonomy and national laws. See Article 115 of the Constitution and Articles 4 & 5 of the Law on Minority Autonomy.

74 See Chen Sixi, *supra* note 63, at 19.

75 Besides the exclusive legislative powers reserved by the Law on Law-making, the Law on Administrative Penalties is perhaps the only law which limits rule-making powers in relation to the imposition of administrative penalties affecting personal liberty and freedom.

76 See Qu Yaoguang, 'On Conflicts of Legislation in Our Country', (no. 5, 1995) *Legal Science in China* (*Zhongguo Faxue*) 41, at 42; Guo Daohui, *supra* note 44, at 23. Thus, one provisional regulation issued by Fujian Province was able to prescribe crime and punishment when dealing with the issues of compulsory education, despite the fact that criminal matters are treated by the Constitution as a subject matter of basic law reserved for the full NPC. See Article 5 of the Provisional Regulations on Popularising Compulsory Education, quoted in Qu Yaoguang, *ibid.*, at 42. See also the discussion on exclusive legislative powers below.

or annul laws and regulations issued by lower authorities, but such power, at least as far as the SCNPC is concerned, has never been exercised.[77]

Outside this three-level framework, regulations and rules are sometimes issued by authorities without apparent legislative competence. One example is that of rules and regulations issued by the Central Military Commission. Nowhere has the Constitution granted any legislative power to the Central Military Commission, yet, as at the end of 2003 the Commission had issued more than 130 separate regulations, and another 30 were issued jointly with the State Council. The total number of rules and regulations issued by its subordinate authorities had reached 2,500.[78] Indeed, the Provisional Regulations of the People's Liberation Army on Legislative Procedures were issued by the Chairman of the Commission in April 1990.[79] This practice seems to have caused little concern to the state legislative authorities. In its suggestions for amending the Constitution in 1993, the Central Committee of the CPC took the view that 'the Central Military Commission can issue and has issued many military rules and regulations for internal use by the army; the Constitution thus needs no new provisions on this matter.'[80]

Clearly, the constitutional provisions on law-making need some clarification and the practice of legislative delegation needs to be regulated. As mentioned early, scholars and officials hoped that a law on law-making would be able to address the ambiguities and provide a clearer practical guidance in a coherent and systematic way – a central task of the Law on Law-making. The 2000 Law on Law-making appears to have had a rather mixed success.

First, Article 2 of the Law clearly intends to bring all laws, regulations and government rules under the scope of the law, and hence to uphold the integrity of the legal system and the unity of law. However, military rule-making is excluded and only the general principles of the Law are to be applicable to such rule-making.[81] Nevertheless, Article 93 confirms that military authorities have rule-making powers, even though, as pointed out above, it is doubtful whether such power has any constitutional foundation.

---

77 See Keller (1994), *supra* note 45, at 737. The SCNPC has never explored measures to control delegated legislation either. See Qu Yaoguang, 'The Messy Situation with Delegated Legislation Needs Urgent Rectification', (no. 12, 1994) *The Voice of Productive Force* (*Shengchanli Zhisheng*) 37, at 39.

78 See *China Law Yearbook 2004* (*Zhongguo Falü Nianjian 2004*) (Beijing: China Law Yearbook Press, 2004), at 102. Chinese scholars put the total number of military rules at close to 20,000. See Zhu Yangming, 'On the Basis of Military Legislation', (no. 3, 1995) *Legal Science in China* (*Zhongguo Faxue*) 33, at 34.

79 In April 2003 these Provisional Regulations were replaced by the Regulations on the Making of Military Regulations and Military Rules, issued by the Central Military Commission. See *China Law Yearbook 2004, id.*, at 103.

80 See Zhu Yangming, *supra* note 78, at 34.

81 See Article 93 of the Law on Law-making.

Secondly, although Article 7 of the Law, which basically reiterates the provisions in Article 58 and 67 of the Constitution, continues the distinction of 'basic law' and 'other laws' without a definition, Article 8 of the Law now provides a detailed list of exclusive legislative powers to be exercised only by the NPC and SCNPC.[82] Although the exercise of some of these powers may be delegated to the State Council by the NPC and SCNPC, the State Council is barred from enacting laws on such matters as those relating to crimes and criminal penalties, the deprivation of political rights of citizens, coercive measures and penalties which restrict personal freedom, and the judicial system. This is a very important development in terms of human rights protection. It is also important to note that the phrase 'coercive measures which restrict personal freedom' was inserted at the last minutes by the NPC[83] and this insertion significantly expands the scope of personal security and liberty issues, which are now off-limits to the State Council. Further, with these absolute exclusive powers vested in the NPC and SCNPC, the legality of the arbitrary distinction between administrative (e.g. re-education through labour) and criminal penalties is seriously challenged.

However, the Law fails to distinguish between the role and functions of the full NPC and those of the SCNPC. Further, as the role of supervision of law now largely falls on the SCNPC, it is perhaps time to consider the constitutional recognition of the SCNPC as the main legislature, rather than pretending that the NPC still has much to do with law-making. Indeed, the NPC itself is no longer primarily involved in law-making; most of its infrequent meetings are devoted to the annual reports by the SCNPC, the State Council, the Supreme People's Court and Procuratorate as well as to personnel arrangements and changes in key state positions.

Thirdly, on the question of the delegation of legislative power, the Law now requires a clear definition of purpose and scope when delegation decisions are made, and delegated powers are prohibited from being further delegated to other authorities.[84] This again is an important development in controlling the exercise of the open-ended delegation of powers. However, the Law fails to impose a requirement for defining time periods for the exercise of each delegated power; it only states that delegation shall cease after the relevant laws have been enacted by the NPC or the SCNPC. It even fails to indicate whether regulations issued under the delegated power would

---

82 The list seems to have been drawn heavily from academic studies.

83 See 'Report on the Examination and Deliberation by the Law Commission of the Ninth NPC on the Draft Bill of the Law on Law-making', *supra* note 36. Article 8 of the 1999 Draft had an even more wide scope for exclusive legislative powers. Thus under the 1999 Draft compulsory measures on property, e.g. search and seizure, confiscation, freezing of property and other compulsory forms of taking of property, are all exclusive legislative powers of the NPC and SCNPC. It is regrettable that these were omitted from the Law as they are also important for the protection of human rights (that is, a human right to property).

84 Article 10 of the Law on Law-making.

still be valid when such delegation has ended.[85] There is also a confusion created by the Law itself. Article 9 speaks of delegating powers to the State Council and Article 65 mentions the delegation of powers to SEZs; the Law fails to indicate whether or not the NPC or the SCNPC could delegate its powers to a province, an autonomous region, or a directly administered municipality etc., or whether these bodies continue to have plenary legislative powers without the need of delegation, as Article 64 seems to suggest.[86] Even on exclusively legislative matters the use of the term 'basic systems' is also bound to cause confusion and uncertainty.

Finally, Chapter Five of the Law establishes a legislative hierarchy and lays down some basic rules for dealing with conflicts and inconsistencies between laws. Under Articles 78 and 79, laws and regulations form the following hierarchy in terms of their legal effect:

- the Constitution;
- laws (by the NPC and the SCNPC);
- administrative regulations (State Council);
- local regulations, regional autonomous regulations and specific regulations; and
- government rules.

Here, the underlying principles are three-fold: (1) the legal effect of legislative documents depends on the administrative status of the issuing authority; (2) at the same level, laws or regulations enacted by legislatures have a higher authority than regulations and rules issued by government authorities; and (3) special regulations (e.g. autonomous regulations or SEZ regulations) prevail over general ones in their specified areas of application.

Under the above principles the Law fails to address an important question, namely the conflict between departmental rules and local government rules, as a ministry is of the same administrative status as a province. Article 82 provides that all departmental rules and local government rules have equal effect and shall be implemented within their corresponding jurisdictions. The law-makers apparently failed to recognise that their jurisdictions often overlap. Although the Law attempts to provide some kind of mechanism for dealing with possible conflict,[87] the practicability

---

85 See Article 11 of the Law on Law-making.

86 See Article 64 of the Law on Law-making.

87 Under Article 86 when provisions of local regulations and departmental rules on the same matter are inconsistent, the State Council shall provide its opinion on the matter and if the State Council is of the opinion that the local regulations shall apply, it shall advise so; if it is of the opinion that the departmental rules shall apply, it shall refer the matter to the SCNPC for determination. Where provisions on the same matter stipulated in different departmental

of these rules is seriously questionable. In short, the Law maintains the *status quo* as established by the Constitution and the various legislative delegation; it only offers very limited clarification and imposes some useful limitations on law-making at the secondary and tertiary levels.

4.2. Questions Relating to *Guizhang* and Other Normative Documents

For a long time the legal status of *guizhang* (governmental/departmental rules) issued by government authorities was unclear and controversial. The Law on Law-making now brings *guizhang* within the scope of law-making. The inclusion of *guizhang* is significant as they are the most pervasive form of regulation in China, yet they had been refused recognition by many scholars as 'law'[88] and at the same time excluded from judicial review of administrative discretion.[89] The issuance of the Law should probably end the debate as to whether *guizhang* are law and hence resolve the question of their absolute status within the Chinese legal system. However, as discussed above, the Law fails to provide practical guidelines for resolving the question of relative status between local government rules and centrally issued departmental rules.

There is another major controversy regarding the legal status of many 'notices', 'directives', 'instructions', 'rules' and other forms of normative documents[90] issued by commissions and ministries of the State Council as well as governments at provincial level. This question of legal status of such documents was made even more confusing when the Regulations on Administrative Reconsideration were upgraded into the Law on Administrative Reconsideration (ARL) in 1999. Under

---

rules or in both departmental regulations and local government rules, are inconsistent, the matter shall be determined by the State Council. On 18 May 2004, the Supreme People's Court put out a document (Fa (2004) No. 96), entitled Minutes of A Meeting on the Application of Laws and Rules in Adjudicating Administrative Litigation Cases, requesting all courts to consult the document in adjudicating cases. Items I (3) and (4) provide some rather complicated rules for the resolution of conflicts between local regulations/rules and centrally issued departmental rules. The underlying principles can be summarised as: (1) the rule which derives from a higher-level enabling law or is authorised by a higher authority prevails; (2) for rules dealing with foreign trade and foreign investment, centrally issued rules prevail; (3) rules strictly dealing with local situations prevail; (4) if doubts exist, the matter shall be reported through the court hierarchy to the Supreme People's Court for resolution (The Supreme People's Court may then consult the relevant authorities as stipulated in the Law on Law-making). However, the document was not issued as a judicial interpretation; its legal status is in fact ambiguous – it is not binding, but lower courts are asked to consult the document in adjudicating cases.

88 See Li Buyun, *supra* note 28; and Jiang Chaoyang, 'Departmental Rule-Making in the PRC', in Otto, Polak, Chen & Li, *supra* note 22, at 105-116.

89 For more systematic treatment of *guizhang* in administrative law, see Chapter 6 below.

90 See Zhang Chunfa, 'Several Questions Concerning Government Rules', in (no. 1, 1991) *Studies in Law* (*Faxue Yanjiu*) 15, at 15.

Article 7 of the ARL, in cases where provisions made by various departments of the State Council, provisions made by governments at county level and above as well as their functional departments, and provisions of villages and towns, are relied upon for administrative decision-making, and the applicant disputes their legality, these provisions may be reviewed by administrative reconsideration organs. Here, how do the relevant authorities distinguish such 'provisions' from 'rules' (*guizhang*) made by these authorities? There are no provisions for distinguishing the two in the ARL. The Law on Law-making has also failed to provide any rules on the making of 'normative documents' or to define their legal status in the Chinese legal system.[91]

4.3. Role of the Communist Party

As discussed in Chapters Two and Three, the legal basis for the pervasive involvement and authority of the CPC in the legal system is ambiguous. Its actual control mechanism is little known both inside and outside China. What is known is that the CPC has a Politico-Legal Committee which has direct control over major national legal affairs including law-making. Further, all state and government authorities have Party committees within their structure which form the core leadership and are directly involved in the work of their respective organisations. However, the actual capacity to intervene and the extent to which they can do so in law-making is unclear to outsiders and disputed by them.[92]

Institutionally certain efforts have been made to formally separate the Party from legislative authorities. Among these the most crucial official effort was the decision by the Sixth Session of the Fifth NPC on 23 February 1979 to establish a Law Commission (*Fazhi Weiyuanhui*) in accordance with Article 27 of the 1978 Constitution (which allowed the NPC and the SCNPC to establish special committees as deemed necessary).[93] The significance of the establishment of the Commission needs some further explanation. Under the 1954 Constitution (Article 34), laws were to be drafted by a Bills Commission of the NPC. However, this Commission soon disappeared and it officially ceased to exist under the 1975 Constitution. In the subsequent period the law-making function was virtually controlled by the Politico-Legal Committee of the Central Committee of the CPC. Immediately after

91 In the 1995 Draft 'normative documents' were clearly included in the scope of the draft law.

92 This uncertainty is largely caused by the Party's reluctance to permit reports of the Party's role in law-making. For different views on the role of the Party in law-making compare, in particular, Keller, *supra* note 48, at 655-660, and Murray Scot Tanner, 'The Erosion of Communist Party Control over Lawmaking in China', (June 1994) 138 *The China Quarterly* 381.

93 The Commission was renamed *Fazhi Gongzuo Weiyuanhui* in September 1983. See *China Law Yearbook 1987*, first English edition (Singapore: Butterworths 1989), at 4-5.

the fall of the 'Gang of Four' it was officially held that law should not be drafted by a specialised organ, but by many organs through the mass-line policy. A draft had first to be examined and approved by the Central Committee of the CPC before being passed to the NPC for 'approval' and promulgation. It was also the official view that more important laws, such as a Civil Code and Criminal Code, must be drafted by the Politico-Legal Committee of the Central Committee of the CPC.[94] This view was challenged in early 1979, and the re-establishment of a Bills Commission in the NPC was urged.[95] The significance of the establishment of the Law Commission was that it officially ended the direct role of the Party in legislative procedures and in theory made the NPC, the SCNPC and special commissions thereunder the sole legislative organs.[96]

It would, however, be mistaken to think that the CPC has now departed from the legislative scene. As already explained in Chapter Three, it has now become a sort of 'convention' that the Party has full control over the revision of the Constitution. In fact, this so called 'convention' entails some wide-ranging but ambiguous principles: all principal matters involving the legislative work of the NPC and its Standing Committee must first be approved by the Central Committee of the CPC, and guidelines and decisions on law-making, major or minor, made by the Central Committee must be implemented by legislatures.[97] In 1991 the CPC issued its *Several Opinions on Strengthening Leadership in State Law-Making*, which was seen as the first ever CPC document defining the scope and procedures for CPC involvement

94 See Zhao Chunpi, Deputy Head of the Politico-Legal Committee of the Central Committee of the CPC and Minister of Public Security, 'An Address to the Forum of the Politico-Legal Committee of the Central Committee of the CPC On Legal Construction', *People's Daily* (*Renmin Ribao*), 29 Oct. 1978, at 2.

95 See Zhou Xinmin & Chen Weiding, 'Some Opinions on Legislative Procedures', *People's Daily* (*Renmin Ribao*), 5 January 1979, at 3.

96 There are however incidents in which the Party has issued 'normative' legal documents together with legislative authorities. See, for instance, Provisions on Disclosure of Important Personal Details of Leaders (jointly issued by the General Office of the Central Committee of the CPC and the State Council on 24 March 1997, in *People's Daily* (*Renmin Ribao*), internet edition, 25 March 1997); Provisions on Prohibiting Waste by Party and State Organisations (jointly issued by the Central Committee of CPC and the State Council on 25 May 1997, in *People's Daily* (*Renmin Ribao*), internet edition, 11 July 1997); and Decisions on Prohibiting Unlawful Levies on Enterprises (jointly issued by the Central Committee of CPC and the State Council on 7 July 1997, in *People's Daily* (*Renmin Ribao*), internet edition, 18 July 1997).

97 See Hang Li, *supra* note 62; Qing Qianhong & Li Yuan, 'The Influence of the Chinese Communist Party on Law-making', initially published in 2003 in <www.chinapublaw.com/emphases/20030613120104htm>, reprinted in <www.usc.cuhk.edu.hk/wk.asp> (last accessed 25 September 2006).

in law-making.[98] This document, according to Chinese scholars, defines the CPC involvement of law-making as follows:

First, all constitutional revisions and all legislative bills concerning major political, economic and administrative matters must be deliberated by the Politburo and the full plenary session of the Party's Central Committee before they can be scheduled for deliberation by the NPC or the SCNPC. Secondly, before drafting starts on any legislative proposal concerning any political matters, the Party Committee of the NPC or the SCNPC must first submit its legislative guidelines and principles to the Central Committee of the CPC for examination and approval. Thirdly, all other legislative bills concerning political, economic and administrative matters must first be submitted by the Party Committee of the NPC or the SCNPC to the Politburo or its Standing Committee for examination and approval. Finally, the Central Committee of the CPC is to exercise centralised leadership over law-making. Under this leadership requirement all draft bills of the NPC and the SCNPC must be submitted by the Party Committee of the NPC or the SCNPC to the Central Committee of the CPC for examination and approval. Draft bills prepared by other state authorities, if they need to be deliberated and enacted by the NPC or the SCNPC, must also be subject to the same procedures.[99]

If the above principles are to be strictly implemented, the Central Committee of the CPC would then become the *de facto* legislature, while the NPC and the SCNPC remain the *de jure* legislatures. My own various interviews in China seem to suggest that the CPC (apart from the Party Committees within the NPC and the SCNPC) does not really have such a pervasive role in law-making, except in areas of major political and economic importance.

The Law on Law-making is, as expected, silent on the role of the CPC in law-making processes. Nevertheless, for the first time in their existence, the 'Four Fundamental Principles' have been rather mysteriously enacted into a provision of law,[100] no longer being a mere political statement in the Preamble of the Constitution. The inclusion of the 'Four Fundamental Principles' into Article 3 of the Law is mysterious because these principles had never appeared in any of the earlier drafts (including the 1999 Draft). The present author has not seen any explanations as to how and why they are now incorporated into a legal provision. As discussed in Chapter Three, China has

---

[98] See *id*. I have not been able to locate a copy of this document. The following discussion is based on discussions in Hang Li, and Qing & Li. Among these two insightful articles on the CPC in law-making, the article by Hang Li is a more elaborate one, which also discusses the influence of individual CPC leaders in law-making in China.

[99] *Ibid*.

[100] Article 3 of the Law on Law-making provides that '[l]aw-making shall observe the basic principles of the Constitution, take economic construction as its central task, follow the socialist road, adhere to the people's democratic dictatorship, uphold the leadership of the Communist Party of China, be subject to the guidance of Marxism-Leninism, Mao Zedong Thought and Deng Xiaoping Theory, and persevere in reform and the open-door policy.'

followed the practice found in other socialist countries, that is, that the leadership role of the Party is to be recognised in the Preamble of the Constitution, with its actual exercise of power to be carried out through extra-constitutional methods. The incorporation of the 'Four Fundamental Principles' into a legal provision raises a serious question: do the law-makers now intend to make the *de facto* leadership of the Party a *de jure* one?

4.4. Supervision

With the multitude of legislative authorities and the lack of quality control, there are bound to be inconsistencies and conflicts among laws, rules and regulations, and indeed some scholars claim that inconsistency exists in every single piece of legislation, and that conflict of law is commonplace among laws, rules and regulations issued by central and local authorities,[101] with the most serious problem being in the areas of government rules (*guizhang*).[102]

For the purpose of maintaining the integrity of the legal system and the unity of law, the Constitution and other organic laws have created some provisions for dealing with conflicts of laws,[103] such as prior approval being necessary before legal effect is taken in cases of autonomous regulations, filing with the SCNPC and the State Council, which would allow superior authorities to examine possible conflicts, and the possibility of rescission by standing committees at a higher level of rules and regulations issued by lower authorities.[104] Although the Constitution theoretically prohibits any laws or administrative or local regulations from contravening the Constitution,[105] there are neither mechanisms nor practical procedures for citizens to challenge the constitutionality or legality of these laws and regulations,[106] nor has the SCNPC ever invalidated any such laws or regulations. In practice, conflicts of law are mostly resolved through extensive informal co-ordination among various

101 Li Yahong, 'Some Thoughts on Central-Local Legislative Relationship during the Transitional Period', (no. 1, 1996) *Legal Science in China* (*Zhongguo Faxue*) 23, at 26.

102 Qu Yaoguang, *supra* note 78, at 43. Qu gives many examples of conflicting laws in China. This is so despite the fact that all *fagui* must be reported to the State Council and the Standing Committee of the NPC for recording. *Guizhang* need no authority of approval as they are, theoretically, made in accordance with laws and *fagui*. They are, however, required to be reported to the State Council and standing committee of the people's congresses of the relevant province for the record.

103 For more detailed discussions, see Chen Yanqing, *supra* note 71.

104 See *supra* note 22.

105 See the Preamble and Article 5 of the 1982 Constitution.

106 The Administrative Litigation Law specifically excludes the review of administrative regulations. See Article 12 of the Administrative Litigation Law (1989).

authorities, including prior approval by superior authorities and party control over legislative affairs.[107]

For the purpose of strengthening supervision over law and law-making, two mechanisms have been established by the Law on Law-making. In the first place, Article 89 systematically codifies the present practice and legal requirements on the filing of law and regulations for the record, as already contained in various laws and regulations. With all laws and regulations filed, largely with central authorities, Article 88 sets out provisions governing the power of a higher authority to alter or even annul laws, regulations and rules enacted by a lower authority. The second mechanism, through Article 90, is to make the SCNPC a kind of constitutional committee responsible for review of conflicts among laws and regulations. Although the Law stops short of establishing a constitutional committee, as advocated by many scholars and contained in the expert draft of the Law on Law-making,[108] it is significant that some practical procedures and mechanisms have finally been established for the review of legislation.

However, constitutional review of legislation, as established by Articles 90 and 91, suffers a number of serious defects. First, Article 88 (1) provides that the NPC has the power to alter or annul improper laws enacted by the SCNPC, but the SCNPC is the actual reviewing authority under Article 90. How then is the NPC to actually conduct its supervision over laws enacted by the SCNPC? Secondly, organisations and citizens are entitled to make suggestions to the SCNPC for review of administrative regulations, local regulations, autonomous regulations and specific regulations, but they do not have a right to demand this, nor can they request the SCNPC to conduct a review of laws – only the State Council, the Central Military Commission, the Supreme People's Court, the Supreme People's Procuratorate, or standing committees of the people's congresses of provinces, autonomous regions or directly administered municipalities can do so.[109] Finally, and more importantly, the Law fails to define any criteria for such a review or for making requests for such a review; Article 90 and 91

---

[107] See Leung & Sun, *supra* note 57, at 11; Chen Yanqing, *supra* note 71, at 29.

[108] See Li Buyun, *supra* note 28, and the Expert Draft. According to Chinese scholars this remains an aspirational goal among academics. See 'Constitutional Experts: a major step towards constitutional review', in <www1.people.com.cn/GB/14576/14528/2590424.html> (last accessed 24 June 2004).

[109] See Article 42 of the Law on Law-making. Article 90 of the Law on Law-making, however, provides that '[w]here … social organisations, enterprises, institutions as well as citizens are of the opinion that certain administrative regulations, local regulations, autonomous regulations and specific regulations contravene the Constitution or laws, they may submit, in writing, suggestions to the Standing Committee of the National People's Congress for review of these. The working organ of the Standing Committee shall examine the matters and, where necessary, refer them to relevant special committees for review and opinion.' Clearly, individuals have no right to request constitutional review of laws, but only of administrative regulations and rules.

only speak of 'contravening' – an important term without definition, although the need for definition has been consistently advocated by scholars.[110]

Despite all these shortcomings in the Law on Law-making, and after much controversy and public debate,[111] the SCNPC finally moved in 2004 to establish some mechanisms on the supervision of law-making.

As mentioned in Chapter Two, a specialised unit within the Legislative Affairs Committee of the SCNPC was established in May 2004 to strengthen the work of the filing for the record of laws and regulation and of reviewing these laws and regulations.[112] In December 2005, the Working Procedures on Filing for Record and Review of Administrative Regulations, Local Regulations, Regulations of Autonomy Regions and Special Economic Zones, initially issued in 2003, were revised and a new set of Working Procedures on Filing for Record and Review of Judicial Interpretations was issued by the SCNPC.[113] These working procedures further establish some specific procedures for the constitutional review of regulations and rules and bring the SEZs' regulations as well as judicial interpretations within the scope of legislative review.[114] The Supervision Law of 2006, as also discussed in Chapter Three, again demands the implementation of the supervisory powers of the SCNPC and its local counterparts. Most recently the SCNPC decided in 2007 to transfer the task of legislative planning from its General Office to the Legislative Affairs Committee.[115] Although this move is not a direct measure in the supervision of law-making, it surely has the potential to ensure the consistency of law-making.

---

110 Both the 1995 Draft and the Expert Draft attempted to define the meaning of 'contravening' and 'inconsistency'. On scholars' advocacy for such definitions, see various chapters in Li Buyun, *supra* note 34.

111 See discussions in Chapter 3 on constitutional cases.

112 See 'Standing Committee of the NPC Clarifies Constitutional Review Process', available at <www.xinhuanet.com/politics/2005-12/20/content_3944117.htm> (last accessed 20 December 2005). According to the *People's Daily*, this special unit is also in charge of interpretation of laws. See 'Standing Committee of the NPC Established an Office for Legislative Review and Filing for Record', in <www1.people.com.cn/GB/14576/14528/2587708.html> (last accessed 24 June 2004). While the establishment of the specialised unit was widely publicised, as some Chinese scholars have pointed out, we know very little about the functions and working procedures of the unit. See Hu Jianmiao & Gao Chunyan, 'Constitutional Review of Law and Regulation in China – Problems and Solutions', in (no. 3, 2006), *Printed Newspaper and Journal Articles (D411 Constitutional & Administrative Law)* 46, at 52.

113 These are seen as internal working procedures (Hu Jianmiao & Gao Chunyan, *id.*, at 52) and none of them has been published.

114 See Hu Jianmiao & Gao Chunyan, *supra* note 112, at 52; and 'The Standing Committee of the NPC Clarifies Constitutional Review Procedures', *supra* note 112.

115 See 'Major Adjustment Made by the National Legislative Authority Regarding the Law-Making System', available at <www.legaldaily.com.cn/misc/2007-03/01/content_547023.htm> (last accessed 2 March 2007).

These initiatives, small steps as they might be,[116] are important in ensuring some degree of unity of law, but they are far from establishing a constitutional review mechanism in its true meaning.

4.5. Interpretation of Law

As Chinese laws (*falü*) are mostly made in general and vague terms, their interpretation by various authorities effectively forms an important source of law. Without these interpretations, Chinese law is unusable, if not meaningless.

The Constitution provides that the SCNPC exercises the power to interpret the Constitution and laws;[117] otherwise, the Constitution has little to say about statutory interpretation. Chinese jurisprudence commonly divides authoritative interpretation into three categories: legislative, administrative and judicial. Generally speaking, legislative interpretation means interpretation given by legislative authorities on laws and rules issued by themselves; administrative interpretation refers to interpretations given by administrative authorities of these rules and regulations; and judicial interpretations are those issued by the Supreme People's Court and the Supreme People's Procuratorate in their adjudicative and procuratorial work.[118] This jurisprudential division of the power of statutory interpretation is reflected in the 1981 Resolution of the Standing Committee concerning the Strengthening of Legal Interpretive Work,[119] which provides some more detailed, but still very general, provisions on dividing the power of legal interpretation.

According to the Resolution the SCNPC shall, through interpretation or the making of decrees (*faling*), supplement or clarify the scope of application of laws and decrees. The Supreme People's Court and the Supreme People's Procuratorate shall interpret questions of law arising out of specific applications of law in their adjudicative or procuratorial work respectively. If the interpretations by the two organs differ fundamentally, the matter shall then be referred to the SCNPC for interpretation or decision. Questions of law arising out of specific application of law in areas other than adjudicative or procuratorial work shall be interpreted by the State Council or its responsible departments. The standing committees of people's congresses at the level of province shall supplement or clarify the scope of

---

116 See 'The Establishment of the Constitutional Review and Filing for Record Unit Should Be Reported', in <www1.people.com.cn/GB/14576/14528/2590398.html> (last accessed 24 June 2004).

117 Article 67 (1) and (4) of the Constitution.

118 See Shen Zongling, *supra* note 44, at 224; Xu Xianming (ed.), *A Textbook on Jurisprudence* (*Falixue Jiaocheng*) (Beijing: China University of Political Science and Law Press, 1994), at 241-243.

119 Adopted on 10 June 1981 by the 19th Meeting of the Standing Committee of the 5th NPC. The 1981 resolution is a revised version of the Resolution concerning Legal Interpretation adopted by the same Committee in 1955.

application of local regulations they themselves have issued, and the governments at the level of province and their responsible departments shall interpret questions of law arising out of the specific application of these rules and regulations.

Several points need to be clarified about this Resolution. First, although the Resolution was adopted before the 1982 Constitution, jurists in China do not see it as contravening the constitutional provisions, despite the fact that the Resolution clearly constitutes 'virtual abdication of responsibility for legal interpretation' by the Standing Committee.[120] Indeed, until this day the Resolution remains the only guideline in dividing responsibilities for legal interpretation.

Secondly, the Resolution only deals with the interpretation of laws, decrees, local regulations promulgated by legislative authorities (i.e. by standing committees and people's congresses at and above the level of province). It does not deal with the interpretation of administrative regulations or government rules. This arrangement was made for doctrinal reasons. As a legislative body, the SCNPC has no jurisdiction over administration, thus lacking jurisdiction over the interpretation of administrative regulations which are made for the purpose of administration in accordance with the Constitution.[121]

Thirdly, as a result of this doctrinal consideration, the State Council and its commissions and ministries have acquired exclusive control over administrative regulations and rules, not only the making but also the interpreting of them. This power was further extended by a 1993 State Council Circular to cover detailed rules and regulations issued by the State Council or its subordinates for the implementation of national laws.[122] This Circular, imitating the 1981 Resolution, assigns the power of supplementation and clarification of administrative regulations to the State Council itself, and leaves the interpretation of questions of law arising out of specific application to its subordinates.

Fourthly, although the SCNPC still possesses the exclusive power of legislative interpretation over national law, it has so far produced many supplementary provisions to many national laws, but not so many on specific national laws.[123] Perhaps it is simply impractical for the Committee, which is convened bi-monthly, to carry

---

120 Keller, *supra* note 45, at 741.

121 See Keller, *supra* note 45, at 742; and Shen Zongling, 'On Legal Interpretation', (no. 6, 1993) *Legal Science in China* (*Zhongguo Faxue*) 57, at 60. This is so even though the Chinese leadership has never formally recognised the doctrine of 'separation of powers'.

122 See the Circular Concerning Procedures and Powers for the Interpretation of Administrative Regulations, issued by the General Office of the State Council on 3 March 1993. This Circular is supplemented by a circular of the same title and issued by the same authority on 10 May 1999.

123 Shen Zongling, *supra* note 121, at 61; Cai Dingjian & Liu Xinghong, 'On Legislative Interpretation', (no. 6, 1993) *Legal Science in China* (*Zhongguo Faxue*) 36, at 39. The Criminal Law is an exception, for which the SCNPC has issued several interpretations on specific articles of the Law since 2001.

out the task of interpretation when it has already been overloaded with legislative tasks.[124] In practice all requests for interpretation of national laws to the SCNPC are referred to the LAC of the SCNPC. However, the LAC itself is not a legislative authority, nor is it vested with the power for legal interpretation; thus, its interpretation has no legal effect, though it is used as guidance in practice.[125]

After all this, what has emerged as the most important and active interpretation authority in China has been the Supreme People's Court.[126] The judicial activism of the Supreme People's Court is, however, not without theoretical and practical problems. Theoretically, the Court is only authorised to interpret questions of law arising out of specific application, while ambiguities and other questions of the law can only be clarified by the SCNPC. However, the Court has often issued interpretations on a specific law soon after the law has come into effect, and sometimes the interpretation is in a much more detailed form than the original law, dealing with it almost article by article.[127] These interpretations can hardly be said to be judicial interpretations arising out of specific applications of law;[128] in fact, they have commonly been issued after extensive consultation with legislative and various relevant

124 Shen Zongling, *supra* note 121, at 62; Cai & Liu, *id*., at 39.

125 Cai & Liu, *supra* note 123, at 41. The lack of constitutional and, indeed, legal status of the Legislative Affairs Committee is sometimes totally ignored in law-making. For instance, The Several Provisions Concerning the Implementation of the Criminal Procedure Law was jointly issued by the LAC with the Supreme People's Court, Supreme People's Procuratorate, Ministry of Public Security and Ministry of State Security on 19 January 1998.

126 In 1994, the Supreme People's Court published its first collection of judicial interpretations. This collection contains over 1720 documents interpreting national laws issued from October 1949 to June 1993, but mostly issued after 1979. See, Supreme People's Court, *A Complete Collection of Judicial Interpretations by the Supreme People's Court of the PRC* (*Zhonghua Renmin Gonghe Guo Zuigao Renmin Fayuan Sifa Jieshi Quanji*) (Beijing: Press of the Supreme People's Court, 1994). The Supreme People's Procuratorate is only slightly less active in judicial interpretation, but that is mainly because it is only concerned with criminal justice, whereas the Supreme People's Court has comprehensive jurisdiction over all legal issues.

127 For instance, the 270-article Civil Procedure Law came into effect in April 1991. An interpretation containing 320 articles was issued by the Supreme Court in July 1992. Similarly, the 156-article General Principles of Civil Law came into effect in January 1987 and by April 1988 the Supreme Court had issued its own comprehensive 200-article interpretation. A similar situation exists in relation to administrative litigation law, succession law, and many other areas of law.

128 Qu Yaoguang, *supra* note 76, at 43; Yuan Jieliang, 'On Problems of the Institution of Legislative Interpretation', (no. 4, 1994) *Legal Science in China* (*Zhongguo Faxue*) 24, at 25. See also Li Siqi, 'The Erosion of Legislative Power by the Judicial Power – on Judicial Interpretations by the Supreme People's Court', available from <www.cuhk.edu.hk/wk.asp> (last accessed 8 June 2007), who also openly criticises the practice as unconstitutional.

administrative authorities.[129] There was then also the question whether other courts might be competent to issue their own interpretations.

To avoid being seen to be exceeding its constitutional power the Supreme People's Court then made some efforts to limit the exercise of such interpretative power. Thus, a 1987 Supreme Court document made the judicial interpretation the exclusive authority of the Supreme People's Court, and deprived other courts of the power to issue judicial interpretations.[130] Later in 1996, Chinese courts were instructed by the Supreme People's Court not to cite judicial interpretations in, much less used as a legal basis for, making judicial decisions (although they were required to implement the judicial interpretations).[131] Lower courts nevertheless used them in judicial reasoning.[132]

In 1997 the Supreme People's Court finally decided that it did not need to pretend that it was not a law-making authority by issuing the Several Provisions on Judicial Interpretation.[133] Under these Provisions judicial interpretations are to be made by the Supreme People's Court only.[134] They also reverse the 1996 instruction by requiring the lower courts to cite relevant judicial interpretations if they are relied upon in decision-making.[135] More significantly, Article 5 of the Provisions declares

---

129 Interview with staff from Research Section of the Supreme People's Court. The reason for this consultation is largely due to the practical difficulties in delimiting legislative and judicial interpretation. The need for consultation has now been formally instituted by the Provisions on Judicial Interpretation, issued by the Supreme People's Court on 23 March 2007.

130 See A Reply from the Supreme People's Court that Local Courts at Various Levels Shall Not Make Judicial Interpretation Documents, issued on 31 March 1987, in *A Complete Collection of Judicial Interpretation by the Supreme People's Court of the PRC, supra* note 126, at 3. This Reply begs the question, what is judicial interpretation. By logic, all judicial decisions are judicial interpretations of the law, or as Common law lawyers would say, the 'discovery of the meaning of the law'.

131 A Reply from the Supreme People's Court on How to Cite Laws and Normative Documents in Legal Documents Made by People's Courts, issued on 28 October 1996, in *A Complete Collection of Judicial Interpretations by the Supreme People's Court of the PRC, supra* note 126, at 28.

132 Zhou Daoluan, 'A Review of Judicial Interpretation in New China and Some Thoughts on Improving Judicial Interpretation', in *A Complete Collection of Judicial Interpretations by the Supreme People's Court of the PRC, supra* note 126, at 14.

133 Issued on June 23, 1997, effective on 1 July 1997. Similar provisions were earlier issued by the Supreme People's Procuratorate on 9 December 1996. The Several Provisions have now been replaced by the Provisions on Judicial Interpretation, issued on 23 March 2007. Earlier, on 10 May 2006, the Supreme People's Procuratorate issued its Provisions on Judicial Interpretation, which also replace its 1996 Provisions. The following discussions are based on the new Provisions.

134 Article 2. These Provisions do not make such a power exclusive, but are silent on whether the lower courts have any authority to issue judicial interpretation.

135 Article 27.

that judicial interpretations by the Supreme People's Court are to have the effect of law. This Article clearly contravenes the constitutional division of law-making powers; hence, the legal effect of it is constitutionally questionable. On the other hand, as some Chinese scholars have rightly argued, without these 'interpretations', it is practically impossible to enforce national laws framed in general principles and vague terms.[136] On the other side of the coin, however, the power to interpret laws by the Court is severely restricted. The Court has no authority to interpret administrative regulations, government rules, or local rules and regulations; it can only interpret laws promulgated by the NPC and its Standing Committee (except for the Constitution).[137] Although the Court may resist unreasonable interpretation, it has to defer the question of interpretation of these rules and regulations to the issuing authorities.[138]

The provisions on the interpretation of law in the Law on Law-making represent one of the most disappointing aspects of the Law. Section 4 of Chapter 2 contains six short articles on the interpretation of law, only dealing with interpretation by the SCNPC. The Law is totally silent on administrative, adjudicative and procuratorial interpretations of law. The reasons for this omission are unclear.[139] Hence all those constitutional and practical problems outlined above will persist. Further, reflecting the ambiguous attitude towards the involvement of the LAC in legislative interpretation and, perhaps, also the struggle for prestige and vested interests, Article 55 of the Law provides that the working organ (i.e. the LAC) of the SCNPC may examine and reply to inquiries concerning relevant concrete issues of law and report them to the SCNPC for recording. This perhaps is one of the most ambiguous provisions in the Law, which is certain to create more confusion than to clarify the status of legislative interpretation of law by LAC, and could potentially undermine the effort to maintain the integrity of the legal system and the unity of law.

The filing for recording system is another important means designed to maintain the integrity of the legal system and the unity of law. However, because of the failure to address administrative interpretation, it is doubtful whether the State Council's interpretations of law and regulations will be seen as part of the legislative

---

136 Chen Yanqing, *supra* note 71, at 31. In fact, the Supreme People's Court makes no effort to hide the fact that it is making laws. Under the Provisions, judicial interpretations are to be made in accordance with annual plans, not out of the demands of concrete cases. See Section II of the Provisions, especially Articles 9-12.

137 See the 1981 Resolution discussed above. See also Zhou Daoluan, 'On Judicial Interpretation and Its Standardisation', (no. 1, 1994) *Legal Science in China* (*Zhongguo Faxue*) 87, at 87; Zhou Daoluan, *supra* note 132, at 2. Zhou Daoluan was then a vice-president of the Supreme People's Court.

138 *Id*. See also Keller, *supra* note 45, at 753.

139 In all drafts since 1993, including the 1999 Draft, there were provisions which would also deal with judicial interpretation and there were also provisions to abolish the 1981 Resolution on interpretation of law.

documents that must be filed for recording. As mentioned above, adjudicative and procuratorial interpretations of law were only formally required to be filed for recording in 2005.[140]

5. Procedural Issues

As discussed in Chapter Two, legal developments in post-Mao China, in particular, the law-making programs, have been pragmatic and utilitarian. This is not wrong in itself. However, pragmatism and utilitarianism may be exercised either in an authoritarian or even totalitarian manner, or may allow a democratic and participatory process. Herein lies the importance of the law-making process.

Until 2000 when the Law on Law-making was enacted, law-making procedures varied between different authorities and there were no uniform rules for all authorities.[141] All these various rules established some basic requirements for the various stages of law or rule making, including initiating, drafting, submission for inclusion on the agenda, deliberation and consultation, adoption and promulgation.[142] The Law on Law-making essentially codifies these practices and, by doing so, institutionalises and attempts to unify procedural practices.

There are some major improvements in the Law over the practice. First, public participation in law-making has now been emphasised as one of the basic principles in law-making.[143] Although specific rules for public participation are mostly lacking, the Law nevertheless requires law and regulation-making authorities to hold symposiums (*zuo tanhui*), public hearings (*tingzheng*) and public debates

---

[140] See *supra* note 114.

[141] Thus, procedures for law-making at the NPC and its Standing Committee are governed by two different sets of procedural rules, i.e. Procedural Rules of the Standing Committee of the NPC of the PRC (1987) and Procedural Rules of the NPC of the PRC (1989). In the State Council there are the Provisional Regulations on Procedures for Administrative Rule and Regulation Making (1987) (now replaced by a new set of Regulation, see *infra* note 148) and Circular Concerning Procedures and Powers for the Interpretation of Administrative Rules and Regulations (1993). Most of the provincial law-making authorities have also issued their own procedural rules.

[142] See Mao Di, *supra* note 61, at 61; Li Yede & Zhang Xingxiang, 'How Are China's Administrative Rules and Regulations Formulated?' (no. 4, 1997) *China Law* 58; Gu Angran, *An Outline of Law-making in New China* (*Xin Zhongguo Lifa Gaishu*) (Beijing: Publishing House of Law, 1995), ch. 7; Zhou Wangsheng, 'One the Processes and Ten Drafting Steps', (no. 6, 1994) *Legal Science in China* (*Zhongguo Faxue*) 19. Since there was no clear procedural guidance, there was no universally agreed division of law-making processes among scholars. For some western studies on the law-making process, see Frances Hoar Foster, 'Codification in Post-Mao China', (1982) 30 *Am. J. Comp. L.* 395; Murray Scot Tanner, 'How a Bill Becomes a Law in China: Stages and Processes in Lawmaking', (1995) *The China Quarterly* 37.

[143] See Article 5 of the Law on Law-making.

(*lunzheng*) and to conduct public consultation through other means.[144] Compared to the past practice and the system of expert drafting,[145] the Law has a much less elitist approach toward public participation. Secondly, publication of law, though already practiced by most authorities, is now made a legal requirement. The Law also defines which published laws and regulations are to be official versions of law for practical purposes.[146] Thirdly, efforts have also been made to balance sufficient deliberation at the NPC or the SCNPC with speedy resolution of major disagreements. Thus major disagreements are to be resolved by special committees, or a bill is to be dropped after two years of indecision.[147] Finally, the roles of special commissions and especially of the Law Commission of the NPC have now been substantially enhanced; essentially they are now the focal points where technical issues and major disagreements will be resolved.

The Law on Law-making also attempts to unify, to a certain degree, procedural rules for law-making by various authorities. First, Article 74 requires that the procedures for enacting the department rules of the State Council and local governmental rules are to be stipulated by the State Council in reference to provisions in Chapter Three (which stipulate procedures for administrative regulation-making) of the Law. Accordingly, the State Council issued, on 16 November 2002, the Regulations Governing the Procedures of the Making of Administrative Regulations,[148] and Regulations Governing the Procedures of the Making of Government Rules (*Guizhang*).[149] Further, even though local legislatures are still allowed to make their own procedural rules, they can do so only with reference (*canzhao*) to the procedures for the NPC and the SCNPC.[150] While this requirement seems to be rather simple, it could actually cause some major practical problems. For instance, most local procedural rules require a legislative bill to be deliberated at two separate sessions of local Standing Committees before being put to the vote, whereas the procedures for the SCNPC require deliberation at three separate sessions.[151] If local

---

144 See Articles 34 and 58 of the Law on Law-making.

145 See also Zhu Jingwen, 'Public Participation in Law-Making in the PRC', in Otto, Polak, chen & Li, *supra* note 22, at 141-156; and Li Buyun, *supra* note 28.

146 See Articles 52, 53, 62, 70, and 77 of the Law on Law-making.

147 See Article 38 and 39 of the Law on Law-making.

148 These Regulations replace the Provisional Regulations governing the Procedure of the Making of Administrative Regulations, issued in 1987.

149 Earlier, on 14 December 2001, the State Council had issued Regulations on the Filing of Government Rules, which replaced the 1990 Provisions on the Filing of Government Rules.

150 See Article 68 of the Law on Law-making.

151 See Article 27 of the Law on Law-making. The Procedural Rules of the Standing Committee (1987) first instituted the so-called 'two-examination' procedure. It was only in 1998 that the Council of Chairmen of the SCNPC decided to extend the time for deliberation by adopting a 'three-examination' procedure; that is, important and complicated bills need to be examined

legislatures are also to be required to implement the 'three examination' system, it could potentially and unnecessarily delay adoption of local regulations. These regulations are often implementing rules, which perhaps need speedy passage so as to adapt national law and regulations to the specific locality. Until this day, it is unclear whether local legislatures have changed their practice in accordance with the requirements imposed by the Law on Law-making.

On the other hand, the Law fails to mention anything about legislative planning which, in current practice, heavily dictates the legislative programs of the SCNPC, the State Council and local legislatures at provincial level.[152] Also, the Law is silent on the compilation of law and regulations and their periodic review. The latter is perhaps one of the most important and pressing issues facing all those authorities which have issued laws, regulations and rules. Finally, unlike earlier drafts, the Law does not attempt to regulate the use of legal terminology at all. Thus the confusing use of such terms as regulations (*tiaoli*), resolutions (*jueyi*), decisions (*jueding*), measures (*banfa*), etc., will continue.

6. Concluding Remarks

It appears that efforts have been made in the Constitution to divide legislative powers and thus to create an hierarchical order of legislation in China, with the idea of upholding legislative unity while allowing local diversity to meet local conditions and to encourage local initiatives for reform. In reality, however, this complex legislative division (including legal interpretation) has resulted in disorder rather than order, and inconsistencies and conflicts of law. There are many factors to which one may attribute this chaotic situation. To start with, the constitutional division of power is far too vague and general and, thus any granting of legislative power is bound to be exercised by the relevant authorities to enhance their own status in this highly hierarchical society, both politically and administratively. The primary legislation is no more concise and precise for practical purposes. Interpretation, which in fact often entails supplementation of law, thus becomes a necessity for those organisations responsible for implementing and enforcing law. Secondly, the lack of experience and training and of theoretical guidance for law-makers,[153] coupled

---

by three Standing Committee meetings before being put to the vote. See Li Peng, 'Speech at the 2nd Meeting of the 9th NPC's Standing Committee on April 29, 1998', in *People's Daily* (*Renmin Ribao*), internet edition, 1 May 1998.

152 Again, in all early drafts (including the 1999 Draft), there were provisions governing legislative planning.

153 For an examination of the lack of experience, training and theoretical guidance, see Ann Seidman & Robert B. Seidman, 'Drafting Legislation for Development: Lessons from a Chinese Project', (1996) *Am. J. Comp. L.* 1.

with the demand for the urgent establishment of a legal system for a transitional market, have resulted in the experimental nature of law and law-making, which, as with economic reforms, the central authority clearly prefers to have carried out in confined areas. Thus, local experiments have been implicitly allowed, if not encouraged. The instrumental use of law to implement policies, which is a main function of the State Council, also makes it acceptable and practical for the State Council to have great power in law-making. Finally, the present reform in China, politically, economically and administratively, is essentially an experimental process of redistribution of state powers. It should therefore not be surprising that local authorities as well as functionaries are taking up every opportunity to enhance their own status and prestige in a status conscious society.

Also importantly, the law-making practice has been largely undemocratic, authoritarian and elitist. There is a general failure to recognise that an important aspect of democracy is to initiate and to participate in law-making; to limit public consultation to technical arrangements after guiding principles have been set down is no democracy.[154] The increasing involvement of 'legal experts' in law and rule-making is an important development to ensure the technical quality of the law. Further, academic studies published by those involved in law-making have made the law-making processes relatively more transparent. But this practice is not necessarily democratic; it remains elitist, if not also authoritarian.

The intention of the Law on Law-making is clear: to achieve what the Chinese call 'the integrity of the legal system and the unity of law'; that is, the consistency, coherence and uniformity of law in China. By codifying law-making procedures, the Law on Law-Making does make the Chinese law-making processes much more democratic, transparent and accountable. The establishment of the supervisory mechanisms is particularly important as it will, to a certain extent, ensure greater certainty, consistency and quality and the avoidance of conflict of laws and rules. However, as discussed above, the Law on Law-Making on the whole leaves too many questions unanswered and too many important issues unaddressed. Many of these are issues of major significance in constitutional law, but the Law was adopted by the full NPC, which has the power to amend the Constitution. This simply means that the 'integrity of law' in China will continue to be only an aspiration in the foreseeable future.

---

154 This is not to suggest that gaps do not exist in other countries between this ideal and reality.

Chapter Six

Administrative Law

1. Introduction

In the early 1980s there were only a few legal scholars in China with some vague ideas about administrative law.[1] Administrative law, as a branch of legal science, was not included in the curricula of tertiary legal education until 1981 by the Ministry of Justice. It first became an elective subject in 1983 and then a compulsory one in 1986. The first textbook on the subject in the PRC, *An Outline of Administrative Law*,[2] was only published in 1983,[3] and by 1984 there were only about 100 people nationwide involved in teaching and researching administrative law.[4] It has, however, since become one of the most rapidly developing areas of law and legal studies in the post-Mao period. By 1989, when the Administrative Litigation Law was enacted, no less than 20 textbooks on administrative law had been published.[5] By the mid-1990s, theories on administrative law were described as 'exploding'.[6]

---

1 Wen Zhengbang (ed.), *Chinese Legal Science Approaching the 21st Century* (*Zouxiang Ershiyi Shiji de Zhongguo Faxue*) (Congqing: Congqing Press, 1993), at 201. Other Chinese scholars described the subject in 1989 as a long forgotten and most confusing and confused area of law. This confusion and ignorance of administrative law was said to be caused by the non-separation of procedural and substantive administrative law, and the practice of giving party and state policies precedence over law. See Zhang Shangshuo, 'Administrative Law Science in New China', (no. 3, 1989) *Journal of Zhongnan Institute of Political Science and Law* (*Zhongnan Zhengfa Xueyuan Xuebao*) 18, at 18-19.

2 *Xingzhengfa Gaiyao*, edited by Wang Mincan and Zhang Shangshuo but with contributions by 13 scholars and published by the Publishing House of Law in Beijing.

3 There were several internally circulated textbooks on administrative law in the 1950s. See Zhang Shangshuo, *supra* note 1, at 19-20.

4 Zhang Huangguang, Liu Suguang & Su Shangzhi, *Basic Principles of Administrative Law* (*Xingzhengfa Jiben Yuanze*) (Taiyuan: Shanxi People's Press, 1984), at 35.

5 See Zhang Shangshuo, *supra* note 1, at 20.

6 Wen Zhengbang, *supra* note 1, at 201.

Institutionally, the people's courts first moved to establish specialised court divisions for administrative litigation.[7] By the late 1990s there were 3,224 such divisions within the court system, with a total of 12,215 judges specialised in administrative law.[8] From the time of the implementation of the Administrative Litigation Law in 1990 to the end of 2004 the courts had adjudicated 1,246,270 administrative cases, with the annual caseload increasing by 17% on average from 1987 on.[9] Complainants won between 17% and 30% of their cases.[10]

Administrative legislation has also developed rapidly since the late 1980s. First came the adoption of the Administrative Litigation Law in 1989. This was followed by the Administrative Reconsideration Regulations (1990),[11] the Administrative Supervision Regulations (1990),[12] the Provisional Regulations on Public Servants (1993),[13] the State Compensation Law (1994), the Administrative Penalties Law (1996), and the Administrative Licensing Law (2003). The provisions of these laws and regulations have been further supplemented and clarified by various

---

7 The 1980 Sino-Foreign Joint Venture Income Tax Law was the first law in post-Mao China to permit lawsuits against administrative decisions. The 1982 Civil Procedural Law (for Trial Implementation) authorised the courts to use civil procedures to adjudicate administrative cases (Article 3). In the second half of 1986 some local courts began to establish specialised divisions for administrative litigation. In January 1987, the Supreme People's Court issued a Notice on the Establishment of Administrative Litigation Divisions. This Notice formally launched the establishment of such special divisions nationwide. The Supreme People's Court itself established an administrative division in September 1988. See Chapter 4 in Zhu Jingwen (ed.), *A Report on Legal Development in China: Data Bank and Assessment Criteria* (*Zhongguo Falü Fazhang Baogao: Shujuku Yu Zhibiao Tixi*) (Beijing: Renmin University Press, 2007).

8 Ma Huaide (ed.), *Chinese Administrative Law* (*Zhongguo Xingzhengfa*) (Beijing: China University of Political Science and Law Press, 1997), at 15. After 1988 economic-related administrative cases were all decided by administrative divisions of the courts, except those concerning intellectual property which were first adjudicated by economic law divisions of the courts and later by specialised intellectual property divisions. See Editorial Board of China Today, *Adjudication in China Today* (*Dangdai Zhongguo de Shenpan Gongzuo*), vol. 1 (Beijing: Press of China Today, 1993), at 189-190, & 440-441.

9 Calculated on the basis of Table 4-07 and Chart 4-33 in Zhu Jingwen, *supra* note 7. A Supreme People's Court survey suggests that the majority of administrative cases relate to administrative decisions concerning economic activities, particularly those relating to fines, confiscation of property, suspension or cancellation of licence, and orders issued to stop production. See *Adjudication in China Today*, *supra* note 8, at 440-441.

10 Up to 1996, complainants were winning around 30% of the cases, but this success rate began to declined from 1996 and, by the end of 2003, it had declined to 17% (remaining so at the end of 2004). See Chart 4-37 in Zhu Jingwen, *supra* note 7.

11 Substantive amendments were made in 1994, and in 1999, these were superseded by the Administrative Reconsideration Law.

12 The Regulations were superseded in 1997 by the Administrative Supervision Law.

13 They were superseded in 2005 by the Law on Public Servants.

implementing rules issued by the State Council, its commissions and ministries, the Supreme People's Court and the Supreme People's Procuratorate.[14] Despite different concepts of administrative law among Chinese scholars,[15] they all agree that a basic framework of administrative law has now been established in China.

This Chapter first reviews the major developments in administrative law in China. This is followed by an analysis of contemporary Chinese conceptions of administrative law. Individual aspects of administrative law, namely administrative decision-making and its control and supervision mechanisms, procedural remedies for individuals, and state liability for maladministration, are then examined one by one.

2. Historical Development of Administrative Law in China

The ancient Chinese bureaucracy is recognised as the oldest continuous one, though not the oldest one, in the world.[16] Together with a sophisticated and well-established bureaucratic system there were institutional laws setting out the functions of government offices and limiting and defining the powers and duties of officials as well as establishing a rather sophisticated system of delegation of powers and accountability.[17] Indeed, administrative law was undisputedly one of the two most developed branches of official law in traditional China,[18] although, for reasons of accessibility, complexity and academic interest, it is not as well known in the West as the traditional penal law.[19] The conception of administrative law in traditional China was quite different from that in contemporary China, but keeping governments accountable, not to the people but to the emperor, was one of its major functions. Indeed, even though the emperors were theoretically supreme and above the law, they themselves nevertheless on the whole observed the law; in particular, they

---

14 See, for instance, a large collection of such supplementary rules and regulations in volume 3 of *A Complete Collection of Legislative, Judicial and Administrative Interpretations [of Laws] in the People's Republic of China* (*Zhonghua Renmin Gongheguo Lifa Sifa Xingzheng Jieshi Quanshu*) (Beijing: Yanshi Press, 1997). For other supplementary rules and regulations, see the annual publication of *A Complete Collection of Laws in the PRC* (*Zhonghua Renmin Gongheguo Falü Quanshu*) (Changchun: Jilin People's Press).

15 See Section 3 on Chinese conceptions of administrative law below.

16 See Eugene Kamenka, *Bureaucracy* (Oxford: Basil Blackwell, 1989), at 22-39.

17 Geoffrey MacCormack, *The Spirit of Traditional Chinese Law* (Athens & London: The University of Georgia Press, 1996), at 20-22.

18 The term 'official law' mainly refers to official enactments by imperial governments in traditional China. The term is also used in contrast to a large body of unwritten law governing private and civil matters. See MacCormack, *id.*, ch. 2.

19 MacCormack, *supra* note 17, at 18-19.

were bound to respect the laws inherited from the past and repeatedly confirmed by their imperial forebears.[20]

Chinese scholars generally trace the history of administrative law back to 1700 BC.[21] The Book of High Offices (*Shangshu*), originally written during the Shang (1700–1200 BC) and Zhou (1200–211 BC) dynasties and containing rules on punishments and rewards for high officials, is said to be the earliest historical record evidencing the institutionalisation of state administration.[22] The Rites of Zhou (*Zhou Li*) of the Zhou Dynasty, also known as Zhou Officials (*Zhou Guan*), outlined the system of administration at the time. One of its chapters, entitled Six Rules (*Liu Dian*), is said to be the first effort in Chinese history in which administrative rules and principles were systematically codified, defining powers and duties for state officials.[23] *Zhou Li* was thus said to be the first Chinese code of administrative law.[24] By AD 738, after 16 years of drafting, the process of the codification of a self-contained and separate administrative code, the Six Rules of Tang (*Tang Liu Dian*), had been completed. This Code provided detailed provisions regarding the establishment of state organs, the appointment of state officials, and the functions and obligations of state organs and their officials. From then on the practice of separating administrative law from the often penal-dominated comprehensive codes continued.[25] The *Tang Liu Dian* was also to become the model for a comprehensive administrative code in the successive dynasties. The last such code, the Collected Rules of the Great Qing (*Da Qing Hui Dian*), first drafted in the fifteenth century and last revised in the eighteenth century, was operative until 1911. These separate administrative codes were further supplemented by various individual statutes that also dealt with state administration.[26]

According to a contemporary authority on Chinese legal history, Professor Zhang Jinfan of the China University of Political Science and Law, the coverage of traditional administrative law may be divided into the following nine categories: (1) rules relating to structures, powers and their limitations, the functions and the working procedures of both the central and local administrative organs; (2) rules relating to the selection, functions and duties, examination, punishments and rewards,

---

20 MacCormack, *supra* note 17, at 21-22.

21 According to MacMormack, it was the Qin (Ch'in, 221-207 BC) state that laid down the administrative basis through legal rules which were built on and refined by succeeding dynasties. See MacCormack, *supra* note 17, at 20.

22 Zhang Jinfan, *A Collection of Papers on Legal History* (*Fashi Jianlüe*) (Beijing: Press of the Masses, 1990), at 171.

23 Zhang Jinfan, *id.*, at 143.

24 Zhang Jinfan, *id.*, at 173.

25 Zhang Jinfan (ed.), *Chinese Legal History* (*Zhongguo Fazhi Shi*) (Beijing: Press of the Masses, 1984), at 204.

26 Zhang Jinfan, *supra* note 22, at 159.

remuneration, promotion and transfer, and entitlement to holidays of officials; (3) rules relating to the forms, procedures and functions of official document-making; (4) rules concerning the supervision of state administration and administrative penalties; (5) rules concerning taxes, revenues and state or official-run industries; (6) rules governing education, science and technology development; (8) rules regulating religion and the administration of temples; and (9) rules for the administration of minority areas.[27] Although the focus of the traditional administrative law was on delimiting the functions of state offices and departments, and defining the powers and duties of officials, which often incorporated Confucianist ethics but was backed by severe penal sanctions, an administrative supervision system began to emerge during the Warring States period (475–221 BC).[28] It was firmly established as early as the Western Han (206 BC – AD 24), and continued throughout the dynasties.[29]

Efforts to separate the judiciary from administration, however, only occurred during the Qing reform, during which imperial orders were given to establish an administrative court. The 1890 Japanese Administrative Litigation Law, which was modelled on German and Austrian laws, was introduced to officials in charge of this task.[30] The idea was however not brought to realisation during the Qing reform. The 1912 Provisional Constitution of the Republic of China (*Zhonghua Minguo Linshi Yuefa*) was the first legislation which specifically required that administrative litigation be separated from the functions of the ordinary courts.[31] In March 1914 the Yuan Shikai government issued the Order for the Organisation of a Court of Administrative Justice (*Xingzheng Yuan*). In May of the same year it issued the Regulations governing Administrative Litigation. These were followed by the Law on Administrative Litigation, issued in July of the same year.[32] The Nationalist government continued the process of separating administrative litigation from

---

27 Zhang Jinfan, *supra* note 22, at 170.

28 Zhang Jinfan, *supra* note 22, at 214.

29 Zhang Jinfan, *supra* note 22, at 159-167.

30 Susan Finder, 'Like Throwing an Egg Against a Stone? Administrative Litigation in the People's Republic of China', (1989) 3 *J. of Chinese Law* 1, at 1-2.

31 Article 49 of the Provisional Constitution of the Republic of China. See Wang Lianchang (ed.), *Administrative Law* (*Xingzheng Faxue*) (Beijing: China University of Political Science and Law Press, 1994), at 31.

32 Wang Lianchang, *id.*, at 31-2. Although an administrative litigation system was thus established, it had little effect on the society. See Finder, *supra* note 30, at 2.

ordinary courts by initially establishing the *pingzheng yuan*,[33] and an administrative court after 1928.[34] Like its predecessor, it had no major impact before 1949.[35]

The pre-PRC Communist authorities concerned themselves more with gaining powers than with controlling them. Thus major legislation in the area of administrative law mainly dealt with the establishment of government organisations and their administration.[36] Even though some 3,000 administrative rules and regulations were issued from 1937 to 1949, dealing with various aspects of administration, these 'laws' were mainly concerned with implementing Party policies, gaining political power and improving the efficiency of government.[37] Nevertheless, an administrative supervision system was established during the Shan Gan Ning Border Area period (1937–1947), though it did not function properly.[38]

The Common Program of the Chinese People's Political Consultative Conference provided that '[t]he people or people's organisations shall have the right to file charges with the people's supervisory organs or people's judicial organs against any state organs or any public functionaries that violate the law or are negligent in the performance of their duties.'[39] The first formal constitution of the PRC, the 1954 Constitution, also provided that '[c]itizens of the People's Republic of China have the right to bring complaints against any person working in organs of state for transgression of law or neglect of duty, by making a written or verbal statement to any organ or state at any level. People suffering losses by reason of the infringement

---

33 This may be roughly translated as Administration Balancing Court.

34 See He Qinghua & Li Xiuqing, *Foreign Law and Chinese Law – An Examination of Transplanting Foreign Law into China in the 20th Century* (*Zhongguofa Yu Waiguofa – Ershishiji Zhongguo Yizhi Waiguofa Fansi*) (Beijing: Press of China University of Political Science and Law, 2003), 112-141. It should be pointed out that it was a highly contentious issue during the late Qing and early KMT legal reform whether to establish separate courts for administrative litigation. See Shen Daming, 'The Debate on the Administrative Litigation System in the Early KMT Period and Its Significance', May 2007, available from <www.civillaw.com.cn/article/default.asp?id=32943> (last accessed 16 June 2007).

35 Finder, *supra* note 30, at 3.

36 The earliest such law was the 1931 Organic Law of the South Fujian Soviet Republic Government. Other such legislation included Temporary Organic Regulations for Local Soviet Republic Governments of China (1931); the Organic Law of the Central Soviet Republic of China (1934), and the Principles of Administration for Shan Gan Ning Border Areas (1941). See Pi Chunxie (ed.), *Textbook on Chinese Administrative Law* (*Zhongguo Xingzhengfa Jiaocheng*) (Beijing: China University of Political Science and Law Press, 1988), at 30-31.

37 Pi Chunxie, *id.*, at 31.

38 Zhu Weijiu (ed.), *Legal Supervision Over Government* (*Zhengfu Fazhi Jiandu Lun*) (Beijing: China University of Political Science and Law Press, 1994), at 161.

39 Article 19 of the Common Program, adopted on 29 September 1949 as a provisional constitution. An English text can be found in Liu Suinian & Wu Qungan (eds), *China's Socialist Economy – An Outline History (1949–1984)* (Beijing: Beijing Review Press, 1986), at 487-500.

of their rights as citizens by persons working in organs of state, have the right to compensation.'[40] Clearly, the establishment of mechanisms for supervision over administration, for administrative litigation and for compensation was envisaged in the early stages of the PRC. Under the Common Program people's governments at or above the level of county were required to establish supervisory organs. Thus a People's Supervision Commission within the Council of Government Administration (now the State Council) was established in 1949. By 1954 about 4000 supervisory organs had been established nationwide, with around 20,000 cadres especially charged with the work of supervision of government administration.[41] Under the 1954 Constitution the Commission was later renamed the Ministry of Supervision within the State Council. However, this Ministry was abolished in 1959.[42] Mechanisms for administrative litigation and compensation were only to be developed in the 1980s.

Although Chinese scholars generally take the 1950s as a period in which administrative law was initially established, they also recognise the limited role it played and the restrictions on its development. Chief among these were the fundamental problems in the political system, including the fusion of the Party and the state, the denial of checks and balances as a government principle, the lack of the principle of *ultra vires*, and the practice of a personality cult that led to the words of the leaders replacing law and policy.[43] Nevertheless, from 1949 to 1956 a large number of laws dealing with state administration were issued.[44]

As discussed in Chapter Two, the 1957 Anti-rightist Movement – a movement seen by many Chinese scholars as essentially the beginning of the denial of democracy and rule of law[45] – marked the beginning of the end of efforts to rebuild a legal system in China. Thus the periodical publication of the *Collection of Laws of the People's Republic of China* (*Zhonghua Renmin Gongheguo Falü Huibian*)

---

40 Article 97 of the 1954 Constitution.

41 Yang Yifang & Chen Hanfeng (eds), *A Legal History of the People's Republic of China* (*Zhonghau Renmin Gongheguo Fazhishi*) (Haerbin: Helongjing People's Press, 1997), at 170-171.

42 See a Decision to Abolish the Ministry of Justice and the Ministry of Supervision, adopted by the First Plenary Session of the Second NPC on 28 April 1959.

43 Zhao Zhenjiang (ed.), *Forty Years of the Chinese Legal Systems* (*Zhongguo Fazhi Sishinian*) (Beijing: Beijing University Press, 1990), at 203.

44 Different scholars give varying numbers for issued regulations and rules, depending on their own methods of calculation and sources. Thus 829 pieces of such laws are identified by some Chinese scholars as having been issued from 1949–1956: Zhao Zhenjiang, *supra* note 43, at 200, while others have cited over 500 pieces of administrative law dealing with administrative structural issues and management between 1954 to 1957: Pi Chunxie, *supra* note 36, at 32. Still others believe that more than 870 administrative rules and regulations were issued from 1949–1957: Lin Feng, *Administrative Law Procedures and Remedies in China* (Hong Kong/London: Sweet & Maxwell, 1996), at 7.

45 Zhao Zhenjiang, *supra* note 43, at 204.

ceased in 1962, and so in 1966 did the State Council Gazette. During the Cultural Revolution (1966–1976) neither the Standing Committee of the NPC nor the State Council issued any significant administrative laws, but the major disruption to administrative law development came from the tight fusion of the Party and the Government. During this period, administrative instructions, orders or measures were often issued by the Central Committee of the Party alone, or jointly with the State Council. Regulations and rules made by the commissions or ministries of the State Council were often issued or endorsed by the Party. Sometimes the Military Commission of the Party also acted as an issuing authority.[46]

The present administrative law system is thus essentially a product of post-Mao China under the reformist leadership of Deng Xiaoping and his successors. It is claimed by Chinese scholars that the term 'administrative rules and regulations' (*xingzheng fagui*) was first used by Zhao Zhiyang, then the Premier of the State Council, in his Government Report to the Fourth Plenary Session of the 5th NPC in 1981.[47] However it was the 1982 Constitution, confirming the need for administrative litigation and the right to compensation for infringement of civil rights by state organs or functionaries,[48] that again provided a foundation for the development of administrative law.

Although administrative law developed rapidly in the 1980s, most administrative laws, regulations and rules were about the restructuring of government organisations and the institutionalisation of state administration. Checks and balances were not the major concerns of the time. The promulgation of the Administrative Litigation Law in 1989 signified a new concept, and began a new period of administrative law development in China. Thereafter, the control of power, if not the protection of individual rights, became a major academic focus, which is still being gradually translated into legislation and, to a certain degree, practice.

3. Changing Conceptions of Administrative Law in Contemporary China

There is no doubt that the re-emergence of administrative law has formed part of the effort to construct a government by law in post-Mao China. Initially, administrative law was conceived mainly as a body of law in which state administration was to be institutionalised, administrative functions and powers were to be defined and allocated among various administrative functionaries, such functions and powers were to be carried out effectively and efficiently, and the exercise of such powers

---

46 Yang & Chen, *supra* note 41, at 189-190.

47 Pi Chunxie, *supra* note 36, at 33.

48 See Article 41 of the Constitution.

was to be controlled.[49] Thus, one early text stated that 'administration is one of the basic functions of the state and a kind of organised activity for administering state affairs in order to realise the ideals of the ruling class.'[50] And 'administrative law is a general term referring to all the legal rules and regulations concerning the state administration.'[51] There was little discussion about the protection of individuals against the abuse or misuse of government powers, about checks and balances for government powers, and about redress and remedies for abuse and misuse of such powers. In fact, early textbooks also specifically rejected the idea of administrative law as being a law concerning checks and balances. It was argued that there was no fundamental conflict of interest between the government and the people; thus, the starting point and the ends of administrative law were to serve the people. 'Serving the people is the foundation of all the administrative rules and regulations in our country, and thus naturally becomes the theoretical basis of our administrative law.'[52]

This concept of administrative law is to be understood in the historical context of the times. For Deng Xiaoping the major problems inherent in the Party and state leadership and the cadre (bureaucratic) system were bureaucratisation, over-concentration of power, patriarchal methods, life tenure in leading posts, and privileges of various kinds.[53] Thus his major concern was the efficiency of government and not government accountability, at least not towards the governed. To deal with these problems, regulations were to be worked out to define the scope of powers allocated to particular posts, to regulate the political and material benefits of cadres at all levels, and to establish specific organisations to exercise supervision over the exercise of these powers and functions.[54] Indeed, on several occasions he unambiguously rejected the theory of separation of powers as a means for checks and balances of government powers.[55]

---

49 See Conita S.C. Leung, 'Conceptual and Constitutional Bases for Chinese Administrative Law', (1992) 17 (no. 58/59) *Bulletin of the Australian Society of Legal Philosophy* 175, at 177-178. See also Wen Zhengbang, *supra* note 1, at 207-208. Chinese scholars often describe such a concept of administrative law as a 'theory of administration' (*Guanli Lun*).

50 Ying Songnian & Zhu Weiju, *General Principles of Administrative Law* (*Xingzhengfa Zonglun*) (Beijing: Press of the Working People, 1985), at 5.

51 Ying & Zhu, *id.*, at 18.

52 Ying & Zhu, *id.*, at 102.

53 See Deng Xiaoping, 'On the Reform of the System of Party and State Leadership', in *Selected Works of Deng Xiaoping (1975–1982)* (Beijing: Foreign Languages Press, 1984), at 309. This speech by Deng was seen as a programmatic document guiding the reform of the political system. See Commentary by World Economic Herald, translated in (Spring 1987) (Vol. XX, no. 1) *Chinese Law and Government*, at 15.

54 Deng Xiaoping, *id.*, at 316.

55 See *Deng Xiaoping On Democracy and Legal Construction* (*Deng Xiaoping Lun Minzhu Yu Fazhi Jianshe*) (Beijing: Law Publishing House, 1994), at 35-38.

With this concept of administrative law and its emphasis on redefining the role of the state *vis-à-vis* the economy, a major difficulty soon emerged in relation to distinguishing administrative law from economic law; the latter being a Soviet-invented concept focusing on the role of the state in managing economic relations. Scholars of administrative law and economic law then began to battle for 'territory'.[56] By 1987, they settled on the 'agreement' that the scope of administrative law was to be confined to political spheres, i.e. to the areas of administrative organisation, administrative liability and administrative litigation, leaving the state management of the economy to the legal field they called 'administrative economic law'.[57] Since then administrative law has enjoyed rapid development, and different conceptions of administrative law began to emerge.

The adoption of the 1989 Administrative Litigation Law prompted some major rethinking of the nature of administrative law.[58] Nowhere is this shift of conception more clearly evidenced than in the preceding and subsequent discussions on the guiding principles of administrative law. In a standard university textbook on administrative law published in 1985[59] three fundamental principles guiding the development of administrative law were summarised: (1) the principle of implementing the Party's basic lines and policies; that is, administrative law is the main channel through which the Party's policies are institutionalised; (2) the principle of socialist democracy; that is, the purpose is to institutionalise the 'principle of democratic centralism' into law; and (3) the principle of socialist legality; that is, administration must be carried out in accordance with law.[60] Absent from the list are the principles of control or supervision of power.

In textbooks published in the 1990s scholars began to argue that principles of administrative law were unique and different from those of constitutional law or of administrative management, in that they were not political.[61] The above three principles were therefore rejected. It was argued that legality (*ultra vires*), reasonableness and fairness were the central principles of administrative law, which should

---

56 See Jianfu Chen, *From Administrative Authorisation to Private Law: A Comparative Perspective of the Developing Civil Law in the People's Republic of China* (Dordrech/Boston/London: Martinus Nijhoff Publishers, 1995), at 56-66.

57 See Jianfu Chen, *id.*, at 65.

58 Thus 1989 was seen as the beginning of a totally new development stage in the Chinese administrative law. See Luo Haocai, Jiang Ming'an, *et al.*, 'The Present Situation and Future Development of Administrative Law Research', (no. 1, 1996), *Legal Science in China* (*Zhongguo Faxue*) 41, at 42.

59 Ying & Zhu, *supra* note 50.

60 Ying & Zhu, *supra* note 50, at 112.

61 Ma Huaide, *supra* note 8, at 19.

govern all aspects of administration, including the granting, exercise, supervision and control of state administrative powers.[62]

There are now many 'theories' regarding the essence and the nature of administrative law, variously termed as a 'theory of administration' (*guanli lun*), a 'theory of control' (*kongquan lun*), a 'theory of balance' (*pingheng lun*), a 'theory of service' (*fuwu lun*), a 'theory of public powers' (*gonggong quanli lun*), etc.[63] Among these the 'theory of administration' (*guanli lun*), 'theory of control' (*kongquan lun*), and 'theory of balance' (*pingheng lun*) are most representative, others being variations of these.

As mentioned above, before 1987 the focus of administrative law was on administrative organisations and the general principles of administrative activities, including the structure and the nature of administrative organs, their classification and composition, their powers and working principles, as well as the management of public servants. At the time scholars generally emphasised that the function of administrative law was to secure the smooth operation of state administration, while supervision and control of administrative powers were neglected.[64] Thus opponents to such a conception of administrative law often referred to it as a 'theory of administration' or a 'theory of securing power'.[65]

The 'theory of control of power' is a result of Western influences. In contrast to the 'theory of administration', it basically advocates that the central task of administrative law is to provide mechanisms for the control of administrative, especially discretionary, powers. Its fundamental premise is that 'Power without checks and balances is destined to corrupt,'[66] clearly a paraphrase of Lord Acton's

---

62 See e.g. Luo Haocai (ed.), *Administrative Law* (*Xingzhengfa Xue*) (Beijing: Beijing University Press, 1996), at 30-35; Ma Huaide, *supra* note 8, at 19-25; and Wang Lianchang, *supra* note 31, at 43-57. See also Lin Feng, *supra* note 44, 23-27.

63 See Yang Xiejun, 'Some Comments on Various Basic Theories of Administrative Law', (no. 2, 1996) *Legal Science in China* (*Zhongguou Faxue*) 64, at 65; Pi Chunxi & Liu Yujie, 'A Review of Administrative Law Studies in 1996', (no. 1, 1997) *Jurists* (*Faxue Jia*) 29; 'The Search for a Theoretical Foundation of Administrative Law', (no. 5, 1996) *Peking University Law Journal* (*Zhongwai Faxue*) 51-60; and Luo Haocai (ed.), *A Theory of Balance of Contemporary Administrative Law* (*Xiandai Xingzhengfa de Pingheng Lilun*) (Beijing: Beijing University Press, 1997). See also Lin Feng, *supra* note 44, at 3-6. Here Lin identifies no less than ten 'definitions' of administrative law advocated by Chinese scholars. As all these theories are thin, some Chinese scholars insist that they can be better described as 'opinions' or 'views'. See Yang Xiejun, *id.*, at 65. For a more recent evaluation of these 'theories', see Yang Haikong & Zhang Zhiyuan, *A Study of the Basic Theories of Administrative Law in China* (*Zhongguo Xingzhengfa Jiben Lilun Yanjiu*) (Beijing: Beijing University Press, 2004), at 64-91.

64 Luo & Jiang, *supra* note 58, at 41.

65 See Yang & Zhang, *supra* note 63, at 69-70.

66 'The Road to Rule by Law – A Summary of Legal Construction and Democratic Developments since the 14th Congress', *People's Daily* (*Renmin Ribao*), internet edition, 3 September 1997.

famous dictum: 'Power tends to corrupt, and absolute power corrupts absolutely.'[67] Since its first emergence in around 1989 there has been some serious resistance to the acceptance of this theory. Many Chinese scholars believe that the political and social reality in China does not allow the total acceptance of such an idea. Politically, the politico-economic system in China is one in transition and necessarily includes the elements of both a planned and a market economy. In this system, administrative law cannot only focus on the control of power, but must also support state planning activities and authorities. Furthermore, in social terms, for administrative officials to accept the idea of being constrained by administrative law requires a period of adjustment. Administrative law in this transitional economy has to make compromises with traditional practice.[68] As one scholar put it: '[o]ur socialist administrative law theory cannot be the study of power control'.[69] Nevertheless, scholars in this 'school of thought', especially young scholars, have persisted, and by the turn of this century this theory had begun to gain mainstream acceptance among academics in China.[70]

There is a sharp contrast between the 'theory of administration' and the 'theory of power control'. In the latter, the essential function of administrative law is to control government power, to prevent, and to provide remedies for, violation of law and maladministration. In the former, administrative law is a means of administration with the purpose of securing the validity and legality of state administration.[71] Although few nowadays openly declare that administrative law is to secure powers for administrative organs, opposition to the 'theory of power control' has been persistent until quite recently.[72] Essentially, it is seen as having a fatal flaw, namely that it cannot guarantee that the administrative organs will positively and efficiently perform their functions.[73] To those who advocate the 'theory of administration', it is wrong to assert that administrative law only concerns the exercise and control of administrative powers; it also grants administrative powers and authority to administrative organs. Further, it is wrong to insist that securing administrative power is necessarily and diametrically oppose to the control of power; administrative

---

67 See Ronald C. Keith, *China's Struggle for the Rule of Law* (New York: St Martin's Press, 1994), at 80.

68 Pi Chunxi & Feng Jun, 'Some Considerations on the Loopholes in the "Theory of Balance" – The Direction for Improvement', (no. 2, 1997) *Legal Science in China* (*Zhongguo Faxue*) 40, at 48.

69 Ying & Zhu, *supra* note 50, at 103.

70 Yang & Zhang, *supra* note 63, at 69.

71 Pi & Feng, *supra* note 68, at 47.

72 Pi & Feng, *supra* note 68, at 47; Yang & Zhang, *supra* note 63, at 69.

73 Zhou Hanhua, 'Administrative Law-Making and Contemporary Administrative Law – the Developing Direction of Chinese Administrative Law', (no. 3, 1997) *CASS Journal of Law* (*Faxue Yanjiu*) 19, at 23.

law is capable of performing both functions. To deal with the problem of avoiding responsibilities in administration and to prevent Party interference in administration, it is necessary for administrative law to have the function of securing administrative powers.[74] It is clearly difficult for the two sides to be reconciled. A new theory was hence required and soon emerged.

The most influential and, to a certain extent, most controversial theory in China today is that of the 'theory of balance'. It was devised in the 1990s by Professor Luo Haocai, then a professor of law at Beijing University, who went on to become a Vice President of the Supreme People's Court, and is now a Vice-President of the Chinese People's Political Consultative Conference.[75] According to this theory, the essential relationship regulated by administrative law is a rights/duty relationship between an administrative organ and another party (a natural person or an organisation). This relationship has undergone some major changes in human history. In ancient times (in the Chinese terminology, in slave and feudal societies), it was one of inequality: citizens were the objects of administration in relation to administrative organs. Administrative law was thus a law of administration (*guanli fa*); it provided powers for administrative authorities and imposed duties on citizens. In modern times (in Chinese terminology, in capitalist societies) and under the Rule of Law and separation of powers, administrative law has undergone a major change from being a law of administration to being one of control. That is, the theoretical foundation of modern administrative law was established on the basis of a need for the control of administrative powers and the protection of the rights of citizens.[76] Although the theoretical foundation of modern administrative law is sound and it has played an important role in the historical development of administrative law, according to Luo and his colleagues this theory now needs major improvements. It has been particularly incapable of dealing with the conflict between democracy and efficiency and often sacrifices efficiency in order to maintain democracy. It is

---

74 Yang Xiejun, *supra* note 63, at 72-73.

75 With two students of his, Luo first systematically discussed the theory in an article published in 1993: Luo Haocai, Yuan Shuhong, & Li Wendong, 'Theoretical Foundation of Contemporary Administrative Law', (no. 1, 1993) *Legal Science in China* (*Zhongguou Faxue*) 52. In 1996, with Shen Kui, Luo further clarified certain theoretical points in responding to various criticisms of the theory: Luo Haocai & Shen Kui, 'A Theory of Balance: A Thought on the Nature of Modern Administrative Law – Some Further Discussions on the Theoretical Foundation of Contemporary Administrative Law', (no. 4, 1996) *Peking University Law Journal* (*Zhongwai Faxue*) 1; and Luo Haocai (ed.), *A Theory of Balance of Contemporary Administrative Law* (*Xiandai Xingzhengfa de Pingheng Lilun*) (Beijing: Beijing University Press, 1997). Thereafter many other scholars joined forces and further developed this theory. The more recent views and theories on this 'school of thought' are published in Luo Haocai (ed.), *The Development Trend in the Modern Administrative Law System* (*Xiandai Xingzhengfa de Fazhang Qushi*) (Beijing: Law Press, 2004). See also discussions in Yang & Zhang, *supra* note 63, at 65-68.

76 Luo, Yuan, & Li, *supra* note 73, at 52-53.

thus not conducive to rapid social and economic development.[77] They maintain that administrative powers must both be controlled and protected, and that citizens' rights must be similarly protected as well as restrained. Thus the relationship between administrative powers and citizens' rights is one of mutual control and balance. Administrative law is therefore neither a law of administration nor a law of control, but rather a law to secure and guarantee a balance between administrative powers and citizens' rights.[78] The theoretical foundation of contemporary administrative law is hence a 'theory of balance'. In the relationship between administrative organs and another party, the powers and duties between them should be balanced overall. In other words, law must give consideration not only to individual interests, but also to the interests of the state and the general public. In this sense the theory of balance may also be termed a 'theory of due consideration' (*jiangu lun*).[79] Since there is a power imbalance between the administrative organs and other parties, the 'theory of balance' places equal emphasis on administrative supervision, the protection of citizens' rights and the provision of administrative remedies.[80] In other words, control of power is an important function of administrative law but not the sole purpose of it.[81]

According to Luo and his supporters, an administrative law built upon the theory of administration is simply a reflection of the law of a planned economy, and the latter itself is a target of reform. On the other hand, an administrative law focusing on control of power does not meet the needs of China, nor its actual situation. Only an administrative law under the theory of balance would be able to clarify the relationship between government and enterprises, to transform the functions of government, and to promote and enhance the establishment and development of a socialist market economy in China.[82]

Since the initial emergence of the 'theory of balance' it has attracted a great deal of attention and aroused some intensive discussion among Chinese scholars,[83] with

---

77 Luo, Yuan, & Li, *supra* note 73, at 53-54.

78 Luo, Yuan, & Li, *supra* note 73, at 54.

79 Luo, Yuan, & Li, *supra* note 73, at 54.

80 Luo, Yuan, & Li, *supra* note 73, at 54.

81 It is in fact on this basis that a new approach within the 'theory of balance' has emerged, with the argument that the theory of balance is a means to control power by balancing administrative power and citizens' rights. See Yang & Zhang, *supra* note 63, at 66.

82 Luo, Yuan, & Li, *supra* note 75.

83 A special seminar was held in Beijing University in 1996. See 'The Search for a Theoretical Foundation for Administrative Law', (no. 5, 1996) *Peking University Law Journal* (*Zhongwai Faxue*) 51.

some supporting it,[84] others criticising it,[85] and still others making suggestions for improvement.[86]

There have been a number of major criticisms of the basic premises upon which the 'theory of balance' has been constructed. First, the characterisation of administrative law in different historical stages is criticised as being too general and sweeping, and as ignoring different situations and developments in different countries.[87] Secondly, it is argued that the 'theory of balance' is based on the presumption that there is no fundamental conflict between the interests of the individuals, the public and the state, and that presumption is false.[88] Thirdly, the conceptual foundation of a specific branch of law must be unique to it. The 'theory of balance' as a 'theory of due consideration' is declared not to be unique to administrative law and thus it cannot be a theoretical foundation for administrative law.[89] Finally, and more importantly, it is argued that the distinction between the balance of powers and control of powers is unclear. In reality the notion of 'overall balance' can only mean a 'compromise' of citizens' rights.[90] Further, it lacks clear criteria for the power balance; the power/duty relationship between an administrative organ and another party can never be balanced and, in any case, achieving a balance is not a unique function of administrative law.[91] 'Due consideration' or 'balance' cannot be used as

84 See, for instance, Yuan Shuhong, 'Contemporary Administrative Law Is by its Nature a Law of Balance', (no. 5, 1996) *Peking University Law Journal* (*Zhongwai Faxue*) 51; Jiang Ming'An, 'Delegation of Powers, Separation of Powers and Control of Powers – The Reasons for the Existence of Administrative Law on the Theory of Balance', (no. 5, 1996) *Peking University Law Journal* (*Zhongwai Faxue*) 51; Yang Haikong, 'The Theoretical Foundation of Administrative Law – Government Under Law', (no. 5, 1996) *Peking University Law Journal* (*Zhongwai Faxue*) 53.

85 See, for instance, Yang Zhongwen & Liu Chuanping, 'Control of Power – Balance of Power: On the Nature of Administrative Law', (no. 2, 1997) *Journal of Seeking Truth from Facts* (*Qiushi Xuekang*) 55; Cheng Yi, 'The Problems with the "Theory of Balance"', (no. 4, 1996) *Administrative Law Review* (*Xingzheng Faxue Yanjiu*) 38; Ye Bifeng, 'Several Issues concerning the Theoretical Foundation of Administrative Law', (no. 5, 1997) *Law Review* (*Faxue Pinglun*) 18.

86 See, for instance, Pi & Feng, *supra* note 68, at 40.

87 Pi & Feng, *supra* note 68, at 43-44.

88 Yang Xiejun, *supra* note 63, at 68.

89 Yang Xiejun, *id.*, at 68.

90 Cheng Yi, *supra* note 85, at 38.

91 Xue Gangling, 'On the Purposes, Means and System of Administrative Law', (no. 3, 1997) *Journal of China University of Political Science and Law* (*Zhengfa Luntan*) 94, at 95. See also Yang Xiejun, *supra* note 63, at 69-72.

a criterion to substitute for the notion of 'justice' and 'fairness'.[92] Thus, the 'theory of balance' is impractical and inoperable.[93]

These criticisms clearly expose the weakness of the theory. However, its emergence is best understood in the context of contending theories and of the search for a new theoretical foundation for administrative law which could be accommodated within the present political system, while also providing mechanisms for control of power. It is precisely in this context that the 'theory of balance' has been a most attractive one, as it is neither conservative nor radical. It does not reject the notion of control of power, but at the same time it is able to avoid its perceived negative aspect, namely the sacrifice of efficiency, in order to maintain democracy. It thus meets the needs of China, namely to control the abuse of power, while still not being seen as hindering rapid social and economic development.[94] Although the notion of 'balance' cannot substitute for that of 'justice' and 'fairness' as the ends of law, the vague concept of 'balance' can allow various means and mechanisms to be introduced for the purpose of control of powers. Here, it seems to me, the 'theory of balance' is sensitive in approaching the ends of law in a politically delicate environment.

Furthermore, the 'theory of balance' is not without constitutional foundation. After all, the Constitution insists that any exercise of individual rights must be balanced against the interests of the state, the society and the collective, and the interests of others.[95] Also, Article 1 of the Administrative Litigation Law, which provides that the administrative law is enacted to protect the rights and interests of citizens, legal persons and other organisations, and to safeguard and supervise the administration organs in the exercise of their authority and functions, also seems to be a reflection of the 'theory of balance'. The emphasis Wang Hanbin gave to the due purpose of the ALL (to protect rights and to safeguard administrative organs), when he delivered the Explanation of the (Draft) Administrative Litigation Law of the PRC to the NPC in 1989, also re-enforces this view.[96] Although scholars advocating a 'theory of control of power' insist that such an interpretation is unacceptable, and

---

92 Cheng Yi, *supra* note 85, at 41.

93 Cheng Yi, *id.*, at 41.

94 Pi & Feng, *supra* note 68, at 48-49. Precisely for the same reason it was also severely criticised as a typical reflection of the culture of compromise. See Lü Taifeng, 'On the New Revolution of the Administrative Law Science', (no. 6, 1995) *Journal of Zhengzhou University* (*Zhengzhou Daxue Xuebao*), at 47.

95 See Article 51 of the 1982 Constitution.

96 Wang Hanbin, 'Explanation of the (Draft) Administrative Litigation Law of the PRC', delivered at the 2nd Session of the Seventh NPC on March 28, 1989, translated in (no. 3, 1991) *Chinese Law and Government* 35, at 35.

that the sole purpose of the ALL is to protect citizen's lawful rights and interests,[97] they seem to confuse a moral argument with a legal interpretation.

Whatever the controversy about this 'theory of balance',[98] and despite its various weaknesses, it is undoubtedly the most prominent, most sophisticated, most influential and, perhaps, most realistic theory on administrative law in contemporary China,[99] although by no means universally supported.[100]

4. Administrative Decision Making and Reconsideration

4.1. The Concept of Administrative Acts

A central concept in the Chinese administrative law is that of the administrative act (*xingzheng xingwei*). An administrative act refers to an action taken by an administrative authority in performing its administrative functions or exercising an administrative power.[101] It is the originator of legal consequences and hence the foundation of administrative law.[102] Put simply, administrative acts refer to rule- and decision-making activities by administrative authorities.

Chinese scholars often classify administrative acts into internal and external acts, depending on the parties affected by the acts, or into rule-making, enforcement or administrative adjudicative acts (*xingzheng sifa xingwei*), depending on the nature of the acts, or individually into licensing acts, permitting acts or punishing acts, etc.[103] Central to an understanding of the Chinese administrative law, however, is the distinction between abstract and concrete administrative acts,[104] with the two

---

97 See Zhang Shuyi, 'A Re-examination of Several Controversial Issues in the Administrative Litigation Law (draft)', (no. 3, 1989) *Jurisprudence* (*Faxue*) 8, translated in (no. 3, 1991) *Chinese Law and Government* 47.

98 Thanks to the controversy the theory has in fact been developed largely in response to various criticisms. Here perhaps is a lesson for China: academic freedom does produce practical results. In a sense, as pointed out by Yang & Zhang (*supra* note 63, at 75), it was the debate on the 'theory of balance' that first provided an opportunity for the development of administrative law and its theories in China.

99 See Yang & Zhang, *supra* note 63, at 68.

100 Yang & Zhang, *supra* note 63, at 77.

101 See Luo Haocai (ed.), *Administrative Law* (*Xingzhengfa Xue*) (Beijing: Beijing University Press, 1996), at 105-106. See also Ying Songnian (ed.), *Law on Administrative Acts* (*Xingzheng Xingwei Fa*) (Beijing: People's Press, 1993).

102 Luo Haocai (1996), *id.*, at 105-107.

103 See Luo Haocai (1996), *id.*, at 114-124. See also Yang & Zhang, *supra* note 63, at 199-200; Lin Feng, *supra* note 44, at 29-41.

104 It should be pointed out that this distinction, though firmly embedded in the Chinese administrative laws, has been controversial, particularly in recent years. The distinction has

kinds of acts attracting different supervision and control mechanisms and legal remedies. The former refers to those activities aimed at the general public, which can be repeatedly carried out; while the latter are those administrative activities of administrative organs which are aimed at specified events or individuals, and can only be carried out once.[105] A common example given by Chinese scholars is the following: in a case where a pricing bureau imposes a fine on a certain iron and steel company for its unlawful practice, the penalty is a concrete administrative activity, while the penalty clause formulated by the price bureau is an abstract administrative activity.[106] In other words, an abstract administrative act refers to the formulation of general rules and policies applicable to the general public, whereas a concrete administrative act is the exercise of powers or discretion with respect to a particular person, or an organisation or a specific social event.[107] Abstract administrative acts therefore effectively mean rule-making activities by administrative authorities. As discussed in the previous chapter on law-making, such activities are regulated by an increasing number of procedural rules issued by various rule-making authorities and, more recently, by the Law on Law-making.[108] The existing framework for administrative control and remedies mainly covers concrete administrative acts.

For practical purposes the notion of 'concrete administrative acts' has been applied in all major administrative legislation without any official definition.[109] Existing legislation now includes at least the following concrete administrative acts: the granting or refusal of permits or licences; decisions relating to rewards,

---

been heavily criticised both in and outside China, principally because it has caused some major difficulties in the practice of administrative law, in its failure to make a large section of administrative activities (e.g. abstract actions) accountable in law. Some Chinese scholars now advocate that this distinction should be abolished in law and that legal scholars should stop using this distinction in their writing. See Yang & Zhang, *supra* note 63, at 203-206. However, until the distinction is abolished in Chinese law it is the most important distinction in the practice of Chinese administrative law.

105 Xiao Xun, 'Several Questions Concerning the Administrative Litigation Law', *People's Daily* (*Renmin Ribao*), 10 March 1991, at 5, translated into English in FBIS-CHI-91-056, at 22-26.

106 Xiao Xun, *id.*, at 5.

107 See Luo Haocai (1996), *supra* note 101, at 116-117. See also Edward J. Epstein, 'Administrative Litigation Law: Citizens Can Sue the State but not the Party', (1 June 1989) *China News Analysis* 1, at 5.

108 See discussion in Chapter 5 on Law-making

109 E.g. Article 5 of the Administrative Litigation Law and Article 1 of the Administrative Reconsideration Law. Although the State Compensation Law and the Administrative Penalties Law do not apply the term 'concrete administrative acts', the concept is implicitly applied in defining the scope of application of the laws (see Articles 2 and 15 of the State Compensation Law and Articles 2 and 8 of the Administrative Penalties Law). See also Luo Haocai (1996), *supra* note 101, at 105. Similarly, the Administrative Licensing Law does not use the term – the Law only deals with 'concrete administrative actions' as understood in Chinese jurisprudence.

punishments, appointments or dismissal, or payments by administrative authorities; the levy of charges and fees; the imposition of administrative penalties; the use of compulsory administrative measures (e.g. freezing of property or restrictions on personal freedom); and decisions of administrative adjudication.[110] Since the term is not defined by any law, its scope can be expanded by direct legal provisions either through amending the existing laws or by enacting new laws.

In the absence of a legislative definition, the Supreme People's Court endeavoured to provide some guidance on concrete administrative acts. According to the Court,

> 'concrete administrative acts' refer to unilateral actions or conduct directed to specific matters and the rights and interests of specific citizens, legal persons or other organisations, and carried out by state administrative organs and their officials, organisations authorised by laws, organisations or individuals entrusted by the administrative organs to exercise their powers or duties during the performance of their administrative functions.[111]

This definition, however, immediately attracted some severe criticism from Chinese scholars. In particular, it was criticised for being too narrow in defining reviewable actions.[112] Facing increasing criticism from scholars, the Supreme People's Court issued another set of interpretations in 2000, which replaced the above Opinions.[113] The new Interpretations have abandoned the efforts to define the notion of 'concrete administrative actions'. Instead, a general definition of 'administrative actions' is provided. As has been pointed out by some Chinese scholars,[114] in spite of the good intentions of the Court to respond to criticisms and to expand the scope of reviewable actions, the Court in fact has failed in its legal duty to provide clear guidance on an essential legal notion that clearly needs clarification, if not definition. As such, uncertainties in administrative litigation and review will continue in the foreseeable future, until and unless the relevant laws are revised and the distinction is abolished by law.

---

110 See Article 11 of the Administrative Litigation Law; Article 6 of the Administrative Reconsideration Law.

111 Article 1 of the Opinions of the Supreme People's Court on Some Issues Relating to the Implementation of the Administrative Litigation Law (For Trial Implementation), adopted on 29 May 1991 and issued on 11 June 1991. An English translation appears in Lin Feng, *supra* note 44, at 332-345.

112 See Yang & Zhang, *supra* note 63, at 199.

113 See Interpretation on Certain Questions Concerning the Implementation of the Administrative Litigation Law of the PRC, issued on 8 March 2000.

114 See Yang & Zhang, *supra* note 63, at 200.

4.2. The Legal Framework

Procedural justice is seen in the West as the core of democracy. The essence of justice, we are reminded, is largely procedural.[115] 'The history of liberty has largely been the history of procedural safeguards', Justice Frankfurter declared.[116] 'It is procedure that spells much of the difference between rule by law and rule by whim or caprice'.[117] In other words, means is as important as ends, if not more so. In the case of China, the legal framework providing procedural justice is fragmented and weak, but its importance is being increasingly recognised. This recognition is reflected in the changing conceptions of administrative law.

The initial conception of administrative law as a 'law of administration', focusing heavily on the structure and jurisdiction, rather than on the processes of government or on the procedural protection of individual rights, still commands a certain influence among scholars and officials, and so the efforts to draft a law governing administrative processes, or to set out certain procedural standards for administrative decision-making, have been difficult to bring to fruition. Indeed, in spite of scholars advocating the drafting of an administrative procedural law for many years,[118] the making of such a law still has to make its way onto the legislative agenda of the NPC or its Standing Committee.[119] That is not to say, however, that there has been no law

[115] K.C. Davis, *Administrative Law Text*, 3rd edition (St Paul Minn: West Publishing Co. 1972), at 192, cited in Michael D. Bayle, *Procedural Justice: Allocating to Individuals* (Dordrecht/Boston/London: Kluwer Academic Publishers, 1990), at 1.

[116] Quoted in Bayle, *id.*

[117] Quoted in Bayle, *id.*

[118] See *A Study on Administrative Procedure Law* (*Xingzheng Chengxu Fa Yanjiu*), being a special issue of the *Administrative Law Review* (*Xingzheng Fa Yanjiu*) (June 1992). See also Jianfu Chen, 'Some Thoughts on Certain Fundamental Issues in Relation to the Making of an Administrative Procedure Law', (no. 2, 1996) *Administrative Law Review* (*Xingzheng Fa Yanjiu*) 58. According to Chinese scholars, a draft bill has been prepared by the Administrative Law Research Group within the Legislative Affairs Committee of the Standing Committee of the NPC and has been submitted to the Legislative Affairs Committee for consideration. See Wang Wanhua, 'The Choice of Chinese Law-making and the Legislative Outline of an Administrative Procedures Law', (no. 8, 2005) *Reprinted Newspaper and Journal Materials: D411 Constitutional and Administrative Law* (*Xianfaxue Xingzhengfaxu*) 3.

[119] The latest legislative plan, the 2007 law-making plan, includes the revision of the State Compensation Law and the making of a law on compulsory administrative measures, but not the administrative procedures law. See 'The Standing Committee outlines its 2007 law-making plan', in <www.legaldaily.com.cn/mis/2007-03/02/content_548464.htm> (last accessed 2 March 2007). In fact, whether China should enact a uniform law on administrative procedures is still an issue under debate. See Jiang Ming'an, 'Eight Major Relationships concerning the Administrative Procedure Legislation', (no. 4, 2006) *Reprinted Newspaper and Journal Materials: D411 Constitiutional and Administrative Law* (*Xianfaxue Xingzhengfaxu*) 23.

in China governing the processes of administrative decision-making.[120]

The earliest regulations governing the administrative decision-making process were the Provisional Regulations Governing the Protection of Invention and Patents, issued by the Council of Government Administration in 1951.[121] Under these Regulations applicants were granted the right to be given reasons and to have access to all the materials upon which the original decisions were made. These Regulations also provided applicants with rights to internal reconsideration and to litigation in courts. However, these procedural requirements were isolated and were soon to be abolished when the above Regulations were replaced in 1963 by the Regulations on Rewarding Invention and Regulations on Rewarding Improvements in Science and Technology.[122]

Serious discussions on procedural justice began in the mid-1980s, which also coincided with the emergence of advocacy for regulating administrative decision-making.[123] Although a comprehensive code on administrative procedures is yet to be produced, certain individual laws or regulations have been issued governing various kinds of administrative decision-making processes. These rules have been drafted in line with the distinction between abstract and concrete administrative acts. Most procedural requirements are incorporated into various individual regulations dealing with aspects of state administration, such as the Regulations Concerning Punishment in the Administration of Public Order,[124] the Land Management Law of the PRC, the Provisional Regulations Governing the Settlement of Labour Disputes in State-owned Enterprises, and the Administrative Penalties Law.[125] Internal reviews of administrative decisions are regulated by the Administrative Reconsideration Law (1999).[126] As with the Civil Code, it is likely that more individual laws and regulations incorporating procedural requirements will be made before a comprehensive procedural law is drafted.[127]

---

120 Indeed a recent collection of such rules amounts to nearly 900 pages. See Wang Wanhua (ed.), *A Collection of Administrative Procedural Laws in China* (*Zhongguo Xingzheng Chengxufa Huibian*) (Beijing: China Legal System Press, 2004).

121 Yang & Chen, *supra* note 41 at 169.

122 Yang & Chen, *id.*, at 169-172.

123 See Jianfu Chen, *supra* note 118.

124 Now replaced by the Law concerning Punishment in the Administration of Public Order, adopted by the Standing Committee of the National People's Congress on 28 August 2005 and effective from 1 March 2006.

125 See Luo Haocai (1996), *supra* note 101, at 301.

126 Prior to the 1999 Law, they were regulated by the Regulations on Administrative Reconsideration issued in 1991.

127 The Administrative Penalties Law (1996), which incorporates detailed procedural requirements for decision-making, is a good indication that China may well adopt a piecemeal approach towards regulating administrative decision-making. Interviews with Chinese scholars and

4.3. Procedural Requirements

As mentioned above, there is no generally applicable law governing the procedures of administrative decision-making, but the 1996 Administrative Penalties Law (APL) and the 2003 Law on Administrative Licensing (LAL) so far stipulate the most comprehensive procedural requirements. Although these may not necessarily be the most representative of procedural requirements in China, the problems they deal with, namely the misuse and abuse of administrative powers and the lack of procedural control of administrative decision-making, are identical in nature to the problems that a comprehensive code on administrative processes would cover. These laws may thus well be the blueprints for future legislation in this area. We therefore now turn to an examination of the APL and LAL as representing the emerging requirements for procedural justice in China.

In the early period of the PRC the power to impose administrative penalties was granted to administrative organs by the Council of Government Administration, and the procedures for such decision-making and the prescription of the kinds of penalties were decided by the administrative organs themselves.[128] Although various regulations were issued by the bureaucracy imposing strict penalties, typically, as in other areas of the exercise of administrative powers, there were few provisions controlling the possible misuse or abuse of such powers.[129] In the early post-Mao period an increasing number of laws and regulations were issued, prescribing various kinds of 'administrative' penalties.[130] Since there was no law governing the prescription of penalties, nor for the application of such penalties, and since such prescription and use of penalties fall exclusively within the domain of administrative powers, several major problems soon emerged. First, an increasing number of penalties were prescribed by various administrative authorities, many of which had no authority to do so. Secondly, enforcement of such penalties was carried out by a large number of authorities, many having no such jurisdiction at all. Thus, one offence was often penalised by several administrative authorities. Thirdly, without

---

legislative officials also confirm such an approach. See also Ma Huaide, 'Problems within the Administrative Permit System and a Legislative Proposal', (no. 3, 1997) *Legal Science in China* (*Zhongguo Faxue*) 40. As mentioned above (*supra* note 119), there is currently a legislative plan to enact a law on administrative compulsory measures which will also define procedures for making compulsory measures.

128 Yang & Chen, *supra* note 41, at 164.

129 Yang & Chen, *supra* note 41, at 164-165.

130 By the time the Administrative Penalties Law was adopted in 1996, over 100 types of administrative penalties had been prescribed by various laws and regulations. See Dingjian Cai, 'Introduction to the Administrative Penalty Law of China', (1996) 10 *Columbian Journal of Asian Law* 259, at 259. These laws and regulations are collected in a 1000-page volume: Editorial Board, *A Handbook of Legal Sources on Administrative Penalties* (*Xingzheng Chufa Falü Yiju Shouce*) (Beijing: Press of the Chinese Legal System, 1997).

a control mechanism, penalties were often arbitrarily enforced and the aggrieved parties had few legal remedies for redress.[131] The APL was thus enacted in 1996 to deal with these problems.[132] It is not itself designed to impose penalties: administrative penalties will continue to be prescribed by laws and administrative regulations and rules.[133] In this sense it is a procedural rather than a substantive law.

Similarly, the practice of establishing and imposing various administrative licensing requirements suffered the same shortcomings in the administrative system. There is no doubt that administrative licensing is a major government function involving government organs issuing formal legal permission to conduct business or other activities. However, as a result of the monetary incentive to impose licences or approval requirements, more and more licensing matters were created and implemented, especially in the 1980s and 1990s, either by the central government and its various subordinates, or by local governments and their agencies at various levels.[134] It is clear that such uncontrolled licensing has been a major source of corruption.

To constrain the tendency of bureaucracies to subject the economy to unnecessary and excessive administrative licensing requirements, to streamline the creation and enforcement of administrative licensing, and to ensure the effectiveness and efficiency of administrative management, China began to draft a national law in 1996.[135] After seven years of work and deliberation the Law on Administrative Licensing (LAL) was adopted on 27 August 2003 by the NPC Standing Committee as part of government reform.[136] The Licensing Law aims to help the government to stop closed-door deals, and to prevent and check corruption in the issuing of administrative licences, given the fact that in recent years most of the corrupt officials

---

131 See Chao Zhi, Secretary-General of the Standing Committee of the NPC, 'Explanations on the (Draft) Administrative Penalties Law of the PRC', delivered to the 4th Plenary Session of the 8th NPC on 12 March 1996, (1996) 3 *Gazette of Standing Committee of the National People's Congress of the PRC* (*Zhonghua Renmin Gongheguo Quanguo Renmin Daibiao Dahui Changwu Weiyuanhui Gongbao*) 15, at 15. See also Dingjian Cai, *supra* note 130, 259.

132 Chao Zhi, *id.*, at 15.

133 Most notably, Law concerning Punishment in the Administration of Public Order; Law on Public Demonstration and Assembly; Emergency Law, Law on the Administration of Entering and Leaving the Country of Foreigners, Law on the Administration of Entering and Leaving the Country of Chinese Nationals; Regulations on *Laojiao*, Provisional Measures on *Laojiao*, Law on Land Management, Environment Protection, etc. For a comprehensive collection of these laws and rules, see *A Handbook of Legal Sources on Administrative Penalties*, *supra* note 130.

134 There were no less than 4,000 matters requiring licensing from the State Council authorities alone in China in 2003. See Yang & Zhang, *supra* note 63, at 319.

135 See 'The Background on the Making of the Administrative Licensing Law', in <news.xinhuanet.com/zhengfu/2003-08/28/content_1048857.htm> (last accessed 17 June 2007). For a more detailed study on the making of the Law, see Yang & Zhang, *supra* note 63, at 330-342.

136 It took effect on 1 July 2004.

behind bars were involved in such acts, as well as to increase the transparency of administrative approval procedures, and to narrow the scope of activities requiring a licence, the dangerous expansion of which has seriously hampered China's efforts to build a market economy.

Essentially, both LAL and APL are procedural laws,[137] with the clear aim of controlling administrative powers in imposing licensing requirements or penalties, by means of setting out a clear scope of legal authority and clear procedures for exercising such authority. As the procedural requirements are similar in both laws,[138] the following discussion on the procedural requirements that now exist in China is based on the APL.

The APL is quite comprehensive, consisting of 64 articles in eight chapters. It starts with a chapter which provides the general principles of the law. This is followed by provisions governing the types of penalties and their prescription by law. Chapter Three then defines the enforcement authorities, and is followed by a chapter on their jurisdiction and the application of penalties. Chapter Five provides procedures for decision-making on penalties. Chapter Six deals with the enforcement of penalties imposed through legal procedures. Reflecting the efforts to control the misuse or abuse by administrative organs and personnel, liabilities for administrative organs and personnel violating the Law in imposing or enforcing administrative penalties are codified separately in Chapter Seven. The last chapter deals with the operation of the Law and its relationship with the previously issued laws and regulations. The APL is best understood from the fundamental principles that run through the Law.

(1) Legality

The APL makes it clear that the prescription, imposition and enforcement of administrative penalties must have a legal basis and must be carried out in accordance with the procedures prescribed in the Law.[139] It is worth noting here that the imposition and enforcement of administrative penalties are seen as concrete administrative actions,[140] and thus subject to administrative litigation.

First, the power to impose administrative penalties is now more strictly controlled. Restrictions on personal freedoms as a kind of penalty are reserved as an exclusive prerogative of the NPC or its Standing Committee.[141] Even though

---

[137] Yang & Zhang, *supra* note 63, at 335.

[138] Of course there are differences between the two laws. For instance, the LAL makes a major effort to ensure that licensing procedures will not be unnecessarily burdensome on applicants and that decisions will be made efficiently (mostly with a deadline).

[139] See Articles 2 and 3 of the APL.

[140] Luo Haocai (1996), *supra* note 101, at 201.

[141] Article 9 of the APL.

administrative rules and regulations may impose any kind of penalties other than restricting personal freedoms, once laws have already imposed such penalties, administrative rules and regulations may only provide for detailed implementation within the scope provided by the enabling laws.[142] Similar requirements also apply to local rules. However, local rules are also excluded from imposing such penalties as revocation of enterprise business licences.[143] Governments at provincial level and ministries and commissions under the State Council are only allowed to provide detailed rules dealing with specified acts and types of penalties within the scope already provided by laws and administrative regulations. In the absence of such laws and regulations, they are only allowed to impose warnings or fines of limited amounts. No other normative documents are allowed to impose administrative penalties.[144] This allocation of legislative power is interpreted to mean that it is mainly the central legislative authorities and government that have the power to impose administrative penalties; local authorities, either through local laws or government rules, have only the power to supplement centrally issued provisions.[145] Although some Chinese scholars see this strict allocation of powers to impose penalties, and hence its inflexibility, as one of the major problems with the APL,[146] it is perhaps the only possible and effective response to the flourishing of administrative penalties in present-day China. The APL further specifies the common types of administrative penalty, namely: warnings, fines, confiscation of unlawfully acquired property and income, order of cessation of business production and operation, temporary withholding or revocation of licences or permits, and administrative detention.[147] This list is however not exhaustive, as the APL allows laws and administrative regulations to impose other types of penalty.[148]

Secondly, administrative penalties can only be enforced by authorities specifically authorised by law and within their authorised scope.[149] Under the Law, the State Council, or provincial governments authorised by the State Council, are to designate an administrative organ in charge of enforcing administrative penalties – with the

142 Article 10 of the APL.

143 Article 11 of the APL.

144 Articles 12, 13 & 14 of the APL.

145 See Luo Haocai (1996), *supra* note 101, at 206. See also Chao Zhi, *supra* note 131, at 16.

146 Zhou Hanhua, *supra* note 73, at 31.

147 Article 8 of APL.

148 Article 8 of the APL. *Laojiao* as administrative detention, for instance, is not in the list. It is certainly a commonly used type of administrative penalty. From interviews with Chinese scholars, it is understood that *Laojiao* was deliberately left out as the Criminal Law was then being revised. At the time it was unclear whether *Laojiao* would be incorporated into the Criminal Law or be abolished altogether. In the end, *Laojiao* was also left out in the revision of the Criminal Law. See Chapter 7 on Criminal Law.

149 Article 15 of the APL.

exception of restriction of personal freedoms, which can only be enforced by the police force.[150] Other enforcing authorities include organisations authorised by laws or administrative regulations to manage public affairs, or other organisations entrusted by administrative organs in accordance with the laws and administrative regulations. Such entrustment can only be made to institutions with responsibility for managing public affairs. Such entrusted institutions must have personnel familiar with the laws, regulations and rules and their professional trades and, if technical inspection or confirmation is required to be carried out, they must be qualified for the required inspections or confirmation.[151] Further, the entrusting authorities have the responsibility of supervising the entrusted organs and will assume the consequences of acts done by the entrusted organs.[152] Finally, the imposition of legally prescribed penalties and the enforcement of such penalties must be carried out in accordance with the procedures prescribed by the APL. These procedures incorporate elements of the Western concept of natural justice, that is, fairness and openness, proportionality; double jeopardy, and the principle of remedies.

(2) Fairness and Openness

Perhaps the most impressive element of the APL is the incorporation of the principle of fairness and openness,[153] which is implemented by detailed rules in Chapter Five governing the decision-making processes.

To ensure openness, the Law first requires transparency by requiring that all laws and regulations imposing penalties must be published; unpublished documents shall not be used as a legal basis for imposing penalties.[154] Secondly, enforcement personnel are required to disclose their own identities when imposing penalties.[155] Thirdly, Article 42 requires that a hearing procedure shall be instituted in cases where there are serious penalties, including the order of cessation of production or business operation, revocation of licences or permits, or imposition of a large fine. Under this procedure, a hearing must be open to the public unless the case involves state secrets, business confidentiality or personal privacy.[156] To ensure that a hearing is actually carried out, persons or organisations affected by the penalties must be informed of the right to a hearing before a penalty decision is made. Further, the

150 Article 16 of the APL.

151 Articles 17, 18 & 19 of the APL.

152 Article 18 of the APL.

153 See Article 4 of the APL.

154 Article 4 of the APL.

155 Article 34 of the APL.

156 Article 42(3) of the APL.

affected party, who must request such a hearing within three days of being notified of such a right, shall not be responsible for the costs in relation to such a hearing.[157]

Specific provisions are also enacted to ensure that fairness is not an empty principle. The right to know, including the right to know the reasons and legal basis of the penalty decision and to be informed of one's rights under the Law[158] before a penalty decision is made, are provided in Article 31. The same is required to be stated in the penalty decision.[159] Article 32 provides the right to be heard, and imposes on the administrative authority which imposes the penalty an obligation to investigate the facts, reasons and evidence raised by the person receiving the penalty. Article 41 further provides that a decision to impose a penalty without informing the affected party of the right to know and the right to be heard is invalid, unless the person affected by the decision has waived these rights. To guarantee the exercise of such rights, no administrative authority is allowed to increase the penalty simply because the affected party offers a defence.[160] To avoid possible prejudice, it is required that investigation must be carried out by at least two persons and that a decision to impose penalties shall be made by the person in charge of the administrative authority, not by those persons who investigate the case.[161] It is also required that, if a hearing is held, the hearing must be chaired by a person not involved in the investigation of the case. Further, the affected party has a right to request the withdrawal of the chairperson if he/she considers that person has a direct interest in the case.[162] Finally, the principle of proportionality also applies, that is, punishment must fit the 'crime'.[163] For this purpose, certain mitigating factors are listed in Article 27.[164] In addition to these legal provisions, Chinese scholars also hold that the principle of reasonableness also requires that no irrelevant factor is taken into account in making penalty decisions and the intention to impose a penalty must fit the purpose of administration.[165] The latter may be interpreted to mean that a penalty must be imposed in good faith and not out of personal malice or prejudice.

---

157 Article 42 of the APL.

158 For instance, the right to request a hearing under Article 42 and the right to administrative reconsideration and to appeal to court under Article 45.

159 Article 39 of the APL.

160 Article 32 of the APL.

161 Articles 37 & 38 of the APL.

162 See Article 42 (4) of the APL.

163 Article 4 of the APL.

164 These are: (1) if a person voluntarily eliminates or alleviates the endangering consequences of the unlawful act; (2) if the unlawful act is done under duress; (3) if a person cooperates with the administrative authority in its investigation and the consequential punishment; (4) if mitigation is provided by law.

165 See Luo Haocai (1996), *supra* note 101, at 207.

(3) Double Jeopardy

The incorporation of the principle of double jeopardy is to deal with the common problem of one unlawful act being penalised by many different administrative authorities.[166] Thus the APL specifically provides that 'for the same unlawful act, no administrative organ shall impose fines twice.'[167] However, the Law does not prohibit the imposition of two different kinds of penalty for the same unlawful act, nor prohibit the imposition of administrative penalties in addition to criminal sanctions should the unlawful act also be a criminal offence.[168]

(4) Principle of Remedies

Chinese scholars also hold that there is a principle which provides that where there are no legal remedies, there should be no penalties. In other words, on every ground on which a penalty may be imposed, there must be a legal channel for reconsideration and/or appeal.[169] Indeed, the APL specifically provides a right to defence against the imposition of administrative penalties and a right to administrative reconsideration and appeal to court. It further provides a right to compensation if the affected party suffers damages due to the unlawful imposition of administrative penalties.[170]

(5) Evaluation

In summary, the APL (and the LAL), which has now incorporated many procedural protection mechanisms known in Western legal systems, is an impressive law in terms of providing procedural protection to people subject to administrative penalties, and of restraining government discretionary power in decision-making. The APL does however have some major problems. The most serious forms of administrative penalties are those under the *Laojiao* regulations. It is unclear whether decisions regarding penalties under these regulations would be subject to public hearing. Further, and more fundamentally, it is questionable whether many of the administrative penalties should be classified as administrative in nature, when personal freedoms may be restricted for up to four years. In fact, the incorporation of many of the criminal procedural law principles seems to indicate that they are in

---

[166] See Luo Haocai (1996), *id.*, at 208.

[167] Article 24 of the APL.

[168] See Luo Haocai (1996), *supra* note 101, at 208-209. However, if the criminal punishment involves a fine or imprisonment, the total amount of the fine or the term of imprisonment shall be reduced by those already imposed by the administrative authority. See Article 28 of the APL.

[169] See Luo Haocai (1996), *supra* note 101, at 208.

[170] See Article 6 of the APL.

fact treated as offences rather than unlawful acts. However, the real challenge has always been about the faithful implementation of the law.

The strict procedure for imposing administrative penalties and the requirement of separating the imposition and collection of fines have apparently led to a drastic decrease in penalties being imposed by administrative organs. So drastically, in fact, that some scholars are calling for a better implementation of the APL so that penalties are in fact imposed whenever they are within the scope of the law.[171]

Most importantly, the promulgation of the APL and the LAL have initiated government efforts to reduce and restrict powers that can be exercised by administrative authorities, in part as measures to curb widespread corruption and abuse of power. While these measures introduce some checks on administrative powers, they do not offer much in the way of balances. What is also important, however, is the requirement imposed by the two laws that all administrative regulations, rules and *guizhang* must be reviewed, revised and repealed (if necessary) to ensure their compliance with the laws.[172] Indeed, massive reviews, revisions and repeals have been conducted by both the State Council and its subordinate authorities since 1996.[173] These efforts amount to much more than streamlining administration; they return much social (in the case of APL) and economic (in the case of LAL) freedom to ordinary people in China.

---

[171] Wang Wangjun & Yao Yongqing, 'Why Administrative Penalties Have Decreased', (no. 10, 1997) *Democracy and the Legal System* (*Minzhu Yu Fazhi*) 48, at 48.

[172] See Article 64 of the APL and Article 83 of the LAL.

[173] To comply with the APL, the State Council revised some 210 regulations and rules and abolished some 30 of its various rules on administrative penalties. See Chapter 3 in Zhu Jingwen, *supra* note 7. To implement the LAL, the State Council and its subordinate authorities reviewed some 3,674 licensing requirements and had some 1,806 approval items taken off the approval list, amounting to just over half of the required approval items. Local governments at the provincial level did similarly. See 'A Visit to the State Council Administrative Examination and Approval Reform Office', in <news.xinhuanet.com/zhengfu/2004-06/content_1555928.htm> (last accessed 15 September 2004); and 'State Council and Its Departments Abolished and Adjusted 1806 Approval Items', in <news.xinhuanet.com/politics/2007-06/19/content_6261163.htm> (last accessed 19 June 2007). In between, there was also a massive review of laws, regulations and rules after China's accession to the WTO. See Zhu Jiangwen, *id*. Starting from February 2007 a new round of review of administrative regulations, rules and *guizhang* started, to be completed by November 2007. See Notice of the General Office of the State Council to Conduct Review of Administrative Regulations, Rules and *Guizhang*, issued as Guobanfa No. 12 (2007) on 25 February 2007.

4.4. Internal Review of Administrative Decisions

(1) Overview

With the assertion in the early days of the PRC that there was no fundamental conflict of interest between the state and the people, it is not surprising that much emphasis was placed on internal rather than external review of administrative decisions. According to Chinese scholars,[174] the earliest regulations dealing with administrative review were the Measures on Establishing Financial Inspection Organs within the Ministry of Finance,[175] the General Principles Governing the Activities of the Taxation Review Committee and the Provisional Regulations on Stamp Duty.[176] These regulations provided reconsideration (*fuyi*) of administrative decisions by a superior authority. More importantly, the then Taxation Review Committee was a semi-independent tribunal composed of representatives from the government, the taxation office, industrial organisations, trade unions and experts.[177] Further, during the same period an administrative re-examination (*fucha*) system was also instituted internally, which allowed decisions to be re-examined by the decision-making authority or its superior upon an application by an affected person.[178] Following these regulations there were many more issued by the government that provided internal review of administrative decisions.[179]

Reconsideration as an internal review mechanism seemed, however, to have disappeared altogether by the 1960s and 1970s. According to Professor Luo, among all administrative regulations issued during these twenty years, only one piece of regulation, the Provisional Regulations Governing the Investigation and Handling of Maritime Accidents,[180] provided a channel for administrative reconsideration.

The 1980s saw the rapid development of administrative reconsideration. By the end of 1990 over 100 laws and administrative regulations had provided for administrative reconsideration as an internal review mechanism.[181] However, this

---

174 See Luo Haocai (1996), *supra* note 101, at 358; Yang & Chen, *supra* note 41, at 168.

175 Issued by the Council of Government Administration on 15 November 1950.

176 Both were issued by the Council of Government Administration on 15 December 1950.

177 Yang & Chen, *supra* note 41, at 168.

178 See for instance the 1951 Provisional Customs Law of the PRC, issued by the Council of Government Administration. See further discussions in Yang & Chen, *supra* note 41, at 168.

179 See examples in Luo Haocai (1996), *supra* note 101, at 358.

180 Issued by the Ministry of Transportation in 1971, see Luo Haocai (1996), *supra* note 101, at 359.

181 Luo Haocai (1996), *supra* note 101, at 359.

mechanism was only institutionalised in 1990 when the Administrative Reconsideration Regulations were issued.[182]

It seems that administrative reconsideration has been widely practised. In the five years since the implementation of the ARR in 1991, 150,000 cases were dealt with under the Regulations. Of these, 23% of the original decisions were rejected or amended.[183] Since the promulgation of the ARL, thousands of cases have been dealt with by the various administrative authorities under the State Council: 2630 (2001), 2288 (2002), 1760 (2003), and 1757 (2004).[184] Early statistics seem to suggest that by 1996 a large number of cases adjudicated by courts had gone through reconsideration processes: 90% of administrative litigation cases had gone through administrative reconsideration before court proceedings and 85% of disputes concerning public orders had been settled through reconsideration.[185] However recent reports suggest that 70% of administrative litigation cases have been initiated without having first gone through administrative reconsideration.[186]

(2) Nature

Administrative reconsideration is a remedial mechanism through internal supervision within the bureaucratic hierarchy. It is a process internal to the bureaucratic organ within which the original decisions are made.[187] The weakness of this mechanism is

---

182 Issued by the State Council on December 24, 1990, effective on 1 January 1991, and amended on September 2, 1994. On 29 April 1999 the Standing Committee of the NPC adopted the Administrative Reconsideration Law (ARL), which superseded the Regulations when the Law became effective on 1 October 1999. On 29 May 2007, the State Council issued its Regulations for the Implementation of the Administrative Reconsideration Law of the PRC, which took effect on 1 August 2007.

183 Cao Kangtai, 'Implementing the Administrative Litigation Law and Promoting Administration by Law', (no. 4, 1995) *Administrative Law Review* (*Xingzhengfa Yanjiu*) 7, at 8. This rate of success by complainants seems to have remained quite stable until now. See Yang & Zhang, *supra* note 63, at 534-535.

184 See Table 3-7 in Zhu Jingwen, *supra* note 7. In fact, nationwide the number of reconsideration appeals has declined quite significantly since 2002. See Yang & Zhang, *supra* note 63, at 533-534.

185 Luo Haocai (1996), *supra* note 101, at 359. Luo however does not specify the period of time regarding these statistics. It may be assumed that he refers to the period from 1990 when the Administrative Litigation Law came into force to 1996 when the textbook was written. Other sources seem to indicate a much lower rate for the period. For instance, another study indicates that only 38% of administrative litigation concerned appeals against administrative reconsideration decisions. See Cao Kangtai, *supra* note 183, at 8.

186 See 'An Interpretative Reading of the Regulations for the Implementation of the Administrative Reconsideration Law', in <www.lawbook.com.cn/fzdt/newshtml/21/20070609222351.htm> (last accessed 10 June 2007).

187 Luo Haocai (1996), *supra* note 101, at 354-357.

apparent. Further, the head of the administrative organ remains responsible for the organ's activities, and retains veto authority over any reconsideration decision.[188]

As the mechanism is wholly controlled by the bureaucratic hierarchy, it is not surprising that it has been jealously guarded by the bureaucracy as an alternative approach to administrative accountability and as a defence against the intrusion of external (judicial) review of administrative acts.[189] It is perhaps not a coincidence that administrative reconsideration was institutionalised soon after the Administrative Litigation Law (ALL) was enacted in 1989.

(3) Scope

As a general rule, only concrete administrative acts may be reviewed.[190] Article 6 of the ARL lists reviewable acts, which include restrictions on personal freedom, the imposition of fines, the taking of compulsory measures, the suspension, withholding or refusal of business licences and permits, interference in business operations, the payments of pensions or compensation for the deceased, failure to perform administrative obligations, the breach of personal rights or property rights, and other concrete administrative acts which infringe the legitimate rights and interests of citizens and organisations. Further, under Article 37 of the Administrative Litigation Law, all decisions subject to judicial review are also allowed for administrative reconsideration.[191]

A major improvement made by the ARL over the ARR is the expansion of the scope for reconsideration. Under Article 10 of the ARR the following were not subject to the reconsideration mechanism: administrative rules and regulations

---

188 See Pitman B. Potter, 'Editor's Introduction', (no. 3, 1991) *Chinese Law and Government*, a special issue on *The Administrative Litigation Law of the PRC: Changing the Relationship Between the Courts and Administrative Agencies in China*, at 11; and Yang & Zhang, *supra* note 63, at 538. Under the ARL (Article 3), the unit in charge of legal affairs within an administrative authority is the organ responsible for handling administrative reconsideration. Since the unit is not an independent authority (in fact, it is not even required to exercise its reconsideration power independently under the ARL), but forms part of the administrative hierarchy within the administrative authority, it is not surprising that the head of the administrative authority may indirectly exercise a veto power. In fact, Article 28 of the ARL specifically requires that a reconsideration decision needs to be approved by the head of the administrative authority or by a collective decision of the authority before it can be handed down.

189 For a discussion of the tension between bureaucratic interests and efforts to institutionalise judicial review of administrative acts, see Pitman B. Potter, 'The Administrative Litigation Law of the PRC: Judicial Review and Bureaucratic Reform', in Pitman B. Potter (ed.), *Domestic Law Reforms in Post-Mao China* (New York/London: M.E. Shaper, 1994), at 273-276.

190 Article 2 of the ARL.

191 This in reality may not expand the scope of administrative reconsideration as the review scope of both laws is identical (comparing Article 6 of ARL with Article 11 of the ALL).

and other universally binding decisions and orders,[192] decisions relating to rewards, punishment, appointment or dismissal of public servants,[193] decisions regarding civil dispute settlement through arbitration, mediation or other means,[194] and state acts in respect of national defence or foreign affairs.[195] Most of these exemptions have now been abolished by the ARL, and all concrete administrative actions are now reviewable. Additionally, Article 7 of the ARL now provides that, when applying for administrative reconsideration over concrete administrative acts, an applicant may request the reviewing authority to examine the legality of provisions (*guiding*) issued by organs of the State Council, governments at and above the county level and their departments, and by township governments. However, governmental rules (*guizhang*) issued by ministries and commissions of the State Council and by local people's governments are excluded from such review. Here a major ambiguity has been created by law: it is quite unclear what is the exact scope of 'provisions' to be subjected to the review of legality. It is equally unclear whether these 'provisions' will now be subject to judicial review.

The ARL provides that the reconsideration authority shall address issues of both legality and merit (appropriateness) of a decision under review.[196] This, in contrast with administrative litigation, permits broader re-examination of bureaucratic decisions than is available under the ALL's judicial review provisions, which only allow a review of legality. As such, the reviewing authority is empowered to uphold or quash the original decision, or to make a new decision. The authority is also empowered to request the original organ to correct the deficiencies in the original decision or to make a new decision.[197] Finally, the reviewing authority may order compensation in accordance with relevant laws and regulations.[198]

(4) Jurisdiction

The administrative reconsideration mechanism is also a part of the power structure; thus the jurisdiction of reconsideration is divided in accordance with the vertical and

---

192 These are seen as abstract administrative actions.

193 These are subject to other regulations governing public servants.

194 These matters are governed by the Civil Procedures Law (1991). Under the 1994 revision of the ARR, decisions relating to the use rights or ownership of land, mines, forests and other natural resources are subject to reconsideration. Clearly these acts are more in the nature of administrative than civil disputes.

195 This exclusion could potentially be extremely wide as neither 'national defence' nor 'foreign affairs' is defined. Further, as both foreign affairs and national defence are subject to the protection of State Secret Law, it is even difficult to know, in the first place, whether any decisions in dispute actually relate to foreign affairs or national defence.

196 Article 3 of the ARL.

197 Article 28 of the ARL.

198 Article 29 of the ARL.

horizontal distribution of administrative powers. As such, provisions on jurisdiction are highly complex and, as was the case under the ARR, could potentially be used as means of ignoring the request for reconsideration.[199] As a general rule, review authority lies with the next higher authority in the same bureaucratic hierarchy.[200]

However, the authority to review decisions made by governments at the provincial level (including ministries and commissions of the State Council) lies with the original decision-making organ; although when appealing a reconsideration decision an applicant may then apply further to the State Council for a final decision or lodge a suit with a people's court.[201] When a decision is made by an organisation which is empowered by law to undertake administrative acts, the application may be made to the people's government or department under the State Council, which is directly in charge of the relevant organisation.[202] If a decision is made jointly by two administrative organs, the review authority lies with their common superior.[203] Finally, if the reconsideration application is against a decision made by an administrative organ which has been abolished, the application shall be made to the administrative organ at the next highest level which continues to exercise the functions of the abolished organ.[204]

(5) Process

As a general rule, an individual or an organisation that thinks their legitimate rights and interests have been infringed upon by a concrete administrative act, has the right to apply for administrative reconsideration. Such a right is inheritable. In cases of an individual, his/her right to administrative reconsideration may be exercised by his/her close relatives if he/she dies, or be exercised by his/her legal representative on his/her behalf where he/she has no civil capacity or only has restricted civil capacity.[205] The extent of 'close relatives' is not defined by the ARL, but according to the Supreme People's Court 'close relatives' include spouses, parents, children, brothers and sisters, grandparents and grandchildren.[206] In cases of a legal person or an organisation, if it ceases to exist the right to administrative reconsideration

---

199 On the other hand, the complex provisions are themselves a response, by delineating jurisdiction in detail, to the problem of administrative authorities declining to exercise review jurisdiction as a way of ignoring requests for reconsideration.

200 Articles 12-15 of the ARL.

201 Articles 14 & 16 of the ARL.

202 Article 15 (3) of the ARL.

203 Article 15 (4) of the ARL.

204 Article 15 (5) of the ARL.

205 Article 10 of the ARL.

206 See Interpretation of the Supreme People's Court on Certain Issues concerning the Implementation of the 'Law of the People's Republic of China on Administrative Litigation' (2000).

may be exercised by the legal person or organisation which succeeds it.[207] Other persons and organisations with interests in the application may also participate in the case as third parties. Applicants or third parties may entrust (an) agent(s) to attend administrative reconsideration on their behalf.[208]

Such an application must be made within 60 days from the date the applicant learns that a concrete administrative act has been taken unless otherwise provided by law or regulations, or the applicant is prevented from doing so due to *force majeure* or other special circumstances.[209] The reviewing authority must, within five days upon receipt of the application, decide either to accept or reject the application or direct the applicant to another authority for consideration if it has no jurisdiction on the matter.[210] Should the reviewing authority fail to reply or reject the application without proper reasons, the ARL imposes an obligation on its superior authority to compel the reviewing authority to reply or to accept the application, or the superior authority itself may directly accept the case for handling.[211]

In upgrading the ARR to the ARL, a major improvement has been made in clarifying the burden of proof. Under the ARR the acceptance of an application was conditional upon the establishment of a *prima facie* case (including reasons for reconsideration) for claim by the applicant, without which a case could be dismissed.[212] That is to say, the ARR itself did not directly impose a burden of proof on the applicant (nor did it impose a burden on the respondent agency to establish the correctness of its decision); rather it appeared to have imposed on the applicant at least a burden of persuasion.[213] Under the ARL, there is no longer the requirement for *prima facie* evidence. As long as the application meets the legal requirements, the case will have to be accepted.[214] More importantly, the respondent agency is now required

---

207 Article 10 of the ARL.

208 Article 10 of the ARL.

209 Article 9 of the ARL. This represents a major extension. Under the ARR, an applicant had only 15 days to make an application for reconsideration (Article 29 of the ARR).

210 Article 17 of the ARL. Again, this is a major improvement. Under the ARR the time limit was ten days (Article 34 of the ARR).

211 Article 20 of the ARL.

212 Articles 33 and 34 of ARR.

213 Potter (1991), *supra* note 188, at 17.

214 Article 17 of the ARL. However, under Article 21 of the State Council Regulations for the Implementation of the Administrative Reconsideration Law of the PRC (2007), evidence must be supplied by the applicant (1) to prove he/she has requested action in cases where the application is against administrative inaction, (2) to prove damage in case where administrative compensation is also applied for, and (3) where laws or administrative regulations require applicants to supply evidence. Item (3) potentially undermines the ARL as it gives the State Council (by itself) the power to stipulate the burden of proof, whereas the ARL does not authorise it to do so.

to produce its evidence, legal basis and other materials for decision-making as well as a response to the application.[215] Furthermore, the applicant is now given wide access to these materials, unless these materials relate to state secrets, commercial confidentiality or personal privacy.[216]

Reconsideration is generally conducted in writing. However the ARL allows the reviewing authority to adopt any other means that it deems necessary for such a review, or that have been requested by the applicant, such as an investigation or an interview with the applicant, the respondent or a third party.[217] A review decision must be made within two months from the date of receipt of the application, and the decision becomes legally effective immediately upon service.[218] Generally, a reconsideration decision is final. However, a dissatisfied party may appeal to the court under the administrative litigation system, which will review the legality of the decision.[219] Such an appeal to the court must be made within 15 days upon receipt of the decision.[220]

5. Administrative Supervision

5.1. Overview

Supervision over administration is carried out through a number of channels, both internal and external, by Party organisations, legislative authorities, judicial authorities, as well as administrative authorities. To start with, appointments of administrative officials ('cadres' in the Chinese terminology) are subject to monitoring by Party authorities at different levels, and the performance of these appointees is subject to an institutionalised system of cadre evaluation (*ganbu kaohe*).[221] Although such monitoring and evaluation focuses as much on political attitudes and ideological stands as on administrative competence and integrity, this system does provide

---

[215] Article 23 of the ARL.

[216] Articles 23 & 24 of the ARL.

[217] Article 22 of the ARL.

[218] Article 31 of the ARL.

[219] Articles 5 & 30 of the ARL suggests that decisions made after administrative reconsideration by a provincial level government, confirming the right of ownership in or the right to the use of natural resources such as land, mineral resources, waters, forests, mountains or hills, grassland, wasteland, tidal flats and sea areas, or such a decision regarding the survey, delimitation or readjustment of administrative division or regarding land requisition, is final and may not be appealed to court.

[220] Article 19 of the ARR.

[221] See Yasheng Huang, 'Research Note: Administrative Monitoring in China', (no. 143, 1995) *The China Quarterly* 828, at 829-834.

a mechanism of internal supervision, at least allowing the central authorities to have a more accurate picture of its bureaucratic organisations during the period of decentralisation and reform.[222] Perhaps more importantly as an internal supervision mechanism, a petition system (*xinfang zhidu*) exists and operates both in the Party and the government hierarchy.[223] Under this system, aggrieved parties may, through letters or visits to officials and petition offices, petition the government for redress, or expose cases of unlawful behaviour, or simply communicate public opinion on economic or other reforms.[224] In terms of controlling corruption it seems to have worked quite well. It was reported that in the mid-1980s, 80% of the cases of illicit conduct by cadres under investigation were revealed through the petition system.[225] The fundamental flaw in this system is that the *xinfang* office can, and often does, return the complaint to the bureau against which the complaint was filed. Consequently, it has frequently led to reprisals against complainants.[226]

Institutionally there are the Ministry of Supervision and its corresponding organisations at different levels of the government. Parallel to the Ministry of Supervision is the Party Discipline Inspection Commission. The administrative division of the two organisations relates more to the identity of the cadre than to the nature of the activities.[227] This parallel mechanism is not necessarily duplicative, but a deliberate policy of the Party which believes 'supervision by Party members should be integrated with the law' and emphasises that 'the Party should supervise itself'.[228]

---

222 Yasheng Huang, *id.*, at 841-842.

223 *Xinfang* was first established in the early 1950s. See further Finder, *supra* note 30. Thereafter it was conducted informally until October 1995 when the State Council finally issued its Regulations on Petition (*Xinfang Tiaoli*). The 1995 Regulations have now been replaced by a new set of Regulations on Petition, adopted by the State Council on 5 January 2005 and effective from 1 May 2005.

224 Yasheng Huang, *supra* note 221, at 834-835.

225 Yasheng Huang, *supra* note 221, at 835.

226 Finder, *supra* note 30, at 4-5. Of course, Chinese law specifically prohibits such reprisals. See Article 3 of the 2005 Regulations on Petition. Article 22 of the 2005 Regulations still retains the practice of having the petition transferred to the relevant authorities for handling, and such transference will only be barred if the petition reveals crimes or corruption (Article 23).

227 Yasheng Huang, *supra* note 221, at 836.

228 See Political Report delivered by Jiang Zemin to the 15th Party Congress on 12 September 1997. Although Jiang did mention 'democratic management and supervision', he did not refer to checks and balances. Instead he emphasised the need to integrate the supervision through party mechanisms with that by law. He further emphasised the importance of supervision over the implementation of Party and state policies as well as the importance of all party organs adhering to the principle that 'the party should supervise itself.' For an English text of the Report, see *China Daily*, internet edition, <www.chinadaily.net/cndy/history/15/fulltext.html>.

Although it might be the good intention of the Party to use party supervision as an effective mechanism to combat corruption and other forms of malpractice by party members, such emphasis does raise the question of whether the law is superior to the Party in China.

In this section, the focus is on legal mechanisms for administrative supervision, while other forms of supervision will be referred to in the relevant discussion below.

5.2. Legal Mechanisms for Administrative Supervision

In post-Mao China administrative supervision was first institutionalised by the Regulations on Administrative Supervision in 1990.[229] There have also been other individual measures or regulations issued by various ministries or local governments, supplementing or implementing the Law on Administrative Supervision.[230]

The central task of a supervisory organ is to supervise the observance of law, administrative regulations, government decisions and orders as well as administrative disciplines, by government departments at the same level and their personnel appointed by administrative authorities. It also deals with complaints by government officials against administrative sanctions they have received.[231] The purposes of such supervision are to ensure that administrative policies and orders are carried out smoothly and effectively, and that efficient and clean government is established.[232]

Supervisory organs are established within the state administrative hierarchy. These organs are specifically charged with powers and duties in administrative supervision.[233] One important feature of their structure is that the local bureaus of supervision are subject to dual leadership by their superior as well as their corresponding local governments.[234] This structure immediately raises the question of their independence, particularly when they are supposed to supervise the work of government departments at the same level. In practice, the work of the supervisory organs relies heavily on the cooperation and support of their supervised departments.[235] Furthermore, the Law specifically requires that all major supervisory decisions or

---

229 Issued by the State Council on 9 December 1990. The Regulations have now been superseded by the Law of the PRC on Administrative Supervision (LAS), adopted by the 25th Meeting of the Standing Committee of the NPC on 5 September 1997 and effective on the same date.

230 E.g. Measures for Supervisory Organs in Handling Appeals from Administrative Sanctions, issued by Ministry of Supervision on 30 November 1991; Supervision Regulations for Public Security Organs, issued by the State Council on 4 June 1997.

231 Article 18 of the LAS.

232 Article 1 of the LAS.

233 Article 2 of the LAS.

234 Article 7 of the LAS.

235 Yasheng Huang, *supra* note 221, at 836-837.

proposals must be approved by the government at the same level, as well as the superior supervisory authority.[236] In any case, a superior supervisory organ can always assume jurisdiction that is allocated to its subordinate organs.[237] Further, a superior supervisory organ has the power to request its subordinate organs to change or withdraw their decisions, or may change or abolish these decisions by itself.[238] In this respect the Party Discipline Inspection organisations seem to be particularly powerful and active in dealing with important cases concerning the conduct of Chinese cadres.[239]

Supervision is initiated in two ways. First, supervisory organs can identify aspects of government activities for close scrutiny.[240] Secondly, supervisory organs have established a Reporting System (*Jubao Zhidu*) in which citizens may report any malpractice in governments on a confidential basis.[241] These reports may also initiate the scrutiny of government. Again, as a reflection of its lack of independence, decisions to investigate any major activities of government departments must be filed with the government at the same level and the superior supervisory organ.[242] For the purpose of investigation, a supervisory organ has the right to access to relevant documents, financial accounts and other materials. It may ask the administrative organisation under scrutiny to explain relevant questions and may order activities that have violated the law, regulations or administrative disciplines to be stopped.[243] However, upon conclusion of the investigation, a supervisory organ is only empowered to make suggestions;[244] it can only make decisions to impose disciplinary sanctions upon officials in accordance with regulations on personnel management, or decisions ordering the return, confiscation or recovery of property obtained by officials in violation of administrative disciplines.[245]

---

236 Article 34 of the LAS. One observer has noted that 'the Ministry would not be able to investigate officials at ministry level without the approval of the premier or a vice-premier, nor would the local branches be able to investigate bureau-level officials without the top leader of the relevant ministry or provincial government.' See Yasheng Huang, *supra* note 191, at 836-837.

237 Article 17 of the LAS.

238 Article 40 of LAS.

239 Yasheng Huang, *supra* note 221, at 836-837.

240 This is often done in accordance with instructions from the Ministry of Supervision, which identifies areas for close scrutiny each year. See e.g. Opinions Regarding the 1996 Supervision over Implementation of Law, issued by the Ministry of Supervision on 15 January 1996.

241 See Article 6 of the LAS. See also *Jubao* Regulations issued by various organisations. For further discussions on *Jubao*, see Zhu Weijiu, *supra* note 38, at 459-465.

242 Articles 29, 30 & 31 of the LAS.

243 Article 19 of the LAS.

244 Article 23 of the LAS.

245 Article 24 of the LAS.

On the whole, the supervision system is more a disciplinary enforcement organisation than a supervisory system.[246] Its fatal flaw is its lack of any meaningful independence and power of decision-making. As such, it is perhaps is not even a toothless tiger; it is a paper tiger.

6. Administrative Litigation

6.1. Overview

In post-Mao China, the Electoral Law of the NPC and Local People's Congresses (1979) was probably the earliest ad hoc substantive law to allow the court to review administrative decisions.[247] The 1982 Constitution, in general terms, suggests the possibility of administrative litigation and confirms the right to compensation for infringement of civil rights by state organs or functionaries.[248] Procedural guidance was first provided by the 1982 Provisional Civil Procedure Law, which specifically provided that the Law was applicable to the settlement of administrative disputes when substantive laws granted courts jurisdiction over such disputes.[249] Since these developments an increasing amount of individual legislation has provided the legal basis for administrative litigation.[250]

The adoption of the Administrative Litigation Law (ALL) in 1989 signalled the separation of procedural and substantive administration law,[251] and the formal institution of a distinct procedure parallel to the civil and criminal procedures. The ALL, however, is one of the most controversial pieces of legislation ever enacted

246 This perhaps explains why many administrative law textbooks in China do not even cover the topic at all.

247 Epstein, *supra* note 107, at 2.

248 See Article 41 of the Constitution.

249 Article 3. The 1983 Provisional Civil Procedure Law was superseded by the 1990 Civil Procedure Law. Under this provision, the court would only accept administrative disputes if the original administrative decision was made under a law which specifically provided the mechanism for judicial adjudication. See further Article 3(2) of the Reply by the Supreme Court on the Question of Whether the People's Courts Should Accept Cases Appealing against Administrative Penalties Imposed by Industrial and Commercial Administrative Bureaus, issued on 19 March 1983. Quoted in *Adjudication in China Today*, *supra* note 8, at 446.

250 By the end of 1988 no less than 130 laws had provided the right for administrative litigation. See *Adjudication in China Today*, *id.*, at 189.

251 Zhang Shangshuo, *supra* note 1, at 18-19.

in post-Mao China.[252] It is essentially a product of academic efforts[253] as well as a compromise among various authorities having vested interests, including the court, bureaucratic authorities and the reformist intellectual constituency.[254] Yet the drafting process was one of the most public. It involved initial approval by the Party, followed by expert drafting and various public discussions and debates. The drafting processes are thus, as Potter has pointed out,[255] a good indication of the law-making process in post-Mao China.[256] Even after three years of public discussions and debates, when the ALL was adopted it was variously described by its opponents as 'a law exceeding historical development' and thus 'unsuitable for the Chinese situation';[257] 'a law with a premature birth by twenty years'. and 'a result of [bourgeois] liberalisation'.[258] The controversies and their compromise solutions have hounded the implementation of the ALL since its implementation in 1990.

6.2. Scope

Deciding the scope of the court's jurisdiction on administrative cases was seen as one of the most important issues in drafting the Administrative Litigation Law.[259] According to Wang Hanbin, the drafting committee used the following principles in deciding the scope:

> (1) Based on the Constitution and the spirit of the Thirteenth Party Congress, and with the safeguarding of the legal rights and interests of citizens, legal persons, and other organisations as the starting point, the

---

252 Perhaps the other piece of comparably controversial legislation is the State Enterprise Bankruptcy Law 1988.

253 The initial drafting task was entrusted to the Administrative Law Research Group – an expert group established within the Legal Affairs Committee of the NPC's Standing Committee – under the direction of Professors Jiang Ping, Luo Haocai and Ying Songnian. See Potter, *supra* note 189, at 274.

254 The term 'legal reform constituency' is used by Potter to refer to groups of legal specialists who share common interests in pushing forward legal reforms. See Potter, *supra* note 189, at 273.

255 Potter, *supra* note 189, at 276.

256 The drafting processes have been excellently described and analysed by Potter: Potter, *supra* note 189, at 273-276. See also Finder, *supra* note 30, at 5-10, and Wang Hanbin, *supra* note 96, at 35-36.

257 Quoted in Luo Haocai, 'Using Administrative Litigation Functions to Promote the Implementation of the Administrative Litigation Law', (no. 4, 1995) *Administrative Law Review* (*Xingzhengfa Yanjiu*) 2, at 3.

258 Quoted in Pi Chunxi, 'An Important Law that Needs Serious Implementation', (no. 4, 1995) *Administrative Law Review* (*Xingzhengfa Yanjiu*) 12, at 12.

259 Wang Hanbin, *supra* note 96, at 36-37.

> scope for accepting administrative cases by the People's Courts is to be enlarged appropriately.[260]
> (2) We shall handle correctly the relationship between adjudicative authority and administrative authority. The People's Court should hear administrative cases in accordance with the law and should not interfere in the administrative conduct of administrative organs under the law and statutes and regulations.[261]
> (3) In light of our country's actual situation, administrative law is still imperfect and the administrative tribunals (divisions) of the People's Courts are still insufficient. The stipulation in the Administrative Litigation Law that 'common people can sue officials' is an issue that is conceptually rather new. It is a question for which there is no custom and to which we have not adapted, and yet it is an enduring issue. Therefore, the scope for acceptance of cases should not yet be set too widely but shall be expanded step by step in order to benefit the implementation of the administrative litigation system.[262]

The scope of court jurisdiction is thus defined narrowly. In principle, a court is only empowered to inquire into the legality (not the merits or appropriateness) of specific (concrete) administrative acts,[263] which include the examination of the following: (1) sufficiency of evidence in decision-making; (2) proper application of laws and regulations; (3) proper observance of statutory procedures; (4) acting within power; and (5) proper use of official power.[264]

The specific grounds for judicial review are identified by Article 11 of the ALL, which include restrictions of personal freedom, the imposition of fines, the taking of compulsory measures, the suspension, withholding or refusal of business licences and permits, interference in business operations, the payments of pensions or compensation for the deceased, failure to perform administrative obligations, and the breach of personal rights or property rights.[265] Four categories of administrative actions are specifically excluded from court jurisdiction, namely state acts involving national defence and foreign affairs, decisions concerning rewards, punishments, appointments, and removals concerning their working staff, the legality of administrative laws and regulations or decisions and orders having universal binding

260 Wang here was referring to court jurisdiction provided by various laws before the ALL.

261 Clearly this statement is to be understood in the context of 'theory of balance', as discussed in section 3.

262 Wang Hanbin, *supra* note 96, at 36-37.

263 See Article 5 of the ALL.

264 See Article 54 (2) of the ALL.

265 As pointed out earlier in *supra* note 191, these grounds are identical with those of administrative reconsideration.

force,[266] and all decisions for which the law provides that final adjudication is to be conducted by administrative authorities.[267] Further, it is doubtful whether specific administrative activities infringing upon the political rights of citizens, legal entities, or other organisations, such as freedom of the press, are reviewable when the court is not specifically empowered to do so by clear legal provisions.[268]

Since the ALL only provides jurisdiction to courts over 'concrete administrative actions' undertaken by administrative organs, all decisions made by other state organs, that is the procuratorates, legislatures or the Party itself and other social organisations would fall outside the court's jurisdiction.[269] The exemption of the Party units was said to be consistent with efforts under way at the time the law was drafted to separate the party from government administration.[270] Since the Party and the state are not clearly separated,[271] it is questionable, in theory at least, whether the Party can be exempted from court jurisdiction altogether. In terms of other social organisations, some Chinese scholars argue that when a non-administrative organ (such as a club, an association) enjoys some administrative powers and functions entrusted by the law and regulations, it can still qualify as a defendant. With the exception of this special case, when any non-administrative organ carries out administrative activities in the course of exercising administrative powers and functions, the administrative organ which entrusts or allows such should act as a defendant.[272]

---

266 This is of course what the Chinese scholars referred to as 'abstract administrative actions'. It is explained that the power to review and supervise rule-making has been vested with people's congresses and their standing committees at all levels by the Constitution (i.e. Articles 67 and 89 of the Constitution) and the Organic Law of Local People's Congresses and Local People's Governments at All Level. In fact, under the distinction between 'abstract administrative actions' and 'concrete administrative actions', the whole category of 'abstract administrative actions' is excluded from court scrutiny. See Xiao Xun, *supra* note 105, at 22-26. As mentioned before, the 1991 ARL now allows certain 'abstract administrative actions' for administrative reconsideration, but it remains unclear whether such actions may also be subject to court litigation. So far, answers from Chinese scholars seem to be negative. See Yang & Zhang, *supra* note 63, at 511.

267 Article 12 of the ALL.

268 Xiao Xun, *supra* note 105, at 22-26.

269 Epstein, *supra* note 107, at 1.

270 Potter, *supra* note 188, at 5. See also Potter, *supra* note 189, at 278.

271 The decision of the Party to close the World Economic Herald in Shanghai in the aftermath of the June event in 1989 is a good example of the non-separation of the Party and state administration.

272 Xiao Xun, *supra* note 105, at 22-26. An example Xiao referred to was the sanitation and anti-epidemic station which is not an administrative organ but is entrusted with administrative power of punishment by the Law on Food Hygiene (Trial Implementation).

6.3. Inter-relationship between Administrative Reconsideration and Litigation

As discussed above, there was, and still is, a tension between the internal and external review of administrative decisions. With the existence of an internal review system parallel to judicial review there is the possibility of the bureaucracy trying to shield itself from judicial scrutiny through its own mechanism, i.e. administrative reconsideration. Both the ARL and the ALL provide some indication of how the relationship will be handled.

First, the court jurisdiction is over legality, not merits or appropriateness of administrative decisions; the latter is within the realm of administrative reconsideration.[273] A court thus can only uphold, quash or partially quash an administrative decision. There is however an exception. Under Article 54 (4), a court may alter an administrative decision on administrative penalty if such a penalty is manifestly unfair. Based on this provision, a prominent administrative scholar in China, Professor Ying Songnian, has suggested that a court may inquire into the reasonableness of administrative decisions under certain circumstances.[274]

Secondly, when a matter is within the jurisdiction of both, the applicant has the freedom to choose his/her course of action, but if an administrative litigation has been initiated, the same person would not be allowed to apply for reconsideration. Correspondingly, if an application has been accepted for reconsideration or the law requires the party to undertake reconsideration before litigation, the person is not entitled to initiate a court action during the processes of reconsideration.[275]

Thirdly and perhaps most significantly, provisions exist in the ALL to prevent the frequently used tactic by bureaucratic organs of trying to circumscribe judicial reviews by simply ignoring the request for reconsideration. The ARR permitted appeal to the court only where the applicant was dissatisfied with the reconsideration decision (including a decision not to accept a reconsideration application);[276] there was no mention of resort to judicial review in the event of a failure by a reconsideration organ to respond to an application. The ARR only provided that the authority at a higher level should order a review authority to respond to the application.[277] Thus, under the ARR, it was possible for a reconsideration organ to simply ignore reconsideration applications and leave the applicants without any channel for redress. Articles 37 and 38 of the ALL are therefore significant in strengthening the role of the courts

---

[273] Indeed the courts were expressly warned not to overstep into the realm of administrative reconsideration or to substitute themselves for administrative organs in making decisions. See Wang Hanbin, *supra* note 96, at 38.

[274] Ying Songnian, 'China's Administrative Procedure System', (no. 4, 1997) *China Law* 81, at 82.

[275] Article 16 of the ARL.

[276] Articles 9 and 36 of ARR.

[277] Article 35 of the ARR.

in curtailing a possible abuse of the reconsideration mechanism by administrative authorities. These two articles provide that plaintiffs may file suit directly, without undergoing administrative reconsideration, unless specifically required by law, and they may institute court proceedings if a reconsideration authority has failed to respond within two months. While these provisions are significantly qualified by the fact that many regulations require administrative reconsideration as a prerequisite to filing for judicial review, the ALL (together with the ARL[278]) has the potential to curtail abuses of administrative reconsideration in other ways.[279]

6.4. Process

Similar to other procedural laws, the ALL adopts a collegiate trial system,[280] allows the request for withdrawal of judicial personnel[281] and public hearings,[282] and implements a two-tier appeal system.[283] Similarly, court jurisdiction is allocated on the basis of geographical location of cases as well as the seriousness of cases.[284] There are however two distinct features of the ALL that provide some strong protection for the plaintiffs.

First, the burden of proof falls wholly on the respondent, that is, the administrative decision-making organ. Once a lawsuit is instituted it is up to the decision-makers to prove the legality of the decision and to establish a legal basis for such a decision.[285] Further, the respondent is prohibited from collecting evidence from the applicant or the witnesses on its own authority;[286] such authority lies with the courts.[287] In a country like China where freedom of information is still a relatively novel idea, the evidence rule,[288] if properly implemented, has the potential to overcome some serious deficiencies in the Chinese administrative law system.

---

278 The provisions in Articles 37 and 38 of the ALL have now been incorporated into Article 19 of the ARL.

279 Potter, *supra* note 188, at 5.

280 Under this cases are heard by a bench composed of an odd number of judges or judges and layperson assessors. See Article 46 of ALL.

281 Under this parties may challenge judicial personnel on the grounds of bias. See Article 47 of the ALL.

282 Unless the cases involve 'state secrets' or private affairs of individuals or otherwise provided by law. See Article 45 of the ALL.

283 Under this the second hearing is final and there can be no further appeal.

284 See Chapter 3 of the ALL.

285 Article 32 of the ALL.

286 Article 33 of the ALL.

287 Article 34 of the ALL.

288 Evidence rules are further clarified by the 2000 Interpretation (see *supra* note 113) and the Provisions on Certain Issues Relating to Evidence in Administrative Litigation issued by the

Secondly, unlike for civil procedures, mediation is not applicable in court processes,[289] and withdrawal of a case (even if the respondent has agreed to amend the original decisions) requires the approval of the court.[290] This non-applicability of mediation does not mean that the parties concerned cannot reconcile differences among themselves.[291] In fact, reconciliation is actively encouraged by the courts.[292] The exclusion of mediation reflects the concern of the law-makers with the power imbalance of the parties and the conception of public administration as not being of the nature of private rights. Reconciliation is allowed in order to enhance the efficiency of court work, and the requirement of approval for withdrawal is to prevent complainants from being subjected to coercion by government authorities.[293]

When the courts are dealing with matters on which there are no provisions in the ALL, the courts may use the Civil Procedure Law as reference.[294]

6.5. The Question of *Guizhang*

With the arbitrary distinction and ambiguous delineation of 'abstract' and 'concrete' administrative actions, submitting the subordinate administrative rules or *guizhang*[295] to judicial review became one of the most divisive struggles between the courts and the administrative authorities during the drafting process.[296] Although these rules (*guizhang*) must not conflict with state laws and regulations, inconsistencies are inevitable as they vary from locality to locality and are mostly issued by authorities with vested interests. In practice they are perhaps more important than the state laws, as in most areas of law the principal laws and administrative regulations leave a great deal of room for implementation by *guizhang*. Other laws have now also begun to give *guizhang* a legitimate legal status by allowing *guizhang* to create legal

---

Supreme People's Court on 1 October 2002.

289 Article 50 of the ALL.

290 Article 51 of the ALL.

291 Xiao Xun, *supra* note 105, at 22-26.

292 Luo Haocai (1996), *supra* note 101, at 401.

293 Luo Haocai, *id.*, at 400-401.

294 See Article 114 of the Opinions of the Supreme People's Court Concerning Some Issues Relating to the Implementation of the Administrative Litigation Law (For Trial Implementation), adopted on 29 May 1991 and issued on 11 June 1991. As mentioned earlier, these Opinions have been replaced by the 2000 Interpretation (see *supra* note 113). The 2000 Interpretation contains the same provisions (Article 97).

295 *Guizhang*, as discussed in the previous chapter on law-making, refers to rules issued by government departments at both central and local levels in accordance, theoretically, with laws and regulations. Their precise nature, whether as rule-making (abstract administrative acts) or as an exercise of discretionary powers (concrete administrative acts) is unclear and controversial.

296 Epstein, *supra* note 107, at 8.

rights and duties.[297] Clearly, the exclusion of *guizhang* from court scrutiny would leave a huge area of administrative discretion without legal remedies.

The ARR expressly excluded direct reconsideration of the validity of *guizhang*,[298] but allowed reliance on them in reviewing the legality and merits of 'concrete' administrative acts.[299] The ARL makes a little concession, by allowing the reconsideration authorities to review '*guiding*' but not '*guizhang*'. Under the ALL, the validity of *guizhang* is clearly excluded from judicial review,[300] but it does not require the court to rely on them for decision making either. Instead, courts are required to 'consult' (*canzhao*) *guizhang* in reaching their decisions.[301] *Canzhao*, according to Wang Hanbin, is a compromise solution and means that:

> [w]ith regard to *guizhang* that conform to laws and administrative regulations and rules, the courts should consult them in hearing cases. With regard to *guizhang* that do not conform or do not entirely conform to the principle and spirit of the laws and administrative regulations and rules, the court may handle these with flexibility.[302]

This 'flexibility', according to Potter, would unavoidably enable the courts to make some sort of determination of legality of *guizhang*, as a court's decision to consult them hinges on an evaluation of whether they comply with higher-level administrative laws and regulations.[303] Others suspect that, 'in the end, this may be no compromise at all because in other laws the meaning of "make reference to" has been understood as following them.'[304]

Chinese scholars too are divided about the actual status of *guizhang*.[305] Some insist that *guizhang* are in their nature law with binding force.[306] *Canzhao* does not mean

297 See for instance Article 13 of APL.

298 Article 10 (1) of the ARR.

299 Article 41 of ARR.

300 Article 12 (2) of ALL.

301 Article 53 of the ALL.

302 Wang Hanbin, *supra* note 96, at 40.

303 Potter, *supra* note 188, at 7.

304 Epstein, *supra* note 107, at 8.

305 For a summary of various views, see Cui Zhuolan, 'A Discussion on the Reviewability of *Guizhang*', (no. 1, 1996) *Studies in Law* (*Faxue Yanjiu*) 140; and Luo Haocai (ed.), *Judicial Review in China* (*Zhongguo Sifa Shencha Zhidu*) (Beijing: Beijing University Press, 1994), at 461-478.

306 Zhang Chunfa, 'Several Issues Relating to *Guizhang*' (no. 1, 1991) *Studies in Law* (*Faxue Yanjiu*) 15, at 15.

'making reference' only, it means 'following them'.[307] Others believe that *canzhao* implicitly allows judicial review of these rules and, if the meaning of *canzhao* is ambiguous, it should be removed from the law.[308] If the latter view is taken, such 'review' would be limited, since Article 53 (2) of the ALL specifically requires the Supreme People's Court to submit the issue of inconsistency among *guizhang* to the State Council for interpretation and resolution.[309] A more realistic interpretation, which also seems to be the practice of the Chinese courts, is that *canzhao* entails an assessment of the quality and consistency of *guizhang* with their enabling laws and regulations, and a decision of their applicability in a specific case, but this does not amount to a review of the general validity of the *guizhang* concerned.[310] Increasingly, however, more and more scholars are calling for revisions to allow the court to review the validity of *guizhang* and other 'abstract administrative actions.'[311]

6.6. A Mixed Result

The ALL, while historically important in single-handedly changing the conception of administration law in the PRC, is a generally weak law plagued by many problems, in theory and in practice. Some Chinese scholars have this to say about the ALL:

> There are operational barriers in the system. Its ability to settle administrative disputes is limited. Its efficacy in achieving justice by subjecting administration to rules of law is not good. It is incapable of regulating the relationship between an individual and the government. Its function in promoting democracy and constitutionalism is weak.[312]

---

307 Zhang Chunfa, *id.*, at 17; Meng Xianfei, 'Application of Law in Administrative Litigation', (no. 6, 1989) *Studies in Law* (*Faxue Yanjiu*) 10, 13.

308 Cui Zhuolan, *supra* note 305, at 143.

309 There are arguments among scholars that such a requirement is unconstitutional, as it interferes with independent adjudication as guaranteed by the Constitution. See Cui Zhuolan, *id.*, at 144.

310 Luo Haocai (1994), *supra* note 305, at 465. This view was finally confirmed by Item 1 of the Minutes of A Meeting on the Application of Laws and Rules in Adjudicating Administrative Litigation Cases. The Minutes were formally issued by the Supreme People's Court as Fa (2004) No. 96 on 18 May 2004, requesting all courts to consult the document in adjudicating cases. Since the document was not issued as a judicial interpretation, its legal status is in fact ambiguous – it is not binding but lower courts are asked to consult the document in adjudicating cases.

311 See Yang & Zhang, *surpa* note 63, 342, and 574-586.

312 Wang Zhenyu & Wang Jingcheng, 'An Analysis on Problems in Our Administrative Litigation System and Their Solutions', (no. 3, 1997) *Jilin University Journal of Social Science* (*Jilin Daxue Shehui Kexue Xuebao*) 79, at 79. Similar assessment was also made by the Standing Committee of the NPC. See 'A Report on the Inspection of the Implementation of the Administrative Litigation Law', delivered to the 29th Meeting of the Standing Committee of the 7th NPC on 25 December 1992, in (no. 7, 1992) *Gazette of the Standing Committee of the National People's*

Early limited statistics available from China seem to support the above arguments. In a general survey conducted in 1992, it was found that 13.7% of the population had never heard of administrative litigation; 21.7% had never known anyone around them who sued the government; and 41% of them had never heard of any case in which citizens won in litigation against the government.[313] Further, the high rate of case withdrawal also indicates the difficulties in using the ALL for protection. During 1989 to 1992 the rate of withdrawing administrative litigation cases was 35%. This was increased to 41% in 1993. In some areas the rate was as high as 52%.[314] However, as mentioned at the beginning of this Chapter, the huge number of cases adjudicated by courts seems to suggest a much more mixed result after some 25 years of litigation. Even the recent lower rate of complainant success at 17% is nevertheless compatible with the situations in the developed world. In any case, the lower rate of success by complainants could also, though not necessarily, be explained by an improvement in the quality of government work.

7. Administrative Liability

7.1. Overview

As mentioned earlier, the need to compensate for state liability was recognised in 1954,[315] and such a need was re-affirmed in the 1980s.[316] However, there had been no specific criteria, nor procedures for state compensation until the adoption of the State Compensation Law (SCL) in 1994.[317]

The efforts to implement the constitutional requirements for state compensation emerged when the ALL was being drafted. There were apparently differences in opinion as to the scope of state compensation, and the danger of delaying the adoption of the ALL because of such differences, and so it was decided that it

Congress of the People's Republic of China (*Zhonghua Renmin Gongheguo Renda Changweihui Gongbao*) 105-111. See also Yang & Zhang, *supra* note 63, at 574-577.

313 Wang & Wang, *id.*, at 80.

314 Wang & Wang, *id.*, at 80-81.

315 See e.g. Article 99 of the 1954 Constitution.

316 See e.g. Article 41 of the 1982 Constitution; Article 33 of the 1981 Economic Contract Law (now replaced by the 1999 Contract Law); Article 121 of the 1986 General Principles of Civil Law; Article 42 of the 1986 Regulations concerning Punishments in the Administration of Public Order (now replaced by the 2005 Law concerning Punishments in the Administration of Public Order); and 1987 Maritime Code. See also Jiang Bixin, 'Of China's Present State Compensation System', (no. 1, 1995) *China Law* 80, at 80-81.

317 Adopted by the 7th Meeting of the Standing Committee of the 8th NPC on 12 May 1994, and effective on 1 January 1995. An English translation appears in Lin Feng, *supra* note 44, at 364-371.

would only contain some very general provisions, leaving details to be provided by a separate compensation law.[318] The drafting work by a group of experts on a state compensation law began almost immediately after the adoption of the ALL. Within three years a draft was completed and distributed nationwide for discussion and comments. Many suggestions and technical revisions were made by the Legislative Affairs Committee of the NPC's Standing Committee and the Law Commission of the NPC before the SCL was finally adopted by the Standing Committee of the NPC in 1994.[319]

7.2. The Scope

Strictly speaking the SCL is not a general state compensation law as suggested by its title; it provides for two specific kinds of compensation, i.e. administrative and criminal compensation on specific grounds. Administrative compensation covers compensation for infringement upon personal and property rights by administrative organs and their personnel, while the right to criminal compensation arises when such infringement is caused by state bodies or their personnel involved in criminal investigation, prosecution, adjudication and prison management.[320] Infringement upon personal rights includes illegal detention or wrongful arrest or imprisonment, infliction of bodily injury caused by illegal use of force of weapons, and other bodily injury or death caused by illegal acts. Violation of property rights includes property losses caused by unlawful orders to cancel licences or permits, illegal use of penalties or imposition of fines and charges, illegal seizure or confiscation of property and other property damages caused by illegal acts.[321] 'Illegal acts' do not include any personal acts of the state personnel which do not relate to their exercise of powers and functions or any acts specifically excluded by law.[322]

The SCL is a typical example of the positive grant of entitlement on specific grounds. Thus, infringement of personal rights or violation of property rights by legislative organs, military organisations, political party organisations, social organisations and enterprises are not covered by the law.[323] In line with the approach of the ALL, damage caused by abstract acts (i.e. the generally applicable rules and regulations)

---

318 Pi Chunxi, Zhang Huangguang & Sun Lihai, 'State Compensation Law – a Complete, Systematic and Scientific State Compensation System', *Guangming Daily* (*Guangming Ribao*), 8 June 1994, at 4.

319 Jiang Bixin, *supra* 316, at 81.

320 See Articles 3, 4, 15 & 16 of the SCL.

321 *Id.*

322 Articles 5 (1) & (3) and 17 (4) & (6) of the SCL.

323 Certain acts in the nature of civil law may, however, be covered by torts provisions in the General Principles of Civil Law and dealt with by the Civil Procedure Law instead of the Administrative Litigation Law.

and state acts (i.e. acts done for the purpose of defence and foreign affairs) are excluded from the scope of the law. The narrow scope of the SCL, coupled with various problems in the law and in practice, has prompted some Chinese scholars to call the SCL a 'State Non-Compensation Law'.[324]

7.3. The Process

Claims for compensation are to be made by any aggrieved individuals, legal persons and other organisations to the organs liable for compensation, i.e. the actual organisations causing the infringement of personal and property rights. Alternatively, such claims may be filed when applying for administrative reconsideration or administrative litigation.[325] In cases of multiple infringing organs,[326] compensation claims may be made to any one of the infringing organs.[327] A decision on compensation must be made by the organ liable for compensation within two months upon receiving the application for compensation. Where an administrative organ liable for compensation fails to make a decision within the time limit or the claimant is dissatisfied with the decision, the claimant may file a lawsuit in a people's court within three months after the above time limit in the case of administrative compensation.[328] In the case of criminal compensation, an application is to be made to the next higher agency for a review within the same system. An unsatisfactory review decision can be further appealed to a compensation committee of the people's court at the corresponding level of the reviewing authority.[329] A decision by a compensation committee of a court is binding and final.[330]

There have been various indications that the government is taking the SCL rather seriously. Thus rules and measures have been issued by different organisations to facilitate the process for settling compensation claims.[331] Special committees are

---

[324] See Yang & Zhang, *supra* note 63, at 546. For a good analysis of the problems with the law and its practice, see Yang & Zhang, *id.*, at 546-560.

[325] Articles 7, 9, 19 & 20 of the SCL.

[326] In such cases they are jointly liable for compensation: Articles 7 & 19 of the SCL.

[327] Article 10 & 20 of the SCL.

[328] Article 13 of the SCL.

[329] Articles 21 & 22 of the SCL.

[330] Article 23 of the SCL.

[331] See e.g. Supreme People's Procuratorate Notice on Preparing for Serious Implementation of the State Compensation Law, issued on 30 May 1994; Supreme People's Procuratorate Further Notice on Preparing for Serious Implementation of the State Compensation Law, issued on 26 October 1994; Supreme People's Procuratorate Measures for Criminal Compensation (Trial Implementation), issued by the Supreme People's Procuratorate on 2 December 1994; Interim Provisions Governing the Work of Criminal Compensation, issued by the Supreme People's Procuratorate on 18 November 1997 (now replaced by Provisions Governing the Work of Criminal Compensation, issued by the Supreme People's Procuratorate on 6 November 2000);

required to be established within all potentially liable organisations.[332] And to facilitate the implementation of the SCL, a series of judicial interpretations have also been issued in the last few years.[333]

Compensations are mainly to be made by payment of indemnities for direct financial losses and the returning or restoring of property.[334] In the case of infringement of personal freedoms, compensation is also to be made in relation to salary losses, calculated on the basis of the previous year's average daily wage set by the state for workers.[335] The SCL provides for no punitive damage or compensation for emotional anguish.

---

the Notice concerning the Implementation of the State Compensation Law, issued by the General Office of the State Council on 22 December 1994; Administrative Measures governing the Costs for State Compensation, issued by the State Council on 25 January 1995; Measures on Administrative and Criminal Compensation by Judicial Administrative Organs, issued by the Ministry of Justice on 8 September 1995; Interpretation of Several Problems concerning the Implementation of State Compensation Law, issued by the Supreme People's Court on 6 May 1996; Tentative Provisions on Procedures for Adjudicating Compensation Cases by Compensation Committees of People's Courts, issued by the Supreme People's Court on 6 May 1996; Several Provisions concerning the Adjudication of Administrative Compensation Cases, issued by the Supreme People's Court on 29 April 1997; and Interpretation of Several Issues Concerning Joint Compensation by the Supreme People's Court and Supreme People's Procuratorate, jointly issued by the Supreme People's Court and Supreme People's Procuratorate on 27 June 1997.

332 See Notice concerning the Implementation of the State Compensation Law, issued by the General Office of the State Council on 22 December 1994; and Article 23 of the SCL.

333 These include Interim Provisions governing Case Filing concerning Criminal Compensation and Non-Criminal Compensation Cases (Trial Implementation), issued by the Supreme People's Court on 4 February 2000; Interpretation of Certain Issues concerning Compensation in Civil and Administrative Cases, issued by the Supreme People's Court on 16 September 2000; Interim Provisions governing the Causes of Action concerning Criminal Compensation and Non-Criminal Compensation Cases (Trial Implementation), issue by the Supreme People's Court on 4 February 2000; Provisions on Confirmation of Cases in the Adjudication by the People's Court on State Compensation (Trial Implementation), issued by the Supreme People's Court on 10 August 2004; and Notice of the Supreme People's Court and the Supreme People's Procuratorate on the Determination of Organs Responsible for Criminal Compensation, jointly issued by the Supreme People's Court and the Supreme People's Procuratorate on 5 July 2005.

334 Article 25 of the SCL.

335 Article 26 of the SCL.

8. Concluding Remarks

Despite various shortcomings,[336] especially the exclusion of the Party from external scrutiny and the heavy reliance on internal review and supervision, the rapid development in administrative law represents one of the most significant forms of progress in legal development in post-Mao China. The importance of this rapid development is to be understood in the Chinese constitutional context. As discussed in Chapter Three on constitutional law, the control of governments is only vaguely provided for in the Constitution. In particular, the Communist Party operates with the Constitution, not under it. In terms of establishing a rule of law in China, it is therefore extremely important that checks and balances be established through individual statutes, most notably through administrative law.

The idea that a citizen can sue the government and that a government is liable for its maladministration is revolutionary in a legal culture where government officials had the status of parents and parents were perceived to be infallible. Even though the Party is reluctant to subject itself to external (such as judicial) supervision, great efforts have been made by the Party to make its members and organisations more accountable.[337] These efforts, though they may be seen as desperate responses to the increasing discontent among the population, and the subsequent threat of social instability, because of the widespread corruption among Party and state officials,[338] do subject Party members and officials to closer scrutiny, stricter discipline and a higher degree of accountability. With the efforts now focusing on regulating the processes of administrative decision-making, it is not unreasonable to be optimistic

---

336 For a more comprehensive evaluation of administrative law in China, see Yang & Zhang, *supra* note 63.

337 See a 731-page collection on Party discipline: *A Selection of Party Rules of the Communist Party of China* (1978–1996) (*Zhongguo Gongchandang Dangnei Fagui Xuanji 1978–1996*) (Beijing: Publishing House of Law, 1996). More recently the Party has issued many rules dealing with appointments, promotion, clean government etc. See e.g. Regulations on Party Disciplinary Sanctions (Trial Implementation) (1997), in *People's Daily* (*Renmin Ribao*), internet edition, 18 April 1997; Several Criteria on Clean Government for Communist Party Leaders (Trial Implementation) (1997), in *People's Daily* (*Renmin Ribao*), internet edition, 18 April 1997; Provisions on Penalising the Violation of the Provisions Regulations concerning the Appointment and Promotion of Party and State Leaders (1997), in *People's Daily* (*Renmin Ribao*), internet edition, 16 July 1997; and Implementing Measures on Several Criteria for Clean Government for Communist Party Leaders (Trial Implementation) (1998), in *People's Daily* (*Renmin Ribao*), internet edition, 9 January 1998.

338 Although the mass demonstrations in late 1986 and early 1989 were caused by many factors, such as the demands for greater freedom and concern regarding inflation, there was no doubt that official corruption was among the most important causes leading to these demonstrations.

that the Chinese administration will become not only more efficient[339] but also more transparent and accountable. Procedural justice may finally be seen to be as important as substantive justice.

Finally, it should be pointed out that administrative law has not only been developed rapidly in the last 20 years or so, it is still advancing at a rapid pace. As already mentioned earlier, a law on compulsory administrative measures is currently on the legislative agenda.[340] The ALL is likely to be revised in the not too distance future,[341] and the calls to revise to SCL look like being heeded by the legislature too.[342] Most administrative law scholars are optimistic that a comprehensive code on administrative procedures will one day be adopted in China.[343]

339 Improvement of government efficiency has always been an argument for regulating the decision-making process. See *A Study on Administrative Procedure Law, supra* note 104.

340 Under the 2007 legislative plan of the SCNPC, the law on administrative compulsory measures is to be adopted in 2007 if the bill is 'ripe'.

341 Interesting, the revision to the ALL was on the 2003 legislative plan of the SCNPC (see Yang & Zhang, *supra* note 63, at 569), but has since not reappeared on the annual legislative plans.

342 Barely five years after the promulgation of the SCL, calls for revision had already appeared in China and continue today. See Yang & Zhang, *supra* note 63, at 546-547.

343 Based on personal interviews conducted in the last many years.

Chapter Seven

Criminal Law

1. Introduction

Criminal law has always been a prominent branch of law in the Chinese legal system. Traditional Chinese law was commonly identified with criminal law, although this interpretation has now increasingly been recognised to be inaccurate. Modern legal reform too started with the reform of the criminal law.[1] In all communist legal reforms, developing the criminal law has always been a major part of the effort.

However, it took some 29 years for the communist authorities to finally produce a comprehensive criminal code.[2] It then took another 18 more years to bring the code closer to internationally accepted standards for criminal justice.[3]

This chapter first reviews the PRC's first criminal code and its developments since 1979. It then analyses the basic principles now embodied in the present code. This is followed by an examination of specific crimes and punishments. Some concluding remarks are made on the development of the criminal law in the PRC.

The focus of this chapter is on the revised criminal law, which is analysed to highlight the major developments of this branch of law.

---

1 See Chapter 1 on legal history.

2 The Criminal Law was first adopted at the 2nd Plenary Session of the 5th National People's Congress (NPC) on 1 July 1979 and became effective on 1 January 1980.

3 A comprehensive revision to the Criminal Law was adopted on 14 March 1997 at the Fifth Plenary Session of the 8th NPC. An English Text of the revised law can be found in Jianfu Chen & Suiwa Ke (eds), *China Criminal Laws: Commentary and Translation* (CCH Asia Pte Limited, 2000). The revised Law came into effect on 1 October 1997.

2. The 1979 Criminal Law and Its Development

The Criminal Law of the PRC (1979) was one of the first major codes to be promulgated in the post-Mao China.[4] Although supposed to be a comprehensive code along a European Continental model, it consisted of only very general, ideology-ridden, vague and ambiguous principles in 192 articles, with a strong Soviet influence.[5] This particular feature of the 1979 Criminal Law can best be understood from its drafting history.

The initial drafting work, aimed at drafting some guiding principles for criminal law, was begun by the Legal Committee of the Central Government in 1950. The earliest draft, consisting of 157 articles and entitled Draft Outline of the Criminal Law of the PRC, was completed in July 1950.[6] As a result of the adoption of the 1954 Constitution and the establishment of the NPC, the drafting work was taken over by the Law Office of the NPC's Standing Committee in October 1954.[7] By June 1957 the Law Office had completed its 22nd draft and submitted it to the NPC for deliberation. It was decided by the NPC that this draft, after the incorporation of suggestions made by representatives to the NPC, would be adopted for trial implementation. This did not happen, as the nation-wide political campaign of the Anti-rightist Movement was soon launched.[8] Efforts to draft a criminal law

---

4 Although there was no comprehensive criminal code, China was not without criminal law before 1979. Starting from the Instruction on Suppressing Counter-Revolutionary Activities (jointly issued by the Council of Government Administration and the Supreme People's Court in July 1950, later formally issued by the Central Government as the Regulations of the PRC on Punishing Counter-Revolution, in February 1951), there were various regulations on punishment for corruption, crimes undermining state currency and the crime of leaking state secrets. There were also various administrative rules, regulations and orders containing penal provisions. See Lan Quanpu, *Thirty Years of the Development of Law and Regulations in Our Country* (*Sanshi Nian Lai Woguo Fagui Yange Gaikuang*) (Beijing: Press of the Masses, 1982), at 55-65; and Jerome Alan Cohen, *The Criminal Process in the People's Republic of China, 1949–1963: An Introduction* (Cambridge, Massachusetts: Harvard University Press, 1968), ch.VI.

5 The 1979 Law was a mixture of the Soviet Criminal Codes of 1926 and 1960 and China's own innovations. There was a second-hand German influence through the Soviet codes. See Harold J. Berman, Susan Cohen & Malcolm Russell, 'Comparison of the Chinese and Soviet Codes of Criminal Law and Procedure', (1982) (vol. 73, No. 1) *Journal of Crim. L. & Criminology* 238.

6 Zhang Youyu & Wang Shuwen, *Forty Years of Legal Science in China* (*Zhongguo Faxue Sishinian*) (Shanghai: Shanghai People's Press, 1989), at 216.

7 Before this, the Legal Committee of the Central Government had finished another draft in 76 articles, entitled Guiding Principles of the Criminal Law of the PRC. See Zhang & Wang, *supra* note 6, at 217.

8 See Zhang & Wang, *supra* note 6, at 218; and Criminal Research Group, the Law Institute of the Chinese Academy of Social Sciences, *Lectures on the Criminal Law*, translated in (Vol. XIII, No. 2, 1980) *Chinese Law and Government*, at 8.

were only resumed in May 1962; rapid progress was apparently made and by 1963 the 33rd draft of the criminal law was completed and submitted to the Standing Committee of the Politburo and to Mao Zedong for examination.[9] However, the drafting work was again to be interrupted by nation-wide political movements and not resumed until 1979.

In March 1979, the Legislative Affairs Committee (LAC) of the Standing Committee of the NPC (SCNPC) was established, and the newly established LAC decided to use the above-mentioned 33rd draft as its basis for drafting the code.[10] After a short period of just four months the Criminal Law was adopted by the NPC. Thus the 1979 Criminal Law was essentially a product of the 1950s and 1960s – a period when Chinese legal science was being established by borrowing heavily from Soviet scholarship and legal experience.[11] It is therefore not surprising that the 1979 Criminal Law embodied strong Soviet influence, though it also reflected the then political policy for ensuring social stability, order and economic development.

Major deficiencies in the 1979 Criminal Law soon became apparent when implementation of the law began. To start with, provisions in the 1979 Criminal Law were soon found to be too general and lacking in precision for actual implementation. Secondly, various anti-crime campaigns launched in China since the early 1980s required the imposition of severe punishments for targeted crimes (e.g. rape, murder, smuggling, drug trafficking etc.). Thirdly, the deepening of economic reform also led to certain economic crimes that were not anticipated in the 1979 Criminal Law.[12]

To deal with the above deficiencies, major supplementation began to emerge. Barely a year and half after the implementation of the 1979 Criminal Law, the Deci-

---

9 *Lectures on the Criminal Law, supra* note 8, at 8-9.

10 Zhang & Wang, *supra* note 6, at 220; Peng Zhen, 'Explanations on the Draft Criminal Law and Draft Criminal Procedure Law', delivered to the 8th Meeting of the Standing Committee of the 5th NPC on 7 June 1979, in Peng Zhen, *On Political and Legal Work in New China* (*Lun Xinzhongguo De Zhengfa Gongzuo*) (Beijing: Press of the Central Committee's Documents, 1992), at 146.

11 In terms of criminal law science, the efforts of Chinese scholars in the first few years of the 1950s were concentrated on the study of Soviet criminal law theories, Soviet codes and the translation of Soviet codes and textbooks. It was natural that drafts of criminal law in the 1950s were largely modelled on the Soviet Code of 1926. Although Chinese scholars began to write their own textbooks on criminal law, these textbooks were then based on the Chinese criminal law drafts. Thus Soviet influence continued and spread through the Chinese textbooks on criminal law. See Zhang & Wang, *supra* note 6, at 216-218. See also discussions in Chapter 2.

12 See Wang Hanbin, 'Explanations on the Draft Revision of the Criminal Law of the PRC', delivered to the 5th Plenary Session of the 8th NPC on 6 March 1997, in Huang Taiyun and Teng Wei (eds), *A Practical Guide and Interpretation of the Criminal Law of the PRC* (*Zhonghua Renmin Gongheguo Xingfa Shiyi Yu Shiyong Zhinan*) (Beijing: The Redflag Press, 1997), at 670.

sion Regarding the Handling of Offenders Undergoing Reform Through Labour and Persons Undergoing Rehabilitation Through Labour Who Escape or Commit New Crimes, and the Provisional Regulations on the Punishment of Crimes of Servicemen in Violation of Duty were issued by the SCNPC on 10 June 1981. Thereafter, numerous 'Decisions', 'Provisional Regulations' and 'Supplementary Provisions' were issued by the SCNPC, amending or supplementing the 1979 Law.[13] Many new offences were also created by various non-criminal statutes issued by the NPC, its Standing Committee or even the State Council.[14] Clearly, the Criminal Law had become too fragmented and unsystematic. Further, certain supplementary provisions violated the principles of the 1979 Criminal Law. For instance, the 1982 Decision of the Standing Committee on Severely Punishing Criminals Who Gravely Endanger the Economy and the 1983 Decision of the Standing Committee on Severely Punishing Criminals Who Gravely Endanger the Public Security of the Society clearly took retrospective force, whereas the 1979 Criminal Law prohibited the retrospective application of the criminal law.[15]

Further, provisions on analogy, counter-revolutionary crimes and the death penalty attracted severe criticism from many intellectuals and human rights organisations.[16] Chinese scholars then began to question the wisdom of including provisions on analogy and counter-revolutionary crimes and the extensive application of the death penalty.[17]

---

13 By the time of the 1997 revision, 22 such Decisions, Provisional Regulations or Supplementary Provisions had been issued. See Wang Hanbin, *supra* note 12, at 670-80. For a list of these Decisions, Provisional Regulations or Supplementary Provisions, see Ma Kechang & Ding Muying (eds) *The Revision and Improvement of the Criminal Law* (*Xingfa De Xiugai Yu Wanshan*) (Beijing: Press of the People's Court, 1995), at 2-3.

14 By early 1995, more than 70 non-criminal statutes prescribing criminal punishment had been issued. For a summary of these provisions, see Ma & Ding, *supra* note 13, at 2. By the time of the 1997 revision, more than 130 provisions contained in various non-criminal statutes had provided criminal liabilities. See Wang Hanbin, *supra* note 12, at 671. These provisions created no less than 103 criminal offences. See Lin Yagang & Jia Yu, 'On the Character of Special Criminal Laws and Their Incorporation into the Criminal Code', in (no. 1, 1997) *Peking University Law Journal* (*Zhongwai Faxue*) 79, at 80. Together with the supplementary provisions, no less than 230 offences had emerged since 1979. See Chen Xingliang, 'Dual Task for Criminal Revision: Change in Values and Adjustment of Structure', (no. 1, 1997) *Peking University Law Journal* (*Zhongwai Faxue*) 55, at 60.

15 See Article 9 of the 1979 Criminal Law.

16 See e.g. Lawyers Committee for Human Rights, *Criminal Justice with Chinese Characteristics* (New York, 1993); and numerous reports by Amnesty International, Human Rights Watch, etc.

17 See various volumes of the *China Law Yearbook* (published by the Press of China Law Yearbook, Beijing), which summarise major academic studies on various branches of law in China. These issues are to be further discussed below.

Under these circumstances, the need to comprehensively revise the 1979 Criminal Law required little justification. Indeed, as soon as the 1979 Law came into effect some scholars had already called for the revision of the law.[18] According to Wang Hanbin, then Vice-Chairman of the SCNPC, the decision to revise the Law was made in 1982 and preliminary guidelines for the revision were established in 1988 by the SCNPC.[19] However, specific revision work was mainly carried out by a Criminal Law Revision Group established in 1994 within the LAC of the SCNPC, consisting of scholars and practitioners.[20] This substantial work was completed in three years.[21]

Although various ideas for revising the 1979 Criminal Law were advanced by Chinese scholars, ranging from a complete overhaul to the rejection of any comprehensive revision,[22] the guidelines for the 1997 Revision apparently offered an easy path. First, the revision was to incorporate various Decisions and Supplementary Provisions issued by the SCNPC since 1979. Secondly, the revision was to ensure the continuity and stability of the Law; thus provisions without 'major' problems would not be revised. Thirdly, general and vague provisions were to be elaborated and clarified.[23] In short, the revision was to rationalise, systematise, clarify and elaborate the 1979 Law.

Following the major revision made to the Criminal Procedure Law (CPL) in 1996, a comprehensive revision of the Criminal Law was finally adopted in March 1997. The original law of 192 articles was now expanded to include 452 articles in total. The categorisation of crimes was overhauled, with many new offences being created to meet the prevailing circumstances for the orderly development of a socialist market economy. Certain fundamental principles of justice, e.g. *nullum crimen, nulla poena sine lege* (and the consequential abolition of the provision on analogy), equality before the law, and proportionality, were now for the first time expressly incorporated into the criminal law.

---

18 As early as 1980 some scholars had already called for the revision of the 1979 Criminal Law. See Zhang Mingkai, 'On Properly Dealing with Several Relations in Revising the Criminal Law', (no. 1, 1997) *Peking University Law Journal* (*Zhongwai Faxue*) 65, in his footnote 3, at 71.

19 Wang Hanbin, *supra* note 12, at 670. The revision was often interrupted by various factors. See Ma Kechang, 'Srengthen the Reform Force, Revise and Perfect the Criminal Law', (no. 5, 1996) *Law Review* (*Faxue Pinglun*) 1, at 1.

20 Cao Zidan & Hou Guoyun (eds), *A Precise Interpretation of the Criminal Law of the PRC*, (*Zhonghua Renmin Gongheguo Xingfa Jingjie*) (Beijing: China University of Political Science and Law Press, 1997), at 1.

21 Chinese officials have, however, insisted that the 1997 revision was a result of 15 years of drafting. See Wang Hanbin, *supra* note 12, at 671.

22 See a collection of essays by 86 Chinese scholars: Ma & Ding, *supra* note 13.

23 See Wang Hanbin, *supra* note 12, at 671-672.

Although the revision was heralded as 'a major and significant measure to improve the criminal law and criminal justice',[24] it is disappointing in many aspects, as will be shown in the following analyses. It should also be pointed out here that the revised Criminal Law has since been amended by the SCNPC six times, not including the various interpretations issued by the SCNPC, the Supreme People's Court and the Supreme People's Procuratorate.[25]

3. General Principles

3.1. An Overview

Following the Continental style of the German model, the 1979 Criminal Law was divided into two parts: General Principles (*zongze*) and Specific Provisions (*fenze*). The General Principles define the purposes and application scope of the Law as well as notions of crime and criminal liability. They also provide rules on sentencing, parole and statutory limitations. Specific Provisions define and elaborate various crimes and offences and their consequent penalties. This overall structure is retained in the 1997 revised Criminal Law.

---

24 *People's Daily* Commentator, 'A Major and Significant Measure to Improve the Criminal Law and Criminal Justice', *People's Daily* (*Renmin Ribao*) (internet edition), 4 April 1997.

25 The post-1997 amendments include Amendment I (12 December 1999), aimed at strengthening the economic order by way of imposing heavier punishments on economic crimes (affecting Articles 162 (1), 168, 174, 180, 181, 182, 185, & 225(3)); Amendment II (31 August 2001), aimed at punishing illegal occupation of and damage to forest land (affecting Article 342 only); Amendment III (29 December 2001), tightening provisions on terrorism and imposing more severe punishment on terrorist activities (affecting Articles 114, 115, 120, 125, 127, 191 & Article 291(1)); Amendment IV (28 December 2002), aimed at cracking down on the manufacture and sale of fake and shoddy medical apparatus and the smuggling of waste, punishing the use of child labour and dereliction of duty of judicial officials, and protecting valuable trees and plants and their products (affecting Articles145, 155, 344, 345, 399, & Article 244(1)); Amendment V (28 May 2005), targeting credit card fraud (affecting Article 196, 177(1) & 369); and Amendment VI (29 June 2006), being the most significant one since 1997. It mainly concerns crimes endangering public security, crimes against enterprise administration order, crimes undermining financial management order, crimes of harming the interests of listed companies and investors, and commercial embezzlement. Heavier punishments are imposed on offenders and more severe criminal liabilities are incurred by persons-in-charge/in authority involved in such crimes. 18 articles were revised (134, 135, 139, 161, 162, 163, 164, 169, 175, 182, 185, 186, 187, 188, 191, 262, 303, 312, 399) and 8 sub-articles were added. According to the SCNPC 2007 legislative plan, there is an Amendment VII that has been scheduled for deliberation for the August session of the SCNPC. See '2007 Legislative Plan and Supervision Plan', in <npc.people.com.cn/GB/28320/41246/41337/5422052.html> (last accessed 20 June 2007).

The structure of the first part, the General Principles, is intact, and the 1997 revision to the provisions of this part has been minimal. However, the incorporation of some fundamental principles of justice into the General Principles constitutes the most significant progress and development in criminal law since 1979.

3.2. *Nullum Crimen, Nulla Poena Sine Lege* and the Abolition of Analogy

The 1979 Criminal Law did not expressly provide the principle of *nullum crimen, nulla poena sine lege*; instead, Article 79 allowed the application of the Law by analogy, subject to the approval of the Supreme People's Court.[26] Many Chinese scholars and officials have, however, insisted that *nullum crimen, nulla poena sine lege* or its 'spirit' is one of the basic principles of Chinese criminal law.[27] The existence of analogy was said to be supplementary to the Law and represented a flexible application of the 'old and rigid' principle of *nullum crimen, nulla poena sine lege.*[28]

This Chinese argument is, however, not convincing. As pointed out above, the 1979 Criminal Law was based on the 33rd draft from 1963, which itself was developed from various drafts completed in the 1950s and early 1960s. The principle of *nullum crimen, nulla poena sine lege* was severely criticised after the Judicial Reform Movement in 1952 as being one of the bourgeois legal principles that gave aid and comfort to landlords and counter-revolutionaries at the expense of the public interest and, as such, had to be rejected by socialist law.[29] The discussion on this principle did not resume until after the promulgation of the 1979 Law.[30] Further, the use of analogy is conceptually inconsistent with the principle of *nullum crimen, nulla poena sine lege.*

Analogy was an ancient legal institution in China. According to Shen Jiaben, the founding father of modern law reform in China, the practice of interpreting the law by analogy started in the Han Dynasty (206–8 BC) and was sanctioned by law

---

26 Article 79 of the 1979 Criminal Law provided that '[a] person who commits crimes not explicitly defined in the Specific Provisions of the criminal law may be convicted and sentenced, after the approval of the Supreme People's Court has been obtained, according to the most similar article in this Law.'

27 See e.g. Wang Henbin, *supra* note 12, at 672; Su Huiyu, *Criminal Law* (*Xingfa Xue*) (Beijing: China University of Political Science and Law Press, 1994), at 32; Lan Quanpu, *supra* note 4, at 69; Zhao Zhenjiang (ed.), *Forty Years of the Chinese Legal System* (*Zhongguo Fazhi Sishinian*) (Beijing: Beijing University Press, 1990), at 338; Huang & Teng, *supra* note 12, at 4; and Ma & Ding, *supra* note 13, 31-32.

28 *Id.*

29 Shao-chuan Leng, *Justice in Communist China: A Survey of the Judicial System of the Chinese People's Republic* (New York: Oceana Publications, Inc., 1967), at 42, 160 and 176; Cohen (1968), *supra* note 4, at 330.

30 See List of Publications (1949–1985) in Gao Mingxuan (ed.), *A Summary of Criminal Law Research in the New China* (*Xinzhongguo Xingfa Yanjiu Zongshu*) (Henan: Henan People's Press, 1986), at 757-971.

in the Sui Dynasty (AD 589–618).[31] However, as the conservatives who opposed the abolition of analogy argued, the practice had perhaps started much earlier.[32] Meijer apparently agreed that the argument based on the *Li Ji* and the *Book of History* by the conservatives was more accurate.[33] It is clear, in any case, that analogy was codified in the earliest extant written code, the Tang Code (*Tang Lü Shuyi*, first published in AD 753).[34] The long history of the practice of analogy is thus said to have created an 'analogy complex' in the Chinese mentality.[35] The nature and the actual use of analogy in traditional China, namely to create new categories of crimes retrospectively, or simply to elaborate the 'most appropriate' punishment, is however disputed among scholars.[36]

In spite of strong opposition from conservative forces,[37] analogy was formally abolished and the principle *nullum crimen, nulla poena sine lege* introduced into Chinese criminal law during the law reforms in the dying days of the Qing Dynasty.[38]

The Chinese communist justice system did not, however, accept this principle. The Statute of the Chinese Soviet Republic on the Punishment of Counter-Revolutionary Crimes – the first comprehensive legislation under the communist rule defining

---

31 See Section IV of The Commissioner for the Revision of the Laws, Shen Jia-pen Presents by Memorial the Draft of the Criminal Law, in M.J. Meijer, *Introduction of Modern Criminal Law in China*, 2nd edition (Hong Kong: Lung Men Bookstore, 1967), at 195-196. A similar view is also held by some modern scholars. See for instance, Mary Buck, 'Justice for All: The Application of Law by Analogy in the Case of Zhou Fuqing', (no. 2, 1993) 7 *J.Chinese L* 113, at 117.

32 See Meijer, *id.*, at 94.

33 See Meijer, *supra* note 31, at 68.

34 See Buck, *supra* note 31, at 117.

35 Chen Xingliang, '*Nullum Creme Noena Peona Sine Lege* in Modern Times', (no. 2, 1996) *Studies in Law* (*Faxue Yanjiu*) 11, at 40.

36 See Buck, *supra* note 31, at 117. One of the authorities on traditional Chinese penal law, Professor Geoffrey MacCormack, clearly holds the view that the reasoning by analogy employed by the imperial judicial officials was similar to statutory interpretation in the West and was not in conflict with the principle *nulla poena sine lege*. See Geoffrey MacCormack, *The Spirit of Traditional Chinese Law* (Athens & London: The University of Georgia Press, 1996), at 172-74.

37 See Meijer (1967), *supra* note 31, at 94.

38 Article 3 of the Chapter on Rights and Duties of the Subjects of the Principles of Constitution (1908, never formally promulgated) for the first time in Chinese history provided that '[a] subject shall not be liable to arrest, imprisonment or punishment except as prescribed by law'. The New Criminal Law issued by the Qing government in 1910 for the first time formally provided in law the principle of *nullum crimen sine lege* (Article 10 thus contained the principle of 'no offence, no punishment without previous legal provision'. See Meijer (1967), *supra* note 31, at 71.) Article 1 of the Criminal Code of the KMT issued in 1935 provided the same. See Chen Xingliang, *supra* note 35, at 39. See also Ma & Ding, *supra* note 13, at 70.

criminal acts – explicitly revived the application of law by analogy.[39] The principle of analogy was reaffirmed by the first comprehensive criminal law in the PRC, the 1951 Regulations of the PRC on the Punishment of Counter-Revolutionary Crimes.[40]

The need for analogy in the communist criminal justice system was justified on the grounds of the temporary lack of comprehensive laws. Thus in the 1957 *Lectures on the General Principles of the Criminal Law of the PRC* edited by the Teaching and Research Office for Criminal Law of the Central Political-Legal Cadres' School, it was said that analogy would be abolished when the criminal law was established.[41] This moderate view on analogy was however to be severely criticised by 1958,[42] when the non-retroactivity of the criminal law, together with other fundamental principles of criminal justice, were systematically denounced.[43]

Abolition of analogy only began to be seriously debated again after 1988.[44] Central to the debate were differing interpretations of the three major issues: the legal position and the trend towards the *nullum crimen, nulla poena sine lege* in the world's major legal systems; the possibility of the co-existence of this principle with analogy; and preference in cases of conflict between *nullum crimen, nulla poena sine lege* and analogy.[45] Those who argued for the abolition of analogy believed strongly that *nullum crimen, nulla poena sine lege* was a universal principle upheld in all major legal systems under the Rule of Law, that it and analogy were mutually exclusive and, thus, that the upholding of *nullum crimen, nulla poena sine lege* necessarily required the abolition of analogy in criminal law.[46] Opponents were not

---

39 See Article 38. An English translation of the Statute can be found in W.E. Butler (ed.), *The Legal System of the Chinese Soviet Republic 1931–1934* (New York: Transnational Publishers Inc., 1983), at 204-207.

40 Article 16. An English translation of the Act can be found in Shao-Chuan Leng & Hungdah Chiu, *Criminal Justice in Post-Mao China: Analysis and Documents* (Albany: State University of New York Press, 1985), at 177-182.

41 The Lectures are extracted in Cohen (1968), *supra* note 4, at 336. This view was perhaps influenced by developments in the Soviet Union, where the principle of analogy was a key part of the 1926 Russian Criminal Code, but was criticised in the late 1930s and finally discarded by the Soviet Union in 1958. See Berman, Cohen & Russell, *supra* note 5, at 249.

42 See Fan Ming, 'Some Opinions about *Lectures on the General Principles of Criminal Law of the PRC*', CFYC, 4:73 (1958), translated in Cohen (1968), *supra* note 4, at 339.

43 See Cohen (1968), *supra* note 4, at 15.

44 Ma & Ding, *supra* note 13, at 56. Up to the mid-1980s scholarly discussion on analogy mainly concentrated on the justification and the proper use of analogy; there was only some isolated discussion on abolishing it. See Gao Mingxuan, *supra* note 30, at 126-37; and Zhao Bingzhi & Xiao Zhonghua, 'A Discussion on the Debate About the Abolition of Analogy in Criminal Law', (no. 4, 1996) *Jurists* (*Faxue Jia*) 54.

45 Zhao & Xiao, *supra* note 44, at 57.

46 See e.g. Zhao & Xiao, *supra* note 44; Hu Yunteng, 'Abolition of Analogy and the Scientific Nature of Criminal Law', (no. 5, 1995) *Studies in Law* (*Faxue Yanjiu*) 55; and Chen Xingliang,

convinced by these arguments, believing that the impossibility of making a perfect criminal code necessarily required the application of the law by analogy. They also believed that *nullum crimen, nulla poena sine lege* was not a principle in Common law countries and that its importance had decreased in all other countries.[47]

The final decision to abolish analogy was perhaps first of all influenced by the fact that the revised Criminal Law, after incorporating various supplements and decisions over the last 18 years, would become relatively comprehensive and the coverage of the Law would be greatly expanded. Secondly, Article 79 on analogy in the 1979 Law had been rarely used by courts. Thus it was deemed possible to abolish analogy and to incorporate *nullum crimen, nulla poena sine lege* into the revised law.[48]

Article 3 of the revised Criminal Law now provides that '[a]ll criminal acts expressly stipulated by law as crimes shall be determined as such and punished according to the law; acts not expressly defined by law as criminal shall not be judged so and shall not be punished.'

3.3. Equality Before the Law and Marxism-Leninism-Mao Zedong Thought as a Guiding Ideology for Criminal Law

Article 4 of the 1979 Criminal Procedure Law, which was issued at the same time as the 1979 Criminal Law, provided that '[a]ll citizens are equal in the application of the Law. No privilege whatsoever is permissible before the Law.' This principle of 'equality before the law' was not, however, provided in the 1979 Criminal Law.

The omission of this principle is perhaps attributable to the upholding of Marxism-Leninism-Mao Zedong Thought as the guiding ideology for criminal law,[49] which strongly emphasised the class nature of law. Under this ideology, criminal law was an important weapon for class struggle, aimed primarily at attacking 'counter-revolutionaries and other criminals who seriously undermined social order and socialist construction'.[50] According to Mao's theory on correctly handling two kinds of social contradictions, i.e. those between the enemies and

---

supra note 35.

47 See Hou Guoyun, '*Nullum Crimen, Nulla Poena Sine Lege* in a Market Economy and the Value of Criminal Analogy', (no. 3, 1995) *Studies in Law* (*Faxue Yanjiu*) 61; Hou Guoyun, 'On the Retention or Abolition of Analogy', in Ma & Ding, *supra* note 13, at 56-68.

48 Wang Hanbin, *supra* note 12, at 672. According to Chinese scholars, in the 18 years of implementation of the 1979 Criminal Law only a few more than 70 cases were decided by analogy and most of them concerned minor offences. See Ma & Ding, *supra* note 13, at 7; Hou Guoyun, *supra* note 47, at 64.

49 See Article 1 of the 1979 Criminal Law.

50 See discussions in Cohen (1968), *supra* note 4, at 71-96.

the people and those among the people,[51] criminals were mainly enemies of the state who must be dealt with severely by criminal law. The 'people', though they might also be punished by the criminal law, had to be treated differently from the 'enemies'.[52] Under this ideology, it was not surprising that equality before the law was repudiated as an anti-Party bourgeois concept in the late 1950s and during the Cultural Revolution.[53]

Equality before the law as a legal principle re-emerged in the post-Mao era. However, there were also heated debates in the late 1970s and early 1980s as to whether equality before the law meant only equality in the application of the law or also included the making of law. Further, the major concern of upholding the principle was to prevent privilege being accorded to officials of all ranks; that is, law was to attack 'tigers and flies' alike. The emphasis was not as much on protection as on punishment.[54] Thus the principle was not included in the substantive law (the Criminal Law) but was incorporated into procedural law (the Criminal Procedure Law) or organic laws (the Organic Laws of the Court and the Procuratorate).[55] The debate in the late 1970s and early 1980s also led to the reinstatement of the equality principle in the 1982 Constitution.[56]

The new Article 4 of the revised Criminal Law now provides that '[a]ll are equal in the application of law. No privilege whatsoever is permissible beyond the law.' Like the previous equality provisions in other laws, the emphasis is on the application of law and on the elimination of official privileges.[57] It is also important to note that Marxism-Leninism-Mao Zedong Thought as a guiding principle of criminal law has now been formally dropped, which presumably means the final burying of the class nature of the criminal law.[58]

---

51 For Mao's theory, see his thesis on Problems Relating to the Correct Handling of Contradictions Among the People, translated in Cohen (1968), *supra* note 4, at 83-88.

52 Lan Quanpu (1982), *supra* note 4, at 70-71.

53 See Leng & Chiu, *supra* note 40, at 104.

54 See the collection of papers debating the principle: Office for Research Materials, Law Institute of the Chinese Academy of Social Science (ed.), *On Equality Before the Law* (*Lun Falü Mianqian Renren Pingdeng*) (Beijing: Publishing House of Law, 1981). See further discussions in Leng and Chiu, *supra* note 40, at 104-108.

55 See Article 5 of the Organic Law of the Courts and Article 8 of the Organic Law of the People's Procuratorates. All these laws were adopted at the same session of the NPC during which the Criminal Law was also adopted.

56 See Article 33 of the 1982 Constitution. See also discussions in Chapter 3.

57 See interpretations by scholars in China: Huang & Tend, *supra* note 12, at 4-5; and Cao & Hou, *supra* note 20, at 5-6.

58 Chinese scholars have, however, insisted that, since the Four Fundamental Principles are constitutional principles, the Criminal Law issued under the Constitution would logically still include this principle. See Huang & Tend, *supra* note 12, at 1; and Cao & Hou, *supra* note 20, at 3-4.

3.4. Proportionality (*Zuixing Xiang Shiying*)

One of the guiding principles incorporated in the 1979 Criminal Law was the policy of combining punishment with leniency,[59] which meant 'leniency to those who confess and severity to those who resist' in the determination of sentences.[60] However, the Law did not provide specific aggravating and mitigating circumstances to guide the court in sentence determination. This was to allow law enforcement to be adapted to the needs of the political situation of the time.[61] As with the concerns regarding equality before the law, such a policy can provide, and did provide, loopholes in the law for officials in power to escape legal sanctions or avoid severe punishment.[62] Further, the emphasis on confession was also potentially in conflict with the presumption of innocence.[63]

As has been the fate of Marxism-Leninism-Mao Zedong Thought as a guiding principle, the principle of combining punishment with leniency has also been abolished. Article 5 of the 1997 revised Criminal Law now provides that 'the severity or leniency of punishment shall be proportionate to the crime committed by the criminal and the consequent criminal liability [prescribed by law].' This is what Chinese scholars refer to as the principle of proportionality (*zuixing xiang shiying yuanze*).

The Chinese principle of proportionality is fundamentally based on the theory developed by the 18th century Italian scholar Cesare Beccaria in his seminal work *On Crimes and Punishments*.[64] The incorporation of this principle, according to

---

59 See Article 1 of the 1979 Criminal Law.

60 See Leng & Chiu, *supra* note 40, at 129.

61 *Ibid*.

62 Zhang Jun, 'The Three Basic Principles of the Criminal Law', *People's Daily* (*Renmin Ribao*) (overseas edition), 26 April 1997, internet edition.

63 The presumption of innocence was partially incorporated into the Criminal Procedure Law when it was revised in 1996. See Article 7 of the Criminal Procedure Law (as revised in 1996). See also discussions in Chapter 8.

64 See Hu Xuexiang, 'The Problems in the Principle of Proportionality and Their Solutions', (no. 3, 1994) *Law Review* (*Faxue Pinglun*) 18; Liao Zengyun, 'Basic Principles that Should Be Clearly Adopted in Our Criminal Law', (no. 1, 1990) *Legal Science in China* (*Zhongguo Faxue*) 54; Chen Xingliang, 'On the Development and Improvement of Our Criminal Law', (no. 3, 1989) *Legal Science in China* (*Zhongguo Faxue*) 53; Li Shaoping & Deng Xiuming, 'Some Theoretical Considerations on Improving the Law on Crimes and Punishments', (no. 1, 1996) *Modern Law Science* (*Xiandai Faxue*) 9; and Hu Xuexiang, 'Improving the Legislative Structure on Punishment', (no. 2, 1996) *Modern Law Science* (*Xiandai Faxue*) 124. For Beccaria's theory on proportionality, see Cesare Beccaria, *On Crimes and Punishments*, translated by Henry Paolucci (Indianapolis/New York: The Bodds-Merrili Co. Inc., 1963). For a more recent translation by Richard Davies, Virginia Cox and Richard Bellamy, see Richard Bellamy (ed.), *Beccaria On Crimes and Punishments and Other Writings* (Cambridge: Cambridge University Press, 1995).

explanations given to the NPC by Wang Hanbin, is to make sure that serious crimes are punished heavily and light crimes leniently. It is also to make sure that there will be a balance between various provisions of the Law in punishing crimes.[65] Thus, this principle encompasses the following aspects: First, the principle of proportionality is the basis for the General Provisions in dealing with issues of preparation to commit a crime, attempted crimes, incomplete crimes, joint offence, recidivism, and voluntary surrender. Secondly, the Specific Provisions of the Law is to have a balanced approach in defining punishments for criminal offences according to the seriousness of the crime. Thirdly, the nature of the crime and its social harm will be the main factors in judicial determination of punishment.[66] This last point is important; it means that the principle of proportionality in China at present is not purely a reflection of the backward-looking philosophy of retributive justice (*lex talionis*, 'an eye for an eye; a tooth for a tooth'). The traditional forward-looking utilitarian views on justice, such as the educational function of the criminal law, are not discarded. Indeed, Article 57 of the 1979 Criminal Law is retained without any revision. This article requires that in individual sentence determination, courts shall consider the facts of a crime, its nature and circumstances as well as its harm to the society.[67] This article, however, gives judges great latitude in imposing punishment. To achieve the intended purpose of avoiding the misuse of leniency, the revised Law now further elaborates a number of articles dealing with aggravating and, in particular, mitigating circumstances. Thus, Article 63 specifically provides that the imposition of punishment below the minimum punishment prescribed by the law must be approved by the Supreme People's Court.[68] Article 67 now defines voluntary surrender as not only voluntary surrender to the authority after committing a crime, but also includes the truthful confession of crimes committed. Further, any criminal suspects, criminal defendants or convicted criminals who voluntarily and truthfully confess crimes not yet discovered by the judicial authorities will also be treated leniently.[69] A new article, Article 68, provides lenient punishment for offenders who provide information or other assistance to investigatory organisations in solving crimes committed by other people.

Despite the above improvement in the criminal law in dealing with leniency, the revised Criminal Law continues to be weak in terms of elaborate and detailed provisions on aggravating and mitigating circumstances. Thus a proper application of the principle of proportionality is a crucial point in the actual operation of the Criminal Law.

---

65 See Wang Hanbin, *supra* note 12 at 672.

66 Huang & Teng, *supra* note 12 at 5-6.

67 Article 57 is renumbered as Article 61 in the revised Criminal Law.

68 Under Article 59 of the 1979 Criminal Law this was to be approved by the judicial committee of a people's court.

69 Article 67 is a revised version of Article 63 of the 1979 Criminal Law.

3.5. 'White Collar' Crime – 'Unit Criminality' (*Danwei Fanzui*)

Imposing criminal liability upon corporations is almost exclusively a tradition of the Common law.[70] Corporate criminal liability has only recently been advocated in European Continental countries as a means of controlling the excesses of the increasingly powerful economic entities.[71] The development of criminal liability of corporations as legal persons in all legal systems, however, has followed a long and slow path. The difficulties associated with corporate criminal liability are apparent. To start with, a corporation as an abstraction is conceptually without its own mind; thus there are difficulties in locating *mens rea* in imposing criminal liability. Further, it has no physical existence of its own. Thirdly, most forms of criminal punishment, such as incarceration, are clearly inapplicable to a corporation. Finally, the principle of *ultra vires* in corporation law certainly does not help in developing a theory of corporate criminal liability. However, for all practical purposes these difficulties are now largely overcome in both Civil and Common law jurisdictions.[72]

The Chinese legal system is no exception. When the Criminal Law was enacted in 1979 it did not expressly provide for, nor absolutely exclude, the criminal responsibility of a legal person. Some provisions seemed to hold only the individual liable;[73] others tended to hold both the legal person and the individual liable.[74] However, the prevailing criminal law theory at that time did not seem to lend much support to arguments for corporate criminal liability.[75] This was because, according

---

70 L.H. Leigh, *The Criminal Liability of Corporations in English Law* (London: London School of Economics and Political Science, 1969), at 1.

71 L.H. Leigh, 'The Criminal Liability of Corporations and Other Groups: A Comparative View', (1982) 80 *Michigan Law Review* 1508, at 1508.

72 See further discussions in Leigh (1969), *supra* note 70; Leigh (1982), *supra* note 71; Elkins, 'Corporations and the Criminal Law: An Uneasy Alliance', (1976) 65 *Ky.L.J.* 73; 'Developments in the Law – Corporate Crimes: Regulating Corporate Behaviours through Criminal Sanctions', (1979) 92 *Harvard Law Review* 1227; and Leonard Orland, 'Reflections on Corporate Crime: Law in Search of Theory and Scholarship', (1980) 17 *American Criminal Law Review* 501.

73 For instance, Article 131 provided that: 'The rights of the person, the democratic rights and the other rights of citizens are to be protected and are not to be unlawfully infringed by any person or any organ. When the circumstances of unlawful infringement are serious, those persons directly responsible are to be given criminal sanctions'.

74 For instance, Article 121 provided that: 'Those directly responsible for violating tax laws and regulations, evading taxes or resisting taxes, if the circumstances are serious, in addition to making up the tax due and paying any fine possibly imposed in accordance with the tax laws and regulations, are to be sentenced to not more than three years of fixed-term imprisonment or criminal detention'. This article does not specify the subject of crime (i.e. who commits the crime). If it is a legal person which violates tax laws, it seems that the criminal punishment of imposing fines may apply to the legal person itself.

75 See Yang Chuanxi, *et al.*, *General Principles of Criminal Law* (Beijing: Beijing University Press, 1981), at 139-140; and *Chinese Encyclopaedia – Law* (*Zhongguo Dabaike Quanshu – Faxue*)

to Chinese theory, crimes could only be committed with consciousness, and legal persons themselves could not commit any intentional criminal activities. Any such criminal activities could only be committed by the natural persons who constitute the legal person, and thus only these natural persons should be responsible for crimes committed by themselves.[76]

However, the emergence of economic crimes committed by enterprises as a result of economic reforms began to change judicial attitudes and practice towards corporate criminality. In 1985, the Resolutions of the Supreme People's Court and the Supreme People's Procuratorate Concerning Certain Questions on the Practical Application of the Law in the Present Adjudication of Cases of Economic Crimes (Trial Implementation) expressly affirmed the criminal liability of legal persons guilty of certain economic crimes.[77] For instance, the Resolutions provide that, if any state organ, association, institution, enterprise or collective economic entity is engaged in smuggling, illicit speculation, seeking illegal profits and bribing, criminal liability will be imposed on the person in charge of the legal person and on the person directly involved in the crime, and the property of the legal person involved in the crimes will be confiscated.[78] Furthermore, two articles (Articles 49 and 110) of the General Principles of Civil Law seem to indicate that crimes may be committed by legal persons and criminal liability may be imposed on legal persons in accordance with law.[79] However, the wording of these provisions is still very vague.

In 1987 the Customs Law of the People's Republic of China was adopted by the SCNPC. Article 47 (3) of the Customs Law states that: 'Where an enterprise, an undertaking, a state organ or a social organisation is guilty of smuggling, the judicial organ shall pursue the criminal liability of the person in charge of the respective unit and the person directly answerable for the offence and shall impose a fine on the unit and confiscate the smuggled goods and articles, the means of transport used to carry them and the illegal incomes obtained therefrom'. This provision is interpreted by some Chinese scholars as meaning that the Chinese legislation for

(Beijing/Shanghai: The Chinese Encyclopaedia Press, 1984), at 128.

76 Yang Chuanxi, *ibid.*, at 141.

77 See section 2 (2) of the Resolutions of the Supreme People's Court and the Supreme People's Procuratorate Concerning Certain Questions on the Practical Application of the Law in the Present Adjudication of Cases of Economic Crimes (Trial Implementation).

78 *Ibid.*, at 190.

79 Article 49 states that: 'Should any one of the following circumstances apply to an enterprise legal person, it shall assume liability and, in addition, its legal representative may be subject to administrative sanction or a fine; if a crime is constituted, criminal liability shall be investigated and determined according to the law: …'. Article 110 states that: 'If it is necessary to investigate and determine administrative liability with regard to a citizen or legal person bearing civil liability, such administrative liability shall be investigated and determined. If a criminal offence is constituted, the criminal liability of the citizen or of the legal representative of the legal person shall be investigated and determined'.

the first time expressly adopted the so-called 'dual punishment' principle.[80] This legislative approach was later followed by two other pieces of legislation adopted by the SCNPC: Article 9 of the Supplementary Rules of the SCNPC on the Severe Punishment of Corruption and Bribery Offences (1988) provides that: 'Any enterprise, institution, authority or body that offers rebates and handling charges to a state functionary, member of staff of a collective economic body or any other person holding public office for unlawful advantages in breach of state regulations shall be fined where severity justifies it. The officer-in-charge directly responsible and other persons directly responsible shall be sentenced to imprisonment or criminal detention of not more than five years ...', and Article 5 of the Supplementary Rules of the SCNPC on the Punishment of Smuggling (1988) states that: 'Any enterprise, institution, state authority, or association that engages in the smuggling of goods and articles specified in Articles 1 to 3 of the present Rules shall be fined; the directly responsible officer-in-charge and other directly responsible persons shall be punished in accordance with the provisions of the present Rules governing smuggling offences committed by individuals'. By 1997, no less than 13 Decisions and Supplementary Provisions had provided corporate criminality.[81] However, there was no law regarding the general concept of crimes committed by legal persons, nor general guidelines for the criminality of legal persons. There were also no procedural rules concerning prosecuting legal persons. It was still unclear whether a legal person, in general, could be a defendant in criminal procedures.

Along with the legislative and judicial developments came the challenge to the traditional criminal theory that denied corporate criminal liability. In around 1982, some scholars began to advocate corporate criminality.[82] At that point two theories, 'affirmative theory' (*Kending Shuo*) and 'negative theory' (*Fouding Shuo*) in the Chinese terminology, existed in opposition to each other.[83]

Generally, the 'negative theory' offered little new; it concentrated on the difficulties of imposing criminal liability on legal persons.[84] Scholars of the 'affirmative theory'

---

80 See Zhu Huaron & Lin Jianhua, 'On Our Legislation and Perfecting the Legislation Concerning Crimes Committed by Legal Persons', (no. 5, 1988) *Journal of China University of Political Science and Law* (*Zhengfa Luntan*) 26; Yang Chunxi, 'Legislative Improvement on Corporate Criminality', (no. 5, 1995) *Legal Science in China* (*Zhongguo Faxue*) 35.

81 Lin Yagang & Jia Yu, 'On the Characters of Special Criminal Laws and Their Incorporation into the Criminal Code', (no. 1, 1997) *Peking University Law Journal* (*Zhongwai Faxue*) 79, at 81.

82 According to some scholars, the challenge first appeared in 1982, and intensified in 1984 when the Party decided that enterprises should become legal persons, and economic crimes were more frequently committed by enterprises and other economic entities. See Zhu & Lin, *supra* note 80 at 25; and Gao Mingxuan, *supra* note 30 at 199.

83 Gao Mingxuan, *supra* note 30 at 199.

84 Gao Mingxuan, *supra* note 30 at 206-213; Ma Junju, *On the Institution of Legal Person* (*Faren Zhidu Tonglun*) (Wuhan: Wuhan University Press, 1988), at 299; Chen Zhixian, 'On Criminal

school argued that the decision-making organ of a legal person was just like that of the human brain, and thus decisions made by the organ reflected the intention and the will of the legal person.[85] It was further argued that, if legal persons could perform intentional civil legal action, there was no reason why a legal person could not perform criminal activities with consciousness and be held liable for the criminal actions.[86] Further, scholars in this group argued that since the decision-making power was in the hands of the decision-making organ of the legal person, which generally made its decisions on the basis of majority voting, it would be wrong to punish the person in charge of the legal person (such as the director or manager) for the activities committed by the legal person through the legal person's decision, which the person in charge might actually have voted against.[87] Also, if the person in charge, as an innocent person, was not punished, nor the legal person, then the result would be that a crime would be left unpunished.[88] If a crime was left unpunished, it was further argued by the scholars in this group, the criminal law's purpose of preventing crime would be circumvented.[89] Only the punishment imposed on legal persons could prevent legal persons from committing crime and serve the educational purposes of criminal law.[90] Regarding the punishments for crimes committed by legal persons, these scholars argued that both the person in charge (the person participating in decision-making or directly performing the criminal actions) and the legal person should be held liable and be punished.[91] They argued that some provisions for supplementary punishment such as fines and confiscation of property were most appropriate for legal persons.[92]

Law Issues Concerning Legal Persons', (no. 6, 1986) *Political Science and Law* (*Zhengzhi Yu Falu*), at 41; Zhao Bingzhi, 'Certain Considerations as to Why Legal Persons Cannot Become Subjects of Crime', (no. 5, 1989), *Studies in Law* (*Faxue Yanjiu*) 57.

85 Gao Mingxuan, *supra* note 30, at 202.

86 Chen Zhixian, *supra* note 84, at 41.

87 *Ibid.*, at 42.

88 *Id.*

89 Chen Zhixian, *supra* note 84, at 43.

90 See Gao Mingxuan, *supra* note 30, at 204.

91 *Ibid.*, at 204-205. Chinese scholars in this group called this kind of punishment the 'principle of dual punishment' (*Liangfa Yuanze*), i.e. both the legal person and the individual should be punished.

92 *Ibid.*, at 205. Punishments in the Criminal Code are divided into principal punishments and supplementary punishment. Principal punishments include Control; Criminal Detention; Fixed-term Imprisonment; Life Imprisonment; and The Death Penalty. The types of supplementary punishments are Fines; Deprivation of Political Rights; and Confiscation of Property. Under the Chinese Criminal Law, supplementary punishment may also be applied independently. See, Articles 27, 28, and 29 of the 1979 Criminal Law of the People's Republic of China.

Although in the mid-1980s only a few scholars argued for corporate criminal liability, legal literature in the PRC had by the late 1980s shifted attention to discussions on improving current criminal legislation.[93] This seems to suggest that there was then consensus among Chinese jurists on affirming the criminal liability of legal persons.

Among various legislative proposals advanced by advocates for corporate criminal liability, three main ideas can be identified. First, there was the proposal that the General Part of the current Criminal Law be amended to expressly provide criminality of legal persons and that individual acts and regulations be made to provide for specific crimes and punishments.[94] The second group suggested that the Criminal Law be wholly amended to both provide for criminal liability of legal persons in general, and for specific crimes and punishments in detail.[95] The third opinion advocated the making of a special code on criminal liability of legal persons which would provide general principles of criminal liability of legal persons and guidelines for the imposition of punishments upon them.[96]

A major development in the 1997 Revision has been the adoption of corporate criminal liability as advocated by the 'affirmative school'. A new section entitled 'Unit Crimes' (*Danwei Fanzui*), is now found in Chapter One of the General Part. Article 30 of the revised Criminal Law now provides that '[c]ompanies, enterprises, institutions, state organs and social organisations when committing acts endangering the society shall assume criminal liability when prescribed by the law.' Article 31 further provides that '[w]hen a unit commits a crime, it shall be fined. At the same time, the person in charge of the unit and other directly responsible persons shall be liable to be punished by the criminal law unless otherwise provided by the Specific Provisions of the Law or by other laws.' In the Specific Provisions of the revised Criminal Law there are 81 articles prescribing unit criminal liability.[97] It

---

93 See Shu Yongbao & Chen Yonglu, 'Causes of and Counter-measures Towards Crimes by Legal Persons', (no. 2, 1989) *Political Science and Law* (*Zhengzhi Yu Falu*), at 63; Zhao Junru & Li Shenglong, 'Discussions on Legislation on Crimes by Legal Persons', (no. 3, 1989) *Modern Law Science* (*Xiandai Faxue*), at 55-58; Zhou Yuan, 'Suggestion on Legislation on Duality of Liability of Crimes by Legal Persons', (no. 1, 1990) *Modern Law Science* (*Xiandai Faxue*), at 54-57; Cuei Qingsen, 'On Crimes by Legal Persons', (no. 5, 1990) *Studies in Law* (*Faxue Yanjiu*), at 14-22; Li Mingliang, 'Personal Opinions on Methods of Legislating on Crimes by Legal Persons', (no. 2, 1991) *Modern Law Science* (*Xiandai Faxue*), at 61-62; Zhang Wen, *et al.*, 'A Further Study on Several Questions regarding Corporate Criminality', (no. 1, 1994) *Legal Science in China* (*Zhongguo Faxue*) 57; Li Xihui, 'Some Considerations on Restructuring Criminal Legislation on Corporate Crimes', (no. 1, 1994) *Journal of China University of Political Science and Law* (*Zhengfa Luntan*) 16; and Ma & Ding, *supra* note 13, at 74-82.

94 Zhao & Li, *supra* note 93.

95 Zhou Yuan, *supra* note 93; and Cuei Qingsen, *supra* note 93.

96 Li Mingliang, *supra* note 93.

97 Based on my own calculation.

should be pointed out that the revised Criminal Law uses the term 'Unit Crime' instead of 'corporate crime'. The reason is that many organisations are not necessarily a corporation but may nevertheless commit a criminal offence; thus the term 'Unit' is designed to encompass not only companies, but also other unincorporated organisations.[98]

3.6. Territorial and Extraterritorial Application

The Criminal Law is applicable to offences committed by any person (Chinese or foreigner alike), including offences committed aboard ships or aircrafts of the PRC if either the commission or the effect takes place within the territory of the PRC.[99] However, the criminal responsibility of foreigners who enjoy diplomatic privilege and immunity will be resolved through diplomatic channels.[100] Further, flexible implementation of the Law in minority autonomous regions is allowed.[101] Finally, the Law is not applicable in Hong Kong or Macau unless otherwise declared by the NPC in accordance with emergency powers stipulated in the Basic Laws of Hong Kong and Macau.

The Chinese Criminal Law has always maintained its extraterritoriality. Under the 1979 Criminal Law an offence committed by a Chinese national outside China would not be punished by the Criminal Law if the act was not punishable by the law of the place where it was committed, or if the minimum punishment under the Chinese law was imprisonment for less than three years, unless the Chinese national committed a more serious offence (e.g. counter-revolutionary crimes) as specified in Article 4.[102] The revision has now greatly expanded the extraterritorial application. The revised Criminal Law now applies to all offences committed outside China by a Chinese national if the maximum punishment under the Chinese law is imprisonment of three years or more. Further, any offences committed by Chinese state personnel or military personnel are covered by the Criminal Law.[103] The expansion of the extraterritorial application is targeted at the increasing number of Chinese students and business people now studying or working abroad.[104] The

---

98 Liu Shengrong, 'Corporate Crimes or Unit Crimes', (no. 6, 1992) *Legal Science in China* (*Zhongguo Faxue*) 77; Cao & Hou, *supra* note 20, at 31-32.

99 Article 6 of the revised Criminal Law.

100 Article 11 of the revised Criminal Law.

101 Article 90 of the revised Criminal Law.

102 See Articles 4 & 5 of the 1979 Criminal Law.

103 See Article 7 of the revised Criminal Law. 'State personnel', under Article 93 of the revised Criminal Law, includes all state personnel working in state-owned companies, enterprises and institutions as well as those assigned by the state to work in non state-owned companies, enterprises, institutions and social organisations.

104 See Huang & Teng, *supra* note 12, at 8.

extraterritorial application to foreigners committing offences against China outside the country has remained the same; that is, the law is applicable if an offence is committed by a foreigner against China or a Chinese national and the minimum punishment prescribed by the law is imprisonment for not less than three years, unless the act is not punishable by the law of the place where it is committed.[105] Further, even if an offence has been tried by a foreign state, the extraterritorial application of the law remains. However, if the offender has been punished by a foreign state, the punishment may be entirely waived or partially mitigated.[106] This provision clearly rejects the principle of double jeopardy as far as crimes committed outside China are concerned.[107]

In terms of retroactivity, the revised Law re-affirms the principle of non-retrospectivity; that is, that offences committed before the revision shall be pursued by the previous law, but if the new law does not consider the act an offence, or provides a lighter punishment, the revised Law shall be applied.[108]

4. Crime and Punishment

4.1. An Overview

The Chinese Criminal Law defines any act which endangers state sovereignty and territorial integrity and security, splits the state, jeopardises the political powers of the people's democratic dictatorship and socialist system, undermines social and economic orders, encroaches upon state property, collective property of the working masses or the privately owned property of citizens, infringes upon the personal, democratic and other rights of citizens or any other act which endangers society and is punishable according to law as a criminal offence, except those offences which are obviously of a minor nature and whose harm is negligible.[109] Following this definition and according to Chinese jurisprudence, there are three basic criteria for determining criminality. First, a criminal offence is an act that endangers society. Secondly, such an act violates the criminal law. Thirdly, such an act is punishable by the criminal law.[110] The Chinese law also requires the existence of *mens rea* (either

---

105 Article 8 of the revised Criminal Law.

106 Article 10 of the revised Criminal Law.

107 See Cao & Hou, *supra* note 20, at 11.

108 See Article 12 of the revised Criminal Law.

109 See Article 13 of the revised Criminal Law. The original Article 10 has been revised to abolish the more ideological terms (e.g. 'socialist revolution' and 'proletariat dictatorship' etc.) and to emphasise the protection of economic order.

110 See Leng & Chiu, *supra* note 40, at 124; Cao & Hou, *supra* note 20, at 15; Huang & Teng, *supra* note 12, at 15; and *Lectures on the Criminal Law*, *supra* note 8, at 23-24. This concept

intention or criminal negligence); an act which results in harmful consequences due to irresistible or unforeseeable factors rather than due to intention or negligence is not a criminal offence.[111]

These provisions defining the concept of crime are not substantially revised; nor are the original eight types of crimes stipulated in the 1979 Criminal Law substantially amended or supplemented. Thus the revised Law now contains ten types (in ten chapters) of crime:

(1) Crime endangering state security;

(2) Crime endangering public security;

(3) Crime undermining the socialist market economic order;

(4) Crime infringing the personal rights or democratic rights of citizens;

(5) Crime encroaching upon property;

(6) Crime disrupting social order and its administration;

(7) Crime endangering the interests of national defence;

(8) Crime of bribery and embezzlement;

(9) Crime of malfeasance; and

(10) Crime in violation of military duties.[112]

While the structure of the Law in stipulating crime is not significantly changed, the Specific Provisions of the Criminal Law for these crimes has been substantially expanded through the incorporation of various decisions and supplementary provisions issued by the NPC between 1979 and 1997. Thus, 'crime undermining the socialist market economic order' is further divided into eight sections dealing with eight sub-divisions of the crime, while 'crime disrupting social order and its administration' is subdivided into nine sections. Further, 'crime against marriage or the family' is now incorporated into 'crime infringing on the personal rights or democratic rights of citizens'. At the same time the 'crime of bribery and embezzlement' has been separated from malfeasance and become an independent category of crime. Finally, and of symbolic significance, 'counter-revolutionary crime' is now renamed

---

of criminality is identical to that articulated in the 1950s. See 1957 Lectures in Cohen (1968), *supra* note 4, at 328-334.

111 See Articles 14-16 of the revised Criminal Law.

112 According to the classification of the Supreme People's Procuratorate, these ten crims include 414 criminal offences. See Supreme People's Procuratorate Opinion on the Names of Offences in the Specific Provisions of the Criminal law, issued on 25 December 2007. A copy of the Opinion (including the specific classifications) is available in *China Law Yearbook 1998* (*Zhongguo Falü Nianjian 1998*) (Beijing: China Law Yearbook Press, 1998), at 692-699.

'crime against state security'. 'Crime endangering the interests of national defence' and 'crime in violation of military duties' form a new category in the criminal law through incorporation of the NPC's earlier decisions.

Criminal punishment remains the same. There are five types of 'principal punishment' (*zhuxing*):

- Control and supervision (*guanzhi*) (from three months to two years);[113]
- Criminal detention (*juyi*) (from one month to six months);[114]
- Fixed term imprisonment (from six months to 15 years and up to 20 years when the death penalty is commuted to fixed term or in cases of combined punishment for more than one crime);[115]
- Life imprisonment;
- The death penalty.

In addition, there are three types of 'supplementary punishment' (*fujia xing*):

- Fines (there is no specified monetary limits);
- Deprivation of political rights (including right to election, freedom of speech and press, the right of protest, the right to hold a position in state organs, and the right to hold a leading position in a state-owned company, enterprise, institution or people's organisation, for one to five years, but with permanent deprivation for those sentenced to death or life imprisonment);[116]
- Confiscation of property.

These supplementary punishments may also be imposed independently of the principal punishment.

---

113 Article 38 of the revised Criminal Law. 'Control' as a form of punishment was developed as a measure of controlling counter-revolutionaries. See Cohen (1968), *supra* note 4, ch.V. Before the enactment of the Criminal Law in 1979, it was often used indefinitely. Thus, when the Criminal Law was being drafted, there were debates whether *guanzhi* should be incorporated into the Criminal Law as a form of punishment. See Gu Angran, *Socialist legal System and Legislative Work* (*Shehui Zhuyi Fazhi He Lifa Gongzuo*) (Beijing: China University of Political Science and Law Press, 1989), at 190-191. During the 1997 revision many scholars again debated whether control should be abolished altogether. See Ma & Ding, *supra* note 12, 32 & 42; Cao Zidan, 'On the Basis for the Existence of *Guanzhi* in Our Country', (no. 1, 1990) *Legal Science in China* (*Zhongguo Faxue*) 61; Jiang Lihua, 'On the Retention and Improvement of *Guanzhi* as a Punishment', (no. 1, 1990) *Legal Science in China* (*Zhongguo Faxue*) 66; and Cao Jianglun & Liu Defa, 'A Suggestion to Abolish *Guanzhi* as a Punishment in Our Criminal Law', (no. 1, 1990) *Legal Science in China* (*Zhongguo Faxue*) 71.

114 Article 42 of the revised Criminal Law.

115 Article 45 of the revised Criminal Law.

116 Articles 54-55 of the revised Criminal Law.

In addition to the above types of punishment, deportation may be applied as an independent or supplementary penalty to a foreigner who commits a crime.[117] Further, the convicted criminal may also be required to compensate the economic losses of their victims.[118] Finally, the court has the discretionary power to exempt a convicted person from criminal punishment where the crime is minor and does not require punishment. But in such a case the offender may be reprimanded or ordered to make a statement of repentance or formal apology, or to pay compensation for losses, or be subjected to administrative penalties or sanctions by the competent authority.[119]

Among these principal and supplementary types of punishment, the death penalty has been the most controversial form of punishment for many years.[120]

4.2. Counter-Revolutionary Crimes and Crimes against State Security

'Counter-revolution' had for a long time been the primary targeted crime in the Chinese communist justice system before the 1997 revision of the Criminal Law. The provisions on 'counter-revolution' in the 1979 Criminal Law were vague and sweeping, reminiscent of the 1926 Russian Criminal Code.[121] In particular, Article 90 of the 1979 Criminal Law contained a catch-all provision which defined 'crimes of counter-revolution' as '[a]ll acts endangering the People's Republic of China committed with the goal of overthrowing the political power of the dictatorship of the proletariat and the socialist system.' Although this provision itself did not stipulate specific penalties, the 1979 Law contained 12 articles specifying punishment for various kinds of 'counter-revolutionary crimes'. Indeed, 'counter-revolution' attracted the most severe punishment prescribed in the 1979 Criminal Law. Sixty percent of the provisions prescribing the death penalty, 45% of the provisions imposing life imprisonment, and 37% of the provisions stipulating imprisonment for ten or more years concerned the crime of counter-revolution.[122]

Although many of the subcategories of 'counter-revolutionary crimes' may be seen as acts endangering social order and security, such as causing explosions, setting fire etc. (Article 100), many other 'counter-revolutionary' acts were clearly aimed at political activities, such as organising or leading 'counter-revolutionary' groups (Article 98), and propagandising for and inciting the overthrow of the political power of the dictatorship of the proletariat and the socialist system (Article 102). Indeed, the essential element of all 'counter-revolutionary' crimes was the aim of

---

117 Article 35 of the revised Criminal Law.

118 Article 36 of the revised Criminal Law.

119 Article 37 of the revised Criminal Law.

120 The death penalty will be discussed further below.

121 Berman, Cohen & Russel, *supra* note 5, at 252-253.

122 Lan Quanpu, *supra* note 4, at 73.

'counter-revolution', which clearly was a political rather than a legal concept. As such it is not surprising that provisions on 'counter-revolutionary' crimes attracted much criticism both within China and abroad. For this reason socialist countries, such as North Korea, Vietnam and the former Soviet Union, all replaced 'counter-revolutionary crimes' with 'crimes against the state' or some similar category many years ago.[123]

In China, discussions on redefining 'counter-revolutionary crimes' began in the mid-1980s. One of the views emerging from these discussions on abolishing this category was the recognition that the concept blurred legal acts and political views and, thus, created difficulties in judicial practice. Further, it was argued that if 'counter-revolutionary crime' was not redefined as an ordinary crime, China would not be able to pursue criminals who had escaped abroad. More recently it was recognised that the concept of 'counter-revolution' would not be compatible with the practice of 'One Country Two Systems' – a policy meant to be implemented for unification with Hong Kong, Macau and Taiwan.[124] The first specific sign of the introduction of the concept of crimes against state security as a substitute for counter-revolution emerged in February 1993 in the promulgation of the Law on State Security. The Law was intended to curb domestic and foreign activities that pose security threats, but it did not use the term 'counter-revolution' itself.[125]

The final revision in 1997 is, however, a major disappointment. 'Counter-revolutionary crime' is indeed redefined as 'crime endangering state security' and all reference to the term 'counter-revolution' has now been deleted from the Law.[126] Essentially, however, the revision is a matter of renaming, restructuring and supplementing, as the majority of the previous provisions on 'counter-revolutionary crimes' have been retained.[127] Thus acts of inciting the overthrow of political power

---

123 As early as 1958 the Soviet Union had discarded the concept of 'counter-revolutionary crimes'. See Bermen, Cohen & Russell, *supra* note 5, at 252.

124 See Cao & Hou, *supra* note 20, at 87; Ma & Ding, *supra* note 13, at 8; 'Criminal Law Called to Revise', (24-30 April 1989) *Beijing Review* 7; Cao Zidan & Hou Guoyun, 'On Redefining "Counter-revolutionary Crimes" "Crimes Endangering State Security"', (no. 2, 1991) *Legal Science in China* (*Zhongguo Faxue*) 9; Zhang & Wang, *supra* note 6, at 242-243; Gao Mingxuan, Zhao Bingzhi & Wang Yong, 'A Review of the Criminal Legislation in the Past Ten Years and Prospect', (no. 2, 1989) *Legal Science in China* (*Zhongguo Faxue*) 66; and Zhang Sihan, 'On Crimes Endangering State Security', *People's Daily* (*Renmin Ribao*) (overseas edition), 14 June 1997, internet edition. See also Lawyers Committee for Human Rights, *supra* note 16, at 79; Albert Chen (1992), at 188.

125 See Lawyers' Committee for Human Rights, *supra* note 16, at 80.

126 See Chapter One of the Specific Provisions of the revised Criminal Law. As discussed in Chapter 3, similar words were also removed from the Constitution through the 1999 Constitution Revision.

127 Although the total number of provisions in this chapter has been reduced from 15 to 12 articles, this reduction has only been achieved by removing some provisions to chapters on

and the socialist system continue to be a major crime in the revised Law.[128] The ambiguous provision on the crime of colluding with foreign states in plotting to harm the sovereignty, territorial integrity and security of the state remains, so does the vague provision on the crime of stealing, secretly gathering or providing state secrets and intelligence for foreign organisations or foreigners.[129] The revised law also adds a provision to make it a crime for state personnel to desert their position and escape to foreign countries to engage in activities endangering state security.[130] Apparently, this provision is aimed at those who were sent to work or study abroad and then decided to stay by, for example, applying for refugee status in a foreign country. In China's own words, these provisions are aimed at acts of joint efforts to westernise China.[131]

The punishment for these crimes continues to be very harsh. The majority of the 12 crimes endangering state security can attract the death penalty. In addition, confiscation of property is applicable to all 12 crimes endangering state security.[132]

4.3. Crimes Endangering Public Security and Social Order

Crimes endangering public security refer to those acts that endanger the lives of the general public and damage public property and facilities.[133] Reflecting the traditional idea of collective rights over individual rights, crimes endangering public security have always been seen as the most dangerous form of crime among the 'ordinary crimes'.[134] It is not surprising that immediately after the provisions on crimes endangering state security come the provisions on crimes endangering public security.

In response to the continuing increase of crimes and the rising incidence of certain serious crimes (such as the hijacking of airplanes and organised terrorism) at the time,[135] this Chapter Two has been extensively expanded; in fact, the total

---

crime endangering public security and crime against social order and administration. See Wang Hanbin, *supra* note 12, at 675.

128 See Article 105 of the revised Criminal Law.

129 Article 102 and Article 111 of the revised Criminal Law.

130 Article 109 of the revised Criminal Law.

131 Zhang Sihan, *supra* note 124.

132 See Article 102-113 of the revised Criminal Law.

133 See Li Guangcan (ed.), *On Criminal Law of the People's Republic of China* (*Zhonghua Renmin Gonghe Guo Xingfa Lun*), vol. 2 (Changchun: Jilin People's Press, 1981), at 98-101; Cao & Hou (1997), *supra* note 20, at 97.

134 Li Guangcan, *id.*, at 98. The term 'ordinary crimes' is used by Chinese scholars to contrast with 'counter-revolutionary crimes'.

135 See Chu Huaizhi, 'The Contradiction between Crimes and Punishments and the Reform of the Criminal Law', (no. 5, 1994) *Legal Science in China* (*Zhongguo Faxue*) 107. As pointed

number of provisions has been more than doubled (from 11 to 26 articles) with 15 new offences being created. In addition to the previous offences (such as setting fire, breaching dikes, causing explosions, and sabotage) against public lives (that is, an offence which is not aimed at a particular person or persons), public property (such as factories, farms, mines etc.) and facilities (such as public transport facilities, power stations and public communications facilities), the revision creates the following new offences: organising, leading and actively participating in terrorist activities (Article 120); hijacking air traffic facilities (Article 121);[136] hijacking boats and vehicles (Article 122); using violence on airplanes to endanger the safety of air traffic (Article 123); illegally selling weaponry (Article 126); illegally owning, possessing and lending weaponry (Article 128); failure to promptly report the loss of weaponry (Article 129); illegally bringing weaponry, knives, explosive and poisoning materials into public places or onto public traffic facilities (Article 130); violation of traffic regulations and causing major accidents by transport personnel (Articles 131-133); failure to rectify safety problems thus causing major accidents in work sites (Article 135);[137] negligence in the building industry (including designing, building and supervision) (Article 137); failure to take measures for the safety of school and education facilities (Article 138);[138] and failure to take action for fire safety after being instructed to do so (Article 139).

In the post-Mao era maintaining social stability and order has been one of the top priorities for the leadership; it is part of the effort of creating a social environment conducive for economic development. Again, many *ad hoc* legislative responses to specific situations had led to the creation of a large number of individual statutes and penal provisions in other statutes, supplementing the original Chapter 6 on crimes against social order and its administration. The new Chapter Six now absorbs all these provisions, and has thus now become the longest and most complicated chapter in the whole Criminal Law. Altogether, Chapter 6 proscribes 116 offences in 91 articles, with 63 offences being new creations of the revised Criminal Law.[139] It should be pointed out that, in addition to the penal provisions in Chapter 6, there is also the 2005 Law concerning Punishment in the Administration of Social Order (replacing the Regulations concerning Punishment in the Administration of Social Order) which imposes administrative penalties on minor acts in violation of social order and its administration.

Chapter Six now deals with penalties for all acts which violate social order and its administration; that is, acts endangering stability, peace and order in the

out earlier (*supra* note 25), provisions on terrorism were further revised in 2001.

136 This article incorporates the Standing Committee Decision on Severe Punishment on Hijacking Air Traffic Facilities of 28 December 1992.

137 This Article incorporates Article 92 of the Labour Law (1994).

138 This Article incorporates Article 73 of the Law on Education (1995).

139 Cao & Hou, *supra* note 20, at 262.

proper operation and running of state organisations, enterprises and institutions, and proper order for scientific research and teaching.[140] It is divided into nine sections. Section One deals with violations against public order. In addition to the previously proscribed crimes of obstructing state personnel from carrying out their functions, hooliganism and gambling, it now also includes two previously 'counter-revolutionary' crimes, namely inciting the masses to resist or to sabotage the implementation of the laws and decrees, and organising and using superstitious sects and secret organisations in violation of law. It also creates a number of new offences, including the illegal production and sale and purchase of police uniforms and car numbers, the illegal production, sale and use of espionage equipment, computer offences, stealing and insulting dead bodies, and offences in violation of demonstration and assembly laws.

Section Two creates a new subcategory of crime (Crime hindering judicial functions).[141] This section collects various provisions in the previous law and further prohibits all acts hindering the performance of judicial powers, including the violation of court proceeding orders, attacking judicial personnel and violation of prison order. Section Three on Crimes Violating Border Administration again collects various provisions dealing with the violation of border administration as well as the Supplementary Provisions on Severe Punishment of Organising and Transporting People to Illegally Cross the Border.[142] Section Four penalises acts violating the administration of cultural relics, historical records and places of historical interest. Section Five deals with acts endangering public health. Except for Article 332, which deals with the violation of border health and quarantine regulations,[143] this Section collects penal provisions from various statutes, such as the Law on the Prevention of Infectious Diseases,[144] Border Health Quarantine Law,[145] Measures for Dealing With Medical Accidents,[146] Administrative Regulations on Blood Products,[147] and the Quarantine Law on the Import and Export of Animals and Plants.[148] Section Six penalises violation of environmental protection and natural resource administration.

---

140 Cao & Hou, *supra* note 20, at 262.

141 The 1979 Criminal Law did deal with a number of offences relating to the performance of judicial functions, such as perjury (Article 148), refusal to carry out court judgements or orders (Article 157), escape from detention or prison (Articles 96 and 160). Scholars had argued for establishing a separate section on crimes hindering judicial functions for a number of years before the 1997 revision. See Zhang & Wang *supra* note 6, at 243.

142 The Supplementary Provision was issued by the Standing Committee on 5 March 1994.

143 Originally Article 178.

144 Issued on 21 February 1989 by the Standing Committee.

145 Issued 2 December 1986 by the Standing Committee.

146 Issued by the State Council on 29 June 1987.

147 Issued by the State Council in January 1997.

148 Issued on 30 October 1991.

Again this section collects various penal provisions in the original Criminal Law as well as individual statutes. Section Seven on the Trafficking and Production of Drugs retains the original provisions and incorporates the Decision on Prohibition of Drugs.[149] Section Eight deals with crimes relating to prostitution. It incorporates the original provisions as well as the Decision on the Prohibition of Prostitution.[150] The final section incorporates the Decision on the Punishment of the Smuggling, Production, Sale and Circulation of Pornographic Materials.[151]

Clearly these new offences in relation to public security and social order have been created on an *ad hoc* basis, and many of them are legislative responses to major incidents that have occurred in China in the first 20 years of reform.

4.4. Crimes Undermining the Socialist Market Order and Economic Crimes

Economic development has since 1978 remained a top priority for the post-Mao leadership. Crimes against such development are thus treated seriously and punished heavily. As economic policy has been liberated considerably since 1979,[152] many kinds of economic activities that were non-existent (e.g. private enterprises, share markets, real estate, insurance and the futures market etc.) have now been permitted, leading to the rise of crimes that were not anticipated in the original criminal law. Further, the dual system, that is the co-existence of a market economy with the continuing control by the government authorities of many forms of economic activity (such as the existence of licence and approval systems) has also led to a drastic increase in many types of economic crime and corruption. Thus some scholars have argued that the main task of the criminal law should be shifted from targeting 'counter-revolutionary' crimes to economic crimes.[153] The government response had been the issuing of many individual statutes on an *ad hoc* basis, to supplement the 1979 Criminal Law. The 1997 Revision of crimes against the socialist market order and other economic crimes has been designed to incorporate these individual statutes and other penal provisions in various ordinary statutes issued by the NPC and its Standing Committee.

The revised Chapter Three is now divided into eight sections in 92 articles with 89 offences. Section One deals with the production and sale of fake and substandard products. This section mainly incorporates the Standing Committee's Decision on

149 The Decision was issued by the Standing Committee on 28 December 1990.

150 The Decision was issued by the Standing Committee on 4 September 1991.

151 The Decision was issued by the Standing Committee on 28 December 1990.

152 For a discussion on the evolution of economic reform policy, see Jianfu Chen, *From Administrative Authorisation of Private Law: A Comparative Perspective of the Developing Civil Law in the People's Republic of China* (Dordrecht/Boston/London: Martinus Nijhoff Publishers, 1995), ch. 3.

153 See Gao, Zhao & Wang, *supra* note 124, at 72.

the Punishment of the Production and Sale of Fake and Substandard Products.[154] Section Two deals with crimes of smuggling, with its provisions mainly coming from the Supplementary Provisions on the Punishment of Smuggling Crimes[155] and the Decision on the Punishment of the Smuggling, Production, Sale and Circulation of Pornographic Materials.[156] Section Three on Crimes Undermining Company and Enterprise Administrative Orders is a relatively new creation. The provisions were first created by the Standing Committee's Decision on the Punishment of Crimes in Violation of Company Law which was issued on 28 February 1995 after the Company Law was adopted on 29 December 1993. The Revision is mainly based on the above Decision, but it also creates a number of offences.[157] Section Four deals with crimes undermining financial administrative orders. The original 1979 Criminal Law proscribed counterfeiting or trafficking in counterfeited national currency (Article 122) and counterfeiting cheques, share certificates or valuable securities (Article 123). These provisions were supplemented by the above-mentioned supplementary provisions on smuggling crimes, and by decisions on crimes against company law. Most importantly, they were supplemented by the Decision on the Punishment of Crimes Undermining Financial Order.[158] The revised Criminal Law now incorporates all these decisions and supplementary provisions as well as further proscribing other crimes in the financial market, such as fraud in bank loans (Article 175), internal trading (Article 180), fabricating and circulating false information about exchange markets (Article 181), etc. Section Five specifically deals with financial fraud. Again, its provisions are mainly derived from the Decision on the Punishment of Crimes Undermining Financial Order. Section Six prohibits acts endangering the collection and administration of taxes. Apart from Articles 201 and 202, which are revised from the original Article 121, provisions in this section come from the Supplementary Provisions on Punishing the Evasion and Refusal of Taxes[159] and the Decision on the Punishment of the Fabricating, Counterfeiting and Illegal Sale of Value-added Tax Receipts.[160] Section Seven punishes the violation of intellectual property by incorporating the Supplementary Provision on the Punishment of Counterfeiting Registered Patents[161] and the Decision on Punishing Crimes in

154 Issued on 2 July 1993.

155 Issued by the Standing Committee of the NPC on 21 January 1988.

156 Issued by the Standing Committee of the NPC on 28 December 1990.

157 These include Articles 164-169.

158 Issued by the Standing Committee of the NPC on 30 June 1995.

159 Issued by the Standing Committee of the NPC on 4 September 1992.

160 Issued by the Standing Committee of the NPC on 30 October 1995.

161 Issued by the Standing Committee of the NPC on 23 February 1993.

Violating Copyright.[162] It further penalises the violation of trade secrets.[163] Section Eight prescribes punishment for violation of market order. This section contains 13 crimes, the majority of which are new creations of the revision.

Further, to demonstrate the government's determination to eliminate corruption, this is now dealt with in a separate chapter, Chapter Eight. The new chapter now expands the original two provisions (Articles 155 and 185) to 15 articles, largely through the incorporation of the Supplementary Provisions on the Punishment of Corruption.[164]

The encroachment on property as an economic crime is separately dealt with in Chapter Five. This chapter also creates some new offences (e.g. illegal use of telecommunication facilities owned by others) and incorporates provisions from other statutes (e.g. Decisions on the Punishment of Crimes in Violation of Company Law).

As pointed out earlier,[165] these provisions on economic crimes have undergone some rather significant revisions in the last few years since the revised Criminal Law was adopted in 1997.

4.5. Crimes Endangering Personal Rights and Democratic Rights

'Crimes endangering personal rights and democratic rights' refers to the violation of personal security, other associated rights (e.g. reputation and dignity), and democratic rights guaranteed by the Constitution (e.g. the right to election, right of appeal, freedom of correspondence, etc.).[166] Chapter Four in the revised Criminal Law now incorporates provisions from Chapter Four in the original criminal law, some provisions in the original Chapter Eight and the Decision on Severely Punishing the Selling and Kidnapping of Women and Children (4 September 1991) issued by the Standing Committee. This Chapter now covers murder and manslaughter, causing bodily injuries, rape (including all sexual intercourse with girls under 14) and molesting or humiliating women through violence or threats, illegal detention or deprivation of personal freedom, kidnapping, selling or buying women and children, falsely accusing or framing another person with the intention to cause the person to be penalised for crime, forced labour in violation of labour laws, illegal searching of another person or residence, insulting or defaming another person, the use of torture by judicial and prison officials, inciting racial hatred or discrimination and insulting minority nationals in publications, illegal deprivation of freedom of

---

[162] Issued by the Standing Committee of the NPC on 5 July 1994.

[163] Article 219. This is a new creation in the revision, which further supplements the provision on trading secrets first provided in the Law of the PRC Against Unfair Competition (1993).

[164] Issued by the Standing Committee on 21 January 1988.

[165] See *supra* note 25.

[166] Cao & Hou, *supra* note 20, at 216.

religion and serious violation of minority customs, serious violation of freedom of correspondence, abusing power and using public office for private gain, carrying out retaliation and frame-ups against complainants, activities endangering elections, interference in freedom of marriage, bigamy, and domestic violence.

The notable improvement in this chapter is the clarification of ambiguous provisions (such as those on hooliganism), and the further supplementation of provisions in detailed form, thus making the provisions more definite and easier to implement.

4.6. Dereliction of Duty

Chapter Nine deals with dereliction of duty by state personnel during their performance of state duties. It amends and expands the original Chapter Eight by incorporating various supplementary provisions issued by the Standing Committee, including the Supplementary Provisions on the Punishment of Crimes in Violation of Company Law, Decision on the Punishment of Fabricating, Counterfeiting and Illegal Sale of Value-added Tax Receipts, Decision on the Punishment of Production and Sale of Fake and Substandard Products, Supplementary Provisions on the Severe Punishment of Organising and Transporting People To Illegally Cross the Border, the Decision on Severely Punishing the Selling and Kidnapping of Women and Children, Decision on the Prohibition of Prostitution, and penal provisions of other statutes (e.g. Education Law and Law on the Protection of Cultural Relics).

4.7. Crimes Undermining the Interests of National Defence and Military Duties

Two new chapters have now been incorporated on crimes undermining the interests of national defence (Chapter Seven) and military duties (Chapter Ten).

Chapter Seven on crimes endangering the interests of national defence is completely new. It covers the use of violence to interfere with military personnel in carrying out their duties, causing damage to military facilities and installations, knowingly supplying substandard equipment to military forces, forcibly entering into and violating orders in military 'prohibited areas', impersonating military personnel, inciting the deserting of military personnel or knowingly employing military deserters, fraudulently supplying unqualified personnel to the army, illegally producing, selling and buying, or fabricating military marks and documents, supplying false information to the military during war, and refusal or intentional delay in supplying military purchase orders during war.

Crimes in violation of military duty are broadly defined as violations of duty by servicepersons which endangers state military interests.[167]

---

167 Article 420 of the revised Criminal Law.

Crimes in violation of military duty were first codified in the Interim Regulation on the Punishment of the Crimes of Servicemen in Violation of Duty.[168] The new Chapter Ten incorporates and supplements this Interim Regulation.

4.8. Administrative Sanctions v. Criminal Punishments

One of the major problems in the Chinese criminal justice system is its artificial and arbitrary distinction between administrative sanctions and criminal punishments.[169] This distinction has caused many problems in human rights protection, as the imposition of administrative sanctions is out of the control of the due process and beyond the supervision of the judiciary. Among the most criticised institutions of administrative sanctions are Shelter and Investigation (*Shourong Shencha*), and Re-education through Labour (*Laojiao*). After much debate, Shelter and Investigation was formally abolished in 1996 during the revision of the Criminal Procedure Law. During the revision of the Criminal Law suggestions were also made by scholars to have the *Laojiao* system reformed or abolished.[170]

The *Laojiao* system was first initiated by the Communist Party Central Committee in the 1950s as a measure to combine labour and education to deal with 'historical counter-revolutionaries' and other 'bad elements' of the society.[171] It was then formally established by the SCNPC's Decision Relating to *Laojiao* Problems and regulated by the Supplementary Provisions of the State Council on *Laojiao*.[172] The Provisions were implemented by the Ministry of Justice through the Trial Implementation Measures on *Laojiao*, issued in January 1982. Under this regime of regulation, *Laojiao* was used to detain people whose offence was not serious enough to warrant criminal punishment, yet too serious to be dealt with under the Regulations concerning Punishment in the Administration of Social Order (since upgraded to a Law). Although it was theoretically not a criminal penalty, a person could be detained for up to 4 years by a decision of a local *Laojiao* Administration Committee, comprising representatives from the bureaus of civil administration, labour and justice, but in fact mainly administered by the local Public Security

---

168 Issued on 10 June 1981.

169 For a discussion on the various forms of administrative sanctions, see Randall Peerenboom, *China Modernizes: Threat to the West or Model for the Rest?* (New York: Oxford University Press, 2007), at 94-97.

170 See e.g. Tao Jigang, 'Some Thoughts on the Law on Re-education through Labour', (no. 3, 1995) *Journal of the China University of People's Police* (*Zhongguo Renmin Jingcha Daxue Xuebao*) 12; Chen Xingliang, *supra* note 14, at 56-60.

171 Instructions on Completely Wiping Out Hidden Counter-revolutionary Elements, issued by the Central Committee of the Party in 1955.

172 The Decision was issued in August 1957 and re-published in November 1979. The Supplementary Provisions were issued in November 1979.

organs.[173] Clearly it was arbitrary to define such loss of freedom as an administrative sanction.

The legality of such an institution was openly questioned in 1996 when the NPC adopted the Law on Administrative Penalties. Article 9 of the Law provides specifically that all restraint of personal freedom must be prescribed by law. Article 10 then adds that administrative rules and regulations can only prescribe penalties other than the restraint of personal freedoms. Since the State Council is only constitutionally empowered to issue administrative rules and regulations, the legal basis for *Laojiao* was clearly questionable. Thus it was suggested that the *Laojiao* should either be abolished or be absorbed into the Criminal Law by establishing a new category of punishment, namely, police orders (similar to community based orders in the West).[174] These opinions were ignored by the authorities, and the revision of the Criminal Law chose not to deal with the issue of *Laojiao* at all.

However, the controversy did not die after the revision of the Criminal Law in 1997; in fact, it has continued until this day.[175] Also importantly, Article 8 of the 2000 Law on Law-making establishes a detailed list of exclusive legislative powers to be exercised only by the NPC and SCNPC. Although the exercise of some of these powers may be delegated to the State Council by the NPC and SCNPC, the State Council is barred from enacting laws on such matters as those relating to crimes and criminal penalties, the deprivation of political rights of citizens, coercive measures, and penalties which restrict personal freedom. Clearly, under the Law on Law-Making, the legality of the arbitrary distinction between administrative (e.g. re-education through labour) and criminal penalties is seriously challenged unless it is clearly authorised by the NPC or the SCNPC.

With pressures for reform, both from within and without, the SCNPC finally made a concrete move toward reforming the *Laojiao* in 2005. In March 2005 the Legal Affairs Committee of the SCNPC finally submitted a draft law on the correction of unlawful behaviour to the SCNPC; the latter then formally included the deliberation of the proposed law in its 2005 legislative plan.[176] Under the proposed scheme, the maximum incarceration period would be capped at 18 months and judicial remedies would also be made available. However, more than two years have passed and we are still waiting for an outcome of this proposed reform.

---

173 Tao Jigang, *supra note* 170, at 12; Ma Kechang, *supra* note 19, at 7-8.

174 Ma Kechang, *supra* note 19, at 7-8; Chen Xingliang, *supra* note 14, at 56-60.

175 For a discussion of the recent controversy over *Laojiao* and different opinions on its reform, see Peerenboom, *supra* note 169, at 209-210.

176 See 'Our Laojiao System Is Facing Reform towards Correction of Unlawful Behaviour', available <news.xinhuanet.com/legal/2005-03/02/content_2636013.htm> (last accessed 19 June 2007). According to the SCNPC 2007 legislative plan, a first deliberation of the proposed law will be conducted in the October SCNPC session. See '2007 Legislative Plan and Supervision Plan', in <npc.people.com.cn/GB/28320/41246/41337/5422052.html> (last accessed 20 June 2007).

4.9. The Death Penalty

Reflecting the idea of relying heavily on criminal punishment to maintain social stability and order, the death penalty was widely prescribed in imperial Chinese codes and frequently used in practice.[177] A reduction in the application of the death penalty thus became one of the major aspects of criminal law reform at the turn of the 20th century. The Qing reform managed to reduce capital offences from more than 800 in total to about 20.[178] The KMT governments continued the reform regarding the death penalty. The various criminal codes issued by different governments retained about 20 capital offences, most of which related to violent crimes.[179] Communist justice however began with a show of violence and frequent summary executions, especially against 'counter-revolutionaries'. This practice continued until well after the founding of the PRC as the campaign to eliminate 'counter-revolutionaries' continued, although Mao and the authorities from time to time called for caution in the application of the death penalty.[180]

According to Peng Zhen the 1979 Criminal Law significantly reduced capital offences as originally contained in the previous drafts.[181] Even so, the 1979 Criminal Law prescribed 28 capital offences in 15 articles.[182] Chinese authorities obviously realised the severity of such a penalty, and thus the death penalty with a two-year suspension period was introduced from the very early period of the PRC's justice system.[183] At the same time a policy of cautious application was introduced.[184] However, this policy has hardly been translated into practice; indeed, Decisions and

---

177 See Stephen B. Davis, 'The Death Penalty and Legal Reform in the PRC', (1987) 1 *Journal of Chinese Law* 303, at 306-308.

178 See Ma & Ding, *supra* note 13, at 115; See also Meijer (1967), *supra* note 29, at 28-35.

179 Ma & Ding, *supra* note 13, at 115-116.

180 See Peng Zhen, *supra* note 10, at 151. See also Kang Yunshen, 'On Ma Zedong's Creative Contribution to the Marxist-Leninist Theory on the Death Penalty', (no. 6, 1991) *Journal of China University of Political Science and Law* (*Zhengfa Luntan*) 29.

181 Peng Zhen, *supra* note 10, at 151.

182 Ma Kechang, *supra* note 19, at 5. 60% of the provisions prescribing the death penalty related to the crime of counter-revolution. See Lan Quanpu, *supra* note 4, at 73.

183 The death penalty with a two-year suspension period is a unique innovation of the PRC; it is said that the idea came from Mao Zedong and formed an important contribution to the Chinese justice system. See Gao, Zhao & Wang, *supra* note 124, at 68; Zhang Youyu, 'Mao Zedong's Creative Contribution to the Development of Marxist Legal Theory', in China Law Society (ed.), *A Collection of Articles on Ma Zedong's Legal Theories* (*Ma Zedong Xixian Faxue Lilun Lunwen Xuan*) (Beijing: Law Publishing House, 1985), at 25; 1979 *Lectures on Criminal Law*, *supra* note 8, at 34; Kang Yunshen, *supra* note 180, at 32. This policy of suspension for two years was first explained by the *People's Daily* on 1 June 1951. See Davis, *supra* note 177, at 314.

184 Peng Zhen, *supra* note 10, at 151.

Supplementary Provisions by the Standing Committee promulgated during various anti-crime campaigns had by March 1997 increased the application of the death penalty to no less than 80 offences, contained in over 50 criminal law provisions.[185] Some scholars have thus argued that the incorporation of all capital offences into the code would make the Chinese Criminal Law a 'Death Penalty Code'.[186]

If the death penalty has caused concern for the authorities, it has certainly been seen as one of the areas for reform by scholars.[187] However, few Chinese scholars advocate the abolition of the death penalty, the majority of them arguing for restrictions and restraint in its use and, ultimately, abolition in the future.[188] For these scholars, China's reputation and international trends are among the

---

[185] Shen Deyong, 'Our Criminal Law Should Establish a "Limited Use" Principle on the Death Penalty', *Legal Science in China* (*Zhongguo Faxue*) 27, at 28; Xing Yan, 'Criminal Law Revision: Minor or Major Revision or No Revision At All', in (no. 1, 1997) *Peking University Law Journal* (*Zhongwai Faxue*) 49, at 50. No one knows the exact number of death penalties handed down in China each year as the number is treated as a 'state secret'. Western media often put the number as between 1,000 and 3,000. See Lawyers Committee for Human Rights, *supra* note 15, at 82; 'Death penalty pressure', *The Australian*, 9 September 1998, at 10. In mid-March 2004, for the first time, Chinese media reported that some 10,000 people were sentenced to immediate execution each year in China, not including people sentenced to death with a two-year suspension. See '41 deputies suggested that the Supreme People's Court should re-centralise the approval power over the death penalty', originally published in the *Zhongguo Qingnian Bao* (*China Youth Daily*), and re-published in the *Renmin Ribao*, 16 March 2004, website edition: <www.people.com.cn/GB/shehui/1060/2388561.html> (last accessed 22 March 2004). One of the most notorious cases that has attracted international condemnation was the one concerning workers Bian Hanwu, Xu Guoming and Yan Xuerong, who were arrested for allegedly setting fire to a train during demonstrations in Shanghai in 6 June 1989. They were charged on June 11, sentenced to death on 14 June and executed on 21 June 1989 after an appeal on 20 June to the Shanghai High People's Court. The whole process took only two weeks. See Lawyers Committee For Human Rights, *supra* note 16, at 83-84.

[186] Chu Huazhi, 'Criminal Law Revision and Criminal Law Policy', in (no. 1, 1997) *Peking University Law Journal* (*Zhongwai Faxue*) 49, at 53.

[187] See Ma & Ding, *supra* note 13, at 105-124; Cui Qingsen & Liao Zengyun, 'On Limited and Cautious Use of the Death Penalty', (no. 2, 1989) *Studies in Law* (*Faxue Yanjiu*) 69; Gao, Zhao & Wang, *supra* note 124, at 75-76; Wang Fengzhi, 'Several Questions on the Abolition or Retention of the Death Penalty', (no. 4, 1995) *Journal of China University of Political Science and Law* (*Zhengfa Luntan*) 23; Seh Deyong, *supra* note 185; Ma Kechang, *supra* note 19, at 5-7; Chen Xingliang, *supra* note 14, at 57-58; Zhang Mingkai, *supra* note 18; Jia Yu, 'Reduction of Capital Offence – An Important Aspect of Criminal Law Reform', (no. 1, 1997) *Politics and Law* (*Zhengzhi Yu Falü*) 7. One of the most comprehensive studies on the death penalty in China is Hu Yunteng, *To Abolish or to Continue: A Theoretical Study on the Death Penalty (Quan yu Fei: Sixing Jiben Lilun Yanjiu)* (Beijing: China Procuratorial Press, 2000). A summary of this study in English is published in Hu Yunteng, 'Application of the Death Penalty in Chinese Judicial Practice', in Jianfu Chen, Jan Michiel Otto, & Yuwen Li (eds), *Implementation of Law in the PRC* (The Hague/London/New York: Kluwer Law International, 2002), at 247-276.

[188] See *id.* Ma & Ding, *supra* note 13, at 22-23; Hu Yunteng, *id.*, at 264-266.

major considerations for restraint.[189] Although some of them advocate the gradual abolition of the death penalty, their targeted timetable has undermined their own argument.[190] Some have pointed out that, according to statistics from one province, 90% of death penalties were imposed for the crimes of murder, robbery, rape, serious bodily injuries and major theft, and that only ten offences seem to have attracted the death penalty frequently.[191] Some have further pointed to the huge discretion in imposing the death penalty. For instance, it has been pointed out that more than 20 offences attract penalties ranging from criminal detention to the death penalty.[192] Many of them clearly see the death penalty as an inappropriate form of punishment for economic crimes.[193]

However, these opinions have not been accepted by the authorities. The policy on the death penalty in the 1997 revision was neither to reduce nor to increase the death penalty.[194] This confirmed the fear of some of the scholars that the revised Criminal Law looks like a 'death penalty code': Among the 542 articles in total, 76 articles contain the death penalty. Further, many of these articles deal with more than one offence, and thus there are many more offences in the revised criminal law that can attract the death penalty.[195] By any criteria, it is a major disappointment in the reform of criminal law.

As in the case of administrative sanctions, the death penalty debate continues in China, and this has also led to some significant reform in 2006. As mentioned above, there is a general consensus among academics and officials that the death penalty needs to be applied cautiously, whether the abolition of it is politically unrealistic or not. However, the problem with the death penalty is not just that it is too common; its application lacks strict control. Under the original 1979 Criminal Law all death penalty sentences had to be reviewed by the Supreme People's Court before their actual execution. However, the final review powers were delegated to High Courts at the provincial level by the Supreme People's Court in the 1980s during

---

189 *Supra* note 187.

190 For instance, one scholar argued that the death penalty should be gradually abolished, but that it would take about one hundred years to do so. See Ma & Ding, *supra* note 13, at 120.

191 Chen Xingliang, *supra* note 14, at 57.

192 Chu Huazhi, *supra* note 186, at 54.

193 Ma & Ding, *supra* note 13, at 110; Cui & Liao, *supra* note 187, at 71; Ma Kechang, *supra* note 19, at 6.

194 Wang Hanbin, *supra* note 12, at 679. The death penalty for people under 18 years was however reduced to life imprisonment in order to satisfy China's international obligation under the UN Convention on the Rights of the Child, which was ratified by the Standing Committee in November 1991.

195 Based on my own examination and calculation of the revised Criminal Law. According to the calculation of Hu Yuntent, the total number of offences attracting the death penalty under the revised Criminal Law is 68. See Hu Yunteng (2002), *supra* note 187, at 264.

the 'anti-crimes campaigns'.[196] Under this delegated system, many death penalty sentences were simply not reviewed in any meaningful sense. The reason is simple: most cases involving the death penalty were tried by an Intermediate Court in the first instance and appealed to a High Court. In this way, the High Court was both the appeal court and the court exercising the final review power. In March 2004 the Supreme People's Court finally indicated that it would reclaim the final review power over the death penalty.[197] In October 2006 the Organic Law of the People's Courts of the PRC was revised by the SCNPC, re-instating the review power to the Supreme People's Court. Thus in December 2006 the Supreme People's Court finally decided to reclaim this power,[198] with effect from 1 January 2007. While this is only a small step toward the reform of the death penalty in China, it is in fact a life-saving measure under the current system.[199]

5. Concluding Remarks

Comparing the 1979 Chinese Criminal Law with the Soviet Criminal Code of 1960, Berman and his colleagues noted a striking difference in the style of the two sets of codes, namely, in the profuse moralism of the Chinese, and the stern formalism of the Soviet code.[200] They believed that the then Soviet codes embodied the law of a revolution that had settled down, whereas the Chinese code embodied the law of a revolution that was still boiling.[201] Clearly, the 1979 Chinese Criminal Law as amended in 1997 now represents a formalistic approach towards crime and punishment. It also signals the stabilisation of a revolution.

---

196 The delegation was made through eight Supreme People's Court Notices issued between 1980 and 1997. A list of these notices are appended to the Decision of the Supreme People's Court on the Relevant Issues concerning the Uniform Exercise of the Death Penalty Review Power, issued by the Supreme People's Court on 28 December 2006.

197 See 'The Death Penalty Review Power at Provincial Level Should Be Given a "Sudden Death"', *Nanfang Weekend* (*Nanfang Zhoumo*), 14 October 2004, available in <www.nanfangdaily.com.cn/zm/20041014/xw/tb/200410140001.asp> (last accessed 18 October 2004).

198 Decision of the Supreme People's Court on the Relevant Issues concerning the Uniform Exercise of the Death Penalty Review Power, *supra* note 196.

199 Under the delegated system the Supreme People's Court retained the review power over the death penalty for crimes against state security and for corruption. According to Chinese source, between 10% and 20% of cases reviewed by the Supreme People's Court ended in changes in sentences. See 'How Far China Is from the Abolition of the Death Penalty', in <news.xinhuannet.com/global/2004-06/01/Content_1502050htm> (last accessed 1 June 2004).

200 Berman, Cohen & Russel, *supra* note 5, at 239.

201 Berman, Cohen & Russel, *supra* note 5, at 257.

However, the 1997 revision is also a major disappointment. Although the revision strives to deal with, and has been quite successful in dealing with, a number of technical deficiencies in the criminal justice system (e.g. the fragmentation of the criminal law, the vagueness and ambiguities of the provisions, and the imbalance in punishments among criminal offences), it fails to address some of the fundamental problems, chief among them being 'counter-revolutionary' crimes, the artificial distinction between administrative sanctions and criminal penalties, and the death penalty. The removal of counter-revolutionary crime as a legal category may be seen as a step forward. The retention of most of the counter-revolutionary crime provisions, without the subjective label of 'counter-revolution', is however a major failure. One must be concerned whether in this way it actually legitimises the punishment of political crimes (e.g. advocacy for changing the socialist system) as they are now treated as 'ordinary' crimes. The problem of the artificial distinction between administrative sanctions and criminal penalties is simply unaddressed, as is the question of the death penalty.

Perhaps China needs to consider comprehensively revising the Criminal Law again.

Chapter Eight

Criminal Procedure Law

1. Introduction

As discussed in Chapter Six, the importance of procedure in administering law and justice was not appreciated until recently. It is therefore not surprising that when the Criminal Procedure Law (CPL) of the People's Republic of China was issued in 1979[1] it became one of the pieces of legislation most criticised by both Chinese and Western scholars. Its comprehensive revision at the 4th Plenary Session of the 8th National People's Congress (NPC)[2] in 1996 thus signified a major development towards a deeper understanding of the notion of Rule of Law and justice. Although the revision of the CPL has been only a moderate step towards improving the criminal justice system in China and its outcome was mainly a result of major compromises between opposing views among scholars, officials and various forces in the Chinese legal system, the progress made in the revision, in the view of the present author, represents one of the most significant advances in the Chinese legal system since the establishment of the PRC in 1949.

This chapter first provides an overview of the major deficiencies of the CPL before the revision, both on its face value and in its implementation, and of the criticisms it had attracted from the time of its adoption in 1979. It then analyses, in detail, specific problems in the original CPL and the major changes made in the 1996 revision. It concludes by pointing out some difficulties in the actual implementation of the law in China, and the current plan for further revision.

---

1 The Criminal Procedure Law of the People's Republic of China was adopted at the 5th National People's Congress on 1 July 1979, effective from 1 January 1980.

2 The Decision concerning the Revision of the Criminal Procedure Law was adopted by the 5th National People's Congress at its 4th Plenary Session, 17 March 1996. See (no. 3, 1996) *Gazette of the Standing Committee of National People's Congress of the PRC* (*Zhonghua Renmin Gongheguo Quanguo Renmin Daibiao Dahui Changwu Weiyuanhui Gongbao*), at 25-47. An English translation of the revised Criminal Procedure Law can be found in Jianfu Chen & Suiwa Ke (eds), *China Criminal Laws: Commentary and Translation* (Singapore: CCH Asia Pte Limited, 2000).

2. An Overview of the Major Deficiencies of the CPL

The CPL, based on drafts prepared in the mid-1950s and early 1960s,[3] was one of the first seven major laws enacted in post-Mao China.[4] The purpose of its enactment was two-fold: to elaborate the constitutional provisions regarding the division of powers and responsibilities among the people's courts, the people's procuratorates and the public security organs; and to provide working procedures for criminal adjudication. Although the CPL was supposed to be a comprehensive code, its provisions were short, vague and, in many instances, ambiguous. Its deficiencies, both on its face value and in its actual practice, were soon to become apparent and thus to attract severe criticism, particularly from Western human rights organisations.[5] Fundamentally, many important 'due process' principles, such as the presumption of innocence, judicial independence, adequate right to legal counsel, etc., were absent from the CPL; many other provisions of the CPL fell far short of minimum requirements for the administration of justice.[6]

---

3 In particular it was based on a draft prepared in 1963. See Wang Guo'ou, Wang Yizhen & Wang Cunhou (eds.), *An Outline of the Criminal Procedure Law* (*Xingshi Susongfa Gailun*) (Beijing: Beijing University Press, 1981), at 50-52; and Peng Zhen, 'Explanations on the Drafts of the Seven Laws', delivered to the Second Plenary Session of the Fifth NPC on 26 June 1979, in Peng Zhen, *On Political and Judicial Work in the New China* (*Lun Xinzhongguo De Zhengfa Gongzuo*) (Beijing: Press of the Chinese Communist Party Documents, 1992), at 157.

4 The other six laws include a substantial criminal code, an organic law for local people's congresses and local governments, two organic laws for the people's courts and people's procuratorates respectively, and a law on Sino-foreign equity joint ventures.

5 There were many reports of human rights violations in relation to criminal processes under the 1979 CPL in China by international human rights organisations. See e.g. Amnesty International (1991), *China – Punishment Without Crime: Administrative Detention* (ASA 17/27/91; Amnesty International, 1992), *Torture in China* (ASA 17/55/92, Amnesty International, 1996), *China: No One Is Safe*, ASA 17/01/96; Lawyers Committee for Human Rights, *Criminal Justice with Chinese Characteristics: China's Criminal Process and Violations of Human Rights* (New York, 1993); and *Reports of the Australian Human Rights Delegation to China*, First Report, July 1991 and Second Report, November 1992 (Canberra, Australian Government Publishing Service).

6 By minimum requirements I mean those provisions embodied in the Universal Declaration of Human Rights (1948) and the International Covenant on Civil and Political Rights (ICCPR) (1966). Many of the principles in these two documents are elaborated in other UN Conventions, e.g. UN Convention Against Torture and Other Cruel, Inhuman or Degrading Treatment or Punishment, and principles adopted by various UN agencies and endorsed by the UN General Assembly, e.g. General Comments made by the UN Human Rights Committee under the ICCPR, the UN Body of Principles for the Protection of All Persons Under Any Form of Detention or Imprisonment, GA Resolution 43/179 (1988); Basic Principles on the Role of Lawyers, endorsed by the UN Resolution 45/121 (1990), Basic Principles on the Independence of the Judiciary, endorsed by the UN GA Resolution 40/146 (1985), and many more.

This deficient law was made even worse by many decisions of the Standing Committee of the NPC (SCNPC), issued during various anti-crime campaigns,[7] and by the inability or unwillingness of the law-enforcement organs to act within the law. Indeed, no sooner had the CPL been implemented than the realisation arose of the inability of the judiciary to handle criminal cases according to the law: In February 1980 – one month after the CPL came into effect – the SCNPC authorised the standing committees at the provincial level to approve extensions of time limits for handling criminal cases as prescribed by the CPL.[8] Such authorisation was again granted by the SCNPC in September 1981 for handling criminal cases during the period of 1981–1983.[9] Thereafter no less than 20 revisions (in the form of Decisions and Supplementary Provisions) concerning criminal and criminal procedure matters were made by the SCNPC alone before the end of 1995.[10] Many of these provisions had serious implications for the protection of human rights and the administration of justice in China.[11] Some of them, such as the Decision of the SCNPC on the Procedures for Rapid Adjudication of Cases Involving Criminal Elements Who Seriously Endanger Public Security (1983),[12] were criticised by Chinese scholars as being a blatant violation of the Chinese Constitution.[13]

With these supplementary provisions, many of them issued specifically for anti-crime campaigns with *ad hoc* policy orientation, the deficiencies of the CPL were no longer restricted to its vagueness and ambiguities, but also involved internal contradictions and confusion. This fact, together with the inability or unwilling-

7 For discussions on the anti-crime campaigns, see 'Note: Concept of Law in the Chinese Anti-Crime Campaign', (1985) 98 *Harvard Law Review* 1890; and Deborah E. Townsend, 'The Concept of Law in Post-Mao China: A Case Study of Economic Crime', (1987–1988) 24 *Stanford Journal of International Law* 227.

8 See Decision of the Standing Committee of the NPC Regarding the Questions of Implementation of the Criminal Procedure Law (12 Feb. 1980). A copy of the Decision can be found in Huang Shengye (ed.), *A Lawyer's Handbook* (*Lüshi Shouce*) (Beijing: Press of the Economic Daily, 1996), at 1284.

9 See further discussions in Shao-Chuan Leng & Hungdah Chiu, *Criminal Justice in Post-Mao China: Analysis and Documents* (Albany: State University of New York Press, 1985), at 87.

10 Huang Taiyun, 'Major Reforms in the Criminal Processes – An Outline of the Major Revisions to the Criminal Procedure Law', (no. 2, 1996) *Legal Science in China* (*Zhongguo Faxue*) 29, at 30. Texts of these Decisions, Supplementary Provisions and many other judicial documents issued by the Supreme People's Court, the Supreme People's Procuratorate and the Ministry of Public Security concerning the implementation of the CPL can be found in Huang Shengye, *supra* note 8.

11 See *supra* note 5; and Leng & Chiu, *supra* note 9.

12 The Chinese text of the Decision can be found in *A Complete Collection of Laws of the PRC* (*Zhonghua Renmin Gonghe Guo Falü Quanshu*) (Jilin: Jilin People's Press, 1989), at 222; An English translation can be found in Leng & Chiu, *supra* note 9, at 232.

13 See Cui Min, 'A Summary of the Discussions on Revising and Perfecting the Criminal Procedure Law', (no. 1, 1995) *Modern Law Science* (*Xiandai Faxue*) 92, at 96.

ness of the law-enforcement organs to act within the law, meant that the practical consequences for the society were serious abuses of human rights, including the wide-spread application of so-called administrative sanctions, prolonged detention without trial, and the disregard for minimum procedural protection.[14] Thus, fundamental concerns about human rights in China can easily be traced to the structure and functioning of the PRC's criminal justice system.[15]

Gellat, writing on behalf of the Lawyers Committee on Human Rights, provided the following overall assessment of the CPL and its implementation before the 1996 revision:

> The 1979 CPL is a detailed document that provides procedures for the criminal process which were completely absent during the PRC's first 30 years. Nevertheless, the procedure law contains numerous defects that on their face violate international standards of fair judicial process. In addition, the authorities frequently violate the provisions of the procedural law. They take advantage of ambiguities in the law or simply disregard legal protection existing in the formal criminal process. They also commonly circumvent such protection by use of administrative, 'non-criminal' sanctioning methods. These abuses occur perhaps most frequently and egregiously in political cases, but also in ordinary criminal cases.[16]

3. Major Changes in the 1996 Revision

3.1. An Overview

To be fair, it should be noted that the CPL was a product of a particular historical time. First, the CPL was adopted before the promulgation of the 1982 Constitution which provided some general principles for the administration of justice that were absent from the 1978 Constitution under which the CPL was drawn up. Further, the promulgation of the CPL coincided with the re-establishment of the law enforcement institutions, namely, the public security organs, the people's procuratorates and the courts, the latter two having been effectively 'smashed' during the so-called Cultural Revolution (1966–1976).[17] The inability of the judicial organs to act in accordance with the law was to be expected, although the abuse of the criminal process is another

---

14 See discussions on specific topics below.

15 Lawyers Committee for Human Rights, *supra* note 5, at 1.

16 *Id.* at 9-10.

17 The People's Procuratorates were officially abolished in 1969; their functions were assigned to the public security organs by the 1975 Constitution. See Zhao Zhenjiang (ed.), *Forty Years of the Chinese Legal System* (*Zhongguo Fazhi Sishinian*) (Beijing: Beijing University Press, 1990), at 368. See also discussions in Chapter 4.

matter. Finally, in the late 1970s, legal research and study had just resumed after the Cultural Revolution, as had the debates on certain fundamental 'due process' principles. The applicability of these principles in China was then, and to a certain extent still is, a hotly contested and unsettled issue.

With the development of legal research and the 'open door' policy which brought in foreign influences, Chinese scholars soon recognised the deficiencies in their law and began to argue for the inclusion of many Western criminal procedural principles into the CPL.[18] Many problems in the implementation of the CPL also came to the attention of scholars and officials.[19] Thus the issue of revising the CPL became a topic of academic discussion and official consideration.[20]

The first formal forum to discuss the revision of the CPL was held in January 1991 in Beijing, organised by the LAC of the SCNPC. A report on the forum was prepared and submitted to the Central Committee of the Communist Party of China. Several seminars were later held in various locations among Chinese scholars. In September 1993 it was officially announced by the Director of the LAC, Mr. Gu Angran, that a formal decision had been made by the SCNPC to include the revision of the CPL in the Legislative Agenda of the NPC.[21] Thereafter, the LAC formally entrusted the drafting work to Professor Chen Guangzhong of the China University of Political Science and Law, who then organised a group of scholars and Ph.D students to carry out the drafting work.[22] This work was efficiently completed in

---

18 For a summary of major debates, see Chen Guangzhong, 'Forty Years of the Chinese Criminal Procedure Science', *Journal of the China University of Political Science and Law* (*Zhengfa Luntan*), Pt I in no. 4, 1989, at 5-14, Pt. II in no. 5, 1989, at 1-8. The whole article was reprinted in Zhang Youyu & Wang Shuwen (eds.), *Forty Years of the PRC's Legal Science* (*Zhongguo Faxue Sishinian*) (Shanghai: Shanghai People's Publishing House, 1989), at 251-287. These debates will be further reviewed in the following discussions on the specific issues.

19 One Chinese scholar described the problems in the criminal process in the following way: 'Those (laws) that have been published are not implemented; and those not published are enforced'; 'those who see the patients do not give prescriptions and those who give prescriptions do not see the patients – the separation of hearing from decision'. See Zhao Zhenjiang, *supra* note 17, at 380-384.

20 As early as mid-1985, the Legislative Affairs Committee (LAC) of the SCNPC had indicated that the revision of the CPL was already under consideration. See Gu Angran, 'Some Major Issues in the Drafting of Criminal and Criminal Procedure Laws – a speech delivered to the training class for law-making cadres, May 1985', in Gu Angran, *The Socialist Legal System and Legislative Work* (*Shehui Zhuyi Fazhi He Lifa Gongzuo*) (Beijing: China University of Political Science and Law Press, 1989), at 206. One of the major academic gatherings to discuss the 'perfecting' of the CPL was the 1986 Guangzhou Conference, at which over 100 procedure law specialists came together to discuss a wide range of issues concerning the improvement of the CPL. See Zhao Zhenjiang, *supra* note 17, at 373-375.

21 Cui Min, *supra* note 13, at 92.

22 This was said to be the first time that the drafting of law had been entrusted to scholars in China. *Ibid.*

about six months.[23] Thereafter many more symposiums were held to discuss the revision of the CPL, either organised by scholars or by the LAC. In October 1995 the LAC issued a draft Bill and Explanations on Several Major Issues Concerning the Revision of the CPL. These two documents then formed the basis for further academic discussion.[24] At the same time the draft Bill was twice submitted to the SCNPC for deliberation.[25] Thus it can be said that the revision of the CPL was a product of major joint efforts by scholars and law-makers.

The revision was a major one: 70 out of the original 164 articles were revised, 2 articles abolished and 63 articles added to the CPL, thus making the CPL much more comprehensive and precise. The significance of the revision lies, however, not in the total number of articles revised, but in that, to some extent, certain fundamental 'due process' principles were incorporated in the CPL for the first time – when the revision was officially adopted by the NPC in 1996.

3.2. Preliminary Detention and 'Shelter and Investigation'

The original 1979 CPL divided the criminal processes into four stages: pre-trial, trial, appeal, and execution. The pre-trial stage included three steps: filing a case (*li'an*), investigation, and institution of prosecution. These three pre-trial steps concerned mainly two principal acts: detention and arrest,[26] and investigation, and were to be carried out by the public security organs and the people's procuratorates.

The Chinese pre-trial process under the 1979 CPL was very different from that in the West; it was a process during which the investigatory organs were supposed to have completed investigation of the defendant's crime, and complete and reliable evidence should have been collected.[27] In order for the investigatory

---

23 Cui Min, *supra* note 13, at 92.

24 Major issues discussed by academics were: (1) the overall desirability of the draft Bill; (2) requirements for approval of arrest; (3) the scope of criminal investigation by the people's procuratorates; (4) the scope of private prosecution; (5) exemption from prosecution; (6) the time at which lawyers and other defenders should be allowed to enter into the criminal process; (7) the methods for court trials; (8) the status and procedural rights of crime victims; (9) time limits for handling of cases; (10) the means of investigation by the people's procuratorates; and (11) the review of death penalty cases. See Wei Tong, 'A Report of the Discussions on the Revision of the CPL', (no. 1, 1996*) Journal of the China University of Political Science and Law* (*Zhengfa Luntan*) 89, at 89.

25 Gu Angran, 'Explanations on the Revision of the Criminal Procedure Law of the PRC', delivered at the 4th Plenary Session of the 8th NPC on March 12, 1996, in (no. 3, 1996) *Gazette of the Standing Committee of National People's Congress of the PRC* (*Zhonghua Renmin Gongheguo Quanguo Renmin Daibiao Dahui Changwu Weiyuanhui Gongbao*), at 85.

26 The CPL distinguished two kinds of detention, detention (*juliu*) and arrest (*daibu*). The former referred to preliminary apprehension of a suspect by the public security organs and the latter to formal arrest with approval of the procuratorate. See Articles 39 & 41 of the 1979 CPL.

27 See Article 100 of the 1979 CPL.

organs to complete the above tasks, the CPL provided very generous time limits for each of the investigation stages. A public security organ might first detain an active criminal or a major suspect in any of the following circumstances: (a) if he/she was in the process of preparing to commit a crime, was committing a crime or was discovered immediately after committing a crime; (b) if he/she was identified as having committed a crime by the victim or by an eye witness at the scene; (c) if he/she was discovered to have criminal evidence on his/her person or at his/her residence; (d) if, after committing the crime, he/she attempted to commit suicide or to escape or was a fugitive; (e) if he/she might possibly destroy or falsify evidence or collude with others to devise a consistent story; (f) if his/her identity was unclear and there was strong suspicion that he/she was a person who went from place to place committing crimes; or (g) if he/she was carrying on 'beating, smashing and looting' and gravely undermining work, production or the social order.[28]

If a public security organ considered it necessary to arrest the detained person, it was required, within three days after detention, to submit a request to the people's procuratorate for review and approval. Under special circumstances, the time for requesting review and approval might be extended by from one to four days. The people's procuratorate was to make its decision to approve arrest or not within three days after receiving the application for approval of arrest from the public security organ.[29] If the arrest requested was not approved, the detained person had to be released immediately.[30] If the above procedure was not followed by the public security organ or by the people's procuratorate, the detained person or his/her family had the right to demand release, and the detained person had to be released immediately.[31] Under these provisions, the maximum period of detention before a formal arrest could not exceed ten days. Once the suspect was arrested, the period of holding a defendant in custody during investigation might not exceed two months. Where the circumstances of a case were complex and the case could not be concluded before the expiration of the period, the period might be extended by one month with the approval of the people's procuratorate at the next level up.[32] In the event of an especially major or complex case that still could not be concluded after the extension, the Supreme People's Procuratorate was to request the NPC's Standing Committee to approve postponement of the hearing of the case.[33] After the expira-

---

28 Article 41 of the 1979 CPL. See also Article 6 of the Detention and Arrest Regulations of the PRC (1979). These Regulations were abolished when the revised CPL took effect on 1 January 1997.

29 Article 48 of the 1979 CPL. See also Article 8 of the Detention and Arrest Regulations of the PRC (1979).

30 Article 48 of the 1979 CPL.

31 *Ibid.*

32 Article 92 of the 1979 CPL.

33 *Ibid.* Here a legal loophole apparently existing for indefinite detention before a trial.

tion of the above time limits, the people's procuratorate was to make a decision to initiate a public prosecution, to exempt the person from prosecution or to quash the case, if the investigation was carried out by the procuratorate.[34] If the investigation was carried out by a public security organ, the public security organ was, upon the expiration of the above time limits, to draft an opinion recommending prosecution or an opinion recommending exemption from prosecution and transfer it together with the materials in the case file and the evidence to the people's procuratorate at the same level for review and decision.[35] Upon receiving the case transferred from the public security organ, the decision to initiate a prosecution or to exempt from prosecution was to be made by the people's procuratorate within one month. In major or complex cases there might be an extension of one and a half months.[36] In cases where supplementary investigation was required, it was to be completed within one month.[37]

Clearly, the maximum duration of detention before trial as provided by the 1979 CPL was a far cry from any international standard for preliminary detention. However, even this over-generous allowance, with a possibility of indefinite detention for major and especially serious cases, was extended during the so called 'Rapid Adjudication of Cases Seriously Endangering Public Orders' campaigns in the 1980s. According to Item 1 of the Supplementary Provisions Regarding the Question of the Time Limits for Handling Criminal Cases,[38] the time limit for holding a defendant in custody during investigation as stipulated in the first paragraph of Article 92 of the Criminal Procedure Law (i.e. two months plus an extension of one month) could be extended by two months with the approval or decision of the people's procuratorate at the level of province, autonomous region or municipality. This extension, theoretically, only applied to cases of major criminal groups or major and complex cases in which criminals went from place to place committing crimes. Also if, during investigation, a defendant was found to be associated with another major and serious crime, the supplementary investigation might be conducted with the approval or decision of the people's procuratorate. In such cases, the custody period might be recalculated.[39]

The matter was made much worse in practice by the Chinese 'ingenious' distinction between 'administrative' and 'criminal' sanctions. Put simply, administrative sanctions are those penalties provided by administrative regulations and administered

---

34 Article 93 of the 1979 CPL.

35 *Id.*

36 Article 97 of the 1979 CPL.

37 Article 99 of the 1979 CPL.

38 Issued by the SCNPC in July 1984. A copy of the Chinese text can be found in *A Complete Collection of Laws of the PRC, supra* note 12, at 223.

39 Item 3 Supplementary Provisions Regarding the Question of the Time Limits for Handling Criminal Cases, *id.*

and executed by administrative organs.[40] Limited judicial supervision was only available after the promulgation of the Administrative Litigation Law in 1989 and the Administrative Penalties Law in 1996. The most notorious and widely used form of administrative sanctions was the so-called 'Shelter and Investigation' provision (*Shourong Shencha*).

'Shelter and Investigation' was first established in 1961 and intended as a form of preventive detention, not as a punishment,[41] and was a widely used alternative measure by the public security organs to detain people and thus to bypass the procedures for arrest and detention as provided in the Arrest and Detention Regulations (abolished in 1997) and the 1979 CPL.[42] However its precise legal nature was unclear and it was a very controversial institution for many years.[43]

Several serious problems were identified by Chinese scholars. Chen Weidong, from the Department of Law of the People's (Renmin) University, and Zhang Tao, from the Law Institute of the Chinese Academy of Social Sciences, for instance, provided excellent analyses of the theoretical and practical problems associated with the institution of 'Shelter and Investigation'.[44] First, with regard to the nature of 'Shelter and Investigation', they examined various relevant documents on the subject and then concluded that, in its form 'Shelter and Investigation' was an administrative measure of investigation of a coercive nature, but in its nature it was used to combat criminal activities committed by minor offenders, or other criminal activities, in order to deal with cases of suspects where it was not possible to clarify major criminal acts and obtain the necessary evidence within the time limits laid down for criminal detention in the CPL. It was thus obviously inappropriate to define such extended 'criminal detention' as being of an 'administrative' nature.[45] Secondly, and again relying on those documents, they believed that the scope of

---

40 See *Chinese Encyclopaedia – Law* (*Zhonggu Dabaike Quanshu – Faxue*) (Beijing/Shanghai: Press of the Chinese Encyclopaedia, 1984), at 670-671.

41 Amnesty International (1991), *supra* note 5, at 6-7.

42 In every large and medium-sized city in China there were several 'Shelter and Investigation' Centres and, each year, hundreds of thousands of people were detained under this institution. See Amnesty International (1991), *supra* note 5, at 6.

43 See *id.*, at 5-14.

44 Chen Weidong and Zhang Tao, 'Research into Several Problems with Shelter and Investigation', (no. 2, 1992) *Legal Science in China* (*Zhongguo Faxue*) 82; and Chen Weidong and Zhang Tao, 'A Further Talk on Why Shelter and Investigation Should Not Be Abolished', (no. 3, 1993) *Legal Science in China* (*Zhongguo Faxue*) 113.

45 The following documents were discussed by the authors: The 1985 Notice on the Strict Control of the Use of Shelter and Investigation (issued by the Ministry of Public Security); Relevant Situations concerning Shelter and Investigation (issued by the Ministry of Public Security); and A Reply to Several Questions Concerning Propaganda of Shelter and Investigation (issuing authority not specified). None of these documents was made public.

application and the legal authority for such application were unclear.[46] Finally, they outlined several major problems in the use of 'Shelter and Investigation', which included its widespread use, detention exceeding time limits, poor management of the system, and unlawful practices of investigation involved in its application.[47] Despite all these 'shortcomings', Chen and Zhang, however, believed that 'Shelter and Investigation' should continue to be available to the public security organs, but that the system should be improved through legislation. They insisted that as 'Shelter and Investigation' was used before the start of criminal proceedings it had nothing to do with criminal procedure law. They further asserted that 'Shelter and Investigation' filled a gap between punishment in order to maintain public order and coercive measures in criminal proceedings and, therefore, naturally should be regulated by the State Council and implemented by public security organs.[48]

Scholars who opposed the use of such an extra-legal form of sanction also questioned its nature and its legal basis, its constitutionality and legality, its scope of operation and its abuse in practice, but put more emphasis on the importance of the protection of individual rights. Wang Xinxin from the Department of Law of the People's University, for example, declared:

> Under various regulations issued by the State Council and the Ministry of Public Security, 'Shelter and Investigation' applies to those who roam around committing crimes or criminal suspects, when investigation into their crimes and the collection of evidence have not been completed. In the cases of criminal suspects without necessary evidence, the deprivation of personal freedom by 'Shelter and Investigation' in order to complete investigation is a violation of the fundamental principles of the Constitution and criminal procedure law. In its nature, it is a presumption of guilt. Furthermore, such practice shifts the burden of investigation within statutory limits from judicial organs to the suspects. Therefore provisions concerning criminal detention and arrest and for the protection of citizens' rights and statutory process and time limits are rendered meaningless by 'Shelter and Investigation'. 'Shelter and Investigation' also deprives those who should not be detained of their personal freedom. Therefore the contents of 'Shelter and Investigation' are also in violation of the Constitution and criminal procedure law.[49]

46 Chen & Zhang (1992), *supra* note 44, at 82-83.

47 *Id.*, at 83.

48 Chen & Zhang (1993), *supra* note 44, at 113-114. See also Cheng Rongbing, 'Coercive Measures and Shelter and Investigation', (no. 5, 1994) *Legal Science in China* (*Zhongguo Faxue*) 38.

49 Wang Xinxin, 'Shelter and Investigation Should Be Abolished – A Discussion with Comrades Chen Weidong and Zhang Tao', (no. 3, 1993) *Legal Science in China* (*Zhongguo Faxue*) 110, at 112.

Wang made it very clear that 'Shelter and Investigation' must be abolished because 'Shelter and Investigation' itself was a serious violation of citizens' rights as provided for by the Constitution.'[50]

Whatever the nature of this extra-legal form of detention, the public security organs preferred the 'Shelter and Investigation' provision to the two mechanisms for detention as provided in the CPL.[51] Further, many Chinese scholars agreed on the explanation for the widespread use of this institution: the time limit provided for arrest by the CPL was too short to fulfil the task of clarifying crime facts in order to have a suspect arrested.[52] Officials too were concerned and now openly admitted that such an institution of prolonged detention administered solely by public security organs violated the CPL provisions and lacked supervision and control.[53] With this understanding it was not surprising that major reforms in the 1996 revision concerning preliminary detention involved re-defining the requirements for arrest, extending the duration for detention, and abolishing the 'Shelter and Investigation' practice.

Under Article 40 of the 1979 CPL one of the requirements for arrest approval was that 'major crime facts have been clarified'. This, as discussed above, was said to be one of the major reasons that caused the prolonged detention and the use of 'Shelter and Investigation'. Article 27 of the Decision concerning the Revision of the Criminal Procedure Law now changed the requirement to be that 'there is evidence of crime' (Article 60 of the revised CPL). 'Clarification' of crime facts and adequacy of evidence are now matters to be inquired into and dealt with during the trial process.[54] The revision also strengthens the preventive institutions, thus making detention and arrest the last means of coercive action. Hence Article 26 of the Decision adds eight articles (Articles 51-58 of the revised CPL) to the CPL to strengthen the procedures for obtaining a guarantor or a bond and thus awaiting trial out of custody, and allowing a suspect to live at home under surveillance. Further, the duration of preliminary detention by public security organs in major cases where the persons are suspected of going from place to place committing crimes, or repeating crimes or committing crimes in a group, has been extended to one month, thus allowing the investigatory organs to have sufficient time to complete

---

50 *Id.*, at 110. In the same article, Wang also questioned the constitutional basis for the State Council to regulate matters concerning criminal procedural matters.

51 This was the widespread practice termed by Chinese scholars as 'those (laws) that have been published are not implemented; and those not published are enforced'. See Zhao Zhenjiang, *supra* note 17, at 380.

52 Cui Min, 'A Comment on the Major Changes to the Criminal Procedure Law', *Guangming Daily* (*Guangming Ribao*), 28 March 1996, at 6; see also Lawyers Committee for Human Rights, *supra* note 5, at 13-14.

53 Gu Angran, *supra* note 25, at 86.

54 See discussions on trial process below.

their investigation. With these provisions in place, the 'Shelter and Investigation' is formally abolished. A few more words need to be added regarding the abolition of 'Shelter and Investigation': as discussed above, 'Shelter and Investigation' is not in fact a measure provided by the CPL; the revision of the CPL has thus not actually affected the operation of this form of administrative detention. The abolition of 'Shelter and Investigation' was therefore announced in the 'Explanations on the Revision of the CPL of the PRC', delivered by Gu Angran at the 4th Plenary Session of the 8th NPC,[55] not in the Decision concerning the Revision of the Criminal Procedure Law.

3.3. The Presumption of Innocence

The presumption of innocence is defined by the *Chinese Encyclopaedia* as 'one of the principles of criminal procedure law in some bourgeois countries, which means that a defendant should be deemed as an innocent person before he/she is found guilty in accordance with law.'[56] This principle, according to the *Encyclopaedia*, was initiated by the bourgeoisie during periods of revolution to oppose the feudalist presumption of guilt. It has thus played some positive and 'progressive' roles in the struggle against autocratic feudalism.[57] In short, it was a bourgeois principle which had once been progressive in the evolution of society. The ambiguity is apparent: As a bourgeois principle it should be rejected by a socialist legal system; yet, as it has played some positive and progressive roles, arguably it may still have some positive elements that a socialist legal system could adopt. Indeed, this ambiguity has allowed strenuous debates on the presumption of innocence in the 1950s and again since the 1980s.

Although Chinese scholars assert that the presumption of guilt is a feudalist criminal practice, they are also able to locate many legal provisions from the ancient codes of law to support the assertion that certain elements of presumption of innocence, in particular the emphasis on evidence and lenient treatment in cases of doubt, existed in traditional China.[58] However it was not codified as a criminal procedure principle before the KMT Criminal Procedure Code (1935), a piece of legislation largely borrowed from Continental European and Japanese legal systems. That law, together with all KMT laws, was abolished when the PRC was founded in 1949. When serious legal efforts resumed after the adoption of 1954 Constitution, academic debate began on many theoretical and practical issues, including

---

55 See *supra* note 25, at 86.

56 *Chinese Encyclopaedia – Law, supra* note 40, at 625.

57 *Ibid.*

58 See e.g. Ning Hanling, 'On the Presumption of Innocence', in *Enquiring Into Legal Theories* (*Faxue Tanwei*) (Chongqing: Chongqing Press, 1986), at 99. This article was first published in (no. 4, 1982) *Social Sciences in China* (*Zhongguo Shehui Kexue*).

the presumption of innocence. That debate was however short-lived, as the 1957 Anti-Rightists Movement was soon to denounce those who advocated bourgeois theories as 'rightists', and to silence all serious theoretical debates.[59]

Legal reform in the late 1970s created a more receptive environment for 'bourgeois' theories and practice, but the 1979 CPL did not adopt the doctrine. Instead, Article 4 of the CPL, reflecting the Party policy of 'seeking truth from facts', provided that in conducting criminal proceedings, the people's courts, the people's procuratorates and the public security organs must rely on the masses and 'must take facts as the basis, and law as the criterion.' This provision, according to Chinese officials, did not support or reject any 'presumption'.[60] In reality, people were presumed guilty until proved innocent.[61] Nevertheless an ambivalent attitude, although characterised by some Chinese scholars as 'empty talk',[62] left room for academic debate. Thus, after more than twenty years of silence the debate on the presumption of innocence resumed in the 1980s.

The debate resumed even before the promulgation of the CPL in 1979. The *People's Daily* led the way by publishing an article advocating the inclusion of the presumption of innocence into the CPL which was then being drafted.[63] After this many academic articles were published on the topic, either advocating or rejecting the doctrine, or trying to find a third position on the controversial principle to accommodate some elements of the doctrine.[64]

---

59 For discussions on the debate in the 1950s, see Timothy A. Gellat, 'The People's Republic of China and the Presumption of Innocence', (1982) 73 *The Journal of Criminal Law and Criminology* 259, esp. 267-281; and G.V. Thieme, 'The Debate on the Presumption of Innocence in the People's Republic of China', (1984) *Review of Socialist Law* 277, esp. 278-283. For a Chinese treatise on the debate, see Guo Daohui, Li Buyun, & Hao Tiechuan (eds), *A Record of Legal Debate in Contemporary China* (*Zhongguo Dangdai Faxue Zhengming Shilu*) (Changsha: Hunan People's Press, 1998).

60 See Lawyers Committee on Human Rights, *supra* note 5, at 14.

61 *Id.*, at 14.

62 *Id.*, at 14.

63 Tian Cai, 'A Question Worth Investigating', *People's Daily* (*Remin Ribao*), 17 February 1979, at 3. Ironically, the debate in the 1950s was also first silenced by the *People's Daily*, which accused those advocating the doctrine of using specious theory to help counter-revolutionaries and other criminals escape criminal responsibility. See Gellat, *supra* note 59, at 275.

64 For detailed discussions, see Thieme, *supra* note 59; and Gellat, *supra* note 59; Chen Guangzhong (Pt II), *supra* note 18, at 2-3; Zhang Lingjie, Zhang Xun & Wang Mingyuan, 'On the Principle of the Presumption of Innocence', (no. 4, 1991) *Studies in Law* (*Faxue Yanjiu*) 34; Chen Jianguo, 'The Principle of the Presumption of Innocence Should be Written into the Criminal Procedure Law', (no. 5, 1994) *Legal Science in China* (*Zhongguo Faxue*) 35; and Fan Fenglin, 'Several Thoughts on the Presumption of Innocence', (no. 5, 1994) *Legal Science in China* (*Zhongguo Faxue*) 36. For a concise summary of arguments for and against the doctrine, see Tian Cai, *supra* note 63, at 3, Guo, Li & Hao, *supra* note 59, 300-320.

The third position seeks to avoid the controversy of a wholesale adoption or a total rejection of the doctrine. It advocates critical adaptation of certain positive elements of the doctrine. Specifically, it argues for the limited adoption of the doctrine in the following sense: (1) no one should be deemed guilty until declared so by a court of law; (2) when a person cannot be proved guilty, he/she should be treated as innocent; (3) in doubtful cases, legal interpretation should be made in favour of the accused.[65] This third position, characterised in Chinese as '*Zuiyi Congwu*' (presumption of innocence in doubtful cases) was proposed by some scholars as a compromise to be included in the 1996 revision of the CPL.[66]

The third position seems to have triumphed in the revision of the CPL. Article 7 of the Decision concerning the Revision of the Criminal Procedure Law adds a new provision to the CPL, which provides that '[n]o one shall be deemed guilty until a judgment has been passed by a people's court in accordance with the law.' (Article 12 of the revised CPL). This, according to Professor Chen Guangzhong who was in charge of drafting the revision, was designed deliberately to avoid the controversy of the doctrine.[67] Clearly, it is not a total endorsement of the presumption of innocence, but it is a significant improvement over the 1979 CPL provisions. Further, Article 34 of the Decision applies the new term 'criminal suspect' to all persons suspected of committing crimes, but before the institution of prosecution. The change of terminology re-enforces the rejection of presumption of guilt, but does not necessarily support the adoption of the presumption of innocence.

With this compromise arrangement in the revision it can be expected that the principle of the presumption of innocence will continue to be controversial in China. However, if the essence of this principle is to afford better protection to the accused against over-eager prosecutors or police officials who find it easier to intimidate the accused on the basis of a presumption of guilt,[68] then the practical significance of this revision will depend on the reform of other aspects of the procedure law, such as the law on evidence and the trial process. Indeed, other reforms in the revision, to be discussed below, seem to indicate a good understanding among Chinese reformers of this fundamental due process principle.

65 Chen Guangzhong (Pt II), *supra* note 18, at 3. See further Tang Guanda, 'The Presumption of Innocence Should be Concretely Analysed', (no. 1, 1980) *Studies in Law* (*Faxue Yanjiu*) 62; Liao Zengyun, 'Views on the Principle of Presumption of Innocence', (no. 5, 1980) *Studies in Law* (*Faxue Yanjiu*) 32; Chen Guangzhong, 'The Principle of the Presumption of Innocence Should be Critically Adopted', (no. 4, 1980) *Studies in Law* (*Faxue Yanjiu*) 34.

66 See Cui Min, *supra* note 13, at 94.

67 See Chen Guangzhong and Yan Duanzhu, *A Draft and its Explanation on the Revision of Criminal Procedure Law* (Beijing: China Fangzheng Press, 1995), at 107. See also Huang Taiyun, *supra* note 10, at 32.

68 Leng & Chiu, *supra* note 9, at 96.

3.4. Exemption from Prosecution

Article 101 of the 1979 CPL provided that '[i]n cases where, according to the provisions of the Criminal Law, it is not necessary to impose a sentence of criminal punishment or an exemption from criminal punishment may be granted, a people's procuratorate may grant Exemption from Prosecution (*Mianyu Qisu*).' To grant Exemption from Prosecution, three requirements had to be met: a) the crime facts were clear; b) the evidence was sufficient and certain; c) no criminal punishment was necessary or an exemption from criminal punishment might be allowed according to the Criminal Law.[69] This is what the Chinese scholars called a 'unique Chinese institution' of Exemption from Prosecution.[70] Its origin, according to a Chinese authority on CPL, could be traced to the Decision on Dealing with Detained Japanese War Criminals From the Sino-Japan War, issued by the SCNPC on 25 April 1956, which for the first time granted the people's procuratorate the power to exempt people from prosecution.[71]

A decision by a people's procuratorate to exempt someone from prosecution was different from a decision not to prosecute. Article 104 of the 1979 CPL provided that when any of the circumstances provided in Article 11 of the CPL applied, the people's procuratorate should make a decision not to prosecute. Circumstances provided in Article 11 included: (a) if the circumstances were clearly minor, the harm was not great, and the act was thus not deemed to be a crime; (b) if the period of limitation for prosecuting the crime had expired; (c) if an exemption from criminal punishment had been ordered in a special amnesty decree; (d) if, according to the Criminal Law, a crime was to be handled only upon complaint and there had been no complaint or the complaint had been withdrawn; (e) if the defendant was deceased; or (f) if other laws or decrees provided for exemption from investigation of criminal responsibility.

The difference between a decision to exempt someone from prosecution and a decision not to prosecute was that the person exempted from prosecution was guilty of a crime but was exempted from punishment, whereas in the latter case the person was not guilty of any crime, or the law would not pursue any criminal punishment on specific legal grounds.[72] The problem was therefore, as Gellat has pointed out, that the public prosecutor rendered a decision on guilt, usurping the role of the courts and acting before the suspect was legally entitled to counsel.[73] Further, in cases where the investigation was conducted by the procuracy, the people's procuratorate assumed all three functions of investigation, prosecution,

69 Wang, Wang & Wang, *supra* note 3, at 213-214.

70 Chen Guangzhong (Pt II), *supra* note 18, at 5.

71 *Ibid.*

72 Wang, Wang & Wang, *supra* note 3, at 215.

73 Lawyers Committee for Human Rights, *supra* note 5, 21.

and adjudication, which were clearly required by the CPL to be divided among the three law-enforcement organs, the public security, the procuratorate and the court.[74] The Exemption from Prosecution also lacked supervision, which led to the abuse of this legal institution through the use of the device to exempt guilty persons from prosecution, as a result of corruption, or to record an Exemption from Prosecution for innocent people.[75]

For these reasons, calls to abolish the practice had been made and debated in China for some time. The debate was heated but inconclusive.[76] Opponents to the abolition arguments asserted that this practice was a reflection of the judicial policy of 'combining punishment with leniency (*Chengban Yü Kuanda Xiangjiehe*)'; it was only an exercise of discretionary power by the procuratorate; and it was economically efficient.[77] As in the debate on the presumption of innocence, a compromise solution was proposed during the revision process. This solution was to abolish the Exemption from Prosecution provision, but at the same time to expand the scope of decisions not to prosecute.[78] Again the compromise solution was adopted. Articles 58-61 of the Decision concerning the Revision of the Criminal Procedure Law have now abolished the Exemption from Prosecution. The scope of decisions not to prosecute under Article 104 of the 1979 CPL has now been expanded to include cases 'where the circumstances of crime are minor and, according to the Criminal Law, it is not necessary to impose a sentence of criminal punishment, or criminal liability is to be exempted.'[79]

The abolition is a step forward, but the compromise solution is not without some fundamental problems. The major problems with the Exemption from Prosecution identified by the SCNPC included, first, that the practice of Exemption from

---

74 See Article 5 of the 1979 CPL.

75 See further Cui Min, *supra* note 52, at 6; Shi Huifang, 'An Opinion on Abolishing the Institution of Exemption from Prosecution', (no. 1, 1995) *Journal of the China University of Political Science and Law* (*Zhengfa Luntan*) 33; and Lawyers Committee for Human Rights, *supra* note 5, 24-25.

76 Chen Guangzhong (Pt II), *supra* note 18, at 5. See further Xu Yichu, 'My Opinion on the Exemption from Prosecution', (no. 3, 1989) *Studies in Law* (*Faxue Yanjiu*) 74; Song Yinghui & Wu Jie, 'A New Study into the Exemption from Prosecution', (no. 1, 1992) *Studies in Law* (*Faxue Yanjiu*) 24; Wang Mingyuan, 'Several Questions on the Exemption from Prosecution', (no. 2, 1992) *Legal Science in China* (*Zhongguo Faxue*) 75; Shi Huifang, *supra* note 75; Wang Hongxiang, 'Upholding and Perfecting the Exemption from Prosecution', (no. 5, 1994) *Legal Science in China* (*Zhongguo Faxue*) 42; Cui Min, 'Abolishing the Exemption from Prosecution', (no. 5, 1994) *Legal Science in China* (*Zhongguo Faxue*) 44.

77 See Chen Guangzhong (Pt II), *supra* note 18, at 5; Cui Min, *supra* note 13, at 95; Huang Taiyun, *supra* note 10, at 36-37.

78 Huang Taiyun, *supra* note 10, at 37; and Cui Min, *supra* note 13, at 95.

79 Article 58 of the Decision concerning the Revision of the Criminal Procedure Law. Now Article 142 of the revised CPL.

Prosecution violated the principles of Rule of Law, as a person could be found guilty without adjudication by a court; and secondly, that some innocent persons could be given a decision of Exemption from Prosecution, which then violated the lawful rights of the persons concerned, while some who deserved criminal punishment could be exempted from prosecution.[80] Under the new provision a person whom the procuratorate decides not to prosecute can nevertheless be regarded as being guilty of a minor crime, and this guilty verdict is not delivered by a court. Further, the phrase 'the circumstances of crime are minor' will in practice be subject to interpretation. There is then no guarantee that 'persons who deserve criminal punishment' will not escape from prosecution. Thus the actual operation of the new provision may easily defeat the original intention of the revision of the law in this regard. It may also severely undermine the new provision on the presumption of innocence.

3.5. Right to Counsel

The 1982 Constitution provides an ambivalent right of defence. Article 125 states that '[a]ll cases handled by the people's courts, except for those involving special circumstances as specified by law, shall be heard in public. The accused has the right of defence.' It is unclear in the Chinese language (*youquan huode bianhu*) whether such a right of defence includes a right to counsel, although it does do so in practice. More importantly, it is unclear whether such a right is only limited to trials in court or also allowed during pre-trial investigations. More detailed rules regarding the right of defence were provided in the CPL. Article 8 of the 1979 CPL repeated the above constitutional clause but further added that 'the people's courts have the duty to guarantee that defendants obtain defence.' The right to counsel – a lawyer, or relative or other citizen – was specifically provided for by Article 26 of the 1979 CPL. However, the 1979 CPL was again silent on whether the defendant had a right to counsel in pre-trial processes; it only provided that the court was required, seven days before the opening of the court session, to deliver to the defendant a copy of the bill of prosecution and to inform him/her that he/she might appoint a defender, or, when necessary, to designate a defender for the defendant (Article 110). Although a right to counsel before trial was not guaranteed by the law, it is difficult to see any technical barrier to a defenders' participation in pre-trial investigations. Chinese scholars, however, interpreted Article 110 to mean that defenders were only allowed to enter into the criminal process seven days before the trial.[81] It was

---

80 Gu Angran, *supra* note 25, at 89.

81 See e.g. Zhang Wei, 'Several Issues Regarding the Involvement of Lawyers in Criminal Procedure', (no. 5, 1994) *Legal Science in China* (*Zhongguo Faxue*) 39, at 39; Chen Guangzhong & Xiong Qiuhong, 'Some Opinions on the Revision of the Criminal Procedure Law – Pt I', (no. 4, 1995) *Legal Science in China* (*Zhongguo Faxue*) 91, at 92.

in fact the usual practice that defence lawyers were only involved in the criminal process several days before the trial.[82]

The inadequate protection for timely access to a defence lawyer has long been of concern to Chinese scholars.[83] The issue was strongly debated for many years,[84] but the controversial issue was not whether lawyers should be allowed earlier participation in the criminal process, but how much earlier they should be allowed.[85] Not surprisingly, the major opposition to lawyers' early participation came from investigatory organs. They argued that early participation of lawyers in the criminal process would unduly interfere with investigatory conduct, particularly in secret investigations.[86] In response to this concern from the investigatory organs, a compromise was proposed: lawyers should be allowed early participation, ideally, immediately after the first questioning of the accused by the public security, but such participation should be limited to providing legal assistance and collecting materials for the defence. Further, certain supervisory powers should be granted to the public security organs to control the access to lawyers by defendants.[87]

Again, the SCNPC decided to accept the compromise solution. Article 41 of the Decision concerning the Revision of the Criminal Procedure Law adds a new provision, as Article 96 of the revised CPL, which provides that '[a]fter the first questioning or the imposition of coercive measures, a criminal suspect has a right to appoint a lawyer to provide him/her legal consultation and to present petitions (*Shensu*) or complaints (*Konggao*) on his/her behalf. When a suspect is arrested the appointed lawyer may apply for bail (obtaining a guarantor and awaiting trial out of custody, *Qubao Houshen*) on his/her behalf. When the case involves state secrets, the appointment of a lawyer by the suspect must be approved by the investigatory organs.' This article further provides that '[t]he appointed lawyer has a right to ask for the names of the alleged crimes from the investigatory organ, and may interview the suspect under detention to acquaint himself/herself with the

82 See Leng & Chiu, *supra* note 9, at 92; Lawyers Committee for Human Rights, *supra* note 5, at 29-30; and Zhang Tao & Chen Weidong, 'A Discussion of the Time for Defence Lawyers to Participate in the Criminal Process', (no. 2, 1990) *Legal Science in China* (*Zhongguo Faxue*) 43, at 43.

83 See Chen Guangzhong (Pt I), *supra* note 18, at 13.

84 Lawyers Committee for Human Rights, *supra* note 5, at 36.

85 See Chen Guangzhong (Pt I), *supra* note 18, at 13; Hong Bing, 'Major Measures to Perfect the Criminal Procedure System', (no. 3, 1996) *Politics and Law* (*Zhangzhi Yu Falü*) 13, at 15; Huang Taiyun, *supra* note 10, at 34; Zhang & Chen, *supra* note 82, at 43; Zhang Wei, *supra* note 81, at 39.

86 *Ibid.*; and Lawyers Committee for Human Rights, *supra* note 5, at 36-37.

87 See e.g. Chen & Xiong, *supra* note 81 at 93; Li Baoyue, 'A Discussion on the Time When Lawyers Should Participate in the Criminal Process', (no. 4, 1994), *Legal Science in China* (*Zhongguo Faxue*) 98, at 100; and Xu Yichu, 'Criminal Processes and Human Rights Protection', (no. 2, 1996) *Studies in Law* (*Faxue Yanjiu*) 89, at 92.

circumstances of the case. When interviewing the suspect under detention, the investigatory organ may, according to the circumstances and the needs of the case, have representatives present. When the case involves state secrets, the interview of a suspect by a lawyer must be approved by the investigatory organ.' To strengthen the right to a defence counsel, Article 16 of the Decision adds a new provision to Article 26 of the 1979 CPL as the new Article 33 of the revised CPL, which provides that '[i]n a case of public prosecution, a criminal suspect has the right to appoint a defence counsel when his/her case is transferred [to the people's procuratorate] for review and prosecution. The accused in cases of private prosecution may appoint a defence counsel at any time.' This revised article also imposes an obligation on the people's procuratorate to inform the accused of his/her right to appoint a defence counsel in cases of public prosecution within three days of receiving the case from an investigatory organ, and on the people's court to do the same in cases of private prosecution within three days after it accepts the private prosecution. The rights of a defence lawyer are provided in the new Article 36 (revising Article 29 of the 1979 CPL): 'When the people's procuratorate begins to review and prosecute a case, a defence lawyer may consult, extract and copy prosecution materials and other expert and technical assessment materials in relation to the case. He/she may also interview and correspond with the criminal suspect. Other defence counsels may also, with the permission of the people's procuratorate, consult, extract and copy prosecution materials and other expert and technical assessment materials in relation to the case, and interview and correspond with the criminal suspect.' This article also provides similar rights for defence counsel after the court has accepted the case for adjudication. Two more articles (Articles 37 and 38 of the revised CPL) are added by Article 20 of the Decision which empower the defence lawyer to collect relevant materials from witnesses, crime victims and their relatives and other persons, and impose an obligation on the defence lawyer not to help the crime suspect or the accused to conceal or destroy evidence or to obtain or alter evidence by threat or inducement, or to engage in any other activities interfering with judicial proceedings.

The above provisions clearly try to distinguish the roles of defence lawyer during investigation and after prosecution, and limit the scope of activities of the defence lawyer during investigation. The rationale, according to Chinese scholars, is to strike a balance between the protection of citizens' rights and the prevention of interference in criminal investigation.[88] However, a range of discretionary powers has been granted to the investigatory organs, such as the presence of personnel from investigatory organs in interviews, and the approval of the appointment of lawyers in cases involving 'state secrets'. The question remains then as to how much these powers will be exercised in good faith.

---

[88] Huang Taiyun, *supra* note 10, at 35.

3.6. The Trial Process

The trial process, both on paper and in practice, had been a flawed one since it was re-institutionalised by the 1979 CPL. Its problems ranged from the passive role for lawyers to the lack of judicial independence, starting from the preliminary examination through to the passing of judgments. A Chinese scholar severely criticised the trial process thus:

> Many shortcomings of the criminal trial process have been documented. For instance, the practice of judges reviewing, examining and discussing the case based on materials supplied by the procuratorate before the trial has led to the prejudice of judges and the consequence of 'verdict first, trial second' (*Xian Ding Hou Shen*); the discussion and decision by the judicial committee and the practice of the first instance court seeking instructions from a higher court have caused the problems of 'trial judges not making decisions and decision-makers not trying the case' (*Shenzhe Bu Pan, Panzhe Bu Shen*) and 'higher courts deciding and lower courts delivering' (*Shangpi Xiapan*); because judges are required to present evidence to prove the guilt of the accused there is the phenomenon of 'non-separation between adjudicature and prosecution' (*Kong Shen Bu Fen*) and 'the *ultra vires* of adjudicature' (*Shenpan Yuewei*), etc. All these practices weaken, or even diminish the function of defence, thus rendering court trial a formality only.[89]

Some Chinese scholars thus described the trial process as a process of legitimising the conclusion which had already been drawn before the trial.[90] This kind of a practice led to the judicial reality of the presumption of guilt.[91]

These problems were deeply rooted in the fundamental political system (e.g. the lack of judicial independence) and the lack of an established legal tradition (e.g. the minimal role played by lawyers in society and in litigation). However, the majority

---

89 Zhang Zhiming, 'A Further Thought on the Reform of the Trial Process', (no. 4, 1995) *Studies in Law* (*Faxue Yanjiu*) 93, at 94-95. Similar criticisms were made by many other Chinese scholars. See e.g. Li Jianmin, 'Several Thoughts on the Reform of the Criminal Trial Process', (no. 1, 1995) *Studies in Law* (*Faxue Yanjiu*) 84, at 85; Huang Taiyun, *supra* note 10, at 37; and Xie Youping, 'Ideal and Reality: A Comment on the Revised Criminal Procedure Law', (no. 2, 1996) *Modern Law Science* (*Xiandao Faxue*) 9, at 10-11. The Chinese trial process had been equally severely criticised by Western scholars and human rights activists, if not more so. See e.g. Leng and Chiu, *supra* note 9, ch. 5; and Lawyers Committee for Human Rights, *supra* note 5, esp. 38-60.

90 Chen Guangzhong & Xion Qiuhon, 'Some Opinions on the Revision of the Criminal Procedure Law – Pt II', (no. 5, 1995) *Legal Science in China* (*Zhongguo Faxue*) 85, at 85; and Hong Bing, *supra* note 85, at 56.

91 Li Xuekuan, 'Some Legal Considerations on the Functions of Defence Lawyer in Our Country', (no. 6, 1995) *Legal Science in China* (*Zhongguo Faxue*) 90, at 94.

of Chinese scholars blamed the inquisitorial system for causing such problems. According to them, the inquisitorial system China adopted was an 'extreme' one in which judges played an extremely active and powerful role both in preliminary examination and in the actual trial process.[92] Thus the debate on reforming the trial process was centred on the merits and shortcomings of the inquisitorial and adversarial systems and the comparison between the two.[93] Though there were scholars advocating a wholesale adoption of the adversarial system and others strongly resisting such a move, many scholars soon agreed that adopting certain elements from the adversarial system was an appropriate approach to reform of the trial process.[94] This approach was then adopted by the NPC.

Four major changes were made by the 1996 revision.[95] First, under Article 108 of the 1979 CPL a court would open a session and adjudicate the case only if, after preliminary examination of the case initiated by the public prosecution, the court had decided that the facts of the crime were clear and the evidence was complete. If the principal facts were not clear and the evidence insufficient, the court might remand the case to the people's procuratorate for supplementary investigation. It was this requirement that led to the practice of 'verdict first, adjudication second'. Now the new provision, Article 150 of the revised CPL, provides that a court shall open its session and adjudicate the case if the bill of prosecution contains alleged crime facts, a list of the evidence, names of witnesses and copies or photos of the principal evidence. This provision thus substantially reduces the extent of preliminary examination by the court; the question of sufficiency of evidence is now a matter for debate and determination during a court session. Further, supplementary investigation is not to be initiated by a court; it is to be applied for by the procuratorate and to be approved by a court during a court session. The maximum period allowed for supplementary investigation is limited to one month (Articles 165-166 of the revised CPL).

Secondly, the functions of the collegiate panel and the judicial committee are re-defined. Under the original CPL, cases other than minor criminal matters were required to be adjudicated by a collegiate panel consisting of judges and people's

---

92 See e.g. Xie Youping, *supra* note 89, at 11; and Zhang Zhiming, *supra* note 89, 94.

93 See e.g. Chen Guangzhong, *et al.*, 'The Market Economy and the Future of the Science of Criminal Procedure Law', (no. 5, 1993) *Legal Science in China* (*Zhongguo Faxue*) 3; Li Jianmin, *supra* note 89; Zhang Zhiming, *supra* note 89; Wang Shaonan, 'Establishing a Direction for Trial Process Reform', (no. 1, 1995) *Studies in Law* (*Faxue Yanjiu*) 77; Zhang Xiu, 'Choices for the Reform in the Trial Process for Public Prosecution Cases', (no. 2, 1996) *Studies in Law* (*Faxue Yanjiu)* 96. See also an excellent summary of major debates on criminal procedure law: Wang Minyuan & Liu Donghua, 'A Comment on and Summary of the Study of Criminal Procedure Law', (no. 1, 1996) *Studies in Law* (*Faxue Yanjiu*) 51, esp. 57-61.

94 See e.g. Zhang Zhiming, *supra* note 89; Wang & Liu, *supra* note 93; Xie Youping, *supra* note 89; and Chen & Xiong (Pt II), *supra* note 90.

95 Gu Angran, *supra* note 25, at 88.

assessors.[96] However, judicial committees were established at all levels of the people's court.[97] Their functions were vaguely defined as being 'to sum up judicial experience and to discuss important or difficult cases and other issues relating to judicial work.'[98] Under Article 107 of the 1979 CPL, all major and difficult cases were to be submitted to the judicial committee for discussion and decision, and the collegiate panel had to carry out the decisions of the committee. Other than this, the CPL was silent on the relationship between the collegiate panel and the judicial committee. In reality, many courts relied on the judicial committees to discuss and decide cases regardless of the importance of the cases concerned and sometimes before a trial by court.[99] Under Article 149 of the revised CPL, after deliberation a collegiate panel must render a judgment. Only when the collegiate panel decides that it is unable to make a decision in difficult, major or complex cases may it request the president of the court to transfer the case to the judicial committee for discussion and decision. In other words, cases will not be decided by a judicial committee before trial and difficult, major or complex cases will no longer be automatically submitted to judicial committees for deliberation and decision. This provision is thus designed to resolve the problem of 'trial judges not making decisions and decision-makers not trying the case' (*Shenzhe Bu Pan, Panzhe Bu Shen*).[100]

Thirdly, instead of the trial judge presenting evidence to the court and questioning the witnesses, the revised CPL now requires the prosecutors and defenders to present evidence to the court, and questioning and debating on the evidence and the alleged crime facts will be mainly left to the prosecutors and the defenders.[101] In short, the trial judges will be taking a much more passive role, concerning themselves mainly with the maintenance of court order and orderly debate, thus leaving much more room for meaningful defence. Finally, a new summary procedure is established to deal with minor criminal offences.[102] This would allow the court to concentrate

---

96 Article 105 of the 1979 CPL.

97 Article 11 of the Organic Law of the PRC (as revised). See also discussions in Chapter 4.

98 *Ibid.*

99 China University of Political Science and Law (ed.), *Research Into and Discussions on Theoretical and Practical Problems of Criminal Procedure* (Beijing: Law Publishing House, 1987) at 205-206.

100 Cui Min, *supra* note 52, at 6.

101 See Articles 155-161 of the revised CPL.

102 Articles 174-179 of the revised CPL. These procedures are now further regulated by the Certain Opinions on the Application of Summary Procedures in the Adjudication of Pubic Prosecution Cases, issued jointly by the Supreme People's Court, the Supreme People's Procuratorate and the Ministry of Justice on 14 March 2003. Since the summary procedures resemble plea bargaining, to a certain extent, and are generally seen as being inconsistent with an inquisitorial system, they have become quite controversial at present. See Randall Peerenboom, *China Modernizes: Threat to the West or Model for the Rest?* (New York: Oxford University Press, 2007), at 204-208.

its human and other resources on the more adversarial proceedings which would certainly be more time-consuming and, perhaps, more expensive.

With these revisions there is little doubt that the quality of trials should improve considerably. However, a crucial issue relating to the quality of court trials has not been addressed, namely the issue of judicial independence – the 'most glaring deficiency in the PRC's trial process'.[103] Judicial independence has been a subject of debate since the 1950s in the PRC.[104] The 1954 Constitution – the first constitution in the PRC – provided that 'people's courts shall conduct adjudication independently and shall be subject only to the law'.[105] However, advocating judicial independence was denounced as Rightist thought and severely criticised in the late 1950s and during the Cultural Revolution. The 1975 and 1978 Constitutions thus abolished the 1954 provision. The present Constitution – the 1982 Constitution – stipulates an ambiguous principle: 'The people's courts shall, in accordance with the law, exercise judicial power independently and are not subject to interference by administrative organs, public organisations or individuals.'[106] On the other hand, the 1982 Constitution upholds the so-called Four Fundamental Principles, among which is the upholding of the leadership of the Communist Party. This constitutional arrangement, particularly when compared with the 1954 constitutional provision, seems to suggest that judicial independence, such as it is, is subject to Party leadership. Indeed, Party leadership over the judiciary has been constantly asserted in China. Sometimes such leadership involves the requirement of Party approval for specific cases,[107] despite the fact that a review and approval system by Party committees was officially abolished in 1979.[108]

---

[103] Lawyers Committee for Human Rights, *supra* note 5, at 52.

[104] Of course there was no discussion on this sensitive issue during the Cultural Revolution (1966–1976). For a discussion on the debate in the 1950s, see Jerome Alan Cohen, 'The Chinese Communist Party and "Judicial Independence": 1949–1959', (1969) 82 *Harvard Law Review* 967. For discussions on the debate since the 1980s, see Hikota Koguchi, 'Some Observations About 'Judicial Independence' in Post-Mao China', (1987) 7 *Boston College Third World Law Journal* 195; Margaret Y.K. Woo, 'Adjudication Supervision and Judicial Independence in the PRC', (1991) 39 *The Am. J. Comp. L.* 95; and Guo, Li & Hao, *supra* note 59. For an English translation of Chinese views, see Liao Kuangsheng, 'Independent Administration of Justice' and the PRC Legal System', (Vol 16, 1983) *Chinese Law & Government* 123.

[105] Article 78 of the 1954 Constitution. The same was also provided by Article 4 of the Organic Law of the People's Courts of the PRC (1954).

[106] Article 126 of the 1982 Constitution. Article 4 of the 1979 Organic Law of the People's Courts of the PRC repeats the same.

[107] See Chen Guangzhong (Pt I), *supra* note 18, at 11-12; Bian Jianlin, 'Direct Contesting and the Reform of the Trial Process', (no. 6, 1995) *Legal Science in China* (*Zhongguo Faxue*) 96, at 97.

[108] Leng & Chiu, *supra* note 9, at 99. The Party Review and Approval System was abolished by the Instruction of the Central Committee of the Chinese Communist Party Concerning the

The 1979 CPL was silent on the issue of judicial independence. Scholars thus proposed that the 1954 constitutional provision be inserted into the revised CPL.[109] The NPC, however, opted to repeat the 1982 constitutional provision in the revision.[110] With the issue of judicial independence unresolved there are good reasons to doubt the effect of the above-mentioned reforms in the trial process, as many of the problems identified by Chinese scholars are, in one way or another, linked with Party intervention in criminal adjudication, especially in politically sensitive cases and in rural areas.[111]

4. Other Revisions

A number of other revisions are also notable. Now the scope of cases to be directly investigated by the people's procuratorates has been narrowed.[112] The status of crime victims is now defined and certain rights in the trial process are provided.[113] Further, the function of judicial supervision in criminal processes by the people's procuratorates is strengthened.[114] Finally, when the revised CPL came into effect on 1 January 1997 three measures were abolished: the 1979 Regulation on Detention and Arrest; the very much criticised Decision of the Standing Committee of the NPC on the Procedures for Rapid Adjudication of Cases Involving Criminal Elements Who Seriously Endanger Public Security (1983); and the Supplementary Provisions of the Standing Committee of the NPC Regarding the Question of the Time Limits for Handling Criminal Cases (1984).

5. Concluding Remarks

Adjudication by an independent institution is a relatively new development in the modern legal history of China. There was no independent judiciary in traditional China; adjudicature was part of administration. The first modern adjudicature system in a Continental European style, separate from administrative organs, was

Full Implementation of the Criminal Law and Criminal Procedure Law. For a full text in English, see the Appendix in Hikota Koguchi, *supra* note 104, at 208-233.

109 Cui Min, *supra* note 13, at 94.

110 Article 5 of the revised CPL.

111 See more detailed discussions in Lawyers Committee for Human Rights, *supra* note 5, esp. at 52-61.

112 See Article 18 of the revised CPL.

113 See Articles 37, 40-41, 82, 87-88, 145, & 182 of the revised CPL.

114 See Articles 8, 87, 112, & 169 of the revised CPL.

only established at the turn of the 20th century.[115] Although the old judicial system established by the Kuomintang Government was abolished in 1949, the new one continued to be based on the Continental European system. To mention this here is to remind readers that there is no legal tradition to back up the operation of a relatively independent judiciary in the PRC. The compromise revision of the CPL should be understood with this background in mind.

Legal developments in China since 1978 can always be assessed from two quite different perspectives: how far has China travelled towards a Rule of Law, and how far a distance still lies ahead towards such a goal. The present revision to the CPL, in my view, should be seen as very positive and encouraging, rather than being dismissed as consisting of half-hearted measures.[116]

In assessing the CPL reform, or any other legal reforms in China, one should also bear in mind the constraints imposed by the present political system in China. As Gellat has pointed out,

> changes in many areas beyond the legal arena will be required to bring about substantial improvements in the human rights situation in the PRC. An overarching concern is of course the subservience of the legal system to the arbitrary dictates of the Communist Party, a problem that cannot by any means be resolved solely by reforms within the legal system. Without fundamental political changes there can be no independent judiciary or an autonomous bar – key elements of the rule of law.[117]

The practical significance of these revisions will depend on the actual endeavour of law-enforcement agents and lawyers. As a Chinese scholar has rightly pointed out, 'a just law does not guarantee the justice of law.'[118] The adoption of many of the Western practices, e.g. the presumption of innocence, early participation by lawyers, elements of the adversarial system, etc.,[119] requires a change in the approach and thinking of judicial personnel. The strengthening of the defence role in trials,

---

115 See discussions in Chapter 1.

116 Some of the conspicuous omissions in the revision are, however, very unfortunate. For example, the revised CPL continues to be silent on the legal validity of illegally obtained evidence (such as confession through torture etc.), despite strong advocacy by scholars to address the issue in the revision. See Cui Min, *supra* note 13, at 94; Yang Duan, 'Appropriately Resolving the Issue of Validity of Illegal Evidence', (no. 5, 1994) *Legal Science in China* (*Zhongguo Faxue*) 41. Another issue not addressed is the absence of rules against self-incrimination.

117 Lawyers Committee for Human Rights, *supra* note 5, 85.

118 Xie Youping, *supra* note 89, at 13.

119 As discussed in Chapter 1, these principles have a rather short history in China; they were all first introduced to China during the Qing and KMT reforms and their initial introduction was extremely controversial. See also Li Chunlei, *A Study of the Transformation of the Criminal Procedure Law in Modern China* (1895–1928) (*Zhongguo Jindai Xingshi Susong Zhidu Biange Yanjiu 1895–1928*) (Beijing: Beijing University Press, 2004).

the limitation of the powers of investigatory organs, and the more adversarial trial process demand higher judicial and professional standards. Effective measures must be found to prevent interference in judicial work, including interference from the Party and administrative organs.[120] The crucial concern will be whether lawyers will be able to limit the operation of the various qualifications and restrictions now existing in the CPL on the implementation of the fundamental 'due process' principles. Clearly, these qualifications and restrictions have the potential to be abused by the investigatory organs. In order to address the concerns that were raised when the CPL was under revision, the critical issue for lawyers is to argue strongly and forcefully that these qualifications and restrictions must remain strictly limited; they should not allow such qualifications and restrictions to be used as a back door or a loophole in the CPL to circumvent the fundamental 'due process' principles now incorporated in the law.

The implementation of the revised CPL so far has indeed been rather disappointing and there have been many difficulties, chief among them being the huge difficulties encountered by lawyers who genuinely want to pursue justice and fairness for defendants. As Peerenboom correctly points out, these difficulties are not ones that can easily be overcome by a revision of the Law, they are political, economic and cultural.[121]

There are however encouraging signs emerging from China. First, recent academic studies on the CPL are becoming increasingly sophisticated and focused on both particular aspects of the law as well as on specific practical issues.[122] These studies help law-makers and law enforcement forces to better understand not only the proper operation of the Law, but also the specific difficulties and problems in law and in practice. Further, law-makers seem to accept that the various compromises made in revising the 1979 CPL are part of the cause of the generally unsatisfactory operation of the Law. Thus in October 2003 the SCNPC formally decided to start a new round of revision by including the revision of the CPL in its five-year legislative plan. This then prompted Professor Chen Guangzhong, who was pivotal in the 1996 CPL reform, to establish an expert group to start a new expert draft. In 2006, after three years of work, this group produced its expert draft in 450 articles.[123] While

---

120 Xie Youping, *supra* note 89, at 13.

121 For an evaluation of the implementation of the revised CPL so far, see Peerenboom, *supra* note 102, at 199-204.

122 See e.g. Chen Guangzhong (ed.), *The Procedure on Criminal Re-trial and the Protection of Human Rights* (*Xingshi Zaishen Chengxu yu Renquan Baozhang*) (Beijing: Beijing University Press, 2005); Xiong Qiuhong, *The Changing Science of Criminal Procedural Law* (*Zhuanbianzhong De Xingshisusong Faxue*) (Beijing: Beijing University Press, 2004); and Xiang Zexuan, Wu Xiaocheng, Luo Rui, *On Legal Supervision and Remedies of Criminal Procedural Law* (*Falü Jiandu Yu Xingshi Susong Jiujilun*) (Beijing: Beijing University Press, 2005).

123 The Draft (in a bilingual format) and its accompanying explanations have now been published. See Chen Guangzhong (ed.), *Expert Draft on Further Revision of the Criminal Procedural Law*

Professor Chen emphasises that any revision must be undertaken within the current constitutional framework and must aim at retaining the existing structure of the CPL, the expert draft nevertheless stresses human rights protection in criminal procedures, the absorption of international criminal justice principles as found in international treaties (including the two covenants on human rights) that China has ratified, the resolution of practical difficulties and problems, and the balancing of procedural justice with substantive justice.[124] Their proposed draft doubles the existing provisions, from 225 to 450 articles. According to the 2007 SCNPC legislative plan, a first deliberation of this CPL draft revision will be conducted during the October 2007 SCNPC session.[125] If the revision is to be conducted along the lines suggested by the expert group we should see some significant improvements in the CPL, which will come even closer to internationally accepted standards for criminal justice. If this is the case, we certainly should have enough reason to be optimistic about the future of criminal processes in China, at least in terms of the law on paper.

---

of the PRC and Its Explanations (*Zhonghua Renmin Gongheguo Xingshi Susong Fa Zaixiugai Zhuanjia Jianyigao Yu Lunzheng*) (Beijing: China Legal System Press, 2006).

124 See 'Underlying Principles for the Further Revision of the Criminal Procedure Law', in Chen Guangzhong, *id.*, at 1-16.

125 See '2007 Legislative Plan and Supervision Plan', in <npc.people.com.cn/GB/28320/41246/41337/5422052.html> (last accessed 20 June 2007).

Chapter Nine

Civil Law: Development and General Principles

1. Introduction

Contemporary civil and commercial law in the PRC is mainly a product of the 20th century. In particular its emergence in the form of state positive law was a result of modern law reform by way of borrowings from European Continental law. In terms of structure, terminology and techniques, early borrowing brought in by the Qing and KMT reforms were retained to a certain extent in civil legislation in the PRC, but the conceptions and nature of civil law in the PRC until quite recently differed radically from those in Qing and KMT legislation as a result of the introduction of Marxist ideology into the study of civil law relations. This ideology also severely affected the development of civil law in China for the first 35 years of the PRC, and certain difficulties in civil law development still remain as a result of this. Thus, although civil law is seen as a basic law, parallel to criminal law and just below the Constitution in the hierarchy of Chinese legislation, it remains relatively underdeveloped despite the fact that most legislation in post-Mao China relates to civil and commercial matters. In a sense the development of civil law resembles that of the economy – rapidly developing, yet lacking coherence and consistency and largely *ad hoc*.

This Chapter will first provide a brief overview of the historical heritage of civil law in China. It will be followed by an outline of the emergence of modern civil law and the contemporary legal framework governing civil and commercial relations. The civil law institutions as codified in the General Principles of Civil Law will be outlined, but specific institutions, namely property, family and contracts will each be analysed in separate chapters.

2. Historical Heritage of Civil Law in China

As discussed in Chapter One, there was no recorded attempt to draw up a distinct code governing civil matters in Chinese history until the introduction of Western law towards the end of the Qing Dynasty. Traditional state positive law was concerned mainly with state interests and the protection of a hierarchical order of social life;

there was no conception of civil law, as understood in contemporary societies, of the claims and suits of citizens as between themselves, in which the state has an interest, as an arbitrator, a stakeholder or an impartial adjudicator.[1] In this historical context, it is not surprising that civil law, as a distinct and separate branch of law, was underdeveloped, unsystematic and often difficult to distinguish from penal provisions.[2] In fact, the notion of '*Minfa*' (civil law) has only a short history in China; and the term itself is, according to many Chinese jurists, a Japanese translation of the European Continental concept of civil law, introduced into China by Japanese scholars who served as advisers for legal reform to the Imperial Court of the *Qing* Dynasty (1644–1911) at the turn of the 20th century.[3] These Japanese scholars also helped to draft the first ever distinct civil code in Chinese history (though it was never promulgated).

The first complete Civil Code (in five Books), distinct from criminal matters, was enacted by the KMT government between 1929–1930.[4] It was largely based on the Qing draft but enacted under the guidance of Sun Yatsen's revolutionary ideas.[5] While the KMT Civil Code is not applicable in Mainland China, certain features of it have remained in the PRC's civil law to this day. For this reason, the principal features of the KMT Civil Code are outlined below.

---

1 Alice E.-S. Tay, 'Law in Communist China – Part 1', (1969) 6 *Syd. L. Rev.* 153, at 160-161. See also discussions in Chapter 1.

2 That is not to say that there were no civil law provisions. In fact, there were many 'rules' concerning civil matters. In an academic study (Li Zhimi, *Ancient Chinese Civil Law* (*Zhongguo Gudai Minfa*) (Beijing: Publishing House of Law, 1988)), the author has been able to identify 'rich sources' of traditional Chinese civil law, containing laws and rules governing the legal status of civil law subjects (social and economic organisations and individuals), marriage and family, rights *in rem*, contracts, torts and limitations of civil actions. However, the 'rich sources' referred to in the study are primarily Confucian classics and teachings and only secondarily such elementary provisions governing civil matters as were scattered in penal codes, penal statutes and customs. Professor Li also concedes that it was the concept of *li* (propriety), not law, which played a primary role in dealing with civil matters and that different rules were applied to persons of different political, social and family status. A more recent study on the history of civil law in China, a book runs into more than 1,300 pages, contains all sorts of rules governing civil relationships. See Zhang Jinfan (ed.), *A General History of the Chinese Civil Law* (*Zhongguo Minfa Tongshi*) (Fuzhou: Fujian People's Press, 2003).

3 See e.g. Tong Rou, *et al.*, *Chinese Civil Law* (*Zhongguo Minfa*) (Beijing: Publishing House of Law, 1990), at 1-2; Wang Liming, Guo Minglei & Fang Liufang, *A New Approach to Civil Law* (*Minfa Xinlun*) (Beijing: Press of the China University of Political Science and Law, 1987), vol. 1, at 1-2; Liu Shiguo, *et al.*, *An Outline of Chinese Civil Law* (*Zhongguo Minfa Yiaolun*) (Shenyang: Liaoning University Press, 1992), vol. 1, at 7-8; and Liu Shiguo, 'On Civil Matters and the Law Governing Civil Matters', (no. 5, 1992) *Law Science* (*Falü Kexue*) at 45.

4 The Civil Code of the Republic of China, hereinafter referred to as the KMT Civil Code.

5 Foo Ping-sheung, 'Introduction', in *The Civil Code of the Republic of China* (Shanghai: Kelly & Walsh, Ltd, 1930), at xii.

First of all, the Civil Code of 1929–1930, although based on the Qing draft and hence under the strong influence of the Japanese Civil Code, and at second hand of the German Civil Code, was influenced by many other sources of foreign law. It was not a Japanese jurist but a European, Professor Jean Escarra, at that time of Grenoble University, who was the major adviser to the Law Revision and Codification Commission. Many contemporary codes of the world were consulted by the lawmakers. Apart from the Japanese Civil Code of 1896, the German Civil Code of 1896 and the French Civil Code of 1804,[6] other codes consulted included, in particular, the Swiss Civil Code of 1907 and the revised Swiss Code of Obligations of 1911, the Brazilian Civil Code of 1916, the Soviet Family Code of 1918; the Civil Code of Soviet Russia of 1922; the Siamese Civil Code of 1923–1925; the Turkish Commercial Code of 1926; the draft Italian Commercial Code of 1925; and the draft Franco-Italian Code on Obligations and Contracts of 1927.[7]

Secondly, as was pointed out in Chapter One, the KMT Civil Code tried to balance modernisation and the preservation of tradition by recognising the general validity of customs as well as codifying some very ancient and socially deep-rooted customs into the code.[8]

Finally, although the KMT Civil Code followed the models of Japan and Germany in some respects, it did not follow their division between civil and commercial law as the Qing reform did. The decision to fuse commercial law with civil law was a

---

6 According to Escarra, the influence of the French Civil Code was mainly due to advisers to the Codification Commission, although the Code itself was not among the models studied carefully by drafting members for possible adoption. Escarra listed several reasons for this. First, the code dated 1804 was too old for the Chinese, who were anxious to know the most recent fruits of Western jurisprudence. Secondly, the Code was a very refined product of a great civilisation which made it very difficult to impose upon yet another ancient civilisation. Thirdly, the Code was also a product of a century of subtle and blended jurisprudence and so almost impossible for foreigners to adopt. See Jean Escarra, *Chinese Law: Conception and Evolution, Legislative and Judicial Institutions, Science and Teaching*, translated from a 1936 French edition by Gertrude R. Browne (Seattle: University of Washington, 1961), at 248-249, in his footnote 66.

7 See George W. Keeton, 'The Progress of Law in China', (1937) 19 *J. Comp. Leg.* 197, at 209; Tien-Hsi Cheng, 'The Development and Reform of Chinese Law', (1948) 1 *Current Legal Problems* 170, at 187; and Escarra, *supra* note 6, at 248.

8 Such as the institutions of *Yung-tien* (*Yong-dian*) (a long-term lease) and *Dien* (*Dian*) (a *usufructuary* mortgage). It should be pointed out that this approach towards customary law was not taken because of KMT ideology but was based on an historically unprecedented and massive survey of customary law and practice initially conducted by the Qing reform and later resumed by the KMT reform. Together the survey lasted for more than three decades and produced nearly 1,000 volumes of reports. For a comprehensive study of this survey, see Gui Hongming, *A Study of the Civil Customary Law Survey during the Late Qing and Early KMT* (*Qingmo Minchu Minshangshi Xiguan Diaocha Zhi Yanjiu*) (Beijing: Law Press, 2005).

reasoned one.[9] Essentially, it was based on the arguments about China's situation in relation to the absence of a merchant class, and on the examination of the legal systems of countries other than the Continental ones. Nevertheless, the decision to fuse civil and commercial matters into one single code did not prevent the KMT from making some special laws on commercial matters. The final result was that commercial and civil matters were generally included in the Civil Code, but certain more important commercial matters, i.e. Negotiable Instruments, Insurance, Commercial Companies, and Maritime Law, were separated out as special codes of the civil law.[10] This arrangement was prompted by four considerations. First, certain practices of the business world were seen as rapidly evolving, and it was recognised that amendments might be necessary from time to time. It is always easier to amend a statute on a single matter than to amend a comprehensive code. Then, in the area of maritime law, many administrative rules were involved, but these rules would be beyond the scope of a civil code. Thirdly, elaborate drafts had already been prepared on these subjects in the form of separate laws; it was easier and it would save time to revise them as such, rather than to insert them in the Code. Lastly, the insertion of the above four items in the Code would have made the Code too bulky and too difficult to handle.[11]

Although the KMT laws were all abolished by the new government in 1949, the general structure and divisions of the KMT Civil Code and its fusion of civil and commercial law have rarely been questioned by scholars in Mainland China.[12] In fact, the KMT Civil Code is one of the principal sources from which civil law and civil law science have been developed in the PRC.[13]

---

9 In the Examination Report to the Central Political Council, detailed reasons were put forward for the adoption of the suggestion. A full Chinese text of the detailed reasons can be found in Cheng Yüpo, *General Principles of Civil Law* (*Minfa Zongze*), 7th edition (Taipei: Shanmin Shuju, 1988), at 35-37; and *Journal of the Legislative Yuan* (*Li-Fa Ch'uan K'an*), vol. 1, at 23-25.

10 All these four laws were promulgated in 1929.

11 See Foo Ping-sheung, *supra* note 5, at xviii.

12 There are, however, some Chinese scholars in the PRC who maintain that family and marriage law is beyond the scope of civil law. See further discussion below.

13 While the ideological foundations for legal development since 1949 have been radically altered, the present civil codification is nowadays considered by many Chinese scholars to be a continuing process that started more than 100 years ago. See Liang Zhiping, in 'The Sixth Civil Law Forum – Chinese Culture and Chinese Civil Code', 13 May 2004, China University of Political Science and Law, available at <www.ccelaws.com/mjlt/default.asp> (accessed 10 June 2004). As a result of increasing legislation and studies on company law, negotiable instruments and other aspects of commercial law, the majority of Chinese scholars in the PRC have clearly adopted the KMT theory which treats commercial law as supplementary to civil legislation. See e.g. Zhu Xanfang and Liang Fang, 'Research into the System of Civil Law Science', (no. 1, 1991) *Journal of Political and Legal Science* (*Zhengfa Xuekan*), at 28-32; Wang Liming, 'The Fusion of Civil and Commercial Law – On the Relations Between Our Civil and Commercial

3. The Emergence of Modern Civil Law in the PRC

3.1. A Politico-Economic Context

For the first 35 years of the PRC Marxist ideology imposed some formidable barriers to the development of civil law in China. First, following the footsteps of the former Soviet Union and other socialist countries, civil law was defined as a branch of socialist law regulating property and personal non-property relationships, with its main 'method of regulation assuming a commodity form'.[14] This linking of civil law with the politico-economic concept of a 'commodity economy'[15] was soon found to be a fundamental barrier to the development of civil law in the PRC, as the existence of such a 'commodity economy' was not formally recognised until post-Mao China.[16]

Secondly, when Chinese scholars successfully argued that a 'commodity economy' did exist to a certain extent in a socialist country and, hence, that there was a limited usefulness for civil law in China,[17] its development soon met another serious hurdle – the role of government in a socialist country in civil law relations. This question was directly reflected in the two inter-related debates on the nature and the scope of civil law. Specifically, the question was one of whether civil law was of the nature of public law or private law, and whether there was a branch of 'economic law' alongside 'civil law'.[18] Essentially the debate on the nature of civil law was about whether the state had any role to play in economic activities,

---

Law', in Tong Rou (ed.), *Several Civil Law Issues Involved in Economic Structural Reform* (*Jingji Tizhi Gaige Zhong De Ruogan Minfa Wenti*) (Beijing: Press of Beijing Teacher's University, 1985), at 38-53; and Yang Zhenshan, 'Market Economy and Our Civil and Commercial Law', (no. 4, 1993) *Journal of the China University of Political Science and Law* (*Zhengfa Luntan*), at 1-8. Although there is no major disagreement on fusing civil and commercial law into one single civil code, scholars and law-makers in China have still to agree on which part of the commercial law should be treated separately and issued as special laws of the civil code. See 'A Summary of the 1997 Civil and Economic Law Section of the China Law Society Annual Conference', (no. 6, 1997) *Legal Science in China* (*Zhongguo Faxue*) 118, at 118-119. At the present one of the most contentious issues in the effort to enact a comprehensive civil code is whether intellectual property should be included in a civil code. See also the various current civil code drafts (and the sources of laws listed in the drafts) discussed below.

14 See detailed discussions in Jianfu Chen, *From Administrative Authorisation to Private Law: A Comparative Perspective of the Developing Civil Law in the PRC* (Dordrecht/Boston/London: Martinus Nijhoff Publishers, 1995), at 50-52.

15 This term has, of course, now been replaced by that of a 'socialist market economy'.

16 There was occasional recognition of the existence of a 'commodity economy' in Mao's China and hence periodically a push towards the development of civil law. See further discussions below.

17 See detailed discussion in Jianfu Chen, *supra* note 14, at 50-52, and 75-87.

18 See detailed discussion in Jianfu Chen, *supra* note 14, at 52-66.

and the debate between 'civilists' and 'economists' was a debate about the proper scope and method of state involvement or intervention in economic arenas. It was thus a debate between private autonomy and state intervention, between the universality of private law and the *ad hoc* approach of administrative rule towards individual situations. In short, it was 'a struggle between more administrative and more individualistic views of (private) law.'[19] Such debates only died down, but were not necessarily settled, after the adoption of the notion of 'socialist market economy' in 1992.[20]

Finally, the linkage between civil law and the politico-economic notion of a 'commodity economy', or more recently, 'socialist market economy', has simply meant that the development or the fate of civil law in the PRC has depended largely on the Party's emphasis on economic development and its tolerance towards economic freedom, or, in contemporary Chinese terminology, 'politico-economic reforms'.[21] The constantly changing reform policy has thus determined the *ad hoc* development of the civil law in China in the last three decades or so.

It is in this politico-economic context that attempts to enact a comprehensive civil code have often been interrupted but continue until this day.

3.2. The First Attempt at Codification in the PRC

As discussed in Chapter Two, the need to make new laws and to establish a new judicial system was first recognised by the 'Common Program' of 1949, but significant legislative activities were only to occur after the adoption of the 1954 Constitution. The emphasis placed on socialist construction at the 1956 Party Congress saw the explicit recognition of the need for law that included a civil code, and so the first attempt to draw up a civil code took place. A Research Office under the Standing Committee of the National People's Congress (SCNPC) started the drafting work in 1954,[22] resulting in the making of a draft divided into four books, with 525 articles in total.[23]

---

19 Alice Tay & Eugene Kamenka, 'Public Law – Private Law', in S. I. Benn & G.F. Gaus (eds), *Public and Private in Social Life* (London: Croom Helm, 1993), at 81. See detailed discussion in Jianfu Chen, *supra* note 14, at 52-66. In such debates, 'economic law' is defined as a branch of law dealing with vertical economic relationships among participants of unequal status, while 'civil law' would deal with economic relations among equal and autonomous parties.

20 See discussion in Jianfu Chen, *supra* note 14, Chapter 2.

21 I have analysed in detail the relationship between economic reform and the development of civil law in Jianfu Chen, *supra* note 14, Chapter 3.

22 Gu Angran, *The Socialist Legal System and Legislative Work* (*Shehui Zhuyi Fazhi He Lifa Gongzuo*) (Beijing: China University of Political Science and Law Press, 1989), at 101; Zhao Zhenjiang, (ed.), *Forty Years of the Chinese Legal System* (*Zhongguo Fazhi Sishi Nian*) (Beijing: Beijing University Press, 1990), at 242. Tong Rou, 'The General Principles of Civil Law of the PRC: Its Birth, Characteristics, and Role', (1989) 52 *Law and Contemporary Problems* 151, at 152.

23 See Liang Huixin, 'The Chinese Inheritance of Foreign Civil Laws' (undated), published in

The 1956 draft, in its structure and in terms of civil law institutions, was largely based on the first Soviet Civil Code – the Civil Code of the Russian Soviet Federated Socialist Republic (the RSFSR Civil Code) of 1922,[24] the latter itself being based on the German Civil Code.[25] In a clear break from the tradition of civil codes, the draft adopted the RSFSR Civil Code approach of applying the notions of ownership (instead of rights *in rem*) and citizens (instead of natural persons), and of emphasising the special protection of public ownership.[26] This should not be surprising. At that time the influence of Soviet law was overwhelming, and thus the first attempt at codification saw the emergence of a new foreign model, that of the Soviets – a foreign influence that was to last until quite recently.

3.3. The Second Attempt

As discussed in Chapter Two too, the first effort to draft comprehensive codes was abruptly ended by political campaigns (i.e. the Anti-Rightists Movement of 1957 and the 'Great Leap Forward' of 1958). It was not to resume until 1962 when the necessity for the development of a commodity economy was recognised by the Party.[27] The second attempt to develop a civil code was thus carried out between 1962 and 1964.[28] The result was a draft of a civil code which was issued and circulated for comments by the SCNPC on 1 July 1964.[29]

<www.iolaw.org.paper32.asp> (accessed 27 July 2004). According to another scholar the draft contained five books in 433 articles. See Zhao Zhenjiang, *id.*, at 242. According to Liang Huixin the draft was completed in December 1956. The various civil code drafts in the PRC are now published in a 3-volume collection: He Qinghua, Li Xiuqing, & Chen Yu (eds), *A Complete Collection of Draft Civil Codes in the New China* (*Xin Zhongguo Minfadian Cao'an Zonglan*) (Beijing: Law Press, 2003). Apparently different books were drafted by different groups and completed at different times. The different number of total articles being quoted by different scholars apparently was caused by the use of different versions of the different books of the draft code.

24 The RSFSR Civil Code was adopted on 11 November 1922 and took effect on 1 January 1923. It was superseded in 1964 but was still in effect when China started its codification efforts.

25 See Liang Huixin, *supra* note 23.

26 See Liang Huixin, *id.*

27 Gu Angran, *supra* note 22, at 102.

28 Zhang Youyu & Wang Shuwen, (eds), *Forty Years of the PRC's Legal Science* (*Zhongguo Faxue Sishi Nian*) (Shanghai: Shanghai People's Publishing House, 1989), at 328.

29 On the front page of the copy of the draft I have there is a short handwritten note which says that the draft (of 1 July 1964) is a revised draft (of 1 June 1964) with the deletion of a chapter on 'family property relations'. Prior to the July draft there were also drafts dated March 1963, 8 June 1963 and 9 July 1963 respectively. Additionally, there were also two expert drafts (by the then Beijing Institute of Political Science and Law and the Law Institute of the Chinese Academy of Social Sciences, both 1963), a further draft code dated 1 November 1963, as well as drafts on lease, construction relationships, account settlement, and taxation. See *A*

This draft was divided into 15 chapters in three books – General Principles (Articles 1-24), Property Ownership (Articles 25-63), and Property Transactions (*Caichan Liuzhuan*) (Articles 64-262) – with 262 articles in total. The draft was unique in that it was drafted more like a political statement than a legal code; legal terms, such as legal person and legal personality, obligation, tort and civil remedy were all missing from the draft. Although it was drafted after the falling off of the Sino-Soviet relationship and hence constituted an intentional effort not to follow the Soviet model, the scope of the contents nevertheless reflected the conception of economic law developed in the Soviet Union; that is, civil law relationships were conceived as vertical economic relationships between the state and economic entities, rather than as horizontal relationships between equal parties.[30] It represented an extreme example of pursuing Chinese characteristics and rejecting virtually all things foreign.

The second effort to make a civil code lasted an even shorter time than the previous one, and a new attempt was only to emerge after the 'Cultural Revolution'.

3.4. The Third Attempt

The third attempt to make a civil code started in 1979, with the establishment of a Civil Law Drafting Group within the Legislative Affairs Committee (LAC) of the SCNPC. The Group held its first meeting in Beijing on 3 November 1979 and its second meeting six days later. At the second meeting the drafting of a civil code officially began.[31] The Group clearly worked efficiently because by 1982 four different versions of a draft code had been completed,[32] all based on the 1962 Fundamental Principles of Civil Legislation of the USSR, the 1964 Civil Code of the RSFSR, and the revised Hungarian Civil Code of 1978.[33] All these three codes were in the German tradition, despite their socialist orientation.

Complete Collection of Draft Civil Codes in the New China, *supra* note 23, Volume Two. The July 1964 draft has been the most discussed one.

30 See J. Chen, *supra* note 14, at 41-44.

31 See Zhou Zhenxiang & Shao Jingchun, (eds), *A Chronicle of Forty Years of Construction of the Chinese New Legal System* (*Xi Zhongguo Fazhi Jianshe Sishinian Yaolan*) (Beijing: Press of the Masses, 1990), at 448.

32 See Wang Hanbin, 'Explanation on the General Principles of the Civil Law of the PRC', in *China Law Yearbook 1987*, first English edition (Singapore: Butterworths, 1989), at 147-152. The first draft with 501 articles was dated 15 August 1980, the second with 426 articles dated 10 April 1981, the third with 510 articles dated 31 July 1981, and the fourth with 465 articles dated 1 May 1982. See *A Complete Collection of Draft Civil Codes in the New China*, *supra* note 23, Volume Two, at 371-626. The fourth draft was translated by Professor William C. Jones, and published in (1984) 10 *Rev. Soc. L.* 193.

33 See Liang Huixing, *supra* note 23.

Two major factors were soon to interrupt the drafting process. First, a piecemeal approach towards legislation advocated by Deng Xiaoping quickly began to take hold. In fact, as early as November 1979 Peng Zhen, then Vice-Chairman of the SCNPC and Secretary of the Politico-Legal Group of the Central Committee of the CPC, instructed the Civil Law Drafting Group that a civil code and individual laws concerning civil law matters could be drafted at the same time.[34] Similar instructions were repeated in the following years,[35] and soon a 'retail' policy, i.e. to make and promulgate individual laws instead of a comprehensive code, was pursued.[36] Secondly, a 'war' was being waged between civil law and economic law scholars, making the drafting of a civil code impossible as each side tried to claim its own disciplinary 'territory'.[37]

In retrospect, the 'retail' policy was a rather positive step: at the time, legal scholarship was still dominated by the Soviet influence and a new generation of scholars who were exposed to wider legal systems was yet to emerge. If a code was to have been enacted, it would have been one along the lines of the Soviet model, a model soon to be proven inappropriate for a market economy. Perhaps more importantly, the ideological shackles in attitudes towards foreign law and comparative law were yet to be broken in the 1990s.[38]

The 'retail' policy resulted in a large number of laws concerning civil matters. Indeed, the Contract Law (1981),[39] the Foreign Economic Contract Law (1986),[40] the Marriage Law (1981),[41] the Succession Law (1986), and the General Principles of Civil Law (GPCL) (1986)[42] were all enacted in quick succession.

---

34 Gu Angran, *supra* note 22, at 110.

35 See e.g. Peng Zhen, 'An Address to the Forum on Civil Code Drafting', *People's Daily* (*Renmin Ribao*), 15 May 1981, at 4.

36 Gu Angran, *supra* note 22, at 110. The formal drafting process for a civil code was 'suspended' in 1982.

37 For a discussion of this debate between civil law and economic law, see Jianfu Chen, *supra* note 14, at 56-66.

38 For a discussion on the changes of attitude towards foreign law, see Chapter 2.

39 Repealed and replaced by the 1999 Contract Law.

40 Repealed and replaced by the 1999 Contract Law.

41 Substantially revised in 1999.

42 In addition, many independent codes in the nature of commercial law have also been enacted, including the Maritime Law of 1992, the Company Law of 1993, the Insurance Law of 1995, and the Securities Law of 1998.

3.5. Present Status of Civil Codification

Having been 'suspended' in 1982, the drafting of a comprehensive civil code did not resume until 1998.[43] The initial resumption involved the establishment by the SCNPC, in January 1998, of a drafting group consisting of 9 prominent scholars and practitioners.[44] In March 1998 a three-step strategy was adopted: (1) an enactment of a uniform contract law; (2) a law on rights *in rem* (property) to be enacted in 4-5 years; and (3) a comprehensive civil code to be completed by 2010.[45] The first major result of this three-step strategy was the adoption of the 1999 Contract Law, which now serves as a uniform contract code and replaces the 1981 Contract Law and the 1985 Foreign Economic Contract Law.

When China was admitted to the WTO in November 2001 the SCNPC decided to change its strategy, requiring the draft of a civil code to be submitted for deliberation in 2002. For this purpose, six scholars were entrusted with drafting specific books.[46] Individual books of the code were indeed completed by 2002.[47] After several meetings a comprehensive draft, often referred to as the September Civil Code Draft, was completed in 2002 and submitted to the SCNPC for consolidation and revision. To the great shock of the scholars involved in the drafting, the LAC of the SCNPC abandoned the Books on Contract, Family, Succession and Intellectual Property completely. Instead, the existing Contract Law, Marriage Law, Adoption Law and

---

43 It was first reported in 1997 that a consensus had emerged among jurists, the Law Commission of the NPC, the LAC of the SCNPC and the Supreme People's Court, that the time was now ripe for a new attempt to draft a comprehensive civil code, with the goal of having it completed by the year 2005. See 'Drafting a Civil Code Will Soon Be on the Agenda', (no. 2, 1997) *Legal Science in China* (*Zhongguo Faxue*) 122, at 122.

44 The 9 scholars were Jiang Ping (China University of Political Science and Law), Wang Jiafu (Law Institute of CASS), Wei Zhengying (Beijing University), Wang Baoshu (Law Institute of CASS), Liang Huixing (Law Institute of CASS), Wang Liming (Renmin University), Xiao Xun (retired member of the Legislative Affairs Committee of the SCNPC), Wei Yarong (retired member of the Legislative Affairs Committee of the SCNPC), and Fu Zongwei (retired judge of the Supreme People's Court). See Liang Huixing, 'The Process of Chinese Civil Codification and Its Major Controversies', a paper delivered at the Sino-Japan Civil Law Symposium, Shangdong University, 25-26 October 2003, available from <www.iolaw.org.cn/paper/paper266.asp>.

45 See Liang Huixing, *supra* note 23.

46 They were Liang Huixing (Law Institute of CASS, in charge of the General Principles, Obligations and Contracts), Wang Liming (Renmin University, in charge of Personal Rights and Torts), Tang Dehua (Supreme People's Court, in charge of Civil Liability), Zheng Chengshi (Law Institute of CASS, in Charge of Intellectual Property), Wu Changzheng (China University of Political Science and Law, in charge of Family and Inheritance), and Fu Zongwei (retired judge, in charge of private international law). See Liang Huixing, *supra* note 23; and Liang Huixing, *supra* note 44.

47 See Liang Huixing, *supra* note 23.

Succession Law were incorporated into the Draft Code without change, and on this basis the LAC produced its own Draft Civil Code (for Deliberation). This Draft was submitted to the SCNPC for deliberation in December 2002.[48] Thus the draft before the SCNPC was in fact largely a collection of existing laws, with the Books on Rights *in rem* and torts being the new parts.[49]

In 2002, however, the 'plan' was changed once again. Instead of adopting the whole civil code, the SCNPC decided to take a 'step-by-step' approach, that is, to adopt individual books, with the Book on Rights *in rem* as the first one to be taken out of the draft code for deliberation by the SCNPC for possible adoption,[50] and the idea of a comprehensive civil code was then shelved for the time being.[51]

This last 'pause' in the rush to enacting a comprehensive civil code was largely unexpected and was seen as a setback by many scholars heavily involved in the drafting work. However, this has not been the end of the efforts to enact a civil code in China. Far from it, it simply means that the 'step-by-step' approach continues. In fact, in the five-year legislative plan for the Tenth NPC, adopted in 2004 with the approval of the Central Committee of the CPC,[52] three separate civil laws (rights *in rem*, torts, and private international law) were included.[53] With the Law on Rights *in rem* having been adopted in March 2007, the major focus is now on torts and private international law. Indeed, in addition to the draft law on torts prepared by the LAC of the SCNPC as part of the 2002 draft civil code, there are already three expert drafts on torts that have been completed and published.[54] It is the general

---

48 See Liang Huixing, *supra* note 44.

49 See Explanation on the Draft Civil Code, delivered by Gu Anrang at the 31st Session of Standing Committee of the Ninth NPC on 23 December 2002.

50 Liang Huixing, *Struggling for China's Civil Code* (*Wei Zhongguo Minfadian er Douzheng*) (Beijing: Law Press, 2002), at 197. The Law on Rights *in rem* was indeed adopted on 16 March 2007.

51 See Liang Huixing, *supra* note 44.

52 See 'Five-year Legislative Plan of the NPC Formally Launched', in <www.people.com.cn/GB.14576/28320/39478/2953165.htm> (last accessed 20 June 2007).

53 A full text of the five-year legislative plan is available from <news.xinhunet.com/zhengfu/2004-01/09/content_1268128.htm> (last accessed 20 June 2007).

54 All these drafts are available from People's (Renmin) University Law School website: <www.civillaw.com.cn/special.asp?id=62> (last accessed 20 June 2007). This however does not mean that the legislative process on torts is going to be easy and that the law will be enacted soon. In comparison with the Law on Rights *in rem*, disagreements on the proposed law on torts are generally seen as of a technical nature ('Professor Wang Liming on the Future Civil Code', in <www.civillaw.com.cn/Article/default.asp?id=31765> (last accessed 21 June 2007)). However, scholars and law-makers disagree on many issues, from general scope to the appropriate foreign models. For a good summary on the disagreements, see Yang Lixin, 'Certain Contentious Theoretical Issues concerning the Enactment of a Law on Torts', in <www.civillaw.com.cn/Article/default.asp?id=23933> (last accessed 20 June 2007).

consensus in China that, once all separate civil laws are enacted or revised, they will be put together as a comprehensive civil code, hopefully by 2010.[55]

4. An Abstract Conceptual Framework on Civil Matters

One of the most important features of private law is its abstraction: law, its rules and principles, its provisions and requirements are oriented towards commonly accepted values rather than *ad hoc* situations, and towards abstract right-and-duty-bearing units. In its abstraction, private law becomes a specific structure relatively independent from social, economic and political changes, yet its principles are able to deal with a wide range of social relations over a long period of time. Such abstraction is also the basis on which private law becomes universally applicable and on which parties to private law relations are treated on an equal footing.

Following the European Continental tradition, Chinese civil and commercial legislation has on the one hand taken a formalist and abstract approach, despite ideological differences underlying the law and law-making. On the other hand, because of the delay in enacting a comprehensive civil code, legislation has taken an *ad hoc* approach towards specific situations, and hence the legal framework governing civil and commercial matters has been fragmented and unsystematic. Without a comprehensive civil code, the GPCL (General Principles of Civil Law) is the only, albeit simplistic, piece of legislation that provides some general principles for creating and defining the structure of civil law, as well as establishing the basic abstract civil law institutions.[56] The actual regulation of specific civil and commercial relations is done through a large body of civil and commercial laws, regulations, measures and judicial interpretations.

Article 2 of the GPCL provides that 'civil law regulates property relations and personal relations on an equal footing among citizens and legal persons, and between citizens and legal persons.' This definition clearly reflects the 'commodity relations theory' advocated by the late Professor Tong Rou of the Chinese People's University

---

55 See 'The Adoption of the Law on Rights *in rem* is a Major Step Towards a Civil Code', in <www.civillaw.com.cn/Article/default.asp?id=31640> (last accessed 21 June 2007); and 'Professor Wang Liming on the Future Civil Code', *id.*

56 Adopted at the 4th Plenary Session of the 6th NPC on 12 April 1986, the GPCL took effect on 1 January 1987. The GPCL is supplemented by a detailed Supreme People's Court explanation: Views of the Supreme People's Court on Questions Concerning the Enforcement of the 'General Principles of the Civil Law of the PRC' (Trial Implementation), adopted by the Judicial Committee of the Supreme People's Court on 26 January 1988. An English text appears in *Statutes and Regulations of the PRC* (Hong Kong: UEA Press Ltd & Institute of Chinese Law (Publishers) Ltd, loose-leaf service).

and many other scholars.[57] While in the politico-economic sphere China has now moved from a 'commodity economy' to a 'socialist market economy', the GPCL is yet to be revised. Thus the notion of a 'socialist market economy' has pushed ahead civil law development in many areas such as contract and property, and the GPCL has become increasingly out of date, yet it remains the only set of general principles governing, theoretically, all civil law relationships.

Under the 'commodity relations theory', the 'property relations' regulated by civil law refer to ownership relations and exchange relations in economic activities which are carried out by persons in production, allocation, transfer, and consumption of material goods.[58] 'Personal relations' refers to social relations having direct concern with the rights of a person's name and honour, such as rights of authorship, invention, discovery, publication rights, patent rights, etc.[59] Scholars advocating this theory emphasise that parties to civil law relations are on an equal footing and have certain freedoms in forming civil law relations.[60] Largely for this reason, the theory has wide support from Chinese scholars.[61] As pointed out earlier, such a linkage between a private law institution and a politico-economic concept means that the scope of civil law in, and even the relevance of civil law to, China is to be determined by the attitude of the authority – the Party – towards a commodity economy. Indeed, jurists supporting this theory explicitly state that the range of commodity relations determines the extent of utilisation of civil law.[62] Even at a technical level this 'commodity relations theory' would exclude family law relations (including law of marriage and inheritance) from the scope of civil law in the PRC,

---

57 Professor Tong Rou was a prominent civil law expert in China. He published very extensively on civil law topics in Chinese journals. He was (before his death in 1991) also chief-editor or co-author of several textbooks for tertiary law schools. Among these textbooks are: *General Principles of Civil Law* (*Minfa Yuanli*) (Beijing: Publishing House of Law, 1983), revised and reprinted in 1987 (this second printing was translated into English by Professor William C. Jones, entitled *Basic Principles of Civil Law in China*, and published by M. E. Sharpe, Inc., 1989), *An Introduction to Civil Law* (*Minfa Gailun*) (Beijing: Press of Chinese People's University, 1982), *Chinese Civil Law Science – General Principles of Civil Law* (*Zhongguo Minfaxue – Minfa Zongze*) (Beijing: Press of the Chinese People's University of Public Security, 1990); and *Chinese Civil Law* (*Zhongguo Minfa*) (Beijing: Publishing House of Law, 1990). Beside the above English translation, the other work of his in English is 'The General Principles of Civil Law of the PRC: Its Birth, Characteristics, and Role', in (1989) 52 *Law and Contemporary Problems* 151. For the various civil law theories, see Jianfu Chen, *supra* note 14, at 50-65.

58 *Basic Principles of Civil Law in China*, *id.*, at 15.

59 *Ibid.*

60 *Id.*, at 15-16 and 20-23.

61 Liu Qishan *et al.*, *New Research into Civil Law Problems* (*Minfa Wenti Xintan*) (Beijing: Press of China University of Public Security, 1990), at 17.

62 See *Basic Principles of Civil Law in China*, *supra* note 57, at 7; and Zhu & Liang, *supra* note 13, at 28.

although they traditionally have a place in civil codes in European Continental countries, because family relations are seen as established by the fact of marriage and based on blood-ties, rather than on commodity relations.[63]

With this definition and conception of civil law there are several civil law concepts and institutions, namely, legal personality, civil acts, civil rights and liabilities which are central to the understanding of the civil law, its structure and scope, and its principles and techniques.

Legal personality is an abstract civil law institution in which all natural persons and legal entities are treated as 'legal persons' with certain capacities and incapacities in conducting civil acts, regardless of their social position, political background and geographical location. 'Civil acts' refers to lawful transactions and activities (such as entering into a contract or performing a duty required by law) which create, change and terminate civil and commercial relations.[64] Civil law rights and liabilities are thus the consequences of such civil acts. Again following Continental tradition, these consequences are governed by the two fundamental civil law institutions of obligations and property. Together with legal personality they form the three pillars of modern Chinese civil law.[65]

---

63 See Tong Rou, 'Building Up China's Own Civil Law Theory and System', (no. 3, 1988) *Guangdong Legal Science* (*Guangdong Faxue*), at 1-7. At first glance, the Roman law structure is strongly evidenced in the civil codes of (former) socialist countries. A large part of such codes is devoted to the law of obligations which largely encompasses contracts and torts. Laws on family and succession are treated separately, both dealing with property rights as well. Copyright and other forms of intellectual property are only dealt with by civil codes in principle; details are worked out in separate codes and enactments. Such an exclusion is clearly opposed by many other scholars who criticise the theory for failing to include personal relations (such as marriage, family and inheritance relations) not based on 'commodity exchange'. See e.g. Jin Ping, 'On Objects Regulated by Our Civil Law', in Tao Xijin, (ed.), *A Collection of Civil Law Papers* (*Minfa Wenji*) (Shanxi: Shanxi People's Press, 1985), at 64-77; Wang, Guo & Fang, *supra* note 3, at 7-22; Liu Qishan, *supra* note 61, at 25-30; Liu Shiguo, *supra* note 3, 19-24; Nie Tienchu, 'A Theoretical Discussion on Civil Law Relationships', (no. 5, 1991) *Hebei Law Science* (*Hebei Faxue*), at 1-4. Many 'theories' held by these scholars may well be described as 'variations' or 'revised versions' of the 'commodity relations theory'.

64 See Art. 54 of the GPCL. This Chinese definition is conceptually flawed, as a tortious act is clearly a civil law act which leads to tortious liabilities. If all civil acts are to be lawful acts, no tortious liabilities would be able to be established under the Chinese civil law, which clearly is not the case.

65 Peng Wanlin (ed.), *Civil Law Science* (*Minfa Xue*) (Beijing: China University of Political Science and Law Press, 1994), at 14.

5. Civil and Commercial Law Institutions

5.1. Legal Personality

(1) Legal Personality, Legal Capacity, and Rights and Duties

Although an abstract approach to defining the positions of individuals and legal entities under civil law is evidenced in the GPCL, the GPCL institution of legal personality has some quite different conceptual approaches to this highly abstract institution. The Chinese institution of legal personality is in fact best understood in a comparative law context.

The notion of 'legal personality' is variously interpreted by jurists. In a narrow sense the term 'legal personality' is used to mean that a natural person or an organisation is recognised as a 'person' in the eyes of the law or a juridical unit, and in a broad sense, to indicate different capacities of 'persons' under the law. Common law jurists generally use the term in a broad sense to mean the sum total of capacities as well as incapacities, rights and duties, and powers,[66] while Civil law jurists more commonly apply it in a narrow sense to mean the quality of being a person under the law.[67]

'Legal capacity' is the power of a 'person' to acquire and exercise rights and assume liabilities.[68] It is defined in European Continental legal science through the notion of 'capacity for acts' (*Handlungsfähigkeit*).[69] This is the attribute of personality, of being able to perform certain classes of acts, and a condition precedent to the

---

66 See e.g. Albert Kocourek, *Jural Relations* (Indianapolis: The Bobbs-Merrill Company Publishers, 1927), at 291-292; R. H. Graveson, *Status in the Common Law* (London: The Athlone Press, 1953), at 111-112.

67 See e.g. Hans Kelsen, *Pure Theory of Law*, (translated from the second German edition by Max Knight) (Berkeley/Los Angeles: University of California Press, 1967), at 172; and Ernest J. Schuster, *The Principles of German Civil Law* (Oxford: the Clarendon Press, 1907), at 17-20.

68 See generally, Carleton Kemp Allen, *Legal Duties* (Oxford: The Clarendon Press, 1931), at 28-70; Roscoe Pound, *Jurisprudence* (St Paul, Minn: West Publishing Co., 1959), vol.IV, at 262-405; Kelsen, *supra* note 67, at 145-192.

69 In contrast, there is no simple or straightforward legal theory regarding a person's capacity in common law jurisprudence, as a result of its pragmatic approach to specific rights and duties and to specific capacities and incapacities of a person. Early analytical jurisprudence in Common law, however, sometimes employed the notion of 'status' as a convenient method of exposition, to cluster a complex of rights and duties, of capacities and incapacities. But the notion of 'status' is both controversial and without a precise meaning. See George Whitecross Paton, *A Textbook of Jurisprudence*, (4th edition by G.W. Paton and David P. Derham) (Oxford: The Clarendon Press, 1972), at 399; and Pound, *supra* note 68, at 262. Since legally imposed enabling or disabling conditions have largely disappeared in modern legal systems, the ambiguous term of 'status' has become quite misleading and of little practical significance.

exercise of particular rights.[70] It is, however, only a latent and potential ability in the 'person';[71] whether or not it can be translated into actual advantages depends on the person's specific rights and powers as provided by law and his/her or its actions in exercising the ability.

In German jurisprudence and in those systems following the German model, legal capacity is further divided into capacity for rights (*Rechtsfähigkeit*) and capacity for acts (*Handlungsfähigkeit*).[72] Under these legal systems, to say a person or an entity has a capacity for rights is merely to say that he/she or it is a 'person' under the law or, in other words, has legal personality. The capacity for acts is the power or ability of a person to cause legal consequences through his/her or its own acts and conduct. In modern law, where legal personality is recognised for all human beings and most associations of human beings, it is, in legal systems which follow the German model, the notion of capacity for acts which actually divides persons into different classes (i.e. persons with full, partial, or no capacity for acts), in accordance with the person's natural capacities (i.e. capacity for judgment or will) or with legal attributes recognised by law in the case of legal persons.

In other words, rights are powers over certain and specific things or powers to enter into certain specific transactions, while capacity is a general qualification or possibility to acquire or exercise rights, and the capacity for acts defines a person's capacities and is a legal prerequisite for actually enjoying rights and assuming liabilities. Capacity for acts affects capacities in general, but not specific rights and duties.

(2) Natural Persons in Chinese Civil Law

The legal position of natural persons under Chinese civil law is dealt with in Chapter Two on Citizens (Natural Persons) of the GPCL. Its approach appears to be that of the German one, i.e. a citizen's legal position is to be determined by his/her civil legal capacity (i.e. capacity for rights) and capacity for civil acts.[73] Though the law distinguishes three sets of separate legal concepts, i.e. civil legal capacity, capacity

---

70 See David M. Walker, *Principles of Scottish Private Law*, 4th edition (Oxford: The Clarendon Press, 1988), vol. I, at 204; and Allen, *supra* note 68, at 47.

71 Allen, *supra* note 68, at 47.

72 Regarding the capacity for acts, German law further distinguishes the capacity for legal transactions, capacity for wrongs, and capacity for crimes. See generally, Schuster, *supra* note 67, at 17-20; Rudolf Huebner, *A History of Germanic Private Law*, (translated by Francis S. Philbrick) (New Jersey: Rothman Reprints, Inc, 1968), at 41-42; E. J. Cohn, *Manual of German Law* (New York: Oceana Publications, Inc., 1968), vol. I, at 63-64; Allen, *supra* note 68, at 45-47; Pound, *supra* note 68, at 276; and Norbert Horn, Hein Kötz & Hans G. Leser, *German Private and Commercial Law: An Introduction*, (translated by Tony Weir) (Oxford: The Clarendon Press, 1982), at 71-74.

73 Articles 9-15 of the GPCL.

for acts, and rights and duties, these concepts are not defined by the law itself. The gap has to be filled by Chinese jurisprudence. While all citizens are equal in respect of having civil legal capacity, which they enjoy from birth and which only ceases on death,[74] their capacities for civil acts differ according to their age groups and mental condition.[75]

Although this approach appears to be a German one, the Chinese law on legal personality of natural persons is not a direct and wholesale copy of German law. It has some unique features that have resulted from the influence of jurisprudence from the former Soviet Union and some particular Chinese considerations.

For a start, under the German Code, or indeed all major Western civil codes and the KMT Civil Code, 'persons' are divided into 'natural persons' (*Ziranren* in the KMT code) and 'juristic persons' (*Faren* in the KMT code), while the Chinese GPCL uses the word 'citizens' (*Gongmin*) together with 'juristic (legal) persons' as subjects of civil law throughout the enactment.[76] The difference between the two is that the term 'natural person', literally designates any person regardless of the nationality of that person, while the word 'citizen', as generally understood, means a person with a certain nationality.

The replacement of the term 'natural person' by the word 'citizen' has historical and ideological reasons as well as practical implications.

Historically the term 'natural person' is alien to the Chinese legal culture. There was no distinction between 'natural persons' and 'legal persons' in Chinese traditional law, although 'individuals' (*Geren*) and 'organisations', such as family-clans, were in some statutes treated differently and separately.[77] The first formal recognition of the distinction between 'natural persons' and 'legal persons' came in the KMT Civil Code which, for the first time in Chinese history, introduced the legal institution of juristic persons to China. The term 'natural persons' thus began to be applied before 1949 and is still used by jurists in Taiwan. When the KMT laws were abolished in the PRC, the term 'natural persons' also ceased to be used.

Ideologically it was Soviet law and jurisprudence which first rejected the term 'natural persons' on the grounds that the ideas of the natural law school (to which the term 'natural persons' was attributed) were incompatible with Marxism-Leninism.[78] For this reason the Soviet Union first replaced the term 'natural persons' with the

---

74 Articles 9 and 10 of the GPCL.

75 Articles 11-13 of the GPCL.

76 The only exception occurs in the title of Chapter Two, where the term 'natural persons' is bracketed in addition to the word 'citizens'. Until quite recently, Chinese textbooks too have used the word 'citizens' instead of the term 'natural persons'. Only the more recent textbooks have begun to use the term 'natural persons' in disregard of GPCL usage.

77 Li Zhimi, *supra* note 2, at 21-27.

78 See Olimpiad S. Ioffe, *Soviet Civil Law* (Dordrecht: Martinus Nijhoff Publishers, 1988), at 27-28.

word 'citizens' in the RSFSR Civil Code of 1922.[79] Following the Soviet model, jurists in the PRC also adopted the term 'citizens'.[80]

Chinese jurists today argue that the attributes of human beings have two aspects: natural and legal. The natural aspect means a person is born and exists according to natural biological law. In this respect, he/she is a natural person. The legal aspect means that the legal status (i.e. legal capacity and capacity to act) of a [natural] person is granted by state law, and the contents and scope of legal capacity are determined by the will of the state. They maintain that a [natural] person does not obtain legal capacity by virtue of birth; the legal status of a slave in a slave-owning society and in Roman law is cited to support this argument.[81] They therefore hold that the term 'natural persons' blurs what only the term 'citizens' can accurately reflect, namely the legal aspect of attributes of a human being.[82] These arguments indicate a fundamental conceptual difference between Western law and Chinese law – the legal personality of a person in China has to be *granted*, not merely to be *recognised*, by the state.

The use of 'citizens' instead of 'natural persons' requires a basic inquiry into the legal capacity of foreigners and stateless persons. The GPCL does not define the word 'citizens'. However, the application of the GPCL to foreigners and stateless persons is addressed separately. Article 8 provides that '*[u]nless otherwise stipulated by the law*, the provisions of this Law with regard to citizens apply to foreign nationals and stateless persons within the territory of the PRC.' This has led many scholars in the PRC to interpret the word 'citizens' to mean persons with PRC nationality.[83] The reasons for the use of two terms at one time are, they explain, first, to allow the possible application of Chinese civil law to foreigners and stateless persons as extended by Article 8; and secondly, it is a result of the consideration that the retention of both terms at the same time would facilitate research exchanges and communications

---

79 The word 'citizens' appeared in the first draft of the RSFSR civil code, while the term 'natural persons' was still applied in Soviet jurisprudence. However, by the time of the second draft, this replacement was also applied in Soviet jurisprudence. See Ioffe, *supra* note 78.

80 For instance the first civil law textbook in the PRC, *Fundamental Issues of Civil Law in the PRC* (*Zhonghua Renmin Gonghe Guo Minfa Jiben Wenti*), (edited by the Teaching Section of Civil Law of the Central Judicial Cadres' School, published by the Publishing House of Law, Beijing, 1958, hereinafter referred to as the *1958 Civil Law Textbook*), uses the word 'citizens' instead of the term 'natural persons'.

81 See Tong Rou, *Chinese Civil Law Science – General Principles of Civil Law*, *supra* note 57, at 87-88. These arguments have been quite consistent in the PRC regime. See, for instance, the *1958 Civil Law Textbook*, at 60-61; *Basic Principles of Civil Law in China*, *supra* note 57, at 50-51; Wang, Guo & Fang, *supra* note 3, at 145-146; and Liu Shiguo, *supra* note 3, at 51.

82 *Ibid.*

83 Major civil law textbooks published in the PRC after the promulgation of the GPCL maintain that the word 'citizens' in the law means Chinese citizens. See reference in *supra* note 3; and Liang Huixin, *Civil Law* (*Minfa*) (Chengdu: Sichuan People's Press, 1989), at 71.

between China, where the word 'citizens' has long been used, and other foreign legal systems where the term 'natural persons' has been traditionally applied.[84] However, there are other scholars who disagree. They maintain that the GPCL actually equates the concept of 'citizens' with that of 'natural persons' because of the heading, where the term 'natural persons' is bracketed after the word 'citizens'.[85]

Chinese jurists have further elaborated on the legal status of foreigners and stateless persons in China. According to them, two principles are implied in Article 8, i.e. the 'principle of national treatment' and the 'principle of reciprocity'.[86] By extending the provisions concerning citizens to foreigners and stateless persons, the 'principle of national treatment' is incorporated, which enables foreigners and stateless persons to have the same legal status as Chinese citizens. By attaching the words '*unless otherwise stipulated by the law*' to Article 8, a 'principle of reciprocity' is incorporated which permits discrimination against and restrictions on foreigners' legal capacities in China if the law of the original country of the foreigners imposes any discrimination or restrictions on Chinese citizens' legal capacities.[87] Furthermore, even in cases where Chinese civil law is applied to foreigners and stateless persons, the 'principle of national treatment' can only be applied in a qualified manner; that is, Chinese law may impose restrictions and/or conditions upon foreigners and stateless persons even if the foreign country does not impose similar restrictions or conditions.[88] Here Chinese jurists seem to have confused the concept of legal capacity with that of rights.[89] This confusion further reduces the degree of abstraction

---

84 Tong Rou, *Chinese Civil Law Science – General Principles of Civil Law*, *supra* note 57, at 88-89.

85 Editorial Board of *Studies in Law*, *A Summary of Civil Law Research in the New China* (*Xin Zhongguo Minfaxue Yanjiu Zongshu*) (Beijing: Press of Chinese Social Sciences, 1990), at 71.

86 See e.g. Tong Rou, *Chinese Civil Law Science – General Principles of Civil Law*, *supra* note 57, at 88-89; and *Lectures on the General Principles of Civil Law* (*Minfa Tongze Jiangzuo*), edited by the Supreme People's Court Training Class on the General Principles of Civil Law, and published by Beijing Bureau of Culture (1986), at 94-95 (Hereinafter cited as the *Supreme Court Lectures*).

87 *Ibid.*

88 Chinese jurists explicitly point out that the 'principle of national treatment' will only be applied to ordinary civil law activities, but the qualification ('unless otherwise stipulated by the law') will be applied to issues of particular importance, such as the right to operate enterprises, the right to contract cultivated land, etc. See *Supreme Court Lectures*, *supra* note 86, at 95.

89 As mentioned above, *supra* note 54, the enactment of a private international law is currently on the agenda of the five-year legislative plan and, hopefully, matters relating to the application of civil law can be clarified in the forthcoming law. It should also be pointed out that, despite the odd arrangement in the GPCL, there has been no reported case where foreigners are deprived of the enjoyment of protection by the Chinese civil law, though the right to conduct commercial activities is restricted by various foreign investment laws, just as it is in most other countries.

of Chinese civil law, and therefore, further diminishes the strength of private law principles as a specific structure relatively independent from political, economic and social changes in China.

Technically, however, the Chinese approach to the legal status of foreigners and stateless persons deviates little from the law of France,[90] Japan,[91] and the KMT,[92] but it is quite different from the laws of Germany[93] or Switzerland.[94] However, it is with the Soviet law that China shares not only its technical arrangement,[95] but also its jurisprudential explanation and emphasis on qualified national treatment and the principle of reciprocity,[96] as well as the ideological basis for the rejection of the term of 'natural person'.

Specific Chinese considerations are also reflected in the GPCL. Although citizens are endowed with civil legal capacity from the moment of birth until death under the GPCL,[97] a foetus has no civil legal capacity under the law.[98] In Western civil codes and the KMT Civil Code the protection of the interests of the foetus is provided to varying degrees,[99] but neither the GPCL nor the Supreme People's Court's views

---

90 Article 11 of the French Civil Code: 'A foreigner enjoys in France the same civil rights as those which are or will be accorded to Frenchmen by treaties of the nation to which such a foreigner belongs.'

91 Article 2 of the Japanese Civil Code: 'Aliens shall enjoy private rights except where prohibited by law, ordinance, or treaty.'

92 Article 2 of the Law Governing the Application of the General Principles of the Civil Code: 'Within the limits prescribed by law or ordinances, a foreigner has the capacity of enjoying rights.'

93 The German Civil Code places no restrictions upon aliens' capacity for rights.

94 The Swiss Civil Code recognises all persons as being subjects of rights and having equal capacity to have rights and duties (Article 11).

95 Article 122 of the Fundamental Principles of Civil Legislation of the USSR and the Union Republics provides that '[f]oreign citizens shall enjoy civil law capacity in the USSR equally with Soviet citizens. Individual exceptions may be established by USSR law. Reciprocal limitations may be established by the USSR Council of Ministers in respect of citizens of those states in which there are special limitations on the civil law capacity of Soviet citizens.' Article 123 provides a similar rule for stateless persons.

96 See O.N. Sadikov, (ed.), *Soviet Civil Law* (New York: M.E. Sharpe, Inc., 1988), at 54.

97 Article 9 of the GPCL.

98 Among major Western civil codes, the Swiss Civil Code presents an exception. Paragraph 2 of Article 31 of the Code provides that 'Between conception and birth the child is held to have legal capacity, conditional on his being born alive.'

99 The French Code protects the right of the foetus to an inheritance provided he/she is subsequently born alive (Article 725); the German Code protects the right of inheritance (paragraph 2 of Article 1923) and a right to damages for the wrongful death of the person bound to provide maintenance (paragraph 2 of Article 844); the Japanese Code protects the right to third party claims (Article 712) and the right to inheritance (Article 886); and the

on the GPCL recognises the interests of the foetus. The only protection appears to be the protection of the right to inheritance provided by the 1985 Inheritance Law,[100] but the nature of this protection, according to Chinese scholars, is not to recognise the civil legal capacity, but merely to provide protection in advance for the future interests of the potential child.[101] Given the fact of the widespread practice of abortion as a means of population control, the lack of provision for the general protection of a foetus' interests in the GPCL appears to be a deliberate arrangement. Scholars' arguments for the legal nature of this protection are also consistent with the population control policy.

Furthermore, the classification of citizens' capacity for acts in the GPCL also contains some rather unusual Chinese 'legal inventions'. Under the GPCL, citizens are divided into three categories, i.e., those with full capacity, those with limited capacity, or those with no capacity for civil acts, according to their ages and intellectual abilities.

A citizen at the age of eighteen attains majority and becomes a person with full capacity for civil acts. He/she can then independently participate in civil law relations.[102] A citizen between sixteen and eighteen years of age may also be deemed to be a person with full capacity for civil acts if his/her main source of livelihood is income derived from his/her own work.[103] The recognition of full capacity on the basis of source of income is rather a peculiar 'legal invention' by the GPCL.[104] The rationale behind the legislation is, according to Chinese scholars, 'to mobilise the enthusiasm among youth to participate in the cause of socialist construction'.[105] On the other hand, marriage does not enable a minor to acquire full capacity to civil acts, or to be emancipated from guardianship, or to attain a precipitated majority,

---

KMT Code protects all personal interests of a foetus provided he/she is subsequently born alive (Article 7).

100 Article 28 of the Inheritance Law (1985) provides that 'When the left-over [residual] property is divided, a portion should be set aside for an embryo to inherit. If the embryo is dead, that portion should be handled according to legal inheritance.'

101 Tong Rou, *Chinese Civil Law Science – General Principles of Civil Law*, *supra* note 57, at 96.

102 Article 11 of the GPCL.

103 *Ibid.* Chinese labour law and practice generally allow a person over the age of 16 to participate in paid employment, but employment of children under sixteen years old is prohibited by the Provisions on Prohibition of Employing Child Labourers (1991) and the PRC Law on the Protection of Minors (1991).

104 Soviet law grants minors over 15 years of age the capacity to independently enter into small household transactions, to receive and dispose of their wages or scholarships, and to enforce their copyright and patent rights; it does not, however, give these minors full capacity for acts. See Article 13 of the RSFSR Civil Code.

105 Wang, Guo & Fang, *supra* note 3, at 24.

although this is achieved under modern civil codes and the KMT Civil Code,[106] and even under Soviet law.[107] Legally, a minor is not allowed to get married under Chinese law,[108] although in reality marriages between minors or with a minor as one party are not uncommon, particularly in rural areas. The lack of any provision dealing with their capacity for civil acts seems to be unrealistic, though consistent with the current birth control policies.

Clearly, the GPCL has followed the German methods quite closely. Conceptually, however, Chinese civil law on the legal personality of natural persons is still very much built on the Soviet model, the latter itself being influenced by the German model but with a different ideology behind the legal provisions and legislative structure. Prevailing policy considerations towards *ad hoc* situations, such as economic development and birth control policies, have also had an impact in the Chinese civil law.

(3) Legal Persons in Chinese Civil Law

With the KMT laws having been abolished, the term 'legal persons' was only occasionally used in the PRC in the 1950s. It only re-emerged in post-Mao China as a direct response to the inadequate protection of business autonomous interests brought about by economic reforms, in particular in the reform of state-owned enterprises.[109]

As a legal term, '*faren*' ('legal persons') first re-emerged in the 1981 Economic Contract Law of the People's Republic of China.[110] The term was not defined by the Law nor was it explained by any legislative organs. Since then, however, this term, without a legal definition or any clarification of its meaning, has been frequently used in the Party's documents and the laws of the PRC, particularly in the areas concerning business transactions and foreign-related economic activities.

---

106 Article 13 of the KMT Civil Code provides that 'a minor who marries acquires thereby the disposing capacity.' Article 14 of the Swiss Civil Code provides that 'marriage constitutes majority.' Article 476 of the French Civil Code provides that 'a minor is emancipated as a matter of law by marriage.' Article 753 of the Japanese Civil Code provides that 'A minor who marries acquires majority.'

107 Under Article 11 of the RSFSR Civil Code, a minor acquires full dispositive capacity from the moment of marrying if the marriage is allowed by the law.

108 The marriageable age under Chinese Marriage Law (1980) is 22 for males and 20 for females.

109 See detailed discussions in Jianfu Chen, *supra* note 14, Chapter 3.

110 Article 2 of the Economic Contract Law of the PRC (1981) states that: 'Economic contracts are agreements reached by *legal persons* to define their mutual relations in regard to their rights and duties so as to realise certain economic goals'. This was the first time the term '*faren*' was officially used in the PRC law in the post-Mao era. The Economic Contract Law has now been superseded by the 1999 Contract Law.

The concept of 'legal persons' was further extended in 1983 when enterprises were legally described as legal persons represented by factory directors with the power 'to exercise the lawful functions of possessing, utilising and disposing of the state property entrusted to them by the state for management, in order to independently organise production and management activities, and to shoulder the responsibility stipulated by the state ... to raise or answer lawsuits in courts independently.'[111]

In 1986 the GPCL formally established the institution of legal personality, which applies to both foreign and domestic enterprises. The GPCL is, however, hardly a useful piece of legislation for solving practical problems, nor is it helpful for clarifying much theoretical dispute. The provisions of the GPCL on legal persons start with a definition of legal person, followed by some generally applicable requirements for being a legal person in the PRC. The GPCL then proceeds to lay down further general provisions for enterprises, institutions, social organisations and joint operations as legal persons, though the law does not explicitly distinguish between different types of legal persons. Detailed provisions governing legal persons are to be found in individual statutes issued at different times under various policy guidelines. Huge gaps left by such a legislative approach are to be expected.

A legal person is defined by the GPCL as 'an organ which possesses civil legal capacity and capacity for civil acts and which, according to the law, independently enjoys civil rights and assumes civil obligations'.[112] According to the same article, the civil capacity and capacity for civil acts of a legal person arise from the time of its establishment and cease to exist upon the termination of the legal person. The emphasis on independently enjoying civil rights and assuming civil liabilities in the Chinese definition of legal person clearly shows the economic rationale behind the establishment of this civil law institution. It is also apparent that the Chinese definition resembles that in the former Soviet Union.[113]

The Chinese definition, however, does not tell us what a legal person is; rather it identifies those capacities an organisation would have *after* it is granted the status of legal person by the law. It is the requirements further set out by the GPCL that say more about what a legal person is under Chinese law. These requirements are as follows: '(1) it [a legal person] is established in accordance with the law; (2)

---

111 Article 8 of the Provisional Regulations of State-owned Industrial Enterprises (1983) (now repealed).

112 Article 36 of the GPCL.

113 Article 11 of the Fundamental Principles of Civil Legislation of the USSR and the Union Republics (1981) states: 'Organisations which possess separate property, may acquire property and personal non-property rights and bear duties in their own name, and be plaintiffs or defendants in court, *arbitrazh*, or arbitration tribunals, shall be juridical persons.' Article 23 of the RSFSR Civil Code (1964) states: 'Juridical persons are such organisations as possess separate property, and may in their own name acquire property and personal rights and be subject to liabilities, and be plaintiffs and defendants in cases in court, or before an institutional or chosen arbitration court.'

it must possess the necessary property or funds; (3) it must have its own name, organisational structure and premises; (4) it must be capable of independently bearing civil liability'.[114] The latter three of these requirements have been referred to by some jurists in the PRC as the characteristics of a Chinese legal person.[115] While these requirements have been worded differently in various civil code drafts drawn up before the GPCL, the basic features have essentially remained the same since the first civil law textbook was published in the PRC.[116] These requirements again resemble Soviet jurisprudence and Soviet law.[117]

The nature of 'legal person' as expressed in Chinese jurisprudence further indicates that, despite the use of similar terminologies and techniques, the Chinese institution of legal personality for economic entities, like that for natural persons, is quite different from German-model legal systems.

Although there are many contending theories in the West on the nature of legal personality,[118] particularly in countries with a civil law system,[119] it can be asserted that the importance and, hence, the essence of legal personality is that such a legal institution is able to effectively reduce the subjects of rights to 'legal individuality and abstract equality, so that even the state can appear in litigation only as another

---

[114] Article 37 of the GPCL. For detailed analysis of these requirements, see Jianfu Chen, *supra* note 14, at 98-103.

[115] See e.g. Luo Yuzhen, *General Principles of Civil Law* (*Minfa Tonglun*) (Wuhan: Press of Central-China Teachers' University, 1986), at 68-69; and Ma Junju, *On the Institution of Legal Personality* (*Faren Zhidu Tonglun*), Wuhan: Wuhan University Press (1988), at 3-5. Besides these three characteristics, the fourth character of a legal person is commonly held to be that a legal person is a social organisation.

[116] See the *1958 Civil Law Textbook, supra* note 80.

[117] See Sadikov, *supra* note 96, at 55-57.

[118] For a summary of these theories, see Jianfu Chen, *supra* note 14, at 104-105.

[119] On the extensive and intensive debate on the nature of legal personality in civil law countries, some jurists in Common law countries have suggested that all the arguments may have been based on the wrong questions in the debate. Instead of asking what is the nature of legal personality, it is suggested that jurists should ask questions as to the kinds of entities recognised by the law, the kinds of relations these entities may enter into and, if the law is ambiguous towards such entities, how they should be recognised by law. See e.g. David P. Derham, 'Theories of Legal Personality', in Leicester C. Webb (ed.), *Legal Personality and Political Pluralism* (Melbourne: Melbourne University Press, 1958), at 11-15; and H.L.A. Hart, 'Definition and Theory in Jurisprudence', (1954) 70 *L.Q. Rev.* 37. This dichotomy of views in fact reflects the different approaches to the same problems in Common and Civil law jurisdictions. To the Common law lawyers, the concern is with practical solutions to various demands, while the Civil law lawyers are concerned with the necessary formalism in the formation of legal entities. See Alice E.-S. Tay, 'Introduction: The Juridical Person in Legal Theory, Law and Comparative Law', in Alice Tay & Conita Leung (eds), *Legal Persons and Legal Personality in Common Law, Civil Law and Socialist Law* (being a special issue of the *Indian Socio-Legal Journal*, 1992), at 4.

individual subject, as having rights and duties *vis-à-vis* the citizen in the same way as the citizen has rights and duties *vis-à-vis* it.'[120]

Chinese jurists in the 1980s began to engage in a nineteenth century jurisprudence battle which was considered to have died down more than thirty years before.[121] However, in sharp contrast with the West, Chinese jurists did not disagree so much with each other on the nature of legal personality, rather they clashed on other matters concerning legal persons which have caused little controversy in the West, such as the nature of the property of a legal person, and the competence to be a legal person.

This is not because Chinese jurists have accepted or rejected Western theories on the nature of legal personality. It is because many other theoretical and practical problems have been created by the pragmatic adoption in the Chinese socialist legal system of the Western 'bourgeois' notion of legal personality, for the purpose of economic reform in a *socialist* public ownership system. Problems have also been caused by the lack of other correlative laws, such as the absence of a corporation law until the mid 1990s, almost ten years after the promulgation of the GPCL.

Chinese jurisprudence sees a legal person, analogous to a natural person, as a subject of civil law relations. According to Chinese jurisprudence, legal personality is an institution recognised by the law, and such an institution personifies certain social organisations in legal relations. These organisations are creatures of law in the same way as natural persons.[122] To a Chinese scholar, 'legal personality is a kind of legal institution. Like other institutions of civil law, it was created by the emergence of a commodity economy and develops together with the commodity economy'.[123] This view on legal personality is very well summarised in the following:

> Although both natural persons and legal persons are subjects of civil relations and have similar civil legal capacities and character, they cannot be assimilated to each other. The legal personality has always been an independent concept of civil law; it grows with the development of a commodity economy, and eventually becomes a perfect legal institution. … The existence of legal personality is a kind of historical reality. [Its existence is] based on the economic conditions of a certain society and decided by the

---

[120] Eugene Kamenka & Alice E-S. Tay, 'Beyond the French Revolution: Communist Socialism and the Concept of Law', (1971) 21 *U. Toronto L.J.* 109, at 132.

[121] Derham, *supra* note 119, at 1.

[122] See e.g. Bai Youzhong, 'On the Character and Origin of the Legal Person', (no. 3, 1983) *Studies in Law* (*Faxue Yanjiu*), at 60; Huang Zhuozhu, 'On the Qualification of the Legal Person of State Enterprises in China', (no. 1, 1984) *Studies in Law* (*Faxue Yanjiu*), at 25; and Wang Junyan, 'On the Character and Legal Status of Companies', (no. 1, 1986) *Studies in Law* (*Faxue Yanjiu*), at 60.

[123] Ma Junju, *supra* note 115, at 32.

> state will of that society. It is an important legal tool of a ruling class for maintaining and developing the economy.[124]

To say that legal personality is a legal device of the state is to state a truism. It does not answer the question as to what the basis is on which legal personality is attributed to associations of persons by the state. To add that legal personality is a product of a commodity economy says nothing about the nature of legal personality. Treating legal personality as a legal tool and as being a product of the will of the ruling class, the Chinese 'theory' effectively rejects the real essence of this private law institution, namely, treating individuals and organisations as well as the state as equal and abstract subjects of rights.

Seen as a legal institution, legal personality is created by the law, and legal persons, like natural persons, enjoy legal rights and bear legal obligations as provided by the law. Thus, in terms of legal capacity and capacity for acts, both natural persons and legal persons are of non-natural origin, as both are created by the law. In fact, there is no such concept as the natural rights of human beings in the Chinese tradition or within Chinese Communist legal concepts. All rights are created and protected by the law.[125] Consequently, it does not seem obvious to Chinese jurists that a special theory is required to explain the 'phenomenon' of legal personality for communities and associations.

The classification of Chinese legal persons also departs significantly from that in European Continental systems. The Chinese classification appears to distinguish between profit-seeking and non-profit-seeking legal persons, which, to some degree, resembles the division of corporations and foundations in the European continental systems. However, Chinese 'corporations' are further divided essentially in accordance with forms of ownership. These divisions are much closer in nature to those of the Soviet Union.[126]

Specifically, two categories of legal persons are provided for by the GPCL, namely, enterprise legal persons on the one hand,[127] and on the other hand organisations (*Jiguan*), institutions (*Shiye Danwei*) and associations (*Shehui Tuanti*).[128] In addition,

---

124 Tong Rou, *Chinese Civil Law*, *supra* note 57, at 94-95.

125 See *Chinese Encyclopaedia – Law* (*Zhongguo Dabaike Quanshu – Faxue*) (Beijing/Shanghai: The Chinese Encyclopaedia Press, 1984), at 485.

126 See Article 24 of the RSFSR Civil Code and Article 11 of Fundamental Principles of Civil Legislation of the USSR and the Union Republics. For a discussion of Soviet classification, see Ioffe, *supra* note 78, at 38-46. It should be pointed out that this is still true in relation to the GPCL. With the rapid development of enterprise laws (such as the Company Law), the Soviet remnants have largely been jettisoned in Chinese law. See further discussion in Chapter 13.

127 Articles 41-49 of the GPCL.

128 Article 50 of the GPCL.

joint operations (*Lianying*) between enterprises and/or institutions may also acquire the status of legal person.[129]

Enterprise legal persons specifically mentioned in the GPCL include enterprises under the ownership of the whole people (*Quanmin Suoyouzhi Qiye*), i.e. state-owned enterprises (SOEs); enterprises under collective ownership (*Jiti Suoyouzhi Qiye*); and enterprises with foreign investment.[130] Missing from the list of the GPCL are Chinese private business entities. In fact, major Chinese private business entities, such as individual industrial and commercial households and rural contracting households at the time of the enactment of the GPCL, are dealt with in Chapter Two of the GPCL, 'Citizens (Natural Persons)'. This arrangement in the GPCL seems to suggest that a privately-owned domestic business is effectively excluded from obtaining the status of legal person. Apparently this situation led to many problems in protecting the interests of private business, and especially had serious consequences in light of the rapid development of the private economy.[131] Thus an amendment to the 1982 Constitution was made in April 1988, which expressly provides that 'the state protects the lawful rights and interests of the private economy and provides guidance, supervision and control.'[132] Subsequently, the 1988 Provisional Regulations of the People's Republic of China on Private Enterprises have allowed some private enterprises to obtain the status of legal person,[133] and the 1988 Administrative Regulations of the People' Republic of China Governing the Registration of Enterprise Legal Persons provide a special category, 'private enterprises', for the purpose of registration of legal persons.[134] This practice clearly reflects the pragmatic approach towards law-making in the PRC. In fact, the Legal Persons Registration Regulations also create another special category: 'any type of enterprise which is legally required to register as an enterprise legal person'.[135] This is apparently to provide for any other contingencies which might arise through further developments in economic reform.

The GPCL does not contain definitions for 'organisations, institutions and associations as legal persons'. However, Chinese legal literature interprets them to include those non-profit-seeking organs which are funded by the state, such as

129 Articles 51-53 of the GPCL.

130 Article 41 of the GPCL.

131 See Chapter 13 for legal developments in this area.

132 See Article 11 of the 1982 Constitution (as amended).

133 See discussion in Chapter 13 below.

134 Article 2 (5) of the 1988 Administrative Regulations of the People's Republic of China Governing the Registration of Enterprise Legal Persons. Hereinafter referred to as the Legal Persons Registration Regulations.

135 Article 2 (6) of the Legal Persons Registration Regulations.

administrative, educational, health or academic institutions.[136] Profit-seeking entities created by these institutions are treated as enterprise legal persons.[137]

Joint operations[138] are economic entities formed by enterprises or between an enterprise and an institution.[139] However, only those which meet the necessary legal requirements may acquire the status of legal person.[140]

These classifications of legal persons clearly destroy, or at least undermine, the effect of the abstract and formalistic approach to legal personality found in the European Continental models.

The status of the state under civil law in socialist countries has always been ambiguous. On the one hand, the concept of 'subject of civil law' does not cover the state; on the other hand, the state is often the subject of civil law participating in civil relations.[141] The same can be said about the legal status of the state under the Chinese civil law. For instance, the state can be an heir to property under wills, and the state will be the owner of the property of deceased persons if there are no heirs.[142] Again, the state acquires buried or hidden property when its ownership is unclear.[143] More actively, the state has issued treasury bonds (*Guoku Quan*) to its citizens and therefore has effectively established obligatory (debtor-creditor) relations with its citizens. Finally, the state, theoretically at least, exercises property rights as the owner of property 'belonging to the whole people'.

The state as a subject of civil law is however absent from the GPCL. The law-makers explain that the relationship between the state and enterprises is not based on equality, but on domination and subordination, and that it should be left to be dealt with by economic and administrative law.[144] It is not explained, however, whether the same is true in the relationship between the state and its citizens in civil law relations.

Despite the apparent omission of the state as a civil law subject from the GPCL, some Chinese jurists have tried to construe the state as a 'special subject of civil

---

136 See Luo Yuzhen, *supra* note 115, at 81; Tong Rou, *Chinese Civil Law supra* note 57, at 99-100; and Tong Rou, *Chinese Civil Law Science – General Principles of Civil Law*, *supra* note 57, at 157.

137 See Article 27 of the Legal Persons Registration Regulations.

138 Some translations use the term 'joint ventures', for instance, Professor William Jones's translation of the *GPCL*. See (1987) 13 *Rev. Soc. L.*, at 370.

139 Article 51 of the GPCL.

140 Legal status of these joint operations are analysed in Chen, *supra* note 14, Chapter 9.

141 See Ioffe, *supra* note 78, at 28-30.

142 Articles 16 and 32 of the Inheritance Law of the People's Republic of China (1985).

143 Article 79 of the *GPCL*.

144 Wang Hanbin, *supra* note 32, at 148.

law'.[145] Such a view can be traced back to that held in the 1950s. The 1958 Civil Law Textbook contained a short paragraph on the legal status of the state under civil law:

> [B]ecause of the establishment and the development of ownership by the whole people, our state also participates in civil law relations with the capacities of a civil law subject. Our state is the only owner of the property belonging to the whole people. In issuing treasury bonds and in foreign trade, the state also directly participates in civil law relations. Our state, however, is not a legal person. Our state establishes the institution of legal personality, lays down criteria and limitations for being a legal person, and provides supervision to them. It itself is not organised as, nor does it carry out its activities in accordance with, the institution of legal personality. It only participates in civil law relations as a special civil law subject under certain circumstances.[146]

This textbook however did not elaborate on the notion of 'special subject of civil law'.

Although jurists in China today echo the view that the state is a special subject, in contrast with citizens (natural persons) and legal persons, the approach taken by these scholars has been closely linked with the idea of separating state functions. According to these jurists, a state exercises two functions, political and economic, and hence has a dual status, that is, as a sovereign power holder and as a property owner. These two functions and the dual status can always be separated. As a sovereign it is a subject of administrative law, and as a property owner it is a subject of civil law.[147] Once the state participates in civil law relations in the capacity of state property owner, the state only has equal status with other participants, and civil law rules, such as equality among parties and compensation at equal value, apply. No special privileges are allowed for the state in civil law relations.[148] The special nature of the state as a subject of civil law lies not in its legal status in relation to other parties, but

145 See e.g. Wu Wenhui, 'On the State as a Special Subject of Civil Law', (no. 5, 1987) *Law Review* (*Faxue Pinglun*), at 70-71; Tong Rou, *Chinese Civil Law Science – General Principles of Civil Law, supra* note 57, at 185-192; Wang Liming, 'On the State as a Civil Law Subject', (no. 1, 1991) *Studies in Law* (*Faxue Yanjiu*), at 59-66 and 46; Min Bing, 'Several Issues Concerning Civil Law Subjects', (no. 1, 1992) *Journal of the South-Central Institute of Political Science and Law* (*Zhongnan Zhengfa Xueyuan Xuebao*), at 17-24; and Ma Junju & Lu Xiaowu, 'On the State as a Civil Law Subject in a Market Economy', (no. 5, 1993) *Law Review* (*Faxue Pinglun*), at 1-5.

146 *The 1958 Civil Law Textbook, supra* note 80, at 72.

147 See e.g. Tong Rou, *Chinese Civil Law, supra* note 57, at 156; Ma & Lu, *supra* note 145, at 1.

148 Tong Rou, *Chinese Civil Law, supra* note 57, at 159; Wang Liming, *supra* note 145, at 61; Min Bing, *supra* note 145, at 21-22; and Ma & Lu, *supra* note 145, at 1.

in its scope and the contents of civil law capacities. According to these scholars, the state is a *special* subject because, firstly, it and only it represents the interests of the whole people and therefore it has some civil law capacities that other parties do not have (such as issuing state treasury bonds). Secondly, it uses the state treasury for assuming civil liabilities. Thirdly, its capacity as a civil law subject is provided and recognised by itself. Finally, it assumes sovereign immunity in foreign countries and has some special protection under civil law, such as exemption from compulsory execution of judgments, and exemption from statutes of limitation in recovering state property.[149] Scholars also emphasise that state-owned enterprises and state institutions are independent legal persons separate from the state itself; the state only becomes a subject of civil law when it participates in civil law relations in its own name.[150] Herein lies the importance of arguing for the state to be a special subject of civil law: On the one hand, the two functions of the state are separate; therefore sufficient autonomy and equal status are given to state enterprises and institutions in economic relations with the state. On the other hand, the state will be able to release itself from any civil liabilities caused by these enterprises and institutions.[151]

Regarding the omission of the state as a civil law subject in the GPCL, it is argued that this issue need not be specifically provided by written law. As long as the state observes civil law rules and principles it automatically relinquishes its status in constitutional and administrative laws. It is however conceded that the issue of whether the state participates in civil law relations in the capacity of an ordinary legal person or as a special subject of civil law, has to be determined by civil law.[152] This is, however, exactly the problem that has been left unresolved by the GPCL and other civil law regulations in the PRC.

5.2. Property

Property is, in any legal system, one of the most important civil and commercial law institutions, yet it has been one of the most under-developed areas of law in China until very recently. While the traditional conception of property is not particularly conducive to the development of a modern legal institution of property, the socialist ideology concerning public ownership, coupled with the rigid European Continental structure and approach, played an essential role in preventing the development of this particular branch of law. Not surprisingly, there were only some fragmented

---

149 Wu Wenhui, *supra* note 145, at 70; Tong Rou, *Chinese Civil Law Science – General Principles of Civil Law*, *supra* note 57, at 189-191; Wang Liming, *supra* note 145, at 64; Min Bing, *supra* note 145, at 22; and Ma & Lu, *supra* note 145, at 2-3.

150 Tong Rou, *Chinese Civil Law Science – General Principles of Civil Law*, *supra* note 57, at 187-188.

151 Tong Rou, *Chinese Civil Law*, *supra* note 57, at 157-158; and Ma & Lu, *supra* note 145, at 2.

152 Wang Liming, *supra* note 145, at 62.

and elementary laws on property until the adoption of the Law on Rights *in rem* in 2007. While the Law on Rights *in rem* is comprehensive, it is not a complete code of property rights. The GPCL continues to provide some supposedly commonly applicable rules on property. However, the underlying philosophy and the fundamental notions applied in the two principal laws on property are radically different. Thus major inconsistency continues within the Chinese legal system. All these issues are to be dealt with systematically in the next chapter on property.

5.3. Civil Law Obligations

(1) An Overview

Following the European Continental tradition, the institution of 'civil obligations' is seen by scholars in China as one of the three pillars of modern civil law.[153] However, unlike in major civil codes in this tradition, this institution is not expressly established in the GPCL. It is rather fused and disguised in two separate chapters dealing with civil rights and civil responsibilities respectively.[154] These two chapters provide general principles on civil obligations.

An obligation is defined as 'a particular relationship involving rights and duties created between parties in accordance with the stipulations of a contract or provisions of the law.'[155] This seemingly concise definition is deceptively simple. It covers the institution of contracts and several statutory sub-institutions including torts, unjust enrichment, *negotiorum gestio* (*wuyin guanli*, management of affairs without authority), and other types of action as may be provided by law.[156]

Certain important and generally applicable principles governing obligations are briefly covered by the GPCL, but spread over different sections of the two chapters without any clear structural rationale.[157] Thus Section 2 of Chapter 5, entitled 'Obligation Rights', defines obligations by shares and joint obligations. The former refers to a situation where parties separately enjoy rights or assume liabilities in accordance with their predetermined share;[158] the latter covers situations in which,

---

153 See *supra* note 65.

154 See Chapters 5 and 6 GPCL. Few explanations have been given as to why the GPCL did not treat 'obligations' as a separate civil law institutions. Perhaps it was seen as one of those issues the law-makers were 'not certain of' and, thus, 'not ripe' for inclusion in the GPCL. Wang Hanbin, *supra* note 32, at 147.

155 Article 84 of the GPCL.

156 See Tong Rou, *Chinese Civil Law*, *supra* note 57, at 307-308; Peng Wanlin, *supra* note 65, at 448-451.

157 Epstein has suggested that this irrationality in structure is caused by the awkward distinction between civil rights and civil responsibilities. See Edward J. Epstein, 'Tortious Liability for Defective Products in the People's Republic of China', (1988) 2 *J. Chinese L.* 285, at 294.

158 Article 86 of the GPCL.

in accordance with a provision of the law or an agreement among parties, any obligee may demand the fulfilment of obligations by the obligors, with the obligors who have fulfilled the obligation having a right to demand other joint obligors to compensate them for the share they are liable for.[159] This Section also contains a provision on security for obligations.[160] The article provides four methods of securing an obligation, namely, guarantees by agreement, designation of property as collateral, a deposit, and a lien, with parties allowed to choose any of them in accordance with law or by agreement among the parties. A law on security, however, was only issued in 1997. A legal duty to satisfy civil law obligations is stipulated in Chapter 6 on Civil Responsibilities.[161] The same article also allows payment by instalments upon the consent of the obligee or a court order, or compulsory payment through a court order. *Force majeure* is recognised as a legitimate excuse from obligations (in contract or in torts) unless otherwise stipulated by law,[162] while a no-fault liability is also anticipated by the GPCL.[163]

Although Chinese scholars have been able to construct an abstract obligation institution in their textbooks along the lines of the civil law tradition, the current civil law is unsystematic, with provisions spread over chapters dealing either with civil rights or duties. Certain abstract definitions do exist in the GPCL, but most are *ad hoc* regarding individual sub-institutions of obligations, with the main provisions being oriented towards general principles of contracts and torts. Moreover, each of the sub-institutions of obligations is dealt with by either individual statutes or regulations, or by judicial interpretations. The GPCL, instead of clearly defining the rights and duties in obligatory relationships, only lays down a foundation for development and co-ordination among individual statutes and regulations. Finally, even though consensus exists among scholars on the institution of obligations, there is disagreement as to whether certain sub-institutions such as torts should be separate from obligations, as torts and other statutory obligations are seen as having rather different conceptual and policy foundations from those of contracts.[164] Besides these general principles, the GPCL provisions address specific kinds of obligations, which are again spread through different sections of the law.

---

159 Article 87 of the GPCL.

160 Article 89 of the GPCL.

161 Article 108 of the GPCL.

162 Article 107 of the GPCL.

163 Article 106 of the GPCL.

164 See e.g. Wang Liming, 'After Unity There's Separation: The Relationship Between Torts and Obligations', (no. 1, 1997) *Jurisprudence Frontiers* (*Faxue Qianyan*) 92.

(2) Civil Obligations Established by Contracts

Section 2 of Chapter 5 of the GPCL, though entitled 'Obligation Rights', contains major provisions on the rights created by obligations established by contracts, whereas liabilities caused by such obligations are dealt with in Section 2 of Chapter 6. These provisions are further implemented and supplemented by a set of contract laws governing different kinds of contracts.[165]

(3) Civil Obligations Created by Torts

Article 106 the GPCL provides that 'Citizens or legal persons who through their own fault infringe upon state or collective property or upon another person, or who harm another person, shall assume civil liability.' Although this article is commonly held to be the Chinese definition of 'torts', an alien term introduced into China through law reforms early this century,[166] it is meant to be a general definition of civil liability covering not only torts but also civil liabilities caused by other kinds of civil acts.[167]

Article 106 nevertheless defines the constituent elements of torts, that is, damage, causation and fault. Although Chinese jurisprudence follows the German civil law tradition in distinguishing 'fault' (*guocuo*) from 'unlawfulness' (*weifa*), with the former referring to the state of mind (i.e. intention, negligence) of the actor and the latter the violation of legal provisions,[168] it is commonly held by Chinese scholars that fault alone without the act being unlawful would not lead to civil liabilities.[169] It is however doubtful whether Chinese judicial practice actually takes consideration of this dichotomy at all.[170] On the other hand, as mentioned earlier, the GPCL does allow no-fault liability.[171]

On the basis of these principles, specific tortious liabilities are separately codified in Section 3 of Chapter 6, which first classifies liabilities according to specific rights infringed, and then lists in an *ad hoc* fashion some specific types of torts. These rights include rights to personal or real property and intellectual property, name, portrait, or reputation or honour, and personal safety.[172] *Ad hoc* types of torts listed by the GPCL include torts caused by state workers, substandard products, hazard-

---

[165] We shall deal with these provisions systematically in Chapter 12.

[166] See Wang Jiafu (ed.), *Chinese Civil Law – Civil Obligations* (*Zhongguo Minfaxue – Minfa Zhaiquan*) (Beijing: Publishing House of Law, 1994), at 411.

[167] See Tong Rou, *Chinese Civil Law supra* note 57, at 46-48.

[168] Wang Jiafu, *supra* note 166, at 461. See also Epstein, *supra* note 157, at 295.

[169] See Wang Jiafu, *supra* note 166, at 461; Peng Wanlin, *supra* note 65, at 520-524.

[170] Wang Jiafu, *supra* note 166, at 461.

[171] Article 106 of the GPCL.

[172] See Articles 117-120 of the GPCL.

ous activities and industries, environmental pollution, roadwork, construction, domesticated animals, excessive self-defence, emergencies, and persons without full civil capacity.[173] All these provisions are clearly intended to be implemented or supplemented by individual statutes and, indeed, many of them have been so implemented.

(4) Other Obligations Arising from Statutes

With general definitions on obligations and civil liabilities having been provided, the *ad hoc* obligations in contracts or torts are clearly not meant to be exhaustive. Other obligations can be created by statutes. Two specific kinds of obligations are further dealt with by the GPCL.

Unjust enrichment is defined as 'improper benefits obtained without a legal basis and for which damage is caused to another party.'[174] Such illegally gained profits or benefits must then be returned to the party which suffered such damage. Although unjust enrichment is a traditional civil law institution, the incorporation of it in the GPCL is held by some Chinese scholars as to provide a legal basis for upholding socialist morality.[175]

Negotiorum gestio (management of affairs without authority) is a unique civil law institution. It is defined by Article 93 of the GPCL which provides 'If a party undertakes management or a service without a legal or agreed obligation in order to avoid harm to the interests of another party, it shall have the right to demand from the benefiting party compensation for the necessary expenses incurred thereby.' If unjust enrichment is to provide a legal basis for promoting socialist morality, one wonders whether *negotiorum gestio* actually undermines socialist morality, or if the adoption of this 'bourgeois' legal institution was only a realistic admission that socialist morality needs materialist support.

(5) Enforcement of Civil Liabilities

Once a civil liability is caused by breach of contract, by torts or other statutory events, such a liability may be assumed by one or a combination of several of the following ten methods: cessation of the infringement, removal of the obstacles, elimination of the danger, return of property, restoration to the original conditions, repair, reconstruction or replacement, compensation for damage, the making of a default payment, eradication of the effect and restoring reputation, and making an apology.[176]

---

173 See Articles 121-133 of the GPCL.

174 Article 92 of the GPCL.

175 Peng Wanlin, *supra* note 65, at 536.

176 Article 134 of the GPCL.

In addition to the above, a court is also empowered to make use of admonitions, to order the signing of a statement of repentance, and to confiscate property unlawfully obtained in the pursuit of unlawful acts. It may even impose a fine or detention in accordance with law, even though the case in question is of a civil law nature.[177] Indeed, the GPCL opens the door for the pursuit of administrative sanctions or criminal penalties in civil law cases when Article 110 provides that 'If it is necessary to investigate and determine administrative liability with regard to a citizen or legal person bearing civil liability, such administrative liability shall be investigated and determined. If a criminal offence is constituted, the criminal liability of the citizen or of the legal representative of the legal person shall be investigated and determined.'

6. Concluding Remarks

The GPCL establishes, or tries to establish, an abstract and formalistic approach and structure in line with European Continental models, but such efforts are largely undermined by the underlying socialist ideology which closely links legal concepts with politico-economic notions – a legacy of the lasting Soviet influence – and the fragmented treatment of civil law institutions. With Soviet influence still strongly evident in Chinese jurisprudence at the time, the GPCL provisions on the legal personality of natural persons are of a different nature from those of German law, despite the fact that the form and terminology of the latter have apparently been followed by the GPCL. The linkage between the politico-economic notion of a 'planned commodity economy' or 'socialist market economy' and civil law initially facilitated the revival of 'bourgeois' civil law institutions, but it is also responsible for major deficiencies in the civil law system. It can be said that the whole system and most civil law institutions established by the GPCL are fundamentally flawed. Indeed, as Jones has pointed out, the GPCL as a whole is an unworkable piece of legislation for settling specific disputes.[178]

The GPCL, instead of providing guiding principles for the development of civil law, has clearly become a liability. Fortunately, Chinese jurists and law-makers have pushed ahead in developing separate laws (on contracts, property, company etc.), in part, in disregard of the constraints imposed by the GPCL. Despite its historical contribution to the initial development of the civil law in post-Mao China, the GPCL has also become an embarrassment with regard to the current status of Chinese law. It is high time that the NPC seriously considered revising and updating the Law.

177 Article 134 of the GPCL.

178 William C. Jones, 'Some Questions Regarding the Significance of the General Provisions of Civil Law of the People's Republic of China', (1987) 28 *Harv. Int'l L.J.*, at 309.

Chapter Ten

Civil Law: Property

1. Introduction

Property law is one of the most significant components of any legal system. From a current law and development perspective the protection of private property constitutes one of the most essential components of the rule of law. And from the perspective of foreign investors in China, it is of great importance in that it defines property rights, including ownership, rights to operate property (state-owned or private), land use rights as well as mortgage rights. All are major legal considerations in investment decision-making and in ensuring smooth investment and trade operations and their legal protection. From a socio-legal perspective, property law penetrates into every corner of society, affecting the basic rights and the capacity of every single citizen and resident. In terms of comparative law, the codification of property rights in a socialist country demands significant innovation and its result could easily challenge some of the conventional views on the classification of legal systems/families.

Ideologically, the politico-economic notion of property rights introduced from the former Soviet Union has proven to be the most stubborn impediment to the establishment of a legal regime on property rights in China. The Soviet notion emphasised public ownership and its priority over other forms of property rights, and treated the sacred nature of public ownership as the essential feature of a socialist property rights regime.[1] It is not surprising, therefore, that private property in the PRC was only declared inviolable by the most recent constitutional revision in 2004.[2] Under socialist ideology, which is still rhetorically upheld in the state Constitution,[3] the reform of the state-owned enterprises and the rural land system,

---

1 See Jianfu Chen, *From Administrative Authorisation to Private Law: A Comparative Perspective of the Developing Civil Law in the PRC* (Boston/London/Dordrecht: Martinus Nijhoff Publishers, 1995), at 144-149.

2 On the evolution of the constitutional protection of private property, see Chapter 3.

3 The present Constitution, as amended in 2004, still upholds public ownership as being sacred while private property is only declared inviolable. See discussions in Chapter 3.

and the protection of private property have all been severely frustrated, and so was the drafting of a law on property rights, for more than half a century.[4]

Politico-economically, the most fundamental challenge in establishing a socialist market economy is two-fold: political reforms and the restructuring of the property rights system. Political reforms in China have been slow and have always lagged behind economic reforms, although such reforms are being pushed ahead indirectly by administrative law reforms, sometimes referred to by Chinese scholars as 'effective constitutional reforms'. While economic reform has been carried out rapidly, it has nevertheless been an incremental, trial and error process, a process which continues today. This process, from a legal viewpoint, is in fact pre-determined by the slow and difficult reform of the property rights regime in China.[5] In one sense, economic reforms since 1978 have essentially been the process of a reform of the property rights system. And, as will be seen, the final enactment of the Law on Rights *in rem* in March 2007 represents a climax in politico-economic reform.

This chapter first reviews the historical development of a modern property law in China. The concepts and conceptions of property law under the General Principles of Civil Law (GPCL) and the Chinese Constitution are then examined. This is followed by an analysis of the conceptual framework of property rights as evidenced in the 2007 Law on Rights *in rem* as well as other laws relating to property rights. In particular, an examination of the very torturous process of enacting the Law on Rights *in rem*, and of the political and academic controversies that erupted during the drafting process will shed light on the contemporary legal framework of property rights in China.

2. Property Rights in Traditional China and Modern Property Law under the KMT

There was no systematic codification of property rights in traditional China until the introduction of Western law at the turn of the 20th century. Although some scholars are able to identify many provisions of law governing property rights, or even a system of rights *in rem* in traditional China,[6] the concept of property rights

---

4 For a detailed study of these issues, see Jianfu Chen, *supra* notes 1; and Jianfu Chen, 'Civil Codification, Foreign Influence and 'Local Conditions' in China', 2005 (2:1) *Chinese Cross Currents* 82.

5 For detailed discussions on the relationship between politico-economic reform and the development of property rights in China, see Jianfu Chen, *supra* notes 1, at 144-149.

6 See e.g. Li Zhimi, *Ancient Chinese Civil Law* (*Zhongguo Gudai Minfa*) (Beijing: Publishing House of Law, 1988), at 72-114; and Li Yusheng, 'A Comparative Study on the Traditional Chinese Law and the Rights *in rem* in Modern Civil Law – On the Relevant Rights *in rem* Provisions in the Draft Civil Code of the PRC', available from <www.iolaw.org.cn/shownews.asp?id=15252> (last accessed 19 January 2007).

was significantly different from that of the West. Essentially, private property rights were not rights enforceable or maintainable against others and the state, but rights granted, and therefore, always subject to intervention by the sovereign authority, which always had the power to confiscate or transfer property. As Powelson has argued whenever there was a change of dynasty there were changes in the system of property through confiscation and transfer, particularly of the essential means of production in an agrarian society, namely land.[7] Furthermore, private property was not freely alienable in the same way as it was in the West. For instance, inheritance of personal property was regulated by law to pass through the patriarchal line at death; testamentary succession was rarely allowed and was not formally established until the adoption of the KMT Civil Code in 1929–1930.[8] In short, while there were rules on property in traditional China, they were scattered in different legal sources and customary law and practice. Property was neither securely nor systematically protected.

The KMT revolution did not end the imperial practice of confiscation and the transfer of property with each change of dynasty: indeed, a re-distribution of social wealth was one of the aims of the Three Principles of Dr. Sun Yatsen. However, a modern legal system of property rights was, for the first time in Chinese history, established during the KMT rule through the Civil Code of 1929–1930.

The property rights system under the KMT Civil Code was an almost wholesale adoption of the German Civil Code, largely through the influence of the Japanese Civil Code which itself was based on the German Civil Code. Like the German Code, Book III of the KMT Civil Code was entitled 'Rights *in rem*' (*wuquan*). It deals with ownership, possession, *superficies* (*dishangquan*),[9] *servitudes* (*diyiquan*),[10] mortgages, pledges, the right of retention (lien), *yung-tien* and *dien*.[11] Again as in the German Code, the notion of 'things' was dealt with in Book One on General

7 See John P. Powelson, 'Property in Chinese Development: Some Historical Comparisons', in James A. Dorn & Wang Xi (eds.), *Economic Reform in China: Problems and Prospects* (Chicago/London: The University of Chicago Press, 1990), at 165-179.

8 Liu Chunmao *et al.*, *Chinese Civil Law Science – Property Succession* (*Zhongguo Minfa Xue – Caichan Jicheng*) (Beijing: Press of the University of the Chinese People's Public Security, 1990), at 15-18.

9 *Superficies* is defined as 'the right to use the land of another person with the object of owning thereon structures or other works or bamboos or trees'. See Article 832 of the KMT Civil Code.

10 *Servitude* is defined as 'the right to use the land of one person for the convenience of another person.' See Article 851 of the KMT Civil Code.

11 *Yung-Tien* and *dien* are, however, Chinese traditional institutions. *Yung-Tien* means a right to cultivate or raise livestock permanently on the land of another person by paying rent (Article 842 of KMT Civil Code). *Dien* refers to the right to use an immovable of another person and to collect the fruits therefrom by paying a particular price and by taking possession of the immovable (Article 911 of KMT Civil Code).

Principles, but unlike in the German Code, there was no definition of 'things'. Nevertheless, 'things' under the KMT Code were interpreted to mean 'corporeal objects' only.[12] Rights between persons *inter se* were dealt with in Book II on Obligations. Intellectual property rights were treated separately by individual statutes outside the Civil Code.

Although the KMT Civil Code as such has had little practical effect in Mainland China, it has been a major theoretical foundation and a structure upon which Chinese scholars have been making efforts to establish a modern institution of property rights today.

3. Socialist Concepts and Conceptions of Property Rights in the PRC

3.1. An Overview

The Chinese Communist revolution was accompanied by a change in the property system through confiscation and transfer – the nationalisation of private property. Once again history repeated itself – private property in China was subject to the exercise of wanton sovereign powers. However, the communist revolution differed from that of the KMT in that private property was relegated to a minor part of the national economy, if not totally abolished. With politicisation making incursions into every sphere of life, including the legal and economic, the development of property law in the PRC took a radically different path from that taken by the KMT.

In all former socialist countries there was a tension between the conception of socialist public ownership and state policies regarding enterprise autonomy. Everywhere in socialist countries there were two preoccupations. First there was the question regarding who was allowed to own property and the scope of property to be owned by the person (legal or natural) concerned. The second and more important concern was to decide in which organs socialist [public] ownership was to be vested.[13] The law of property in former socialist countries was therefore more precisely a law of ownership.[14] In particular, the central concerns of jurists in

---

12 Cheng Yüpo, *General Principles of Civil Law* (*Minfa Zongze*), 7th edition (Taipei: Sanmin Shuju, 1989), at 192-193.

13 See Viktor Knapp, 'Socialist Countries' and F.H. Lawson, 'Comparative Conclusions' in *Int'l Enc. Comp. L.*, vol. vi (Property and Trust), ch. 2 (Structural Variations in Property Law), S.3 and S.8 respectively.

14 In fact, the 1981 Fundamental Principles of Civil Legislation of the USSR and Union Republics only had one section on Ownership (Section II). Part Two of the RSFSR Civil Code of 1964 (as amended), though entitled Law of Property, dealt only with various forms of ownership. Perhaps it is for this reason, the book, *Soviet Civil Law*, (O.S. Ioffe, Dordrecht: Martinus Nijhoff Publishers, 1988), contains a chapter on the law of ownership but not a chapter on the law of property.

socialist countries were such issues as whether, under public ownership, SOEs had any property rights over property which they were authorised to manage and, if so, what kinds of property rights they had and how these rights could be separated from state ownership rights. At the theoretical level, the tension is caused in part by a rigid adherence on the part of socialist jurists to the Civil law principles that there must be an owner, and only one owner, of a property; the fragmentation of ownership frequently met with in the Common law system is strongly resisted in socialist countries.

For many years Chinese scholars repeated the fruitless efforts undertaken in other socialist countries to theorise the notion of the 'right to operation', and effectively, the preoccupation with the issues associated with the notion of 'right of operation' had held up the whole development of the institution of property in China until very recently.

3.2. A Politico-Economic Concept of Property Rights

In examining property law in the PRC, two different terms, '*suoyouzhi*' and '*caichan suoyouquan*', have to be distinguished. These two terms are reminiscent of the two different definitions of the term 'ownership' as used in other socialist countries.[15] The term '*suoyouzhi*', literally meaning ownership system, refers to the politico-economic system of the state, e.g. ownership by the whole people and the collective ownership of the working people.[16] The term '*caichan suoyouquan*', literally meaning rights of property ownership, denotes property rights of the property owner as provided by the law.[17] In legal literature, a third term, '*suoyouquan*', literally meaning rights of ownership, is frequently used by Chinese jurists interchangeably with '*caichan suoyouquan*'.[18] A more general term '*caichanquan*' is also used in Chinese literature and legislation. This term is here translated as 'property rights'.

Under the 1982 Constitution the basis of the socialist economic system is defined to include the public ownership of the means of production and collective ownership by the working people.[19] While this remains unchanged in the current Constitution (as amended), major changes have been made since 1988 in relation to other forms of 'capitalist' ownership in the national economy, and to the protection of private

15 See Knapp, *supra* note 13, at 35-36.

16 See Article 6 of the 1982 Constitution of the PRC.

17 See Article 71 of the GPCL.

18 For instance, the *Chinese Encyclopaedia – Law* (Beijing/Shanghai: The Chinese Encyclopaedia Press, 1984, at 572-573) uses '*suoyouquan*' and '*caichan suoyouquan*' interchangeably under the entry of '*suoyouquan*'. There is no entry under '*caichan suoyouquan*'.

19 Article 6 of the 1982 Constitution.

property.[20] However, in line with the preoccupation with the notion of ownership in socialist countries, the Constitution continued, at least until the 2004 Constitutional revision, to refer to the rights of property ownership (*suoyouquan*) instead of the more universally understood term of property rights (*caichanquan*).[21]

The relationship between ownership and ownership rights is that the latter is the reflection of the former in legal form and the former, therefore, determines the nature and contents of the latter.[22] In practice, this means that state property (i.e. property under ownership by the whole people) is owned by the whole people,[23] who are theoretically represented by the state through the National People's Congress and local people's congresses at different levels.[24] It also means that the property of a collective organisation of the working people (i.e. the property under collective ownership by the working people) is owned by the collective.[25]

3.3. The System of Property Rights before the GPCL of 1986

In the former socialist countries it was common to classify property as means of production or consumer goods. Also common to these countries was the principle that 'public ownership' must replace capitalist ownership. The central concern of property law in these countries, as mentioned earlier, may be summarised as a concern for 'who can own what under what conditions'. In other words, socialist property law had little interest in other types of right *in rem*. Differences in practice between socialist countries were matters of degree, pace and method in transforming capitalist ownership into socialist ownership and of the toleration of private ownership within a defined scope.[26]

Despite the fact that in the first years the PRC government undertook more moderate measures to transform capitalist ownership and had a more tolerant attitude towards private property than was the Soviet practice, few laws were actually made to protect private property rights and to govern and regulate property relations among citizens. The 1954 Constitution provided that '[t]he State protects the right

---

20 See discussions in Chapter 3. For a concise summary of changes in property protection under the Chinese constitutional law, see Wang Kai, 'Historical Changes of Property Protection under the Constitution in New China (1949–2004), available at <www.iolaw.org.cn/shownews?id=14704> (last accessed 12 September 2006).

21 See revision to Article 13 of the Constitution in 2004.

22 Luo Yuzhen, *General Principles of Civil Law* (*Minfa Tonglun*) (Wuhan: Press of Central-China Teachers' University, 1986), at 178.

23 Article 73 of the GPCL.

24 Article 2 of the 1982 Constitution.

25 Article 74 of the GPCL.

26 See John N. Hazard, *Communists and Their Law: A Search for the Common Core of the Legal Systems of the Marxian Socialist States* (Chicago/London: the University of Chicago Press, 1969), at 145-222.

of capitalists to own means of production and other capital according to law.' At the same time, however, the law called for the control of the negative aspects of capitalist industry and the gradual transformation of capitalist to socialist ownership.[27] However, even this limited protection was short-lived: capitalism was eliminated within the first fifteen years of the PRC.[28] The protection of the private ownership of the means of production was formally dropped in the 1975 Constitution.

The PRC's first comprehensive treatise on civil law, the 1958 Civil Law Textbook,[29] was strongly influenced by Soviet perceptions and developments. Property matters were dealt with in chapters on ownership rights and obligations, the latter encompassing contracts and torts. There was no discussion on rights *in rem* other than ownership. Ownership rights were defined to include the rights to possess, use and dispose of property.[30] Common ownership, which might be in the form of co-ownership by shares (i.e. each owner had a specified share in the property) or the form of joint ownership (i.e. each had an equal but indivisible share in the property), was allowed, but only between cooperative organs or between individuals.[31] The concept of rights *in rem* and the attributive power of ownership to reap benefit (*shouyiquan*), as contained in the KMT law, were criticised as the products of semi-colonialism and semi-feudalism, and as being used as a disguise for exploitation.[32] The 1958 Civil Law Textbook nevertheless emphasised that some or all of the three attributes of ownership (i.e. rights to possess, use and dispose of property) might be separated from ownership rights without the owner being deprived of such rights.[33]

With regard to the question of SOEs, the PRC adopted the Soviet theory of the rights of operational administration, together with the implementing mechanism of 'economic accountability.'[34] According to the 1958 Civil Law Textbook, SOEs were

---

27 See Article 10 of the 1954 Constitution.

28 Hazard, *supra* note 26, at 179.

29 *Fundamental Issues of Civil Law of the PRC* (*Zhonghua Renmin Gonghoguo Minfa Jiben Wenti*), edited by the Teaching Section of Civil Law of the Central Judicial Cadres' School (Beijing: Press of Law, 1958). Hereinafter referred to as the 1958 Civil Law Textbook.

30 *Id.*, at 123.

31 *Id.*, at 120-121.

32 *Id.*, at 118-119.

33 *Id.*, at 124.

34 For Soviet theories on the right of operational administration and 'economic accountability', see Ioffe, *supra* note 14, at 92-95, 102-105, and 106-108; O. S. Ioffe & Peter B. Maggs, *Soviet Law in Theory and Practice* (New York: Oceana Publications, Inc., 1983), at 162-171; Gyula Eörsi, *Comparative Civil (Private) Law* (Budapest: Akadémiai Kiadó, 1979), at 311-312; Harold J. Berman, *Justice in the U.S.S.R.: An Interpretation of Soviet Law*, revised edition (Cambridge, Massachusetts: Harvard University Press, 1962), reprinted in 1982, at 110-117; and A.K.R. Kiralfy, 'Attempts to Formulate a Legal Theory of Public Ownership', (no. 8, 1957) *Soviet Studies* 236.

legal persons. The independently controlled property of these legal persons was the property entrusted to them by the state for operational administration through the mechanism of independent economic accounting (*jingji duli hesuan*).[35] The right of operational administration was interpreted as having a threefold meaning. First, state organs and SOEs, within the scope of their authorities, had the power to control (*zhipei*) property entrusted to them for management in accordance with policies, laws and decrees. Secondly, state organs and SOEs might participate in civil law transactions in the capacity of a legal person and independently assume external civil liabilities. Thirdly, the contents of the rights of operative administration included the right to possess, use and dispose of state property for the purpose of implementing state plans. However, ownership rights in such property remained with the state; the state organs and SOEs could not acquire ownership rights over such property.[36] The resemblance to the Soviet concept is apparent. Moreover, in the Chinese concept state organs and SOEs were treated together, which evidenced an even stronger administrative approach than that in the Soviet Union.

In the 1960s, as a result of the Sino-Soviet split, attempts were made to modify or even to replace Soviet terminologies, but this often led to greater confusion. For instance, the 1964 Draft Civil Code provided that ownership included the right to operationally manage, use, reap benefit from and dispose of property owned.[37] It further provided that state property included property entrusted to state organs, SOEs and state institutions for operational administration.[38] It then provided that:

> In accordance with provisions of laws and decrees and the principle of 'Unitary Leadership but Management at Different Levels' (*tongyi lingdao, fenji guanli*), the state authorises state organs, SOEs and institutions to exercise the rights contained in Paragraph 2 of article 26 [that is the right to operationally manage, use, reap benefit from and dispose of property].

In the first few years after the Cultural Revolution the property rights theory of the 1950s made a comeback, though with modifications and expansion. The 1981 and 1982 drafts of the civil code dropped the notion of obligations; instead, both drafts contained parts on ownership rights, contracts, torts, intellectual property and inheritance. Although the provisions on ownership rights were considerably

---

35 The *1958 Civil Law Textbook, supra* note 29, at 68-69. The Textbook did not explain the concept of 'independent economic accounting'. However, the term was apparently an adopted Soviet one.

36 *Id.*, at 138-139.

37 Para. 2 of Article 26 of the 1964 Draft Civil Code. The various drafts (from the 1950s onward) are now collected in He Xinhua, Li Xiuqing, and Chen Yi (eds), *A Complete Collection of Civil Code Drafts in the New China* (*Xinzhongguo Minfadian Cao'an Zonglan*) (Beijing: Law Press, 2003), three volumes.

38 Para 2 of article 32 of the 1964 Draft Civil Code.

expanded, their concerns remained the same; that is, to determine who could own what under state ownership, collective ownership and personal ownership. Ownership rights were again defined to include the rights to possess, use and dispose of property owned.[39] Again, common ownership was divided into co-ownership by shares and joint ownership.[40] As in the 1958 Civil Law Textbook, SOEs were granted the right to possess, use and dispose of property entrusted for their management.[41]

When the notion of the 'right of operational administration' re-emerged during the post-Mao reform, it also largely reflected the concept of the 1950s. For instance, Paragraph 3 of Article 85 of the 1981 draft Civil Code provided that all SOEs were state property, and Article 86 provided that:

> Within the scope of state authorisation, state organs, SOEs and institutions exercise the rights of possession, use, and disposal over the state property entrusted to them for operational administration.

Similar provisions could also be found in the 1982 draft Civil Code.[42] Finally, a 1984 Party Decision replaced the term 'rights of operational administration' with the term 'rights of operation'.[43]

Major developments in property law theories appear to have taken place around 1984. The *Chinese Encyclopaedia – Law*, published in 1984, defined 'property rights' as 'the rights of civil law subjects having economic interests.'[44] More specifically, property rights here included rights *in rem* (*wuquan*), with ownership as the main kind, 'quasi-rights *in rem*' (*zhunwuquan*),[45] obligations and intellectual property rights.[46] Rights *in rem* were defined as the right to directly control and dispose of a thing and to exclude interference by others. It also classified ownership rights to include *superficies* (*dishangquan*), *servitudes* (*diyiquan*), mortgages (*diyaquan*), pledges (*zhiquan*), the right of retention [lien] (*liuzhiquan*), the right of *dien* (*dianquan*),

---

39 Articles 72 and 61 of the 1981 and 1982 draft civil codes respectively.

40 Articles 101 and 99 of the 1981 and 1982 draft civil codes respectively.

41 Articles 86 and 82 of the 1981 and 1982 draft codes respectively.

42 Articles 81 and 82 of the 1982 draft civil code.

43 See detailed discussions in Chapter 3 in Jianfu Chen, *supra* note 1.

44 The *Chinese Encyclopaedia – Law*, *supra* note 18, at 33.

45 The Encyclopaedia did not define the term 'quasi-rights *in rem*'. But in the entry for 'rights *in rem*', it explained that: 'In some countries' civil codes, intellectual property rights and other rights attached to intellectual property are called quasi-rights *in rem*. These rights have certain features of rights *in rem*, but they are in fact not rights *in rem*. In some other countries, property rights which may be governed by civil law rules concerning rights *in rem*, such as mining rights, fishing rights, are called quasi-rights *in rem*. Therefore, rights *in rem* under civil law are called original rights *in rem* or ordinary rights *in rem*, and quasi-rights *in rem* are called special rights *in rem*.' See the *Chinese Encyclopaedia – Law*, *supra* note 18, at 628-629.

46 *Id*., at 33.

and the right of *yung-tien* (*yongdianquan*).[47] It is clear that both the definition of property rights and rights *in rem* and the classification of rights *in rem* were direct copies of those under the KMT Civil Code.[48] The right of ownership was defined by the Encyclopaedia as 'an owner's right to possess, use, reap benefit from, and dispose of property owned and the right to exclude interference from other people.'[49]

Although the contributors to the Encyclopaedia were leading authorities in the PRC's legal circles, the fresh approach taken by the Encyclopaedia did not lead Chinese scholars to any systematic discussion on the institution of rights *in rem* until after the promulgation of the GPCL.[50]

The absence of debate, however, did not signify agreement among scholars. In fact, the 1984 draft of the GPCL indicated major uncertainties and disagreements among scholars: indeed the entire Chapter Three on Property (Things) was left blank, to be drafted in the future.[51] The 1984 draft contained no provisions regarding ownership rights either.

Major theoretical innovations appeared in the 1985 draft of the GPCL. Instead of dealing with different kinds of ownership or rights *in rem*, the draft was divided into General Principles, Citizens, Legal Persons, Partnerships, *Civil Rights* (*minshi quanli*), Juristic Acts and Agency, Civil Liabilities (*minshi zeren*), and Limitations of Actions. According to Article 47, the law protected all kinds of civil law rights, including ownership rights, obligatory rights [*zhaiquan*, creditors' rights], intellectual property rights, succession rights, personal rights, and other civil rights created by law and contracts, such as the right of use, the right to manage land under contract (*chengbao quan*), the right of operation, the right of pledge (*diya quan*), and neighbourhood rights (*xianglin quan*). This theoretical innovation was later adopted by the GPCL.

3.4. The System of Property Rights under the GPCL

The legal concept of property rights is dealt with in Chapter Five of the GPCL, entitled 'Civil Rights'. This chapter is divided into four sections, entitled Ownership Rights and Property Rights Relating to Ownership Rights, Obligatory Rights, Intellectual Property Rights, and Personal Rights. Ownership rights are defined as 'referring

---

47 *Id.*, at 628.

48 For the classification of rights *in rem* under the KMT Civil Code, see Books III, Rights *in rem*, of the Code. The KMT Code does not define the concept of rights *in rem*, but identical definitions are contained in all textbooks on civil law: e.g. Cheng Yüpo, *supra* note 12, at 49-53.

49 The *Chinese Encyclopaedia – Law*, *supra* note 18, at 572.

50 I could find no systematic discussion of rights *in rem* in any of the major legal journals or textbooks published in the PRC in 1984, 1985 and 1986.

51 In the Table of Contents, Chapter Three was entitled 'Property (to be drafted)'. In the text of the draft itself, Chapter Three was entitled 'Things (to be drafted)'.

to the rights of an owner, in accordance with the law, to possess, use, reap benefit from, and dispose of his own property'.[52] 'Property rights relating to ownership rights' are set out in Articles 80 to 83. These include the rights of state-owned or collectively-owned units to use and reap benefit from land owned by the state according to law (land use rights, *tudi shiyong quan*); rights of citizens or collectives to manage land according to contract (rights over land under contract, *tudi chengbao jingying quan*); rights of state-owned or collectively-owned units or citizens to exploit mineral resources owned by the state (mining rights, *caikuangquan*); rights of state-owned enterprises to operate and manage property entrusted to it by the state, that is, the right of operation (*jingying quan*), and limitations on property rights over immovable property in such matters as the damming of water, drainage, access, ventilation and natural lighting (rights of neighbourhood, *xianglin quan*). There is also the right of succession in this section, but jurists in China have made it clear that the right of succession is neither a right of ownership, nor an obligatory [creditors'] right; nor is it a kind of right *in rem*.[53] In fact, succession is seen as a different branch of law outside the scope of civil law. The inclusion of the right of succession in that section, according to Professor Tong Rou, is the result of purely technical considerations aimed at linking the GPCL to the Succession Law that had been issued before the formation of the GPCL.[54]

Although the GPCL structure appears to be innovative, jurists' conceptions of property rights are somewhat in line with a Civil law approach, as evidenced in the *Chinese Encyclopaedia – Law*. This Civil law attitude towards property rights became even more prominent among scholars after the promulgation of the GPCL, despite the socialist 'innovative' approach of the GPCL itself towards property rights.

Clearly, legal thinking and theoretical conceptions of property rights did not match the legal reality as reflected in the GPCL, nor was the elementary GPCL property institution able to deal with social reality. In particular, the practical difficulties relating to the property rights of SOEs, which were required to act as independent legal persons while the state retained ownership over such property, remained problematic. It is therefore not surprising that for many years, both before and after the promulgation of the GPCL, great efforts were made by civil law scholars in debating the nature of the property rights of SOEs, a debate that was to become one of the most extensive and intensive academic discourses in post-Mao China. With the deepening of economic reforms and the continuing difficulties of SOEs to adjust to a market economy, many Chinese scholars finally came to the conclusion

52 Article 71 of the GPCL.

53 Tong Rou, *Explanations and Answers to Difficult Questions and Problems in the GPCL* (*Zhonghua Renmin Gongheguo Minfa Tongze Yinan Wenti Jieda*), Issue no. 1 (Beijing: Press of China University of Political Science and Law, 1986), at 40.

54 *Ibid*.

that the GPCL institution of property rights required fundamental restructuring to bring it in line with a civil law model, centred on the notion of rights *in rem*.[55]

4. The New Rights *in rem*

4.1. The Making of the Law on Rights *in rem*

Officially the drafting of the 2007 Law on Rights *in rem* started in 1993; thus the process may be said to have taken 13 years to complete.[56] This statement is accurate in that new drafting of a law on rights *in rem* started at that time, but it is inaccurate in that rights *in rem* have always been part of the effort to draft a civil code in the PRC. As pointed out in Chapter Nine, the first attempt to draft a civil code occurred in the 1950s, an attempt that was followed by efforts in the 1960s and 1980s and which continues today. In this sense, the enactment of a law on rights *in rem* has taken some 50 years.

Until very recently, the term *Wuquan* (rights *in rem*) was alien for most, ordinary Chinese people.[57] It was referred to as the 'exclusive patent rights' of academics or a 'lone resident' in some law school classrooms.[58] The term 'rights *in rem*' did not appear in the various civil code drafts prepared in the 1950s, 1960s and 1980s, but these drafts always contained a chapter or book on property or ownership rights. While academic works used the term from time to time, and often interchangeably with the term 'property rights', serious studies on rights *in rem* only appeared during the heated debate on the nature of the right to operate state-owned enterprises. These studies, particularly during the first stage of urban reform in the 1980s and 1990s, produced various theories that attempted to define the legal nature of the rights

---

55 For a detailed analysis of this debate, see discussions in chapters 7-9 of Jianfu Chen, *supra* note 1.

56 See Wang Zhaoguo, 'Explanations on the Draft Law on Rights *in rem* of the PRC', delivered at the Fifth Session of the Tenth NPC on 8 March 2007, available from <www.npc.gov.cn/zgrdw/common/zw.jsp?label=WXZLK&id=360472&pdmc=1502> (last accessed 24 April 2007).

57 A story reported in the *Democracy and Legal System* (*Minzhu Yu Fazhi*, no. 7, 2007, at 6), though humorous, reveals much about the alien nature of this term: a Beijing resident was asked what *Wuquan* meant. He replied that, 'well, mankind has human rights. So I suppose things have their own rights too. No wonder my computer keeps freezing these days, I think it demands rights from me.'

58 'How the Law on Rights *in rem* was Made', (no. 7, 2007) *Democracy and Legal System* (*Minzhu Yu Fazhi*), at 5. Since the draft was published for public consultation, *wuquan* became one of the three most popular social terms used in 2005. See *id*., at 6.

granted to SOEs.[59] After some years of fruitless debate Chinese scholars came to realise that they needed to have a structure for rights *in rem* before continuing the debate on the right to operation, which was by then increasingly seen as an instance of a right *in rem*. As a result, rights *in rem* emerged as an academic discipline that accompanied the first signs of a legislative effort to codify a separate law on such rights.[60]

As pointed out in Chapter Nine, the first formal decision to enact a law on rights *in rem* occurred in 1998, when a three-step strategy was adopted for the final adoption of a civil code by 2010. As soon as the decision was made, an outline of the law on rights *in rem* was proposed by Professor Liang Huixing (of the Institute of Law, the Chinese Academy of Social Sciences). Almost immediately, major disagreement erupted between Professor Liang and Professor Wang Liming (of the People's University). According to Liang, Wang disagreed with the proposed provisions on usufruct, co-ownership, servitudes (neighbouring rights in real property), and the so-called construction building distinction rights (condominiums). As a result, Professors Liang and Wang were each entrusted by the Legislative Affairs Committee (LAC) of the Standing Committee of the NPC (SCNPC) to lead a team to undertake their own drafting.[61] Thus, instead of one drafting team, there were two. Very efficiently, Liang completed a draft law on rights *in rem* in October 1999, and Wang completed his in December 2000.[62] On the basis of these two drafts the LAC of the SCNPC compiled its first preliminary draft in May 2001. After some discussions among academics, the LAC completed its first official draft at the

---

59 For a detailed examination of the various theories on the right to operation and efforts to define the right as a right *in rem*, see Jianfu Chen, *supra* note 1, ch. 7.

60 See Jianfu Chen, *supra* note 1, at 194. See also Cao Zhi, 'Explanations on the Draft Legislative Plan of the Standing Committee of the Eighth NPC', delivered on 9 December 1993 at the Seminar on Law-making convened by the Standing Committee of the NPC, available from <www.e-cpcs.org/yhyj_readnews.aspx?id=2033&cols=151813> (last accessed 23 April 2007), which referred to the enactment of a code on rights *in rem*.

61 See Liang Huixing, *Struggling for China's Civil Code* (*Wei Zhongguo Minfadian er Douzheng*) (Beijing: Law Press, 2002), at 152 & 185. In fact, the disagreement between Liang and Wang went far beyond these technical issues. For a good discussion on this disagreement, see Frank Xianfeng Huang, 'The Path to Clarity: Development of Property Rights in China' 2004 (17) *Column J. Asian L* 191, at 204-211.

62 See Liang Huixing, *id.*, at 185. Revised versions of these drafts were published: Liang Huixing, *A Proposed Draft of a Chinese Civil Code with Explanations – Rights in rem* (*Zhongguo Minfadian Cao'an Jianyigao Fu Liyou – Wuquan Bian*) (Beijing: Law Press, 2004); Wang Liming, *A Proposed Draft Chinese Law on Rights in rem and Explanations* (*Zhongguo Wuquanfa Caian Jianyigao Ji Shuoming*) (Beijing: Press of Chinese Legal System, 2001); Wang Liming, *Academic Draft of Chinese Civil Code and Legislative Explanations – Rights in rem* (*Zhongguo Minfadian Xueze Jianyigao Ji Lifa Liyou – Wuquan Bian*) (Beijing: Law Press, 2005). Hereinafter, these drafts are referred to as Liang's draft and Wang's draft.

end of 2001, and this draft was then officially circulated to academic institutions, government departments and judicial organisations for comment.[63]

When the LAC submitted the Draft Civil Code (for Deliberation) to the SCNPC for deliberation in December 2002, the above draft law on rights *in rem* constituted the Book on Rights *in rem*. Thus the deliberation on the draft civil code in 2002 is commonly seen as the first deliberation of the law on rights *in rem*.[64] When the SCNPC changed its 'plan' in 2002 to take out the Book on Rights *in rem* for separate enactment, further revision was undertaken, and in August 2004 a revised draft was produced,[65] which was then submitted to the SCNPC for a second deliberation in October 2004.[66] A third deliberation then occurred in June 2005. As a matter of practice, a draft would normally be adopted after deliberation at three SCNPC sessions. This however was not to be the case here; the SCNPC decided in July 2005 that the draft should be published for nationwide public consultation. The draft was duly published on 10 July 2005, with the consultation to last until 10 August 2005. While the consultation only lasted for the short period of one month, it led to a remarkable level of political and academic interest, receiving an unprecedented response of 11,543 submissions from the general public.[67] The next deliberation was then held in October 2005, and the SCNPC indicated repeatedly after this that it intended to submit the draft law for adoption to the plenary session of the NPC in 2006, in accordance with its five-year (2003–2008) legislative plan.[68]

Up to this stage the debate had been mostly of a technical and practical nature.[69] This was soon to change. At the end of 2005, when the drafting of the law was approaching its completion, an open letter was published by a constitutional law scholar (and later supported by some 700 retired high-ranking government officials and

---

63 Liang Huixing, *supra* note 61, at 191-196.

64 See 'The Making of the Law on Rights *in rem*: Eight Deliberations in Five Years for the Law on Rights *in rem*', available from: <news.thebeijingnews.com/0923/2007/03-19/018@005230.htm> (last accessed 20 April 2007).

65 'The Legislative Processes of the Chinese Law on Rights *in rem*', available from <npc.people.com.cn/GB.14957/3530674.html> (last accessed 3 January 2006).

66 See 'The Making of the Law on Rights *in rem*', *supra* note 64.

67 See Xinhua News Agency website: <news.xinhuanet.com/legal/2005_09/06/content_3448478.htm> (last accessed 6 September 2006).

68 See 'Prospect of Law in 2006', *People's Daily*, 28 December 2005. The NPC at the time seemed to be rather determined to have it adopted in 2006. Thus, when an official indicated in January 2006 that the adoption might be once again delayed (see Xinhua News Agency: <fc.zj.com/news/gddt/126241.html>), the NPC was quick to emphasise that the deliberation was continuing (see Xinhua News Agency: <news.xinhuanet.com/legal/2006-01/17/content_4063621.htm>).

69 For a summary and analyses of these issues, see Chu Jianyuan, & Shen Weixing (eds), *A Study on the Difficult Issues in the Enactment of a Law on Rights in rem* (Beijing: Qinghua University Press, 2005).

academics), questioning whether the proposed law on rights *in rem* upheld socialism and, hence, whether it violated the Chinese Constitution.[70] This last minute debate then effectively delayed the legislative process for at least a year. While there were merits in some of the technical analyses, the open letters were largely misconceived and misguided, as the 2004 constitutional revision had already elevated the protection of private property, declaring it 'inviolable'. The letters were also at odds with the 2004 revised Constitution, which had for the first time applied the term 'property rights' and cleared the last hurdle to the enactment of a code on rights *in rem*.[71] In this context, it is not unfair to say, as a Chinese scholar has rightly pointed out, that the theoretical foundation of the letters remained that of the 'socialist conception of law' of the former Soviet Union, which had been gradually, but not completely, jettisoned from the Constitution through the revisions of 1988 to 2004.[72] However one sees this political debate, it is clear that because the proposed law touched the issue of ownership rights, it demanded a more thorough politico-economic reform at a constitutional level than had been achieved by the time the law on rights *in rem* was being drafted.[73] As such, the legislative process itself was a process of 'legal thought liberation'.[74] Not surprisingly, the next deliberation did not take place until 10 months later in August 2006, and this was followed by a sixth deliberation in October 2006.[75] After the seventh deliberation in December 2006, the SCNPC finally decided to submit the revised draft to the full session of the NPC in March 2007 for

---

70 Professor Gong Xiantian, a constitutional law scholar based in Beijing University Law School, first published an Open Letter addressed to the Chairman and members of the SCNPC on 12 August 2005. A copy of the letter is available at <www.chinaelections.org/NewsInfo.asp?NewsID=45986> (last accessed 20 June 2007). Knowing that the draft law was to be debated and adopted by a full session of the NPC in March 2007, he published a second Open Letter on 9 December 2006, addressed to all NPC deputies. This second letter was soon supported by more than 700 (mostly retired) scholars and former officials. See 'Beijing University Law Professor: Five Aspects of the Law on Rights *in rem* Violate the Constitution', available at <www.hicourt.gov.cn/news/news_detail.asp?newsid=2006-12-21-9-20-11> (last accessed 20 June 2007). In addition to constitutional issues, the second letter (on personal file) also contained some detailed technical analyses of the provisions that Professor Gong believed needed major revision before adoption. It should be pointed out that his criticism that the proposed law on rights *in rem* might effectively legalise illegally obtained property (such as through corruption) attracted widespread support (see Gong Xiantian First Interview after the Incident of Stopping the Law on Rights *in rem*', available at <news.xinhuanet.com/legal/2006-03/17/content_4312171.htm>, last accessed 23 March 2006), which ultimately led to some changes in the draft (see discussion below).

71 See discussion in Chapter 3.

72 See Sun Xianzhong, 'A Review of the Effects of the Adopted Western Civil Law in China', (no. 3, 2006) *China Legal Science* (*Zhongguo Faxue*) 166, at 169.

73 'How the Law on Rights *in rem* Was Made', *supra* note 58, at 6.

74 'How the Law on Rights *in rem* Was Made', *supra* note 58, at 7.

75 See 'The Making of the Law on Rights *in rem*', *supra* note 64.

deliberation and adoption. The adoption of the Law on Rights *in rem* on 16 March 2007[76] signifies a legislative process that can truly be described as extraordinary and unprecedented in the PRC's history. Without doubt the new Law is one of the most significant legal developments in the history of the PRC, representing a climax in a half century-long attempt at legal modernisation.

4.2. The Law on Rights *in rem*

(1) Structure of the Law

The Law on Rights *in rem* is one of the most comprehensive laws ever enacted in the PRC. It is arranged in five divisions, and comprises 19 chapters and 247 articles in total. Division One on General Provisions contains three chapters, dealing with general principles, the establishment, alteration, transfer and lapse of rights *in rem*, and the protection of rights *in rem* respectively. Division Two on Ownership Rights provides common stipulations on ownership rights, which are followed by provisions on state, collective and private ownership rights, building ownership rights, neighbouring relationships, common ownership, and special regulations on the attainment of ownership rights. Division Three on Usufruct Rights deals with the rights to possess, to use, and to reap benefit from property, and also includes special provisions on land contract rights, construction land use rights, residential land use rights, and servitudes. The next division is on security interests in property, which include mortgage rights, pledges, and lien. The last division is on possession.

While the various published drafts vary significantly in contents, they are surprisingly similar in structure. The initial expert draft prepared by the group led by Liang Huixing contained 435 articles in 12 chapters, and the expert draft by the team led by Wang Liming contained 575 articles in six chapters.[77] Liang's published version (2004) contains 422 articles, and Wang's published version (2005) contains 381 articles. The initial draft of the LAC contained 191 articles in 10 chapters.[78] The official version (July 2005) published for public consultation contains 268 articles in 19 chapters. In terms of structure, the major differences between Liang and Wang lay in whether state, collective and private ownership rights should be stipulated separately and differently, and whether land contract rights and residential land use rights should be singled out for treatment. In comparison, the initial LAC's draft did not provide provisions on security interests in property rights.[79] The final law, as a compromise between Liang's and Wang's drafts, is nevertheless closer to Wang's in

---

76 Adopted with 2799 votes in favour, 52 against, and 37 abstentions. See 'The Making of the Law on Rights *in rem*', *supra* note 64.

77 See Liang Huixing, *supra* note 61, at 185-190.

78 Liang Huixing, *id.*, at 191.

79 Liang Huixing, *id.*, at 185-192.

structure; it is, however, a significantly shortened version in terms of contents when compared to the expert drafts. Most strikingly, if the unique provisions on state, collective and private ownership rights, and on separate treatment of land use rights (i.e. land contract rights, condominiums, and residential land use rights) are taken out, the similarity, in structure and language, between the Chinese Law on Rights *in rem* and the Book on Rights *in rem* in the KMT Civil Code is unmistakeable. In this sense, the Law on Rights *in rem* is indeed a 'socialist' law in a Civil Law tradition.

(2) Definition and Scope of the Rights in rem

The general principles in Chapter One of the Law largely repeat the constitutional provisions on equal protection of all property under different ownership forms and to all market players in China. Importantly, this Chapter also defines 'things' (or property) to include both movable and real property, as well as the 'rights' that have been defined by law as being the 'objects' of rights *in rem*. 'Rights *in rem*' are defined to mean the rights by the right-holder to directly and exclusively control specific 'things' (property); it includes ownership rights, usufruct and security interests in property.[80] On the one hand the reference to 'rights' in the definition of 'things' means that the notion of 'rights *in rem*' covers more than 'rights over things' and opens the door for some contractual rights to be defined as 'rights *in rem*'. On the other hand it may just be a practical compromise to accommodate the inclusion of the land contract rights in the Law, as it has been controversial whether the land contract right is, in its nature, a contractual right or a 'right *in rem*'.[81] Consequently it is difficult to ascertain whether this inclusion is an innovation, or simply an odd compromise in legislation.

(3) Establishment, Alteration, Transfer and Extinguishment of Rights in rem

As in other countries, the establishment, alteration, transfer and extinguishment of rights *in rem* in real property must be registered, unless otherwise provided for by the law, with the exception of natural resources owned by the state.[82] Details on registration certificates will be the *prima facie* evidence of rights over the registered property.[83] Such registration will be uniform throughout the nation, with specific

---

80 See Article 2 of the Law on Rights *in rem*.

81 This clearly was one of the major disagreements between Liang Huixing and Wang Liming. Liang saw land contract rights as contractual rights, whereas Wang believed that land contract rights had now been firmly established as a distinct legal institution of property rights backed by a set of laws and policies and should thus be recognised in property law. See Liang Huixing, *supra* note 61, at 185-194.

82 Article 9 of the Law on Rights *in rem*.

83 Articles 16 & 17 of the Law on Rights *in rem*.

laws and administrative regulations to be issued separately for this purpose;[84] and before the national law and administrative regulations are issued, local authorities may issue local rules to govern registration.[85] The establishment, alteration, transfer and extinguishment of rights *in rem* in real property may also be established by contracts, unless otherwise provided for by law or by other agreements; and the absence of registration of the rights *in rem* will not affect the legal validity of the contracts concerned.[86] The establishment and transfer of rights *in rem* over movables take effect upon the delivery of the movables. However, ships, aircraft and automobiles must be registered in order to defend themselves against claims from a *bona fide* third party.[87] Rights *in rem* may also be established, altered, transferred or extinguished by other legal processes, such as court adjudication, arbitration awards, expropriation by government, inheritance and wills.[88]

(4) Methods of Protection

As in other civil law areas, disputes about rights *in rem* may be resolved through mediation, conciliation, arbitration and litigation and civil law remedies, including the return of the property, repair, remaking, replacement or restoration to the original state of damaged property, and claims for damages. All are available individually or jointly. Additionally, administrative or criminal liabilities may also be imposed if administrative or criminal laws are violated.[89] Article 37 of the Law on Rights *in rem* also refers to 'other civil liabilities' in the case of violation of rights *in rem*. This effectively means that all other remedies and liabilities stipulated in the GPCL will be applicable. Under the GPCL other remedies or liabilities available from a court may include the issuance of a reprimand, the signing of a statement of repentance, re-possession of property, confiscation of property and the imposition of fines.[90]

(5) Ownership Rights

Ownership rights are defined, as in the GPCL, as rights to possess, use, reap benefit from, and dispose of real property and movables,[91] as well as the right to establish usufruct and security interests over the property.[92] Certain real property and movables,

---

84 Article 10 of the Law on Rights *in rem*.

85 Article 246 of the Law on Rights *in rem*.

86 Article 15 of the Law on Rights *in rem*.

87 Articles 23-24 of the Law on Rights *in rem*.

88 Articles 28-31 of the Law on Rights *in rem*.

89 Article 32-38 of the Law on Rights *in rem*.

90 See Article 134 of the GPCL.

91 Article 39 of the Law on Rights *in rem*.

92 Article 40 of the Law on Rights *in rem*.

to be defined by law separately, may only be exclusively owned by the state and no organisation or individual may acquire ownership of them.[93] Expropriation (*zhengshou*) for the public interest of real property, in accordance with legal procedures, is allowed, and compensation will be paid. In case of emergency, movables may also be taken over for use (*zhengyong*) in accordance with the law, but they shall be returned after use and compensation shall be paid (including compensation for damage or loss).[94] While the Law stipulates an obligation for compensation in the case of expropriation or taking over, it does not use the internationally familiar phrases of 'just term' or 'adequate compensation.' Instead, the Law stipulates the need to guarantee the livelihood of peasants in cases of the expropriation of collective land, and to guarantee housing conditions in cases of the expropriation of housing of individuals, in addition to compensation.[95] If these provisions are interpreted strictly to the spirit of the letter, it would not be unreasonable to suggest that the Law does, after all, stipulate an obligation of 'adequate compensation' in a practical sense.

While the Law continues the socialist tradition of distinguishing ownership rights under different forms of ownership, that is, state ownership, collective ownership and private ownership,[96] it does not attempt to provide a different degree of protection of these rights. Property rights may be categorised under different forms of ownership, but they enjoy equal protection under the Law – a point emphasised by Professor Wang Liming as the 'real characteristic of the Chinese Law'.[97] As such, Chapter Five on State, Collective and Private Ownership Rights is in fact about the property scope of ownership rights under different forms of ownership (including defining the scope of property for exclusive state ownership) and, importantly, the methods of exercising state and collective ownership rights.

With the commercialisation of housing in China the need to clearly distinguish joint ownership and private ownership in residential buildings and building blocks has been strongly felt, and there have been increasing incidents of disputes in relation to the use of joint property and facilities, and fee charges for such use. Not surprisingly, Chapter Six on Condominiums (but oddly entitled 'Construction Building Distinction Ownership Rights of Owners'[98]) attracted many responses during the

---

93 Article 41 of the Law on Rights *in rem*.

94 Article 44 of the Law on Rights *in rem*.

95 See Articles 42-44 of the Law on Rights *in rem*.

96 This may be seen as a response to the political controversy caused by the open letters discussed above.

97 According to Professor Wang Liming, '[a]mong laws on rights *in rem* in various countries, China is the first one to provide "equal protection" as a fundamental principle in the Law. This is the real Chinese characteristic'. Quoted in 'A Chinese Kind of Law on Rights *in rem*', (no. 7) 2007 *Democracy and Legal System* (*Minzhu Yu Fazhi*), at 8.

98 This term is apparently adopted from the Japanese Civil Code. See Wang's draft, *supra* note 62, at 201, and Liang's draft, *supra* note 62, at 103.

public consultation. Under Article 70, a unit owner has exclusive ownership rights over the unit he/she owns, and has joint ownership rights and joint management rights with other unit owners in relation to all other parts of the building or building block. Two important conditions are imposed on unit owners in relation to the exercise of the ownership rights or co-ownership and management rights. First, the exercise of ownership rights must not endanger the safety of the building or damage the lawful rights and interests of other unit owners in the building.[99] This restriction is clearly important, considering that it is not uncommon for unit owners to alter their apartment structure without giving much thought to the overall structural safety of the building. Secondly, a unit owner may not escape their obligations towards other parts of the building or block under joint ownership by waiving their rights to these parts of the building or block.[100] This, once again, was designed to deal with the situation where unit owners refuse to pay levies or other fees for maintenance and repair of joint property. All major decisions concerning the property and facilities under joint ownership are to be made by a single or two-third majority of all owners.[101] For this purpose, an Owners Meeting and an Owners Committee may be established.[102]

Restrictions on the use of real property and certain entitlements in the nature of rights to access to adjacent land are codified in Chapter Seven, entitled 'Neighbourhood Relationships'. Here the provisions are generally brief, providing, on the one hand, access rights to adjacent land in defined circumstances such as road access, connection of water, gas, electricity and other facilities and, on the other hand, prohibiting the endangering or damaging of neighbouring property in the exercise or use of real property. Interestingly, Article 85 explicitly recognises the effect of local customs in the absence of law or administrative regulations. This perhaps is the first major Chinese law that gives such explicit recognition to the validity of local practices.

Chapter Eight deals with common ownership, which includes joint ownership and co-ownership by shares over real property and movables.[103] The provisions mainly concern the management and disposal of the property under common ownership. Importantly, the Law respects agreements in relation to the management, liabilities and disposal of property among the co-owners. Thus, the provisions in the Law may be understood as 'gap filling' or 'back up' provisions that are applicable to cases where agreements are unclear or where there is no agreement among co-owners. Also importantly, unless the law provides otherwise or the third party knows that

[99] Article 71 of the Law on Rights *in rem*.

[100] Article 72 of the Law on Rights *in rem*.

[101] Article 76 of the Law on Rights *in rem*.

[102] Article 75 of the Law on Rights *in rem*.

[103] See Article 93 of the Law on Rights *in rem*.

the co-owners do not have a joint and several liability relationship, co-owners are jointly liable to the third party for debts caused by the property under common ownership, although internally among the co-owners such liabilities may be assumed in accordance with a prior agreement or, in the absence of an agreement, by shares in the case of co-ownership by shares.

Provisions on the acquisition of ownership rights are codified in Chapter Nine. These provisions deal with the ownership rights of property that has been disposed of by persons who have rights to disposal, ownership rights over lost property, and ownership rights over naturally derived interests in a property. In general, the interest of the *bona fide* third party is protected in the case of property disposed of by a person without such a right.[104] In the case of lost property (including flowing, buried or hidden property), a person who has found the property has no right to keep it, and the property will belong to the State if the owner is not found.[105] The holder of usufruct rights has the right over naturally derived interests, not the property owner.[106]

(6) Usufruct

Usufruct refers to the right to possess, use and reap benefit from real property and movables that are owned by another person.[107] This right may also be established over natural resources owned by the state or collectives on a user-pay principle, unless otherwise provided by law.[108] While there is little disagreement on the definition and the general principles on usufruct rights among Chinese scholars, there have been (as alluded to above in the discussion of the legislative processes,) major disagreement as to the scope of usufruct rights, and which of these rights need to be singled out for particular treatment. In this part, the Chinese law is unique. In addition to servitudes as commonly found in civil codes, the Law on Rights *in rem* further singles out land contract rights, construction land use rights, and residential land use rights. Each of the additional instances of usufruct is clearly of particular interest to Chinese people as they are the result of reforms toward the establishment of a market economy and the commercialisation of almost everything valuable. As a result this Division Three on Usufruct is perhaps more Chinese than other parts of the law, even though the term 'usufruct' and 'servitudes' are not familiar words to ordinary Chinese people.

104 Article 106 of the Law on Rights *in rem*.

105 Articles 109-113 of the Law on Rights *in rem*.

106 Article 116 of the Law on Rights *in rem*.

107 Article 117 of the Law on Rights *in rem*.

108 Articles 118-119 of the Law on Rights *in rem*.

The term 'land contract rights'[109] is not defined in the Law, but it specifically refers to rural land contracting, a system that has been gradually established in China during the post-Mao reforms, and that culminated in the enactment of the Rural Land Contracting Law of 2002.[110] However, legal protection for this right has not been able to stop land 're-adjustment', i.e. the taking or expropriation by the government for commercial development. Consequently, violence in protest against such land taking has been increasing steadily in the last decade or so, and has attracted wide attention in the west.[111] With the increasing and widening income gap between urban and rural residents[112] and the increasing incidents of violent protests, the Chinese government has recently finally realised that increasing attention must be paid to the so-called 'three rural issues' (*sannong wenti*, peasant, village and agriculture problems). Informing many of the suggested solutions for the provision of security for land contract rights was the belief that such a right should be elevated to the status of a property right; others went even further by suggesting a full privatisation of rural land.[113] Not surprisingly the lawmakers in China favoured the inclusion of land contract rights in the Law on Rights *in rem*. However, there is little new in the Law on Rights *in rem* concerning land contract rights; the Law, for the most part, repeats what had already been codified in the 1986 Land Management Law (as revised in 1988, 1998 and 2004) and the 2002 Rural Land Contracting Law. The real significance lies in the fact that the largely contractual rights have now been

---

109 A more direct translation of the Chinese term (*tudi chengbao jingying quan*) would be 'right to land contract and management'.

110 For a good discussion of the land contract rights, including their historical evolution and the practical reality of modern China, see Zhu Keliang, Roy Prosterman, Ye Jianping, Li Ping, Jeffrey Riedinger & Quyan Yiwen, 'The Rural Land Question in China: Analysis and Recommendations Based on a Seventeen-Province Survey', 2006 (38) *Journal of International Law and Politics* 761.

111 According to the Ministry of Land and Resources, some forty million farmers have lost their land in the last decade, and another 15 million are facing a similar fate in the coming years. According to the Ministry of Public Security, there were some 87,000 protests, riots and other 'mass incidents' relating to land loss in 2005, representing a 6.6% increase from 2004 but a 50% increase from 2003. See 'China Grapples With the Thorny Issue of Rural Land Rights', available at <english.people.com.cn/200609/01/eng2006091_298824.html> (last accessed 2 May 2007). The conflict increased despite the fact that, on 30 April 2004, the State Council had issued an Urgent Notice concerning the Appropriate Settlement of Contemporary Rural Land Contracting Disputes.

112 Income analysis suggests that the current rural-urban income ratio represents the worst urban-rural income gap in the modern history of China. See Zhu, Prosterman, Ye, Li, Riedinger & Quyan, *supra* note 110, at 764.

113 See Cai Jiming and Fang Cao, 'A Comparative Analysis of Different Proposals for Rural Land Reform', originally published in Social Sciences Research, no. 4, 2005, available at <www.usc.cuhk.edu.hk/wk.asp> (last accessed 2 May 2007).

elevated to property rights.[114] Whether this will just be of symbolic significance or will lead to real practical differences will only be tested by time.

Provisions on construction land use rights consolidate and update, in a uniform code, the principles on the acquisition of construction land, registration, change of land use purposes, ownership rights to buildings and facilities on construction land, transfer, mortgages and protection of construction land use rights as originally established in the 1986 Land Management Law (as amended 1988, 1998, & 2004) and its 1998 Implementation Rules, the 1994 Urban Real Estate Law, the 1990 Provisional Regulations of the PRC concerning the Grant and Assignment of the Use Right to State Land in Urban Areas (State Council), and a whole range of other administrative regulations. Some operational rules, such as the required clauses in a construction land use rights contract, are also provided in this Chapter. An important provision is Article 149, which provides that land use rights on residential construction land will be automatically extended upon the expiry of the land use period, as defined in the original land use rights contract. This provision is stipulated to re-assure Chinese residents who have bought commercial apartments, and to provide some certainty upon the expiry of 70 years of land use rights. However, the Law is silent on whether such automatic extensions will be free of charge or upon payment of a new use fee. Thus it is not a complete assurance, nor does it lead to absolute certainty.

Residential land in rural China has always been different from urban construction land. Put simply, housing land in the countryside has always been allocated to rural residents free of charge. These rural residents, however, only enjoy a right to occupancy and use; they do not have ownership rights. Chapter 13 on Residential Land Use Rights, which contains only four short articles, does not break any new ground. In fact, Article 153 specifically provides that the acquisition, exercise and transfer of housing land use rights are subject to land management laws and other state regulations.

Chapter 14 on Servitudes is new and provides the typical Civil law type of property rights that are similar to, but not entirely identical with, easement in Common law. Interestingly, despite the fact that the term 'servitudes' is largely unfamiliar to Chinese people without formal legal training,[115] the Law does not provide a definition of servitudes. Instead Article 156 provides that a servitude right holder is entitled to, in accordance with contractual agreements, the use of the real estate belonging to another person so as to improve the interests and efficiency of his/her own real estate. Servitudes may only be established by written contracts, and the

---

114 Article 127 of the Law on Rights *in rem* specifically provides that land contract rights are established when the contracts on land contracting take effect.

115 For this reason Liang's draft decided not to use the term at all; instead, it used the term 'use right to adjacent land', which catches the essence of servitudes. See Liang's draft, *supra* note 62, at 275.

Law stipulates the essential contractual clauses required for a servitude contract.[116] It is discretionary for the contractual parties to decide whether they want to have the contract registered. However, in the absence of such a registration, a servitude contract may not be a defence against a claim by a *bona fide* third party.[117] While a servitude may be established as an independent usufruct, it goes with the land use rights holders, including land contract rights holders, construction land use rights holders, and residential land use rights holders.[118] It may not be used independently for a mortgage, nor transferred independently by other usufruct rights unless the contract states otherwise.[119] Clearly, 'servitudes' under the Law on Rights *in rem* refers only to praedial servitudes (rights over land); it does not refer to personal servitudes, despite the fact that it is arranged under Division Three on Usufruct.

(7) Security Interests

As a matter of general civil law principle, contractual arrangements only give rise to contractual obligations in a Civil law system. However, certain exceptions have always been allowed, whereby such arrangements will create interests in property (rights *in rem*).[120] Typical examples of such exceptional instances include mortgages, pledges and lien. In the PRC, security interests were first codified in the Law of the PRC on Security Interests in 1995. The 1995 Law lays down general principles on security interests (and the contracts that create security interests in property), followed by specific provisions on guarantee, mortgage, pledges, lien and deposits as security in civil transactions such as sales, loans, transportation and contracting for process and assembly. These provisions have now been consolidated, revised, and expanded to form Division Four on Security Interests in the Law on Rights *in rem*. In this way these security interests are reconfirmed as a form of property rights. The principal purpose of the Law on Rights *in rem* is therefore to define the nature of these interests in an unambiguous manner. It is also important to note that under Article 178 of the Law on Rights *in rem*, when provisions in the 1995 Security Interests Law and the Law on Rights *in rem* are inconsistent, the provisions in the latter prevail.

Division Four starts with some general provisions that are applicable to all forms of security interests. The re-codification could be said as to have an almost 'scientific' arrangement in that they are consolidated into a single coherent section. This is in contrast to the 1995 Security Interests Law, which placed them under the

116 Articles 156-157 of the Law on Rights *in rem*.

117 Article 158 of the Law on Rights *in rem*.

118 Articles 162-163 of the Law on Rights *in rem*.

119 Articles 164-165 of the Law on Rights *in rem*.

120 See Andrew Borkowski, *Textbook on Roman Law* (London: Blackstone Press Limited, 1994), at 170.

different sections of each kind of security interest. Essentially, security interests are to be established by contracts and, unless otherwise prohibited by law, freedom of contract is allowed and upheld.[121] A contract establishing security interests is defined as a collateral contract to a main contract and, as such, if the main contract is held to be invalid, the collateral contract will also be rendered ineffective – unless otherwise provided by law.[122] An important point to note is that under Article 173 the scope of security includes the principal debts and interest thereon, penalties for contractual breach, damages, costs for property maintenance and safekeeping, and costs to realise the value of the security interests, unless the scope of security is otherwise stipulated by the contract creating the security interests.

In contrast to the 1995 Security Interests Law, the Law on Rights *in rem* only singles out three kinds of security interests for specific treatment: mortgage, pledges and lien. As a result the 1995 Security Interests Law continues to be applicable to guarantees and deposits, but the general principles of the Law on Rights *in rem* apply to cases in which there is an inconsistency between the legal stipulations of the two laws. The provisions on these three kinds of security interests are not significantly different between the two laws.

The Law on Rights *in rem* does not provide a definition of mortgage; instead it states that, for the purpose of securing the performance of obligations, if a debtor or a third party, without transferring possession, designates property as security against the claims of a creditor, and the debtor fails to perform his/her obligations, or where the prior agreed circumstances for the realisation of the mortgage value occur, the creditor is entitled to a priority right of compensation.[123] This is not dissimilar in substance to the provisions in Article 33 of the 1995 Security Interests Law, which provides a definition of mortgage. The major improvements in relation to mortgage lie in the more detailed provisions regarding the waiver of priority rights for compensation,[124] methods and timing for the valuation of mortgaged property,[125] and the maximum claim that can be made on mortgages.[126]

Similarly, the Law on Rights *in rem* contains no definition of pledges. However, Article 208 stipulates the consequences in incidents regarding pledged property if the debtor fails to perform his/her contractual obligations for the realisation of the value of the pledged property. In substance, it is similar to the provisions of Article 63 of the 1995 Security Interests Law, which provides a definition of pledge. The approach to lien in the Law on Rights *in rem* is the same; that is, while it does not

---

121 See Chapter 15 of the Law on Rights *in rem*.

122 Article 172 of the Law on Rights *in rem*.

123 Article 179 of the Law on Rights *in rem*.

124 Article 194 of the Law on Rights *in rem*.

125 Articles 195-196 of the Law on Rights *in rem*.

126 Articles 202-207 of the Law on Rights *in rem*.

provide a definition of lien, Article 230 outlines the legal consequences of failing to perform mature obligations, consequences that are in line with the provisions of Article 82 of the 1995 Security Interests Law. An important addition to the provisions on lien, however, is Article 239, which provides that if a mortgage or pledge has been established over a movable, and the movable is 'liened', the lien holder has a priority right for compensation.

As in the 1995 Law, Articles 179, 208 and 230 suggest that any property (real or movable) may be used as a mortgage, but pledges and liens are only established over movables.

(8) Possession

Division Five on Possession is surprisingly short, consisting of only five short articles.[127] It does not even stipulate what constitutes a possession. The use of the word 'possession' instead of 'possession right' may imply that it refers to a factual situation rather than a legal entitlement, thus distinguishing it from the instance of possession as a part of ownership rights.[128]

This Division starts with Article 241, which provides that, in relation to possession arising out of a contract, the use, right to reap benefit from, liability for contractual breach shall be regulated by the contract; disputes in which the contract is missing or where contractual provisions are unclear are to be dealt with by relevant laws. However, it is entirely unclear where the relevant laws are located, as the Law on Rights *in rem* is the principal law governing possession and other property rights. The other four articles mainly deal with the right to demand the return of the possessed property, to claim for damages, and to request the clearance of an obstacle to possession. Presumably, these provisions deal with unlawful possession. In relation to the right to request the return of an unlawfully possessed property, there is a short one-year statutory limitation on the exercise of this right.[129]

5. Concluding Remarks

With the adoption of the Law on Rights *in rem* one may say that Chinese property law, after a long detour along the socialist road, has finally come of age. However, from the above outline, it is clear that while the Law is comprehensive in coverage it is thin in substance. In large part (i.e. construction land use, contract land use,

---

127 Wang's draft contains 19 articles on possession and Liang's draft 16 articles. Thus, the Law on Rights *in rem* has ignored most of the expert draft provisions. The reason for this rejection is entirely unclear, as possession is largely a technical issue involving little ideological debate.

128 In contrast, Article 940 of KMT Civil Code clearly defines 'possession' as a factual situation.

129 Article 245 of the Law on Rights *in rem*.

security interests, possession, and so on), it breaks little new ground. In many parts, the Law simply consolidates and updates the provisions of other laws. While it includes those in which consensus had been reached,[130] it also leaves many other provisions out, and in this regard it is clearly a compromise resulting from the amalgam of different schools of thought. As such it urgently needs supplementary laws and the revision of other laws, to ensure consistency in the legal system on rights *in rem*.[131] Much more importantly, the GPCL needs to be revised and updated to jettison the last remnants of Soviet jurisprudence from the law.

Despite certain shortcomings, the Law now lays down an outline and a structure of legal principles governing property rights (especially in the general notion of usufruct), allowing further development to occur. Most importantly, the Law now firmly and comprehensively establishes the notion of 'property rights' in the Chinese legal system. This, in a nominally socialist country, represents no less than a revolution in legal thought and legal development.

---

130 As pointed out by Professor Wang Liming, himself heavily involved in the drafting process, at least three major issues were left unaddressed: the definition of 'public interest', the litigation status of the property management committee, and the transferability of rural residential land. See 'Dean Wang Explains Details of the Law on Rights *in rem* in Guangzhou', available at <www.civillaw.com.cn/Article/default.asp?id=32003> (last accessed 23 June 2007).

131 Indeed, in a seminar given to the Legislative Affairs Office of the State Council after the adoption of the Law on Rights *in rem*, Professor Wang listed the following laws that needed urgent enactment or revision: new laws on the management of state assets, expropriation or taking of property, and real property registration, and revisions to the Law on Property Management, Land Management Law, and the Urban Real Estate Law. See Wang Liming, 'The Implementation of the Law on Rights *in rem* and the Improvement of its Supplementary Laws', available at <www.civillaw.com.cn/article/default.asp?id=33490> (last accessed 23 June 2007)

Chapter Eleven

Civil Law: Family

1. Introduction

Family is seen in many countries as a basic unit of society, and China is not the only country that frequently resorts to 'family values' as a cure-all solution to many perceived or real 'social problems'. Even in the more individualistic societies, such as the UK, US and Australia, conservative politicians have never been hesitant to resort to 'family values' as election campaign slogans. However, China is perhaps one of the few countries to have continuously been a particularly family-oriented society throughout its history.[1] Indeed, as discussed in Chapter One, the concept of family has been one of the fundamental concepts in Confucianism, and the state has generally only been regarded as an extension of the family. In this tradition individuals were nothing more than members of a family or a social group. The traditional Chinese family system was also a hierarchical system. Members were differentiated according to criteria of generation, age, degree of relationship and sex, with one's status determining one's different rights, obligations and duties.

As revolutionary forces, both the Kuomintang (KMT) and the Communist Party of China (CPC) saw the traditional family as a basically feudal social cell which had to be transformed completely. Thus, despite ideological differences, both the KMT and the CPC made great efforts, through state law and Party poli-

---

[1] This was partly sanctioned by state law. Among the ten most serious criminal offences (the 'Ten Offences', *Si-e*) in traditional China, the majority related to the family. The 'Ten Offences' were: 1. Rebellion (*moufan*); 2. Treason against the sovereign (*moudani*); 3. Betrayal to the enemy (*moupan*); 4. Perverse offences against parents and other seniors (*e-ni*) (to beat or to murder one's grandparents or parents, to murder one's paternal uncles or their wives, father's sisters, elder brothers and sisters, mother's parents, husband, or husband's grandparents or parents); 5. Massacre (*budao*) (to murder three or more persons in one family, to dismember someone for the purpose of black magic); 6. Disrespect to the emperor (*dabujing*); 7. Filial impiety (*buxiao*); 8. Discord in families (*bumu*) (to murder or to sell a fourth degree relative, etc.); 9. Unrighteousness (*buyi*) (the murder of the local official by the people, the murder of a superior official by subordinates, to murder one's teacher, not to wear mourning for one's husband, etc.); 10. Incest (*neiluan*). See Tung-tsu Ch'ü, *Law and Society in Traditional China* (Paris: Mouton & Co, 1961), at 179.

cies, to modernise the family structure and institutions. The transformation of the Chinese family structure and institutions may well be seen as a typical example of the transplantation of western laws, legal institutions, and legal ideologies into modern Chinese history.

This transformation has not been without resistance and social conflict, nor is the transformation completed. If one considers the present social reality it can be seen that the traditional structure and practice have only been partly broken down and never completely destroyed. Indeed, the recent 'revival' of prostitution, of 'keeping a concubine' (*bao ernai*),[2] of mercenary marriage, of the use of go-betweens and of dowries are all blamed on the revival of feudalist practices. In politics, Chinese leaders have blamed traditional patriarchal practices for the main malpractices found at both the leadership and cadre level, in both the Party system and the government organs.[3] On the other hand, facing the reality of a severely underdeveloped social welfare system, especially for the elderly and children, and of a crisis of values among the young generation as a result of the collapse of the idealistic communist value system, and influenced by the half-understood 'western values', the Chinese leadership has not hesitated to resort to a call for 'traditional values' and 'the rule of virtue'.[4] Thus tradition and modernity often collide.

This Chapter first outlines the traditional family structure and institutions. This is followed by an introduction to modern reforms in these structures and institutions. Thirdly, the present legal framework for family matters is analysed, and through this several fundamental, and sometimes controversial, family law issues are examined, namely freedom of marriage and divorce, the legal treatment of extra-marital affairs, matrimonial property, and domestic violence.

2. An Overview of the Traditional Family and Society

Although the traditional 'ideal family' did exist,[5] consisting of some four to five generations living together as one unit, it was actually rare among ordinary people

---

2 See the discussion in Section 5.3 below.

3 Wang Yubo, *The Patriarchal System in History* (*Lishishang de Jiazhangzhi*) (Beijing: People's Press, 1984), at 3.

4 Indeed, a sort of 'rule by virtue' was incorporated into the Constitution in its 2004 revision. See Jianfu Chen, 'A Great Leap forward or a Symbolic gesture? – The Revision of the Constitution in the PRC', (no. 53, May – June 2004) *China Perspective* 15, at 19.

5 What will be described below are the traditional family structures of the Han Chinese. Although certain features were shared with the practices of minority nationalities in China, marriage and family among the minorities differed significantly, and still differ, from one nationality to another. For family issues among minority nationalities in China, see Colin Mackerras, *China's Minority Cultures: Identities and Integration Since 1912* (New York: St. Martin's Press/ Longman, 1993), esp. chapters 4 & 8. It must also be pointed out that the traditional Chinese

because of practical problems, such as housing, family quarrels and family property disputes.[6] Among the majority of Chinese people the traditional family consisted of five to ten persons living together and sharing their income and property,[7] with the family-head (*jiazhang*) at the centre (usually the father of the family except in the cases where the grandfather or elder brother was head).

The domestic relationship in the family is well described by Baker with the formula: Generation-Age-Sex.[8] Under this system, if it is assumed that the family was only composed of two generations, the father, usually the head of the family, had paternal authority over his children, while children had the duty to practice filial behaviour and to support their parents in old age; the elder brother had some prestige and certain rights to be respected by the junior; and the husband exercised authority over his wife, with the wife's correlative duties being of obedience and faithfulness. Further, age superiority might be overruled by sex: for instance, a younger brother usually had a higher status than his older sister in the family, especially if he was an only son.[9] This kind of relationship is believed to have existed for over five thousand years, with a quite comprehensive patrilineal and patriarchal system existing since the Han Dynasty (206 BC – AD 220).[10]

The family-head had absolute authority and discretion. This kind of power was not only confirmed by the rules of propriety (*li*), which were the major norms regulating domestic relationships, but was also protected by state and customary laws. These rules provided him with arbitrary power over family property and with superior authority over women and children. They provided strict guidelines for family behaviour, as well as for the absolute power of the head in making decisions concerning all aspects of family matters, including the marriage of his children. In an important Confucian classic, the *Li Ji*, there were very detailed rules concerning what each family member should do and what they could not do, from getting up in the morning to going to bed at night. Instructions about posture in walking and

---

family structure was both rigid and flexible: it was rigid in terms of fundamental principles and it was flexible in that its organisational structures varied significantly in different places and at different times. What are briefly described below are the more rigid principles.

6 See M.J. Meijer, *Marriage Law and Policy in the Chinese People's Republic* (Hong Kong: Hong Kong University Press, 1971), at 9. It needs to be pointed out, however, there has always been disagreement among Sinological anthropologists whether the large and complex family in traditional China was simply a myth or actually existed at different time in different places. See Arthur P. Wolf, 'Chinese Family Size: A Myth Revitalised', in Hsieh Jih-chang & Chuang Ying-change (eds), *The Chinese Family and Its Ritual Behaviour* (Taipei: Institute of Ethnology, Academia Sinica, 1985, second printing 1992), at 30-49.

7 *Ibid.*, at 1.

8 Hugh D.R. Baker, *Chinese Family and Kinship* (London and Basingstoke: the Macmillan Press Ltd., 1979), at 15

9 Baker, *id.*, at 15-25. See also Meijier, *supra* note 6, at 6-19.

10 See Wang Yubo, *supra* note 3, at 4 & 21.

gestures in speaking as well as sitting before the head were provided, not to mention the family members' speech. All together, the family-head represented the family to the outside world, controlled the property of the family and attended to the needs of the household, punishing members who violated family and clan norms. Moreover, his ideas and will became the family's, and no one could breach them or argue with him, as the 'family-head could never be wrong'.[11]

Family property, which included the land and the house as well as the goods of the household, was also under the absolute control of the head: all earnings of family members had to be handed to him, no one was allowed to have private property except he.[12] Even members who settled somewhere else, or were temporarily absent as seasonal workers, sent their surplus earnings home and their property was regarded as family property. Until there was a division of the family (*fenjia*), the property could only be disposed of by the family-head. When a division was effected, property was divided into equal parts for each son, with a part of the property set aside for maintenance of the parents and another part for daughters' dowries.[13]

A discussion of the patrilineal and patriarchal domestic system would not be complete without mentioning the lineage (*zong*) and clan (*zu*) system. The Chinese lineage was defined as consisting of a 'group of males all descended from one common ancestor, all living together in one settlement, owning some property in common, and all nominally under the leadership of the man most senior in generation and age. Together with these males there were, of course, their wives and unmarried daughters.'[14] The clan was an artificial kin group, consisting of 'a deliberate amalgamation into one loose federation of a number of lineages, all of which bore the same surname.'[15] The lineage and clan systems were formed largely to avoid the division of property and thus to form a strong economic force for self-protection, and also to raise the bargaining power of the lineage against the rest of society at large, and against the government in particular.[16]

The lineages and clans were largely regulated by their own customs and rules of propriety concerning all aspects of domestic life. The head of the lineage and the clan had the power to interfere in the life of families in his lineage and clan. From

---

11 Wang Yubo, *supra* note 3, at 42-60; Baker, *supra* note 8, at 15-25. See also Meijier, *supra* note 6, at 6-19

12 Wang Yubo, *supra* note 3, at 44.

13 Meijer, *supra* note 6, at 5-12.

14 Baker, *supra* note 8, at 49.

15 Baker, *supra* note 8, at 68.

16 For detailed discussion on lineage and the clan system, see Baker, *supra* note 8, 49-70; and Wang Yubo, *supra* note 3, 61-79. On the other hand governments constantly kept them in check, as common sense dictated that any uncontrolled growth of lineage and clan would threaten the governments as well. See Maurice Freedman, 'The Family in China, Past and Present', (1961–1962) 34 (4) *Pacific Affairs* 323, at 325.

a legal viewpoint governments in the past saw civil matters, such as the sale of a house, irrigation, etc., as matters that should be handled by the people themselves and actually left the lineages and clans to deal with. A large number of criminal matters were also settled within the clan system, although they had to be brought to the attention of 'magistrates'.[17]

In summary, and in a somewhat simplistic way, we may describe the traditional Chinese society as being basically composed of families instead of individuals, and organised in a hierarchical and paternalistic order. The family unit was part of a higher level organisation, the lineage and clan, in which kinship was the closest link. The concept of the family and its structure were further extended into the state, with the emperor as the head of the 'big family'. These three kinds of hierarchical systems were similar and were mostly regulated by the rules of propriety.

3. Historical Development of Family Law in Modern China

3.1. The Pre-1949 Modernisation of Family Law

As discussed in Chapter One, the structures and the values of traditional China were under stress at the turn of the 20th century,[18] and under attack by reform-minded scholars.[19] Modern legal reforms were both a response to the prevailing social changes and were designed to undermine the foundations of the traditional society. Although conservative forces opposed virtually every aspect of the initial legal reforms, the fiercest opposition was towards such fundamental reforms as in family law, which were seen as challenging traditional institutions and structures, ignoring the traditional values as embodied in Confucian *li*, and undermining the social foundations of centuries-old social morality and customs.[20] To the opponents, legal reforms were inevitable, but they had to be built upon Confucian doctrines

---

17 Meijer, *supra* note 6, at 20-21.

18 In terms of family law reform, the May 4th Movement of 1919 drew a line between traditional and modern China, and in this movement 'the conflict between individual freedom and nationalism with the traditional notions governing the family became of great importance.' See Meijer, *supra* note 6, at 23.

19 Starting from the social reform movement towards the end of the 19th century, family law and, especially, women's position in the 'feudal' families were under severe attack by the reformists who saw the 'basic cells' of the society as representing the very essence of the corrupt feudal system that must be removed. See Zhang Minjie, 'The Study on Chinese Marriage and Family Issues – a review of a century', first published in (no. 3, 2001) *Studies in Social Sciences* (*Shehui Kexue Yanjie*), available from <www.usc.cuhk.edu.hk/wk_wzdetails.asp?id=1571>.

20 See M.J. Meijer, *The Introduction of Modern Criminal Law in China*, 2nd edition (Hong Kong: Lung Men Bookstore, 1967), chs 2 & 5; Guo Chengwei, 'Legal Thought of Shen Jiaben and the Controversies during the Qing Legal Reform', in China University of Political Science and

of virtue, loyalty and filial piety.[21] Despite various concessions being made by the Qing era Law Reform Commissioner, Shen Jiaben, in proceeding to legal reform, the initial reform did not achieve much in the area of family law.

Despite fundamental conflict and differences in ideologies, the KMT and CPC shared the revolutionary ideology that social and political reform must start from the transformation of the 'basic cells' of the society, that is, the family and its structure. The KMT social and political programs included the reform of the Chinese family and inheritance system, which was seen as being feudal and backward, and these programs first contributed substantially to the introduction of a modern family and succession law to China. On the CPC side, Chen Duxiu, Li Dachao and Mao Zedong, all founding members of the CPC, were among the most critical writers attacking the 'feudal' family system, especially marriage, divorce and women's status, in family and society.[22] It is therefore not surprising that a Resolution on Women's Work was adopted at the Second National Congress of the CPC in July 1922. In this Resolution, the political goals that were set were to secure all political rights and freedoms, to protect the interests of working women and children and to eliminate all constraints imposed by all the old rituals and customs.[23] In the draft Constitution of the CPC, dated June 1923, it was declared that 'men and women shall be equal in all public and private law.'[24] On the side of the KMT, and as early as 1921, it was considered that the task of reform was to 'superimpose on the primitive notion of the unity of the clan or the family that of the unity of the nation, composed of the whole body of these families and these clans.'[25] Thus such issues as freedom of marriage, common property during marriage, and the equal right of male and female heirs to share inheritance were all first addressed by the KMT political programs and policies, and later incorporated into Books IV (Family) and V (Succession) of the Civil Code.[26] In terms of legislation it can therefore be said that the traditional family system was formally broken down by the KMT government, while the communist

---

Law, *A Study on the Legal Thought of Shen Jiaben* (*Shen Jiaben Falu Sixiang Yanjiu*) (Beijing: Publishing House of Law, 1990), at 103-121.

21 Meijer (1967), *id*., at 44.

22 See Zhang Minjie, *supra* note 19.

23 See Resolution on Women's Work, adopted by the Second National Congress of the CPC, July 1922, available from the website of the All China Federation of Women <www.women.org.cn>.

24 Draft Constitution of the Communist Party of China, June 1923, available from the website of the All China Women's Federation: <www.women.org.cn>.

25 Introduction to the French translation (of the Civil Code), vol. II, cited in Jean Escarra, *Chinese Law: Conception and Evolution, Legislative and Judicial Institutions, Science and Teaching* (translated from a 1936 French edition by Gertrude R Browne, Seattle: University of Washington, 1961), at 256.

26 See discussions in Chapter 1 on KMT legal reforms.

revolution in this area amounted to a continuation rather than a renewal of the process of modernisation.

While the KMT ideologies were largely based on 'bourgeois' ideas of individualism and liberty, the CPC relied on another Western source, Marxism. Marxist theory sees the family system as one of the social superstructures which are dependent on the economic basis. In this ideological framework, the task of Communist legislation was seen to be the transformation of the society from feudalism to socialism. To fulfil this 'historical' task, land reform, which aimed at a revolution of the economic basis, and family reform, which was to change the basic social cell, became the primary and parallel agendas both in policy-making and legislation.[27] Indeed, in the CPC's first comprehensive policy statement in relation to the liberation of women, the goals that were set were to achieve equal rights for women in land reform, in political rights and freedom and in freedom of marriage, as well as to provide special protection for the working conditions for mothers of infants.[28] Thus the first communist constitutional document, the Provisional Constitution of 1931, declared that: '[T]he purpose of the Soviet Government is to guarantee the fundamental liberation of women. Freedom of marriage is recognised, and measures for the protection of women will provide the material basis to enable them to cast off the bonds of the family by gradual stages, and to participate in economic, political, and cultural life.'[29] Together with the Provisional Constitution there were draft regulations on land reform, labour protection and marriage. Specifically on family matters, the Marriage Regulations of the Soviet Republic were issued on 1 December 1931.[30]

The Regulations, consisting of 7 chapters and 23 articles in total, established the principles of freedom of marriage (Article 1) and complete freedom of divorce (Article 9); prohibited polygamy (Article 2) including concubinage, the practice of foster-daughter-in-law (*tongyangxi*) as well as bigamy by men; and abolished marriage gifts in any form, including dowries (Article 8). They also defined the marriageable age (20 for men and 18 for women (Article 3)); required marriage to

27 It is not surprising, therefore, that both in the Soviet Union and in China the first statutes enacted in the 'private' law sphere were family laws. See W. Müller-Freienfels, 'Soviet Family Law and Comparative Chinese Development', in David C. Buxbaum (ed.), *Chinese Family Law and Social Change in Historical and Comparative Perspective* (Seattle and London: University of Washington Press, 1978), at 325.

28 Outline of the Central Committee of the CPC on the Struggle for Working Women, 8 November 1930. Document on personal file, also available from the website of the All China Women's Federation: <www.women.org.cn>. It should be noted that many *ad hoc* policy statements had already been issued by the CPC well before 1930. See the website of the All China Federation of Women.

29 Article 11. For an English translation, see Meijer, *supra* note 6, at 41. See also Yang Dawei (ed.), *A Textbook of Marriage Law* (*Hunyinfa Jiaocheng*), revised edition (Beijing: Law Publishing House, 1985), at 63.

30 For an English translation of the Regulations, see Meijer, *supra* note 6, at 281.

be registered (Article 8); and imposed a duty on the husband to raise the children after divorce (Article 11), equal sharing among the spouse and the children any property accumulated during marriage (Article 17), the obligation to pay common debts during marriage (Article 18), and an obligation to support the woman until she remarried (Article 20). The positions of illegitimate and legitimate children were also equalised (Article 21), and any violation of the Marriage Regulations were to be punished by criminal laws (Article 22).

There are few materials to show how the Regulations were applied, how people reacted to them and how strictly they were enforced. However, according to a government document, all aspects in relation to marriage, land reform and distribution, labour protection, and property rights (especially for divorced women) met strong resistance and difficulties in implementation.[31] Not surprisingly, a need for revision was therefore felt,[32] and so the Marriage Law of the Chinese Soviet Republic was promulgated on 8 April 1934,[33] repealing the 1931 Regulations.

Although the Law did not greatly differ from the Regulations, some changes were made. First of all the express recognition of *de facto* marriage in Article 9 was a really striking addition to the Regulations. The recognition of 'cohabiting' marriage has lasted until today, though with various problems, and makes the registration of marriage only the official evidence of the existence of a marriage. Secondly, the Law prohibited not only bigamy of men but also of women (Article 2). Thirdly, the husband's obligation to support his ex-wife was limited to cases where the woman lacked 'the capacity to perform work or had no definite occupation', and the duty was removed if the man lacked 'the capacity to do manual work or did not have a definite occupation' (Article 15). Finally, there was an important addition concerning the divorce of wives of army personnel (Article 11). These women could only divorce their husbands when consent was obtained from their husbands, or after a period of non-communication. Similar provisions are to be found in China today.[34]

Basically, these two laws were general principles relating to marriage. Their documents were brief, and the words and phrases applied in them were often political. No clear definitions could be found in either document. None of the articles was concerned with the situation during marriage, such as the relationship between spouses. This legislative style reflected more the political attitude of the

---

31 See Order No. 6 of the Provisional Central Government concerning the Organisation and Work on the Protection of Women and the Establishment of the Committee on Improving the Life of Women, 20 June 1932. Document on personal file, also available from the website of the All China Women's Federation: <www.women.org.cn>.

32 Meijer, *supra* note 6, at 42.

33 For an English Translation, see Meijer, *supra* note 6, at 281.

34 In fact, these were already provided by Article 18 of the Regulations on the Preferential Treatment for the Workers and Peasants Red Amy, November 1931.

party towards the family as a social institution, rather than the intention to regulate private matters in any detailed form.

New legislation was introduced after the 1934 Law, during the period of the United Front against the Japanese invasion. In this period the CPC occupied several border areas, which became autonomous regions after the truce with the KMT in 1937. As a result, legislation in various border areas mirrored those in the Civil Code of the Republic of China.[35] A new set of regulations, the Interim Regulations of Shan-Ji-Lu-Xiang Border Area on Penalising Offences Against Marriage, was also enacted 'in accordance with the principle of the criminal law of the Republic of China on offences against marriage.'[36] It was during this period, and through the incorporation of KMT legislation, that situations arising during marriage were dealt with for the first time in Communist legislation, leading to a totally new and genuine change in the legal treatment of the family.

3.2. The 1950 Marriage Law

After the founding of the People's Republic of China, among the first pieces of legislation on 'private matters' was the 1950 Marriage Law. According to the Report to the Central People's Government delivered by the then Chairman of the Legal Committee,[37] Chen Shaoyu,[38] the drafting work started in the winter of 1948 and lasted for one and a half years, and most of the articles were revised more than 20 times, and even up to 40 times. Others who participated in the drafting work or gave instructions were the Judicial Committee of the Party, the Democratic Women's Association, judicial organs and administrative authorities, as well as Mao Zedong

---

35 Indeed, Article 1 of the Marriage Regulations of Jinchaji (Chin-Ch'a-Chi) Border Area (1941) expressly stated that: 'These Regulations are enacted in accordance with the legislative spirit of the Book of the Family of the Civil Code of the Republic of China and are adapted to the circumstances prevailing in the Border area.' This provision remained in the re-promulgated Marriage Regulations of Jinchaji (Chin-Ch'a-Chi) Border Area of 1943. Earlier, the Marriage Regulations of Shan-Gang-Ning Border Area (1939) contained many provisions which were clearly adapted from the Civil Code. All these documents are available from the website of the All China Federation of Women <www.women.org.cn>. English translations of the 1939 and 1943 Regulations can be found in Meijer, *supra* note 6, Appendixes III and V. For further discussions, see also Müller-Freienfels, *supra* note 27, at 352.

36 Article 1 of the Interim Regulations of Shan-Ji-Lu-Xiang Border Area on Penalising Offences Against Marriage, 5 January 1943. Document on personal file, but also available from the website of the All China Women's Federation: <www.women.org.cn>.

37 A Report on the Drafting and Reasons for Drafting of the Marriage Law of the PRC, in *Teaching Reference Materials on Marriage Law* (*Hunyinfa Jiaoxue Cankao Ziliao*), edited and published by the Northwest Institute of Political Science and Law (1982), at 66-113.

38 His real name was Wang Ming. He was one of the founding members and early leaders of the Communist Party of China.

and other important members in the government.[39] Marriage laws in socialist countries as well as the theory of Marxism on marriage and domestic relationships were consulted and studied. In addition, old collections of case laws and customs and the KMT Civil Code were critically studied as references. All in all, the Law was claimed to be the 'result of mass participation in drafting work.'[40]

The Law consisted of eight chapters and 27 articles in total.[41] Although the term 'Marriage Law' was still applied, it was effectively a family law in its contents. In addition to those items which had existed in the previous legislation in the 1930s, there were certain important developments. First, in Article 1, the basic elements of a conjugal family, i.e. man, woman and children, appeared together. This was the first time that this kind of law seemed to preserve a conjugal family, rather than just to regulate the contracting and dissolution of marriage. Secondly, also for the first time, a chapter (Chapter Three) on the rights and duties of the husband and wife appeared. It is also interesting to note that this chapter provided that: 'Husband and wife are in duty bound to love, respect, assist, and support each other, to form a harmonious union, to perform labour and be productive, to raise children and to struggle for the happiness of the family and the building of the new society.'[42] This is a mixture of moral and revolutionary duties presented in a legal form. Finally, Chapter Four on the relationship between parents and children was a new creation. Also, Article 13 for the first time touched on the relationship between parents and adopted children in marriage law. These provisions, and, indeed the whole law, again indicated the recognition of the family, although it still needed to be transformed. Despite the continuing ideological emphasis, the 1950 Law was closer to the KMT legislation in its contents, scope and methods than the early communist legislation in the 1930s.

---

39 Recent research indicates that the drafting work was entrusted to a drafting group within the Women's Committee of the CPC's Central Committee. The drafting group was led by Deng Yingchao (wife of Zhou Enlai) and was composed of six members. Among these only one member had prior legal education. See Huang Chuaghui, *Marriage under Heaven: A History of the Three Marriage Laws in the PRC* (*Tianxia Hunyin: Gongheguo Sanbu Hunyinfa Jishi*) (Shanghai: Wenhui Press, 2004), at 39.

40 *Ibid.*, at 66-68. These contrast sharply with comments by some scholars in the West. For instance, Chiu commented that 'there is nothing new in these laws. They are either inhibitory of things that are legally non-existent in China, or declaratory of heretofore existing laws, or else they are imported from Russia. Besides, in these laws public duties are confused with private duties, morality with law and criminal matters with civil matters. Furthermore, the Articles are in conflict with one another and the whole thing displays an ignorance of the technique of legislations.' See Vermier Y. Chiu, *Marriage Law and Customs of China* (Hong Kong: the Chinese University of Hong Kong, 1966), at 191.

41 For an English translation of the Law, see, Meijer, *supra* note 6, at 300.

42 Article 8 of the 1950 Marriage Law.

The 1950 Law remained effective in theory until a new marriage law was issued in 1980. However, most literature remained silent on how the law was applied, except for the mention of mass participation in enforcing the law during 1950–1953.[43] It was said that millions of cadres and activists were trained during this mass movement, with 70% of the mainland area being reached by propaganda concerning the Law, and thousands of villages being used as models to enforce the law.[44] Like all other legislation, the 1950 Marriage Law was largely ignored in the 1960s and 1970s, as the Party and indeed the whole nation was preoccupied with seemingly more important political issues than enforcing laws and regulations.

3.3. The 1980 Marriage Law and Its Recent Reform

(1) The 1980 Marriage Law

The 1980 Marriage Law, based on a revision of the 1950 Marriage Law,[45] was an extremely brief piece of legislation, consisting of 5 chapters and 37 articles. It was, however, significantly different from the previous one. The purpose of the law was to consolidate and develop socialist marriage and family relationships, as well as to facilitate the realisation of the 'Four Modernisations' by providing social stability

---

43 Government documents issued during this period of time also indicated tremendous difficulties in and resistance to the implementation of the new marriage law. See Notice of the Central Committee of the CPC to All Members of the CPC concerning the Guarantee of the Implementation of the Marriage Law (1952), Joint Notice of the All China Union, the Central Committee of Chinese Youth League, the All China League of Youth, the All China League of Scholars, and the All China Federation of Women to the Various Associations and Communities of the People on the Support of the Marriage Law (1950), Instructions of the Government Council of the Central People's Government on Inspection of the Implementation of the Marriage Law (1951), Instructions of the Government Council of the Central People's Government concerning the Implementation of the Marriage Law (1953), and other documents. All these documents are collected in All China Federation of Women (ed.), *Important Documents on Chinese Women's Movement* (*Zhongguo Funiu Yuandong Zhongyao Wenxian*) (Beijing: People's Press, 1979).

44 Yang Dawei, *supra* note 29, at 77.

45 Promulgated by the Standing Committee of the 5th NPC on 10 September 1980 and effective on 1 January 1981. It was drafted by a revision group consisting of representatives from the All China Women's Federation, the Supreme People's Court, the Supreme People's Procuratorate, Ministry of Civil Affairs, Ministry of Health, National Leading Group for Birth Control, Commission on Nationalities Affairs, Political Department of the Army, the National Trade Union and the League of Communist Youth. See Explanations on the Draft Marriage Law of the PRC, delivered by the Vice Chairman of the Legislative Affairs Committee of the Standing Committee of the NPC, Mr Wu Xingyu, to the Third Plenary Session of the 5th NPC on September 2, 1980, in All China Women's Federation, *Handbook on Marriage Law* (*Hunyinfa Shouce*) (Beijing: Publishing House of Law, 1980), at 9-11. Major revisions were then undertaken in 2001.

conducive to economic development.[46] Thus, in addition to the basic principles (freedom of marriage, equality between the sexes, monogamy, and the prohibition of third party intervention in marriage, of mercenary marriage and of dowries) already laid down in the previous marriage law and regulations, the protection of the rights of the elderly, children and women, and the implementation of birth control became principles of the Law.[47] The marriageable age was increased from 20 for men and 18 for women to 22 and 20 respectively.[48] Further, birth control was now not only a state policy to be promoted but also made a duty of both partners.[49] With this additional obligation being imposed by law, as the Report explained, the State would therefore be able to curtail, as it did and still does, the right to have a child, even if a couple are legally married.[50] In order to deal with the problem of the very poor state welfare system far more detailed provisions were introduced concerning family property and the duty of supporting family members, including familial responsibility for three generations and siblings.[51] Finally, 'breakdown of affection' (*ganqing que yi polie*) was introduced as a sole ground for divorce.[52] The introduction of this phrase was intended, as explained by the Report mentioned above, to give courts greater flexibility and discretion in deciding divorce cases.[53]

Parallel to the 1980 Law were the 1980 Marriage Registration Measures, which replaced those issued by the Ministry of Civil Affairs in 1955. The 1980 Measures were, however, soon repealed by a new set of regulations issued in 1986 by the same Ministry. These regulations were intended to strictly implement the 1980 Law, dealing with the registration of marriage and remarriage (*zaihun*), divorce and restoration of marriage (*fuhun*).[54] The speedy revision of the 1980 Measures was designed to strengthen the registration process (both institutionally and procedurally), to emphasise rights and duties of the intending spouses, as well as to deal with some new problems such as bigamy and *de facto* marriage, which were claimed to have

46 See State Council Circular Concerning the Serious Implementation of the New Marriage Law (10 December 1980), and State Council Further Circular Concerning the Implementation of the Marriage Law (12 December 1981), in Ma Yuan (ed.), *A Practical Collection of Laws concerning Chinese Women* (*Zhongguo Funü Falü Shiyong Quanshu*) (Beijing: Publishing House of Law, 1993), at 541 & 542 respectively.

47 See Article 2 of the 1980 Marriage Law.

48 See Article 5 of the 1980 Marriage Law.

49 See Articles 2 & 12 of the 1980 Marriage Law.

50 See Explanations on the Draft Marriage Law of the PRC, *supra* note 45, at 11.

51 See Article 14-18 of the 1980 Marriage Law.

52 Article 25 of the 1980 Marriage Law.

53 See Explanations on the Draft Marriage Law of the PRC, *supra* note 45, at 11-12.

54 Restoration of marriage relates to remarriage of the same partners whose divorce was usually caused by political movements during the Cultural Revolution of 1966–1976.

been 'revealed' by the open door policy.[55] The changing social environment again prompted the issuing of a new set of Marriage Registration Regulations by the Ministry of Civil Affairs in February 1994.[56] The 1994 Regulations were intended to strengthen the administration and supervision of marriage registration. The new Regulations also introduced pre-marriage health examinations, to be implemented by local governments at the provincial level.[57] While the Regulations strengthened the right of the parties to have their marriage or divorce registered, and provided them with an appeal right under the Law of Administrative Reconsideration and the Administrative Litigation Law, they also imposed financial penalties on parties who had obtained marriage registration by fraud or cheating.[58]

(2) The Reform of the 1980 Marriage Law

Proposals for reform had begun to emerge not long after the promulgation of the Marriage Law of 1980. According to some Chinese scholars the first initiative to revise the Marriage Law was raised in a collection of papers edited by the China Marriage Law Association in 1990 and entitled *Contemporary Chinese Marriage and Family Problems*.[59] Thereafter the call for reform of the Chinese law on marriage and the family began to emerge in academic circles.[60] In 1993 the Internal Affairs Committee of the NPC convened a meeting on the necessity and feasibility of Marriage Law revision, attended by representatives from the Supreme People's Court, the State Family Planning Commission, the Ministry of Civil Affairs, the All China Women's Federation and legal experts. This meeting concluded that the revision of the Marriage Law was both necessary and feasible.[61] A formal decision to revise the Marriage Law was made by the Standing Committee of the NPC (SCNPC) in October 1995 at its 16th Meeting, and the Legislative Affairs Committee (LAC) was entrusted with the task of investigating and collating existing laws, administrative regulations and judicial interpretations, as well as relevant foreign legislative

---

55 For more detailed discussions on the speedy revision, see Michael Palmer, 'The People's Republic of China: New Marriage Regulations', (no. 1, 1987–1988) 26 *Journal of Family Law* 39.

56 These Regulations have now been replaced by a new set of Regulations issued by the State Council in 2003.

57 Articles 9 & 10 of the Marriage Registration Regulations (1994).

58 Articles 24 of the Marriage Registration Regulations (1994).

59 See *NPC News* (*Zhongguo Renda Xinwen*) (internet edition): <zgrdxw.peopledaily.com.cn>, 30 August 2000.

60 See Wu Changzhen, 'Ideas and Concepts for Revision of the Marriage Law of China', (no. 3, 1997) *China Law* 72, at 72.

61 *NPC News* (*Zhongguo Renda Xinwen*) (internet edition): <zgrdxw.peopledaily.com.cn>, 18 July 2002.

precedents.[62] It was made clear that although the proposed revision would deal with various deficiencies in the Marriage Law of 1980, as well as various 'new' problems said to have emerged in the 1980s and 1990s,[63] the fundamental philosophical change would be a shift from transforming marriage and family relations into maintaining the stability of such relations.[64]

Initial academic discussions suggested that the reform was aimed at three major issues. First, marriage law would be expanded to cover all family matters and would thus become a family code. Secondly, provisions on the invalidity of marriage, which were then absent from the Marriage Law, would be added and, similarly, certain policies on birth control and reproduction would be translated into law. Thirdly, provisions on family and matrimonial property and on conditions of marriage and divorce would all be elaborated. On divorce, the sole ground of the 'breaking down of affection' would be replaced by 'the breaking down of marriage';[65] a terminology which would give courts greater discretion in granting or refusing divorce by taking the whole marriage situation into consideration.[66]

In June 1996 the Ministry of Civil Affairs began to prepare for the drafting of a new marriage law, and in November of the same year a leading group and a working office on the revision of the Marriage Law was established, commissioned by the SCNPC and consisting of representatives from the Ministry of Civil Affairs, the Supreme People's Court and the All China Women's Federation.[67] Within a period of little more than one year, four different (trial) drafts of a Marriage and Family Law had been completed by this Leading Group.[68] However, their work was carried out 'in secret'.[69] In June 1997, after the second trial draft had been completed, the Ministry of Civil Affairs organised a seminar in Beijing, which was attended by legal scholars and sociologists, to discuss the draft. It was at this event that for the first time the drafting work on the new marriage law came out into the open, and immediately prompted a heated nation-wide debate that was to last until the adoption of the Revision to the Marriage Law in 2001.

---

62 'How to Assess the Divorce Rate', *People's Daily* (*Renmin Ribao*), internet edition, 7 October 1997, and *NPC News* (*Zhongguo Renda Xinwen*) (internet edition): <zgrdxw.peopledaily.com.cn>, 31 August 2000.

63 These 'new' problems included irresponsibility in the relationship, the increase in the divorce rate, and family violence. See Wu Changzhen, *supra* note 60, at 73.

64 'How to Assess the Divorce Rate', *supra* note 62.

65 Wu Changzhen, *supra* note 60, at 74.

66 'How to Assess the Divorce Rate', *supra* note 62.

67 See Huang Chuaghui, *supra* note 39, at 60; and *NPC News*, *supra* note 59.

68 *NPC News* (*Zhongguo Renda Xinwen*) (internet edition): <zgrdxw.peopledaily.com.cn>, 31 August 2000.

69 See Huang Chuaghui, *supra* note 39, at 158.

Two related reform proposals fundamentally changed the course of debate, and delayed the process of reform. First, it was suggested that the revised law should stress family responsibility, loyalty and obligations between the spouses, as well as other aspects of family morality.[70] Secondly, as a result of such emphasis, the notion of 'fault', such as unfaithfulness in marriage, should be re-introduced, at least in deciding the division of matrimonial property in divorce proceedings.[71] The underlying philosophy of these reform proposals seemed to be a partial return to that of the 1950s,[72] and these proposals immediately caused some very emotional debate in the Chinese media and among academics as well as ordinary people, on the very significant issue of the relationship between morality and law.

In June 1999, the above-mentioned Leading Group completed its first official Expert Draft of the Marriage and Family Law, which consisted of 11 chapters and 147 articles.[73] An unprecedented number of fieldwork visits to various provinces in China, and random and media polls, seminars etc. were then conducted by the LAC of the SCNPC and the All China Women's Federation, seeking views on the revision of the law from experts, academics, and ordinary citizens.[74] With this expert draft in place, the LAC then began its own review. Meanwhile, debate on the fusion of law and morality raged in China, focusing on the proposals for the establishment of a right of the spouse, the rights and duties to be faithful during marriage, the legal treatment of any 'third party' and mistresses ('*ernai*' in Chinese), and the introduction of the notion of 'fault' in divorce proceedings.[75]

In August 2000, a Draft of the Revision of the Marriage Law (*For Consultation*), largely based on the Expert Draft but also taking into consideration drafts by other organisations (such as those by the All China Women's Federation), was issued to seek comment among Party and Central Government officials, and selected local and legal experts.[76] While the Expert Draft attempted to deal with both marriage

---

70 Wu Changzhen, *supra* note 60, at 74.

71 'How to Assess the Divorce Rate', *supra* note 62.

72 See *supra* note 42.

73 This comprehensive draft, dealing with both marriage and family matters, and dated 11 June 1999, was in fact soon to be replaced by a much shorter version (the Second Expert Draft) in 8 chapters and 77 articles. Both draft versions are now collected in Wang Shengming & Sun Lihai (eds), *Selection of Legislative Materials relating to the Revision of the Marriage Law of the People's Republic of China* (*Zhonghua Renmin Gongheguo Hunyinfa Xiugai Lifa Ziliao Xuan*) (Beijing: Publishing House of Law, 2001), at 433-470.

74 See *NPC News*, *supra* note 68; and 'Explanations for the Draft Revision of the Marriage Law of the PRC', delivered by Hu Kangsheng at the 18th Meeting of the Standing Committee of the 9th NPC, 23 October 2000. Full texts of the Explanation were published in *People's Daily*, internet edition, 24 October 2000.

75 See Huang Chuaghui, *supra* note 39, at 166.

76 See 'Explanations to the Draft Revision of the Marriage Law of the PRC', *supra* note 74; and *NPC News*, *supra* note 68.

and family law by incorporating matters relating to adoption and guardianship, the Draft (*For Consultation*) clearly intended to limit itself to the revision of the 1980 Marriage Law, rather than promulgating a new Marriage and Family Law. In October 2000 a Draft Bill on the Revision of the Marriage Law was formally submitted to the SCNPC for deliberation. After the second deliberation (December 2000) by the SCNPC, the SCNPC then decided that the revision would only address the following five issues: polygamy, domestic violence, invalidity of marriage, common property in marriage, and compensation for the no-fault party in a divorce.[77] Also at this meeting the legislature came to the conclusion that the revision of the marriage law was going to be a very complex and difficult process which would require input from academics, the judiciaries and the women's organisations, as well as an understanding of the society's views on the various marriage and family related issues. Thus it was decided that the full text of the Draft Bill would be published for public discussion on 11 January 2001 and all responses were required to be fed back to the SCNPC by 28 February 2001.[78] The Marriage Law was then to undergo an unprecedented scale of consultation, investigation and debate. Indeed, despite the short period designated for consultation, 3,829 submissions were received by the SCNPC by the deadline.[79] It is said that the revision of the Marriage Law attracted the largest participation of ordinary people and legislators and the widest debate in the recent history of China and, hence, was a model example of a successful experiment in democratic law-making.[80]

---

77 See Huang Chuaghui, *supra* note 39, at 167.

78 See 'Notice of the General Office of the Standing Committee of the NPC on Publication of the Draft Bill on the Revision of the Marriage Law for Public Consultation', in *NPC News* (*Zhongguo Renda Xinwen*) (internet edition): <zgrdxw.peopledaily.com.cn>, 11 January 2001. The suggestion of publishing such a draft for public comment was made as early as October 2000, when the draft was being deliberated for the first time by the SCNPC. See *NPC News* (*Zhongguo Renda Xinwen*), internet edition, 27 October 2000.

79 See 'Report on the Solicitation of Opinions on the Draft Bill for the Revision of the Marriage Law', in *People's Daily*, internet edition, 23 April 2001. According to the *People's Daily*, among the people who made submissions, the oldest was 90 years and the youngest only 13. See 'The Adoption of the Bill on the Revision of the Marriage Law', *NPC News* (*Zhongguo Renda Xingwen*) (internet edition): <zgrdxw.peopledaily.com.cn>, 29 April 2001.

80 See 'Focus on the New Marriage Law – Press Conference held by the Legislative Affairs Committee', *People's Daily*, internet edition, 16 May 2001, and 'The Revision of Marriage Law, a Successful Experiment in Democratic Law-making', *NPC News* (*Zhongguo Renda Xinwen*) (internet edition): <zgrdxw.peopledaily.com.cn>, 18 July 2002. It should be pointed out here that participation and consultation processes were more elitist than democratic. The process was largely driven by 'experts' and, until the release of the draft in 2001, consultation was conducted 'internally' among elite scholars and officials. Similarly, legislative intentions were only conveyed to the 'experts' but never publicly expressed. Although ordinary people did have some opportunities to express their views in the media, especially through the internet, few had ever seen any draft nor had any opportunities to have the official positions on the

The Bill on the Revision of the Marriage Law was finally adopted by the SCNPC on 28 April 2001. Among the 137 voting members of the Committee, 127 voted for adoption, one against, and there were 9 abstentions.[81] Considering that the Revised Law attempted to deal with some of the most controversial issues concerning marriage and family (the so-called 'basic cells' of a society) in contemporary China, it was surprising, and counter to common-sense expectations, that the revised Marriage Law took immediate effect upon promulgation by Presidential Order No. 51, on the same day that the Revision Bill was adopted.

(3) Major Controversies concerning the Reform of the Marriage Law

Almost all aspects proposed for the reform of the Marriage Law were deemed controversial by 'experts' and law-makers. Among these, some were perhaps genuinely controversial, such as legal intervention in extra-marital affairs, but others became controversial because of misconceptions, such as those regarding the legal response to domestic violence. The controversial issues may be listed as follows:[82]

- Restrictions on freedom of marriage;
- Restricted grounds for divorce;
- Legal intervention in extra-marital affairs;
- Rights of the Spouse (e.g. whether the law should stipulate a mutual obligation of cohabitation between couples (hence, the question of rape within marriage));
- Civil liabilities for domestic violence;
- Right to privacy between a husband and a wife;

revision explained to them until 2001, just a few months before the draft was put to formal vote for adoption. When they were given the opportunity to comment on the draft, they were only allowed a very short period of some 40 days for a final draft that was more than seven years in the making, and more than ten years under discussion among academic experts.

81 See 'The Adoption of the Bill on the Revision of the Marriage Law', *supra* note 79.

82 See Wang & Sun, *supra* note 73; 'Explanations to the Draft Revision of the Marriage Law of the PRC', *supra* note 74; 'A Report on the Nationwide Opinion Poll on the Revision of the Marriage Law', *NPC News* (*Zhongguo Renda Xinwen*) (internet edition): <zgrdxw.peopledaily.com.cn>, 22 November 2000; 'Experts on Controversies concerning the Revision of the Marriage Law', *People's Daily* (*Renmin Ribao*), internet edition, 14 July 2002; 'Controversies concerning the Revision of the Marriage Law', *People's Daily* (*Renmin Ribao*), 9 August 2000; Hu Kangsheng, 'Marriage and the Family Legal System in Our Country – being Seminar No. 15 of the Standing Committee of the NPC', in *NPC News* (*Zhongguo Renda Xinwen*) (internet edition), 31 August 2000 (A shorter version of the paper is published in English: Hu Kangsheng, 'Major Issues in Amending the Chinese Marriage Law', (Oct 2000) *China Law* 63-66)); Lu Pipi, 'New Marriage Law Sparks Concern', (March 15, 2001) *Beijing Review* 12-17; *People's Daily* (*Renmin Ribao*), internet edition, 9 August 2000.

- Legal response to the rapid increase in foreign-related marriage;
- Property relationships between couples.

There are of course other issues that were also controversial, such as the debate about whether the revised law should emphasise either establishing a legal framework or providing solutions to practical issues, and whether the right to have children should be treated as the right of the couple, or only belong to one of the parties in a marriage.

At the end, the 2001 Revision of the 1980 Marriage Law did not just revise, but also significantly supplemented, many important aspects that were missing from the 1980 Law. The original 37-article Law has now been extended to include 52 articles, with Chapter 5 on Legal Remedies and Legal Liabilities being an entirely new chapter. In a nutshell, the Revision has managed to address the following four issues that were absent from the 1980 Marriage Law: legal treatment of extra-marital affairs; invalid and revocable marriage; property division in divorce; and domestic violence.

4. The Contemporary Legal Framework on Family Matters

4.1. An Overview

It is clear that the latest legal framework on family matters is primarily a product gradually established since the early 1980s. Although the above review of the historical development focuses on the development of the marriage law, family matters are regulated by a number of laws, each regulating a different aspect of the family. Thus, shortly after the promulgation of the Marriage Law in 1980, the Law of Succession (1985) and the Adoption Law (1991 and revised 1998) were issued. The Population and Family Planning Law came into existence in 2002, which now provides some legal guidance on the strict family planning policy in China. Although socialist ideology and the modernisation of family structure are still the major emphasis in the laws, the present legal framework is much more pragmatic in orientation, focusing primarily on promoting social stability and national economic development. The gradual expansion since the early 1980s of the scope of the legal framework to cover issues of property inheritance and adoption, has made it more inclusive and comprehensive but, at the same time, also makes the framework fragmented and task/policy-oriented in an *ad hoc* fashion. There is, however, an advantage to the piecemeal approach, namely that the legal framework is more flexible for adaptation to new situations as a result of rapid economic reform and development.

Since family matters are at the centre of customary law and practice, which vary from place to place and from one nationality to another, most national laws governing family matters specifically allow local variations in implementation, especially in minority autonomous regions. Without exception, all legislatures at the provincial level have issued their own implementation rules and measures governing family matters.[83]

4.2. Marriage

The principal law governing marriage is the 1980 Marriage Law as revised in 2001. However, many practical matters are regulated by registration regulations at the central and local levels.

The Marriage Law first lays down, in Chapter One, some general principles on freedom of marriage (and divorce), gender equality, protection of children and the elderly, obligations on family planning and faithfulness between spouses, and the prohibition of bigamy and domestic violence. Except for the provisions on mutual obligations of faithfulness and the prohibition of domestic violence, many of these principles had all been established by the Constitution (1982) and the 1980 Marriage Law before the 2001 revision.

Chapter Two (on marriage) then establishes conditions for marriage and invalidation of marriage. Article 5 stipulates that marriage must be based on a completely voluntary union and prohibits any interference from any party. Marriageable ages are defined as 22 for men and 20 for women, and the Law specifically *encourages* late marriage and late childbirth.[84] Although the Law uses the word 'encourage', this provision has often been used by local authorities as a legal ground for compulsory enforcement of late marriage and late childbirth.[85] In fact, there have been many other rules issued by local authorities (such as the rules issued by the Army, civil aviation authorities, ministry of education, State Commission of Sports, etc.), which have stipulated a much later marriageable age for men and women.[86] As such, there were arguments to have this particular provision deleted from the Law, but these were not accepted by the law-makers. Importantly, Articles 10, 11 and 12 now formally establish the legal notions of invalid and revocable marriage and their legal consequences, aspects that were conspicuously missing from the 1980 Marriage Law.

---

83 A relatively comprehensive collection of these local rules can be found in the website of the All China Women's Federation: <www.women.org.cn>.

84 Article 6 of the Marriage Law. There is no legal definition of 'late marriage' or 'late childbirth'. According to the Instruction of the Central Party Committee and the State Council on Further Strengthening Birth Control (9 February 1982), 'Late marriage' means a marriage where the ages of the couple are three years older than the legal marriageable ages, that is 25 for men and 23 for women. 'Later childbirth' means the woman has reached 24 years of age when she gives birth to her first child. An extract of the Instruction is contained in Ma Yuan, *supra* note 46, at 597-598.

85 Wang & Sun, *supra* note 73, at 41.

86 Wang & Sun, *supra* note 73, at 97.

Chapter Three (on family relations) is the longest chapter in the Law, clearly indicating the legislative intention of maintaining stability in family relationships. The focus of this chapter is on property relationships and financial maintenance and support among the three generations of family members. The provisions on financial maintenance and support recognise the lack of a comprehensive social welfare system in China, and the provisions on property relationships reflect the reality of increasing wealth accumulated in families, and a concern for social stability that might otherwise be disturbed if the family property relationship is not properly handled, especially upon a divorce.

Chapter Four (on divorce) deals with legal grounds for dissolution of a marriage and its legal consequences. Again, much of the attention of the legal provisions is on property relationships and financial maintenance and support among family members.

Chapter Five, being the new addition brought in by the 2001 revision, provides civil remedies in the case of, and administrative sanctions against, violation of the Marriage Law. It also establishes legal grounds for state intervention in marriage and family matters.

The revision of the 1980 Marriage Law in 2001 also saw the revision of the 1994 Registration Regulations. Although taking a longer than expected time, the new Marriage Registration Regulations were issued on 8 August 2003 by the State Council. The 1994 Registration Regulations were repealed simultaneously upon the implementation of the new Regulations from 1 October 2003.

The 2003 Registration Regulations brought in a number of new changes. First, the requirement for a certificate by the working unit or a neighbourhood committee or a village committee of the applicant, stating the marital status of the applicant, has now been abolished. Instead, applicants are now only required to make a marital status declaration. It certainly is a very welcome reform, as it is now formally recognises that marriage is a matter between two individuals, and their working units should have no right to enforce any of their own considerations (such as those for birth control) in the issuing of such a certificate. Secondly, the compulsory pre-marriage health check has now also been abolished. While this abolition will surely be welcomed by the intending couples, at least in terms of not paying yet another kind of fee or charge, the authority for the State Council to abolish this is doubtful. Although the Marriage Law does not impose a requirement for a pre-marriage health check, Article 12 of the Law on the Health Care for Mothers and Infants (1995) specifically stipulates that a pre-marriage health certificate is required for marriage registration. The 1995 Law was issued by the SCNPC, a higher legislative authority than the State Council. Since the State Council should not annul a legal requirement imposed by the SCNPC, it is not surprising that this abolition soon caused some controversy. The Ministry of Civil Affairs and the Ministry of Health have now both asserted that the abolition simply means that a health examination will not be a compulsory requirement for registration, but all intending couples are encouraged to undertake such a health check on a voluntary basis.[87] Thirdly, the various special provisions for foreign-related marriage registration have now been incorporated into the new Marriage Registration Regulations. Like in other areas of law in China, foreign-related family matters were previously dealt with by separate regulations. Thus, marriage between a mainland Chinese and an overseas Chinese or a Chinese from Hong Kong or Macau was governed by the Provisions Concerning Registration Procedure for Marriages between Overseas Chinese or Chinese from Hong Kong or Macau and Citizens of Mainland China.[88] Intermarriage between Chinese and foreigners was dealt with by the Provisions for the Registration of Marriages Between Chinese Citizens and Foreigners.[89] There was also a set of measures dealing with intermarriage between Chinese citizens and citizens of neighbouring countries.[90] Until 1998 there were no special rules for marriage between a Taiwanese and a mainland Chinese. The 'historical' questions concerning marriage, divorce, financial support and property inheritance between spouses separated since 1949 were addressed by the Several Provisions Concerning Civil Matters Involving Taiwan Residents.[91] These provisions took a pragmatic non-interventionist attitude towards the marital status of the separated parties while retaining as much as possible the property rights of the parties residing in Taiwan. In December 1998 a set of Interim Measures for the Registration of Marriage Between Mainland Chinese and Residents of Taiwan was issued by the Ministry of Civil Affairs, regulating the registration of marriage, divorce and re-marriage between mainland Chinese and residents of Taiwan and the associated documentation requirements. The increasing number of Chinese studying or working overseas then also necessitated

---

87 'Is Pre-marital Health Check Still Compulsory – the Ministry of Civil Affairs Says No', *Xinhua News*, internet edition, 28 August 2003, and 'Ministry of Health Encourages Citizens to Take Care of Pre-marital Health Examination', *Xinhua News*, internet edition, 3 September 2003. For this purpose, the Ministry of Health issued, on 23 June 2004, a Notice on Conducting Free Pre-Marriage Health Checks and Consultations. The Notice recognises that since the implementation of the new Marriage Registration Regulation, less than 10% of intending couples nationwide had undergone pre-marriage health checks. The free service offered by the government does not seem to have improved the situation at all. According to Xinhua News Agency, almost no intending couple in Beijing underwent such a health check since the new Marriage Registration Regulations were introduced. See 'Beijing Pre-marriage Health Check Rate Is Almost Zero – Compulsory Pre-marriage Health Check Will Be Difficult to Resume', available from <news.xinhuanet.com/society/2006-03/30/content_4320546.htm> (last accessed 20 March 2006).

88 Issued by the Ministry of Civil Affairs on 10 March 1983.

89 Issued by the Ministry of Civil Affairs on 26 August 1983.

90 Measures on the Registration of Marriage between Chinese Citizens and Citizens of Neighbouring Countries (for trial implementation), issued by Ministry of Civil Affairs on 17 February 1995.

91 Issued by the Supreme People's Court on 9 August 1988.

some special measures for the registration of their marriages and divorces. These measures were issued in August 1997.[92] They allowed such marriage and divorce to be registered either in China or with diplomatic missions in foreign countries. They also imposed strict proof of marital status for the returned students or workers if they had stayed overseas for over 6 months. As with the provisions governing intermarriage between a Chinese and a foreigner, servicemen, diplomatic personnel, people in the public security forces, and persons engaged in confidential work or in possession of any important confidential information were prohibited from registering their marriage or divorce in the Chinese diplomatic missions in foreign countries. These foreign-related provisions imposed certain strict requirements for documentation and proof of marital status of the intending spouses. They required pre-marriage health examination and proof of occupation and/or reliable economic income of the foreign or Hong Kong or Macau Parties.[93] Servicemen, diplomatic personnel, people in the public security forces, persons engaged in confidential work or in possession of any important confidential information, and those being reformed through labour or serving prison terms were prohibited from marrying foreigners.[94] Although the 2001 revision of the Marriage Law decided not to deal with foreign-related marriage,[95] the 2003 Registration Regulations have now simplified the above various measures and rules and incorporate the basic requirements into the Regulations. As in the case of marriage between Chinese citizens, registration of foreign-related marriage no longer imposes any pre-marriage health examination. The new Registration Regulations do not however abolish any of the above measures/rules. Presumably, they will continue to operate unless they conflict with the new Registration Regulations.

4.3. Succession

Ideologically the idea of property inheritance is incompatible with socialism. Indeed, Marx once proclaimed that the communist revolution would effect the 'abolition of

---

92 Administrative Measures concerning the Marriage Registration of People Going Abroad, jointly issued by the Ministry of Civil Affairs and Ministry of Foreign Affairs on 5 August 1997.

93 Article 2 of the Provisions Concerning Registration Procedures for Marriages between Overseas Chinese or Chinese from Hong Kong or Macau and Citizens of Mainland China; and Article 3 of the Provisions for the Registration of Marriages Between Chinese Citizens and Foreigners.

94 Article 4 of the Provisions for the Registration of Marriages Between Chinese Citizens and Foreigners, and Article 10 of the Measures on Registration of Marriages between Chinese Citizens and Citizens of Neighbouring Countries.

95 It should be pointed out that there was a strong argument among many people and law-makers that a new chapter on 'foreign-related marriage' should be added to the marriage law. Wang & Sun, *supra* note 73.

all right of inheritance.'[96] The reality is that all socialist law has had provisions dealing with property succession. In the case of China inheritance law did not disappear, but its scope gradually expanded, in part to reform the 'feudal' family system and to provide women with equal rights.[97] Institutionally, however, Chinese legislation only briefly touched on the issue of inheritance until the late 1980s; an operative legal framework was mainly established by Supreme People's Court decisions and 'opinions' as well as by academic commentaries.[98]

Like its predecessor, the 1980 Marriage Law briefly touched on the issue of inheritance by providing that 'husband and wife have the right to inherit each other's property. Parents and children have the right to inherit each other's property'.[99] Clearly, the increasing accumulation of private wealth through the policy of allowing the development of individual and private enterprises and the improvement of living standards demanded a more sophisticated legal framework on property succession. Further, the lack of a comprehensive social security system and the corresponding demand for family support among family members also necessitated the regulation of inheritance. The reliance on various Supreme Court decisions and various administrative directives and measures was insufficient to deal with succession issues.[100] Thus the Law of Succession was issued in 1985 by the SCNPC. In addition, the Supreme People's Court issued many *ad hoc* interpretations and opinions on the implementation of the law, including a set of comprehensive opinions.[101] Strangely, the State Council has not issued any implementation regulations on this important piece of law, nor has the 1985 Law been revised until this day.

The first thing to note about the legal framework on property succession is the basic principles embodied in various sections of the Succession Law. These basic principles emphasise the equal entitlement of both sexes;[102] the promotion of mutual support among family members and, hence, the harmony of the family and the

---

96 See Frances Foster-Simons, 'The Development of Inheritance Law in the Soviet Union and the People's Republic of China', (1985) *Am. J. Comp. L.* 33, at 33.

97 Foster-Simons, *id.*, at 37-40.

98 For detailed discussions, see Foster-Simons, *supra* note 96, at 43-49.

99 Article 18 of the Marriage Law (1980). This provision has now been elaborated by the 2001 revision. See the discussion below.

100 For a collection of the judicial documents, see Ma Yuan, *supra* note 46, at 526-566.

101 Supreme People's Court Opinions on Implementing the Law of Succession, issued on 11 September 1985.

102 Article 9 of the Law of Succession. It should be noted here, however, that Article 9 is contained in Chapter Two (Statutory Succession) rather than in Chapter One (General Principles). It is therefore unclear whether this equal entitlement is a general principle of the Law or would only be applicable in cases of statutory succession.

shifting of social welfare burdens to the family unit;[103] and the linking of family support with the right of inheritance.[104] Under these principles the language of the law is extremely vague and flexible, allowing the court and the relevant authorities great discretion in deciding the final distribution of property for succession.

Three types of succession are provided by the 1985 Law, namely statutory, testamentary, and through legacy agreements in return for support.[105] Reflecting the basic principles underlying the Law, Article 5 gives priority to legacy agreements in return for support over statutory and testamentary succession, and testamentary over statutory succession.

A legacy agreement in return for support can be made between individuals or an individual and an organisation under collective ownership.[106] Although when a legacy agreement exists succession is to be dealt with in accordance with the agreement,[107] an organisation which has supported the deceased is nevertheless entitled to be paid for support expenses out of the estate.[108] On the other hand, such a legacy agreement between the deceased and his/her children has no legal effect, as such support is a legal duty under Chinese law.[109]

Although testamentary disposition of property is expressly allowed by the Law, statutory successors who do not have the ability to work and have no income must not be totally deprived of the right to inheritance.[110] Wills depriving the rights of the underaged or the unborn are also invalid. However, there is no provision prohibiting sex discrimination in testamentary disposition of property. Considering the persistence of the traditional idea of male inheritance only, the lack of such a provision can cause major problems in the actual implementation of equal rights for women, particularly in the vast areas of the countryside.[111]

Statutory succession occurs when the property, or a part of it, is not dealt with by testament or legacy agreement either because there is no testament or legacy

---

103 See Articles 10 – 14 of the Law of Succession which emphasise the right to inheritance by those who have a relationship of support or dependence with the deceased.

104 See Articles 7 & 13 of the Law of Succession.

105 Article 5 of the Law of Succession.

106 Article 31 of the Law of Succession.

107 Article 5 of the Law of Succession. Such a right to succession may be denied by a people's court if the legatee has failed to fulfil the obligations under the agreement. See Article 21 of the Law of Succession (1985).

108 Article 16 of the Supreme People's Court Opinions on Implementing the Law of Succession.

109 Zhang Xianchu, 'Family Law', in Wang Chenguang & Zhang Xianchu (ed.) *Introduction to Chinese Law* (Hong Kong/Singapore: Sweet & Maxwell Asia, 1997), at 331.

110 Article 19 of the Law of Succession.

111 As noted above, it is unclear whether Article 9 on equal entitlement to success is applicable in the case of testament or legacy agreements.

agreement, or the testament or agreement is invalid, or the persons entitled to such have died or have disclaimed their entitlement.[112] Estates are to be inherited in two orders. In the first order are the spouse, children and parents; and in the second order brothers and sisters, and paternal and maternal grandparents. Children include legitimate, illegitimate, adopted and step-children who supported or were supported by the deceased. Parents also include natural and adoptive parents as well as step-parents who supported or were supported by the deceased. Brothers and sisters also include blood or half-blood, adopted brothers and sisters and step brothers/sisters who supported or were supported by the deceased. Inheritance by subrogation is also provided.[113] Further, widowed daughters-in-law or sons-in-law who have contributed to the support, as a principal supporter, of the parents-in-law are also to be included in the first order. This provision clearly targets the 'feudal' practice of allowing property only to be inherited within the family of blood relatives.

Estate for inheritance includes all lawful property, both tangible and intangible (e.g. intellectual property).[114] However, partitioning of the estate must be conducted in a way conducive to production and livelihood, and must not diminish the usefulness of the estate.[115] Serious criminal conduct, including the murder of the deceased or other successors, abandoning or maltreating the deceased, acts of forging, tampering with or destroying the will, are legal grounds for disinheritance.[116]

A critical issue concerning succession is the delineation and division of property ownership between spouses. Neither the original 1980 Marriage Law nor the 1985 Law on Succession has much to say on this important issue. This issue is now addressed by the Marriage Law as revised in 2001.[117]

4.4. Adoption

Although adoption was protected by the 1980 Marriage Law,[118] there was no legal framework dealing with this important family issue until 1991 when the Adoption Law was promulgated.[119] Without a national legal framework, adoption relations were largely established through notarisation, particularly after the issuance of the

[112] Article 27 of the Law of Succession.

[113] Article 10 of the Law of Succession.

[114] Article 3 of the Law of Succession.

[115] Article 29 of the Law of Succession.

[116] Article 7 of the Law of Succession.

[117] See discussions in Section 5.4 below.

[118] Article 20 of the Marriage Law (1980), now Article 26 of the Marriage Law as amended in 2001.

[119] Adopted by the Standing Committee on 29 December 1991, effective on 1 April 1992. This Law was amended by the same authority on 4 November 1998 and the amended Law became effective on 1 April 1999.

Provisional Measures for the Notarisation of the Adoption of Children, issued by the Ministry of Justice.[120] Criteria and procedures for adoption were often inconsistent between various administrative rules and measures issued by different administrative authorities and local governments.[121]

The Adoption Law is applicable to the adoption of Chinese children by Chinese citizens as well as by foreigners.[122] Adoption is limited to minors under the age of 14 who are orphans bereaved of parents, or abandoned infants, or children whose parents cannot be ascertained or found, or children whose parents are unable to rear them due to unusual difficulties.[123] Under the 1991 Law an adopter has to be childless, capable of rearing and educating the adoptee, and to have reached the age of 35 – this last age requirement has now been reduced to 30 after the 1998 revision of the Law.[124] He/she may only adopt one child. In the case of a single male adopting a child, the age difference between them must be no less than forty years.[125] Certain exceptions are made to these strict requirements. Thus, adoption requirements for a collateral relative by blood up to the third degree of kinship are substantially relaxed, and overseas Chinese adopting a collateral relative by blood up to the third degree of kinship need not meet the requirement of childlessness.[126] The adoption of orphans or disabled children or children now in welfare institutions and whose parents could not be found is not restricted by the requirements of the adopter being childless and of allowing only one child for each adopter.[127]

One of the major policy concerns in the Law is to prevent the circumvention of family planning policies through adoption. Thus Article 3 specifically provides that adoption shall not contravene laws and regulations on family planning. Article 19 further provides that a person having placed out a child for adoption may not bear

---

120 See Jing Jian, 'Explanations on the Draft Adoption Law', delivered to the 20th Meeting of the Standing Committee of the 7th NPC on 21 June 1991, in (no. 7, 1991) *Gazette of the Standing Committee of the NPC of the PRC (Zhonghua Renmin Gongheguo Quanguo Renmin Daibiao Dahui Changwu Weiyuanhui Gongbao)* 8, at 9.

121 *Id.*

122 The original draft law had a special chapter on adoption by foreigners. The whole chapter was however replaced by Article 20, which applies the Law to adoption by foreigners. Nevertheless, separate measures were later issued jointly by the Ministry of Justice and Ministry of Civil Affairs: Implementing Measures for Adoption by Foreigners in China (issued and effective on November 3, 1993). These Implementing Measures were later replaced by Measures on the Registration of Adoption of Children in the PRC by Foreigners, issued by the State Council on 12 May 1999 and effective on promulgation.

123 Article 4 of the Adoption Law.

124 Article 6 of the Adoption Law.

125 Article 9 of the Adoption Law.

126 Article 7 of the Adoption Law.

127 Article 8 of the Adoption Law. Initially under the 1991 Law such relaxation of adoption requirements was only applicable to the adoption of orphans or disabled children.

any more children in violation of family planning, on the grounds of having placed out their child for adoption. This article clearly concerns not only family planning but also the practice of placing a female infant out for adoption in order to have a male child under the one child policy.

Although the Adoption Law is apparently simple and requirements imposed therein do not seem to be particularly stringent, the Law establishes a registration system through which actual control of adoption is achieved.[128] Such registration is regulated by two sets of measures, namely the Measures on the Registration of the Adoption of Children by Chinese Citizens (Domestic Adoption Measures), and the Measures on the Registration of the Adoption of Children in the PRC by Foreigners (Foreign Adoption Measures), both issued by the State Council on 12 May 1999 and effective on promulgation. The focus of the Domestic Adoption Measures is on documentation requirements to ensure that such adoption is voluntary, that the identity of all parties is clearly established, and that no family planning law or regulation is violated or circumvented.

Adoption by foreigners is a much more complicated, time-consuming and, often, expensive process than is indicated under the Foreign Adoption Measures. To start with, foreigners wanting to adopt must meet the legal requirements imposed by two legal systems (China and home country of the prospective parents), must go through official channels and licensed agencies (required under Article 4 of the Foreign Adoption Measures and often supplemented by bilateral agreements),[129] and must undertake complex documentation, authentication, and emigration and immigration processes. In addition to such documentation on marital status, health (including family health history), and good character test (e.g. no criminal record), evidentiary documents on occupation, income and assets are required. A prospective child for adoption is selected by the Chinese agency through a 'match' between the requirements by the prospective parents and the children available for adoption. In most cases children adopted by foreigners are girls. Although the Foreign Adoption Measures only encourage prospective parents to make donations to social welfare institutions,[130] such a donation, which can amount to several thousand US dollars, is in practice compulsory before the adoption processes can be completed. Perhaps most importantly, prospective parents must understand that foreign adoption in China is still a very sensitive issue and publicity about such adoptions is not tolerated by the Chinese agency.

---

128 Article 15 of the Adoption Law (as revised in 1998). The original 1991 Law only imposed registration requirements on the adoption of orphans and abandoned children. For this kind of adoption the revised Law further required a public announcement before registration.

129 On the Chinese side the official agency is the China Centre for Adoption Affairs under the Ministry of Civil Affairs.

130 Article 14 of the Foreign Adoption Measures.

4.5. Family Planning

China is not just a large country, it is a hugely over-populated one. According to the last population census, as of 1 November 2000, the total population amounted to more than 12.66 billion.[131] This did not include people born outside family planning and hence not officially declared during the census.[132] Population increase, on such a huge base, is almost frightening: between 1962 to 1972 (when family planning policies began to be introduced), some 300 million people were added to the total Chinese population.[133] Even with strict family planning policies and, sometimes, draconian local measures, the Chinese population increased by 126.58 million between the fourth national census (1 July 1990) and the fifth census (1 November 2000).[134] The unsustainability of such population growth is beyond question: China has some 21% of the total global population, but occupies only 7% of the world's cultivated land, and possesses only one fourth of the world's per capita water resources.[135]

Family planning through strict birth control has become one of the most important strategic policies in China since the early 1970s.[136] This policy, according to the Chinese white paper on family planning, is not only vital for the survival and development of China, but also important for the stability and prosperity of all human society. With the increasing realisation of the global impact of population on the environment and on natural resources, family planning *per se* deserves little criticism.[137]

Strategically important though it is, there had been no national legal framework on birth control until 2001, when the Population and Birth Control Law was adopted.[138] Various laws and regulations did exist, however, at both central and local levels. The 1980 Marriage Law imposed a legal duty on couples to practise

---

131 Public Notice on Major Statistics of the Fifth National Census (2000), *People's Daily* (*Renmin Ribao*), 29 March 2001, at 1.

132 Under the Chinese family planning practice, all couples require a family planning certificate before they can legally give birth to a child.

133 Section 1 of the Chinese White Paper on family planning, *Family Planning in China*, issued by the Information Office of the State Council of the PRC, August 1995.

134 Public Notice on Major Statistics of the Fifth National Census (2000), *supra* note 131, at 1.

135 See the website of the National Population and Family Planning Commission of China: <www.sfpc.gov.cn>.

136 Nation-wide family planning policy began to be implemented in China after 1973. See *Family Planning in China*, *supra* note 133.

137 Any justification for family planning does not, however, automatically justify all measures for its implementation. In this context, the Chinese White Paper on family planning is misconceived; it focuses on justifying the need for family planning rather than addressing the problems involved in its implementation.

138 Adopted by the 25th Meeting of the Standing Committee of the Ninth National People's Congress on 29 December 2001, and effective from 1 September 2002.

birth control and to delay marriage.[139] The 1982 Constitution elevated birth control to a fundamental state policy in order to limit population growth within national economic and social development plans.[140] The Adoption Law, as mentioned above, prohibits any violation of birth control laws, regulations and policies through the practice of adoption, and the Law for the Protection of the Rights and Interests of Women (1992) provides various protections for women practising birth control.[141] The Criminal Law (1997) imposes severe penalties on persons who perform illegal operations on women in violation of birth control measures.[142] In practice, specific implementation of birth control was, and still is, carried out by many *ad hoc* policies and significantly varying local measures.[143] Local authorities were and still are the principal enforcers of the birth control policy.[144]

The Population and Birth Control Law was jointly drafted by the State Family Planning Commission and the Legislative Affairs Office of the State Council in accordance with the Decision of the Central Committee of the Party and the State Council on Strengthening the Work of Population and Birth Control and Stabilising a Low Birth Rate.[145] The legislative intention is to translate state policy on birth control into law, to establish a national legal framework on the basis of local experience,

---

139 Articles 2, 5 & 12 of Marriage Law (1980). Now Article 2, 6 & 16 of the revised Marriage Law (2001).

140 Article 25 & 49 of the Constitution.

141 See Articles 26, 35, 42, 46, & 47 of the Law for the Protection of the Rights and Interests of Women.

142 Article 336 of the Criminal Law (as amended in 1997).

143 A relatively comprehensive collection of these policies and local rules is in Ma Yuan (ed.), *supra* note 46, Part Four. It should however be pointed out that many of the local measures have now been replaced by new local measures implementing the Population and Birth Control Law of 2001. There is little doubt that provincial level local governments are fully competent in rule-making in this area. In the case of minority areas the Nationality Autonomous Law specifically authorises local governments to issue birth control measures appropriate to local situations (Article 44).

144 Indeed, the Village Committee and Neighbourhood Committee are specifically authorised by law to implement state birth control policies: Article 22 of the Organic Law of the Village Committee (1987, as amended in 1998) and Article 3 of the Organic Law of the Neighbourhood Committee (1989).

145 'Explanations on the Draft Law on Population and Birth Control', delivered at the 21st Meeting of the Standing Committee of the 9th NPC on 24 April 2001, in (no. 1, 2002) *Gazette of the Standing Committee of the NPC of the PRC (Zhonghua Renmin Gongheguo Quanguo Renmin Daibiao Dahui Changwu Weiyuanhui Gongbao)*, at 8. An English translation of the Decision itself can be found on the website of the UN Economic and Social Commission for Asia & the Pacific: <www.unescape.org/pop/databse/law-china/chtitle.htm>. This website contains many other Chinese laws and regulations (both at central and local levels) on family planning and birth control, but many of the local regulations contained therein are no longer valid.

and to establish social security and compensation mechanisms to encourage family planning and to penalise violations of birth control policy.[146]

Under the Law, the State Council is responsible for overall population planning, which should form part of the national social and economic development plans, and governments at the various levels are responsible for the implementation of such plans.[147] The 'one-child' policy is to be encouraged, but local authorities at the level of province may allow a second child for a couple under certain circumstances which must be stipulated in local rules.[148] This relaxation of the 'one-child' policy represents a realistic attitude towards local measures and practices in relation to the strict enforcement of such a policy.[149] The Law provides various rewards for couples who delay their marriage and giving birth, or who practise other birth control methods. However, such rewards are to be implemented by local governments.[150] Severe penalties are laid down by the Law for violation of family planning and birth control policies.[151] In order to unify the various practices at local levels of imposing different fines for child birth beyond the legal allowance (i.e. one child, or two children under special circumstances per couple), the Law now requires such couples to pay a social maintenance levy, the standard of which is to be regulated by the State Council.[152]

Although the Law now finally establishes a national legal framework on birth control, it contains mainly general principles. Specific practice continues to vary

---

146 *Id.*

147 Article 9 of the Population and Birth Control Law.

148 Article 18 of the Population and Birth Control Law.

149 As from the end of 2001 practically all provinces had allowed the birth of a second child under certain circumstances, such as a second child for a rural couple if their first child is a girl, a second child for a couple if both of them are only children, and a second child for couples if their first child is disabled without a chance of growing up to be a full capacity labourer. See 'Report of the Law Commission of the NPC on the Revision of Major Issues concerning the (Third) Draft of the Population and Birth Control Law', delivered at the 25th Meeting of the Standing Committee of the 9th NPC on 27 December 2001, in (no. 1, 2002) *Gazette of the Standing Committee of the NPC of the PRC (Zhonghua Renmin Gongheguo Quanguo Renmin Daibiao Dahui Changwu Weiyuanhui Gongbao)*, at 14-15. One of the most serious consequences emerging from this one-child policy and the exceptions allowed under the policy (and, of course, the traditional preference for male children, the lack of social security system, the availability of modern sex detection technologies, etc.) has been the huge sex imbalance in the Chinese population. According to Chinese sources, the ratio between female and male births in 1982 was 100:108.5. This ratio has since increased steadily and at the end of 2005 the ratio had become 100:118.88. This means that there are 37 million more men than women in China today. See '37 Million More Men than Women', Xinhua News Agency, 6 July 2007: <news.xinhuanet.com/politics/2007-07/06/content_6334993.htm> (last accessed 6 July 2007).

150 Chapter 4 of the Population and Birth Control Law.

151 Chapter 6 the Population and Birth Control Law.

152 Articles 41 and 45 of the Population and Birth Control Law.

according to local measures, the making of which is clearly mandated by the Law itself.[153] As such, any monitoring of family planning and birth control practice must be undertaken at the local level rather than at the central level, and the authorities at the local level have often been the subject of criticisms regarding the use of draconian measures and malpractices.[154] Herein then lies a very fundamental flaw of the Law: it offers little to prevent local authorities from taking harsh measures towards the implementation of family planning policies, and little protection for those whose human rights are seriously violated by local authorities in implementing such measures.

5. The Law as an Instrument for and in Response to Social Change

5.1. An Overview

From the above historical review and analysis of the modern Chinese legal framework on family matters, certain salient features and characteristics can be identified. First of all, family matters have more often than not been treated as state matters, and domestic units have been required to serve social interests in general, and Party policies in particular. The ambition of the authorities (Communist or Republican) to regulate domestic relationships arose from their final goal of a complete change in social structure and in the social system. Secondly, the contents of these laws are usually general principles and models of conduct, and the terminology in these laws is vague, with few clear definitions or concrete details, and language is sometimes emotional, and not uncommonly political. This form of wording can better serve the frequently changing policies, as interpretations can easily be changed, and it can also give more power and flexibility to the courts to meet different situations in different areas and at different times. It also indicates the fundamental attitude of the Party to the use of laws as an instrument of government. In a more broad sense, this attitude is itself a reflection of the traditional attitude towards law, i.e. that law is a secondary instrument for ruling a state. Finally, mass movements have often been used in Communist China to enforce these laws. In these movements family reactions against official policies have been simply labelled as either 'feudalist practice' or 'bourgeois thought' and have been turned into thought problems instead of legal affairs. On the other hand, as in the most recent reform of the marriage law, moral problems are turned into legal questions, available for legal intervention.

---

153 See Articles 9, 15, 18, 26, 29, & 31.

154 In a US Congress Committee hearing in 1998, horrendous stories were told about forced abortion and sterilisation programs practised at the local level, including the forced abortion of nine months' pregnancies, compulsory sterilisation and even the destruction of the houses of those who violated the one-child policy. See *The Age*, internet edition, 15 June 1998.

The instrumental use of law is not always a harmful practice, although it often causes social conflict and tensions. These conflicts are most clearly evidenced in the areas of freedom of marriage and divorce, extramarital affairs, family relationships, and domestic violence. In this regard the instrumental use of law has led to the introduction of revolutionary ideas (e.g. freedom of marriage and divorce), confusion between morality and law (legal intervention in extramarital affairs), and responses to social change (property in divorce and domestic violence).

5.2. Freedom of Marriage and Divorce

The concept of freedom of marriage and, correspondingly, freedom of divorce, although not first introduced in Communist China, is in every sense of the word a very revolutionary one in modern China. This idea has caused a very sharp break in the continuity of traditional ideas as well in their practice. The new idea has not only attacked the old form of marriage but, and more importantly, has vitally struck at the traditional essence of marriage – the concept of marriage as an arrangement between families, rather than two individuals. One can better recognise the revolutionary nature of the notion of the two freedoms in the context of marriage and divorce in traditional practice.

In traditional China, marriage was primarily a matter concerning two families, and not at all an affair of two individuals. In the Book of Rites (*Li Ji*), marriage was described as a custom 'to unite the two families with a view to harmonising the friendship between them' (*jie lianxing zhihao*).[155] Marriage was also intended to serve the function of ensuring the continuity of the clan, i.e. to produce sons for the family. Thus marriage was much more important to the parents than to the intended couple. The relationship concluded by marriage was not that between man and wife, but one of kinship. The bride became a member of the man's family – the daughter-in-law, and only secondarily a wife.[156]

If marriage was to promote unity and harmony between two families, divorce was then 'to cut off friendship between two families' (*ju lianxing zhihao*), and so divorce again primarily concerned family and clan.

While mutual consent for divorce under certain conditions was possible,[157] and specific grounds for a wife to initiate divorce was provided in some traditional laws,[158] traditional divorce institutions on the whole existed more to protect the rights of the husbands (such as the right to divorce a wife who failed to produce a son) and to enforce the duties of the wife (such as the obligation to be faithful and chaste to

---

155 See Chiu, *supra* note 40, at 4.

156 See Geoffrey MacCormack, *The Spirit of Traditional Chinese Law* (Athens & London: The University of Georgia Press, 1996), at 88.

157 Tai Yen-hui, 'Divorce in Traditional Chinese Law', in Buxbaum, *supra* note 27, at 81.

158 Tai Yen-hui, *id.*, at 98-99.

her husband while he was alive, and sometimes after his death).[159] In this context, the traditional conception of the permanency of marriage and of consistency in affection and loyalty, as expressed in a well-known Chinese proverb – 'A good horse will not serve two masters; a good woman will not marry two husbands' (*Haoma bushi er zhu; haonu bujia er fu*)[160] – entailed more a burden on women than a desire for the stability of the family. It is also in this context that, throughout China's long history, the concept of divorce has eventually become associated with the concept of disgrace and immorality. While divorced women were presumed to have failed to fulfil their filial duties to the family and their obligations to propriety, divorced men could be seen as the strong ones who arbitrarily abandoned the weak, and so divorced women could also be sympathised with as victims.

Modern Chinese legislation has emphasised freedom of marriage from the very beginning of its legislative history. In contemporary China, Article 49 of the present Constitution provides that 'violation of the freedom of marriage is prohibited'. Article 2 of the 1980 Marriage Law provides that freedom of marriage is one of the principles of the Law, and Article 3 of the same law emphasises that: 'marriage upon arbitrary decision by a third party, mercenary marriage and interference in freedom of marriage are prohibited'.[161] Although there is no express prohibition against receiving gifts, it is probably covered by the provision that 'the exaction of money and gifts in connection with the marriage shall be prohibited.'[162] Other regulations implementing the constitutional provision and the Marriage Law simply confirm the principle of freedom of marriage without exception.

The principle of freedom of marriage can be, and actually has been interpreted to include two aspects. One is that it should be free from interference from other parties; the other is that in the choice of a spouse it must be free from considerations such as social status, economic factors, etc., other than the consideration of affection. 'Freedom of marriage' is however interpreted as an instrument to protect marriage on the basis of love, rather than as a goal for people to pursue.[163] As such, this freedom is not an absolute but a relative one: marriage is not only a private matter, but also a matter concerning the interests of others, of the later generation

159 See MacCormack, *supra* note 156, at 90-99.

160 See Chiu, *supra* note 40, at 59.

161 These provisions have remained the same after the 2001 revision of the Marriage Law.

162 Article 3 of the 1980 Marriage Law, which has remained the same after the 2001 revision.

163 Yang Dawei, 'On Freedom of Marriage', in The Law Society of China (ed.), *A Collection of Papers on Law on Chinese Legal Science (I)* (*Zhongguo Faxue Wenji*) (Beijing: Law Publishing House, 1984), at 213.

as well as of the society.[164] Thus this freedom is not only regulated by law, but also restricted by morality and social interests.[165]

As mentioned earlier, the first communist regulation on marriage, the 1931 Marriage Regulations of the Soviet Republic, provided express and absolute freedom of divorce, which was re-affirmed by the 1934 Marriage Law of the Chinese Soviet Republic. Although this freedom has not been explicitly provided by later marriage legislation, it is interpreted as being an extension of the freedom of marriage, or the other side of the same coin.[166] Further, most of the marriage laws and regulations in modern China expressly allow voluntary divorce or provide very general grounds for divorce. The original 1980 Marriage Law allowed divorce by mutual consent and established some further grounds for divorce initiated by one party. The 2001 revision of the Marriage Law then elaborated these grounds. The present divorce provisions can be summarised as follows:

(a) divorce by mutual consent shall be granted and registered (Article 31);

(b) in the case of divorce initiated by one party, a procedure of mediation is required; if mediation fails and mutual affection has completely broken down, divorce shall be granted. Divorce will also be allowed if mediation fails in cases where one party is involved in bigamy or cohabiting with another person, or family violence or maltreatment is involved, or one party is a gambler or drug addict, or the parties have been separated for two years or more, or there are other circumstances causing incompatibility between the husband and the wife. Further, if one party is declared to have disappeared, and the other party files for divorce proceedings, the divorce shall be allowed (Article 32);

(c) in case of divorce from a serviceperson, consent must be obtained from that person unless the serviceperson is at serious fault (Article 33); and

(d) during the period of pregnancy and within one year after birth, the husband is not allowed to initiate divorce unless the court decides otherwise (Article 34).

---

164 This consideration has been a strong argument for those who demand further restrictions on freedom of divorce (being the other side of the same coin of freedom of marriage). See Nie Siyi, 'Controversies Caused by the Draft Bill on the Revision of the Marriage Law', *People's Daily* (*Renmin Ribao*), overseas edition, 15 August 1998, at 5. See also the discussion below on freedom of divorce.

165 Yang Dawei, *supra* note 163, at 216; Gu Maochuan, 'Marriage Is Not a Game', *People's Daily* (*Renmin Ribao*), internet edition, 7 October 1997.

166 Bai Ji & Li Fushen, 'On Freedom of Divorce', (no. 1, 1997) *Journal of China University of Political Science and Law* (*Zhengfa Luntan*) 59, at 59.

At first glance these provisions are quite liberal, imposing few restrictions on freedom of marriage and divorce. However, for a long time legislative policy and judicial practice seem to have undermined these liberal provisions, and social practices themselves tend to be quite different from legal requirements, particularly in the area of divorce.

On the policy side, flexibility has been left in the implementation of the Marriage Law, which requires compulsory mediation for divorce cases initiated by one party.[167] Such mediation has frequently led to the result of 'reconciliation'. Further, until quite recently, political marriage was encouraged, although in different forms throughout the years.[168] Because of the birth control policy, until the revision of the Law in 2001 it was not uncommon for people over the marriageable age to be refused permission to register,[169] while due to corruption among bureaucrats cases of under-age marriages being registered have not been unheard of either. Party policies, although varying from time to time, treat the family as the basic social unit, connected with the interests of the whole state. Stability of the family has thus been seen as a fundamental factor in social stability, and the latter is seen as extremely important to the government. Therefore, maintaining marriage stability, and hence social stability, is taken as one of the guiding principles in dealing with marriage and divorce cases.[170]

Court practice, which can reasonably be said to reflect the Party's policy, had, at least until the revision of the Marriage Law in 2001, tended to concentrate on finding causes of the breakdown of affection and on assessing the rights and wrongs of each party from the viewpoint of 'socialist' morality, rather than on judging whether affection had really broken down and granting divorce accordingly. As a result horrendous cases where divorce proceedings took 15, 20 and even 30 years to settle (not necessarily in a granting of divorce) were often reported in the Chinese media.[171] Sometimes, grounds for divorce had little to do with those stated in the laws, but emphasis was put on morality and the social interest. In one case the court even said to the plaintiff: 'We have mentioned many times to you that your marriage

---

167 See Article 25 of the Marriage Law (1980), now Article 32 in the 2001 revised Law.

168 Mao Jian, 'Should Political Ideas Be Considered in Marriage?', (no. 1, 1981) *Democracy and Legality* (*Minzhu Yu Fazhi*), at 23-25.

169 This was largely caused by working units refusing to issue a consent letter for marriage registration. As discussed earlier, this requirement has now been abolished.

170 See Certain Opinions on Handling Cases of Persons Living Together as Husband and Wife Without Marriage Registration, issued by the Supreme People's Court on 13 December 1989.

171 See e.g. Zhang Yujia, 'Rethinking on the Issue of Marriage Between Old People', (no. 7, 1987) *Democracy and Legality* (*Minzhu Yu Fazhi*), at 34-36; Wang Linuo, 'A Broken Family Has Been Preserved for Thirty Years', (no. 7, 1987) *Democracy and Legality* (*Minzhu Yu Fazhi*), at 34-36.

is dead. But now that your case is well known in society we have great difficulty in giving that decision'.[172] It is not uncommon for social pressure to prevail over legal grounds. When the Supreme People's Court finally issued its practical guide on divorce in 1989,[173] setting out 14 grounds on which a 'breakdown in affection' could be established, the courts seemed to be more interested in identifying fault in marriage than strictly implementing the Law. In fact, the courts were specifically required to determine who was the party at fault in their decisions on divorce.[174]

Socially, and expectedly, traditional practices die hard. The use of go-betweens and the demand for dowries and marriage banquets were never uncommon,[175] and are still practised.[176] Even though a 'breakdown in affection' was the only ground for divorce under the original marriage law, some surveys have indicated that no more than 20% of the people believe that a marriage should be dissolved simply because of this.[177] Meanwhile long condemned 'feudalist' or 'bourgeois' practices, such as bigamy, concubinage, extra-marital affairs, foster-daughters-in-law, exchange marriages etc., have all 're-appeared'.[178] Divorces caused by third party involvement

---

172 Wang Wanli, 'What Could I Do?', (no. 4, 1988) *Democracy and Legality* (*Minzhu Yu Fazhi*), at 4. In this case, the male plaintiff, Wang, was forced by his parents to become engaged with a woman in 1974. In the same year, he went to study in a university and started to persuade the woman to cancel the engagement. All effort failed and they got married in 1978. In 1981, he initiated the divorce. Since then, social pressure from all directions was put on him and in 1985 his salary was reduced by 25% and in 1986 he was sent back to his hometown in order to be reconciled with his wife. All this was because he had a high status and worked in the city while his wife was only a country-woman, and this led most people to draw the conclusion that he was abandoning a weak person – a typical reflection of the persistence of traditional ideas.

173 See Concrete Opinions on How to Determine the Breaking Down of Mutual Affection Between a Husband and a Wife in Handling Divorce Cases by Court, issued by the Supreme People's Court on 13 December 1989.

174 See Zhang Xianchu, *supra* note 109, at 315.

175 For some social survey results on this, see Shi Binghai, 'New Problems Facing Family Research', (no. 6, 1987) *Jurisprudence Monthly* (*Faxue*) 42; Gao Chaijin, 'New Problems facing Families in Town after the Reform', A paper presented to the National Conference on Marriage Law in Xiamen in 1986; *Law Year Book of China* (*Zhongguo Falü Quanshu*) (Beijing: Law Publishing House, 1987); and Michael Palmer, 'China, People's Republic of: Reacting to Rapid Social Change', in (1989–1990) 28 *Journal of Family Law* 438.

176 In fact, when the Supreme People's Court issued its Interpretation (II) of Certain Issues in the Application of the Marriage Law on 26 December 2003, it formally recognised dowries as part of the property to be settled in divorce proceedings. See Article 10 of the Interpretation (II).

177 'The Law Will Safeguard Marriage', *People's Daily* (*Renmin Ribao*), internet edition, 7 October 1997.

178 Ma Yuan, *supra* note 46, at 87; Mo Lijun, 'On Legislative Improvements on Divorce Grounds in Our Marriage Law', (no. 5, 1997) *Legal Science* (*Falü Kexue*) 88, at 89. Exchange marriage

or caused by giving birth to a daughter also increased rather dramatically in the 1980s and 1990s,[179] and continue today. Not surprisingly, some scholars came to openly declare that the present stage of socialism in China has not yet provided any realistic basis for marriage and divorce to be mainly based on affection.[180]

The actual practice of freedom of marriage and divorce has thus been a mixed picture. On the one hand there has indeed been an increase in divorce,[181] but on the other hand, divorce is not easy[182] and divorcees are subject to social stigma, just as they were in traditional China.[183]

However, it was the increase in the divorce rate, not the absolute number of divorces, and especially the increase in the divorce rate in the coastal areas,[184] that pre-occupied the minds of the expert group in charge of revising the 1980 Marriage Law, and prompted them to consider restricting divorce or imposing further conditions. Debate on divorce thus started in the 1990s.

---

means that one family marries its daughter to another family in exchange for a daughter from the other family to marry their own son.

179 Mo Lijun, *id.*, at 90.

180 Deng Hongbi, 'Some Considerations for Improving Our Marriage and Family System (Part I)', in (no. 1, 1997) *Modern Law Review* (*XiandaiFaxue*) 41, at 44; Mo Lijun, *supra* note 178, at 90.

181 An analysis of 20 years of divorce statistics shows that there were two peaks of divorce, in 1981 and 1987. There was a 30% increase in 1981, and then another 15-20% increase for three years from 1987. From 1991 to 1999 the divorce rate maintained a stable increase of around 4.4%. See Li Ping, 'A Brief Analysis of Divorce Cases in the Last Twenty Years', *People's Court Daily* (*Renmin Fayuan Bao*), internet edition, 3 October 2000. However, statistics compiled (on the basis of the *2000 Yearbook of China Statistics*) by the State Commission on Population and Family Planning indicated a much lower rate: the divorce rate increased from 0.95% in 1985 to 1.9% in 1997 and stabilised at that for 1998 and 1999. Available from <www.sfpc.gov.cn> (last accessed (16 September 2004). It should also be pointed out here that statistics in China are not reliable, even those from official authorities. For instance, a Shanghai researcher recently discovered that divorce statistics contained in the Yearbook of China Statistics compiled by the China Statistics Bureau in fact doubled the divorce rate, as divorces were always calculated twice because they involved couples. See 'Shanghai Scholar Finds Flaws in Divorce Statistics: Divorce Rate to Be Halved', available in <news.xinhuanet.com/local/2007-01/25/content_5649849.htm> (last accessed 25 January 2007).

182 There is a Chinese saying, which goes like this: If you do not want peace for a day, invite some friends for a banquet; if you do not want peace for a year, start moving your home; and if you do not want peace for a whole life, start your divorce. See Huang Chuanhui, *supra* note 39, at 206.

183 See *supra* note 160.

184 According to the *People's Court Daily*, nearly a quarter of marriages ended in divorce in the coastal provinces. See Zhang Hong, 'It Is Difficult Not to Be Confused about Extramarital Affairs', *People's Court Daily* (*Renmin Fayuan Bao*), internet edition, 26 November 2000.

A restriction on divorce that was strongly advocated was to demand the change of the grounds from 'breakdown in affection' to 'breakdown in family relations' or 'breakdown in marriage relations', a terminology which would give courts greater discretion in granting or refusing divorce by taking the whole marriage situation into consideration.[185] The argument was that marriage was the state recognition of a marriage relationship, not the recognition of affection, and the 14 grounds established by the Supreme People's Court in 1989 related to marriage relationships, not affection.[186] It was further argued that, since the law did not require affection as a marriage reason, why should a breakdown in affection be the grounds for divorce?[187] The expert drafts also aimed at restricting freedom of divorce by further elaborating divorce grounds in the Law, as well as by proposing a three-year separation as one of the criteria.[188] The imposition of such restrictions was defended on the grounds that 'such restrictions will maintain family and social stability as well as be conducive to the healthy development of the next generation'.[189]

However, the move to restrict freedom of divorce was met with strong resistance. Opponents made it clear that such restrictions would damage the freedom of divorce that had been won with a hard fight.[190] To many, freedom of divorce was a symbol of social and cultural development and any restriction would be 'cruel'.[191] They declared that any restriction on freedom of divorce would be a step back both in law and in morality, and the dissolution of marriage in which affection between spouses had gone was not only moral but also a symbol of advanced civilisation.[192] One of the most passionate arguments was mounted by Xu Anqi, a sociologist based in Shanghai. She declared that '[f]reedom of divorce is an indispensable part of freedom of marriage, and any restriction on freedom of divorce or move back to divorce on the basis of fault is a step back in cultural advancement and a development opposed to modern civilisation in the world.'[193] Xu attributed the increase of divorce to the rising living standards, the pursuit of quality marriage, more choice and freedom

---

185 'How to Assess the Divorce Rate', *supra* note 62.

186 See Wu Changzhen, *supra* note 60, at 74; and Hu Kangsheng, 'Major Issues in Amending the Chinese Marriage Law', (Oct 2000) *China Law* 63, at 65.

187 Wang & Sun, *supra* note 73, at 37.

188 See Expert Drafts in Wang & Sun, *supra* note 73. Others proposed a two-year separation as a ground for divorce.

189 Nie Siyi, *supra* note 164, at 5.

190 Nie Siyi, *supra* note 164, at 5.

191 See 'Opinions Split on Marriage Law', *China Daily*, internet edition, 12 September 2000.

192 'It Is a Step Back to Use Restriction of Divorce to Protect Weak Women', *Wenhui Daily* (*Wenhui Bao*), 7 September 2000, republished in *People's Daily*, internet edition, 22 November 2000.

193 Xu Anqi, 'Restriction on Divorce Should not be the Main Objective in the Revision of the Marriage Law', *Legal Daily* (*Fazhi Ribao*), internet edition, 12 October 2000. See also, 'Can the Law Save Shaky Marriages?', (November 27, 2000) *Beijing Review* 23-25.

in choosing partners, and the smaller size of families.[194] She further pointed out that divorce was in fact not easy at all. Xu rejected the argument that divorce would have a very negative impact on the children affected. She argued that her research showed that only 5% – 10% of divorces had a negative impact on the children, while 10% – 15% actually had a positive impact. As to extramarital affairs as the reason for divorce, Xu rightly argued that it was also the main reason for divorce in the 1950s and 1960s.[195]

On the question of elaborating divorce grounds, while some opponents to a restriction of freedom of divorce agreed to the incorporation of judicial interpretations into law instead of the imposition of any further restrictions on freedom of divorce,[196] others believed that the grounds established by the 1980 Marriage Law were considered ones, and the 14 grounds listed by the 1989 Supreme People's Court Opinions were not necessary reasons for breaking up the marriage relationship. They argued that the listing of these in the revised Law might in fact be interpreted as expanding the grounds for divorce.[197]

Law-makers also disagreed on whether 'breakdown in affection' should continue to be a ground or condition for divorce, and whether it should be replaced by 'breakdown in the marriage relationship'.[198] Some law-makers were concerned about adding a rule on several years of separation before divorce, believing it was too long and could lead to domestic violence and social instability. Others believed that this rule would simply give the economically well off yet another legal ground for divorce and for looking to new love and would cause instability in the family.[199]

In the end there was a typical Chinese solution – a compromise. Freedom of marriage (by logical extension, freedom of divorce) was upheld, and 'breakdown in affection' was retained as the principal reason for divorce. A two-year separation rule was added and some less controversial grounds for divorce as initially contained in the 1989 Supreme Court Opinions were also incorporated into the revised Law.[200]

---

194 Xu Anqi 'To Protect Freedom of Divorce: Restriction on Divorce Should not be the Main Objective in the Revision of the Marriage Law', *Southern Weekend Weekly* (*Nanfang Zhoumo*)), internet edition, 21 September 2000.

195 Xu Anqi, *supra* note 193.

196 See 'Revision of the Marriage Law: An Insider (Wu Changzhen) Talks about the Key Issues', (March 15, 2001) *Beijing Review* 14, at 15.

197 Hu Kangsheng, *supra* note 186, at 65.

198 'Observations on the Deliberation of the Marriage Law Revision bill at the Standing Committee of the NPC', *People's Daily (Renmin Ribao)*, internet edition, 27 Oct 2000. 'How Should the Marriage Law Be Revised', *Legal Daily* (*Fazhi Ribao*), internet edition, 31 October 2000

199 *Id*; Wang & Sun, *supra* note 73, at 37.

200 See Article 32 of the Marriage Law (as revised in 2001).

5.3. Extramarital Affairs

Issues relating to extramarital affairs are almost always discussed in the context of the emergence of the '*bao ernai*' phenomenon. *Bao ernai* generally refers to the phenomenon of a married man keeping a mistress or several mistresses outside wedlock. It is an extra-marital affair but differs in that (1) it is generally a long-term relationship; (2) the man normally supports the mistress(es) financially so as to keep the mistress(es) exclusively to himself; (3) the relationship is often based on exchange of sex for money or power; and (4) it is a phenomenon that it is widespread among corrupt officials and the new rich in society.[201] Hu Kangsheng, Deputy Director of the LAC of the SCNPC, defines '*bao ernai*' as 'the use of material benefits, like money, to maintain opposite sex companions.' He further lists the following forms as examples: (1) maintaining a mistress through the provision of housing, a car, living expenses etc.; (2) maintaining a prostitute on a long-term basis, and sometimes in the name of 'rescuing a prostitute to become a good woman'; (3) maintaining long-term sexual partners in the guise of secretaries, babysitters, etc., and (4) open cohabitation by husband, wife and concubine.[202] It is, in a sense, the revival of the concubinage practised in traditional China, except that it is against the law now and appears in all kinds of guises (personal secretary, personal assistant, business associate etc.). In a similar vein, but much less commonly, some powerful or rich women, or the spouses of rich men, also keep secret lovers, either as revenge for their husband's behaviour or in pursuit of lust or a 'new life' style. The latter is then referred to as *bao erye* ('keeping a second man').

It is unclear how widespread the phenomenon of *bao ernai* is, but it is clear that it is increasing rather rapidly. According to Hu Kangsheng, the Women's Federation in Guangdong Province experienced a 7.3% increase in such complaints in 1997, but a 48% increase in 1998.[203] It was reported that 95% of cases of economic corruption in Guangdong Province contained an element of 'maintaining a mistress', and statistics from one city in Sichuan indicated that 65% of divorce cases had a third party involvement.[204] It is therefore not surprising that 'maintaining a mistress' was seen not only as ruining social morality, but also as corrupting government officials,[205] and hence that there was a need to address the issue by law.

Dealing with extra-marital sex by law is not a new issue in China; it was hotly debated whether it should be criminalised when the KMT Civil Code was being

---

201 See Hu Kangsheng, *supra* note 82.

202 See Hu Kangsheng, *supra* note 186, at 63. (China Law is published in bilingual form. The English text above has been modified according to the Chinese texts.)

203 *Id.*, at 63

204 Nie Siyi, *supra* note 164; 'No Leeway for Bigamists: Chinese Legislators', *China Daily*, internet edition, 28 October 2000.

205 'No Leeway for Bigamists: Chinese Legislators', *id.*

drafted in the late 1920s.[206] The current Chinese Criminal Law proscribes the crime of bigamy, which is defined as occurring if 'one, having a spouse, marries again, or marries another with the knowledge of the other's having a spouse'.[207] The Supreme People's Court Interpretation also prescribes that the crime of bigamy would have been committed if a person having a spouse cohabits with another in the name of husband and wife, or one cohabits with another in the name of husband and wife in the knowledge of the other having a spouse.[208] However, the phenomenon of '*bao ernai*' does not generally constitute bigamy.

It was in the above context that demands for reform began to emerge. Initially, the Expert Group made two suggestions. The first was that family responsibility, loyalty and obligations between the parties, and other aspects of family morality should be stressed in the law.[209] Secondly, that as a result of such emphasis the notion of 'fault', such as unfaithfulness in marriage, should be re-introduced, at least in deciding the division of matrimonial property in divorce proceedings. It was argued that 'if someone begins to look for new love because his/her economic status has changed, then the other party whose interests have been damaged should have a right to economic compensation.'[210] Obviously, this approach was a partial return to that of the 1950s.[211] Such a legal provision could lead to invasion of privacy, but it was argued that 'freedom means that you can do what the law allows you to do, and privacy refers to matters you do not want others to know, and that do not impair the interests of others. However, it is unlawful to do anything that is prohibited by law, and non-disclosure of matters which damage others or are in violation of law interferes with judicial justice.'[212]

On these principles the legal requirements for 'mutual faithfulness' in marriage and legal sanctions against those involved in extra-marital sex in divorce proceedings were contained in early drafts. These provisions caused some very emotional debates in the Chinese media and among academics. Ironically, both provisions were proposed by those who claimed to be feminists, for the purpose of maintaining marriage, and hence, social stability. Outspoken scholars loudly protested against such provisions, denouncing them as a backward step in legal development, confusing social morality with legal obligations, and the marriage situation with social

---

206 Philip C.C. Huang, *Code, Custom, and Legal Practice in China: The Qing and the Republic Compared* (California: Stanford University Press, 2001), at 185.

207 Article 258 of the Criminal Law (as amended in 1997).

208 See *supra* note 170.

209 Wu Changzhen, *supra* note 60, at 74.

210 'How to Assess the Divorce Rate', *supra* note 62.

211 See *supra* note 42.

212 Nie Siyi, *supra* note 164, at 5

stability. To the younger generation any legal treatment of purely moral issues was simply unacceptable.[213]

However, more radical reform proposals soon emerged. There were suggestions that the revised marriage law should directly prohibit extramarital sexual intercourse.[214] To ease legal requirements there was a suggestion to define a six-month period of cohabitation as a criterion for convictions for bigamy.[215] There was also a proposal to amend the Criminal Law by adding a new crime called 'sexual bribery' for soliciting and accepting 'sexual service,'[216] a practice that was said to have existed in China since time immemorial.[217] To many of the supporters, criminal law was the most appropriate channel for dealing with such matters.[218]

Most radically, a proposal also emerged to establish, in law, the right of the spouse to impose an obligation of chastity upon the husband or wife.

The so-called 'right of the spouse' was strongly advocated by the 'marriage experts' and incorporated into the expert drafts, without actually being defined. It was mostly discussed in the context of extra-marital affairs. According to some academics,

---

213 See 'Revision of the Marriage Law Causes Great Controversy', *People's Daily* (*Renmin Ribao*), internet edition, 15 August 1998; 'Extra-marital love elicits controversy', *China Daily*, internet edition, 6 October 1998; 'Farewell, My Concubine, as China Plans to Outlaw Hanky-panky', *The Age*, 8 October 1998, at 17; and 'Major Points for the Revision of the Marriage Law', *People's Daily*, internet edition, 9 August 2000.

214 See Wang & Sun, *supra* note 73, at 45.

215 See Hu Kangsheng, *supra* note 82. The six months criterion was proposed by the All China Women's Federation. See 'Bigamy and Maintaining a Mistress Should be Stopped – A Proposal from the All China Federation of Women' *Legal Daily* (*Fazhi Ribao*) internet edition, 21 September 2000.

216 "Professor: Sexual Bribery Must Be Made a Crime in China', *China Daily*, internet edition, 8 December 2000. Current Chinese Criminal Law only defines bribery as accepting money or goods. As in the debate on extramarital affairs, strong objections were soon to emerge, that it was 'in essence an ethical problem.' See 'Professor: Time Not Ripe to Make "Sexual Bribery" a Crime in China', *China Daily*, internet edition, 12 December 2000. On this debate, see 'Who Should Be Punished in Sexual Bribery', *Beijing Youth Daily* (*Beijing Qingnian Bao*), 19 December 2000 (republished in <www.people.com.cn>); 'When Sexual Bribery Should Be Criminalised', *People's Daily* (*Renmin Ribao*), 20 December 2000, at 9; 'Sexual Bribery Is Horrendous, but Punishment Is Difficult to Mete Out', *Beijing Evening News* (*Beijing Wanbao*), 20 December 2000 (republished in <www.people.com.cn>); 'Judicial Treatment of Sexual Bribery', *Procuratorial Daily* (*Jiancha Ribao*), 20 December 2000 (republished in <www.people.com.cn>); and 'Legislation Against Sexual Bribery: Legal Experts Disagree', *Procuratorial Daily* (*Jiancha Ribao*), 12 December 2000. (republished in <www.people.com.cn>).

217 'A Look at Sexual Bribery in Ancient China', *People's Court Daily* (*Renmin Fayuan Bao*) internet edition, 17 January 2001.

218 See also 'Issues in Focus for New Marriage Law', <www.china.org.cn/english/1993.htm>.

> The right of the spouse is a right to personal status as husband and wife in wedlock, a general name for the special rights and obligations enjoyed and assumed by husband and wife in a marriage. It means that both the husband and wife have equal rights to the use of their own names, determination of residence, living together, loyalty to each other and management of property.[219]

This definition was by no means universally agreed by the Chinese scholars who supported the inclusion of such a notion in the revised Marriage Law. According to one of the chief scholars writing on the subject, there were at least three kinds of definition on the right of the spouse: that it was a right for a spouse to demand companionship, love and assistance from the other spouse; that it was a right of status, in which one belongs to the other in a spousal relationship; and that it was a personal right covering all personal interests derived from a marriage relationship.[220] Miao defined it as a right based on the status of being a spouse, entailing all personal interests relating to the fact of being a spouse, and all other rights and duties necessary to sustaining a normal spousal relationship.[221]

Scholars often started from the definition of 'Consortium' as contained in the Oxford Companion to Law,[222] as confirmation of the existence of such a right, with its origin and development in Anglo-Saxon Common law.[223] On this basis it was advocated that such a right would cover all personal and property rights based on the status of being a spouse, including the right to name, residence, cohabitation, mutual faithfulness, and agency for daily matters for each other.[224]

Opponents were quick to point out that: 'To talk about extramarital affairs, adultery and bigamy together is to confuse moral sanctions with legal penalties or to upgrade moral regulations to legal provisions. It is ignorant to expect criminal sanctions for violations of morality.'[225] They further pointed out that if third party liability was to be pursued in divorce cases it effectively encouraged people, in judicial practice, to

---

219 *Id.*

220 Miao Wenquan, 'On the Meaning and Value Analysis of the Rights of the Spouse', (no. 4, 2000) *Politics and Law* (*Zhengzhi yu falu*) 50, at 50.

221 *Id.*

222 Which refers to the right of each spouse to the companionship, affection, and assistance of the other. See David M Walker (ed.), *The Oxford Companion to Law* (Oxford: Clarendon Press, 1980), at 275.

223 See Miao Wenquan, *supra* note 119, at 50; Ma Qiang, 'On the Right of the Spouse', (no. 2, 2000) *Legal Forum* (*Faxue Luntan*) 49, at 49.

224 Ma Qiang, *id.*, 50-52.

225 'Morality and Law – No. 2 of a Series of Comments on the Revision of the Marriage Law', *People's Daily* (*Renmin Ribao*) (overseas edition), 20 December 2000; at 10.

catch 'adultery', and hence to cause major concerns for privacy.[226] Others reminded people that such revisions would amount to a backward step in legal development,[227] and a violation of the spirit of the rule of law.[228] To the opponents, the revision of the marriage law had been misdirected to the so-called 'hot issues' such as bigamy, extra-marital affairs etc.; the real issue, they argued, was freedom of marriage, or more precisely, freedom of divorce.[229] Not surprisingly, they demanded that the word 'faithfulness' should be removed from the draft law altogether.[230] However, supporters for such a right believed that 'one of the functions of legal provisions is their directional influence.'[231]

Technically, it was also pointed out that if compensation was to be given by the party at fault in divorce proceedings, then (1) how were the fault and the wrongdoing party to be determined; (2) what was the nature of the compensation ('emotional compensation' or 'compensation for mental anguish'); and (3) should the third party also be liable for joint liability.[232] Still others questioned the wisdom of the proposal of six-month cohabitation as a criterion for determining bigamy, fearing such a provision would simply encourage the man to drop his mistress for a new woman before the six-month period expired.[233] It was also argued that extramarital affairs were a result of western values of individualism and sexual ideas, not a necessary result of men having more money. Based on her study of several thousand divorce cases, Xu pointed out that less than 5% of such divorces were caused by the fact that the men had more money and began to have mistresses.[234] She therefore went further and opposed the idea of providing the party without fault, women, and under-aged children with special protection to penalise the party at fault and make them pay for their mistakes.[235]

Opponents argued that most rights that might be covered by the notion of spousal rights, as defined by jurists, had been provided by the marriage law already, and thus the hidden agenda of advocating such a notion was to outlaw extramarital affairs

---

226 Nie Siyi, *supra* note 164, at 5

227 *Id.*

228 'Morality and Law', *supra* note 225, at 10.

229 Wen Yibing, 'What Issues Need to Be Dealt With by the Marriage Law', *People's Court Daily (Renmin Fayuan Bao)*, internet edition, 31 Jan 2001.

230 See Wang & Sun, *supra* note 73, at 29.

231 'Revision of the Marriage Law: An Insider (Wu Changzhen) Talks about the Key Issues', *supra* note 196, at 14.

232 See Hu Kangsheng, *supra* note 186, at 66.

233 'Issues in Focus for New Marriage Law', *supra* note 218.

234 Xu Anqi, *supra* note 194.

235 Xu Anqi, supra note 193.

and extramarital sex.[236] Liang went further, accusing the jurists of having a modern disease, that is, of being too eager to use law to interfere with private life.[237] Other opponents rightly pointed out that the establishment of a right of the spouse would undermine efforts to deal with domestic violence as well as the question of rape in marriage.[238] Still others simply declared it was a most ridiculous idea to make sex an exclusive right and a duty.[239] The essence of the right of the spouse was, one scholar pointed out, a right to sexual intercourse and such a right was a most fundamental personal rights. Such a right must only belong to oneself and not be alienated by a single promise (marriage) to another. In this, moral issues (extramarital affairs) should not be dealt with by legal provisions.[240] Even the more sympathetic opponents would have preferred the widening of the meaning of bigamy, either through the revision of the marriage law or judicial interpretation, or the revision of the criminal law to cover all *bao ernai* cases, rather than using a new notion.[241]

These opponents' views were seen by the members of the Expert Group as the result of a misunderstanding of the notion of 'right of the spouse'. Thus, a leading member in the Group, Professor Wu Changzhen argued that '[t]he emphasis on mutual loyalty between a husband and wife partially results from long-lasting debates over the right of a spouse. This right essentially is related to the right one spouse has over the other. There has always been some misunderstanding of that right, narrowly recognising it as a sex-related right. As a result, some people naturally confuse mutual loyalty between a husband and wife with sexual monopoly. This is a lopsided viewpoint.'[242]

Law-makers were in a dilemma: 90% of those involved in the drafting of the Expert Drafts were women, but 80% of the NPC deputies (law-makers) were men.[243] On the one hand they could not agree on how to deal with extra-marital affairs, and on the other hand they did not want to be seen as male chauvinists. Some believed it was a moral issue, others insisted that the law must step in when morality has

---

236 Liang Hongbo, 'Spousal Right Is Not Appropriate for Our Time', *Chinese Women Daily* (*Zhongguo Funu Bao*), 13 September 2000, republished in *People's Daily*, internet edition, 22 November 2000.

237 *Id.*

238 'How Wide Should the Law Be in Regulating Marriage and Family', *People's Court Daily* (*Renmin Fayuan Bao*), internet edition, 31 October 2000.

239 Wang & Sun, *supra* note 73, at 30.

240 'Peace and Harmony – No. 1 of a Series of Comment on the Revision of the Marriage Law', *People's Daily* (*Renmin Ribao*), 20 December 2000, at 10.

241 See Wang & Sun, *supra* note 73, at 45.

242 'Revision of the Marriage Law: An Insider (Wu Changzhen) Talks about the Key Issues', *supra* note 196, at 14.

243 Nie Siyi, *supra* note 164, at 5

failed to deal with an issue.[244] On the question of compensation, some law-makers rightly pointed out that it would be difficult to determine whose fault had led to a 'breakdown in affection' and hence the actual implementation of the compensation provisions.[245] Others believed that the marriage law, being of the nature of civil legislation, should not deal with crimes or criminal punishment, and that such matters should be dealt with through amendments to the Criminal Law.[246] Woman judges too were strongly opposed to the reforms proposed by the 'feminist' academics, arguing that such a move was neither scientific nor feasible, and that the marriage law or any other law could only have a limited role in social life.[247]

Misunderstanding or not, law-makers finally decided that a compromise position was the way to go, that is, to lay down an obligation of mutual faithfulness and cohabitation,[248] but not to legislate for rights of the spouse. It was the law-makers' view that although 'faithfulness' is a moral issue, it could nevertheless be declared in law, without attaching any legal sanctions or having it used for judicial judgement.[249]

The revised Law now imposes a legal obligation on spouses to be faithful to each other and prohibits a married person from cohabiting with any other person than his/her spouse.[250] Further, in addition to criminal sanctions against bigamy, the Law provides the party without fault a right to seek compensation for damages in divorce proceeding.[251]

Although the new law has been swiftly, and apparently retrospectively, applied by Chinese courts, especially in cases of '*bao ernai*',[252] there are many practical difficulties in deciding what amounts to 'continuing and stable cohabitation' between a

---

244 Nie Siyi, *id*; 'How Should the Marriage Law Be Revised', *Legal Daily* (*Fazhi Ribao*), internet edition, 31 October 2000.

245 'How Should the Marriage Law Be Revised', *id*.

246 'Hot Issues in the Revision of the Marriage Law', *People's Daily* (*Renmin Ribao*) 26 December 2000, 3.

247 See Wang & Sun, *supra* note 73, at 135.

248 Hu Kangsheng, *supra* note 82.

249 See Wang & Sun, *supra* note 73, at 30. This then became the position taken by the Supreme People's Court in interpreting the revised Marriage Law. See Article 3 of the Interpretation (I) of the Supreme People's Court on Certain Issues concerning the Application of the Marriage Law, issued 27 December 200. Article 3 specifically requires a court not to accept a case solely on the basis of Article 4 (mutual faithfulness requirement) of the revised Marriage Law.

250 Articles 3 & 4 of the revised Marriage Law.

251 Articles 12 & 46 of the revised Marriage Law.

252 On 10 May 2001, a Beijing Court applied the revised Law in a case dealing with the question of '*bao ernai*'. Thereafter, the Law was soon applied by courts in Anshan, Fuzhou, Hangzhou, Shenzhen, Shenyang, Nanjing, etc. See 'The Revision of the Marriage Law, a Successful Experiment in Democratic Law-making', *NPC News* (*Zhongguo Renda Xinwen*) (internet edition): <zgrdxw.peopledaily.com.cn>, 18 July 2002. See also 'Unclear Issues in the Implementation of the New Marriage Law', *People's Daily* (*Renmin Ribao*), internet edition, 22 June 2001.

married person and another.[253] For practical purposes there is an immediate conflict between obtaining evidence and protection of privacy. The latter could also lead to questions of infringement of personal rights, such as personal dignity.[254] On this point, the experience in Taiwan is perhaps of some help. The mutual obligation of spouses to cohabitate (*tongju*) was first introduced to China by the KMT Civil Code.[255] Recent studies seem to indicate that this provision was misused (if not abused) by husbands to force their wives to return home, even though domestic mistreatment was claimed by the wives.[256]

5.4. Property in Marriage and Divorce

With rapid economic development, rising living standards and the accumulation of private wealth (especially among private entrepreneurs), it was generally agreed among law-makers and academics that there is need for clear rules on property division in divorce cases, and for giving better protection to women. It was also recognised that, with the increasing accumulation of wealth, re-marriage between the elderly met with major objections from their children, fearing the loss of their inheritance.[257] However, this agreement was soon overshadowed by disagreements on the required length of a marriage before property could be treated as common property, and the kinds of property that should be treated so.[258] Most controversial was the introduction of prenuptial agreements, often criticised as a preparation for divorce even before getting married.[259] Indeed, according to a survey conducted by the All China Women's Federation, 57% of those surveyed saw the prenuptial

---

253 See also 'Unclear Issues in the Implementation of the New Marriage Law', *id.*

254 Obtaining evidence to prove bigamy is not easy; there have been cases where either the evidence (such as a video recording or photos taken secretly) was rejected by courts as illegal evidence, or the wives were actually penalised for infringing the personal rights of their husbands or mistresses. See 'Catching Adultery: the new difficult topic in marriage law', *Legal Daily* (*Fazhi Ribao*), internet edition, 16 October 2000. This problem was only intensified after the implementation of the new marriage law. It was further aggravated because of the ban on private investigation, a ban imposed by the Ministry of Public Security in 1993. See Mao Lei, 'Proof of Evidence in Divorce Compensation Is Hard', *People's Daily* (*Renmin Ribao*), 15 May 2002, at 10. The newly issued Supreme People's Court interpretation of Civil Evidence (issued by the Supreme People's Court on 21 December 2001) now allows secret video and audio recordings to be used as evidence.

255 See Huang, *supra* note 206, at 184. This obligation remains in the Civil Code in Taiwan. See Article 1001 of the Civil Code of the Republic of China, in *Major Laws of the Republic of China on Taiwan* (Tainan: Magnificent Publishing Co., 1991), at 301.

256 Huang, *id.*, at 179.

257 'Morality and Law', *supra* note 225, at 10.

258 Nie Siyi, *supra* note 164.

259 'Peace and Harmony', *supra* note 240.

notarisation of property agreements as a violation of traditional family ideas, while 43% nevertheless believed it was necessary.[260]

It should also be pointed out that prenuptial notarisation of property agreements is relatively new in China. In the case of Beijing, it only emerged in the 1990s, but mainly among the marriages of middle-aged or elderly couples. It has not been common among young couples.[261]

The property regime proposed by legal experts and government departments included the following:[262]

> A contractual regime, which may be one of the following: (a) unity of property: all property (acquired before and after marriage) of the spouses shall be co-owned by the spouses; (b) community property: all property (acquired before and after marriage) belongs to both spouses but is managed by one of them according to contractual agreement; (c) separation of property: all property (acquired before and after marriage) shall be owned and managed by each of the spouses separately.
> Proprietary property: certain property (such as property before marriage, inheritance, intellectual property etc.) may only belong to one of the spouses.
> Statutory property: Property acquired during marriage, except proprietary property and in the absence of contractual agreement, shall be co-owned by both spouses.

In order to deal with gender discrimination it was also proposed that the revised law should directly provide that married women in rural areas should be allowed to have equal rights with others in the distribution of land and allocation of contracting rights for cultivation land.[263]

These proposals are not strictly controversial, but encountered major difficulties in at least three areas: (1) housing, (2) private companies, (3) contract land in rural areas.[264]

The Revised Law took an easy way out: first, Chapter 3 on Family Relationship now defines, in more detailed provisions, joint property and individual property during and after marriage. Furthermore, for the first time the Law now recognises

---

260 'Opinion Divided Among Chinese on Prenuptial Notarisation of Property', *People's Daily* (*Renmin Ribao*) internet edition, 4 August 2000.

261 'Should "You and Me" Be Clearly Defined Before Marriage', *People's Daily* (*Renmin Ribao*), 7 August 2000.

262 Hu Kangsheng, *supra* note 186, at 65.

263 See Wang & Sun, *supra* note 73, at 48.

264 Hu Kangsheng, *supra* note 186, at 65.

the legal validity of prenuptial agreements.[265] However, the more difficult questions on the division of property are largely left undefined. Practical rules on these matters are therefore largely dealt with by the interpretations of the Supreme People's Court.[266]

5.5. Domestic Violence

Domestic violence exists in all societies and countries. The issue often invokes emotion, which in turn is sometimes inflamed by exaggeration and sensationalisation by the media.[267] In the case of China a widely cited survey result, said to be the one conducted by the All China Women's Federation, suggested that domestic violence existed in some 30% of Chinese families, and that among the 270 million families, around 100,000 families were dissolved as a result of domestic violence each year.[268] This turned out to be completely inaccurate; the actual figure in fact referred to the percentage of women citing domestic violence as their reasons for their making complaints to women's written complaint centres (*xinfang*), not to the society in general.[269] This of course is not to say that domestic violence should be tolerated or ignored; every case of domestic violence is one too many and must be dealt with seriously by law.

Although the original 1980 Marriage Law prohibited ill-treatment and desertion of one family member by another, it had little to say about the forms of domestic violence, nor provided any legal remedies. The major difficulties in dealing with domestic violence have been the traditional view that 'ugliness in the family should not be leaked outside', and 'a good judge is not able to judge family matters'.[270] In terms of law, although the Criminal Law does deal with intentional injuries and maltreatment, in cases where domestic violence only leads to minor injuries there

---

265 See Article 19 of the revised Marriage Law.

266 Especially by Interpretation (II) (2003), *supra* note 176.

267 In Australia, for instance, when a major newspaper, *The Age*, started a series on domestic violence, the headlines ran like these: 'Epidemic of violence on women', 'The war against women', etc. See *The Age* series starting from 3 June 1993.

268 See NPC News, internet edition, 27 April 2001; *People's Daily*, internet edition, 20 November 2000; 'Morality and Law', *supra* note 225, at 10, and Lu Pipi, 'New Marriage Law Sparks Concern', (15 March 2001) *Beijing Review* 12, 13; 'Ban on Family Violence Urged in China', China.org.cn, 14 September 2000, and many other media articles. There were also claims that the percentage of families where domestic violence exist is in fact much higher. See 'On the Reality, Harms and the Prevention of Domestic Violence', in All China Women's Federation website: <www.women.org.cn>, 17 March 2003.

269 See Xu Anqi, 'Media Misleading Areas in the Revision of the Marriage Law', in *People's Daily* (*Renmin Ribao*) (internet edition), 20 November 2000.

270 'Morality and Law', *supra* note 225, at 10.

will be difficulties in applying the criminal law.[271] Because of these views the debate on domestic violence has often been misconceived as a social problem, not a legal concern.[272] It is misconceived in that that all injuries, mental or physical, caused to another person are a violation of law, no matter what relationship the persons might have under the law.

In the absence of a national law, local governments began to take their own initiatives in the late 1990s. Thus Hunan Province took the lead by issuing its own Resolution of the Standing Committee of Hunan People's Congress on the Prevention and Punishment of Family Violence on 31 March 2000.[273] This was subsequently followed by other provinces. Under these circumstances, the revision of the national law went rather smoothly.

The Revised Law now specifically prohibits domestic violence,[274] and much of the new chapter (Chapter 5 on Legal Remedies and Liabilities) is about the legal consequences of domestic violence, ill-treatment, and the desertion of family members. Domestic violence is also specified as a ground for divorce[275] and for compensation during divorce proceedings.[276]

6. Concluding Remarks

Like in any other country, there is a gap between the law and social reality in China. There are many factors that contribute to this disparity. Essentially, however, Party and state policies are often inconsistent and undermine each other. The present economic policies, which emphasise the importance of the family unit and shift state welfare burdens to the family, and the one-child birth control policy, obviously re-enforce the traditional values of the family rather than reforming them. In very poor economic and social welfare situations the pursuit of survival will inevitably prevail over high spiritual goals, whether they be communist or bourgeois. The frequent condemnation of the deterioration of morality needs a further examination of the causes of these social phenomena.

---

271 See 'Domestic Violence Should Be Explicitly Proscribed – Second Proposal on the Revision of the Marriage Law by the All China Federation of Women', *Legal Daily* (*Fazhi Ribao*), internet edition, 28 September 2000.

272 See Xiaoqing Feng, 'A Review of the Development of the Marriage Law in the People's Republic of China', (2002) 79 *U. Detroit Mercy L. Rev.* 331, at 393; Hu Kangsheng, *supra* note 82.

273 See 'Major Points for the Revision of the Marriage Law', *People's Daily* (*Renmin Ribao*), internet edition, 9 August 2000.

274 Article 3 of the revised Marriage Law.

275 Article 32 of the revised Marriage Law.

276 Article 46 of the revised Marriage Law.

There is an added difficulty in family reform. The transplanted western law, whether in the name of communist ideology or of the modernisation of Chinese law, faces the formidable task of fighting a five-thousand-year long tradition in an underdeveloped country and with poorly educated people in the vast rural areas. Such a task is clearly a major undertaking, fraught with difficulties. Revolution may have been spread all over the country, but it needs much more than ideological education to reach the heart of the ordinary people.

Further, in the Chinese context one must thus be sensitive in assessing the progress made and the remaining problems in contemporary policy and law. Western feminist scholars have been very critical of the communist policy on the family and, especially, on women. Thus, Stacey asserts that from the beginning the CPC wanted nothing more for women than a stable family life in the nature of a democratic patriarchal style, making socialism and patriarchy mutually co-operative.[277] This interpretation of the CPC's intention in family law reform misses the point: the present problems are more a result of the conflict between modernity and tradition than of hypocrisy in the CPC's policy. The social reality has to be assessed in the context of development; that is, in the progress made from a traditional patriarchal society, rather than through a direct comparison with western countries or according to western criteria.

Finally, it is also important to recognise realistically the power of the law. Certainly law can be, and has always been, used as an instrument for social change. But there is a limit to what law can do and there is a boundary beyond which law shall not enter. The attempt to use law to intervene in extramarital affairs is an issue in point. Extramarital affairs are not unique to China, nor are they unique to contemporary China. This is more often than not a moral issue rather than a legal one. More importantly, it is an issue of discrimination and disadvantage, the solution to which lies with anti-discrimination laws, women's protection laws, and more fundamentally, government initiatives to address the issues relating to discrimination and disadvantage, and equitable distribution and re-distribution of wealth. Any attempt to fuse morality with law is bound to be controversial,[278] and

277 Judith Stacey, *Patriarchy and Socialist Revolution in China* (Berkeley/Los Angeles/London: University of California Press, 1983), at 266.

278 In fact, the fusion of morality and law arose once again recently. In October 2006, a local court in Guangdong Province awarded damages to a young woman for the loss of 'right of chastity'. In this case, the young woman had a relationship with her boss for several years. When she fell pregnant, it was then discovered that the man was in fact a married man without any intention of marrying her. She then sued the man for cheating her 'chastity' and claimed damages for the loss of 'right of chastity' – a traditional notion of 'chastity' fused with a modern notion of 'right' which has never existed in modern Chinese law – and won compensation of 10,000 *yuan*. This decision immediately caused fierce debates that are still going on in China today. See the cover story in (no. 11, 2007) *Democracy and Legal System* (*Minzhu Yu Fazhi*), at 4-12.

indeed, any attempt to allow law to readily and easily enter into a citizens' bedroom must be questionable.

Chapter Twelve

Civil Law: Contracts

1. Introduction

The civil law institution of contracts in the form of customary law has a history at least as long as the known history of China.[1] State regulation, more often with regard to the control and use of contracts than to their contents, appeared as early as the Western Zhou (11–771 BC).[2] However, a comprehensive code on contracts did not appear until the KMT Civil Code was promulgated between 1929–1930.[3] Despite its extremely long history, contract law in present-day China is largely a product of the 1980s and 1990s.

As a legal institution contracts have been emphasised as a focal point for legal measures for economic reform, to be utilised for assuming and dividing legal liabilities, as well as for asserting economic autonomy. Despite their importance in economic and legal reform, this area of law was for a long time largely composed of underdeveloped, fragmented and essentially *ad hoc* legislation until the enactment of a uniform law on contracts in 1999.

This Chapter first provides a brief review of contract law development in the PRC, explaining the evolution of the conception of contract law in line with politico-economic development in post-Mao China. It then outlines the legal framework on contracts in contemporary China, focusing on the generally applicable principles now governing the formation, performance and contracting practices. Through this examination it will be shown that contract law in China most closely reflects the

---

1 It is claimed by some Chinese scholars that contracts existed even before the creation of the Chinese written language. See Zhao Yuhong, 'Contract Law', in Wang Chenguang & Zhang Xianchu (eds), *Introduction to Chinese Law* (Hong Kong: Sweet & Maxwell Asia, 1997), at 235.

2 Li Zhimi, *Ancient Chinese Civil Law* (*Zhongguo Gudai Minfa*) (Beijing: Publishing House of Law, 1988), at 116.

3 Following the Continental tradition, the KMT Civil Code contained a separate Book (Book II) on Obligations covering both torts and contracts.

ideological transformation from a planned economy to a market-oriented one, as well as the corresponding bureaucratic changes in post-Mao China.

2. The Development of Contract Law in the PRC

The slow development of contract law is better understood in the context of the evolving politico-economic system and the struggle for power within the bureaucratic structure than in terms of Chinese tradition or history.[4] Put crudely, contracts were for a long time simply seen as a means for economic transactions, hence their usefulness and the extent of their use was largely determined by the prevailing politico-economic systems[5] and their development often encountered strong resistance from bureaucratic authorities vested with the power of examination and approval for economic activities. In this situation the first set of regulations on contracts in the PRC, the Provisional Measures concerning the Making of Contracts among Governmental Institutions, State-owned Enterprises and Cooperatives, was issued in September 1950. Thereafter, several more provisional regulations were issued, governing various specific kinds of contractual transactions.[6] One of the main reasons for the initial issuance of contract regulations was the recognition of the co-existence of public and private economies. Socialist transformation however soon led to the domination of public ownership, and so contracts were mainly used as a means for implementing state economic plans, rather than for regulating transactions among individuals and economic entities.[7]

The first major contract law in post-Mao China was the Economic Contract Law (ECL).[8] As it was issued at the initial stage of economic reform, it had the strong flavour of a planned economy. Thus Article 1 of the Law defined the purpose of the

---

4 See Pitman B. Potter, 'Law-Making in the PRC: The Case of Contracts', in J.M. Otto, M.V. Polack, J. Chen & Y. Li (eds), *Law-Making in the People's Republic of China* (The Hague/London/Boston: Kluwer Law International, 2000), at 189-203; and Pitman B Potter, *The Economic Contract Law of China: Legitimation and Contract Autonomy in the PRC* (Seattle & London: University of Washington Press, 1992).

5 Wang Jiafu, *et al.* (eds), *Contract Law* (*Hetong Fa*) (Beijing: China Social Science Press, 1986), at 5-11; Pi Chunxie & Shi Zhiyuan (eds), *An Outline of Economic Contract Law* (*Jingji Hetong Fa Gailun*) (Beijing: People's Press, 1987), at 33-44.

6 See Wang Jiafu, *id.*, at 141-143.

7 See Wang Jiafu, *id.*, at 141-147.

8 Initially issued by the 4th Plenary Session of the 5th NPC on 13 December 1981 and effective on 1 July 1982, and comprehensively revised by the Standing Committee of the 8th NPC on 2 September 1993. The ECL has now been repealed by the 1999 Contract Law. Before the promulgation of this major contract law there were several provisional regulations issued by different government departments, such as the Tentative Provisions on Basic Clauses of Industrial, Commercial and Agricultural Economic Contracts (issued by the State Administra-

Law as being to protect the social economic order, to promote economic efficiency and to guarantee the implementation of state plans. Its application was confined to domestic economic contracts between legal persons.[9] The implementation of the 'open door' policy then necessitated the promulgation of a second major set of contract regulations, the Foreign Economic Contract Law (FECL).[10] As indicated by its title, it was only applicable to foreign-related economic transactions. In 1986, the General Principles of Civil Law (GPCL) were issued,[11] which provided certain governing principles for all kinds of contracts. Piecemeal, task-oriented development continued after the promulgation of the GPCL. Thus in 1987 the Law on Technology Contracts (LTC) was issued,[12] regulating contracts for technology development, transfer, consultancy and services. Together, the three separate contract laws were often referred to as the 'three pillars' of contract law in China.[13] In addition, the Supreme People's Court issued many explanations relating to the implementation of the various contract laws (not just for the 'three pillars' of the contract law).[14] In the foreign-related area, China also became a party to the United Nations Convention on Contracts for the International Sales of Goods (the CISG Convention, ratified by China in 1986). Finally, this contract law system was supplemented by many administrative regulations which governed and regulated specific contracts, such as contracts on the sale of specific kinds of goods, insurance, leases, and transport.

---

tion of Industry and Commerce in 1980), and the Provisional Regulations on Contracts for Mining Products (issued by the State Economic Commission in 1981).

9 See Article 2 of ECL.

10 Issued by the Standing Committee of the 6th NPC on 21 March 1985 and effective on 1 July 1985. The FECL has now been replaced by the 1999 Contract Law.

11 Adopted by the 4th Plenary Session of the 6th NPC on 12 April 1986, effective on 1 January 1987.

12 Adopted by the Standing Committee of the 6th NPC on 23 June 1987 and effective on 1 October 1987. The LTC has now been repealed by the 1999 Contract Law.

13 See Wang Liming, 'An Inquiry into Several Difficult Problems in Enacting China's Uniform Contract Law', (1999) 8 *Pacific Rim Law and Policy Journal* 351, at 352.

14 See e.g. Opinions of the Supreme People's Court on Certain Issues relation to the Implementation of the Economic Contract Law, issued on 17 September 1984; Interpretation of the Supreme People's Court on Certain Issues relating to the Application of the Economic Contract Law in Adjudicating Economic Contract Disputes, issued on 21 July, 1987; Interpretation of the Supreme People's Court on Certain Issues relation to the Implementation of the Foreign Economic Contract Law, issued on 7 October 1987; and many more. For a comprehensive collection of these interpretations, see Lei Xian (ed.), *A Practical Book on Sino-Foreign Contracts* (*Zhongwai Hetong (Qiyue) Falü Shiyong Quanshu*) (Beijing: China Economic Press, 1994), at 655-758. Since the three contract laws were repealed by the 1999 Contract Law, it can be assumed that these interpretations are no longer applicable.

To further complicate this system, many local governments also issued their own contract rules.[15]

At this stage it should be pointed out that the three principal laws on contracts represented rather different ideological orientations. The 1981 ECL and the 1987 LTC clearly reflected the planned economy ideology first imported from the former Soviet Union.[16] On the other hand, the 1985 FECL had already allowed much more freedom and autonomy for parties to form, conclude and perform contracts, more in line with western capitalist practice than with socialism. In fact it was the 1985 FECL (together with the various joint venture laws) that initially started a sort of 'plural' approach to drawing experience from foreign and international sources. As such, the 1985 FECL, though evidencing some continuing influences from the former Eastern European countries, clearly reflected influences of international treaties and practices.[17]

Under this 'three pillars' system, the application of a specific contract law depended on two factors: whether there was foreign participation, and the subject matter of the contract. Economic contracts, defined as 'agreements for achieving specific economic purposes and for defining the rights and obligations of each party',[18] were regulated by one of the above two economic contract laws, depending on whether there was a foreign party to the contract or not. Contracts other than 'economic agreements' were regulated by the GPCL or by specifically applicable contract rules. Although foreign-related contracts were governed by the FECL, a contract between a joint venture, or a wholly foreign-owned enterprise, and a Chinese business entity was regulated by the ECL, as a joint venture or a wholly foreign-owned enterprise generally acquired the status of a legal person in China.[19]

Theoretically the GPCL had a higher status in the Chinese hierarchical order of legal sources than the FECL and TCL and related central and local regulations, as the former was a basic law adopted by the full NPC. This meant that the GPCL not only served a gap-filling function, but stipulated governing principles for all

---

15 The most comprehensive collection of Chinese contract laws is the 1471-page handbook: Lei Xian (ed.), *id.*

16 So was the 1986 GPCL which, as discussed in Chapter 9, was mainly drawn from the Fourth Draft of the Civil Code (prepared in the 1960s) and hence heavily modelled on laws of the former Soviet Union and other former Eastern European countries.

17 See discussions in Potter (2000), *supra* note 4, at 191-194.

18 See Article 2 of ECL.

19 The Economic Contract Law originally applied only to Chinese legal persons. When it was amended in September 1993 its scope of application was expanded to include legal persons of equal status, other economic entities, individual industrial and commercial households and rural contractors and thus was made applicable to domestic contracts concluded with foreign investment enterprises.

kinds of contracts and, at least theoretically, overruled any inconsistent provisions in individual contract laws. This, however, was hardly the case in practice.

Clearly, the 'three pillars' system was a complicated one, fraught with many practical problems. Practically, as pointed out by Wang Liming, it suffered 'from duplicative, inconsistent, and even contradictory provisions' and lacked 'some of the most fundamental rules and institutions of standard contract relations'.[20] But much more fundamentally, as discussed in Chapter Three, significant progress in reforming the politico-economic system had been made in the early 1990s, and thus a contract law based entirely or partially on a planned market ideology was seen as clearly out of date and out of step with reform efforts.

The initial legislative response to the changed politico-economic ideology was the making of some major revisions to the 1981 Economic Contract Law in 1993.[21] Even though the revision was reasonably comprehensive, the result was a half-cooked meal. The revision removed references to 'state planning' and 'state policy'; however the revised law was, as Potter has pointed out, still largely a policy driven document.[22] Technically there were still many inconsistencies between the 'three pillars' of the contract law and uncertainties in determining which law would apply in a particular transaction. Further, there were also western pressures (especially from the US) on China to unify its contract law and practice, to fall more in line with international practices.[23] Most importantly, a certain consensus among Chinese scholars had also emerged, demanding that contract law treat all parties on an equal footing, and that the fundamental principle of contract be that of 'freedom of contract.'[24] Thus, new efforts to enact a uniform code on contracts started almost immediately after the revision of the 1981 Economic Contract Law.

While the efforts to draft a uniform contract code are often seen as having emerged in the early 1990s, it should be pointed out that such drafting has always been part of the task of enacting a comprehensive civil code. In other words, the initial drafting can be said to have started as early as the 1950s.[25] The 'three pillars' of contract legislation came about principally as a result of the piecemeal approach towards the making of the civil code, rather than as an effort in the making of a contract law.

The first specific effort to draft a uniform contract code started in early 1993 when the Legislative Affairs Committee (LAC) of the NPC's Standing Committee

---

20 See Wang Liming, *supra* note 13, at 352.

21 For a detailed discussion of the 1993 revision of the 1981 Economic Contract Law, see Potter (2000), *supra* note 4, at 193-196.

22 See Potter (2000), *supra* note 4, at 195-196.

23 Potter (2000), *supra* note 4, at 191.

24 See detailed discussions in Wang Liming, *supra* note 13.

25 Xiao Bing, 'The Process of Drafting a Contract Code', (no. 1, 1997) *Jurisprudence Frontiers* (*Faxue Qianyan*) 184, at 184. See also discussions in Chapter 9.

(SCNPC) formally commenced the drafting work. Three major justifications were advanced by the SCNPC for making a uniform contract law. First, in the then exiting legal framework for contracts many provisions were too vague and general; these provisions needed clarification as well as supplementation. Further, inconsistencies in relation to contract formation, damages and statutory limitations existed among the three pillars of the contract law as well as other contractual regulations. Secondly, supplementary stipulations on fraud in contracts were required, as an increasing incidence of contractual fraud was occurring in economic activities. Thirdly, certain newly emerged types of contract, such as financial leasing contracts, brokerage contracts and partnership contracts still lacked legal regulation.[26] One can easily add the lack and inconsistency of provisions on freedom of contracts and formation of contracts as further reasons for the making of a uniform contract law.

Three major guiding principles were established for drafting a uniform contract law. First, the uniform contract law would be based on the GPCL and the practical experience of the existing three pillars of the contract law. It would provide uniform principles governing all contracts. Various administrative and judicial interpretations on contracts would also be absorbed into the uniform law. Secondly, the continuation and stability of the existing legal framework on contracts would be upheld. Thirdly, newly emerging contractual issues would be addressed, general and vague provisions would be clarified and supplemented, and international experience would be taken into consideration.[27] Further, the full performance of contracts would be emphasised.[28] In other words the new code would not only be uniform for all contracts, but also practical and precise through the incorporation of the existing laws and practice, including the jurisprudence of the Supreme People's Court.

The drafting of the new Code was carried out efficiently. By August 1993, a draft of the Major Provisions of the Contract Law was produced by the Civil Law Office of the LAC of the SCNPC. In early 1995 twelve academic institutions, including the Law Institute of the Chinese Academy of Social Sciences, Beijing University, the People's University, the China University of Political Science and Law, and Yantai University, joined forces to form an academic drafting group, which produced a Proposed Draft.[29] In July 1995 the Civil Law Office of the LAC produced another Tentative Draft, which was circulated among scholars and practitioners for comment.

---

26 See 'Explanations on Several Questions Regarding the Contract Law (Draft for Consolidating Opinions)', General Office of the SCNPC, 14 May 1997. Similar explanations were given to the Fourth Meeting of the SCNPC, 24 August 1998, in *People's Daily* (*Renmin Ribao*), internet edition, 25 August 1998.

27 See *id*.

28 See *id*.

29 Xiao Bing, *supra* note 25, at 185. This expert draft, The Contract Law of the People's Republic of China (Proposed Draft), was published in (no. 2, 1995) *Civil and Commercial Law Review* (*Minshang Fa Luncong*), at 439-539.

Upon receiving comments and suggestions, the Office produced its Second Draft in October 1995. In late May 1996 the LAC then organised a special symposium, attended by scholars and practitioners, to discuss the above Proposed Draft by scholars, and the Second Draft by the Civil Law Office. This special symposium then led to the completion of the Third Draft by the LAC.[30] The draft code was scheduled for adoption at the Fifth Plenary Session of the 8th NPC in March 1997.[31] The original schedule was however soon jeopardised by major disagreements among various state departments, which were more a struggle for power than actual disagreements in any technical sense, on provisions governing technology and financing contracts.[32] Nevertheless, drafting work continued. In May 1997 a new Draft for Consolidating Opinions by the LAC was issued and circulated among scholars and practitioners.[33] Again it was scheduled for adoption at the First Plenary Session of the 9th NPC in March 1998, but failed to be included in the agenda. Although the same disagreements were blamed for the failure,[34] it is more likely that the political struggle for leadership and personnel changes left little time for any specific legislative agenda.[35] However, quite unexpectedly, a revised draft was put to the Fourth Meeting of the SCNPC in August 1998 for deliberation. On 4 September 1998 the full text of the draft was issued by the SCNPC for public consultation, the results of which had to be sent back to the SCNPC by 15 October 1998.[36] Finally, after four separate sessions of examination and deliberation by the SCNPC, the Contract Law was finally adopted by the 2nd Session of the 9th NPC on 15 March 1999.[37] The Law came into force on 1 October 1999, and the ECL, FECL and LTC were simultaneously repealed. The new Law now applies to all contracts entered into between individuals, legal persons, and other organisations, which clearly includes foreign persons (natural

---

30 Xiao Bing, *supra* note 25, at 185; and Liang Huixing, 'On the Third Draft of the Uniform Contract Law of China', (no. 1, 1997) *Jurisprudence Frontiers* (*Faxue Qianyan*) 186, at 186.

31 Jiang Ping, 'Drafting the Uniform Contract Law in China', (1996) 10 *Columbia J. of Asian Law* 245, at 245.

32 Interview with officials from the LAC of the SCNPC in early 1997.

33 The draft on my personal file is dated 14 May 1997.

34 Interview with officials from the LAC of the SCNPC in early 1998.

35 Indeed, the Plenary Session did not include any legislative agenda at all.

36 'The General Office of the Standing Committee of the NPC issued the Contract Law (Draft) for consolidating opinions', *People's Daily* (*Renmin Ribao*), internet edition, 5 September 1998. A full text of the draft was published in the *People's Daily* (*Renmin Ribao*), internet edition, on 7 September 1998. Clearly there had been many drafts of the uniform contract law circulated for discussion. To avoid confusion, all reference in this Chapter to the draft contract law refers to this draft unless otherwise indicated.

37 For more detailed analysis of the making of the 1999 Contract Law, see Potter (2000), *supra* note 4, at 199-202.

or legal). As such, a uniform code on contracts came into existence for the first time in the PRC.[38]

Equally importantly, the long process of eliminating the Soviet influence in private law, initially started with the FECL, now finally reached its climax. No longer were the civil code drafts of the 1950s and 1960s used as the foundation for drafting the 1999 Contract Law; instead, the German Civil Code, the Japanese Civil Code and the KMT Civil Code were all studied carefully and followed to varying degrees.[39] Furthermore, the UNIDROIT Principles of International Commercial Contracts (1994) and the UN Convention on Contracts for the International Sale of Goods (1980) were followed closely, and in some places copied article by article.[40] Additionally, Common law was also looked into for inspiration.[41]

3. Present Legal Framework on Contracts

The enactment of the 1999 Contract Law, on face value, only repealed the 'three pillars' of the contract law then existing in China. In reality, many more administrative regulations, local rules and judicial interpretations were also rendered ineffective. As a result the legal framework on contracts is now streamlined and straightforward. The 1999 Contract Law contains the principal rules, and the 1986 GPCL will continue to serve a gap-filling function as a stand-by law.[42] As in any other area of law in

---

38 Until the last stage of the legislative process, the term 'uniform contract code' was used by scholars and law-makers, but it was abandoned when the official draft was put to the SCNPC for formal deliberation. It should also be pointed out that the supposedly uniform contract law may not be universal in practice: Part II of the 1999 Contract Law provides specific provisions on 15 types of specific contracts apparently chosen on an *ad hoc* basis. Article 124 of the Law seems to suggest that provisions in Part II on specific contracts prevail over the general principles stipulated in Part I. Further, Article 123 provides that if other laws contain provisions on contract, these other provisions shall apply. Article 123 also presents a legal dilemma for lawyers: the Contract Law was adopted by a full session of the NPC and, as a result, it has the highest legal status in the Chinese law hierarchy. However, the Law itself authorises 'other laws', which may not be a law enacted by the full NPC, to override the provisions in the Contract Law. In case of conflict between the Contract Law and another law (which also deals with contracts), it would be extremely difficult for a court to decide which law should be applied.

39 See Liang Huixing, *supra* note 30.

40 See Liang Huixing, *supra* note 30.

41 In any case, the decision to follow the CISG Convention would already ensure some Common law influence. As pointed out by Potter, the principles of the CISG drew heavily from the US Uniform Commercial Code. See Potter (2000), *supra* note 4, at 191.

42 It should be pointed out that Article 2 of the 1999 Contract Law specifically excludes the application of the Law to agreements defining status relationships, such as agreements relating to marriage, adoption and guardianship, etc. These agreements/contracts will continue to be

China, judicial interpretations will then provide further practical guidance. In fact, soon after the adoption of the Law, the Supreme People's Court issued its first part of the interpretation on the application of the Contract Law.[43] This Interpretation (I) mainly clarifies certain procedural issues concerning the relationship between the previous contract laws and regulations and the new Contract Law, the scope of application of the Law, the time limit for filing a law suit, the determination of validity of a contract, subrogation of rights, the right to annul certain contractual transactions or legal actions, and the third party in a contract. As indicated in the title of the Interpretation (I), further interpretations clarifying substantial issues as contained in, or omitted from, the principal law are to be issued by the Court. However, other than some *ad hoc* (and mostly brief) interpretations on specific contract law issues, no further comprehensive interpretation has yet been issued.

Reflecting its status as a comprehensive basic law, the 1999 Contract Law is divided into three parts: General Provisions, Specific Provisions and Supplementary Provisions, consisting of 23 Chapters and 428 articles. Part I is further divided into eight chapters, dealing with general principles, formation, legal effect, performance, alteration and transfer, termination, liabilities for breach, and other stipulations. These provisions (Articles 1-129) apply to all kinds of contracts. Part II on Specific Provisions (Articles 130-427) regulates 15 specific types of contract, namely sale and purchase of goods; the supply of electricity, water, gas and heating; gifts; loans; leasing; lease financing; hiring of work; construction projects; transportation; technology; storage; warehousing; trusts; commissioning agencies; and brokerage. The last Part of the Supplementary Provisions contains one article only, which serves the purpose of repealing the ECL, the FECL, and the LTC upon the implementation of the Contract Law on 1 October 1999.

Although the General Provisions closely follow the structure of the ECL, provisions in this part are now elaborated and much more precise. Three significant changes merit particular comment. First, a contract is no longer defined as an agreement between legal persons or units, but is defined as an agreement between citizens, legal persons and other organisations of equal status, which creates, modifies and terminates creditor's rights and obligation relationships.[44] This definition finally extends Chinese contract law to agreements between individuals. Further, the

---

regulated by other laws such as the Marriage Law, the Adoption Law, and the Succession Law. This exclusion was added to the Law in the last minute. See 'Report on the Examination of the Draft Contract Law of the PRC', delivered at the Second Session of the Ninth NPC on 14 March 1999. A copy of the Report is published in (no. 2, 1999) *Gazette of the Standing Committee of the NPC of the PRC* (*Zhonghua Renmin Gongheguo Quanguo Renmin Daibiao Dahui Changwuweiyuanhui Gongbao*), at 157-158.

43 Interpretation (I) of the Supreme People's Court on Certain Issues concerning the Application of the Contract Law of the PRC, issued on 19 December 1999.

44 See Article 1 of the 1999 Contract Law.

definition seems to incorporate Articles 84 and 85 of the GPCL on definitions of the civil law institution of obligations, thus re-emphasising contracts as part of the institution of obligations. By doing so it paves the way for future incorporation of the contract law into a civil code. Secondly, the Law for the first time in the PRC introduces, and provides detailed rules on, offer and acceptance.[45] These rules, consisting of 23 articles in total (Articles 13-35), regulate the definitions of offer, invitation to treat, promise, withdrawal, revocation and rejection of offer, mode and time of acceptance, and modified acceptance. These rules on offer and acceptance follow the UNIDROIT Principles of International Commercial Contracts very closely,[46] or even copy them article by article. Also, as in the UNIDROIT Principles, there is no concept of consideration in the Law, which then provides the possibility of irrevocable offer. Finally, there is no longer a general distinction between domestic and foreign-related contracts, although several provisions on the governing law and choice of law in relation to foreign-related contracts do exist in the Law;[47] however, they exist to deal with practical issues rather than reflecting any differentiated treatment.

The Specific Provisions on particular contracts chosen on a seemingly *ad hoc* basis follow a similar approach to that in the KMT Civil Code. This arrangement already existed in the ECL. The reason for creating special categories of contract in the ECL was, however, quite unique. It was said to be that each of them was a special concern of a different central government ministry.[48] This simply means that such an arrangement in the ECL reflected the departmentalised and compartmentalised interests of the Chinese bureaucracy, inherent in a planned politico-economic system.[49] This arrangement can thus be seen as a major flaw in the ECL. The continuation of such an arrangement in the Law requires some justification at a time when China is emphasising its orientation towards a market economy; otherwise it undermines the universality of the contract law and continues to fragment the legal framework

---

45 The lack of rules on offer and acceptance was seen as a major flaw in Chinese contract law. See Jiang Ping, *supra* note 31, at 249.

46 It was in fact an express policy of the SCNPC to follow the provisions of the UNIDROIT Principles: interview with Chinese officials of the LAC of the SCNPC in December 1997. See also *supra* notes 39 & 40.

47 See e.g. Articles 126, 128 and 129 of the 1999 Contract Law. More specifically, these issues are now dealt with by the Provisions on Certain Issues concerning the Application of Law in Adjudicating Foreign-related Civil and Commercial Contractual Disputes, issued by the Supreme People's Court on 11 June 2007.

48 Lucie Cheng & Arthur Rosett, 'Contract with a Chinese Face: Socially Embedded Factors in the Transformation from Hierarchy to Market, 1978–1989', (no. 2, 1991) 5 *J. of Chinese Law* 143, at 206.

49 On this politico-economic system, see Jianfu Chen, *From Administrative Authorisation to Private Law: A Comparative Perspective of the Developing Civil Law in the PRC* (Dordrecht/Boston/London: Martinus Nijhoff Publishers, 1995), Chapter 5.

on contractual relationships. However, such a justification for singling out these 15 specific types of contract for particular treatment has not yet been given.[50]

4. General Principles of the Contract Law

As Potter has pointed out, the contract law has been particularly reflective of the tensions in the Chinese economic reforms and the intense ideological struggles involved in moving towards a market oriented economy.[51] Indeed, as discussed above, the evolution of the contract law in post-Mao China reflects rather precisely the development of the politico-economic system, as well as the continuing reform of the bureaucratic power structure. Within the area of contract law itself, it is the general principles of the contract law that best encapsulate the essence of this transformation. The following discussion on the basic principles in the present contract law further illustrates the tensions and transformations of socialist ideologies since reform started in 1978.

4.1. Equality of Parties

Equality of parties in civil relations has been, for many years, a battleground for politico-economists and jurists in China. The battle strikes at the heart of the politico-economic system and hence at the legal system in relation to civil legislation. The whole battle has reflected the process of the transformation from a planned to a market economy, which itself redefines the role of the state (represented by its various bureaucratic authorities) in economic management and activities.[52]

As one of the most prominent civil law authorities in China, Professor Wang Jiafu, has pointed out, the ECL, reflecting the then politico-economic structure, contained two kinds of legal provisions: those of civil law and those in the nature of administrative law. The former referred to provisions regulating the contractual relations of equal parties on the basis of voluntariness, and the latter to those provisions (such as Chapters 5 & 6 of the ECL) that guaranteed the possibility of state intervention in economic activities.[53] These provisions not only impaired the

---

50 Among the three different drafts of the uniform contract law on personal file, each covers different individual types of contract. Most notably, the May 1997 draft of the SCNPC further covered contracts on consultancy, services, tourism, partnership, and employment. The academic draft has the widest coverage of specific contracts (24 types in total), including contracts on the sale of houses, transfer and assignment of land use rights, business operations, banking transactions, publications, entertainment, guarantees, and insurance.

51 Potter (2000), *supra* note 4, at 190.

52 See detailed discussions in Jianfu Chen, *supra* note 49, chapters 2 & 5. See further discussion in Chapter 13 on business entities.

53 Wang Jiafu, *supra* note 5, at 151.

implementation of freedom of contract, but were at odds with the GPCL, which emphasises equality of parties in civil relationships.[54]

The Contract Law now defines a contract as an agreement between equal parties and stresses that parties enjoy equality of position in contractual relations.[55] The Law also prohibits one party from imposing its will on the other.[56] This provision could and should be interpreted to mean that state authorities as contractual parties have no right to force anyone, natural person or legal person, to enter into a contract. These provisions come directly, though not word-for-word, from the GPCL, and hence make the GPCL provisions relevant in practice.

4.2. Freedom of Contract

Freedom of contract was one of the most discussed principles for enacting a uniform contract law.[57] It was not explicitly stipulated in the 'three pillars' of contract laws. Nevertheless, there were provisions which were based on, and which indirectly guaranteed, the principle of freedom of contract. Further, the extent of, and restrictions on, this principle as provided in different sets of contract law differed significantly.

The initial ECL of 1981 was most restrictive in contract formation and performance. Although Article 9 provided that a contract was formed as soon as the parties to the contract achieved agreement on the principal clauses of the contract through consultation in accordance with the law,[58] Article 4 prohibited the making of any contract that would violate state plans, and such a contract was rendered invalid by Article 7. The 1993 revision substantially removed these mandatory planning requirements and emphasised compliance with the principles of equality and mutual benefit, and of achieving agreement through consultation. The revised ECL also prohibited the imposition by either party of its own will on the other party, and other illegal interference in contract formation and performance.[59] Thus parties were given much greater freedom in establishing contractual relationships. However, Article 4 of the revised ECL continued to provide some open-ended prohibitions, vaguely phrased as 'illegal activities', acts 'disrupting the social or economic order', acts 'damaging the state or public interest', or 'seeking illegal income under cover of economic contracts'. Further, the state retained the right to issue mandatory plans to enterprises, in which case a contract could only be formed in accordance with the relevant laws and regulations in relation to the implementation of such economic

54 See Article 2 of the GPCL.

55 Articles 2 & 3 of the 1999 Contract Law.

56 Article 3 of the 1999 Contract Law.

57 See Wang Liming, *supra* note 13.

58 This Article remained the same after the 1993 revision.

59 Article 5 of the ECL as revised in 1993.

plans.[60] Also reflecting these restrictions on freedom of contract, the ECL stipulated mandatory provisions on damages for breach of contract, instead of allowing parties to make contractual arrangements for such damages.[61]

In contrast, the FECL provided much greater freedom in contractual arrangements. Although Article 5 of the FECL insisted that Chinese law must apply to joint venture contracts and contracts for Sino-foreign joint exploration and the development of natural resources, under the same article and Article 6 there were possibilities for applying foreign law and international conventions and international customs to other kinds of foreign related contracts. Specifically, under Article 5 parties might choose applicable laws for their contracts. Such a choice could be made even after disputes had already arisen.[62] Further, where Chinese law did not make provisions, international customary law would apply. Importantly, under Article 6 international agreements ratified by China prevailed over Chinese domestic law.[63] Although foreign related contracts would be invalid if they violated Chinese law or the public interest of the society, most of the restrictions imposed by the ECL did not exist in the FECL. In strong contrast to the ECL, the FECL specifically allowed parties to stipulate damages for breach of contract by the parties.[64]

The GPCL, in terms of freedom of contract, stands between the ECL and FECL. It emphasises equality between contractual parties as well voluntary participation, equity, compensation at equal value and honesty and trustworthiness.[65] It also requires parties to respect social moral principles, not to harm the common interest of society, or to damage state economic plans or disrupt the social economic order.[66] It invalidates any economic contracts that contravene state planning directives.[67]

A rather important restriction on freedom of contract was that all kinds of economic contract were required to be in a written form.[68] Further, when the approval of a contract by state authorities was required either by law or by administrative

60 Article 11 of the ECL as revised in 1993. The original Article 11 imposed a much stricter obligation on enterprises to abide by such mandatory plans. Reflecting the effort to rule the country in accordance with law, the implementation of state mandatory plans was now, after the 1993 revision, to be achieved through laws and administrative rules, instead of the direct imposition of such plans.

61 See Chapter 4 of the ECL as revised in 1993.

62 See Article 2(4) of Interpretation of the Supreme People's Court on Certain Issues Relating to the Implementation of the Foreign Economic Contract Law (1987).

63 A similar provision is also provided by Article 142 of the GPCL.

64 Article 20 of FECL.

65 See Articles 2 & 4 of GPCL.

66 Article 7 of GPCL.

67 Article 58 (6) of GPCL.

68 Article 3 of ECL; Article 7 of FECL; and Article 9 of LTC.

regulations, such a contract was only formed after the required approval has been granted.[69]

Quite clearly equality as guaranteed by law is seriously undermined if parties subject to different contract laws enjoy a different degree of freedom of contract. More importantly, if China is to practice a market economy, there is little justification (saving some limited but well defined circumstances where restrictions of freedom of contract may be justified) for not providing freedom of contract and equality of economic players in all economic fields.

Interestingly, even though the 1999 Contract Law is heavily influenced by the UNIDROIT Principles, it approaches this fundamental principle in an indirect way, instead of providing an explicit principle of freedom of contract. Specifically, the Law contains a number of provisions which either endorse or restrict freedom of contract. Thus Article 4 emphasises voluntariness in contracting, and prohibits unlawful interference by any individual or organisation in contract-making. As mentioned above, Article 3 prohibits the imposition of the will of one party upon the other. These two articles have their origin in Article 5 of the ECL. Article 5 of the Law is the provision most close to the principle of freedom of contract. It provides that parties shall determine their rights and duties according to the principle of fairness. This provision seems to be the first such provision giving qualified endorsement of freedom of contract. The detailed rules on offer and acceptance, as mentioned above, can be seen as further enforcing the idea of freedom of contract.[70] Further, the Law now permits contracts to be concluded in writing, orally or in other forms, unless laws or administrative regulations require otherwise.[71] However, where the State, in accordance with its needs, assigns mandatory tasks or tasks relating to state orders for goods, relevant legal persons and other organisations must only conclude contracts between themselves in accordance with the rights and obligations stipulated in relevant laws and administrative regulations. More generally, and as with the then existing contract laws before 1999, freedom of contract is restricted by the requirement that, in making or performing a contract, parties must abide by laws and administrative regulations, respect social morality, and must not disrupt the social economic order or harm the public interest of the society.[72] At face value, these provisions reflect the general trend in the West, where freedom of contract is increasingly qualified by doctrines of equity and unconscionability. The problem with the Chinese provisions is that the qualifications and restrictions on freedom

69 Article 7 of FECL and Article 91 of GPCL. There was no such direct requirement in the ECL and the LTC, but the GPCL requirement is applicable in these cases. In practice, most foreign-related contracts, such as joint venture contracts, require government approval.

70 See Potter (2000), *supra* note 4, at 198.

71 See Article 10 of the 1999 Contract Law.

72 Article 7 of the Contract Law. Again, this article has its origin in Article 4 of ECL and Articles 6 & 7 of the GPCL.

of contract are broad, open-ended and undefined. The notions of social morality and social economic order have no limit in scope, nor are they ever defined by Chinese law. These provisions could, in the end, virtually extinguish any potential for a uniform contract law in terms of freedom of contract. In this context the Law on freedom of contract is disappointing, breaking little new ground in upholding such an important contract principle.

4.3. Performance of Contract

Restrictions on freedom of contract are further reflected in the requirements for contract performance. All the pre-1999 Chinese contract laws emphasised actual performance. Thus parties to a contract were required to fully discharge their obligations as stipulated in the contract; neither party was permitted to arbitrarily amend or dissolve the contract.[73] *Force majeure* and other impossibilities of contract performance were however allowed as legitimate grounds for discharge of contract.[74] Mutual agreement to alter or terminate a contract was also permitted.[75] However, in the case of domestic economic contracts the ECL specifically required that such mutual agreement must not harm the state or public interest.[76] Further, in the case of a breach by one party, the injured party might require the party in breach to continue performance of the contract after compensation for such breach.[77]

Once again, and as in the case of freedom of contract, provisions in the 1999 Contract Law on performance on the one hand follow the UNIDROIT Principles quite closely, but on the other hand lean heavily towards full performance in accordance with the principle of good faith.[78] The real progress made in the Law lies in the elaboration and expansion of the provisions on contract performance, and on liabilities for breach of contract.[79] Further, Article 77 of the Law, which allows parties to alter the contract upon reaching agreement through consultation,[80] may provide some relief from the strict requirement for full performance and thus restore part of the implicit principle of freedom of contract.

---

73 Article 6 of the ECL; Article 16 of the FECL; and Article 88 of GPCL.

74 Article 26 of ECL; Article 29 of FECL; Article 107 of GPCL.

75 Article 26 of ECL; Article 28 of FECL. The GPCL is silent on this point.

76 Article 26 of ECL.

77 Article 31 of ECL.

78 See Article 8 of the 1999 Contract Law. It should be pointed out that the UNIDROIT Principles and the CISG Convention themselves lean much more towards actual performance of contracts than would normally be required under Common law.

79 See Article 60-76 of the 1999 Contract Law.

80 However, if alteration of contract requires approval, registration or other formality in accordance with laws or administrative regulations, such laws or administrative regulations must be complied with. See Article 77 of the 1999 Contract Law.

4.4. Breach of Contract and Damages

The variations on freedom of contract from the pre-1999 contract laws are also reflected in the way the issue of damages in breach of contract is addressed. In the FECL and GPCL, damages recoverable in the case of breach were generally limited to the actual loss sustained as a result by the other party, and parties might stipulate a fixed amount of default payment in their contract.[81] The ECL however provided detailed and mandatory provisions on damages which left little freedom for the contractual parties,[82] a stipulation clearly reflecting a planned economy policy.

The 1999 Contract now rather closely follows the UNIDROIT Principles in this regard.[83] The Law allows both compensatory damage and liquidated damage, the latter to be set out (either as a fixed monetary amount or by a calculation formula) when forming a contract.[84] A duty to mitigate damages in the case of breach of contract is imposed on the innocent party. The innocent party has no right to claim compensation for any additional damages as a result of the failure to take immediate mitigating measures to prevent the damages from extending.[85]

5. Concluding Remarks

There is no doubt that the making of the 1999 Contract Law is a far-reaching effort to wrestle with China's rapidly developing 'socialist market economy', as well as to ensure that China's approach to contracts corresponds more closely to international norms. It is not simply an attempt to reorganise China's range of contract legislation, but a systematic redesigning of the form and context of the whole body of Chinese contract law. It successfully establishes a reasonably unified framework for all contract activities; it eliminates the distinctions between domestic and foreign-related contractual relationships, and between civil law and economic law, in regulating contractual relationships. It also updates many aspects of the 'three pillars' of the contract law, which had become either outdated or inconsistent with later legal developments since their adoption.

It also seems to be a sound decision to model the uniform contract law on the UNIDROIT Principles of International Commercial Contracts. These Principles

81 Articles 19 & 20 of FECL; Article 112 of GPCL.

82 Articles 33-41 of ECL.

83 See Articles 107-122 of the 1999 Contract Law. Thus, as in the UNIDROIT Principles and the CISG Convention, repair, replacement, re-making, return of goods and price reduction are all made part of damages for breach of contract. See Article 111 of the 1999 Contract Law.

84 See Article 114 of the 1999 Contract Law.

85 Article 119 of the 1999 Contract Law. While the FECL (Article 22) and the GPCL (Article 114) provided the same, the ECL was silent on this general duty.

have been drafted for the purpose of international unification of private law by absorbing common elements from various legal systems.[86] It is, however, difficult to understand the reluctance of the Chinese law-makers to explicitly provide the principle of freedom of contract. This reluctance is particularly at odds with the frequent assertion that a market economy is fundamentally based on freedom of contract and economic equality.

86 On these aspects, see UNIDROIT, *UNIDROIT Principles of International Commercial Contracts* (Rome, 2004). This book provides both texts and commentary.

Chapter Thirteen

Law on Business Entities

1. Introduction

The evolving Chinese law on business entities typically reflects the tension between socialist ideology and 'bourgeois' legal institutions. At the centre of the legal framework are the 'bourgeois' private law institution of legal personality, and a politico-economic structure heavily dictated by the changing socialist ideology. The two do not sit comfortably together.

On the one hand the conventional conception of socialist civil law, by virtue of its 'sacred' principle of upholding socialist public ownership and transforming or eliminating forms of private economy, has long involved certain principles opposing those of the 'bourgeois' private law, such as economic equality and freedom. Since the inception of communism as an ideology in China the whole politico-economic system has been built upon the distinction between forms of ownership, relations of subordination, and geographical location. Economic entities have not been treated as abstract and autonomous subjects of rights and duties on an equal footing. Thus, instead of a uniform legal framework for business entities, different enterprises in China have been subject to various individual laws and regulations on specific forms of enterprises. These laws have effectively established a system of legal persons in which economic entities are differentiated and accorded different legal status and legal capacities according to such variable factors as forms of ownership and departmental and regional subordination relations. This differentiation also existed at a higher level until very recently, in the Chinese Constitution of 1982.

On the other hand, such inequality has become increasingly at odds with the declared principle of equality among civil law parties in a market economy. For many years great efforts have been made to reform the fundamental politico-economic structure, and hence to provide equal treatment for all business entities, both through civil legislation,[1] and partly through constitutional revisions undertaken since 1988.[2]

---

1 Meng Qinguo, 'Civil Legislation during Economic Structural Reform', (no. 6, 1988) *Social Sciences in China* (*Zhongguo Shehui Kexue*) 82, at 83.

2 See discussions in Chapter 3.

Indeed, economic equality was formally written into the General Principles of Civil Law (GPCL) (Articles 2-4) in 1986. As discussed in Chapter Nine on civil law, the establishment of the civil law institution of legal personality was meant to provide formal legal status to economic entities, to establish a uniform legal framework applicable to all economic entities, and to lay down a foundation upon which further details could be built. This apparent principle of equality is not, however, followed consistently in the remaining provisions of the GPCL, nor in other laws and regulations. In fact, the generally applicable Company Law was not enacted until December 1993, and only took effect in July 1994.

The promulgation of the Company Law in 1993 was one of the most significant efforts of Chinese law-makers to implement the principle of economic equality under the civil law. However, this supposedly generally applicable law has a rather narrow scope of application. Laws on different business entities thus continue to apply until an enterprise is transformed into a company, having met the strict requirements under the Company Law.[3] Further, although efforts have been made to converge the two distinct legal frameworks governing foreign-related and domestic businesses, foreign investment business entities continue to be regulated by a separate set of laws, at least until after China's transitional period (2001–2008) for WTO membership has expired. The civil law provisions on legal persons, though out of date, continue to be the unifying force for laws on business entities, at least theoretically.

This Chapter first outlines the differentiated structure of business entities under the Chinese Constitution and other laws governing business activities. It then examines the Individual Sole Investment Law, the Partnership Enterprise Law, and the Company Law. Foreign investment enterprise laws will be discussed in Chapter 17.

2. Business Entities in Transition

2.1. An Overview

Under the original 1982 Constitution of the PRC, socialist public ownership, which includes ownership by the whole people and collective ownership by the working people, was the basis of the socialist economic system; individual economy was then

---

3 The transformation of enterprises into companies was never meant to be a swift and sweeping process. See Wang Zhongyu (then Chairman of the State Economic and Trade Commission), 'To Firmly Carry Out Enterprise Reform', *People's Daily* (*Renmin Ribao*), 5 June 1994, at 2. Even if an enterprise is transformed into a company, it is unclear whether the various enterprise laws will continue to apply concurrently, as the Company Law is silent on this point. For certain practical purposes, such as obtaining bank loans and government assistance, it has been clear that the form of ownership and the business, the size of the enterprise, geographical location and administrative subordination relationships are all still relevant.

only allowed as a complement to the socialist public economy.[4] In addition, the Constitution also stipulated protection of foreign investment in China. Correspondingly, the GPCL divided enterprise legal persons into state-owned enterprises, collective enterprises, Sino-foreign joint ventures and wholly foreign-owned enterprises,[5] each of which was then (and still is largely) subject to different sets of enterprise law. Provisions are also laid down in the GPCL regarding individual enterprises, but without stipulating any clear legal status.[6] In 1988 Article 11 of the Constitution was amended to further 'permit a private economy to exist and develop within the limits prescribed by law.' This amendment and the subsequent State Council Provisional Regulations on Private Enterprises (1988) thus legalised a new form of business entity – private enterprise – which had existed for many years outside the law.[7] Here, the private economy refers to the economy in the form of private enterprises as defined by the Law. The rapid development of the private economy[8] then necessitated further elevation of the role of the non-public economy in the state economic system. Through the 1999 constitutional revision the individual and private economies are no longer defined as a complement to the socialist public economy; they are treated as 'an important component of the country's socialist market economy.'[9] Further, the 1999 revision tried to treat the individual and private economies on an equal footing, whereas the previous provisions seemed to accord a different degree of state control over them.[10]

Because of the specific meaning of the individual and private economies, and the continuing flourishing of the private sector in different business forms and structures, such as sole proprietorship and partnerships, there was a clear need to accord constitutional protection to these new forms of the private economy; hence a new phrase 'other non-public economy' was inserted into Article 11 of the Constitution through the 2004 revision. Though the phrase is an ambiguous one, it is meant to embrace the various existing and emerging forms of private business,

4 Articles 6 and 11 of the original 1982 Constitution.

5 Article 41 of the GPCL.

6 See Articles 26-29 of the GPCL and discussions below.

7 This practice clearly reflects the pragmatic approach towards law-making in the PRC. In fact, Article 2 (6) of the Regulations Concerning the Administration of the Registration of Enterprise Legal Persons (1988) also creates another special category: 'any type of enterprise which is legally required to register as an enterprise legal person'. This is apparently designed to meet the need for any other requirements which may be brought about by further developments in economic reform. A similar approach is also taken by the Provisions concerning Enterprise Registration Classification, jointly issued by the State Statistics Bureau and the State Administration for Industry and Commerce on 28 September 1998.

8 See discussion in Section 2.9 below.

9 See 1999 amendment to Article 11.

10 See discussions in Chapter 3, and further discussion below.

including foreign investment in China. In addition to providing protection, the 2004 revision further adds that the state will also provide encouragement and support to the development of the non-public economy. In this way the private sector has finally achieved equal status with its public counterparts in many economic activities, at least in theory.[11]

The most recent constitutional changes are yet to be fully incorporated into the legal framework governing business entities. In any case, the Constitution has not provided full equality to all forms of economy, nor has the politico-economic system been completely transformed. Thus economic and business entities continue to be further differentiated and subject to different individual statutes and administrative regulations, depending on administrative subordination relations,[12] the location of the enterprise concerned,[13] forms of investment,[14] or even the size of the business.[15]

---

[11] Article 7 of the Constitution however still states that '[T]he state-owned economy, i.e. the sector of the socialist economy under the ownership of the whole people, is the leading force in the national economy. The State ensures the consolidation and growth of the State-owned economy.' And indeed, in some important economic activities, such as obtaining bank loans, the state sectors continue to have priority over the private sectors. See further discussions below.

[12] That is, the various ministries and commissions of the State Council and local governments often issue departmental and local rules that regulate enterprises under their respective jurisdictions. Such rules often define business scope and conduct, the right to establishment, and conditions for such establishment. While many of these rules have now been repealed, many others continue to operate. See discussion in section 2.9 below.

[13] E.g. Law of the PRC on Township and Village Enterprises (adopted by the Standing Committee of the NPC on 29 October 1996, effective from 1 January 1997); Rural Collective Enterprise Regulations of the PRC (issued by the State Council on 3 June 1990); Urban Collective Enterprise Regulations of the PRC (issued by the State Council on 9 September 1992); Certain Measures Governing Individual Industrial and Commercial Households in Rural Areas (originally issued by the State Council on 27 February 1984, but since repealed) and Provisional Regulations Governing Individual Industrial and Commercial Households in Urban Areas (issued by the State Council on 5 August 1987).

[14] Law of the PRC on Sino-foreign Joint Equity Enterprises (initially adopted by the 2nd Session of the 5th National People's Congress on 1 July 1979); Law of the PRC on Enterprises with Wholly Foreign-owned Investment (initially adopted at the 4th Session of the 6th National People's Congress on 12 April 1986); and Law of the PRC on Sino-foreign Co-operative Enterprises (initially adopted by the 1st Session of the 7th National People's Congress on 13 April 1988). All these laws have since been revised several times and will be discussed in Chapter 17 below.

[15] E.g. Provisional Regulations Concerning Leasing Management of Small-sized State-owned Industrial Enterprises (issued by the State Council on 5 June 1988); Provisional Measures Concerning Invigorating Large and Medium-sized State-Owned Enterprises (issued by the State Economic Commission and the State Commission for Economic Structural Reform, and approved by the State Council on 11 September 1985); State Council Notice on Further Invigorating Large and Medium-sized State-Owned Enterprises (issued by the State Council

Indeed, the latest business registration classification, issued in 1998, continues to partially reflect the above differentiation of enterprises. Under the Provisions concerning Enterprise Registration Classifications,[16] enterprises are to be registered under three categories (Article 2):

(1) domestic investment enterprises, which are further divided into state-owned enterprises, collective enterprises, shareholding cooperatives, joint operations, limited liability companies, companies limited by shares, private enterprises and other enterprises;

(2) Hong Kong, Macau, Taiwan investment enterprises, which are divided into equity joint ventures (Hong Kong or Macau, Taiwan investment), contractual joint ventures (Hong Kong or Macau, Taiwan Investment), sole investment enterprises by Hong Kong, Macau or Taiwan Investors, and companies limited by shares with Hong Kong, Macau or Taiwan investment; and

(3) foreign investment enterprises, which include Sino-foreign equity joint ventures, Sino-foreign contractual joint ventures, wholly foreign-owned enterprises, and companies limited by shares with foreign investment.

These laws and administrative regulations not only lay down provisions governing organisational structures, but also provide, together with many other administrative measures and regulations, detailed rights and duties as well as advantageous or discriminatory treatments. The results of such a legislative structure are threefold: first, the legal status of many economic entities is ambiguous. Secondly, many legislative gaps regarding the legal status of such enterprises as joint operations or enterprise groups have been left unresolved as a result of the lack of an abstract and general approach towards the legal status of economic entities. Thirdly, and most importantly, an unequal and unfair environment for economic competition among different economic entities has been created by these laws, administrative measures and regulations,[17] although since 1994 when the Company Law was implemented,

on 16 May 1991), and most recently the Law of the PRC on the Promotion of Medium- and Small-Sized Enterprises (adopted by the Standing Committee of the NPC, 29 June 2002, and effective from 1 January 2003).

16 See *supra* note 7.

17 For detailed discussions on the root of the unequal treatment of these entities, see Jianfu Chen, *From Administrative Authorisation to Private Law: A Comparative Perspective of the Developing Civil Law in the People's Republic of China* (Dordrecht/Boston/London, Martinus Nijhoff Publishers, 1995), Chapter 5. See also the discussion in section 2.9 below. It should be pointed out at this point that although the non-public economy has been subject to various forms of discrimination, the private sectors, as compared to the public sector, do have a higher degree of freedom in business decision-making and, hence, in heading off competition in the market.

increasing efforts have been made to provide a level play field for all business entities, with limited success.[18]

2.2. The 'Individual Households' (*Getihu*) (the 'Two Households')

An Individual Industrial and Commercial Household is defined as a citizen or citizens 'who, within the scope permitted by the law and following examination, approval and registration according to the law, engage(s) in industrial or commercial business.'[19] A Rural Contracting Household is, according to the same law, 'a member or members of a collective rural economic organisation who, within the scope permitted by the law, engage(s) in commodity business in accordance with the provisions of a contract.'[20]

Under the GPCL the difference between the two 'Households' seems to be that, first, 'Individual Households' are treated rather as business entities, while 'Contracting Households' are regarded more as being contractual arrangements.[21] Secondly, 'Individual Households' own their 'business' property, but 'Contracting Households' have only a contractual right to use the 'business property', that is the land and farming implements which are owned by the collective. Finally, eligibility for membership of these two 'Households' is different. Rural collective property may be contracted to any members of that collective, while conditions for 'Individual Households' membership are separately prescribed by administrative rules.[22]

Despite these differences the two 'Households' share similar problems concerning their legal status under civil law.

Both 'Households' are dealt with by the GPCL under Chapter Two on Citizens (Natural Persons). However, both 'Households' are clearly expected to be, and actually

18 See further discussion in Section 2.9 below.

19 Article 26 of the GPCL. For the convenience of discussion, 'Individual Industrial and Commercial Households' are hereinafter referred to as 'Individual Households'.

20 Article 27 of the GPCL. Also for convenience, 'Rural Contracting Households' are hereinafter referred to as 'Contracting Households'.

21 Article 26 of the GPCL requires an 'Individual Household' to be registered, and allows it to adopt a business name. The GPCL says nothing about 'Contracting Households' in this regard.

22 People allowed to engage in 'Individual Households' business are urban unemployed persons or rural residents who are able to run a business, or other persons permitted by state policies. See Article 2 of the Provisional Regulations Concerning the Administration of Individual Industrial and Commercial Households in Cities and Townships. See also Zou Zhenlü, *Individual Industrial and Commercial Households* (*Geti Gongshang Hu*) (Beijing: Publishing House of Law, 1986), at 22. In practice, these restrictions are not strictly enforced, at least not any more.

often are, run on a family basis.[23] The central question, as has often been asked by Chinese jurists,[24] is in what capacity (i.e. as natural persons or legal persons) the two 'Households' participate in civil law relations. Until now jurists in China have failed to provide a satisfactory answer on the basis of the existing law. Instead, many treat the two 'Households' as 'special subjects' of civil law or 'quasi-legal persons' (*zhun faren*), said to be different from the traditional subjects of civil law, i.e. legal and natural persons (citizens).[25] According to these scholars the two 'Households' in most cases have only legal capacity as accorded to citizens (natural persons) by law. These two 'Households' may, however, participate in civil law relations, such as signing contracts with third parties and appearing in court proceedings, in the name of the 'Households'. Furthermore, they are also treated as business entities rather than individuals for such legal purposes as taxation and registration. Chinese jurists have, moreover, failed to explain any possible legal implications of being a 'special subject of civil law', a term not used by any legislative enactments at all. The reality seems to be that the two 'Households' will be treated in most cases as business entities, but as individuals in the case of assuming civil liabilities; that is, assuming unlimited liabilities with either personal or family property.[26]

It must be pointed out that while the two 'Households' are still an important force in the private sector, they are no longer as prominent as they were in the early days of the post-Mao reforms, due to a combination of factors. The introduction of new forms of private enterprise in 1988, the corporatisation of enterprises allowed by the Company Law of 1994, the introduction of sole investment enterprises, and most recently the allowance of the establishment of one-person companies since 2005,

---

23 Article 29 of the GPCL provides: 'The debts of Individual Industrial and Commercial Households and Rural Contracting Households shall, where such enterprises are individually operated, be met by the property of the individual. *Where operation is by a family*, they shall be met by the property of the household.'

24 See e.g. 'A Summary of Discussions on Legal Problems Concerning the Individual Economy', *Daily of the Chinese Legal System* (*Zhongguo Fazhi Bao*), 24 October 1986, at 3; Xie Shisong, 'On Legal Problems Concerning the Individual Economy', (no. 2, 1986) *Politics and Law* (*Zhengzhi Yu Falü*) 28; Xu Ming & Guo Liming, 'On the Legal Status of "Households"', (no. 1, 1988) *Law Magazine* (*Faxue Zazhi*) 40; Luo Yuzhen (ed.), *General Principles of Civil Law* (*Minfa Tonglun*) (Wuhan, Centre-China Teacher's University Press, 1986), at 58-65; Wang Liming, Guo Minglei & Fang Liufang, *A New Approach to Civil Law* (*Minfa Xinlun*), vol. 1 (Beijing: Press of the China University of Political Science and Law, 1987), at 190-201; Li Youyi, *et al.*, *Civil Law Science* (*Minfa Xue*) (Beijing: Beijing University Press, 1988), at 64-69; Liang Huixin, *Civil Law* (*Minfa*) (Chengdu: Sichuan People's Press, 1989), at 91-95; Tong Rou, *et al.*, *Chinese Civil Law Science – General Principles of Civil Law* (*Zhongguo Minfaxue – Minfa Zongze*) (Beijing: Press of the University of the Chinese People's Public Security, 1990), at 134-138; and Tong Rou, *et al.*, *Chinese Civil Law* (*Zhongguo Minfa*) (Beijing: Publishing House of Law, 1990), at 84-86.

25 *Id.*

26 *Id.*

coupled with their own success and growth, have all contributed to the transformation of the two 'Households' into private enterprises and private companies. Further, the overall environment has not been particularly conducive for their operation either, such as the difficulty in raising funds, the levying of government charges and fees, discrimination in taxation and entry to the market etc.[27] Thus the total number of the two 'Households' decreased from 31.69 million in 1999 to 23.5 million in 2004, a reduction of some 1.35 million annually.[28]

2.3. Private Enterprises (*Siying Qiye*)

The term 'private enterprise' refers to 'a privately funded economic entity which employs at least eight persons.'[29] This definition has to be understood from recent developments in private enterprise in China.

Private enterprises first grew out of the growth of Individual Industrial and Commercial Households without any benefit of the law. According to Article 5 of the State Council Provisions Concerning Certain Policies on the Non-Agricultural Individual Economy in Cities and Township,[30] an 'Individual Household' could employ, with the approval of industrial and commercial administrative bureaus, two helpers and no more than five apprentices. This restriction on employment by 'Individual Households' was further confirmed by Article 4 of the Provisional Regulations Concerning the Administration of Individual Industrial and Commercial Households in Cities and Townships (1987).[31] However, many 'Individual Households' had actually employed more than seven people before 1988. According to official Chinese sources, at the end of 1987 there were 115,000 Individual Households, each

27 On this, see '"Individual Households" Number Decreased by Millions Indicating a Difficult Environment', 21 September 2006, available in <news.xinhunet.com/fortune/2006-09/21/content_5120824.htm> (last accessed 28 September 2006); and 'Who Made the Two Households Decrease by 8.1 Million?', 21 August 2006, available in <news.xinhunet.com/comments/2006-08/21/content_4988208.htm> (last accessed 28 September 2006).

28 See 'Who Made the Two Households Decrease by 8.1 Million?', *id*. It should be pointed out that government and private research statistics are almost always inconsistent. According to the government statistics, the total number of the 'Two Households' increased by 1.8 million during 2005–2006 to reach 25.05 million by the end of June 2006 (see 'The Total Number of the Two Households Reached 25 Million, and the Total Number of All Kinds of Enterprises Reached 83 Million', available in <news.xinhunet.com/fortune/2006-09/28/content_5150116.htm> (last accessed 28 September 2006)). According to the *Blue Book of the Private Economy*, the total number continued to decline, with the total standing at 24.64 million at the end of June 2006 (See '"Individual Households" Number Decreased by Millions Indicating a Difficult Environment', *id*).

29 Article 2 of the Provisional Regulations of the People's Republic of China on Private Enterprises (1988).

30 Issued by the State Council on 7 July 1981.

31 Issued by the State Council on 5 August 1987.

of which employed more than eight persons, with a total employment of 1,847,000 persons.[32] At the same time some small but unprofitable state-owned or collective enterprises had already been sold to individuals.[33] These enterprises then operated, as mentioned before, without a constitutional base or a legal framework until 1988. This reality effectively forced the Communist Party to admit the need to formulate laws to regulate the private sector and to protect legitimate interests as well as to provide 'effective guidance, supervision and control.'[34]

The 1988 Constitutional Amendment and the enactment of the 1988 Provisional Regulations on Private Enterprises were apparently responses to the above call from the Party. The former restriction on number of employees by individual enterprises was adopted by the 1988 Provisional Regulations as a criterion for distinguishing private enterprises from 'Individual Households'.

Since a private economy and therefore private enterprises were only legalised in 1988, the GPCL of 1986 contains no provisions on private enterprises. Consequently the legal status of private enterprises is governed by administrative regulations, i.e. the 1988 Provisional Regulations on Private Enterprises issued by the State Council.

According to Articles 6-9 of the 1988 Provisional Regulations on Private Enterprises, these enterprises are divided into three types: sole investment enterprises,[35] partnership enterprises,[36] and limited liability companies.[37] Among these, only limited liability companies are accorded the status of legal person.[38]

This sector has grown rapidly since permission for the establishment of private enterprises was granted. At the end of 2006 there were more than 49.4 million such enterprises, employing some 63.96 million people, with a total fixed asset investment of over 4,830 billion *yuan*.[39]

---

32 *People's Daily* (*Renmin Ribao*), 16 March 1988, at 1. Cited in Wang Junyan & Sun Xiaoping, 'On the Nature, Characteristics and Legal Status of Private Enterprises', (no. 1, 1989) *Studies in Law* (*Faxue Yanjiu*), at 17.

33 Wang & Sun, *id.*, at 17.

34 See 'Advance Along the Road of Socialism with Chinese Characteristics', Report Delivered by Zhao Ziyang at the Thirteenth National Congress of the Communist Party of China on 25 October 1987, in *Documents of the Thirteenth National Congress of the Communist Party of China (25 October – 1 November 1987)* (Beijing: Foreign Languages Press, 1987), at 39.

35 'A sole investment enterprise refers to an enterprise which is funded and managed by one person.' (Article 7).

36 'A partnership enterprise refers to an enterprise which is jointly funded and managed by two or more persons, who assume joint responsibility for its profits and losses.' (Article 8).

37 'A limited liability company refers to an enterprise in which investors are liable for company obligations only to the amount of their investment contributions, and the company is liable for company obligations only to the amount of its total assets.' (Article 9).

38 Article 10 of the 1988 Provisional Regulations on Private Enterprises.

39 See 'The Mixed Development of the Private Economy', *People's Daily* (*Renmin Ribao*), overseas edition, 2 February 2007, at 1.

2.4. Collective Enterprises (*Jiti Qiye*)

The legal status of collective enterprises has been theoretically clear since the GPCL and other laws specifically granted the status of legal persons to these enterprises.[40] Therefore legal problems relating to collective enterprises were rarely discussed by Chinese jurists in the 1980s. However around 1990, when the Chinese government decided to make specific and comprehensive laws governing collective enterprises, Chinese jurists suddenly discovered that the reality was not as clear-cut as the theory would have suggested. In particular, they now saw that in many cases it was unclear who was the investor in a particular collective enterprise and who had ownership rights over the property of collective enterprises. Scholars also found that there were no clear-cut criteria for distinguishing collective from private enterprises.[41] Property rights disputes were reported to have occurred frequently concerning collective enterprises and, as a result, Chinese jurists recognised that: 'It can well be said that among all legal issues concerning enterprises, no other issues have been more unclear and complicated than those concerning legal problems relating to collective enterprises.'[42]

Regarding the legal status of collective enterprises, the doubt was not about whether collective enterprises were legal persons, but about who actually owned the property of collective enterprises. The conventional view that the property of collective enterprises belonged to the working people as a collective was, Chinese jurists argued, a direct translation of the politico-economic concept of collective ownership. In dealing with property rights relations under civil law, it was maintained that there had to be a specific organisation or individual in whom property rights were vested. In the case of collective enterprises, the concept of 'working people as a collective' was no clearer than the concept of 'the whole people' was in the case of state-owned enterprises (SOEs). Therefore, property rights relations in collective enterprises were in no way clearer than those in SOEs.[43] Chinese scholars rightly pointed out that all disputes concerning property rights in SOEs were equally relevant to cases of collective enterprises.[44]

Two sets of regulations were issued governing collective enterprises in rural and urban areas in 1990 and 1991 respectively. These regulations have, however, only

---

40 See e.g. Article 41 of the GPCL and Article 2 of the Regulations Concerning the Administration of the Registration of Enterprise Legal Persons (1988).

41 See *China Law Yearbook 1991* (*Zhongguo Falü Nianqian*) (Beijing: Press of China Law Yearbook, 1991), at 845.

42 Zhao Xudong, 'On the Legal Person Status of Collective Enterprises', (no. 1, 1991) *Legal Science in China* (*Zhongguo Faxue*), at 62.

43 *Id.*, at 63-65. See also Keun Lee, *Chinese Firms and the State in Transition: Property Rights and Agency Problems in the Reform Era* (New York: M.E. Sharpe, Inc., 1991), at 103-108.

44 *Ibid.*; and Lin Rihua & Leng Tiexun, 'On Legal Problems Relating to Rural Collective Enterprises', (no. 1, 1991) *Law Review* (*Faxue Pinglun*), at 43.

made the property rights relations even more confusing. According to Article 18 of the Regulations on Rural Collective Enterprises, the property of a rural enterprise belongs to all the peasants of the village or town which has established the enterprise concerned. Although a rural collective enterprise may obtain legal person status, it has only the right to possession and use of the property of the enterprise.[45] In the case of urban collective enterprises the property of an enterprise belongs to the working people as a collective.[46] Urban collective enterprises may obtain legal person status in the same way as state-owned enterprises, and have the right to possess, use, reap benefit from and dispose of the property of the enterprises.[47]

Under these two regulations the position of collective enterprises in relation to property rights is no different from that of state-owned enterprises.[48] It should be pointed out that, with the deepening of economic reform, and in particular *de facto* privatisation, the importance of collective enterprises has decreased dramatically in the last 20 years or so.

2.5. State-owned Enterprises (SOEs)

The legal status of SOEs is theoretically clear. In 1983 they were granted the status of legal persons, represented by factory directors with the power 'to exercise the lawful functions of possessing, utilising and disposing of the state property entrusted to them by the state for management, to organise production and management activities independently, and to shoulder the responsibility stipulated by the state ... to raise or answer lawsuits in courts independently.'[49] Their managerial powers, collectively described as the 'right of operation', were conferred by the State Enterprise Law issued in 1988. These powers, under Chapter Three of the State Enterprise Law, include the right to arrange by themselves the production of goods or the provision of services, to request the adjustment of mandatory plans, and to reject additional assignments outside any mandatory plan, to sell their own products outside plan quotas, to choose their suppliers and purchase goods and materials required for production,

---

45 Articles 10 and 24 (1) of the Regulations of the PRC on Rural Collective Enterprises (1990).

46 Article 4 of the Regulations of the PRC on Urban Collective Enterprises (1991). On 25 December 1994 the State Administration of State-owned Assets issued its Interim Measures on Determination of State-owned Property Rights in Collective Enterprises. Under these Measures any property invested by the State in collective enterprises would be asserted as state property, but they are silent as to who owns the property that belongs to the collective enterprises.

47 Articles 6 and 21 (1) of the Regulations of the PRC on Urban Collective Enterprises (1991).

48 See detailed discussions in Tian Guoqiang, 'Property Rights and the Nature of Chinese Collective Enterprises' (2000) 28 *Journal of Comparative Economics* 247.

49 Article 8 of the Provisional Regulations of State-owned Industrial Enterprises (1983) (now replaced by the State Enterprise Law of 1988).

to set their own prices other than those controlled by the state, to negotiate and sign contracts with foreign parties, to control their retained funds, to lease or assign their fixed assets, to decide wages and bonuses, and to recruit and dismiss their staff and workers.[50] In addition, SOEs are empowered to reject the exaction of manpower, materials and financial resources by any state organs or units.

Certain conditions are however imposed on the exercise of these managerial powers. First, SOEs must promote socialist ideals and morality as well as adhere to the socialist road.[51] Secondly, the policies and guiding principles of the Party and the state must be fully implemented under the supervision of Party personnel within the enterprises.[52] Thirdly, the government or government department-in-charge retains and exercises the power of issuing mandatory plans which must be implemented fully by the SOEs.[53] In addition, major construction and technical transformation must be approved by the government or government department.[54] Finally, foreign exchange, material supplies, allocation of resources, and transportation and communications are all controlled by the government or government departments for all practical purposes.

The reality is that the State Enterprise Law was largely, if not completely, ignored. One year after the implementation of the State Enterprise Law, a Chinese jurist described the situation in the following words:

> [Enterprises' rights and powers as provided by] the State Enterprise Law have not been properly implemented; enterprises' status of legal person has not been taken seriously; and the exercise of the right of operation has been impeded by various restraints and obstacles. More specifically, administrative organs have ignored all provisions of the State Enterprise Law by stressing and relying on their own administrative orders and administrative measures; thus they have encroached upon enterprises' rights of operation at their own will; policies of some administrative organs have been changing constantly; thus enterprises have been left without 'rules' to go by. These practices have also caused economic losses to enterprises. Worse still, some organs and individuals, ignoring the various orders and regulations, impose various apportions of charges upon or even extort from enterprises at their own will under various excuses; thus enterprises have sustained heavy losses. The ordeal they have suffered simply cannot be expressed in words.[55]

---

50 Articles 22-32 of the State Enterprise Law.

51 Articles 4-5 of the State Enterprise Law.

52 Article 8 of the State Enterprise Law.

53 Article 55 of the State Enterprise Law.

54 *Ibid.*

55 Luo Mingda & Bian Xiangping, 'On Problems in and Countermeasures for Enforcing the Enterprise Law', (no. 5, 1989) *Law Review* (*Faxue Pinglun*), at 9.

Faced with the mounting difficulties in implementing the State Enterprise Law, in 1992 the State Council issued its Regulations on Changing the Operating Mechanisms of State-owned Industrial Enterprises, with the aim of enforcing the State Enterprise Law by way of clarifying powers that had been granted to SOEs. However, the situation did not become better for many years after the implementation of the State Enterprise Law.[56]

To Chinese jurists and economists the root of the problems lies with the system of property rights.[57] Fundamentally, it is unclear, under Chinese civil law and its jurisprudence, whether SOEs have their *own* powers and rights in controlling the property under their management. To Chinese jurists the fundamental feature of, and the most important requirement for, being a legal person is the possession of *independent* property. This view inevitably comes into great conflict with the intention of the reform policy in China. It has been emphasised throughout the whole process of economic reform that the purpose of the reform is to extend some decision-making powers to enterprises and thus to invigorate their productivity, but not to change the socialist system of economy. Deng Xiaoping clearly summarised the basic reform policy of the Party and the state:

> Our modernisation programme is a socialist programme, not anything else. All our policies for carrying out reform, opening to the outside world and invigorating the domestic economy, are designed to develop the socialist economy. We allow the development of individual economy, of joint ventures with both Chinese and foreign investment and of enterprises wholly-owned by foreign businessmen, but socialist public ownership will always remain a predominant form of economy.[58]

This reform policy was re-affirmed at the 15th Party Congress in September 1997, although at the same time the Party called for exploring various methods for the

---

56 See 'An Inspection Report on the Implementation of the State Enterprise Law', delivered by Yang Bao at the 29th Meeting of the Standing Committee of the 7th NPC on 25 December 1992, in (no. 7, 1992) *Gazette of the Standing Committee of the NPC of the PRChina* (*Zhonghua Renmin Gongheguo Quanguo Renmin Daibiao Dahui Changwu Weiyuanhui Gongbao*), at 97-105; 'Enterprise Law: Four Years on a Rough and Bumpy Road', *Legal Daily* (*Fazhi Ribao*), 31 January 1993, 2; and 'Enterprises Are Not the Flesh of "Tangzeng"', *Legal Daily* (*Fazhi Ribao*), 22 March 1994, at 7.

57 See *China Youth Daily* (*Zhongguo Qingnian Bao*), 26 August 1991, at 1; 4 September 1991, at 1; Gu Peidong, 'Some Legal Considerations for Deepening Enterprise Reform', *Guangming Daily* (*Guangming Ribao*), 23 May 1997, at 3; and Wu Jianbin, 'Establishing a Scientific Foundation for Our Modern Enterprise System', (no. 1, 1998) *Legal Science in China* (*Zhongguo Faxue*) 30.

58 Deng Xiaoping, *Fundamental Issues in Present-Day China* (Beijing: Foreign Languages Press, 1987), at 101.

realisation of the domination of socialist public ownership.[59]

Despite the upholding of the socialist rhetoric, *de facto* privatisation of SOEs has been carried out, with the exception of large state corporations directly under supervision of the State Asset Supervision and Administration Commission of the State Council or its local counterparts. This was done initially through corporatisation after the enactment of the Company Law in 1994, the sale of unprofitable SOEs to domestic private enterprises, and more recently by way of mergers with and acquisition by foreign investors.[60]

2.6. Joint Operation (*Lianying*) & Enterprise Groups (*Qiye Jituan*)

Joint operations and, later, enterprise groups, emerged as a pragmatic solution to counter the rigid enterprise structuring in accordance with the forms of ownership and the regional and administrative subordination relationship. Their principal purpose, at least initially, was to diversify ownership in enterprises, to breakdown regional and administrative barriers and to promote increased scale of production in enterprise development.[61] In short, they came about as a method of circumventing the rigid socialist ideology underlying the then politico-economic system in the 1980s.

A jointly operated enterprise can be defined in broad terms as a partnership formed between two or more economic entities for the purpose of undertaking business operations or forming closer economic ties.

The GPCL provides specifically for enterprises jointly operated between enterprises (presumably including private enterprises, collectively-owned enterprises and state-

---

59 See 'Holding High the Great Banner of Deng Xiaoping Theory for the All-round Advancement of the Cause of Building Socialism with Chinese Characteristics to the 21st Century', a Political Report delivered by Jiang Zemin at the 15th National Congress of CPC on 12 September 1997.

60 Initially, this was authorised by some interim measures (such as the Interim Provisions on Utilising Foreign Funds to Restructure State-owned Enterprises (2002); Notice on Certain Issues concerning the Transfer to Foreign Investors of State Shares and Legal Person Shares in Listed Companies (2002); Opinion on Standardising the Transformation of State Owned Enterprises (2003); Interim Measures on the Transfer of State Owned Property Rights in Enterprises (2003); Administrative Measures on the Acquisition of Listed Companies (2002); Interim Provisions for the Acquisition and Merger of Domestic Enterprises by Foreign Investors (2003); and other measures), but the practice has since by formalised by the Administrative Measures on Strategic Investment in Listed Companies by Foreign Investors (2005) and the Provisions on the Merger and Acquisition of Domestic Enterprises by Foreign Investors (2006).

61 See detailed discussion in Jianfu Chen, *supra* note 17, at 252-269. See also Lisa A. Kerster & Jin Lu, 'The Transformation Continues: The Status of Chinese State-Owned Enterprises at the Start of the Millennium', 12 (3) (2001) *NBR Analysis*, available from <www.nbr.org/publications/issue.esp?&id=202> (last accessed 27 June 2007), especially at 12-15.

owned enterprises), or between an enterprise and an institution. The subsequent legal treatment of a jointly operated enterprise is differentiated on the basis of the degree of affiliation between or among its members. Where joint operations lead to the formation of a new economic entity which is able to assume civil liability independently and which possesses all other qualifications for legal person status, legal person status will be conferred upon approval and registration by a competent authority, i.e. the local bureau of the SAIC.

Under the Provisional Administrative Regulations on the Registration of Enterprise Groups, which was promulgated on 6 April 1998 by the State Administration for Industry and Commerce, an enterprise group is defined as a joint entity of enterprise legal persons, which has a definite size, regards the parent and its subsidiary companies as the principal body, takes the group articles of association as the standard for joint activities, and is constituted by a parent company, subsidiary companies, mutual shareholding companies and other member enterprises or institutions.

An enterprise group itself does not have enterprise legal person status; however, all its members must be legal persons. The parent company must be a registered holding enterprise and a subsidiary company must be an enterprise in which the parent company has all the shares or has a controlling shareholding. Other members must either have a mutual shareholding with the parent company or have formed production operations and cooperative connections with the parent-subsidiary company.

2.7. Foreign-invested Enterprises (FIEs)

As mentioned above, foreign-related business is regulated by a separate legal framework. Despite the continuing reforms towards universal treatment of all economic entities under the principles of national treatment, the separate system will be retained, at least for the foreseeable future, and this system will be discussed in Chapter 17.

2.8. Rural Cooperatives

Rural cooperatives emerged in the early 1980s when the 'family contracting' system was first introduced. Initially the 'family contracting' system concentrated on agricultural production, but surplus rural labour soon led to the establishment of various kinds of township and village enterprises, many of them in the nature of collective cooperatives. For some time shareholding cooperatives seemed to be the mainstream form in this development, although without much legal basis.

Shareholding cooperatives (*Gufen Hezuo Qiye*[62]) are direct products of post-Mao reform. In this form of enterprise shares are held by employees, and such shares are not transferable to outsiders. Remuneration of workers is decided by their

---

[62] Also translated as 'partnership shareholding firms'.

performance and the shares they hold. They are neither traditional cooperatives, nor partnerships, nor joint stock companies, but a hybrid of all of them.

This enterprise form first emerged in the early 1980s in rural areas in Zhejiang and Guangdong provinces, and was later adopted by collective enterprises in light industries in cities.[63] Its development has been very rapid. By 1995 there were over three million such enterprises in rural areas and over fourteen thousand in cities.[64] With a large number of small-sized collective and state-owned enterprises facing bankruptcy and, at the same time, strong ideological resistance to the idea of bankruptcy and privatisation, shareholding cooperatives were favoured and encouraged as a form for the re-organisation of such enterprises.[65]

This new form of enterprise, however, did not fit into any existing legal framework governing enterprises. Although certain government rules were issued to facilitate the development of shareholding cooperatives,[66] there was a total lack of legal framework. As such, there was considerable controversy as to whether it was a new form of enterprise, or was simply a new name under which an enterprise was formed as either a partnership, or a joint stock company or a cooperative.[67] Its legal status and its form of liability were all in doubt.

---

63 'Actively Promote the Development of Shareholding Cooperatives', *People's Daily* (*Renmin Ribao*), internet edition, 8 August 1997. See also 'Explanations on the Draft Law on the Peasant Specialised Cooperative Organisations', delivered by Li Chuanting at the 22nd Session of the Standing Committee of Tenth NPC on 24 June 2006. A copy of the text is available from <www.npc.gov.cn/zgrdw/common/zw.jsp?label=WXZLK&id=354949> (last accessed 29 June 2007). For a detailed study, see Eduard B. Vermeer, 'Development of the Shareholding Cooperative System and Property Rights in China', Eduard B. Vermeer & Ingrid d'Hooghe (eds), *China's Legal Reforms and Their Political Limits* (UK: Curzon Press, 2002), at 123-156.

64 *Ibid.*

65 Opinions on Guiding the Development of Shareholding Cooperatives in Cities, issued by the State Structural Reform Commission, 6 August 1997, in *People's Daily* (*Renmin Ribao*), internet edition, 7 August 1998. See also Ricky Tung, 'The Bankruptcy System of Mainland China's State-Owned Enterprises', (no. 1, 1997) 33 *Issues & Studies* 23, at 41.

66 Certain Tentative Provisions on Shareholding Cooperatives Among Peasants, issued by the Ministry of Agriculture on 12 February 1990; Circular concerning Promoting and Improving the System of Shareholding Cooperatives, issued by the Ministry of Agriculture on 24 December 1992; Provisional Measures on Shareholding Cooperatives in Light Industries, issued by the Ministry of Light Industry on 1 March 1993. In addition to these policy documents, there were some local rules, such as the Shenzhen Regulations on Companies in the Form of Shareholding Cooperatives (1994); the Shanghai Provisional Measures on Collective Shareholding Cooperatives in Cities and Towns (1994).

67 See e.g. Ma Yaojin, 'A Shareholding Cooperative Is Not an Independent Enterprise Form', (no. 2, 1997) *Journal of China University of Political Science and Law* (*Zhengfa Luntan*) 98; Gu Gongyun, 'Several Difficult Questions Concerning Legislation on Shareholding Cooperatives', Part I in (no. 8, 1997) *Legal Science* (*Faxue*) 49, Part II in (no. 9, 1997) *Legal Science* (*Faxue*) 39.

By the late 1990s efforts were made to regulate shareholding cooperatives in a fashion similar to a company, at least for those in cities. Defined as a new form of enterprise, a shareholding cooperative was granted the status of an independent legal person, with its liability limited to its total assets, and shareholders' liability limited to their subscribed shares.[68] It was required to establish a board of director and to appoint a general manager in charge of daily operations.[69]

Faced with mounting difficulties and discontent among rural residents, the Chinese government finally decided to tackle the so-called '*san nong*' problems (three rural problems – agriculture, peasants, and villages). As part of this effort the Central Government started drafting a law on rural cooperatives in December 2003, in order to clarify the legal status, standardise enterprise structures, and resolve some practical difficulties in relation to rural cooperatives.[70] This then led to the enactment of the Law on Peasant Specialised Cooperative Organisations in 2006.[71] Under this new Law rural cooperatives are now finally granted the status of legal persons.[72] It is, however, unclear how widely this Law may apply to cooperatives. The use of 'peasant' instead of 'rural' perhaps was intended to apply the Law to such cooperatives established by peasants in cities.

2.9. Towards a Modern Enterprise System

Clearly the different enterprise laws have a particular ideological orientation at the particular time when each was adopted. One could be tempted to think that many of the discriminating provisions in the different laws have often been ignored in practice. This may have been true from time to time, but these laws have provided a legal foundation upon which thousands of departmental and local rules have been issued, which have differentiated and discriminated between enterprises with different forms of ownership or regional/administrative subordinate relationships. These rules have in fact been the real barriers to equality in economic activities, particularly those adverse to the private sector. While there is no doubt that the politico-economic environment for the private sector has gradually improved, its development in China has been a thoroughly uphill battle.

---

68 Article 4 of the Opinions on Guiding the Development of Shareholding Cooperatives in Cities (1997).

69 Article 8 of the Opinions on Guiding the Development of Shareholding Cooperatives in Cities (1997).

70 See 'Explanations on the Draft Law on the Peasant Specialised Cooperative Organisations', *supra* note 63.

71 Adopted at the 24th Session of the Standing Committee of the Tenth NPC on 31 October 2006, and effective from 1 July 2007. The Law is now further implemented by the Administrative Regulations on the Registration of the Peasant Specialised Cooperative Organisations, issued by the State Council on 28 May 2005.

72 See Article 4 of the Law of the PRC on Peasant Specialised Cooperative Organisations.

By the late 1980s the differentiated treatment of business entities was no longer a question of law; it had penetrated deeply into almost every sphere of economic activity, so that almost no economic entity could survive without its economic nature being decided and without its being affiliated to some superior administrative and regional organ. A Chinese scholar described the situation in the following words:

> Under the current system, enterprise planning, material supply and taxation burdens are all decided in accordance with the form of ownership. Without the nature of ownership for a given company being determined, it is impossible to lay down operating conditions for that company. Under the current labour system which regulates labour relations according to forms of ownership, it is difficult to decide working conditions and welfare for workers without first clarifying the nature of ownership of the company. Today, planning is still in a predominant position and production plans, material allocation, product sales and quotas for loans are all allocated through vertical and regional administrative networks, without which a company is not able to obtain these materials and loan quotas nor have access to a market. A company may not even be able to get itself registered since, under current registration rules, a company without an administrative organ-in-charge is usually not accepted for registration.[73]

Such differential treatment entailed political, economic and legal discrimination against non-state sectors. It created, as a Hong Kong journal commented,[74] some truly adverse circumstances for non-state sectors. However, against all odds, the private sector proved to be the most vigorous in growth during the reform period. Official statistics showed that the SOEs' share in national industrial output value decreased from 78% in 1981 to 55% in 1991; during the same period, industrial output of collective enterprises increased from 21% to 35%, and that of the private sector, including foreign-funded enterprises, climbed from 0.7% to 10%.[75] By the end of 1992 the share of national industrial output by various sectors of the economy had again changed significantly: The SOEs' share had again decreased to 48.3%, while collective enterprises increased their share to 38.2% and the private sector's share increased to 13.5%.[76] With regard to employment and registered capital as at the end of 1991, the two 'Households' employed 22,580,000 people with a registered capital of 48.82 billion *yuan*, and private enterprises employed 1,839,000 persons

---

73 Zhao Xudong, 'Certain Problems in Chinese Corporate Legislation', (no. 1, 1991) *Journal of China University of Political Science and Law* (*Zhengfa Luntan*), at 43.

74 See *Mirror Monthly* (Hong Kong), March 1994, at 36-37, translated in *Inside China Mainland*, May 1994, 34-37, at 36.

75 *People's Daily* (*Renmin Ribao*) (overseas edition), 7 August 1992, at 1; and *Beijing Review*, 24-30 August 1992, at 6.

76 'The Reform of the Property Rights System Has Achieved Positive Progress', *People's Daily* (*Renmin Ribao*), 25 February 1994, at 2.

with 12.32 billion *yuan* of registered capital. The two 'Households' and private enterprises turned over 17.9 billion *yuan* in tax to the state, amounting to 7.6% of the total taxes the state collected in 1991.[77]

After the Southern China tour by Deng Xiaoping in January 1992, the development of individual and private enterprises was again singled out for encouragement by the Central Government and various authorities.[78] By the end of 1996 the SOEs' share in industrial output further decreased to 32%, while that of the non-state sector jumped to 24%.[79] At the end of 1997 there were 2.85 million individual enterprises with 257.4 billion *yuan* in registered capital and employing 54.4 million people, while the number of private (excluding foreign invested) enterprises increased to 960,000 with a registered capital of 514 billion *yuan* and employing 13.5 million people. The two sectors contributed 54 billion *yuan* in tax to the State, amounting to 7% of national tax levied on industry and commerce.[80]

Even within the state sector the township collective enterprises contributed to the bulk of growth. In 1995 44% of added value in the industrial sector came from township collective enterprises, which also contributed 34% of China's exports.[81] Despite all kinds of protection, one third of the SOEs ran at a loss during the first 20 years of reform.[82]

However, even after some twenty years of reform the private economy was still perceived by many as inferior to the public economy.[83] Nevertheless, the rapid development of the non-public sectors continued and they grew much faster than the GDP. Between 1992 and 2002 the individual and the private sectors grew at an

---

77 See *supra* note 75.

78 See e.g. 'Further Encouragement for the Healthy Development of the Private Economy' and 'Beijing Encourages the Development of the Individual Economy', both in *People's Daily (Renmin Ribao)* (overseas edition), 16 May, 1992 at 1 and 2 respectively; and 'Further Relaxation in Restrictions on Employment and Business Scope Led to Good Developmental Trends in the Individual and Private Economy', *People's Daily* (*Renmin Ribao*) (overseas edition), 20 August, 1992, at 1.

79 See *People's Daily* (*Renmin Ribao*), internet edition, 5 April 1997; and 'How the Domination of the State Economy Is Reflected', *People's Daily* (*Renmin Ribao*), internet edition, 12 November 1997.

80 *People's Daily* (*Renmin Ribao*), internet edition, 11 May 1998.

81 See Report on the Township Enterprises, Their Future Reform and Development, issued by the Ministry of Agriculture, in *People's Daily* (*Renmin Ribao*), internet edition, 24 April 1997.

82 In 1996, 37.7% of SOEs ran at a loss: *People's Daily* (*Renmin Ribao*), internet edition, 5 April 1997. In 1997, losses suffered by industrial enterprise nationwide amounted to 134.1 billion *yuan*. Among them, the SOEs lost 74.4 billion *yuan*, a share of 55.5% of the total. See Statistical Communique on Socioeconomic Development in 1997, (11-17 May 1998), *Beijing Review* 14, at 15-16.

83 'To Promote the Individual and Private Economy', *People's Daily* (*Renmin Ribao*), internet edition, 10 May 1998.

average rate of 33% and 31% respectively. The share of the two sectors in the GDP increased from less than 1% in 1979 to more than 20%. If foreign investment is included, the three sectors accounted for over one third of the GDP.[84] By the end of 2002 there were 23,775,000 and 2,430,000 registered businesses in the individual and private sectors respectively, employing 47,430,000 and 34,090,000 people respectively, and accounting for some 33% of employment at the township level.[85] If the collective economy is also included in the non-public sector, the non-public economy then represented 74% of GDP.[86]

This rapid development of the private sector occurred despite continuing discrimination and disadvantage. Thus in 2003 a Chinese scholar summarised the problems and conflicts in terms of (1) difficulties in classification of enterprises; (2) conflicting rules on internal decision-making powers; (3) the uncertainties in decision-making powers in relation to external business operations; (4) the application of several sets of enterprise laws at the same time and to the same enterprises; (5) the ambiguities in property rights; and (6) complications in enterprise registration.[87]

These developments in the private sector of the economy have highlighted, and will continue to highlight, the stagnation in the reform of the fundamental economic administration system and the deficiencies of the legal system built on this economic base. As late as 2004 a high ranking government official, Hu Kangsheng, Director of the LAC of the SCNPC summarised the problems thus:

> At the present there are still many systemic barriers to the development of the non-public economy. There are still restrictions for the non-public sectors in market access, investment and fund raising. Some government departments still impose much stricter criteria for business registration, operation, establishment of projects etc. on the non-public sectors than those on the enterprises under public ownership. Some non-public enterprises still cannot acquire land-use rights and loans on equitable terms. Some local and departmental officials continue to interfere with non-public enterprises, impose unreasonable requirements, erect artificial barriers and even deliberately cause difficulties for their operation. ...[88]

---

84 Hu Kangsheng, 'To Resolutely Promote the Development of the Non-Public Economy', *People's Daily* (*Renmin Ribao*) 6 April 2004, at 10. By contrast, in early 1999, it accounted for 15 per cent of the national GDP. See 'Constitutional Amendments Propel China's Reform and Opening-up', *China Daily*, internet edition, 17 March 1999.

85 Hu Kangsheng, *id*., at 10.

86 Tian Guoqiang, *supra* note 48, at 248.

87 Jiang Tianbo, 'Several Considerations on Legislation on Enterprise Entities', 6 November 2003, in China Government Law Info net: <www.chinalaw.gov.cn>.

88 Hu Kangsheng, *supra* note 84, at 10. See also 'Non-public Sectors enter into a golden period and most barriers have been removed', Xinhua News Agency, 17 December 2003: <news.xinhuanet.com/fortune/2003-12/17/content_1235833.htm>.

It is truly a system of inequality.

It would be unfair to imply that the government has been indifferent to these problems. It is in any case in the interest of the government to see the private sectors thriving and developing, if only for the sake of overall economic development. Indeed, by the early 1990s the Central Government had fully recognised these fundamental problems in the politico-economic system.[89] Thus a general reform policy was introduced to establish a modern enterprise system.[90] Although there were different interpretations of what a 'modern enterprise system' was,[91] it seemed to be the consensus among economists and legal scholars that it involved comprehensive reform, including the need to clarify property relations among and within enterprises, to change enterprise operating mechanisms, to transform government functions and to reduce administrative interference in economic management, and to encourage the development of all economies under different forms of ownership.[92]

---

89 See 'An Important Step Towards a Modern Enterprise System – An Interview with the Director of the State Administration of Industry and Commerce, Liu Minxue', *Legal Daily* (*Fazhi Ribao*), 15 February 1994, at 2.

90 See Li Peng's speech at the annual meeting of the World Economic Forum in Davos, Switzerland on 30 January 1992, *People's Daily* (*Renmin Ribao*), 1 February, 1992, at 4. An English translation of his speech appears in *Beijing Review*, 17-23 Feb. 1992, at 11-13, at 12; Li Peng's speech at the National Working Conference of Economic Structural Reform, *People's Daily* (*Renmin Ribao*), (overseas edition), 13 January 1992, at 1; 'Main Points of Economic Reform for 1992,' *People's Daily* (*Renmin Ribao*), (overseas edition), 30 March 1992, at 3; 'Enterprise Reform Is at the Centre of Economic Structural Reform', *People's Daily* (*Renmin Ribao*), (overseas edition), 25 June 1992, at 2; He Wei, 'The Key to the Deepening of Reform is to Transform Government Functions', (no. 3, 1992) *Reform* (*Gaige*), at 100-103; 'State Council Approves the Main Points of Economic Structural Reform', *People's Daily* (*Renmin Ribao*), 26 March 1993, at 3; Decision of the CPC Central Committee on Some Issues Concerning the Establishment of a Socialist Market Economic Structure, an English translation appears in *Beijing Review*, 22-28 November 1993, at 12-31; and Report on the Work of the Government, delivered by Li Peng on 10 March 1994, an English translation appears in *Beijing Review*, 4-10 April 1994, at I-XV.

91 See 'What Are the Characteristics of a Modern Enterprise System?' *Economic Daily* (*Jingji Ribao*), 15 March 1994, at 5.

92 See e.g. Wang Zhongyu (Chairman of the State Economic and Trade Commission), 'To Firmly Carry Out Enterprise Reform', *People's Daily* (*Renmin Ribao*), 5 June 1994, at 2; Modern Enterprise System Investigation Group, 'Establishing a Modern Enterprise System in a Socialist Market Economy', *People's Daily* (*Renmin Ribao*), 21 December 1993, at 5; 'Transformation of Mechanisms and Structural Reform – An Interview with Professor Liu Shibao', *Economic Daily* (*Jingji Ribao*), 18 February 1994, at 5; Dai Yannian, 'Spotlight on China's Modern Enterprise System', *Beijing Review*, 28 February – 6 March 1994, at 4-5; Chen Jiagui, 'Establishing a Modern Enterprise System is a Great Revolution in Enterprise Systems', *People's Daily* (*Renmin Ribao*), 4 March 1994, at 5; Zheng Yanning, 'Three Points on the Understanding of Establishing a Modern Enterprise System', *People's Daily* (*Renmin Ribao*), 11 March 1994, at 5.

From a legal perspective, to establish a 'modern enterprise system' simply means to restructure the legal framework for enterprises, making the company law the core of such a framework, but supplemented by laws on sole proprietorship and on partnership, in which the distinctions between enterprises under different forms of ownership, administrative subordination and geographical location are to be totally disregarded.[93] In other words, a modern enterprise legal framework should divide enterprises according to forms of investment and methods for liability, rather than forms of ownership and classification of trades.[94]

By 1999 when the Law of the PRC on Individual Sole Investment Enterprises was adopted, the legal framework for this 'modern enterprise system' was indeed established. But the uphill battle for the private sector was far from over. With the last revision of the Constitution having been completed in 2004, the State Council then began a new round of encouraging the development of the private sector by issuing two important documents: the Decision of the State Council on the Reform of the Investment System,[95] and the Certain Opinions on the Encouragement, Support and Guidance for Economic Development of the Individual, Private and other Non-public Sectors.[96] The former provides the principle of equality for all economic sectors in investment decision-making, and the latter contains concrete measures for equality in market entry, financial support and all economic activities. Among the measures contained in the 2005 Opinions is a demand that all government departments and local governments review their rules and documents and have all discriminatory rules repealed. By May 2007 this task was apparently completed. According to the Chinese media more than 1.6 million sets of documents were reviewed nationwide,[97] and among them some 6,428 were found to be restricting the development of the non-public sectors. Thus 4,184 was repealed, 329 revised, with another 875 still to be repealed and more than 300 to be revised.[98] One can easily

93 See Wang Jianping, *et al.*, 'On Criteria for Distinguishing Forms of Enterprises', (no. 2, 1997) *Journal of the China University of Political Science and Law* (*Zhengfa Luntan*) 92; and Wu Jianbin, 'A Scientific Legal Foundation to Building a Modern Enterprise System', (no. 1, 1998) *Legal Science in China* (*Zhongguo Faxue*) 30.

94 'Explanations on the Draft Sole Investment Law', delivered at the 9th Session of the 9th NPC, 26 April 1999, in (no. 5, 1999) *Gazette of the Standing Committee of the NPC* (*Zhonghua Renmin Gongheguo Quanguo Renmin Daibiao Dahui Changwu Weiyuanhui Gongbao*) 419, at 419.

95 Issued as Guofa [2004] No. 20 on 16 July 2004.

96 Issued as Guofa [2005] No. 3 on 19 February 2005.

97 Compared to the total number of laws, regulations and rules issued by the various legislatures and governments at different levels (see Chapter 5), it is clear that most of these documents are the so-called 'Red Head' documents that have not been formally published, despite the emphasis on legal transparency since the Law on Law-Making took effect in 2000.

98 See 'Legal Protection for the Non-Public Sectors Becoming Increasingly Perfect', *People's Daily* (*Renmin Ribao*), overseas edition, 30 May 2007, at 1.

imagine the kind of barriers that had existed to the development of the non-private sectors. Amazingly, the non-public sectors (not counting the foreign investment sector) had survived and, in fact, continued to thrive. In 2005, the total industrial output by the private sector amounted to 2,000 billion *yuan*, realising a total profit of 983.7 billion *yuan* and paying a total tax of 567.2 billion *yuan*. They now account for 65% of the GDP.[99] Even more importantly, private enterprises now account for 80% of all enterprises in the 53 state-level hi-tech development zones, 66% of all patents, 74% of all technological innovation, and 82% of all new products.[100]

3. Individual Sole Investment Enterprises (Sole Proprietorship) (*Geren Duzi Qiye*)

The distinction between the two 'Households' and non-legal person private enterprises was, as mentioned above, arbitrary. Although the Private Enterprise Regulations allow the establishment of sole investment enterprises (sole proprietorship), the Regulations are more concerned about enterprise forms on the basis of ownership than about business operations. This situation did not change until the Law of the PRC on Individual Sole Investment Enterprises was adopted by the SCNPC on 30 August 1999.[101] The Law is enacted as part of the effort to establish a 'modern enterprise system', in which enterprises are to be classified according to methods of investment and liabilities, disregarding forms of ownership and business trade.[102] The principal purpose of the Law is to provide a legal framework for the two 'Households' and private enterprises that operated neither as legal persons nor as partnerships. It is also meant to break the arbitrary distinction between private and individual enterprises by the number of employees.[103] The Law does not apply to state-owned, collective or foreign investment enterprises.

Article 2 of the Individual Sole Investment Enterprise Law defines a sole investment enterprise as a business entity which is invested in by a natural person who owns the enterprise's property and bears unlimited liability with respect to the obligations of the enterprise by way of his/her property.

Article 9 of the Law seems to suggest that sole investment enterprises may engage in business in any field of industry, construction, transportation, commerce, catering, the service industry, the repair trade and scientific and technological consultancy, unless prohibited by law or administrative regulations. If a special permit is required

---

99 See 'Legal Protection for the Non-Public Sectors Becoming Increasingly Perfect', *id.*

100 See 'Private Economy Promotes Technological Innovation and Localisation of Technologies', *People's Daily* (*Renmin Ribao*), overseas edition, 13 January 2007, at 1.

101 The Law became effective on 1 January 2000.

102 'Explanation on the Draft Sole Investment Law', *supra* note 94, at 419.

103 *Id.*, at 421.

for any particular business operation, such a permit must be produced upon applying for establishment and registration. To form a sole investment enterprise the individual must apply to the local registration organ for approval.[104]

Sole investment enterprises may be formed by any individual except those who are prohibited by law and administrative regulations and rules from engaging in profit earning activities.

4. The Partnership Law

4.1. An Overview

Although partnership as an enterprise form is not new in China,[105] it was only regulated by some sketchy provisions in the GPCL until quite recently.[106] The promulgation of the Partnership Enterprise Law (1997) represents the latest effort to rationalise the fragmented and rudimentary enterprise law.[107]

The GPCL contains six articles on individual partnership and enterprise partnership.[108] It also anticipates the possibility of enterprise partnerships under the section on joint operations (*lianying*).[109] The GPCL provisions on individual partnership stipulate joint liability for the debts of a partnership by partners, but leave all other substantive issues, such as capital contribution, distribution of profits, responsibility for debts, entry into and withdrawal from the partnership, operation and termination of partnership to be decided by written partnership agreements. The GPCL provisions allow joint operations meeting legal person requirements to gain legal person status.[110] Presumably the remaining joint operations would be treated as partnership enterprises. Otherwise these provisions provide no guidance

104 The registration of sole proprietorships is governed by the Measures on the Administration of the Registration of Sole Investment Enterprises, issued by the State Administration of Industry and Commerce on 13 January 2000.

105 At the end of 1995, there were 120,000 partnership enterprises in China. See Huang Yicheng, 'Explanations on the Draft Partnership Enterprise Law of the PRC', delivered to the 22nd Meeting of the Standing Committee of the 8th NPC on 23 October 1996, in (no. 1, 1997) *Gazette of Standing Committee of the NPC of the PRC* (*Zhonghua Renmin Gongheguo Quanguo Renmin Daibiao Dahui Changwu Weiyuanhui Gongbao*), at 12.

106 Like in the case of company law, some local governments moved ahead of central government in issuing their own partnership regulations. See e.g. Shenzhen Partnership Regulations (1994).

107 The Law was initially adopted by the Standing Committee on 23 February 1997 and became effective on 1 August of the same year.

108 See Articles 30-35 of the GPCL.

109 See Articles 51-53 of the GPCL.

110 Article 51 of the GPCL.

for such partnership enterprises. Despite rapid development, and strong encouragement for it by the government, joint operations and the subsequent development of enterprise groups (*qiye jituan*) have largely operated outside the Chinese legal framework, with ambiguous legal status.[111]

Clearly the sketchy provisions in the GPCL were not adequate for dealing with partnership as an emerging and rapidly developing enterprise form. The Economic and Financial Commission of the NPC thus established a drafting group for partnership law in May 1994.[112] After three years of extensive consultation the Commission formally submitted its draft to the SCNPC for adoption in October 1996. The draft underwent substantial revision by the Law Commission of the NPC and the SCNPC in the ensuing four months until it was finally adopted in February 1997.[113]

The 1997 Partnership Enterprise Law, although important in sanctioning a new legal form of enterprise structure, suffered some significant defects, such as the lack of provisions on limited partnerships, tax liabilities, foreign partners in partnerships and bankruptcy of partnership enterprises, and the very narrow scope of application. The rapid development of partnership enterprises,[114] the need for private investment, the increasing importance of encouraging venture capital investment in the push for high tech development, and the rapid expansion of professional services (e.g. accountancy, law firms etc.) further highlighted the defects of the 1997 Law in practice and demanded an urgent revision of the Law.[115] This was done in 2006.

The 2006 revision, undertaken by the Economic and Financial Commission of the NPC, was comprehensive. It took over two years before a draft was submitted,

---

111 See discussions in Section 2.6 above.

112 Huang Yicheng, *supra* note 105, at 12.

113 See Li Yining, 'An Examination Report of the Law Commission of the NPC on the Draft Partnership Law of the PRC', delivered to the 24th Meeting of the Standing Committee of the 8th NPC on 19 February 1997, in (no. 1, 1997) *Gazette of the Standing Committee of the National People's Congress of the PRC* (*Zhonghau Renmin Gongheguo Quanguo Renmin Daibiao Dahui Changwu Weiyuanhui Gongbao*), at 17-20; and Que Ju, 'A Written Report on the Revision of the Draft Partnership Law', in (no. 1, 1997) *Gazette of the Standing Committee of the National People's Congress of the PRC* (*Zhonghau Renmin Gongheguo Quanguo Renmin Daibiao Dahui Changwu Weiyuanhui Gongbao*), at 21-22.

114 By the time of the adoption of the 1997 Partnership Law, there were some 60,000 partnership enterprises. 60,000 more were established since the Law came into force. Thus there are currently some 120,000 partnership enterprises, employing some 2 million people in China. See 'China Revises Law to Open Further Space for Partnership Enterprises', in <news.xinhuanet.com/politics/2006-08/27/content_5013377.htm> (last accessed 28 August 2006).

115 See 'China Revises Law to Open Further Space for Partnership Enterprises', *id*; and 'On the Revision of Partnership Law', in <aixin.njmu.edu.cn/Law/003xffd/200605/6645.html> (last accessed 19 September 2006).

in April 2006, to the SCNPC for deliberation.[116] The passage of the revision through the SCNPC was smooth;[117] it underwent three sessions (April, June and August sessions of the SCNPC in 2006) of deliberation and was adopted on 27 August 2006. The revised Law took effect on 1 June 2007.

4.2. The Partnership Enterprise Law

As mentioned above, the Partnership Enterprise Law is seen as a major component of a modern enterprise legal framework governing all actors and players in the market.[118] The original 1997 Law had defined a 'partnership enterprise' as a profit-making organisation established in China by a partnership agreement concluded among all partners who jointly contributed capital, undertook business as partners, shared profits and risks and assumed unlimited joint and several liability for the debts of the partnership enterprise.[119] The revised Law now provides a circular definition of partnership enterprises, defining them as ordinary partnership enterprises and limited partnership enterprises established in China by natural persons, legal persons and other organisations.[120] This defect of a circular definition is remedied, however, by provisions defining the forms of liabilities. Thus in an ordinary partnership all partners will bear unlimited liability unless otherwise provided by law. In limited partnerships ordinary partners continue to bear unlimited liability while limited partners will assume a limited liability in accordance with their subscribed share of investment.[121] There are no further definitions on ordinary or limited partnerships. However the conditions for establishment suggest that ordinary partnerships are those established by two or more natural persons with full civil capacity, while limited partnerships are to be established by between two to fifty partners, with at least one partner being an ordinary partner (that is, a natural person).[122]

Article 2 seems to suggest that there are two kinds of partnership under the revised Law: ordinary partnerships and limited partnerships. The actual situation

---

116 See Wang Xiang, 'An Introduction to the Revision of the Partnership Law', available from <www.npc.gov.cn/zgrdw/common/zw.jsp?label=WXZLK&id=352015&pdme=110106> (last accessed 31 August 2006); and 'On the Revision of Partnership Law', *id.*

117 At the three sessions deliberations on the draft were overwhelmingly positive, with only a few members questioning whether the time was ripe for the revision of the Partnership Law. Others were all supportive and focused on technical aspects of the draft revision. For deliberation speeches, see <www.npc.gov.cn> (last accessed 21 September 2006) under the Standing Committee meetings (21st, 22nd and 23rd sessions in April, June and August 2006 respectively).

118 See also Huang Yicheng, *supra* note 105, at 13.

119 Article 2 of the original 1997 Partnership Enterprise Law.

120 Article 2 of the revised Partnership Enterprise Law.

121 Article 2 of the revised Partnership Enterprise Law.

122 Articles 14 & 61 of the revised Partnership Enterprise Law.

may not be as clear-cut as the Law has suggested. The phrase in Article 2 'unless otherwise provided by law' in relation to ordinary partnerships implies that ordinary partnerships may contain special provisions that would further distinguish them. Indeed, Section 6 of Chapter One of the revised Law, which is an entirely new section, creates an odd category of ordinary partnership called 'special ordinary partnerships'.[123] These in fact relate to professional service partnerships such as legal and accountancy firms, medical clinics, and architecture design firms, etc. This legislative arrangement requires some further explanations. Under the original draft of the 1997 Partnership Law submitted by the Economic and Financial Commission, the Partnership Law would be applied to all other organisations taking the form of partnership by analogy. The Law Commission of the NPC however took the view that such enterprises were partnerships of a different nature and that they should be subject to the GPCL and special laws and regulations on such professions.[124] The Law Commission's view apparently triumphed in the final version of the Law as adopted in 1997. With legal and accountancy firms, medical clinics, asset evaluation organisations, architectural design firms etc. being excluded from the Law, the significance of the Law was severely diminished. As mentioned above, one of the reasons for the revision of the Law was to regulate the ever-increasing number and types of professional service organisations. Thus the draft revision submitted by the Economic and Financial Commission contained a new chapter on 'limited liability partnerships'. Even though the available deliberation speeches contained no objection to this phrase, and indeed members of the SCNPC preferred the phrase 'limited liability partnerships', the final revision text submitted to the SCNPC in August 2006 changed the phrase 'limited liability partnerships' to the odd 'special ordinary partnerships' without much explanation.[125]

The 'special ordinary partnerships' are special in two aspects, namely forms of liability and requirements for insurance. Otherwise provisions for ordinary partnerships continue to apply. Under Article 57, if a partner or several partners have created debts for the partnership enterprise, either intentionally or by gross negligence, the partner or partners will be liable for unlimited liability, and other partners in the enterprises will only assume their liability in proportion to their share of property in the enterprise. All partners will assume joint and several liabilities for debts caused by professional conduct. Article 59 then requires that 'special partnership enterprises' must establish professional risk funds and take out professional risk insurance. Specific regulations on the funds and insurance are to be issued separately by the State Council.

---

123 Not surprisingly, members of the SCNPC questioned whether the Partnership Law intended to provide two or three types of partnership. See deliberation speeches, *supra* note 117.

124 Li Yining, *supra* note 113, at 17-20.

125 See deliberation speeches, *supra* note 117.

The whole of Chapter 3 on limited partnership is new, or more precisely resurrected from the early drafts of the 1997 Partnership Law. The original draft of the 1997 Law contained special provisions on limited partnerships and specifically allowed legal persons to form partnerships.[126] These provisions would, therefore, supplement and clarify the GPCL provisions on joint operations and enterprise groups. The Law Commission of the NPC however took a different view, insisting that not sufficient experience had been gained in dealing with limited partnerships. Thus it recommended that all provisions on limited partnerships be deleted and the requirement of bearing unlimited liability be inserted as a qualification for establishing a partnership enterprise.[127] This effectively meant that no enterprises with legal person status would be able to form a partnership; hence, those joint operations and enterprise groups which did not meet legal persons requirements would still lack a clear legal framework governing their legal status, organisational matters and forms of liability. In the absence of a legal framework on limited partnership and under pressure for high tech development, especially for venture capital investment in these areas, local authorities went ahead with their own local regulations on limited partnerships.[128] Not surprisingly, the 2006 revision revisited the whole issue of limited partnership with enthusiastic support from members of the SCNPC.[129]

As mentioned above, limited partnerships are to be established by between two and fifty partners, with at least one partner being an ordinary partner, unless otherwise provided by law.[130] The original draft of the 2006 revision did not impose any restrictions on the total number of partners in a limited partnership. During the

[126] See Huang Yicheng, *supra* note 105, at 13-16.

[127] Li Yining, *supra* note 113, at 17-20.

[128] See Partnership Regulations of Shenzhen Special Economic Zone (1994), Regulations of Zhongguanchun Science Park (Beijing, 2000), Administrative Measures on Limited Partnerships (Beijing, 2001), Interim Measures of Zhuhai Municipality on Venture Capital Investment in Science and Technology (2001), and Interim Administrative Measures of Hangzhou Municipality on Limited Partnerships (2001). For a discussion on these local regulations, see Ma Zhongfa, 'On Limited Partnerships and the Improvement of the Partnership Enterprise Law', in <www.lawyerbridge.com/LAW/20057/0621495385201.html> (last accessed 19 September 2006). In fact, some government investment rules, though not using the phrase 'limited partnership', had also allowed the practice, at least in terms of liability by contractual arrangement. See e.g. Article 4 of the Provisions for the Administration of the Establishment of Foreign Investment Venture Capital Enterprises jointly issued on 30 January 2003 by the then MOFTEC (now MOC), the Ministry of Science and Technology, the State Administration for Industry and Commerce, the State Administration of Taxation and the State Administration of Foreign Exchange (The Provisions replaced the Interim Provisions on the Establishment of Foreign Investment Venture Capital Enterprises issued jointly by MOFTEC, the Ministry for Science and Technology and the State Administration for Industry and Commerce on 28 August 2001).

[129] See deliberation speeches, *supra* note 117.

[130] Article 61 of the revised Partnership Enterprise Law.

deliberation of the draft members of the SCNPC raised the possibility of business people using partnerships as an illegal means for fundraising, and therefore demanded that the total number of partners allowed should be limited by law.[131] It is however unclear how the 'magic' number fifty was chosen in the final version.

Chapter Three should be seen as additional to, rather than the only rules on limited partnerships. In fact, Article 60 makes it clear that matters not regulated by Chapter Three shall be governed by Section 1-5 of Chapter Two on ordinary partnerships. Thus Chapter Three mainly regulates the rights, obligations and conduct of the limited partners in a limited partnership, and these must be clearly listed in the partnership agreement. While in general the limited partners assume limited liability, they will be held liable for unlimited liabilities in a particular transaction if a third party has sufficient reason to believe that the limited partners are ordinary partners in the transaction.[132] It should also be noted that limited partners are liable for debts of the partnership enterprise even though the debts were incurred before the partners joined the enterprise.[133] Further, a limited partner that changes its status to an ordinary partner in the enterprise will have unlimited joint and several liability for debts incurred during the time it was still a limited partner.[134] On the other hand, a limited partner will assume unlimited joint and several liability for debts incurred while it was an ordinary partner in the partnership enterprise.[135]

Under Article 64 limited partners may make capital contributions in cash, in kind or in the form of intellectual property rights, land use rights or other property rights. Under Article 16 ordinary partners may also use labour as a contribution. There is no minimum capital requirement for establishment. However a business name, a place of business and the possession of necessary means to engage in the partnership business are required for such establishment.

Specific internal arrangements are to be decided by partnership agreements. However the Law stipulates certain matters that must be dealt with in the agreement. These include the purposes and scope of the partnership, capital contribution and its methods, and time limits for payments, methods of distributing profits and sharing risks, methods of admission and retiring from the partnership, and methods of operation of the partnership enterprise. Although freedoms are given to such arrangements, the Law is strict in terms of liability. Indeed, the whole approach of the Law focuses on how liabilities will be borne by partners.

For a considerable time, partnerships were subject to double taxation; that is, the partnership enterprise paid income tax and partners were also required to pay

---

131 See 'China Revises Law to Open Further Space for Partnership Enterprises', *supra* note 114; and deliberation speeches, *supra* note 117.

132 See Article 76 of the revised Partnership Enterprise Law.

133 See Article 77 of the revised Partnership Enterprise Law.

134 See Article 83 of the revised Partnership Enterprise Law.

135 See Article 84 of the revised Partnership Enterprise Law.

tax on income. This practice was only eliminated by a circular of the State Council in 2000.[136] The revised Law now formally stipulates that only the partners are liable for income tax, in accordance with law.[137]

The establishment of a partnership seems to be a right. This seems to be further stressed by the 2006 revision, in which provisions on registration have now been relocated to Chapter One on General Principles.[138] Under Article 10 a decision by a registration authority[139] on whether to register a partnership enterprise must be decided within twenty days of receiving an application, and if a decision can be made on the spot, such a decision must be made and a business licence must be issued on the spot. There does not seem to be any requirement for government approval for establishment. However, a licence issued by a registration authority is a precondition for engaging in business in the name of the partnership.[140] State sole investment companies, state-owned enterprises, listed companies and other units and social organisations of a public interest nature may not become an ordinary partner in a partnership,[141] a provision clearly designed to prevent these enterprises and organisations from bearing unlimited liabilities.[142] The capacity of foreigners and foreign enterprises to establish a partnership enterprise in China is not clear. The original revision draft provided that 'foreign enterprises or foreign individuals establishing a partnership enterprise or joining a partnership enterprise, hence becoming an ordinary partner, shall conform to the relevant legal provisions of the state.'[143] However, in terms of pursuing unlimited liabilities and regulating and controlling foreign investment, that provision was seen as inadequate and needed further consideration.[144] Thus the revised Law, in Article 108, now provides that 'The administrative measures governing the establishment by foreign enterprises

136 See 'On the Revision of Partnership Law', *supra* note 115.

137 Article 6 of the revised Partnership Enterprise Law.

138 See Articles 9-13 of the revised Partnership Enterprise Law. These provisions were in Chapter 2 on Establishment in the 1997 Law.

139 Under the Administrative Measures on the Registration of Partnership Enterprises of the PRC (issued by the State Council on 19 November 1997), the registration authority is the local office of the State Industry and Commerce Administration. These Measures were revised by the State Council and re-issued on 9 May 2007. The registration authorities remain the same.

140 Article 11 of the revised Partnership Enterprise Law.

141 Article 3 of the revised Partnership Enterprise Law.

142 See 'On the Revision of Partnership Law', *supra* note 115.

143 See deliberation speeches, *supra* note 117; and 'Foreign Businesses Establishing Partnerships to be Regulated by State Council Measures', in <www.chinaacc.com/new/184/186/2006/8/xu0731444241828600211616-0.htm> (last accessed 19 September 2006).

144 See deliberation speeches, *supra* note 117; and 'Foreign Businesses Establishing Partnerships to be Regulated by State Council Measures', *supra* note 143.

or foreign individuals of partnership enterprises in China shall be formulated by the State Council.' That is to say that foreign businesses may not be able to establish partnership enterprises until the State Council issues its specific rules.[145]

On the whole, the revised Partnership Enterprise Law now conforms to much of the international practice in partnership law. However, the revised Law also contains some odd provisions. For instance Article 6 of the original 1997 Partnership Enterprise Law provided that 'When engaging in business activities, a partnership enterprise must abide by the law and administrative regulations and comply with professional ethics.' The revised Law, in Article 7, now provides that 'A partnership enterprise and its partners must abide by the law and administrative regulations, comply with social morality and business ethics, and bear social responsibilities.' These provisions may reflect the current political environment, which emphasises social morality, but no one knows how they could be actually enforced. Indeed, as some members of the SCNPC have commented, perhaps no one knows what social morality or business ethics actually means.[146]

5. Company Law

5.1. An Overview

Clearly, as explained earlier, the differentiated treatment of business entities on the basis of ownership, administrative subordination, geographical location or the size of business, conflict with the underlying philosophy of a market economy which emphasises equal treatment and fair competition in economic activities. Moreover, despite the absence of a company code, company shares and debentures began in the 1980s to be traded in a number of regional stock markets in the PRC. The need for a company law was soon recognised by law-makers, and thus efforts to draft a company law began to emerge in 1983, first jointly by the State Planning Commission and the State Commission for Economic Structural Reform, and later by the LAC of the SCNPC.[147] Ideological disagreements and theoretical controversy regarding the nature of SOEs' property rights, however, delayed the legislative process for many years. To deal with the urgent need for company law, local company laws were issued

---

[145] It can however be assumed that previous foreign investment laws allowing contractual arrangements for limited partnership, such as the Provisions for the Administration of the Establishment of Foreign Investment Venture Capital Enterprises (2003), will continue to operate before the State Council issues its new rules.

[146] See deliberation speeches, *supra* note 117.

[147] See 'A Historical Leap Forward', *Guangming Daily* (*Guangming Ribao*), 18 January 1994, at 4.

in the early 1990s,[148] which were followed by a set of national policy directives.[149] The latter, although providing for national standards, were not legislative enactments.

On 29 December 1993 the SCNPC finally adopted the Company Law of the PRC.[150] The event was seen by the Chinese press as a 'historical leap forward'.[151] The Company Law, according to the then Vice-chairman of the State Commission for Economics and Trade, Chen Qingtai, was the 'most important' piece of legislation for regulating business entities.[152] Whether 'historical' or not, the Law was the first of its kind in the PRC's legal history. It had been ten years in the making and represented the most significant effort to provide a uniform legislative framework for business entities and activities in the PRC.

As at the time the Chinese government had determined to begin the transformation of its troublesome state-owned enterprises into shareholding companies, the Company Law focused particularly on the restructuring of state-owned enterprises. The supposedly generally applicable law also had a rather narrow scope of application. Laws for different business entities thus continued to apply until an enterprise was transformed into a company that met the strict requirements under the Company Law. Further, as mentioned above, although efforts were made to convert the two distinct legal frameworks governing foreign-related and domestic businesses, foreign investment business entities continued to be regulated by a separate set of laws. The GPCL provisions on legal persons, rather than the Company Law, thus continued to be the unifying force for laws on business entities. Moreover, the Company Law was not applicable to foreign investment companies limited by shares.

Not surprisingly, the Company Law was soon amended on 25 December 1999. However, the revision was minimal, affecting only Article 67 on the supervisory boards of sole state investment companies, and Article 229 on hi-tech companies. Another minor revision was also undertaken in August 2004, removing the second clause of Article 131, which dealt with the issuance of company shares.

---

148 E.g. Tentative Provisions of Shenzhen Municipality on Companies Limited by Shares 1992, and Tentative Provisions of Shanghai Municipality on Companies Limited by Shares 1992.

149 During May, June and July 1992, a set of 15 policy documents regulating the experiment of securitisation was jointly issued by the State Commission for Economic Structural Reform, the State Planning Commission, the Ministry of Finance, the People's Bank of China and the Office of Production of the State Council. Among these documents were Suggestions on Standards for Limited Liability Companies and Suggestions on Standards for Companies Limited by Shares. These two documents can be found in (no. 16, 1992) *Gazette of the State Council of the PRC* (*Zhonghua Renmin Gongheguo Guowuyuan Gongbao*), at 554-592.

150 Promulgated by the President of the PRC on the same day. The Law became effective on 1 July 1994.

151 See *supra* note 147.

152 See *Daily of the Legal System* (*Fazhi Ribao*), 19 January 1994, at 2.

More comprehensive revision took place in October 2005. Although the 2005 revision was not as ambitious as academics had hoped for,[153] it deleted 46 articles, added 41 and had another 137 articles revised among the total of 229 articles. The revisions focused on issues relating to corporate capitalisation and governance, incorporating substantial adjustments to various aspects of the Law including registered capital requirements, corporate governance, protection of shareholders' rights, introduction of one-person companies and, for the first time, the principle of 'piercing the corporate veil', the abolition of the mandatory requirement for companies to have public welfare fund reserves (5%-10% of the company's profit to be distributed in the year), etc. The Law is now applicable to both domestic and foreign investment companies. However, the revision has not completely abolished the dual-track legal systems applying to domestic and foreign-investment companies. Foreign investment business entities will, while governed by the Company Law, continue to be regulated by a separate set of laws.

As in other major areas of law, the Company Law is further implemented by a large number of regulations and rules on registration and other practical issues.

5.2. Structure and Scope of the Company Law

The Company Law is divided into thirteen chapters and 219 articles in total. Broadly, the Law regulates the organisational structure and business activities of companies. Companies covered by the Law include limited liability companies (*Youxian Zeren Gongsi*, LLCs) and companies limited by shares (joint-stock companies) (*Gufen Youxian Gongsi*, CLSs) established in China in accordance with the Law.[154] Additionally, the Law also provides special stipulations on one-person companies and sole state investment companies. The previous provisions on state enterprise restructuring and transitional provisions for companies established under local laws, administrative regulations and policy directives are now all removed.[155]

---

153 Academics had hoped for a complete re-writing of the Company Law. In fact, a group of academics, led by Professor Wang Baoshu of Qinghua University, established a Research Group on Company Law Revision in 2001, and by May 2004, the Group had already published a proposed draft of a new company law. See Wang Baoshu (ed.), *Chinese Company Law: Proposed Revision Draft* (*Zhongguo Gongsifa: Xiugai Cao'an Jianyigao*) (Beijing: Social Sciences Press, 2004).

154 Article 2 of the Company Law.

155 Under the original 1994 Company Law, these companies had to be restructured and transformed within a 'specific period of time' that would be defined by the State Council. This period was later specified as 31 December 1996. See Circular on Standardisation of LLCs and CLSs in Accordance with the Company Law, issued by the State Council on 3 July 1995, and the Circular on the Implementation Opinion Regarding the Registration of the Existing Limited Liability Companies and Companies Limited by Shares, issued by the State Administration of Industry and Commerce on 22 August 1995. By November 1997 there were 414,400 companies, with a total registered capital of 1592.36 billion *yuan*, re-structured or established under the new

The Company Law does not provide definitions of LLC or CLS. Instead it defines how liabilities will be assumed by a company or its shareholders. Thus, in the case of an LLC, the shareholders will assume limited liability equal to their capital contribution, and in a CLS the shareholders assume liability equal to the amount of subscribed shares.[156] Both kinds of company are defined as enterprise legal persons.[157] This reference to the concept of 'enterprise legal person' means that all requirements regarding 'enterprise legal persons' as laid down in Chapter Three of the GPCL apply to companies regulated by the present Law.

Article 218 of the 2005 revised Company Law provides that the Law applies to domestic companies as well as LLCs and CLSs established in China by foreign investors, unless laws governing foreign investment provide otherwise. The inclusion of foreign investment CLSs within the coverage of the Company Law finally removes the confusion caused by the previous Company Law, which did not cover foreign investment CLSs. Nevertheless, as pointed out above, it continues the current parallel legal system by subjecting foreign investment companies to a set of separate laws and regulations especially applicable to them, in addition to the Company Law.

5.3. Limited Liability Companies

(1) Establishment

Articles 23-36 of the Law prescribe conditions under which an LLC can be established in the PRC. The general trend in this regard since the initial enactment of the Law has been towards easing the conditions, though not removing the restrictions, on establishment. Under Article 24 an LLC may not have more than fifty shareholders. When the Law still required a minimum of two shareholders to establish LLCs,[158] an exception had been allowed for a state investment institution or an organisation authorised by the State, as sole investor.[159] Companies established by sole state investment are defined as 'solely state-owned companies' (*Guoyou Duzi Gongsi*) and are generally regulated by Section 4 (Articles 65-71) of Chapter 2 of the Law. Also under the original 1994 Company Law, companies engaged in manufacturing special products or in special industries as defined by the State Council could only

---

Company Law. See 'Restructured and Newly Established Companies Number Over Four Hundred Thousand', *People's Daily* (*Renmin Ribao*), internet edition, 7 November 1997.

156 Article 3 of the Company Law.

157 Article 3 of the Company Law.

158 Under Articles 19 (1) & 20 of the original 1994 Law, an LLC may only be established by more than two but less than 50 shareholders. Since the introduction of the one-person companies by the 2005 revision, the minimum shareholder requirement is thus removed from the Law.

159 Article 20 of the original 1994 Law. Now Article 65 of the revised Law (2005).

be established in the form of 'solely state-owned companies'.[160] This requirement has now been removed, in line with the government policy of allowing equal and fair competition among all economic entities.[161] The investors in this kind of company are now defined as State-owned Assets Supervision and Administrative authorities at the central and local government level,[162] in line with the State Council Provisional Regulations on the Supervision and Administration of State-owned Assets in Enterprises.[163]

Two major improvements were also made during the 2005 revision, to ease the establishment of companies – relaxation on capitalisation and the allowance of the establishment of one-person companies. The original 1994 Company Law required an LLC to have a minimum registered capital ranging between 100,000 and 500,000 *yuan*, depending on the types of business the company engaged in. Further, State laws or administrative regulations could also prescribe a higher amount for specific businesses.[164] Equally strict was the requirement that the registered capital of the company had to be the actually paid up capital as recorded with company registration authorities.[165] Now the incorporation threshold is significantly lowered to 30,000 *yuan* and this threshold will apply to all companies (except one-person companies) regardless of the types of business they conduct, unless laws and regulations provide otherwise.[166] Although, compared with the 'one-dollar company' allowed in most developed countries, this registered capital requirement is still very high, it is a big step forward in China's modernisation of its company law, given that the government has long seen the imposition of tight requirements on registered capital as an effective way of controlling company quality. Further, the revised Law also broadens the methods by which registered capital may be contributed. Shareholders are permitted to make their contributions in cash, in kind, in industrial property rights, land use rights and other non-cash assets that can be monetarily valued and legally transferred (except those excluded by laws and regulations). Instead of capital contribution in the form of intangible assets not being permitted to exceed 20% of the total registered capital, as under the original 1994 Law, shareholders' non-cash contribution, such as intellectual property rights, may now constitute up to 70% of the company's registered capital. All non-cash assets must be valued and

---

160 See Article 64 of the original 1994 Company Law.

161 See Item 1 (2) of the Certain Opinions on the Encouragement, Support and Guidance for Economic Development of the Individual, Private and other Non-public Sectors (2005), *supra* note 96.

162 See Article 65 of the Company Law.

163 Issued by the State Council on 27 May 2003.

164 Article 23 of the original 1994 Company Law.

165 See Articles 23 & 34 of the original 1994 Company Law.

166 See Article 26 of Company Law.

verified.[167] Finally, the registered capital of an LLC may be contributed within two years after its establishment, provided that the initial contribution will not be lower than 20% of the company's registered capital and not lower than the minimum registered capital requirement (30,000 *yuan*). Holding companies are allowed to pay registered capital within five years of establishment.[168]

Section 3 (Article 58-64) in Chapter Two is an entirely new section inserted into the Law during the 2005 revision. This Section, for the first time in the PRC, allows the formation of one-person companies, though with some stringent requirements. To constrain the sole shareholder from taking advantage of the company's assets for personal use,[169] one-person companies are required, in addition to complying with the rules set out for an LLC, to abide by a number of special provisions. These include that it must have a minimum registered capital of 100,000 *yuan* (rather than 30,000 *yuan* as for other LLCs), and must pay the registered capital in full at the time of incorporation (rather than within two years as for other LLCs); it must produce annual financial and accounting reports at the end of each year and have them audited; a natural person may only set up one one-person company and the company is not allowed to invest in other one-person companies. Where the shareholder fails to prove that their assets are independent from the assets of the company, the shareholder shall be personally liable for the company's debts.[170]

The aim of lowering the incorporation threshold has been to encourage investment, promote economic development and increase employment. This is backed up by the introduction of the principle of piercing the corporate veil to minimise any negative impact on creditor protection, which may be weakened because of the granting of the lower incorporation threshold.

(2) Organisational Structure

A company's organisational structure generally consists of a shareholders' meeting, a board of directors, the manager, and a supervisory board.[171] While technically

---

167 Article 27 of the Company Law

168 See Article 26 of the Company Law.

169. The opposition to the introduction of the one-person companies was strong. At the final deliberation of the draft revision there were still members of the SCNPC demanding the exclusion of this section, fearing the abuse of the company form for personal advantage. Thus the introduction of the stringent conditions came about. See 'Report of the Law Commission of the NPC on the Revision of the Draft to Revise the Company Law', in (no. 7, 2005) *Gazette of the Standing Committee of the NPC of the PRC* (*Zhonghua Renmin Gongheguo Quanguo Renmin Daibiao Dahui Changwu Weiyuanhui Gongbao*) 578, at 580.

170 See Articles 59, 63 & 64 of the Company Law.

171 For small-sized companies or companies with a small number of shareholders, an executive director and an executive supervisor may suffice without the need for the establishment of a board of directors and a supervisory board. See Articles 51 & 52 of the Company Law.

the functions of a shareholders' meeting, a board of directors etc., are not radically different from their counterparts in the developed economies, there are some notable requirements that were introduced by the 2005 revision. First, the original 1994 Company Law required employee representation on the board of directors in state-owned companies. This representation may now also be allowed in other LLCs under Article 45 of the 2005 revised Company Law. Clearly it is a hesitant and indirect response to demands for improving labour conditions by potentially allowing some voices of employees in the management of a company. It is a hesitant response because of the use of the dubious word 'may' instead of the clear word 'should' or 'must'. In the case of the supervisory board, however, no less than one third of the board members must be employees' representatives.[172] Secondly, while the functions of company managers are still legislated by law, these can now be overruled by a company's Articles of Association,[173] allowing more autonomy in company management. On the other hand, however, if a Communist Party organisation is to be established in a company, such a company must provide the requisite conditions for its activities.[174] Finally, for smaller companies where there is only an executive director without a board of directors, the functions of the executive director may also be decided by the Articles of Association.[175] All these clearly indicate some major efforts to allow autonomy and freedom to companies in their business operations, while making certain efforts to ensure that employees' voice may also be heard.

5.4. Companies Limited by Shares

(1) Establishment

As in the case of LLCs, the trend is towards relaxing restrictions on establishment and allowing more autonomy in business operations. However, CLSs have a wider social impact than LLCs because they raise funds from the society in general. Understandably, the control over their establishment and operation is always stricter than that over LLCs.

CLSs may be established by means of promotion or of share offer.[176] Where the company is established by promotion, the promoters (no less than two but not more

---

The requirement for the establishment of a supervisory board or an executive supervisor apparently follows that of the German model. It should be pointed out that the Law (either in its original or revised version) does not quantify 'small number' or 'small size'.

172 See Article 52 of the Company Law.

173 See Article 50 of the Company Law.

174 Article 19 of the Company Law, which is applicable to both LLCs and CLSs.

175 See Article 51 of the Company Law.

176 Article 78 of the Company Law.

than 200 promoters, of which more than half must have their domicile in China[177]) are to hold all of the issued shares; where the company is to be established by share offer, the promoters subscribe to only part of the shares to be issued, and a public offering is held for the remaining shares. Under the original 1994 Company Law shares could be offered only to the public, after the subscription by the promoters.[178] They can now be offered to specific targets under Article 78 of the 2005 revised Law. These specific targets generally mean institutional investors. Under the Securities Law (Article 10), all public offers of shares must first be approved by the China Securities Regulatory Commission or other State Council authorised authorities.[179] As in the case of LLCs, the minimum registered capital for CLSs has now been reduced from 10 million *yuan* to five million, unless laws and administrative regulations prescribe a higher minimum amount of registered capital.[180] In the case of establishment by promotion, the registered capital means the total paid-up capital. However, in the case of establishment by share offer, capital contribution is allowed to be paid in instalments, as long as the initial payment is not less than 20% of the required minimum registered capital.[181] Promoters are permitted to make capital contributions in cash, in kind, in industrial property rights, land use rights and with other non-cash assets that can be monetarily valued and legally transferred, except for those excluded by laws and regulations, so long as they do not exceed 70% of the company's registered capital.[182]

Clearly, the establishment of CLSs is still under rather strict control, but the conditions for establishment have been considerably relaxed.

(2) Organisational Structure

CLSs have a similar organisational structure to that of LLCs, and each of the company authorities exercises similar powers. However, the establishment of a board of directors and a supervisory board is compulsory for all CLSs without exception. Further, all

---

177 See Article 79 of the Company Law. Under the original 1994 Company Law (Article 75), the minimum number of promoters was five, without a maximum limit. The maximum number of promoters is set to meet the requirement set out under Article 10 of the Securities Law (also revised in 2005). The lower minimum number of promoters is clearly set to ease the establishment of a CLS.

178 See Article 74 of the original 1994 Company Law.

179 Originally, the establishment of CLSs had to be approved by the State Council authorities. In the case of establishment by promotion, such an approval system has now been changed to a registration system, no longer requiring prior approval.

180 See Article 78 of the original 1994 Company Law and Article 81 of the 2005 revised Company Law.

181 Article 81 of the Company Law.

182 See Article 83 of the Company Law.

listed companies are now required to appoint independent directors, although the Law leaves detailed regulations to be issued by the State Council.[183]

5.5. Corporate Governance

Considering that enterprise reform has, for a long time, been largely utilised to diversify ownership, improve productivity and invigorate state-owned enterprises, it is not surprising that corporate governance is in fact a relatively new concept in Chinese company and securities laws. As a result, the stock markets in China gained a reputation of being 'home to shoddy companies and shady trading practices'.[184] Questions about corporate governance have been raised by many Chinese and foreign academics and practitioners in China in the last many years. The rapid development of the securities industry, where the great majority of investors are individuals as minority shareholders, has now forced the government and securities regulatory authorities to take this issue seriously. The need for a sound corporate governance system is both economic and political. Politically, no government wishes to see market scandals leading to social instability.

Not surprisingly, strengthening corporate governance is an issue much emphasised recently by the government in the campaign of shaking up its industrial structure, stabilising its share markets and protecting shareholders' rights and interests. The focus in revising the Company Law in 2005 was two-fold: easing the restrictions on company establishment, and at the same time placing a much greater emphasis on corporate governance in terms of corporate finance and accounting, protection of minority shareholders and disclosure of information, and placing heavy liabilities on companies and their senior managers in cases of violation of the law and misconduct. Additionally, civil remedies through private lawsuits and fiduciary duties (duties of loyalty and due diligence in the Chinese terminology) have now finally been codified into the revised Company Law.[185] Thus listed companies are required to strictly abide by the Company Law and corporate governance regulations and rules on the protection of shareholders' interests, including implementing an independent director system for listed companies, complying with rules for procedures for shareholders' meetings, rules for associated transactions, information disclosure, investment consultation, profit distribution, asset restructuring, fund-raising, and

183 See Article 123 of the Company Law.

184 Andrew Batson, 'China Bets on Blue-Chip IPOs to Lay Strong Market Foundation', *The Wall Street Journal*, 10 August 2006, at 19.

185 For a detailed analysis of the revised Company Law on corporate governance, see Craig Anderson & Bingna Guo, 'Corporate Governance under the New Company Law (Part 1): Fiduciary Duties and Minority Shareholders Protection', (April 2006) *China Law & Practice* 17; & 'Corporate Governance under the New Company Law (Part 2): Shareholder Lawsuits and Enforcement', (May 2006) *China Law & Practice* 15. See also Roman Tomasic (ed.), *Corporate Governance: Challenges for China* (Beijing: Law Press, 2005).

rules for the conduct of major shareholders and senior managerial personnel, etc. Directors, supervisors or senior managerial personnel shall be liable for compensation if they act in violation of laws, regulations or the company's Articles of Association, and cause the company losses.

Shareholders are, for the first time, granted the right to bring an action against wrongdoing directors and managers. Articles 152 and 153 provide that a shareholder who has held one-tenth of the company's shares for a period of at least 180 days, or shareholders whose shares together account for one-tenth of the company's shares, have the right to request the supervisory board to bring an action against directors or senior managerial personnel for any violation of laws, regulations or the company's Articles of Association. If the supervisory board fails to act within 30 days from the date of receiving their request, they may bring the case directly to court. All shareholders are entitled to bring actions against directors or senior managerial personnel who, in violation of laws, regulations and articles of association, harm their interests.

To strengthen corporate governance, the principle of piercing the corporate veil has, for the first time in the PRC, been introduced into the 2005 revised Company Law. The aim is to curb the practice by shareholders of abusing the privileges of incorporation of a company to avoid fulfilling their liabilities, and to protect creditors' interests. Paragraph 3 of Article 20 of the Law provides that where a shareholder uses the independent corporate legal personality and limited liabilities of shareholders to evade liabilities, and thus seriously damages the interests of the creditors, he/she shall assume unlimited liability for the company's debts.

In fact, in terms of listed companies many of these new provisions in the Company Law and the Securities Law had earlier been included in the Code of Corporate Governance for Listed Companies,[186] which was seen as a major step taken by the CSRC in the corporate governance campaign. The requirement for independent directors in listed companies, rules on associated parties and related party transactions, information disclosure and transparency, the use of independent business accounting, rules on dealing with conflict of interests etc., were all first introduced by the Code.[187]

With the revision of the Company Law and Securities Law now completed and the laws improved,[188] the real test for corporate governance will be the enforcement of the law.[189] In this, past experience does not give investors much confidence.

---

186 Issued as Zhengjianfa [2002] No. 1 on 7 January 2002,

187 For further discussions, see Donald C. Clarke, 'The Independent Director in Chinese Corporate Governance', 36 (1) (2006) *Delaware Journal of Corporate Law* 125.

188 The Code on corporate governance is, however, yet to be updated in line with the revision of the Company Law and the Securities Law.

189 In fact, a lengthy Notice on Certain Issues Concerning the Special Campaign to Strengthen Corporate Governance in Listed Companies was issued on 9 March 2007 by the China Securities

6. Concluding Remarks

There is no doubt that the Chinese legal framework on business entities is still in evolution and remains largely fragmented. Although the process to establish a modern enterprise system, consisting of the three pillars of law (Company Law, Partnership Law and Sole Investment Enterprise Law) has now been completed, the largely fragmented enterprise laws made under different ideological orientations continue to operate. The published result of the latest review of regulations on enterprises indicates that there is still a long way to go before all Chinese enterprises may enjoy equal treatment, or as Chinese scholars have emphasised, be granted 'national treatment'.[190]

However, the present difficulties and problems facing non-public enterprises, and the current legislative situation, must be understood in the context of gradual reform. Compared to some 25 years ago, China today is almost a haven for private enterprise. Also importantly, the most recent reforms seem to be well coordinated, reasonably comprehensive and balanced. It all started with the 2004 constitutional revision. The changed politico-economic ideology under the Constitution after the 2004 revision is clearly reflected in the State Council documents on the reform of the investment system and the opinions on promoting the private sector. The revisions made to the Partnership Law and the Company Law (and the Securities Law to be discussed in the next Chapter) further followed through many of the initiatives contained in the State Council documents.

Perhaps it is unrealistic to expect China to abolish the classification of enterprises in accordance with forms of ownership, and to abolish all other enterprise laws, leaving the three pillars of the modern enterprise law as the universally applicable laws.[191] But as long as China abolishes the differentiated treatment in business establishment, operation and market entry and support, the private sector will continue to thrive. After all, as Deng Xiaoping said, who cares what the colour of the cat is, as long as it catches mice.

Regulator Commission to formally launch a new campaign on corporate governance that will be completed by the end of October 2007, though only applicable to listed companies.

190 See '"Individual Households" Number Decreased by Millions Indicating a Difficult Environment', *supra* note 27.

191 Equally, it is unrealistic to expect China to revise and update all these laws, considering the heavy schedule of the Chinese legislatures.

Chapter Fourteen

Securities Law

1. Introduction

Anyone who visited China in 2006–2007 could not help but have the impression that urban Chinese people belonged to two camps – those who were in, and those who were not but wanting to be in, the securities market. In any case both groups were talking about the market. The share market in China, it seems, is exactly like that in any capitalist country, where the lucky ones make quick money, but overall the haves get even more. In other words, a share market is a share market; it is the same everywhere and fulfils the same economic and financial functions in society. These are however not the initial reasons that share markets emerged in socialist China during the post-Mao reform era.

In fact, the government sanctioned securities market initially emerged in post-Mao China not as a capitalist vehicle for investment, and not even principally for the purpose of fund-raising.[1] It was proposed as a capitalist means for a socialist solution to tackling a fundamental dilemma in urban economic reform – to maintain socialism while invigorating the highly unproductive and unprofitable state-owned enterprises, or more precisely, to allow capitalist practices within a socialist politico-economic context. Recognising this context is important in our understanding of the rapidly developing legal framework governing securities and their market. It is also this context that explains why China opened its capital market to the outside world only recently, and also allows us to understand why shares are still divided into A-Shares, B-Shares, H-Shares etc. and subject to different sets of regulations. Finally it explains the slow and limited development of the securities derivatives

---

1 It was true, though, that in 1981 China began issuing State Treasury Bonds. This move was clearly contrary to China's long-held policy of being 'free from external and internal debts'. It is also true, as will be discussed, that the earliest enterprises to issue 'shares' had the aim of raising funds. However, none of these experiments were moves towards a securities market in the true sense. One must not forget that the Chinese were not yet rich and there was not much idle money sleeping in the bank accounts, even though the Chinese did save at a relatively high rate compared to their counterparts in the West.

market in China, as the latter only became meaningful when the development of the securities industry began to be an end in itself.

This Chapter first examines the reasons behind the initial emergence of the securities market in post-Mao China. It then introduces the legal framework governing the securities market, focusing on the evolution of this highly complicated network of regulations. It further outlines the institutional setting of the regulatory authorities and that for market players. Through these analyses we will see that the securities market is still in transition, if not still in its infant stage of development.

2. Early Experiences and Their Politico-Economic Functions

It is well-known that economic reform in post-Mao China started with rather successful reform in the countryside by adopting the family contracting system. With rapid economic development and growth many have however forgotten the tremendous difficulties and major controversies in the early 1980s, when urban industrial reform started. Looking at the hugely diversified ownership system in the present Chinese economic system and the increasing share of the private sector in the economy, one also easily forgets the overwhelming domination of the state-owned enterprises (SOEs, but then still called state-run enterprises) in the industrial sector. In fact the whole politico-economic reform in post-Mao China has been centred on the reform of the SOEs, and the most innovative politico-economic theories were largely about approaches to SOE reform.

The reality was that China rightly rejected the idea of large scale privatisation and the 'Big Bang' approach adopted in the former East European countries, fearing social unrest and instability in a huge yet still poor country. Instead, China adopted a gradual but nevertheless rather swift transformation approach to reforming the SOEs. In constitutional law that meant gradual changes taking place in redefining the essence of socialism and politico-economic ideology, through a series of constitutional revisions.[2] In general policy and legal reform the approach was first to tolerate the existence and development of the private sector, and then to encourage such development. On SOEs specifically, the initial response was to grant the 'right to operation' to SOEs. Even though this was not particularly innovative, essentially repeating a failed practice in the former socialist countries, major controversy erupted in politico-economic and legal circles. Despite enormous efforts by legal scholars to theorise the notion of 'right to operation' and to convert such an essentially administratively authorised autonomy into a civil law notion of property rights, the 'right to operation' largely failed to invigorate the SOEs or to improve their productivity and efficiency. By the mid-1980s scholars had come to the conclusion that the reform required was one that needed to be applied to the politico-economic

---

2 See the discussion in Chapter 3.

system and, in legal areas, to the ownership and property rights system. This however could only be done within a socialist context; that is, full-scale privatisation was not the acceptable solution. Instead, the professed solution was to diversify ownership both in the overall economic system and within the SOEs themselves.[3]

The proposed approach was the securitisation of the SOEs.

According to some scholars, the idea of securitising SOEs was first proposed to the Chinese Government by the World Bank.[4] The suggestion to institute a socialist joint-stock ownership system was contained in a report of a World Bank mission to China in 1983.[5] The mission first examined various SOE reform policies that had already taken place in China. Although it saw some good results from these policies, it believed that changes in the state-enterprise relationship had been only marginal and that the fundamental problem remained the same; that is, the problem of the proper relationship between the state and SOEs.[6] It was the World Bank mission's view that the recognition that 'ownership right can be separated from operating right' (and hence the 'right to operation') was an important step taken by the Chinese Government to deal with the relationship between the state and SOEs; but it also believed that the ultimate control of property remained in the state under this principle. Such development still left unresolved the question of the proper degree of SOE autonomy and the measure of state control over activities of autonomous SOEs.

To address the difficulties in implementing enterprise autonomy, the World Bank mission looked into, among other issues, three alternative approaches to enterprise control and management: giving direct control of SOEs to their workers, giving control of SOEs simply to their managers, and giving strategic decision-making authority to boards of directors. The mission clearly favoured establishing boards of directors within SOEs to exercise strategic decision-making powers. However, it pointed out that the mere establishment of boards of directors was not enough. More importantly, these boards had to be made not only profit-oriented, but also free from direct intervention by state administrative organs. Here the mission recognised that such goals were in direct conflict with the nature of the SOEs. This conflict had to be resolved, and they found that:

---

3 For detailed discussions, see Jianfu Chen, *From Administrative Authorisation to Private Law: A Comparative Perspective of the Developing Civil Law in the PRC* (Dordrecht/Boston/London: Martinus Nijhoff Publishers, 1995), Chapters 3 & 7.

4 Xiao Liang, 'A Review of Studies on Economic Restructuring and the Question of Ownership', (no. 3, 1986) *Social Science in China* (*Zhongguo Shehui Kexue*) 1; and Yew-kwang Ng and Yang Xiaokai, 'Why China Should Jump Directly to Privatisation', *World Economic Herald* (*Shijie Jingji Daobao*), 6 February 1989, at 12.

5 World Bank, *China: Long-Term Development Issues and Options* (Baltimore/London: The Johns Hopkins University Press, 1985), see particularly 164-171.

6 *Id.*, at 164.

> A possible solution might be to spread the ownership of each state enterprise among several different institutions, each in some way representing the whole people, but with an interest mainly in the enterprise's profits rather than directly in its output, purchases, or employment. Examples of such institutions, in addition to central and local governments, are banks, pension funds, insurance companies, and other enterprises ... In China, such a system of socialist joint stock ownership could perhaps be created initially by suitable dispersion of the ownership capital of existing state enterprises. Over time, it could be reinforced by a more diversified pattern of investment finance, with a variety of state institutions acquiring financial interests in existing and new enterprises.[7]

This proposal seemed to suggest a two-stage process for securitising SOEs: in the first stage, ownership of SOEs' property was to be dispersed among different institutions, each of which would represent the whole people. In the second stage, securitisation of SOEs would be reinforced by a more 'diversified pattern of investment finance'. This 'diversified pattern of investment finance' in the World Bank Report context meant that vertical flows of finance and compartmentalised reinvestment, as then existed, would be supplemented with and eventually replaced by horizontal flows.[8] 'Horizontal flows' of investment finance would allow SOEs to enter new kinds of activities, as well as allowing investment between economic units. To achieve efficient and large horizontal flows, the mission further suggested the use of financial institutions functioning as intermediaries between the suppliers and the users of investment resources.[9] These financial institutions would be similar to commercial banks, investment trusts, development finance companies and other intermediaries in capitalist countries, but with the difference that 'they would be dealing with flows of funds that were to a large extent socially owned – by government organs, state enterprises and other state institutions, or collectives.'[10] Enterprise ownership would also be diversified by the use of diversified flows of funds.[11]

In proposing the institution of a joint-stock ownership system the World Bank mission did recognise that the state might wish to exercise direct control or supervision over strategic and key enterprises such as defence-related industries, basic public services and natural resource exploitation, and therefore they suggested that these enterprises be identified and be exempted from securitisation.[12]

---

7 *Id.*, at 166.

8 *Id.*, at 172. 'Compartmentalised reinvestment' means that SOEs can only reinvest their retained profits in specified and limited areas of economic activities.

9 *Id.*, at 173.

10 *Ibid.*

11 *Id.*, at 175.

12 *Id.*, at 168-169.

In the same report the mission called for the Chinese Government to encourage and promote the development of collective and individual enterprises, and therefore to achieve diversification of the whole ownership system in China.[13]

Although it appears that the World Bank saw the joint-stock system more as an alternative form of management than as a direct measure to reform the socialist ownership system, there was little doubt that the proposed securitisation was capable of leading to such reform. However, it was also clear that such securitisation was a process which stopped short of privatisation. The mission was more concerned with the way public ownership was exercised than with the public ownership system itself. In other words, what the World Bank wanted to do, through the use of financial institutions as intermediaries, and the separation of government administrative and economic functions, was to limit direct administrative interference in the operation of SOEs.[14] However, some economists suggested that the proposal of the World Bank to securitise (instead of privatising) SOEs was to have them peacefully evolve into privatised enterprises by developing diversified ownership forms, and by doing so, to avoid strong ideological opposition to privatisation in China.[15] Whether the World Bank mission had such an intention in mind is anyone's guess; it is however true that the World Bank proposal was interpreted by many Chinese scholars as an attempt to change the nature of the socialist public ownership system in China. It thus prompted strong ideological opposition to securitisation, and disagreement about what was the best business and economic structure for China, as well as intense debate about the property rights of joint-stock companies.[16]

Perhaps the World Bank was the first to formally propose the securitisation of the SOEs, but a joint-stock system had started in China before the World Bank report in 1985. In fact, the experiment with issuing bonds and/or shares began in the early 1980s for the primary purpose of raising funds for collective enterprises.[17] The first city to experiment with the joint-stock system was the heavy industry city

---

13 *Id.*, at 169-170.

14 These ideas became much clearer in the 1990 World Bank report on China: *China: Between Plan and Market* (Washington, DC, 1990), at 72-77. In this Report (at 75), the World Bank expressly admits that '[t]he role of the government as owner, ... has somehow to be maintained but separated from its role as an economic regulator with a range of other objectives.'

15 Ng and Yang, *supra* note 4, at 12.

16 See Jianfu Chen, *supra* note 3, at 207-220.

17 See Henry R. Zheng, *China's Civil and Commercial Law* (Singapore: Butterworths, 1988), at 355; Xu Jing'an, 'The Stock-Share System: A New Avenue for China's Economic Reform', in Bruce L. Reynolds (ed.), *Chinese Economic Reform: How Far, How Fast?* (Boston: Academic Press, Inc., 1988), at 219; Chen Ziqiao, 'The Way to Invigorate Enterprises – Joint-stock System in China', (no. 3, 1988) *Legal Construction* (*Fazhi Jianshe*), at 6-8; 'Preliminary Achievements of Reform through the Joint-stock System in China', *People's Daily* (*Renmin Ribao*) (overseas edition), 20 May 1992, at 2; Z. Jun Lin, Qu Xiaohui & Chen Feng, 'Experimentation of the Share-capital System and Economic Development in China', (1993) 21 *Asian Profile*, at 455-465;

of Shenyang, capital of Liaoning Province in northeastern China.[18] An investment company in Baoan County, Shenzhen, was the pioneer company in China to issue shares to the general public in 1983.[19] The joint-stock company (*gufen gongsi*) structure was first adopted by the Beijing Tianqiao General Merchandise Joint-Stock Company in July 1984.[20] Official sanctions for such moves began with the 1983 Interim Provisions of the State Council on Several Policy Issues Concerning the Urban Collective Economy.[21] These Provisions granted collective enterprises the power to issue shares to their own employees in order to raise funds. Under these Provisions there was a 15% ceiling on the rate of return of the money invested, and 'shares' were to be gradually redeemed from profits.[22]

Further developments occurred in 1985 and 1986 with stock exchange markets being established and operated by state banks in Shenyang, Shanghai, Beijing and other cities located in twelve provinces including Henan, Hebei, Anhui, and Hubei provinces and in Inner Mongolia.[23] Experimentation with securitisation of SOEs was authorised by a State Council Circular of 1985.[24] This Circular provided that 'a few large-sized SOEs may issue stocks to their own employees' as a measure to raise funds. The Circular allowed some small SOEs to be transformed into collective enterprises by means of issuing stocks.[25] In 1986 the first over-the-counter market (in Shanghai) was authorised by the People's Bank of China. Also in 1986 Guangdong, Xiamen, Shenyang and Beijing issued securities regulations providing detailed rules for the issuance of stocks and bonds by various types of enterprises, including SOEs.[26] In actual practice, however, these early experiments were mainly confined to small

---

and Robert Nottle, 'The Development of Securities Markets in China in the 1990s', (1993) 11 *Company and Securities Law Journal*, at 503-523.

18 Chen Ziqiao, *supra* note 17, at 6. The early experiment in Shenyang, however, mainly involved bonds and debentures issued to enterprise employees for the purpose of raising funds.

19 *People's Daily* (*Renmin Ribao*), *supra* note 17. For a comprehensive examination of the development of China's stock markets, see Carl E. Walter & Fraser J. Howie, *Privatizing China: Inside China's Stock Markets*, 2nd edition (Singapore: John Wiley & Sons (Asia) Pte Ltd, 2006).

20 *Ibid.*

21 Issued by the State Council on 14 March 1983.

22 Item 15 of the Interim Provisions.

23 See *supra* note 17. See also Howard Chao & Yang Xiaoping, 'The Reform of the Chinese System of Enterprise Ownership, (1987) 23 *Stan. J. Int'l L.* 365, at 379; and Yue Haitao, 'China Opens the Securities Market', *Beijing Review*, February1-7, 1988, at 20.

24 Minutes of the All-China Conference of Experimental Locations for Economic Reform, issued by the State Council.

25 Item 2 of Minutes of the All-China Conference of Experimental Locations for Economic Reform.

26 See discussions in Chao & Yang, *supra* note 23, at 379; and Henry Zheng, *supra* note 17, at 355-363.

and medium-sized collective enterprises,[27] and 'shares' were often in the nature of bonds and debentures and did not provide ownership rights.[28]

Nevertheless, these developments soon led some reformist scholars to predict that, as in the case of the household contracting system replacing production brigades in the rural areas, stock companies would eventually replace all SOEs.[29] Contrary to this prediction, the year 1987 saw some significant restrictions on the use of stocks as a means of raising funds. In March 1987 the State Council issued Interim Regulations on the Administration of Enterprise Bonds. Under Articles 12 and 13 of these Regulations the People's Bank of China, in cooperation with State planning and financial authorities, was to set an annual quota for issuing bonds, and all issuance was to be approved by a People's Bank of China at an appropriate level. Soon after these Regulations the State Council issued a Notice regarding the strengthening of the administration of shares and bonds.[30] Under this Notice the issuance of shares was restricted, and only approved collective enterprises were allowed to issue shares on an experimental basis. SOEs were allowed to issue bonds only. This Notice, however, made an exception for those SOEs which had already gained approval to issue shares and still needed to do so. The reasons for imposing restrictions were, according to the Notice, uncontrolled spending outside state plans as a result of the unchecked issuance of stocks, and the corrupt practice of forcing ordinary people to purchase stocks. There was, however, little doubt that ideological opposition to the securitisation of SOEs played a role in the decision to tighten the control of stock experimentation.[31]

Later in the same year, the Party changed its perception again. Discussing the need to invigorate SOEs in his report to the 13th National Congress of the Communist Party of China, Zhao Ziyang, then the Secretary-General of the Party, directly contradicted the above State Council Notice by announcing that:

> Various forms of a system of shares in enterprises have appeared during the reform. These include purchase of shares by the state, collective purchase by departments, localities [local organs] and other enterprises and purchase by individuals. This system is one means of organising property for socialist enterprises and shall be further implemented on a trial basis. The property

---

27 See Xu Jing'an, *supra* note 17, at 220; and Yuan Jianguo, 'The Stock System and Stock Legislation in China', (no. 1, 1991) *Legal Science in China* (*Zhongguo Faxue*), at 54.

28 Yue Haitao, *supra* note 23, at 20; and Ajit Singh, 'The Stock Market in a Socialist Economy', in Peter Nolan & Dong Fureng, (eds), *The Chinese Economy and Its Future: Achievements and Problems of Post-Mao Reform* (Cambridge: Polity Press, 1990), at 167.

29 See e.g. Li Yining, 'Some Thoughts on the Reform of the Ownership System in Our Country', *People's Daily* (*Renmin Ribao*), 26 September 1986, at 5.

30 'The State Council Requires Various Regional Governments to Strengthen the Administration of Shares and Bonds', *People's Daily* (*Renmin Ribao*), 7 April 1987, at 3.

31 See *supra* note 16.

rights of certain small state-owned enterprises can be sold to collectives or individuals.[32]

After that the experimentation with securitisation continued, with the blessing of the Central Government. In April 1990 the Shenzhen Stock Exchange was formally opened after more than one year of preparation.[33] Then in December 1990 the Shanghai Stock Exchange opened its doors to the public.[34] Late in 1990 a State Trading Automated Quotation System (STAQS) was set up in Beijing and began operation. The quotation system provided a national computerised network linking major cities that had stock markets.[35] In 1991 tentative steps were also taken to attract foreign investors to participate in the Chinese securities markets. For instance an international symposium on foreign participation in the Chinese securities market was held in Beijing, attended by officials from Chinese government agencies and the World Bank and individual participants from the US, the UK, Australia, Japan, Germany, South Korea, Hong Kong and Taiwan.[36] For the purposes of foreign participation, the above two Exchange Centres began to issue special 'B-type' shares exclusively to foreign investors in 1991,[37] and from 1993 on the listing of H-shares overseas was also permitted.[38] Enterprises outside the two regions could have their shares traded

---

32 The report is available from *Documents of the Thirteenth National Congress of the Communist Party of China (October 25-November 1, 1987)* (Beijing: Foreign Languages Press, 1988), at 34. The English translation has been modified by myself according to the original text in Chinese.

33 *Chinese Youth Daily* (*Zhongguo Qingnian Bao*), 4 July, 1991, at 1.

34 *Beijing Review*, 24 February – 1 March 1992, at 16. It is interesting to note that the Shanghai Stock Exchange was said to be the largest in Asia before 1949. See Yuwa Wei, 'The Development of the Securities Market and Regulation in China', (2005) 27 *Loy. L.A. Int'l & Comp. L. Rev.* 479, at 488.

35 Wang Poming, 'The Current Situation and Perspectives on the Prospects of China's Securities Market', in *Conference Papers of the 1991 International Symposium on Foreign Participation in China's Securities Market (13-14 September 1991, Beijing)* (Beijing: Beijing Investment Consultants Inc., 1991), at 11.

36 See Preface to *Conference Papers of the 1991 International Symposium On Foreign Participation in China's Securities Market, id.*

37 'B' shares, formally known as '*Renminbi* special category shares', are registered shares of *Renminbi* par value available exclusively to foreign investors for trading in foreign exchange. See Article 2 of Provisional Measures of Shenzhen Municipality for the Administration of *Renminbi* Special Category Shares (December 1991) and Articles 2 and 14 of Administrative Measures of Shanghai Municipality Governing *Renminbi* Special Category Shares. See further discussions in s. 6.2 below.

38 Tsingtao Brewery was the first Chinese company to be listed in Hong Kong (H-shares) in 1993. See CSRC, *China's Securities and Futures Markets* (2006), August 2006, available from <www.csrc.gov.cn/en/jsp/detaill.jsp?infoid=1153810173100&type=CMS.STD> (last accessed 3 August 2006), at 4. (Hereinafter referred to as the CSRC Report 2006).

in these two centres with the approval of the State Council.[39] Another exchange centre was planned in 1992 to be established in North China and intended to form a national network with the Shanghai and Shenzhen Stock Exchanges.[40] By the end of 1993 there were some 3800 enterprises adopting the shareholding system, of which 47% issued shares to their own employees, 46% issued shares to other legal persons (enterprises), and 7% issued shares to the general public. By the end of March 1994 barely five months after the implementation of the Company Law, 244 companies had listed in the two Exchanges.[41] Guangdong, Fujian and Hainan provinces were soon approved by the Central Government to experiment in the shareholding system on a large scale.[42] Thus was born the Chinese securities market.

However, the development in the late 1980s and earlier 1990s was not smooth sailing. The rapid and continuing development after 1987 led to what the Chinese called a 'share craze' phenomenon.[43] In response, a more cautious, and sometimes conflicting, approach was taken by the Government. In March 1992 a national conference on enterprise securitisation, co-sponsored by the State Commission for Economic Structural Reform and the Office of Production of the State Council, was held in Shenzhen. At the end of this conference it was decided that experimentation with the stock system had to be further and firmly pursued.[44] In the same month the State Council endorsed the Main Points for 1992 Economic Reform proposed by the State Commission for Economic Structural Reform. The further promotion of various forms of shareholding was among the main points.[45] By contrast, the final report of the 1992 national conference on enterprise securitisation, approved by the State Council, took a much more cautious approach. In this final report, the enthusiastic response from the public towards the stock market was criticised as an 'over-heated reaction'. The final report set out a general guideline for further experimentation: 'firmly pursuing the experiment but not on a large scale; carrying

---

39 'Experiment with Securitisation Must Be Carried Out in Accordance with Regulations', *People's Daily* (*Renmin Ribao*) (overseas edition), 22 May 1992, at 2

40 *People's Daily* (*Renmin Ribao*) (overseas edition), 13 March 1992, at 3. There was also a proposal from Chinese economists to establish an Exchange in Chengdu for the western region. See 'A Summary Report on the Symposium on the Theories and Practice of Securitisation in China', *Guangming Daily* (*Guangming Ribao*), 11 March 1994, at 3. This did not actually eventuate.

41 'Securitisation Has Invigorated State-owned Enterprises', *Legal Daily* (*Fazhi Ribao*), 25 January 1994, at 1; and 'China Stocks List Abroad', *Beijing Review*, May 30-June 6, 1994, at 28.

42 *Ibid.*

43 'Stocks: New Excitement in China's Economic Life', *Beijing Review*, 10-16 August 1992, at 14-17. See also 'Chinese Investors Flock to Market', *The Australian*, 12 August 1992, at 31; and 'More Forms Pledge Eases Share Frenzy', *The Sydney Morning Herald*, 13 August 1992, at 9.

44 *People's Daily* (*Renmin Ribao*) (overseas edition), 6 March 1992, at 1.

45 *People's Daily* (*Renmin Ribao*) (overseas edition), 30 March 1992, at 3.

out the experiment but in good order.'[46] More specifically, this report classified shareholding enterprises into four types: enterprises with shares held by legal persons, enterprises with shares held by their employees, enterprises with shares issued to the public but not traded in exchange centres, and enterprises whose shares were traded in exchange centres. Accordingly, Chinese government authorities decided that the experiment on a national scale should be primarily with the first two types of enterprises. The experiment with the third type should be restricted to Guangdong, Fujian and Hainan Provinces, and the experiment with the fourth type should be confined to Shanghai and Shenzhen. Enterprises outside these two regions wanting to have their shares traded in these two centres had first to seek approval from the State Council.[47] In December 1992 the experiment with the third type was authorised to be carried out nationwide by the State Council Notice Concerning Macro-Administration of the Securities Market.[48] This Notice also announced the establishment of the State Council Securities Committee and the China Securities Regulatory Commission (CSRC). These two authorities were to jointly administer and supervise the development of the securities market and a regulatory structure for the market. The administrative functions of the People's Bank, the State Planning Commission, the Ministry of Finance, the State Commission for Economic Structural Reform and the two Exchanges in Shenzhen and Shanghai were also delineated by the Notice.[49] This Notice could be seen as the first step towards a regulated development of the securities market. Indeed, the Main Points for Economic Structural Reform in 1993 emphasised that experimentation with securitisation had to be carried out in an orderly fashion in accordance with approved plans and under strict policy guidelines.[50] The Party had now taken a cautious approach and emphasised that the public listing of SOE shares had to be strictly examined and approved and the number had to remain small.[51]

These cautious and sometimes conflicting policies reflected the Chinese government's indecisiveness and grave concerns about losing control over the use of capitalist measures to serve socialism, in particular the use of capitalist means to reform the SOEs. Not surprisingly, enormous ideological, politico-economic and legal controversies erupted. Politico-economists were busy advancing various theories to justify the practice of capitalism in a socialist country and to assure both

---

46 'Experiment with Securitisation Must Be Carried Out in Accordance with Regulations', *supra* note 39, at 2.

47 *Ibid.*

48 See Item 2 of the Notice Concerning Macro-Administration of Securities Market.

49 See Item 1 of the Notice Concerning Macro-Administration of Securities Market.

50 Main Points of Economic Structural Reform (1993), (no. 5, 1993) *Gazette of the State Council of the PRC* (*Zhonghua Renmin Gongheguo Guowuyuan Gongbao*), at 191-192.

51 See paragraph 6 of the Decision of the CPC Central Committee on Some Issues Concerning the Establishment of a Socialist Market Economic Structure (1993).

the authorities and the Chinese people that this capitalist tool would not change the nature and essence of socialism.[52] In legal circle too, major theoretical efforts were made to bring about an all-embracing civil law theory to allow the diversification of ownership, while allowing the state to continue its legal control over the securitised property of SOEs.[53]

3. The Coming of Age of the Securities Market and Its Regulation

Whatever the controversies, the experimentation with securitisation and the stock market continued. Indeed, the securities industry grew at an astonishing speed, spreading and flourishing nationwide, and soon became very over-heated and largely speculative. There was not only a stock investment bubble; there were many poor quality and nearly bankrupt companies also entering the market by dishonest means, and investors lost money when the bubble finally burst. Adding to the problem was the confusion in regulation. As mentioned above, in October 1992 the State Council formed the Securities Committee and its executive arm, the China Securities Regulatory Commission (CSRC), to take charge of overall supervision and regulation of the securities market in China. These two authorities shared their regulatory powers with the People's Bank of China and several other powerful government departments. The existence of multiple regulators led to an inconsistent legislative framework and weak and ineffective supervision.[54]

Before long government officials realised that such developments required not just strict but also consistent and coherent nationwide legal regulation. Legal scholars also realised that they had a more urgent task than theorising about ownership and property rights. That task was to draft laws and regulations governing the securities market. Indeed, the experimentation with the stock system had been carried out without national laws, although regional legal structures did exist.[55] Thus began the

52 See Jianfu Chen, *supra* note 3, at 207-212.

53 See Jianfu Chen, *supra* note 3, at 212-220.

54 By the end of 1998 no less than 250 regulations for the securities industry had been issued, among which some were soon out of date and some were in conflict with each other.

55 The most comprehensive regional legal structures for stock markets were those of Shenzhen and Shanghai. In Shenzhen, major regulations included: Provisional Measures on Share Issuing and Trading (May 1991), Provisional Regulations for the Administration of Securities Institutions (June 1991), Provisional Measures for the Administration of *Renminbi* Special Category Shares (December 1991), Detailed Rules for Implementing the Provisional Measures for the Administration of *Renminbi* Special Category Shares (December 1991), Detailed Rules for the Implementation of a Centralised Entrustment System for Share Trading (December 1991), Operating Rules of the Shenzhen Securities Exchange for Trading and Clearing of B Shares, Provisional Rules for the Registration of Special *Renminbi*-denominated Shares (1992), Tentative Provisions on Companies Limited by Shares (March 1992), and Provisional

creation of relevant laws and regulations as well as of policies,[56] in particular the making of a Company Law and Securities Law.

In fact, when forming the State Council Securities Committee and the CSRC, the National People's Congress (the NPC) also established another committee in 1992 to draft a uniform and comprehensive securities law. The drafting obviously proceeded quite efficiently. By August 1993 an initial draft law had been submitted to the Standing Committee of the NPC (SCNPC) for preliminary examination, and a second deliberation was conducted in December 1993. The various authorities at the national and local levels having been consulted, a revised draft was completed in June 1994.[57] At this time it was first reported that the Securities Law would be issued by the end of 1994.[58] This of course did not happen.

Meanwhile, the Company Law was adopted in December 1993 and became effective on 1 July 1994. As discussed in the previous Chapter, the Law regulated both limited liability companies and companies limited by shares. Chapter 4 of the 1993 Company Law provided some general provisions governing the issuing and transfer of company shares and, interestingly, referred to many other laws and

---

Regulations of Shenzhen Municipality on Companies Limited by Shares (1992). In Shanghai, major regulations included: Administrative Measures Governing Securities Trading (November 1990), Administrative Measures Governing *Renminbi* Special Category Shares (November 1991), Detailed Implementing Rules for the Measures for the Administration of Special *Renminbi*-denominated Shares (November 1991), Supplementary Operating Rules for the Trading Market (Special *Renminbi-denominated* Shares) of the Shanghai Securities Exchange (February 1992), and Provisional Regulations of Shanghai Municipality on Companies Limited by Shares (1992). Most of these regulations have now ceased to operate after the establishment of a national regulatory framework, to be discussed below.

56 During May, June and July 1992, a set of 15 policy documents was jointly issued by the State Commission for Economic Structural Reform, the State Planning Commission, the Ministry of Finance, the People's Bank of China and the Office of Production of the State Council. This set of policies filled a legal vacuum by providing guiding principles for the experiment of securitisation, standard rules for setting up companies limited by shares and limited liability companies; rules governing general management, accounting, labour and wages, taxation, auditing, financial management, material supplies, administration of state property, registration, share issuing and trading. See *People's Daily* (*Renmin Ribao*) (overseas edition), 19 June 1992, at 1. Part of these documents can be found in (nos 16-18, 1992) *Gazette of the State Council of the PRC* (*Zhonghua Renmin Gongheguo Guowuyuan Gongbao*). Most of these documents have now also ceased to be operational after the establishment of a national regulatory framework.

57 See 'Introduction: an Important Law in Regulating the Securities Market', available from NPC's website: <www.npc.gov.cn/zgrdw/common/zw.jsp?label=WXZLK&ID=pdmc=010501> (last accessed 17 January 2006).

58 See 'Securities Law Is Being Speedily Revised', *Legal Daily* (*Fazhi Ribao*), 5 January 1994, at 3.

regulations or rules that were yet to be issued by national legislative authorities or the State Council.[59]

The promulgation of the Company Law effectively put heavy pressure on the SCNPC to speed up its work on the Securities Law. The SCNPC then began yet another round of consultations with various government authorities. The Asian Financial Crisis in 1997 further prompted the SCNPC to speed up the process.[60] Thus in October 1998 the draft came back to the SCNPC for formal deliberation, and finally, after deliberations at five different sessions of the SCNPC, and with six years in the making, the Securities Law was finally adopted on 29 December 1998 and became effective from 1 July 1999. For the first time China had a national framework regulating the securities market.

The market, meanwhile, was soon to undergo some major upheavals. As mentioned earlier, China's securities market then was plagued by chronic liquidity problems, lack of comprehensive regulations and supervision, and the generally low quality of listed companies. The major problems in the Chinese market were recognised by the government. However it was the Asian Financial Crisis that prompted the Chinese government to launch a nationwide campaign to clean up and restructure the securities market. Some securities companies were suspended, some were merged. Some troubled companies were de-listed. Subsequently, the market was depressed for 20 consecutive months, until 19 May 1999 (the so-called '5.19' market opportunity) when the market once again revived.

In February 2001 China opened its B-share market to domestic individual investors holding legally obtained foreign currencies, as one of the many efforts made by the government in relation to entering the WTO.[61] In the same year, on China's accession to the WTO, the CSRC announced the following WTO-related commitments: (1) foreign securities organisations would be allowed to participate in B-share transactions without the need to use Chinese intermediaries; (2) representative offices in China of foreign securities organisations would be allowed to join the Chinese stock exchanges as special members; (3) the establishment of joint ventures to participate in the management of securities investment funds would be allowed, with foreign equity to be limited to 33%, which could be extended to 49% three years after China's WTO accession; and (4) three years after China's accession to the WTO, Sino-foreign joint venture securities companies (with foreign equity limited to 33%) would be allowed to engage (without Chinese intermediaries) in dealing in A-, B- and H-shares, and in government and company bonds, as well as in the promotion of investment.[62] These commitments have now all been fulfilled.

---

59 See e.g. Articles 135 and 155 of the 1993 Company Law.

60 See 'Introduction: an Important Law in Regulating the Securities Market', *supra* note 57.

61 See CSRC Report 2006, *supra* note 38, at 10.

62 See CSRC announcement, <www.csrc.gov.cn/cn/search/search_detail.jsp?infoid=1059654766100&type=CMS.STD> (last accessed 3 August 2006).

In December 2002 China gave foreign qualified institutional investors (FQII) conditional access to its domestic equity markets, including to A-shares and traded government and corporate bonds. At the end of January 2006 China opened its A-share market to foreign strategy investors, bringing closer the time when A-shares would ultimately merge with B-shares. As of the end of 2005 there were 34 Qualified Foreign Institutional Investors (QFII), 7 joint ventures securities companies and 20 joint venture fund management companies licensed by the Chinese government to operate in China.[63]

At the end of 2005 there were some 116 securities companies (with 3,090 retail branches nationwide),[64] 1,381 listed companies (of which 1,240 companies issued A-shares only, 23 issued B-shares only, 86 issued both A- & B-shares, and 32 companies issued both A- & H-shares)[65] and 73.36 million securities investment accounts, largely held by individual investors in China.[66] The aggregate market capitalisation reached 3,243 billion *yuan* (with 1,063 billion *yuan* in tradable shares), equivalent to 17.79% of China's GDP.[67] At the same time there were also 3 futures exchanges and 183 futures brokerage companies, with a total two-way turnover of commodity futures value amounting to 13,450 billion *yuan*.[68]

It seems that the securities market in China has now finally come of age, though the volatile movement of the market in mid-2007 seems to suggest that there is still some way to go before the Chinese market becomes mature. However, it should be pointed out that the financial derivatives market in China is currently a very underdeveloped market, with warrant being the only financial derivative traded on the stock exchange.[69]

4. Legal Framework

The gradual development of the securities industry has been a trial and error process that continues today, and the market, along with mechanisms for corporate governance and investment protection (especially that of minority investors), is yet to fully develop. Similarly, laws regulating the industry and its conduct and activities, though relatively comprehensive by Chinese standards, are far from perfect and remain largely *ad hoc* and piecemeal in approach, despite the enactment

---

63 See CSRC Report 2006, *supra* note 38, at 3-4.

64 See CSRC Report 2006, *supra* note 38, at 22.

65 See CSRC Report 2006, *supra* note 38, at 17.

66 See CSRC Report 2006, *supra* note 38, at 3.

67 See CSRC Report 2006, *supra* note 38, at 3 & 14.

68 See CSRC Report 2006, *supra* note 38, at 4.

69 See CSRC Report 2006, *supra* note 38, at 38.

of the Securities Law in 1998; many are inherently contradictory and others are provisional in nature if not already out of date. In short, like the market itself, this body of laws and regulations is yet to mature and, worse still, remains transitional and highly unstable in nature.

It is unstable not in terms of national legislation, but because of the constant changes being made to the secondary legislation, which forms an important part of the regulatory framework and provides the actual practical measures and guidance for the conduct and operation of the market.

4.1. Primary National Legislation

As mentioned earlier, the securities market was initially regulated by local regulations, principally those issued by Shanghai and Shenzhen authorities, where experimentation first formalised. The enactment of the Company Law in 1993 and the Securities Law in 1998 signalled the establishment of a uniform national legal framework on companies and securities. Within the short span of fifteen years a national legal framework consisting of the Company Law (1993), the Securities Law (1998) and the Securities Investment Fund Law (2003) was established. Additionally, the Criminal Law, initially promulgated in 1979 but comprehensively revamped in 1997, further supplements the national legal framework on securities by providing severe legal penalties for the violation of the law.

(1) The Securities Law

Since its promulgation in 1998 the Securities Law has undergone two revisions. The first took place on 28 August 2004, involving only two articles. Article 28 was amended to allow the price of shares to be determined by negotiation between the issuer and the underwriter, and Article 50 was amended to move the power of approval of listing corporate bonds from the CSRC to the stock exchanges. The second revision of 27 October 2005 is, however, substantial and comprehensive. Of the original total 214 articles, some 40% have been revised (including rewording), 27 articles have been removed, and 53 new articles have been added (including 8 articles transferred from the Company Law). The principal aim has been to solve the problems of the poor quality of listed companies and irregularities in securities companies, to improve the securities issuance, trade and registration systems, and to strengthen corporate governance and market supervision.[70] In addition to the various technical revisions, significant amendments to the Securities Law affect issues relating to separate operations among banking, insurance and securities

---

[70] See 'Explanations on the Revision of the Securities Law of the PRC', delivered by Zhou Zhengqing at the 15th session of the Standing Committee of 10th NPC on 24 April 2005, in (no. 7, 2005) *Gazette of the Standing Committee of the NPC* (*Zhonghua Renmin Gongheguo Quanguo Renmin Daibiao Dahui Changwuweiyuanhui Gongbao*), at 611-619.

industries, spot trading, money and securities finances, and permit state-owned companies and banking funds to enter the stock market. The revised Securities Law took effect on 1 January 2006.

The revised Securities Law is divided into 12 chapters and 240 articles. As a comprehensive code it sets out in detail the standard practice for share offering and trading, and a code of conduct and liabilities for violations of the Law. It deals with all aspects of the securities industry, covering listed companies, stock exchanges, brokerages, registration and settlement agencies, service agencies, self-regulatory associations, and government regulatory bodies. However, issues relating to overseas listings by Chinese companies and B-share activities are not covered by the Securities Law; these matters continue to be governed by other applicable regulations and rules issued by the State Council, the CSRC and other government authorities (such as the State Administration of Foreign Exchange).[71]

(2) The Company Law

The revision of the Company Law and the Securities Law in 2005 was conducted simultaneously, and was thus a much better coordinated exercise. As a result the Company Law's provisions on the issuance of shares and bonds have now been incorporated into Chapter One of the Securities Law, and provisions on company listing, suspension and termination of listing have been incorporated into Chapter Three of the Securities Law. The Company Law therefore focuses on regulating the organisational structure, governance, and business activities of companies.

(3) The Securities Investment Fund Law

Investment funds as an instrument of investment were introduced into China in the early 1990s, with the first fund created in 1991. Closed-end funds were allowed in 1998 and in late 2001 open-ended funds were launched. Since then this industry has developed rapidly (with a setback during the Asian financial crisis and the SARS outbreak). By the end of 2005 there were 54 closed-end funds and 154 open-ended funds under the management of 53 fund management companies. These funds held 44% and 17% respectively of the total tradable share capitalisation in China.[72]

In the early stages, investment funds operated in China on a self-regulating basis without much legal status. In 1997 the first national law, the Provisional Measures on the Administration of Securities Investment Funds, was issued to regulate China's securities investment fund industry. In order to boost investors' confidence and to attract more investors, especially institutional investors, to enter into the securities market, and to help the development of the investment fund industry, the legislative process for a national securities investment fund law was started in 1999. After

71 See Article 239 of the Securities Law.

72 See CSRC Report 2006, *supra* note 38, at 27.

four years of drafting, discussion and revision, the Law of the People's Republic of China on Securities Investment Funds was finally passed by China's top legislator on 28 October 2003.[73]

The new Law regulates the functions and roles of securities investment funds, formally establishes the regulatory system, emphasises the protection of investors' rights and interests, sets the market entry threshold, specifies the liabilities of practitioners, and imposes penalties for violations of the law by fund managers and fund trustees as well as securities administrative officials.

(4) The Criminal Law

The Criminal Law provisions, in particular those dealing with the violation of the 'socialist market order', back up the operation of the company and securities laws as well as laws governing business activities and conduct by imposing heavy criminal and financial penalties for violations of the relevant laws. It should be pointed out that many of the securities regulations refer to criminal sanctions as contained in the Criminal Law, and the Criminal Law is constantly revised to secure and maintain a desired order in the market economy.

4.2. Secondary Legislation: Administrative Regulations and Rules

It is important to note that even though the above laws are meant to be comprehensive codes, they only establish a basic legal framework for securities regulation and general principles for such regulation. For most practical purposes and the actual operation of the industry, there are still hundreds of regulations, measures, and rules issued by the CSRC and other state authorities to implement the laws.[74] These secondary regulations must not be overlooked. It also needs to be noted that the Securities Law does not expressly abolish any previous securities regulations or rules. This means that these previous regulations and rules continue to apply so long as they do not conflict with the Securities Law. In order to establish a consistent securities legal system the CSRC has in recent years made great efforts to examine and tidy up all existing regulations, many of them having been abolished and others revised, but the process is an on-going one and far from systematic. As a result it is an extremely difficult process to identify and determine the status of validity of the many hundreds of secondary rules and regulations.[75]

---

73 The new Law was promulgated on the day of its adoption and became effective from 1 June 2004.

74 According to the CSRC, there were more than 300 departmental rules, guidelines and codes at the end of 2005. See CSRC Report 2006, *supra* note 38, at 45.

75 In fact, official websites, such as those of the CSRC or the Shanghai Stock Exchange, are entirely unreliable for determining the accurate status of secondary legislation. There is only one very burdensome way of reviewing the status, which is to cross-examine all available

The Company Law suffers the same defect as the Securities Law; its actual implementation relies on the many hundreds of administrative regulations and rules governing specific aspects of company establishment, registration and business operation, mostly issued by the General Administration for Industry and Commerce and the Ministry of Commerce (especially relating to foreign investment in China). The implementation of the Criminal Law, too, is further aided by the many 'interpretations' issued by the Supreme People's Court and the Supreme People's Procuratorate. It must be pointed out that although the Supreme People's Court and the Supreme People's Procuratorate nowadays publish selected cases, these cases do not establish precedents as understood in a Common law jurisdiction.

For these reasons, a 'mini' legal framework, consisting of administrative regulations, departmental rules and court interpretations, exists for each of the technical issues involved in issuance, trading, listing and other securities-related activities.[76]

5. Institutional Setting

5.1. Regulatory Authorities

While the China Securities Regulatory Commission has taken centre stage for administering and supervising the development and activities of the securities market since 1998, it is not strictly the sole authority in charge of the industry. Several other authorities continue to perform important functions in this industry.

(1) The State Council Authority – The China Securities Regulatory Commission

As mentioned earlier, the State Council securities regulatory authority initially comprised the State Council Securities Committee (the SCSC) and the China Securities Regulatory Commission (the CSRC). The SCSC was the State authority responsible for exercising centralised market regulation and administration, and the CSRC was the executive arm of the SCSC, responsible for conducting uniform national supervision and administration over all securities markets. Both the SCSC and the CSRC were established in October 1992.

---

rules and regulations and constantly follow up announcements of the abolition of laws by the relevant state authorities. This is so in the case of CSRC, even though various notices on the abolition and revision of its regulations and rules have been issued. For these notices, see the CSRC website: <www.csrc.gov.cn>.

76 These regulations and rules are outlined below. For detailed discussions of these rules and their operation, see Jianfu Chen, 'Securities Regulations in the People's Republic of China', being *Booklet I: Commentary*, in Gordon Walker, James D. Fox & Ian Ramsay (eds), *International Securities Regulation: Pacific Rim* (New York: Oceana Publications/Oxford University Press, 2007).

Since their establishment the powers and functions of the SCSC and the CSRC have been gradually expanded. In November 1993 the SCSC and the CSRC were authorised to take charge of experimental futures work. From August 1997 the Shanghai and Shenzhen stock exchanges came under the CSRC's supervision and administration, and by November of the same year the functions of the People's Bank of China in supervision and administration of the securities operation organisations were also passed over to the CSRC. In April of 1998, and as part of the State Council structural adjustment, the SCSC and CSRC were merged into one single authority – the China Securities Regulatory Commission – as the sole State Council securities regulatory authority responsible for the uniform administration and supervision of securities and futures markets throughout the country.

The main duties, powers and functions of the CSRC are defined by the Securities Law,[77] and include rule-making, regulation, supervision and administration, and investigation and imposition of penalties.

Initially, when performing the above duties, the CSRC had the power to investigate and to gather evidence; to question the parties to any case or other related units or individuals; to inspect and make copies of securities documents or seal them up for safekeeping; to investigate fund accounts and securities accounts of the parties to a case or other related units or individuals, and, where necessary, to apply to a court to have funds and securities frozen. These power are now expanded by the revised Securities Law to include the power to conduct on-site inspection of issuers, listed companies, securities companies, securities investment fund management companies, securities services organisations, stock exchanges and securities registration and settlement organisations, the power to freeze or seize corporate or individual capital, stocks, bank accounts and other property or evidential materials in cases of suspected illegal activity (without the need to go through a court, but in accordance with its own Implementation Measures on the Power to Freeze and Seize [Assets], issued by CSRC on 30 December 2005), and the power to suspend for 15 days the trading activity of persons suspected of stock manipulation or insider trading, with a permissible 15-day extension for complicated cases. No unit or individual under examination or investigation may refuse to co-operate with the authority or obstruct the investigation or conceal information.[78] Further, the CSRC is authorised to share information with other financial supervision and administration authorities of the State Council, and all relevant state authorities are required to cooperate with the CSRC in its performance of its supervision, inspection and investigation functions.[79]

---

77 See Article 179 of the Securities Law.

78 See Articles 180 & 183 of the Securities Law.

79 See Article 185 of the Securities Law.

Such a wide range of, powers, duties and functions has made the CSRC a very powerful authority. It now enjoys and exercises administrative, supervisory, regulatory, disciplinary, quasi-judiciary as well as legislative powers.

(2) Branch Offices of the CSRC

The Securities Law authorises the establishment of branch offices (*paichu jigou*) by the CSRC where needed.[80] Branch offices may only perform their supervisory and administrative functions within the scope of their delegated authority from the CSRC. The first established were 10 offices located respectively in Tianjin, Shenyang, Shanghai, Jinan, Wuhan, Guangzhou, Shenzhen, Chengdu, Xi'an and Beijing, and formally began their work from 1 July 1999. At the end of 2005 there were some 36 branch offices (referred to as bureaus) spread throughout the nation's provinces, autonomous regions, directly administered municipalities and cities with separate planning, and two supervisory offices in Shanghai and Shenzhen where the stock exchanges are located.[81]

(3) Share Issue Examination and Verification Commission

The Share Issue Examination and Verification Commission (also referred to as the Public Offering Review Committee) is established by, and subject to, the CSRC. It has 25 members, 5 from the CSRC and 20 from other administrative authorities, trade organisations, research institutes and universities. All Commission members are appointed by the CSRC. The membership term is one year, with the possibility of up to three continuous terms.[82]

The Commission is responsible for examination and verification of applications for the issue of shares, company bonds and other types of stocks. It votes on applications and submits examination opinions to the CSRC for final approval. The organisational structure, functions and responsibilities, activities and working procedures are regulated by the Measures on the Share Issue Examination and Verification Commission (2006), which replaced the Provisional Measures on the Share Issue Examination and Verification Commission (issued by the CSRC on 5 December 2003).[83]

---

80 See Article 7 of the Securities Law.

81 See CSRC Report 2006, *supra* note 38, at 50.

82 See Articles 6 and 7 of the Measures on the Share Issue Examination and Verification Commission, issued as Order No. 31 by the CSRC on 9 May 2006.

83 As a result of the issuance of the new Measures, it can be assumed that the Detailed Working Rules of the Share Issue Examination and Verification Commission (issued by the same body on 11 December 2003) have also been repealed.

(4) State Auditing Authorities

State auditing authorities are responsible for the supervision of auditing of the activities of stock exchanges, securities companies, securities registration and account settlement organisations, securities trading services organisations, and securities supervisory and administrative bodies.

(5) The People's Bank of China

Initially when the securities industry and market were developed in China, the People's Bank of China was one of the major regulators. Along with the reform of the functions of the People's Bank, especially the change in its nature from an all-purpose bank to a policy (central reserve) bank, and the establishment of the specialised regulatory authorities; most of the Bank's functions and authorities in the securities industry have now been transferred to the CSRC. However, the Bank continues to regulate finance-related matters in the securities industry. Further, regulations and rules issued by the Bank before the transfer of powers and functions remain valid unless and until they are replaced or repealed by later rules.

(6) Stock Exchanges

When the Chinese stock exchanges were first established they were defined as non-profit-seeking legal persons, a status confirmed by the Securities Law of 1998. The 2005 revised Securities Law now defines stock exchanges as 'self-governing legal persons which provide the venue and facilities for centralised trading of securities and are responsible for organising and supervising securities trading'.[84] The establishment and dissolution of a stock exchange is to be decided by the State Council itself.

While the stock exchanges are not strictly regulatory authorities and their articles of associations are subject to the examination and approval of the CSRC, they do exercise many functions and powers directly authorised by the Securities Law, including rule-making for listing, trading, membership and other relevant matters, the power to suspend the market, supervision over information disclosure, imposition of restrictions on trading and penalties.[85]

Trading activities in the stock exchanges are governed by the Trading Rules of Shanghai Stock Exchange and the Trading Rules of Shenzhen Stock Exchange respectively, both of which are revised from time to time.

Although there are only two stock exchanges in China, the trading system has now reached most cities through its 2,400-plus retail branches. As of the end of 2005 there were 834 companies and 878 equities listed on the Shanghai Exchange, with a

---

84 Article 102 of the Securities Law.

85 See Articles 113, 114, 115, 118 & 121 of the Securities Law.

total market capitalisation of RMB 2,310 billion *yuan*. It had a total membership of 156, including 4 overseas special members and special B-share trading seats for 39 overseas securities companies. At the same time there were 544 companies and 586 equities listed in the Shenzhen Exchange with a total market capitalisation of RMB 933 billion *yuan* and a total membership of 177 (including 4 overseas special members and special B-share trading seats for 19 overseas securities companies).[86]

(7) Securities Industry Associations

Securities industry associations are defined by the Securities Law as self-regulating social body legal persons.[87] The Securities Association of China (SAC) was founded on 28 August 1991. All securities companies are required to join a securities industry association. The articles of association of a securities industry association must be formulated by a members' meeting and reported to the CSRC for the record. Its functions are stipulated by Article 176 of the Securities Law, which include education, professional training, and dispute resolution among members or between members and clients.

As of the end of 2005 the SAC had a total membership of 282, including 116 securities companies, 33 securities investment fund management companies, 3 financial assets management companies, and 86 securities investment consulting institutions.[88]

5.2. Securities Companies

The securities companies have been the focus of reform since 2004 when the CSRC formally launched its campaign to strengthen the supervision of such companies.[89] Not surprisingly the 2005 revised Securities Law has now fundamentally revamped the provisions on securities companies – of the total 29 articles in the original Chapter 6, 'Securities Companies', 13 have been revised, 9 removed, and 13 added. The old classification of securities companies into comprehensive and brokerage types has now been abolished. A new system of securities investor protection funds has been established. The methods of deposition of trading settlement funds have been changed. Greater emphasis is placed on the protection of investors' assets by the revised Securities Law, and the supervision and administrative power of securities regulatory authorities over the securities companies have been strengthened. In short, the revised Securities Law aims to make securities companies more accountable in their business conduct and operation, and submits them to strict supervision

86 See CSRC Report 2006, *supra* note 38, at 35-36.

87 Article 174 of the Securities Law

88 See CSRC Report 2006, *supra* note 38, at 32.

89 See CSRC Report 2006, *supra* note 38, at 25.

and administration, so as to avoid the repetition of the securities scandals in the last few years.[90]

As mentioned above, the old classification that divided securities companies into comprehensive and brokerage companies has now been abolished. A legally established securities company may now engage in all or part of the following businesses,[91] provided that specific requirements for specific businesses are met by the company: securities brokerage; securities investment consultation; financial consultation relating to securities trading and securities investment; securities underwriting and sponsoring; self-managed securities business; securities asset management; and other securities business.

The Securities Law provisions on the securities companies are supplemented and implemented by many other rules and regulations,[92] effectively creating a mini legal framework of its own.

5.3. Securities Depository and Clearing Organisations

A depository and clearing house is referred to in China as a securities registration and account settlement organisation, which is defined by Article 155 of the Securities

---

90 As mentioned in Chapter 13, the Chinese stock markets gained a reputation of being a 'home to shoddy companies and shady trading practices.' See Andrew Batson, 'China bets on blue-chip IPOs to lay strong market foundation', *The Wall Street Journal*, 10 August 2006, at 19.

91 Article 125 of the Securities Law.

92 The principal rules include the following: Administrative Measures on Securities Companies, issued by the CSRC on 28 December 2001 and effective from 1 March 2002; Measures on the Inspection of Securities Companies, issued by the CSRC on 12 December 2000 and effective on the same day; Procedures for the Verification of On-line Entrusted Business of Securities Companies, issued by the CSRC on 29 April 2000 and effective on the same day; Guidelines for the Internal Control of Securities Companies, issued by the CSRC on 25 December 2003 (which repealed an earlier set of Guidelines issued on 31 January 2001); Notice on Issues relating to Increasing Capital and Shares by Securities Companies, issued by the CSRC on 23 November 2001; Provisional Measures on the Administration of Corporate Bonds of Securities Companies (CSRC Order No. 25), issued initially on 19 August 2003 and revised on 15 October 2004; Administrative Measures on Share-pledged Loans of Securities Companies, issued by the CSRC on 4 November 2004, which repealed the 2000 measures under the same title; Administrative Measures on Short-term Financing Bonds of Securities Companies, issued by the People's Bank of China on 18 October 2004 (PBOC Announcement [2004] No. 12); and Provisional Measures on Securities Companies Engaging in the Business of Asset Management for Clients, issued by the CSRC on 18 December 2003 and taking effect from 1 February 2004. Clearly, all the detailed rules and regulations were issued before the major revision of the Company Law and the Securities Law in 2005. These rules and regulations initiated many of the changes that have now been incorporated into the revised Company Law and the Securities Law of 2005. However, some of the provisions in these rules and regulations may not be consistent with the Company Law and the Securities Law and are now subject to revision and amendment, or even repeal. Caution must therefore be used in following up regulatory development in this area.

Law as a non-profit-seeking legal person. As in the case of securities companies, the Securities Law brings the securities registration and account settlement organisations under centralised and uniform operational control, and their establishment and dissolution, as well as the articles of association and the operational rules, are subject to the examination and approval of the CSRC.[93]

The functions of these organisations are defined by the Securities Law to include the establishment of securities accounts and settlement accounts; custody and transfer of securities; registration in the register of securities holders; settlement and delivery of traded listed securities; allotment of securities rights and interests on the authority of the issuer; handling inquiries related to the above services; and other services approved by the CSRC.[94]

Currently, the China Securities Depository and Clearing Corporation Ltd (CSDCC), which was established in March 2001, is the only registration and settlement institution in China. It took charge of all registration and settlement business of securities from October 2001, and has thus established a unified securities registration and settlement system. It is also responsible for registration and settlement businesses of all other instruments listed in stock exchanges and open-ended funds. It applies the T+1 settlement method for A-shares and T+3 for B-shares.[95]

5.4. Securities Trading Services Organisations

Securities trading services organisations include investment consultancy organisations, financial consultancy organisations, credit rating organisations, asset valuation organisations and accounting firms providing securities services. Their establishment must have approval from the CSRC and the relevant competent departments in charge.[96]

Professional personnel of investment consultancy organisations, financial consultancy organisations and credit rating organisations must possess specialised knowledge of securities and have had at least two years' professional experience in the securities industry. Like such organisations in other countries, these organisations and their personnel are prohibited from engaging in certain activities, including making securities investments for the principals; agreeing on the share of investment gains or losses with the principals; the purchase or sale of shares in a listed company that uses the services of the said consultancy organisation; using media or other means to provide or disseminate fraudulent or misleading information to investors; or other conduct prohibited by laws or administrative regulations.[97]

---

93 See Articles 155 & 158 of the Securities Law.

94 See Article 157 of the Securities Law.

95 See CSRC Report 2006, *supra* note 38, at 25-26.

96 See Article 169 of the Securities Law.

97 See Article 171 of the Securities Law.

They are also subject to various reporting obligations to ensure that their audited reports, asset valuation reports, financial consultancy reports, credit rating or legal opinions for securities issuance, listing and trading and other such documents are authentic, accurate and complete.

The Securities Law does not provide detailed rules governing these organisations. Thus, once again, their establishment, conduct, and operation are subject to various departmental rules.[98]

As of the end of 2005 there were 53 fund management companies, 108 investment consultancy institutions (advisers) and 70 accounting firms engaged in securities businesses.[99]

5.5. Listed Companies

The management and operation of listed companies is governed by the Company Law which provides a general framework of principles governing activities of companies, including finance, accounting, and corporate governance, secondary legislation issued by company registration authorities to implement the Company Law, and specific rules issued by the CSRC (such as rules on takeover of listed companies). Detailed and often *ad hoc* rules are issued to regulate specific aspects of company activities, such as the important issues of listing and delisting,[100] public offering of shares,[101] major assets changes,[102] and corporate governance.[103]

---

98 These include the Provisional Administrative Measures on Consultations on Securities and Futures Investments and the Detailed Rules for the Implementation of the Provisional Administrative Measures on Consultations on Securities and Futures Investments, issued by the CSRC on 30 November 1997 and 23 April 1998 respectively.

99 See CSRC Report 2006, *supra* note 38, at 25-27.

100 E.g., the Implementing Measures on Suspension and Termination of Listing of Loss-making Listed Companies, issued by the CSRC on 22 February 2001; the Supplementary Provisions on the Implementation of the (Amended) Implementing Measures on Suspension and Termination of the Listing of Loss-making Listed Companies, issued by the CSRC on 18 March 2003; and the Measures on Inspection of Listed Companies, which replace the Measures on Implementing the Systems of Inspection of Listed Companies issued on 20 December 1996.

101 E.g. Administrative Measures on Initial Public Offering and Listing of Shares, issued by the CSRC on 17 May 2006, and effective on 18 May 2006.

102 E.g. Notice on Regulating Acts Involving Major Assets Purchase, Sale and Replacement by Listed Companies, which was issued by the CSRC on 10 December 2001 and repealed an earlier Notice on Regulating Acts Involving Major Assets Purchase, Sale and Replacement by Listed Companies (*Zhengjian Gongsizi* [2000] No. 75); and Administrative Measures on Repurchasing Public Shares by Listed Companies (Trial Implementation) (Zhengjian fa [2005] No. 51), issued by the CSRC on 16 June 2005 and effective on the same day;

103 As discussed in the previous chapter, various corporate governance rules have now been codified into the Company Law; nevertheless, the CSRC issues its own Code of Corporate Governance For Listed Companies (the present version was issued in 2002, yet to be revised

Listed companies are further classified into 13 categories according to the principle that a listed company will be classified into the trade category to which the highest proportion of its business is related. Specific classification is contained in the Guideline for Industrial Classification of Listed Companies in China, issued by the CSRC in April 2001.[104]

6. Issuing of Securities

6.1. The Changing System of Share Issuance

Since the PRC issued its first set of regulations on public share issuance and corresponding polices in 1993[105] the share issuance regulatory system has gone, roughly speaking, through four stages: quota control, target control, a channel system, and a sponsorship system, which indicates a progression from administrative authorisation to a more market oriented mechanism.[106]

The first stage was a centralised quota control (1993–1995) system. At this stage the State Council securities administrative department formulated a total quota for the nation, and distributed it among administrative zones at provincial level and industries according to their importance to the national economy and their needs. The provincial governments or competent departments of industries then themselves determined which enterprises could issue shares. During this period 10.5 billion shares were issued in total, 5 billion in 1993 and 5.5 billion in 1995. About 200 enterprises (mainly state-owed enterprises) participated in the share issuance, with capitalisation of some 40 billion *yuan* in total.

---

after the revision of the Company Law and Securities Law in 2005), as well as information disclosure rules. Since the promulgation of the revised Company Law and Securities Law, a new campaign on corporate governance was formally launched in March 2007 that are to be completed by the end of October 2007. See the lengthy Notice on Certain Issues Concerning the Special Campaign to Strengthen Corporate Governance in Listed Companies, issued on 9 March 2007 by the CSRC.

104 The CSRC first issued the Guideline for the Classification of Listed Companies in China on 7 April 1999. Although the 2001 Guideline does not expressly abolish the old one, the 1999 Guideline is assumed to have become automatically invalid.

105 Provisional Regulation on the Administration of the Issuing and Trading of Stocks, issued by the State Council on 22 April 1993. While this set of regulation remains valid, most of its contents are now out of date.

106 See 'Comment on the Evolution of the Supervision and Administration System for Share Issuance in China', available from Xinhua News Agency: <news.xinhuanet.com/coments/2004-09/18/content_1993887.htm> (last accessed 2 August 2006). The following summary is based on this article, and statistics contained in the following paragraphs are drawn from it.

The second stage represented a target control (1996–1999) system. During this time the State Council securities administrative department determined the total number of enterprises (the index) that could issue shares in a given period, while limiting the total value of shares, and assigned the index to various provincial governments and industries. The provincial governments or competent departments of industries would then select and recommend enterprises to the securities administrative departments according to the assigned index. The latter would verify the cases and determine which enterprises met the prescribed conditions to issue shares. In this period some 700 enterprises completed share issuance, with capitalisation of around 400 billion *yuan*. After 1 July 1999, when the Securities Law took effect, no more new indexes were issued, yet the 1997 index remained in place until 2001.

The third stage introduced the channel control (2001–2004) system. From March 2001 China began to implement a 'pass-way system'; that is, all comprehensive type securities companies were given certain 'channels' (i.e. the number of enterprises it might recommend to the stock exchange to issue shares). Generally a securities company with a lead underwriter qualification could have 2 to 9 channels. In this period some 200 enterprises took part in share issuance, with total capitalisation of about 200 billion *yuan*.

Since October 2004 China has implemented a sponsorship system, which represents the fourth stage.[107] Under this system, the government has given up its power to control the number of share issuers. Enterprises intending to issue shares need to find a securities company to act as their sponsor (*baojian ren*) in applying for share issuance, and the sponsors become responsible for review of the issuer's application documents and information disclosure, and for supervising the conduct of the issuer during the course of share issuance. The sponsor will bear joint liability for any wrongs on the part of the issuers that occur during the share issuance process. The sponsorship system is designed to assign a first gate-keeper to be in control of the quality of listed companies.[108] This system is further formalised in the newly revised Securities Law.[109]

From the above we can see that the quota control, target control and channel control system have all involved a high level of government interference, and the sponsorship system still falls within the orbit of a government verification system.

---

107 See Notice on Certain Issues Concerning the Trial Establishment of a Sponsorship System for Initial Share Issue (Order No. 162, 2004). This Notice has now been repealed by the Administrative Measures on Share Issue and Consignment Sale (2006).

108 For a more detailed examination of the sponsorship system, see Mao Baigen & Roland Sun, 'Upgrading the Sponsorship System: The CSRC Makes Moves to Enhance Market Quality', (April 2004) *China Law & Practice* 85.

109 See Article 11 of the Securities Law.

We can also see a significant attempt on the part of the Chinese government to reduce administrative interference in the stock market.

6.2. Types of Shares

Shares in China are classified into A-shares, B-shares, H-shares, N-shares, L-shares and S-shares, depending on the types of investors who are eligible for purchasing shares and the places where the shares may be listed. The importance of the classification of shares is declining due to the opening of the B-shares market to domestic individual investors in early 2001, and more recently the opening of the A-shares market to foreign strategy investors, and China's accession to the WTO. The two markets are however yet to be fully merged into one.

A-shares

A-shares are registered shares issued by enterprises established in the PRC. Until recently these shares could only be owned or traded by PRC citizens on domestic stock markets. A-shares are denominated, sold and purchased in *Renminbi*.

B-shares

B-shares, officially known as '*Renminbi* Special Category Shares', are registered shares offered inside China. They are denominated in *Renminbi* but are subscribed for and traded in foreign currency. Initially, PRC citizens and entities inside China were not permitted to own or trade in B-shares, as the creation of B-shares was meant to create a parallel securities market for foreign investors in China. On 19 February 2001 the CSRC decided to open China's B-share market to domestic individual investors. Domestic institutional investors are, however, still excluded.

As of the end of 2005 there were 109 listed companies that had issued a total of 19.47 billion B-shares, raising 38.08 billion *yuan* in total.[110]

H-shares and other shares

'H-shares' in the narrow definition refers to shares issued by mainland companies on the Hong Kong market. More generally, they refer to shares which are issued and traded exclusively on foreign stock markets by companies incorporated in the PRC. As a general term, 'H-shares' covers H-shares, N-shares, L-shares and S-shares for shares listed in Hong Kong, New York, London and Singapore respectively.

110 See CSRC Report 2006, *supra* note 38, at 10.

Tradable and non-tradable shares

With regard to the ability to circulate shares, these are also classified in China into two broad categories: non-tradable and tradable shares. With the guiding ideology of maintaining the dominant position of state-owned entities, most shares in China were non-tradable until recently. By the end of 1998 the total non-tradable equity of listed companies was around 166.5 billion *yuan*, i.e. 65.89% of the total equity of all listed companies. As at the end of 2005 the 1,381 mostly state-owned listed companies had a combined market capitalisation of 3,243 billion *yuan* (US$ 405 billion), of which about 67% were non-tradable, and among the non-tradable shares the state owned some 74%.[111] However, this situation is expected to change within the foreseeable future. A pilot scheme to convert the non-tradable to tradable shares was launched by the CSRC in April 2005, and by March 2006 there were 768 listed companies (accounting for 57% of all listed companies) in the scheme. This pilot scheme was expected to be completed by the end of 2006,[112] but there has been no report on the completion.

6.3. The Mini Legal Framework

Despite a series of reforms in relation to the issuing of shares, public offering of securities is still firmly controlled by the government by way of prescribing criteria as well as imposing approval requirements, both of which are undertaken by the CSRC or the departments authorised by the State Council. As such, there are a host of departmental rules under the Securities Law, which effectively constitute a rather complicated and constantly changing mini legal framework controlling the issuing of shares in China.[113]

---

[111] See CSRC Report 2006, *supra* note 38, at 5-6.

[112] *Ibid.*

[113] The principal rules on the issuing of shares and bonds include: the Measures on Administration of the Initial Public Issuing and Listing of Shares, issued by the CSRC (Order No. 32) on 17 May 2006 and effective the next day (these Measures repealed several CSRC notices including the 2003 Notice on Further Regulation of Work Related to the Initial Public Offering and Listing of Shares; the Administrative Measures on Securities Issuance and Consignment Sale, issued by the CSRC (Order No. 37) on 17 September 2006 and effective from the 19th of the same month (which also repealed a series of CSRC prior rules and notices); the Provisional Measures on the System of Sponsorship of the Issuing and Listing of Securities, issued by the SCRC (Order No. 18) on 28 December 2003 (effective from 1 February 2004); the Measures on Guidance Work for the Initial Public Issuing of Shares, issued by the CSRC on 16 October 2001 and effective on the same day; the Measures on the Administration of the Issue of Securities by Listed Companies, issued by the CSRC on 6 May 2006 (Order No. 30) (the Measures replaced several sets of previous measures and notices of the CSRC, including the Measures on the Administration of the Issue of New Shares by Listed Companies 2001, the Notice on Making Efforts in the Work of Issuing New Shares by Listed Companies 2001, and the Notice on Issuing Additional Shares by Listed Companies 2002); and the Provisional

6.4. Information Disclosure

Certain strict disclosure requirements are set out in the Securities Law. The disclosure requirements apply to a wide range of parties and to all major documents and reports that are submitted and issued, including share listing reports, prospectuses, methods of corporate bond offering, financial accounting reports, annual reports and mid-term reports, interim reports, etc.

Issuers and listed companies have an obligation to continuously disclose information and to ensure that all disclosed information is true, accurate and complete and does not contain false information, misleading representation or major omissions. If they fail to do so the issuers will bear compensation liability for investors' losses therefrom; the directors, supervisors, senior managerial personnel and other directly responsible persons of the issuer or the listed company, and the sponsor, underwriter and controlling shareholders or actual controlling parties who are at fault will bear several and joint liability for compensation with the issuer or the listed company.[114]

Again, specific rules on information disclosure are issued by the CSRC in the form of departmental rules and Codes on Information Disclosure for the various reporting obligations.[115]

7. Trading of Securities

According to the Securities Law, securities that are not issued and paid for through legal means are prohibited from being traded. All listed trading of securities must be conducted publicly at stock exchanges or other securities trading centres approved by the State Council. Trading must conform to the method of centralised price competition or other methods approved by the CSRC, and in accordance with the

---

Measures on the Administration of Bonds of Securities Companies, issued by the CSRC on 29 August 2003 (amended on 15 October 2004).

114 See Article 69 of the Securities Law.

115 E.g. Administrative Measures on Information Disclosure by Listed Companies, issued by the CSRC on 30 January 2007 and effective on promulgation (as a result, several interim measures and notices issued by the CSRC have now been repealed); Code No. 17 on the Information Disclosure of Companies that Issue Shares to the Public – Special Rules on the Contents and Format of the Prospectuses Issued by Foreign Investment Companies Limited By Shares issued by the CSRC on 19 March 2002; Code No. 20 on the Contents and Format of Information Disclosed by Public Securities Issuing Companies – Application Documents for Issuing Bonds by Securities Companies, Code No. 21 on the Contents and Format of Information Disclosed by Public Securities Issuing Companies – Prospectus of Securities Company Bonds, Code No. 22 on Contents and Format of Information Disclosed by Public Securities Issuing Companies – Announcement on the Listing of Bonds by Securities Companies, and Rules on Information Disclosure on the Private Sale of Bonds by Securities Companies, etc.

principle that the highest and earliest offers have priority. Previously securities trading could only be conducted through spot transactions, but the new Securities Law now allows other forms stipulated by the State Council, in addition to spot trading. This revision is designed to leave room for future development, especially in areas of financial and other securities derivatives.

With regard to the listing of shares and company bonds, many of the rules on initial offering are applicable. In terms of trading regulation the focus is on the prevention of insider trading and other fraudulent practices. Thus the Securities Law bans certain organisations and persons from engaging in securities trading,[116] either to avoid conflicts of interest or insider trading, or as a penalty for violation of the Securities Law. These provisions of the Securities Law have now been further elaborated by the Provisions on the Banning of Entry into the Securities Market.[117] Insider trading,[118] manipulation of the market[119] and fraudulent practices[120] are all prohibited by the Securities Law.

8. Special Rules on B-Shares

As mentioned earlier, in 1991 the Shanghai and Shenzhen stock exchanges began to offer and trade in B-shares, which for the first time provided foreign investors with a legal channel to invest in China's equity markets. Certain domestic or overseas securities dealers were designated as brokers specially licensed to accept foreign investors' consignments for trading. In 1994 these stock exchanges began to offer special seats for B-share trading, and overseas securities dealers were allowed to engage in floor trading via the seats.

For quite some time before the establishment of a national regulatory scheme B-shares were regulated by the Shanghai and Shenzhen securities authorities. The CSRC is now responsible for the regulation and supervision of issuance and trading, and of related activities, concerning B-shares.

In December 1995 the first piece of national law on B-shares, the Regulations of the State Council on Foreign Capital Shares Listed in China by Companies Limited

116 See Article 43 and 45 of the Securities Law.

117 Issued by the CSRC on 7 June 2006 and effective on 10 July 2006. These Provisions repealed an earlier set of Interim Provisions on the Banning of Entry into the Securities Market, issued by the CSRC on 3 March 1997

118 See Article 74 (defining 'insiders') and Article 75 (defining 'inside information') of the Securities Law.

119 See Article 77 (defining 'acts of manipulation') of the Securities Law.

120 See Article 79 (defining the scope of fraud) of the Securities Law.

by Shares, was promulgated with immediate effect.[121] In May 1996 the Detailed Rules for the Implementation of the Regulations of the State Council on Foreign Capital Shares Listed in China by Companies Limited by Shares were also issued by the then State Council Securities Committee (now CSRC), and took effect on the same day as the B-share Regulations. Since then a number of rules and regulations concerning B-share companies and the issuing and trading of B-shares have been issued by the CSRC on an *ad hoc* basis. More recently efforts have been made to establish a uniform and systematic legal framework for securities law which would provide a wider coverage, without the distinction of various types of shares. One example is the Measures on the Administration of the Issue of New Shares by Listed Companies promulgated on 28 March 2001.[122]

The number of foreign currency holders in China has grown greatly in recent years, and their savings have increased sharply. These residents' savings have largely been used by domestic banks to buy bonds overseas. In order to prevent excessive capital outflow and to prepare for entering the WTO, the CSRC decided on 19 February 2001 to open China's B-share market to domestic individual investors.[123] As also mentioned earlier, China's WTO membership has led to the gradual opening up of the A-share market to foreign investors, although under certain strict conditions. Thus it is expected that the B-shares and A-shares markets will eventually merge into one.

9. Legal Liabilities for Violations of the Securities Law

Like the Company Law, the Securities Law contains a lengthy chapter (Chapter 11 in 48 Articles) setting forth detailed and harsh penalties for various kinds of violations of the Securities Law. Although most penalties are administrative and civil punishments, including warnings, forfeiture of unlawful income, fines, and

121 The Regulations, as subsidiary legislation of the national Company Law, repealed the Administrative Measures of Shanghai Municipality Governing *Renminbi* Special Category Shares (issued on November 22, 1991) and the Provisional Measures of Shenzhen Municipality for the Administration of *Renminbi* Special Category Shares (issued on December 5, 1991). Although there is no express repeal of the many implementing and ancillary rules under these two local Measures, it can be assumed that such local implementing and ancillary rules have also been repealed by implication

122 These Measures have now been replaced by the Securities Issue Measures of 2006. The 2001 Measures replaced the Provisional Measures on the Issue of B-shares for Capital Increased by Foreign Capital Share (B-share) Companies (1999).

123 See Notice on Certain Issues Relating to Investment in Listed Foreign Capital Shares by Individuals Residing Inside China, jointly issued by the CSRC and the State Administration of Foreign Exchange on 21 February 2001.

revocation of business licences, some of these Articles also impose criminal liability on activities which are serious in their circumstances.

10. Concluding Remarks

Several concluding remarks may be made about the Chinese securities regulation and its development so far.

Importantly, the development of a securities market has witnessed a major transformation in the politico-economic system in post-Mao China. It has been a potent symbol of not just a socialist market economy but also of a capitalist economy. The perception of a securities market and the conception of its functions in the economy have undergone some highly significant changes in politico-economic and legal circles, to the extent that most people have forgotten the initial perceived functions that a securities market might perform in a socialist country.

However, while there is now a uniform scheme for securities regulation, consisting of the several principal national laws on companies, securities and securities investment funds and administered by the CSRC, actual regulation of the securities market is still largely governed by a large body of *ad hoc* rules that are not necessarily consistent, nor up-to-date. Although the 2005 revision of the Company Law and the Securities Law has now provided a clearer delineation between company law and securities law, there is still overlapping between the two branches of law, which are still administered by two different state authorities. The lack of timely revision of secondary rules to reflect the changes in the 2005 revision of the Company Law and the Securities Law is a rather serious problem that will probably continue for a few years to come.

Whatever the changes, there continues to be a strong element of government control. Most listed companies are still state-owned[124] and the emphasis of the rules

[124] This however may change in the coming years. Since 2002 China has allowed foreign investors to acquire state-owned listed companies (see Notice Regarding Issues Relating to the Transfer of State-owned Shares and Legal Person Shares of Listed Companies to Foreign Investors (2002); Interim Provisions on the Use of Foreign Capital to Reform State-owned Enterprises (2002), and Interim Provisions on the Merger and Acquisition of Domestic Enterprises by Foreign Investors of 2003 (the 2003 Interim Provisions have now been replaced by Provisions on the Merger and Acquisition of Domestic Enterprises by Foreign Investors (2006)). After the recent reform of converting non-tradeable state-owned shares to tradeable shares, the State Council State Assets Administration (in conjunction with the CSRC) issued the following three sets of regulations on 30 June 2007: Interim Measures on the Administration of the Transfer of State-owned Shares in Listed Companies, Interim Provisions on the Administration of State-owned Enterprises Transferring Shares in Listed Companies, and Interim Provisions on the Administration of the Identification of State-owned Shares in Listed Companies. These regulations were issued to facilitate the controlled transfer of state-owned shares in listed companies in accordance with market and state needs.

and regulations is still placed heavily on the monitoring, supervisory, approval or veto functions of the CSRC. While the CSRC is making strenuous efforts to address serious concerns about government intervention by providing detailed operational rules, such efforts do not change the nature of the regulations.

The continuing strict government control and supervision needs to be understood not only through the realisation that the securities market is still at an early stage of development, but also by recognising that a sound system of corporate governance is yet to be established in China. The recent emphasis on information disclosure is an important part of the government's efforts to shift supervision of the market from government control to market forces by way of improving corporate governance. However, significant improvement in corporate governance lies not just in enforcing information disclosure, the appointment of independent directors, the establishment of several and joint civil liabilities, the imposition of severe criminal liabilities etc. Fighting against corruption, market fraud, and other misconduct in the market must be facilitated by a political reform that would establish some checks and balances among authorities and persons holding state powers.

Finally, whatever the problems the Chinese securities market and industry are facing, they must be understood from a developmental perspective. After all, the securities market has only been established in the People's Republic for a very short time and a sound (modern) corporate system is yet to be established in China. Despite all the difficulties in the last years, the trend in China has been clear: a shift from government control to that of market forces by way of improving corporate governance, but such a shift is yet to be completed and the market is yet to mature.

Chapter Fifteen

Enterprise Bankruptcy Law

1. Introduction

Enterprise bankruptcy, particularly the bankruptcy of state-owned enterprises (SOEs), has been the source of political controversy and struggle ever since its possibility was raised in post-Mao China.[1] Traditionally, it is strongly believed by the Chinese that 'a debt must be paid' (*qianqian huanzhai*) and that 'a father's debt must be paid by his sons' (*fuzhai zihuan*).[2] Thus, the idea of bankruptcy does not sit comfortably with the traditional conception of debts and repayment. Politically also, the idea of bankruptcy is both alien and contradictory to socialism, as property is meant to be predominantly owned by the 'whole people' or 'collectively owned'. Further, without strict separation of government and enterprises, bankruptcy processes are bound to be interfered with by administrative authorities. Thus the adoption of the Enterprise Bankruptcy Law of the People's Republic of China (hereinafter referred to as the 2006 Enterprise Bankruptcy Law) by the Standing Committee of the National People's Congress (SCNPC) on 27 August 2006 represents one of the most significant legal developments in establishing a legal framework governing and regulating a market economy.[3] While the new Enterprise Bankruptcy Law is not a complete code on bankruptcy, it is the most comprehensive one so far promulgated in the PRC on this matter.

---

1 For an excellent record of this political struggle, see Cao Siyuan, *The Storm Over Bankruptcy* (*Pochan Fengyun*) (Beijing: Zhongyan Bianyi Press, 1996). This text is translated in *Chinese Law and Government*, nos 1 & 2, 1998. See also Ta-kuang Chang, 'The Making of the Chinese Bankruptcy Law: A Study in the Chinese Legislative Process', (no. 2, 1987) 28 *Harvard Int'l L. J.* 333; and Ricky Tung, 'The Bankruptcy System of Mainland China's State-owned Enterprises', (no. 1, 1997) 33 *Issues & Studies* 23.

2 See An Jian & Wu Gaosheng (eds), *A Practical Text on Enterprise Bankruptcy Law* (*Qiye Pochanfa Shiyong Jiaocheng*) (Beijing: China Legal Publishing House, 2006), at 1.

3 The 2006 Enterprise Bankruptcy Law became effective from 1 June 2007 and replaced the 1986 Enterprise Bankruptcy Law.

Officially, the drafting of the 2006 Enterprise Bankruptcy Law started in 1994; thus the process took some 12 years to complete.[4] In reality, the initial idea of enacting such a law had emerged much earlier than 1994, and the history of this law-making reflects not only the gradual changes in the politico-legal system in China, but also the triumph of market ideologies over socialist ideals. This Chapter reviews the legislative history of the 2006 Enterprise Bankruptcy Law, focusing on the major issues contested during the drafting processes. It also examines the limits, new developments, and significance of the new Law in China's drive towards a market economy.

2. A Historical Review of Bankruptcy Law in China

China's bankruptcy law can be traced back to as early as 1906 when the first bankruptcy law was formulated during the Qing Dynasty as 'the Bankruptcy Rules', although this was abandoned one year later. In 1915 the Republic of China completed a draft bankruptcy law, which was promulgated and implemented in 1935.[5] After the founding of the PRC in 1949 the 1935 Bankruptcy Law was abolished, as were all other laws enacted by the Republic of China. In order to deal with issues relating to unpaid debts by private enterprises at that time, the Supreme People's Court and the Ministry of Justice jointly issued, in October 1955, the Reply on Two Issues Concerning the Procedures for Repayment of Debts by Bankrupt Private Enterprises. In January 1957 the Supreme People's Court again issued the Reply on Several Issues Concerning Bankruptcy Liquidation.[6] Soon, however, socialist transformation was declared complete and private enterprises largely ceased to exist. Thereafter for a period of some 30 years the PRC did not have, and indeed did not need, any bankruptcy law under its socialist planned economy.[7]

---

4 See Jia Zhijie, 'Explanations on the Draft Enterprise Bankruptcy Law of the PRC', delivered at the Tenth Meeting of the Standing Committee of the Tenth NPC on 21 June 2004, available from <www.people.com.cn/GB.14576/28320/34543/34546/259854.html> (last accessed 24 July 2004).

5 See Cao Siyuan, 'The Legislation and Implementation of China's Bankruptcy Law in the Past Ten Years', *Modern China Study* (Issue No. 2, 1997) available at <www.usc.cuhk.edu.hk/wk_WZdetals.asp?id=1028> (last accessed 12 September 2006).

6 See An & Wu, *supra* note 2, at 4.

7 As pointed out by Wang Weiguo, under the socialist planned economy the transfer of funds and supply of materials between enterprises were not conducted on the basis of credits and debts in any meaningful sense; they were established simply as 'adjustment in accordance with state plans'. See Wang Weiguo, 'The Adoption of Enterprise Rescue in China: A Comparative View', in Wang Weiguo & Roman Tomasic (eds), *Reform of PRC Securities and Insolvency Laws* (*Zhongguo Zhenquanfa Pochanfa Gaige*) (Beijing: Press of the China University of Political Science and Law, 1999), at 9.

After China began its economic reform and open-door policy in the late 1970s the question of debt repayment re-emerged. Thus, Article 180 of the 1982 Civil Procedure Law (Trial Implementation)[8] established, in its Chapter 17 on Execution Measures, a priority order for debt repayment in situations where an enterprise's assets would not be sufficient for such repayment. However the word 'bankruptcy' did not appear in the Law. Scholars were among the first to float the idea of bankruptcy in a socialist country. Chief among them was Cao Siyuan, a prominent Chinese scholar, who in 1980 began to promote the idea of China re-introducing a bankruptcy law.[9] Officially, the Proposal on Several Issues concerning Scientific and Technological Advancement and the Promotion of Economic Development, drafted by the State Council Centre for the Study of Technology and Economics, was the first formal draft document to advocate the use of bankruptcy as a means to jettison 'backward' enterprises and to promote technological advancement for enterprises.[10] In May 1984 some NPC deputies attending the Second Session of the Sixth NPC moved a motion in favour of enacting a bankruptcy law. In December 1984 the State Council agreed that a drafting team be established by the State Council's Economic Law Research Centre in collaboration with other government departments.[11] In January 1985 Cao Siyuan was appointed by the State Council as the head of the China bankruptcy law drafting team. In January the following year a draft bankruptcy law, together with a draft law on bankruptcy assistance, was submitted to the State Council and was approved.[12] But when the law was submitted to the SCNPC for its deliberation, it stirred up a storm of debate:[13] Opposition opinions dominated the meeting of the SCNPC (of the 50 members speaking at the meeting, 41 voted against and only 9 for the law). The draft thus failed, but debate continued and went nationwide. After a year-long discussion and debate, on 2 December 1986 a heavily watered down version of the law (after heavy editing from 11,000 words down to 4800 words), the Law of the People's Republic of China on Enterprise Bankruptcy (Trial Implementation) (hereinafter referred to as the 1986 Enterprise Bankruptcy Law) was finally adopted by the SCNPC.[14] However, it took nearly another three years before the Law took effect.[15] Nevertheless, this enactment of a bankruptcy law

---

8 Now replaced by the 1991 Civil Procedure Law.

9 See *supra* notes 1 & 5.

10 An & Wu, *supra* note 2, at 5.

11 An & Wu, *supra* note 2, at 5.

12 See Cao Siyuan, *supra* note 5.

13 Within a year some 357 articles were published in China. See Cao Siyuan, *supra* note 5. See also *supra* note 1.

14 With 101 votes for, 9 abstentions, and none against. See Cao Siyuan, *supra* note 5.

15 Under Article 43 of the 1986 Enterprise Bankruptcy Law, the Law would only be effective three months after the implementation of a yet to be enacted Law on State Industrial Enterprises.

in 1986 signalled the country's transition from a socialist planned economy to a market-oriented one, although its primary objective was to improve the efficiency and productivity of SOEs, rather than to jettison loss-making enterprises.[16]

While the enactment of the 1986 Enterprise Bankruptcy Law represented a major ideological breakthrough in socialist practice, the Law was soon proven to be of limited usefulness. First, the Law applied only to SOEs 'which have suffered serious losses and are unable to clear their debts within a fixed period of time because of poor management'.[17] The dramatic growth in the private economic sector soon exposed the serious limitations of the 1986 Law. Even among SOEs the major and important public utilities and enterprises could not be declared bankrupt if the government was providing them with financial assistance. Similarly protected from bankruptcy proceedings were enterprises which had obtained guarantees that their debts would be paid within six months of a bankruptcy petition having been filed.[18] Secondly, the bankruptcy law was far too general and vague, with only 6 chapters and 42 articles in total, and thus difficult to implement. The definition of bankruptcy quoted above was itself unclear and left much room for government intervention.[19] Thus, even though 40% of SOEs were reported to be running at a loss up to the end of 1991,[20] no SOE had been declared bankrupt despite the fact that the 1986 Bankruptcy Law

---

The latter law was finally enacted on 13 April 1988, taking effect from 1 August 1988. Hence, the 1986 Enterprise Bankruptcy Law took effect on 1 November 1988.

16 Wang Weiguo, *supra* note 7, at 9.

17 Article 3 of the 1986 Enterprise Bankruptcy Law.

18 Article 3 of the 1986 Enterprise Bankruptcy Law.

19 In fact, Article 3 of the 1986 Enterprise Bankruptcy Law specifically provided that 'Upon a bankruptcy application being lodged by a creditor against an enterprise, should the higher level department in charge request re-structuring to be carried out, and in addition if the enterprise and the creditor meet and reach a conciliated agreement, the bankruptcy procedures shall be suspended.' The language of Article 3 of the 1986 Enterprise Bankruptcy Law, as Tomsic and Wang have pointed out, effectively subjected bankruptcy to government discretion. See Roman Tomasic & Margaret Wang, 'The Long March towards China's New Bankruptcy Law', in Roman Tomasic (ed.), *Insolvency Law in East Asia* (Hampshire, UK: Ashgate Publishing Limited, 2006), at 99.

20 See *Beijing Review*, 26 August – 1 September 1991, at 5. Another report indicated that a third of SOEs were in the red and a further third were plagued by 'hidden' debts. See *Beijing Review*, 10-16 August 1991, at 4. The percentage given by the State Council was lower. According to the State Council, as at the end of 1991, 29.7% of SOEs were running at a loss totalling 31 billion *yuan* with the situation worsening in the first quarter of 1992. See State Council Notice concerning Deepening the Work of Turning Enterprises from Loss into Profit, in (no. 13, 1992) *Gazette of the State Council of the PRC* (*Zhonghua Renmin Gongheguo Guowuyuan Gongbao*), at 445. The situation in 1993 and 1994 was no better. In 1993, 32% of SOEs had actual losses with another 30% having potential losses: 'An Overview of Reforming State-owned Enterprises', (no. 6, 1993) *Search* (*Qiusuo*), at 23-24, translated in (March 1994) *Inside China Mainland*, at 26-32.

had been in effect since November 1988.[21] The fundamental difficulty in enforcing the 1986 Enterprise Bankruptcy Law was that decisions to liquidate SOEs had always been made by local governments or administrative authorities rather than by the SOEs themselves or their creditors according to their financial status.[22]

In light of the problems with the 1986 Enterprise Bankruptcy Law and difficulties in its implementation, further political and legal efforts began to emerge in 1991. First, a new Civil Procedure Law was adopted on 9 April 1991 (and effective on the same day), which contained a new chapter on bankruptcy debt repayment procedures and was applicable to all enterprises with legal person status.[23] Further, in November 1991 the Supreme People's Court issued its Notice on Certain Issues concerning the Implementation of the Enterprise Bankruptcy Law (Trial Implementation). Then in July 1992 the Supreme People's Court further issued its Opinions on Certain Issues concerning the Application of the Civil Procedure Law of the PRC, which elaborated the Civil Procedure Law provisions on bankruptcy debt repayment in Chapter 16 on Enterprise Legal Person Bankruptcy Debt Repayment Procedures (Articles 240-253). With these legal actions in place, serious efforts to enforce the 1986 Enterprise Bankruptcy Law began to be made in the first half of 1992.[24] Thus we saw a major increase in court cases on bankruptcy: 428 in 1992, 710 in 1993, 1625 in 1994, and 2385 in 1995.[25]

The above statistics indicate a major increase in bankruptcy cases in the Chinese courts. It is however unclear how many of these cases involved SOEs. The then widely discussed 'triangular debt' (*Sanjiao Zhai*) problem seemed to suggest that there was not much success with the SOEs. 'Triangular debts' were debts between enterprises and banks. Their peculiar nature was that enterprises found themselves in a circle in which each owed debts to and owned credits from the others. But in this circle, none of them was able or willing to pay their debts, as none of them could claim back their credits from the others to pay their own debts. Therefore they were deadlocked debts. As a result, banks stopped providing loans as they were unable to collect repayment of their previous loans and the related interest

21 See *Beijing Review*, 26 August – 1 September 1991, at 5. It is, however, possible that some SOEs were closed down but not reported as such in the official media. See *infra* note 42.

22 Wang Xinxin, 'On Operative Mechanisms of the Bankruptcy Law and Problems in Enforcing the Law', (no. 6, 1991) *Legal Science in China* (*Zhongguo Faxue*), at 90; 'Why Is It So Difficult to Declare Enterprises Bankrupt?', *Legal Daily* (*Fazhi Ribao*), 8 March 1994, at 7. All governments were reluctant to have enterprises declared bankrupt as such a declaration would be seen as a failure in their work and might negatively affect their career development. See Cao Siyuan, *supra* note 5.

23 This chapter, however, contains only 8 articles. It could not solve the problem of the lack of specificity on procedural and substantive matters concerning bankruptcy practice.

24 It is reported that 15 SOEs went bankrupt in the first half of 1992. See *People's Daily* (*Renmin Ribao*), (overseas edition), 7 August 1992, at 1.

25 Cao Siyuan, *supra* note 5.

from enterprises; this in turn left enterprises without sufficient operating funds for the purchase of materials, for production, and even for the payment of salaries to their employees. Taking into consideration that the property of SOEs at the time amounted to some 70% of national fixed capital, and that their profits and taxes supposedly amounted to 80% of national financial income, and that 90% of SOEs were said to be involved in this 'triangular debt' problem to some degree,[26] the severity of the problem becomes clear.[27] Although Chinese economists identified many reasons for this 'debt crisis', the fundamental cause was that debt collection could not be enforced upon the property of SOEs since they were seen as state property.[28] One Chinese newspaper commented on the property situation in SOEs as follows:

> Yours is mine and mine is yours; after all it is the state's. I owe you and you owe me; after all we all owe the state. Delaying repayment of debts is seen as reasonable and denying debts is seen as profitable.[29]

Since SOEs were unable to resolve their debts, although they were legal persons solely responsible for their own profits and losses, the central government had to step in with administrative measures and financial assistance. A Leading Group on Clearing the 'Triangular Debt', headed by the then Vice-premier Zhu Rongji, was established in 1990 within the State Council, with similar Groups established in provincial governments and ministries, and a number of national and regional conferences were held to resolve the debt crisis.[30] In 1991 and 1992 the State Council injected 51 billion *yuan* to deal with the 'triangular debt' problem, and it was then claimed that the deadlock had been broken, and the official assistance from the State Council to clear the debts ended on 23 December 1992.[31] However, the same

---

[26] *China Youth Daily* (*Zhongguo Qingnian Bao*), 17 August 1991, at 3. The figure concerning SOEs' profits and taxes is however doubtful. See Jianfu Chen, *From Administrative Authorisation to Private Law: A Comparative Perspective of the Developing Civil Law in the People's Republic of China* (Dordrecht/Boston/London: Martinus Nijhoff Publishers, 1995), at 132-135.

[27] Total 'triangular debt' as at the end of March 1991 stood at 142.8 billion *yuan*. See *China Youth Daily* (*Zhongguo Qingnian Bao*), 5 August 1991, at 3.

[28] Extreme measures, such as kidnapping factory directors' children, kidnapping debtors and using torture upon them, as well as hunger-strikes by, ironically creditors, were used by some enterprises to recover their credits. See a series of reports published in *China Youth Daily* (*Zhongguo Qingnian Bao*), 22 August 1991, at 1; 26 August 1991, at 1; 28 August 1991, at 1; 4 September 1991, at 1; 6 September 1991, at 1; and 9 September 1991, at 1.

[29] *China Youth Daily* (*Zhongguo Qingnian Bao*), 28 August 1991, at 1.

[30] See State Council Notice concerning Clearing 'Triangular Debts' Nationwide, in *China Law Yearbook 1991* (*Zhongguo Falü Nianjian*) (Beijing: China Law Yearbook Press, 1991), at 275.

[31] *People's Daily* (*Renmin Ribao*) (overseas edition), 18 August 1992, at 1; *People's Daily* (*Renmin Ribao*) (overseas edition), 26 December 1992, at 1.

reports also noted that new 'triangular debts' were also emerging in some provinces, despite the repeated government declaration of its intention not to help to resolve any new debts incurred in 1992, since which time local governments would have to be responsible for any debts they incurred.[32]

The root of the problem lay in the system of property rights.[33] The government was warned by economists in China that without a reform of the system of property rights in SOEs, the 'triangular debt' could become a 'black hole' where money might simply 'disappear'.[34] Indeed, the 'triangular debt' not only re-appeared, but increased in some provinces in the early 1990s. For instance, in Liaoning Province 'triangular debts' increased from 22 billion *yuan* in early 1991 to 47 billion *yuan* in 1994.[35] A new cycle of government intervention thus began.[36] However, neither could the government afford, nor it was willing, to fill this 'black hole' for ever. A trade-off between enterprise autonomy and self-responsibility (with limited liability), in lieu of full privatisation, was to be worked out through enterprise reform in the form of corporatisation.

In December 1993, the Company Law was enacted.[37] The Company Law, for the first time, provided some uniform criteria for enterprise bankruptcy, without

---

32 The work to clear 'triangular debts' was officially declared finished and the Leading Group was dissolved at the end of 1992 after a total injection of 55.5 billion *yuan*. See 'Report on the Work to Clear "Triangular Debts" Nationwide', in (no. 4, 1993) *Gazette of the State Council of the PRC* (*Zhonghua Renmin Gongheguo Guowuyuan Gongbao*), at 166-171.

33 As discussed in Chapter 10, a property law, the *Law on Rights in rem*, was adopted by the National People's Congress on 15 March 2007, which will become effective on 1 October 2007. Under Articles 55 and 67 of the *Law on Rights in rem*, property rights of the state-owned property are to be exercised by the State Council or local governments, but only their rights as capital contributors in the enterprises, in accordance with prior agreements or in proportion to their shareholding in the enterprises. While the owners of state-owned property are now clearly defined as the whole people represented by governments at different levels, it is difficult to see how the actual exercise of such rights might change in practice, when the state holds the majority shareholding in an enterprise.

34 See *China Youth Daily* (*Zhongguo Qingnian Bao*), 26 August 1991, at 1; 4 September 1991, at 1. In fact, the so-called 'triangular debt' was not a new phenomenon in China; it had already happened in the 1950s. Experiences in the 1990s made economists much less confident than politicians. During a period of ten years (1980–1990s) the amount of total 'triangular debt' had multiplied 40 times. See *China Youth Daily*, 17 August 1991, at 3, and 9 September 1991, at 1.

35 See 'Triangular Debt Reappears', *Wenhua Po* (Hong Kong), 14 March 1994, at 2, translated in *Inside China Mainland*, May 1994, at 44-5.

36 *Id.*; 'Report on the Work of the Government', delivered by Li Peng on 10 March 1994, in *Beijing Review*, 4-10 April 1994, I-XVI, at VIII; 'State Began Clearing Up Debts for Key Industries in North-east Region', *Economic Daily* (*Jingji Ribao*), 20 May 1994, at 2.

37 The Company Law has since been amended three times in December 1999, August 2004 and October 2005 respectively. See discussion in Chapter 13.

regard to types of enterprise ownership, while also establishing the notion of limited liability. Thus, if a company is unable to discharge matured liabilities and is declared bankrupt by a people's court, the court is required to organise shareholders, interested parties and relevant professionals to form a liquidation committee in accordance with the law.[38]

Also importantly, in the absence of a comprehensive code on bankruptcy local legislative authorities went ahead to enact their own rules. Guangdong Province was the first one to issue bankruptcy regulations on 14 May 1993, and this was followed by similar regulations issued by Shenzhen (10 November 1993). Local regulations on the liquidation of foreign investment enterprises were also issued in Shenzhen, Shanghai, Beijing and other places. On 9 July 1996 the Measures on Liquidation Procedures for Foreign Investment Enterprises were promulgated by the then Ministry of Foreign Trade and Economic Cooperation (now Ministry of Commerce).

Other national laws and regulations also contain provisions or possibilities for bankruptcy, including all the enterprise laws as well as the Commercial Bank Law (1995) and the Insurance Law (1995). More importantly, the State Council began its 'planned' bankruptcy (often referred to, ironically, as 'policy bankruptcy' or 'administrative bankruptcy') trial in early 1994.[39] Initially the trial was to be conducted in 10 cities. However, because of the financial support provided by the Central Government many more local governments wanted to participate in the trial scheme and the trial was thus conducted in 18 cities selected by the State Structural Reform Commission, with seven billion *yuan* injected by the State into these cities to help bankrupt enterprises to repay their debts.[40] Before long, the scheme was extended to 58 cities (including all provincial capital cities) and then to 111 cities by 1997,[41] and by 1998, it was applicable to all SOEs nationwide.[42]

---

38 Article 189 of the original 1993 Company Law.

39 This was formally launched by the State Council Notice on Relevant Issues concerning the Trial of State-owned Enterprise Bankruptcy in Certain Cities, issued by the State Council on 25 October 1994. A Chinese text is available from *A Complete Collection of Laws of the PRC* (*Zhonghua Renmin Gongheguo Falu Quanshu*), volume 5 (Changchun: Jilin People's Press, 1995), at 551-553.

40 Cao Siyuan, *supra* note 5.

41 See Li Shuguang, 'Bankruptcy Law in China: Lessons of the Past Twelve Years', available from <www.asiaquartely.com/content/view/95/40> (last accessed 30 November 2006). See also Supplementary Notice on Relevant Issues concerning the Trial of State-owned Enterprise Bankruptcy, Merger and Re-employment of workers in Certain Cities, issued by the State Council on 2 March 1997. A Chinese text is available from *A Complete Collection of Laws of the PRC* (*Zhonghua Renmin Gongheguo Falu Quanshu*), volume 8 (Changchun: Jilin People's Press, 1998), at 545-549.

42 An & Wu, *supra* note 2, at 179.

With these policies, national laws and local regulations in place, 1996 saw bankruptcy cases in the courts jump to 6,232, a 161% increase on the year before, which surpassed the combined number of cases of the previous seven years (1989–1995).[43]

More importantly, with experience in bankruptcy practice, it was clearly recognised that the 1986 Enterprise Bankruptcy Law conflicted with the new Company Law, Partnership Law and the Sole Investment Enterprise Law, and was outdated. Many provisions of the 1986 Enterprise Bankruptcy Law allowed, if they did not promote, government interference and control over bankruptcy procedures, and were obviously an obstacle to China's transition to a market-oriented economy. A new round of debates regarding the 1986 Enterprise Bankruptcy Law thus began, and so did the efforts to adopt a more comprehensive, up-to-date bankruptcy law.

In 1994 a draft bankruptcy law, consisting of 193 articles and covering all types of enterprise legal persons, was submitted to the SCNPC for deliberation and approval. Unfortunately the draft was held up in the national legislature and grounded there for more than a decade, never being scheduled for deliberation. The reasons were explained by the Finance and Economic Commission of the NPC in a speech at the submission of another draft Enterprise Bankruptcy Law to the SCNPC for first deliberation in 2004 as being that 'there were different opinions as to when it would be the right time to issue the law, and because of other considerations such as the lack of a corresponding social security system'.[44]

Meanwhile, in an effort to remedy the limitations of the 1986 Enterprise Bankruptcy Law so as to provide practical guidance to courts dealing with the increasing number of bankruptcy cases involving enterprises under different forms of ownership, the Supreme People's Court issued, on 7 July 2002, the Provisions on Certain Issues Relating to the Adjudication of Enterprise Bankruptcy Cases (hereinafter referred to as the 2002 Provisions). The 2002 Provisions,[45] containing 14 parts and 106 articles with detailed rules on enterprise bankruptcy proceedings, applied to any enterprise with legal person status, regardless of the type of ownership of the enterprise involved. In the absence of a comprehensive national bankruptcy law, these Provisions then acted as a *de facto* enterprise bankruptcy law.

---

43 Cao Siyuan, *supra* note 5. As in many other areas of law, statistics quoted by Chinese scholars are often different and often given without reference to sources. The following are two sets of total numbers of national of bankruptcy cases quoted by two prominent scholars in bankruptcy law: 98 (1989), 32 (1990), 117 (1991), 428 (1992), 710 (1993), 1,625 (1994), 2,583 (1995), 5,875 (1996) & 5,396 (1997) (Li Shuguang, *supra* note 41). 98 (1989), 32 (1990), 117 (1991), 428 (1992), 710 (1993), 1,625 (1994), 2,583 (1995), & 6,232 (1996) (Cao Siyuan, *supra* note 5).

44 See 'Explanations on the Draft Enterprise Bankruptcy Law of the PRC', *supra* note 4.

45 Effective from 1 September 2002.

The work of drafting a comprehensive enterprise bankruptcy law resumed in 2003 under the five-year legislation plan of the Standing Committee of the 10th NPC. The Finance and Economics Commission again took responsibility for the job. A new team was set up and the drafting work went smoothly and efficiently. In November 2003 a draft was completed and was sent to provinces, municipalities, autonomous regions and other relevant departments of the State Council for comment. After wide consultation with judges, local governments, enterprises and bankruptcy experts, on 28 May 2004 the Finance and Economics Commission submitted the draft to the General Office of the SCNPC and the State Council for approval. On 15 June 2004 a finalised draft (containing 164 articles in 11 chapters[46]) was submitted to the SCNPC for deliberation. After 12 years of drafting, discussion and deliberation, the Enterprise Bankruptcy Law of the People's Republic of China was finally adopted by the SCNPC on 27 August 2006,[47] and thus the PRC finally achieved its first comprehensive bankruptcy law.

3. Current Legal Framework on Bankruptcy

The 2006 Enterprise Bankruptcy Law is far more comprehensive than the 1986 Enterprise Bankruptcy Law. In an attempt to modernise China's bankruptcy rules it provides a wider legal structure for the country's increasingly market-driven economy. The objectives of the Law are 'to standardise enterprise bankruptcy procedures, to provide fair settlement of debts and credits, to protect the rights and lawful interests of creditors, and to safeguard the economic order of the socialist market economy.'[48] As such, the 2006 Enterprise Bankruptcy Law provides the principal legal framework regulating enterprise bankruptcy matters, both procedurally and substantively.

Like all other Chinese laws the 2006 Enterprise Bankruptcy Law, comprising 12 chapters and 136 articles, starts with general principles which define the purposes and scope of application of the law, court jurisdiction, and relationships with other existing laws. It is then followed by procedural rules on application for and acceptance of bankruptcy cases (Chapter Two). Chapters Three, Four and Five on Administrators, Property of Debtors, and Bankruptcy Costs and Debts of a Public Interest Nature contain both procedural and substantive requirements on these matters. Chapter Six on Declaration of Creditors' Rights again deals with largely procedural issues. However, Chapter Seven on Creditors' Meetings and Creditors' Committees covers both procedural and substantive issues. Chapter Eight and Nine, on Re-organisation and Conciliation respectively, form the principal rules on alternatives to bankruptcy

---

46 See 'Explanations on the Draft Enterprise Bankruptcy Law of the PRC', *supra* note 4. The final law contains 136 articles in 12 chapters.

47 With 157 votes for, 2 against and 2 abstentions. See An & Wu, *supra* note 2, at 9.

48 Article 1 of the 2006 Enterprise Bankruptcy Law.

and represent major improvements over the 1986 Enterprise Bankruptcy Law. Chapter Ten on Liquidation switches to procedural rules. Again, like all other Chinese laws, Chapter Eleven stipulates legal liabilities and legal consequences for breaches of the Bankruptcy Law and for causing bankruptcy in the first place. While Chapter Twelve looks short, it either extends the application of the Law to 'other organisations' not covered by the Law, or authorises or requires the State Council to issue implementation measures on specific matters, such as bankruptcy of financial institutions, and transitional arrangements for SOEs. Although bankruptcy law is defined as a special civil procedural law,[49] many substantive issues are in fact dealt with in the Bankruptcy Law, especially those relating to the 'institutions' of administrator and re-organisation, both of which are new mechanisms established by the 2006 Law.

When compared to the 1986 Enterprise Bankruptcy Law, the present Law represents some major legislative progress in this area. First, the scope of application of the Law has been extended to cover all types of enterprises that have legal person status, including SOEs and private enterprises, as well foreign investment enterprises, whether limited liability companies or companies limited by shares; whereas the 1986 Enterprise Bankruptcy Law applied to Chinese SOEs only. Secondly, in replacing the old system which put the government in charge of almost every stage of the bankruptcy process, the new Law implements a bankruptcy administrator system, allowing law firms, accounting firms, bankruptcy liquidation firms and other intermediary organisations to run formal enterprise bankruptcy procedures, which makes the handling of the bankruptcy process more professional and brings the Chinese bankruptcy law closer to international practice. Thirdly, the Law introduces a new re-organisation procedure, allowing insolvent enterprises and enterprises facing insolvency to continue to run their assets and businesses, so as to restructure them into viable businesses, instead of going into liquidation. And finally, while not ignoring workers' interests, the new Law tries to accord with international practice by providing better protection for creditors' interests, giving them more certainty and confidence in their right to recover their investment and claims when the debtor goes into bankruptcy.[50]

It should be pointed out that the 2006 Enterprise Bankruptcy Law is not the only law governing bankruptcy in China. The Company Law (as amended in 2005), the Civil Procedure Law (1991), the General Principles of Civil Law (1986) and the various enterprise laws continue to apply, especially where matters are not covered by the 2006 Law. Some foreign-related matters also continue to be regulated

---

49 See An & Wu, *supra* note 2, at 14.

50 See 'Explanations on the Draft Enterprise Bankruptcy Law of the PRC', *supra* note 4; 'Regulating Bankruptcy Procedures and Dealing with Credits and Debts Fairly – Three Experts Explain the New Enterprise Bankruptcy Law', *People's Court Daily* (*Renmin Fayuan Bao*), 6 September 2006, at 5.

by special measures. So, the Measures on Liquidation Procedures for Foreign Investment Enterprises (1996) will continue to serve as the primary legal tool for initiating liquidation proceedings by foreign investment enterprises in the PRC. Also importantly, the Provisions on Certain Issues related to the Adjudication of Enterprise Bankruptcy Cases are still valid judicial interpretations that will guide judicial practice in the near future.[51]

4. Breakthrough, Compromise & Limitations

4.1. Scope of the Law & Transitional Arrangements for SOEs

Defining the scope of application of the law was one of the major contentious issues that arose during the drafting process. As one of the initial objectives of the new law was to achieve some degree of unification and uniformity of law on enterprise bankruptcy, it has been clear from the very beginning that all enterprises, regardless of the form of ownership and the size of the enterprise, would be governed by the new law. However, disputes soon arose as to whether the proposed law should also regulate bankruptcy of the so-called Industrial and Commercial Households[52] and individuals. Chinese media reports suggest that by 2004 it had already been accepted that personal bankruptcy would not be included in the new law;[53] however,

---

51 It should however be pointed out that the 2002 Provisions were issued before the 2006 Enterprise Bankruptcy Law. Thus, many provisions may no longer be applicable. Also, any new interpretations issued by the Supreme People's Court will automatically supersede any conflicting provisions in the 2002 Provisions. So far (August 2007), three sets of new interpretations have been issued by the Supreme People's Court: the Provisions of the Supreme People's Court on Appointment of Administrators in Adjudicating Enterprise Bankruptcy Law (issued on 12 April 2007), the Provisions of the Supreme People's Court on the Determination of Remuneration for Administrators in the Adjudication of Enterprise Bankruptcy Cases (issued on 12 April 2007), and the Provisions of the Supreme People's Court on the Question of the Application of Law in relation to Bankruptcy Cases that Have not Yet Been Concluded by the Time of the Implementation of the Enterprise Bankruptcy Law of the PRC (issued on 25 April 2007). All these interpretations became effective from 1 June 2007 when the Enterprise Bankruptcy Law took effect in June 2007.

52 See 'Explanations on the Draft Enterprise Bankruptcy Law of the PRC', *supra* note 4; and An & Wu, *supra* note 2, at 11-13. As of 2004, there were some 23 million Industrial and Commercial Households in China (see 'Explanations on the Draft Enterprise Bankruptcy Law of the PRC', *supra* note 4). The Industrial and Commercial Households are essentially individual family businesses. See discussions in Chapter 13.

53 The reasons for this exclusion include that there was no major need for personal bankruptcy as Chinese consumption was generally constrained by the traditional idea of high saving, that there was no personal property and credit standing registration system, and that commercial banks were yet to establish their internal operating systems. See 'Ten Years of Bankruptcy

debate continued as to the inclusion of partnerships (and their partners) and sole investment enterprises (and their investors).[54] The drafting team took the view that the existence of a personal property registration system and a good credit standing environment would be a prerequisite for personal bankruptcy practice so as to prevent people from using bankruptcy as a means to avoid debts.[55] Thus, in the draft submitted to the SCNPC in 2004 the proposed law would cover all enterprise legal persons, partnership enterprises and their partners, sole investment enterprises and their investors, and other profit-seeking organisations. The 2006 Enterprise Bankruptcy Law as adopted by the NPC, however, narrows down its application to enterprise legal persons only.[56] At the same time Article 135 of the Law extends the application to liquidation of 'other organisations' 'by reference'. The meaning of this article is ambiguous, leaving many practical issues to be clarified by judicial interpretation or other implementation measures.[57] As such, the new Enterprise Bankruptcy Law does not expand the combined coverage of the 1986 Enterprise Bankruptcy Law and the 1991 Civil Procedure Law. However, the new Law unifies the jurisdictional issues and thus avoids some conflicts of laws.[58] With this narrow scope of application, the new Law is described by one of the Chinese scholars who also participated in the drafting as 'half of a bankruptcy law'.[59]

In the Chinese legal system the phrase 'enterprise legal persons' is an ideologically neutral term and covers all enterprises which qualify as 'legal persons' under the General Principles of Civil Law (1986). As an ideologically neutral phrase it disregards the socialist practice of classifying enterprises according to forms of ownership, or the Chinese bureaucratic practice of classifying enterprises according to their size, geographic location or administrative subordination relationship.[60] In other words, and for practical purposes, it means that the 2006 Enterprise Bankruptcy Law will be applicable to all companies and most foreign investment enterprises, but not to partnerships or individuals.

Law Drafting and Continuing Debate', in <finance.sina.com.cn> (last accessed 2 December 2004).

54 See *id.*

55 See 'Explanations on the Draft Enterprise Bankruptcy Law of the PRC', *supra* note 4. These were also the views held by those academics who advocated a narrow scope for the bankruptcy law to regulate enterprises only. See An & Wu, *supra* note 2, at 11-12.

56 See Article 2 of the 2006 Enterprise Bankruptcy Law.

57 Ju Wei, in 'Regulating Bankruptcy Procedures and Dealing with Credits and Debts Fairly – Three Experts Explain the New Enterprise Bankruptcy Law', *supra* note 50.

58 Ju Wei, *ibid.*

59 Li Shuguang, in 'An Analysis of the Three Hot Issues', <www.chinareviewnews.com> (last accessed 11 September 2006).

60 See discussions in Chapter 13.

While the Law is entitled 'bankruptcy' law, it is in fact about both bankruptcy and what the Chinese scholars refer to as 'enterprise rehabilitation' (*Qiye Zaisheng*) (i.e. conciliation and re-organisation).[61] Together, the three processes are collectively referred to as 'debt settlement' (*Zhaiwu Qingli*).[62] Accordingly, the 2006 Enterprise Bankruptcy Law establishes three different procedures – bankruptcy, conciliation, and re-organisation – the application scope of each being the same, that is, to enterprise legal persons, but the conditions for invoking them are not. Under Article 2 of the Enterprise Bankruptcy Law, debt settlement will be conducted according to the Law where an enterprise legal person is unable to repay its debts as they become due, and its assets are insufficient for the settlement of all debts, or where it is clearly insolvent. Where an enterprise legal person finds itself in this situation, or if there is a clear possibility of it being insolvent, re-organisation may be conducted. A debtor may apply to the people's court for re-organisation, reconciliation or bankruptcy liquidation, but a creditor may only apply for re-organisation or bankruptcy liquidation.[63] On the other hand an administrator must apply to a court for bankruptcy if the assets of the enterprise legal person are insufficient to pay debts after liquidation, or if the enterprise legal person has been disbanded.[64] It is within the exclusive power of a people's court to decide whether such an application for bankruptcy, conciliation or re-organisation is to be accepted.[65] If it is accepted, relevant procedures start. The 2006 Enterprise Bankruptcy Law does not, however, provide any detailed criteria for a court on which to base its decision of accepting or rejecting an application, other than referring to the extremely vague provisions in Article 2 of the Law.

The effects of an acceptance of a bankruptcy case are that the enterprise is no longer allowed to make any debt repayments to individual creditors, all preservation measures over the enterprise's assets will be cancelled, and enforcement procedures and civil proceedings or arbitration proceedings relating to the enterprise will be suspended (but will resume after the administrator has taken over the administration of the assets).[66] Contracts entered into by the enterprise prior to the court's acceptance of the bankruptcy case, but still pending full performance by the parties, may be continued or rescinded, depending on the decision of the administrator. If the administrator does not notify the other contracting party within two months from the date on which the court accepts the bankruptcy application, or does not reply within 30 days from the date of receiving a reminder by the other contracting

61 Zou Hailin, 'An Analysis and the Application of Enterprise Rehabilitation Procedures in China', in (no. 1, 2007) *Journal of China University of Political Science and Law* (*Zhengfa Luntan*) 48, at 48. For conciliation and re-organisation, see the discussion below.

62 See Articles 2 & 7 of the 2006 Enterprise Bankruptcy Law.

63 Article 7 of the 2006 Enterprise Bankruptcy Law.

64 Article 7 of the 2006 Enterprise Bankruptcy Law.

65 Articles 10, 71, & 96 of the 2006 Enterprise Bankruptcy Law.

66 See Articles 16, 19 & 20 of the 2006 Enterprise Bankruptcy Law.

party, the contract concerned will be deemed rescinded. Where the administrator decides to continue performing the contract, the other contracting party is obliged to do so, but it may request a security from the administrator and may rescind the contract if the administrator fails to satisfy such a request.[67]

Since the 2006 Enterprise Bankruptcy Law does not provide any criteria for a court to accept or reject an application for bankruptcy liquidation, the 2002 Provisions will continue to provide judicial guidance in the near future. Under the 2002 Provisions a people's court will reject an application if it discovers that the debtor is not insolvent, or that the enterprise applicant has concealed or transferred its assets, or is making the application in order to evade repayment of debts, or discovers that the purpose of the creditor applicant is to damage the debtor enterprise's commercial reputation and to undermine fair competition.[68] A case may also be turned down by the people's court even after having been accepted if the court later finds that the applicant does not meet legal requirements, or that major assets of the enterprise applicant are missing and the enterprise is unable to explain their whereabouts. A court decision may be appealed to the people's court at the next highest level within 10 days from the date on which such a ruling is received.[69]

Since bankruptcy fraud, such as enterprises dodging their debts by declaring bankruptcy after dividing up their business and changing licences, is seen as a very serious problem,[70] several mechanisms are established by the Law to prevent such fraud from occurring. Thus, any of the following transactions undertaken by an enterprise within one year prior to the bankruptcy proceedings may be revoked by the court:

- gratuitous transfers of assets;
- transactions made at a clearly unreasonable price;
- providing a guarantee with assets for non-secured debts;
- prepayment of debts that are not due; or
- any waiver of creditor rights.[71]

Similarly, any debt settlement with any individual creditor during the six months prior to a court decision to accept a bankruptcy application may be set aside by a

---

67 See Article 18 of the 2006 Enterprise Bankruptcy Law.

68 Article 12 of the 2002 Provisions.

69 Article 14 of the 2002 Provisions.

70 Wang Xinxin, in 'Regulating Bankruptcy Procedures and Dealing with Credits and Debts Fairly – Three Experts Explaining the New Enterprise Bankruptcy Law', *supra* note 50, at 5; Li Shuguang, *supra* note 41.

71 Article 31 of the 2006 Enterprise Bankruptcy Law.

court unless such settlement adds value to the debtor's assets.[72] Finally, any actions to conceal or transfer assets for the purpose of debt evasion or to fabricate debts that are imaginary or fictitious, or false admission of debts are by law invalid.[73] In any of these circumstances, the administrator has the right to recover any assets so lost.

Although the 2006 Enterprise Bankruptcy Law became effective on 1 June 2007, it does not apply to SOEs that have already been included in the State Council 'policy bankruptcy' plan.[74] Under the current State Council plan (2005–2008),[75] policy bankruptcy will continue until the end of 2008, and 2,116 SOEs, involving a total debt of 227.16 billion *yuan* owed to financial institutions and 3.51 million workers, have been included in the current plan.[76] This significant exclusion means that the full impact of the new Enterprise Bankruptcy Law will not be felt until at least 2009.

The application of the 2006 Enterprise Bankruptcy Law to cases that are currently pending in the court system, about 10,000 cases in total at the moment,[77] is a more complicated situation. The Provisions of the Supreme People's Court on the Question of the Application of the Law in relation to Bankruptcy Cases that Have not Yet Been Concluded by the Time of the Implementation of the Enterprise Bankruptcy Law of the PRC, issued by the Supreme People's Court on 25 April 2007, seems to suggest three guiding principles. First, all proceedings that would have been completed by 1 June 2007 would continue to be upheld by the court. Secondly, continuing proceedings after 1 June will be subject to the new Law as long as the new procedural provisions are applicable (such as converting bankruptcy proceedings to conciliation or re-organisation processes). Thirdly, the new Law will not be retrospectively applied in relation to substantive matters (such as the determination of legal validity or the revoking of commercial transactions prior to the filing of bankruptcy cases) in adjudicating these 10,000 pending cases.

---

72 Article 32 of the 2006 Enterprise Bankruptcy Law.

73 Article 33 of the 2006 Enterprise Bankruptcy Law.

74 Article 133 of the 2006 Enterprise Bankruptcy Law.

75 See Opinion on Further Improving the Work of State-owned Enterprise Policy Bankruptcy, issued by the Leading Group on National State-owned Enterprise Merger, and Bankruptcy and Re-employment of Workers and endorsed by the State Council on 16 January 2006. A Chinese text is available from An & Wu, *supra* note 2, at 306-309.

76 *Id.*, at 307. By the end of April 2004 some 3,377 SOEs were closed under the 'policy bankruptcy' plan, involving a total debt of 223.8 billion *yuan* owed to financial institutions and 6.2 million workers and staff. In total, the Central Government had injected 49.3 billion *yuan* as bankruptcy assistance. See An & Wu, *supra* note 2, at 181.

77 See 'Supreme People's Court Answering Questions from Journalists in relation to Relevant Judicial Interpretations on the Enterprise Bankruptcy Law', 27 April 2007, available at <www.lawbook.com.cn/fzdt.newshtml/21/20070427224005.htm> (last accessed 29 April 2007).

4.2. Administration

While the old law contained provisions on the liquidation committee/group to be appointed by a people's court, it did not provide anything on administrators. Further, the old liquidation system contained many shortcomings: the liquidation committee was established rather late in the bankruptcy process, there were areas without supervision, and its composite members mainly came from administrative authorities in charge of the enterprise, government financial authorities and some professionals, and thus it had a very strong administrative flavour, allowing local protection and affecting fairness and justice.[78] The need for some kind of independent administration of bankruptcy liquidation was well recognised by law-makers and scholars and, in fact, had been introduced in some local practice prior to the enactment of the 2006 Enterprise Bankruptcy Law.[79] Thus the introduction of the mechanism of administrator did not cause much debate at all.

The 2006 Enterprise Bankruptcy Law devotes a whole chapter to rules governing and regulating the powers, functions and duties of administrators. Under Article 13, an administrator must be appointed by the court when the court accepts a bankruptcy case. Since applications for bankruptcy, conciliation or re-organisation are of a different nature and will invoke different procedures under the new Law, Article 13 seems to suggest that administrators are only used in bankruptcy processes.[80] This clearly is not the case: Chapter Eight (on Re-organisation) frequently refers to the roles of the administrator in the re-organisation process.

An administrator is to be appointed by the court having jurisdiction over the bankruptcy case.[81] Once appointed the administrator may not resign from the position without a proper reason and such a resignation will need the approval of the appointing court.[82] An administrator is to report to the appointing court and

---

78 See Article 24 of the 1986 Enterprise Bankruptcy Law. See also Qiang Xiaochen, in 'Regulating Bankruptcy Procedures and Dealing with Credits and Debts Fairly – Three Experts Explaining the New Enterprise Bankruptcy Law', *supra* note 50, at 5; and Supreme People's Court, 'Person-in-charge of the Second Civil Law Chamber of the Supreme People's Court Answers Journalists' Questions regarding the Provisions of the Supreme People's Court on the Appointment of administrators in Adjudicating Enterprise Bankruptcy Law and Provisions of the Supreme People's Court on the Determination of Remunerations for Administrators in the Adjudication of Enterprise Bankruptcy Cases', 17 April 2007, available from <www.lawbook.com.cn/fzdt/newshtml/21/20070417091519.htm> (last accessed 17 April 2007).

79 See 'Explanations on the Draft Enterprise Bankruptcy Law of the PRC', *supra* note 4.

80 Thus, some Chinese scholars refer them to as 'bankruptcy administrators'. See An & Wu, *supra* note 2, at 26-27.

81 Article 22 of the 2006 Enterprise Bankruptcy Law. The court is also to determine the remuneration for its work, but specific measures for such determination are to be issued separately by the Supreme People Court. See Article 22 of the 2006 Enterprise Bankruptcy Law. The measures were indeed issued by the Supreme People's Court in April 2007. See *supra* note 51.

82 See Article 29 of the 2006 Enterprise Bankruptcy Law.

is subject to the supervision of the creditors' meeting and creditors' committee.[83] As such, a creditors' meeting may apply to the court for a new appointment if it considers the administrator to be incompetent or unable to perform their duties fairly and lawfully.[84] This provision is interpreted by some Chinese scholars as having vested the creditors' meeting with a partial veto power over the appointment of the administrator,[85] even though the law is silent as to whether a court is under any legal obligation to grant such an application from the creditors' meeting.

As mentioned above, this mechanism was adopted as a means to ensure independent administration and thus to prevent administrative interference in bankruptcy or other related proceedings. The 2006 Enterprise Bankruptcy Law nevertheless leaves much room for potential interference by administrative authorities. Under Article 24 an administrator may be a liquidation team comprising relevant departments and organisations, or an intermediary such as a law firm, accounting firm or bankruptcy liquidation firm, etc. That is to say that the 'old' liquidation group under the 1986 Enterprise Bankruptcy Law may simply be appointed as an administrator under the new Law, and hence this defeats the principal objective of the new mechanism.[86] Further, the 2006 Enterprise Bankruptcy Law does not provide professional qualification requirements or an examination system for such administrators. It was the legislative authority's view that professional training will be a prerequisite for obtaining such a professional qualification, not a universal examination.[87] In light of the recent trends towards professionalism in many areas of professional practice (lawyers, accountancy, securities brokerage, auditing etc.), one wonders whether it was the last attempt by administrative authorities to retain some kind of control over bankruptcy and/or re-organisation.

In light of the importance of administrators in bankruptcy proceedings and partly in response to the above concerns, on 12 April 2007 the Supreme People's Court issued two sets of rules on administrators – the Provisions of the Supreme People's

---

83 Article 23 of the 2006 Enterprise Bankruptcy Law.

84 Article 22 of the 2006 Enterprise Bankruptcy Law.

85 See An & Wu, *supra* note 2, at 27.

86 This is indeed now confirmed by Article 3 of the Provisions of the Supreme People's Court on the Question of the Application of Law in relation to Bankruptcy Cases that Have not Yet Been Concluded by the Time of the Implementation of the Enterprise Bankruptcy Law of the PRC. Article 24 of the 2006 Enterprise Bankruptcy Law, however, proceeds to provide that the following persons may not act as administrators: (1) a person who has been convicted of a criminal offence; (2) a person whose relevant practising certificate has been revoked; (3) a person who is an interested party to the case; and (4) any other person who is deemed unsuitable to act as an administrator by the People's Court. Item (3) then seems to contradict Article 24 as the liquidation team composed of relative departments and organisations clearly has an interest in the bankruptcy case. It is doubtful whether a court will invoke Item (3) to decline the appointment of the liquidation team as an administrator.

87 Qiang Xiaochen, *supra* note 78, at 5.

Court on the Appointment of Administrators in Adjudicating Enterprise Bankruptcy Law, and the Provisions of the Supreme People's Court on the Determination of Remuneration for Administrators in the Adjudication of Enterprise Bankruptcy Cases – both of which took effect on 1 June 2007 when the 2006 Bankruptcy Law became operational. Under these Provisions High Courts at provincial level, or Intermediate Courts designated by the relevant High Courts, will establish lists of administrators, which may be law firms, accounting firms, bankruptcy liquidation firms, other intermediaries, and individual professionals. While these Provisions elaborate grounds for the dismissal of administrators, they do not, like the 2006 Enterprise Bankruptcy Law, establish specific professional qualifications required for inclusion in the lists. However, to prevent corrupt practices in the determination of the lists of administrators and in the appointment of administrators in specific cases, certain mechanisms such as public notification of preliminary determination, a large selection committee, a point system for judging applicants, a system for random selection or tendering for specific cases, and a filing-for-record system, have been established by the Provisions.

The functions and duties of an administrator under the Chinese law are largely similar to those practised in developed industrial countries.[88]

4.3. Bankruptcy Property and Order of Priority

Defining, determining and ascertaining an enterprise's assets are some of the most critical aspects of any bankruptcy or bankruptcy-related proceedings, and are important measures in preventing bankruptcy fraud. Additionally, in the case of China and also increasingly in Western welfare societies, protection of employees' benefits is nowadays a point of contention in bankruptcy negotiations and proceedings.

Under Article 30 of the 2006 Enterprise Bankruptcy Law an enterprise's assets include all assets that belong to the enterprise at the time of the commencement of the bankruptcy proceedings, and any asset obtained by the enterprise thereafter but before the conclusion of bankruptcy proceedings. It will also include capital contribution subscribed but not yet fully paid-up by capital contributors of the enterprise (even though such capital contribution may not be due yet under the

88 Under Article 25 of the 2006 Enterprise Bankruptcy Law an administrator is to perform the following functions: taking over the administration of all assets, seals and accounts and documents of the enterprise; investigating the status of the enterprise's assets and preparing an asset status report; deciding on the enterprise's internal management matters; deciding on the enterprise's daily expenditure and other necessary expenditure; deciding on the continuation or suspension of the enterprise's business before the first creditors' meeting is convened (subject to the approval of the court); managing and disposing of the enterprise's assets; representing the enterprise in litigation, arbitration or any other legal proceedings; proposing the convening of creditors' meetings; and performing any other duties that the Court deems relevant. In addition to these functions, the Law also grants, in various places, certain other powers to the administrators.

original capital contribution agreement),[89] and any income and assets of the enterprise recovered from the enterprise's senior management personnel which they obtained by abusing their positions.[90] Under Article 5, such assets also include those located overseas but owned by the enterprise.[91]

Before a court accepts an application for bankruptcy liquidation, a creditor is allowed to offset a debt it owed to the enterprise prior to the bankruptcy proceedings, unless its claim against the enterprise is obtained from another party after the bankruptcy proceedings have commenced, or it has created a debt to the enterprise while knowing that the latter is insolvent, or while knowing of the bankruptcy application (unless the debt was created due to statutory provisions or was incurred one year before the bankruptcy application).[92]

For liquidation purposes, the enterprise's assets will be disposed of through auction in accordance with the distribution plan formulated by the administrator and approved by a creditors' meeting or by the court, unless the creditors' meeting decides otherwise.[93]

Deciding the order of priority in debt repayment in bankruptcy proceedings, in particular for the purpose of protecting employees' benefits and interests, turned out to be one of the most contentious issues, and hence one of the principal reasons causing the delay of the adoption of the bankruptcy law.[94] In the end, a compromise was reached under which the so-called 'old debts old method, and new debts new method' principle will be applied to employees' wages and benefits.[95] Under this principle, the 'new method' will deal with debt repayment in accordance with the following rules:

Exempt property: In early drafts of the bankruptcy law, the term 'exemption rights' (*Bie Chu Quan*) was used to define which property would be exempt from bankruptcy claims. Because of the awkward term, which is also alien in Chinese law, this term

---

89 Article 35 of the 2006 Enterprise Bankruptcy Law.

90 Article 36 of the 2006 Enterprise Bankruptcy Law.

91 See discussions in Section 4.5 below.

92 Article 40 of the 2006 Enterprise Bankruptcy Law.

93 Article 112 of the 2006 Enterprise Bankruptcy Law.

94 Li Yongjun, 'Procedural Structure of the Bankruptcy Law and the Balance of Interests', in (no. 1, 2007) *Journal of the China University of Political Science and Law* (*Zhengfa Luntan*) 17, at 27. See also 'Explanations on the Draft Enterprise Bankruptcy Law of the PRC', *supra* note 4. Other scholars describe this issue as the most difficult and most contentious issue during the drafting of the law. See An & Wu, *supra* note 2, at 177.

95 Wang Xinxin, in 'Regulating Bankruptcy Procedures and Dealing with Credits and Debts Fairly – Three Experts Explain the New Enterprise Bankruptcy Law', *supra* note 50, at 5.

was dropped in the final draft.[96] Nevertheless, Article 109 of the 2006 Enterprise Bankruptcy Law provides that '[h]olders of interests secured by specific assets of the bankrupt enterprise shall be entitled to a priority right of repayment in respect of such specific assets.' This provision, according to Chinese scholars, establishes the notion of 'exemption rights' in an indirect way,[97] and as such security collateral would not constitute bankrupt property, unless the value of the collateral is higher than that of the claims.[98]

Priority Payment: In accordance with Article 43, bankruptcy expenses[99] and debts of a public interest nature[100] may be settled against an enterprise's assets at any time. A literal reading of this provision would suggest that such expenses and debts could also be claimed against security collateral. It is therefore uncertain whether security collateral will be exempt from such claims, as the Law does not actually apply the term 'exemption rights'.

Other payments: all other debts will be repaid (if there are sufficient assets for doing so) in accordance with the following order of priority:

- employees' wages and benefits;[101]
- other social security expenses and taxes owed by the enterprise;

---

96 Wang Xinxin, 'Exemption Rights in the Newly Enacted Bankruptcy Law', (no. 1 2007) *Journal of the China University of Political Science and Law* (*Zhengfa Luntan*) 31, at 31. For a more systematic treatment of the notion of *bie chu quan*, see An & Wu, *supra* note 2, at 144-149.

97 *Ibid.*

98 In fact, Article 28 of the 1986 Enterprise Bankruptcy Law specifically provided that such collateral would not be regarded as bankruptcy property.

99 These include litigation expenses for the bankruptcy case, expenses incurred in the management, sale and distribution of the enterprise's assets, and expenses for the performance of the administrator's duties, the administrator's remuneration and expenses for staff employment. See Articles 41 & 113 of the 2006 Enterprise Bankruptcy Law.

100 These include debts arising from the resumption of the contractual performance of a contract which is yet to be fully performed by both parties; debts arising under a *negotiorum gestio* of the debtor's assets; debts arising from unjust enrichment by the debtor; labour costs and social security premiums payable for the continuation of the debtor's business, and any other debt arising therefrom; debts arising from damages caused to others when the administrator or its personnel performed its duties; and debts arising from damages caused to others by the debtor's assets. See Articles 42 & 113 of the 2006 Enterprise Bankruptcy Law.

101 These benefits include medical subsidies, disability subsidies, disability subsidies and pensions for survivors, basic aged pension insurance and basic medical insurance expenses owed by the enterprise that are to be included in the individual workers' accounts, and other statutory compensation to workers. Wages of the directors, supervisors and senior management personnel are to be calculated on the basis of the average wage of the enterprise's workers. See Article 113 of the 2006 Enterprise Bankruptcy Law.

– ordinary claims.[102]

The so-called 'old method' then makes an exception for employee wages and benefits that had accrued before the publication (28 August 2006) of the 2006 Enterprise Bankruptcy Law. Specifically, such wages and benefits are to be treated as claims secured by the enterprise's specific assets.[103] Any debts (including employees' benefits and interests) accrued after the publication of the Law will be paid in accordance with the new rules established by the 2006 Enterprise Bankruptcy Law.

If the bankrupt enterprise's assets are insufficient to satisfy all claims at the same level of priority, the claims are to be settled on the basis of *pro rata* distribution. But if the enterprise's assets cannot even pay off all expenses on the administration of bankruptcy processes, then the administrator must seek a Court ruling to terminate the bankruptcy procedures.

4.4. Alternatives to Bankruptcy

As mentioned before, although the law is entitled 'bankruptcy law', the 2006 Enterprise Bankruptcy Law is not only about bankruptcy, but is also about 'enterprise rehabilitation'; that is, conciliation and re-organisation. While conciliation has always been available in Chinese bankruptcy proceedings, re-organisation is a relatively new mechanism introduced into Chinese law and it is described as the 'core of the whole bankruptcy law'.[104]

(1) Conciliation

Under Articles 17 & 18 of the 1986 Enterprise Bankruptcy Law, within three months of a court accepting a bankruptcy case initiated by creditors a higher level department in charge of the enterprise could apply to the court for re-structuring of the enterprise, and after the submission of a re-structuring application a draft conciliation agreement had to be submitted to a creditors' meeting for consideration. Under Article 202 of the Civil Procedure Law (1991), an enterprise and the creditors' meeting could also settle their debts by a conciliation agreement. However, neither Law provided any detailed guidelines on practical issues, such as the rights and obligations of the debtors and creditors. Further, different conciliation procedures existed for different kinds of enterprises. Most importantly, for SOEs conciliation largely depended on a decision by the administrative authorities in charge of the

---

102 Article 113 of the 2006 Enterprise Bankruptcy Law.

103 See Articles 109 & 132 of the 2006 Enterprise Bankruptcy Law, and See 'Supreme People's Court Answering Questions from Journalists in relation to Relevant Judicial Interpretations on the Enterprise Bankruptcy Law', *supra* note 77.

104 Li Shuguang, *supra* note 59.

enterprise, rather than on one by the enterprise itself.[105] The much more detailed provisions on conciliation in the 2006 Enterprise Bankruptcy Law are therefore a welcome rectification of these deficiencies in the earlier law.

Under the new Law conciliation is available to both insolvent enterprises and enterprises at a high risk of insolvency,[106] aimed at achieving a quick compromise regarding unsecured claims so as to avoid protracted bankruptcy proceedings. Unlike re-organisation, conciliation may only be initiated by the debtor enterprise, and the enterprise may directly apply to the court for conciliation or apply after the court has accepted the bankruptcy application but before the enterprise is declared bankrupt.[107] In all cases there must be a draft conciliation agreement. A proper interpretation of these provisions would clearly exclude administrative interference in the conciliation process.

On the other hand much of the conciliation process is in the hands of the court and the creditors. Thus the people's court is required to make a ruling for conciliation when the application complies with the law, to announce the ruling, and to convene a creditors' meeting to discuss the draft conciliation agreement.[108] Whether conciliation succeeds or fails depends almost entirely on the decision of creditors, as the draft conciliation agreement requires the approval of a majority of the creditors with voting rights, representing two-thirds or more of the total unsecured creditor rights, before it is submitted to the court for final approval.[109] If the conciliation agreement fails at the creditors' meeting, or is passed by the creditors' meeting but rejected by the people's court, the court will terminate the conciliation process and declare the enterprise bankrupt.[110] An approved conciliation agreement is legally binding on the enterprise and on all creditors (i.e. those who hold unsecured creditor rights at the time of acceptance of a bankruptcy application by the court).[111] In the event that the enterprise is unable to repay its debts or does not do so, as stipulated in the conciliation agreement, the creditors concerned may apply to the people's court for termination of the conciliation agreement. The court will render a ruling

105 For detailed analysis, see An & Wu, *supra* note 2, at 109-112.

106 See Article 7 of the 2006 Enterprise Bankruptcy Law.

107 See Article 95 of the 2006 Enterprise Bankruptcy Law.

108 Article 96 of the 2006 Enterprise Bankruptcy Law.

109 Articles 97 & 98 of the 2006 Enterprise Bankruptcy Law. On the other hand Article 105 allows debtors and creditors to reach a conciliation agreement during bankruptcy proceedings without the need to apply to a court for conciliation, but such a voluntary conciliation agreement still needs court approval before it acquires legal effect and before the bankruptcy proceedings can be terminated.

110 Article 99 of the 2006 Enterprise Bankruptcy Law.

111 Article 100 of the 2006 Enterprise Bankruptcy Law.

to that effect and declare the enterprise bankrupt. The bankruptcy proceedings then will resume.[112]

Unlike the practice in many other countries, the conciliation process in China may not be converted, at a later stage, into a re-organisation process. Thus, a decision on undertaking conciliation or re-organisation at the beginning of the process is a critical one. The reason for this legislative arrangement is said to be purely a consideration of procedural costs.[113]

(2) Re-organisation

The 1986 Enterprise Bankruptcy Law did contain provisions on conciliation and re-structuring (*Zhengdun*). However both of these, as pointed out above, were in their nature administrative processes, or at least had a very strong administrative flavour.[114] Thus the re-organisation, as codified in the 2006 Law, is in its nature a new procedure. While the introduction of re-organisation was heralded as a significant development in China's bankruptcy legislation, the idea was not included in the original proposal when the new bankruptcy law was being drafted. In March 1995 the American re-organisation law was first introduced to a symposium on the first draft of the bankruptcy law held in Chengdu, Sichuan Province. It was after this introduction that scholars began to advocate the inclusion of re-organisation into Chinese bankruptcy law.[115]

Although there was little dispute as to whether China should introduce the scheme of re-organisation into the new bankruptcy law, there were heated debates as to its scope of application. In particular there were some strong arguments about whether re-organisation should be limited to companies limited by shares or only to listed companies, considering the cost, the complexity of the procedures and the potential delay if the enterprise ended in bankruptcy as a result of a failure in re-organisation.[116] Further, because of the complicated procedures and high costs, re-organisation had in effect only applied to large-sized enterprises in the various trial practices since 1995, while medium and small sized enterprises had only utilised

[112] Article 104 of the 2006 Enterprise Bankruptcy Law.

[113] Li Yongjun, *supra* note 94, at 21-22.

[114] It was described by some Chinese scholars as a combination of conciliation and re-organisation, conducted by government departments, but conforming to neither conciliation nor re-organisation in a legal sense. See An & Wu, *supra* note 2, at 79.

[115] Wang Weiguo, *supra* note 7, at 11.

[116] Li Yongjun, *supra* note 94, at 19-20. See also 'Explanations on the Draft Enterprise Bankruptcy Law of the PRC', *supra* note 4.

conciliation.[117] Nevertheless, the law-makers finally decided that re-organisation would be available to all enterprise legal persons.[118]

The whole scheme on bankruptcy administration is designed to save insolvent but not yet hopeless enterprises from bankruptcy liquidation. To serve this purpose the Law allows not only enterprises with a high probability of insolvency, but also insolvent enterprises, to restructure their debts instead of directly going into bankruptcy liquidation.[119]

Under Article 70 of the 2006 Enterprise Bankruptcy Law, either the debtor or the creditors may apply directly to a people's court for re-organisation. In cases where creditors apply for bankruptcy liquidation, the enterprise or the investors whose capital contributions represents one-tenth or more of the registered capital of the enterprise may also apply to the people's court for re-organisation after the court has accepted the bankruptcy application but prior to the enterprise being declared bankrupt. The court is required to give a ruling for re-organisation whenever the application meets the requirements of the Enterprise Bankruptcy Law.[120]

In comparison to bankruptcy procedures, the debtor enterprise has considerable freedom in managing its assets during re-organisation. However, the court plays a very strong role, being vested with many approval powers. Thus an enterprise only enters the re-organisation period after the court approves the re-organisation application.[121] While the enterprise is now allowed to continue to manage its assets and run its business under the supervision of an administrator, the enterprise needs to apply to the court for approval for such operations.[122] As for conciliation, a re-organisation plan must be submitted to the court and the creditors' meeting for approval within six months after the commencement of the re-organisation (with a possibility of an extension of three months if the court approves). Failure to submit such a plan will lead to the re-organisation procedure being terminated by the court and the enterprise will be declared bankrupt.[123]

Again as in the conciliation process, the re-organisation plan needs first to be given approval by the creditors' meeting and then final approval by the court.[124] The voting procedures are more complicated than those for conciliation. Creditors are divided into groups according to the category of creditor rights, and the plan must be passed by each of these groups (by a simple majority of creditors

---

117 Ju Wei, *supra* note 50, at 5.

118 See Articles 2 & 7 of the 2006 Enterprise Bankruptcy Law.

119 See Article 2 of the 2006 Enterprise Bankruptcy Law.

120 See Article 71 of the 2006 Enterprise Bankruptcy Law.

121 See Article 72 of the 2006 Enterprise Bankruptcy Law.

122 See Article 73 of the 2006 Enterprise Bankruptcy Law.

123 See Article 79 of the 2006 Enterprise Bankruptcy Law.

124 See Article 86 of the 2006 Enterprise Bankruptcy Law.

in the same voting group present at the meeting, whose creditor rights represent two-thirds of the total creditor rights of the group).[125] Re-voting by a voting group that failed to obtain a majority for the plan can be organised by the enterprise or the administrator after negotiation with such a group. In the event that the voting group refuses to re-vote or fails to pass the plan a second time, the last resort for the enterprise or the administrator is to apply to the people's court for approval of the plan, if it believes that the plan meets the prescribed conditions of the Enterprise Bankruptcy Law.[126]

Where the re-organisation plan is rejected at the creditors' meeting or by the court, the court will terminate re-organisation proceedings and declare the enterprise bankrupt.[127] Once again, detailed criteria for a court to accept or reject an application for re-organisation or an application for approval of a re-organisation plan are yet to be provided by implementation measures or judicial interpretation.

4.5. Financial Institutions

During the drafting of the 2006 Enterprise Bankruptcy Law there were different opinions on whether to include financial institutions within the coverage of the new law, or to have a separate bankruptcy law for them. Those against the inclusion of financial institutions in the law based their arguments on considerations of the financial institutions' special nature and the serious social impacts of their bankruptcy, while those supporting the inclusion were more concerned with the integration of the bankruptcy law system, the time-consuming effort of drafting another set of law (given that it took 12 years to draft the new enterprise bankruptcy law!), the reality of bankruptcy risks facing financial institutions, and the necessary balance between market entry and market exit.[128] Obviously the latter opinion won the day, but only after some major concessions were made by the proponents. As a result, there is only one article on financial institutions with the effect of having them included in the Law, but for practical purposes they will be governed by a separate law in the form of State Council regulations.[129] Furthermore, also under Article 134, only bankruptcy or re-organisation is available to financial institutions and, importantly, only the State Council's financial regulatory authorities (not debtors nor creditors) may initiate any of these procedures.

---

125 See Articles 82, 84 & 86 of the 2006 Enterprise Bankruptcy Law.

126 See Article 87 of the 2006 Enterprise Bankruptcy Law.

127 See Article 88 of the 2006 Enterprise Bankruptcy Law.

128 See Wang Xinxin, "Connecting Financial Institution Bankruptcy Regulation with the International Track", *People's Daily* (overseas edition), 28 September 2006, at 5.

129 Under Article 134, the State Council is authorised to issue implementation measures for the bankruptcy of financial institutions, which include commercial banks, securities companies, insurance companies and other financial institutions.

4.6. Cross-Border Bankruptcy

The 2006 Enterprise Bankruptcy Law for the first time declares that a Chinese bankruptcy proceeding will be binding on all assets held outside the territory of China by the debtor. Correspondingly the Law provides that China will recognise and enforce an effective bankruptcy judgment or ruling of a foreign court that involves assets in China held by a debtor, provided that it will 'not violate the basic principles of Chinese law, threaten national sovereignty, security and public interest, and not impair the lawful rights and interests of creditors in China.'[130] The new provision is said to be in response to the increasing number of foreign-related claims and debts in China that have been brought about by the recent strong inflow of international capital and multinational companies, and of Chinese companies going overseas.[131]

Article 5 is only a provision in principle. According to Professor Li, a member of the Enterprise Bankruptcy Law drafting team, to make it enforceable the provision will be fleshed out with detailed special extraterritorial bankruptcy procedures, judicial interpretations, and judicial cooperation agreements,[132] and in future there may be separate extraterritorial bankruptcy regulations.

In terms of the current practice, the actual execution upon property situated outside China relies on multilateral or bilateral judicial assistance agreements.[133]

5. Concluding Remarks

Without much doubt the new Enterprise Bankruptcy Law is a major improvement, and a much more comprehensive code than the previous one enacted in 1986. Its promulgation has attracted a great deal of attention worldwide and has been largely welcomed both in China and abroad. However, its comprehensiveness lies mainly in terms of the wider scope of application and the introduction of new mechanisms. While it provides general principles, it lacks practical details. As it stands it is not a practical piece of law.

Even if detailed practical criteria and guidance are later provided by implementation measures or judicial interpretations, as is often the case in most areas of law, the actual realisation of the objectives of the Law will still depend on the effective, fair and consistent application of the Law, the true independence of the courts, well trained judges and professionals, and the economic and political environment in

---

130 See Article 5 of the 2006 Enterprise Bankruptcy Law.

131 Li Shuguang, 'Extraterritorial Bankruptcy in China Will Have a Legal Basis', *People's Daily* (overseas edition), 22 September, 2006, at 5.

132 Li Shuguang, *id.*, at 5.

133 See An & Wu, *supra* note 2, at 37.

China. Fundamentally, as pointed out by one Chinese scholar, once the implementation of the new Enterprise Bankruptcy Law starts, 'inappropriate administrative interference must be actively resisted and resolved. The dominant position and the absolute authority of the court must be clearly established so as to rectify the wrong positioning of courts being an appendix to the government in bankruptcy cases.'[134] While it might sound strange to place so much faith in the judiciary in bankruptcy proceedings, it is perhaps the only means available in China at the moment to transform the bankruptcy proceedings from an administrative exercise into a truly independent and professional process.

Despite all these shortcomings the adoption of a comprehensive bankruptcy law represents yet another major ideological breakthrough in post-Mao China. Perhaps this is the most significant aspect of the new Law.

134 Wang Xinxin, *supra* note 70, at 5.

Chapter Sixteen

Intellectual Property Law

1. Introduction

There is always a tension between regulation and protection when it comes to issues concerning intellectual property (IP), in China just as elsewhere. Furthermore, attitudes towards IP are conditioned by the cultural setting of the countries concerned. This means that particularly in a socialist country the regulation of these issues is not simply a question of equity and balance of interests; but that there is always a political dimension involved as a part of general social control.

Regulation of IP issues occurs in many forms, from the censorship of publications and requirements for technology registration, to IP licensing control and official approval of other contractual arrangements. Such regulation is more often than not a prerequisite for protection. For instance registration of patents and trademarks, and to a lesser extent copyright, is almost universally a precondition for protection. China is no exception to this. However the power of regulation is exercised by a myriad of government authorities at the central and local levels in China.

Although IP protection has developed rapidly in China, it has only done so recently and largely in response to Western pressure, and as a means of attracting foreign capital, know-how and other investment. In fact, until quite recently China, like many other Asian countries, had sought to curtail the protection of IP rights.[1] As late as in 1981 China declared that all products of technological innovation and invention were the common heritage of mankind.[2] This attitude towards IP rights and technological innovation only began to change when it clearly became an obstacle to China's ambition to attract advanced foreign technologies and expertise and, more recently, after realising that IP protection was also crucial for the development of China's own hi-tech markets and economy. Thus a modern legal framework for IP protection started slowly but developed solidly and rapidly after China began to implement its 'open door' policies in the late 1970s. While formal legal development

---

1 See Michael D. Pendleton, 'Intellectual Property Regimes of Selected Asia-Pacific Jurisdictions', in K.C.D.M. Wilde & M. Rafiqul Islam (eds), *International Transactions* (Sydney: The Law Book Company, 1993), at 361.

2 *Id.*, at 362.

has been rapid, impressive and in some ways admirable, the implementation of legal protection of IP rights in China is far from perfect, and the protection promised on paper has largely remained there until this day.

This Chapter mainly concerns the protection of IP in China; issues relating to IP regulation are only dealt with if they are relevant to this examination. It begins with a review of the rapid growth of the IP market and legal development in relation to IP protection. It goes on to deal with the legal framework for different kinds of IP rights, followed by an examination of the administrative and judicial mechanisms for the enforcement of the IP protection law. The gap between rights on paper and the reality of IP protection will, however, be analysed as a part of the case studies in Chapter Eighteen.

2. Rapid Development of the IP Market and Legal Framework on Protection

With a long history of civilisation and a record of some of the world's greatest inventions, including the Great Four Inventions (papermaking, gunpowder, printing and the compass), it is not particularly surprising to learn that traditional China had legal provisions regulating IP issues. However, as in the case of civil law in general, such provisions were more about social control and the protection of the interests of the Imperial Court than about IP rights.[3] Again in line with civil law development, the first modern legal system on IP protection was established through the law reforms made during the Qing and Guomindang (KMT) periods at the turn of the 20th century. However, these 'old' laws were abolished when the PRC was founded in 1949. While there were some *ad hoc* regulations on IP protection in the first 30 years of the People's Republic, such as the 1957 Interim Regulations concerning the Protection of Copyright in Published Works and the 1963 Provisional Regulations on Trademarks, there was very little in the sense of a comprehensive legal regime for IP protection by the time China launched its economic reform programs and opened its doors to foreign investment in the late 1970s. The contemporary legal system for IP protection is therefore a product of the last 25 years or so, and continues to evolve until this day.

The first move towards IP protection occurred in 1979 as part of China's efforts to attract foreign investment, when China promulgated its Law on Sino-foreign Joint Ventures.[4] In March 1980 China submitted its application for membership

[3] For a good summary of intellectual property protection in traditional China, see Qu Sanqiang, *Fundamentals of Intellectual Property Law* (*Zhishi Chanquanfa Yuanli*) (Beijing: Procutorial Press, 2004), Chapter 3; and Qu Sanqiang, *Copyright in China* (Beijing: Foreign Languages Press, 2002), Chapter 1.

[4] This Law was further implemented by a set of Implementation Rules issued in 1983. The two laws, both revised twice since their issuance (see *infra* notes 50 & 51), allow foreign parties

to the World Intellectual Property Organisation (WIPO) and became a member in June of the same year.[5] Serious legal efforts began to emerge in 1982 with the promulgation of the Trademark Law, which replaced the very weak Provisional Regulations of 1963, and its implementing rules in 1983. Two years later, a Patent Law was promulgated, which, together with its implementation rules, became effective in 1985. The General Principles of Civil Law of 1986 formally recognised IP rights as civil law rights. The Copyright Law was adopted in 1990 and its implementation rules as well as the Computer Software Protection Regulations were issued in 1991. Amid foreign concerns about the weak protection offered by China, and as a result of Western pressure (in particular that from the United States),[6] 1992–1993 saw some major amendments being made to the Trademark Law and the Patent Law, an amendment to the Criminal Law (to make the counterfeiting of registered trademarks a criminal offence), the issuance of the Law against Unfair Competition (which protects trade secrets), the promulgation of new implementing rules for the Patent Law as well as the ratification of the Berne Convention for the Protection of Literary and Artistic Works and the Universal Copyright Convention in 1992. Besides these two conventions, China had earlier ratified the Paris Convention for the Protection of Industrial Property (in 1984), the Madrid Agreement Concerning the International Registration of Trademarks and the Treaty on Intellectual Property in Respect of Integrated Circuits (both in 1989), the Convention for the Protection of Producers of Phonograms Against Unauthorised Duplication of Their Phonograms, and the Patent Cooperation Treaty (both in 1993). With these developments as its legal foundation, China declared to the world that it had established a basic legal framework on IP protection by the mid-1990s,[7] but much improvement was yet to be achieved in the second half of the 1990s and continues today.

---

to use industrial property rights as an investment contribution, while promising, in general terms, legal protection for such foreign interests in the joint ventures.

5 See the State Council White Paper, *Intellectual Property Protection in China*, issued by the Information Office of the State Council in June 1994 (hereinafter referred to as the *1994 IP White Paper*). A Chinese text of the White Paper appears in *Peoples Daily* (*Renmin Ribao*), 17 June 1994, at 1 & 3. An English translation can be found in *Beijing Review*, 20-26 June 1994, at 8-17.

6 See Richard L. Thurston, 'Country Risk Management: China and Intellectual Property Protection', (1993) 27 *Int'l Lawyer* 51. American pressure has led to the signing of many agreements with specific implementation plans. See e.g. Memorandum of Understanding on Intellectual Property Rights (January 1992); An Action Plan for Enforcement (February 1995); and Letter of Agreement (1996). For further discussions, see Qu (2002), *supra* note 3. The effectiveness of foreign pressure on the improvement of IP protection in China is however a controversial issue. See Andrew Mertha, *The Politics of Piracy: Intellectual Property in Contemporary China* (Ithaca/London: Cornell University Press, 2005), Chapter 1. In the context of Sino-US relationship, IP diplomacy is described as a 'defining characteristic' and a 'constant' in the bilateral relationship: Mertha, at 2.

7 See *1994 IP White Paper*, *supra* note 5.

Indeed, a set of rules on Customs enforcement of IPR was only issued in 1995,[8] followed by specific regulations on the protection of business secrets in 1995,[9] the protection of well-known trademarks in 1996,[10] the protection of new plant varieties in 1997,[11] and a new amendment to the Criminal Law in 1997 (allowing private prosecution of IP violations). These laws and their implementation rules, together with some individual regulations on specific issues, as well as many international conventions have further strengthened the basic legal framework for IP protection in China.[12] Such a rapid development of a legal system has been remarkable. A former Director-General of WIPO, Dr. Arpad Bogsch, was reported to have said in 1994 that '[t]he change is from nothing to everything and the whole world admires what China achieved in a very short time.'[13]

China's efforts to join the World Trade Organisation (WTO), and its membership of it since 2001, have led to a new wave of legal reform in IP protection as well as in foreign trade and investment law. Thus, the protection of layout designs of integrated circuits appeared in late 2001.[14] At the same time all major laws on IP protection underwent comprehensive revision to match and meet the requirements of the relevant

---

8 Regulations of the People's Republic of China on Customs Protection of Intellectual Property (1995). These regulations have now been replaced by a new set of regulations of the same title, issued on 2 December 2003 and effective since 1 March 2004. Bilingual texts of most Chinese IP laws are available from CCH, *China Laws for Foreign Business – Business Regulation*, Volume 2, Singapore: CCH Asia Pacific (loose-leaf service).

9 Certain Provisions on the Prohibition of Activities Infringing upon Commercial Secrets, issued by the State Administration of Industry and Commerce, 23 November 1995, and revised on 3 December 1998.

10 Provisional Regulations on Identification and Administration of Well-known Trademarks, issued by the State Administration for Industry and Commerce in August 1996 (revised in April 2003).

11 Regulations on the Protection of New Plant Varieties, issued by the State Council on 20 March 1997, effective on 1 October 1997. China also ratified the International Convention for the Protection of New Varieties of Plants in August 1998.

12 For a recent detailed introduction to the system for the protection of IP and its development in China, see the *1994 IP White Paper*, *supra* note 5; *New Progress in China's Protection of Intellectual Property Rights*, Information Office of the State Council of the PRC, April 2005 (hereinafter referred to as the *2005 IP White Paper*, an English version is available at <news.xinhuanet.com/english/2005-04/21/content_2858667.htm>); Li Chunmao (ed.), *Chinese Civil Law: Intellectual Property* (Beijing: China Public Security University Press, 1997); Qu Sanqiang (2004), *supra* note 3.

13 'IP Protection, From Nothing to Everything', (18-24 April 1994) *Beijing Review* 5, at 6. Dr Bogsch was also reported to have said that 'China has accomplished all this at a speed unmatched in the history of intellectual property protection'. See the 1994 IP White Paper, *supra* note 5, at 10.

14 The Regulations for the Protection of the Layout Design of Integrated Circuits, issued by the State Council on 19 April 2001 and effective from 1 October 2001, and the Detailed Implementing Rules for the Regulations for the Protection of the Layout Design of Integrated

international treaties (including the TRIPs agreement of the WTO): the Trademark Law and its implementing rules were revised on 27 October 2001 and 3 August 2002 respectively, the Patent Law and its implementing rules were amended on 25 August 2000 and 15 June 2001 respectively, and the Copyright Law and its implementing rules on 27 October 2001 and 2 August 2002 respectively. A new set of regulations on customs protection of IP was issued by the State Council in 2003[15] and a new set of implementation rules by the General Administration of Customs (GAC) in 2004.[16] Specialised rules on the protection of pharmaceutical products, computer software, video-audio products, internet copyright protection, etc. have also been issued since the 1990s. Most recently the Standing Committee of the NPC (SCNPC) ratified, on 29 December 2006, the WIPO Copyright Treaty 1996 and the WIPO Performance & Phonograms Treaty 1996. Together with many judicial interpretations on various aspects of IP protection issued by the Supreme People's Court,[17] and local regulations on IP protection (especially of well-known marks), the present IP protection regime is indeed a far cry from that which existed in the late 1970s.

Institutional development has been equally remarkable. In January 1991 rules were issued for the setting up of arbitration commissions for technology transfer contracts. In June 1991 Shanghai, Tianjin, Guangdong, Sichuan, etc. took the lead in setting up such commissions[18] and soon most provinces did the same. To strengthen the implementation of IP laws, the Beijing Intermediate and High Courts, the Guangdong, Shanghai, Hainan, and Fujian High Courts and the Shenzhen Intermediate Court took the initiative in establishing specialised chambers for IP protection,[19] and by 1999 most high courts in China had done the same.[20] The Supreme People's Court itself established such a chamber in October

Circuits, issued by the State Intellectual Property Office on 18 September 2001 and effective from 1 October 2001.

15 See *supra* note 8.

16 Implementing Measures for the Regulations of the People's Republic of China on Customs Protection of Intellectual Property, adopted by the GAC on 22 April 2004, issued by the same on 25 May 2004, and effective on 1 July 2004. These measures replaced an earlier set of rules issued in 1995.

17 Between 1978 and 2004, the Supreme People's Court issued a total of 47 pieces of judicial interpretation in the area of IP protection, and 26 of these were issued since 2000. See 'The Situation in Judicial Protection of IP by the People's Courts', available from <www.chinaiprlaw.cn/file/200502014166.html> (last accessed 3 February 2005).

18 *China Law Yearbook 1992* (*Zhongguo Falü Nianjian*) (Beijing: China Law Yearbook Press, 1993), at 63-64.

19 'We Protect Foreign Registered Trademarks', *People's Daily* (*Renmin Ribao*) (overseas edition), 19 April 1994, at 2; 'Our Intellectual Property Protection Law Is Basically Complete', *People's Daily* (*Renmin Ribao*), 9 May 1994, at 3.

20 See 'Situation in Judicial Protection of IP by the People's Court', *supra* note 17. A full list of courts that had established such specialised chambers as of 2004 is available at <www.

1996.[21] By 2006 most intermediate courts in China had also done so: there are now 172 courts that have established special IP chambers and 140 special IP collegiate panels, with 1667 specialised IP judges.[22] In total, jurisdiction over patents, new plant varieties and computer layout has been granted to 62, 38 and 43 intermediate courts respectively, with 17 basic courts having also been granted jurisdiction over certain IP civil disputes.[23] Specialist master or bachelor degree programs have been introduced in many universities, including the prestigious Beijing University and Renmin University, to train specialists for intellectual property protection.[24]

Administratively, specialised authorities have been set up by the State Council to be in charge of different aspects of IP issues. These now include the State Intellectual Property Office (SIPO) (for patents and international cooperation for IP protection), the Trademark Bureau of the State Administration for Industry and Commerce (SAIC) (for trademarks), State Administration of Copyrights, and the General Administration of Customs (for Customs enforcement and protection of IP). To coordinate the fragmented enforcement of IP laws by different state authorities the State Council established, in January 2005, a cross-jurisdictional working group, formally called the Leading Working Group on State Intellectual Property Strategy-Making, headed by Vice Premier Wu Yi and composed of vice-ministers of relevant ministries as well as leaders from the State Council IP authorities.[25] Its tasks are to coordinate IP protection and enforcement nationwide (both horizontally and vertically), to supervise the handling of major IP infringement cases, and to consult foreign investment enterprises on a regular basis.[26]

---

chinaiprlaw.cn/file/200107311402.html> (last accessed 3 February 2005).

21 'Judicial Protection for Intellectual Property Rights Strengthened in Our Country', *People's Daily* (*Renmin Ribao*), internet edition, 17 July 1997.

22 See Cao Jianming, 'Speech by the Vice-President of the Supreme People's Court', delivered at the National Conference on IP Adjudication, 18 January 2007, available at <www.chinaiprlaw.cn/file/2007020210142htm> (last accessed 15 February 2007). See also 'IP Cases increase and IP judicial protection preliminarily established', available from <news.xinhuanet.com/legal/2007-01/18/content_5622505.htm> (last accessed 18 January 2007).

23 See Cao Jianming, *id.*

24 'Our Patent Work Is at a New Stage', *People's Daily* (*Renmin Ribao*), 24 December 1993, at 3; and the 1994 IP White Paper, *supra* note 5, at 10.

25 See 'State Council Decided to Establish a Leading Working Group on the Making of a State Intellectual Property Strategy', in <www.sipo.gov.cn/sipo/ywdt/120050117_38734.htm> (last accessed 2 February 2005). The fragmented structure of IP administration and enforcement is itself a rather complicated story of politics and economics in China, which has been well researched and discussed by Mertha, *supra* note 6, ch. 3.

26 See 'Sino-US IP Round Table: Progress in IP Protection in Our Country'', in <www.chinaprlaw.cn/file/200501154051.html> (accessed 1 February 2005). See also the website: <ipr.mofcom.gov.cn>. It is unclear, however, whether this Leading Working Group is meant to be a temporary or permanent authority. In July 1994 a State Council IP Working Conference was

In addition to the legislative, administrative and institutional development there are the various public campaigns against IP infringement that are organised by the different government authorities from time to time.[27]

If the initial catalyst for establishing an IP protection regime came from the need to attract foreign investment as well as foreign pressure in the 1980s and 1990s, the continuing efforts to improve the legal framework are caused as much by the need to protect China's own IP development and achievements as by foreign pressure. Indeed, the improvement of IP protection has a rather clear correlation with the IP market status in China, as indicated by the following tables in relation to trademarks, patents and import and export technology contracts/trade in new and high tech products.[28]

Development of IP Market in China: Table 1 – Trademarks

	1979[29]	1993[30]	2001[31]	2003	2005
Accumulated total number of trademark registrations at the end of the year	32,589[32]	411,161[33]	1,450,000[34]	1,973,000[35]	2,499,000[36]

established with similar structure and responsibilities. The Notice of the State Council on the Establishment of a State Council Intellectual Property Working Conference and Division of Work among Relevant Departments (issued 11 July 1994) did not set a time framework, and it is unclear whether the Working Conference has stopped functioning and whether this new Working Group is meant to replace the Working Conference.

27 See further discussion in Section 7.2 below.

28 Under the Copyright Law and its Implementation Rules, copyright registration is voluntary; thus any available statistics do not reflect the actual status of publications in China.

29 Trademark registration resumed in 1979.

30 Major IP law changes made.

31 China became a member of the WTO and further IP law changes were made.

32 *2005 Annual Report of China's Trademarks*, SAIC, 2006. The report is available from <www.saic.gov.cn> (last accessed 15 August 2006). See also 'Trademark: A Sharp Knife in Market Competition', *Legal Daily* (*Fazhi Ribao*), 25 February 1994, at 5.

33 With 59,466 being trademarks from overseas. See 'We Protect Foreign Registered Trademarks', *supra* note 19; and the 1994 White Paper, *supra* note 5, at 13.

34 Jianfu Chen (ed.), *China Business Law Guide* (Singapore: CCH International, loose-leaf service), para. 60-010.

35 Li Shunde, 'Chinese Legal Framework on Intellectual Property Protection', available at <www.chinaiprlaw.cn/file/200501224095.html> (last accessed 3 February 2005).

36 Among which 443,000 were registered foreign trademarks. See *2005 Annual Report of China's Trademarks*, *supra* note 32. According to the same source, as of the end of 2005 the accumulated total number of applications for registration was 4,219,640.

Table 2 – Patents

	1985[37]–1998	1993	2001	2003	2005
Accumulated total number of patent approvals at the end of the year	430,884[38]	175,000[39]	1,370,00[40]	1,931,118[41]	2,761,189[42]

The latest available statistics, of 2006, indicate continuing growth. There were 573,178 applications for patents filed in that year, of which 268,002 were granted. Among the applications, 82.1% were domestic applications, with the following details:[43]

2006	*Total*	*Domestic*	*Foreign*
Applications accepted	573,178 (20.3% ↑) 476,264 (2005)	470,342 (22.8% ↑) 383,157 (2005)	102,836 (10.4% ↑) 93,107 (2005)
Approvals granted	268,002 (25.2% ↑) 214,003 (2005)	223,860 (30.4% ↑) 171,619 (2005)	44,142 (4.1% ↑) 42,384 (2005)

Table 3 – New & High-Tech Product Trade

	1979–1993 (accumulated total)[44]	2001[45]	2003 (billion)[46]	2005 (billion)[47]
Annual technology import/ export[48]	Total tech import contracts: 7,000 worth US$ 48 billion	Total tech import contracts: 3900 Worth US$ 9.091 billion	Total: US$ 229.34 Import: US$ 119.18 Export: US$ 110.16	Total: US$ 415.96 Import: US$ 197.71 Export: US$ 218.25

37 Patent Law became effective in 1985.

38 See *Intellectual Property Yearbook of China 2003* (*Zhongguo Zhishi Chanquan Nianjian*) (Beijing: Press of Intellectual Property, 2003), Table 5, at 232.

39 See 'Our Patent Work is at a New Stage', supra note 24. The total number of applications increased to 370,000 by the end of February 1994: 'To Perfect the Patent System and to Establish Transfer Markets', *Economic Daily* (*Jingji Ribao*), 14 April 1994, at 3; and the 1994 White Paper, *supra* note 5, at 13.

40 Calculated on the basis of the *2005 Annual Reports*, State Intellectual Property Office, available from: <www.sipo.gov.cn/sipo_English/ndbg/nb/ndbg2005> (last accessed 15 August 2006).

41 *Id.*

42 This includes 503,674 foreign patents registered in China. See *2005 Annual Reports, supra* note 40.

43 See '57 thousand patent applications for 2006 and 80% are domestic', available from <www.chinaiprlaw.cn/file/200701169950.html> (last accessed 17 January 2007).

44 1993 alone saw the signing of foreign-related technology transfer contracts worth US$ 8.26 billion. See 'Our Intellectual Property Protection Law Is Basically Complete', *supra* note 19.

In 2005 there were 573 publishing houses in China, and 222,473 books were published, with a total printing of 6.402 billion copies. There were 1,931 newspapers published, with a total printing of 41.26 billion copies, and 9,468 journals with a combined printing of 2.759 billion copies.[49]

The number of applications shown in the above Tables is much larger than the number of approved registrations, the majority of approved registrations being domestic applications. Clearly China has had some significant interest in protecting IP (though its value is yet to be fully recognised), and foreign pressure is only one of the reasons for doing so.

3. Trademarks

3.1. Legal and Administrative Framework

Trademarks are regulated and protected by a host of laws and regulations. At the centre are the Trademark Law of the PRC[50] and its Detailed Rules for the Implementation of the Trademark Law of the PRC.[51] These two principal laws are implemented by many administrative regulations, departmental rules and judicial interpretations.[52]

In 1996 a total of 7,312 contracts of technology imports and exports, with a total contract value of US$ 19.951 billion, were signed. See 'An Account of China's Technology Trade in 1996', in *Almanac of China's Foreign Economic Relations and Trade 1997/98* (Beijing: China National Economic Publishing House, 1997), at 62.

45 Source: Ministry of Commerce: <kjs.mofcom.gov.cn/aarticle/bn/br/200208/20020800034976.html> (last accessed 29 August 2006).

46 *Id.*

47 *Id.*

48 Until 2001 (inclusive) the statistics of the Ministry of Commerce referred to Technology import contracts and value. From 2002 (inclusive), such statistics refer to the value of import and export products.

49 See *People's Daily* (overseas edition), 29 August 2006, at 2.

50 Initially promulgated by the SCNPC on 23 August 1982, first revised on 22 February 1993 and revised for the second time on 27 October 2001.

51 First issued by the State Council on 10 March 1983, amended four times on 3 January 1988, 15 July 1991, and 23 April 1995, and most recently revised and re-promulgated on 3 August 2002.

52 The principal regulations and rules include the following: Regulations on the Recognition and Administration of Well-known Trademarks (initially issued by the SAIC on 14 August 1996 as Provisional Regulations, revised and re-issued on 17 April 2003); Rules for the Evaluation and Review of Trademarks (first issued by the SAIC in 1995, revised and re-issued on 17 September 2002, further revised and re-issued on 26 September 2005); Regulations concerning the Administration of Trademarks in Foreign Trade (jointly issued by MOFTEC and the SAIC on 25 August 1995); Measures on the Registration and Administration of Collective

Other laws that contain provisions on the regulation and protection of trademarks (in fact, intellectual property in general) include the General Principles of Civil Law (1986), the Law against Unfair Competition (1993), the Foreign Trade Law (1994, revised 2004), and the Criminal Law (1979, revised 1997).

As mentioned before, China is also a party to the Paris Convention for the Protection of Industrial Property (since 1985) and the Madrid Agreement for the International Registration of Marks (since 1989) and the Protocol thereunder (since 1995).[53] While China only ratified the Nice Agreement concerning the International Classification of Goods and Services for the Purposes of the Registration of Marks in August 1994, this International Classification system had been adopted for use in China since November 1988.[54]

The overall responsibilities for trademark registration and administration are vested with the SAIC (through its Trademark Bureau) and its local equivalents. The Ministry of Commerce (formerly the Ministry of Foreign Trade and Economic Cooperation, MOFTEC) is also involved in the administration of all foreign trade related trademarks. Two authorities within the SAIC are directly responsible for trademark matters: the Trademark Bureau and the Trademark Evaluation and Review Board (TERB). The Bureau is a decision-making authority and the TERB is an internal review mechanism.

3.2. The Trademark System

The Trademark Law provides that any visible symbol including word, design, letter, number, three dimensional mark, colour combination or combination of all of the above elements, may be registered in China,[55] as long as such a mark is so distinctive that it is capable of identification and does not conflict with legal rights and interests

---

Trademarks and Certification Marks (issued by the SAIC on 17 April 2003, and replacing an earlier set of similar rules issued on 20 December 1994); Administrative Measures on Trademark Agencies (issued by the SAIC on 2 December 1999); various judicial interpretations issued by the Supreme People's Court, including the Interpretations of the Supreme People's Court on Certain Issues concerning the Application of Laws in the Adjudication of Civil Dispute Cases related to Trademarks (issued on 12 October 2002), and the Interpretation on Certain Issues concerning the Application of Law in the Adjudication of Civil Dispute Cases relating to Computer Network Domain Names (issued on 17 July 2001 and effective from 24 July 2001); and various rulings by the SAIC on specific issues relating to trademark registration, alteration, and protection.

53 The Agreement and the Protocol are implemented by the Measures on the Implementation of the Madrid System for International Registration of Trademarks, issued by the SAIC on 17 April 2003 and replacing an earlier set of the measures issued in May 1996.

54 See Notice of the SAIC on Implementing an International Classification of Commodities for the Purposes of Registration of Trademarks, issued 15 September 1988 and becoming effective on 1 November 1988.

55 See Article 8 of the Trademark Law.

obtained by others prior to the registration.[56] Initially the original Trademarks Law only recognised trademarks for goods and services; collective marks and certification marks were only included in the Law after the revision in 2001.

A collective trademark is defined as a sign used to indicate membership qualifications of a certain organisation and registered by the organisation for use in commercial activities. A certification trademark is defined as a sign owned and controlled by another organisation which controls a certain commodity or service and which authorises the use of such a sign to the commodity or service so as to indicate the origin of place, raw materials, methods of production, quality or other specific character of the commodity or service.[57] Collective and certification marks are apparently seen as being different from commodity and service marks and the Trademarks Law specifically allows the industry and commerce authority of the State Council to issue special provisions in relation to their registration and administration.[58] While the Regulations concerning the Administration of Trademarks in Foreign Trade were issued before the 2001 Trademark Law revision, and thus do not refer to collective or certification marks, the latter could be seen as having been included in 'other trademarks approved and registered by the Trademark Bureau of SAIC'.[59]

For a mark to be registered, it must be distinctive for the particular class of goods or services to which it applies.[60] This essentially means that it must be different from other marks. It must also show something which is not generic to the product it represents, or which is indicative of quality rather than brand.[61] Applicants for registration need to specify both the mark to be registered and the class of goods or services to which it is to apply.[62]

The Trademark Law specifically prohibits the use of official symbols or names or inspection imprints or racially discriminatory symbols as trademarks.[63] Specific examples of such marks are provided in the Law.[64] Further, if a trademark under application for registration for an identical or similar product is a copy, imitation or a translation of a well-known trademark that has not been registered in China and may easily cause confusion, the trademark may not be registered or used. Likewise,

---

56 See Article 9 of the Trademark Law.

57 See Article 3 of the Trademark Law.

58 *Ibid.*, and these were duly issued in 1994 and revised in 2003. See *supra* note 52.

59 Article 4 of the Regulations concerning the Administration of Trademarks in Foreign Trade.

60 Article 9 of the Trademark Law.

61 Article 11 of the Trademark Law.

62 Article 19 of the Trademark Law.

63 Article 10 of the Trademark Law.

64 See Article 10 & 11 of the Trademark Law.

if a trademark under application for registration for non-identical or non-similar products is a copy, imitation or a translation of a well-known trademark registered in China and may mislead the public and possibly cause harm to the rights and interests of the registrant of the well-known trademark, the trademark may not be registered or used.[65] On the other hand the revised Trademark Law now allows the use of letters as trademarks,[66] and this may lead to the recognition of the registrability of surnames.

Special protection is accorded to famous or well-known trademarks even if they are not registered in China. The original Trademark Law did not contain any provisions on well-known marks, and the 1993 revision continued to neglect this important issue, despite the fact that China acceded to the Paris Convention for the Protection of Industrial Property in 1984.[67] In the absence of an explicit legal protection, certain protection was provided in certain circumstances on a case-by-case basis. The first formal legal protection came in 1996 in the form of the Provisional Regulations on the Recognition and Administration of Well-known Trademarks.[68] These Provisional Regulations were followed by the Notice on Certain Issues relating to Applications for the Recognition of Well-known Trademarks,[69] which clarified certain practical issues for the recognition of well-known marks. The 2001 revision of the Trademark Law finally added provisions on the protection of well-known trademarks.[70] In April 2003 the SAIC further issued the Provisions on Recognition and Protection of Well-known Trademarks, which replaced the 1996 Provisional Regulations as mentioned above.

The Trademark Law (as revised in 2001) does not provide a definition for well-known marks; it does however provide a list of factors to be considered in recognising a well-known trademark. The factors include the public knowledge, the duration of its usage, publicity efforts of the trademark holder, and the protection it has received as a well-known mark.[71] Under the 2003 Well-known Trademark Provisions a well-known trademark is defined as one that is widely known to the relevant public and has a relatively high reputation in China. 'Relevant public' includes consumers using goods or services carrying the trademark, proprietors producing such goods or providing such services, and sellers and other persons involved in sales activities.[72]

---

65 See Article 13 of the Trademark Law.

66 See Article 7 of the Trademark Law.

67 Well-known marks are protected by the Paris Convention, Article 6*bis*.

68 Issued on 14 August 1996 by the SAIC, but now superseded by a new set of Regulations issued in 2003. See *supra* note 52.

69 Issued on 28 April 2000 by the SAIC.

70 See Articles 13 & 14 of the Trademark Law as revised in October 2001.

71 See Article 14 of the Trademark Law.

72 Article 2 of the Well-Known Trademark Provisions.

In strong contrast to the 1996 Provisional Regulation, a well-known trademark is not necessarily one that has been registered in China; an unregistered mark may also come under the protection of the Well-known Trademark Provisions, as long as it can be proven to be 'well-known'. As such, Chinese government authorities no longer need to take the initiative in assessing and recognising well-known marks, as they did in batches every year before the new Provisions. It also means that the sole purpose of registering well-known trademarks is for settling disputes involving trademark infringement.

As is the case in every other country, the principal problems concerning well-known marks relate to the reproduction or imitation of trademark symbols, or the registering of a well-known trademark as a company name. Thus the protection provided by the Well-known Trademark Provisions focuses on objections to registration and use of such a reproduction or imitation, if a claim to a well-known mark can be established. For this purpose Article 3 of the Well-known Trademark Provisions provides a long and open-ended list of materials that may be used as evidence for proving that a trademark is well known, which is not radically different from Article 14 of the Trademark Law.

In cases where a well-known trademark has been used by another as a company name, once a claim to a well-known mark has been established the de-registration of such a company name is to be handled in accordance with the Administrative Measures on the Registration of Enterprise Names.[73]

It is not compulsory to register a trademark for goods sold on the Chinese domestic market unless otherwise provided by law (such as for tobacco and pharmaceutical products).[74] However, goods bearing no trademark or goods with an unregistered mark must show the name and address of the seller on the goods and the packaging. Registered marks receive certain protections under the law. Unauthorised use of a mark which is identical or similar to a registered mark for the same or a similar category of goods or services to which the registered mark applies is prohibited. Unregistered marks are not generally protected by the law although, as mentioned above, famous or well-known marks and marks which have been registered in some other countries with which China has treaty arrangements do enjoy some special protections even if they are not registered in China.

Procedures for trademark registration with the Trademark Bureau may be conducted by the applicants themselves or entrusted to a trademark agent. Where the applicant is a foreign national or a foreign organisation, application for registration and other trademark-related matters must be entrusted to a qualified Chinese

73 These Measures were issued by the SAIC on 22 July 1991 (with the approval of the State Council). They are further implemented by the Implementing Measures on the Registration of Enterprise Names, initially issued by SAIC on 8 December 1999, and revised on 14 June 2004.

74 See Article 7 of the Implementation Rules.

trademark agency.[75] Chinese is the official language and all materials in a foreign language must have a Chinese translation. Trademark agencies are regulated by the Administrative Measures on Trademark Agencies (1999).

3.3. Domain Names

As in other countries the question of domain names as an IP issue has only recently become a concern. China began its formal regulation and protection in 2002 by the issuance of the Administrative Measures on China Internet Domain Names,[76] which established a registration and protection system for domain names.

'Domain name' is defined in the Chinese law as characters and symbols of a hierarchical structure which distinguish a computer on the internet and correspond to the computer's internet protocol address. Registered domain names are protected from infringement. The Ministry of Information Industry (largely through the China Internet Network Information Centre) is responsible for the administration of China's internet domain names.

Any organisation or individual may apply for registration of domain names. The principle in domain name registration is 'first come, first registration'. Administrative organisations for domain name registration are generally prohibited from reserving domain names. However, in the interests of the state and the public they may provide 'necessary protection for certain reserved characters'.[77]

To apply for domain name registration applicants are required to submit true, accurate and complete information, sign a user registration agreement with the domain name registration service organisation, and pay a registration fee (and an ongoing fee is payable to maintain a domain name). Upon registration the applicant becomes the holder of the domain name, and bears liability for infringement on the lawful rights and interests of other parties when holding or using the said domain name.[78]

Here one needs to note that while people may create various kinds of domain names, domain names containing certain meanings are prohibited from being registered and used. These prohibited contents include: violation of the fundamental principles of the Constitution, undermining State security, divulging State secrets, subverting State power or damaging national unity, harming the dignity or interests of the State, inciting ethnic hatred or racial discrimination or damaging inter-ethnic unity, sabotaging state religious policy or propagating heretical teachings or feudal

---

75 Article 18 of the Trademark Law.

76 Issued by the Ministry of Information Industry. These Measures have now been replaced by a new set of Measures of the same title issued on 5 November 2004 and effective from 20 December of the same year (Order No. 30).

77 See Article 25 of the Domain Name Measures.

78 Article 28 of the Domain Name Measures.

superstition, disseminating rumours, disturbing the social order or disrupting social stability, propagating obscenity, pornography, gambling, violence, murder or fear, or inciting the commission of crimes, insulting or libelling others or infringing upon the lawful rights and interests of others, or other contents prohibited by laws or regulations.[79] The scope of prohibition is thus vague but extremely wide.

With the rapid development of the internet and the increasing recognition of commercial value in domain names, there has been a steady increase since the 1990s, in China and elsewhere, of disputes relating to the use of trademarks, brand names or other commercial names as domain names. In their nature, most of these cases involve trademark infringements and unfair competition caused by domain name registration.[80] The settlement of such disputes is not easy, not simply because such disputes are new to the legal systems, but because the nature of the disputes does not sit comfortably in any particular branch of law, such as trademark or competition law. The conventional understanding of trademark protection is closely associated with goods or services, while competition is not always the reason a particular name is registered as a domain name. To make things even more complicated, domain registration is largely regulated and conducted by professional organisations rather than by state authorities.[81] Not surprisingly, when domain disputes first went to Chinese courts in the 1990s, the courts found themselves struggling with establishing a legal basis for decision-making (both in terms of jurisdiction and substantive issues). Faced with this new legal challenge, and after several years of study,[82] the Supreme People's Court finally issued the Interpretation on Certain Issues concerning the Application of Law in the Adjudication of Civil Dispute Cases relating to Computer Network Domain Names.[83] While this Interpretation does not

79 See Article 27 of the Domain Name Measures.

80 For an analysis of some recent cases, see Gary Soo, 'Domain Name Protection in China: Practice under the Current Regime', (September 2004) 11 (3) *Murdoch University Electronic Journal of Law*, available <www.murdoch.edu.au/elaw/issues/v11n3/soo113_text.html> (last accessed 18 August 2005).

81 In the case of China, while the Ministry of Information Industry has powers over all internet regulation, registration and dispute settlement for domain names is conducted by the China Internet Network Information Centre (CNNIC) and its agencies. While the establishment of the CNNIC (3 June 1997) has the approval of the State Council and, administratively, it belongs to the Chinese Academy of Sciences and it is under the leadership of the Ministry of Information Industry in terms of business development, it is not a government department or agency. See homepage of CNNIC: <www.cnnic.net.cn>.

82 See 'On the Understanding and Applicability of the Interpretation on Certain Issues concerning the Application of Law in the Adjudication of Civil Dispute Cases relating to Computer Network Domain Names', <www.chinaiprlaw.cn/file/200109121072.html> (last accessed 18 August 2005).

83 Issued on 17 July 2001 and effective from 24 July 2001.

address all relevant issues it does clarify many ambiguities over the nature of domain names, the application of laws, and jurisdiction over domain name disputes.

The basic approach of the Interpretation is to define certain registrations or uses of domain names as tortious or unfair competition. Essentially, if a domain name or the main part of a domain name constitutes a copy, imitation, translation or transliteration of a well-known trademark owned by another, or such a domain name is so similar or identical to a registered trademark or domain name belonging to the another that it may cause misleading identification, then such registration or use of the domain name will constitute a tort or unfair competition if the holder of the domain name does not have any rights over the domain name or has no valid reason for such registration, and the registration or use of the domain name by the defendant is malicious.[84] Clearly, 'malice' is the key ingredient and an issue likely to cause contention.

There are only certain activities that can easily be defined as 'malicious', such as the registration or use of a well-known trademark, or a similar or identical mark owned by another as a domain name for commercial purposes, in order to offer to sell, rent or transfer the domain name at a high price, so as to obtain improper profits; or registering a domain name without using it or without any intention to use it so as to prevent the lawful right holder from registering the domain name. However, the Interpretation has taken an open-ended approach to the issue of 'malice' by including the catch-phrase 'other malicious activities'.[85] This open-ended approach on the one hand reflects the general Chinese legal drafting style, and on the other hand indicates the uncertainties about future developments in this area. It also gives courts almost unlimited powers of discretion.

Anyone undertaking activities that are held to be tortious or unfair in competition will bear civil liabilities in accordance with laws governing torts or the prohibition of unfair competition (e.g. the Trademark Law, the General Principles of Civil Law and the Unfair Competition Law). The court of jurisdiction is an intermediate court in the place where the torts occurred, or where the defendant resides. These courts are required to accept cases filed in compliance with the provisions of Article 108 of the Civil Procedure Law. In addition to court settlement, domain name disputes may also be handled by a domain name dispute resolution institution or heard by an arbitration institution.

84 See Article 4 of the Interpretation.

85 See Article 5 of the Interpretation.

4. Patents

4.1. Legislative and Administrative Framework

Similar to the legal framework on trademarks, the principal laws governing patents are the Patent Law of the PRC[86] and the Implementing Regulations for the Patent Law of the PRC.[87] These two laws are then further implemented by many departmental rules, local measures and judicial interpretations.[88]

Certain aspects of the protection of foreign patents in the PRC are governed by the Paris Convention for the Protection of Industrial Property, to which the PRC acceded on 14 November 1984, and which took effect on 19 March 1985, and the Patent Cooperation Treaty to the World Intellectual Property Organisation, of which the PRC became a member state from 1 January 1994. Additionally, China is also a party to the following international treaties relating to patents: the Locarno Agreement Establishing an International Classification for Industrial Designs 1968 (since September 1996); the Washington Treaty on the Protection of Intellectual Property in Respect of Integrated Circuits 1989 (since May 1989); the Budapest

86 Initially promulgated 12 March 1984 by the SCNPC. The Patent Law has now undergone three major revision processes: September 1992, August 2000, and July 2001. It should also be noted here that the Patent Law is currently in the process of another round of revisions. According to the Chinese media, this round will be a major one, to be completed by 2008. The focus of the new revision will be on simplification of patent application and examination, incorporation of international standards on granting patents, improvements in patent protection, and possibly, new rules on biological and genetic resources. See *China Daily*, 24 November 2005, available from <www.chinadaily.com.cn/english/doc/2005-11/24/content_497552.htm> (last accessed 5 December 2005).

87 Initially issued by the Patent Office on 19 January 1985 with the approval of the State Council, and amended in 1992 by the Patent Office. In 2001, these Regulations were replaced by the present ones issued by the State Council on 15 June 2001, which became effective from 1 July 2001. Further amendments (to Articles 101 and 108) were made on 28 December 2002.

88 The principal rules include the following: Provisions on the Investigation and Punishment of Activities involved in Passing Off Patents by Patent Administrative Organs (issued on 6 January 6 1999); Certain Provisions concerning the Application of Law in the Adjudication of Patent Dispute Cases (issued by the Supreme People's Court on 22 June 2001); Rules of the Patent Office of the PRC on Administrative Reconsideration (issued on 10 January 1995 and becoming effective on 1 February 1995, which replaced the 1991 Rules of the Patent Office of the PRC for Administrative Reconsideration); Regulations for the Protection of New Plant Varieties (issued by the State Council on 20 March 1997 and effective on 1 October 1997); and the implementing rules (for agriculture, issued 16 June 1999, and for forestry, issued 8 August 1999); Regulations for the Protection of the Layout Design of Integrated Circuits (issued by the State Council on 19 April 2001 and effective from 1 October 2001); Detailed Implementing Rules for the Regulations for the Protection of the Layout Design of Integrated Circuits (issued by the State Intellectual Property Office on 18 September 2001 and effective from 1 October 2001); and various national and local regulations issued with respect to dispute resolution and other matters.

Treaty on the International Recognition of the Deposit of Microorganisms for the Purposes of Patent Procedures 1977 (since July 1995); the Strasbourg Agreement concerning International Patent Classification (since June 1997); and the International Convention for the Protection of New Varieties of Plants 1961 (since April 1999).

The authority for the administration of patents has evolved in the last twenty years or so. Initially a patent office, the China Patent Office (CPO), was established in January 1980 as a division of the SAIC, with the responsibility of accepting patent applications and handling patent examination and registration. In March 1993 this Office was upgraded in the Chinese administrative hierarchy to an administrative authority directly under the State Council. During the 1998 State Council structural reform the State Intellectual Property Office (SIPO) was established. The original idea of this establishment was to centralise all IP work in one authority, but this idea is yet to be realised, and perhaps never will be.[89] With the establishment of the SIPO the CPO became an authority under the SIPO. In addition to administering patents by its CPO, the SIPO is also responsible for foreign cooperation and exchange for all IP-related matters. At the local level corresponding IP offices have been established in most provinces.[90]

While the CPO is the only authority responsible for acceptance, examination and approval of patent applications nationwide, the Patent Law now empowers patent departments of the people's governments in provinces, autonomous regions and directly administered municipalities to administer the patent work in their respective jurisdictions. However, the Law is silent on the scope of the power and functions of the local patent departments.

With regard to international patents, the CPO has been recognised since January 1994 as an Acceptance Office, International Searching Authority and International Preliminary Examination Authority of the Patent Cooperation Treaty.

The CPO is both a functional and policy authority in relation to the administration of the patent system nationwide. It accepts and examines patent applications as well as adjudicates patent disputes. It is also responsible for keeping up to date with the patent laws and regulations, providing guidance to local patents offices and promoting knowledge about patent protection. It is also the designated authority for international communications, cooperation and exchange on patent work, and for foreign-related intellectual property work.[91]

---

89 For an interesting and detailed discussion on the politics of establishing SIPO as a unifying IP authority and its failure, see Mertha, *supra* note 6, at 110-117.

90 See SIPO website: <www.sipo.gov.cn>.

91 *Id.*

4.2. The Patent System

As in the case of trademark protection, the scope of patent protection has undergone a process of gradual expansion since the promulgation of the 1984 Patent Law, both as a result of international cooperation and pressure and of domestic development in technologies.

The 1984 Patent Law provides for the protection of 'inventions', which include inventions, practical and new models and designs.[92] While this formula remains the same today, the original Law specifically excluded the grant of patents to foods, beverages and condiments, pharmaceutical products and substances made by means of a chemical process.[93] These exclusions were only abolished by the 1992 Amendment to the Patent Law. While the 1992 Amendment did not address the issue of patentability of bi-organisms *per se*, the revised Implementing Regulations for the Patent Law of the PRC extended patent protection to new bi-organisms.[94] Also importantly, the 1992 revision extended terms of protection, from 15 years to 20 years for inventions, and from 5 to 10 years for utility models and industrial designs.[95] Other revisions made in 1992 related to compulsory licensing and priority rights, in part to bring the Patent Law in line with TRIPS requirements.

In 2000, more extensive revisions in relation to judicial and administrative protection and law enforcement were introduced in the second revision of the Patent Law. The focus of the 2000 revision of the Patent Law was on the administrative structure, the procedures for application and examination of patents, the strengthening of the protection of patents, the review of and appeal against patent-related decisions, and the settlement of patent-related disputes. A specific technical issue that has finally been resolved is the ownership of patent rights in relation to an invention by employees during the course of their employment. Under Article 6 of the revised Patent Law such patent rights belong to the employing units unless a contract between the employing unit and the inventor or designer provides otherwise. In other words, Chinese Patent Law now finally allows contractual arrangements on the ownership of patent rights in relation to an invention or design by employees during the course of their employment.

---

92 See Articles 1 & 2 of the Patent Law.

93 See Article 25 of the Patent Law (1984). However, processes used in producing them (including animal and plant varieties) are patentable under the Law.

94 See Article 25 of Implementing Regulations, as revised in 1992.

95 See Article 42 of the Patent Law. The original Law provided a term of five years for utility models and new designs, with a possibility of extension for another three years. In accordance with the Public Announcement on Extending the Terms of Patent Rights for Certain Inventions, issued by the State Intellectual Property Office on 10 December 2001, for inventions whose applications were made before 31 December 1992 and whose patent rights were still valid by 11 December 2001, the term of protection would be extended to 20 years.

Article 22 of the Patent Law sets out criteria for the grant of patent rights, under which an invention or a practical and new model must possess the nature of novelty, creativity and practicability.

Novelty means that before the application no identical invention or practical and new model has been published, used or known to the general public, nor have patent rights for such been applied for and the application recorded by the relevant authorities.

Creativity indicates significant substantive features and notable progress in the invention or the practical and new model, as compared to existing technology before the application.

Practicality requires the invention or the practical and new model to be capable of being manufactured or used, and that it can produce positive results.

However not all technologies or innovations will be granted patent rights. Thus scientific discoveries, rules and methods for intellectual activities, methods for the diagnosis or treatment of diseases, animal and plant varieties, and substances obtained by means of nuclear transformation are explicitly excluded from the grant of patent rights.[96]

Once patent rights are granted the extent of protection is then determined by the terms of claims, and the interpretation of such terms of claims may also be aided by the description and appended drawings to the patent application.[97] As mentioned above, the term of protection for inventions is 20 years, and for utility models and industrial designs 10 years, both calculated from the date of application.[98]

Even though patent rights may be granted, the protection of the rights may nevertheless be qualified or restricted under certain circumstances. Thus Article 63 of the Patent Law provides a number of exclusions from the general rule of protection for patent rights, including the use of the patent solely for scientific research and experimentation. Further, if a patented product or product derived directly from a patented process is used and sold without knowingly lacking the patentee's authorisation, the user or seller will not be liable for compensation if it is able to prove the legal source of the product. Additionally, compulsory licensing may be mandated or authorised under certain circumstances, including for the purpose of a national emergency or public interest.[99] Under Article 72 of the Implementing Regulations, any unit may apply for compulsory licensing if the relevant patent rights have been granted for more than three years. In 2005, in response to the

---

96 See Article 25 of the Patent Law.

97 See Article 56 of the Patent Law.

98 See Article 42 of the Patent Law.

99 See Articles 48-50 of the Patent Law. These provisions are now further implemented by the Measures on the Implementation of Patent Compulsory Licensing, issued by the SIPO on 13 June 2003 and effective from 15 July of the same year.

Declaration on the TRIPS Agreement and Public Health,[100] the SIPO issued the Measures on Compulsory Patent Licensing concerning Public Health.[101] These Measures, in accordance with Article 49 of the Patent Law, allow the compulsory licensing of patents when there is an emergency in public health due to the outbreak of infectious diseases.

4.3. Layout Design in Integrated Circuits

The topography or layout design in integrated circuits (IC) is a relatively new addition to IP protection contents.[102] The World Intellectual Property Organisation (WIPO) did not fully address the issue until its adoption of the 1989 Washington Treaty on the subject. It is, however, WTO's TRIPs agreement that now imposes universal obligations for the protection of layout design in IC. While there is no doubt that there was pressure on China from US-led western countries to provide legal protection for layout design in IC, and there is an international obligation under TRIPs for China to do so, perhaps the most direct incentive came from China's own interest in expanding its rapidly developing IC industry. As Hatano has pointed out, while China was a latecomer, in 2002 it took some 15 percent of the total world IC market, worth US$ 18 billion, and that share was expanding rapidly.[103] As a matter of state policy, China has set itself the goal of becoming a major world development and production base for the IC industry by 2010, and of meeting its own domestic demand in 5-10 years' time as from 2000.[104] There is then clearly a high degree of self-interest in protecting layout design in IC in China.

At present the major laws in this area consist of the Regulations for the Protection of the Layout Design in Integrated Circuits,[105] and the Detailed Implementing Rules for the Regulations for the Protection of the Layout Design in Integrated Circuits.[106] In addition, the Supreme People's Court issued its Notice on Adjudication by Courts of Cases concerning Layout Design in IC on 30 October 2001, which set out court jurisdiction, and the scope of cases that courts may accept for adjudication. The

---

[100] Adopted on 14 November 2001.

[101] Issued on 29 November 2005 and effective 1 January 2006.

[102] Indeed, the US Semiconductor Chip Protection Act of 1984 is said to be the first such formal legal protection to emerge in the world. See Daryl G Hatano, 'China's Semiconductor Chip Protection Law – a Work in Progress', Paper presented to the 4th Annual Advanced Patent Law Institute, Berkeley Centre for Law and Technology, 4 December 2003, available from <www.sia-onlin.org/downloads/china_chip_protection_law.pdf> (last accessed 16 June 2005).

[103] See Hatano, *id.*

[104] See Articles 1 & 2 of the Certain Policies for the Encouragement and Development of the Software and Integrated Circuit Industry, issued by the State Council on 24 June 2000.

[105] Issued by the State Council on April 19, 2001 and effective from October 1, 2001.

[106] Issued by the State Intellectual Property Office on 18 September 2001 and effective from 1October 2001.

SIPO also issued its Measures on Administrative Law Enforcement for the Layout Design in Integrated Circuits.[107]

The 'layout design in an integrated circuit' is defined by the State Council Regulations as a three-dimensional configuration in an integrated circuit which has two or more components, with at least one of these being an active component, and has part or all of the interconnected circuitry, or a three-dimensional configuration which is prepared for the production of integrated circuits. To be under protection the layout design must be unique and original, i.e. it must be an intellectual achievement of the designer and must not be considered conventional among designers of layout and manufacturers of integrated circuits. However, where a layout design consists of several conventional designs and the combination as an integrated unit satisfies the aforesaid requirements on layout design, the layout design is under protection.

Exclusive rights to layout design include the right to duplicate the whole design or any part of the design that is creative, and the right to make commercial use of the design and of the integrated circuit containing the design, or commodities containing the said integrated circuit. Only registered layout designs are under protection, but such protection is not extended to the conception, handling process, methods of operation or mathematical concepts.[108]

However, the SIPO is vested with powers to give unilateral permission for the use of a layout design under certain special circumstances, such as where there is a state emergency or a public interest need, or where a holder of the exclusive rights is found to have engaged in unfair competition. Those who acquire unilateral permission must pay for the use of the layout design to the exclusive rights holder. The amount of payment is to be negotiated by the two parties. If no agreement can be reached the SIPO will make a ruling. Any party that disagrees with the ruling may lodge a lawsuit in a court within three months from the date of receiving the ruling.

The protection period of the exclusive rights is ten years, commencing from the date of the application for registration of the layout design, or the date on which the layout design was put to commercial use, whichever is earlier. In all cases the protection period of the exclusive rights is to be ended 15 years from the time of its creation, no matter whether it has been registered or put to commercial use or not.

Since registration is a pre-condition for protection, there is a potential conflict between registration and the protection of trade secrets. Thus Article 15 of the State Council Regulations provides that '[w]here a layout design for which registration is applied involves national security or major national interests and confidentiality is required, the handling of the application shall be conducted in accordance with

---

107 Issued on 28 November 2001 and effective on the same day.

108 See Articles 5, 7 & 8 of the State Council Regulations. Under the Detailed Implementation Rules the state authority for such registration is the SIPO. See Article 2 of the Detailed Implementation Rules.

relevant provisions stipulated by the State.' While the US Semiconductor Industry Association has sought assurances from China that 'major national interests' would be interpreted to include trade secrets and allowing applicants to withhold such trade secrets in their application,[109] it is unclear whether this provision could actually provide such protection in practice.

4.4. New Varieties of Plants

The 1984 Patent Law specifically excluded patent protection for plants and animals. The 1992 revision retained this exclusion. Thus, for quite some time it was uncertain whether patent protection would be granted to new varieties of animals and plants. This ambiguity was clarified when, in 1997, the Regulations for the Protection of New Plant Varieties were issued by the State Council.[110] On 23 March 1999 China formally lodged its instrument of accession to the International Convention for the Protection of New Varieties of Plants (1978),[111] and at the same time China also joined the International Union for the Protection of New Varieties of Plants (UPOV). The processes used in producing animal and plant varieties were accorded patent protection through the revision of the Patent Law in 2000. In 2001 the Supreme People's Court issued the Interpretation on Certain Questions concerning the Adjudication of Disputes on New Plant Varieties,[112] which defined court jurisdiction in relation to disputes on new varieties of plants. In 2007 the Supreme People's Court again issued Certain Provisions concerning the Specific Application of Law in the Adjudication of Dispute Cases concerning the Infringement of Rights for New Plant Varieties.[113] It should be noted that the 2007 Interpretation supplements, but does not replace, the 2001 Interpretation. Additionally, China is also bound by the WTO's TRIPS Agreement, Article 27:3(b) of which specifically demands the protection of new plan varieties 'either by patents or by an effective *sui generis* system or by any combination thereof.'

As a result of these legal developments a large number of applications for protection of new varieties of plant have been lodged in China. According to the Ministry of Agriculture 3,207 applications had been lodged at the end of 2006, among which 114 applications came from foreign entities, and a total of 747 applications had been approved. Since the issuance of the Regulation, 62 kinds of plants and 789 kinds of

---

[109] See Hatano, *supra* note 102.

[110] Issued by the State Council on 20 March 1997 and effective on 1 October 1997. These Regulations were followed by implementing rules (for agriculture, issued 16 June 1999, and for forestry, issued 8 August 1999) issued by the Ministry of Agriculture and Ministry of Forest respectively.

[111] The accession to the Convention was approved by the Standing Committee of the NPC in August 1999.

[112] Issued on 5 February 2001, and effective from 14 February 2001.

[113] Issued on 12 January 2007, effective from 1 February 2007.

forestry plants have been included in the national list of protected plant varieties.[114] There have also been many cases under investigation by the Chinese courts.[115]

According to the State Council Regulation, a new plant variety means a cultivated plant variety or a developed one based on a discovered wild plant. Further, such a variety must possess the characteristics of novelty, distinctness, uniformity and stability in order to meet the requirements for protection, and its denomination must be adequately designated.[116]

Novelty is largely a question of prior commercial sales. Under the Regulations, novelty is defined to mean that the propagating material of the new plant variety in respect of which variety rights are applied for has not been sold prior to the filing of the application, or has not been for sale, with the consent of the breeder, for more than one year in China, or that the propagating material of vines, forest trees, fruit trees and ornamental plants have not been for sale for more than six years, or the propagating material of other plant varieties for more than four years in a foreign country.[117]

Distinctness requires the new variety to be able to noticeably distinguish itself from any other plant variety known prior to the application.[118] Uniformity means that the variety is uniform in its relevant features or characteristics after propagation, although expected variation is allowed.[119] Stability refers to the ability to keep its relevant features or characteristics unchanged after repeated propagation, or at the end of a particular cycle of propagation.[120]

Interestingly, the administrative responsibility for new plant varieties is assigned to the Ministries of Agriculture and Forestry, instead of to any IP authorities.[121] A grant of 'variety rights' entails the exclusive rights to production, sale and commercial use (e.g. propagating materials of the protected variety for commercial purposes) of a new plant variety,[122] except for exploitation of the protected variety for breeding and other scientific research, or the use for propagating purposes by farmers, on their own holdings, to propagate material of the protected variety harvested on their

---

114 'China Steps up Efforts to Protect New Plant Varieties', in <english.people.com.cn/200604/24/eng20060424_260677.html> (last accessed 24 August 2006).

115 As at the end of 2006 some 800 cases of violation were being investigated, with 460 cases having been taken to court. *Id.*

116 See Article 2 of the Regulations.

117 See Article 14 of the Regulations.

118 See Article 15 of the Regulations.

119 See Article 16 of the Regulations.

120 See Article 17 of the Regulations.

121 See Article 3 of the Regulations.

122 Article 6 of the Regulations.

own holdings.[123] Compulsory licensing is also permitted for reasons of national or public interest.[124] The protection for vines, forest trees, fruit trees and ornamental plants lasts for 20 years, and for all others 15 years.[125]

The Chinese regulations and the Convention are largely consistent, though with some variations in terms of length of protection.[126] While compulsory licensing and exclusion of protection for the national or public interest are permissible under international treaties, the added elements of shorter periods of protection have led some to conclude that the Chinese protection for plant varieties is actually rather weak.[127] This 'defect' in Chinese regulations is in fact remedied by the fact that China is bound by multilateral and bilateral treaties which prevail over domestic regulations.

5. Copyright

5.1. Legislative and Administrative Framework

As a politically tightly controlled country, China has traditionally focused on the control of publications in its laws, rather than on the protection of them.[128] While this 'tradition' continues today, copyright protection has increased and improved significantly, partly due to western pressure and WTO requirements, and partly due to domestic needs as a result of the commercialisation of intellectual achievements. Nevertheless, copyright is an area in IP with the strongest tension between regulation and protection.

In terms of protection, the Copyright Law of the PRC[129] and the Regulations of the PRC on the Implementation of the Copyright Law[130] establish the principal legal framework, which, as in the case of trademarks and patents, is complemented by

123 Article 10 of the Regulations.

124 Article 11 of the Regulations.

125 Article 34 of the Regulations.

126 See Chengfei Ding, 'Protection for New Plant Varieties of American Business in China after China Enters the WTO', (2001) 6 *Drake J. Agric. L.* 333, at 341.

127 *Ibid.*, at 343.

128 See Qu Sangqian (2002), *supra* note 3.

129 As the first copyright statute in the history of the People's Republic of China it was enacted by the SCNPC on 7 September 1990 and came into effect on 1 June 1991. It was revised on 27 October 2001 to incorporate requirements under the Berne Convention.

130 Initially issued in 1991, it was replaced by the new set of regulations issued on 2 August 2002 and effective from 15 September 2002.

various departmental rules, either to implement the principal laws or to supplement them.[131]

Again, as in other areas of IP protection, China is a party to several international conventions on copyright, including the Berne Convention for the Protection of Literary and Artistic Works 1886 (since October 1992); the Universal Copyright Convention 1952 (since October 1992); the Geneva Convention for the Protection of Producers of Phonograms against Unauthorised Duplication of Their Phonograms 1971 (since April 1993); the WIPO Copyright Treaty 1996;[132] the WIPO Performance & Phonograms Treaty 1996;[133] and the UNESCO Convention on the Protection and Promotion of the Diversity of Cultural Expressions 2005.[134]

It is clear that the legal framework for copyright is both *ad hoc* and fragmented; it largely reflects the process of a gradual expansion of the scope of copyright protection, as well as responsive efforts to deal with uncertainties in the original Copyright Law as well as western pressure on specific IP rights issues.

Administrative responsibility (for both control and protection) is vested with the National Copyright Administration (NCA) and its local equivalents at provincial level. While the Copyright Law only refers to administrative powers for the NCA and its local equivalents, Article 47 of the Copyright Law and Article 37 of its Implementing Regulations also grant investigation and prosecution powers to local copyright administration departments in relation to copyright infringement as defined by Article 47 of the Copyright Law, when such infringement also jeopardises the public interest. It also grants the NCA the power to investigate and prosecute infringing acts which have a significant nationwide effect. However, the requirement under the original 1991 regulations that copyright disputes and infringements

---

131 The principal rules include the following: Measures on the Administrative Protection of Internet Copyright (issued by the National Copyright Administration on 30 April 2005 and effective on 30 May 2005); Provisions for the Implementation of International Copyright Treaties (issued by the State Council on 25 September 1992, and effective on 30 September 1992); Regulations on Computer Software Protection (first issued by the State Council on 24 May 1991 and revised and re-issued in December 2001); Measures for the Registration of Computer Software Copyright (issued on 2 February 2002 by the National Copyright Administration); Interpretation of the Supreme People's Court on Certain Issues Concerning the Application of Laws in the Hearing of Cases Involving Computer Network Copyright Disputes (initially issued on 19 December 2000 and revised on 2 January 2004); Interpretation of the Supreme People's Court on Certain Issues Related to the Application of Laws in the Adjudication of Civil Dispute Cases concerning Copyright (issued on 12 October 2002 and effective from 15 October of the same year); and other judicial interpretations on the adjudication of intellectual property rights disputes.

132 Ratified on 29 December 2006 by the SCNPC.

133 Ratified on 29 December 2006 by the SCNPC.

134 Ratified on 29 December 2006 by the SCNPC.

involving foreigners shall be handled by the NCA has been abolished under the new Implementing Regulations.

The NCA is in fact an external organisational name for the General Administration of Press and Publications when the latter exercises powers in relation to copyright administration. Like the organisation administering patents, the NCA has undergone several organisational changes. The General Administration of Press and Publications was established in November 1949. It operated directly under the Central Government until it was abolished in November 1954. A Press and Publications Bureau was then established within the Ministry of Culture in 1954. In June 1985 a National Copyright Bureau was also established within the Ministry of Culture. The two bureaus then became one organisation using two names for the exercise of two different powers. In January 1987 the State Council decided to abolish the Press and Publications Bureau and to establish the Administration for Press and Publications directly under the State Council. This new Administration then shared the same organisational structure with the National Copyright Administration (i.e. one organisation with two names). In 2000 the Administration for Press and Publications was renamed General Administration of Press and Publications (GAPP). The GAPP and the NCA have since operated under two external names but exist as one organisation.[135]

Part of the administrative functions of the NCA are in fact being exercised by the Copyright Protection Centre of China (CPCC), established in September 1998 and defined as 'a social copyright management and social service organisation', under the direct leadership of the NCA. The Centre then took over the management from NCA of the Copyright Agency of China (CAC), the Software Registration Centre of China (SRCC) (now deregistered), the Remuneration Collection and Distribution Centre for the Use of Copyright of China (RCDCUCC) (now deregistered), and the Editorial Office of Copyright Journals (now re-named China Copyright). It is also responsible for copyright registration, copyright agencies, legal services, copyright authentication, and information and services.[136]

In order to combat rapidly spreading copyright infringements in China, a national anti-piracy organisation – the Anti-Piracy Commission – was set up on 25 October 2002. The Commission is subject to the Copyright Association of China, and is responsible for co-ordinating local anti-piracy alliances and handling anti-piracy related matters, such as investigation, evidence collection and filing of court actions, upon the request of copyright owners.[137]

---

[135] See GAPP website: <www.gapp.gov.cn>.

[136] See <www.ccopyright.com.cn>.

[137] See <www.ccopyright.com.cn/crorganise/cro_xhfzjg_fdbwyh.htm>.

5.2. The Copyright System

The original Copyright Law of 1990 left many uncertainties as to the kinds of subject matter to be protected and the scope of protection to be accorded. While some of the problems and unanswered questions were addressed by the Implementing Regulations, and especially by the revisions of the Copyright Law and its Implementing Regulations in 2001 and 2002 respectively, other issues were dealt with by special regulations – theoretically forming part of various implementing regulations for the Copyright Law, such as regulations on computer software and internet publications. Additionally, regulations on audio-video products, film, TV programs and other performing works etc. also provide additional protection against piracy of such products/programs. Thus, although the Copyright Law and its Implementing Regulations are meant to provide comprehensive coverage of copyrights protected in China, the protection of more specialised copyright or copyright-related matters is in fact further supplemented by separate legislation. As mentioned above, this fragmented approach reflects the gradual improvement of copyright protection in China not by design, but more by necessity, in order to balance China's inexperience with international demands.[138]

Article 3 of the Copyright Law, as revised in 2001, defines the protected subject matter (works) for copyright protection to include literary works, oral works, musical, dramatic and folk art, dance and acrobatic artistic works, works of fine art and architectural works, photographic works, film works and other similar works, engineering designs, product designs, maps, schematic diagrams and other graphic works and model works, computer software, and other works stipulated by laws and administrative regulations.

The scope of the protected subject matter is further extended by Article 12 of the Law, which accords protection to adaptations, translations, annotations and collations of pre-existing works. Article 14 further extends protection to 'edited' works (*bianji zuopin*), which are defined as the compilation of several works, extracts of works or data and other material that does not constitute a work, but the selection or editing of which displays a work of creativity. Specific meanings of the protected 'works' are explained by Article 4 of the Implementing Regulations, as revised in 2002.

However, protected works do not include any work whose publication or distribution is prohibited by law,[139] nor is the Copyright Law applicable to legislative, administrative or judicial documents, current affairs news reports or calendars, general digital tables, general tables and formulae.[140]

---

[138] After all, the Copyright Law of 1990 was the first such law in the PRC since its founding in 1949, and its enactment came about largely due to western pressure.

[139] See Article 4 of the Copyright Law.

[140] See Article 5 of the Copyright Law.

Copyright in a protected work is not the only right protected by the Copyright Law; it also protects copyright-related rights and interests. The term 'copyright-related rights and interests' is not defined by the Copyright Law, but is defined by the Implementing Regulations to mean 'publishers' rights relating to the format and design of books and periodicals, performers' rights relating to performances, producers' rights relating to audio-visual recordings, and rights held by radio or television stations in relation to radio or television programs.'[141] These are effectively what the Civil Law system refers to as 'neighbouring rights'.[142] These rights are, in their nature, independent of the copyright embodied in the protected works, thus forming separate protection for persons and entities that produce copyrighted works.

As part of the protection for 'neighbouring rights', broadcasts of cinematographic works and video works by television stations are required to have the express authorisation of the copyright owner, and a payment at freely negotiated rates is also legally required.[143] An important part of this 'neighbouring rights' protection is the rather extensive protection accorded to audio-video products, an area where, despite extensive legal protection, violation of copyright has been fairly rampant until this day. However, effective protection comes more from separate legal regulations than from the Copyright Law.[144]

An individual author is generally assumed to be the copyright owner of a work, unless the subject matter is cinematographic, television, video and sound recordings, in which case copyright is vested in the producers of such works. Copyright holders are protected for their personal (moral) rights and related property rights. These rights are detailed in Article 10 of the Copyright Law and are not significantly different from international standards. Copyright holders may authorise a copyright collective management organisation to exercise these rights. The organisation may claim the rights in its own name for the copyright holder, and may also participate in litigation or arbitration activities pertaining to the copyright or related rights.

Moral rights, that is, the right of copyright holders to obtain attribution, to revise their works, and to protect their works from misrepresentation or distortion, are to be protected perpetually. While the Copyright Law does not specifically indicate whether authors are permitted to contract to forgo the exercise of their moral rights, the Berne Convention specifically precludes any assignment of moral rights. Since China is a party to the Convention, this is perhaps also true in China.

Other rights, including the right of publication, are to be protected for the author's lifetime and 50 years after his/her death if the author is an individual citizen. In

---

141 See Article 26 of the Implementing Regulations.

142 See Qu Sanqiang (2004), *supra* note 3, at 158.

143 See Article 45 of the Copyright Law.

144 Most of these are in the form of control and regulation rather than protection. See further discussion in Section 5.3 below.

the case of a joint work of individuals, the copyright protection period will end on December 31 of the fiftieth year after the death of the last surviving joint contributor. For works of entities, and film and film-like works, or where the copyright holder is an entity, the right of publication and other rights will be protected for 50 years, concluding on December 31 of the fiftieth year after a work's initial publication. If, however, a work is not published within 50 years of its creation, the copyright will no longer be protected.

Article 2 of the Copyright Law specifically provides that works of 'Chinese citizens, legal persons and other organisations of China, whether published or not' will be protected. Although this is not specifically addressed in Article 2, authors from Hong Kong, Taiwan and Macao will be regarded as Chinese and be protected on the same basis as those of mainland authors. The status of foreigners in the Copyright Law is, however, not entirely clear.

Under Article 2 of the Copyright Law foreign works will be protected if they are 'first published' in the PRC. The 2001 revision extends such protection to works of persons without nationality. The Implementing Regulations have adopted the Berne Convention definition for 'first published' – a foreign work, if initially published overseas but released in China within 30 days of initial publication, will still be regarded as 'first published' in China.[145] The definition of publication provided in the Regulations includes distribution of a work, which in turn is defined as providing enough reproductions of a work to reasonably satisfy public demand. It remains uncertain, however, whether unpublished foreign works will attract copyright protection. On the other hand, the Copyright Law states that the works of 'foreign persons' and 'persons without nationality' published outside China may enjoy protection under bilateral agreements signed between China and the country, or the usual country of domicile, of the author, or under international conventions to which both China and the aforesaid country are participants. It nevertheless remains unclear whether 'foreign persons' will be interpreted to exclude protection for foreign corporations, as opposed to natural persons. The Implementing Regulations suggest that copyright can be granted to either an individual citizen or a corporation deemed to be the author of a work.[146]

5.3. Audio Video Products

The foundation for the protection of audio video products is laid down by the General Principles of Civil Law and the Copyright Law. The WIPO Convention for the Protection of Producers of Phonograms against Unauthorised Duplication of Their Phonograms, which China acceded to in April 1993, is also relevant in this area. More specific mechanisms for protection are established by special regulations issued by

---

145 See Art 25 of the Implementing Regulations.

146 See Article 9 of the Implementing Regulations.

the State Council and its various ministries and administrative authorities. Among these are the Regulations on the Administration of Audio-Visual Products, issued by the State Council on 25 December 2001 and effective on 1 February 2002.[147]

The State Council Regulations on the Administration of Audio-Visual Products are not in themselves about copyright protection. Instead, they establish a rather strict mechanism of control and administration of the publication, production, duplication, importation, wholesaling, retailing, and rental of audio-video products. Specifically, all audio-video related activities are subject to a licensing system[148] which serves a dual purpose – (indirect) administrative protection of copyright and other commercial rights in audio-video products, and regulation and censorship of publications.

Under the State Council Regulations, the administration of audio-video products is subject to no less then three authorities. Administrative departments at the national and local levels responsible for publications are in charge of the supervision and administration of the publishing, production and duplication of audio-visual products. Administrative departments at the national and local levels responsible for cultural affairs are in charge of the supervision and administration of the importing, wholesaling, retailing and rental of audio-video products. The supervision and administration of business activities related to audio-video products are the responsibility of industry and commerce authorities.[149] Contents censorship is undertaken by press authorities (for publication of audio-video products) and departments for culture (for the importation of audio-video products).

As a means of copyright protection, all audio-video products, when published, are required to include, in a prominent position on their audio-visual products and packaging, information indicating clearly the name and address of the publishing organisation, the audio-visual product publishing number, the time of publication,

---

147 As mentioned before, these Regulations replaced an earlier set of regulations issued on 25 August 1994 by the State Council.

148 See Art 5 of the Regulations on the Administration of Audio-Visual Products. This licensing system is further implemented by Administrative Measures on the Publication of Audio-Video Products (issued by the General Administration of the Press and Publications on 17 June 2004 (replacing an earlier set of Measures issued on 1 February 1996)), the Administrative Measures on the Importation of Audio-Video Products jointly issued by the Ministry of Culture and the General Administration of Customs on 17 April 2002, effective on 1 June 2002 and replacing an earlier set of Measures issued on 30 April 1999), the Administrative Measures on the Wholesaling, Retailing and Rental of Audio-Video Products (issued by the Ministry of Culture on 28 March 2002, effective on 10 April 2002 and replacing an earlier set of Measures issued on 30 January 1996), and the Administrative Measures on Sino-foreign Cooperative Enterprises Engaged in the Distribution of Audio-visual Products (jointly issued by Ministry of Commerce and the Ministry of Culture on 9 February 2004, effective retrospectively from 1 January 2004 and replacing an earlier set of Measures jointly issued by MOFTEC and the Ministry of Culture 10 December 2001).

149 Article 4 of the Regulations on the Administration of Audio-Visual Products.

and the copyright owner. For imported products the import licence numbers must also be clearly indicated.[150] Further, production of audio-video products can only be undertaken by enterprises having obtained an Audio-Video Product Production Licence, and no audio-video publishing organisation may commission any organisation that does not hold such a licence to produce audio-visual products.[151] Similarly, a licence is required to engage in the duplication of audio-video products, their importation, wholesaling, retailing and rental.[152] In other words, a rather strict system of licensing, product authenticity disclosure as well as production and duplication authorisation has been established for audio-video publication and business operations. Piracy of audio-video products is subject to penalties through these regulations as well as IP protection laws. Clearly, if the regulations were strictly enforced and observed, copyright in audio-video products would enjoy good protection in China.

In reality, the piracy of CDs, DVDs and other audio-video products is rampant and constitutes perhaps the most serious problem in IP rights infringement in China. Not surprisingly, there have periodically been many campaigns to crack down on piracy in this area.[153] As in the case of the regulations on audio-video products, these campaigns often serve a dual purpose – to crack down on illegal publications (such as pornographic materials) as well as on copyright infringements.

5.4. Computer Software

The protection of computer software is internationally a relatively recent issue. As China did not start its legal efforts in this area until the late 1980s, Chinese law started straight from a copyright approach. The debate as it has occurred in western countries, as to whether computer software should be protected by copyright law or patent law, was largely a non-issue as, by the time China intended to legislate for such protection, it had largely been accepted internationally that copyright protection was a preferable approach to software.

The first effort to protect computer software appeared in the 1990 Copyright Law. However, the special nature of software, such as its short life span of usefulness or technological advantage, was recognised by the legislators. Thus, Article 53 of the original 1990 Law specifically provided that special rules on computer software protection would be issued separately by the State Council. The Regulations on Computer Software Protection were indeed issued by the State Council on 6 April

[150] Article 12 of the Regulations on the Administration of Audio-Visual Products.

[151] Article 19 of the Regulations on the Administration of Audio-Visual Products.

[152] Articles 21, 27 & 32 of the Regulations on the Administration of Audio-Visual Products.

[153] See e.g. the 2006 Action Plan for the Regulation and Rectification of Audio-Video Markets, issued by the Ministry of Culture, 6 March 2006; Notice of the Ministry of Culture on the Crackdown on Illegally Imported Audio-Video Products, 14 July 2006. See further discussions in Section 7.2 below.

1992.[154] The then Ministry of Engineering and Electronics Industries supplemented the Regulations by issuing the Measures for Computer Software Copyright Registration in April 1992.[155] These two sets of administrative regulations, together with the Copyright Law, provide the basic legal framework for the protection for computer software in China today.

Computer software is defined to mean computer programs and related documents and files, which are developed independently by the developer and already have been set down on some type of tangible medium.[156] Its protection is, at present, not extended to include thoughts, processing procedures, operational methods and mathematical concepts,[157] while in the 1992 Regulations discoveries, principles, and algorithms in the development of software were also excluded from protection.

The term of software protection for a natural person copyright holder is his/her lifetime plus 50 years after his/her death, commencing from the date on which the development of the software is completed. Where the copyright holder is a legal person or an entity, the term of software protection is 50 years commencing on the date of first publication. However, if the software has not been released within 50 years from the date on which the software development is completed, it shall no longer receive protection by these Regulations.[158] Software copyright of a natural person may be inherited (except for the right to receive acknowledgment for the development of the software).[159]

Initially, under the 1992 Regulations, protection for software was conditional upon registration with a Chinese administrative authority. This compulsory requirement has now been removed, and registration of computer software is now simply an optional method of protection.[160] Under the 2002 Registration Measures the NCA is in charge of administering software copyright registration for the whole nation and the China Copyright Protection Centre is designated by the NCA as the authority responsible for actual registration.[161] The Centre may establish local branches with the approval of the NCA.

---

[154] These Regulations were re-issued by the State Council on 20 December 2001 and the new regulations became effective from 1 January 2002.

[155] These Measures have now be replaced by a new set of measures of the same title, issued by the NCA on 22 February 2002, revised on 18 June 2004.

[156] See Articles 3 & 4 of the Software Regulations.

[157] See Article 6 of the Software Regulations.

[158] See Article 146 of the Software Regulations.

[159] See Article 15 of the Software Regulations.

[160] This compulsory requirement was contained in Chapter 3 of the 1992 Regulations; the whole chapter was abolished when the 2001 Regulations were issued.

[161] It should be noted that the new Measures govern not only registration of software copyright, but also registration of licensing contracts and assignment contracts of such copyright. Although registration is no longer compulsory as a result of the above-mentioned revision

While copyright holders are protected for all property rights, a lawful holder of software enjoys certain rights in using and copying software which do not infringe the copyright. These include the right to install software into a computer, the right to make back-up copies of software for personal use and the right to alter software to tailor it for a particular computer environment.[162] Furthermore, Article 17 of the Software Regulations gives two exceptions to the prohibition of unauthorised and free use of software. These are where software is being used for studying and where software is being used for scientific research, through means of installation, display, transmission or storage. In such cases software may be used without the approval of, or compensation being paid to, the software copyright holder.

An interesting point in relation to software protection is a discriminatory provision in the current Regulations. Software developed by Chinese citizens and entities is eligible for protection no matter whether the software is published or not, or where it is published. Foreign software or software developed by stateless persons is only eligible for protection if the software is first published in China. If a foreign or a stateless software developer has published software outside China, the software will be protected in China only if the foreigner's home country or the stateless person's habitual country of residence and China are parties to a bilateral or multilateral copyright treaty.[163]

5.5. Computer Network Publications

When international copyright conventions were established, the word 'internet' was unheard of. Thus, the protection of copyright in a digital age (principally the internet) is internationally a new issue. While the notion 'rights related to copyright' may be able to cover certain issues concerning the transmission of copyrighted works via the internet, such a notion is clearly inadequate for providing copyright protection in the internet age. The WIPO therefore took the leadership in adopting the WIPO Copyright Treaty and the WIPO Performances and Phonograms Treaty in December 1996,[164] collectively referred to as the WIPO Internet Treaties. While the Treaties do not themselves grant rights, they set some minimum standards for members to follow.

In China, issues relating to copyright on the internet became a major contentious issue during the revision of the Copyright Law in 1998–1999. After much discussion in the Chinese media and due consideration by Chinese authorities on the subject,

---

of the Regulations on Computer Software Protection, the Registration Measures nevertheless encourage such registration and declare that priority protection will be given to software which has been registered in China. See Article 2 of the 2002 Registration Measures.

162 See Article 16 of the Regulations.

163 See Article 5 of the Regulations.

164 Which became effective on 6 March 2002 and 20 May 2002 respectively.

including the suggestion by NPC deputies for a separate Network Copyright Law, the State Council finally decided not to provide detailed provisions on this subject. Instead, it decided to conduct further research.[165] The Copyright Law therefore only provides, in Article 58, that protective measures for the rights of computer software and information network broadcasting shall be separately formulated by the State Council. This approach left the Chinese courts in a difficult position when they faced litigation on copyright infringement via the internet. The Supreme People's Court then led the way by issuing, in 2000, the Interpretation of the Supreme People's Court on Certain Issues Concerning the Application of Laws in the Hearing of Cases Involving Computer Network Copyright Disputes.[166]

With some 45.6 million computers connected to the internet and over 100 million internet users by the end of June 2005,[167] a Supreme People's Court interpretation was clearly not adequate for copyright protection, as it could only interpret existing laws. The NCA and the Ministry of Information Industry then jointly issued, in 2005, the Measures on Administrative Protection of Internet Copyright,[168] providing some relief to copyright holders in the form of administrative penalties. Finally, in May 2006 the State Council issued Regulations on the Protection of Information Network Transmission Rights,[169]making such protection the latest addition to copyright protection.

Together, the above regulations, measures and interpretations form the principal legal framework for internet copyright protection.

China had not yet signed any of the WIPO Internet Treaties when the State Council Regulations were issued. These Regulations were, however, according to the Legal Office of the State Council,[170] enacted on the principle that they would conform with the minimum requirements contained in the WIPO Internet Treaties. The State Council Regulations specifically provide that information network transmission rights (right of making available/right of communication under the WIPO Internet Treaties) are protected by both Copyright Law and the Regulations. Under the Regulations, any organisation or individual providing the works, performances or audio and video products of others to the public via an information network must

---

165 See Qu Sanqiang (2004), *supra* note 3, at 73.

166 Initially issued on 19 December 2000 and revised on 2 January 2004 by the Supreme People's Court.

167 See Press Conference by the Legal Office of the State Council on the Regulations on Protection of Information Network Transmission Rights, 29 May 2006, available from <www.law_lib.com/fzdt/newshtml/21/20060529145029.htm> (last accessed 15/906).

168 Issued on 30 April 2005 and effective on 30 May 2005.

169 Issued on 18 May 2006 and effective on 1 July 2006.

170 See Press Conference by the Legal Office of the State Council on the Regulations on Protection of Information Network Transmission Right, *supra* note 167. China ratified the WIPO treaties in December 2006. See *supra* notes 132 & 133.

obtain the consent of the rights holders and pay remuneration, unless otherwise provided by the laws and administrative regulations.[171] The Regulations prohibit the evasion or removal of technical measures for the protection of copyright, or the intentional deletion or alteration of management information for works, or the provision of works, products or performance to the public, knowing the digital management information therein has been deleted or altered illegally.[172]

For the purposes of these Regulations, 'information network transmission right' is defined to mean the right to provide works, performances or audio and video products through wired or wireless methods to the public so as to give the public the right to access works, performances or audio and video products at their selected time and venue. 'Technical measures' include effective technology, devices or parts used for the prevention and restriction of the browsing of works, performances and audio and video products, or the provision of works, performances, audio and video products through information networks to the public without the permission of rights holders. And 'digital rights management information' refers to explanatory information on the works and the authors, performances and the performers, audio and video products and the producers, information on works, performances, audio and video products rights holders and information on usage requirements, and numerals or codes which represent the aforesaid information.[173]

However, the Regulations provide a long list of exceptions to the above protection, including the provision/reporting/presentation of speeches made in public assemblies, translation of works into minority languages, the conversion of works into Braille for visually impaired persons and the provision of current affairs articles on political and economics affairs. Additionally, qualified exceptions are made for libraries, archives, museums, art museums etc., that are conducted for the purposes of nine-year compulsory education or national education planning, and for works in relation to cultivation and breeding, the prevention and treatment of illnesses, disaster prevention and mitigation and poverty alleviation, as well as adaptation for basic cultural requirements.[174]

The Regulations impose serious legal sanctions, including fines and, ultimately, criminal penalties, against violations of the information network transmission rights.

The Measures on the Administrative Protection of Internet Copyright apply to acts of uploading, storing, linking or searching works and audio-visual products in internet information services based on the instructions of internet content providers without editing, amending or selecting such stored or transmitted contents. The Measures extend the application of the Copyright Law to acts of direct provision of

---

171 Article 2 of the Regulations.

172 Articles 4 & 5 of the Regulations.

173 Article 26 of the Regulations.

174 Articles 7, 8 & 9 of the Regulations.

internet content in internet information services.[175] The Measures further extend the application of Implementation Measures on Administrative Punishment for Copyright Violations to violations of right of communication on information network in internet information services.[176] Under these Measures, an internet contents provider must take immediate action to remove the relevant contents if the provider is notified by a copyright holder of infringement of his/her copyright. Otherwise, the provider is liable for compensation and other copyright infringement penalties.[177]

It should be noted, however, that the Measures were issued before the State Council Regulations, and were enacted by authorities at a lower level. This means that if there are any inconsistencies between the Regulations and the Measures, the Regulations prevail.

Under the Supreme People's Court Interpretation, copyright protection is extended to works circulated to the public through the internet. The copyright holders of such works are entitled to use, or to permit another party to use, their work, as well as to receive remuneration.

The reprinting or publishing on the internet of excerpts from works previously published in the press or circulated on the internet does not constitute copyright infringement so long as remuneration is paid in accordance with the relevant provisions, and sources are cited. But if the copyright holder has stipulated, or newspapers, journals or the internet service provider has stipulated on behalf of the copyright holder, that the re-publication of the work or excerpts from it is prohibited, or if the reproduction or publishing on the internet of excerpts exceeds the relevant limitations on the publishing and re-printing of works, copyright infringement will be constituted.[178]

In line with China's approach to holding internet service providers responsible for internet contents, the Interpretation puts these providers under a legal obligation to prevent copyright infringement on the internet. Thus, when an internet service provider is aware of an internet user infringing someone's copyright, or when it has been warned by the copyright holder with substantiated evidence of infringement, it must adopt appropriate measures to remove the infringing content and eliminate the consequences of the copyright infringement. Failing to do so, the internet service provider will bear joint and several liabilities with the internet user for the infringement.[179] Furthermore, when a copyright holder requests the internet service provider to supply information about the infringing party in order to pursue the

175 Article 2 of the Measures.

176 Article 4 of the Measures.

177 See Articles 5 & 12 of the Measures.

178 Article 3 of the Interpretation.

179 Articles 4, 5, 6 & 7 of the Interpretation.

infringing party's liability, and has shown their identification, copyright certification or proof of the circumstances of infringement, the internet service provider must give such information. Refusal to do so without due reason will render the internet service provider liable for infringement.[180] The Interpretation relies on torts provisions in the General Principles of Civil Law as well as the Copyright Law in providing legal remedies and penalties.

6. Competition Law & Commercial Secrets

The use of competition law to protect intellectual property rights is not new in the developed world; it is, however a rather recent development in China. The promulgation of the Law of the PRC against Unfair Competition (the Unfair Competition Law) in 1993 signifies the beginning of this new legal development.

Most recently, on 12 January 2007, the Supreme People's Court issued its long-awaited Interpretation on Certain Questions concerning the Adjudication of Civil Cases in Unfair Competition, which took effect on 1 February 2007. The Interpretation not only clarifies many ambiguities in the various relevant laws, but more importantly provides many practical details to guide the judiciary in adjudicating such civil cases.

While the Unfair Competition Law was intended to provide a comprehensive legal framework for ensuring fair competition in business operations, its two most lengthy articles are about additional protection of intellectual property. Article 5 of the Law thus prohibits the following unfair business practices:

- faking the registered trademarks of others;
- using, without prior permission, the same or similar names, packages or decorations of well known brand name products so as to mislead buyers;
- using, without prior permission, the names of other enterprises so as to mislead buyers;
- forging or counterfeiting the identification marks, marks indicating good quality products and other quality marks on commodities or falsifying the place of origin or using other false indicators to mislead people with regard to quality.

Article 10 of the Unfair Competition Law addresses specifically the difficult issue of protecting commercial secrets by prohibiting the following business practices:

- obtaining the commercial secrets of other proprietors by theft, inducement, coercion or other illicit means;

[180] Article 8 of the Interpretation.

- revealing, using or allowing others to use commercial secrets obtained by the means mentioned in the above;
- revealing, using or allowing others to use commercial secrets of other proprietors which are in their possession by violation of agreements or by virtue of a request to keep secrets by the owners concerned.

Here, 'commercial secrets' are defined to mean technical and management information which is unknown to the public and can produce economic benefits, and which is of practical value to other proprietors and has therefore been kept secret.

The same article further holds a third party liable for infringement if he/she obtains, uses or reveals the commercial secrets of others when he/she knew or should have known of the act to be in violation of the law.

These provisions on the protection of commercial secrets are further implemented by the Certain Provisions on the Prohibition of Activities Infringing upon Commercial Secrets.[181] These Provisions further define 'technical and management information' to include, but not limited to, designs, processes, formulae of products, processes of production, manufacturing techniques and methods, management secrets, lists of clients, information on sources of commodities, production and sales strategies as well as the bottom price of a bid and the contents of a bidding document.[182]

Both the Unfair Competition Law and the Certain Provisions provide for heavy civil liabilities for infringement of commercial secrets. However the most severe penalty came from the Criminal Law revision in 1997, when infringement of commercial secrets was made a criminal offence which could attract imprisonment of between three and seven years.[183] It should also be pointed out that legal obligations to maintain commercial secrets are also provided for by the General Principles of Civil Law (1986),[184] the Labour Law (1994),[185] and other regulations (such as the Regulations on the Protection of Computer Software).[186]

Statistics from No. 2 Intermediate Court in Tianjin indicates that, among all commercial secrets cases, 95% related to technological secrets, and 80% were leaked by employees.[187]

---

181 Issued by the SAIC on 23 November 1995 and revised on 3 December 1998 by the same authority.

182 Article 2 of the Certain Provisions.

183 Article 219 of the Criminal Law.

184 See Article 118 of the General Principles of Civil Law.

185 See Article 102 of the Labour Law.

186 See Article 30 of the Regulation.

187 See 'Internal and External Worries for IP Protection for Chinese Enterprises', Xinhua News: <news3.xinhuanet.com/focus/2006-04/07/content_4348971.htm> (last accessed 11 November 2006).

7. Implementation and Enforcement Mechanisms

7.1. Overview

There is little doubt that the legislative and regulatory framework for intellectual property protection in China, though leaving much room for improvement, is close to meeting international standards. It is equally clear, however, that the actual protection is far from being ideal, and certainly a great deal of protection still remains only on paper.[188] This does not mean that there has been no legal mechanism for implementation and enforcement of IP protection laws. In fact, there are various forms and mechanisms available, ranging from periodical public campaigns to raise public awareness of IP rights, internal review and administrative penalties and customs enforcement of law, to judicial sanctions against violations of the law.

While these mechanisms, to be discussed below, are not all of the same nature or of equal legal and practical effect, they complement each other and, as a whole, form a comprehensive scheme for the implementation and enforcement of IP rights. As complementary mechanisms none is exclusive, and theoretically each has the potential to remedy the weakness in another mechanism. As is the case in any other country, however, the ultimate protection lies with the public attitude towards the law and the effectiveness of the judiciary.

7.2. Public Campaigns and Public Awareness

While public campaigns may not be seen as legal enforcement in a strict sense, these campaigns nevertheless affect the implementation and enforcement of law in both the short and the long term. In the short term, laws are often strictly enforced during these campaigns for political reasons or otherwise and, more importantly, coordinated enforcement of law is achieved. In the longer term, public awareness of IP rights achieved through such campaigns is perhaps the ultimate guarantee for respect and protection for IP.

There are different kinds of public/political campaigns for law and order conducted from time to time. The so-called Strike Hard campaigns have attracted the most attention both inside and outside China because of the heavy use of the death penalty, lack of strict observation of procedural requirements, and the severe punishments imposed on identified crimes.[189] There are also *ad hoc* campaigns to

---

188 Not surprisingly, western media and companies routinely complain that 'product piracy is rampant in China'. See e.g. 'Chinese Use Courts to Sink Pirates', *The Australian*, 29 August 2006, IT Business Section, at 5.

189 See H.M. Tanner, *Strike Hard! Anti-Crime Campaigns and Chinese Criminal Justice, 1979–1985* (New York: Cornell University, 1999). For western criticism on these campaigns, see various reports by Amnesty International on the campaigns.

publicise the newly adopted laws or to enforce specific laws.[190] An important and a most persistent campaign for law is in the form of the Popularising Law (*Pufa*) Campaigns which have been conducted for over 20 years on a five-year plan basis since 1985.[191] These campaigns are seen by some as being one of the six elements of ruling the country according to law.[192]

Among the campaigns for implementation of law in specific areas are those on IP protection. The IP rights enforcement campaigns are both independent and a part of the larger campaigns of Popularising Law (*Pufa*), and each can be seen as enforcing the other.

Initially, 'crackdown' campaigns were conducted on IP violations, apparently on an *ad hoc* basis. But my own various field studies in China seem to suggest that these *ad hoc* campaigns have often coincided with the annual visits by US IP or trade negotiation delegations. More recently such campaigns have become a more regular feature. In April 2001 the SIPO, the SAIC, and the NCA jointly initiated the World IP Day in China, set for 26 April each year. In 2004 this was further extended to IP Protection Week (19-26 April), during which various media outlets are mobilised to promote IP knowledge, academic conferences and seminars are held, major cases are publicised, and often 'crackdown' campaigns on IP violation are waged.[193] In 2004, the State Council approved a Special Action Plan for IP Rights Protection, which authorised a full-year (September 2004-August 2005) campaign for IP protection.[194] This full year campaign was later extended to the end of 2005.[195] On 27 March 2006 the State Council (through its General Office) launched a new round of campaigns when it issued the Outline of Actions for

---

190 See Troyer, Ronald J. 'Publicising New Laws: The Public Legal Education Campaign', in Ronald J. Troyer, John P. Clark and Dean G. Royek (eds), *Social Control in the People's Republic of China* (New York: Praeger, 1989), at 70-83.

191 See the dedicated website on this topic established by the Ministry of Justice: <www.legalinfo.gov.cn>; see also Troyer, *id.*, at 70-83; M. Exner, 'Convergence of Ideology and the Law: The Functions of the Legal Education Campaign in Building a Chinese Legal System', (August, 1995) *Issues and Studies*, 68-102.

192 These six elements are law-making, administrative enforcement of law, judicial administration of law, legal supervision, legal services, and *Pufa*. See Jing Yuanshu, 'Retrospect and Prospect of *Pufa* Work', available at <www.iolaw.org.cn/shownews.asp?id=11599> (last accessed 8 April 2005). On general *Pufa* campaigns, see Chapter 18 on Implementation of Law.

193 See Ministry of Commerce, 'Intellectual Property Protection in China – part 4 (Publicity Activities for Improving the Public Awareness of IPR Protection in China', available at <kjs.mofcom.gov.cn/stati/colum/ztxx/dwmyxs/q.html/4> (last accessed 22 August 2006); Notice on Conducting Activities for the 2005 'IP Protection Week', available at <ipr.mofcom.gov.cn/article/200412/20041200323438_1.xml> (last accessed 14 February 2005).

194 Notice on Issuing a Special Action Plan for IPR Protection, issued by the General Office of the State Council on 26 August 2004.

195 See 2005 IP White Paper, *supra* note 12, Section I.

Intellectual Property Protection (2006–2007).[196] This was followed by a specific action plan for 2006 issued, also in March 2006, by the National Intellectual Property Rights Working Group.[197] The Outline sets out principles for coordinated actions against IP infringement, and the Action Plan maps out various activities, from law/rule-making, special enforcement actions plans, publicity activities, to international cooperation throughout the year. On 1 February 2007 the SIPO issued the 2007 Action Plan for Intellectual Property Protection[198] to further implement the State Council Outline of Actions (2006–2007), thus continuing the latest campaign for IP protection formally launched in 2006.

As part of the public campaigns against IP infringements, major cities are required to establish a dedicated IP infringement complaints centre. As of the end of August 2006, 50 such Centres had been established and put into operation. There is also a nationwide dedicated complaints telephone line (123312) and a special internet complaints 'window' (<www.ipr.gov.cn>).[199] The Ministry of Commerce has also established an IP Rights Protection Webpage, with special funds having been set aside to improve the site for the next three years.[200]

Although it is difficult to evaluate the overall effect of these campaigns,[201] it is certain that these campaigns have achieved at least some short term results.

Often the 'achievements', as announced by the Chinese government, seem to be rather impressive. For instance, in the latest 100-day crackdown on pirated movies and computer software (starting from 25 July 2006), it was claimed that Chinese authorities had confiscated some 50 million CDs and DVDs after 15,000 shops and street vendors were closed down by the government, with some 8,500 fine notices being issued as administrative penalties.[202] Significantly, these campaigns attract some

---

196 A copy of the Outline is available at <doc.ipr.gov.cn/ipr/doc.info/Article.jsp?a_no=2817&col_no=9&dir=200604> (last accessed 15 August 2006).

197 A copy of the Action Plan 2006 is available at <www.ipr.gov.cn/ipr.en/info/Article.jsp?a_no=3326&col_no=102&dir=200604> (last accessed 15 August 2006).

198 A copy of the Action Plan 2007 is available at <doc.ipr.gov.cn/ipr/info/article.jsp?a_no=66277&col_no=9&dir=200704> (last accessed 4 June 2007).

199 See *People's Daily*, 29 August 2006. The requirement to establish 50 such Centres was made by the above-mentioned Outline of Actions for IPR Protection (2006–2007), Item IV (13).

200 'China Will Establish an IP Rights Protection Website in Three Years', in <news.xinhuanet.com/politics/2006-09/02/conten_5039830.htm> (last accessed 3 September 2006).

201 According to the US Trade Representative, they are largely ineffective even though in the short term they result in high numbers of seizures of infringing materials. See US Trade Representative, *2005 Report to Congress on China's WTO Compliance*, 11 December 2005, available at <www.ustr.gov> (last accessed 15 August 2006), 71.

202 See Wu Handong (ed.), *The Blue Book of IPR in China* (*Zhongguo Zhishi Chanquan Lanpishu*) (Beijing: Peking University Press, 2007), at 65. These figures were also reflected in the results of the survey conducted by International Data Corp on behalf of the Business Software Alliance, which indicated that the software piracy rate in China was down from 86% in 2005 to 82%

coordinated political support and actually do crack down on pirate and counterfeit markets during the campaigns. More importantly, the campaigns make people feel that it is dangerous to produce, sell and buy pirated or counterfeit products. Thus a Ministry of Commerce web survey indicates the following interesting statistics:[203] while 42% of people claimed to understand basic IP rights and 45.4% to understand them fully, 26% often bought pirated DVDs, software and books and 49.8% occasionally did so. While 9.4% of people often bought counterfeit brand clothes and bags and 41.3% occasionally did so, 40.1% also agreed that buying counterfeit and pirated goods infringed others' intellectual efforts and should be resisted. An overwhelming 83.9% believed that IP protection was a prerequisite for national economic development and technological innovation. The cheap prices and the relatively high quality of counterfeited and pirated goods are clearly the principal reason that people buy them, as 44.3% of the people acknowledged.

7.3. Internal Review and Administrative Sanctions

As explained above, each kind of IP right is administered by a different administrative authority, and the effort to consolidate the administrative structure (through the establishment of the SIPO) seems to have faded and is unlikely to be renewed in the near future. As a result, internal review mechanisms exist in a different administrative setting for different kinds of IP rights.

For trademarks, internal reviews exist at both registration and infringement stages. For registration matters there is the Trademark Evaluation and Review Board (*Shangbiao Pingshen Weiyuanhui*,[204] TERB) which, on application, may review the decisions by the Trademark Bureau. These decisions include rejection of an objection to trademark registration, rejection of an application for trademark registration, or a decision to cancel trademark registration.[205]

Infringements of trademarks are handled by the Trademark Bureau (or its local departments) of the SAIC. The SAIC and its local departments have the power to investigate a complaint lodged by a rights holder or any interested party and the parties involved must provide assistance with the investigation.[206] While the Trademarks Law prefers a conciliated settlement,[207] other remedies available to the SAIC and its

---

in 2006. See *Fourth Annual BSA and IDC Global Software Piracy Study* (2007). The study is available from <www.bsa.org> (last accessed 30 May 2007).

203 <gzly.mofcom.gov.cn/website/survey/zgb/ivtg_statistics.jsp?seq_no=1146> (last accessed 31 August 2006).

204 This Chinese term has been translated into different English names. The SAIC website translates this as the Trademark Review and Adjudication Board. Other translations include Trademark Evaluation and Review Committee, Trademark Review Committee etc.

205 See Article 2 of the Rules on Evaluation and Review of Trademarks (2005).

206 Article 55 of the Trademark Law.

207 See Article 53 of the Trademark Law.

local departments include ordering the infringer to cease the infringing conduct, confiscation or destruction of counterfeit goods, and imposing fines of up to 300% of the profit gained from the infringement, or 100,000 *yuan*. The infringer may also be required to pay compensation to the trademark registrant for any financial losses suffered.[208] Investigation of trademark infringement may also be initiated by the SAIC (or its legal departments), and any infringement amounting to a criminal offence must be transferred to a judicial authority in accordance with the law.[209]

In both cases, the ruling of the TERB or SAIC (or its local authorities) may be appealed to a court of law.[210]

As in the case of the trademark mechanism, the internal review of decisions of the Patent Office is handled by a special board, the Patent Re-examination Board (*Zhuanli Fushen Weiyuanhui*). The Board is responsible for all appeals relating to refusals to approve patent applications, refusals by the Patent Office to entertain opposition, and requests for invalidation of existing patents.[211]

Infringements of patent rights are handled by the Patent Office or its local counterparts. Again, conciliation is preferred.[212] And, as with the handling of trademarks, administrative remedies include an order to cease the infringing conduct, confiscation of illegal income, and the imposition of a fine of up to 300% of the profit gained from the infringement, or 50,000 *yuan*.[213]

Decisions by the Patent Re-examination Board and the Patent Office may be appealed to a court.[214]

In relation to copyright protection, the Copyright Law contains no clause on the registration of copyright subject matter.[215] In the Implementing Regulations a new Article 25 provides a voluntary filing-for-record scheme for copyright exclusive usage contracts or contracts of transfer. As such, the internal (administrative) mechanisms are mainly about protection against infringement and contractual disputes.

Article 7 of the Copyright Law vests power to control copyright matters at the national level in the NCA. The copyright administrative departments at provincial level (including in autonomous regions and directly administered municipalities) are vested with the power to administer copyright matters in their respective

208 See Article 53 of the Trademark Law.

209 Article 54 of the Trademark Law.

210 Articles 43 and 53 of the Trademarks Law.

211 Article 41 of the Patent Law, and Articles 64 of its Implementation Rules.

212 Article 57 of the Patent Law.

213 Article 58 of the Patent Law.

214 Articles 41 and 57 of the Patent Law.

215 Copyright protection for computer software is however different, where registration is optional.

jurisdictions. The Implementing Regulations define such administrative powers to include the power to investigate and handle copyright infringement cases.

Acts of copyright infringement are defined in Articles 46 and 47, and available administrative remedies include an order to cease infringement, to remove influences, to make public apologies, to pay compensation for damages, the confiscation of illegal income and infringing materials, the confiscation of the main materials, tools and equipment used in the production of the infringing materials, and the imposition of a fine of up to 300% per cent of any illegal income, or a fine of up to 100,000 *yuan*.[216] Rules on administrative penalties for copyright infringement and the procedures are provided in the Measures on Implementing Copyright Administrative Penalties, which were issued by the NCA on 3 July 2003 and effective from 1 September of the same year, replacing the 1997 measures under the same title. An administrative penalty decision may be appealed to a court.[217]

It should be pointed out that the various secondary legislations on different aspects of intellectual property rights (e.g. computer software, new plant varieties, etc.) also contain administrative sanctions against infringement, but the severity of such administrative penalties is limited to those provided by the principal laws as explained above. Further, administrative reconsideration of all penalties decisions are available under the Law on Administrative Reconsideration and the various administrative reconsideration measures issued by different administrative authorities.

7.4. Customs Protection

Customs enforcement of intellectual property law is the first frontier for IP protection in trade and investment, and hence a critical mechanism for the protection of foreign IP rights. This mechanism is therefore highly important in this age of global trade and globalisation. The 1992 US-China Memorandum of Understanding on IP protection represented the first serious international demand that China must protect IP rights in its Customs processes. That saw the issuance, in 1994, of a Notice of the General Administration of Customs on Strengthening IP Protection in Customs Administration.[218] However, Customs IP protection mechanisms were not formally introduced until 1995 when the Regulations on Customs Protection of Intellectual Property were issued by the State Council, and the Implementing Measures of the Customs for the Protection of Intellectual Property Rights were issued by the GAC. In 1997 the GAC and the Chinese Patent Office jointly issued the Regulations on Certain Issues Concerning the Implementation of Customs Protection on Patent

---

216 Articles 46 and 47 of the Copyright Law, and Article 36 of its Implementing Regulations.

217 Article 55 of the Copyright Law.

218 See 'Ten Years of Customs Protection of IP Rights', <www.legaldaily.com.cn/xwzx/2004-02/21/content_94050.htm> (last accessed 21 April 2004).

Rights.[219] As part of the WTO induced legal reform, 2003 and 2004 saw some major revamping and improvements to the mechanisms introduced by the issuance of the revised Customs IP protection regulations; i.e. the Regulations of the PRC on Customs Protection of Intellectual Property,[220] and Measures on the Implementation of the Regulations of the PRC on Customs Protection of Intellectual Property.[221]

The Customs Protection Regulations apply to IP rights in relation to goods entering or leaving Chinese territory, which receive the protection of Chinese laws and regulations, including trademarks, copyright, and copyright-related rights and patents.

The Customs of the PRC is responsible for the Customs protection of intellectual property. The general scheme for Customs protection is a two-step mechanism. In the first place a rights holder applies to the GAC for filing their intellectual property rights on the GAC's record so as to request the Customs to protect their intellectual property rights in relation to goods to be imported or exported. An application for filing must provide details, supported with certification documents (if any) including details on manufacturers, importer/exporter of the goods concerned, as well as the licensing status for use of the intellectual property rights, their main features, prices, and other relevant details of the goods etc. A successful filing-for-record is valid for 10 years,[222] and may be renewed.[223]

An effect of a Customs file entry is that when an IP rights holder discovers that goods suspected of infringing intellectual property rights are about to enter into or exit from China, they may apply to Customs at the relevant port to have the suspected goods impounded.[224]

In making an application for having suspected goods impounded the rights holder must submit to the relevant Customs office details and evidence of the infringement, including the name of the consignee or consignor of the suspected goods, the name and specifications of the suspected goods, the name of the likely port of entry or exit, time of entry or exit, means of transport, etc. In addition, the rights holder must also provide Customs surety money in an amount not exceeding the value of the said goods. The money will be used to pay compensation if the applicant causes undue losses to the consignee or consignor, and to pay for the storage, custody and disposal costs incurred by Customs after impounding the

219 Issued on 11 March 1997.

220 Issued by the State Council on 2 December 2003, effective on 1 March 2004, and replacing the 1995 Regulations.

221 Issued by the General Administration of Customs on 25 May 2004, effective from 1 July of the same year, and replacing the 1995 Implementing Measures.

222 For details, see Articles 7 of the Customs Protection Regulations.

223 Article 10 of the Measures.

224 Article 12 of the Regulations.

said goods.[225] On the other hand, if Customs finds imports or exports suspected of infringing intellectual property rights, it should notify the rights holder and the latter may apply to Customs to have the suspected goods impounded following the normal application procedures and the provision of a surety.[226]

Upon receiving the application of the rights holder and the surety, Customs will impound the suspected goods, notify the rights holder, and issue a Customs impoundment warrant to the consignee or consignor of the said goods.

If a consignee or consignor considers that their imports or exports do not violate the IP rights of the applicant, they must submit a written explanation with the relevant evidence to Customs. If the alleged infringement involves a patent, the consignee or consignor may provide Customs with a surety in an amount equivalent to the value of the goods concerned, and request Customs to release the goods. If the rights holder has failed to lodge a lawsuit on the matter with a court, the surety will be returned to the provider.[227]

After having impounded the goods, if Customs does not receive a court notice of enforcement within the prescribed period of time, the impounded goods must be released. Customs will also release impounded goods where the consignee or consignor has provided a surety and requests Customs to release the goods, or where it is satisfied that the consignee or consignor has sufficient evidence to prove that the goods do not infringe IP rights.[228]

But if it is confirmed that the impounded goods have infringed IP rights, the impounded goods will be confiscated by Customs. In such cases Customs will issue a written notification to the rights holder with all the relevant information concerning the goods found to have infringed intellectual property rights.[229]

Confiscated goods will be disposed of by Customs according to the following rules: if they may be made available for the use of social welfare, the goods will be given to the relevant welfare organisation; if the IP rights holder is willing to buy the goods, the goods will be sold to the rights holder; if the goods can neither be used for social welfare and the IP rights holder does not have the desire to buy them, the goods will be put up for auction after removing the relevant infringing features, and the proceeds will be turned over to the Treasury, or if the infringing features are impossible to remove, the goods will be destroyed.[230]

Official statistics from China, as shown below, indicate some limited success in the customs enforcement of law, considering the relatively low number of cases

[225] Articles 13 & 14 of the Regulations.

[226] Article 16 of the Regulations.

[227] See Articles 18 and 19 of the Customs Protection Regulations.

[228] Article 24 of the Regulations and Article 17 of the Measures.

[229] Article 27 of the Regulations.

[230] See Article 27 of the Regulations and Article 30 of their Implementing Measures.

handled by the Customs authorities in relation to the huge volume of foreign trade in China.

Table 4 – Customs IP Enforcement Case (1996–2005)[231]

Year	*Total*	*Total value (million yuan)*	*Trademark*	*Copyright*	*Patent*
1996	705	15.8	38	659	8
1997	193	32.21	92	85	16
1998	233	52.69	139	67	27
1999	225	92.02	178	42	5
2000	295	56.7	235	3	57
2001	330	134.9	308	1	21
2002	573	95.62	557	2	14
2003	756	67.97	741	1	14
2004	1051	84.17	1009	16	26
2005	1210	99.78	1106	67	37
Accumulated total	5571	731.86	4403	943	225

7.5. Judicial Enforcement – Civil and Criminal Sanctions

The above discussion indicates that administrative sanctions are far too light to have any real impact on the prevention of IP infringement. While the statistics from GAC seem to be impressive, they in fact represent an extremely small quantity of goods in the overall volume of foreign trade.[232] This suggests that if IP rights are to be properly protected in China, the judiciary's role will be critical.

In fact, as in other countries, judicial enforcement of rights and protection against violations of law is the most powerful mechanism available. However, it is not necessarily the most effective and efficient one. Thus it is used in all countries as the last resort. While China is often said to be a country disfavouring litigation, some foreign lawyers working in China have claimed that 'China is the most litigious country in the world in terms of intellectual property lawsuits.'[233] Whether this observation is accurate or not, there is evidence suggesting that some IP rights

[231] Compiled on the basis of statistics published by the GAC: <www.customs.gov.cn/YWStaticPage/2559/c6179711.htm> (last accessed 12 September 2006).

[232] On both points, see the discussion in Chapter 18 on Implementation of Law.

[233] J Benjamin Bai (a lawyer with a global law firm, Jones Day), quoted in 'Chinese Use Courts to Sink Pirates', *supra* note 188, at 5.

holders are willing to go to court to protect their rights, as shown in the following statistics in relation to cases handled by courts.[234]

Table 5 – First instance IP Civil Cases 1998–2002

	Cases accepted					
Details	*1998*	*1999*	*2000*	*2001*	*2002*	*Sub-total*
Copyrights	571	750	963	1117	1824	5225
Trademarks	527	460	393	482	707	2569
Patents	1162	1485	1596	1597	2081	7920
Tech Contracts	1175	942	1146	1238	1318	5819
Invention/Discovery					3	3
New Varity of Plants					32	32
Others IP	658	645	714	831	236	3084
Total	4093	4282	4811	5265	6201	24652

	Cases decided					
Details	*1998*	*1999*	*2000*	*2001*	*2002*	*Sub-total*
Copyrights	546	654	989	1063	1776	5028
Trademarks	456	487	401	445	611	2400
Patents	1114	1420	1562	1567	1796	7459
Tech Contracts	1181	1007	1109	1167	1260	5724
Invention/Discovery					3	3
New Varity of Plants					24	24
Others IP	699	592	729	799	179	2998
Total	3996	4160	4790	5041	5649	23636

(Source: *Intellectual Property Yearbook of China 2003*, Beijing: Press of Intellectual Property (2003), Table 51, at 276)

Between 1993 and 1997, Chinese courts settled 16,894 cases concerning IP rights disputes.[235] According to the Supreme People's Court, in the five years from 2002 to

234 For unclear reasons the Supreme People's Court does not publish systematic statistics on IP enforcement (or for that matter, any systematic adjudication and enforcement statistics). The following statistics are therefore extracted from many different sources; they are sometimes overlapping and sometimes inconsistent with each other.

235 Supreme Court Work Report, delivered at the First Session of the Ninth National People's Congress on 10 March 1998, see *People's Daily* (*Renmin Ribao*), internet edition, 24 March 1998.

2006 Chinese courts accepted a total of 54,321 first instance civil cases with 52,437 actually having been settled, representing a 145.9% and 142% increase from the previous five-year period (1997–2001). At the same time the courts accepted 13,170 second instance civil cases with 12,700 being settled.[236]

In addition, between 2000 and 2004 there were 2,462 arrest warrants approved by the People's Procuratorates at different levels, involving IP infringement in 1,539 cases, among which 2,491 persons in 1,500 cases were prosecuted.[237]

It should also be pointed out that the great majority of the court cases concerned domestic parties. Thus, in 2002 and 2003 only around 2% and 2.9% of the cases involved foreign parties (including parties from Hong Kong, Macao and Taiwan).[238] In 2005, among the civil cases (13,393 in total), only 268 cases were foreign related, accounting for only 2% of all civil cases. There were also 108 cases that related to IP from Hong Kong, Macao and Taiwan. Clearly, foreign parties are yet to be a real force in the use of judicial remedies in China.[239] Also importantly, in the last years around half of the civil cases were settled by mediation (and in 2005 that accounted for about 54.1% of all cases settled by the judiciary).[240]

While the overall situation in judicial enforcement in IP protection is far from perfect, there seems to have been some improvement, at least in terms of the number of cases that have gone to court.[241] This improvement can be largely attributed to the Supreme People's Court, which has issued a large number of judicial interpretations,[242] including the most recent policy document, Opinions on Strengthening the Work of Intellectual Property Rights Adjudication So as to Provide Judicial Guarantee for the Construction of a Creative Country.[243] These interpretations provide practical

---

236 'IP Cases Increase and IP Judicial Protection Preliminarily Established', available from <news.xinhuanet.com/legal/2007-01/18/content_5622505.htm> (last accessed 18 January 2007).

237 '1,710 IPR Violations Handled since 2000', in <www.chinaiprlaw.cn/file/200501234114.html> (accessed 3 February 2005). See US Trade Representative, *2005 Report to Congress on China's WTO Compliance*, 11 December 2005, available at <www.ustr.gov> (last accessed 15 August 2006).

238 See Cao Jianming, 'New Development in Judicial Protection of Intellectual Property', (no. 4, 2004) *Intellectual Property* (*Zhishi Chanquan*) 9, at 10.

239 Transcripts of a Web Forum on IP Protection, 23 May 2006, available from <www.legaldaily.com.cn/misc/2006-05/23/content_320062htm> (last accessed 8 September 2006).

240 *Id.*

241 According to Chinese statistics, between 1985 and 2004 Chinese courts accepted 69,636 first instance IP civil cases with 66,385 having been settled (See 'Situation in Judicial Protection of IP by the People's Court', *supra* note 17). When compared with statistics for 1993–2004 as quoted above, this suggests that there were very few cases between 1985 and 1993.

242 See *supra* note 17.

243 Issued on 11 January 2007 by the Supreme People's Court.

mechanisms for law enforcement as well as addressing deficiencies in the existing laws.[244]

Like elsewhere, Chinese courts provide civil remedies and impose criminal sanctions. While all principal IP laws, the Civil Procedural Law, and the Criminal Law provide IP rights holders the right to have access to courts, most of the practical issues are only addressed by various interpretations issued by the Supreme People's Court.[245] These Interpretations clarify court jurisdiction, specific kinds of IP infringements that may be accepted for court litigation, the application and scope of civil and criminal penalties, rules of evidence, burden of proof, calculation of compensation, limitations of action, and other detailed guidance to resolving practical issues. While they are supposed to be interpretations by the judiciary, they are effectively supplementary laws for all practical purposes.

In general, civil litigation against IP infringements is within the jurisdiction of the court in the place where the infringing act is committed, or the place where the offending goods are stored, or the place where the offending goods are sealed up or under seizure, or the place where the defendant resides. In the case of several defendants and involving different places of infringement, the plaintiff may choose the people's court in the place where one of the defendants has committed the infringing acts to handle the case. But if there is only one defendant, the case shall come within the jurisdiction of the court in the place where that defendant committed the infringing act. Civil jurisdiction is generally limited to the courts at the intermediate level and above, however, criminal and administrative jurisdiction may be exercised by basic level courts.

The people's courts have the power to impose various kinds of penalties on IP infringements, such as ordering the infringing party to stop infringement, remove obstacles, eliminate risks, compensate losses and dispel effects caused by the infringement; and imposing a fine and forfeiting offending goods, forged trademarks,

---

244 For instance, the clarification of ambiguities in the Criminal Law, to be discussed below.

245 These include: The Interpretations of the Supreme People's Court on Certain Issues Related to the Application and Law in Adjudication of Civil Cases of Trademark Disputes (issued on 12 October 2002 and effective from 16 October 2002); Certain Provisions on Issues relating to the Application of Laws in Handling Cases of Patent Disputes (issued by the Supreme People's Court on 19 June 2001); the Interpretation of the Supreme People's Court on Certain Issues related to the Application of Laws in the Adjudication of Copyright Civil Dispute Cases (issued on 12 October 2002); Interpretations on Certain Issues Related to Concrete Application of Laws in Handling Criminal Cases Involving Infringement upon Intellectual Property (jointly issued on 8 December 2004 by the Supreme People's Court and the Supreme People's Procuratorate); Interpretations on Certain Issues Related to the Concrete Application of Laws in Handling Criminal Cases Involving Infringement upon Intellectual Property (II) (jointly issued by the Supreme People's Court and the Supreme People's Procuratorate on 5 April 2007); and the Opinions on Strengthening the Work of Intellectual Property Rights Adjudication So as to Provide Judicial Guarantees for the Construction of a Creative Country (issued on 11 January 2007 by the Supreme People's Court).

and property, materials, tools and equipment used specially for the manufacture of offending goods. However, the court does not generally impose civil sanctions on an act of infringement that has been penalised by the administrative department in their administrative enforcement of law, although the latter action itself could often be a subject-matter for court appeal.

The original 1979 Criminal Law was rather weak in punishing IP infringements. The 1997 revamped Criminal Law incorporated various *ad hoc* criminal provisions then existing in different IP protection laws (such as the Patent Law and the Law Against Unfair Competition). The Criminal Law now contains seven different IP offences, namely, using fake trademarks, selling products with fake trademarks, manufacturing and selling illegally manufactured fake trademark symbols, counterfeiting patents, copyright infringement, selling duplicated works that infringe on IP rights, and infringement of commercial secrets.[246] Additionally, many IP infringements can also be prosecuted and convicted as crimes of manufacturing and selling fake and shoddy commodities, or as crimes of conducting illegal business. While the Criminal Law imposes sanctions against IP infringement, it often uses vague terms such as 'serious circumstances' etc. To overcome practical difficulties and to unify practice, the Supreme People's Court in 1998 issued the Interpretations on Certain Issues Related to Concrete Application of Laws in the Adjudication of Criminal Cases of Illegal Publications, which set out criteria for cases that could be regarded as 'serious circumstances'. More recently, on 8 December 2004, the Supreme Court, jointly with the Supreme People's Procuratorate, issued another set of Interpretations on Certain Issues Related to the Concrete Application of Laws in Handling Criminal Cases Involving Infringement of Intellectual Property. The purpose was on the one hand to crack down on intellectual property right infringements that had become widespread, rapidly increasing and out of control, and on the other hand to fulfil China's WTO commitments on complying with the TRIPS Agreement requirements to criminalise serious IP infringements and improve the system for providing damages for such infringements. As a result the criteria for 'serious circumstances' set in the 1998 Interpretations have been lowered.

The principal approach of the 2004 Supreme Court Interpretations is to provide detailed criteria, in most cases with a specific monetary amount, for determining the meaning of such terms as 'serious circumstances', 'other serious circumstances', 'particularly serious circumstances', 'relatively large amount', 'great amount of illegal income', 'major damages', 'particularly serious consequences' etc., as used in the Criminal Law without clear definitions. Both the Criminal Law and the Interpretation provide heavy monetary fines as well as imprisonment of up to seven years for IP infringements. Most recently, on 5 April 2007, the Supreme People's Court and the Supreme People's Procuratorate jointly issued the Interpretations on Certain Issues Related to the Concrete Application of Laws in Handling Criminal Cases Involving

246 See Arts 213-220 of the Criminal Law.

Infringement of Intellectual Property (II). These Interpretations have once again lowered the threshold for criminal prosecution, clarifying remaining ambiguities of certain legal terms, and increasing the amount of fines that the court can impose.

However, lowering the threshold for criminal prosecution does not address all the deficiencies of the Criminal Law in relation to IP infringements. There is much room for improvement. Most IP laws have been amended since 1997 when the Criminal Law was revamped; thus it is not difficult to find a mismatch between the Criminal Law and other IP laws. Definitions in the Criminal Law are not only vague; often they are narrow in scope of application. Some important new IP developments since 1997 (e.g. the internet) are missing from the law, and more generally, there are internal inconsistencies in the Law.[247]

8. Concluding Remarks

This Chapter has outlined some remarkable achievements in law-making, institution-building and the making of efforts to uphold laws that have been enacted and promulgated in IP areas. It is however important to point out that what has been outlined is generally only what is on paper. The reality is an entirely different matter. Indeed, China has constantly been accused of being a rampant violator of IP rights.[248] As will be discussed in Chapter Eighteen, the issue of implementing and enforcing law is complex, and is complicated by a variety of factors and players in the processes; thus one perhaps could not and should not expect any quick fix for the IP protection situation in China in the near future. Essentially, as will be argued in Chapter Eighteen, China will only enforce its IP laws until and unless it has its own interest in doing so.

It is generally understood that the largest industrial firms in China spent less than 2 percent of their sales revenue on designing new goods and technologies. This represented less than one-tenth of the funding for R & D normally devoted by technology firms in the United States, Europe and Japan.[249] As a result, Chinese firms are now paying hefty prices for foreign technology. According to the Vice Minister for Science and Technology, Shang Yong, royalties now paid to foreign firms amount to 20% of the mobile phone sales price and 30% of the computer sales price, and for each DVD machine sold, the Chinese firm only makes US$ 1 in profit,

---

[247] For an analysis of these issues, see Shang Aiguo & Bao Yonghong, 'A Discussion on the Deficiencies of the Criminal Law on IP Protection and Their Improvement', (no. 40, 2004) *Journal of Heilongjiang Administrative Cadre Institute of Politics and Law* (*Heilongjiang Zhengfa Guanli Ganbu Xueyuan Xuebao*) 47-50.

[248] The reality of the protection of IP rights in China will be further examined in Chapter 18 on Implementation of Law.

[249] Peter S. Goodman, 'China's Weak Ally on Piracy', *Washington Post*, 4 June 2005, at D01.

and 10 *yuan* for each TV sold.[250] Whatever the real price that Chinese firms are paying, stronger IP protection will force Chinese firms to undertake their own R & D and hence foster China's own technological innovation. A stronger technological market will in turn demand better IP protection – a positive cycle that China now desperately needs.

China is also now realising that it could lose out economically if IP is not protected. According to a Chinese official source, between 2002–2004 some 15% of well known trademarks had been registered by foreign companies, resulting in an economic loss of some US$ 150-200 million.[251]

Some companies are now realising that it is in their own economic interest to not only develop, but also to protect their IP rights. As a result, it is very encouraging to see that more and more Chinese firms are now beginning to establish their own in-house legal departments or to expand their existing ones, so as to protect their own IP rights.[252]

Governments too are now realising that a long-term economic future depends on technological innovation and competitiveness. Thus the Ministry of Commerce has now decided that it will concentrate in the next 3-5 years on cultivating and promoting 300 Chinese brand names.[253] More generally, an increasing number of laws, regulations and policies have been issued to encourage high tech development in China. At the national level there are the Law on the Advancement of Science and Technology[254] and the Law on the Promotion of the Transformation of Scientific and Technological Results.[255] From the very beginning of the post-Mao economic reform and open door policy, tax and other financial incentives have been provided for the development and importation of new and high technologies. Most recently, in 2003 the State Council issued its Outline for the Medium and Long Term Development of Science and Technology, which provides a blueprint for science and technology development in the next 15 years and identifies specific areas for funding (amounting to hundreds of billions in government funding at different levels) and for policy, finance and tax incentives, support and encouragement.[256] However, the achievement

250 See 'Only 0.03% of Chinese Enterprises Own Their Own IP Rights', in Xinhua news: <www.xinhuanet.com/st/2006-03/22/content_4332493.htm> (last accessed 23 March 2006).

251 '15% of Well-known trademarks registered by foreigners', in <www.legaldaily.com.cn/bm/2006-07/24/content_357373.htm> (accessed 18 December 2006), and 'US$ 200 Million Loss in Three Years Due to Registration of Chinese Trademarks by Foreigners', in <www.legaldaily.com.cn/bm/2006-10/31/content_441580.htm> (accessed 18 December 2006).

252 'Chinese Use Courts to Sink Pirates', *supra* note 188, at 5.

253 'China Will Establish an IP Rights Protection Website in Three Years', *supra* note 200.

254 Adopted by the SCNPC 2 July 1993, and effective 1 October 1993.

255 Adopted by the SCNPC on 15 May 1996, and effective 1 October 1996.

256 See Xu Guanghua (Minister of Science and Technology), 'Report on the State Council Efforts to Strengthen Innovation Capacity and IP Protection', delivered at the 21st Session of the

so far has been limited. As of the end of April 2006 fewer than 0.03% of Chinese businesses had their own core technologies in products they produced. The great majority of enterprises had no patents or trademarks.[257] As of September 2006, only some 25% of large Chinese firms conducted research and development and their spending on R & D accounted for only 0.56% of their income.[258]

In short, China is taking concrete measures to develop its own IP, though with mixed results so far, and this will be a crucial ingredient in the actual protection of IP rights in the future.

Standing Committee of the NPC on 27 April 2006. A full text is available at <www.npc.gov.cn/zgrdw/rdgb_qg/regb.jsp> (last accessed 16 August 2006). China is currently drafting the Outline of Strategies for State Intellectual Property Rights, and the Eleventh Five-Year Plan for Intellectual Property Rights. See IP Action Plan 2007, *supra* note 198.

257 See 'Only 0.03% of Chinese Enterprises Own their Own IP Rights', *supra* note 250; Xu Guanghua, *is*; 'China Must Face Up to IP Competition', *People's Daily* (*Renmin Ribao*), 22 May 2006, 1.

258 See 'Only 0.03% of Chinese Enterprises Own their Own IP rights', *supra* note 250.

Chapter Seventeen

Foreign Trade and Investment Law

1. Introduction

These days business executives often claim that in terms of doing business you are either in China or you are nowhere. This is of course an exaggeration. But it is indicative of the increasing importance of China in the world's economy. Indeed, China is now one of the most significant trading countries, and its economy threatens to overtake the largest economy in the world, that of the US, in the not too distant future. Most importantly, its consistent double-digit (or near) growth rate in the last years has also made the Chinese economy the fastest growing economy in the world. Since its accession to the WTO, GDP has grown more than 10% annually.[1] Foreign trade has grown even faster, at 21.8%, 37.1%, 35.7%, 23.2%, and 23.8% in the successive years from 2002 to 2006,[2] with a huge annual trade surplus. China has also been one of the largest recipients of foreign direct investment (FDI) inflow for many years,[3] and certainly is going to stay that way for many years to come.

---

1 More precisely, 9.1%, 10%, 10.1%, 10.4% and 10.7% in the successive years from 2002 to 2006. See 2006 National Economic and Social Development Statistical Announcement, 30 April 2007, available <www.fdi.gov.cn/pub/FDI/zgjj/tzhj/hgjj/gmjjyshfz/t20070430_77928.htm> (last accessed 8 July 2007). See also 'China's Growth Skyrockets', *The Australian*, 21 January 2004, at 36, which contains growth rates from between 1984 and 2003.

2 See 2006 National Economic and Social Development Statistical Announcement, *id*. Foreign trade now accounts for some 20% of China's economic growth. See 'A Comment on the Present Economic Situation: Foreign Trade Grows Steadily and Open Door Opens even Wider', in <news.xinhuanet.com/newscenter/2007-08/01/content_6462583.htm> (last accessed 2 August 2007).

3 See annual World Investment Reports issued by the World Bank. As at the end of 2006, China had approved a total of 594,000 foreign investment enterprises, with a total utilised foreign capital of US$ 691.9 billion. These enterprises paid the government a total of 795 billion *yuan* in tax in 2006 alone, amounting to 21.12% of the total tax revenue of the state (See 'Explanation on the Draft Enterprise Income Tax Law of the PRC, delivered at the Fifth Plenary Session of the Tenth NPC on 8 March 2007). Together with tariffs and other import-related taxes, foreign economic related tax now amounts to 40% of China's total tax revenue. Foreign related

Just barely 30 years ago China was a negligible and isolated player in the world economy. Although Chinese scholars boasted that China traded with 160 countries in 1976,[4] the nature of foreign trade was then import-substitution, to facilitate the realisation of self-reliance, and so emphasis was placed on the importation of complete plants and equipment for heavy industry.[5] The total value of imports and exports in 1980 amounted to just a little over US$ 38 billion for a population of nearly one billion.[6] Exports amounted to less than one percent of total world exports in 1980.[7] Further, up to 1979 trade was monopolised by the Ministry of Foreign Trade, and conducted exclusively through eight national trading corporations, each responsible for specific categories of commodities. Finally, trade was largely conducted according to state mandatory plans or bilateral governmental agreements.[8] Similarly, in terms of foreign investment China only gradually opened to the world after the visit to China by President Nixon in 1971. Foreigners did not do business or invest in China until the late 1970s.[9]

Until the launch of the 'Open Door' policy in the late 1970s there was no legal framework for direct foreign investment, nor anything meaningful regarding foreign trade, nor indeed any need for such. Foreign trade and investment only became a phenomenon in the 1980s and so the present legal framework on foreign trade and investment is purely a product of the 1980s, which developed throughout the 1990s and continues to evolve until this day.

This Chapter first provides an overview of the evolution of the legal framework governing foreign trade and foreign investment in China. This is followed by an examination of the laws regulating both foreign trade and investment. It concludes

---

industries now employ some 149 million people (See 'A Comment on the Present Economic Situation: Foreign Trade Grows Steadily and Open Door Opens even Wider', *supra* note 2).

4 Wang Linsheng ad Chen Yujie, 'Economic Relations with Foreign Countries', in Yu Guangyuan (ed.), *China's Socialist Modernisation* (Beijing: Foreign Languages Press, 1984), at 685.

5 In fact, the Common Program of 1949 specifically declared that '[a]ll legitimate public and private trade shall be protected. Control shall be exercised over foreign trade and the policy of protecting trade shall be adopted.' See Article 37 of the Common Program. See further discussions in Wang Shaoxi & Wang Shouchun, *Chinese Foreign Trade* (*Zhongguo Duiwai Maoyi*) (Beijing: People's University of China Press, 1994), at 20-24.

6 *Almanac of China's Foreign Economic Relations and Trade 1997/98* (Beijing: China National Economic Publishing House, 1997), at 454.

7 *Almanac of China's Foreign Economic Relations and Trade 1997/98, id.*, at 456.

8 See Wang & Wang, *supra* note 5, at 706-709. See also Nicholas R. Lardy, 'The Open-door Strategies: An Outside Perspective', in Ross Garnaut & Liu Guoguang (eds), *Economic Reform and Internationalisation: China and the Pacific Region* (Sydney: Allen & Unwin, in association with the Australian National University, 1992), 137-148.

9 A. J. Easson & J. Li, *Taxation of Foreign Investment in the People's Republic of China* (Deventer/Boston: Kluwer Law and Taxation Publishers, 1989), at 3.

that the reform of the legal framework is yet to be completed, despite the huge efforts made since China was admitted to the WTO in 2001.

2. A Process of Gradual Transformation

While scholars in the 1990s were able to claim that without foreign trade and investment China would not be able to establish a socialist market economy,[10] this had not been the official position in the early period of post-Mao China.

As discussed in Chapter Two, when Deng Xiaoping came to power in 1977–1978, China was on the edge of economic collapse, and the legitimacy of the Communist leadership was in question. The announcement of the 'four modernisations' program was a direct response to the crisis. However, there was no agreement as to how the 'four modernisations' could be realised. Nevertheless, it was clear to Deng Xiaoping that to fund the ambitious modernisation program and to raise the standard of living, China needed not only foreign technology and foreign capital, but also foreign management expertise, marketing experience and marketing networks. He thus launched the 'Open Door' policy. But after three decades of 'self-reliance' and 'self-sufficiency' under the influence of the conventional understanding of socialism, ideological opposition to such a policy was to be expected. Deng Xiaoping was not only pragmatic, he was also realistic. Thus he neither pushed for 'Big Bang' therapy, nor did he try to change the politico-economic system as defined in the Constitution overnight. He undertook a gradual process of transformation, politically, economically and administratively.

This gradual trial and error approach to the implementation of the 'Open Door' policy led to practices that still have some ramifications in the present legal framework for foreign trade and investment.

Initially all reform measures were tightly controlled; the 'door' to China was only open to those with officially issued tickets. In terms of law and regulations, a rather strict examination and approval system was first established, the power of which was often exercised by different departments of the government, and then began to be gradually reduced and, in some aspects, dismantled. Over the whole thirty years of post-Mao reform there was therefore a gradual process of reducing restrictions and control. However, this process is far from completed, especially in relation to foreign investment in the service sectors. Thus the present 'socialist market economy' is better described as a 'managed economy'. But the overall direction has been towards liberalisation, especially after China became a WTO member in 2001.

The 'Open Door' policy was first introduced in confined areas, partly reflecting the need to allow the Central Government to retain tight control of the planned

10 See e.g. Fang Sheng, 'Open Up to the World and Utilise Capitalism', *People's Daily* (*Renmin Ribao*), (overseas edition), 24 February 1992, at 4.

and gradual implementation of the policy, and partly due to the lack of knowledge, experience and confidence in dealing with international economic relations after a long period of isolation. The establishment of Shenzhen Special Economic Zone (SEZ) in 1979 signified the beginning of this practice in post-Mao China. Essentially, 'special' economic zones or areas have served the purpose of testing within some confined areas the experiences of Taiwan and other Asian countries in the operation of Export Processing Zones, and subsequently applying the successful experience to the whole nation.[11] The overall trend towards liberalisation has been a process of expanding and opening up more and more areas for foreign investment. Thus, soon after the establishment of the first SEZ in Shenzhen, another three SEZs came into existence (Shantou, Zhuhai and Xiamen) in 1980. The designation of these areas as special economic zones was largely attributed to the fact that local residents had had a long history of foreign contact, overseas immigration and involvement in commercial activities, and that they are geographically close to Hong Kong, Macau and Taiwan. The obvious success of the SEZs led the government in 1984 to extend 'special' policies to a further fourteen Coastal Open Cities (Dalian, Qinhuangdao, Tianjin, Yantai, Qingdao, Lianyungang, Nantong, Shanghai, Ningbo, Wenzhou, Fuzhou, Guangzhou, Zhangjiang and Baihai). In February 1985 three more coastal areas were opened up for investment: the Changjiang (Yangtze) River Delta Open Economic Zone, the Zhujiang River Delta Open Economic Zone and the Southern Fujian Delta Open Economic Zone. Hainan Island became a province in 1988, and China's largest SEZ. In 1990 several regulations were issued by the Shanghai Municipal Government regarding the development and opening of the Shanghai Pudong New Area. Two years later the State Council again decided to open a number of border cities, as well as all the capital cities of inland provinces and autonomous regions. In addition, 15 free-trade zones, 32 state-level economic and technological development zones, and 52 new and high-tech industrial development zones were established in large and medium-sized cities. More recently, financial incentives and other forms of assistance have been granted to investors so as to encourage investment in the Central-Western region of China.[12] As a result a variety of 'open' zones and areas with different degrees of autonomy and economic freedom have been formed in China.[13]

It is however difficult to define an SEZ or a special investment area. For practical purposes these areas may be seen as places where foreign investors enjoy various economic preferential treatments and non-financial concessions relating to economic

---

11 Easson, & Li, *supra* note 9, at 2-5. See also Paul Chao, 'China's New Economic Zones: A Model for Development?', (1994) 10 *J. of Developing Societies*, at 59-73.

12 See Jianfu Chen, 'Great Western Development', (December 2000) 3 (12) *China Law Update* 3.

13 For a more detailed description of SEZs and other 'open' areas, see Jianfu Chen (ed.), *China Business Law Guide* (Singapore: CCH Asia Pacific, loose-leaf service), para. 87-015.

freedom, including reduced income tax rates, special concessions for import and export duties, flexible labour management, special fees for land use, better access to domestic markets, as well as simplified administrative processes regarding examination and approval of foreign investment projects. These special preferential treatments and concessions are not only provided by national laws and measures, but also by local regulations and rules. With practically the whole country now open for business, the significance of such 'special' investment areas is dramatically decreasing, but not completely diminished.[14] A unified national legal system, in terms of treating all investors in all areas equally, is still to be established.

The implementation of the 'Open Door' policy has followed a trial and error approach until this day, reflecting the constantly changing perceptions of the need and usefulness of foreign investment. Thus for most of the post-Mao reform period regulations and rules have constantly been issued as 'interim' or 'provisional' measures which are then subject to revision from time to time. This approach is also reflected in the use of state industrial policies and local guidelines, issued often on an *ad hoc* basis, with foreign investment being guided into high priority areas by way of offering investment incentives (financial or otherwise) and/or relaxation of control.[15] These policy documents also serve the purpose of transparency by dividing and defining areas or projects into those encouraged, restricted and prohibited.

Chinese laws relating to foreign business and interests has been developed separately and has been largely insulated from the development of domestic laws until very recently. This mainly reflects the lack of experience in dealing with foreign economic relations, but has also partly been for the purpose of offering special incentives to attract foreign capital, know-how and market expertise. Thus, at the national level, there have effectively been two legal systems in China, although efforts are being made to unify the two. Further, China has been very active in signing bilateral investment protection agreements and/or avoidance of double taxation agreements with other countries, as well as participating in various international agreements affecting international transactions. These agreements form an important part of the legal framework.

Although the whole development trend has been towards liberation, reduction of control and relaxation of restrictions, the most significant and thorough reform was undertaken during China's tortuous 13-year long negotiations for WTO membership and, since 2001, as part of its efforts to meet the requirements laid

---

14 After all, all relevant laws and regulations granting special incentives and treatments are still valid and have not yet been abolished.

15 See 'State Council Held Working Conference on the Utilisation of Foreign Capital', *Economic Daily* (*Jingji Ribao*), 8 March 1994, at 2. See also, David Bachman, 'China Hails the "Socialist Market Economy"', (July-August 1993) 20 *The China Business Review* 34, at 43; and Dong Shizhong, Danian Zhang & Milton R. Larson, *Trade and Investment Opportunities in China: The Current Commercial and Legal Framework* (Westport, Connecticut: Quorum Books, 1992), at 149-150.

down in the Protocol on Accession of the PRC (10 November 2001) and the WTO agreements. While the WTO-induced reform, described by some as the 'third wave' of legal reform in China,[16] has led to many general legal reforms, the most efficient, effective and significant ones have been those concerning foreign trade and foreign investment.[17] The WTO-induced reform is also different from the previous attempts in that it is much less *ad hoc* or piecemeal in approach.

Not surprisingly, this gradual trial and error approach has produced an extremely complicated and constantly changing system of regulations and rules, issued not only by the national legislature and the State Council, but also by various departments under the State Council. Conflicts and contradictions are of course to be expected. The WTO-related reforms have now significantly streamlined and simplified this system. However, although China has been a WTO member for more than six years, the legal framework on foreign trade and investment is still, as it has always been, in a state of flux. This is especially so in relation to trade in services, as China has been allowed a long and varied period of transition for full liberalisation.

3. Law on Foreign Trade

3.1. Evolution of the Legal Regime Governing Foreign Trade

The establishment of the State Commission for the Control of Import and Export Affairs in July 1979 signified the beginning of the reform of the foreign trade system.[18] Since then various reforms in the trading system have been carried out, by way of granting trading powers to local governments and to enterprises and through the reform of the licensing and quota systems. The initial goals of reform were to achieve the following:

(1) The separation of government administration from enterprise management, with the original national trading corporations to be replaced by a much larger number of enterprises with foreign trade powers directly under MOFERT,[19]

---

16 See Jerome A. Cohen, 'Opening Statement before the First Public Hearing of the US-China Security Review Commission', Washington, DC, 14 June 2001 (copy on file with author).

17 See Jianfu Chen, 'China and WTO: Legal Implications and Challenges' (November 2001) 4 (11) *China Law Update* 7.

18 Wang & Wang, *supra* note 5, at 709.

19 The Ministry of Foreign Economic Relations and Trade (MOFERT) was established in 1982 by merging the then Ministry of Foreign Trade, the Ministry of Foreign Economic Relations, the Foreign Investment Control Commission and the State Commission for the Control of Import and Export Affairs. This Ministry was renamed Ministry of Foreign Trade and Economic Cooperation (MOFTEC) in March 1993. In March 2003, MOFTEC was merged with the Ministry of Domestic Trade to become Ministry of Commerce. See website of the Ministry of Commerce: <www.mofcom.gov.cn>.

and specialised trading agencies under the State Council and other ministries to be established. Government bodies were then to continue to perform administrative tasks including unified leadership over foreign trade, working out policies and plans, supervising enterprise managers and their business activities and dismissing incompetent personnel;

(2) Decentralisation of authority of the import and export corporations to the provinces and the municipalities with the establishment of local foreign trade corporations;

(3) The granting of trading authority directly to certain major enterprises; and

(4) The reduction of items under state quota and/or licensing control.[20]

A further impetus for reforming the trade system arose in 1986 when China began to push for the 'resumption' of its GATT membership.[21] Efforts to meet GATT/WTO requirements included tariff reductions, the publication of many 'internal' regulations concerning foreign trade, and the reduction of quotas and licensing control.[22] Such efforts involved pressure from the United States and other Western countries.[23]

The reforms demanded during China's negotiation for WTO membership emphasised the improvement of macro-control of foreign trade through exchange rates, taxation and loans, the reduction of administrative interference, the abolition of mandatory trade plans, the transformation of foreign trade enterprises in line with modern company structures, and the unification of policy and regulations on foreign trade in line with international rules and practices and an increase in their transparency.[24] During this period the long-awaited Foreign Trade Law was issued in 1994. This then led to another round of reform, implementing principles

---

[20] See Suggestions for the Reform of the Foreign Trade System, Ministry for Foreign Economics and Trade, 14 August 1984, in *A Selection of Economic Law Materials* (*Jingjifa Ziliao Xuanbian*) (Vol. 2) (Beijing: Press of the Masses, 1986), 316-321. See also Wang Jianmin, 'The "Open Policies" and Internationalisation', in Garnaut & Liu, *supra* note 8, at 29-37; and Lardy, *supra* note 8.

[21] Three major decisions for reform were taken by the State Council in 1988, 1990 and 1994 respectively: Decision on Certain Questions on Quickening and Deepening Foreign Trade System Reforms (1988); Decision on Certain Questions on Further Reforming and Improving the Foreign Trade System (1990); and Decision on Further Deepening Reform of the Foreign Trade System (1994).

[22] See 'Minister Wu on Foreign Investment in China', (18-24 March 1996) *Beijing Review*, at 12.

[23] See 'Join the Club', *Far Eastern Economic Review*, 17 March 1994, at 42-44.

[24] 'Wu Yi Answers Questions on Foreign Exchange and Trade Reforms', *Economic Daily* (*Jingji Ribao*), 31 December 1993, at 1; and State Council Decision on Further Deepening Reform of the Foreign Trade System (1994).

as codified in the Law by revising administrative regulations and rules on foreign trade enterprise licensing, foreign trade agencies, anti-dumping, anti-subsidies, and safeguard measures.[25] However, the system established by the 1994 Foreign Trade Law was still one characterised as a 'controlled' system, by way of controlling the participation in foreign trade, establishing a wide range of requirements for licences and quotas, and installing indirect restrictions on trade through commodity inspection and quarantine. The system was also one consisting of a huge number of *ad hoc*, often confusing and not infrequently conflicting rules, issued by different authorities under the State Council.

The post-WTO reform in foreign trade started with a major review of all existing regulations and rules, resulting in the abolition of hundreds of them, with the rest being updated, as well as new regulations and rules being issued.[26] Two significant reforms were carried out in relation to the granting of trading rights and the imposition of licensing and quota requirements, each of which continued the long and slow process of reform.[27]

Interestingly, the Foreign Trade Law was only revised in 2004, almost three years after China joined the WTO. The 2004 revision of the Foreign Trade Law, adopted on 6 April 2004, was quite comprehensive: 29 articles having been revised, 35 articles (including three new chapters) added and 2 articles abolished, in a law that originally contained only 44 articles. Major revisions focused on three aspects. First, all rules that did not comply with the WTO Accession Protocol and WTO agreements were revised. Secondly, new mechanisms and procedures were established so that China might fully enjoy its rights as a WTO member. Thirdly, all out-of-date provisions were updated.[28] The 2004 revised Law contains some major improvements over the original Foreign Trade Law, including further liberalisation of trading rights, and the introduction of automatic licensing for free-trade goods, further strengthening of the protection of intellectual property in trade, and the establishment of a mechanism for the investigation of violations of foreign trade orders. As a consequence China

---

25 'A Historical Event in Foreign Trade – Minister Wu Yi Answers Questions Regarding the Newly Adopted Foreign Trade Law', *People's Daily* (*Renmin Ribao*), 14 May 1994, at 2; and State Council Decision on Further Deepening Reform of the Foreign Trade System (1994).

26 See Jianfu Chen, 'An Emerging New Legal Framework on Foreign Trade', (April 2002) 5 (4) *China Law Update*, at 7-12; Jianfu Chen, *supra* note 17. In fact, as soon as China was admitted to the WTO a comprehensive review of laws, regulations and rules was conducted. During the review, the State Council and its subordinate authorities reviewed a total of more than 2,300 regulations and rules, with 830 having been repealed and another 325 revised. See 'We Have Basically Established a Legal System Complying with WTO Requirements', *People's Daily* (*Renmin Ribao*), 11 December 2002, at 6.

27 See discussions in Section 3.5 below.

28 See Yu Guangzhou, 'Explanations on the Draft Revision to the Foreign Trade Law of the PRC', delivered at the 6th Session of the Standing Committee of the 10th NPC on 22 December 2003.

has asserted that it has fully implemented its WTO commitments and that its law now fully complies with WTO rules and standards.[29] While licensing and quotas still exist, the new legal framework can be properly described as one of regulation instead of control and restriction. As is the case with the WTO in general,[30] the current system in China is fairer and freer, but certainly not free and, to many, not fair either.[31] But it is also much more transparent, stable, coherent, and specific for practical purposes.[32]

3.2. The Regulatory Framework

As mentioned above, for many years, the regulatory framework for foreign trade, consisting of many overlapping or even conflicting 'interim' regulations and measures, had been highly complicated and, often, *ad hoc*. The adoption of the long-awaited Foreign Trade Law in 1994 pushed the legal framework towards a more transparent, coherent and specific system for practical purposes.

However the legal regime under the 1994 Foreign Trade Law (FTL) was still a very complicated one.[33] The FTL only laid down some general principles for governing foreign trade activities, and established an administrative framework regulating foreign trade. This principal law was then implemented or supplemented by over

---

29 See *People's Daily* Editorial, 10 April 2004.

30 The WTO has often been mistakenly perceived as pursuing free trade or ensuring fair trade. It does not. It is always about 'freer' and 'fairer' trade. See Jianfu Chen & Gordon Walker, 'Introduction: Towards a Fairer Order by Rules', in Jianfu Chen & Gordon Walker (eds), *Balancing Act: Law, Policy and Politics in Globalisation and Global Trade* (Sydney: The Federation Press, 2004), at 9.

31 The largely fixed rate of currency exchange between US and Chinese dollars and the implementation of an export tax rebate system in China are seen by many in the West (especially in the US) as unfair trade policies in China and have thus caused long-standing disputes between China and the US. It is claimed that the Chinese dollar (the *yuan*) is undervalued by as much as 40%. See Nipa Piboontanasawat, 'Dragon's Roaring Surplus Adds Fuel to US Fire over Chinese Exports', *The Age*, Business Section, 11 July 2007, at 1. However, China has as usual taken some gradual measures to reform both – pegging the Chinese *yuan* to a basket of foreign currencies of China's major trading partners (instead of the US dollar alone) and reducing the items and rates for export tax rebate. See Jianfu Chen, *supra* note 13, para. 30-010 and para. 52-700. See also Peter Morici, 'Why China Won't Revalue', 28 June 2007, available from <weazlsrevene.blogspot.com/2007/06/and-when-chinese-revaleu-dollar-plunges.html> (last accessed 30 June 2007).

32 For a comprehensive review of foreign trade reform, see Liu Mingxing and Ma Xiaoye, 'A Comprehensive Review of the Reform of the Chinese Foreign Trade System', available from <www.usc.cuhk.hk/wk_wzdetailss.asp?id=2953> (last accessed 10 March 2004).

33 For an analysis of this highly complicated legal regime at the time of the adoption of the 1994 Foreign Trade Law, see Jianfu Chen, 'China: Constitutional Changes and Legal Developments', in Alice Tay & Conita Leung, *Greater China: Law, Society and Trade* (Sydney: LBC, 1995), at 159-163.

150 regulations and measures issued by the State Council, the then MOFTEC (now Ministry of Commerce), the General Administration of Customs, and other commissions and ministries under the State Council.[34] Together, they maintained a tightly controlled system of foreign trade by way of limiting trade participation and imposing tariff and non-tariff barriers for trade and protection. Furthermore, and for all practical purposes, the principles laid down in the FTL could only be understood as goals for reform, while the protection mechanisms were the real rules which foreign traders with China had to cope with. Worse still, many of the rules and measures for managing trade in China often remained 'internal'.

While the WTO-induced reform has been the most far reaching and comprehensive, aimed at making the laws, regulations and rules transparent, streamlined and consistent, the legal framework has remained an extremely complicated system. At the centre of the present legal regime is the 1994 Foreign Trade Law (FTL) as revised in 2004. As in the case of the original 1994 law, the revised FTL only lays down certain general principles governing foreign trade activities. This principal law is implemented and supplemented by a large number of regulations and measures issued by the State Council.[35] The State Council regulations generally set out the administrative framework on specific aspects of foreign trade, as well as laying down detailed conditions for the conduct of foreign trade in the areas concerned. Specific and practical rules and measures are issued by the Ministry of Commerce (MOC, formerly the MOFTEC), the General Administration of Customs (GAC) and other commissions and ministries responsible for inspection, quarantine, and other aspects of foreign trade. The largest number of newly issued regulations and measures are those at this level, and these regulations and measures are mostly issued in accordance with the results of the negotiations for China's accession to the WTO.[36]

---

34 There was no precise calculation of the number of rules and measures affecting foreign trade at the time. A computer search of the Laws and Regulations of the PRC Database (provided by the State Legal Information Centre in Beijing) under the heading of 'Foreign Trade and Economy' showed more than 150 such rules at the end of 1996. If such a calculation is to include rules under other relevant headings, e.g. Customs, Taxation, etc., the total number would be much larger.

35 The most important State Council regulations include the following: Regulations of the PRC on Import and Export Tariffs (2003); Goods Import and Export Regulations of the PRC (2001); Regulations of the PRC on the Administration of the Import and Export of Technology (2001); Anti-dumping Regulations of the PRC (2001, revised 2004); Anti-subsidy Regulations of the PRC (2001, revised 2004); Regulations of the PRC on Safeguard Measures (2001, revised 2004); and Regulations of the PRC on Place of Origin of Import and Export Goods (2004).

36 For a full list of the most important laws, regulations and rules governing foreign trade, see Jianfu Chen, *supra* note 13, para. 80-030. Most of these laws, regulations and rules are published in a bilingual format in *China Law for Foreign Business – Business Regulations* (Singapore: CCH Asia Pacific, loose-leaf services).

Although 'free trade' or 'liberalisation of trade' seem to be the catchwords in these regulations, foreign trade is far from being free; the essence of the regulatory framework is still to maintain a managed system of foreign trade through both tariff and non-tariff measures for trade and protection. For practical purposes the protection and controlling mechanisms are the real rules that have the most significant impact in practice.

In short, although WTO principles and rules now provide some objective criteria and standards to assess regulatory reforms and the actual operation of the regulatory framework, one can only realistically expect that it will take some time before China fully discharges its WTO commitments and complies with all WTO requirements. In any case, China is still in the transitional period allowed by its Accession Protocol. Before that concludes one must be prepared for a continuing struggle with this regulatory framework as well as its implementation.

3.3. General Principles

When the FTL was adopted in 1994 it did not replace the previously existing regulations (but required revisions to be made to them), nor did it provide its own detailed rules. As was pointed out by the then Minister Wu Yi, the Law had only codified fundamental principles and policies and established a rough administrative framework, with the details to be gradually worked out.[37] Another major feature of the original 1994 FTL was to allow local variations in implementation in order to encourage local initiatives, while establishing uniform laws and measures to be maintained throughout China.[38] Upholding a unified system while also allowing local initiatives has been a constant feature of Chinese law, and this arrangement in the FTL was to allow the Central Government to implement a trial and error practice, while at the same time retaining overall control over the activities of foreign trade. However, this practice only served to make the already complicated system even more difficult to operate.

The new regime under the 2004 revised FTL, though still only containing very basic principles, now provides some clearer guidance for the administration and operation of the law.

The FTL defines foreign trade as the import and export of goods and technology and international trade in services.[39] Import and export of goods is further defined under the Goods Import and Export Regulations as the import of goods into and export of goods out of the People's Republic of China. The basic principles for

---

37 'A Historical Event in Foreign Trade – Minister Wu Yi Answers Questions Regarding the Newly Adopted Foreign Trade Law', *supra* note 25.

38 Article 4 of the 1994 FTL.

39 Article 2 of the FTL.

implementing a unified system of administration in relation to the import and export of goods are then defined by the law.

(1) A Unified System for Fair and Free Trade

Under the unified system, the Ministry of Commerce under the State Council (MOC) is designated as the overall and principal authority in charge of foreign trade throughout the whole country.[40] In practice, some of its specific functions are carried out by certain designated authorities at the local level.

In addition to upholding a unified system for foreign trade, the FTL declares that foreign trade must be fair and free in accordance with the law.[41] The term 'fair and free trade' is not defined by the FTL. Articles 32 and 33 of the FTL do, however, specify certain acts as unfair and as disturbing the foreign trade order, including acts of monopoly, selling goods at an unreasonably low price, bidding in collusion, bribing, false advertising, etc. Anyone involved in such acts will be penalised accordingly.

Unfair competition in foreign trade is further controlled by the Law against Unfair Competition (1993), the Anti-Dumping Regulations of the People's Republic of China (2001, revised 2004), the Anti-Subsidy Regulations of the People's Republic of China (2001, revised 2004), and the Regulations of the People's Republic of China on Safeguard Measures (2001, revised 2004).

It must be pointed out once again that, while free trade remains one of the objectives of the FTL and the Goods Import and Export Regulations, many of the laws deal with and regulate the control of trade through licensing, quotas and other non-tariff measures.

(2) State Intervention according to Law

Article 15 of the FTL allows free import and export of goods and technology except of those that are either restricted or prohibited by law or administrative regulations. Articles 16 and 17 of the FTL then authorise the State to restrict or prohibit the import or export of goods or technology in defined circumstances. Lists of goods and technologies whose trade is restricted or prohibited must be published and adjusted by the State Council authorities in charge of foreign trade. Temporary restriction or prohibition of trade outside the scope of Articles 16 and 17 is also allowed with the approval of the State Council.[42] For trade in goods, restriction and prohibition are to be implemented through a quota and licensing system and, for trade in technologies, through licensing administration.[43]

---

40 Article 3 of the FTL.

41 Article 4 of the FTL.

42 Article 18 of the FTL.

43 Article 19 of the FTL.

Furthermore, international trade in services may be restricted or prohibited for any of the following reasons: the protection of national security, the public interest, social morals, public health and safety, animals and plants and the environment; establishing or accelerating specific domestic service industries; ensuring the balance of the state's foreign exchange revenue and expenditure; or implementing laws, administrative regulations, or international obligations assumed by China.[44]

(3) State Promotion of Foreign Trade

Both the original 1994 and the revised 2004 FTL provide that the State may promote foreign trade by the establishment of foreign trade development funds and risk funds, the provision of financial loans, tax refunds for exports, and other measures deemed necessary for such promotion.[45] The very complicated and controversial export tax rebate scheme is established according to these provisions.

Put simply, export tax refunding is a scheme through which export goods are made free from export duties and indirect taxes in order: (1) to make export goods more competitive; and (2) to avoid double tax for these goods. Indirect taxes generally include VAT and Consumption tax. In a sense, the export tax refund scheme is a form of indirect export subsidy that is allowed under WTO rules.[46] However, if such a refund exceeds duties and taxes, it could amount to an 'illegal' export subsidy. The fundamental problem with the Chinese export tax refund scheme is that the scheme (both in terms of refund rates and eligibility criteria for refund) has been in a state of constant change, but this has not been caused by changes in tax rates, which have remained relatively stable. Thus the export tax refund scheme is not just a mechanism to make export goods tax-neutral, it has been used as a 'macro' economic policy.[47] As such, it is not surprising that its practice has been controversial.

(4) Reciprocity and Retaliation

The FTL specifically stipulates that China will take similar measures if any country imposes discriminatory restrictions or bans on Chinese goods.[48] This principle is

---

44 Article 26 of the FTL.

45 See Chapter 6 of the FTL (Article 33-37 of the revised FTL).

46 Article VI (4) of GATT provides that '[n]o product of the territory of any contracting party imported into the territory of any other contracting party shall be subject to anti-dumping or countervailing duty by reason of the exemption of such product from duties or taxes borne by the like product when destined for consumption in the country of origin or exportation, or by reason of the refund of such duties or taxes.'

47 For a comprehensive analysis of the law and policy on export tax refunds (with a collection of relevant documents), see He Zhidong (ed.), *A Practical Guide to the Current Export Tax Refund/Exemption* (*Xianxing Chukou Tuimianshui Caozuo Zhinan*) (Beijing: China Machine Press, 2002).

48 Article 7 of the FTL.

implemented by the Goods Import and Export Regulations. The Goods Import and Export Regulations offer most favoured nation status or national treatment to signatories and participants of treaties and agreements concluded or participated in by China in accordance with such treaties and agreements, and to other parties in accordance with the principles of mutual benefit and equity.[49] Immediately after this Article 6 of the Goods Import and Export Regulations makes it clear that if, in respect of the import and export of goods, any country or region adopts prohibitive, restrictive or other measures of a discriminatory nature against China, China will adopt corresponding measures against that country or region according to the specific situation.

Other than laying down the above basic principles, the FTL is hardly a useful piece of legislation. Indeed, all measures to regulate, control and promote foreign trade have to be further implemented by administrative regulations.

3.4. Operational Mechanisms

(1) A Unified National Framework Existing at Three Levels.

As already mentioned above, this 'unified' national legal framework exists at three levels, and as such the regulatory framework looks rather complicated and even confusing. However, legislation at each level seems to serve certain specific functions. Generally speaking, the primary legislation (i.e. the FTL) lays down the governing principles. These principles, though generally conforming to WTO principles, are hardly operational without further implementing rules. At the second level the State Council regulations then set out specific mechanisms (e.g. licensing and quota control, state trading, designated trading, and safeguard measures) and define specific authorities for implementing the principles contained in the national legislation. The specific methods of operation of these mechanisms are then provided at the tertiary level, i.e. by the Ministry of Commerce (formerly MOFTEC) and other ministries and commissions. Because of the goal of national unity of law, the legal framework on foreign trade seems to leave very little room for local discretion. As a matter of practice, foreign trade laws and regulations are enacted only by national authorities.

(2) Differential Treatment

Although trade regulations are nationally unified, differentiated treatment is accorded to different commodities or technologies. At least three kinds of differentiation exist. First, goods and technologies are classified into those whose import and export is freely allowed, restricted or prohibited, and different rules apply accordingly. The various commodities and technologies subject to restriction, prohibition and

---

49 Article 5 of the Goods Import and Export Regulations.

other lesser degrees of control are also published in specific lists. All these lists are, of course, subject to adjustment from time to time.[50] Secondly, trading of certain commodities is only allowed by designated enterprises or is monopolised by state trading enterprises, and specific rules exist to regulate such trading.[51] Finally, special rules continue to govern the import and export of certain commodities, such as machinery and electronic products, agricultural products, textile and wool products, etc.

(3) A Graded Administrative System

The actual administration of the regulations and rules is conducted by a graded system in accordance with specific authorisation. A principal method of foreign trade control is that of licensing and quota control. While the Ministry of Commerce (MOC) is the principal authority in charge of such control throughout China, it may authorise, and in fact does authorise, its own representative offices or provincial licensing offices to issue import/export licences under the so-called graded administration; that is, certain categories of commodities must have their licences directly issued by MOC, while the Special Commissioner Offices of MOC and the provincial bureaus of commerce are each authorised by MOC to issue licences within their authorised scope and in accordance with the MOC rules. Issuance of licences beyond this authority, or without approval documents, or in excess of quotas, is strictly forbidden. Any licence issuing authority that violates the regulations of import/export licensing control will be penalised by MOC. Further, such imports/exports will not be able to pass Customs control.

3.5. Trade Barriers

Trade barriers exist in all countries, and without them there would be little reason for the existence of the WTO. Thus the primary objective of the WTO is defined as being to substantively reduced tariffs and other trade barriers and to eliminate discriminatory treatment in international trade.[52] Trade liberalisation means nothing other than the reduction and, ultimately, the elimination of trade barriers.

Trade barriers are generally classified as tariff and non-tariff barriers. While one of the major objectives in trade law reform in China is always managing trade, the whole process could also be seen as one of the gradual reduction of trade barriers, with major success in some areas (e.g. tariffs) but only limited success in others (e.g. licensing and other non-tariff controls).

---

[50] See Article 18 of the FTL.

[51] See Article 11 of the FTL.

[52] See Preamble of the GATT.

(1) Tariffs

Tariffs exist in almost all countries, for the purpose of either raising state revenue or of controlling foreign trade. The present goal of GATT/WTO is not to eliminate tariffs, but to reduce them. Chinese reform has been quite remarkable in this area, in order to meet GATT/WTO membership requirements.

Tariff control is governed by the Customs Law,[53] the Import and Export Tariff Regulations,[54] and the Customs Import and Export Tariff Schedule,[55] and administered by the General Administration of Customs and the Customs Tariff Commission directly under the State Council. This clear legal regime makes tariff control in China exceptionally transparent as compared to other aspects of foreign trade management.

Tariff reduction in the 1990s has been sweeping and steep. In 1992, after tariff reduction on 40 commodities, the average tariff rate on imports was around 66%. Successive reductions followed in 1992, 1993, 1994.[56] In April 1996 tariffs on 4,900 items were cut by an average rate of 40%, bringing the average tariff down from 35.9% to 23%. This was followed by tariff reductions on 4,874 commodities by an average of 26%, which took effect from 1 October 1996, thus taking the average tariff down further from 23% to 17%.[57] This second cut in 1996 was to implement the formal announcement by the then Chinese President, Jiang Zemin, in November 1996 at the APEC Informal Leadership Meeting (in Subic Bay) in the Philippines that the average import tariff rate was to be further cut to 15% by the year 2000.[58] Since then, further substantial tariff reductions have been made. In January 2004 China announced yet another cut, bringing down the average tariff rate from 11% to 10.4%.[59]

---

53 Adopted by the Standing Committee on 22 January 1987, effective on 1 July 1987, and revised on 8 July 2000.

54 First adopted by the State Council in 1985 and frequently revised since then.

55 First issued by the State Council in 1985 and frequently revised since then. The Schedule is prepared in conformity with the International Customs Cooperation Council Nomenclature (CCCN) system.

56 Reduction was carried out twice in 1992 on 225 and 3,371 commodities respectively. 1993 saw further reductions on 2,898 commodities, followed by reductions on 234 items. See Wang & Wang, *supra* note 5, at 101; and Sun Weixing & Wang Guoxiang (eds), *A Handbook on International Trade* (*Guoji Shangmao Shouce*) (Beijing: China foreign Economic Relations and Trade Press, 1994), at 2179.

57 See *People's Daily* (*Renmin Ribao*), internet edition, 26 September 1997.

58 'Speech by President Jiang Zemin of the People's Republic of China at the Fourth APEC Informal Leadership Meeting', in *Almanac of China's Foreign Economic Relations and Trade 1997/98*, *supra* note 6, at 2.

59 See 'China Cutting Average Tariff Rate to 10.4%', available from <www.china.org.cn/english/2004/Jan/83793.htm> (last accessed 10 July 2007).

Under China's WTO commitment, its average tariff rate is to be cut to 9.8% by 2010.[60]

While the average tariff rate in China is still relatively high compared to the 3%-4% in developed nations, in the short time span of 15 years China has managed to cut its average tariff rate from 66% to just over 10%. This is a remarkable achievement by any criteria. At around 10% tariffs do not really constitute a significant trade barrier any more.

(2) Non-tariff Control

Non-tariff barriers to trade also exist in all countries. Some are more regulated (such as the use of anti-dumping/subsidy and safeguard measures), others are more ingenious in their disguise (such as unreasonable Customs practices and quarantine measures). In China the two primary means for the control and restriction of trade were for a long time restrictions of the right to trade and the imposition of licensing and quotas. Both of these have been subjected to extensive reform, with one being more successful than the other.

Right to Trade

For a long time in China only authorised persons (natural or legal) were allowed to engage in foreign trade. This mechanism of control is of course not new in China, but its reform in the past thirty years has been remarkable.

One of the early economic policies in the PRC was to control foreign trade. Thus privately controlled foreign trade companies were among the first to be nationalised in the process of nationalisation. In 1949 the Ministry for Trade was established and, in the following year, 7 trading companies (commonly referred to as Foreign Trade Corporations, FTCs) were established exclusively for foreign trade. The number was then increased to 15 in 1953, while private trading companies were subject to a process of nationalisation, initially in the form of joint operations. State-controlled foreign trade amounted to 66.88% of the total foreign trade in 1950, but by 1957, 99.9% of foreign trade was controlled by the state FTCs.[61] Thereafter, foreign trade was monopolised by the state and conducted according to mandatory plans until the mid 1980s.

Reforms in the foreign trade system, initially started in 1984, witnessed a gradual process of diversification and decentralisation of foreign trade powers, thus breaking the monopoly of trade by the Ministry of Foreign Trade. Increasing numbers of FTCs began to be established by various ministries under the State Council and governments at provincial level, and foreign-invested enterprises were granted trading rights for importing and exporting equipment and materials needed for

---

60 See *id*.

61 Wang & Wang, *supra* note 5, at 17-18.

their own operations. By 1987 more than 2,200 FTCs had been established with government approval.[62] The continuing reforms, carried out to meet GATT/WTO membership requirements, saw a subsequent explosion in the number of FTCs being established throughout China.[63]

The expansion of foreign trade rights was accompanied by reforms in the management of FTCs. First came the introduction of a contractual responsibility system, which was soon, but gradually, replaced by an economic accountability system under which FTCs were responsible for their own profits and losses. The guaranteed foreign exchange resources and subsidies for FTCs and mandatory plans for foreign trade were also gradually abolished. As the principal conduit for foreign trade, FTCs began, from 1991, to lose their state subsidies and, in exchange, gained greater business independence. Instead of importing and exporting according to state plans they could act as independent agents for companies that wished to import or export, and charge commissions. Under the 1994 Foreign Trade Law they gained even wider autonomy and became responsible for their profits and losses for the first time. These reforms thus made FTCs competitive profit-seeking enterprises rather than government-subsidised institutions.[64]

Although FTCs were now made market-oriented entities, the government did not abandon its control over them. Under Article 9 of the original 1994 Foreign Trade Law, all FTCs, referred to as foreign trade operators in the Law, had to obtain their business permission from foreign trade authorities under the State Council before engaging in the business of import and export of goods and technologies. This requirement was however waived for foreign investment enterprises for import and export of their business-related equipment, raw materials or goods.[65] In September 1996 MOFTEC issued the Provisional Measures on the Trial Establishment of Sino-foreign Joint Venture Foreign Trade Companies on a Pilot Basis, and thus

---

[62] Wang & Wang, *supra* note 5, at 87.

[63] According to Minister Wu Yi, then Minister for MOFTEC, there were some 2,000 enterprises and 100 research institutions that had been authorised to directly conduct foreign trade at the end of 1993. See 'On the Trade Deficit at the End of the Year – An Interview with Minister Wu Yi', *People's Daily* (*Renmin Ribao*), 30 December 1993, at 2. If the Chinese report is accurate, the number increased dramatically in 1994. According to the *People's Daily*, there were more than 7,000 [domestic] enterprises, in addition to more than 170,000 foreign investment enterprises, that had the right to directly conduct foreign trade in 1994: 'An Historical Event in Foreign Trade – Minister Wu Yi Answers Questions Regarding the Newly Adopted Foreign Trade Law', *supra* note 25, at 2. The foreign trade yearbook contains a list of the 5,000 largest FTCS: *Almanac of China's Foreign Economic Relations and Trade 1997/98*, *supra* note 6, at 973-992.

[64] See Wang & Wang, *supra* note 5, 80-104.

[65] See *Almanac of China's Foreign Economic Relations and Trade 1997/98*, *supra* note 6, at 156-157.

for the first time Sino-foreign joint ventures for foreign trade were allowed to be established in China, though with some extremely tight conditions.[66]

The most significant step in this continuing reform was the transformation of the approval system for foreign trade rights into a 'Registration and Verification' system through the Provisions on Issues Relating to the Administration of Qualifications for Import and Export Operations.[67] Under this system foreign trade operation qualifications were classified into two major categories: a general right to engage in foreign trade in goods and technologies, and the right to engage in the export of self-produced products and the import of self-use equipment and materials. All types of enterprises which met prescribed conditions were allowed to apply for a foreign trade certificate, and all applicants were to be assessed against uniform criteria under simplified procedures.

The revised Foreign Trade Law concludes this long process of reform by introducing a 'filing-for-record' system.[68] Under this system, all enterprises, organisations and, for the first time, individuals, that have completed industry and commerce registration or other formalities for business operation are permitted to engage in foreign trade activities, provided that they have completed procedures of 'filing-for-record' with the Ministry of Commerce or its entrusted organs. That is to say, state control over the participation in foreign trade has now finally been dismantled, and the term 'free trade' has gained one more meaning in China for those wishing to engage in the import/export business.

Licensing and Quotas

A licensing system for foreign trade in goods existed for a short period in the early days of the People's Republic. However, when foreign trade was monopolised by the state, such a need ceased to exit and no licence was required for import or export of commodities from the early 1950s until the early 1980s.[69] With decentralisation and diffusion of foreign trade powers, a licensing system was re-introduced to control possible excessive imports of foreign goods and exports of under-priced Chinese commodities.[70] Until 1994 when the Foreign Trade Law was adopted the import and

---

66 These measures were to implement the promise given by the Chinese president, Jiang Zemin, at the Third Informal Leadership Meeting of APEC in October 1995, during which Jiang announced that Sino-foreign joint ventures for foreign trade would be allowed to be established in Pudong (Shanghai) and selected locations. See *People's Daily* (*Renmin Ribao*), internet edition, 11 July 1997.

67 Issued by the then MOFTEC on 10 July 2001.

68 See Article 9 of the FTL.

69 Wang Chaoying, Meng Xiangang & Zang Yaomin (eds), *Practical Answers to Foreign Trade Law* (*Duiwai Maoyi Fa Shiwu Wenda*) (Beijing: China Commerce Press, 1994), at 93.

70 The licensing system was first introduced in 1980 through the Provisional Measures concerning the Management of Imports in Foreign Trade and Provisional Measures on the Export

export of technologies was subject to a separate administrative process through the Administrative Regulations on Contracts for the Import of Technologies and their Implementation Rules, issued by the State Council in 1985 and by the MOFTEC in 1988 respectively. The 1994 FTL dealt with the control of imports and exports of both goods and technologies.

The 1994 FTL first established a differentiated treatment of goods according to a three-category classification – goods and technologies whose import and export was to be free, restricted, or prohibited by law or administrative regulations.[71] This system continues under the 2004 revised FTL.[72] Under this system, a licensing and/or quota system has been established for restricted goods.[73] Thus, freedom of foreign trade only refers to goods and technologies not under state control.

Under the FTL the Chinese government is able to restrict or prohibit foreign trade in almost all areas according to its own perceived needs, which are to be reflected in and decided by national industrial policies and, therefore, to be adjusted from time to time.[74] The licensing and quota system has however been improved in that it is now relatively transparent. Indeed, the FTC specifically requires that the lists of restricted or prohibited goods or technologies be published by foreign trade authorities,[75] and rules on the distribution of quotas are to be made public by the State Council.[76]

Overall, the number of items of goods and technologies subject to licensing and/or quota control has been significantly reduced in the last twenty years or so. However, Articles 16 and 17 (on restricted and prohibited goods), which authorise the State Council and its subordinate authorities to impose licensing and quota control, are framed in extremely vague language, and thus give the administrative authorities almost absolute discretionary power to free or control foreign trade.

Other Trade Barriers

Licensing and quotas are, of course, not the only means that a country may use to control its trade. Commodities inspection and quarantine, for example, are imposed by all nations for the protection of the public interest, health and national security. The problem is that such mechanisms can also be misused or even abused, and thus

---

Licensing System, both jointly issued by the Import and Export Control Commission and Ministry for Foreign Economic Cooperation and Trade. See Wang, Meng & Zang, *supra* note 69, at 93.

71 Article 15 of the 1994 FTL.

72 Articles 14, 16 & 17 of the revised 2004 FTL.

73 Article 19 of the FTL.

74 See Article 16 of the FTL.

75 Article 18 of the FTC.

76 Article 21 of the FTC.

become in practice mechanisms for non-tariff barriers to foreign trade. The need for commodities inspection and quarantine is well recognised, so the question is therefore whether such a system is fair and reasonable. The criteria are in themselves hardly objective.[77]

The FTL also authorises the restriction of trade for reasons of 'the public interest' and 'public morals'. This in practice often means restrictions for political reasons. A typical example is the restriction on publications – an area described by American politicians as one of the most closed markets in the world for the US publishing industries,[78] hence one of the reasons contributing to intellectual property violations.[79]

4. Direct Foreign Investment

4.1. The Development of Foreign Investment Law and Policies

As mentioned earlier, there was little to talk about regarding foreign investment in China at the time the 'Open Door' policy was launched. Even when the policy was launched, foreign investment was largely confined and channelled to the special investment areas (such as SEZs). And just as in other areas of economic activity, various forms of foreign investment often appeared and developed, permitted by *ad hoc* policies ahead of legislative sanctions. As foreign investment proliferated in China, so did the volume of Chinese laws and regulations, both at the central and at the local level. These laws and regulations then gradually established a special legal regime for foreign investment enterprises. Until this day a unique feature of these laws and regulations is that they deal with specific types and specific aspects of foreign investment; there is no uniform code for foreign investment.

The gradual liberalisation of foreign investment policies might have often taken place ahead of legislative sanctions, but various forms of restrictions and control were never far from the scene. Indeed, most of the WTO defined trade-related investment measures (TRIMs) accompanied this development. Thus there were strict foreign exchange controls, a centrally controlled examination and approval system for foreign investment, requirements for product export and foreign exchange

---

77 For discussions on commodity inspection and quarantine, see Jianfu Chen, *supra* note 13, paras 80-710 – 80-840, and paras 81-310 – 81-500 respectively.

78 Statement of Eric H. Smith (President of the International Intellectual Property Alliance), in *Roundtable: Intellectual Property Protection as Economic Policy: Will China Ever Enforce its IP Laws?*, transcripts of the Roundtable are available from <www.cecc.gov> (last accessed 19 May 2005)

79 Statement of Diane Watson, US Congresswoman from the State of California, in *Hearing before the U.S.–China Economic and Security Review Commission, June 7-8, 2006*. Transcripts published in July 2006, and available from <www.uscc.gov> (last accessed 31 August 2006).

balance, requirements for the introduction and transfer of advanced technologies, requirements for the use of local content and of Chinese banking and insurance facilities. There were also all kinds of other restrictions issued from time to time, either codified in law and regulations or contained in industrial policies. Like in many other developing countries, investment incentives, financial or otherwise, were offered to foreign investors as a means of compensating for the strict control and restrictions.

Once again it has been the WTO-induced reform that has compelled China to remove the various TRIMs by revising all existing laws on foreign investment. However, this reform has not changed the two fundamental features of the Chinese foreign investment law. First, the foreign investment law and regulations still constitute a separate legal regime from the general domestic legal system. Certainly efforts to unify foreign investment law began to appear in the late 1980s and were partly achieved with the introduction of uniform taxation for all kinds of foreign investment enterprises in 1991, the promulgation of a uniform company law in December 1993, the introduction of a number of tax regulations (e.g. regulations on consumption and business taxes) applicable to both domestic and foreign investment enterprises, and most recently the adoption of a unified enterprise income tax law in 2007. Nevertheless, the process towards a unified legal system is far from complete, largely because of the 'gradual liberalisation' policy negotiated and accepted for China's WTO membership, especially in relation to the opening up for investment in the service sectors and the removal of barriers to access to the market. Secondly, the initial design of dividing foreign investment into different forms (equity joint venture, cooperative (contractual) joint venture, and wholly foreign-owned enterprises) continues. The WTO-induced reform, unlike that in foreign trade law, has not led to a fundamental redesign of the law in this area. In fact, the gradual liberalisation of investment in the trade service sectors has only made the system even more complicated and confusing.

Nevertheless, specific commitments agreed during the WTO negotiations were quickly implemented, by way of revising and updating all principal foreign investment laws and the implementing rules thereunder. The major revisions may be summarised as follows:

- allowing a foreign investment enterprise to purchase raw materials, fuel and other requirements from both domestic and international markets;
- allowing various items of insurance required by a foreign investment enterprise to be covered by insurance companies within the Chinese territory;
- allowing further freedom for a foreign investment enterprise to sell in the domestic market;
- abolishing the requirement for a foreign investment enterprise to keep a balance between its foreign exchange income and expenditure; and

- abolishing the requirement that a foreign investment enterprise must utilise advanced technology and equipment or export all or the majority of its products.[80]

In short, in the absence of a comprehensive code of investment, and with the continuation of an *ad hoc* approach towards foreign investment and the separate treatment of foreign-related business entities, the legal framework governing foreign investment in China is highly complex and, as a result of China's WTO membership, transitional for various kinds of investment vehicles.

4.2. The Regulatory Framework

Three principal factors continue to make the regulatory framework on foreign investment particularly complicated. First, in the absence of a comprehensive code of investment, an *ad hoc* approach towards foreign investment and the separate treatment of foreign-related business entities continues. Secondly, while certain overall control mechanisms do exist, for practical purposes such control mechanisms are implemented by tertiary legislation, oriented towards particular sectors/industries or geographical areas. Thirdly, China's WTO transitional arrangement has led to a huge number of departmental rules dealing with particular sectors, and these rules are changed from time to time in accordance with the timetable of the transitional arrangement. In a nutshell, this legal framework may be best understood through the following:

(1) Principal Forms of Foreign Investment Defined by National Law

Although foreign investment may take place in different forms, such as counter-trade, representative offices, etc. foreign investors in China often adopt joint ventures (equity or contractual) or wholly-owned subsidiaries as their investment vehicles; that is, the so-called *sanzi qi ye* (the 'three investment enterprises'). These three principal foreign investment forms are all defined and governed by three pieces of national legislation, and each of these is further elaborated by three separate sets of detailed implementing rules issued by the State Council. Many aspects of regulation as contained in the principal laws and implementing rules are further supplemented by governmental rules (ministerial rules), the majority of which are issued by MOFTEC and its successor the Ministry of Commerce, and, sometimes also by local governmental rules.

80 For a detailed outline of these revisions, see Jianfu Chen & Lijian Hong, 'China Watch', *China Law Update*, December 2000 (at 10-11); April 2001 (at 2-5), May 2001 (at 2-7); & September 2001 (at 11).

(2) Ad Hoc *and Transitional Rules on Investment in the Service Sectors*

For most of China's 'Open Door' practice, the service sectors were largely closed to foreign investment. China's WTO negotiations and membership then forced it to open up these service sectors and to reduce barriers to access to the markets. However, China has only agreed to 'gradual liberalisation', albeit with firm commitments in accordance with specific timetables.[81] As China's commitments are made for specific services, and each with different timetables for 'full liberalisation', a large number of *ad hoc* and transitional rules have been issued to implement these commitments. Since China currently is in a transitional period, these *ad hoc* rules are often issued as 'interim' measures to serve a transitional function and are revised from time to time in accordance with the agreed timetables.

(3) Changing Policies to Meet Changing Needs

With an emphasis on legal certainty and stability, state policy guidelines have been increasingly used to guide foreign investment into servicing the constantly changing needs, or the perceived needs, of the country. Thus various state industrial policies and occasional local guidelines have been issued on an *ad hoc* basis, and foreign investment is then guided into high priority areas. These policy documents also serve the purpose of transparency by dividing and defining areas or projects into those that are encouraged, restricted or prohibited.[82] Foreign investment projects that do not meet these needs will have difficulty obtaining approval from Chinese authorities or will be excluded from enjoying any preferential policies for encouraging foreign investment.

(4) Locality Variations Permitted for Now

As explained earlier, the 'Open Door' policy has been implemented only 'gradually' through the various 'special' areas (e.g. SEZs, economic and technological development zones, hi-tech development zones, etc.). The special policies, mostly in the form of preferential treatment, will continue to apply, although with diminishing importance as a result of the nationwide implementation of the 'Open Door' policy.[83]

---

81 These details are contained in Annex 9 (Schedule of Specific Commitments on Services) of the Protocol on the Accession of the PRC.

82 Among the many policy documents, the following three are the most important ones: Regulations on Foreign Investment Guidelines (last revised 1 April 2002); Guideline Catalogue of Foreign Investment Industries (last revised 30 November 2004); and Catalogue of Priority Industries for Foreign Investment in the Central and Western Regions (last revised 23 July 2004).

83 The new Enterprise Income Tax Law, adopted on 16 March 2007 (and to take effect on 1 January 2008), for the first time establishes a uniform tax scheme for both domestic and foreign investment enterprises. However, Article 57 of the Law specifically allows a transitional

This practice has become a policy problem in recent years, as the accession of China to the WTO demands uniformity of law and policy throughout the nation, as well as national treatment for foreign investment.[84] In other words the various preferential treatments and concessions currently offered in accordance with the nature of each 'special investment area' will ultimately be abolished.

4.3. Equity Joint Ventures (EJVs)

Equity joint ventures (EJVs) are governed by the 1979 Law on Sino-foreign Equity Joint Ventures.[85] The Equity Joint Venture Law is supplemented by the Detailed Implementation Rules (1983)[86] and many other measures and rules regulating various aspects (i.e. registration, labour relations, profit sharing, foreign exchange balance, capital contribution, etc.) of joint ventures.[87] There is no doubt that the regulatory regime for EJVs is the most comprehensive of the laws governing the forms of foreign investment in China.

An EJV is an independent legal entity (legal person) of limited liability, with each party sharing profits and losses in accordance with the proportion of its contribution to the registered capital of the venture. The foreign party shall in general contribute at least 25% of the registered capital.[88] Contribution to the venture can be made in the form of cash, materials and advanced equipment, industrial technologies,

---

period (yet to be defined by the State Council) for the continuing operation of the various preferential policies and laws applied in the various 'special zones and areas'.

84 In fact, many Chinese business people running their own private businesses have increasingly complained that what the foreign investment enterprises have enjoyed is not 'national treatment' but 'extra' national treatment or 'policies superior to national treatment'. They have become increasingly vocal in arguing for these 'privileges' to be abolished. See 'Non-public Sectors Enter into a Golden Period and Most Barriers Have Been Removed', Xinhua News Agency, 17 December 2003: <news.xinhuanet.com/fortune/2003-12/17/content_1235833.htm> (last accessed 6 January 2004); 'Legal Protection for the Non-Public Sectors Becoming Increasingly Perfect', *People's Daily* (*Renmin Ribao*), overseas edition, 30 May 2007, at 1; 'Private Economy Promotes Technological Innovation and Localisation of Technologies', *People's Daily* (*Renmin Ribao*), overseas edition, 13 January 2007, at 1; and 'China's Parliament Adopts Enterprise Income Tax Law', <english.people.com.cn/200703/16/eng20070316_358252.html> (last accessed 8 June 2007).

85 Initially issued on 1 July 1979, amended in 1990 to provide more flexibility and powers to foreign parties in terms of controlling a joint venture, and further amended on 15 March 2001 to meet WTO requirements.

86 Initially issued 20 September 1983, and most recently revised 22 July 2001.

87 For more detailed analysis on the law and practice of EJVs, see Jianfu Chen, *supra* note 13, paras 25-010 – 26-540.

88 Article 4 of the EJVs Law. 'Registered capital' is the capital subscribed by the parties to the joint venture and registered with the registration authorities.

buildings, premises and land-use rights.[89] For obvious reasons, the Chinese party often offers land-use rights and buildings as part of its contribution.

An EJV is controlled by a board of directors. The position of chairperson of the Board was only opened to foreign investors by the 1990 Amendment. The chairperson is the legal representative of the joint venture,[90] but the powers of the chairperson are not defined by the Law or its Implementation Rules. Article 30 of the Implementing Rules grants the powers of daily operation of the venture to the general manager, who is also responsible for carrying out the decisions of the Board meetings.

Despite the rigidity of its legal requirements, the EJV was and perhaps still remains the most popular form of direct foreign investment, as the involvement of Chinese partners often facilitates the penetration of Chinese domestic markets and dealings with the Chinese bureaucracy.

4.4. Contractual (Co-operative) Joint Ventures (CJVs)

Although the form of Contractual joint ventures (CJVs) had already been quite popular, the Law on Contractual Joint Ventures did not appear until 1988,[91] with detailed implementation rules on the Law appearing in 1995.[92] However not many detailed implementation measures and regulations have been issued on a number of specific aspects of CJVs, and in practice the rules and regulations on EJVs have been, and continue to be, applied to contractual joint ventures 'by reference'.[93]

Under Article 2 of the CJV Law, parties to a CJV shall prescribe in their contracts the provisions on investment or terms for co-operation, distribution of earnings or products, sharing of risks and losses, methods of business management, and the ownership of property on the expiry of the contract term. In other words, the contract negotiated between the parties plays a vital role both in establishing and operating the joint venture. Although a CJV is primarily a contractual arrangement, Article 2 of the CJV Law also provides the possibility of a CJV obtaining the status of legal person, that is, in the Chinese context, of taking the form of a limited liability company.[94]

---

[89] Article 5 of the EJV Law and Articles 22-29 of its Implementing Rules.

[90] Article 34 of the Implementation Rules.

[91] Initially promulgated on 13 April 1988 and revised on 31 October 2000.

[92] Regulations for the Implementation of the Sino-foreign Joint Cooperative Ventures Law, issued by MOFTEC (with approval from the State Council) on 4 September 1995 and effective on the same date. For unknown reasons these Regulations have not yet been revised since China joined the WTO.

[93] For more detailed analysis on the law and practice of CJVs, see Jianfu Chen, *supra* note 13, paras 26-010 – 26-170.

[94] See Article 14 of the CJV Implementation Regulations.

Under the CJV Law, a CJV must have either a board of directors or a joint management body, which will decide all major issues involving the joint venture in accordance with the CJV contract. In addition, with the unanimous agreement of the members of the board of directors or the joint management body and the approval of a competent authority, the parties to a CJV may contract the management of the venture to a third party.[95]

The unique advantages of forming a CJV, as compared with EJVs, include its greater flexibility in joint venture arrangements and the fact that there are fewer restrictions as to economic activities and capital contribution.[96]

4.5. Wholly Foreign-owned Enterprises (WFOEs)

A wholly foreign-owned enterprise (WFOE) refers to an enterprise established within China with capital provided totally by foreign investors. It does not include branches of foreign enterprises or other economic entities.[97] Again, WFOEs appeared in China well before the Law on Wholly Foreign-owned Enterprises was issued in 1986.[98] Detailed implementation rules were only issued in December 1990.[99]

For a long time the establishment of WFOEs was subject to various restrictions. Thus the original WFOE Law specifically required that the establishment of WFOEs must benefit the development of the Chinese national economy and must utilise advanced technology and equipment, or that the enterprises export all, or the majority of, their products.[100] The same article also anticipated (and still does) the State Council imposing restrictions on the establishment of WFOEs. Article 4 of the original Implementation Rules indeed prohibited the establishment of WFOEs in the following areas: (1) newspapers, publishing, broadcasting, television or films; (2) domestic commerce, foreign trade or insurance; (3) post and telecommunications; (4) other industries which the Chinese government prohibits a WFOE from establishing. Article 5 of the original Implementation Rules further listed areas in which the establishment of WFOEs would be restricted.[101] In addition, Article 6 of the Implementation Rules stipulated certain situations in which the establishment

---

95 Article 12 of CJV Law.

96 Under Article 18 of the CJV Implementation Regulations, if the CJV is to obtain legal person status, the capital contribution by the foreign party shall not normally be lower than 25% of the total registered capital of the CJV.

97 Article 2 of the PRC Law on Wholly Foreign-owned Enterprises.

98 Initially issued on 12 April 1986, revised on 31 October 2000.

99 Initially issued on 12 December1990, revised on 12 April 2001. For detailed examinations of the law and practice of WFOEs, see Jianfu Chen, *supra* note 13, paras 26-510 – 26-900.

100 Article 3 of the original WFOE Law. The export requirement was relaxed to 50% of the value of total product output for the year and the achieving of a foreign exchange balance or surplus: Article 3 of the original Detailed Implementation Rules.

101 These include public utilities, transport facilities, real estate, trust investment and leasing.

of WFOEs would not be approved.[102] It is, however, unclear how strictly these prohibitions and restrictions were actually enforced.

The 2000 revision of the WFOE Law abolished the compulsory requirement for advanced technologies or the exportation of products. Instead it provides that the State *encourages* the introduction of advanced technologies and the export of products. The 2001 revision of the Implementation Rules then abolished the original Articles 4 and 5. In their place, Article 4 of the revised Implementation Rules simply provides that '[b]usiness and industries in which the establishment of sole foreign investment enterprises is prohibited or restricted shall be decided in accordance with State provisions on Foreign Investment Guidelines and the Guideline Catalogue of Foreign Investment Industries.' The original Article 6 of the Implementation Rules continues as Article 5 in the revised Rules.

The close control of WFOEs by foreign investors means better protection of intellectual property, and flexibility in terms of the location and duration of business. Although WFOEs are generally encouraged in coastal areas, sometimes even over joint ventures, inland local authorities may not regard them as being as favourable as joint ventures, particularly in terms of domestic sales.

4.6. Foreign Investment in the Service Sectors

As explained earlier, foreign investment in the service sectors was heavily restricted, with all kinds of market access barriers or outright bans. During the long negotiations for its membership in the WTO, China eventually made some major concessions, but only agreed to a process of gradual liberalisation. The specific concession and commitments China made in relations to the removal of restrictions and access barriers include the gradual liberalisation in the following areas/aspects:

- Ownership restrictions: that is, whether foreign majority ownership or wholly foreign-owned subsidiaries are allowed;
- Forms of investment: that is, whether foreign investors have full freedom in choosing their forms of investment (i.e. equity joint venture, contractual joint venture or subsidiary etc.);
- Geographic restrictions: that is, whether foreign investment is restricted to specific cities and investment areas;
- Scope of business: that is, whether foreign investment enterprises are allowed to conduct all business or only specific kinds/scopes of business in the industry;

102 These include projects considered likely to harm China's sovereignty or the public interest, to endanger China's national security, to violate China's laws or statutory regulations, to cause environmental pollution, or to fail to conform with the requirements for developing China's national economy.

- National treatment: that is, whether any limitations on national treatment are imposed on foreign investment enterprises; and
- Qualifications of investors: that is, whether specific qualifications (i.e. business experience, registered capital, business track record, professional credentials, etc.) are imposed.[103]

These specific commitments are to be implemented in accordance with various firm timetables (up to eight years in some cases) for the removal or reduction of the various restrictions. It should be pointed out that some restrictions (such as majority Chinese ownership in certain important service sectors) will remain after the expiry of the existing timetables. Also importantly, the rules already issued seem to suggest that China will continue to exercise major control and impose restrictions on foreign investment in the service sectors through stipulations on matters (e.g. professional and financial qualifications of Chinese partners) that are not covered by the specific commitments and the regulations of establishment, examination and approval, registration and operation.

As a result of the commitment to gradual implementation, a large number of separate rules have been issued (and constantly revised in accordance with the agreed timetable) on the following service sectors and on the regulation of the related investment enterprises: holding companies; research and development enterprises; merchandising enterprises; shipping companies; international freight agencies; railway freight companies; foreign trade companies; financial institutions; financial leasing companies; construction enterprises; medical institutions; travel agencies; educational institutions; real estate development enterprises; insurance companies; trust and investment companies; telecommunications services; venture capital investment; leasing companies; financial securities organizations; foreign law firms; civil aviation; advertising agencies; accounting firms; employment services; commodity inspection; urban planning and utilities construction; petroleum exploration and exploitation cooperation; internet information services; film and cinema theatre services, audiovisual services, and logistics services.[104]

The hugely complicated framework on investment in services, in a nutshell, deals with the following issues:

- *Conditions for establishment*: These often define maximum foreign ownership allowed, forms of investment (joint venture, contractual cooperation, wholly

---

[103] For details, see Annex 9 (Schedule of Specific Commitments on Services) in the Protocol on the Accession of the People's Republic of China. The Annex does not use the above headings, instead, it uses the usual WTO headings of Market Access, National Treatment, etc. Nevertheless, these are the principal issues dealt with by Annex 9.

[104] For a collection of these rules (up to September 2002), see MOFTEC, *Collection of Rules and Regulations on Foreign Investment in Service Trade* (Beijing: China Legal Publishing House, 2002).

owned subsidiary, etc.) and, sometimes, geographical limitations on foreign investment. So far, conditions contained in the newly issued rules largely conform to WTO negotiation results.

- *Qualifications for participation*: Often qualifications on both Chinese and foreign investors are laid down. These qualifications concerns credit standing, professional qualifications and requirements, business experience, total assets of foreign companies and registered capital requirements, profit-making situation prior to application, and legal system (such as the existence of a sound regulatory system for banking supervision etc.) in the home country of the foreign investors.
- *Business scope*: Business scope is often limited by the rules in accordance with China's liberalisation commitment. Such business scope is also registered in the business and legal person registration.
- *Procedures for application, examination and approval*: In most cases, examination and approval are conducted at the provincial level and often with time limits set for examination and approval authorities to complete their processes. As such, applications are normally submitted to the provincial level authorities. Sometimes, however, examination and approval by multiple authorities is required.
- *Penalty clauses*: Most of the new rules contain severe penalties for violation of the relevant laws and rules.[105]

It should be noted that since the commitment for liberalisation is a gradual one, with specific timetables, most of the newly issued rules on trade in services are 'interim' or 'transitional' in nature. Upon the start of each stage of liberalisation these rules are either revised, or a new set of rules is issued (so far, the latter has been the main practice).

5. Concluding Remarks

After some thirty years of the 'Open Door' policy, the achievements China has made in attracting foreign investment and in promoting foreign trade (especially in exports) have been remarkable, and particularly so when compared with other former socialist countries. With increasing experience, and hence confidence, in dealing with foreign trade and business, the legal framework for foreign trade and investment has now been greatly liberalised, and has become more transparent

105 For details analysis of these rules, see Jianfu Chen, *supra* note 13, paras 27-010 – 27-540.

and accessible, although this achievement has not been made without persistent international pressure from mainly Western countries.

While policy and law regarding foreign trade and investment have been greatly liberalised, foreign-related business is still controlled and managed by the state. This is especially so in areas of non-tariff barriers to trade, and the continuing *ad hoc* management of foreign investment in the service sectors. The Chinese trade system was once branded by frustrated American trade negotiators as a 'capitalist export regime with socialist import rules.'[106] While the import rules are no longer 'socialist' in the sense of planning and control, they are certainly still part of a managed system, either via the control of currency values or other non-tariff measures. In the area of investment in the service sectors the whole system is still characterised as an *ad hoc* 'examination and approval' one. However, all in all, the current legal framework on trade and investment is a much freer and fairer system than that existed just before China's admission to the WTO.

[106] 'A Lighter Shade of Red: Is China's Trade Picture Really Improving?', *Far Eastern Economic Review*, 28 April 1994, at 79.

Chapter Eighteen

Implementation of Law

1. Introduction

By any criteria the 'lawless' days in China have gone, even though a 'complete' legal system is yet to be completed by 2010.[1] However, having laws is one thing; having them properly implemented is another. Few would dispute that law acquires its life and performs its intended social functions through processes of implementation and enforcement, without which it has little meaning in any given society. The Rule of Law is not simply about the making of law.[2] Even if the law concerned is equitable and just, it still needs to be implemented and administered impartially, equitably and independently. It is through the operation and functioning of law in society that justice, fairness and human rights protection are achieved or abused.

The concentration of efforts on law-making during the early period of post-Mao 'legal construction' is understandable: without law there is little that can be said about justice and fairness. However, now that a massive quantity of laws has been enacted rapidly and efficiently, the issue of implementation of law can no longer be ignored. As many Chinese scholars and practitioners have asserted, 'a just law does not guarantee the justice of law' and a refusal to obey the law creates a worse situation than one where there is no law to go by.[3]

This Chapter examines the problems and difficulties involved in implementing laws in China. It starts with a brief introduction to the nature and the complexity of the implementation of law in general. This is followed by two case studies, one of the much-publicised problems in intellectual property protection, and the other the question of '*Zhixing Nan*' (problems and difficulties in the enforcement of court rulings and decisions) in China. An analysis of the various identified problems and

---

1 See the discussion in Chapter 5 on Sources of Law and Law-making.

2 The use of capital letters for 'Rule of Law' is not to imply that there is one commonly accepted version of rule of law, but to say that for the purpose of this discussion I have taken an idealised version of rule of law, which is hardly fully practised in any country.

3 See e.g. Zhao Sanying, 'On Rule of Law in a Market Economy', *Economic Daily* (*Jingji Ribao*), 2 May 1994, at 5.

their causes follows. It is concluded that for law to become alive and to be respected, much more fundamental reform in the politico-economic system is required.

2. Implementation of Law – Its Nature and Complexity

As an academic topic the implementation of law has been researched more often by scholars in public policy or public administration than by legal scholars.[4] As a result, implementation is often conceptualised as pressure politics (a system of pressures and counter-pressures), a social and political phenomenon, an administrative control process, or an inter-governmental bargaining process. In short, it is more often seen as a political game than as a legal issue.[5] However it is conceived, implementation is undoubtedly a very complicated process in the administration of law. This process necessarily includes general policy programs, detailed rules, generally applicable measures and concrete individual decisions by executive organs and other state authorities, as well as the specific enforcement of law and judgements by the judiciary, the legal profession, the police, and other law-enforcement/administrative organisations. Moreover, the political, economic, social and cultural settings are equally relevant, if not more important.

In China the process is made even more complicated because of the complex inter-relationship between the various institutions and actors, where separation of powers has never been formally recognised, nor practised with any conviction or consistency.[6] Indeed, the relationships between the three branches of the state in China are far from clear, and constantly in a state of flux. There is no shortage of demands for independence, nor lack of instances of *ultra vires* (or more precisely, the overstepping of authority) by various authorities. Among the three branches

4 This is not to say that there are no legal studies on this topic. In fact, there is now an increasing (but still limited) number of such studies, among them being Donald C. Clarke, 'Power and Politics in the Chinese Court System: The Enforcement of Civil Judgement', (1996) 10 (1) *Columbia Journal of Asian Law* 1; Stanley B. Lubman, *Bird in a Cage: Legal Reform in China After Mao* (Stanford, California: Stanford University Press, 1999); Xiaoying Ma & Leonard Ortolano, *Environmental Regulation in China: Institutions, Enforcement and Compliance* (New York: Rowman & Littlefield, 2000); Randall Peerenboom, 'Seek Truth from Facts: An Empirical Study of Enforcement of Arbitral Awards in the PRC', (2001) 49 (2) *Am. J. Comp. L.* 249; Xia Yong (ed.), *Towards the Age of Rights: A Perspective on Civil Rights Development in China* (*Zouxiang Quanli de Shidai*) (Beijing: Press of China University of Political Science and Law, 1995); Jiang Mingan (ed.), *Survey Report on the Development and Progress of China's Administrative Rule of Law* (Beijing: Law Publishing House, 1998); and Jianfu Chen, Yuwen Li & Jan Michiel Otto (eds), *Implementation of Law in the People's Republic of China* (London/Boston/The Hague: Kluwer Law International, 2002).

5 See J. Chen, 'Implementation of Law in China – an Introduction', in Chen, Li & Otto, *supra* note 4, at 2.

6 This is not to say that separation of powers is a practical reality in China.

of state powers, the judiciary is neither the exclusive nor the principal dispute arbitrator, nor even the final arbitrator (or, in the words of Dworkin, 'the capital of law's empire') in dispute resolution. Although in no country is the judiciary the only or exclusive dispute arbitrator, the somewhat arbitrary distinction made in China between administrative and criminal penalties means that not only are the administrative authorities involved in the administration of law, they also exercise substantial judicial powers that are normally exercised by the judiciary in most western countries.[7] Further, perhaps more as a result of a struggle to gain power or control rather than to establish checks and balances, the Chinese legislatures have in the last few years moved to exercise 'supervisory powers', not only over the executive, but also over the judiciary, and hence are increasingly involving themselves in the implementation of law.[8] Finally, these three authorities are not the only ones exercising state power: the Chinese Communist Party, though not a constitutional authority, is the *de facto* supreme power – a title nominally granted to the National People's Congress by the Constitution. In terms of implementation of law, two more forces are now increasingly visible, namely the media and the legal profession, both of which have also claimed a certain degree of independence and self-regulation. Adding to the complexity is the system of ADR (Alternative Dispute Resolution, e.g. arbitration and mediation), which is conducted by non-state authorities and is preferred by ordinary people and practitioners, either as a result of economic considerations or because of the continuing influence of traditional legal culture.

In this complex system it would be inaccurate to assert that there is no implementation of law in China, or that all implementation has the same serious problems. In fact, if secondary law-making by the various state authorities (such as the judiciary) and government authorities (such as the State Council and its subordinate authorities) is seen as part of the implementation of law, we may in fact say that implementation of law has been, in general, rather successful.[9] However, if we confine ourselves to the consideration of translating rights on paper into those in reality, we then face some tremendous difficulties and problems. Two examples will illustrate this. One major issue has been the lack of effective protection of intellectual property rights, which has been a constant struggle in China's diplomatic relations with especially the US and other western countries. A more general issue has been the difficulties in enforcing court rulings and decisions, which have been widely and persistently

---

7 On the distinction between administrative and criminal penalties, see discussions in Chapters 6 & 7. Of course it is not uncommon in modern times for legislatures in various countries to increasingly invoke institutions other than the court to implement new laws for 'social engineering' purposes. See Ann Seidman & Robert B. Seidman, *State and Law in the Development Process: Problem Solving and Institutional Change in the Third World* (New York: St. Martin's Press, 1994), at 134.

8 See the discussion in Chapter 3 on Constitutional Law.

9 See the discussion in Chapter 5 on Sources of Law and Law-making.

discussed by Chinese academics and practitioners for many years. The two case studies related to these issues, which are presented below, will illustrate the extent of the problems in law implementation and enforcement in China, in the sense of translating paper rights into real remedies.

3. Implementation of Law – the Case of IP Protection

Chapter 16 on intellectual property law has described the tremendous progress in law-making, institution-building and politico-legal efforts undertaken for the protection of intellectual property rights. This progress must be properly acknowledged and the genuineness of the politico-legal efforts to uphold the law should not be seriously questioned. In fact, the laws in the book are generally seen as being reasonable and as meeting international requirements.[10] The general view emerging from a recent US Congress Commission hearing confirms this, although further required improvements are also identified.[11] However, no one can seriously deny that China has been one of the major violators of IP rights in the world, and that the good laws have, so far, only remained true in the book

The practical reality of IP protection has been a long-running issue and will remain contentious between China and developed countries, especially the United States and the EU. In 1994 Microsoft claimed that 98% of the software sold under its name in China was fake.[12] The International Intellectual Property Alliance in Washington estimated that American businesses lost more than US$ 800 million

---

10 In fact, a prominent Chinese IP scholar has pointed out recently that there have been views among some Chinese officials and academics that Chinese law on IP protection is too strict and sets too higher a standard for a developing country like China. See Zheng Chenxi, 'The Kind of IP Strategy China Needs', *Economic Reference News* (*Jingji Cankao Bao*), 17 April 2004, at 5; and Zheng Chensi, 'China's IP Protection Is Far from Enough', available from <www.chinaiprlaw.cn/file/200041029456.html> (last accessed 3 February 2005). Others have also argued that all countries protect IP rights in accordance with their own specific national interests and no country should provide protection which does not accord with the level of its own development of science, the economy and culture. See Wang Xianlin, 'Abuse of IP Rights by Multinational Companies in China', *Business Watch Magazine* (*Shangwu Zhoukan Zazhi*), 3 November 2005, available from <www.sina.com.cn> (last accessed 5 November 2005). The idea of development by copying others' technologies seems to still have some support in China. See Tian Lipu & Li Shunde, 'Are China's IP Protection Problems World Perils?', in <www.chinaiprlaw.cn/file/2004012103808.html> (accessed 3 February 2005). The author also sees Western IP policy as a possible means of Western colonialism/imperialism.

11 See *Hearing before the U.S.–China Economic and Security Review Commission*, June 7-8, 2006. Transcripts published in July 2006, and available from <www.uscc.gov> (last accessed 31 August 2006).

12 'Pirates' Lair: U.S. Pressures Beijing over Copyright Protection', *Far Eastern Economic Review*, 19 May 1994, at 55.

in sales in 1993 due to piracy in China.[13] An IP protection guide for US companies, prepared by the US Department of Commerce and dated January 2003, asserted that China continued to be a haven for counterfeiters and pirates. On average, according to the US Department of Commerce, 20 percent of all consumer products on the Chinese market are counterfeit. If a product sells, it is claimed, it is likely to be illegally duplicated.[14] In 2004 the US insisted that its companies were losing some US$ 24 billion a year due to piracy in China and that this piracy had caused some US$ 50 billion in business losses worldwide.[15] The US Embassy in Beijing recently estimated that American, European and Japanese companies now lose more than US$ 60 billion a year due to Chinese IP piracy.[16] Similarly, 70% of European companies do not think that Chinese IP protection is adequate, and many Japanese companies take the same view.[17] A 2006 survey conducted by the American Chamber of Commerce found that 41 percent of US companies with operations in China believed that counterfeiting of their products had increased in 2005.[18]

Counterfeiting and piracy are of course, not just a problem in China; they are a widespread problem in global trade.[19] However, China is seen as a most significant country for counterfeiting and piracy for the US, where the value of IP accounts for almost half of its GDP,[20] and its copyright industries generate over 50% of their revenue from outside the US, contributing over US$ 89 billion in exports and foreign sales to the US economy.[21] The following statement by the US-China Economic and

13 *Ibid.*

14 US Department of Commerce, International Trade Administration, *Protecting Your Intellectual Property Rights (IPR) in China: A Practical Guide for U.S. Companies*, January 2003, available from <www.mac.doc.gov/China/Docs/BusinessGuide/IntellecturalPropertyRights.htm> (accessed 15 February 2005).

15 Quoted in Tian & Li, *supra* note 10.

16 Desmond Lachman, 'China Impervious to US Trade Tactics', *Australian Financial Review*, 5 December 2006, available at <www.aei.org/publications/pubID.25255/pub_detail.asp> (last accessed 17 January 2007).

17 See Tian & Li, *supra* note 10.

18 'Chinese Use Courts to Sink Pirates', *The Australian*, 29 August 2006, IT Business Section, at 5. See also *Hearing before the U.S.-China Economic and Security Review Commission, supra* note 11, at 43.

19 It is claimed that 'counterfeiting now accounts for five percent to seven percent of world trade. It shows no signs of abating, is highly lucrative, and represents a growth industry for criminal cartels as well as terrorists.' See Opening Statement by the Commission Chairman, *Hearing before the U.S.-China Economic and Security Review Commission, supra* note 11, at 8.

20 See Opening Statement by the Commission Chairman, *Hearing before the U.S.-China Economic and Security Review Commission, supra* note 11, at 7.

21 Statement of Eric H. Smith (President of the International Intellectual Property Alliance), at *Roundtable: Intellectual Property Protection as Economic Policy: Will China Ever Enforce its*

Security Review Commission Chairman explains why IP issues are now one of the most thorny issues in US-China diplomatic relations.

> China is widely viewed as the model country for intellectual property piracy and for good reason. U.S. companies lose an estimated $2.5 billion a year due to piracy of copyrighted materials. Roughly 95 percent of all CDs and DVDs manufactured in China are counterfeit. Amazingly, counterfeit products account for 15 to 20 percent of all products made in China and approximately eight percent of its GNP. Moreover, many of these counterfeit products end up re-entering our domestic U.S. market. U.S. Immigration and Customs Enforcement estimates that nearly 70 percent of all pirated goods it seizes at our borders originate in China.[22] ...The theft and piracy of software in China is equally staggering. The business Software Alliance estimates that for every two dollars' worth of software purchased legitimately, one dollar's worth is obtained illegally.[23] ... The Motion Picture Association of America estimates that in 2005 its member companies lost approximately $244 million in revenues to Chinese piracy.[24] The cost of Chinese piracy to the entire property rights community was more than $2.3 billion, with losses of more than 10.6 billion over the last five years. Also, according to the MPAA, piracy has reached almost 100 percent of the retail market in China with private DVDs of the latest U.S. theatrical release available within days of international release (*footnotes added*).[25]

IP Laws? Transcripts of the Roundtable are available from <www.cecc.gov> (last accessed 19 May 2005).

22 Which actually represents more than ten times that of any other US trading partner. See US Trade Representative, *2006 Special 301 Report*, available from <www.ustr.gov> (last accessed 15 August 2006).

23 It is claimed that the software piracy rate in China is around 90%, costing the US software publishers US$ 1.4 billion in 2004. See Statement by Eric H Smith (President of International Intellectual Property Alliance) at *Roundtable: Intellectual Property Protection as Economic Policy: Will China Ever Enforce its IP Laws? supra* note 21.

24 It is claimed that the piracy rate in motion pictures is 95% in China, costing the US motion picture industry more than US$ 1 billion (not including losses from internet piracy) between 1998 and 2004. See Statement by Eric H Smith (President of the International Intellectual Property Alliance) at *Roundtable: Intellectual Property Protection as Economic Policy: Will China Ever Enforce its IP Laws? supra* note 21. However, a recently published survey by the Motion Picture Association of America indicated that 'illegal copying in Britain, France, Mexico and Russia each costs the movie makers considerably more than piracy in China, and that within the US itself the loss is more than four times the loss from China.' See Rowan Callick, 'Patents Face Great Wall of Piracy', *The Australian*, 17 July 2006, available <www.theaustralian.news.com.au> (last accessed 17 July 2006).

25 See Opening Statement by the Commission Chairman, *Hearing before the U.S.–China Economic and Security Review Commission, supra* note 11, at 8-9.

The co-chair of the Commission, Richard D'Amato, also had this to say:

> There is no question that China is a rampant violator of intellectual property rights. … the underdeveloped legal system has not provided the necessary protection when rights, particularly intellectual property rights, are violated, and is overwhelmed by the economic imperatives of development and employment pressures, and provincial political authorities. … It remains unclear whether the Chinese government is committed to engaging with the IPR infringement issue or whether Chinese development is dependent on such infringement. … In the five years since China has joined the WTO, there has been no tangible improvement in the protection of intellectual property.[26]

There are, however, areas where effective enforcement of IP law and protection has been achieved. Thus, a journalist living in China described the jealous guarding against any infringement of the Beijing Olympic logo:

> One can gain a brief insight into how effective Chinese policing of intellectual property rights becomes, by considering the zeal with which Beijing is protecting its great current brand – the 2008 Olympic Games. The event is not exactly an invention, of course, but it is potentially a big earner, one in which the leadership is investing the prestige of the country and of its ruling Communist Party. The Games' lively logo, a version of the Chinese characters for Beijing reshaped as a running figure, and its mascots, the Five Friendlies, are being assiduously protected against piracy.[27]

This strong and successful protection, along with the widespread and continuing serious problems in general IP protection, have led many to question the political will of the Chinese government, despite the huge efforts by the government in law-making, institutional building and *ad hoc* efforts for IP protection. Many US Congress Members and other speakers at the June 2006 Congress Hearing pointed to the fact that China had been able to effectively protect the Beijing Olympic logo and that it had generally come down hard on counterfeited pharmaceutical goods.

---

26 See Statement of C. Richard D'Amato, at the *Hearing before the U.S.–China Economic and Security Review Commission, supra* note 11, at 18-19. Similarly, a US Trade Representative report to the Congress describes the violation as massive in scale, rampant, with the situation unchanged from 2004 or even getting worse etc. See US Trade Representative, *2005 Report to Congress on China's WTO Compliance*, 11 December 2005, available at <www.ustr.gov> (last accessed 15 August 2006), esp. 63-73.

27 See Callick, *supra* note 24.

Therefore, as the Commission Chairman, Larry M. Wortzel, pointed out, China can enforce laws when the government sees it in its interest to do so.[28]

It is not just politicians and business people who complain about Chinese IP protection in practice; many academics hold similar views on the situation. Thus Professor Daniel C. K. Chow described counterfeiting in China thus:

> In terms of size, scope, and magnitude, counterfeiting in China is considered by many to be the most serious counterfeiting problem in world history. … China is also a leading exporter of counterfeit products to other countries in Asia, Europe, and the United States. … local governments are either directly or indirectly involved in supporting the trade in counterfeit goods and are often reluctant to punish counterfeiters. … It is no exaggeration to say that some local areas in China are entirely supported by trade in counterfeit goods and that local residents are ready to use any means necessary to protect their illegal trade.[29]

To make things even more irritating, counterfeit and pirated goods are not just sold in China; they are being exported to other countries. According to Chow, 66% of US Customs seizures in 2003 came from China (49% in 2002), and at the same time no other country accounted for more than 3%. If Hong Kong were included (through which many counterfeits produced in China are transhipped), China would have accounted for 75% in 2003. In fact, according to his estimate, China in reality accounted for more than 80% in 2003.[30] Another source has put China's share at 63% in 2004, 69% in 2005, and 81% in 2006.[31]

Of course such statistics must always be treated with caution. In most cases they are estimates calculated by those with vested interests. So it is not surprising that disputes about these statistics are not uncommon – not only in China but also in other countries. For instance, the Australian Institute of Criminology recently lashed out at the music and software sectors, accusing them of failing to explain how they reached financial loss statistics used in lobbying activities and in court cases.[32]

Nevertheless, despite the great efforts for IP protection that have been made in the last twenty years, Chinese practice is not perceived as having met international standards, and certainly not those of the US. While the extent of the counterfeiting

---

28 See Opening Statement by the Commission Chairman, *Hearing before the U.S.-China Economic and Security Review Commission*, *supra* note 11.

29 See Statement by Professor Chow at *Roundtable: Intellectual Property Protection as Economic Policy: Will China Ever Enforce its IP Laws?*, *supra* note 21.

30 *Id.*

31 See *2006 Special 301 Report*, *supra* note 22; and *2007 Special 301 Report*, available at <www.ustr.gov/…/Reports_Publications/2007/2007_Special_301_Review/asset_upload_file230_11122.pdf> (last accessed 5 June 2007) at 18.

32 See 'Piracy Stats Don't Add Up', *The Australian*, 7 November 2006, at 33.

and piracy and the seriousness of the implementation problems are disputed,[33] China has not simply indulged in boasting of its achievements in IP protection and its legal and policy development.[34] It has always frankly admitted that it has some serious problems in realising what has been set out on paper.[35]

4. Enforcement of Law – the Case of '*Zhixing Nan*'

One of the most important aspects of the implementation of law is the enforcement of court judgements and rulings. The power to compel obedience to its judgements and orders not only distinguishes a court of law from other semi-judicial organisations, but also defines the authority of the court.[36] One may also argue that the authority of law ultimately rests upon the court's ability to enforce its own judgements and rulings. This is indeed how many Chinese scholars and officials see the issue:

> Who shall make the final judgement on the question of whether the conduct of a citizen or an organisation is lawful? According to the Constitution and provisions of law, the People's Court is the only organ which represents the State for the purpose of exercising adjudication powers. The judgement of a people's court is the final result of a series of activities involved in the enforcement of law. The execution of effective court judgements is the most

---

33 See, for instance, Tian & Li, *supra* note 10; and Transcripts of a Web Forum on IP Protection, 23 May 2006, available from <www.legaldaily.com.cn/misc/2006-05/23/content_320062htm> (last accessed 8 September 2006).

34 See e.g. State Council White Paper, *Intellectual Property Protection in China*, issued by the Information Office of the State Council in June 1994. A Chinese text of the White Paper appears in *Peoples Daily* (*Renmin Ribao*), 17 June 1994, at 1 & 3. An English translation can be found in *Beijing Review*, 20-26 June 1994, at 8-17; *New Progress in China's Protection of Intellectual Property Rights*, issued by the Information Office of the State Council of the PRC, April 2005, an English version is available at <news.xinhuanet.com/english/2005-04/21/content_2858667.htm>.

35 See e.g, Notice on Issuance of the Minutes of the 2005 IP Protection Joint Conference, jointly issued by the Economic Crimes Investigation Bureau of the Ministry of Public Security, the Trademarks and Fair Trading Bureaus of the State Administration for Industry and Commerce, the Coordination Bureau of the State Intellectual Property Office, the Second Criminal Trial Chamber of the Supreme People's Court, and the Investigation Supervision Bureau of the Supreme People's Procuratorate, 24 October 2005; and Xu Guanghua (Minister of Science and Technology), 'Report on the State Council Efforts to Strengthen Innovation Capacity and IP Protection', delivered at the 21st Session of the Standing Committee of the NPC on 27 April 2006. A full text is available at <www.npc.gov.cn/zgrdw/rdgb_qg/regb.jsp> (last accessed 16 August 2006).

36 See Neil J. Williams, *Supreme Court Civil Procedure* (Sydney: Butterworths, 1994), at 340.

basic requirement to guarantee the implementation of law, and to safeguard the dignity and authority of the state law.[37]

Here, however, lies a major weakness in the actual practice of the Chinese legal system, which recently has become the focus of politico-legal efforts to overcome the so-called '*Zhixing Nan*' problems. Most notably, the Civil Procedure Law and the Criminal Procedure Law were revised in 1991 and 1996 respectively, with the clear aim of improving the implementation of the law in terms of both strengthening the law enforcement apparatus and providing practical procedural rules. Intensive efforts have been made in the last few years, especially in the area of enforcing civil and economic judgements and rulings, often as a part of general judicial reform efforts.[38] Reflecting the traditional practice of using political campaigns for intensified efforts, 1999 was declared a 'Year for Enforcement [of Judicial Judgements and Rulings]' (*Zhixing Nian*) by the Supreme People's Court.[39] And, at this point, the Communist Party joined in by issuing Document no. 11 (1999) of the Central Committee of the Communist Party of China, entitled Notice of the Central Committee of the Communist Party of China on Transmitting the Report of the Party Committee of the Supreme People's Court on Resolving Certain Problems Causing 'Enforcement Difficulties' Facing the Courts, and Document No. 17 (1999) of the Central Disciplinary Inspection Committee [of the Communist Party of China], entitled Notice concerning Handling Seriously the Violation of Law and Discipline in Dealing with '*Zhixing Nan*' Encountered by the People's Courts (jointly issued by the Disciplinary Inspection Committee of the Central Committee of the Communist Party of China and the Ministry of Supervision).[40] In 2002, the Political Report of

---

37 Nin Wen, 'Law Must Not Issue Rubber-Stamp [empty promises]', *People's Daily* (*Renmin Ribao*), internet edition, 22 April 1998.

38 Among these, the most important are the Provisions on Certain Issues Concerning the People's Court Enforcement Work (Trial Implementation), issued in July 1998 by the Supreme People's Court. These Provisions aim at one particular aspect of the implementation of law – the execution of effective court judgements, rulings and other legal documents. For a discussion of these Provision, see Jianfu Chen, 'Enforcement of Civil Judgements and Rulings', (July 1999) 2 (7) *China Law Update* 3; and Jianfu Chen, 'Judicial Reform in China', (May 2000) 3 (5) *China Law Update* 3.

39 1999 was also declared by the Supreme People's Court as a 'Year for Quality Trials'.

40 Documents on personal file. Although Document 11 has not been issued publicly, it has been widely quoted in the Chinese media and by judicial leaders at various levels in their public speeches. See, for example, Xiao Yang (President of the Supreme People's Court), 'To Promote Reform, to Ensure Judicial Justice, and to Stride into the New Century with a Completely New Image', in (no. 1, 2000) *Gazette of the Supreme People's Court of the PRC* (*Zhonghua Renmin Gongheguo Zuigao Renmin Fayuan Gongbao*) 13, at 13. Document No. 17 was recently published in the *People's Daily*, internet edition: <www.peopledaily.com.cn/GB/news/6056/2002514/728120.html>.

the Party delivered at the 16th National Congress of the CPC directly demanded that the *Zhixing Nan* problems must be resolutely resolved.[41]

These intensive efforts highlight the concerns among the leadership of the Party, the government and the judiciary regarding problems encountered by the judiciary and litigants in enforcing effective judgements and rulings. They also indicate the seriousness of the present problems in this area.[42] Although it is difficult to know the precise situation and reliable statistical information is hard to find in China,[43] we do know several aspects of the situation.

Firstly, although there has been no attempt to define or clarify the meaning of '*Zhixing Nan*', we know it is largely about the difficulties in the enforcement of civil judgements, decisions and rulings. These problems are often summarised as 'Si Nan' (four difficulties): difficulties in finding the person upon whom execution of judgement is to be carried out; difficulties in finding the property to execute judgement; difficulties in taking action against the property (if it is found); and difficulties in finding any authorities to assist the enforcement.[44] The term was said to have been first used in a 1987 national conference on court work, and was then adopted by the Supreme People's Court Work Report to the NPC in 1988 and has since never been off the agenda from the Supreme People's Court Work Reports to the NPC.[45] It is one of the most persistently publicised issues in Chinese legal circles and the public media, and a cause of widespread concern among ordinary citizens in China.[46]

---

41 See Tong Zhaohong (ed.), *Civil Enforcement: Investigation and Analysis* (*Minshi Zhixing: Diaocha yu Fenxi*) (Beijing: Press of the People's Court, 2005), at 1.

42 This is clearly evidenced in the annual reports presented by the Supreme People's Court to the National People's Congress and the frequent and prominent coverage of the topic in the Chinese legal press.

43 See also Clarke, *supra* note 4. It should be pointed out that, as illustrated in Chapter 16, not only are official statistics difficult to find, they are often (if available) neither comprehensive nor reliable, nor are they consistent. They are certainly not published in any particular source, but only fragmented statistics are contained in different places. Often these numbers are contained in official speeches without any reference to sources. As such, few could be verified as to their accuracy and so must be treated with caution. They probably indicate a trend rather than an accurate situation at any particular time.

44 See Huang Songyou (Vice-President of the Supreme People's Court), 'The Authority of Enforcement Mechanisms Urgently in Need of Legislative Support', *Legal Daily* (*Fazhi Ribao*), 16 May 2007, available at <www.legaldaily.com.cn/0705/2007-07/05/content_653451.htm> (last accessed 6 July 2007). According to Chinese judges, the 'Si Nan' summary was first given by Party Document No. 11 (1999) (*supra* note 40). See Tong Zhaohong, *supra* note 41, at 3.

45 See Tong Zhaohong, *supra* note 41, at 2.

46 For instance, during the NPC meeting in March 2003, an on-line survey indicated that resolving the problems in *Zhixing Nan* was the top issue that Chinese people hoped the NPC would address. See Tong Zhaohong, *supra* note 41, at 1.

Secondly, we know that difficulties in enforcing judgements and rulings were already identified as major problems in judicial work in the very early years of the PRC.[47] We also know that complaints from litigants were almost identical to those of today. Consider the following statement:

> According to reports from all regions of North China, there is a great accumulation of unexecuted cases at the level of the court of first instance. … In some of the cases, it has been two or three years since judgement; in some, the party frequently runs to the court to apply for execution but the problem is not resolved; in some, the party asks, 'Is there any law in the court?' and 'Does the judgement count for anything?'[48]

Identical statements in newspapers, academic journals and judicial reports can easily be found in present-day China.[49]

Thirdly, we know that the problems worsened in the late 1980s and the 1990s.[50] Without systematic and comprehensive statistical information we can only rely on various speeches by judicial leaders and the extensive coverage of the issue in the Chinese public media and legal press, which do provide some indications as to the extent of the problem and the nature of the difficulties in judgement enforcement. The basic situation around 1998, when concentrated efforts began to be made and the important Provisions on Certain Issues Concerning the People's Court Enforcement Work (Trial Implementation) were issued, may be summarised as follows:[51]

---

[47] For various judicial documents concerning enforcement problems in the early years of the PRC, see Research Office of the Supreme People's Court (ed.), *A Complete Collection of Judicial Interpretations of the Supreme People's Court of the PRC (1949–1993)* (*Zhonghua Renmin Gongheguo Zuigao Renmin Fayuan Sifa Jieshi Quanji*) (Beijing: Press of the People's Court, 1994), at 1871–1883; and The Execution Work Office of the Supreme People's Court (ed.), *A Collection of Practical Documents on Compulsory Execution* (*Qiangzhi Zhixing Shiwu Wenjian Huibian*) (Beijing: Publishing House of Law, 1999).

[48] 'Instructions on Enforcement Work by People's Courts at Various Levels', issued by the North China Division of the Supreme People's Court, 1953, in *A Complete Collection of Judicial Interpretations of the Supreme People's Court of the PRC*, *id.*, at 1880. The above English translation is adopted from Clarke, *supra* note 4, at 1.

[49] See Section 5 below.

[50] See Clarke, *supra* note 4, at 27-34; Qi Suji & Ma Changming, 'On Several Issues for Improving Compulsory Enforcement of Law in Our Country', (1997) 83 (3) *Law Review* (*Faxue Pinglun*) 35, at 35; and Tong Zhaohong, *supra* note 41.

[51] 1995–1997 Statistics are drawn from the following sources: Speech by Li Guoguang (Vice President of the SPC) on 8 October 1997, Speech by Xiao Yang (President of SPC) on 7 May 1998, and Speech by Li Guoguang (Vice President of the SPC) on 3 August 1998. Full texts of these speeches can be found in *A Collection of Practical Documents on Compulsory Execution*, *supra* note 47, at pp. 103-107, 107-108, and 112-116, respectively. 1998–1999 statistics are drawn from *China Law Yearbook* 1999 & 2000. 2000–2001 Statistics are drawn from the Supreme People's Court Reports delivered to the NPC (March 2001 and March 2002).

Year	*Number of new cases brought for enforcement*	*Monetary amounts involved*	*Number of cases actually enforced*	*Percentage (among all pending cases) of actual enforcement*
1995	1,360,000	n/a	1,190,000	75.00%
1996	1,680,000	n/a	1,420,000	73.98%
1997	1,840,000	n/a	1,460,000	67.98%
1998	2,201,000	249.1 billion *yuan* (new)	2,078,000	79.49%
1999	2,590,000 (new)	351.2 billion *yuan* (new)	2,645,000	71.12%
2000	n/a	306.4 billion *yuan* (enforced)	2,640,000	n/a
2001	n/a	315 billion *yuan* (enforced)	2,540,000	n/a

At least since 1987 serious efforts to work out specific measures for tackling problems in enforcement began to emerge from the Supreme People's Court when the annual national court work meetings engaged in special deliberation on these issues.[52] Thereafter the subject has never been off the agenda for such national conferences, nor from the Supreme People's Court reports to the National People's Congress. We also know that the problems, described as a '20-year fever' that refuses to recede,[53] persist until this day,[54] and continue to be the focus of the media, the state authorities, deputies to the NPC, and the general public.

Fourthly, although the Supreme People's Court is particularly concerned about the high proportion of unexecuted judgements, the amount of money involved explains why the issue has become a national one and a major concern among the Party, government and judicial leadership. According to the *People's Daily*, at the end of July 1998 there were 9,882 judgements in civil disputes, involving several billion *yuan*, pending execution in Beijing alone.[55] Similarly, in Hainan Province there were, at the end of February 1999, some 7,000 unexecuted judgements and rulings, involving over 10 billion *yuan*.[56] Nationwide, at the end of June 1999 (around the time the Communist Party of China stepped in), there were more than 850,000

52 See Qi & Ma, *supra* note 50, at 35.

53 'The Central Disciplinary Committee's and Other Authorities' Joint Measures Aimed at the Root of the Enforcement Problems', in <www.legalinfo.gov.cn/misc/2006-06/23/content_339808.htm> (last accessed 5 July 2007).

54 Indeed shortly after the politico-legal campaigns of 1999, '*Zhixing Nan*' again became a topic for reports in the *People's Daily*. See *People's Daily* (*Renmin Ribao*), internet edition, 14-15 May 2002. Most recently the Supreme People's Court launched yet another major campaign in January 2006, to last for six months, to clear up un-enforced judgements and decisions. See 'Supreme Peoples Court Launched A War to Clear Up Accumulated Enforcement Cases', <www.legalinfo.gov.cn/misc/2006-01/24/content_257084.htm> (last accessed 6 July 2007).

55 *People's Daily*, internet edition, 13 September 1998.

56 *People's Daily*, internet edition, 26 April 1999.

cases for enforcement of decisions/judgements which were still pending, involving some 250 billion *yuan* in claims.[57] In the latest six-month campaign (January – June 2006), courts in China identified 1.64 million cases whose enforcement had been overdue for more than a year, involving 568.8 billion *yuan*, and among which the courts managed to enforce 780,000 cases, involving 216 billion *yuan* during the campaign.[58] Although we neither know how reliable these statistics are, nor have the sources to verify them, they do indicate the severity of the problem. Further, the problem is not simply the huge backlog of cases and the extremely large monetary claims involved, but also the long periods of delay in the execution of court judgements, or simply the inability of the judiciary to enforce its judgements, rulings and orders at all.

Fifthly, and more seriously, there have been many reports concerning violence against judicial personnel who were carrying out enforcement orders. It was reported recently that in Jiangsu Province 35% of judicial enforcement officials had been attacked by mid-1990s by parties subject to enforcement, twenty-two vehicles were damaged, and in sixty-four instances judicial enforcement officials were rounded up and illegally detained (in some cases for up to fifty hours) by local parties involved in the original civil disputes.[59] There are also instances in which the actions of local police arresting judicial enforcement officials were clearly orchestrated by local government.[60] Between 1995 and 1998 statistics from twenty-one provinces and municipalities indicated that there were 3,473 incidents of violence against the enforcement of judgements, 2,378 judicial personnel were injured and four died as a result.[61] In 2006 in one province alone (Henan Province), there were 108 instances in which violent resistance to court enforcement occurred.[62]

---

57 'Editorial', (no. 18, 1999) *Democracy and Law* (*Minzhu yu Falü*), at 1.

58 See 'Court Summing Up Experiences in Clearing Up Unexecuted Judgements', *Legal Daily* (*Fazhi Ribao*), 21 September 2006; and Huang Songyou, *supra* note 44.

59 Hou Guoyun & Lu Erping, 'Dangers, Causes and Responses to Enforcement Difficulties under a Market Economy', (1996) (no. 1) *Journal of China University of Political Science and Law* (*Zhengfa Luntan*) 75, at 75.

60 Hou & Lu, *id.*, at 76.

61 *Legal Daily* (*Fazhi Ribao*), internet edition, 25 August 1999. According to the *People's Daily*, such violence has occurred in all provinces and autonomous regions with the exception of Shanghai. See 'Enforcement by Court Meets with Local Protectionism', in *People's Daily* (*Renmin Ribao*), internet edition, 15 May 2002, It is therefore not surprising that violence against enforcement of law has been one of the major ongoing concerns of the Supreme People's Court for many years. See 'Work Report of the Supreme People's Court', delivered at the Fifth Plenary Session of the Ninth National People's Congress, 11 March 2002, in *People's Daily* (*Renmin Ribao*), internet edition, 20 March 2002.

62 'Henan Judge Beaten in Hubei – Reasons and Background', Legal Daily Web: <202.99.23.215:8080/search/detail.jsp?dataid=376845&tableclassid=4_1> (last accessed 6 July 2007).

Finally, we also know that serious enforcement problems also exist in other areas of law, although these problems have not been so widely discussed and publicised in China.[63] For instance, in the area of criminal law there have always been major concerns about overzealous enforcement and persistent violations of the Criminal Procedure Law.[64] However, there are also reports of non-enforcement of the criminal law. In 1997, a certain Cheng Keyun in Jiangsu Province was accused of robbery, hooliganism, intentional injury, and other serious crimes. When his file was transferred to a local procuratorate for prosecution, serious questions were raised by the prosecutors who examined the cases: all the alleged crimes were committed between 1992 and 1995, but according to the file Cheng was sentenced to six years' imprisonment in May 1991 and this criminal sentence would not have been completed until January 1997. How was he able to commit these serious crimes while serving his sentence, without any record of his being on bail or of having some other way of serving the sentence outside prison? This soon alarmed the provincial leaders in charge of politico-legal affairs and an investigation was ordered, which revealed that Cheng had been released immediately after being sentenced and had not served a single day of his six-year sentence. The reason was simple: the relevant persons – the presiding judge and court clerk, the police and the prison officers – had all been bribed by Cheng. Cheng was later found guilty of a number of serious criminal offences and sentenced to death and executed.[65] In another case in Hunan Province a young woman was sexually assaulted and had the courage to report the case, but although one of the men was apprehended, no legal action was taken until three years later when she petitioned the local chief procurator, and a prosecution followed. While corruption in the local police force

63 According to Chinese judges, difficulties in enforcement are concentrated in four types of cases: where peasants are involved as parties, where the government authorities are involved as parties, financial cases, and cases concerning compensation and the 'three payments' (support to parents, to children and to ex-spouses). See Tong Zhaohong, *supra* note 41, at 7-11.

64 As discussed in Chapter 8, the revised Criminal Procedure Law was promising in terms of protection of the rights of criminal defendants and, indeed, there are reports of the positive impact of the law in judicial practice. See also Jianfu Chen, 'A Moderate Step in a Right Direction – The Revision of the Criminal Procedure Law in the PRC', (1997) 3 (1) *Journal of Chinese and Comparative Law*, at 139-166. However, the overall situation is far from perfect. According to an inspection report by the Standing Committee of the NPC, three years after the implementation of the revised *Criminal Procedure Law*, prolonged detention far beyond legal limitation was still a widespread phenomenon, forced confession was practised in many places, and lawyers still found it very difficult to meet their clients, to examine prosecution files and documents and to verify evidence presented by the prosecution. See *News of the National People's Congress*, internet edition, 29 December 2000.

65 See 'The Evil Relationship between a Judge, the Police and a Death Penalty Prisoner', (no. 18, 1999) *Democracy and Law* (*Minzhu yu Falü*), at 32-34.

was not clearly stated, it was certainly implied.[66] It should also be pointed out that it is not only enterprises or individuals that refuse to comply with court rulings and decisions – governments are not much better in abiding by the law. In October 2005 a judge of the High Court of Hainan Province told a Xinhua News Agency journalist that government authorities and state institutions in Hainan were among the worst offenders in enforcement cases.[67]

Clearly there are some very serious problems in the implementation of law in general, and in the enforcement of court judgements and rulings in particular. It is therefore not surprising that many Chinese describe court judgements and rulings as 'rubber-stamps' (*falü baitiao*), that many courts describe enforcement as their number one 'headache',[68] and that others describe civil enforcement as 'harder than reaching the sky',[69] or the 'hardest thing on earth'.[70] Still others declare it to be the 'bottleneck' in building the rule of law in China.[71]

5. Enemies Within and Without, Systemic and Institutional

The two case studies above share some common features. First, both of them are high profile issues in China. As such, great efforts by government and state authorities have been made, although without substantial progress having been made in either case. Secondly, neither of them is a new problem – both of them have existed for more than 20 years. Thirdly, the problems and difficulties in both cases are massive in scale and deep in their roots. The failure in IP protection directly implicates the inability of many government authorities to implement the law, and the *Zhixing Nan* is primarily a problem of the inability of the judiciary to enforce its own rulings and decisions. Significantly, the specific problems identified by various studies clearly indicate that the underlying causes are mostly of the same nature. Put simply, these problems are rooted in the politico-economic system in China today.

The individual factors causing the problems are numerous and complex. Clarke, who has conducted a comprehensive survey and analysis of the problems

---

66 See 'Three Years without Justice for a Humiliated Woman', (no. 14, 1999) *Democracy and Law* (*Minzhu yu Falü*), at 19-21.

67 'Court Enforcement Hits Government Wall – Why Government and Institutions Deny Debts', Xinhua News Agency: <news.xinhuanet.com/focus/2005-10/14/content_3613472.htm> (last accessed 14 October 2006).

68 *China Daily*, internet edition, 13 April 1999.

69 See 'Enforcement of Civil Judgements: Harder than Reaching the Sky'. (no. 2, 2004) *China Law and Government Review*, available: <www.chinareview.info/pages/legal.htm#1> (last accessed 13 June 2004).

70 Tong Zhaohong, *supra* note 41, at 2.

71 Tong Zhaohong, *supra* note 41, at 568.

in enforcement of civil judgement, and whose analysis is mostly also applicable to enforcement of court judgements in general,[72] identifies the major causes of the difficulties as those of the legal culture, the anomalous position of the courts in the Chinese polity, the lagging of legal reform behind economic reform and other social changes, and the question of the proper role of the State. Specifically, these factors include the following:

- the control of the finances and personnel of the courts by governments at various levels;
- the generally poor level of education among judicial personnel in the court system;
- the lack of legislation on enforcement and, where it does exist, the lack of precise legal provisions;
- the courts' reluctance to use coercive measures (which is often linked to a traditional culture that judges people not according to legal rights but on moral grounds) and, if they exist at all, the inadequacy of legal means of coercion;
- the lack of interest in execution among the judiciary;
- local protectionism, interference by administrative authorities (which is also linked to local protectionism);
- the insolvency of defendants;
- the lack of cooperation by other units.[73]

Added to these are such factors as the low level of legal consciousness among the public, the on-going economic transition, corruption, the Communist Party's incomplete retreat from day-to-day governance, and the battles for power among the emerging state organs.[74] Further, a comparison of these underlying causes and those identified in the 1950s[75] reveals that many of them already existed in the early years of the PRC.[76] For all practical purposes these factors and problems exist, although sometimes in different forms, in the implementation of law in general

72 Clarke, *supra* note 4.

73 See Clarke, *supra* note 4, at pp. 81-88. See also Lubman, *supra* note 4, ch. 9; Jerome A. Cohen, 'Reforming China's Civil Procedure: Judging the Courts', (1997) 45 *The Am. J. Comp. L.* 793-804; Chen, Li & Otto, *supra* note 4.

74 Peerenboom, *supra* note 4.

75 See *supra* note 48. See also *A Complete Collection of Judicial Interpretations of the Supreme People's Court of the PRC*, *supra* note 47, at 1871–1883.

76 See Yuwen Li, 'Court Reform in China: Problems, Progress and Prospects', Jianfu Chen, 'Mission Impossible: Judicial Efforts to Enforce Civil Judgements and Rulings in China', and

as well. For instance, in relation to implementing IP laws in China, various US government authorities have identified the following problems: lack of transparency (thus difficulty in assessing and ensuring enforcement and actions), heavy reliance on administrative measures (which many see as toothless) rather than on criminal sanctions, too high a threshold for criminal prosecution, light penalties and hence the lack of a deterrent effect of law, lack of coordination among different authorities, and vagueness and ineffectiveness in court rules regarding evidence, expert witnesses, and the protection of confidential information.[77]

It would be wrong to assume that these problems are identified by scholars and commentators operating merely from a western perspective. Many studies by scholars and practitioners in China too have identified similar problems as being the underlying factors causing the difficulties in the enforcement of law in general and of civil judgements in particular.[78] In fact, even Chinese government officials are talking about similar factors as having undermined the implementation and enforcement of law. Thus, as early as 1993 the then President of the Supreme People's Court, Ren Jianxin, categorised the major factors as follows: the inability of enterprises to pay

---

Randall Peerenboom, 'Law Enforcement and the Legal Profession in China', all in Chen, Li & Otto, *supra* note 4, at 55-82, 85-112, and 125-148 respectively.

77 See *Hearing before the U.S.–China Economic and Security Review Commission, supra* note 11; *2005 Report to Congress on China's WTO Compliance, supra* note 26; *Roundtable: Intellectual Property Protection as Economic Policy: Will China Ever Enforce its IP Laws? supra* note 21; and *2006 Special 301 Report, supra* note 22.

78 See He Weifang, 'To Realise Social Justice Through the Judiciary', in Xia Yong (ed.) *Towards an Age of Rights: A Perspective on Civil Rights Development in China* (*Zouxiang Quanli de Shidai: Zhongguo Gongmin Quanli Fazhan Yanjiu*) (Beijing: Press of China University of Political Science and Law, 1995), 209-284; Li Guoqiang, 'On the Internal Factors Causing Difficulties in Enforcement', *People's Court Daily* (*Renmin Fayuan Bao*), internet edition, 18 August 2000; 'On Judicial Enforcement Systems and Theories – a Symposium', (no. 5, 1998) *Politics and Law* (*Zhengzhi yu Falu*) 4; Chang Yi & Chui Jie, 'Several Issues for the Improvement of Compulsory Civil Enforcement'. (no. 1, 2000) *Legal Science in China* (*Zhongguo Faxue*) 97; Jiang Wei & Xiao Jianguo, 'Several Questions concerning the Civil Enforcement System', (no. 1, 1995) *Legal Science in China* (*Zhongguo Faxue*) 67; Qi & Ma, *supra* note 50; Xue Jinian, 'Reforming the Present Enforcement System and Enacting a Law on Enforcement', (no. 2, 1995) *Politics and Law* (*Zhengzhi yu Falu*) 49; Guo Guoyun & Lu Erping, 'On Reasons for and Damages Caused by Problems in Enforcement under the Conditions of a Market Economy and Their Responses', (no. 1, 1996) *Journal of China University of Political Science and Law* (*Zhengfa Luntan*) 75; Li Changqi, Chao Xingyong & Peng Xingshi, 'Local Protectionism in Economic Trials Must Be Stopped', (no. 4, 1998) *Modern Legal Science* (*Xiandai Faxue*) 71; Jing Hanchao, 'On Difficulties in Enforcement and Counter-Measures', (no. 5, 2000) *Journal of China University of Political Science and Law* (*Zhengfa Luntan*) 124; 'Improvement and Reform in Enforcement', *People's Daily* (*Renmin Ribao*), internet edition, 20 February 2002; Chen, Li & Otto, *supra* note 4; and Tong Zhaohong, supra note 41. This last book edited by Tong Zhaohong has contributions by ten senior Chinese judges in charge of or involved in enforcement work in their respective courts.

as they were deeply in debt; interference by local protectionism and departmental protectionism; parties avoiding their obligations; and a small number of decisions that were unfair and thus could not be enforced.[79]

In analysing these issues, the first problem we have concerns transparency.[80] Every experienced China law researcher can attest to the serious problems existing in relation to transparency in the Chinese law enforcement institutions (especially the judiciary) and the clarity of statistics (if available). These problems relate more to the question of research and analysis of enforcement problems, than to enforcement itself. In the absence of accurate and reliable statistics the severity of the problems in implementing laws (such as in IP areas) may be disputed, and the extent of the difficulties in court enforcement may be doubted. Nevertheless, the endless discussions in the public media, academic papers and in official reports confirm the existence of serious problems in this area. The fundamental problem here is the practice of defining enforcement as 'politico-legal', and hence the political sensitivity of any research or of publication of the actual situation.

The lack of transparency and clarity can create confusion in understanding the actual situation of law enforcement, sometimes at the cost of a misunderstanding of the actual efforts being made to enforce the law. For instance, the under-utilisation of the criminal law is often criticised. The USTR pointed out that in 2004, according to statistics provided by China, only 96 out of 51,851 administrative trademark cases (0.2%) and 101 out of 9,691 administrative copyright cases (1%) were transferred for criminal prosecution. The rate in 2001 was 0.2% and 1.5% respectively.[81] It has also been pointed out that up to 2006 there had been no criminal prosecution against any software end-user piracy.[82] Another complaint was that in 2005 the Administrations for Industry and Commerce had only transferred 230 (out 40,000) cases for criminal prosecution, while there was a 24% increase in that year in criminal convictions of IPR offenders.[83] However, these figures do not represent

---

[79] Work Report of the Supreme People's Court, delivered at the First Plenary Session of the Eighth National People's Congress, 31 March 1993, in (no. 2, 1993) *Gazette of the Supreme People's Court of the PRC* (*Zhonghua Renmin Gongheguo Zuigao Renmin Fayuan Gongbao*), at 55. See also Document no. 11 (1999), *supra* note 40.

[80] The Supreme People's Court has in recent years called for openness in trials and in its enforcement work. For instance, in March 1999 the Supreme People's Court issued its Provisions on the Strict Application of Open Trials. In 2006 the Court issued Certain Provisions on the Openness of the Enforcement Work of the Court. And in June 2007 the Court issued once again its Opinion on the Work of Open Trial by Courts. Despite these efforts, there have been no efforts to publish any systematic statistics in relation to courts and their work.

[81] *2005 Report to Congress on China's WTO Compliance*, *supra* note 26, 72.

[82] See *Hearing before the U.S.–China Economic and Security Review Commission*, *supra* note 11, at 10.

[83] Statement of Myron Brilliant, Vice President, East Asia, US Chamber of Commerce, at *Hearing before the U.S.–China Economic and Security Review Commission*, *supra* note 11, at 77.

all criminal prosecutions in relation to IP. According to the Vice President of the Supreme People's Court, Cao Jianming, in a four year period (2000–2004), a total of 1,369 IPR criminal cases (85% related to trademarks, 8.6% concerning trade secrets) were dealt with by Chinese courts nationwide. While the Vice President conceded that the number of criminal prosecution cases was too low and often the penalties were too light (mostly, if imprisonment was imposed, less than three years), he also pointed out that the statistics did not reflect the true extent of criminal prosecution as many IP infringement cases were prosecuted and convicted under crimes of manufacturing and selling fake and shoddy commodities, or crimes of conducting illegal business.[84] Similarly, while Chinese media and official speeches often refer to the total number of cases (and the total monetary amount involved) where rulings and decisions are not enforced, we do not know how many of these are ones that the defendants have the capacity to pay, and how many are simply insolvent so that it is impossible to have the decisions executed. The latter are those that the Chinese judges refer to as 'impossibility of enforcement' rather than '*Zhixing Nan*'.[85] If the two are distinguished, the problems of '*Zhixing Nan*' may not be as bad as the total number suggests.

The lack of a deterrent effect of the law is clearly a serious problem with major implications in our case studies. In relation to IP protection, Chow has pointed out:

> the average fine imposed on the counterfeiter or infringer in 2000 was $794, a figure that is so low as to be considered a cost of doing business in a very lucrative trade. The amount of compensation awarded to brand owners in 2000 stands at $19, a negligible amount. Damages awarded by AICs seek to award the brand owner the profits earned by the counterfeiter after deducting all expenses (as represented by the counterfeiter) and are not based upon economic losses suffered. As for criminal prosecutions, in 2000 only 1 in 500 cases was referred to judicial authorities for criminal prosecutions. Enforcement in China does not create fear in counterfeiters or deterrence.[86]

---

84 Cao Jianming, 'New Development in Judicial Protection of Intellectual Property', (no. 40, 2004) *Intellectual Property* (*zhishi Chanquan*) 9, at 10.

85 See Tong Zhaohong, *supra* note, at 4.

86 *Roundtable: Intellectual Property Protection as Economic Policy: Will China Ever Enforce its IP Laws?*, *supra* note 21. It should be pointed out here that while the majority of cases depend on transfer of administrative authority to the judiciary, private prosecution is available under Art 170 of the Criminal Procedure Law, which was further confirmed by Article 1 of the Interpretation of the Supreme People's Court on Certain Issues relating to the Implementation of the Criminal Procedure Law of the PRC (1998).

The result is that damages actually obtained through court barely cover litigation costs.[87] For instance, in a recent decision by the High Court of Beijing, five western companies holding the well-known brands of LV, Gucci, Burberry, Prada and Chanel sued five retailers and one company operating in the notorious Xushui Street in Beijing, claiming damages of half a million *yuan* against each defendant (with a total claim of 2.5 million *yuan*). These western companies won the case, but damages awarded to each plaintiff were only 20,000 *yuan*.[88]

The lack of deterrent effect and poor law enforcement explains why Chinese enterprises have been rather reluctant to apply for patents and other IP registration. According to official statistics, 99% of enterprises have never applied for patents and 60% of enterprises have no trademark.[89] When asked about enforcing IP law, a company manager replied that '[w]hen IP infringement occurs, if the total value is below 200,000 *yuan*, we normally do not pursue the case as the remedies will not compensate for our efforts.'[90] During my own fieldwork in China in 2005–2006 I was shocked to note that practically none of the small and medium sized enterprises that I visited ever applied for patents. Among these enterprises, a medium-sized enterprise specialising in electronic equipments has a small group of very talented and innovative engineers. They clearly have many good inventions or innovative products, but none were patented. When asked the reason behind their lack of interest in patent protection, the answer was simple – it is not worth it. According to the Chief Engineer of the enterprise, their greatest hope is to maintain the confidentiality of their own inventions before the products get to the market. Even though they do all they can to protect confidentiality, more often than not their designs are stolen by small enterprises, and products by these small enterprises often reach the market before their own, and sometimes even before they themselves have started production. When asked why they did not sue the small enterprises, the answer was equally simple – how do you gather enough evidence to do so? And even if you can, the small enterprises will simply close and the owners will start yet another small enterprise doing exactly the same. According to the Chief Engineer, their profit margins are so small that there is hardly any money for anything else. Furthermore, Chinese consumers seem to have an insatiable taste for anything

---

87 Transcripts of Web Forum on IP Protection, *supra* note 33.

88 'Five Well-known Brand Companies Won Case against Beijing Xushui Street', available at <news3.xinhuanet.com/legal/2006-04/18/content_4440716.htm> (last accessed 15 November 2006).

89 See 'Only 0.03% of Chinese enterprises own their own IP rights', in Xinhua news: <www.xinhuanet.com/st/2006-03/22/content_4332493.htm> (last accessed 23 March 2006); Xu Guanghua, *supra* note 35; 'China Must Face Up to IP Competition', *People's Daily* (*Renmin Ribao*), 22 May 2006, at 1.

90 See 'Internal and External Worries for IP Protection for Chinese Enterprises', Xinhua News: <news3.xinhuanet.com/focus/2006-04/07/content_4348971.htm> (last accessed 11 November 2006).

'new'. It thus makes better economic sense to make small changes (and more often than not, just changes in appearance) periodically, and to make the life cycle of the products short (two to three years), than trying to use the law to protect their inventions and innovations.[91]

In a similar vein, the Supreme People's Court has emphasised to the NPC that, for court rulings and decisions to be adequately enforced, the laws on enforcement need to have deterrent power.[92] There is little doubt that many disputants in civil cases refuse to abide by the court rulings and decisions simply because they know there are few consequences in doing so.[93]

The lack of precise legal provisions for courts to rely on in their implementation and enforcement of law, and the inconsistency among laws rapidly enacted, but enacted at different times and under different ideological orientations, are well known. As discussed in Chapter 16 in relation to IP protection, although the pragmatic practice of laying down only general and vague rules is often rectified by the more detailed provisions issued by the Supreme People's Court, the Court is nevertheless constrained by general principles set out in the laws, the reform of the latter being beyond the powers of the judiciary. In the area of enforcement of court rulings and decisions, the problem of inadequate legal provisions and the reluctance of courts to use coercive measures in civil and economic cases are also linked to legal culture and traditions. Chinese legal culture and the conception of justice are mostly concerned with substantive law, while ignoring procedural matters,[94] and there is a clear emphasis on the alternative settlement of disputes (for example, through mediation rather than litigation). As such, the lack of detailed practical guidance for enforcement of judgements and rulings is not really surprising.

---

91 For the same reason one has to have doubts about the legal measures that are constantly being issued. Thus, while the *Notice on Certain Issues concerning Pre-Installation of Computer Operation Software*, jointly issued by the Ministry of Information Industry, State Copyright Administration and the Ministry of Commerce on 30 March 2006, was welcomed by the American politicians and business people as a very positive measure for the protection of computer software [see *2006 Special 301 Report, supra* note 22; and *Hearing before the U.S.–China Economic and Security Review Commission, supra* note 11], one should also remember that as early as 1995 the Chinese government had required that unlicensed computer software must not been used by any units. See Notice of the State Copyright Bureau on the Prohibition of the Use of Illegally Duplicated Computer Software, 23 August 1995. This Notice was transmitted to all local and central government departments by the General Office of the State Council (with approval of the State Council itself).

92 See 'China Intends to Build Enforcement Mechanisms with Deterrent Effect', Xinhua News Agency: <nes.xinhuanet.com/legal/2006-01/23/content_4090180.htm> (last accessed 24 January 2006); and 'To Build a State Enforcement Mechanism with Deterrent Effect so as to Resolve Enforcement Problems', *Legal Daily* (*Fazhi Ribao*), internet edition, 7 March 2007.

93 Huang Songyou, *supra* note 44.

94 As discussed in Chapter 6 on Administrative Law, this conception is changing, at least in the area of administrative law.

The most commonly identified problems are interference by administrative and Party authorities and local protectionism,[95] which are both deeply rooted institutional problems, and these indicate a clear lack of the concept of judicial independence. Indeed, interference by administrative and party authorities and other local powerful officers is so common that political backing from the Party is often deemed to be necessary for the execution of court judgements.[96] This was frankly admitted by the President of the Supreme People's Court when he stated that '[w]e must closely rely on the leadership of Party committees in the work of enforcement. Enforcement concerns a wide range [of issues] and involves many areas and departments. If we rely on the courts alone, there will be many difficulties and problems as well as restrictions. Courts at all levels must frequently and actively report their work to Party committees, inform them of the problems encountered, and seek their attention and support.'[97] This sentiment is, not surprisingly, echoed at the local levels. Thus the President of the Shangdong Higher People's Court stated that '[t]he court alone is not enough to resolve problems involved in the execution of judgements; it requires support from various sources, especially the support and attention of the Party and government organisations at various levels.'[98] This is so for several institutional reasons. Firstly, courts are seen as one part, and one part only, of the government power structure, and they are not perceived as being different from such other power-holders as administrative authorities. Secondly, local financial authorities are responsible for the salaries and other costs of the courts. Thirdly, many aspects concerning the personnel of the courts, for example,

---

95 See *supra* note 79 and discussions below. See also 'Enforcement by Courts Meets with Local Protectionism', in *People's Daily* (*Renmin Ribao*), internet edition, 15 May 2002. In a recent empirical study by Peerenboom, however, local protectionism has not emerged as statistically relevant, nor does it become a bar to recovery in many cases. This might be caused by technical reasons or the specific focus (arbitration awards) of the research, or the need to use *guanxi* with the courts or local governments. See Peerenboom, *supra* note 4.

96 According to the Supreme People's Court, in some provinces interference by party or government instructions (*pi tiao*) occurs in up to 70% of enforcement cases. See 'Five Major Difficulties in Legislating for Compulsory Enforcement', in *People's Daily* (*Renmin Ribao*), internet edition, 14 May 2002. This *People's Daily* article does not separately explain the percentage of Party interference among these cases, as the article apparently intends to highlight the difficulties caused by 'outside' interference, rather than blaming specific authorities.

97 Speech delivered by Ren Jianxin (then President of the Supreme People's Court) at the first national Court Enforcement Work Conference on 23 April 1996, in *A Collection of Practical Documents on Compulsory Execution*, *supra* note 47, at 88. Although this was a statement made in 1996, there is no shortage of similar statements made by high-ranking judicial officials in China today.

98 *People's Daily* (*Renmin Ribao*), internet edition, 19 May 1999.

the total number of court personnel and the transfer of such personnel, are still controlled by the local Party and administrative authorities.[99]

Local protectionism occurs not only in the form of interference by local administrative and party authorities, it also takes the form of local judicial protectionism, which is defined by some Chinese scholars as a tendency in economic adjudication and enforcement by judicial authorities to render rulings and judgements which favour local parties and local economic interests, but to disregard facts as the basis, and law as the criterion.[100] The problem of such protectionism has been so serious that in 1996 it became the subject matter for special investigation by the Political-Legal Committee of the Central Committee of the Communist Party and the Supreme People's Court[101] and has been a major theme repeatedly reported to the NPC annual conference by the Supreme People's Court.[102] Specific practices include violation of rules on whether or not to exercise jurisdiction, giving in to unlawful interference by local party or administrative authorities (individual or institutional), abuse of the mediation process so as to avoid formal adjudication, using criminal penalties in place of economic remedies, disregard of facts and law, and disregard of requests for execution of judgements by courts from outside the region.[103]

The widespread practice of local protectionism is often seen to be a result of economic reform, and particularly of the process of decentralisation of economic management powers.[104] This decentralisation and the implementation of tax sharing have effectively created an economic federation in China, if not 'economic lords'.[105] In this context, the fact that local economic interests overrule the observation of law is not really surprising.

This explains why there is a serious problem of coordination and cooperation between different regions and why any attempt to achieve this is difficult. Chinese authorities certainly are aware of these problems. Thus, Hong Kong and Guangdong

---

99 Special Investigation Group, Supreme People's Court, 'Investigation Report on Local Protectionism in Judicial Activities', 18 July 1996, at 12-14, document on personal file. See also Zhu Aichun, 'On Administrative Interference in Enforcement', *Legal Daily* (*Fazhi Ribao*), internet edition, 15 January 2000.

100 Li, Chao & Peng, *supra* note 78, at 71.

101 Investigation Report on Local Protectionism in Judicial Activities, *supra* note 99. According to the Report, the investigation was requested by the Political-Legal Committee of the Central Committee of the Communist Party but conducted by the Supreme People's Court.

102 It has also remained a constant theme at annual national judicial conferences since 1988.

103 See Investigation Report on Local Protectionism in Judicial Activities, *supra* note 99. See also Li, Chao & Peng, *supra* note 78, at 71.

104 Zhang Shengzu, 'A Search for Reasons Causing Unfairness in the Enforcement of Law by Courts', *People's Daily*, internet edition, 13 January 1999.

105 On economic decentralisation and the increasing economic powers of local governments, see Jianfu Chen & Lijian Hong, *China Local Business Law Guide* (Singapore: CCH Asia Pacific, loose-leaf services, first published in 1999), at paras 1-070 – 1-090.

Province now have established a special IP group aimed at information sharing and cooperation. The Yangtze Delta (including Hong Kong, Macao, Sichuan, Fujian, Jiangxi, Hunan, Guangdong, Guangxi, Hainan, Guizhou, Yunnan) has established a regional IP cooperative mechanism. Another 16 Provinces (including Beijing, Shanghai, Tianjin, Helongjian, Shangdong, Sichuan) have signed an Agreement on Cooperation in Law Enforcement for Inter-Provincial Patent Protection. And 10 provinces (Beijing, Tianjin, Shanxi, Inner Mongolia, Shanxi, Gansu, Ningxia, Qinghai, Xingjiang, and Hebei) in North China and Central-Western China have issued a declaration for IP protection cooperation. Most of these cooperation agreements were signed in 2004 and 2005. These regional agreements/mechanisms aim for cooperation in information sharing, personnel training, mutual reporting of discovered IP infringement cases, transfer of cases, and joint investigation and gathering of evidence.[106] Different authorities involved in IP protection and administration have agreed that cross-regional and cross-jurisdictional cooperation is the key to the successful protection of IP rights,[107] and some specific measures have been taken by these authorities.[108] These efforts should improve IP law enforcement, but there is a more serious problem, namely that of local economic interests. As Chow has pointed out, some local economies are almost entirely supported by trade in counterfeited and pirated goods.[109] An American journalist thus has this to say on IP enforcement in China: 'Far from an ally in a joint undertaking, China's government actively tolerates and even rewards the stealing of ideas as its anointed development strategy. Local governments see the sales of pirated products as a way to

---

106 See Wu Yi, Speech at the Roundtable on IP Protection with Foreign Investment Enterprises, October 2004, available in <ipr.mofcom.gov.cn/article/200410/20041000294871_1.xml> (last accessed 2 March 2005); 'Great Regional IP Cooperation', in <www.legaldaily.com.cn/bm/2005-11/07/content_215674.htm> (last accessed 8 November 2005).

107 See Notice on the Issuance of the Minutes of the 2005 IP Protection Joint Conference, Economic Crimes Investigation Bureau of the Ministry of Public Security, Trademarks and Fair Trading Bureaus of the General Administration of Industry and Commerce, Coordination Bureau of the State Intellectual Property Office, Second Criminal Trial Chamber of the Supreme People's Court, Investigation Supervision Bureau of the Supreme People's Procuratorate, 24 October 2005.

108 For instance, Interim Provisions on the Strengthening of Cooperation and Coordination in Cracking Down on Illegal Activities that Infringe Upon Proprietary Rights of Trademarks, jointly issued by the Ministry of Public Security and the State Administration of Industry and Commerce on 13 January 2006; Interim Provisions on the Strengthening of Cooperation and Coordination in Cracking Down on Illegal Activities that Infringe Upon Copyright, jointly issued by Ministry of Public Security and State Copyright Bureau on 26 March 2006; Interim Provisions on Enforcement Cooperation for the Protection of Intellectual Property, jointly issued by the Ministry of Public Security and the General Administration of Customs, 24 March 2006.

109 See *supra* note 29.

keep people working.'[110] In these areas, therefore, one simply should not expect local cooperation in IP enforcement. As three judges from the High Court in Zhejiang Province have pointed out, because of the economic impact on enterprises and local governments IP cases often attract the attention of the local Party Committee, People's Congress and local government.[111] One must not forget that the legitimacy of the communist leadership and the future careers of local officials are all heavily dependent on economic development, often only assessed in terms of annual GDP growth. In other words, when local governments are under pressure during the campaigns they will cooperate, but when the campaigns are over there is no reason to expect their continuing efforts, unless such efforts assist economic development in their respective regions.

However, as many Chinese scholars and practitioners have discovered, local economic interest is a critical but not unique reason causing local protectionism.[112] It is actually more a result of the lack of reform than of the implementation of the reform itself. It is the lack of interest in the separation of powers (and hence in judicial independence) and in the de-politicisation of the judiciary that causes local judicial protectionism. In most cases, such protectionism is no more than an extension, or a different form, of interference by local administrative and Party authorities. As the Supreme People's Court has correctly pointed out, '[i]n an absolute majority of cases, local [judicial] protectionism is linked to local protectionist activities of local Party and government authorities and, in some cases, it is directly participated in or even directly orchestrated by local court leaders.'[113] As the Supreme People's Court discovered, it is not uncommon for local Party or government organs to compel courts to act according to various local 'internal documents' or policies by means of threats in the form of cutting court funding or of the removal of judicial personnel from the court.[114]

This lack of reform also directly contributes to various forms of malpractice in the judiciary. Thus, facing a severe funding shortage, many local courts set their own quotas for creating extra revenue through various means such as the levy of fees for

---

110 Peter S. Goodman, 'China's Weak Ally on Piracy', *Washington Post*, 4 June 2005, p. D01.

111 Tong Zhaohong, Chen Huiming, Zhou Gencai, 'A Study of Intellectual Property Trials in Zheijing Province', (no. 2, 2003) *Beijing University Intellectual Property Rights Review* 415, at 417.

112 For example, unlawful interference by local party and administrative authorities; the low professional quality of judicial personnel; traditional ideas resulting from a long history of an agricultural economy based on self-reliance and self-sufficiency; self-protection among judicial personnel (not to offend local authorities); abuse of the adjudication process by local parties so as to exhaust financial and other resources of the party from outside the region. See Li, Chao & Peng, *supra* note 78, at 71.

113 See Investigation Report on Local Protectionism in Judicial Activities, *supra* note 99, at 9.

114 See *id.*, at 7-8.

litigation, or the sharing with litigation parties of debts recovered.[115] This practice often leads to the exercise of jurisdiction by courts in cases over which in fact they have no jurisdiction at all.[116] Such actions can then lead to the refusal of cooperation from other courts for the enforcement of judgements, should the judgements need to be enforced outside the jurisdiction. Then there is also illegal enforcement of judgements by courts when they have exercised undue jurisdiction. In a case reported in the *People's Daily*, a county court, in order to fulfil the revenue creation quota, accepted 10,000 *yuan* as fees for exercising jurisdiction over a case that was clearly out of its jurisdiction. In order to exercise the jurisdiction, the judges, together with the plaintiffs, went to the place of the defendants and kidnapped them. As a result of efforts to prevent one defendant from calling out for help, the defendant was suffocated and died.[117] There are also many instances where the judges' travel, accommodation, etc. costs are covered by parties to a case,[118] and many others where courts arbitrarily increase fees in order to recover costs. Finally, the court itself may also be subject to fee levies by local administrative authorities.[119]

The lack of judicial independence is not simply a result of the rejection of the separation of powers. Throughout my own field research I have been constantly reminded of the fact that the serious problem of the inadequacy of professional qualifications of judicial personnel is one reason that granting independence to the judiciary may actually lead to even worse consequences. It is no secret that judges in the Chinese courts have not been well-educated and qualified in law until very recently.[120] Many of them, particularly in courts at the basic level, are demobilised army officers. The practice of employing such officers clearly reflects a long-held attitude in the communist leadership that law is 'an extension of military force' and that judicial tasks are equivalent to those of the army and the police.[121] Lack of professional qualifications was so serious that in 1994 it was asserted that almost 50% of judges nationwide had not even completed vocational legal education.[122] Although the 1995 Law on Judges does stipulate certain requirements for professional qualifications,[123] the requirements are not high and those who do not obtain

115 See *id.*

116 Zhang Shengzu, *supra* note 104.

117 *People's Daily*, internet edition, 31 July 1998.

118 This practice often leads to the wining and dining of judges and hence judicial corruption. See Cohen, *supra* note 73, at 801.

119 *Legal Daily* (*Fazhi Ribao*), internet edition, 20 June 2000.

120 See Zhang Shengzu, *supra* note 104, 1999. See also Clarke, *supra* note 4.

121 See the discussion in Chapter 2. For an insightful account of the problems associated with the employment of demobilized army officers as judges, see He Weifang, *supra* note 78, at 224-245.

122 He Weifang, *supra* note 78, at 228.

123 See discussions in Chapter 4 on Legal Institutions.

such qualifications are required to undergo training rather than to resign.[124] The introduction of a national judicial examination system in 2000 will certainly eventually improve the overall qualification standard of the judiciary, but the rectification of the deficiencies caused by lack of professional qualifications is not going to be quick[125] and certainly is not going to be thorough, because of the continuing emphasis on political and ideological correctness over professional qualifications.[126] As such the current problems in relation to professional qualifications are so widespread that they can only be seen as a systemic deficiency in the judiciary. Clearly, there is a long way to go before Chinese courts are fully professionalised.

Finally, at the deeper cultural level, there is a serious conceptual problem about law and its role in society. Thus, in the area of IP law, as Professor Qu Sanqiang has pointed out, the fact of IP infringement crimes being placed under 'Crimes against the Socialist Market Economic Order' instead of 'Crimes against Property' indicates a lack of understanding of the nature of IP rights in China.[127] A US law-maker has testified thus:

---

124 The professional qualifications and education of some judges are so poor that many legal documents prepared by them become unenforceable because of bad drafting, in terms of both general language and legal reasoning, and hence become a serious problem of enforcement in themselves. See 'On Internal Causes Leading to Difficulties in Enforcement', *People's Court Daily* (*Renmin Fayuan Bao*), internet edition, 18 August 2000; and Luo Shuping, 'The Quality of Court Adjudicating Documents Is Worrying', (no. 3, 1998) *Sichuan Adjudication* (*Sichuan Shenpang*) 22, at 22. For a recent interesting and comprehensive analysis of the various problems in court judgement writing, see Ma Shufang, 'Judicial Poverty and Counter-Poverty [Measures] – a Comprehensive Analysis of Civil and Commercial Judgements and Documents', originally published in (no. 2006) *Shangdong Adjudication* (*Shangdong Shenpan*) 113-117, reprinted in (no. 2, 2007) *Journal and Newspaper Reprinted Materials* (*Procedural Law and the Judicial System*) 67-72.

125 Indeed, the judiciary is said to be one of the professions in which, for a long time, it had been most easy for non-professionals to be employed. See He Weifang, *supra* note 78, at 228.

126 Speaking at the National Judicial Education Conference, Wei Jianxing, a member of the Standing Committee of the Politburo of the Central Committee of the Communist Party of China, made it clear that the most important qualifications for judicial personnel are political quality and ideological standing. See *People's Daily* (*Renmin Ribao*), internet edition, 17 September 2000. See also 'The Central Political Legal Committee Demands an Overall Rise in the Quality of Judicial Forces under the Guidance of the "Three Representatives"', *Legal Daily* (*Fazhi Ribao*), internet edition, 27 September 2000; and 'Work Report of the Supreme People's Court', delivered at the Fifth Plenary Session of the Ninth National People's Congress, 11 March 2002, in *People's Daily*, internet edition, 20 March 2002.

127 Qu Sanqiang, *Fundamentals of Intellectual Property Law* (*Zhishi Chanquanfa Yuanli*) (Beijing: Procutorial Press, 2004), at 62. For an excellent and much more in-depth study on the development of intellectual property law and the deep-rooted cultural difficulties in its enforcement, see William P. Alford, *To Steal a Book Is an Elegant Offense: Intellectual Property Law in Chinese Civilisation* (Stanford, California: Stanford University Press, 1995).

> It is difficult enough for our government and industry to protect property rights on our own shores, but defending America's IPR in a foreign nation that does not view property rights as an underpinning of its government or culture presents us with a Gordian knot of diplomatic, governmental and economic challenges.[128]

Here then is a clear case of contradiction: law in China is traditionally conceived as a tool for social order and control, whereas the largely transplanted law emphasises the protection of property rights.

All these identified causes, though inter-related, vary in nature, with some being systemic and others structural, and with some being internal to the judiciary while others are external.

6. Politico-Legal Manoeuvres in the Battlefield

In both cases, there has been no lack of responses by authorities of the government, judiciary and even the Party.[129] These responses come in two forms – general legal education and *ad hoc* politico-legal campaigns to raise the awareness of law in the society, as well as *ad hoc* legal and policy responses to specific problems.

There are different kinds of public/political campaigns for law and order conducted from time to time. As mentioned in Chapter 16, the so-called Strike Hard campaigns have attracted the most attention inside and outside China because of the heavy use of the death penalty, lack of strict observation of procedural requirements, and the severe punishments imposed on identified crimes. There are also *ad hoc* campaigns to publicise newly adopted laws or to enforce specific laws.[130] An important and persistent campaign is the series of Popularising Law (*Pufa*) Campaigns, which have been conducted for over 20 years on a five-year plan basis since 1985.[131]

The Popularising Law (*Pufa*) Campaigns may be said to have actually started in 1979 when seven major pieces of law, including the Criminal Law and the Criminal

---

128 Statement by Commissioner Kerri Houston, in *Hearing before the U.S.-China Economic and Security Review Commission, supra* note 11, 34.

129 For measures to enforce IP protection laws and regulations, see Chapter 16 on Intellectual Property Law. For measures on enforcement, see the 782-page collection: *A Collection of Practical Documents on Compulsory Execution, supra* note 47. See further discussions below.

130 Troyer, Ronald J. 'Publicising New Laws: The Public Legal Education Campaign', in Ronald J. Troyer, John P. Clark and Dean G. Royek (eds), *Social Control in the People's Republic of China* (New York: Praeger, 1989), at 70-83.

131 See the dedicated website on this topic established by the Ministry of Justice: <www.legalinfo.gov.cn>; see also Troyer, *id.*, at 70-83; M. Exner, 'Convergence of Ideology and the Law: The Functions of the Legal Education Campaign in Building a Chinese Legal System', (August 1995) *Issues and Studies* 68.

Procedural Law, were adopted, following a decision of the Central Committee of the CPC to publicise these two laws and hence to kick-start the *Pufa* and the Strike Hard Anti-Crime campaigns.[132] The adoption of the Marriage Law in 1980 and a new Constitution in 1982 further intensified the initial public campaign to spread the knowledge of law among the masses.

However, systematic *Pufa* campaigns only started with the National Legal Publicity Education Conference convened in Beijing in June 1985, during which the idea of having a five-year program was discussed.[133] In November 1985 the Five-Year Program concerning Dissemination of Common Legal Knowledge to All Citizens was approved by the Central Committee of the CPC and the State Council. This was followed by the Decision concerning the Dissemination of Common Legal Knowledge to All Citizens, adopted by the NPC on 22 November 1985.[134] The systematic *Pufa* campaigns continue to this day, with similar decisions being issued by the Propaganda Department of the CPC, the Ministry of Justice and the NPC at an interval of every five years. The latest campaign is the fifth five-year campaign, from 2006–2010.[135]

After some twenty years of *Pufa*, these campaigns are now a permanent fixture of the legal scene in China. The Five-Year Plan outlines the focuses and approaches, which are then implemented by special *Pufa* offices established within the governments at different levels in accordance with their own local circumstances. Special budgets are required to be allocated by governments at different levels, and inspections are conducted periodically. All kinds of media outlets are mobilised to conduct such campaigns, sometimes on disseminating knowledge about law, and sometimes on the implementation of specific laws. These campaigns are now seen as being one of the six essential aspects of ruling the country according to law.[136]

Although the actual effect on the general population of the campaigns is yet to be evaluated, the eagerness of urban residents to use law, to threaten disputants with legal action, and to challenge government decisions seems to suggest that it has had some success, at least in urban areas, and especially in the large eastern

---

132 See 'Legal *Popularisation*', Ministry of Justice, available <www.legalinfo.gov.cn/english/LawPopularisatin/lawpopularisation1_1.htm> (last accessed 25 August 2006).

133 See 'Legal Popularisation', *id.*

134 See 'Legal Popularisation', *id.*

135 See Resolution of the Standing Committee of the NPC on Strengthening Legal System Publicity and Education, adopted on 29 April 2006, and the Five-Year Plan for Legal System Publicity and Education among Citizens, jointly issued by the Propaganda Department of the CPC and the Ministry of Justice, 2006.

136 These six aspects are law-making, administrative enforcement of law, judicial administration of law, legal supervision, legal services, and *Pufa*. See Jing Yuanshu, 'Retrospect and Prospect of Pufa Work', available at <www.iolaw.org.cn/shownews.asp?id=11599> (last accessed 8 April 2005).

coastal cities, and demonstrates some significant changes in attitude towards law and conceptions of law. Attitudes towards state law in rural areas, where some 70-80 percent of the Chinese population live and work, are quite different and rarely studied and analysed. A recent case study on rural society and dispute resolution clearly indicates that state law is only one of the many sources and authorities through which disputes are resolved, and more often than not local customs and practice prevail over state law.[137] Other limited studies have also revealed that state laws are yet to fully penetrate the vast countryside in China.[138] In fact, the potential conflict and tension between the largely western style law now being introduced into China, and local customs and practices, especially in minority areas, where they are too often and too readily described as feudalist superstitious practices, are themselves major factors affecting the effective implementation of law. This suggests that 'rights consciousness' and thus the importance of such public law campaigns, is yet to penetrate to rural areas and townships.

In terms of *ad hoc* legal and policy responses, many regulations and measures have been issued to rectify the many identified problems, to raise the standard of actual implementation of law, and to improve the functioning of the various law-implementing/enforcing authorities in both cases. Practically all institutions involved have made, and continue to make, efforts in the battle against improper or inadequate implementation and enforcement of law.[139]

The legislatures – the National People's Congress, its Standing Committee and their local equivalents – being defined as the highest organs of state powers, have increasingly emphasised the exercise of their newly 'discovered' supervisory powers of interpreting laws, inspecting the implementation of selected laws, and supervising the work of the administrative and judicial organs. As discussed in Chapter Three on Constitutional Law, the power to interpret laws is clearly reserved for the legislatures in the Chinese Constitution and, hence, the legislatures have always been part of the implementation institutions in this sense. The practice of sending investigation groups to various provinces to inspect the actual implementation of selected laws at local levels has been conducted for some years and, generally speaking, the effect of such 'supervision' is minimal. Partly as a form of power politics, and partly frustrated by judicial corruption and judicial inability to uphold the law, some local legislatures

137 See Zhao Xudong, *Power and Justice: Dispute Resolution in Rural Societies and Plurality of Authorities* (*Quanli Yu Gongzheng: Xiangtu Shehui de Jiufen Jiejue yu Quanwei Duoyuan*) (Tianjin: Tianjin Ancient Books Publishing House, 2003).

138 See e.g. H. L. Fu, 'The Shifting Landscape of Dispute Resolution in Rural China', in Chen, Li, Otto, *supra* note 4, at 179-195; Tian Chengyou, 'Functions of Customs and Strategies for Dispute Settlement by Basic Level Judges', available at <www.usc.cuhk.edu.hk/wk_wzdetails.asp?id=1696> (last accessed 8 April 2006).

139 These responses in the area of IP protection have been outlined in Chapter 16 on Intellectual Property. The following therefore focuses on legal and policy responses in the area of court enforcement of their own rulings and decisions.

went so far as to attempt to 'supervise' individual cases handled by the judiciary.[140] Justifications for the exercise of such 'supervisory' powers have been largely based on the need for prevention of corruption and the establishment of some kind of checks and balances. However, the appropriateness of vesting interpretative powers in the legislatures, the actual motivation of exercising these 'supervisory' powers, and the constitutional basis for supervising the judiciary in individual cases are all questionable and raise serious questions and concerns about judicial independence in China.[141] Although legislatures in the West are not totally absent from the implementation scene – parliamentary reviews of administrative regulations (and subsequent disallowance of statutory rules), and parliament's prerogative to dismiss judges and other judicial personnel are upheld and practised in most western constitutional systems – the pervasive involvement of the Chinese legislatures in the implementation of law is unprecedented in any western system, and could be seen as contrary to commonly accepted constitutional principles. Further, with the legislatures being defined as a 'supreme power of the state', and accountable to no one, one must watch their acquisition of any specific powers with caution, until and unless the legislatures are called upon to be accountable to certain mechanisms, or to the people they are supposed to represent.[142] In short, the involvement of the legislatures in implementation of law points more to the need for constitutional reform than to actually overcoming problems in the implementation of law.[143]

The executive branch in China is not only powerful in law-making,[144] it is also one of the most important branches of state authority for the implementation of law. Its importance lies in much more than its ability to control judicial and other law-enforcement authorities through such measures as allocation of financial resources and the control of personnel, or through its often undue interference in the administration of justice, or its direct involvement in the administration of law through such authorities as the Ministry of Public Security, the Ministry of State Security and the Ministry of Justice. Much of the actual implementation of most of the laws is in fact carried out by administrative authorities through their secondary

---

[140] See the discussions in Chapter 3 on Constitutional Law.

[141] It should be pointed out that a controversial draft law on supervision of major violations of law in adjudication and procuratorate work, one of the major proposed means to supervise the judiciary in individual cases and submitted to the 12th Meeting of the Standing Committee of the NPC (October 1999), seems to have been shelved.

[142] For detailed discussions on the involvement of the legislature in implementation and enforcement of law, see Cai Dinjian, 'Functions of the People's Congress in the Process of Implementation of Law', in Chen, Li & Otto (eds), *supra* note 4, at 35-53.

[143] As discussed in Chapter 3 on Constitutional Law, the newly enacted Law on Supervision by Standing Committees of the People's Congresses at Various Levels (2006) managed to avoid these crucial questions instead of providing any answers.

[144] See the discussions in Chapters 3 & 5 on Constitutional Law and Law-making respectively.

rule-making, as well as through direct (administrative) enforcement of laws and regulations. The actual practice of administrative enforcement is often problematic. To start with, administrative enforcement of law has often involved informal methods, such as negotiation and mediation, rather than those set out in formal legal stipulations. Although the application of informal methods is often backed up by the threat of formal legal action, such legal action refers almost exclusively to legal penalties. Even if the administrative authorities are willing to act within the legal parameters, the problems of vagueness in law, local protectionism, economic and budgetary constraints, the lack of respect for and knowledge of law, etc. will still often force the administrative authorities to seek extra-legal mechanisms for administrative enforcement of law, or even to abandon attempts at enforcement. Further, seasonal politico-legal campaigns are often employed for the enforcement of law in targeted areas of activities.[145] These practices inevitably raise many questions about the universality, predictability and certainty of law as a requirement of the rule of law, and not infrequently undermine the authority of law itself.

The judiciary (including both the courts and the procuratorates) is the first institution people quickly associate with the notion of implementation and enforcement of law. Impressive efforts have been made and measures taken by the judiciary itself to ensure transparency, fairness and impartiality in law enforcement as well as to eliminate widespread judicial corruption. Collectively, the measures taken are voluminous in number,[146] including: (1) *ad hoc* decisions and rulings oriented toward specific problems; (2) judicial efforts to further clarify existing legal provisions; (3) judicial measures targeting the identified factors causing difficulties in enforcement; and (4) judicial endeavours toward general judicial reform.[147] There is no question that these judicial efforts are crucial in resolving some of the practical difficulties,[148] in making the general vague law practical,[149] and in assisting the establishment of a rule of law in China. Nevertheless, these efforts suffer the same fate as those of the administrative measures.

145 See the various campaigns on IP enforcement discussed in Chapter 16. See also Benjamin Van Rooij, 'Implementing Chinese Environmental Law Through Enforcement' in Chen, Li & Otto, *supra* note 4, at 149-178, where Van Rooij examines administrative enforcement of law in the area of environmental protection law.

146 See *A Collection of Practical Documents on Compulsory Execution*, *supra* note 47.

147 See further discussion in Clarke, *supra* note 4, Y. Li, 'Court Reform in China: Problems, Progress and Prospects', and J. Chen, 'Mission Impossible: Judicial Efforts to Enforce Civil Judgements and Rulings in China', both in Chen, Li & Otto, *supra* note 4, at 55-82, and 85-112 respectively.

148 See e.g. the discussion in Chapter 16 on IP protection.

149 As mentioned in Chapter 5 on law-making, the constitutional foundation for extensive law-making power by the judiciary is questionable.

As mentioned earlier,[150] judicial efforts began in 1987 to deal with the '*Zhixing Nan*' problems. Twenty years later no Chinese authorities have declared a victory in this battle. The recently renewed campaign on clearing up accumulated unexecuted cases is in itself an indirect admission of the failure of the efforts of the last 20 years. The issuance of yet another set of Party documents[151] simply indicates that the problems are as serious as they were, at least as in 1999 when the Party Document No. 11 (1999) was issued.

To be fair, there is no doubt that each of the principal authorities and institutions involved in implementation and enforcement of law has, mostly individually but sometimes jointly, made great efforts to improve the situation in the administration of law in China. Nevertheless significant improvement is still to be achieved. This clearly raises the question of the effectiveness of such efforts and the need to reconsider the whole range of issues at a deeper level.

7. Contradictions in Reform and the Missed Target

The ineffectiveness of the measures, some of which are admirable and many of which have been tried for many years, targeting internal operations and improvements as well as specific problems, suggests that the problems in implementation and enforcement of law are deeply rooted in the politico-economic system.

The involvement of a multitude of organisations and factors in the implementation of law means that difficulties and problems encountered by law-enforcement agencies in the process of the implementation of law often have a variety of causes. More importantly, it logically implies that efforts undertaken by individual authorities will not be able to resolve these problems. It thus points to the conclusion that the

---

150 *Supra* note 45.

151 In January 2006, the Political-Legal Committee of the Central Committee of the Party issued a document entitled Notice on Ensuring the Resolution of Court Enforcement Problems. As a Party document, it has not been publicly issued, but has been frequently referred to in the media and other publicly issued documents. According to the Chinese media, the document acknowledges the persistent and ever increasing severity of the problems in enforcing court rulings and decision, the interference by local governments and authorities, the existence of local protectionism etc. It calls upon Party committees at all level to assist the judiciary in tackling these problems. See 'The Party Central Committee's Political and Legal Committee Issued Notice to Resolve Enforcement Problems', China Court website: <www.chinacourt.org/public.detail.php?id=193356> (last accessed 5 July 2007). In June 2006, the Disciplinary Committee of the Central Committee of the Party, the Supreme People's Court and the Ministry of Supervision also jointly issued a Notice, demanding a stop to all forms of interference in court enforcement work. Again, this document has not been publicly issued. See 'Disciplinary Committee of the Central Committee of the Party, the Supreme People's Court and the Ministry of Supervision Jointly Issued a Notice', Xinhua News Agency: <news.xinhuanet.com/newscenter/2006-06/21/content_4726867.htm> (last accessed 5 July 2007).

next law reform will need to be a comprehensive one which attempts to tackle the root causes of such problems – a task that will be more political than legal.

Perhaps the problem is that the 'medicine' prescribed does not match the 'medical conditions' diagnosed, and the contradictions in the current judicial reform (in general terms, and in relation to enforcement) serve as a good illustration of this problem.

7.1. Contradiction One: Politicisation v. Professionalisation

To resolve the various problems and difficulties requires, first of all, that a genuine respect for law be established. For this it must first be established that there is a neutral, objective, respect-worthy arbitrator for dispute resolution that has the backing of the ultimate power of the state. Hence any talk of a fundamental improvement in implementation of law in China must first consider the establishment of genuine professionalism of the judiciary (including both the court and the procuratorates), and certainly not the politicisation of it. The latter will only re-enforce the view held by so many Chinese people that the judiciary is nothing but a part of the corrupt bureaucracy.

The most obvious aspects of the politicisation of the Chinese judiciary are the requirement that it subject itself to the leadership of the Party (imposed by the Party itself), and the *de facto* requirement of Party membership of judicial personnel.[152] Recent judicial policy documents do not seem to help the gradual separation of the Party from the judiciary at all.[153] These documents specifically and explicitly emphasise that judicial reform may only be carried out in accordance with the principles of upholding the leadership of the Communist Party, that all measures must be beneficial to the strengthening of the position of the Party as the ruling party in China, and that the judiciary must always maintain its political character and political obligations, in the form of upholding Party leadership and being loyal to the Party. These blunt statements of the judiciary being an instrument of the Party do little to help the transformation of the conventional view that law is merely an instrument to implement Party policies. The judiciary is often politicised by its own

---

[152] There are no statistics to show the percentage of party members among the judiciary. Cohen has suggested that 90% or more of the judicial personnel are party members. See Cohen, *supra* note 73, at 797.

[153] See e.g. the Outline of the Five-Year Reform of the People's Courts, issued by the Supreme People's Court in October 1999; the Opinions on Playing Fully the Role of Adjudication to Provide Judicial Protection and Legal Services for Economic Development, issued by the Supreme People's Court on 3 March 2000; the Second Five-Year Court Reform Outline, issued by the Supreme People's Court on 26 October 2005; Implementation Opinion on Deepening the Three-Year Procuratorial Reform, issued by the Supreme People's Procuratorate on 12 September 2005; and Certain Opinions on Judicial Guarantees for the Establishment of a Harmonious Socialist Society, issued by the Supreme People's Court on 15 January 2007.

practices as well, such as the frequent use of political campaigns for the enforcement of judgements and rulings. Clearly, this self-imposed political obligation upon the court may compromise the efforts of the judiciary towards professionalisation, not to mention judicial independence.

The danger of political campaigns and the politicising of judicial tasks in line with the prevailing Party policies is not only that it re-enforces the conception of law as a tool, frequently used for perceived needs and/or on selected targets. The instrumentalist approach is also detrimental to efforts at establishing a true rule of law in China. Political backing, occurring mostly during judicial campaigns, can lead to short-term gains, as evidenced in the present campaigns for implementation of law. Therefore, some scholars have asserted that 'Party involvement may not be bad; in paying due respect to the Party organisation, courts may simply be doing what is necessary to ensure political backing for their judgements.'[154] The problem is that this kind of concession to party involvement and intervention carries the danger of legitimising the use of law as a tool for the ruling party or ruling elite, and hence the danger of continuing loss of respect for law among the general populace. Finally, the requirement for political and ideological correctness in the recruitment of judicial personnel may not necessarily destroy the movement toward professionalism, but it certainly undermines it and re-enforces the politicisation of the judiciary. It is simply wrong to demand that judges must reflect the image of the Party and that courts should serve to implement the central tasks of the Party,[155] when the Party sees its ultimate task as to assert its own leadership over national affairs and when it is accountable to no one.[156]

7.2. Contradiction Two: Judicial Independence v. Economic Fragmentation

Politicisation of the judiciary undermines not only judicial professionalism and professionalisation, but also judicial independence. However, the economic fragmentation resulting from economic reforms in post-Mao China has inevitably led to local protectionism. This actually creates a curious form of 'judicial independence' – local judicial protectionism. Ironically, this kind of 'judicial independence' is a direct result of the lack of actual judicial independence. Although courts in China form a kind of judicial hierarchy with the Supreme People's Court at the helm, court budgets, the general welfare and salaries of judicial personnel, appointment and removal of

---

154 Clarke, *supra* note 4, at 51.

155 This was, indeed, insisted on by the President of the Supreme People's Court, Xiao Yang, when he declared that 'Judges, symbolic of the nation, should represent the image of the Party, the legal system and the State'. See *China Daily*, internet edition, 26 February 1999. See also *supra* note 126.

156 It is no secret that, under the much-publicised Administrative Litigation Law (1989), the court has no jurisdiction over the Communist Party of China in judicial reviews. See discussions in Chapter 6.

judges, etc., are all controlled and decided by local authorities – that is, the local Party committees, local people's congresses and their standing committees and local governments.[157] Within this financial and administrative structure it is not difficult to understand why local courts, willingly or unwillingly, favour local interests. Nor is it difficult to understand how easily local governments can interfere with judicial enforcement of legally effective judgements.

The first Outline of Five-Year Reform of the People's Courts decided on the need to 'explore mechanisms to secure court funding and appointment of personnel'.[158] The second Five-Year Reform Outline declared the same.[159] However, as a matter of common sense, if any reform is to be made in relation to court funding and the appointment of personnel, this will have to be a matter beyond the power of the judiciary itself. It demands fundamental politico-economic and constitutional reform.[160] Not surprisingly, much more than five years have passed and there has been no sign of when a centralised court funding and personnel appointment scheme will be implemented.

7.3. Contradiction Three: Internal Efforts v. External Constraints

As has been outlined earlier, there is no doubt that all state authorities and institutions related to implementation of law are making great efforts to tackle the problems and difficulties. But these efforts are *ad hoc* and mostly aim at specific problems. Thus they are only capable of tackling certain symptoms of the problems, not their fundamental causes. Put simply, all efforts (judicial or otherwise) are of their nature internal, whereas the fundamental causes are often external to the authorities making such efforts. For instance, in the case of the judiciary, the Supreme People's Court may be able to fill some legislative gaps in the existing legal system, but the problems with the existing law itself are beyond the capacity of the court to repair. More importantly, as the Supreme People's Court has itself pointed out, the fundamental causes of local protection lie with the political and constitutional systems, which now lag well behind economic reform. There are also no specific mechanisms to ensure that the

---

157 See Investigation Report on Local Protectionism in Judicial Activities, *supra* note 99, at 12-14.

158 Article 43 of the Outline of Five-Year Reform of the People's Courts refers to possible revision of the Court Organic Law in relation to the court structure. Article 44 calls for actively exploring possible reform in the judicial cadre system so as to strengthen the supervision of the system by the Party and people's congress, and Article 45 mentions the need to actively explore possible reform in the funding system in order to secure court funding. None of these articles contains any details of possible reforms nor explains the direction of such reforms.

159 The second Three-Year Reform Opinion of the Supreme People's Procuratorate says the same.

160 'Enforcement to Be Improved through Reforms', *People's Daily* (*Renmin Ribao*), internet edition, 20 February 2002.

constitution and national law will be properly implemented at the local levels, and there are no effective mechanisms for dealing with conflicts of laws between those issued by the central government and those issued by local authorities.[161] Then there are the practical problems, mentioned above, of local judicial authorities being created by local people's congresses, and of judicial appointment, funding, welfare, etc. being directly controlled by local authorities. Also in this context, the approach of certain authorities is questionable. For instance, there is a question of constitutional legitimacy of local legislatures' attempts to supervise the implementation of law. Instead of pushing towards exercising such supervision, the NPC perhaps would do better to consider a re-arrangement of the constitutional separation of powers, and the establishment of constitutional checks and balances, so as to avoid being directly questioned about its motivation for exercising such powers.

Clearly, most of the problems in the implementation of law cannot be resolved by the individual institutions in isolation: they are, as already pointed out, questions for fundamental and systemic politico-economic and constitutional reforms, as well as institutional and cultural transformation.[162] Herein, however, lies a proper role for Party leadership. It is no secret that the Party is the real authority in major policy-making and political and fundamental constitutional reforms. It is here that the involvement of the Party leadership could enhance judicial independence rather than undermining it. It is here that political initiatives could be translated into lasting judicial progress. However, we have yet to see any such political initiatives for fundamental political and constitutional reform, and this is where the missed target – a fundamental constitutional reform aimed at a radical politico-economic and institutional transformation – lies.[163]

8. Concluding Remarks

In contrast to the impressive achievements that have occurred in law-making, the general situation regarding the implementation and enforcement of law in China may well be described as unsatisfactory, if not dismal or even in crisis. This is so despite great efforts by the various authorities. Typical of the pragmatic solutions

---

161 See Investigation Report on Local Protectionism in Judicial Activities, *supra* note 99, at 12-14; and 'Five Major Difficulties in Legislating for Compulsory Enforcement', in *People's Daily* (*Renmin Ribao*), internet edition, 14 May 2002. As discussed in Chapter 3, some mechanisms are currently being established.

162 See 'Why Is It so Difficult to Eliminate Local Protection', *People's Daily* (*Renmin Ribao*), internet edition, 20 February 2002; and Stanley Lubman, 'The WTO Debate: Chinese Justice on Trial', *The Asian Wall Street Journal*, 9 May 2000, at J10.

163 This is certainly not the only reform that would be required, but an essential one that is wanting.

produced in China, these efforts are *ad hoc*, piecemeal and uncoordinated, and largely avoid the underlying problems in the political system.

It is important to realise, as pointed out by Alford in relation to IP protection, that the effective enforcement of these laws may require the reformulation of the law by taking into account historical and cultural factors in China, and reforms in the current political system.[164] But fundamentally, as Stevenson-Yang and DeWoskin have pointed out (also in relation to IP protection), it is the current politico-economic system that needs urgent repair.[165]

Perhaps, a fundamental re-thinking should start from here.

Of course the *ad hoc* measures and efforts will have some impact on the improvement of the implementation of law in China, at least, in the short term. But in order to change the situation fundamentally a theoretical framework will be needed to guide and develop a comprehensive reform program, and such a reform would need, at the minimum, to address the following: a further strengthening of the various institutions involved in the implementation and enforcement of law, in terms of both their political and social status as well as their economic and financial positions, and a need to improve the professional qualifications and hence professionalism of personnel in such institutions. Such a reform must also define, in clear terms, the functions of the various institutions, as well as establish some clear channels of communication between the various players involved. More importantly, there must not only be coordination, but also checks and balances between and among these institutions (including the Communist Party). Ultimately, this kind of reform will need to be assessed by such criteria as coherence, transparency and accountability in policy-making, and fairness, certainty and impartiality in legal processes. These are not unrealistic ideals; they are essentially about judicial professionalisation. In fact, as early as 1996, the Supreme People's Court had itself pointed out that any comprehensive reform would at a minimum need to include the following aspects:

- the re-establishment of branches of the Supreme People's Court in different regions, so as to provide direct leadership and supervision over local courts and to bypass local authorities;
- the power to establish courts and the centralisation of all judicial appointments under a national authority;
- de-linking of the establishment of courts from administrative divisions; thus courts to be established according to geographical and population needs;

---

164 See Alford, *supra* note 127, esp. Chapters 1-3. See also Graham J. Chynoweth, 'iBrief/Copyrights and Trademarks: Reality Bites: How the biting Reality of Piracy in China is Working to Strengthen Its Copyright Laws', (Winter 2003) *Duke L. & Tech. Rev.* 3.

165 Anne Stevenson-Yang & Ken DeWoskin, 'China Destroys the IP Paradigm', *Far Eastern Economic Review*, March 2005.

- all administration of personnel (including rewards and punishment, transfer and allocation) to be devolved to the courts; and
- funding for courts to be allocated directly by central authorities and administered by the Supreme People's Court.[166]

These reforms, as the Supreme People's Court made clear, would be part of political reform, but are also fundamental as a minimum guarantee for judicial independence and accountability.[167] Sadly, we have yet to see any of these proposals being implemented.

In this context, what can we say about the two case studies? On IP protection, perhaps, three major factors will ultimately determine its fate. First, a strong political will from Chinese governments at all levels. The effective protection of the Beijing Olympic logo is a good example. While the genuine desire of the Central Government for IP protection is not to be seriously doubted, the political will of the local governments is questionable, largely due to economic interests of their own. This then leads to the second factor, namely that IP protection will improve when China has its own sufficient IP interests to protect, and IP protection improvement will only occur in proportion to the weight of these interests.[168] Finally, counterfeiting and piracy may ultimately be destroyed by their own success. No longer are counterfeits and piracy confined to branded clothing, CDs and DVDs; they are now in every industry, including automotives, pharmaceutical goods, skin and health care products and other products that directly affect the health and safety of people. With the steady improvement of living standards and consumption powers there will be a day when consumers revolt against substandard and unsafe products, and that will be the day counterfeits and piracy destroy themselves. As to the '*Zhixing Nan*', it will continue to be a recurring problem until Chinese law and the judiciary are truly respected by the Chinese people, which is not likely to be the case in the near future.

---

166 See Investigation Report on Local Protectionism in Judicial Activities, *supra* note 99, at 17-18.

167 *Id.*

168 In this regard, things are not all gloomy. It is very encouraging to see that more and more Chinese firms are now beginning to establish their own in-house legal departments or to expand the existing ones, so as to protect their own IP rights. See 'Chinese Use Courts to Sink Pirates', *supra* note 18. In other words, China is now forced to change not only by foreign pressures but also because of its own economic interests.

Conclusion

1. Chinese Law Transformed

The detailed discussions in this book suggest that while legal modernisation, and indeed modernisation in general, has not been without flaws and setbacks, the overall movement of law in China has been in the right direction, and the progress made so far has been positive and remarkable.

Ever since the Qing and KMT legal reforms that first introduced Western law and legal systems into China and broke down traditional systems, values and practices, and separated private law from public law, civil law from criminal law, and the legal system from the administrative hierarchy, Chinese law has been transformed into Western law in form, along a Continental civil law model. Indeed, as some Chinese scholars have pointed out:

> For the whole of the 20th century the development of Chinese law and legal science was a process of learning from, making use of, absorbing and digesting, foreign experience. As far as legal institutions, principles and terminologies in the contemporary legal system in China are concerned, almost all were transplanted from foreign countries, although China's own situation was considered. In fact, foreign laws are now an indispensable part of the main body of modern Chinese law.[1]

As a result, Chinese law today is a system with mixed external influences, for which specific foreign sources are difficult to identify, but one that is nevertheless moving towards commonly accepted international practices, albeit operating in a very different political, social and economic context.

More substantially, the heavy utilitarian and instrumentalist attitude towards law, clearly evidenced in the major part of legal modernisation, is losing its hold and is

---

1 See 'Preface' to He Qinghua & Li Xiuqing, *Foreign Law and Chinese Law – An Examination of the Transplanting of Foreign Law into China in the 20th Century* (*Zhongguofa Yu Waiguofa – Ershishiji Zhongguo Yizhi Waiguofa Fansi*) (Beijing: Press of China University of Political Science and Law, 2003).

increasingly being abandoned. The brutal use of law as a weapon for class struggle has gone, and without much doubt gone for good. Even if law may still be seen as an instrument, it is increasingly seen as such for justice, fairness and equality, not simply for creating and maintaining social stability conducive to economic development. This substantive transformation of Chinese law and the Chinese conception of law will ultimately be the most decisive factor in determining the future direction of the development of Chinese law and the fate of the rule of law in China.

2. Towards a Rule of Law?

Legal modernisation in China is however not a finished business; Party and state authorities have now made it clear that a 'complete' legal system is yet to be established by 2010.[2] Legal development in China can thus be assessed from two quite different perspectives: how far China has travelled towards the rule of law, and how great a distance still lies ahead towards such a goal. In terms of law-making and institution building, the achievements of the last 28 years or so are indisputably remarkable and must be acknowledged as such. Indeed, this achievement represents one of the greatest contributions that the Communist Party of China has made in its approximately 86 years of existence.

In assessing legal development and reform in China in terms of the distance that still lies ahead, one must bear in mind China's own legal tradition and social background. We should not forget that on the whole the Chinese political and legal traditions have not been particularly conducive to the establishment of the rule of law, however it is understood. Nor is there a strong legal tradition to back up the operation of a relatively autonomous legal system.

Whether we wish to assess the glass as half empty or half full, we must inevitably assess it in terms of the rule of law. Having now examined almost all substantive branches of law and their development and transformation in the last 28 years (and to a certain extent, the last 100 years), we at this point inevitably reach the question: is China now a country under the rule of law? If not, is China moving towards this end?

Earlier I cast doubt on describing China as a 'rule of law' country,[3] and I remain reluctant to use this label for several reasons. First, the notion has largely originated and been developed in the West, and its nature (and even its contents) is contested. While many scholars have now argued for a broader definition of this notion so as to

---

2 See 'Chinese Legal System Will Be Established on Schedule', available from <www.legaldaily.com.cn/2007-3/13/content_557642htm> (last accessed 14 March 2007).

3 Jianfu Chen, 'To Have the Cake and Eat It Too? China and the Rule of Law', in Guenther Doeker-Mach & Klaus A Ziegert (eds), *Law, Legal Culture and Politics in the Twenty First Century* (Munich: Franz Steiner Verlag Stuttgart, 2004), at 250-272.

accommodate its development in Asian countries, there is a danger that a completely new 'Asian' or 'Chinese' conception that is so alien as to render any comparison and assessment meaningless, is not a helpful solution. Secondly, while we should not deny China the right to use that label, we should not impose western liberal ideas and values on a wholesale scale upon China, or any other non-western country either. Thirdly, the Chinese term '*Fa Zhi*' (法治) – traditionally referring to Legalism, and literally more close to 'rule by law' than 'rule of law' - is largely a scholarly construct; the official term is a mouthful: '*Yifa Zhiguo, Jianshe Shehuizhuyi Fazhi Guojia*' (ruling the country according to law and building a socialist country governed by law), and open to different interpretations, at least literally.[4] Nevertheless Chinese law is still rapidly developing and as such it is perhaps safer to follow the China home-grown phrase than to give it a western label.

I must also, however, submit that we are all conditioned by our educational background and social environment, and the language in which we are trained is normally the medium through which we try to understand 'others'. Here, even though I prefer the Chinese phrase 'ruling the country according to law' to the western notion of 'rule of law', inevitably the nature of 'ruling the country according to law' will be assessed against specific 'rule of law' criteria.[5] In other words, a value judgement is inevitable when assessing the evolution of Chinese law.

If legal development in China is to be assessed against an idealised liberal concept of 'rule of law', the conclusion is likely to be that China is far from being a rule of law country.[6] But in so doing we run into two major risks: we basically assess a non-western country according to western liberal ideas and values, and, more unfairly, we assess a country against ideal criteria that are far from actually being universally practised in western countries. To address the shortcomings of this approach, many scholars have been arguing for a broader definition of 'rule of law'. In this regard the most prominent scholar is Randall Peerenboom. Peerenboom classifies rule of law into thin and thick versions (the latter is further divided into four ideal types), each with a specific set of assessment criteria, so as to accommodate countries at different levels of development.[7] On this basis, Peerenboom argues that the Chinese legal system is moving towards a regime that complies with the basic elements of a thin

---

4 See Chen, *id.*, at 254-260.

5 As such, my preferred phrase of 'ruling the country according to law' perhaps indicates more the current level of development of law than it does the nature of law in China.

6 See e.g. Eric W. Orts, 'The Rule of Law in China', (2001) 34 *Vanderbilt Journal of Transnational Law* 43; Stanley B. Lubman, *Bird in a Cage: Legal Reform in China after Mao* (Stanford, California: Stanford University Press, 1999); Pitman B Potter, *The Chinese Legal System: Globalization and Local Legal Culture* (London & New York: Routledge Cuzon, 2001); and Chen, *supra* note 3.

7 See Randall Peerenboom, *China's Long March toward Rule of Law* (Cambridge: Cambridge University Press, 2002).

rule of law.[8] Furthermore, he also believes that law is used instrumentally in every legal system, even though he tries to distinguish between pernicious instrumentalism and acceptable instrumentalism, the former being rule by law and the latter rule of law.[9] He believes that China has moved away from a purely instrumental conception of law toward a conception of rule of law in which law is meant to bind both government officials and citizens, though he concedes that the goal of a legal system to bind the state and its actors is often not realised in Chinese practice.[10] This is a fair, and perhaps kind, approach to assessing rule of law development in developing countries. However, it runs the risk of allowing countries 'to have their cake and eat it too', as people too often remember the label but forget the contents and context. Most recently Peerenboom has further developed his theories and modified his approach in his new book, *China Modernizes: Threat to the West or Model for the Rest?*[11] In this book, instead of comparing China with western developed countries, he puts China in a comparative context with other developing countries, especially Southeast Asian ones. Once again, Peerenboom has made an extremely sensitive and valuable contribution to helping us understand China, its place in the world and among developing countries.

While admiring the efforts of Peerenboom and many others, I prefer however a simple, although not simplistic, approach that assesses China in its own context. To me, what is important is the substance, not the label itself. Throughout my many years of conducting fieldwork in China it has become clear to me that the rule of law is understood by ordinary people as meaning that '[t]here must be laws for people to follow, these laws must be observed, their enforcement must be strict, and law-breakers must be dealt with' – a notion that contains assessment criteria which have also been held by Party and government officials to be the essence of, or basic requirements for, the rule of law.[12] In this context, the critical questions to be asked would be: according to whose law, to whom are the laws applied, and how are they applied? On these questions, the development so far, and the general trends in China, as discussed in this book, are both promising and reasonably positive.

---

8 *Id.*, at 6 & 558.

9 *Id.*, at 23, footnote 23 therein.

10 *Ibid.*

11 Oxford University Press (New York), 2007. I am most grateful to Professor Peerenboom for kindly letting me have the whole manuscript before its publication.

12 See Item 2, Section V of the 2002 Political Report 'Building a Well-off Society in an All-Round Way and Creating a New Situation in Building Socialism with Chinese Characteristics - a Political Report delivered by Jiang Zemin at the 16th Party Congress, 8 November 2002'. An English text is available from *China Daily*, internet edition, 6 December 2002; and 'There Must Be Some "References" for Implementation of Law', *People's Daily* (*Renmin ribao*), internet edition, 20 February 2002.

Answering the question of 'according to whose law' requires an analysis of how law is made. Rarely would we hear these days that law represents the will of the ruling class. Importantly, the adoption of the Law on Law-making in 2000 has now made the procedures of law-making much more transparent, with mechanisms to ensure the consistency of laws enacted at different levels, and the participation of the general population.[13] While law-making in China has always been of an urban elitist nature, if not urban chauvinist, this too is changing. Increasingly, draft bills are published for public consultation before further revision and adoption. The processes to revise the Marriage Law and to enact the Law on Rights *in rem* are two good examples of such public consultation. Even the Supreme People's Court nowadays publishes its draft interpretations of law before final adoption and promulgation. Also notably, even though the Party still strictly controls the revision of the Constitution, draft revisions to the Constitution have been published for consultation. Further, most bills and proposed revisions are initially drafted by scholars. While scholars' participation in law-making represents more of an urban elitist approach, it cannot be accurately described or easily dismissed as a top-down approach, as many scholars hold no official positions in the government. Most importantly, there are signs that the government is now responding to concerns from ordinary people regarding law-making and the implementation of the constitution. A specific example is the 'Sun Zhigang' case discussed in Chapter Three. The State Council's swift action to repeal the allegedly unconstitutional Measures on Detention and Repatriation may be seen as an indication of state authorities responding to social pressures. This in a traditionally authoritarian society is in itself remarkable. Finally, the Chinese authorities have now also explicitly stressed that the emphasis on law-making will be two-fold: on quality over quantity and with a shift from economic considerations to the social impact of law-making.[14]

Equality before the law is nowadays often emphasised, with demands for the application of the law to both the CPC and high-ranking government officials. It is about this aspect that you hear most complaints from ordinary people in China. Ask any taxi driver in China about law or the rule of law and you will be universally told that there is no law or rule of law. When you point out the rapid legal development in law and legal institutions, the reply is once again universal: that the law is intended to govern and the institutions to control the ordinary people. The reality is of course not so simple, and significant progress has been made. While there is no doubt that the CPC has a firm control over state affairs, it is also clear that major efforts have been made for such control to be exercised through constitutional and legal mechanisms. Thus express constitutional provisions in the 1975 and 1978 Constitutions, which declared that the Party was the 'core of leadership', and which imposed an explicit

---

13 See discussions in Chapter 5.

14 See 'Chinese Legal System Will Be Established on Schedule', *supra* note 2.

obligation on the citizens to support the Party leadership,[15] were abolished. Specific measures for the Party to retreat to the background have also been taken and, for the first time, the 1982 Constitution expressly declares that the Constitution has the supreme authority of law.[16] These changes in the constitutional mechanisms have made it possible for a gradual separation of the Party and Government, in the sense that Party policies are to be translated into state law through legal procedures.[17] Furthermore, while different interpretations may be given to the motivations for the current anti-corruption campaigns, the fact is that a large number of high-ranking officials have fallen from grace, been jailed, or even executed after legal processes.[18] This perhaps indicates that law can apply, and has been applied, to everyone, high and low in official positions, when there is the political will to do so.

As to the question of the fair application of law, the revised Criminal Procedural Law represents a far cry from that of the original law. While talk about the courts and procuratorates upholding Party leadership and supporting Party policies is still commonplace, the motto of the Supreme People's Court has been quietly changed to 'Justice and Effectiveness',[19] and that of the Supreme People's Procuratorate to 'Prosecution for the Public and Enforcement for the People'.[20] Most important are the courts' attitudes towards the practical effect of the Constitution. The long-held view that the provisions of the Constitution might not be directly enforced in a court of law seems to be losing its grip, and the direct enforceability of the constitutional provisions is nowadays recognised by Chinese scholars.[21] Further, as discussed in Chapter Three, it has been argued that Chinese courts can and should make protection of human rights a major consideration in their adjudications, at least when the relevant Chinese

---

15 These provisions included Articles 2 & 3 of both the 1975 and 1978 Constitutions, Article 26 of the 1975 Constitutions and Article 56 of the 1978 Constitution.

16 See the discussion in Chapter 3.

17 This understanding was re-affirmed in the Political Report of the Party at the 14th Party Congress which specifically said that 'the main method for the Party to exercise its political leadership over state affairs is to translate Party policies into state will through legal procedures'. See 'Accelerating the Reform, the Opening to the Outside World and the Drive for Modernisation, so as to Achieve Great Successes in Building Socialism with Chinese Characteristics', in *People's Daily* (*Renmin Ribao*) (overseas edition), 21 October 1992, at 1-3; and Li Peng, 'Speech at the Second Meeting of the Standing Committee of the 9th NPC', 29 April 1998, in *People's Daily* (*Renmin RiBao*), internet edition, 1 May 1998.

18 China has not published any comprehensive data on anti-corruption cases, but reports on high-ranking officials caught by the campaigns are reported on a daily basis by Chinese media outlets.

19 See the website of the Supreme People's Court: <www.court.gov.cn> (last accessed 26 November 2006).

20 See the website of the Supreme People's Procuratorate: <www.spp.gov.cn/site2006> (last accessed 26 November 2006).

21 See the discussion in Chapter 3.

law is not clear, or is ambiguous on particular matters. Most importantly, with or without a practical mechanism for enforcing the supreme law, attempts have been made by Chinese scholars and the Supreme People's Court to use the Constitution as a document with practical consequences. Equally significant is the increasing emphasis on procedural justice as discussed in Chapters Six and Eight.

Even though the principle of separation of powers is not formally recognised in China, the 1982 Constitution clearly stipulates that the power of adjudication may only be exercised independently by the people's courts. The 13-year long debate on the Supervision Law struck at the heart of the question, and highlighted this very fundamental problem in the Chinese polity. Although the adopted Law avoids addressing the question of separation of powers, it probably can be said that the issue, once raised, will not easily go away.

While it is premature to treat these latest developments as representing a firm trend, they are nevertheless emerging signs of a positive development in the right direction. In short, the substantive developments, especially since 1996, that are described in this book, and the emerging signs from China indicate that 'ruling the country according to law' can no longer be accurately described as 'rule by law', and the Chinese authorities' attitude towards law is now much less of a purely instrumentalist nature. Perhaps it is also premature or simply unfair to assess contemporary Chinese law according to the criteria of the 'rule of law'. After all, the 'rule of law' has been developed for some 800 years in the Common law system, whereas China's modern history has been a rather turbulent time. But the overall trend is evidently in that direction.

3. What's Next?

However, the present law and legal system are not free of some serious problems, and as such it would be misleading not to highlight some of the major weaknesses and failures in legal development.

Whether we call it 'westernisation', 'internationalisation', 'rule of law', 'ruling the country according to law', or a 'socialist law with Chinese characteristics', Chinese law has become less Chinese than ever before, both in its form and substance.[22] Law, however, always operates in 'local conditions'; that is, in the unique political, social, economic and cultural context of the country concerned. However much Chinese law has become 'western', the adoption of western law is not necessarily the same

---

22 A prominent scholar, Profess Liang Zhiping, in discussing Chinese civil law has this to say '[i]f Japanese law, Korean law etc. and Chinese law are each compared with their own legal heritage, we may find that Chinese law would stand out as the one most divorced from its own traditions.' See Liang Zhiping, in 'The Sixth Civil Law Forum – Chinese Culture and Chinese Civil Code', 13 May 2004, China University of Political Science and Law, available at <www.ccelaws.com/mjlt/default.asp> (accessed 10 June 2004).

as the introduction of the western values that underpin the western law. Common sense dictates that the incorporation of adopted western law and western values in a non-western country takes time.[23] We must therefore not jump to the conclusion that Chinese law is now western law in a Continental civil law fashion.[24] There is clearly a divorce between western law and western values, which operates at two levels. First, although the study of foreign law continues to be a celebrated cause, there has been little sophisticated study of the context of foreign laws. It is not uncommon to note deputies to the National People's Congress talking about foreign legal stipulations (and they are very knowledgeable), but few ever explain why a particular legal provision exists in one country but not in another. In short, foreign laws are adopted with little understanding of their context. Secondly, legal transplantation in China until now has been largely a process of adoption not adaptation. Until very recently there has been little study on whether there are 'local conditions' or 'local resources' (*bentu ziquan*) for the adoption of foreign law; that is, whether there is an environment in which 'transplanted' law could work in transitional China.[25] Too often local customary laws and practices are dismissed as being 'backwards' or 'old and bad habits', more often impeding economic and legal development than enhancing it, but too few have bothered to explain the reasons for their existence.[26] With the recent emphasis

---

23 Here Taiwan offers a good case study for examining changes of attitudes and values, and difficulties in the operation of adopted foreign laws. See Herbert H.P. Ma, 'The Chinese Concept of the Individual and the Reception of Foreign Law', 1995 (9:2) *Journal of Chinese Law* 207; and Wan Tay-sheng (translated by Sean Cooney), 'The Impact of Modern Western Law on the Chinese in Taiwan', 1999 1 (2) *The Australian Journal of Asian Law* 194.

24 Here I am not suggesting, as Mattei has, that China (along with other East and South East Asian countries) belongs to 'the rule of traditional law' category. See Ugo Mattei, 'Three Patterns of Law: Taxonomy and Change in the World's Legal Systems', 1997 (45) *Am. J. Comp. L.* 5.

25 I am not suggesting that there has been no discourse on the need to adapt foreign laws to local circumstances. The emphasis on 'Chinese characteristics' in itself would in fact demand a consideration of the suitability of any adoption of foreign legal sources. However, such a consideration has been more often politically oriented towards establishing a 'socialist' law than a 'Chinese' law, and most importantly a comprehensive and systematic study of Chinese legal heritage, cultures and traditional practices, and their continuing influences in China is only a very recent phenomenon. See *infra* note 26.

26 The recent signs are however promising, evidencing the emergence of some serious studies on China's own 'local conditions'. Among the most serious scholars on the study of 'local conditions' is the Dean of Beijing University Law School, Professor Zhu Suli (pen name Su Li). For a recent representative work by Zhu Suli, see Su Li, *Roads to Cities – Rule of Law in Transitional China* (*Daolu Tongxiang Chengshi – Zhuanxing Zhong de Fazhi*) (Beijing: Law Press, 2004). For an analysis of his studies, see Albert Chen, 'Socio-legal Thought and Legal Modernisation in Contemporary China: A Case Study of the Jurisprudence of Zhu Suli', in Doeker-Mach & Ziegert, *supra* note 3, at 227-249. Other serious works include: Tian Chengyou, (Vice-President of the Yuannan High Court), *Local Customary Law in Rural Societies (Xiangtu Shehui Zhong de Minjianfa*) (Beijing: Law Press, 2005); Gao Qicai (ed), *Chinese Customary Law* (*Zhongguo Xiguan Fa Lun*) (Changsha: Hunan Press, 1992). Of course, there are scholars who advocate

by the Party on creating a harmonious society, there are some reasons to hope that an environment has perhaps been created for legal scholars and law-makers to pay more attention to potential conflicts between adopted laws and local conditions. If that is to be the case, adaptation not just adoption of law will begin, and thus the transformation of law may finally make Chinese law Chinese, while still meeting commonly accepted international standards for justice and fairness.

Law-in-the-book is not necessarily the same as law-in-action. Herein lies the most glaring failure in modern legal development in China. As discussed in Chapter 18, there is no lack of measures by the Supreme People's Court, the Supreme People's Procuratorate, and many other law-enforcement authorities, although they are often *ad hoc* and experimental. And indeed many of these measures are innovative, admirable and reasonably well implemented, but few have achieved their intended objectives. The tremendous difficulties experienced by Chinese courts in our two case studies in Chapter Eighteen, on enforcing court judgements/decisions and protecting intellectual property, are but two examples of the limitations on fundamental political reform, which cannot be carried out without authorisation from the Party. In short, the problems in this area are massive and deeply rooted in the fundamental politico-economic system of China. The root of these problems is power, or more precisely, the lack of checks and balances of power - a problem described by a Chinese economist as the 'privatisation of public power.'[27] If law cannot be independently enforced, as one Chinese scholar has noted,[28] it is doubtful whether it is important to have law at all.

What China now clearly needs are meaningful mechanisms for checks and balances. As pointed out in Chapters Three and Six, some forms of constitutional and administrative checks have indeed been established, but there is a significant lack of development in power balances. While it is clear that political reform is seriously lagging behind economic reform, it is most difficult to predict when the catch-up will start. What is also clear is that the establishment of balances relies heavily on political reform. Thus, as Chinese scholars have reminded us, the next 'liberation of legal thought' awaits a Party decision to deepen political reform.[29]

---

that 'if Chinese legal culture is to be built upon local resources, then the Chinese culture will never be modernised.' See Ai Yongmin, 'Several Questions on Modernisation of Chinese Law', originally published in 2005 (11) *Social Sciences* (*Shehui Kexue*) 52, reprinted in 2006 (1) *Jurisprudence and History of Laws* (*Falixue Fashixue*) 49, at 53. They believe modernisation of Chinese law simply means harmonising with international practices (at 50).

27 Tang Xiaotian, '"Strictly Rule the Party" and Constitutional Litigation', (No. 2, 2002) *Journal of Jiangsu Administrative College* (*Jiangsu Xingzheng Xueyuan Xuebao*) 104, at 105.

28 Zhao Sanying, 'On Rule of Law in a Market Economy', *Economic Daily* (*Jingji Ribao*), 2 May 1994, at 5.

29 See Guo Daohui, Li Buyun, Hao Tiechuan (eds), *A Record of the Contention on the Science of Law in Contemporary China* (*Zhongguo Dangdai Faxue Zhengming Shilu*) (Changsha: Hunan People's Press, 1998), at 1.

Select Bibliography

1. Sources of Chinese Law and Documents

For the first time in the PRC, the Law on Law-making (2000) (Articles 52, 53, 62, 70, and 77) now defines the official version of laws, regulations and rules. Specifically, the official versions of the laws are those published in the gazettes of the law/rule-making authorities. English translations (not of all laws) are available from many sources, including government websites and commercial publications. However, none is 'official' even though some of the translations are claimed to be 'authorised' or 'endorsed' by law/rule-making authorities.

1.1. Major Official Publications

The following are the major gazettes which contain the official version of laws, regulations, rules, and judicial interpretations:

Gazette of the Standing Committee of the National People's Congress of the PRC (*Zhonghua Renmin Gongheguo Quanguo Renmin Daibia Dahui Changwu Weiyuanhui Gongbao*);

Gazette of the State Council of the PRC (*Zhonghua Renmin Gongheguo Guowuyuan Gongbao*);

Gazette of the Supreme People's Court of the PRC (*Zhonghua Renmin Gongheguo Zuigao Renmin Fayuan Gongbao*);

Gazette of the Supreme People's Procuratorate of the PRC (*Zhonghua Renmin Gongheguo Zuigao Renmin Jianchayuan Gongbao*); and

Gazettes of the various ministries and commissions under the State Council, as well as legislative and administrative authorities at the provincial level.

Most of these gazettes are also published on-line and free on the internet. In addition to Google search, a good entry point is the Chinese Government-on-line: <www.gov.cn>.

1.2. Major Newspapers/News Agencies

Even with an on-line version, the publication of gazettes often takes a few months to appear. This 'deficiency' is rectified by the quick publication of the newly adopted laws, regulations, rules and judicial interpretations by the relevant enacting authorities on their own websites. Additionally, the following newspapers/news agencies are often 'authorised' to publish the full texts of new enactments:

Xinhua News Agency: <www.xinhua.org>.
People's Daily (*Renmin Ribao*): <www.people.com.cn>.
Legal Daily (*Fazhi Ribao*): <www.legaldaily.com.cn>.

Most law school websites in China also provide a free 'quick delivery of laws & regulations' service on their websites.

1.3. Determining the Validity of Laws, Regulations, Rules and Other Legal Documents

Chinese law and other legal documents are nowadays published quickly in many sources, both official and commercial. Finding the latest law is no longer a major research problem, but determining the status of validity of specific laws, regulations and especial departmental and local rules is a constant struggle. It is not at all uncommon that the websites of rule-making authorities contain out of date regulations and rules – they have been either already repealed or revised. There is no simple solution for this problem other than careful research. Fortunately Chinese law and rule making authorities have, in recent years, moved to undertake systematic reviws of legal enactments. The results of these reviews are published in the official gazettes and websites of the reviewing authorities. Further, the Standing Committee of the NPC has increasingly strengthened its work on filing-for-record of all laws, regulations, rules and judicial interpretations, as well as reviwing these legal enactments. As a result, some internet databases of laws now contain annotated notes on the validity of legal enactments. A good example is the database maintained by the Standing Committee of the NPC (<www.npc.gov.cn>). Towards the end of each law contained therein, there is a list of subsequent decisions and other related laws, and explanations of bills. Another excellent service is the law database maintained by the Legal Affairs Office of the State Council (<www.chinalaw.gov.cn>), which also provides a clear indication of the validity of laws, regulations, departmental and local rules and judicial interpretations contained therein.

1.4. Commercial Publications

Almost as soon as China began its efforts to rebuild its legal system, commercial collections of laws appeared. In 1990 the State Council moved to define certain 'authorised' publications as 'official' version of collections of laws. This however did not stop the flourishing of commercial publications. Since the Law on Law-making defines the laws published in official gazettees as the official versions, any commercial publication claiming to be an 'official' version is perhaps doubtful.

Commercial publications of laws are useful for research purposes as they usually provide some 'added value': the inclusion of laws promulgated in the early days of the PRC and policy (sometimes Party policy) documents, and special collections for specific purposes or areas of laws.

(1) Loose-leaf Services

There are many loose-leaf services available, including the following:

Laws and Regulations of the People's Republic of China (*Zhonghua Renmin Gongheguo Falü Fagui*) (Beijing: Law Press), loose-leaf service since 1995 (Chinese).

Laws and Regulations of the People's Republic of China (Beijing: Law Press), loose-leaf service since 2001 (English).

China Laws for Foreign Business (Singapore: CCH Asia), loose-leaf service since 1985 (bilingual).

China Law Reference Service (Asia Law & Practice Ltd, Hong Kong), loose-leaf service since 1996 (bilingual) (now ceased).

Statutes and Regulations of the People's Republic of China (Hong Kong: Institute of Chinese Law (Publishers) Ltd.), loose-leaf service (English) (now ceased).

(2) Collections of Laws in Chinese

There are many commercial publications of collection of laws and regulations published in China. The following include those that are comprehensive in coverage; other more specialised collections are indicated in the footnotes in this book:

Chinese Laws and Regulations (*Zhongguo Fagui*) (Beijing: Press of the Chinese Legal System, 2002), supplemented annually.

A Complete Collection of Laws of the PRC (*Zhonghua Renmin Gongheguo Falü Quanshu*) (Changchun: Jilin People's Press), first published in 1989, supplemented annually since 1990.

A Collection of Normative Interpretations of Laws in the PRC (*Zhonghua Renmin Gongheguo Falü Guifanxing Jieshi Jicheng*) (Changchun: Jilin People's Press, 1990), supplemented annually.

A Complete Collection of Judicial Interpretations of the Supreme People's Court of the PRC (October 1949 – June 1993) (*Zhonghua Renmin Gongheguo Zuigao Renmin Fayuan Sifa Jieshi Quanji*), edited by the Research Division of the Supreme People's Court and published by the Press of the People's Court (1994).

A Complete Collection of Legislative, Judicial and Administrative Interpretations [of Laws] in the People's Republic of China (*Zhonghua Renmin Gongheguo Lifa Sifa Xingzheng Jieshi Quanshu*), six volumes (Beijing: Yanshi Press, 1997).

A Selection of Local Regulations and Rules (*Difangxing Fagui Xuanbian*), two volumes (Beijing: China Economics Press, 1991).

The China Law Yearbook (*Zhongguo Falü Nianjian*) (Beijing: China Law Yearbook Press, first published 1987).

Laws and Regulations of China Database (*Guojia Falü Shujü Ku*), CD and Internet Services, Beijing, State Economic Information Centre.

(3) Collections of Laws in English

There is no up-to-date and comprehensive collection of Chinese laws in English, other than the loose-leaf services mentioned above, or specialised collections referred to in the footnotes in this book. However, most government websites also maintain some selected translations of laws, regulations, rules and judicial interpretations. Further, *China Law and Practice* (a monthly bilingual journal, Hong Kong) publishes full texts of selected newly adopted laws, regulations and judicial interpretations.

2. Academic Works in Chinese

The following do not include all the articles or books referred to in this book; they include only those that are significant for further research and study.

'A Market Economy and the Modernisation of a Legal System – Speeches Given at the Symposium on a Market Economy and the Modernisation of the Legal System', (no. 6, 1992) *Studies in Law* (*Faxue Yanjiu*) 2.

'A Summary of the 1997 Civil and Economic Law Section of the China Law Society Annual Conference', (no. 6, 1997) *Legal Science in China* (*Zhongguo Faxue*) 118.

'A Summary of the Symposium on the Draft Law on Law-Making', (no. 3, 1997) *Legal Science in China* (*Zhongguo Faxue*) 123.

'A Summary of Views Expressed at the Symposium on the Study of Chinese Civil Law-making', (no. 3, 1992) *Legal Science in China* (*Zhongguo Faxue*) 120.

'A Summary Report of the Symposium on New Topics for Civil and Economic Law in a Socialist Market Economy', (no. 4, 1993) *Legal Science in China* (*Zhongguo Faxue*) 119.

'Considerations and Proposals for Strengthening the Work of Supervision by the NPC – A Summary of Newspaper and Journal Discussions', (no. 6, 1990) *Legal Science in China* (*Zhonggu Faxue*) 13.

'Forty Years of the Chinese Criminal Procedure Science', *Journal of the China University of Political Science and Law* (*Zhengfa Luntan*), Pt I in no. 4, 1989, at 5-14, Pt. II in no. 5, 1989, at 1-8.

'Further Emancipating Minds and Making Great Efforts for the Prosperity of Legal Science – A Discussion in Commemorating the 10th Anniversary of the Re-establishment of the China Law Society', (no. 4, 1992) *Legal Science in China* (*Zhongguo Faxue*) 13.

'Further Emancipating Minds and Making Great Efforts for the Prosperity of Legal Research – A Discussion on Deng Xiaoping's Talk during his Southern Tour', (no. 5,1992) *Studies in Law* (*Faxue Yanjiu*) 1.

'Issues in Focus for New Marriage Law', <www.china.org.cn/english/1993.htm>.

'Jurisprudential Debate on the Relationship Between Rights and Duties', in (no. 4, 1991) *Xinhua Digest* (*Xinhua Wenzhai*) 16.

'Major Points of Speech Made in Wuchang, Shenzhen, Zhuhai and Shanghai [by Deng Xiaoping]', *People's Daily* (*Renmin Ribao*), 6 Nov. 1993, at 1.

'On Judicial Enforcement Systems and Theories – a Symposium', (no. 5, 1998) *Politics and Law* (*Zhengzhi yu Falu*) 4.

'Taking Traditions Seriously in Creating the Future – A Report on the Seminar on Recent American Academic Writings on Traditional Chinese Law', (no. 3, 1995) *Studies in Law* (*Faxue Yanjiu*) 84.

'The Search for a Theoretical Foundation of Administrative Law', (no. 5, 1996) *Peking University Law Journal* (*Zhongwai Faxue*) 51.

A Selection of Party Rules of the Communist Party of China (1978–1996) (*Zhongguo Gongchandang Dangnei Fagui Xuanji 1978–1996*) (Beijing: Publishing House of Law, 1996).

A, Tao & Zhu, Huan, 'The Import of Legal Science in the Late Qing Dynasty and its Historical Significance', (no. 6, 1990) *Journal of China University of Political Science and Law* (*Zhengfa Luntan*) 52.

Ai, Yongmin, 'Several Questions on Modernisation of Chinese Law', originally published in 2005 (11) *Social Sciences* (*Shehui Kexue*) 52, reprinted in 2006 (1) *Jurisprudence and History of Laws* (*Falixue Fashixue*) 49.

All China Women's Federation (ed.), *Important Documents on Chinese Women's Movement* (*Zhongguo Funiu Yuandong Zhongyao Wenxian*) (Beijing: People's Press, 1979).

All China Women's Federation, *Handbook on Marriage Law* (*Hunyinfa Shouce*) (Beijing: Publishing House of Law, 1980).

An, Jian & Wu, Gaosheng (eds), *A Practical Text on Enterprise Bankruptcy Law* (*Qiye Pochanfa Shiyong Jiaocheng*) (Beijing: China Legal Publishing House, 2006).

Bai, Ji & Li, Fushen, 'On Freedom of Divorce', (no. 1, 1997) *Journal of China University of Political Science and Law* (*Zhengfa Luntan*) 59.

Bian, Jianlin, 'Direct Contesting and the Reform of the Trial Process', (no. 6, 1995) *Legal Science in China* (*Zhongguo Faxue*) 96.

Building of Political Democracy in China, issued by the Information Office of the State Council, October 2005.

Cai, Dingjian & Liu, Xinghong, 'On Legislative Interpretation', (no. 6, 1993) *Legal Science in China* (*Zhongguo Faxue*) 36.

Cai, Dingjian, 'The Development of Constitutionalism in the Chinese Transitional Period', (no. 4, 2006) *Journal of East China University of Political Science and Law* (*Huadong Zhengfa Xueyuan Xuebao*) 3.

Cai, Dingjian, 'Towards a Private Law Approach to the Implementation of the Chinese Constitution', originally published in (no. 2, 2004) *Social Science in China* (*Zhongguo Shehui Kexue*), re-published in <www.usc.cuhk.edu.hk/wk.asp> (last accessed 12 November 2004).

Cao, Jianglun & Liu Defa, 'A Suggestion to Abolish *Guanzhi* as a Punishment in Our Criminal Law', (no. 1, 1990) *Legal Science in China* (*Zhongguo Faxue*) 71.

Cao, Jianming, 'New Development in Judicial Protection of Intellectual Property', (no. 4, 2004) *Intellectual Property* (*Zhishi Chanquan*) 9.

Cao, Jianming, 'Speech by the Vice-President of the Supreme People's Court', delivered at the National Conference on IP Adjudication, 18 January 2007, available at <www.chinaiprlaw.cn/file/2007020210142htm> (last accessed 15 February 2007).

Cao, Jianming, Sun, Chao, and Gu, Changhao, 'The Socialist Legal System Has to Favour the Liberation and Development of the Productive Forces', 1992 (4) *Legal Science in China* (*Zhongguo Faxue*) 8.

Cao, Kangtai, 'Implementing the Administrative Litigation Law and Promoting Administration by Law', (no. 4, 1995) *Administrative Law Review* (*Xingzhengfa Yanjiu*) 7.

Cao, Quanlai, *Internationalisation and Localisation: the Formation of the Modern Chinese Legal System* (*Guojihua yu Bentuhua – Zhongguo Jindai falü Tixi de Xingcheng*), Beijing: Beijing University Press (2005).

Cao, Siyuan, 'The Legislation and Implementation of China's Bankruptcy Law in the Past Ten Years', *Modern China Study* (Issue No 2, 1997) available at <www.usc.cuhk.edu.hk/wk_WZdetals.asp?id=1028> (last accessed 12 September 2006).

Cao, Zidan & Hou, Guoyun (eds), *A Precise Interpretation of the Criminal Law of the PRC*, (*Zhonghua Renmin Gongheguo Xingfa Jingjie*) (Beijing: China University of Political Science and Law Press, 1997).

Chang, Hanchu, *A History of the Modern Chinese Legal System* (*Zhongguo Jindai Fazhishi*) (Taipei: The Commercial Press, 1973).

Chang, Yi & Chui, Jie, 'Several Issues for the Improvement of Compulsory Civil Enforcement', (no. 1, 2000) *Legal Science in China* (*Zhongguo Faxue*) 97.

Chen, Chunlong, 'A Study on the System of Multi-party Cooperation under the Leadership of the Communist Party and Its Legal Problems', (no. 3, 1995) *Studies in Law & Commerce* (*Fashang Yanjiu*) 8.

Chen, Guangzhong (ed.), *Expert Draft on Further Revision of the Criminal Procedural Law of the PRC and Its Explanations* (*Zhonghua Renmin Gongheguo Xingshi Susong Fa Zaixiugai Zhuanjia Jianyigao Yu Lunzheng*) (Beijing: China Legal System Press, 2006).

Chen, Guangzhong (ed.), *The Procedure on Criminal Re-trial and the Protection of Human Rights* (*Xingshi Zaishen Chengxu yu Renquan Baozhang*) (Beijing: Beijing University Press, 2005).

Chen, Guangzhong and Yan Duanzhu, *A Draft and its Explanation on the Revision of Criminal Procedure Law* (Beijing: China Fangzheng Press, 1995).

Chen, Guangzhong, 'The Principle of the Presumption of Innocence Should be Critically Adopted', (no. 4, 1980) *Studies in Law* (*Faxue Yanjiu*) 34.

Chen, Guangzhong, *et al.*, 'The Market Economy and the Future of the Science of Criminal Procedure Law', (no. 5, 1993) *Legal Science in China* (*Zhongguo Faxue*) 3.

Chen, Guyuan, *An Outline of Chinese History* (*Zhongguo Fazhishi Gaiyao*), 4th edition (Taipei: Sanmin Shuju, 1970).

Chen, Jianfu, 'Some Thoughts on Certain Fundamental Issues in Relation to the Making of an Administrative Procedure Law', (no. 2, 1996) *Administrative Law Review* (*Xingzheng Fa Yanjiu*) 58.

Chen, Jianguo, 'The Principle of the Presumption of Innocence Should be Written into the Criminal Procedure Law', (no. 5, 1994) *Legal Science in China* (*Zhongguo Faxue*) 35.

Chen, Sixi, 'On the Division of Legislative Powers in Our Country', (no. 1, 1995) *Legal Science in China* (*Zhongguo Faxue*) 12.

Chen, Weidong & Zhang, Tao, 'Research into Several Problems with Shelter and Investigation', (no. 2, 1992) *Legal Science in China* (*Zhongguo Faxue*) 82.

Chen, Xingliang, 'Dual Task for Criminal Revision: Change in Values and Adjustment of Structure', (no. 1, 1997) *Peking University Law Journal* (*Zhongwai Faxue*) 55.

Chen, Xingliang, '*Nullum Creme Noena Peona Sine Lege* in Modern Times', (no. 2, 1996) *Studies in Law* (*Faxue Yanjiu*) 11.

Chen, Xingliang, 'On the Development and Improvement of Our Criminal Law', (no. 3, 1989) *Legal Science in China* (*Zhongguo Faxue*) 53.

Chen, Yanqing & Xu, Anbiao, 'Clarify the NPC's External Relations and Invigorate the NPC', (no. 6, 1990) *Legal Science in China* (*Zhongguo Faxue*) 10.

Chen, Yanqing, 'On the Procedures and Limitations of Legislative Supervision in Our Country', (no. 3, 1995) *Legal Science in China* (*Zhongguo Faxue*) 27.

Chen, Zhixian, 'On Criminal Law Issues Concerning Legal Persons', (no. 6, 1986) *Political Science and Law* (*Zhengzhi Yu Falu*) 41.

Chen, Ziqiao, 'The Way to Invigorate Enterprises – Joint-stock System in China', (no. 3, 1988) *Legal Construction* (*Fazhi Jianshe*) 6.

Cheng, Rongbing, 'Coercive Measures and Shelter and Investigation', (no. 5, 1994) *Legal Science in China* (*Zhongguo Faxue*) 38.

Cheng, Yi, 'The Problems with the "Theory of Balance"', (no. 4, 1996) *Administrative Law Review* (*Xingzheng Faxue Yanjiu*) 38.

Cheng, Yüpo, *General Principles of Civil Law* (*Minfa Zongze*), 7th edition (Taipei: Shanmin Shuju, 1988).

China Law Society (ed.), *A Collection of Articles on Ma Zedong's Legal Theories* (*Ma Zedong Xixian Faxue Lilun Lunwen Xuan*) (Beijing: Law Publishing House, 1985).

China University of Political Science and Law (ed.), *Research into and Discussions on Theoretical and Practical Problems of Criminal Procedure* (Beijing: Law Publishing House, 1987).

China University of Political Science and Law, *A Study on the Legal Thought of Shen Jiaben* (*Shen Jiaben Falü Sixiang Yanjiu*) (Beijing: Publishing House of Law, 1990).

Chinese Encyclopaedia – Law (*Zhongguo Dabaike Quanshu – Faxue*) (Beijing/Shanghai: The Chinese Encyclopaedia Press, 1984).

Chinese Society of Legal Science (ed.), *A Selection of Papers on the Constitution* (*Xianfa Lunwen Xuan*) (Beijing: Press of the Masses, 1983).

Chu, Huaizhi, 'The Contradiction between Crimes and Punishments and the Reform of the Criminal Law', (no. 5, 1994) *Legal Science in China* (*Zhongguo Faxue*) 107.

Chu, Huazhi, 'Criminal Law Revision and Criminal Law Policy', in (no. 1, 1997) *Peking University Law Journal* (*Zhongwai Faxue*) 49.

Chu, Jianyuan, & Shen, Weixing (eds), *A Study on the Difficult Issues in the Enactment of a Law on Rights in rem* (Beijing: Qinghua University Press, 2005).

Cong, Xuangong, 'Applying Foreign Things for Chinese Use through Reference and Creation', 1992 (1) *Journal of the China University of Political Science and Law* (*Zhangfa Luntan*) 69.

Cui, Min, 'A Summary of the Discussions on Revising and Perfecting the Criminal Procedure Law', (no. 1, 1995) *Modern Law Science* (*Xiandai Faxue*) 92.

Cui, Min, 'Abolishing the Exemption from Prosecution', (no. 5, 1994) *Legal Science in China* (*Zhongguo Faxue*) 44.

Cui, Qingsen & Liao Zengyun, 'On Limited and Cautious Use of the Death Penalty', (no. 2, 1989) *Studies in Law* (*Faxue Yanjiu*) 69.

Cui, Zhuolan, 'A Discussion on the Reviewability of *Guizhang*', (no. 1, 1996) *Studies in Law* (*Faxue Yanjiu*) 140.

Cui, Zhuolan, Son Bo & Luo Mengyan, 'An Empirical Analysis of the Growth Trend of Local Legislation', originally published in (no. 5, 2005) *Jilin University Journal of Social Sciences* (*Jilin Daxue Shehuixue Xuebao*), reprinted in <www.usc.cuhk.edu.hk/wk.asp> (last accessed 17 July 2006).

Dai, Yanhui, *A Chinese Legal History* (*Zhongguo Fazhishi*), 3rd edition (Taipei: Sanmin Shuju, 1971).

Deng Xiaoping On Democracy and Legal Construction (*Deng Xiaoping Lun Minzhu Yu Fazhi Jianshe*) (Beijing: Law Publishing House, 1994).

Deng, Hongbi, 'Some Considerations for Improving Our Marriage and Family System (Part I)', in (no. 1, 1997) *Modern Law Review* (*XiandaiFaxue*) 41.

Dong, Kaijun & Li, Cheng, 'On Legal Forms of Enterprises', (no. 4, 1992) *Legal Science in China* (*Zhongguo Faxue*) 65.

Duan, Qinguan, 'A Brief Discussion on the Evolution of Legal Ideology in Qin and Han Dynasties', (no. 5, 1980) *Studies in Law* (*Faxue Yanjiu*) 45.

Editorial Board of China Today, *Adjudication in China Today* (*Dandai Zhongguo de Shenpan Gongzuo*), vol. 1 (Beijing: Press of China Today, 1993).

Editorial Board of *Studies in Law*, *A Summary of Civil Law Research in the New China* (*Xin Zhongguo Minfaxue Yanjiu Zongshu*) (Beijing: Press of Chinese Social Sciences, 1990).

Editorial Board, *A Handbook of Legal Sources on Administrative Penalties* (*Xingzheng Chufa Falü Yiju Shouce*) (Beijing: Press of the Chinese Legal System, 1997).

Family Planning in China, issued by the Information Office of the State Council of the PRC, August 1995.

Fan, Fenglin, 'Several Thoughts on the Presumption of Innocence', (no. 5, 1994) *Legal Science in China* (*Zhongguo Faxue*) 36.

Fan, Zhongxin, 'A Comparative Approach to Crimes Against Family Relatives', (no. 3, 1997) *CASS Journal of Law* (*Faxue Yanjiu*) 117.

Fang Shaokun, 'On Correcting Civil Legislation Deficiencies', (no. 1, 1993) *Legal Science in China* (*Zhongguo Faxue*) 29.

Fang, Jian, 'Internationalisation of Law and the Development of Jurisprudence', 1993 (3) *Law Science* (*Falü Kexue*) 9.

Fang, Liufang, 'The Company Examination and Approval System and Administrative Monopoly', (no. 4, 1992) *Legal Science in China* (*Zhongguo Faxue*) 56.

Fundamental Issues of Civil Law in the PRC (*Zhonghua Renmin Gonghe Guo Minfa Jiben Wenti*), (edited by the Teaching Section of Civil Law of the Central Judicial Cadres' School, published by the Publishing House of Law, Beijing, 1958).

Gan, Zangchuan, 'How to Secure the Legitimacy of Reform – From Reliance on Policy to Reliance on Law', (no. 6, 1991) *Studies in Law* (*Faxue Yanjiu*) 3.

Gao, Lu, 'The Emergence of the Notion of "Socialist market Economy"' (no. 1, 1993) *Xinhua Digest* (*Xinhua Wenzhai*) 40.

Gao, Mingxuan (ed.), *A Summary of Criminal Law Research in the New China* (*Xinzhongguo Xingfa Yanjiu Zongshu*) (Henan: Henan People's Press, 1986).

Gao, Mingxuan, Zhao Bingzhi & Wang Yong, 'A Review of the Criminal Legislation in the Past Ten Years and Prospect', (no. 2, 1989) *Legal Science in China* (*Zhongguo Faxue*) 66.

Gao, Qicai, *On Chinese Customary Law* (*Zhongguo Xiguan Fa Lun*) (Changsha: Hunan Press, 1995).

Geng, Cheng, 'The Market Economy and Internationalisation of the Legal System', 1994 (11) *Economic Law* (*Jingji Fazhi*) 2.

Gong, Pixiong, 'Four Great Contradictions Facing the Modernisation of Chinese Law', 1995 *Research and Debate* (*Tansuo Yu Zhengming*) 3.

Gu, Angran, *An Outline of Law-making in New China* (*Xin Zhongguo Lifa Gaishu*) (Beijing: Publishing House of Law, 1995).

Gu, Angran, *The Socialist Legal System and Legislative Work* (*Shehui Zhuyi Fazhi He Lifa Gongzuo*) (Beijing: China University of Political Science and Law Press, 1989).

Gu, Gongyun, 'Several Difficult Questions Concerning Legislation on Shareholding Cooperatives', Part I in (no. 8, 1997) *Legal Science* (*Faxue*) 49, Part II in (no. 9, 1997) *Legal Science* (*Faxue*) 39.

Gui, Hongming, *A Study of the Civil Customary Law Survey during the Late Qing and Early KMT* (*Qingmo Minchu Minshangshi Xiguan Tiaocha Zhi Yanjiu*) (Beijing: Law Press, 2005).

Guo, Daohui, 'Authority, Power or Rights: Some Considerations on the Relationship between the Party and the People's Congress', in (no. 1, 1994) *Studies in Law* (*Faxue Yanjiu*) 3.

Guo, Daohui, Li, Buyun, & Hao, Tiechuan (eds), *A Record of Legal Debate in Contemporary China* (*Zhongguo Dandai Faxue Zhengming Shilu*) (Changsha: Hunan People's Press, 1998).

Guo, Daohui, *The Law-making System in China* (*Zhongguo Lifa Zhidu*) (Beijing: People's Press, 1988).

Guo, Daoxu, 'The Market Economy and the Changes in Legal Theory and Legal Thought', (no. 2, 1994) *Jurisprudence* (*Faxue*) 2.

Guo, Guoyun & Lu, Erping, 'On Reasons for and Damages Caused by Problems in Enforcement under the Conditions of a Market Economy and Their Responses', (no. 1, 1996) *Journal of China University of Political Science and Law* (*Zhengfa Luntan*) 75.

Hang, Li, 'On the Informality and Political Functions of Law-making in China', first published in (no. 2, 2002) *Research in Contemporary China* (*Dandai Zhongguo Yanjiu*), reprinted in <www.usc.cuhk.hk/wk_wzdetails.asp?id=1685> (last accessed 10 May 2004).

Hao, Tiechuan, 'Law Students Studying Abroad in Modern Chinese History and the Modernisation of Chinese Law', (no. 6, 1997) *CASS Journal of Law* (*Faxue Yanjiu*) 3.

He, Hangzhou, 'On Legal Transplant and the Construction of an Economic Legal System', (no. 5, 1992) *Legal Science in China* (*Zhongguo Faxue*) 50.

He, Qinghua & Li, Xiuqing, *Foreign Law and Chinese Law – An Examination of the Transplanting of Foreign Law into China in the 20th Century* (*Zhongguofa Yu Waiguofa – Ershishiji Zhongguo Yizhi Waiguofa Fansi*) (Beijing: Press of China University of Political Science and Law, 2003).

He, Qinghua, Li, Xiuqing, & Chen, Yu (eds), *A Complete Collection of Draft Civil Codes in the New China* (*Xin Zhongguo Minfadian Cao'an Zonglan*) (Beijing: Law Press, 2003).

He, Weifang, 'Difficulties in Establishing the Rule of Law and Solutions', published in <www.sinoliberal.com/hwf/hwf2003010502.htm>.

He, Weifang, 'The Force and Obstacles to Constitutionalism', published in <law-thinker.com/details.asp?id=1754> (last accessed 21/11/04).

He, Zhidong (ed.), *A Practical Guide to the Current Export Tax Refund/Exemption* (*Xianxing Chukou Tuimianshui Caozuo Zhinan*) (Beijing: China Machine Press, 2002).

Hong, Bing, 'Major Measures to Perfect the Criminal Procedure System', (no. 3, 1996) *Politics and Law* (*Zhangzhi Yu Falü*) 13.

Hou, Guoyun & Lu, Erping, 'Dangers, Causes and Responses to Enforcement Difficulties under a Market Economy', (1996) (no. 1) *Journal of China University of Political Science and Law* (*Zhengfa Luntan*) 75.

Hou, Guoyun, '*Nullum Crimen, Nulla Poena Sine Lege* in a Market Economy and the Value of Criminal Analogy', (no. 3, 1995) *Studies in Law* (*Faxue Yanjiu*) 61.

Hu Jianmiao & Gao Chunyan, 'Constitutional Review of Law and Regulation in China – Problems and Solutions', in (no 3, 2006), *Printed Newspaper and Journal Articles (D411 Constitutional & Administrative Law)* 46.

Hu, Xuexiang, 'Improving the Legislative Structure on Punishment', (no. 2, 1996) *Modern Law Science* (*Xiandai Faxue*) 124.

Hu, Xuexiang, 'The Problems in the Principle of Proportionality and Their Solutions', (no. 3, 1994) *Law Review* (*Faxue Pinglun*) 18.

Hu, Yunteng, 'Abolition of Analogy and the Scientific Nature of Criminal Law', (no. 5, 1995) *Studies in Law* (*Faxue Yanjiu*) 55.

Hu, Yunteng, *To Abolish or to Continue: A Theoretical Study on the Death Penalty (Quan yu Fei: Shixing Jiben Lilun Yanjiu)* (Beijing: China Procuratorial Press, 2000).

Hu, Zhixin (ed.), *A History of the United Front of the Communist Party of China* (*Zhongguo Gongchandang Tongyi Zhanxian Shi*) (Beijing: Huaxia Press, 1988).

Hua Yougen, 'The Guiding Principles and Ideological Influence of the Qing Draft of a Civil Code', (no. 5, 1988) *Political Science and Law* (*Zhnegzhi Yu Falü*) 46.

Huang, Shengye (ed.), *A Lawyer's Handbook* (*Lüshi Shouce*) (Beijing: Press of the Economic Daily, 1996).

Huang, Taiyun and Teng, Wei (eds), *A Practical Guide and Interpretation of the Criminal Law of the PRC* (*Zhonghua Renmin Gongheguo Xingfa Shiyi Yu Shiyong Zhinan*) (Beijing: The Redflag Press, 1997).

Huang, Taiyun, 'Major Reforms in the Criminal Processes – An Outline of the Major Revisions to the Criminal Procedure Law', (no. 2, 1996) *Legal Science in China* (*Zhongguo Faxue*) 29.

Intellectual Property Protection in China, issued by the Information Office of the State Council in June 1994.

Jia, Yu, 'Reduction of Capital Offence – An Important Aspect of Criminal Law Reform', (no. 1, 1997) *Politics and Law* (*Zhengzhi Yu Falü*) 7.

Jiang, Bikun et *al.* (ed.), *Constitutional Law* (*Xianfa Xue*) (Beijing: China University of Political Science and Law Press, 1993).

Jiang, Lihua, 'On the Retention and Improvement of *Guanzhi* as a Punishment', (no. 1, 1990) *Legal Science in China* (*Zhongguo Faxue*) 66.

Jiang, Ming'An, 'Delegation of Powers, Separation of Powers and Control of Powers – The Reasons for the Existence of Administrative Law on the Theory of Balance', (no. 5, 1996) *Peking University Law Journal* (*Zhongwai Faxue*) 51.

Jiang, Ming'an, 'Eight Major Relationships concerning the Administrative Procedure Legislation', in (no. 4, 2006) *Reprinted Newspaper and Journal Materials: D411 Constitiutional and Administrative Law* (*Xianfaxue Xingzhengfaxu*) 23.

Jiang, Mingan (ed.), *Survey Report on the Development and Progress of China's Administrative Rule of Law* (Beijing: Law Publishing House, 1998).

Jiang, Ping & Mi, Jian, 'On Civil Law Tradition and Contemporary Chinese Law – Part II', (no. 3, 1993) *Journal of China University of Political Science and Law* (*Zhengfa Luntan*), 1.

Jiang, Tianbo, 'Several Considerations on Legislation on Enterprise Entities', 6 November 2003, in China Government Law Info net: <www.chinalaw.gov.cn>.

Jiang, Wei & Xiao, Jianguo, 'Several Questions concerning the Civil Enforcement System', (no. 1, 1995) *Legal Science in China* (*Zhongguo Faxue*) 67.

Jing, Hanchao, 'On Difficulties in Enforcement and Counter-Measures', (no. 5, 2000) *Journal of China University of Political Science and Law* (*Zhengfa Luntan*) 124.

Kang, Yunshen, 'On Ma Zedong's Creative Contribution to the Marxist-Leninist Theory on the Death Penalty', (no. 6, 1991) *Zhengfa Luntan* 29.

Kong, Qingming, Hu, Liuyuan & Sun, Jiping (eds), *A History of Chinese Civil Law* (*Zhongguo Minfa Shi*) (Changchun: Jilin People's Press, 1996).

Kuang, Yamin, *A Critical Biography of Confucius* (*Kunazi Pingzhuan*) (Jinan: Qiru Press, 1985).

Lan, Quanpu, *Thirty Years of the Development of Law and Regulations in Our Country* (*Sanshi Nian Lai Woguo Fagui Yange Gaikuang*) (Beijing: Press of the Masses, 1982).

Lei, Xian (ed.), *A Practical Book on Sino-Foreign Contracts* (*Zhongwai Hetong (Qiyue) Falü Shiyong Quanshu*) (Beijing: China Economic Press, 1994).

Li, Baoyue, 'A Discussion on the Time When Lawyers Should Participate in the Criminal Process', (no. 4, 1994), *Legal Science in China* (*Zhongguo Faxue*) 98.

Li, Buyun (ed.), *A Comparative Study of Constitutional Law* (*Xianfa Bijiao Yanjiu*) (Beijing: Law Press, 1998).

Li, Buyun (ed.), *Studies in Law on Law-making* (*Lifafa Yanjiu*) (Changsha: Hunan People's Press, 1998).

Li, Changqi, Chao, Xingyong & Peng, Xingshi, 'Local Protectionism in Economic Trials Must Be Stopped', (no. 4, 1998) *Modern Legal Science* (*Xiandai Faxue*) 71.

Li, Chunlei, *A Study of the Transformation of the Criminal Procedure Law in Modern China* (1895–1928) (*Zhongguo Jindai Xingshi Susong Zhidu Biange Yanjiu 1895–1928*) (Beijing: Beijing University Press, 2004).

Li, Chunmao (ed.), *Chinese Civil Law: Intellectual Property* (Beijing: China Public Security University Press, 1997),

Li, Guangcan (ed.), *On Criminal Law of the People's Republic of China* (*Zhonghua Renmin Gonghe Guo Xingfa Lun*), vol. 2 (Changchun: Jilin People's Press, 1981).

Li, Guilian, 'Legal Reforms in Modern China and the Japanese Influence', (no. 1, 1994) *Studies in Comparative Law* (*Bijiaofa Yanjiu*) 24.

Li, Huawei, 'A New Light in Constitutional Review in Mainland China?' available from the China Constitutionalism web: <www.calaw.cn/include/shownews.asp?newsid=2001> (last accessed 12 November 2004).

Li, Jianmin, 'Several Thoughts on the Reform of the Criminal Trial Process', (no. 1, 1995) *Studies in Law* (*Faxue Yanjiu*) 84.

Li, Jingbing, 'On the Significance of and Current Barriers to the Making of a Civil Code', (no. 5, 1992) *Law Science* (*Falü Kexue*) 37.

Li, Maoguan, 'The Legal Controversy Concerning the Separation of Public and Private Law', (no. 22, 1995) *Seeking Truth* (*Qiushi*) 44.

Li, Mingliang, 'Personal Opinions on Methods of Legislating on Crimes by Legal Persons', (no. 2, 1991) *Modern Law Science* (*Xiandai Faxue*) 61.

Li, Shaoping & Deng, Xiuming, 'Some Theoretical Considerations on Improving the Law on Crimes and Punishments', (no. 1, 1996) *Modern Law Science* (*Xiandai Faxue*) 9.

Li, Shuanyuan & Xiao, Beigen, 'Socialist Market Economy and the Direction of Legal Modernisation', 1994 (6) *Hunan Normal University Social Science Journal* (*Hunan Shifan Daxue Shehui Xuebao*) 11.

Li, Shuanyuan, Zhang, Mao & Du, Jian, 'A Study on the Assimilation of Chinese Law [with International Practice]', (no. 3, 1994) *Journal of Wuhan University* (*Wuhan Daxue Xuebao*) (Philosophy & Social Sciences) 3.

Li, Shuguang, 'Bankruptcy Law in China: Lessons of the Past Twelve Years', available from <www.asiaquartely.com/content/view/95/40> (last accessed 30/11/06).

Li, Shuguang, 'Extraterritorial Bankruptcy in China Will Have a Legal Basis', *People's Daily* (overseas edition), 22 September, 2006, at 5.

Li, Shunde, 'Chinese Legal Framework on Intellectual Property Protection', available at <www.chinaiprlaw.cn/file/200501224095.html> (last accessed 3 February 2005).

Li, Siqi, 'The Erosion of Legislative Power by the Judicial Power – on Judicial Interpretations by the Supreme People's Court', available from <www.cuhk.edu.hk/wk.asp> (last accessed 8 June 2007).

Li, Xihui, 'Some Considerations on Restructuring Criminal Legislation on Corporate Crimes', (no. 1, 1994) *Journal of China University of Political Science and Law* (*Zhengfa Luntan*) 16.

Li, Xuekuan, 'Some Legal Considerations on the Functions of Defence Lawyer in Our Country', (no. 6, 1995) *Legal Science in China* (*Zhongguo Faxue*) 90.

Li, Yahong, 'Some Thoughts on Central-Local Legislative Relationship during the Transitional Period', (no. 1, 1996) *Legal Science in China* (*Zhongguo Faxue*) 23.

Li, Yongjun, 'Procedural Structure of the Bankruptcy Law and the Balance of Interests', in (no. 1, 2007) *Journal of the China University of Political Science and Law* (*Zhengfa Luntan*) 17.

Li, Yusheng, 'A Comparative Study on the Traditional Chinese Law and the Rights *in rem* in Modern Civil Law – On the Relevant Rights *in rem* Provisions in the Draft Civil Code of the PRC', available from <www.iolaw.org.cn/shownews.asp?id=15252> (last accessed 19 January 2007).

Li, Zhimi, *Ancient Chinese Civil Law* (*Zhongguo Gudai Minfa*) (Beijing: Publishing House of Law, 1988).

Liang, Huixin, *Civil Law* (*Minfa*) (Chengdu: Sichuan People's Press, 1989).

Liang, Huixing, 'On the Third Draft of the Uniform Contract Law of China', (no. 1, 1997) *Jurisprudence Frontiers* (*Faxue Qianyan*) 186.

Liang, Huixing, 'The Chinese Inheritance of Foreign Civil Laws' (undated), published in <www.iolaw.org.paper32.asp> (accessed 27 July 2004).

Liang, Huixing, 'The Process of Chinese Civil Codification and Its Major Controversies', a paper delivered at the Sino-Japan Civil Law Symposium, Shangdong University, 25-26 October 2003, available from <www.iolaw.org.cn/paper/paper266.asp>.

Liang, Huixing, *A Proposed Draft of a Chinese Civil Code with Explanations – Rights in rem* (*Zhongguo Minfadian Cao'an Jianyigao Fu Liyou – Wuquan Bian*) (Beijing: Law Press, 2004).

Liang, Huixing, *Struggling for China's Civil Code* (*Wei Zhongguo Minfadian er Douzheng*) (Beijing: Law Press, 2002).

Liang, Zhiping, *Customary Law in Qing Dynasty: Society and State* (*Qingdai Xiguan Fa: Shehui yu Guojiao*) (Beijing: China University of Political Science and Law Press, 1996).

Liang, Zhiping, in 'The Sixth Civil Law Forum – Chinese Culture and Chinese Civil Code', 13 May 2004, China University of Political Science and Law, available at <www.ccelaws.com/mjlt/default.asp> (last accessed 10 June 2004).

Liang, Zhiping, *The Pursuit of Harmony in Natural Orders: A Study on Chinese Traditional Legal Culture* (*Xunqiu Ziran Zhixu Zhong De Hexie: Zhongguo Chuantong Falü Wenhua Yanjiu*) (Beijing: China University of Political Science and Law Press, 1997).

Liao, Zengyun, 'Basic Principles that Should Be Clearly Adopted in Our Criminal Law', (no. 1, 1990) *Legal Science in China* (*Zhongguo Faxue*) 54.

Liao, Zengyun, 'Views on the Principle of Presumption of Innocence', (no. 5, 1980) *Studies in Law* (*Faxue Ynajiu*) 32.

Lin, Jie, 'A Question on the Proposition "A Market Economy Is an Economy Under the Rule of Law"' (no. 1, 1994) *Legal Science in China* (*Zhongguo Faxue*) 68.

Lin, Rihua & Leng, Tiexun, 'On Legal Problems Relating to Rural Collective Enterprises', (no. 1, 1991) *Law Review* (*Faxue Pinglun*) 43.

Lin, Yagang & Jia, Yu, 'On the Character of Special Criminal Laws and Their Incorporation into the Criminal Code', (no. 1, 1997) *Peking University Law Journal* (*Zhongwai Faxue*) 79.

Liu Hainian, Li Buyuan & Li Lin (eds), *To Rule the Country according to Law and to Establish a Socialist Rule of Law Country* (*Yifa Zhiguo Jianshe Shehui Zhuyi Fazhi Guojia*) (Beijing: Press of Chinese Legal System, 1996).

Liu, Chunmao *et al.*, *Chinese Civil Law Science – Property Succession* (*Zhongguo Minfa Xue – Caichan Jicheng*) (Beijing: Press of the University of the Chinese People's Public Security, 1990).

Liu, Hehai & Gao, Xingwen, 'On Several Questions concerning Our State Law-making', (no. 2, 1995) *Journal on Politics and Law* (*Zhengfa Luncong*) 3.

Liu, Jinghua, 'Globalisation: An Historical Process Full of Paradoxes', (no. 1, 1995) *Pacific Studies* (*Taipingyan Xuebao*) 70.

Liu, Mingxing and Ma, Xiaoye, 'A Comprehensive Review of the Reform of the Chinese Foreign Trade System', available from <www.usc.cuhk.hk/wk_wzdetailss.asp?id=2953> (last accessed 10 March 2004).

Liu, Qishan *et al.*, *New Research into Civil Law Problems* (*Minfa Wenti Xintan*) (Beijing: Press of China University of Public Security, 1990).

Liu, Shengping *et a.l*, 'The Market Economy and Changes in Legal Ideologies', (no. 4, 1993) *Legal Science in China* (*Zhongguo Faxue*) 3.

Liu, Shengrong, 'The Present Situation of the Legislative Process and Methods to Perfect It', (no. 2, 1995) *Journal of the Central Administrative College for Prosecutors* (*Zhongyang Jianchaguan Guanli Xueyuan Xuebao*) 24.

Liu, Shiguo, 'On Civil Matters and the Law Governing Civil Matters', (no. 5, 1992) *Law Science* (*Falü Kexue*) at 45.

Liu, Shiguo, *et al*, *An Outline of Chinese Civil Law* (*Zhongguo Minfa Yiaolun*) (Shenyang: Liaoning University Press, 1992).

Liu, Xiaobing, 'Some Legal Considerations on Central-Local Relations', (no. 2, 1995) *Legal Science in China* (*Zhongguo Faxue*) 24.

Liu, Zheng, 'Further Constitutional Protection for the Construction of Socialism with Chinese Characteristics', (no. 2, 1993) *Zhongguo Faxue* (*Legal Science in China*) 5.

Liu, Zheng, 'Supervisory Work of the Standing Committee of the NPC – being the second seminar presented at the Standing Committee of the 10th NPC', July 2003, available from the *People's Daily,* internet edition: <www.peopledaily.com.cn> (accessed 30 September 2003).

Lü, Taifeng, 'On the New Revolution of the Administrative Law Science', (no. 6, 1995) *Journal of Zhengzhou University* (*Zhengzhou Daxue Xuebao*) 47.

Lu, Yun, 'Formation and Development of the System of Multi-Party Cooperation', (19-25 March 1990) *Beijing Review 16*

Lu, Yun, 'The Transformation of Legal Models: A Deep Revolutionary Change', (no. 1, 1994) *Legal Science in China* (*Zhongguo Faxue*) 27.

Luo, Haocai & Shen, Kui, 'A Theory of Balance: A Thought on the Nature of Modern Administrative Law – Some Further Discussions on the Theoretical Foundation of Contemporary Administrative Law', (no 4, 1996) *Peking University Law Journal* (*Zhongwai Faxue*) 1.

Luo, Haocai (ed.), *The Development Trend in the Modern Administrative Law System* (*Xinadai Xingzhengfa de Fazheng Quqi*) (Beijing: Law Press, 2004).

Luo, Haocai (ed.), *A Theory of Balance of Contemporary Administrative Law* (*Xiandai Xingzhengfa de Pingheng Lilun*) (Beijing: Beijing University Press, 1997).

Luo, Haocai (ed.), *Administrative Law* (*Xingzhengfa Xue*) (Beijing: Beijing University Press, 1996).

Luo, Haocai (ed.), *Judicial Review in China* (*Zhongguo Sifa Shencha Zhidu*) (Beijing: Beijing University Press, 1994).

Luo, Haocai, 'Using Administrative Litigation Functions to Promote the Implementation of the Administrative Litigation Law', (no. 4, 1995) *Administrative Law Review* (*Xingzhengfa Yanjiu*) 2.

Luo, Haocai, Jiang, Ming'an, *et al.*, 'The Present Situation and Future Development of Administrative Law Research', (no. 1, 1996), *Legal Science in China* (*Zhongguo Faxue*) 41.

Luo, Haocai, Yuan, Shuhong, & Li, Wendong, 'Theoretical Foundation of Contemporary Administrative Law', (no. 1, 1993) *Legal Science in China* (*Zhongguou Faxue*) 52.

Luo, Mingda & Bian, Xiangping, 'On Problems in and Countermeasures for Enforcing the Enterprise Law', (no. 5, 1989) *Law Review* (*Faxue Pinglun*) 9.

Luo, Shuping, 'The Quality of Court Adjudicating Documents Is Worrying', (no. 3, 1998) *Sichuan Adjudication* (*Sichuan Shenpang*) 22.

Ma, Huaide (ed.), *Chinese Administrative Law* (*Zhongguo Xingzhengfa*) (Beijing: China University of Political Science and Law Press, 1997).

Ma, Huaide, 'Problems within the Administrative Permit System and a Legislative Proposal', (no. 3, 1997) *Legal Science in China* (*Zhongguo Faxue*) 40.

Ma, Junju & Lu, Xiaowu, 'On the State as a Civil Law Subject in a Market Economy', (no. 5, 1993) *Law Review* (*Faxue Pinglun*) 1.

Ma, Junju, *On the Institution of Legal Personality* (*Faren Zhidu Tonglun*), Wuhan: Wuhan University Press (1988).

Ma, Kechang, 'Srengthen the Reform Force, Revise and Perfect the Criminal Law', (no. 5, 1996) *Law Review* (*Faxue Pinglun*) 1.

Ma, Shufang, 'Judicial Poverty and Counter-Poverty [Measures] – a Comprehensive Analysis of Civil and Commercial Judgements and Documents', originally published in (no. 2006) *Shangdong Adjudication* (*Shangdong Shenpan*) 113-117, reprinted in (no. 2, 2007) *Journal and Newspaper Reprinted Materials* (*Procedural Law and the Judicial System*) 67.

Ma, Yaojin, 'A Shareholding Cooperative Is Not an Independent Enterprise Form', (no. 2, 1997) *Journal of China University of Political Science and Law* (*Zhengfa Luntan*) 98.

Ma, Yuan (ed.), *A Practical Collection of Laws concerning Chinese Women* (*Zhongguo Funü Falü Shiyong Quanshu*) (Beijing: Publishing House of Law, 1993),

Meng, Qingguo, 'On Studying and Using Western Civil Law', 1993 (2) *Studies in Law* (*Faxue Yanjiu*) 79.

Meng, Xianfei, 'Application of Law in Administrative Litigation', (no. 6, 1989) *Studies in Law* (*Faxue Yanjiu*) 10.

Miao, Wenquan, 'On the Meaning and Value Analysis of the Rights of the Spouse', (no. 4, 2000) *Politics and Law* (*Zhengzhi yu falu*) 50.

Min, Bing, 'Several Issues Concerning Civil Law Subjects', (no. 1, 1992) *Journal of the South-Central Institute of Political Science and Law* (*Zhongnan Zhengfa Xueyuan Xuebao*) 17.

Min, Xianwei, 'A Socialist Market Economy Is Naturally an Economy Under the Rule of Law', (Special Issue, 1994) *Journal of Shandong Normal University* (*Shandong Shifan Daxuebao*) 93.

Mo, Lijun, 'On Legislative Improvements on Divorce Grounds in Our Marriage Law', (no. 5, 1997) *Legal Science* (*Falü Kexue*) 88.

MOFTEC, *Collection of Rules and Regulations on Foreign Investment in Service Trade* (Beijing: China Legal Publishing House, 2002).

New Progress in China's Protection of Intellectual Property Rights, Information Office of the State Council of the PRC, April 2005.

Office for Research Materials, Law Institute of the Chinese Academy of Social Science (ed.), *On Equality before the Law* (*Lun Falü Mianqian Renren Pingdeng*) (Beijing: Publishing House of Law, 1981).

Peng, Wanlin (ed.), *Civil Law Science* (*Minfa Xue*) (Beijing: China University of Political Science and Law Press, 1994).

Peng, Zhen, *On Political and Legal Works in New China* (*Lun Xinzhongguo De Zhengfa Gongzuo*) (Beijing: Press of CPC Documents, 1992).

Pi, Chunxi & Feng, Jun, 'Some Considerations on the Loopholes in the "Theory of Balance" – The Direction for Improvement', (no. 2, 1997) *Legal Science in China* (*Zhongguo Faxue*) 40.

Pi, Chunxi & Liu, Yujie, 'A Review of Administrative Law Studies in 1996', (no. 1, 1997) *Jurists* (*Faxue Jia*) 29.

Pi, Chunxi, 'An Important Law that Needs Serious Implementation', (no. 4, 1995) *Administrative Law Review* (*Xingzhengfa Yanjiu*) 12.

Pi, Chunxie (ed.), *Textbook on Chinese Administrative Law* (*Zhongguo Xingzhengfa Jiaocheng*) (Beijing: China University of Political Science and Law Press, 1988).

Project Group (Law Institute, Chinese Academy of Social Sciences), 'Some Theoretical Considerations and Practical Suggestions Regarding the Establishment of a Legal System for a Socialist Market Economy', (no. 6, 1993) *Studies in Law* (*Faxue Yanjiu*) 3.

Qi Suji & Ma Changming, 'On Several Issues for Improving Compulsory Enforcement of Law in Our Country', (1997) 83 (3) *Law Review* (*Faxue Pinglun*) 35.

Qiao, Congqi, *A Study on Sun Yatsen's Legal Thoughts* (*Sun Zhongsan Falü Shixiang Tixi Yanjiu*) (Beijing: Publishing House of Law, 1992).

Qiao, Wei, 'Guidelines for Building Up a Legal System in the New Era – Comrade Deng Xiaoping's Writings on Building a Legal System', (no. 2, 1984) *Legal Science in China* (*Zhongguo Faxue*) 67.

Qiao, Xiaoyang, 'To Enact a Law on Law-making and to Promote the Ruling of the Country by Law – a speech at the symposium on the draft law on law-making', (no. 3, 1997) *Administrative Law Review* (*Xingzheng Fa Yanjiu*) 1.

Qing, Qianhong & Li Yuan, 'The Influence of the Chinese Communist Party on Law-making', initially published in 2003 in <www.chinapublaw.com/emphases/20030613120104.htm>, reprinted in <www.usc.cuhk.edu.hk/wk.asp> (last accessed 25 September 2006).

Qu, Sanqiang, *Fundamentals of Intellectual Property Law* (*Zhishi Chanquanfa Yuanli*) (Beijing: Procutorial Press, 2004).

Qu, Yaoguang, 'On Conflicts of Legislation in Our Country', (no. 5, 1995) *Legal Science in China* (*Zhongguo Faxue*) 41.

Shang, Aiguo & Bao, Yonghong, 'A Discussion on the Deficiencies of the Criminal Law on IP Protection and Their Improvement', (no. 40, 2004) *Journal of Heilongjiang Administrative Cadre Institute of Politics and Law* (*Heilongjian Zhengfa Guanli Ganbu Xueyuan Xuebao*) 47.

Shen, Daming, 'The Debate on the Administrative Litigation System in the Early KMT Period and Its Significance', May 2007, available from <www.civillaw.com.cn/article/default.asp?id=32943> (last accessed 16 June 2007).

Shen, Kui, 'The Beginning of the Age of Constitutionalism – Questions regarding the First Constitutional Case', published in the Beijing University Law website: <www.law-dimension.com/details.asp?id=758> (last accessed 12 November 2004).

Shen, Zongling (ed.), *Basic Theories of Law* (*Faxue Jichu Lilun*) (Beijing: Beijing University Press, 1988).

Shen, Zongling (ed.), *Studies in Jurisprudence* (*Falixue Yanjiu*) (Shanghai: Shanghai People's Press, 1990).

Shen, Zongling, 'On Legal Interpretation', (no. 6, 1993) *Legal Science in China* (*Zhongguo Faxue*) 57.

Shi, Binghai, 'New Problems Facing Family Research', (no. 6, 1987) *Jurisprudence Monthly* (*Faxue*) 42.

Shi, Huifang, 'An Opinion on Abolishing the Institution of Exemption from Prosecution', (no. 1, 1995) *Journal of the China University of Political Science and Law* (*Zhengfa Luntan*) 33.

Son, Jian & Zheng, Chengliang (ed.), *A Report on Judicial Reforms: Procuratorate and Court Reforms in China* (Beijing: Law Press, 2004).

Song, Rufeng, *Recollections on Participation in Law-making* (*Canjia Lifa gongzuo Suoji*) (Beijing: Press of China Legal System, 1994).

Song, Yinghui & Wu Jie, 'A New Study into the Exemption from Prosecution', (no. 1, 1992) *Studies in Law* (*Faxue Yanjiu*) 24.

Su, Huiyu, *Criminal Law* (*Xingfa Xue*) (Beijing: China University of Political Science and Law Press, 1994).

Su, Li, *Maybe It Is Happening – Legal Science in Transitional China* (*Yexu Zhengzai Fasheng – Zhuanxing Zhong de Faxue*), Beijing: Law Press (2004).

Su, Li, *Roads to Cities – Rule of Law in Transitional China* (*Daolu Tongxiang Chengshi – Zhuanxing Zhongguo de Fazhi*) (Beijing: Law Press, 2004).

Sun, Guohua & Zeng, Bing, 'On the Definition of Law by Vishinsky', (no. 2, 1996) *Jurists* (*Faxue Jia*) 38.

Sun, Weixing & Wang, Guoxiang (eds), *A Handbook on International Trade* (*Guoji Shangmao Shouce*) (Beijing: China foreign Economic Relations and Trade Press, 1994).

Sun, Xianzhong, 'A Review of the Effects of the Adopted Western Civil Law in China', (no. 3, 2006) *China Legal Science* (*Zhongguo Faxue*) 166.

Sun, Xiaoxia, 'On Internationalisation and Nationalisation of Law in a Market Economy Society', (no. 4, 1993) *Journal of Hangzhou University* (*Hanzhou Daxue Xuebao*) 79.

Tang, Guanda, 'The Presumption of Innocence Should be Concretely Analysed', (no. 1, 1980) *Studies in Law* (*Faxue Yanjiu*) 62.

Tang, Xiaotian, '"Strictly Rule the Party" and Constitutional Litigation', (No. 2, 2002) *Journal of Jiangsu Administrative College* (*Jiangsu Xingzhen Xueyuan Xuebao*) 104.

Tao, Jigang, 'Some Thoughts on the Law on Re-education through Labour', (no. 3, 1995) *Journal of the China University of People's Police* (*Zhongguo Renmin Jingcha Daxue Xuebao*) 12.

The Execution Work Office of the Supreme People's Court (ed.), *A Collection of Practical Documents on Compulsory Execution* (*Qiangzhi Zhixing Shiwu Wenjian Huibian*) (Beijing: Publishing House of Law, 1999).

Tian, Chengyou, *Local Customary Law in Rural Societies (Xiangtu Shehui Zhong de Minjianfa)* (Beijing: Law Press, 2005).

Ting, Wei-chih, 'The Phases of Changes in Confucianism', (no. 12, 1978) *Studies in History* (*Lishi Yangjiu*) 25.

Tong, Rou (ed.), *Several Civil Law Issues Involved in Economic Structural Reform* (*Jingji Tizhi Gaige Zhong De Ruogan Minfa Wenti*) (Beijing: Press of Beijing Teacher's University, 1985).

Tong, Rou, 'Building Up China's Own Civil Law Theory and System', (no. 3, 1988) *Guangdong Legal Science* (*Guangdong Faxue*) 1.

Tong, Rou, *et al*, *Chinese Civil Law* (*Zhongguo Minfa*) (Beijing: Publishing House of Law, 1990).

Tong, Zhaohong (ed.), *Civil Enforcement: Investigation and Analysis* (*Minshi Zhixing: Diaocha yu Fenxi*) (Beijing: Press of the People's Court, 2005).

Tong, Zhaohong, Chen, Huiming, Zhou, Gencai, 'A Study of Intellectual Property Trials in Zheijing Province', (no. 2, 2003) *Beijing University Intellectual Property Rights Review* 415.

Tong, Zhiwei & Guo, Yanjun, 'An Important Topic for Constitutional Studies – Comparative Study on State Structure', (no. 5, 1993) *Studies in Law* (*Faxue Yanjiu*) 10.

Wang Junyan & Sun Xiaoping, 'On the Nature, Characteristics and Legal Status of Private Enterprises', (no. 1, 1989) *Studies in Law* (*Faxue Yanjiu*) 17.

Wang, Baoshu (ed.), *Chinese Company Law: Proposed Revision Draft* (*Zhongguo Gongsifa: Xiugai Cao'an Jianyigao*) (Beijing: Social Sciences Press, 2004).

Wang, Chaoying, Meng, Xiangang & Zang, Yaomin (eds), *Practical Answers to Foreign Trade Law* (*Duiwai Maoyi Fa Shiwu Wenda*) (Beijing: China Commerce Press, 1994).

Wang, Chengguan, 'Cross Reference and Absorption Among Laws in Different Countries – An Important Topic for Comparative Law', (1992) (4) *Legal Science in China* (*Zhongguo Faxue*) 39.

Wang, Chengguang & Liu Wen, 'The Market Economy and the Separation of Public and Private Law', (no. 4, 1993) *Legal Science in China* (*Zhongguo Faxue*) 28.

Wang, Dexian, 'The May Fourth Movement and Democratic Constitutionalism', (no. 3, 1989) *Studies in Law* (*Faxue Yanjiu*) 11.

Wang, Fengzhi, 'Several Questions on the Abolition or Retention of the Death Penalty', (no. 4, 1995) *Journal of China University of Political Science and Law* (*Zhengfa Luntan*) 23.

Wang, Hongxiang, 'Upholding and Perfecting the Exemption from Prosecution', (no. 5, 1994) *Legal Science in China* (*Zhongguo Faxue*) 42.

Wang, Jiafu (ed.), *Chinese Civil Law – Civil Obligations* (*Zhongguo Minfaxue – Minfa Zhaiquan*) (Beijing: Publishing House of Law, 1994).

Wang, Jiafu *et al.*, 'On the Rule of Law', (no. 2, 1996) *Studies in Law* (*Faxue Yanjiu*) 3.

Wang, Jiafu, *et al.* (eds), *Contract Law* (*Hetong Fa*) (Beijing: China Social Science Press, 1986).

Wang, Jianping, et al, 'On Criteria for Distinguishing Forms of Enterprises', (no. 2, 1997) *Journal of the China University of Political Science and Law* (*Zhengfa Luntan*) 92.

Wang, Lei, 'On Constitutional Interpretation Organs in Our Country', (no. 6, 1993) *Journal of Chinese and Foreign Legal Science* (*Zhongwai Faxue*) 21.

Wang, Lianchang (ed.), *Administrative Law* (*Xingzheng Faxue*) (Beijing: China University of Political Science and Law Press, 1994).

Wang, Liming, 'After Unity There's Separation: The Relationship Between Torts and Obligations', (no. 1, 1997) *Jurisprudence Frontiers* (*Faxue Qianyan*) 92.

Wang, Liming, 'On the State as a Civil Law Subject', (no. 1, 1991) *Studies in Law* (*Faxue Yanjiu*) 59.

Wang, Liming, *A Proposed Draft Chinese Law on Rights in rem and Explanations* (*Zhongguo Wuquanfa Caian Jianyigao Ji Shuoming*) (Beijing: Press of Chinese Legal System, 2001).

Wang, Liming, *Academic Draft of Chinese Civil Code and Legislative Explanations – Rights in rem* (*Zhongguo Minfadian Xueze Jianyigao Ji Lifa Liyou – Wuquan Bian*) (Beijing: Law Press, 2005).

Wang, Liming, Guo, Minglei & Fang, Liufang, *A New Approach to Civil Law* (*Minfa Xinlun*) (Beijing: Press of the China University of Political Science and Law, 1987).

Wang, Mingyuan, 'Several Questions on the Exemption from Prosecution', (no. 2, 1992) *Legal Science in China* (*Zhongguo Faxue*) 75.

Wang, Minyuan & Liu, Donghua, 'A Comment on and Summary of the Study of Criminal Procedure Law', (no. 1, 1996) *Studies in Law* (*Faxue Yanjiu*) 51.

Wang, Qianghua, 'On the Role of Law in Reform and the Three Legal Reforms in Our History', (no. 5, 1982) *Studies in Law* (*Faxue Yanjiu*) 58.

Wang, Renbo, *Modern China and Its Constitutional Culture* (*Xianzheng Wenhua Yu Jingdai Zhongguo*) (Beijing: Publishing House of Law, 1997).

Wang, Shaonan, 'Establishing a Direction for Trial Process Reform', (no. 1, 1995) *Studies in Law* (*Faxue Yanjiu*) 77.

Wang, Shaoxi & Wang, Shouchun, *Chinese Foreign Trade* (*Zhongguo Duiwai Maoyi*) (Beijing: People's University of China Press, 1994).

Wang, Shengming & Sun, Lihai (eds), *Selection of Legislative Materials relating to the Revision of the Marriage Law of the People's Republic of China* (*Zhonghua Renmin

Gongheguo Hunyinfa Xiugai Lifa Ziliao Xuan) (Beijing: Publishing House of Law, 2001).

Wang, Shuwen, 'On the Guarantee of Constitutional Enforcement', (no. 6, 1992) *Legal Science in China* (*Zhongguo Faxue*) 15.

Wang, Wanhua (ed.), *A Collection of Administrative Procedural Laws in China* (*Zhongguo Xingzheng Chengxufa Huibian*) (Beijing: China Legal System Press, 2004).

Wang, Wanhua, 'The Choice of Chinese Law-making and the Legislative Outline of an Administrative Procedures Law', in (no. 8, 2005) *Reprinted Newspaper and Journal Materials: D411 Constitutional and Administrative Law* (*Xianfaxue Xingzhengfaxu*) 3.

Wang, Weiguo & Tomasic, Roman (eds), *Reform of PRC Securities and Insolvency Laws* (*Zhongguo Zhenquanfa Pochanfa Gaige*) (Beijing: Press of the China University of Political Science and Law, 1999).

Wang, Xinxin, 'Exemption Rights in the Newly Enacted Bankruptcy Law', (no. 1 2007) *Journal of the China University of Political Science and Law* (*Zhengfa Luntan*) 31.

Wang, Xinxin, 'On Operative Mechanisms of the Bankruptcy Law and Problems in Enforcing the Law', (no. 6, 1991) *Legal Science in China* (*Zhongguo Faxue*) 90.

Wang, Xinxin, 'Shelter and Investigation Should Be Abolished – A Discussion with Comrades Chen Weidong and Zhang Tao', (no. 3, 1993) *Legal Science in China* (*Zhongguo Faxue*) 110.

Wang, Zhenyu & Wang, Jingcheng, 'An Analysis on Problems in Our Administrative Litigation System and Their Solutions', (no. 3, 1997) *Jilin University Journal of Social Science* (*Jilin Daxue Shehui Kexue Xuebao*) 79.

Wei, Tong, 'A Report of the Discussions on the Revision of the CPL', (no. 1, 1996) *Journal of the China University of Political Science and Law* (*Zhengfa Luntan*) 89.

Wen, Zhengbang (ed.), *Chinese Legal Science Approaching the 21st Century* (*Zouxiang Ershiyi Shiji de Zhongguo Faxue*) (Congqing: Congqing Press, 1993).

Wen, Zhengbang, 'Some Legal and Philosophical Thoughts on the Market Economy', (no. 4, 1995) *Legal System and Social Development* (*Fazhi Yu Shehui Fazhang*) 1.

Wu, Chunlei, 'On Different Conceptions of Law in Different Historical Periods in Our Country', (no. 1, 1996) *Journal of Gansu Institute of Political Science and Law* (*Gansu Zhengfa Xueyuan Xuebao*) 7.

Wu, Daying & Shen, Zongling, *A Basic Theory of Chinese Socialist Law* (*Zhongguo Shehui Zhuyi Falü Jiben lilun*) (Beijing: Publishing House of Law, 1987).

Wu, Handong (ed.), *The Blue Book of IPR in China* (*Zhongguo Zhishi Chanquan Lanpishu*) (Beijing: Peking University Press, 2007).

Wu, Jianbin, 'Establishing a Scientific Foundation for Our Modern Enterprise System', (no. 1, 1998) *Legal Science in China* (*Zhongguo Faxue*) 30.

Wu, Xieying, Li, Zhiyong & Wang, Ruihe, 'On a Constitutional Ligation System in China' (no. 5, 1989) *Legal Science in China* (*Zhonggu Faxue*) 62.

Xia, Xinhua & Hu, Xucheng (eds), *Modern Chinese Constitutional Movements: A Collection of Historical Records* (*Jindai Zhongguo Xianzheng Licheng: Shiliao Huicui*) (Beijing: Press of China University of Political Science and Law, 2004).

Xia, Yong (ed.) *Towards an Age of Rights: A Perspective on Civil Rights Development in China* (*Zouxiang Quanli de Shidai: Zhongguo Gongmin Quanli Fazhan Yanjiu*) (Beijing: Press of China University of Political Science and Law, 1995).

Xia, Yong, 'Several Theoretical Questions concerning Constitutional Reform in China', (no. 2, 2003) *Social Sciences in China* (*Zhongguo Shehui Kexue*), reproduced in <www.usc.cuhk.edu.hk/wk_wzdetails.asp?id=2150> (last accessed 21/11/04).

Xiang, Zexuan, Wu Xiaocheng, Luo Rui, *On Legal Supervision and Remedies of Criminal Procedural Law* (*Falü Jiandu Yu Xingsh Susong Jiujilun*) (Beijing: Beijing University Press, 2005).

Xiao, Bing, 'The Process of Drafting a Contract Code', (no. 1, 1997) *Jurisprudence Frontiers* (*Faxue Qianyan*) 184.

Xiao, Weiyun (ed.), *One Country Two Systems and the Basic Legal System in Hong Kong* (*Yiguo Liangzhi Yu Xianggang Jiben Falu Zhidu*) (Beijing: Beijing University Press, 1990).

Xiao, Yang, *Market Economy and Legal Construction* (*Shichang Jingji yu Fazhi Jianshe*) (Beijing: Publishing House of Law, 1994).

Xie, Guisheng, 'The Market Economy and the Separation of Public and Private Law', (no. 1, 1994) *Studies in Finance* (*Caimao Yanjiu*) 62.

Xie, Huaishi, 'On Establishing a Civil-Economic Law System Appropriate to the Needs of a Socialist Market Economy', (no. 1, 1993) *Studies in Law* (*Faxue Yanjiu*) 12.

Xie, Hui, 'From a Planned Economy to a Market Economy: A Revolution in Legal Theory', (no. 4, 1994) *Gansu Journal of Theoretical Research* (*Gansu Lilun Xuekang*) 53.

Xie, Youping, 'Ideal and Reality: A Comment on the Revised Criminal Procedure Law', (no. 2, 1996) *Modern Law Science* (*Xiandao Faxue*) 9.

Xing, Yan, 'Criminal Law Revision: Minor or Major Revision or No Revision At All', in (no. 1, 1997) *Peking University Law Journal* (*Zhongwai Faxue*) 49.

Xiong, Qiuhong, *The Changing Science of Criminal Procedural Law* (*Zhuanbianzhong De Xingshisusong Faxue*) (Beijing: Beijing University Press, 2004).

Xiu, Menyou, 'Legislation on Party System in the Western Countries and the Legal Institutionalisation of Our Multi-Party Cooperation', (no. 4, 1993) *Journal of Northwest University* (*Xibei Daxue Xuebao*) 23.

Xu, Anqi 'To Protect Freedom of Divorce: Restriction on Divorce Should not be the Main Objective in the Revision of the Marriage Law', *Southern Weekend Weekly* (*Nanfang Zhoumo*)), internet edition, 21 September 2000.

Xu, Anqi, 'Restriction on Divorce Should not be the Main Objective in the Revision of the Marriage Law', *Legal Daily* (*Fazhi Ribao*), internet edition, 12 October 2000.

Xu, Jiexun & Wu, Shuxing (eds), *A Study on the Implementation of Autonomy Law* (*Shishi Zizhi Fa Yanjiu*), Guilin: Guangxi Nationalities Press (1997).

Xu, Lizhi, 'Commercial Legislation in the Late Qing and Its Characteristics', (no. 3, 1989) *Studies in Law* (*Faxue Yanjiu*) 89.

Xu, Ming & Guo Liming, 'On the Legal Status of "Households"', (no. 1, 1988) *Law Magazine* (*Faxue Zazhi*) 40.

Xu, Xianming (ed.), *A Textbook on Jurisprudence* (*Falixue Jiaocheng*) (Beijing: China University of Political Science and Law Press, 1994).

Xu, Yichu, 'Criminal Processes and Human Rights Protection', (no. 2, 1996) *Studies in Law* (*Faxue Yanjiu*) 89.

Xue, Gangling, 'On the Purposes, Means and System of Administrative Law', (no. 3, 1997) *Journal of China University of Political Science and Law* (*Zhengfa Luntan*) 94.

Xue, Jinian, 'Reforming the Present Enforcement System and Enacting a Law on Enforcement', (no. 2, 1995) *Politics and Law* (*Zhengzhi yu Falu*) 49.

Yang, Chunxi, 'Legislative Improvement on Corporate Criminality', (no. 5, 1995) *Legal Science in China* (*Zhongguo Faxue*) 35.

Yang, Dawei (ed.), *A Textbook of Marriage Law* (*Hunyinfa Jiaocheng*), revised edition (Beijing: Law Publishing House, 1985).

Yang, Duan, 'Appropriately Resolving the Issue of Validity of Illegal Evidence', (no. 5, 1994) *Legal Science in China* (*Zhongguo Faxue*) 41.

Yang, Haikong & Zhang, Zhiyuan, *A Study of the Basic Theories of Administrative Law in China* (*Zhongguo Xingzhengfa Jiben Lilun Yanjiu*) (Beijing: Beijing University Press, 2004).

Yang, Haikong, 'The Theoretical Foundation of Administrative Law – Government Under Law', (no. 5, 1996) *Peking University Law Journal* (*Zhongwai Faxue*) 53.

Yang, Hunglieh, *A History of Chinese Legal Thought* (*Zhongguo Falü Sixiangshi*), vol. II (Beijing: Commercial Publishing House, 1937).

Yang, Jingfan & Yu, Ronggen, *Confucius' Legal Thoughts* (*Kongzi de Falü Sixiang*) (Beijing: Press of the Masses, 1984).

Yang, Xiejun, 'Some Comments on Various Basic Theories of Administrative Law', (no. 2, 1996) *Legal Science in China* (*Zhongguou Faxue*) 64.

Yang, Yifang & Chen, Hanfeng (eds), *A Legal History of the People's Republic of China* (*Zhonghau Renmin Gongheguo Fazhishi*) (Haerbin: Helongjing People's Press, 1997).

Yang, Zhengshan, 'The Central Point for Chinese Legal Reform is the Civil Law', (no. 1, 1995) *Journal of China University of Political Science and Law (Zhangfa Luntan)* 48.

Yang, Zhenshan, 'Market Economy and Our Civil and Commercial Law', (no. 4, 1993) *Journal of the China University of Political Science and Law* (*Zhengfa Luntan*) 1.

Yang, Zhongwen & Liu, Chuanping, 'Control of Power – Balance of Power: On the Nature of Administrative Law', (no. 2, 1997) *Journal of Seeking Truth from Facts* (*Qiushi Xuekang*) 55.

Ye, Bifeng, 'Several Issues concerning the Theoretical Foundation of Administrative Law', (no. 5, 1997) *Law Review* (*Faxue Pinglun*) 18.

Ye, Yonglie, *The History of the Anti-Rightists Movement* (*Fan Youpai Shimo*) (Xining: Qinghai People's Press, 1995).

Ying, Songnian (ed.), *Law on Administrative Acts* (*Xingzheng Xingwei Fa*) (Beijing: People's Press, 1993).

Yu, Jianze, 'On the Multi-party Cooperation and Political Consultation System under the Leadership of Communist Party of China', in (no. 6, 1990) *Legal Science in China* (*Zhonggu Faxue*) 3.

Yu, Ronggen, 'Questioning the Theory of Rule by Man in Confucianism and Rule of Law in Legalism', (no. 4, 1984) *Law Science Quarterly* (*Faxue Jikan*) 60.

Yuan Shuhong, 'Contemporary Administrative Law Is by its Nature a Law of Balance', (no. 5, 1996) *Peking University Law Journal* (*Zhongwai Faxue*) 51.

Yuan, Jieliang, 'On Problems of the Institution of Legislative Interpretation', (no. 4, 1994) *Legal Science in China* (*Zhongguo Faxue*) 24.

Zeng, Ping, 'A Summary of Research on Issues relating to Constitutional Revision', in *Renmin Ribao* website: <www.peopledaily.com.cn/GB/14576/14841/2084188.htm>.

Zhang, Chunfa, 'Several Issues Relating to *Guizhang*' (no. 1, 1991) *Studies in Law* (*Faxue Yanjiu*) 15.

Zhang, Jinfan (ed.), *A General History of the Chinese Civil Law* (*Zhongguo Minfa Tongshi*) (Fuzhou: Fujian People's Press, 2003).

Zhang, Jinfan (ed.), *A Summary of Research in the History of the Chinese Legal System* (*Zhongguo Fazhishi Yanjiu Zongshu*) (Beijing: Press of Chinese People's University of Public Security, 1990).

Zhang, Jinfan, 'Chinese Legal Tradition and the Beginning of Modernisation', (no. 5, 1996) *Journal of China University of Political Science and Law* (*Zhengfa Luntan*) 77.

Zhang, Jinfan, 'On the Legal Thought of Shen Jiaben – Part II', (no. 5, 1981) *Studies in Law* (*Faxue Yanjiu*) 47.

Zhang, Jinfan, *A Collection of Papers on Legal History* (*Fashi Jianlüe*) (Beijing: Press of the Masses, 1988).

Zhang, Jinfan, *et al.* (eds), *A Chinese Legal History* (*Zhongguo Fazhi Shi*) (Beijing: Press of the Masses, 1986).

Zhang, Junhao, 'Market System and Private Law in China', (no. 6, 1994) *Journal of China University of Political Science and Law* (*Zhangfa Luntan*) 34.

Zhang, Lingjie, Zhang, Xun & Wang, Mingyuan, 'On the Principle of the Presumption of Innocence', (no. 4, 1991) *Studies in Law* (*Faxue Yanjiu*) 34.

Zhang, Mingkai, 'On Properly Dealing with Several Relations in Revising the Criminal Law', (no. 1, 1997) *Peking University Law Journal* (*Zhongwai Faxue*) 65.

Zhang, Minjie, 'The Study on Chinese Marriage and Family Issues – a review of a century', first published in (no. 3, 2001) *Studies in Social Sciences* (*Shehui Kexue Yanjie*), available from <www.usc.cuhk.edu.hk/wk_wzdetails.asp?id=1571>.

Zhang, Shangshuo, 'Administrative Law Science in New China', (no. 3, 1989) *Journal of Zhongnan Institute of Political Science and Law* (*Zhongnan Zhengfa Xueyuan Xuebao*) 18.

Zhang, Tao & Chen, Weidong, 'A Discussion of the Time for Defence Lawyers to Participate in the Criminal Process', (no. 2, 1990) *Legal Science in China* (*Zhongguo Faxue*) 43.

Zhang, Wei, 'Several Issues Regarding the Involvement of Lawyers in Criminal Procedure', (no. 5, 1994) *Legal Science in China* (*Zhongguo Faxue*) 39.

Zhang, Wen, *et al*, 'A Further Study on Several Questions regarding Corporate Criminality', (no. 1, 1994) *Legal Science in China* (*Zhongguo Faxue*) 57.

Zhang, Wenxian, 'Inheritance, Transplant and Reform: A Necessity for Legal Development', (no. 2, 1995) *Social Science Fronts* (*Shehui Kexue Zhanxian*) 9.

Zhang, Wenxian, 'Three Points on the Market Economy and Legal Construction', (no. 3, 1993) *Legal Science in China* (*Zhongguo Faxue*) 12.

Zhang, Xiaohui (ed.), *The Implementation of Chinese [National] Law in National Minority Areas* (*Zhongguo Falü zai Shaoshu Minzu Diqu de Shishi*) (Kunming: Yunnan University Press, 1994).

Zhang, Xibao (ed.), *A Legal History of Revolutionary Base Areas* (*Geming Genjudi Fazhi Shi*) (Beijing: Publishing House of Law, 1994).

Zhang, Xiu, 'Choices for the Reform in the Trial Process for Public Prosecution Cases', (no. 2, 1996) *Studies in Law* (*Faxue Yanjiu*) 96.

Zhang, Youyu & Wang, Shuwen, (eds), *Forty Years of the PRC's Legal Science* (*Zhongguo Faxue Sishi Nian*) (Shanghai: Shanghai People's Publishing House, 1989).

Zhang, Youyu (ed.), *A Collection of Papers on the Constitution* (*Xianfa Lunwen Ji*) (Supplementary Volume) (Beijing: Press of the Masses, 1982).

Zhang, Youyu, 'On Strengthening the Socialist Legal System', first published in (no. 6, 1981) *Social Sciences in China* (*Zhongguo Shehui Kexue*), reprinted in *A Collection of Articles on Chinese Legal Science* (*Zhongguo Faxue Wenji*) (Beijing: Press of the Masses, 1984).

Zhang, Zhiming, 'A Further Thought on the Reform of the Trial Process', (no. 4, 1995) *Studies in Law* (*Faxue Yanjiu*) 93.

Zhao, Bing, 'Problems in the Chinese Lawyer and Professional System and the Direction of Reform', available at <www.iolaw.org.cn/whownews.asp?id=15335> (last accessed 15 march 2007).

Zhao, Bingzhi & Xiao, Zhonghua, 'A Discussion on the Debate About the Abolition of Analogy in Criminal Law', (no. 4, 1996) *Jurists* (*Faxue Jia*) 54.

Zhao, Bingzhi, 'Certain Considerations as to Why Legal Persons Cannot Become Subjects of Crime', (no. 5, 1989), *Studies in Law* (*Faxue Yanjiu*) 57.

Zhao, Junru & Li, Shenglong, 'Discussions on Legislation on Crimes by Legal Persons', (no. 3, 1989) *Modern Law Science* (*Xiandai Faxue*) 55.

Zhao, Xudong, 'Certain Problems in Chinese Corporate Legislation', (no. 1, 1991) *Journal of China University of Political Science and Law* (*Zhengfa Luntan*) 43.

Zhao, Xudong, 'On the Legal Person Status of Collective Enterprises', (no. 1, 1991) *Legal Science in China* (*Zhongguo Faxue*) 62.

Zhao, Xudong, *Power and Justice: Dispute Resolution in Rural Societies and Plurality of Authorities* (*Quanli Yu Gongzheng – Xiangtu Shehui de Jiufen Yu Quanwei Duoyuan*) (Tianjin: Tianjin Ancient Books Publishing House, 2003).

Zhao, Zenghai & Fang, Wei, 'The Tenth Five-Year Plan and the Development Strategy of the Chinese Legal Profession', 23 October 2006, available from <www.acla.org.cn/pages/2006-10-23/s36871.html> (last accessed 15/11/06).

Zhao, Zhenjiang (ed.), *Forty Years of the Chinese Legal System* (*Zhongguo Fazhi Sishinian*) (Beijing: Beijing University Press, 1990).

Zhou Yiliang (ed.), *A History of Sino-Japan Cultural Exchange* (*Zhong Ri Wenhua Jiaoliu Shi Daxi*) vol. 2 (*Legal System*) (*Fazhi Juan*) (Hangzhou: Zhejiang People's Press, 1996).

Zhou, Hanhua, 'Administrative Law-Making and Contemporary Administrative Law – the Developing Direction of Chinese Administrative Law', (no. 3, 1997) *CASS Journal of Law* (*Faxue Yanjiu*) 19.

Zhou, Wangsheng, 'One the Processes and Ten Drafting Steps', (no. 6, 1994) *Legal Science in China* (*Zhongguo Faxue*) 19.

Zhou, Wangsheng, *The Science of Legislation* (*Lifa Xue*) (Beijing: Beijing University Press, 1988).

Zhou, Yezhong, 'The Supremacy of the Constitution: The Spirit for the Chinese Movement towards a Rule of Law', (no. 6, 1995) *Review of Law* (*Faxue Pinglun*) 1.

Zhou, Yongkun, 'A Market Economy Demands Equality in Legislation', (no. 4, 1993) *Legal Science in China* (*Zhongguo Faxue*)16.

Zhou, Zhenxiang & Shao, Jingchun, (eds), *A Chronicle of Forty Years of Construction of the Chinese New Legal System* (*Xi Zhongguo Fazhi Jianshe Sishinian Yaolan*) (Beijing: Press of the Masses, 1990).

Zhu, Huaron & Lin, Jianhua, 'On Our Legislation and Perfecting the Legislation Concerning Crimes Committed by Legal Persons', (no. 5, 1988) *Journal of China University of Political Science and Law* (*Zhengfa Luntang*) 26.

Zhu, Jingwen (ed.), *A Report on Legal Development in China: Data Bank and Assessment Criteria* (*Zhongguo Falü Fazhang Baogao: Shujuku Yu Zhibiao Tixi*) (Beijing: Renmin University Press, 2007).

Zhu, Weijiu (ed.), *Legal Supervision Over Government* (*Zhengfu Fazhi Jiandu Lun*) (Beijing: China University of Political Science and Law Press, 1994).

Zhu, Xanfang and Liang, Fang, 'Research into the System of Civil Law Science', (no. 1, 1991) *Journal of Political and Legal Science* (*Zhengfa Xuekan*) 28.

Zhu, Yangming, 'On the Basis of Military Legislation', (no. 3, 1995) *Legal Science in China (Zhongguo Faxue)* 33.

Zou, Hailin, 'An Analysis and the Application of Enterprise Rehabilitation Procedures in China', in (no. 1, 2007) *Journal of China University of Political Science and Law (Zhengfa Luntan)* 48.

3. Academic Works in English

The following do not include all the articles or books referred to in this book; they include only those that are significant for further research and study.

'An Overview of Reforming State-owned Enterprises', (no. 6, 1993) *Search* (*Qiusuo*), at 23-24, translated in (March 1994) *Inside China Mainland* 26.

'Gist of Speeches Made in Wuchang, Shenzhen, Zhuhai and Shanghai [by Deng Xiaoping]', *Beijing Review*, Feb. 7-20, 1994, at 9-20.

'Note: Concept of Law in the Chinese Anti-Crime Campaign', (1985) 98 *Harvard Law Review* 1890.

'Revision of the Marriage Law: An Insider (Wu Changzhen) Talks about the Key Issues', (March 15, 2001) *Beijing Review* 14.

Alford, William P., *To Steal a Book Is an Elegant Offense: Intellectual Property Law in Chinese Civilisation* (Stanford, California: Stanford University Press, 1995).

Anderson, Craig, & Guo, Bingna, 'Corporate Governance under the New Company Law (Part 1): Fiduciary Duties and Minority Shareholders Protection', (April 2006) *China Law & Practice* 17-24; & 'Corporate Governance under the New Company Law (Part 2): Shareholder Lawsuits and Enforcement', (May 2006) *China Law & Practice* 15-22.

Baker, Hugh D.R., *Chinese Family and Kinship* (London and Basingstoke: the Macmillan Press Ltd., 1979).

Barry, Donald D., Feldbrugge, F.J. M. & Lasok, Dominik, (eds), *Codification in the Communist World* (Leiden: A.W. Sijthoff, 1975).

Berman, Harold J., Cohen, Susan & Russell, Malcolm 'Comparison of the Chinese and Soviet Codes of Criminal Law and Procedure', (1982) (vol. 73, No. 1) *Journal of Crim. L. & Criminology* 238.

Berman, Harold J., *Justice in the U.S.S.R.: An Interpretation of Soviet Law*, revised edition (Cambridge, Massachusetts: Harvard University Press, 1962).

Bernhardt, Kathryn & Huang, Philip C.C, *Civil Law in Qing and Republican China* (Stanford: Stanford University Press, 1994).

Blaustein, Albert P., (ed.), *Fundamental Legal Documents of Communist China* (New Jersey: Fred B. Rothman & Co., 1962).

Bodde, Derk & Morris, Clarence, *Law in Imperial China* (Cambridge, Mass: Harvard University Press, 1967).

Brady, James P., *Justice and Politics in People's China: Legal Order or Continuing Revolution?* (London/New York: Academic Press, 1982).

Brown, Ronald C., *Understanding Chinese courts and Legal Process: Law with Chinese Characteristics* (The Hague/Boston: Kluwer Law International, 1997).

Brugger, Bill, *China: Liberation and Transformation 1942–1962* (London: Croom Helm, 1981).

Brugger, Bill, *China: Radicalism to Revisionism 1962–1979* (London: Croom Helm, 1981).

Buck, Mary, 'Justice for All: The Application of Law by Analogy in the Case of Zhou Fuqing', (no. 2, 1993) 7 *J.Chinese L* 113.

Burns, John (ed.), *The Chinese Communist Party's Nomenklatura System: A Documentary Study of Party Control of Leadership Selection 1979–1984* (Armonk, New York/ London: M.E.Sharpe, Inc., 1989).

Butler W.E., (ed.), *The Legal System of the Chinese Soviet Republic 1931–1934* (New York: Transnational Publishers Inc., 1983).

Buxbaum, David C. (ed.), *Chinese Family Law and Social Change in Historical and Comparative Perspective* (Seattle and London: University of Washington Press, 1978),

Cai, Dingjian, 'Constitutional Supervision and Interpretation in the People's Republic of China', (1995) 9 *Journal of Chinese Law* 219.

Cai, Dingjian, 'Introduction to the Administrative Penalty Law of China', (1996) 10 *Columbian Journal of Asian Law* 259.

Cameron, Meribeth E., *The Reform Movement in China 1898–1912* (New York: Octagon Books, 1963).

Cao, Siyuan, *The Storm Over Bankruptcy* (*Pochan Fengyun*) (Beijing: Zhongyan Bianyi Press, 1996), translated in *Chinese Law and Government*, nos 1 & 2, 1998.

Ch'ien, Tuan-Sheng, *The Government and Politics of China* (Cambridge: Harvard University Press, 1950).

Ch'ü, T'ung-tsu, *Law and Society in Traditional China* (Paris: Mouton & Co., 1961).

Chan, Peter P. F., *People's Republic of China: Modernisation and Legal Development*, (London: Oyez Longman, 1983).

Chang, Chin-tsen, '*Li* and Law', (no. 2, 1960) 2 *Chinese Culture* 6.

Chang, Chi-yun, 'Confucianism vs. Communism', (no. 2, 1959) 2 *Chinese Culture* 1.

Chang, Gordon G., *The Coming Collapse of China* (London: Random House, 2001).

Chang, Ta-kuang, 'The Making of the Chinese Bankruptcy Law: A Study in the Chinese Legislative Process', (no. 2, 1987) 28 *Harvard Int'l L. J.* 333.

Chao, Howard, & Yang, Xiaoping, 'The Reform of the Chinese System of Enterprise Ownership, (1987) 23 *Stan. J. Int'l L.* 365.

Chao, Paul, 'China's New Economic Zones: A Model for Development?', (1994) 10 *J. of Developing Societies* 59.

Chen, Albert H.Y, 'Towards a Legal Enlightenment: Discussions in Contemporary China on the Rule of Law' (2000) 17 *UCLA Pacific Basin Law Journal* 125.

Chen, Albert H.Y., *An Introduction to the Legal System of the People's Republic of China*, 3rd edition (Singapore: LexisNexix/Butterworths Asia, 2004).

Chen, Jianfu & Hong, Lijian, *China Local Business Law Guide* (Singapore: CCH Asia Pacific, loose-leaf services, first published in 1999).

Chen, Jianfu & Ke, Suiwa, *China Criminal Law: Commentary and Legislation* (Singapore, CCH Asia, 2000).

Chen, Jianfu, Li, Yuwen & Otto, Jan Michiel (eds), *Implementation of Law in the People's Republic of China* (London/Boston/The Hague: Kluwer Law International, 2002).

Chen, Jianfu, & Walker, Gordon, (eds), *Balancing Act: Law, Policy and Politics in Globalisation and Global Trade* (Sydney: The Federation Press, 2004).

Chen, Jianfu, (ed.), *China Business Law Guide* (Singapore: CCH Asia Pacific, loose-leaf service).

Chen, Jianfu, *From Administrative Authorisation to Private Law: A Comparative Perspective of the Developing Civil Law in the PRC* (Dordrecht/Boston/London: Martinus Nijhoff Publishers, 1995).

Chen, Jianfu, *Chinese Law: Towards an Understanding of Chinese Law, Its Nature and Development* (The Hague/London/Boston: Kluwer Law International, 1999).

Chen, Jianfu, 'Securitisation of State-Owned Enterprises and Ownership Controversy in the PRC', (1993) 15 *The Sydney Law Review* 59.

Chen, Jianfu, 'A Moderate Step in a Right Direction – The Revision of the Criminal Procedure Law in the PRC', (1997) 3 (1) *Journal of Chinese and Comparative Law* 139.

Chen, Jianfu, 'Conceptual Evolution of Socialism with Chinese Characteristics – the Revision of the Constitution in the PRC', 1999 (24) *China Perspectives* 66.

Chen, Jianfu, 'Development and Conception of Administrative Law in China, (1999) 16 (2) *Law in Context* 72.

Chen, Jianfu, 'Internationalisation of Civil and Commercial Law in the PRC', in Kanishka Jayasuriya (ed.), *Law, Capitalism and Power in Asia* (London: Routledge, 1999), at 69-94.

Chen, Jianfu, 'Implementation of Law as a Politico-Legal Battle in China', (2002) 43 *China Perspectives* 26.

Chen, Jianfu, 'A Great Leap Forward or a Symbolic Gesture? – The Revision of the Constitution in the PRC', (2004) 53 *China Perspectives* 15.

Chen, Jianfu, 'To Have the Cake and Eat It Too? China and the Rule of Law', in Guenther Doeker-Mach & Klaus A Ziegert (eds), *Law, Legal Culture and Politics in the Twenty First Century* (Munich: Franz Steiner Verlag Stuttgart, 2004), at 250-272.

Chen, Jianfu, 'Securities Regulations in the People's Republic of China', being *Booklet I: Commentary*, in Gordon Walker, James D. Fox & Ian Ramsay (eds), *International Securities Regulation: Pacific Rim* (New York: Oceana Publications/Oxford University Press, 2007).

Chen, Shouyi, 'A Review of Thirty Years of Legal Studies in New China', (1988) 2 *J.Chinese L.* 181.

Chen, Sixi, 'Formulate a Law on Legislation to Regulate Legislative Activities', (no. 2, 1995) *China Law* 74.

Cheng, Chung-ying, *New Dimensions of Confucian and Neo-Confucian Philosophy* (Albany, State University of New York Press, 1991).

Cheng, Chu-yuan (ed.), *Sun Yat-sen's Doctrine in the Modern World* (Doulder/London: Westview Press, 1989).

Cheng, F.T., 'Law Codification in China', 1924 (6) *J. of Comp. Leg.* 283.

Cheng, Lucie, & Rosett, Arthur, 'Contract with a Chinese Face: Socially Embedded Factors in the Transformation from Hierarchy to Market, 1978–1989', (no. 2, 1991) 5 *J. of Chinese Law* 143.

Cheng, Tien-His, 'The Development and Reform of Chinese Law', (1948) 1 *Current Legal Problems* 170.

Clarke, Donald C., 'Power and Politics in the Chinese Court System: The Enforcement of Civil Judgement', (1996) 10 (1) *Columbia Journal of Asian Law* 1.

Clarke, Donald C, 'Economic Development and the Rights Hypothesis: The China Problem', (2003) 51 *The Am. J. Comp. L.* 89

Clarke, Donald C., 'Statement Before the US-China Security Review Commission', Washington, DC, 18 January 2002 (copy on file with the author).

Clarke, Donald C., 'The Independent Director in Chinese Corporate Governance', 36 (1) (2006) *Delaware Journal of Corporate Law* 125.

Cohen, J. A Edwards,. R.R.& Chen, F-M. C., (eds), *Essays on China's Legal Tradition* (NJ: Princeton, 1980).

Cohen, Jerome A, 'The Chinese Communist Party and "Judicial Independence": 1949–1959', (1969) 82 *Harvard Law Review* 967.

Cohen, Jerome A, *The Criminal Process in the People's Republic of China, 1949–1963: An Introduction* (Cambridge, Massachusetts: Harvard University Press, 1968).

Cohen, Jerome A., 'Opening Statement before the First Public Hearing of the US-China Security Review Commission', Washington, DC, 14 June 2001 (copy on file with author).

Cohen, Jerome A., 'Reforming China's Civil Procedure: Judging the Courts', (1997) 45 *The Am. J. Comp. L.* 793.

Corne, Peter Howard, *Foreign Investment in China: the Administrative Legal System* (Hong Kong: Hong Kong University Press, 1997).

Criminal Research Group, the Law Institute of the Chinese Academy of Social Sciences, *Lectures on the Criminal Law*, translated in (Vol. XIII, No. 2, 1980) *Chinese Law and Government*.

Davis, Stephen B., 'The Death Penalty and Legal Reform in the PRC', (1987) 1 *Journal of Chinese Law* 303.

de Bary, Wm. Theodore, *The Trouble with Confucianism* (Cambridge: Harvard University Press, 1991).

Diamant, Neil J., Lubman, Stanley B. & O'Brien, Kevin (eds), *Engaging the Law in China: State, Society and Possibilities for Justice* (Stanford: Stanford University Press, 2005).

Ding, Chengfei, 'Protection for New Plant Varieties of American Business in China after China Enters the WTO', (2001) 6 *Drake J. Agric. L.* 333.

Documents of the Thirteenth National Congress of the Communist Party of China, Beijing: Foreign Languages Press (1987).

Dong, Shizhong, Zhang, Danian, & Larson, Milton R., *Trade and Investment Opportunities in China: The Current Commercial and Legal Framework* (Westport, Connecticut: Quorum Books, 1992).

Dorn, James A. & Wang, Xi (eds), *Economic Reform in China: Problems and Prospects* (Chicago/London: The University of Chicago Press, 1990).

Dowdle, Michael W., 'The Constitutional Development and Operations of the National People's Congress', (1997) 11 (1) *Columbia Journal of Asian Law* 1.

Easson, A. J., & Li, J., *Taxation of Foreign Investment in the People's Republic of China* (Deventer/Boston: Kluwer Law and Taxation Publishers, 1989).

Edward, R. Randle, Henkin, Louis & Nathan, Andrew J. (eds), *Human Rights in Contemporary China* (New York: Columbia University Press, 1986).

Elvin, Mark, *The Pattern of the Chinese Past* (Stanford: Stanford University Press, 1973).

Eörsi, Gyula, *Comparative Civil (Private) Law* (Budapest: Akadémiai Kiadó, 1979).

Epstein, Edward J., 'Administrative Litigation Law: Citizens Can Sue the State but not the Party', (1 June 1989) *China News Analysis* 1.

Epstein, Edward J., 'Tortious Liability for Defective Products in the People's Republic of China', (1988) 2 *J. Chinese L.* 285.

Escarra, Jean, *Chinese Law: Conception and Evolution, Legislative and Judicial Institutions, Science and Teaching*, translated from a 1936 French edition by Gertrude R. Browne (Seattle: University of Washington, 1961).

Exner, M., 'Convergence of Ideology and the Law: The Functions of the Legal Education Campaign in Building a Chinese Legal System', (August, 1995) *Issues and Studies* 68.

Fairbank, John K. & Liu, Kwang-ching, *The Cambridge History of China*, vol. 11, Late Ch'ing, 1800–1911, Part 2 (Cambridge: Cambridge University Press, 1980).

Fairbank, John K., *The Cambridge History of China*, vol. 10, Late Ch'ing, 1800–1911, Part I (Cambridge: Cambridge University Press, 1978).

Feng, Xiaoqing, 'A Review of the Development of the Marriage Law in the People's Republic of China', (2002) 79 *U. Detroit Mercy L. Rev.* 331.

Finder, Susan, 'Like Throwing an Egg Against a Stone? Administrative Litigation in the People's Republic of China', (1989) 3 *J. of Chinese Law* 1.

Foo, Ping-sheung, 'Introduction', in *The Civil Code of the Republic of China* (Shanghai: Kelly & Walsh, Ltd., 1930).

Foster, Frances Hoar, 'Codification in Post-Mao China', (1982) 30 *Am. J. Comp. L.* 395.

Foster-Simons, Frances, 'The Development of Inheritance Law in the Soviet Union and the People's Republic of China', (1985) *Am. J. Comp. L.* 33.

Freedman, Maurice, 'The Family in China, Past and Present', (1961–1962) 34 (4) *Pacific Affairs* 323.

Fu, Hualing, 'When Lawyers are Prosecuted: The Struggle of a Profession in Transition', available from <ssrn.com/abstract=956500> (last accessed 12 June 2007).

Fundamental Issues of Civil Law in the PRC (*Zhonghua Renmin Gonghe Guo Minfa Jiben Wenti*), (edited by the Teaching Section of Civil Law of the Central Judicial Cadres' School, published by the Publishing House of Law, Beijing, 1958).

Fung, Yu-lan, *A Short History of Chinese Philosophy* (New York: The Free Press, 1966).

Gao, Huanyue, 'Ruling Government Officials through Laws: the Essence of Rule by Law in Ancient China', (no. 4, 1997) *China Law* 98.

Gao, Huanyue, 'The Uniqueness of Ancient Chinese Civil Law', (no. 3, 1997) *China Law* 90.

Garnaut, Ross, & Liu, Guoguang (eds), *Economic Reform and Internationalisation: China and the Pacific Region* (Sydney: Allen & Unwin, in association with the Australian National University, 1992).

Gellat, Timothy A., 'The People's Republic of China and the Presumption of Innocence', (1982) 73 *The Journal of Criminal Law and Criminology* 259.

Gernet, Jacques, *A History of Chinese Civilisation*, 2nd edition translated from French by J.R. Foster & Charles Hartman (New York: Cambridge University Press, 1996).

Gillespie, John and Nicholson, Pip (eds), *Asian Socialism and Legal Change: the Dynamics of Vietnamese and Chinese Reform* (Canberra: Asia Pacific Press, 2005).

Gilpatrick, Meredith P., 'The Status of Law and Law-making Procedures Under the Kuomintang 1925–46', 1950–1951 (10) *Far Eastern Q* 39.

Great Qing Code, translated by William C Jones (Oxford, Clarendon Press, 1994).

Grimheden, Jonas, *Themis v Xiezhi: Assessing Judicial Independence in the PRC under International Human Rights Law*, PhD thesis at Lund University, 2004.

Han, Depei & Kanter, Stephen, 'Legal Education in China', (1984) 32 *Am. J. Comp. L.* 543.

Hatano, Daryl G, 'China's Semiconductor Chip Protection Law – a Work in Progress', Paper presented to the 4th Annual Advanced Patent Law Institute, Berkeley Centre for Law and Technology, 4 December 2003, available from <www.sia-onlin.org/downloads/china_chip_protection_law.pdf> (last accessed 16 June 2005).

Hazard, John N., *Communists and Their Law: A Search for the Common Core of the Legal Systems of the Marxian Socialist States* (Chicago/London: The University of Chicago Press, 1969).

Hearing before the U.S.–China Economic and Security Review Commission, June 7-8, 2006. Transcripts published in July 2006, and available from <www.uscc.gov> (last accessed 31 August 2006).

Hook, Brian (ed.), *The Individual and the State in China* (Oxford: Clarendon Press, 1996).

Hsüeh, Chün-tu, 'The New Constitution', (no. 3, 1975) 24 *Problems of Communism* 11.

Hsu, Francis L.K., *Under the Ancestors' Shadow* (New York: Columbia University Press, 1948).

Hsü, Immanuel C.Y., *The Rise of Modern China*, 5th ed, (New York: Oxford University Press, 1995).

Hu, Kangsheng, 'Major Issues in Amending the Chinese Marriage Law', (Oct 2000) *China Law* 63.

Huang, Frank Xianfeng, 'The Path to Clarity: Development of Property Rights in China' 2004 (17) *Column J. Asian L* 191.

Huang, Philip C.C., *Civil Justice in China: Representation and Practice in the Qing* (Stanford, Calif : Stanford University Press, 1996).

Huang, Philip C.C., *Code, Custom, and Legal Practice in China: The Qing and the Republic Compared* (California: Stanford University Press, 2001).

Idema, W.L. & Zürcher, E. (eds), *Thought and Law in Qin and Han China* (Leiden: E.J. Brill, 1990).

Ioffe O. S., & Maggs, Peter B., *Soviet Law in Theory and Practice* (New York: Oceana Publications, Inc., 1983).

Jiang, Ping, 'Drafting the Uniform Contract Law in China', (1996) 10 *Columbia J. of Asian Law* 245.

Jin, Ren, 'New Approaches of People's Congresses in China to Supervise Law Enforcement', (no. 1, 1997) *China Law* 53.

Jones, W.C., 'Some Questions Regarding the Significance of the General Provisions of Civil Law of the People's Republic of China', (1987) 28 (2) *Harvard International Law Journal* 309.

Jun, Lin, Qu, Xiaohui & Chen, Feng, 'Experimentation of the Share-capital System and Economic Development in China', (1993) 21 *Asian Profile* 455.

Kamenka, Eugene & Tay, Alice E.-S., 'Beyond the French Revolution: Communist Socialism and the Concept of Law', (1971) 21 *U. Toronto L.J.* 109.

Kamenka, Eugene & Tay, Alice E.-S., 'Marxism, Socialism and the Theory of Law', (1985) 23 *Colum. J. Transnat'l L.* 217.

Kamenka, Eugene, *Bureaucracy* (Oxford: Basil Blackwell, 1989).

Keeton, George W., 'The Progress of Law in China', (1937) 19 *J. Comp. Leg.* 197.

Keith, Ronald C., and Lin, Zhiqiu, *Law and Justice in China's New Marketplace* (New York: Palgrave, 2001).

Keith, Ronald C., *China's Struggle for the Rule of Law* (New York: St. Martin's Press, 1994).

Keller, Perry, 'Legislation in the People's Republic of China', (1989) 23 (3) *U.B.C. Law Rev.* 643.

Keller, Perry, 'Sources of Order in Chinese Law', (1994) 42 *Am. J. Comp. L.* 711.

Kent, Ann, *Between Freedom and Subsistence: China and Human Rights* (Hong Kong: Oxford University Press, 1993).

Kerster, Lisa A. & Lu, Jin, 'The Transformation Continues: The Status of Chinese State-Owned Enterprises at the Start of the Millennium', 12 (3) (2001) *NBR Analysis*, available from <www.nbr.org/publications/issue.esp?&id=202>.

Koguchi, Hikota, 'Some Observations About 'Judicial Independence' in Post-Mao China', (1987) 7 *Boston College Third World Law Journal* 195.

Lawyers Committee for Human Rights, *Criminal Justice with Chinese Characteristics: China's Criminal Process and Violations of Human Rights* (New York, 1993).

Lee, Keun, *Chinese Firms and the State in Transition: Property Rights and Agency Problems in the Reform Era* (New York: M.E. Sharpe, Inc., 1991).

Lee, Peter N.S, *Industrial Management and Economic Reform in China, 1949–1984* (Hong Kong: Oxford University Press, 1987).

Lee, Tahirih V., *Law, the State, and Society in China* (New York: Garland Publications, 1997).

Leng, Shao-chuan & Chiu, Hungdah, *Criminal Justice in Post-Mao China: Analysis and Documents* (Albany: State University of New York Press, 1985).

Leng, Shao-chuan, 'The Role of Law in the People's Republic of China as Reflecting Mao Tse-tung's Influence', (1977) 68 *J. Criminal L. & Criminology* 356.

Leng, Shao-chuan, *Justice in Communist China: A Survey of the Judicial System of the Chinese People's Republic* (New York: Oceana Publications, Inc., 1967).

Leung, Conita S.C., 'Conceptual and Constitutional Bases for Chinese Administrative Law', (1992) 17 (no. 58/59) *Bulletin of the Australian Society of Legal Philosophy* 175.

Li, C, 'The Old Law Cannot Be Critically Inherited, It Can Only Be Used as a Mirror', originally published in (No. 3, 1979) *Studies in Law* (*Faxue Yanjiu*) 45, translated in (1980) (6) *Review of Socialist Law* 287.

Li, Yede & Zhang, Xingxiang, 'How Are China's Administrative Rules and Regulations Formulated?' (no. 4, 1997) *China Law* 58.

Liao, Kuangsheng, 'Independent Administration of Justice' and the PRC Legal System', (Vol 16, 1983) *Chinese Law & Government* 123.

Lin, Chris X, 'A Quiet Revolution: An Overview of China's Judicial Reform', 4 (2003) *Asian-Pacific Law & Policy Journal* 180.

Lin, Feng, *Administrative Law Procedures and Remedies in China* (Hong Kong/London: Sweet & Maxwell, 1996).

Lin, R., 'A Little Discussion of the Heritability of Law', 1979 (1) *Studies in Law* (*Faxue Yanjiu*) 13, translated in (1980) (6) *Review of Socialist Law* 280.

Linebarger, Paul M. A., *The Political Doctrine of Sun Yat-sen: An Exposition of the San Min Chu I* (Baltimore: John Hopkins University Press, 1937).

Linebarger, Paul M.A. *The China of Chiang Kai-shek: A Political Study* (Boston: World Peace Foundation, 1943).

Liu Nanping, '"Judicial Review" in China: A Comparative Perspective', (1988) 14 *Rev. of Soc. L.* 241.

Liu, Hui-chen Wang, *The Traditional Chinese Clan Rules* (New York: Association for Asian Studies, 1959).

Liu, James T. C. & Tu, Wei-ming (eds), *Traditional China* (Englewood Cliffs: Prentice-Hall, Inc., 1970).

Liu, Suinian & Wu, Qungan, (eds), *China's Socialist Economy: An Outline History (1949–1984)* (Beijing: Beijing Review Press, 1986).

Lo, Carlos Wing-hung, *China's Legal Awakening: Legal Theory and Criminal Justice in Deng's Era* (Hong Kong: Hong Kong University Press, 1995).

Loeber, Dietrich André, *et al.* (eds), *Ruling Communist Parties and Their Status under Law* (Dordrecht/Boston/Lancaster: Martinus Nijhoff Publishers, 1986).

Lu, Yun, 'Formation and Development of the System of Multi-Party Cooperation', (19-25 March 1990) *Beijing Review 16*

Lubman, Stanley (ed.), *China's Legal Reforms* (Oxford/New York: Oxford University Press, 1996).

Lubman, Stanley B., *Bird in a Cage: Legal Reform in China After Mao* (Stanford, California: Stanford University Press, 1999).

Lubman, Stanley, 'Keynote Speech' (delivered at the international conference *Legal and Political Reform in the People's Republic of China,* Lund, Sweden, 3-4 June 2002) (copy on file with author).

Ma, Herbert H.P., 'The Chinese Concept of the Individual and the Reception of Foreign Law', 1995 (9: 2) *Journal of Chinese Law* 207.

Ma, Xiaoying & Ortolano, Leonard, *Environmental Regulation in China: Institutions, Enforcement and Compliance* (New York: Rowman & Littlefield, 2000).

MacCormack, Geoffrey, *The Spirit of Traditional Chinese Law* (Athens/London: The University of Georgia Press, 1996).

Main Documents of the Second Session of the Fifth National People's Congress of the People's Republic of China (Beijing: Foreign Languages Press, 1979).

Mao, Baigen & Sun, Roland, 'Upgrading the Sponsorship System: The CSRC Makes Moves to Enhance Market Quality', (April 2004) *China Law & Practice* 85.

Mattei, Ugo, 'Three Patterns of Law: Taxonomy and Change in the World's Legal Systems', 1997 (45) *Am. J. Comp. L.* 5.

Meijer, M.J., *Marriage Law and Policy in the Chinese People's Republic* (Hong Kong: Hong Kong University Press, 1971).

Meijer, M.J., *The Introduction of Modern Criminal Law in China,* 2nd edition (Hong Kong: Lung Men Bookstore, 1967).

Mertha, Andrew, *The Politics of Piracy: Intellectual Property in Contemporary China*, Ithaca/London: Cornell University Press (2005).

Michael C. Davis (ed.), *Human Rights and Chinese Values: Legal, Philosophical, and Political Perspectives* (Hong Kong/New York: Oxford University Press, 1995).

Münzel, F., 'Chinese Thoughts on the Heritability of Law: Translations', 1980 (6:3) *Review of Socialist Law* 275.

Needham, Joseph, *Science and Civilisation in China*, multi-volume (Cambridge University Press, since 1954).

Nolan, Peter, & Dong, Fureng, (eds), *The Chinese Economy and Its Future: Achievements and Problems of Post-Mao Reform* (Cambridge: Polity Press, 1990).

Nottle, Robert, 'The Development of Securities Markets in China in the 1990s', (1993) 11 *Company and Securities Law Journal* 503.

O'Brien, Kevin J., 'Agents and Remonstrators: Role Accumulation by Chinese People's Congress Deputies', (June 1994) *The China Quarterly* 359.

O'Brien, Kevin J., *Reform Without Liberalisation: China's National People's Congress and the Politics of Institutional Change* (New York: Cambridge University Press, 1990).

Orts, Eric W., 'The Rule of Law in China', (2001) 34 *Vanderbilt Journal of Transnational Law* 43.

Otto, J M, Polak, M V., Chen, J. & Li, Y. (eds), *Law-Making in the People's Republic of China* (The Hague/London/Boston: Kluwer Law International, 2000).

Owen M. Fiss, 'Two Constitutions', (1986) 11 *Yale J. of Int'l L.* 492.

Palmer, Michael, 'China, People's Republic of: Reacting to Rapid Social Change', (1989–1990) 28 *Journal of Family Law* 438.

Palmer, Michael, 'The People's Republic of China: New Marriage Regulations', (no. 1, 1987–1988) 26 *Journal of Family Law* 39.

Pan, Wei-Tung, *The Chinese Constitution: A Study of Forty Years of Constitution-making in China* (Washington: Institute of Chinese Culture, 1954).

Peerenboom, Randall (ed.), *Asian Discourses of Rule of Law: Theories and Implementation of Rule of Law in Twelve Asian Countries, France and the US* (London/New York: Routledge, 2004).

Peerenboom, Randall, 'Seek Truth from Facts: An Empirical Study of Enforcement of Arbitral Awards in the PRC', (2001) 49 (2) *Am. J. Comp. L.* 249.

Peerenboom, Randall, *China Modernizes: Threat to the West or Model for the Rest?* (New York: Oxford University Press, 2007).

Peerenboom, Randall, *China's Long March toward Rule of Law* (Cambridge: Cambridge University Press, 2002).

Peerenboom, Randall, Petersen, Carole & Chen, Albert H.Y. (eds), *Human Rights in Asia: a Comparative Legal Study of Twelve Asian Jurisdictions, France, and the USA* (New York: Routledge, 2005).

Peerenboom, Randy, 'Assessing Human Rights in China: Why the Double Standard?', (2005) 38:1 *Cornell International Law Journal* 71.

Potter, Pitman B, *The Chinese Legal System: Globalization and Local Legal Culture* (London & New York: Routledge Cuzon, 2001).

Potter, Pitman B, *The Economic Contract Law of China: Legitimation and Contract Autonomy in the PRC* (Seattle & London: University of Washington Press, 1992).

Potter, Pitman B. (ed.), *The Administrative Litigation Law of the PRC: Changing the Relationship Between the Courts and Administrative Agencies in China*, a special issue of *Chinese Law and Government* (no. 3, 1991).

Potter, Pitman B., (ed.), *Domestic Law Reforms in Post-Mao China* (New York/London: M.E. Shaper, 1994).

Potter, Pitman B., *From Leninist Discipline to Socialist Legalism: Peng Zhen on Law and Political Authority in the PRC* (Stanford: Stanford University Press, 2003).

Pound, Roscoe, 'Law and Courts in China: Progress in the Administration of Justice', 1948 (34) *ABAJ* 273.

Pound, Roscoe, 'The Chinese Civil Code in Action', 1955 (29) *Tulane L. Rev.* 277.

Pu, Zengyuan, 'A Comparative Perspective on the United States and Chinese Constitutions' (1989) 30 *Williiam and Mary L. Rev.* 867.

Pye, Lucian W., 'The State and the Individual: An Overview Interpretation', in Brian Hook (ed.), *The Individual and the State in China* (Oxford: Clarendon Press, 1996).

Qu, Sanqiang, *Copyright in China* (Beijing: Foreign Languages Press, 2002).

Reynolds, Bruce L., (ed.), *Chinese Economic Reform: How Far, How Fast?* (Boston: Academic Press, Inc., 1988).

Riley, Mary L. (ed.) *Protecting Intellectual Property Rights in China* (Hong Kong: Sweet & Maxwell Asia, 1997).

Rodan, Garry (ed.), *Political Oppositions in Industrialising Asia* (London/New York: Routledge, 1996).

Rosett, Arthur, 'Legal Structures for Special Treatment of Minorities in the People's Republic of China, (1991) 66 *Notre Dame L. Rev.* 1503.

Roundtable: Intellectual Property Protection as Economic Policy: Will China Ever Enforce its IP Laws?, transcripts of the Roundtable are available from <www.cecc.gov> (last accessed 19 May 2005)

Sadikov, O.N., (ed.), *Soviet Civil Law* (New York: M.E. Sharpe, Inc., 1988).

Schwartz, Benjamin I., *The World of Thought in Ancient China* (Cambridge, Massachusetts: Harvard University Press, 1985).

Seidman, Ann & Seidman, Robert B., 'Drafting Legislation for Development: Lessons from a Chinese Project', (1996) *Am. J. Comp. L.* 1.

Seidman, Ann, & Seidman, Robert B., *State and Law in the Development Process: Problem Solving and Institutional Change in the Third World* (New York: St. Martin's Press, 1994).

Seidman, Ann, Seidman, Robert B., and Payne, Janice, *Legislative Drafting for Market Reform: Some Lessons from China* (New York: St. Martin's Press, 1997).

Selected Works of Deng Xiaoping (1875–1982) (Beijing: Foreign Languages Press, 1984).

Seymour, James D., *China's Satellite Parties* (New York/London: M.E. Sharpe, Inc., 1987).

Soo, Gary, 'Domain Name Protection in China: Practice under the Current Regime', (2004) 11 (3) *Murdoch University Electronic Journal of Law*, available <www.murdoch.edu.au/elaw/issues/v11n3/soo113_text.html> (last accessed 18 August 2005).

Sun, Yatsen, *Fundamentals of National Reconstruction* (published by China Culture Service and printed by Sino-America Publishing Co. Ltd., Taipei, 1953).

Sun, Yatsen, *The Three Principles of the People: San Min Chu I* (With two supplementary chapters by Chiang Kai-shek) (Taipei: China Publishing Co., undated).

Tanner, H.M., *Strike Hard! Anti-Crime Campaigns and Chinese Criminal Justice, 1979–1985* (New York: Cornell University, 1999).

Tanner, Murray Scot, 'How a Bill Becomes a Law in China: Stages and Processes in Lawmaking', (1995) *The China Quarterly* 37.

Tanner, Murray Scot, 'The Erosion of Communist Party Control over Lawmaking in China', (June 1994) 138 *The China Quarterly* 381.

Tanner, Murray Scot, *The Politics of Lawmaking in Post-Mao China: Institutions, Processes, and Democratic Prospects* (Oxford/New York: Oxford University Press, 1999).

Tay, Alice E.-S., and Kamenka, Eugene, 'Public Law – Private Law', in S.I. Benn & G.F. Gaus (eds), *Public and Private in Social Life* (London/New York: Croom Helm St. Martin's Press, 1983).

Tay, A.E-S. & Kamenka, E., 'Marxism-Leninism and the Heritability of Law', 1980 (6) *Review of Socialist Law* 261.

Tay, Alice & Leung, Conita, (eds), *Legal Persons and Legal Personality in Common Law, Civil Law and Socialist Law* (being a special issue of the *Indian Socio-Legal Journal*, 1992).

Tay, Alice E.-S. & Kamenka, Eugene 'Law, Legal Theory and Legal Education in the People's Republic of China', (1986) *N.Y.L.S.J. Int'l & Comp. L.* 1.

Tay, Alice E-S & Leung, Conita S C, (eds), *Greater China: Law, Society and Trade* (Sydney: The Law Book Company, 1995).

Tay, Alice E-S., & Leung, Conita (eds), *Constitution-making and Restructuring in the Present and Former Communist World*, being a special issue of the *Bulletin of Australian Society of Legal Philosophy* (Vol. 17, nos 58/59, 1992).

Tay, Alice, 'The Struggle for Law in China', (1987) 21 *U.B.C. Law Rev.* 561.

The Book of Lord Shang, translated by Dr. J.J.L. Duyvendak (the University of Chicago Press, 1928).

Thieme, G.V., 'The Debate on the Presumption of Innocence in the People's Republic of China', (1984) *Review of Socialist Law* 277.

Thurston, Richard L., 'Country Risk Management: China and Intellectual Property Protection', 1993 (27) *Int'l Lawyer* 51.

Tian, Guoqiang, 'Property Rights and the Nature of Chinese Collective Enterprises' (2000) 28 *Journal of Comparative Economics* 247.

Tideman, Sander G., 'Tibetans and Other Minorities in China's Legal System'. (1988) 14 *Rev. of Soc. L.* 5.

Ting, Wei-chih, 'The Phases of Changes in Confucianism', (no. 12, 1978) *Studies in History* (*Lishi Yangjiu*) 25.

Tomasic, Roman, (ed.), *Insolvency Law in East Asia* (Hampshire, UK: Ashgate Publishing Limited, 2006).

Tomasic, Roman, (ed.), *Corporate Governance: Challenges for China* (Beijing: Law Press, 2005).

Tong, Rou, 'The General Principles of Civil Law of the PRC: Its Birth, Characteristics, and Role', (1989) 52 *Law and Contemporary Problems* 151.

Townsend, Deborah E., 'The Concept of Law in Post-Mao China: A Case Study of Economic Crime', (1987–1988) 24 *Stanford Journal of International Law* 227.

Troyer, Ronald J., Clark, John P., and Royek, Dean G., (eds), *Social Control in the People's Republic of China* (New York: Praeger, 1989).

Tsao, W.Y., *The Constitutional Structure of Modern China* (Melbourne: Melbourne University Press, 1947).

Tu, Wei-ming (ed.), *China in Transformation* (Cambridge, Massachusetts: Harvard University Press, 1994).

Tung, Ricky, 'The Bankruptcy System of Mainland China's State-Owned Enterprises', (no. 1, 1997) 33 *Issues & Studies* 23.

Tung, William L., *The Political Institutions of Modern China* (The Hague: Martinus Nijhoff, 1964).

Turner, Karen G., Feinerman, James V., and Guy, R. Kent (eds), *The Limits of the Rule of Law in China* (Seattle: University of Washington Press, 2000).

Turner, Karen, 'A Case for Contemporary Studies of Classical Chinese Legal History', (vol. 22, no. 4, 1994) *China Exchange News* 25.

US Trade Representative, *2005 Report to Congress on China's WTO Compliance*, 11 December 2005, available at <www.ustr.gov> (last accessed 15 August 2006).

US Trade Representative, *2006 Special 301 Report*, available from <www.ustr.gov> (last accessed 15 August 2006).

van der Valk, M.H., *An Outline of Modern Chinese Family Law* (Peking: Henri Vetch, 1939, reprinted by Ch'eng Wen Publishing Co., Taipei, 1969).

Vermeer, Eduard B. & dHooghe, Ingrid (eds), *China's Legal Reforms and Their Political Limits* (London: RoutledgeCurzon, 2002).

Walter, Carl E. & Howie, Fraser J., *Privatizing China: Inside China's Stock Markets*, 2nd edition (Singapore: John Wiley & Sons (Asia) Pte Ltd, 2006).

Wan, Tay-sheng (translated by Sean Cooney), 'The Impact of Modern Western Law on the Chinese in Taiwan', 1999 1 (2) *The Australian Journal of Asian Law* 194.

Wang, Jiangyu, 'The Rule of Law in China: A Realistic View of the Jurisprudence, the Impact of the WTO, and the Prospects for Future Development', (Decmber 2004) *Singapore Juounal of Legal Studies* 347.

Wang Joseph En-pao, (ed.), *Selected Legal Documents of the PRC* (University Publications of America, 1976).

Wang, Chenguang & Zhang, Xianchu (ed.) *Introduction to Chinese Law* (Hong Kong/ Singapore: Sweet & Maxwell Asia, 1997).

Wang, Guiguo, & Wei, Zhenying (eds), *Legal Developments in China: Market Economy and Law* (Hong Kong: Sweet & Maxwell Asia, 1996).

Wang, Guiguo, 'Economic Integration in Quest of Law', (1995) 29: (2) *Journal of World Trade* 5.

Wang, Guiguo, Tomasic, Roman, *China's Company Law: an Annotation* (Singapore: Butterworths Asia, 1994).

Wang, Liming, 'An Inquiry into Several Difficult Problems in Enacting China's Uniform Contract Law', (1999) 8 *Pacific Rim Law and Policy Journal* 351.

Wei, Yuwa, 'The Development of the Securities Market and Regulation in China', (2005) 27 *Loy. L.A. Int'l & Comp. L. Rev.*479.

Wm. Theodore de Bary, 'The "Constitutional Tradition" in China', (no. 1, 1995) 9 *J. of Chinese L.* 7.

Woo, Margaret Y.K., 'Adjudication Supervision and Judicial Independence in the PRC', (1991) 39 *Am. J. Comp. L.* 95.

Woodhead H.G.W., (ed.), *The China Year Book 1925–1926* (Tientsin: Tientsin Press Limited).

World Bank, *China: Between Plan and Market* (Washington, DC, 1990).

World Bank, *China: Long-Term Development Issues and Options* (Baltimore/London: The Johns Hopkins University Press, 1985).

Wu, Changzhen, 'Ideas and Concepts for Revision of the Marriage Law of China', (no. 3, 1997) *China Law* 72.

Wu, Jianfan, 'Building New China's Legal System', (1983) 22 *Colum. J. Transnat'l L.* 1.

Wu, Yuan-li, Lee, Ta-ling, Michael, Franz Maria Chang, His, Cooper, John F. & Gregor, A. James, *Human Rights in the People's Republic of China* (Boulder/London: Westview Press, 1988).

Xin Ren, *Tradition of the Law and Aaw of the Tradition: Law, State, and Social Control in China* (Westport: Greenwood Press, 1997).

Yeh, Jiunn-Rong, 'Changing Forces of Constitutional and Regulatory Reform in Taiwan', (1990) 4 *J. of Chinese L* 83.

Yen, Hawking L., *A Survey of Constitutional Development in China* (New York: AMS Press, 1968).

Ying, Songnian, 'China's Administrative Procedure System', (no. 4, 1997) *China Law* 81.

Yu, Guangyuan (ed.), *China's Socialist Modernisation* (Beijing: Foreign Languages Press, 1984).

Yu, Xingzhong, 'Legal Pragmatism in the People's Republic of China', (1989) 3 *J. of Chinese L.* 29.

Zhang, Shuyi, 'A Re-examination of Several Controversial Issues in the Administrative Litigation Law (draft)', (no. 3, 1989) *Jurisprudence* (*Faxue*) 8, translated in (no. 3, 1991) *Chinese Law and Government* 47.

Zheng, Chengsi, *Intellectual Property Enforcement in China: Leading Cases and Commentary* (Hong Kong: Sweet & Maxwell Asia, 1997).

Zhu, Keliang, Prosterman, Roy, Ye, Jianping, Li, Ping, Riedinger, Jeffrey, & Quyan, Yiwen, 'The Rural Land Question in China: Analysis and Recommendations Based on a Seventeen-Province Survey', 2006 (38) *Journal of International Law and Politics* 761.

Index